C0-DXA-266

Chicago Public Library

REFERENCE

Form 178 rev. 1-94

CHICAGO PUBLIC LIBRARY
SOCIAL SCIENCES AND HISTORY
400 S. STATE ST.   60605

THE SOURCEBOOK OF COLLEGE AND UNIVERSITY STUDENT RECORDS

A National Guide to Student Attendance, Degree, and Transcript Records at Accredited Post-Secondary Schools.

Another Sourcebook from The Public Record Research Library

PUBLISHED BY BRB PUBLICATIONS, INC.

The Sourcebook of College and University Student Records

ISBN: 1-879792-24-9
Copyright © 1995 by BRB Publications, Inc.

1st Printing, August 1995

All rights reserved. Printed in the United States of America. No part of this book may be used or reproduced in any form or by any means, or stored in a database or retrieval system without the prior written permission of the publisher, except in the case of brief quotations embodied in critical articles or reviews. Making copies of any part of this book for any purpose other than your own personal use is a violation of United States copyright laws. Entering any of the contents into a computer for mailing list or database purposes is strictly prohibited unless written authorization is obtained from BRB Publications, Inc.

This directory is sold as is, without warranty of any kind, either express or implied, respecting the contents of this directory, including but not limited to implied warranties for the directory's quality, performance, merchantability, or fitness for any particular purpose. Neither the publisher nor its dealers or distributors shall be liable to the purchaser or any other person or entity with respect to any liability, loss, or damage caused or alleged to be caused directly or indirectly by this directory.

BRB Publications, Inc.
4653 South Lakeshore, Suite 3 • Tempe, Arizona • 85282
(602) 838-8909 • FAX (602) 838-8324

Cover Design by Robin Fox & Associates
Photographs by Lynn Beshara Sankey

Acknowledgements

We **genuinely wish** to extend a special **thank you** and **our appreciation** to—

All the **Administrators** and **Personnel** at the **Registrars'** and **Admissions' Offices** profiled herein. We enjoyed talking to all of you and learning how your particular departments provide access to student record information. This edition is a direct reflection of your interest and time in helping us assemble this information accurately. Our sincere thanks, to you, from all of us at BRB Publications, Inc.

Carol DuPree, Kim Hornback, Emily Lewis,
Tim Russell, Dan Smith, and Annette Talley, Research Staff
Carl R. Ernst, Editor-in-Chief
Michael Sankey, Publisher
August, 1995

CHICAGO PUBLIC LIBRARY
SOCIAL SCIENCES AND HISTORY
400 S. STATE ST.   60605

Public Record Research Library

1995 Book Titles and Information

At The State...

☐ **THE SOURCEBOOK OF STATE PUBLIC RECORDS** 2nd Edition
ISBN # 1-879792-22-2   Pub 5/95   Pages 320   Price: 29.00

☐ **THE 1995 MVR BOOK** 6th Edition (Published Annually)
ISBN # 1-879792-19-2   Pub 2/95   Pages 272   Price: 18.00

☐ **THE 1995 MVR DECODER DIGEST** 5th Edition (Published Annually)
ISBN # 1-879792-20-6   Pub 2/95   Pages 288   Price: 18.00

At The Court and County Level...

☐ **THE SOURCEBOOK OF FEDERAL COURTS—US DISTRICT & BANKRUPTCY** 2nd Edition
ISBN # 1-879792-25-7   Pub 10/95   Pages 672   Price: 36.00
Includes insert updating all PACER and VCIS data at all court locations.

☐ **THE FEDERAL COURT LOCATOR**
ISBN # 1-879792-18-4   Pages 144   Price: 29.00
This is an up-to-date looseleaf and includes one complete update 6 months after purchase.

☐ **THE SOURCEBOOK OF COUNTY COURT RECORDS** 2nd Edition
ISBN # 1-879792-16-8   Pub 1/95   Pages 540   Price: 33.00

☐ **THE SOURCEBOOK OF COUNTY ASSET/LIEN RECORDS**
ISBN # 1-879792-17-6   Pub 1/95   Pages 464   Price: 29.00

Sources, Retrieval and Unique Searching Aids

☐ **THE SOURCEBOOK OF PUBLIC RECORD PROVIDERS** 3nd Edition
ISBN # 1-879792-13-3   Pub 12/95   Pages 304   Price: 29.00

☐ **THE SOURCEBOOK OF LOCAL COURT & COUNTY RECORD RETRIEVERS** 2nd Edition
ISBN # 1-879792-21-4   Pub 4/95   Pages 544   Price: 45.00

☐ **THE COUNTY LOCATOR (LOCUS)**
ISBN # 1-879792-11-7   Pub 6/93   Pages 928   Price: 25.00
Includes insert updating new ZIP data at locations.

Published by **BRB Publications, Inc**.
4653 S. Lakeshore Suite #3
Tempe, Arizona 85282
(800) 929-3811
FAX (800) 929-3810

*The Sourcebook
of
College and University Student Records*

Table of Contents

Before You Start... vii

How to Use This Book ix

Section One
    Accredited, Degree Granting College and
    University Profiles 1

Section Two
    Accredited, Non-Degree Granting
    Institution Listings 387

Section Three
    State Cross Reference Index 427

Before You Start...

Why a Book About College Records?

Employers, human resource professionals, and pre-employment screening firms recognize the importance of verifying credentials and education. They know that too many times, a business will hire a new employee without verifying what is represented on the employment application and be embarrassed or suffer in some manner later. However, the verification of credentials is not limited to this group. Other users include news reporters, genealogists, financial institutions, and private investigators. A lawful investigation into an individual's past is recommended when considering promotion of, endorsement of, publication of, or strategic alignment with an individual.

This book was compiled and written with the express purpose of making the reader an expert in confirming and/or accessing student attendance records at accredited colleges and universities. This first edition breaks new ground as the only comprehensive reference for searching student record centers at nearly 3,800 degree granting and over 1,750 non-degree granting accredited institutions in the US.

The information contained herein is based upon each institution's response to surveys conducted by our staff. The vast majority of school personnel readily understood the importance of this information and its intended use by professionals and public libraries. Nearly all answered our survey questions, and some information is included even for those few that did not.

Accreditation and Other Resources

These institutions are recognized as accredited by specific accrediting bodies, which in turn, are approved by the Commission on Recognition of Postsecondary Accreditation (COPRA). Please note that the accreditation process is ongoing and the status of each school may be determined or changed on an annual basis. For further information regarding the accreditation process, we suggest you contact COPRA at One Dupont Circle NW #305, Washington DC 20036, (202) 452-1433.

If you are looking for a good overall general description of curriculum, degrees offered, number of students, etc., we can suggest several publications. *The Accredited Institutions of Post Secondary Education* is distributed annually by The Oryx Press, (800) 279-6799, for the American Council On Education and offers extensive details on academics and accreditation. Peterson's Publications, (800) 338-3282, offer several excellent titles including *Peterson's Guide to Four-Year Colleges* and *Peterson's Guide to Two-year Colleges*.

How To Use This Book

The *Sourcebook of College and University Student Records* is divided into three sections.

Section One—Accredited, Degree Granting College and University Profiles

3,778 institutions are listed in alphabetical order. The address and phone number given is the location maintaining the student records or the closest route possible. Also, included are office hours, FAX numbers, types (levels) of degrees granted, and, usually, an indication of how many years back records are maintained. Branch campuses are listed. We have indicated when records are maintained at a different or central location.

The descriptive format falls into three categories: **attendance confirmation**; **degree confirmation**; and **obtaining copies of transcripts.** Each category is then individually dissected as follows:

- Permissible Access Modes
  Phone, FAX, mail, and written requests only are examined

- General Search Requirements
  Items you must submit such as years attended, signed release, Social Security Number, etc.
  Items which are optional, but helpful

- Fees and Payments
  All costs involved

The final paragraph of each profile also contains searching tips that you should be aware of regarding the school. We have included such items as if a school requires the use of a self-addressed stamped envelope (**SASE**), if credit cards are accepted for payment, and any comments or searching aids the schools asked us to print.

Alumni Associations and Adverse Action Record Centers

You will find many profiles include an alumni association address and phone number. However, some schools have no such organization since they are very technically oriented or narrow in their fields of study. (Note: An alumni association is a good place to find a maiden name if you are doing a search and all you have is the married name.)

Also, we have indicated 905 institutions that house an adverse incident record database. This can be the center for student activities, campus police or even the local jurisdictional police. Again, the larger institutions generally have some record center of this type, and the smaller institutions do not.

Section Two—Accredited, Non-Degree Granting Institution Listings

According to the Commission on Recognition of Postsecondary Accreditation, there are 1,760 institutions that, although accredited, do not offer a "degree." These schools offer training and certificates in such fields paralegal studies, beauty or barber related occupations, and other vocational training areas.

Although these institutions are not profiled in-depth in this sourcebook, they are generally quite willing to respond to a professional inquiry concerning students. Some of these schools may be upgrading to meet the educational requirements necessary to offer a degree. We recommend a phone confirmation whenever possible.

Section Three—State Cross Reference Index

This section was designed to aid those searchers not sure which school their subject may have attended. The list, in state order, shows where schools and branch campuses are located by city. This will help indicate when schools are close geographically. As most experienced searchers and investigators know, "searching" usually begins at the local level and this section serves as an excellent research tool. Genealogists will find this list particularly useful.

Getting the Results You Want

School Search Policies Will Vary

Most schools are very willing to cooperate with an employer regarding the placement or hiring of a former student. However, how a record is released and the degree of authority needed to obtain the record are subject to **individual school policy**. Although most schools will confirm attendance over the phone, the policies of the admissions' or registrars' office can, and do, vary significantly from school to school. For example—

- 65 % require a Social Security Number to confirm attendance and/or degree
- 76 % will confirm attendance and/or degree over the phone
- 34 % require a signed release from the student to confirm a degree
- 93 % require a signed release from the student to release a transcript

Using the Phone

Even when a college or university indicates that it does not take telephone calls for information about students and former students, most of these institutions will accept a phone call to confirm or deny information that you already have in your possession. Try this if you have the following kinds of questions—
- Did Sheri Byrkit graduate with a B.S. in Biology in 1990? (yes or no response)

- Did Joe Lambright receive a degree from your school? (looking for a yes-no answer, not the details.

When you call with this kind of request, be sure to identify yourself up front as someone with an obviously proper need to know. For example—
- I'm a reporter doing a story on Steve Gallagher
- I've got a new employee named Carol Fox
- Marc Dauphinais applied for a loan with us (bank)
- I'm about to sign a large contract with Jean Lurtsema

Identifying information

Although it is obvious that you must give the name of the student or graduate in order to obtain information about him or her, you should not overlook the possibility that the person went by another name or name variation while in school. The clear example of this is a married woman, but there is also the possibility that someone who today goes by the moniker C. Alexander Ernst, was just plain Carl A. Ernst when he was in school.

Other Searching Nuances to Keep in Mind
- At larger universities, it will help if you know the student's degree or major. This is especially true if you are trying to obtain information by telephone.
- Older records are usually archived. Whether they are on microfiche or stored in a box in the basement, count on it taking longer for the school to complete your search.
- Branch campuses generally do not maintain official transcript files; however, many, when asked by a requester with a legitimate purpose, will confirm attendance or a degree.
- Some schools allow students to block or restrict access to their records. If this happens to you, a signed release is advised. On the other hand some schools which are restrictive by nature will permit the student to have a release in his or her file to facilitate a background check. It wouldn't hurt to ask if a school indicates they have such a policy.
- Many schools who accept FAX requests ask that a written request follow in the mail. Most school consider any information FAXed back to a requestor to be unofficial or uncertified.

Use Common Sense

When you are requesting your a transcript and have a signed release from the graduate him or herself, make certain that you have all the information the registrar will need to complete your request in a timely manner. This information might include the address and telephone number of the graduate in case the school wants to verify the request directly with the graduate. Also, if the college had an internal identification number system, include that number as well if available.

If a subject or an employee claims to have a four-year (or higher) degree from an institution that offers only a two-year associate's degree, you have an immediate indication of that person's character.

Always include in your letter of request a note that the Registrar should feel free to call you collect or at your free 800 number if she has any questions about your request.

Just as with a telephone call, include in your cover note a proper valid reason for your request, and indicate the urgency of your request as well.

Even if not requested, we advise always to include a prepaid return envelope (SASE) for the results. This, again, is a matter of courtesy that is likely to get you a better than average level of service.

Happy searching!

The Sourcebook of College and University Records

Section One

Accredited, Degree Granting College and University Profiles

Editor's Note: New Telephone Area Code Changes

- Southern Alabama • Effective 1/15/95, the southern half of Alabama (Montgomery area) switched from **Code 205** to **Code 334**. The end of the overlap period is 5/13/95.

- Washington • Effective 1/15/95, all **Code 206** outside Washington counties of King, Pierce, and Snohomish changed to **Code 360**. The end of the overlap period is 7/9/95.

- Arizona • Effective the Spring of 1995, all of Arizona, except for the Phoenix metro area of Maricopa County, changed from **Code 602** to **Code 520**. The overlap period will end 7/95.

- Southwest Florida • Effective May 28, 1995, **Code 941** was created from **Code 813**, except for Tampa which will remain 813. The overlap period ends March 3, 1996.

- Northern Virginia • Effective July 15, 1995, **Code 540** was created from **Code 703**. This will not include the DC Suburban area. The overlap period ends Jan. 27, 1996.

- Connecticut • Effective August 28, 1995, **Code 860** will be created from **Code 203**. The entire state will change except for New Haven and Fairfield counties. The overlap period ends Oct. 4, 1996.

- Southern California • Effective September 2, 1995, **Code 562** will overlay **Code 310** for cellular phones and pagers only.

- Eastern Tennessee • Effective September 11, 1995, **Code 423** will be created from **Code 615**. The overlap period ends Feb. 26, 1996.

- Oregon • Effective November 5, 1995, **Code 541** will be created from **Code 503**. The entire state will change except for the geographic region from Salem to Portland. The overlap period ends Feb. 26, 1996.

A

Abilene Christian University, Registrar, ACU Station Box 7940, Abilene, TX 79699, 915-674-2235 (FAX: 915-674-2238). Hours: 8AM-Noon, 1-5PM. Records go back to 1906. Alumni Records Office: ACU Box 8381, Abilene, TX 79699, 915-674-2622. Degrees granted: Bachelors; Masters; Doctorate. Adverse incident record source: Student Services, 914-674-2630.

Attendance and degree information available by phone, FAX, mail. Search requires name plus social security number, date of birth. Other helpful information: approximate years of attendance. No fee for information.

Transcripts available by FAX, mail. Search requires name plus social security number, date of birth, signed release. Other helpful information: approximate years of attendance. No fee up to five transcripts. More than five are $2.00 each. FedEx service is available.

Major credit cards accepted for payment.

Abilene Intercollegiate School of Nursing, Registrar, 2149 Hickory, Abilene, TX 79601, 915-672-2441. Hours: 8AM-5PM. Records go back to 1945. Alumni records are maintained here also. Call 915-672-2441. Degrees granted: Associate; Bachelors.

Attendance and degree information available by phone, mail. Search requires name plus social security number, date of birth, exact years of attendance. No fee for information.

Transcripts available by mail. Search requires name plus social security number, date of birth, exact years of attendance, signed release. Fee is $4.00.

Abraham Baldwin Agricultural College, Registrar's Office, ABAC 3, 2802 Moore Hwy, Tifton, GA 31794-2601, 912-386-3236 (FAX: 912-386-7006). Hours: 8AM-5PM. Degrees granted: Associate. Adverse incident record source: Public Safety, 912-386-3274.

Attendance and degree information available by phone, FAX, mail. Search requires name only. Other helpful information: social security number, date of birth, approximate years of attendance. No fee for information.

Transcripts available by FAX, mail. Search requires name plus signed release. Other helpful information: social security number, date of birth, approximate years of attendance. No fee for transcripts.

Academy of Art College, Registrar, 79 New Montgomery, San Francisco, CA 94105, 415-274-2251. Hours: 9AM-5PM. Records go back to 1930. Degrees granted: Bachelors.

Attendance and degree information available by phone, mail. Search requires name plus social security number. Other helpful information: approximate years of attendance. No fee for information.

Transcripts available by mail. Search requires name plus social security number, signed release. Other helpful information: approximate years of attendance. First transcript fee is $10.00, and each additional request is $2.00.

Academy of Business College, Registrar, 3320 W Cheryl Dr Ste 155, Phoenix, AZ 85051, 602-942-4141 (FAX: 602-942-9082). Hours: 7:45AM-8PM M-Th, 7:45AM-5PM F. Records go back to 1982. Degrees granted: Associate.

Attendance and degree information available by phone, FAX, mail. Search requires name plus social security number, exact years of attendance. No fee for information.

Transcripts available by FAX, mail. Search requires name plus social security number, exact years of attendance, signed release. Fee is $5.00.

Academy of Chinese Culture and Health Sciences, Registrar, 1601 Clay St, Oakland, CA 94612, 510-763-7787. Hours: 9AM-5PM. Records go back 12 years. Degrees granted: Masters.

Attendance and degree information available by mail. Search requires name plus signed release. Other helpful information: social security number, date of birth, approximate years of attendance. Fee is $5.00. Expedited service available for $5.00.

Transcripts available by mail. Search requires name plus signed release. Other helpful information: social security number, date of birth, approximate years of attendance. Fee is $5.00. Expedited service available for $5.00.

Academy of Court Reporting, Registrar, 614 Superior Ave NW, Cleveland, OH 44113, 216-861-3222. Hours: 8AM-5PM. Records go back to 1978. Degrees granted: Associate.

Attendance and degree information available by mail. Search requires name plus social security number, date of birth, approximate years of attendance, signed release. No fee for information.

Transcripts available by mail. Search requires name plus social security number, date of birth, approximate years of attendance, signed release. Fee is $5.00.

Academy of Court Reporting, (Branch), Registrar, 2930 W Market St, Akron, OH 44313, 216-861-3222 (FAX: 216-861-4517). Hours: 8AM-5PM. Records go back to 1970. Degrees granted: Associate.

Attendance and degree information available by mail. Search requires name plus social security number, date of birth, approximate years of attendance, signed release. No fee for information.

Transcripts available by mail. Search requires name plus social security number, date of birth, approximate years of attendance, signed release. Fee is $5.00.

Academy of Court Reporting, (Branch), Registrar, 630 E Broad St, Columbus, OH 43215, 614-221-7770 (FAX: 614-221-8429). Hours: 8AM-5PM. Records go back to 1975. Degrees granted: Associate.

Attendance and degree information available by mail. Search requires name plus social security number, date of birth, exact years of attendance, signed release. No fee for information.

Transcripts available by mail. Search requires name plus social security number, date of birth, exact years of attendance, signed release. Fee is $5.00.

Academy of Court Reporting, (Branch), Registrar, 26111 Evergreen Rd Ste 101, Southfield, MI 48076, 810-353-4880 (FAX: 810-353-1670). Hours: 8:30AM-7PM. Records go back 5 years.

Attendance and degree information available by phone, FAX, mail. Search requires name plus social security number, approximate years of attendance. No fee for information.

Transcripts available by phone, mail. Search requires name plus social security number, approximate years of attendance. Fee is $2.00.

Academy of the New Church College, Registration, PO Box 717, Bryn Athyn, PA 19009, 215-947-4200. Hours: 8AM-4:30PM. Degrees granted: Associate; Bachelors.

Attendance information available by phone, mail. Search requires name only. No fee for information.

Degree information available by phone, mail. Search requires name plus social security number. No fee for information.

Transcripts available by phone, mail. Search requires name plus social security number, exact years of attendance, signed release. Fee is $3.00.

Students only may receive transcript information over the phone.

Adams State College, Registrar, Alamosa, CO 81102, 719-589-7331 (FAX: 719-589-7522). Hours: 8AM-4:45PM. Records go back to 1925. Degrees granted: Associate; Bachelors; Masters. Adverse incident record source: Public Safety, 719-589-7901: Dean of Students, 719-589-7221

Attendance and degree information available by phone, FAX, mail. Search requires name plus social security number. Other helpful information: approximate years of attendance. No fee for information.

Transcripts available by FAX, mail. Search requires name plus social security number, signed release. Other helpful information: approximate years of attendance. Fee is $2.00.

Unofficial transcript copies are $1.00 each.

Adelphi University, Registrar, South Ave, Garden City, NY 11530, 516-877-3300. Hours: 8:30AM-8PM M-Th; 8:30AM-4:30PM F.

Attendance and degree information available by phone, mail. Search requires name only. Other helpful information: social security number, approximate years of attendance. No fee for information.

Transcripts available by phone, mail. Search requires name plus signed release. Other helpful information: social security number, approximate years of attendance. Fee is $7.50. Expedited service available for $10.00.

Adirondack Community College, Registrar, Queensbury, NY 12804, 518-743-2280 (FAX: 518-745-1433). Hours: 8AM-5PM. Records go back to 1962. Alumni records are maintained here at the same phone number. Degrees granted: Associate.

Attendance and degree information available by phone, FAX, mail. Search requires name plus social security number, date of birth, exact years of attendance. No fee for information.

Transcripts available by written request only. Search requires name plus social security number, date of birth, exact years of attendance, signed release. Fee is $3.00.

Major credit cards accepted for payment.

Adler School of Professional Psychology, Registrar, 65 E Wacker Pl Ste 2100, Chicago, IL 60601-7203, 312-201-5900 (FAX: 312-201-5917). Hours: 9AM-5PM. Records go back to 1970. Alumni records are maintained here also. Call 312-201-5900. Degrees granted: Masters; Doctorate.

Attendance and degree information available by mail. Search requires name plus social security number, exact years of attendance, signed release. No fee for information.

Transcripts available by mail. Search requires name plus social security number, exact years of attendance, signed release. Fee is $5.00.

Major credit cards accepted for payment.

Adrian College, Registrar, 110 S Madison St, Adrian, MI 49221, 517-265-5161 (FAX: 517-264-3331). Hours: 8:30AM-5PM. Records go back to 1859. Alumni records are maintained here also. Call 517-265-5161. Degrees granted: Associate; Bachelors.

Attendance and degree information available by phone, FAX, mail. Search requires name only. Other helpful information: social security number, date of birth, approximate years of attendance. No fee for information.

Transcripts available by FAX, mail. Search requires name plus signed release. Other helpful information: social security number, date of birth, approximate years of attendance. Fee is $2.00. Expedited service available for $2.00.

Agnes Scott College, Registrar, 141 E College Ave, Decatur, GA 30030, 404-638-6137 (FAX: 404-638-6177). Hours: 8:30AM-4:30PM. Records go back to 1889. Alumni records are maintained here also. Call 404-638-6323. Degrees granted: Bachelors; Masters.

Attendance and degree information available by phone, FAX, mail. Search requires name only. Other helpful information: approximate years of attendance. No fee for information.

Transcripts available by FAX, mail. Search requires name plus signed release. Other helpful information: approximate years of attendance. Fee is $1.00.

Aguadilla Regional College, Registrar, PO Box 160, Ramey, PR 00604, 809-890-2681 X242 (FAX: 809-890-4543). Hours: 8AM-4:30PM. Records go back 23 years. Degrees granted: Associate. Adverse incident record source: Dean of Administration, 809-890-2681 X209.

Attendance and degree information available by FAX, mail. Search requires name plus signed release. Other helpful information: social security number. Fee is $1.00.

Transcripts available by mail. Search requires name plus signed release. Other helpful information: social security number. Fee is $1.00.

Aguinas College, Registrar, 4210 Harding Rd, Nashville, TN 37205, 615-297-7545 (FAX: 615-297-7557). Hours: 8AM-3:40PM. Degrees granted: Associate; Bachelors.

Attendance information available by phone, FAX, mail. Search requires name plus social security number. Other helpful information: date of birth. No fee for information.

Degree information available by phone, FAX, mail. Search requires name plus social security number. Other helpful information: date of birth, approximate years of attendance. No fee for information.

Transcripts available by FAX, mail. Search requires name plus social security number, signed release. Other helpful information: date of birth, approximate years of attendance. Fee is $3.00. Expedited service available for $5.00.

Major credit cards accepted for payment.

Aiken Technical College, Registrar, PO Box 696, Aiken, SC 29802-0696, 803-593-9231 (FAX: 803-593-6641). Hours: 7:30AM-7:30PM. Records go back to 1972. Alumni records are maintained here also. Call 803-593-9231 X1263. Degrees granted: Associate. Adverse incident record source: Dean of Students.

Attendance and degree information available by phone, FAX, mail. Search requires name plus social security number, approximate years of attendance, signed release. Other helpful information: date of birth, exact years of attendance. No fee for information.

Transcripts available by FAX, mail. Search requires name plus social security number, approximate years of attendance, signed release. Other helpful information: date of birth, exact years of attendance. Fee is $5.00.

Major credit cards accepted for payment.

Aims Community College, Registrar, PO Box 69, Greeley, CO 80632, 303-330-8008 X440 (FAX: 303-339-6669). Hours: 8AM-5:30PM Summers closed Friday. Records go back to 1967. Degrees granted: Associate. Adverse incident record source: Dean of Student Services, 303-330-8008 X225.

Attendance and degree information available by phone, FAX, mail. Search requires name only. Other helpful information: social security number, date of birth, approximate years of attendance. No fee for information.

Transcripts available by FAX, mail. Search requires name plus signed release. Other helpful information: social security number, date of birth, approximate years of attendance. No fee for transcripts.

Air Force Institute of Technology, Registrar, 2950 P St, Wright-Patterson AFB, OH 45433, 513-255-2816 (FAX: 513-255-2791). Hours: 7:30AM-5PM. Records go back to 1951. Alumni records are maintained here also. Call 513-255-9623. Degrees granted: Masters; Doctorate.

Attendance and degree information available by FAX, mail. Search requires name plus social security number, date of birth, approximate years of attendance, signed release. No fee for information.

School does not provide transcripts. Search requires name plus social security number, date of birth, approximate years of attendance, signed release. No fee for transcripts.

Include a self addressed stamped envelope with mail request.

Alabama Agricultural and Mechanical University, Registrar, PO Box 908, Normal, AL 35762, 205-851-5254 (FAX: 205-851-5253). Hours: 8AM-5PM. Degrees granted: Associate; Bachelors; Masters; Doctorate. Adverse incident record source: Public Safety, 205-851-5555.

Attendance and degree information available by phone, FAX, mail. Search requires name only. Other helpful information: social security number, date of birth, approximate years of attendance. No fee for information.

Transcripts available by FAX, mail. Search requires name plus signed release. Other helpful information: social security number, date of birth, approximate years of attendance. Fee is $3.00.

Alabama Aviation and Technical College, Registrar, PO Box 1209, Ozark, AL 36361-1209, 334-774-5113 (FAX: 334-774-5113). Hours: 7:45AM-4:30PM. Records go back to 1960. Alumni records are maintained here at the same phone number. Degrees granted: Associate.

Attendance and degree information available by phone, FAX, mail. Search requires name plus social security number. Other helpful information: approximate years of attendance. No fee for information.

Transcripts available by FAX, mail. Search requires name plus social security number, signed release. Other helpful information: approximate years of attendance. Fee is $2.00.

Alabama Southern Community College, Registrar, PO Box 2000, Monroeville, AL 36461, 205-575-3156 X 252. Hours: 7:30AM-4:30PM. Records go back to 1965. Degrees granted: Associate.

Attendance and degree information available by phone, mail. Search requires name plus social security number. No fee for information.

Transcripts available by mail. Search requires name plus social security number, exact years of attendance, signed release. No fee for transcripts.

Alabama Southern Community College, (Thomasville), Registrar, Hwy 43 S, Thomasville, AL 36784, 334-575-3156 X252 (FAX: 334-575-5356). Records are not housed here. They are located at Alabama Southern Community College, Registrar, PO Box 2000, Monroeville, AL 36461.

Alabama State University, Registrar, 915 S Jackson St, Montgomery, AL 36101-0271, 334-293-4243 (FAX: 334-834-0336). Hours: 8AM-6PM M-Th, 8AM-5PM F. Records go back to 1874. Alumni records are maintained here also. Call 334-293-4280. Degrees granted: Associate; Bachelors; Masters. Adverse incident record source: Security, 334-293-4400.

Attendance information available by phone, FAX, mail. Search requires name plus social security number. No fee for information.

Degree information available by phone, FAX, mail. Search requires name plus social security number, exact years of attendance. No fee for information.

Transcripts available by mail. Search requires name plus social security number, exact years of attendance, signed release. Fee is $2.00. Expedited service available for $4.00.

Alamance Community College, Registrars Office, Student Services, PO Box 8000, Graham, NC 27253-8000, 910-578-2002 (FAX: 910-578-1987). Hours: 8AM-8PM M-Th; 8AM-5PM F. Records go back to 1959. Degrees granted: Associate. Adverse incident record source: Security Chief, 910-578-2002 X4405.

Attendance and degree information available by phone, FAX, mail. Search requires name only. Other helpful information: social security number, date of birth, approximate years of attendance. No fee for information.

Transcripts available by FAX, mail. Search requires name plus signed release. Other helpful information: social security number, date of birth, approximate years of attendance. Fee is $2.00.

Alaska Bible College, Registrar, College Rd, Box 289, Glennallen, AK 99588, 907-822-3201 (FAX: 907-822-5027). Hours: 8AM-Noon, 1-5PM. Records go back to 1970. Degrees granted: Associate; Bachelors. Adverse incident record source: Alaska State Troopers, 907-822-3263.

Attendance and degree information available by phone, FAX, mail. Search requires name only. No fee for information.

Transcripts available by FAX, mail. Search requires name plus signed release. Fee is $5.00.

Alaska Junior College, Registrar, 800 E Diamond Blvd Ste 3-215, Anchorage, AK 99515, 907-349-1905 (FAX: 907-349-9802). Hours: 8AM-6:30PM. Records go back to 1963. Degrees granted: Associate.

Attendance information available by phone, FAX, mail. Search requires name plus exact years of attendance. Other helpful information: social security number, approximate years of attendance. No fee for information.

Degree information available by phone, FAX, mail. Search requires name only. Other helpful information: social security number, date of birth. No fee for information.

Transcripts available by FAX, mail. Search requires name plus signed release. Other helpful information: social security number, date of birth. Fee is $5.00.

Major credit cards accepted for payment.

Alaska Pacific University, Registrar, 4101 University Dr, Anchorage, AK 99508, 907-564-8210 (FAX: 907-562-4276). Hours: 8AM-5PM. Records go back 35 years. Degrees granted: Associate; Bachelors; Masters.

Attendance and degree information available by phone, mail. Search requires name plus signed release. Other helpful information: social security number, date of birth, approximate years of attendance. Fee is $4.00. Expedited service available for $10.00.

Transcripts available by mail. Search requires name plus signed release. Other helpful information: social security number, date of birth, approximate years of attendance. Fee is $4.00. Expedited service available for $10.00.

Major credit cards accepted for payment.

Albany College of Pharmacy of Union University, Registrar, 106 New Scotland Ave, Albany, NY 12208, 518-445-7221 (FAX: 518-445-7202). Hours: 8:30AM-4:30PM. Records go back to founding date. Alumni records are maintained here also. Call 518-445-7251. Degrees granted: Bachelors.

Attendance and degree information available by phone, FAX, mail. Search requires name only. Other helpful information: social security number, exact years of attendance. No fee for information.

Transcripts available by written request only. Search requires name plus signed release. Other helpful information: social security number. Fee is $3.00.

Albany Law School, Registrar, 80 New Scotland Ave, Albany, NY 12208, 518-445-2330. Hours: 8:30PM-4:30PM. Records go back to 1930. Alumni records are maintained here at the same phone number. Degrees granted: Doctorate.

Attendance and degree information available by phone, FAX, mail. Search requires name plus social security number, approximate years of attendance. No fee for information.

Transcripts available by mail. Search requires name plus social security number, approximate years of attendance, signed release. Fee is $2.00.

Albany Medical College of Union University, Registrar, 47 New Scotland Ave, Albany, NY 12208, 518-262-4970 X5523. Hours: 8AM-4PM. Records go back to 1839. Alumni records are maintained here also. Call 518-262-5970 X5033. Degrees granted: Masters; Doctorate.

Attendance and degree information available by mail. Search requires name plus social security number, approximate years of attendance, signed release. No fee for information.

Transcripts available by mail. Search requires name plus social security number, approximate years of attendance, signed release. Fee is $3.00.

Albany State College, Registrar, 504 College Dr, Albany, GA 31705-2794, 912-430-4638 (FAX: 912-430-2953). Hours: 8AM-5PM. Alumni records are maintained here also. Call 912-430-4600. Degrees granted: Bachelors; Masters. Adverse incident record source: Registrar, 912-430-4638.

Attendance information available by FAX, mail. Search requires name plus social security number, approximate years of attendance, signed release. Other helpful information: date of birth. No fee for information.

Degree information available by phone, FAX, mail. Search requires name plus social security number, approximate years of attendance, signed release. Other helpful information: date of birth. No fee for information.

Transcripts available by mail. Search requires name plus social security number, approximate years of attendance, signed release. Other helpful information: date of birth. Fee is $1.00.

Albertson College, Registrar, 2112 Cleveland Blvd, Caldwell, ID 83605, 208-459-5201 (FAX: 208-454-2077). Hours: 9AM-4PM. Records go back to 1891. Alumni records are maintained here also. Call 208-459-5300. Degrees granted: Bachelors; Masters.

Attendance and degree information available by phone, mail. Search requires name plus date of birth. No fee for information.

Transcripts available by mail. Search requires name plus date of birth, signed release. Fee is $3.00.

Albertus Magnus College, Registrar, New Haven, CT 06511-1189, 203-773-8514 (FAX: 203-773-3117). Hours: 9AM-5PM. Records go back to 1925. Alumni records are maintained here also. Call 203-773-8502. Degrees granted: Associate; Bachelors; Masters. Adverse incident record source: Student Services, 203-773-8541.

Attendance information available by phone, FAX, mail. Search requires name plus social security number, approximate years of attendance. No fee for information.

Degree information available by phone, mail. Search requires name plus social security number, approximate years of attendance. No fee for information.

Transcripts available by mail. Search requires name plus social security number, approximate years of attendance, signed release. Fee is $5.00.

Albion College, Registrar, 611 E Porter St, Albion, MI 49224, 517-629-0477 (FAX: 517-629-0509). Hours: 8AM-5PM. Records go back to 1835. Degrees granted: Bachelors.

Attendance and degree information available by phone, FAX, mail. Search requires name only. Other helpful information: social security number, date of birth, approximate years of attendance. No fee for information.

Transcripts available by FAX, mail. Search requires name plus signed release. Other helpful information: social security number, date of birth, approximate years of attendance. Fee is $3.00. Expedited service available for $13.00.

Albright College, Registrar, PO Box 15234, Reading, PA 19612-5234, 610-921-2381 (FAX: 610-921-2381). Hours: 8AM-4PM. Records go back to 1930. Alumni records are maintained here also. Call 610-921-2381. Degrees granted: Bachelors. Adverse incident record source: Dean of Students, 610-921-2381.

Attendance and degree information available by phone, FAX, mail. Search requires name only. Other helpful information: social security number, approximate years of attendance. No fee for information.

Transcripts available by FAX, mail. Search requires name plus signed release. Other helpful information: social security number, approximate years of attendance. No fee for transcripts.

Albuquerque Technical-Vocational Institute, Records Office, 525 Buena Vista Dr SE, Albuquerque, NM 87108, 505-224-3202. Hours: 8AM-7PM M-Th; 8AM-5PM F. Records go back to 1965. Degrees granted: Associate. Adverse incident record source: Student Services, 505-224-3020.

Attendance and degree information available by phone, mail. Search requires name plus date of birth. Other helpful information: social security number, approximate years of attendance. No fee for information.

Transcripts available by phone, mail. Search requires name plus date of birth, signed release. Other helpful information: social security number, approximate years of attendance. First five transcripts are free; additional ones are $1.00 each.

Alcorn State University, Registrar's Office, 1000 ASU Drive #420, Lorman, MS 39096-9402, 601-877-6170 (FAX: 601-877-6688). Hours: 8AM-5PM M-Th; 8AM-4PM F. Records go back to 1871. Degrees granted: Associate; Bachelors; Masters. Special programs- School of Nursing, Natchez Branch, 601-877-6550. Adverse incident record source: Security, 601-877-6390: Academic Affairs, 601-877-6142

Attendance and degree information available by phone, FAX, mail. Search requires name plus social security number. Other helpful information: date of birth, approximate years of attendance. No fee for information.

Transcripts available by mail. Search requires name plus social security number, date of birth, signed release. Other helpful information: approximate years of attendance. Fee is $2.00.

Major credit cards accepted for payment.

Alderson-Broaddus College, Registrar, Philippi, WV 26416, 304-457-6278 (FAX: 304-457-6239). Hours: 8AM-4:30PM. Records go back to 1895. Degrees granted: Associate; Bachelors; Masters. Adverse incident record source: Student Life.

Attendance and degree information available by phone, FAX, mail. Search requires name only. Other helpful information: social security number, approximate years of attendance. No fee for information.

Transcripts available by FAX, mail. Search requires name plus signed release. Other helpful information: social security number, approximate years of attendance. No fee for transcripts.

Confirm OK if no restriction on release.

Alexandria Technical College, Registrar, 1601 Jefferson St, Alexandria, MN 56308, 612-762-4470 (FAX: 612-762-4501). Hours: 8AM-4:30PM. Records go back to 1965. Degrees granted: Associate.

Attendance and degree information available by phone, FAX, mail. Search requires name plus approximate years of attendance, signed release. Other helpful information: social security number. No fee for information.

Transcripts available by FAX, mail. Search requires name plus approximate years of attendance, signed release. Other helpful information: social security number. Fee is $0.50.

Alfred Adler Institute of Minnesota, Registrar, 1001 Hwy 7 Ste 344, Hopkins, MN 55305, 612-988-4170 (FAX: 612-988-4171). Hours: 8:30AM-4:30pm. Records go back 12 years. Alumni records are maintained here at the same phone number. Degrees granted: Masters. Adverse incident record source: Registrar, 612-988-4170.

Attendance information available by mail. Search requires name plus approximate years of attendance. Fee is $3.00.

Degree information available by mail. Search requires name plus approximate years of attendance, signed release. Fee is $3.00.

Transcripts available by mail. Search requires name plus signed release. Fee is $3.00.

Alfred University, Registrar, Main St, Alfred, NY 14802, 607-871-2122 (FAX: 607-871-2347). Hours: 8:30AM-4:30PM. Records go back to 1925. Alumni records are maintained here also. Call 607-871-2114. Degrees granted: Masters; Doctorate; Ph.D.

Attendance and degree information available by phone, FAX, mail. Search requires name plus date of birth. No fee for information.

Transcripts available by written request only. Search requires name plus date of birth, signed release. Fee is $5.00.

Alfred University, **(New York State College of Ceramics)**, Registrar, Alfred, NY 14802, 607-871-2411. Records are not housed here. They are located at Alfred University, Registrar, Main St, Alfred, NY 14802.

Alice Lloyd College, Registrar, Purpose Rd, Pippa Passes, KY 41844, 606-368-2101 X4502 (FAX: 606-368-2125). Hours: 8AM-4:30PM. Records go back to 1923. Alumni records are maintained here also. Call 606-368-2101. Degrees granted: Bachelors.

Attendance and degree information available by phone, FAX, mail. Search requires name only. Other helpful information: social security number, date of birth, approximate years of attendance. No fee for information.

Transcripts available by written request only. Search requires name plus signed release. Other helpful information: social security number, date of birth, approximate years of attendance. Fee is $2.00. Expedited service available for $2.00.

Allan Hancock College, Registrar, 800 S College Dr, Santa Maria, CA 93454, 805-922-6966 X3277 (FAX: 805-928-7905). Hours: 8AM-6PM M-Th; 8AM-4PM F. Records go back to 1954. Degrees granted: Associate. Adverse incident record source: 805-922-6966 X3277.

Attendance and degree information available by phone, FAX, mail. Search requires name plus social security number, signed release. Other helpful information: date of birth, approximate years of attendance. No fee for information.

Transcripts available by FAX, mail. Search requires name plus social security number, signed release. Other helpful information: date of birth, approximate years of attendance. Fee is $2.00. Expedited transcripts by FAX are $5.00 or $10.00.

Major credit cards accepted for payment.

Allegany Community College, Registrar, Willowbrook Rd, Cumberland, MD 21502, 301-724-7700 X212 (FAX: 301-724-6892). Hours: 9AM-5PM. Records go back to 1961. Alumni records are maintained here at the same phone number. Degrees granted: Associate.

Attendance and degree information available by phone, mail. Search requires name plus social security number. No fee for information.

Transcripts available by mail. Search requires name plus social security number, exact years of attendance, signed release. Fee is $2.00.

Allegheny College, Registrar, 520 N Main St, Meadville, PA 16335, 814-332-2357 (FAX: 814-337-0988). Hours: 8AM-5PM.

Degrees granted: Bachelors. Adverse incident record source: Dean of Students, 814-332-4356.

Attendance and degree information available by phone, FAX, mail. Search requires name plus approximate years of attendance. Other helpful information: social security number, date of birth. No fee for information.

Transcripts available by mail. Search requires name plus approximate years of attendance, signed release. Other helpful information: social security number, date of birth. Fee is $5.00. Major credit cards accepted for payment.

Allen County Community College, Registrar, 1801 N Cottonwood, Iola, KS 66749, 316-365-5116 (FAX: 316-365-3284). Hours: 8AM-5PM. Records go back to 1923. Degrees granted: Associate.

Attendance and degree information available by phone, FAX, mail. Search requires name plus social security number, date of birth. Other helpful information: approximate years of attendance. No fee for information.

Transcripts available by mail. Search requires name plus social security number, date of birth, signed release. Other helpful information: approximate years of attendance. Fee is $2.00. Expedited service available for $2.00.

Major credit cards accepted for payment.

Allen University, Registrar, 1530 Harden St, Columbia, SC 29204, 803-254-4165 (FAX: 803-376-5709). Hours: 9AM-5PM. Records go back 90+ years. Degrees granted: Associate; Bachelors. Adverse incident record source: Student Affairs, 803-376-5714.

Attendance information available by FAX, mail. Search requires name plus social security number, signed release. Other helpful information: date of birth, approximate years of attendance. No fee for information.

Degree information available by FAX, mail. Search requires name plus social security number, signed release. Other helpful information: date of birth, approximate years of attendance. No fee for information.

Transcripts available by mail. Search requires name plus social security number, signed release. Other helpful information: date of birth, approximate years of attendance. Fee is $5.00.

Allentown College of St. Francis de Sales, Registrar, 2755 Station Ave, Center Valley, PA 18034, 610-282-1100 X1354 (FAX: 610-282-2850). Hours: 8:30AM-4:45PM. Records go back to 1965. Alumni records are maintained here also. Call 610-282-1100 X1245. Degrees granted: Bachelors; Masters. Adverse incident record source: Student Affairs, 610-282-1100 X1261.

Attendance and degree information available by phone, FAX, mail. Search requires name only. Other helpful information: social security number, approximate years of attendance. No fee for information.

Transcripts available by mail. Search requires name plus signed release. Other helpful information: social security number, approximate years of attendance. Fee is $3.00.

Alma College, Registrar, Alma, MI 48801, 517-463-7348 (FAX: 517-463-7277). Hours: 8AM-Noon,1-5PM. Records go back to founding date. Degrees granted: Bachelors.

Attendance and degree information available by phone, FAX, mail. Search requires name only. Other helpful information: social security number, date of birth, approximate years of attendance. No fee for information.

Transcripts available by FAX, mail. Search requires name plus signed release. Other helpful information: social security number, date of birth, approximate years of attendance. Fee is $2.00. Expedited service available for $15.00.

Alpena Community College, Registrar, 666 Johnson St, Alpena, MI 49707, 517-356-9021 (FAX: 517-356-0980). Hours: 8AM-4:30PM. Degrees granted: Associate.

Attendance and degree information available by written request only. Search requires name plus social security number, signed release. Other helpful information: date of birth, approximate years of attendance. No fee for information.

Transcripts available by written request only. Search requires name plus social security number, signed release. Other helpful information: date of birth, approximate years of attendance. Fee is $1.00.

Altoona School of Commerce, Registrar, 508 58th St, Altoona, PA 16602, 814-944-6134 (FAX: 814-944-4684). Hours: 8AM-5PM. Records go back to 1960. Alumni records are maintained here also. Call 814-944-6134. Degrees granted: Associate.

Attendance information available by phone, FAX, mail. Search requires name plus social security number. No fee for information.

Degree information available by phone, FAX, mail. Search requires name plus social security number, exact years of attendance. No fee for information.

Transcripts available by FAX, mail. Search requires name plus social security number, exact years of attendance, signed release. No fee for transcripts.

Alvernia College, Registrar, 400 St Bernadine St, Reading, PA 19607, 610-796-8201 (FAX: 610-777-6632). Hours: 8AM-4:30PM. Records go back 34 years. Degrees granted: Associate; Bachelors. Adverse incident record source: Student Services, 610-796-8289.

Attendance and degree information available by phone, FAX, mail. Search requires name plus approximate years of attendance. Other helpful information: social security number. No fee for information.

Transcripts available by mail. Search requires name plus signed release. Other helpful information: social security number, date of birth, approximate years of attendance. Fee is $5.00. Expedited service available for $1.00.

Need to state whether graduated and date. Major credit cards accepted for payment.

Alverno College, Registrar, PO Box 343922, 3401 S 39th St, Milwaukee, WI 53234-3922, 414-382-6370 (FAX: 414-382-6354). Hours: 8AM-5PM. Records go back to 1950s. Alumni records are maintained here also. Call 414-382-6090. Degrees granted: Associate; Bachelors.

Attendance and degree information available by phone, FAX, mail. Search requires name plus signed release. Other helpful information: social security number, approximate years of attendance. No fee for information.

Transcripts available by mail. Search requires name plus signed release. Other helpful information: social security number, approximate years of attendance. Fee is $3.00.

Alvin Community College, Registrar, 3110 Mustang Rd, Alvin, TX 77511-4898, 713-388-4615 (FAX: 713-388-4929). Hours: 8AM-5PM. Records go back to 1949. Alumni records are maintained here also. Call 713-388-4614. Degrees granted: Associate.

School will not confirm attendance or degree information. Search requires name plus social security number, date of birth, signed release. No fee for information. Include stamped envelope.

Transcripts available by FAX, mail. Search requires name plus social security number, date of birth, signed release. No fee for transcripts. Expedite fee is based on cost of service.'

Amarillo College, Registrar, PO Box 447, Amarillo, TX 79178, 806-371-5030 (FAX: 806-371-5066). Hours: 8AM-4:30PM. Records go back to 1929. Alumni records are maintained here also. Call 806-371-5030 X5106. Degrees granted: Associate.

Attendance and degree information available by mail. Search requires name plus social security number, date of birth, exact years of attendance. No fee for information.

Transcripts available by mail. Search requires name plus social security number, date of birth, exact years of attendance, signed release. Fee is $2.00.

Amber University, Registrar, 1700 Eastgate Dr, Garland, TX 75041, 214-279-6511 (FAX: 214-279-9773). Hours: 8AM-4:30PM. Alumni records are maintained here at the same phone number. Degrees granted: Bachelors; Masters.

Attendance and degree information available by mail. Search requires name plus social security number, exact years of attendance, signed release. No fee for information.

Transcripts available by mail. Search requires name plus social security number, exact years of attendance, signed release. Fee is $5.00.

American Academy McAllister Institute of Funeral Service, Inc., Registrar, 450 W 56th St, New York, NY 10019, 212-757-1190. Hours: 9AM-3:30PM. Records go back to 1930. Degrees granted: Associate.

Attendance and degree information available by mail. Search requires name plus social security number, approximate years of attendance, signed release. No fee for information.

Transcripts available by mail. Search requires name plus social security number, approximate years of attendance, signed release. Fee is $3.00.

American Academy of Art, Registrar, 332 S Michigan Ave #300, Chicago, IL 60604-4301, 312-461-0600. Hours: 8AM-3:30PM. Records go back to 1923. Degrees granted: Associate.

Attendance and degree information available by phone, FAX, mail. Search requires name plus social security number, date of birth, signed release. Other helpful information: approximate years of attendance. Fee is $3.00.

Transcripts available by mail. Search requires name plus social security number, date of birth, signed release. Other helpful information: approximate years of attendance. Fee is $3.00.

Major credit cards accepted for payment.

American Academy of Dramatic Arts, Registrar, 120 Madison Ave, New York, NY 10016, 212-686-0250 (FAX: 212-545-7934). Hours: 9AM-2PM, 3-5PM. Records go back to 1885. Degrees granted: Associate.

Attendance information available by FAX, mail. Search requires name plus social security number, date of birth, approximate years of attendance, signed release. No fee for information.

Degree information available by written request only. Search requires name only. No fee for information.

Transcripts available by written request only. Search requires name plus social security number, date of birth, approximate years of attendance, signed release. Fee is $5.00.

Specify day or evening classes.

American Academy of Dramatic Arts West, Registrar, 2550 Paloma St, Pasadena, CA 91107, 818-798-0777 (FAX: 818-798-5047). Hours: 8:30AM-5PM. Degrees granted: Associate.

Attendance and degree information available by phone. Search requires name plus social security number, approximate years of attendance. No fee for information.

Transcripts available by written request only. Search requires name plus social security number, signed release. Other helpful information: date of birth, approximate years of attendance. Fee is $3.00. Expedited service available for $3.00.

American Baptist College, Registrar, 1800 Baptist World Ctr, Nashville, TN 37207, 615-224-7877. Hours: 8AM-4:30PM. Records go back to 1924. Alumni records are maintained here also. Call 615-228-7877. Degrees granted: Bachelors.

Attendance and degree information available by phone, mail. Search requires name plus exact years of attendance. No fee for information.

Transcripts available by mail. Search requires name plus exact years of attendance, signed release. Fee is $2.00.

American Baptist Seminary of the West, Registrar, 2606 Dwight Way, Berkeley, CA 94704-3029, 510-841-1905. Hours: 8AM-4:30PM. Degrees granted: Masters.

Attendance information available by phone, mail. Search requires name plus social security number. No fee for information.

Degree information available by phone, mail. Search requires name plus social security number. No fee for information.

Transcripts available by mail. Search requires name plus social security number, signed release. Fee is $5.00.

American College, Registrar, 3330 Peachtree Rd NE, Atlanta, GA 30326, 404-231-9000 (FAX: 404-231-1062). Hours: 8AM-4:30PM. Alumni records are maintained here at the same phone number. Degrees granted: Associate; Bachelors.

Attendance and degree information available by phone, FAX, mail. Search requires name only. Other helpful information: social security number, date of birth, approximate years of attendance. No fee for information.

Transcripts available by mail. Search requires name only. Other helpful information: social security number, date of birth, approximate years of attendance. Fee is $2.00.

Credit card charge minimum $10.00.

American College, Registrar, 270 Bryn Mawr Ave, Bryn Mawr, PA 19010, 610-526-1462 (FAX: 610-526-1465). Hours: 8:30AM-5PM M-Th, 8:30AM-4PM F. Records go back to 1927. Degrees granted: Masters. Adverse incident record source: Registrar, 610-526-1462.

Attendance information available by phone, FAX, mail. Search requires name plus social security number. No fee for information.

Degree information available by phone, FAX, mail. Search requires name plus social security number, exact years of attendance. Other helpful information: date of birth. No fee for information.

Transcripts available by FAX, mail. Search requires name plus social security number, exact years of attendance, signed release. Other helpful information: date of birth. Fee is $15.00.

Major credit cards accepted for payment.

American College for the Applied Arts, (Branch), Registrar, 110 Marylebone High St, London, England, UK W1M 3DB, 011-44-171-486-1772 (FAX: 011-44-171-935-8144). Hours: 9AM-5:30PM. Records go back to 1976. Alumni records are maintained here at the same phone number. Degrees granted: Bachelors; Masters.

Attendance and degree information available by FAX, mail. Search requires name plus social security number, date of birth, exact years of attendance, signed release. No fee for information.

Transcripts available by FAX, mail. Search requires name plus social security number, date of birth, exact years of attendance, signed release. Fee is $2 p.

American College for the Applied Arts, (Branch), Registrar, 1651 Westwood Blvd, Los Angeles, CA 90024, 310-470-2000. Hours: 9AM-5PM M-Th. Records go back 12 years. Alumni records are maintained here at the same phone number. Degrees granted: Associate; Bachelors.

Attendance information available by phone, mail. Search requires name only. Other helpful information: social security number, date of birth, approximate years of attendance. No fee for information.

Degree information available by phone, mail. Search requires name plus approximate years of attendance. Other helpful information: social security number, date of birth. No fee for information.

Transcripts available by mail. Search requires name plus social security number, date of birth, approximate years of attendance, signed release. Fee is $2.00. Expedited service available for $10.00.

Note if student attended another American College campus. Major credit cards accepted for payment.

American College of Traditional Chinese Medicine, Registrar, 455 Arkansas St, San Francisco, CA 94107, 415-282-7600 (FAX: 415-287-0856). Hours: 9AM-5PM. Records go back to 1980. Degrees granted: Masters. Certification: TCM.

Attendance information available by written request only. Search requires name only. Other helpful information: social security number, date of birth, approximate years of attendance. No fee for information.

Degree information available by phone, FAX, mail. Search requires name only. Other helpful information: social security number, date of birth, approximate years of attendance. No fee for information.

Transcripts available by FAX, mail. Search requires name only. Other helpful information: social security number, date of birth, approximate years of attendance. Fee is $5.00.

American Conservatory Theater, Registrar, 30 Grant Ave, San Francisco, CA 94108, 415-834-3350. Degrees granted: Masters.

Attendance and degree information available by phone, FAX, mail. Search requires name plus signed release. Other helpful information: exact years of attendance. No fee for information.

Transcripts available by FAX, mail. Search requires name plus signed release. Other helpful information: exact years of attendance. Fee is $5.00. Expedited service available for $7.00.

American Conservatory of Music, Registrar, 16 N Wabash Ave Ste 1850, Chicago, IL 60602-4792, 312-263-4161 (FAX: 312-263-5832). Hours: 9AM-6PM. Records go back to 1886. Alumni records are maintained here at the same phone number. Degrees granted: Associate; Bachelors; Masters; Doctorate.

Attendance and degree information available by phone, mail. Search requires name plus exact years of attendance, signed release. Other helpful information: approximate years of attendance. No fee for information.

Transcripts available by mail. Search requires name plus exact years of attendance, signed release. Other helpful information: approximate years of attendance. Fee is $15.00.

Include a self addressed stamped envelope with mail request. Major credit cards accepted for payment.

American Film Institute Center for Advanced Film/TV Studies, Registrar, 2021 N Western Ave, Los Angeles, CA 90027, 213-856-7714 (FAX: 213-467-4578). Hours: 9AM-5:30PM. Records go back 82 years. Degrees granted: Masters.

Attendance and degree information available by written request only. Search requires name plus social security number, date of birth, approximate years of attendance, signed release. Fee is $5.00.

Transcripts available by written request only. Search requires name plus social security number, date of birth, approximate years of attendance, signed release. Fee is $5.00.

American Graduate School of International Management, Registrar, Thunderbird Campus, 15249 N 59 Ave, Glendale, AZ 85306, 602-978-7980. Hours: 9AM-4:30PM. Records go back 49 years. Degrees granted: Masters.

Attendance information available by phone, FAX, mail. Search requires name only. No fee for information.

Degree information available by phone, FAX, mail. Search requires name plus exact years of attendance. No fee for information.

Transcripts available by mail. Search requires name plus approximate years of attendance, signed release. Other helpful information: exact years of attendance. No fee for transcripts.

American Indian Bible College of the Assemblies of God, Registrar, 10020 N 15th Ave, Phoenix, AZ 85021, 602-944-3335 X15 (FAX: 602-943-8299). Hours: 8AM-4:30PM. Records go back to 1958. Degrees granted: Associate; Bachelors. Adverse incident record source: Dean of Students, 602-944-3335 X20.

Attendance information available by mail. Search requires name plus signed release. Other helpful information: approximate years of attendance. No fee for information.

Degree information available by written request only. Search requires name plus signed release. Other helpful information: approximate years of attendance. No fee for information.

Transcripts available by written request only. Search requires name plus signed release. Other helpful information: approximate years of attendance. Fee is $2.00.

Include a self addressed stamped envelope with mail request.

American Institute, Registrar, 3343 N Central Ave, Phoenix, AZ 85012, 602-252-4986 (FAX: 602-252-7440). Hours: 8AM-6PM. Degrees granted: Associate.

Attendance and degree information available by phone, FAX, mail. Search requires name plus social security number, date of birth. Other helpful information: approximate years of attendance. No fee for information.

Transcripts available by written request only. Search requires name plus social security number, date of birth, approximate years of attendance, signed release. Fee is $5.00.
Include program attended in request.

American Institute of Business, Registrar, 2500 Fleur Dr, Des Moines, IA 50321, 515-244-4221 (FAX: 515-244-6773). Hours: 7AM-4:30PM. Alumni records are maintained here at the same phone number. Degrees granted: Associate.

Attendance and degree information available by phone, mail. Search requires name plus approximate years of attendance. Other helpful information: social security number, date of birth. No fee for information.

Transcripts available by mail. Search requires name plus approximate years of attendance, signed release. Other helpful information: social security number, date of birth. Fee is $3.00.

American Institute of Commerce, Registrar, 1801 E Kimberly Rd, Davenport, IA 52807, 319-355-3500 (FAX: 319-355-1320). Hours: 8AM-5PM. Records go back 50 years. Degrees granted: Associate.

Attendance and degree information available by phone, FAX, mail. Search requires name only. Other helpful information: social security number, date of birth, approximate years of attendance. No fee for information.

Transcripts available by mail. Search requires name plus signed release. Other helpful information: social security number, date of birth, approximate years of attendance. Fee is $4.00.
Major credit cards accepted for payment.

American Institute of Commerce, **(Branch)**, Registrar, 2302 W First St, Cedar Falls, IA 50613, 319-277-0220 (FAX: 319-268-0978). Hours: 8AM-5PM.

Attendance information available by written request only. Search requires name plus social security number, signed release. Other helpful information: date of birth, approximate years of attendance. Fee is $4.00.

Degree information available by written request only. Search requires name plus signed release. Other helpful information: social security number, date of birth, approximate years of attendance. Fee is $4.00.

Transcripts available by written request only. Search requires name plus social security number, signed release. Other helpful information: date of birth, approximate years of attendance. Fee is $4.00.

American Institute of Design, Registrar, 1616 Orthodox St, Philadelphia, PA 19124-3706, 215-288-8200 X23 (FAX: 215-288-0466). Hours: 8AM-5PM. Degrees granted: Associate.

Attendance and degree information available by phone, FAX, mail. Search requires name plus social security number, date of birth, exact years of attendance. No fee for information.

Transcripts available by mail. Search requires name plus social security number, date of birth, exact years of attendance, signed release. Fee is $5.00.

American International College, Registrar, 1000 State St, Springfield, MA 01109, 413-737-6212 (FAX: 413-737-2803). Hours: 8:30AM-4:30PM. Records go back to 1885. Alumni records are maintained here also. Call 413-737-7000. Degrees granted: Bachelors; Masters.

Attendance and degree information available by mail. Search requires name plus social security number, exact years of attendance, signed release. No fee for information.

Transcripts available by mail. Search requires name plus social security number, exact years of attendance, signed release. Fee is $3.00.

American River College, Registrar, 4700 College Oak Dr, Sacramento, CA 95841, 916-484-8171. Hours: 7:30AM-8PM M-Th, 7:30AM-5PM F. Records go back to 1955. Alumni records are maintained here also. Call 916-568-3100 X8990. Degrees granted: Associate.

Attendance and degree information available by mail. Search requires name plus social security number, date of birth, exact years of attendance, signed release. No fee for information.

Transcripts available by mail. Search requires name plus social security number, date of birth, exact years of attendance, signed release. Fee is $2.00.

American Samoa Community College, Registrar, PO Box 2609, Pago Pago, AS 96799, 011-684-699-9155. Hours: 8AM-4PM. Records go back to 1976. Alumni records are maintained here at the same phone number. Degrees granted: Associate.

Attendance and degree information available by phone, mail. Search requires name plus social security number, date of birth, exact years of attendance. No fee for information.

Transcripts available by mail. Search requires name plus social security number, date of birth, exact years of attendance, signed release. Fee is $5.00.

American Schools of Professional Psychology, Registrar, 20 S Clark St 3rd Fl, Chicago, IL 60603, 312-201-0200 X610 (FAX: 312-201-1907). Hours: 8:30AM-5PM. Records go back to 1976. Alumni records are maintained here also. Call 312-201-0200 X610. Degrees granted: Masters; Doctorate. Adverse incident record source: Registrar, 312-201-0200 X610.

Attendance and degree information available by phone, FAX, mail. Search requires name plus social security number. No fee for information.

Transcripts available by mail. Search requires name plus social security number, exact years of attendance, signed release. No fee for transcripts.

American Schools of Professional Psychology, **(Georgia School of Professional Psychology)**, Registrar, 990 Hammond Dr NE, Atlanta, GA 30328, 404-671-1200 (FAX: 404-671-0476). Hours: 8:30AM-5:30PM. Records go back to 1990. Degrees granted: Masters; Doctorate. Adverse incident record source: Registrar, 404-671-1200.

Attendance and degree information available by phone, FAX, mail. Search requires name plus social security number. No fee for information.

Transcripts available by mail. Search requires name plus social security number, signed release. No fee for transcripts.
Information released unless restriction on file.

American Schools of Professional Psychology, **(Illinois School of Professional Psychology)**, Registrar, 20 S Clark St, Chicago, IL 60603, 312-341-6500 X0 (FAX: 312-922-1730). Hours: 8:30AM-5PM. Degrees granted: Masters; Doctorate.

Attendance information available by phone, FAX, mail. Search requires name plus social security number. Other helpful information: date of birth, approximate years of attendance. No fee for information.

Degree information available by phone, FAX, mail. Search requires name plus social security number. Other helpful information: approximate years of attendance. No fee for information.

Transcripts available by written request only. Search requires name plus social security number, signed release. Other helpful information: date of birth, approximate years of attendance. No fee for transcripts.

American Schools of Professional Psychology, (Minnesota School of Professional Psychology), Registrar, 3103 E 80th St Ste 290, Bloomington, MN 55420, 612-858-8800 (FAX: 612-858-3515). Hours: 8:30AM-5PM. Records go back 8 years. Degrees granted: Masters; Doctorate.

Attendance and degree information available by phone, FAX, mail. Search requires name plus social security number. Other helpful information: approximate years of attendance. No fee for information.

Transcripts available by FAX, mail. Search requires name plus social security number, signed release. Other helpful information: approximate years of attendance. No fee for transcripts.

Major credit cards accepted for payment.

American Technical Institute, Registrar, PO Box 8, Brunswick, TN 38014, 901-382-5857 (FAX: 901-385-7627). Hours: 9AM-5PM. Records go back to 1985.

Attendance and degree information available by written request only. Search requires name plus social security number, signed release. Other helpful information: date of birth, exact years of attendance. No fee for information.

Transcripts available by written request only. Search requires name plus social security number, signed release. Other helpful information: date of birth, exact years of attendance. Fee is $8.00.

American University, Registrar, 4400 Massachusetts Ave NW, Washington, DC 20016, 202-885-2200 (FAX: 202-885-1046). Hours: 9AM-6PM M-Th, 9AM-5PM F. Records go back to 1973. Alumni Records Office: Penley Campus, 140 Constitution Hall, Washington, DC 20016. Degrees granted: Bachelors; Masters; Doctorate. Adverse incident record source: Dean, 202-885-3310.

Attendance and degree information available by phone, FAX, mail. Search requires name plus social security number, approximate years of attendance. No fee for information.

Transcripts available by FAX, mail. Search requires name plus social security number, approximate years of attendance, signed release. No fee for transcripts.

American University of Puerto Rico, Registrar, PO Box 2037, Bayamon, PR 00621, 809-798-2022.

American University of Puerto Rico, (Branch Campus), Registrar, PO Box 929, Dorado, PR 00646, 809-796-2169.

American University of Puerto Rico, (Branch Campus), Registrar, PO Box 1082, Manati, PR 00701, 809-854-2835.

Amherst College, Registrar, Amherst, MA 01002, 413-542-2225 (FAX: 413-542-2227). Hours: 8:30AM-4:30PM. Records go back to 1800s. Alumni records are maintained here also. Call 413-542-5900. Degrees granted: Bachelors.

Attendance and degree information available by phone, FAX, mail. Search requires name plus social security number, signed release. No fee for information.

Transcripts available by FAX, mail. Search requires name plus social security number, signed release. Fee is $2.00.

Ancilla College, Registrar, PO Box 1, Donaldson, IN 46513, 219-936-8898 (FAX: 219-935-1773). Hours: 8AM-4:30PM. Records go back to 1937. Alumni records are maintained here at the same phone number. Degrees granted: Associate.

Attendance information available by phone, FAX, mail. Search requires name plus social security number. No fee for information.

Degree information available by mail. Search requires name plus social security number. No fee for information.

Transcripts available by mail. Search requires name plus social security number, exact years of attendance, signed release. Fee is $3.00.

Anderson College, Registrar, 316 Blvd, Anderson, SC 29621, 803-231-2120 (FAX: 803-231-2004). Hours: 8:30AM-4:30PM. Records go back to 1945. Alumni records are maintained here also. Call 803-231-2064. Degrees granted: Associate; Bachelors.

Attendance information available by phone, FAX, mail. Search requires name plus social security number, approximate years of attendance. Other helpful information: date of birth. No fee for information.

Degree information available by phone, FAX, mail. Search requires name plus social security number. Other helpful information: date of birth, approximate years of attendance. No fee for information.

Transcripts available by FAX, mail. Search requires name plus social security number, approximate years of attendance, signed release. Other helpful information: date of birth. Fee is $3.00.

Anderson University, Registrar, 1100 E Fifth St, Anderson, IN 46012-3462, 317-641-4160 (FAX: 317-641-3851). Hours: 8AM-5PM. Records go back to 1917. Alumni records are maintained here at the same phone number. Degrees granted: Associate; Bachelors; Masters; Doctorate. Adverse incident record source: Dean of Students, 317-641-4192.

Attendance and degree information available by phone, FAX, mail. Search requires name only. Other helpful information: social security number, date of birth, approximate years of attendance. No fee for information.

Transcripts available by FAX, mail. Search requires name plus signed release. Other helpful information: social security number, date of birth, approximate years of attendance. Fee is $3.00. Expedited service available for $5.00.

Andover College, Registrar, 901 Washington Ave, Portland, ME 04103, 207-774-6126 (FAX: 207-774-1715). Hours: 9AM-5PM. Records go back 69 years. Degrees granted: Associate.

Attendance and degree information available by phone, FAX, mail. Search requires name plus social security number, signed release. Other helpful information: date of birth, approximate years of attendance. No fee for information.

Transcripts available by phone, FAX, mail. Search requires name plus social security number, signed release. Other helpful information: date of birth, approximate years of attendance. Fee is $3.00.

Major credit cards accepted for payment.

Andover Newton Theological School, Registrar, 210 Herrick Rd, Newton Centre, MA 02159, 617-964-1100 X212 (FAX: 617-965-9756). Hours: 8:30AM-4:30PM. Records go back

77 years. Alumni records are maintained here also. Call 617-964-1100 X202. Degrees granted: Masters; Doctorate.

Attendance and degree information available by phone, FAX, mail. Search requires name plus exact years of attendance. Other helpful information: social security number, date of birth. No fee for information.

Transcripts available by mail. Search requires name plus signed release. Other helpful information: social security number, date of birth, approximate years of attendance. Fee is $2.00.

Andrew College, Registrar, 413 College St, Cuthbert, GA 31740-1395, 912-732-2171 (FAX: 912-732-2176). Hours: 8:30AM-Noon, 1-4:30PM. Records go back to 1883. Degrees granted: Associate.

Attendance information available by phone, FAX. Search requires name plus social security number, approximate years of attendance. Other helpful information: date of birth. No fee for information.

Degree information available by phone, FAX. Search requires name plus social security number, date of birth, exact years of attendance. No fee for information.

Transcripts available by FAX. Search requires name plus social security number, approximate years of attendance, signed release. Other helpful information: date of birth, exact years of attendance. Fee is $2.00.

Andrews University, Registrar, Berrien Springs, MI 49104, 616-471-3399 (FAX: 616-471-6001). Hours: 8AM-Noon, 1-5PM. Degrees granted: Associate; Bachelors; Masters; Doctorate.

Attendance and degree information available by phone, FAX, mail. Search requires name only. Other helpful information: social security number. No fee for information.

Transcripts available by FAX, mail. Search requires name plus signed release. Other helpful information: social security number, date of birth. Fee is $5.00. Expedited service available for $10.00. Major credit cards accepted for payment.

Angelina College, Registrar, PO Box 1768, Lufkin, TX 75902, 409-639-1301 (FAX: 409-639-4299). Hours: 8AM-9PM M-Th. Records go back to 1968. Degrees granted: Associate.

Attendance and degree information available by phone, FAX, mail. Search requires name plus social security number. Other helpful information: date of birth, approximate years of attendance. No fee for information.

Transcripts available by FAX, mail. Search requires name plus social security number, signed release. Other helpful information: date of birth, approximate years of attendance. Fee is $2.00.

Angelo State University, Registrar, 2601 West Ave N, San Angelo, TX 76909, 915-942-2043 (FAX: 915-942-2078). Hours: 8AM-5PM. Records go back to 1928. Degrees granted: Associate; Bachelors; Masters. Certification: Teaching.

Attendance and degree information available by phone, mail. Search requires name plus social security number, approximate years of attendance. Other helpful information: date of birth. No fee for information.

Transcripts available by mail. Search requires name plus social security number, approximate years of attendance, signed release. Other helpful information: date of birth, exact years of attendance. Fee is $3.00.

Anna Maria College, Registrar, Paxton, MA 01612-1198, 508-849-3400 X275 (FAX: 508-849-3430). Hours: 8:30AM-4:30PM. Records go back to 1952. Alumni records are maintained here also. Call 508-849-3342. Degrees granted: Associate; Bachelors; Masters.

Attendance and degree information available by phone, FAX, mail. Search requires name plus social security number, approximate years of attendance, signed release. No fee for information.

Transcripts available by mail. Search requires name plus social security number, approximate years of attendance, signed release. Fee is $3.00.

Anne Arundel Community College, Registrar, 101 College Pkwy, Arnold, MD 21012, 410-541-2243/541-2241 (FAX: 410-541-2489). Hours: 8:30AM-8PM M-Th, 8:30-4:30PM F, 9AM-1PM Sat. Records go back to 1961. Alumni records are maintained here also. Call 410-541-2515. Degrees granted: Associate.

Attendance and degree information available by phone, mail. Search requires name plus social security number, exact years of attendance, signed release. No fee for information.

Transcripts available by mail. Search requires name plus social security number, exact years of attendance, signed release. No fee for transcripts.

Anoka Technical College, Registrar, 1355 W Hwy 10, Anoka, MN 55303, 612-427-1880 (FAX: 612-422-0607). Hours: 8AM-8PM M-Th, 8AM-4PM F. Records go back to 1970.

Attendance and degree information available by phone, FAX, mail. Search requires name plus social security number, approximate years of attendance, signed release. No fee for information.

Transcripts available by mail. Search requires name plus social security number, approximate years of attendance, signed release. Fee is $2.00.

Anoka-Ramsey Community College, Records Office, 11200 Mississippi Blvd, Coon Rapids, MN 55433, 612-422-3422 (FAX: 612-422-3341). Hours: 8AM-4:30PM M,T,W,F; 8AM-6:30PM Th. Records go back 65 years. Degrees granted: Associate. Adverse incident record source: Bonnie Anderson, 612-422-3430.

Attendance and degree information available by FAX, mail. Search requires name plus social security number, signed release. Other helpful information: date of birth, approximate years of attendance. No fee for information.

Transcripts available by FAX, mail. Search requires name plus social security number, signed release. Other helpful information: date of birth, approximate years of attendance. No fee for transcripts.

Fees may be instituted in the future.

Anson Community College, Registrar, PO Box 126, Polkton, NC 28135, 704-272-7635 (FAX: 704-272-8904). Hours: 8AM-5PM. Records go back to 1950s. Alumni records are maintained here at the same phone number. Degrees granted: Associate.

Attendance and degree information available by phone, FAX, mail. Search requires name plus social security number. No fee for information.

Transcripts available by FAX, mail. Search requires name plus social security number, exact years of attendance, signed release. No fee for transcripts.

First transcript is free. Others are $1.00 each. Major credit cards accepted for payment.

Antelope Valley College, Registrar, 3041 W Ave K, Lancaster, CA 93536, 805-943-3241 X620. Hours: 8AM-4:30PM.

Records go back to 1929. Alumni records are maintained here at the same phone number. Degrees granted: Associate.

Attendance and degree information available by mail. Search requires name plus social security number, date of birth, exact years of attendance, signed release. No fee for information.

Transcripts available by mail. Search requires name plus social security number, date of birth, exact years of attendance, signed release. Fee is $1.00.

Antioch University, Registrar, 795 Livermore St, Yellow Springs, OH 45387, 513-767-6401. Hours: 8:30AM-4PM. Records go back to 1860. Alumni records are maintained here also. Call 513-767-6381. Degrees granted: Bachelors; Masters; Doctorate.

Attendance and degree information available by phone, mail. Search requires name plus social security number, exact years of attendance. No fee for information.

Transcripts available by mail. Search requires name plus social security number, exact years of attendance, signed release. Fee is $5.00.

Antioch University, (Antioch New England Graduate School), Registrar, 40 Avon St, Keene, NH 03431, 603-357-3122 (FAX: 603-357-0718). Records are not housed here. They are located at Antioch University, Registrar, 795 Livermore St, Yellow Springs, OH 45387.

Antioch University, (Antioch Seattle), Registrar, 2607 Second Ave, Seattle, WA 98121, 206-441-5352 X771 (FAX: 206-441-3307). Hours: 9AM-5PM. Records go back to 1985. Pre-1985 records are housed at Antioch University, 795 Livermore St., Yellow Springs, OH 45387, 513-767-6401. Alumni records are maintained here also. Call 206-441-5352 X5105. Degrees granted: Bachelors; Masters. Certification: Ed.

Attendance and degree information available by phone, FAX, mail. Search requires name plus signed release. Other helpful information: social security number, approximate years of attendance. No fee for information.

Transcripts available by written request only. Search requires name plus signed release. Other helpful information: social security number, approximate years of attendance. No fee for transcripts.

Antioch University, (George Meany Center for Labor Studies), Registrar, 10000 New Hampshire Ave, Silver Spring, MD 20903, 301-431-5410 (FAX: 301-434-0371). Hours: 9AM-4:30PM. Records go back to 1974. Degrees granted: Bachelors. Special programs- Transcript, 513-767-6321.

Attendance and degree information available by phone, FAX, mail. Search requires name plus social security number, approximate years of attendance, signed release. No fee for information.

School does not provide transcripts. Search requires name only. No fee for transcripts.

Transcripts at Yellow Springs location.

Antioch University, (School for Adult and Experiential Learning), Registrar, 800 Livermore St, Yellow Springs, OH 45387, 513-767-6321 (FAX: 513-767-6461). Hours: 9AM-4:30PM T-F, 7AM-3PM Sat. Records go back to 1987. Degrees granted: Bachelors; Masters.

Attendance information available by phone, FAX, mail. Search requires name only. Other helpful information: approximate years of attendance. No fee for information.

Degree information available by phone, FAX. Search requires name only. Other helpful information: approximate years of attendance. No fee for information.

Transcripts available by written request only. Search requires name plus signed release. Other helpful information: approximate years of attendance. Fee is $5.00.

Antioch University, (Southern California (Los Angeles)), Registrar, 13274 Fiji Way, Marina Del Rey, CA 90292, 310-578-1080 (FAX: 310-822-4824). Hours: 9AM-7PM M,W; 9AM-5PM T,Th; 9AM-1PM F. Records go back to 1972. Records prior to 7/85 housed at Administrative Headquarters; Yellow Springs, OH. Alumni records are maintained here also. Call 310-578-1080 X115. Degrees granted: Bachelors; Masters.

Attendance information available by mail. Search requires name plus signed release. Other helpful information: social security number, date of birth, approximate years of attendance. No fee for information.

Degree information available by mail. Search requires name plus signed release. Other helpful information: social security number, date of birth, exact years of attendance. No fee for information.

Transcripts available by mail. Search requires name plus signed release. Other helpful information: social security number, date of birth, approximate years of attendance. Fee is $5.00.

Antioch University, (Southern California (Santa Barbara)), Registrar, 801 Garden St, Santa Barbara, CA 93101, 805-962-8179 (FAX: 805-962-4786). Hours: 8AM-5PM M-Th; 9AM-2PM F. Records go back to 1985. Pre-1985 records are housed at Antioch University, 795 Livermore St, Yellow Springs, OH 45387, 513-767-6401. Degrees granted: Bachelors; Masters.

Attendance information available by phone, FAX, mail. Search requires name only. No fee for information.

Degree information available by phone, FAX, mail. Search requires name only. Other helpful information: social security number. No fee for information.

Transcripts available by mail. Search requires name plus social security number, signed release. Other helpful information: approximate years of attendance. Fee is $5.00. Expedited service available for $15.00.

First and last name while attending is needed.

Antonelli Institute, Registrar, 2910 Jolly Rd, Plymouth Meeting, PA 19462-0570, 610-275-3040 (FAX: 610-275-5630). Hours: 8:30AM-5PM. Records go back to 1938. Degrees granted: Associate.

Attendance and degree information available by mail. Search requires name plus social security number, exact years of attendance. No fee for information.

Transcripts available by mail. Search requires name plus social security number, exact years of attendance, signed release. No fee for transcripts.

Antonelli Institute of Art and Photography, Registrar, 124 E Seventh St, Cincinnati, OH 45202-2592, 513-241-4338 (FAX: 513-241-9396). Hours: 8AM-5PM M-Th, 8AM-4PM. Records go back 8 years. Degrees granted: Associate.

Attendance and degree information available by phone, FAX, mail. Search requires name plus social security number, exact years of attendance, signed release. No fee for information.

Transcripts available by phone, FAX, mail. Search requires name plus social security number, exact years of attendance, signed release. Fee is $5.00.

Appalachian Bible College, Registrar, PO Box ABC, Bradley, WV 25818, 304-877-6428 (FAX: 304-877-5082). Hours: 8AM-Noon, 1-5PM. Records go back to 1950. Alumni records are maintained here at the same phone number. Degrees granted: Associate; Bachelors. Adverse incident record source: Dean of Students.

Attendance and degree information available by phone, FAX, mail. Search requires name only. Other helpful information: social security number, approximate years of attendance. No fee for information.

Transcripts available by written request only. Search requires name plus signed release. Other helpful information: social security number, date of birth. Fee is $2.00.

Transcripts issued to student are unofficial. Official copies to institutions designated by student. Need to know whether graduated before or after 1978.

Appalachian State University, Registrar, Boone, NC 28608, 704-262-2000. Hours: 8AM-5PM. Records go back to 1929. Alumni records are maintained here at the same phone number. Degrees granted: Bachelors; Masters; Doctorate; EDS.

Attendance and degree information available by phone, mail. Search requires name plus social security number, exact years of attendance, signed release. No fee for information.

Transcripts available by mail. Search requires name plus social security number, exact years of attendance, signed release. Fee is $5.00.

Phone confirmations only if release on file.

Aquinas College, Registrar, 1607 Robinson Rd SE, Grand Rapids, MI 49506, 616-459-8281 (FAX: 616-732-4435). Hours: 8:30AM-6PM. Records go back to founding date. Degrees granted: Associate; Bachelors; Masters. Certification: Teaching - MI. Adverse incident record source: Campus Safety, 616-459-8281 X 3754.

Attendance information available by phone, FAX, mail. Search requires name plus signed release. Other helpful information: social security number, date of birth, exact years of attendance. No fee for information.

Degree information available by phone, FAX, mail. Search requires name only. Other helpful information: social security number, date of birth, exact years of attendance. No fee for information.

Transcripts available by FAX, mail. Search requires name plus signed release. Other helpful information: social security number, date of birth, exact years of attendance. Fee is $3.00. Expedited service available for $10.00.

Aquinas College at Milton, Registrar, 303 Adams St, Milton, MA 02186, 617-696-3100 (FAX: 617-696-8706). Degrees granted: Associate.

Attendance and degree information available by phone, mail. Search requires name plus social security number, exact years of attendance. No fee for information.

Transcripts available by mail. Search requires name plus social security number, exact years of attendance, signed release. Fee is $2.00.

Aquinas College at Newton, Registrar, 15 Walnut Park, Newton, MA 02158, 617-969-4400. Hours: 8AM-4PM. Records go back to 1961. Alumni records are maintained here also. Call 617-969-4400 X25. Degrees granted: Associate.

Attendance and degree information available by phone, mail. Search requires name plus social security number, exact years of attendance. No fee for information.

Transcripts available by mail. Search requires name plus social security number, exact years of attendance, signed release. Fee is $2.00.

Aquinas Institute of Theology, Registrar, 3642 Lindell Blvd, St Louis, MO 63108-3396, 314-977-3883 (FAX: 314-977-7225). Hours: 8:30AM-5PM. Degrees granted: Masters; Doctorate.

Attendance and degree information available by phone, mail. Search requires name plus exact years of attendance. No fee for information. Include stamped envelope.

Transcripts available by written request only. Search requires name plus exact years of attendance, signed release. Fee is $5.00.

Arapahoe Community College, Registrar, 2500 W College Dr, PO Box 9002, Littleton, CO 80160-9002, 303-797-5621 (FAX: 303-797-5970). Hours: 8AM-5PM. Records go back to 1966. Degrees granted: Associate. Adverse incident record source: Public Safety, 303-797-5800.

Attendance and degree information available by phone, FAX, mail. Search requires name plus social security number, date of birth, approximate years of attendance, signed release. No fee for information.

Transcripts available by FAX, mail. Search requires name plus social security number, date of birth, approximate years of attendance, signed release. Fee is $2.00.

Arecibo Technological University College, Registrar, PO Box 4010, Arecibo, PR 00613, 809-878-2830. Hours: 8AM-4:30PM. Records go back to 1967. Degrees granted: Bachelors.

Attendance information available by phone, mail. Search requires name plus approximate years of attendance, signed release. No fee for information.

Degree information available by written request only. Search requires name plus signed release. Other helpful information: approximate years of attendance. No fee for information.

Transcripts available by written request only. Search requires name plus signed release. Other helpful information: approximate years of attendance. Fee is $1.00. Expedited service available for $1.00.

Major credit cards accepted for payment.

Arizona College of the Bible, Registrar, 2045 W Northern Ave, Phoenix, AZ 85021, 602-995-2670 (FAX: 602-864-8183). Hours: 7:30AM-4:30PM. Records go back to 1971. Alumni records are maintained here at the same phone number. Degrees granted: Associate; Bachelors. Certification: 1yr Bible. Adverse incident record source: Dean of Students, 602-995-2670.

Attendance and degree information available by phone. Search requires name plus approximate years of attendance. Other helpful information: social security number, date of birth, exact years of attendance. No fee for information.

Transcripts available by mail. Search requires name plus signed release. Other helpful information: social security number, date of birth, approximate years of attendance. Fee is $2.00.

Arizona Institute of Business and Technology, Registrar, 4136 N 75th Ave Ste 211, Phoenix, AZ 85033, 602-849-8208 (FAX: 602-849-0110). Hours: 8AM-8PM M-Th, 8AM-5PM F. Records go back to 1980. Alumni records are maintained here at the same phone number. Alumni Records Office: Suite 104, Phoenix, AZ 85033. Degrees granted: Associate.

Attendance and degree information available by FAX, mail. Search requires name plus signed release. Other helpful information: social security number, date of birth, approximate years of attendance. No fee for information.

Transcripts available by FAX, mail. Search requires name plus signed release. Other helpful information: social security number, date of birth, approximate years of attendance. No fee for transcripts.

Arizona Institute of Business and Technology, **(Branch)**, Registrar, 925 S Gilbert Rd Ste 201, Mesa, AZ 85204, 602-545-8755 (FAX: 602-926-1371). Hours: 7:30AM-8PM M-Th, 8MA-4:30PM F. Records go back to 1983. Degrees granted: Associate.

Attendance and degree information available by FAX, mail. Search requires name plus social security number, signed release. No fee for information.

Transcripts available by mail. Search requires name plus social security number, signed release. No fee for transcripts.

Arizona Institute of Business and Technology, **(Branch)**, Registrar, 4136 N 75th Ave Ste 211, Phoenix, AZ 85033-3172, 602-849-8208 (FAX: 602-849-0110). Hours: 8AM-5PM. Records go back 15 years. Alumni records are maintained here at the same phone number. Degrees granted: Associate.

Attendance and degree information available by FAX, mail. Search requires name plus social security number, signed release. No fee for information.

Transcripts available by FAX, mail. Search requires name plus social security number, signed release. No fee for transcripts.

Arizona State University, Registrar, Tempe, AZ 85287, 602-965-7276. Hours: 8AM-5PM. Records go back to 1885. Alumni Records Office: Alumni Center, Arizona State University, Box 871004, Tempe, AZ 85287-1004. Degrees granted: Bachelors; Masters; Doctorate. Adverse incident record source: Registrar, 602-965-7276.

Attendance and degree information available by phone, mail. Search requires name plus social security number, date of birth, exact years of attendance. No fee for information.

Transcripts available by mail. Search requires name plus social security number, date of birth, exact years of attendance, signed release. Transcript fee is $5.00 for first copy, and $1.00 each additional copy.

Arizona State University West, Registrar, 4701 W Thunderbird Rd, PO Box 37100, Phoenix, AZ 85069-7100, 602-543-8123. Hours: 8AM-6PM M-Th, 8AM-4PM F. Records go back to 1980. Alumni Records Office: Alumni Center, Arizona State University, Box 871004, Tempe, AZ 85287-1004. Degrees granted: Bachelors; Masters. Adverse incident record source: Registrar, 602-543-8123.

Attendance and degree information available by phone, mail. Search requires name plus social security number, exact years of attendance. No fee for information.

Transcripts available by mail. Search requires name plus social security number, exact years of attendance, signed release. Fee is $5.00.

Arizona Western College, Registrar, PO Box 929, Yuma, AZ 85366, 602-726-1050 (FAX: 602-344-7730). Hours: 7AM-5PM M-Th. Records go back to 1962. Degrees granted: Associate.

Attendance information available by written request only. Search requires name plus social security number, signed release. Other helpful information: date of birth, approximate years of attendance. Fee is $2.00.

Degree information available by written request only. Search requires name only. No fee for information.

Transcripts available by written request only. Search requires name only. No fee for transcripts.

Will confirm attendance only.

Arkansas Baptist College, Registrar, 1600 Bishop St, Little Rock, AR 72202, 501-374-7856 (FAX: 501-372-0321). Hours: 8:30AM-4:30PM. Records go back to 1884. Alumni records are maintained here at the same phone number. Degrees granted: Bachelors.

Attendance and degree information available by mail. Search requires name plus social security number, approximate years of attendance, signed release. No fee for information.

Transcripts available by mail. Search requires name plus social security number, approximate years of attendance, signed release. Fee is $3.00.

Arkansas State University, Registrar, PO Box 1570, State University, AR 72467, 501-972-2031. Hours: 8AM-5PM. Records go back to 1909. Degrees granted: Associate; Bachelors; Masters; Doctorate; Specialis.

Attendance and degree information available by phone, FAX, mail. Search requires name plus social security number. Other helpful information: date of birth, approximate years of attendance. No fee for information.

Transcripts available by FAX, mail. Search requires name plus social security number, signed release. Other helpful information: date of birth, approximate years of attendance. Fee is $3.00. Expedited service available for $5.00.

Arkansas State University, **(Beebe Branch)**, Registrar, Drawer H, Beebe, AR 72012, 501-882-8260 (FAX: 501-882-8370). Hours: 8AM-5PM. Records go back to 1920. Degrees granted: Associate. Adverse incident record source: Student Services, 501-882-8245.

Attendance and degree information available by FAX, mail. Search requires name plus social security number, date of birth, approximate years of attendance. No fee for information.

Transcripts available by mail. Search requires name plus social security number, date of birth, approximate years of attendance, signed release. Fee is $1.00.

Arkansas Tech University, Registrar, Russellville, AR 72801, 501-968-0272 (FAX: 501-968-0683). Hours: 8AM-5PM. Records go back to 1909. Alumni records are maintained here also. Call 501-968-0242. Degrees granted: Associate; Bachelors; Masters. Certification: Medical Transcription. Adverse incident record source: 501-968-0222.

Attendance and degree information available by phone, FAX, mail. Search requires name only. Other helpful information: social security number, date of birth, approximate years of attendance. No fee for information.

Transcripts available by mail. Search requires name plus signed release. Other helpful information: social security number, date of birth, approximate years of attendance. Fee is $3.00.

Attendance confirmed only for students currently enrolled.

Arlington Baptist College, Registrar, 3001 W Division St, Arlington, TX 76012-3425, 817-461-8741 (FAX: 817-274-1138).

Hours: 1-4PM. Records go back to 1939. Degrees granted: Bachelors. Certification: Bible.

Attendance and degree information available by phone, FAX, mail. Search requires name only. Other helpful information: social security number, date of birth, approximate years of attendance. No fee for information.

Transcripts available by FAX, mail. Search requires name plus signed release. Other helpful information: social security number, date of birth, approximate years of attendance. Fee is $4.00.

Armstrong State College, Registrar, 11935 Abercorn Ext, Savannah, GA 31419-1997, 912-927-5278 (FAX: 912-921-5462). Hours: 8:15AM-7PM M-Th; 8:15AM-5PM. Records go back to 1935. Degrees granted: Associate; Bachelors. Adverse incident record source: Public Safety, 912-927-2367.

Attendance information available by phone, FAX, mail. Search requires name plus social security number, approximate years of attendance, signed release. Other helpful information: exact years of attendance. No fee for information.

Degree information available by phone, mail. Search requires name only. No fee for information.

Transcripts available by mail. Search requires name plus social security number, approximate years of attendance, signed release. Other helpful information: exact years of attendance. Fee is $2.50.

Armstrong University, Registrar, 2222 Harold Way, Berkeley, CA 94704, 510-848-2500. Hours: 8:30AM-5:30PM M-Th; 8:30AM-4PM F. Records go back to 19yr. Degrees granted: Associate; Bachelors; Masters.

Attendance and degree information available by phone, FAX, mail. Search requires name plus approximate years of attendance, signed release. Other helpful information: social security number, date of birth, exact years of attendance. No fee for information.

Transcripts available by written request only. Search requires name plus social security number, approximate years of attendance, signed release. Other helpful information: date of birth, exact years of attendance. Fee is $5.00.

Art Academy of Cincinnati, Registrar, 1125 St. Gregory St, Cincinnati, OH 45202, 513-562-8749 (FAX: 513-562-8778). Hours: 8:30AM-5PM M,W,Th. Degrees granted: Associate; Bachelors; Masters.

Attendance information available by phone, FAX, mail. Search requires name plus approximate years of attendance. No fee for information.

Degree information available by phone, FAX, mail. Search requires name only. Other helpful information: social security number, approximate years of attendance. No fee for information.

Transcripts available by FAX, mail. Search requires name only. Other helpful information: social security number, approximate years of attendance. Fee is $2.00. Expedited service available for $10.00.

Major credit cards accepted for payment.

Art Center College of Design, Registrar, 1700 Lida St, PO Box 7197, Pasadena, CA 91109, 818-396-2316 (FAX: 818-568-0258). Hours: 8:30AM-4:30PM M-Th; 8:30AM-4PM F. Records go back to 1930. Alumni records are maintained here also. Call 818-396-2305. Degrees granted: Bachelors; Masters.

Attendance and degree information available by phone, FAX, mail. Search requires name plus social security number, date of birth. Other helpful information: approximate years of attendance. No fee for information.

Transcripts available by mail. Search requires name plus social security number, date of birth, signed release. Other helpful information: approximate years of attendance. Fee is $2.00.

Art Institute of Atlanta, Registrar, 3376 Peachtree Rd NE, Atlanta, GA 30326, 404-266-1341 (FAX: 404-266-1383). Hours: 8AM-5PM. Records go back to 1975. Art Institute records available since 1975; formerly Massey Junior College 1949-1975. Degrees granted: Associate; Bachelors.

Attendance and degree information available by phone, FAX, mail. Search requires name plus social security number. Other helpful information: date of birth, approximate years of attendance. No fee for information.

Transcripts available by mail. Search requires name plus social security number, exact years of attendance, signed release. Other helpful information: date of birth, approximate years of attendance. Fee is $2.00.

Art Institute of Boston, Registrar, 700 Beacon St, Boston, MA 02215, 617-262-1223 (FAX: 617-437-1226). Hours: 8AM-5PM. Records go back to 1950. Alumni records are maintained here at the same phone number. Degrees granted: Bachelors.

Attendance and degree information available by phone, FAX, mail. Search requires name plus social security number, date of birth, approximate years of attendance. Other helpful information: exact years of attendance. No fee for information.

Transcripts available by written request only. Search requires name plus social security number, date of birth, approximate years of attendance, signed release. Other helpful information: exact years of attendance. Fee is $3.00. Expedited service available for $15.00.

Art Institute of Fort Lauderdale, Registrar, 1799 SE 17th St, Fort Lauderdale, FL 33316-3000, 305-463-3000 X451 (FAX: 305-523-7676). Hours: 8AM-5PM. Records go back 25 years. Degrees granted: Associate; Bachelors.

Attendance information available by FAX, mail. Search requires name plus social security number, approximate years of attendance, signed release. No fee for information.

Degree information available by phone, FAX, mail. Search requires name plus social security number, approximate years of attendance, signed release. No fee for information.

Transcripts available by mail. Search requires name plus social security number, approximate years of attendance, signed release. Fee is $3.00.

Art Institute of Philadelphia, Records Office, 1622 Chestnut St, Philadelphia, PA 19103-5198, 215-567-7080 (FAX: 215-246-3339). Hours: 8AM-5PM. Records go back 20 years. Degrees granted: Associate.

Attendance information available by phone. Search requires name only. Other helpful information: social security number. No fee for information.

Degree information available by phone, mail. Search requires name only. Other helpful information: social security number. No fee for information.

Transcripts available by mail. Search requires name plus social security number, signed release. Fee is $2.00.

Major credit cards accepted for payment.

Art Institute of Pittsburgh, Registrar, 526 Penn Ave, Pittsburgh, PA 15222-3269, 412-263-6600 (FAX: 412-263-6600 X313). Hours: 7:30AM-7PM M, 7:30AM-5PM T-F. Records go back 30 years. Degrees granted: Associate.

Attendance information available by phone, FAX, mail. Search requires name plus social security number. Other helpful information: approximate years of attendance. No fee for information.

Degree information available by phone, FAX, mail. Search requires name only. Other helpful information: social security number, approximate years of attendance. No fee for information.

Transcripts available by FAX, mail. Search requires name plus social security number, signed release. Other helpful information: approximate years of attendance. Fee is $2.00.

Need maiden name. Major credit cards accepted for payment.

Art Institute of Seattle, Registrar, 2323 Elliott Ave, Seattle, WA 98121-1633, 206-448-0900 X884. Hours: 8AM-4PM. Degrees granted: Associate.

Attendance and degree information available by phone, mail. Search requires name plus social security number. No fee for information.

Transcripts available by mail. Search requires name plus social security number, signed release. Fee is $2.00.

Art Institute of Southern California, Registrar, 2222 Laguna Canyon Rd, Laguna Beach, CA 92651, 714-497-3309. Hours: 8AM-5PM. Records go back to 1979. Alumni records are maintained here at the same phone number. Degrees granted: Bachelors.

Attendance and degree information available by mail. Search requires name plus social security number, signed release. Other helpful information: date of birth. No fee for information.

Transcripts available by mail. Search requires name plus social security number, signed release. Other helpful information: date of birth. Fee is $5.00. Expedited service available for $10.00.

Major credit cards accepted for payment.

Arthur D. Little Management Education Institute, Inc., Registrar, Cambridge, MA 02140-2390, 617-498-6249 (FAX: 617-498-7100). Hours: 8:30AM-5PM. Records go back to 1965. Degrees granted: Masters.

Attendance and degree information available by FAX, mail. Search requires name plus approximate years of attendance, signed release. No fee for information.

Transcripts available by FAX, mail. Search requires name plus approximate years of attendance, signed release. No fee for transcripts.

Asbury College, Registrar, One Macklem Dr, Wilmore, KY 40390-1198, 606-858-3511 X2325 (FAX: 606-858-3511 X3921). Hours: 8AM-5PM. Records go back to 1890. Alumni records are maintained here also. Call 606-858-3511 X2167. Degrees granted: Bachelors. Adverse incident record source: Student Affairs, 606-858-3511 X2322.

Attendance and degree information available by phone, FAX, mail. Search requires name plus social security number, date of birth, exact years of attendance, signed release. Other helpful information: approximate years of attendance. No fee for information.

Transcripts available by mail. Search requires name plus social security number, date of birth, exact years of attendance, signed release. Other helpful information: approximate years of attendance. No fee for transcripts.

Asbury Theological Seminary, Registrar, 204 N Lexington Ave, Wilmore, KY 40390-1199, 606-858-3581 (FAX: 606-858-2248). Hours: 8AM-4:30PM. Records go back to 1923. Alumni records are maintained here also. Call 606-858-2305.

Degrees granted: Masters; Doctorate. Adverse incident record source: Dean of Students, 606-858-2313.

Attendance information available by phone, mail. Search requires name plus approximate years of attendance. Other helpful information: social security number, date of birth, exact years of attendance. No fee for information.

Degree information available by phone, mail. Search requires name plus approximate years of attendance. Other helpful information: social security number, date of birth. No fee for information.

Transcripts available by mail. Search requires name plus exact years of attendance, signed release. Other helpful information: social security number, date of birth, approximate years of attendance. Fee is $3.00. Expedited service available for $5.00.

Asheville-Buncombe Technical Community College, Registrar, 340 Victoria Rd, Asheville, NC 28801, 704-254-1921 X147,148 (FAX: 704-251-6355). Hours: 8:30AM-8PM M,W; 8:30AM-4:30PM T,Th,F. Records go back to 1959. Degrees granted: Associate.

Attendance and degree information available by phone, FAX, mail. Search requires name plus social security number. No fee for information.

Transcripts available by FAX, mail. Search requires name plus social security number, signed release. Other helpful information: approximate years of attendance. No fee for transcripts.

Ashland Community College, Registrar, 1400 College Dr, Ashland, KY 41101-3683, 606-329-2999 (FAX: 606-325-9403). Hours: 8AM-5PM. Records go back to 1940. Degrees granted: Associate.

Attendance information available by phone, FAX, mail. Search requires name plus social security number, signed release. No fee for information.

Degree information available by FAX, mail. Search requires name plus social security number, signed release. No fee for information.

Transcripts available by FAX, mail. Search requires name plus social security number, signed release. Fee is $2.00.

Ashland University, Registrar, 401 College Ave, Ashland, OH 44805, 419-289-5028 (FAX: 419-289-5333). Hours: 7:30AM-5PM. Records go back 75 years. Alumni records are maintained here also. Call 419-289-5040. Degrees granted: Associate; Bachelors; Masters. Special programs- Seminary, 419-289-5907.

Attendance and degree information available by phone, FAX, mail. Search requires name only. Other helpful information: social security number, date of birth, approximate years of attendance. No fee for information.

Transcripts available by mail. Search requires name plus signed release. Other helpful information: social security number, date of birth, approximate years of attendance. Fee is $2.00. Expedited service available for $10.00.

Asnuntuck Community-Technical College, Registrar, 170 Elm St, Enfield, CT 06082, 203-253-3017 (FAX: 203-253-3016). Hours: 8:30AM-4:30PM. Records go back to 1973. Degrees granted: Associate.

Attendance information available by phone, FAX. Search requires name plus social security number, exact years of attendance. No fee for information.

Degree information available by phone, FAX. Search requires name plus social security number, date of birth. No fee for information.

Transcripts available by written request only. Search requires name plus signed release. Other helpful information: social security number. No fee for transcripts.

Assemblies of God Theological Seminary, Registrar, 1445 Boonville Ave, Springfield, MO 65802, 417-862-3344 X5608 (FAX: 417-862-3214). Hours: 8AM-4:30PM. Records go back to 1973. Alumni records are maintained here also. Call 417-862-3344 X5613. Degrees granted: Masters.

Attendance and degree information available by phone, FAX, mail. Search requires name plus social security number, date of birth, signed release. No fee for information.

Transcripts available by FAX, mail. Search requires name plus social security number, date of birth, signed release. Fee is $4.00.

Associated Mennonite Biblical Seminary, Registrar, 3003 Benham Ave, Elkhart, IN 46517-1999, 219-295-3726 X200 (FAX: 219-295-0092). Hours: 8AM-4PM. Records go back to 1958. Degrees granted: Bachelors; Masters.

Attendance and degree information available by phone, mail. Search requires name only. No fee for information.

Transcripts available by mail. Search requires name plus exact years of attendance, signed release. Fee is $3.00.

Assumption College, Registrar, 500 Salisbury St, Worcester, MA 01609, 508-767-7355 (FAX: 508-789-5411). Hours: 8:30AM-4:30PM. Records go back to 1905. Alumni records are maintained here also. Call 508-767-7223. Degrees granted: Bachelors; Masters. Adverse incident record source: Dean of Students, 508-767-7325.

Attendance and degree information available by phone, FAX, mail. Search requires name plus social security number, signed release. No fee for information.

Transcripts available by FAX, mail. Search requires name plus social security number, signed release. Fee is $2.00.

Assumption College for Sisters, Registrar, 350 Bernardsville Rd, Mallinckrodt Convent, Mendham, NJ 07945-0800, 201-543-6528 (FAX: 201-543-9459). Hours: 9AM-4PM. Records go back to 1953. Degrees granted: Associate.

Attendance and degree information available by mail. Search requires name plus social security number. No fee for information.

Transcripts available by mail. Search requires name plus social security number, signed release. No fee for transcripts.

Athenaeum of Ohio, Registrar, 6616 Beechmont Ave, Cincinnati, OH 45230-2091, 513-231-2223 (FAX: 513-231-3254). Hours: 8:30AM-5PM. Degrees granted: Masters.

Attendance and degree information available by phone, FAX, mail. Search requires name only. Other helpful information: social security number, approximate years of attendance. No fee for information.

Transcripts available by FAX, mail. Search requires name plus signed release. Other helpful information: social security number, approximate years of attendance. No fee for transcripts.

Major credit cards accepted for payment.

Athens Area Technical Institute, Registrar, 800 Hwy 29 N, Athens, GA 30601-1500, 706-355-5012 (FAX: 706-369-5753). Hours: 8AM-5PM M-Th, 8AM-4PM F. Records go back to 1967. Degrees granted: Associate.

Attendance and degree information available by phone, FAX, mail. Search requires name plus social security number, exact years of attendance. No fee for information.

Transcripts available by mail. Search requires name plus social security number, exact years of attendance, signed release. Fees have not been established at this time. Please call.

Need former names.

Athens State College, Records Office, 300 N Beaty St, Athens, AL 35611, 205-233-8165 (FAX: 205-233-8128). Hours: 8AM-4:30PM. Records go back to 173yr. Alumni records are maintained here also. Call 205-233-8275. Degrees granted: Bachelors.

Attendance and degree information available by phone, FAX, mail. Search requires name only. Other helpful information: social security number, date of birth, approximate years of attendance. No fee for information.

Transcripts available by mail. Search requires name plus date of birth, signed release. Other helpful information: social security number, approximate years of attendance. Fee is $3.00.

Credit cards are accepted in person only.

Atlanta Christian College, Registrar, 2605 Ben Hill Rd, East Point, GA 30344, 404-669-2093 (FAX: 404-669-2024). Hours: 8:30AM-4:30PM. Records go back to 1937. Alumni records are maintained here also. Call 404-669-2091. Degrees granted: Associate; Bachelors.

Attendance and degree information available by phone, FAX, mail. Search requires name only. Other helpful information: social security number, date of birth, approximate years of attendance. No fee for information.

Transcripts available by FAX, mail. Search requires name plus signed release. Other helpful information: social security number, date of birth, approximate years of attendance. Fee is $2.00. Expedite fee is based on cost of service.'

Maiden name helpful.

Atlanta College of Art, Registrar, 1280 Peachtree St NE, Atlanta, GA 30309, 404-733-5001. Hours: 8AM-5PM M-Th, 8:45AM-3PM F. Records go back to 1970. Alumni records are maintained here also. Call 404-733-5001. Degrees granted: Bachelors.

Attendance and degree information available by phone, mail. Search requires name plus social security number, exact years of attendance. No fee for information.

Transcripts available by mail. Search requires name plus social security number, exact years of attendance, signed release. No fee for transcripts.

Atlanta Metropolitan College, Registrar, 1630 Stewart Ave SW, Atlanta, GA 30310, 404-756-4001 (FAX: 404-756-5686). Hours: 8:30AM-5PM. Records go back to 1974. Degrees granted: Associate.

Attendance and degree information available by phone, FAX, mail. Search requires name plus social security number. Other helpful information: approximate years of attendance. No fee for information.

Transcripts available by FAX, mail. Search requires name plus social security number, signed release. Other helpful information: approximate years of attendance. No fee for transcripts.

Atlantic Coast Institute, Registrar, 5225 W Broward Blvd, Fort Lauderdale, FL 33317, 305-581-2223 (FAX: 305-583-9458).

Hours: 8AM-5PM. Records go back to 1975. Degrees granted: Associate.

Attendance and degree information available by mail. Search requires name plus social security number, signed release. Other helpful information: approximate years of attendance. No fee for information.

Transcripts available by mail. Search requires name plus social security number, signed release. Other helpful information: approximate years of attendance. Fee is $3.00.

Atlantic College, Registrar, PO Box 1774, Guaynabo, PR 00651-1774, 809-720-0596 (FAX: 809-720-1092). Hours: 8AM-5PM. Records go back to 1985. Degrees granted: Associate; Bachelors.

Attendance and degree information available by mail. Search requires name plus social security number, signed release. No fee for information.

Transcripts available by mail. Search requires name plus social security number, signed release. Fee is $5.00.

Atlantic Community College, Registrar, 5100 Black Horse Pike, Mays Landing, NJ 08330-2699, 609-343-5005 (FAX: 609-343-4914). Hours: 9AM-4:30PM. Records go back to 1969. Degrees granted: Associate. Adverse incident record source: Dean of Students, 609-343-5083.

Attendance and degree information available by FAX, mail. Search requires name plus signed release. Other helpful information: social security number, date of birth, approximate years of attendance. No fee for information.

Transcripts available by FAX, mail. Search requires name plus signed release. Other helpful information: social security number, date of birth, approximate years of attendance. Fee is $2.00. Expedited service available for $5.00.

Major credit cards accepted for payment.

Atlantic Union College, Registrar, PO Box 1000, South Lancaster, MA 01561, 508-368-2216 (FAX: 508-368-2015). Hours: 9AM-Noon,1-4PM M-Th; 9-11AM F. Records go back to 1884. Degrees granted: Associate; Bachelors; Masters.

Attendance and degree information available by phone, FAX, mail. Search requires name plus social security number, date of birth. Other helpful information: approximate years of attendance. No fee for information.

Transcripts available by FAX, mail. Search requires name plus social security number, date of birth, signed release. Other helpful information: approximate years of attendance. No fee for transcripts. Expedited fees are $10.00 to $15.00.

Previous or other names used helpful. Major credit cards accepted for payment.

Auburn University, Registrar, 100 Mary Martin Hall, Auburn University, AL 36849, 205-844-4770. Hours: 7:45AM-4:45PM. Records go back to 1960. Alumni records are maintained here also. Call 205-844-2586. Degrees granted: Bachelors; Masters; Doctorate. Adverse incident record source: Campus Security, 205-844-4000.

Attendance and degree information available by phone, mail. Search requires name plus social security number, date of birth, exact years of attendance. No fee for information.

Transcripts available by mail. Search requires name plus social security number, date of birth, exact years of attendance, signed release. Fee is $3.00.

Auburn University at Montgomery, Registrar, 7300 University Dr, Montgomery, AL 36117-3596, 334-244-3614. Hours: 8AM-5PM. Records go back to 1976. Alumni records are maintained here also. Call 334-244-3356. Degrees granted: Bachelors; Masters. Adverse incident record source: Campus Police, 334-244-3424.

Attendance and degree information available by phone, mail. Search requires name plus social security number. No fee for information.

Transcripts available by mail. Search requires name plus social security number, exact years of attendance, signed release. Fee is $3.00.

Audrey Cohen College, Registrar, 345 Hudston St, New York, NY 10014-4598, 212-989-2002 X501 (FAX: 212-924-4396). Hours: 9AM-7PM M-Th; 9AM-5PM F; 11AM-3PM S. Records go back to 1964. Alumni records are maintained here also. Call 212-989-2002 X257. Degrees granted: Bachelors; Masters.

Attendance and degree information available by FAX, mail. Search requires name plus social security number, signed release. No fee for information.

Transcripts available by mail. Search requires name plus social security number, signed release. Fee is $4.00.

Augsburg College, Registrar, 2211 Riverside Ave, Minneapolis, MN 55454, 612-330-1036 (FAX: 612-330-1649). Hours: 8AM-4:30PM. Records go back to founding date. Records for past five years other than transcripts. Alumni Records Office: 2124 S 7th St, Minneapolis, MN 55454. Degrees granted: Bachelors; Masters.

Attendance and degree information available by phone, FAX, mail. Search requires name only. Other helpful information: social security number, date of birth, approximate years of attendance. No fee for information.

Transcripts available by mail. Search requires name plus signed release. Other helpful information: social security number, date of birth, approximate years of attendance. Fee is $2.00.

Augusta Technical Institute, Registrar, 3116 Deans Bridge Rd, Augusta, GA 30906, 706-771-4035 (FAX: 706-771-4016). Hours: 8AM-4:30PM. Records go back to 1961. Degrees granted: Associate.

Attendance and degree information available by phone, mail. Search requires name only. Other helpful information: social security number, approximate years of attendance. No fee for information.

Transcripts available by written request only. Search requires name plus social security number, signed release. Other helpful information: approximate years of attendance. Fee is $2.00.

Augustana College, Registrar, 639 38th St, Rock Island, IL 61201-2296, 309-794-7277 (FAX: 309-794-7422). Hours: 8AM-4:30PM. Records go back to 1900. Alumni records are maintained here also. Call 309-794-7336. Degrees granted: Bachelors.

Attendance and degree information available by phone, FAX, mail. Search requires name plus date of birth. Other helpful information: social security number, approximate years of attendance. No fee for information.

Transcripts available by FAX, mail. Search requires name plus date of birth, signed release. Other helpful information: social security number, approximate years of attendance. No fee for transcripts. Expedited service available for $5.00.

The Sourcebook of College and University Student Records

Augustana College, Registrar, 29th St and Summit Ave, Sioux Falls, SD 57197, 605-336-4121 (FAX: 605-336-4450). Hours: 8AM-5PM. Records go back to 1889. Alumni records are maintained here also. Call 605-336-5230. Degrees granted: Associate; Bachelors; Masters. Adverse incident record source: Student Services, 605-336-4124.

Attendance and degree information available by phone, FAX, mail. Search requires name plus social security number, approximate years of attendance. Other helpful information: date of birth, exact years of attendance. No fee for information.

Transcripts available by FAX, mail. Search requires name plus social security number, approximate years of attendance, signed release. Other helpful information: date of birth, exact years of attendance. No fee for transcripts.

Need written request for FAX-back transcript.

Aurora University, Registrar, 347 S Gladstone Ave, Aurora, IL 60506, 708-844-5464 (FAX: 708-844-5463). Hours: 8AM-9PM M-Th; 8AM-6PM F; 9AM-1PM S. Records go back to founding date. Degrees granted: Bachelors; Masters.

Attendance and degree information available by phone, FAX, mail. Search requires name plus signed release. Other helpful information: social security number, date of birth, approximate years of attendance. No fee for information.

Transcripts available by FAX, mail. Search requires name plus signed release. Other helpful information: social security number, date of birth, approximate years of attendance. Fee is $3.00. Expedited service available for $10.00.

Major credit cards accepted for payment.

Austin College, Registrar, 900 N Grand Ave, PO Box 1177, Sherman, TX 75091-4440, 903-813-2371 (FAX: 903-813-2378). Hours: 8AM-5PM. Degrees granted: Bachelors; Masters.

Attendance information available by phone, FAX, mail. Search requires name only. Other helpful information: social security number, date of birth, approximate years of attendance. No fee for information.

Degree information available by phone, FAX, mail. Search requires name only. Other helpful information: social security number, date of birth, approximate years of attendance. No fee for information.

Transcripts available by FAX, mail. Search requires name plus signed release. Other helpful information: social security number, date of birth, approximate years of attendance. Fee is $2.00. Expedited service available for $2.00.

Austin Community College, Registrar, 1600 8th Ave NW, Austin, MN 55912, 507-433-0510 (FAX: 507-433-0515). Hours: 8AM-4:30PM. Records go back to 1940. Degrees granted: Associate.

Attendance and degree information available by phone, FAX, mail. Search requires name plus signed release. Other helpful information: social security number, date of birth, approximate years of attendance. No fee for information.

Transcripts available by mail. Search requires name plus signed release. Other helpful information: social security number, date of birth, approximate years of attendance. No fee for transcripts.

Austin Community College, Registrar, 5930 Middle Fiskville Rd, Austin, TX 78752-4390, 512-483-7000 (FAX: 512-483-7791). Hours: 8AM-4:30PM. Degrees granted: Associate.

Attendance and degree information available by phone, FAX, mail. Search requires name plus social security number, date of birth, exact years of attendance. No fee for information.

Transcripts available by FAX, mail. Search requires name plus social security number, date of birth, exact years of attendance, signed release. Fee is $5.00.

Austin Peay State University, Registrar, 601 College St, Clarksville, TN 37044, 615-648-7121 (FAX: 615-648-6264). Hours: 8AM-4:30PM. Records go back to 1927. Alumni records are maintained here also. Call 615-648-7979. Degrees granted: Associate; Bachelors; Masters. Adverse incident record source: Admissions, 615-648-7661: Public Safety, 615-648-7786

Attendance and degree information available by phone, FAX, mail. Search requires name plus signed release. Other helpful information: social security number, date of birth, approximate years of attendance. No fee for information.

Transcripts available by written request only. Search requires name plus signed release. Other helpful information: social security number, date of birth, approximate years of attendance. No fee for transcripts.

Austin Presbyterian Theological Seminary, Registrar, 100 E 27th St, Austin, TX 78705-5797, 512-472-6736. Hours: 8:30AM-5PM. Records go back to founding date. Degrees granted: Masters; Doctorate.

Attendance and degree information available by phone, FAX, mail. Search requires name only. Other helpful information: social security number, date of birth. No fee for information.

Transcripts available by mail. Search requires name plus signed release. Other helpful information: social security number, date of birth. Fee is $3.00.

Averett College, Registrar, 420 W Main St, Danville, VA 24541, 804-791-5600 (FAX: 804-799-0658). Hours: 8AM-5PM. Records go back to 1859. Alumni records are maintained here at the same phone number. Degrees granted: Bachelors; Masters.

Attendance and degree information available by phone, mail. Search requires name plus social security number, exact years of attendance. No fee for information.

Transcripts available by mail. Search requires name plus social security number, exact years of attendance, signed release. Fee is $4.00.

Avila College, Registrar, 11901 Wornall Rd, Kansas City, MO 64145, 816-942-8400 X2210 (FAX: 816-942-3362). Hours: 8AM-5PM. Records go back to 1960. Alumni records are maintained here also. Call 816-942-8400 X236. Degrees granted: Bachelors; Masters.

Attendance and degree information available by phone, FAX, mail. Search requires name plus social security number, approximate years of attendance, signed release. No fee for information.

Transcripts available by mail. Search requires name plus social security number, approximate years of attendance, signed release. Fee is $2.00.

Azusa Pacific University, Registrar, 901 E Alosta, Azusa, CA 91702-7000, 818-969-3434 X3391. Hours: 8AM-5PM. Records go back to 1880. Alumni records are maintained here also. Call 818-812-3026. Degrees granted: Bachelors; Masters.

Attendance and degree information available by phone, mail. Search requires name plus social security number, date of birth. No fee for information.

Transcripts available by phone, mail. Search requires name plus social security number, date of birth, signed release. Fee is $4.00.

B

Babson College, Registrar, Babson Park, Wellesley, MA 02157, 617-239-4519 (FAX: 617-239-5618). Hours: 8:30AM-4:30PM. Alumni records are maintained here also. Call 617-239-4562. Degrees granted: Bachelors.

Attendance and degree information available by phone, FAX, mail. Search requires name plus signed release. No fee for information.

Transcripts available by mail. Search requires name plus signed release. No fee for transcripts.

Bacone College, Registrar, 2299 Old Bacone Rd, Muskogee, OK 74403-1597, 918-683-4581 X275-277 (FAX: 918-687-5913). Hours: 8AM-4:30PM. Records go back to 1880. Degrees granted: Associate. Adverse incident record source: Dean, 918-683-4581.

Attendance and degree information available by phone, FAX, mail. Search requires name plus social security number, approximate years of attendance, signed release. Other helpful information: date of birth. No fee for information.

Transcripts available by phone, FAX, mail. Search requires name plus social security number, approximate years of attendance, signed release. Other helpful information: date of birth. No fee for transcripts.

Bainbridge College, Registrar, Hwy 84 E, Bainbridge, GA 31717, 912-248-2504 (FAX: 912-248-2525). Hours: 8AM-6PM M,T,Th; 8AM-5PM W,F. Records go back to 1973. Degrees granted: Associate.

Attendance and degree information available by phone, FAX, mail. Search requires name only. Other helpful information: social security number. No fee for information.

Transcripts available by mail. Search requires name plus social security number, signed release. No fee for transcripts.

Baker College of Flint, Registrar, G-1050 W Bristol Rd, Flint, MI 48507, 810-766-7600 (FAX: 810-766-4049). Hours: 8AM-6PM. Records go back to 1950. Degrees granted: Associate; Bachelors; Masters.

Attendance and degree information available by phone, FAX, mail. Search requires name plus social security number. Other helpful information: date of birth, approximate years of attendance. No fee for information.

Transcripts available by mail. Search requires name plus social security number, signed release. Other helpful information: date of birth, approximate years of attendance. Fee is $2.00. Expedited service available for $5.00.
Major credit cards accepted for payment.

Baker College of Flint, (Baker College of Muskegon), Registrar, 123 E Apple Ave, Muskegon, MI 49442, 616-726-4904 (FAX: 616-728-1417). Hours: 7AM-9:40PM M-Th, 7AM-5PM F. Records go back to 1965. Alumni records are maintained here also. Call 616-726-4904. Degrees granted: Associate; Bachelors; Masters.

Attendance and degree information available by phone, FAX, mail. Search requires name plus social security number, signed release. No fee for information.

Transcripts available by mail. Search requires name plus social security number, signed release. Fee is $2.00.

Baker College of Owosso, Registrar's Office, 1020 S Washington St, Owosso, MI 48867, 517-723-5251 (FAX: 517-723-3355). Hours: 8AM-6PM. Records go back to 1983. Degrees granted: Associate; Bachelors; Masters.

School will not confirm attendance information. Search requires name plus social security number, signed release. Other helpful information: approximate years of attendance. No fee for information.

Degree information available by phone, FAX, mail. Search requires name plus social security number. Other helpful information: approximate years of attendance. No fee for information.

Transcripts available by FAX, mail. Search requires name plus social security number, signed release. Other helpful information: approximate years of attendance. Fee is $2.00. Expedited service available for $5.00.

Baker University, Registrar, 606 W 8th St, PO Box 65, Baldwin City, KS 66006-0065, 913-594-6451 X530 (FAX: 913-594-2500). Hours: 9AM-Noon, 1-5PM. Records go back 137 years. Alumni records are maintained here also. Call 913-594-6451 X526. Degrees granted: Bachelors; Masters. Special programs- School/Professional & Graduate Studies, 913-491-4432. Adverse incident record source: Student Services, 913-594-6451 X484.

Attendance and degree information available by phone, FAX, mail. Search requires name plus social security number, approximate years of attendance. Other helpful information: exact years of attendance. No fee for information.

Transcripts available by FAX, mail. Search requires name plus social security number, exact years of attendance, signed release. Other helpful information: approximate years of attendance. Fee is $4.00. Expedited service available for $16.00.
Name attended under (maiden, etc.) helpful.

Bakersfield College, Registrar, 1801 Panorama Dr, Bakersfield, CA 93305, 805-395-4011. Hours: 8:30AM-4:45PM M-Th, 8:30AM-Noon F. Records go back to 1913. Alumni records are maintained here at the same phone number. Degrees granted: Associate. Adverse incident record source: Security, 805-395-4554: Dean of Students, 805-395-4204

Attendance and degree information available by mail. Search requires name plus social security number, exact years of attendance, signed release. No fee for information.

Transcripts available by mail. Search requires name plus social security number, exact years of attendance, signed release. Fee is $2.00. Expedited service available for $7.00.

Baldwin-Wallace College, Registrar, 275 Eastland Rd, Berea, OH 44017, 216-826-2126 (FAX: 216-826-6522). Hours: 8:30AM-4:30PM. Records go back 40 years. Degrees granted: Bachelors; Masters.

Attendance information available by phone, FAX, mail. Search requires name only. Other helpful information: social security number, approximate years of attendance. No fee for information.

Degree information available by phone, FAX, mail. Search requires name plus social security number. Other helpful information: approximate years of attendance. No fee for information.

Transcripts available by written request only. Search requires name plus signed release. Other helpful information: social security number, approximate years of attendance. Fee is $3.00.
College major also helpful.

Ball State University, Registrar, 2000 University Ave, Muncie, IN 47306, 317-285-1722. Hours: 8AM-5PM. Records go back to 1919. Alumni records are maintained here also. Call 317-

285-1413. Degrees granted: Associate; Bachelors; Masters; Doctorate.
Attendance information available by phone, mail. Search requires name plus social security number. No fee for information.
Degree information available by mail. Search requires name plus social security number, exact years of attendance, signed release. No fee for information.
Transcripts available by mail. Search requires name plus social security number, exact years of attendance, signed release. No fee for transcripts.

Baltimore City Community College, Registrar, 2901 Liberth Heights Ave, Baltimore, MD 21215, 410-333-5525 (FAX: 410-333-7723). Hours: 8AM-5PM. Records go back to 1947. Alumni Records Office: 600 E Lombard St, Baltimore, MD 21201. Degrees granted: Associate. Adverse incident record source: Student Affairs, 410-333-5775.
Attendance and degree information available by phone, FAX, mail. Search requires name plus social security number. Other helpful information: date of birth, approximate years of attendance. No fee for information.
Transcripts available by mail. Search requires name plus social security number, signed release. Other helpful information: date of birth, approximate years of attendance. Fee is $2.00.
Major credit cards accepted for payment.

Baltimore City Community College, **(Harbor)**, Registrar, 600 E Lombard St, Baltimore, MD 21202, 410-333-8395 (FAX: 410-333-8444). Hours: 8AM-4:30PM. Degrees granted: Associate.
Attendance and degree information available by phone, mail. Search requires name plus social security number, exact years of attendance. No fee for information.
Transcripts available by mail. Search requires name plus social security number, exact years of attendance, signed release. Fee is $2.00.

Baltimore Hebrew University, Registrar, 5800 Park Heights Ave, Baltimore, MD 21209, 410-578-6918 (FAX: 410-578-6940). Hours: 9AM-5PM. Records go back to 1920s. Alumni records are maintained here also. Call 410-578-6915. Degrees granted: Associate; Bachelors; Masters; Doctorate.
Attendance and degree information available by written request only. Search requires name plus social security number, signed release. Other helpful information: date of birth, approximate years of attendance. No fee for information.
Transcripts available by written request only. Search requires name plus social security number, signed release. Other helpful information: date of birth, approximate years of attendance. Fee is $5.00.

Baltimore International Culinary College, Registrar, 17 E Commerce St, Baltimore, MD 21202, 410-752-1446 (FAX: 410-545-5000). Hours: 8AM-4:30PM. Records go back to 1972. Alumni records are maintained here also. Call 410-752-1446. Degrees granted: Associate. Adverse incident record source: Registrar, 410-751-1446.
Attendance and degree information available by phone, FAX, mail. Search requires name plus social security number. No fee for information.
Transcripts available by FAX, mail. Search requires name plus social security number, exact years of attendance, signed release. First transcript is free. Additional ones are $2.00 each.

Bangor Theological Seminary, Registrar, 300 Union St, Bangor, ME 04401, 207-942-6781 X36 (FAX: 207-942-4914). Hours: 8AM-5PM. Records go back to 1814. Alumni records are maintained here at the same phone number. Degrees granted: Masters; Doctorate.
Attendance and degree information available by FAX, mail. Search requires name plus date of birth, exact years of attendance. No fee for information.
Transcripts available by FAX, mail. Search requires name plus date of birth, exact years of attendance, signed release. Fee is $3.00.

Bank Street College of Education, Registrar, 610 W 112th St, New York, NY 10025, 212-875-4407 (FAX: 212-875-4753). Hours: 9AM-5PM. Records go back to 1919. Alumni records are maintained here also. Call 212-875-4606. Degrees granted: Masters.
Attendance and degree information available by FAX, mail. Search requires name plus social security number, date of birth, approximate years of attendance. No fee for information.
Transcripts available by mail. Search requires name plus social security number, date of birth, approximate years of attendance, signed release. Fee is $7.00.

Baptist Bible College, Registrar, 628 E Kearney St, Springfield, MO 65803, 417-869-9811 X2219 (FAX: 417-831-8029). Hours: 9AM-5PM. Records go back to 1950. Alumni records are maintained here also. Call 417-869-9811 X2362. Degrees granted: Associate; Bachelors; Masters. Adverse incident record source: Dean, 417-869-9811 X2224.
Attendance information available by phone, FAX, mail. Search requires name plus social security number, signed release. No fee for information.
Degree information available by FAX, mail. Search requires name plus social security number, signed release. No fee for information.
Transcripts available by FAX, mail. Search requires name plus social security number, signed release. Fee is $3.00.

Baptist Bible College and Seminary, Registrar, PO Box 800, 538 Venard Rd, Clarks Summit, PA 18411, 717-586-2400 X217 (FAX: 717-586-1753). Hours: 8AM-5PM. Records go back to 1932. Degrees granted: Associate; Bachelors; Masters; Doctorate.
Attendance and degree information available by phone, FAX, mail. Search requires name plus signed release. No fee for information.
Transcripts available by FAX, mail. Search requires name plus signed release. No fee for transcripts.
Some requests may be expedited.

Baptist Missionary Association Theological Seminary, Registrar, 1530 E Pine St, Jacksonville, TX 75766, 903-586-2501 (FAX: 903-586-0378). Hours: 9AM-4PM. Records go back to 1965. Degrees granted: Associate; Bachelors; Masters.
Attendance information available by phone, FAX, mail. Search requires name only. Other helpful information: approximate years of attendance. No fee for information.
Degree information available by phone, FAX, mail. Search requires name plus approximate years of attendance. Other helpful information: social security number, exact years of attendance. No fee for information.

Transcripts available by FAX, mail. Search requires name plus approximate years of attendance, signed release. Other helpful information: social security number, exact years of attendance. Fee is $2.00.

Barat College, Registrar, 700 E Westleigh Rd, Lake Forest, IL 60045, 708-234-3000 (FAX: 708-234-1084). Hours: 8:30AM-4:30PM. Records go back to 1922. Alumni records are maintained here at the same phone number. Degrees granted: Bachelors. Adverse incident record source: Dean of Students, 708-234-3000.

Attendance and degree information available by phone, FAX, mail. Search requires name plus social security number. No fee for information.

Transcripts available by mail. Search requires name plus social security number, exact years of attendance, signed release. Fee is $3.00. Expedited service available for $6.00.

Barber-Scotia College, Registrar, 145 Cabarrus Ave W, Concord, NC 28025, 704-786-5171 X221 (FAX: 704-793-4950). Hours: 8:30AM-4:30PM. Alumni records are maintained here at the same phone number. Degrees granted: Bachelors.

Attendance and degree information available by mail. Search requires name plus exact years of attendance. No fee for information.

Transcripts available by mail. Search requires name plus exact years of attendance, signed release. Fee is $3.00.

Barclay College, Registrar, 607 N Kingman, PO Box 288, Haviland, KS 67059, 316-862-5252 (FAX: 316-862-5403). Hours: 8AM-5PM. Records go back to 1917. Alumni records are maintained here also. Call 316-862-5252. Degrees granted: Bachelors. Certification: Bible.

Attendance and degree information available by phone, FAX, mail. Search requires name plus approximate years of attendance. Other helpful information: date of birth. No fee for information.

Transcripts available by FAX, mail. Search requires name plus approximate years of attendance, signed release. Other helpful information: date of birth, exact years of attendance. Fee is $3.00. Expedited service available for $5.00.

Bard College, Registrar, Annandale-On-Hudson, NY 12504, 914-758-7458 (FAX: 914-758-4294). Hours: 9AM-5PM. Records go back to 1940. Alumni records are maintained here also. Call 914-758-7407. Degrees granted: Bachelors.

Attendance and degree information available by phone, FAX, mail. Search requires name plus approximate years of attendance. No fee for information.

Transcripts available by mail. Search requires name plus approximate years of attendance, signed release. Fee is $3.00.

Barnard College, Registrar, 3009 Broadway, New York, NY 10027-6598, 212-854-2011. Hours: 9:30AM-4:30PM. Records go back to 1892. Alumni records are maintained here also. Call 212-854-2005. Degrees granted: Bachelors.

Attendance and degree information available by mail. Search requires name plus social security number, date of birth, approximate years of attendance. No fee for information.

Transcripts available by mail. Search requires name plus social security number, date of birth, approximate years of attendance, signed release. Fee is $3.00.

Barry University, Registrar, 11300 NE Second Ave, Miami Shores, FL 33161-6695, 305-899-3948 (FAX: 305-899-3946).
Hours: 8:30AM-5PM. Alumni records are maintained here also. Call 305-899-3175. Degrees granted: Bachelors; Masters; Doctorate. Adverse incident record source: VP Student Services, 305-899-3085.

Attendance and degree information available by phone, FAX, mail. Search requires name plus social security number, date of birth, signed release. Other helpful information: approximate years of attendance. No fee for information.

Transcripts available by mail. Search requires name plus signed release. Other helpful information: social security number, date of birth, approximate years of attendance. Fee is $2.00.

Major credit cards accepted for payment.

Barstow College, Registrar, 2700 Barstow Rd, Barstow, CA 92311, 619-252-2411 (FAX: 619-252-1875). Hours: 8AM-5PM. Records go back to 1964. Degrees granted: Associate. Adverse incident record source: HRDO Office, 619-252-2411.

Attendance and degree information available by mail. Search requires name plus signed release. Other helpful information: social security number, date of birth, approximate years of attendance. No fee for information.

Transcripts available by mail. Search requires name plus signed release. Other helpful information: social security number, date of birth, approximate years of attendance. Fee is $4.00.

Bartlesville Wesleyan College, Registrar, 2201 Silver Lake Rd, Bartlesville, OK 74006, 918-333-6151 (FAX: 918-335-6229). Hours: 8AM-Noon, 1-5PM. Records go back to 1909. Alumni records are maintained here at the same phone number. Degrees granted: Associate; Bachelors. Adverse incident record source: Student Development, 918-333-6151.

Attendance information available by phone, FAX, mail. Search requires name plus signed release. Other helpful information: social security number, date of birth, approximate years of attendance. No fee for information.

Degree information available by phone, FAX, mail. Search requires name plus signed release. Other helpful information: social security number, date of birth, approximate years of attendance. No fee for information.

Transcripts available by FAX, mail. Search requires name plus signed release. Other helpful information: social security number, date of birth, approximate years of attendance. Fee is $2.00. Expedited service available for $4.00.

FAX results available for $4.00. Major credit cards accepted for payment.

Barton College, Office of Registrar, College Station, Wilson, NC 27893, 919-399-6327. Hours: 8:30AM-5PM. Records go back to 1902. Alumni records are maintained here also. Call 919-399-6360. Degrees granted: Bachelors. Adverse incident record source: Student Life Division, 919-399-6364.

Attendance and degree information available by phone, mail. Search requires name plus social security number. No fee for information.

Transcripts available by mail. Search requires name plus social security number, date of birth, exact years of attendance, signed release. Other helpful information: approximate years of attendance. Fee is $5.00.

Major credit cards accepted for payment.

Barton County Community College, Registrar, Rural Rte # Box 136Z, Great Bend, KS 67530, 316-792-2701 (FAX: 316-792-3056). Hours: 7:30AM-4:30PM. Records go back 25 years. Degrees granted: Associate.

Attendance and degree information available by phone, FAX, mail. Search requires name only. Other helpful information: social security number. No fee for information.

Transcripts available by FAX, mail. Search requires name plus signed release. Other helpful information: social security number. Fee is $2.00. Expedited service available for $5.00.

Major credit cards accepted for payment.

Basic Institute of Technology, Registrar, 4455 Chippewa Ave, St Louis, MO 63116-9990, 314-771-1200 (FAX: 314-351-9255). Hours: 9AM-5PM. Records go back to 1964. Degrees granted: Associate.

Attendance information available by phone, FAX, mail. Search requires name plus social security number, approximate years of attendance. No fee for information.

Degree information available by FAX, mail. Search requires name plus social security number, approximate years of attendance. No fee for information.

Transcripts available by mail. Search requires name plus social security number, approximate years of attendance. Fee is $5.00.

Bassist College, Registrar, 2000 SW Fifth Ave, Portland, OR 97201, 503-228-6528 (FAX: 503-228-4227). Hours: 7:30AM-5PM. Alumni records are maintained here at the same phone number. Degrees granted: Associate; Bachelors. Adverse incident record source: Angie McKenna, 503-228-6508.

Attendance and degree information available by phone, FAX, mail. Search requires name plus date of birth, exact years of attendance. Other helpful information: social security number, approximate years of attendance. No fee for information.

Transcripts available by written request only. Search requires name plus date of birth, exact years of attendance, signed release. Other helpful information: social security number, approximate years of attendance. Fee is $5.00. Expedited service available for $7.00.

Major credit cards accepted for payment.

Bastyr University, Registrar, 144 NE 54th St, Seattle, WA 98105, 206-523-9585 X29. Hours: 8AM-4:30PM. Degrees granted: Bachelors; Masters; First Professional Degree.

Attendance and degree information available by phone, mail. Search requires name only. No fee for information.

Transcripts available by mail. Search requires name plus signed release. Fee is $3.00.

Bates College, Registrar, 2 Andrews Rd, Lewiston, ME 04240, 207-786-6096. Hours: 8AM-5PM. Records go back to 1956. Alumni records are maintained here also. Call 207-786-6127. Degrees granted: Bachelors.

Attendance and degree information available by phone, mail. Search requires name plus date of birth, exact years of attendance. No fee for information.

Transcripts available by mail. Search requires name plus date of birth, exact years of attendance, signed release. No fee for transcripts.

Bauder College, Registrar, Phipps Plaza, 3500 Peachtree Rd NE, Atlanta, GA 30326-9975, 404-237-7573. Hours: 8AM-4PM. Records go back to 1970. Degrees granted: Associate.

Attendance and degree information available by phone, mail. Search requires name plus social security number, exact years of attendance. No fee for information.

Transcripts available by mail. Search requires name plus social security number, exact years of attendance, signed release. Fee is $3.00.

Bauder Fashion College-Arlington, Registrar, 508 S Center St, Arlington, TX 76010, 817-277-6666 (FAX: 817-274-9701). Hours: 8AM-4PM. Records go back to 1968. Degrees granted: Associate; Assoc. of Applied Arts.

Attendance and degree information available by phone, FAX, mail. Search requires name plus social security number. Other helpful information: approximate years of attendance. No fee for information.

Transcripts available by mail. Search requires name plus social security number, signed release. Other helpful information: approximate years of attendance. Fee is $10.00.

Bay Path College, Registrar, 588 Longmeadow St, Longmeadow, MA 01106, 413-567-0621 (FAX: 413-567-9321). Hours: 8:30AM-5PM. Records go back to 1897. Alumni records are maintained here also. Call 413-567-0621 X421. Degrees granted: Associate; Bachelors.

Attendance and degree information available by phone, FAX, mail. Search requires name plus social security number, exact years of attendance, signed release. Other helpful information: approximate years of attendance. No fee for information.

Transcripts available by FAX, mail. Search requires name plus social security number, exact years of attendance, signed release. Other helpful information: approximate years of attendance. Fee is $4.00.

Bay State College, Registrar, 122 Commonwealth Ave, Boston, MA 02116, 617-236-8000 (FAX: 617-236-8023). Degrees granted: Associate.

Attendance and degree information available by phone, FAX, mail. Search requires name plus exact years of attendance, signed release. Other helpful information: social security number, date of birth. No fee for information.

Transcripts available by mail. Search requires name plus exact years of attendance, signed release. Other helpful information: social security number, date of birth. Fee is $3.00.

Bay de Noc Community College, Registrar, 2001 N Lincoln Rd, Escanaba, MI 49829, 906-786-5802 (FAX: 906-786-8515). Hours: 8AM-4:30PM. Records go back to 1962. Degrees granted: Associate.

Attendance and degree information available by phone, FAX, mail. Search requires name plus social security number. Other helpful information: date of birth, approximate years of attendance. No fee for information.

Transcripts available by FAX, mail. Search requires name plus social security number, signed release. Other helpful information: date of birth, approximate years of attendance. Fee is $1.00.

Bayamon Central University, Registrar, PO Box 1725, Bayamon, PR 00960-1725, 809-786-3030 (FAX: 809-740-2200). Hours: 8-11:30AM, 1-4:30PM. Degrees granted: Associate; Bachelors; Masters. Certification: Pre-Medical Sciences.

Attendance and degree information available by FAX. Search requires name plus signed release. No fee for information.

Transcripts available by written request only. Search requires name plus signed release. Fee is $3.00.

Bayamon Technological University College, Registrar, Bayamon, PR 00959-1919, 809-786-2885.

Attendance and degree information available by written request only. Search requires name plus signed release. Fee is $3.00.

Transcripts available by written request only. Search requires name plus signed release. Fee is $3.00.

Baylor College of Dentistry, Registrar, 3302 Gaston Ave, Dallas, TX 75246, 214-828-8230 (FAX: 214-828-8346). Hours: 8AM-4:30PM. Records go back to 1905. Alumni records are maintained here at the same phone number. Degrees granted: Doctorate.

Attendance and degree information available by phone, mail. Search requires name plus social security number, exact years of attendance, signed release. No fee for information.

Transcripts available by mail. Search requires name plus social security number, exact years of attendance, signed release. Fee is $4.00.

Release must be in file to receive information by phone.

Baylor College of Medicine, Registrar, One Baylor Plaza, Houston, TX 77030-3498, 713-798-4600 (FAX: 713-798-7951). Hours: 8AM-4:30PM. Alumni records are maintained here at the same phone number. Degrees granted: Doctorate.

Attendance and degree information available by phone, mail. Search requires name plus social security number. No fee for information.

Transcripts available by mail. Search requires name plus social security number, signed release. No fee for transcripts.

Baylor University, Registrar, PO Box 97068, Waco, TX 76798, 817-755-1181 (FAX: 817-755-2233). Hours: 8AM-5PM. Records go back to 1900. Degrees granted: Bachelors; Masters; Doctorate.

Attendance and degree information available by phone, FAX, mail. Search requires name only. Other helpful information: social security number, date of birth, approximate years of attendance. No fee for information.

Transcripts available by FAX, mail. Search requires name plus signed release. Other helpful information: social security number, date of birth, approximate years of attendance. Fee is $5.00.

Beal College, Registrar, 629 Main St, Bangor, ME 04401, 207-947-4591. Degrees granted: Associate.

Attendance and degree information available by FAX, mail. Search requires name plus social security number, date of birth, approximate years of attendance, signed release. Other helpful information: exact years of attendance. No fee for information.

Transcripts available by FAX, mail. Search requires name plus social security number, date of birth, approximate years of attendance, signed release. Other helpful information: exact years of attendance. Fee is $2.00.

Major credit cards accepted for payment.

Beaufort County Community College, Registrar, PO Box 1069, Washington, NC 27889, 919-946-6194 (FAX: 919-946-0271). Hours: 8:15AM-5PM M-Th; 8:15AM-4PM F. Records go back to 1970. Degrees granted: Associate.

Attendance information available by phone, FAX, mail. Search requires name plus social security number, approximate years of attendance. Other helpful information: exact years of attendance. No fee for information.

Degree information available by phone, FAX, mail. Search requires name plus social security number, approximate years of attendance. Other helpful information: date of birth, exact years of attendance. No fee for information.

Transcripts available by mail. Search requires name plus social security number, signed release. Other helpful information: date of birth, approximate years of attendance. Fee is $2.00.

Beaver College, Registrar, 450 S Easton Rd, Glenside, PA 19038-3295, 215-572-2100 (FAX: 215-572-2126). Hours: 8:30AM-8PM M-Th, 8:30AM-5PM F. Records go back to 1949. Alumni records are maintained here also. Call 215-572-2160. Degrees granted: Associate; Bachelors; Masters; Post Bac. Adverse incident record source: Security Dept., 215-572-2800.

Attendance and degree information available by phone, FAX, mail. Search requires name plus social security number, exact years of attendance. No fee for information.

Transcripts available by mail. Search requires name plus social security number, exact years of attendance, signed release. Fee is $5.00.

Becker College, Registrar, 61 Sever St, Worcester, MA 01615, 508-791-9241 (FAX: 508-831-7505). Hours: 8:30AM-5PM. Records go back to 1930s. Alumni records are maintained here also. Call 508-791-9241. Degrees granted: Associate; Bachelors.

Attendance and degree information available by phone, FAX, mail. Search requires name plus exact years of attendance, signed release. Other helpful information: social security number, date of birth. No fee for information.

Transcripts available by FAX, mail. Search requires name plus exact years of attendance, signed release. Other helpful information: social security number, date of birth. Fee is $3.00.

Need maiden name.

Becker College, (Branch), Registrar, 3 Paxton St, Leicester, MA 01524, 508-791-9241 X434 (FAX: 508-892-0330). Hours: 8AM-5PM. Records go back to 1897. Degrees granted: Bachelors.

Attendance information available by phone, FAX, mail. Search requires name plus social security number, exact years of attendance. No fee for information.

Degree information available by phone, FAX, mail. Search requires name plus social security number, exact years of attendance. Other helpful information: date of birth. No fee for information.

Transcripts available by written request only. Search requires name plus social security number, exact years of attendance, signed release. Fee is $3.00.

Bee County College, Registrar, 3800 Charco Rd, Beeville, TX 78102, 512-358-3130 X244 (FAX: 512-358-3971). Hours: 8AM-4:30PM. Degrees granted: Associate.

Attendance and degree information available by mail. Search requires name plus social security number, exact years of attendance. No fee for information.

Transcripts available by mail. Search requires name plus social security number, exact years of attendance, signed release. Fee is $2.00.

Bel-Rea Institute of Animal Technology, Registrar, 1681 S Dayton St, Denver, CO 80321-3048, 303-751-8700. Hours: 8AM-5PM. Records go back to 1970. Degrees granted: Associate.

School will not confirm attendance information.

Degree information available by phone, FAX, mail. Search requires name plus approximate years of attendance. Other helpful information: social security number, date of birth. No fee for information.

The Sourcebook of College and University Student Records

Transcripts available by mail. Search requires name plus approximate years of attendance, signed release. Other helpful information: social security number, date of birth. Fee is $2.00.

Belhaven College, Registrar, 1500 Peachtree St, Jackson, MS 39202, 601-968-5922 (FAX: 601-968-9998). Hours: 8AM-5PM. Records go back to 1900. Alumni records are maintained here also. Call 601-968-5930. Degrees granted: Bachelors. Adverse incident record source: Security, 601-968-5900.

Attendance information available by phone, FAX, mail. Search requires name plus social security number, date of birth, signed release. No fee for information.

Degree information available by written request only. Search requires name plus social security number, date of birth, signed release. Other helpful information: approximate years of attendance. No fee for information.

Transcripts available by written request only. Search requires name plus social security number, date of birth, signed release. Other helpful information: approximate years of attendance. Fee is $3.00.

Bellarmine College, Registrar, 2001 Newburg Rd, Louisville, KY 40205, 502-452-8133 (FAX: 502-456-3331). Hours: 8AM-5PM. Records go back to 1938. Alumni records are maintained here also. Call 502-452-8333. Degrees granted: Associate; Bachelors; Masters.

Attendance and degree information available by phone, FAX, mail. Search requires name plus social security number, approximate years of attendance, signed release. Other helpful information: date of birth, exact years of attendance. No fee for information.

Transcripts available by mail. Search requires name plus social security number, approximate years of attendance, signed release. Other helpful information: date of birth, exact years of attendance. Fee is $3.00.

Belleville Area College, Registrar, 2500 Carlyle Rd, Belleville, IL 62221, 618-235-2700 X214 (FAX: 618-235-1578). Hours: 8AM-7PM M-Th, 8AM-4PM F. Records go back 50 years. Degrees granted: Associate.

Attendance and degree information available by phone, FAX, mail. Search requires name only. Other helpful information: date of birth, approximate years of attendance. No fee for information.

Transcripts available by FAX, mail. Search requires name plus signed release. Other helpful information: date of birth, approximate years of attendance. Fee is $2.00. Expedited service available for $10.00.

Major credit cards accepted for payment.

Bellevue Community College, Registrar, 3000 Landerholm Cir SE, Room B232D, Mainstop B125, Bellevue, WA 98007-6484, 206-641-2761. Hours: 8AM-5PM. Degrees granted: Associate.

Attendance and degree information available by phone, mail. Search requires name plus social security number, date of birth, exact years of attendance. No fee for information.

Transcripts available by mail. Search requires name plus social security number, date of birth, exact years of attendance, signed release. No fee for transcripts.

Bellevue University, Registrar, Galvin Rd at Harvell Dr, Bellevue, NE 68005, 402-293-3780 (FAX: 402-293-2020). Hours: 8AM-5PM. Records go back to 1966. Alumni records are maintained here also. Call 402-293-3707. Degrees granted: Bachelors; Masters.

Attendance and degree information available by phone, FAX, mail. Search requires name only. Other helpful information: social security number, date of birth, approximate years of attendance. No fee for information.

Transcripts available by mail. Search requires name plus signed release. Fee is $3.00.

Bellin College of Nursing, Registrar, PO Box 1700, 929 Cass St, Green Bay, WI 54305, 414-433-3560. Hours: 8AM-4:30PM. Records go back to 1970S. Degrees granted: Associate.

Attendance and degree information available by phone, mail. Search requires name plus social security number. No fee for information.

Transcripts available by written request only. Search requires name plus social security number, signed release. Fee is $4.00.

Belmont Abbey College, Registrar, 100 Belmont-Mount Holly Rd, Belmont, NC 28012-2795, 704-825-6732 (FAX: 704-825-6727). Hours: 8:30AM-4:30PM. Degrees granted: Bachelors; Masters.

Attendance information available by phone. Search requires name only. Other helpful information: social security number, date of birth, approximate years of attendance. No fee for information.

Degree information available by phone. Search requires name only. Other helpful information: date of birth, approximate years of attendance. No fee for information.

Transcripts available by written request only. Search requires name plus signed release. Other helpful information: social security number, date of birth, approximate years of attendance. Fee is $2.00.

Belmont Technical College, Registrar, 120 Fox-Shannon Pl, St. Clairsville, OH 43950, 614-695-9500 (FAX: 614-695-2247). Hours: 8AM-4:30PM. Records go back to 1971. Degrees granted: Associate.

Attendance and degree information available by phone, FAX, mail. Search requires name plus social security number. Other helpful information: approximate years of attendance. No fee for information.

Transcripts available by mail. Search requires name plus social security number, signed release. Other helpful information: approximate years of attendance. No fee for transcripts.

Will FAX "issued to student" only.

Belmont University, Registrar, 1900 Belmont Blvd, Nashville, TN 37212-3757, 615-385-6619 (FAX: 615-386-4415). Hours: 8AM-4:30PM. Records go back to 1955. Degrees granted: Associate; Bachelors; Masters.

Attendance and degree information available by phone, FAX, mail. Search requires name plus social security number, approximate years of attendance, signed release. Other helpful information: date of birth. No fee for information.

Transcripts available by FAX, mail. Search requires name plus social security number, approximate years of attendance, signed release. Other helpful information: date of birth. Fee is $1.00. Expedited service available for $1.00.

Beloit College, Registrar, 700 College St, Beloit, WI 53511, 608-363-2640 (FAX: 608-363-2718). Alumni records are maintained here also. Call 608-363-2218. Degrees granted: Bachelors; Masters.

Degree Granting Institutions

Attendance and degree information available by phone, FAX, mail. Search requires name plus date of birth, approximate years of attendance. Other helpful information: social security number. No fee for information.

Transcripts available by FAX, mail. Search requires name plus social security number, date of birth, approximate years of attendance, signed release. Fee is $2.00.

Bemidji State University, Registrar, 1500 Birchmont Dr NE, Bemidji, MN 56601-2699, 218-755-2020 (FAX: 218-744-4048). Hours: 8AM-4PM. Records go back to 1919. Alumni records are maintained here also. Call 218-755-3989. Degrees granted: Associate; Bachelors; Masters.

Attendance and degree information available by phone, FAX, mail. Search requires name only. Other helpful information: social security number, date of birth, approximate years of attendance. No fee for information.

Transcripts available by FAX, mail. Search requires name plus signed release. Other helpful information: social security number, date of birth, approximate years of attendance. Fee is $2.00.

Benedict College, Registrar, 1600 Harden St, Columbia, SC 29204, 803-253-5143 (FAX: 803-253-5167). Records go back to 1870. Alumni records are maintained here at the same phone number. Degrees granted: Bachelors.

Attendance and degree information available by phone, FAX, mail. Search requires name plus social security number, date of birth, exact years of attendance. No fee for information.

Transcripts available by FAX, mail. Search requires name plus social security number, date of birth, exact years of attendance, signed release. Fee is $5.00.

Benedictine College, Registrar, 1020 N Second St, Atchison, KS 66002, 913-367-5340 X2550 (FAX: 913-367-3673). Hours: 8AM-Noon, 1-5PM. Records go back to 1858. Degrees granted: Associate; Bachelors; Masters. Adverse incident record source: Student Affairs, 913-367-5340 X2550.

Attendance information available by phone, FAX, mail. Search requires name only. Other helpful information: social security number, date of birth, exact years of attendance. No fee for information.

Degree information available by phone, FAX, mail. Search requires name only. Other helpful information: social security number, date of birth, exact years of attendance. No fee for information.

Transcripts available by FAX, mail. Search requires name plus social security number, signed release. Other helpful information: date of birth, exact years of attendance. Fee is $3.00. Expedited service available for $5.00.

Bennett College, Records Office, 900 E Washington St, Greensboro, NC 27401-3239, 910-370-8620 (FAX: 910-272-7143). Hours: 8AM-5PM. Records go back to 1928. Alumni records are maintained here also. Call 910-370-8620. Degrees granted: Bachelors.

Attendance information available by phone, FAX, mail. Search requires name plus social security number. No fee for information.

Degree information available by phone, FAX, mail. Search requires name plus social security number, exact years of attendance. Other helpful information: approximate years of attendance. No fee for information.

Transcripts available by FAX, mail. Search requires name plus social security number, exact years of attendance, signed release. Fee is $2.00.

Need former names. Major credit cards accepted for payment.

Bennington College, Registrar, Bennington, VT 05201, 802-442-5401 X2212 (FAX: 802-442-6164). Hours: 9AM-5PM. Records go back to 1932. Degrees granted: Bachelors; Masters.

Attendance and degree information available by FAX, mail. Search requires name plus date of birth, signed release. Other helpful information: exact years of attendance. No fee for information.

Transcripts available by FAX, mail. Search requires name plus date of birth, exact years of attendance, signed release. Other helpful information: social security number. Fee is $3.00.

Bentley College, Registrar, 175 Forest St, Waltham, MA 02154-4705, 617-891-2177 (FAX: 617-891-3428). Hours: 8:30AM-6:30PM M-Th, 8:30AM-4:30PM. Records go back to 1917. Alumni records are maintained here also. Call 617-891-3444. Degrees granted: Associate; Bachelors. Adverse incident record source: Dean of Students, 617-891-2058.

Attendance and degree information available by phone, FAX, mail. Search requires name plus social security number, signed release. No fee for information.

Transcripts available by FAX, mail. Search requires name plus social security number, signed release. Fee is $2.00.

Berea College, Registrar, Berea, KY 40404, 606-986-9341 X5185 (FAX: 606-986-4506). Hours: 8AM-Noon, 1-5PM. Records go back to 1855. Degrees granted: Bachelors.

Attendance and degree information available by phone, FAX, mail. Search requires name only. Other helpful information: social security number, approximate years of attendance. No fee for information.

Transcripts available by mail. Search requires name plus signed release. Other helpful information: social security number, approximate years of attendance. Fee is $2.00.

Berean Institute, Registrar, 1901 W Girard Ave, Philadelphia, PA 19130-1599, 215-763-4833 (FAX: 215-236-6011). Hours: 9AM-5PM. Records go back to 1940. Alumni records are maintained here at the same phone number. Degrees granted: Associate. Adverse incident record source: Student Affairs, 215-763-4833.

Attendance information available by phone, FAX, mail. Search requires name plus social security number. No fee for information.

Degree information available by phone, FAX, mail. Search requires name plus social security number, exact years of attendance. No fee for information.

Transcripts available by FAX, mail. Search requires name plus social security number, exact years of attendance, signed release. First transcript is free. Additional ones are $5.00 each.

Bergen Community College, Registrar, 400 Paramus Rd, Paramus, NJ 07652, 201-447-7857 (FAX: 201-670-7973). Hours: 9AM-5PM. Records go back to 1968. Degrees granted: Associate.

Attendance information available by FAX, mail. Search requires name plus social security number, signed release. Other helpful information: date of birth, approximate years of attendance. No fee for information.

Degree information available by mail. Search requires name plus social security number, signed release. Other helpful information:

date of birth, approximate years of attendance. No fee for information.

Transcripts available by mail. Search requires name plus social security number, signed release. Other helpful information: date of birth, approximate years of attendance. Fee is $3.00.

Major credit cards accepted for payment.

Berkeley College, Registrar, W Red Oak Lane, White Plains, NY 10604, 201-652-0388 X126 (FAX: 201-670-7735). Hours: 9AM-5PM. Records go back to 1932. Degrees granted: Associate.

Attendance and degree information available by phone, FAX, mail. Search requires name plus social security number, approximate years of attendance, signed release. No fee for information.

Transcripts available by mail. Search requires name plus social security number, approximate years of attendance, signed release. Fee is $5.00.

Berkeley College of Business, (Waldwick Campus), Registrar, 100 W Prospect St, Waldwick, NJ 07463, 201-652-0388 (FAX: 201-670-7737). Hours: 7:30AM-4:30PM. Records go back to 1961. Alumni records are maintained here at the same phone number. Degrees granted: Associate.

Attendance and degree information available by phone, FAX, mail. Search requires name plus social security number, approximate years of attendance. Other helpful information: date of birth, exact years of attendance. No fee for information.

Transcripts available by mail. Search requires name plus social security number, approximate years of attendance, signed release. Other helpful information: date of birth, exact years of attendance. Fee is $5.00.

Berkeley College of Business, (West Paterson Campus), Office of the Registrar, 44 Rifle Camp Rd, West Paterson, NJ 07424, 201-652-1346 X126 (FAX: 201-670-7737). Hours: 8:30AM-4:30PM. Records go back to 1945. Degrees granted: Associate.

School will not confirm attendance information. Search requires name plus social security number, exact years of attendance, signed release. Other helpful information: date of birth. No fee for information.

Degree information available by FAX, mail. Search requires name plus social security number, exact years of attendance, signed release. Other helpful information: date of birth. No fee for information.

Transcripts available by written request only. Search requires name plus social security number, exact years of attendance, signed release. Other helpful information: date of birth. Fee is $5.00.

Need name of campus attended.

Berkeley College of Business, (Woodbridge Campus), Registrar, 430 Rahway Ave, Woodbridge, NJ 07095, 201-750-1800. Hours: 7:30AM-4:30PM. Records go back to founding date. Alumni records are maintained here at the same phone number. Degrees granted: Associate.

Attendance and degree information available by phone, FAX, mail. Search requires name plus social security number, approximate years of attendance. Other helpful information: exact years of attendance. No fee for information.

Transcripts available by written request only. Search requires name plus social security number, approximate years of attendance, signed release. Other helpful information: exact years of attendance. Fee is $5.00.

Berkeley School of New York, Registrar, 3 E 43rd St, New York, NY 10017, 212-986-4343. Records are not housed here. They are located at Berkeley College of Business, (West Paterson Campus), Office of the Registrar, 44 Rifle Camp Rd, West Paterson, NJ 07424.

Berklee College of Music, Registrar, 1140 Boylston St, Boston, MA 02215, 617-266-1400 (FAX: 617-247-8278). Hours: 9AM-5PM. Records go back to 1950. Degrees granted: Bachelors; 4 year Professional Diploma. Adverse incident record source: Dean of Students.

Attendance and degree information available by phone, FAX, mail. Search requires name only. Other helpful information: social security number, date of birth, exact years of attendance. No fee for information.

Transcripts available by FAX, mail. Search requires name plus approximate years of attendance, signed release. Other helpful information: social security number. No fee for transcripts.

Berkshire Community College, Registrar, West St, Pittsfield, MA 01201, 413-499-4660. Hours: 8AM-8PM M-Th; 8AM-4PM F. Records go back 10 years. Degrees granted: Associate.

Attendance information available by phone, mail. Search requires name plus social security number, exact years of attendance. No fee for information.

Degree information available by phone, mail. Search requires name plus social security number. Other helpful information: approximate years of attendance. No fee for information.

Transcripts available by mail. Search requires name plus social security number, signed release. Other helpful information: date of birth, approximate years of attendance. Fee is $3.00.

Bernard M. Baruch College, Registrar, 17 Lexington Ave, New York, NY 10010, 212-802-2182 (FAX: 212-802-2190). Hours: 9:15AM-7PM M-Th; 9:15AM-4:45PM F. Records go back to 1920. Alumni records are maintained here also. Call 212-387-1145. Degrees granted: Bachelors; Masters.

Attendance and degree information available by FAX, mail. Search requires name plus social security number, date of birth, approximate years of attendance, signed release. No fee for information.

Transcripts available by FAX, mail. Search requires name plus social security number, date of birth, approximate years of attendance, signed release. Fee is $4.00.

Berry College, Registrar, 400 Mount Berry Station, Rome, GA 30149-0039, 706-236-2282 (FAX: 706-236-2248). Hours: 8AM-5PM. Records go back to 1902. Alumni records are maintained here also. Call 706-236-2256. Degrees granted: Bachelors; Masters.

Attendance and degree information available by phone, FAX, mail. Search requires name plus social security number. No fee for information.

Transcripts available by FAX, mail. Search requires name plus social security number, signed release. Fee is $3.00. Expedite fee is $5.00 plus FedEx fee of $8.00.

Bessemer State Technical College, Registrar, PO Box 308, Bessemer, AL 35021, 205-428-6391. Hours: 8AM-4PM. Records go back to 1965. Degrees granted: Associate.

Attendance and degree information available by phone, mail. Search requires name plus social security number. No fee for information.

Transcripts available by mail. Search requires name plus social security number, exact years of attendance, signed release. First three transcripts are free. Additional ones are $3.00 each.

Beth HaTalmud Rabbinical College, Registrar, 2127 82nd St, Brooklyn, NY 11214, 718-259-2525. Hours: 9AM-2PM. Records go back to 1990.

Attendance and degree information available by phone, FAX, mail. Search requires name plus social security number, approximate years of attendance, signed release. No fee for information.

Transcripts available by mail. Search requires name plus social security number, approximate years of attendance, signed release. No fee for transcripts.

Beth Hamedrash Shaarei Yosher, Registrar, 4102 16th Ave, Brooklyn, NY 11204, 718-854-2290. Hours: 8AM-5PM. Records go back to 1957.

Attendance and degree information available by phone, mail. Search requires name plus social security number, date of birth, exact years of attendance, signed release. No fee for information.

Transcripts available by mail. Search requires name plus social security number, date of birth, exact years of attendance, signed release. No fee for transcripts.

Beth Medrash Govoha, Registrar, 617 Sixth St, Lakewood, NJ 08701, 908-367-1060 (FAX: 908-367-7487). Hours: 9AM-1:40PM. Records go back to 1970. Degrees granted: Bachelors; Masters.

Attendance and degree information available by FAX. Search requires name plus signed release. Other helpful information: social security number, date of birth, approximate years of attendance. No fee for information.

Transcripts available by FAX. Search requires name plus signed release. Other helpful information: date of birth, approximate years of attendance. Fee is $3.00. Expedited service available for $3.00.

Beth-El College of Nursing, Registrar, 2790 N Academy Blvd Ste 200, Colorado Springs, CO 80917-5338, 719-475-5170 (FAX: 719-475-5198). Hours: 8AM-4:30PM. Records go back to 1907. Degrees granted: Bachelors; Masters. Certification: NNP Forensics.

Attendance and degree information available by phone, FAX, mail. Search requires name plus social security number, approximate years of attendance, signed release. Other helpful information: date of birth. No fee for information.

Transcripts available by FAX, mail. Search requires name plus social security number, approximate years of attendance, signed release. Other helpful information: date of birth. Fee is $2.00. Expedited service available for $2.00.

Major credit cards accepted for payment.

Bethany College, Registrar, Bethany, WV 26032, 304-829-7831 (FAX: 304-829-7108). Hours: 8AM-4:30PM. Records go back to 1900. Degrees granted: Bachelors. Adverse incident record source: Dean of Students, 304-829-7631.

Attendance and degree information available by phone, FAX, mail. Search requires name only. Other helpful information: date of birth, approximate years of attendance. No fee for information.

Transcripts available by FAX, mail. Search requires name plus signed release. Other helpful information: date of birth, approximate years of attendance. Fee is $1.00.

Bethany College, Registrar, 421 N First St, Lindsborg, KS 67456, 913-227-3311 (FAX: 913-227-2004). Hours: 8AM-5PM. Records go back to 1888. Alumni records are maintained here at the same phone number. Degrees granted: Bachelors.

Attendance information available by phone, FAX, mail. Search requires name plus social security number. Other helpful information: date of birth, approximate years of attendance. No fee for information.

Degree information available by phone, FAX, mail. Search requires name plus social security number. No fee for information.

Transcripts available by written request only. Search requires name plus social security number, signed release. Other helpful information: date of birth, approximate years of attendance. Fee is $3.00.

Bethany College of the Assemblies of God, Registrar, 800 Bethany Dr, Scotts Valley, CA 95066, 408-438-3800 X1444 (FAX: 408-438-1621). Hours: 8AM-5PM. Records go back to 1919. Alumni records are maintained here also. Call 408-438-3800 X1470. Degrees granted: Associate; Bachelors. Adverse incident record source: Campus Life, 408-438-3800 X1417.

Attendance information available by phone, FAX, mail. Search requires name plus social security number, date of birth. Other helpful information: exact years of attendance. No fee for information.

Degree information available by phone, mail. Search requires name plus social security number, date of birth, exact years of attendance, signed release. Other helpful information: approximate years of attendance. No fee for information.

Transcripts available by mail. Search requires name plus social security number, date of birth, approximate years of attendance, signed release. Other helpful information: exact years of attendance. Fee is $5.00.

Bethany Lutheran College, Registrar, 734 Marsh St, Mankato, MN 56001, 507-386-5310 (FAX: 507-386-5376). Hours: 8AM-5PM. Records go back to 1911. Alumni records are maintained here also. Call 507-386-5314. Degrees granted: Associate.

Attendance and degree information available by phone, FAX, mail. Search requires name plus social security number, signed release. No fee for information.

Transcripts available by FAX, mail. Search requires name plus social security number, signed release. Fee is $2.00.

Bethany Theological Seminary, Coordinator of Academic Services, 615 National Road W, Richmond, IN 47374-4019, 317-983-1816 (FAX: 317-983-1840). Hours: 8AM-5PM. Records go back to 1905. Alumni records are maintained here also. Call 317-983-1806. Degrees granted: Masters. Certification: Theological Studies.

Attendance and degree information available by phone, FAX, mail. Search requires name only. Other helpful information: social security number, date of birth, approximate years of attendance. No fee for information.

Transcripts available by FAX, mail. Search requires name plus signed release. Other helpful information: social security number, date of birth, approximate years of attendance. Fee is $5.00.

Bethel College, Registrar, 325 Cherry Ave, McKenzie, TN 38201, 901-352-1000 (FAX: 901-352-1008). Hours: 8AM-4:30PM. Records go back to 1842. Alumni records are maintained here also. Call 901-352-1000. Degrees granted: Bachelors; Masters.

Attendance and degree information available by phone, FAX, mail. Search requires name only. Other helpful information: social security number, date of birth. No fee for information.

Transcripts available by FAX, mail. Search requires name plus signed release. Other helpful information: social security number, date of birth. Fee is $2.00.

Bethel College, Registrar, 1001 W McKinley Ave, Mishawaka, IN 46545, 219-257-3302. Hours: 8AM-5PM. Records go back to 1947. Degrees granted: Associate; Bachelors; Masters.

Attendance information available by phone, FAX. Search requires name only. Other helpful information: social security number, date of birth, exact years of attendance. No fee for information.

Degree information available by phone, FAX, mail. Search requires name only. Other helpful information: social security number, date of birth, exact years of attendance. No fee for information.

Transcripts available by written request only. Search requires name plus approximate years of attendance, signed release. Other helpful information: social security number, date of birth, exact years of attendance. Fee is $4.00.

Bethel College, Registrar, 300 E 27th St, North Newton, KS 67117, 316-283-2500 (FAX: 316-284-5286). Hours: 8AM-Noon, 1-5PM. Alumni records are maintained here at the same phone number. Degrees granted: Bachelors.

Attendance and degree information available by phone, FAX, mail. Search requires name plus exact years of attendance. Other helpful information: social security number, date of birth, approximate years of attendance. No fee for information.

Transcripts available by written request only. Search requires name plus social security number, signed release. Other helpful information: date of birth, approximate years of attendance. Fee is $2.00. Expedited service available for $4.00.

Bethel College, Registrar, 3900 Bethel Dr, St Paul, MN 55112, 612-638-6250 (FAX: 612-638-6001). Hours: 8AM-4:30PM. Degrees granted: Associate; Bachelors; Masters. Adverse incident record source: Student Life, 612-638-6300.

Attendance and degree information available by phone, FAX, mail. Search requires name only. Other helpful information: social security number, date of birth, approximate years of attendance. No fee for information.

School does not provide transcripts. Search requires name only. Other helpful information: social security number, date of birth, approximate years of attendance. Fee is $1.00.

Bethel Seminary College, (West), Registrar, 6116 Arosa St, San Diego, CA 92115, 619-582-8188. Hours: 8AM-5PM. Records go back to 1977. Degrees granted: Masters; Doctorate.

Attendance and degree information available by phone, mail. Search requires name plus social security number, exact years of attendance. No fee for information.

Transcripts available by mail. Search requires name plus social security number, exact years of attendance, signed release. Fee is $2.00.

Bethel Theological Seminary, Registrar, 3949 Bethel Dr, St Paul, MN 55112, 612-638-6181 (FAX: 612-638-6002). Hours: 8AM-4:30PM. Records go back to 1930. Records prior to 1930 in archives. Alumni Records Office: Alumni Association, Bethel Theological Seminary, 3900 Bethel Dr, St Paul, MN 55112. Degrees granted: Masters; Doctorate.

Attendance and degree information available by phone, FAX, mail. Search requires name only. Other helpful information: social security number, date of birth, approximate years of attendance. No fee for information.

Transcripts available by FAX, mail. Search requires name plus signed release. Other helpful information: social security number, date of birth, approximate years of attendance. Fee is $2.00. Expedited service available for $10.00.

Bethune-Cookman College, Registrar, 640 Dr Mary McLeod Bethune Blvd, Daytona Beach, FL 32114-3099, 904-255-1401 (FAX: 904-257-5338). Hours: 8:30AM-5PM. Records go back to 1904. Alumni records are maintained here also. Call 904-255-1401. Degrees granted: Bachelors.

Attendance information available by FAX, mail. Search requires name plus social security number, signed release. No fee for information.

Degree information available by phone, FAX, mail. Search requires name plus social security number, signed release. No fee for information.

Transcripts available by mail. Search requires name plus social security number, signed release. Fee is $2.00.

Bevill State Community College, Registrar, PO Box 800, Sumiton, AL 35148, 205-648-3271 (FAX: 205-648-2288). Hours: 8AM-4:30PM. Records go back to 1969. Degrees granted: Associate.

Attendance information available by phone, FAX, mail. Search requires name only. Other helpful information: social security number, date of birth, approximate years of attendance. No fee for information.

Degree information available by mail. Search requires name only. Other helpful information: social security number, date of birth, approximate years of attendance. No fee for information.

Transcripts available by mail. Search requires name plus social security number, signed release. Other helpful information: date of birth, approximate years of attendance. Fee is $3.00. Major credit cards accepted for payment.

Bevill State Community College, (Brewer), Registrar, 2631 Temple Ave N, Fayette, AL 35555, 205-932-3221. Records are not housed here. They are located at Bevill State Community College, Registrar, PO Box 800, Sumiton, AL 35148.

Biblical Theological Seminary, Registrar, 200 N Main St, Hatfield, PA 19440, 215-368-5000 (FAX: 215-368-7002). Hours: 8:30AM-4:30PM. Records go back to 1972. Alumni records are maintained here at the same phone number. Degrees granted: Masters; Doctorate.

Attendance and degree information available by phone, mail. Search requires name plus social security number, exact years of attendance. No fee for information.

Transcripts available by mail. Search requires name plus social security number, date of birth, exact years of attendance, signed release. Fee is $2.00.

Big Bend Community College, Registrar, 7662 Chanute St, Moses Lake, WA 98837-3299, 509-762-6226 (FAX: 509-762-6243). Hours: 8AM-4:30PM. Records go back to founding date. Degrees granted: Associate.

Attendance and degree information available by phone, FAX, mail. Search requires name plus social security number. Other helpful information: date of birth, approximate years of attendance. No fee for information.

Transcripts available by FAX, mail. Search requires name plus social security number, signed release. Other helpful information: date of birth, approximate years of attendance. Fee is $2.00. Major credit cards accepted for payment.

Biola University, Registrar, 13800 Biola Ave, La Mirada, CA 90639, 310-903-4720 (FAX: 310-903-4748). Hours: 8:30AM-4:30PM. Records go back to 1913. Alumni records are maintained here also. Call 310-903-4728. Degrees granted: Bachelors; Masters; Doctorate. Adverse incident record source: Registrar's Office, 310-903-4720.

Attendance and degree information available by phone, FAX, mail. Search requires name plus social security number, date of birth, exact years of attendance. No fee for information.

Transcripts available by mail. Search requires name plus social security number, date of birth, exact years of attendance, signed release. Fee is $6.00. Expedited service available for $9.00. Need student ID number.

Birmingham-Southern College, Registrar, 900 Arkadelphia Rd, Birmingham, AL 35254, 205-226-4698. Hours: 8:15AM-4:45PM. Records go back to 1856. Degrees granted: Bachelors; Masters.

Attendance and degree information available by phone, FAX, mail. Search requires name only. Other helpful information: social security number, date of birth, approximate years of attendance. No fee for information.

Transcripts available by mail. Search requires name plus exact years of attendance, signed release. Other helpful information: social security number, approximate years of attendance. Fee is $3.00. Expedited service available for $3.00.

Bishop State Community College, Registrar, 351 N Broad St, Mobile, AL 36603-5898, 205-690-6421 (FAX: 205-438-5403). Hours: 8AM-5PM. Records go back to 1960. Degrees granted: Associate.

Attendance and degree information available by phone, mail. Search requires name plus social security number, exact years of attendance. No fee for information.

Transcripts available by mail. Search requires name plus social security number, exact years of attendance, signed release. Fee is $1.00.

Bishop State Community College, (Carver), Registrar, 414 Stanton St, Mobile, AL 36617, 334-473-8692 (FAX: 334-471-5961). Hours: 8AM-4:30PM. Degrees granted: Associate.

Attendance and degree information available by mail. Search requires name plus social security number, date of birth, signed release. Other helpful information: exact years of attendance. No fee for information.

Transcripts available by mail. Search requires name plus social security number, date of birth, signed release. Other helpful information: exact years of attendance. Fee is $2.00. Major credit cards accepted for payment.

Bishop State Community College, (Southwest), Registrar, 925 Dauphin Island Pkwy, Mobile, AL 36605-3299, 334-479-7476 (FAX: 334-473-2049). Hours: 8AM-7PM M-Th; 8AM-4:30PM F. Records go back to 1955. Degrees granted: Associate.

Attendance and degree information available by mail. Search requires name plus social security number, approximate years of attendance, signed release. Other helpful information: date of birth, exact years of attendance. No fee for information.

Transcripts available by mail. Search requires name plus social security number, approximate years of attendance, signed release. Other helpful information: date of birth, exact years of attendance. First two transcripts are free. Additional ones are $3.00 each. Major credit cards accepted for payment.

Bismarck State College, Registrar, 1500 Edwards Ave, Bismarck, ND 58501, 701-224-5429 (FAX: 701-224-5550). Hours: 8AM-5PM M-Th, 8AM-4PM F. Alumni records are maintained here also. Call 701-224-5431. Degrees granted: Associate.

Attendance and degree information available by phone, FAX, mail. Search requires name plus social security number, date of birth, approximate years of attendance, signed release. No fee for information.

Transcripts available by phone, FAX, mail. Search requires name plus social security number, date of birth, approximate years of attendance, signed release. No fee for transcripts.

Black Hawk College, Registrar, 6600 34th Ave, Moline, IL 61265, 309-796-1260. Hours: 7:30AM-6PM M-T, 7:30AM-5PM W-F. Records go back to 1966. Alumni records are maintained here also. Call 309-796-1311. Degrees granted: Associate.

Attendance information available by phone, mail. Search requires name plus social security number. No fee for information.

Degree information available by mail. Search requires name plus social security number. No fee for information.

Transcripts available by mail. Search requires name plus social security number, exact years of attendance, signed release. Fee is $5.00.

Major credit cards accepted for payment.

Black Hills State University, Admissions & Records, 1200 University Ave, USB 9502, Spearfish, SD 57799-9502, 605-642-6011 (FAX: 605-642-6214). Hours: 7AM-5PM. Records go back to 1885. Degrees granted: Associate; Bachelors; Masters.

Attendance information available by FAX. Search requires name plus social security number, signed release. Other helpful information: date of birth, approximate years of attendance. No fee for information.

Degree information available by FAX. Search requires name plus social security number, signed release. Other helpful information: date of birth, approximate years of attendance. No fee for information.

Transcripts available by FAX. Search requires name plus social security number, signed release. Other helpful information: date of birth, approximate years of attendance. Fee is $5.00.

Black River Technical College, Registrar, Hwy 304 E, PO Box 468, Pocahontas, AR 72455, 501-892-4565 (FAX: 501-892-3546). Hours: 8AM-4:30PM. Records go back 5 years. Degrees granted: Associate.

Attendance and degree information available by mail. Search requires name plus social security number, date of birth, exact years of attendance, signed release. Other helpful information: approximate years of attendance. Fee is $2.00.

Transcripts available by mail. Search requires name plus social security number, date of birth, exact years of attendance, signed release. Other helpful information: approximate years of attendance. Fee is $2.00.

Blackburn College, Registrar, 700 College Ave, Carlinville, IL 62626, 217-854-3231 X4210 (FAX: 217-854-3713). Hours: 8AM-4:30PM. Degrees granted: Bachelors.

The Sourcebook of College and University Student Records

Attendance and degree information available by phone. Search requires name plus approximate years of attendance. Other helpful information: date of birth. No fee for information.

Transcripts available by mail. Search requires name plus approximate years of attendance, signed release. Other helpful information: social security number, date of birth. Fee is $2.00. Expedited service available for $12.00.

Blackfeet Community College, Registrar, Browning, MT 59417, 406-338-3197 (FAX: 406-338-7808). Hours: 8AM-4PM. Degrees granted: Associate.

Attendance and degree information available by phone, FAX, mail. Search requires name only. Other helpful information: social security number, date of birth, approximate years of attendance. No fee for information.

Transcripts available by written request only. Search requires name plus signed release. Other helpful information: social security number, date of birth, approximate years of attendance. Fee is $1.00.

Blackhawk Technical College, Records, PO Box 5009, Janesville, WI 53547-5009, 608-757-7668 (FAX: 608-757-9407). Hours: 8AM-4:30PM. Degrees granted: Associate. Adverse incident record source: Rock County Sheriff, 608-757-8000.

School will not confirm attendance information. Search requires name plus social security number, approximate years of attendance, signed release. Other helpful information: date of birth, exact years of attendance. No fee for information.

Degree information available by phone, FAX, mail. Search requires name plus social security number, approximate years of attendance. Other helpful information: date of birth, exact years of attendance. No fee for information.

Transcripts available by mail. Search requires name plus social security number, approximate years of attendance, signed release. Other helpful information: date of birth, exact years of attendance. Fee is $3.00.

Bladen Community College, Registrar, PO Box 266, Dublin, NC 28332-0266, 910-862-2164. Hours: 8AM-4:30PM M-Th; 8AM-3PM F. Records go back to 1967. Degrees granted: Associate.

Attendance and degree information available by phone, FAX, mail. Search requires name plus social security number. Other helpful information: approximate years of attendance. No fee for information.

Transcripts available by FAX, mail. Search requires name plus social security number, signed release. Other helpful information: approximate years of attendance. First transcript is free; second one is $2.00; additional ones are $1.00 each.

Blair Junior College, Registrar, 828 Wooten Rd, Colorado Springs, CO 80915, 719-574-1082 (FAX: 719-574-4493). Hours: 7:30AM-7PM. Records go back to 1900. Degrees granted: Associate. Adverse incident record source: Same as above.

Attendance information available by phone, FAX, mail. Search requires name plus social security number, approximate years of attendance, signed release. Other helpful information: date of birth, exact years of attendance. No fee for information. Include stamped envelope.

Degree information available by phone, mail. Search requires name plus social security number, approximate years of attendance, signed release. Other helpful information: date of birth, exact years of attendance. No fee for information.

Transcripts available by mail. Search requires name plus social security number, approximate years of attendance, signed release. Other helpful information: date of birth, exact years of attendance. Fee is $2.00. Expedited service available for $10.00.

Blessing-Rieman College of Nursing, Registrar, Broadway at 11th St, PO Box 7005, Quincy, IL 62301-7005, 217-223-5811 X1486 (FAX: 217-223-6400). Hours: 8:30AM-5PM. Records go back to 1908. Degrees granted: Bachelors.

Attendance and degree information available by phone, FAX, mail. Search requires name only. Other helpful information: social security number, date of birth, approximate years of attendance. No fee for information.

Transcripts available by FAX, mail. Search requires name plus signed release. Fee is $2.00.

Blinn College, Admissions & Records, 902 College Ave, Brenham, TX 77833, 409-830-4140 (FAX: 409-830-4110). Hours: 8AM-5PM. Records go back to 1899. Degrees granted: Associate.

Attendance and degree information available by phone, FAX, mail. Search requires name plus social security number. Other helpful information: approximate years of attendance. No fee for information.

Transcripts available by mail. Search requires name plus social security number, signed release. Other helpful information: date of birth, approximate years of attendance. Fee is $3.00.

Bloomfield College, Registrar, 467 Franklin St, Bloomfield, NJ 07003, 201-478-9000 (FAX: 201-743-3998). Hours: 7:30AM-5PM. Records go back to founding date. Alumni records are maintained here at the same phone number. Degrees granted: Associate; Bachelors.

Attendance and degree information available by phone, FAX, mail. Search requires name plus date of birth, exact years of attendance, signed release. Other helpful information: approximate years of attendance. No fee for information.

Transcripts available by written request only. Search requires name plus date of birth, exact years of attendance, signed release. Other helpful information: approximate years of attendance. No fee for transcripts.

Bloomsburg University of Pennsylvania, Registrar, 400 E Second St, Bloomsburg, PA 17815, 717-389-4263 (FAX: 717-389-4001). Hours: 8AM-4:30PM. Records go back to 1888. Alumni records are maintained here also. Call 717-389-4058. Degrees granted: Associate; Bachelors; Masters. Adverse incident record source: Student Life, 717-389-4063: Campus Police, 717-389-4168

Attendance and degree information available by phone, FAX, mail. Search requires name plus social security number. Other helpful information: date of birth, approximate years of attendance. No fee for information. Include stamped envelope.

Transcripts available by written request only. Search requires name plus social security number, signed release. Other helpful information: date of birth, approximate years of attendance. Fee is $2.00.

Blue Mountain College, Registrar's Office, PO Box 188, Blue Mountain, MS 38610, 601-685-4771 X2 (FAX: 601-685-4776). Hours: 8AM-5PM. Records go back to 1910. Alumni records are maintained here at the same phone number. Alumni Records Office: PO Box 111, Blue Mountain, MS 38610. Degrees granted: Bachelors.

Degree Granting Institutions

Attendance and degree information available by phone, mail. Search requires name plus signed release. Other helpful information: social security number, date of birth, approximate years of attendance. No fee for information.

Transcripts available by written request only. Search requires name plus signed release. Other helpful information: social security number, date of birth, approximate years of attendance. Fee is $2.00.

Blue Mountain Community College, Registrar, PO Box 100, Pendleton, OR 97801, 503-276-1260 (FAX: 503-276-6118). Hours: 8AM-5PM. Records go back to 1916. Degrees granted: Associate.

Attendance information available by phone, FAX, mail. Search requires name plus social security number, approximate years of attendance, signed release. No fee for information.

Degree information available by phone, FAX, mail. Search requires name plus social security number, approximate years of attendance, signed release. No fee for information.

Transcripts available by phone, FAX, mail. Search requires name plus social security number, approximate years of attendance, signed release. Fee is $2.00.

Blue Ridge Community College, Registrar, College Dr, Flat Rock, NC 28731-9624, 704-692-3572 X217 (FAX: 704-692-2441). Hours: 8AM-8PM M-Th; 8AM-4:30PM F. Records go back to 1969. Degrees granted: Associate.

Attendance and degree information available by phone, FAX, mail. Search requires name only. Other helpful information: social security number, date of birth, exact years of attendance. No fee for information.

Transcripts available by mail. Search requires name plus signed release. Other helpful information: social security number, date of birth, exact years of attendance. No fee for transcripts.

Blue Ridge Community College, Registrar, PO Box 80, Weyers Cave, VA 24486, 703-234-9261 (FAX: 703-234-9231). Hours: 8:15AM-5PM. Records go back to 1967. Alumni records are maintained here at the same phone number. Degrees granted: Associate.

Attendance and degree information available by phone, FAX, mail. Search requires name plus social security number. Other helpful information: date of birth, approximate years of attendance. No fee for information.

Transcripts available by mail. Search requires name plus social security number, signed release. Other helpful information: date of birth, approximate years of attendance. Fee is $1.00.

Transcripts must be prepaid.

Bluefield College, Registrar, 3000 College Dr, Bluefield, VA 24605, 703-326-3682 (FAX: 703-326-4288). Hours: 8:30AM-Noon, 1-5PM. Records go back to 1922. Degrees granted: Associate; Bachelors. Adverse incident record source: Student Development.

Attendance and degree information available by phone, mail. Search requires name plus social security number, exact years of attendance. Other helpful information: date of birth, approximate years of attendance. No fee for information.

Transcripts available by mail. Search requires name plus social security number, exact years of attendance, signed release. Other helpful information: date of birth, approximate years of attendance. Fee is $3.00. Expedited service available for $10.00.

Major credit cards accepted for payment.

Bluefield State College, Registrar, 219 Rock St, Bluefield, WV 24701, 304-327-4060 (FAX: 304-325=7747). Hours: 8AM-4PM. Degrees granted: Associate; Bachelors. Adverse incident record source: Student Services, 304-327-4068.

Attendance and degree information available by phone, FAX, mail. Search requires name only. Other helpful information: social security number, approximate years of attendance. No fee for information.

Transcripts available by FAX, mail. Search requires name plus signed release. Other helpful information: social security number, approximate years of attendance. Fee is $3.00.

Bluffton College, Registrar, 280 W College Ave, Bluffton, OH 45817-1196, 419-358-3821 (FAX: 419-358-3323). Hours: 8AM-Noon, 1-5PM. Records go back 96 years. Degrees granted: Bachelors. Adverse incident record source: Student Affairs, 419-358-3248.

Attendance and degree information available by phone, mail. Search requires name plus social security number, approximate years of attendance. Other helpful information: exact years of attendance. No fee for information.

Transcripts available by FAX, mail. Search requires name plus social security number, approximate years of attendance, signed release. Other helpful information: exact years of attendance. Fee is $3.00. FAX transcripts are $15.00.

Bohecker's Business College, Registrar, 326 E Main St, Ravenna, OH 44266, 216-297-7319. Hours: 8AM-7PM M-Th, 8AM-4PM F. Records go back to 1922. Degrees granted: Associate.

Attendance and degree information available by mail. Search requires name plus social security number, approximate years of attendance, signed release. No fee for information.

Transcripts available by mail. Search requires name plus social security number, approximate years of attendance, signed release. Fee is $2.00.

Boise Bible College, Registrar, 8695 Marigold St, Boise, ID 83714, 208-376-7731 (FAX: 208-376-7743). Hours: 8:30AM-4:30PM. Alumni records are maintained here at the same phone number. Degrees granted: Associate; Bachelors. Certification: 1yr bible.

School will not confirm attendance or degree information. Search requires name only. No fee for information.

Transcripts available by FAX, mail. Search requires name plus social security number, signed release. Other helpful information: date of birth, approximate years of attendance. Fee is $5.00.

Major credit cards accepted for payment.

Boise State University, Registrars Office, 1910 University Dr, Boise, ID 83725, 208-385-3486 (FAX: 208-385-3169). Hours: 8AM-4PM. Records go back to 1930. Degrees granted: Associate; Bachelors; Masters; Doctorate.

Attendance and degree information available by phone, FAX, mail. Search requires name plus signed release. Other helpful information: social security number, date of birth, approximate years of attendance. No fee for information.

Transcripts available by FAX, mail. Search requires name plus signed release. Other helpful information: social security number, date of birth, approximate years of attendance. Fee is $3.00. Expedited service available for $10.00.

Boricua College, Registrar, 3755 Broadway, New York, NY 10032, 212-694-1000 (FAX: 212-694-1015). Hours: 9:30AM-

6PM. Records go back to 1976. Degrees granted: Associate; Bachelors.

Attendance information available by FAX, mail. Search requires name plus social security number, signed release. Other helpful information: date of birth, approximate years of attendance. No fee for information.

Degree information available by mail. Search requires name plus social security number, approximate years of attendance, signed release. Other helpful information: date of birth. No fee for information.

Transcripts available by mail. Search requires name plus social security number, date of birth, approximate years of attendance, signed release. Other helpful information: exact years of attendance. Fee is $7.00.

Borough of Manhattan Community College, Registrar, 199 Chambers St, New York, NY 10007, 212-346-8000. Degrees granted: Associate.

Attendance and degree information available by mail. Search requires name plus social security number, signed release. Other helpful information: date of birth, exact years of attendance. No fee for information.

Transcripts available by mail. Search requires name plus social security number, signed release. Other helpful information: date of birth, exact years of attendance. Fee is $4.00.

Bossier Parish Community College, Registrar, 2719 Airline Dr at I-220, Bossier City, LA 71111, 318-746-9851 (FAX: 318-742-8664). Hours: 8AM-4PM M-Th, 8AM-3PM F. Records go back to 1967. Degrees granted: Associate. Adverse incident record source: Student Affairs, 318-746-9851 X64.

Attendance and degree information available by phone, FAX, mail. Search requires name plus signed release. Other helpful information: social security number, approximate years of attendance. No fee for information.

Transcripts available by FAX, mail. Search requires name plus signed release. Other helpful information: social security number, approximate years of attendance. No fee for transcripts.

Boston College, Registrar, Chestnut Hill, MA 02167-3934, 617-552-2300 (FAX: 617-552-4975). Hours: 8:45AM-4:45PM. Records go back to 1863. Alumni records are maintained here also. Call 617-552-3440. Degrees granted: Bachelors; Masters; Doctorate; Graduate Law School. Adverse incident record source: Dean, 617-552-3470.

Attendance information available by phone, FAX, mail. Search requires name plus social security number, approximate years of attendance, signed release. No fee for information.

Degree information available by FAX, mail. Search requires name plus social security number, approximate years of attendance, signed release. No fee for information.

Transcripts available by FAX, mail. Search requires name plus social security number, approximate years of attendance, signed release. Fee is $2.00. Expedited service available for $7.00.

Boston Conservatory, Registrar, 8 The Fenway, Boston, MA 02215, 617-536-6340 X46. Hours: 9AM-5PM. Records go back to 1920. Alumni records are maintained here also. Call 617-536-6340 X28. Degrees granted: Bachelors; Masters.

Attendance and degree information available by phone, mail. Search requires name plus social security number, exact years of attendance. No fee for information.

Transcripts available by mail. Search requires name plus social security number, exact years of attendance, signed release. First transcript is free. Additional transcripts are $5.00 each.

Boston University, Registrar, 147 Bay State Rd, Boston, MA 02215, 617-353-3616. Hours: 9AM-5PM. Records go back to 1800s. Alumni records are maintained here also. Call 617-353-2233. Degrees granted: Bachelors; Masters; Doctorate.

Attendance and degree information available by phone, mail. Search requires name plus social security number, date of birth, signed release. No fee for information.

Transcripts available by mail. Search requires name plus social security number, date of birth, signed release. Fee is $3.00.

Bowdoin College, Registrar, Brunswick, ME 04011, 207-725-3226 (FAX: 207-725-3338). Hours: 8:30AM-5PM. Records go back to 1954. Earlier records in archives. Alumni records are maintained here also. Call 207-725-3266. Degrees granted: Bachelors.

Attendance and degree information available by phone, FAX, mail. Search requires name only. Other helpful information: approximate years of attendance. No fee for information.

Transcripts available by written request only. Search requires name plus signed release. Other helpful information: approximate years of attendance. Fee is $2.00.

Bowie State University, Admissions Records & Reg., 14000 Jericho Park Rd, Bowie, MD 20715, 301-464-6566 (FAX: 301-464-7521). Hours: 8AM-5PM. Records go back 50 years. Alumni records are maintained here also. Call 301-464-6584. Degrees granted: Bachelors; Masters. Adverse incident record source: Public Safety, 301-464-7165.

Attendance information available by mail. Search requires name plus social security number, approximate years of attendance, signed release. Other helpful information: date of birth, exact years of attendance. No fee for information.

Degree information available by phone, mail. Search requires name plus social security number, approximate years of attendance, signed release. Other helpful information: date of birth, exact years of attendance. No fee for information.

Transcripts available by mail. Search requires name plus social security number, approximate years of attendance, signed release. Other helpful information: date of birth, exact years of attendance. No fee for transcripts.

Bowling Green State University, Office of Registration & Records, 110 Administration Bldg, Bowling Green, OH 43403, 419-372-7973 (FAX: 419-372-7977). Hours: 8AM-5PM. Alumni records are maintained here at the same phone number. Degrees granted: Bachelors; Masters; Doctorate.

Attendance and degree information available by phone, mail. Search requires name plus social security number, exact years of attendance. No fee for information.

Transcripts available by mail. Search requires name plus social security number, exact years of attendance, signed release. Fee is $4.00.

Bowling Green State University, (Firelands College), Registrar, 901 Rye Beach Rd, Huron, OH 44839, 419-433-5560. Records are not housed here. They are located at Bowling Green State University, Office of Registration & Records, 110 Administration Bldg, Bowling Green, OH 43403.

Bradford College, Office of the Registrar, 320 S Main St, Bradford, MA 01835, 508-372-7161 X261 (FAX: 508-521-0480). Hours: 8:30AM-4:30PM. Records go back to 1920. Degrees granted: Bachelors. Adverse incident record source: Dean of Students, 508-372-7161 X222.

Attendance information available by phone, FAX, mail. Search requires name plus approximate years of attendance. Other helpful information: social security number, date of birth. No fee for information.

Degree information available by phone, FAX, mail. Search requires name only. Other helpful information: social security number, date of birth, approximate years of attendance. No fee for information.

Transcripts available by mail. Search requires name plus approximate years of attendance, signed release. Other helpful information: social security number, date of birth, exact years of attendance. Fee is $3.00.

Bradford School, Registrar, 6170 Busch Blvd, Columbus, OH 43229, 614-846-9410 (FAX: 614-846-9656). Hours: 8AM-5PM. Records go back to 1940s. School was previously called Office Training School and Columbus Business University. Degrees granted: Associate.

Attendance and degree information available by phone, FAX, mail. Search requires name plus social security number, exact years of attendance. No fee for information.

Transcripts available by written request only. Search requires name plus social security number, exact years of attendance, signed release. Fee is $2.00. Expedited service available for $2.00.

Bradford School, Registrar, 707 Grant St, Gulf Tower, Pittsburgh, PA 15219, 412-391-6710. Hours: 7AM-4PM. Records go back to 1957. Degrees granted: Associate.

Attendance information available by phone, mail. Search requires name plus social security number. No fee for information.

Degree information available by phone, mail. Search requires name plus social security number, exact years of attendance. No fee for information.

Transcripts available by mail. Search requires name plus social security number, exact years of attendance, signed release. Fee is $10.00.

Need to know student's program.

Bradley Academy for the Visual Arts, Registrar, 625 E Philadelphia St, York, PA 17403-1625, 717-848-1447 (FAX: 717-845-6016). Hours: 7:30AM-5:30PM. Records go back to 1988. Alumni records are maintained here also. Call 717-848-1447. Degrees granted: Associate.

Attendance information available by phone, FAX, mail. Search requires name plus social security number. No fee for information.

Degree information available by phone, FAX, mail. Search requires name plus social security number, exact years of attendance. No fee for information.

Transcripts available by mail. Search requires name plus social security number, exact years of attendance, signed release. No fee for transcripts.

Bradley University, Registrar, 1501 W Bradley Ave, Peoria, IL 61625, 309-677-3101 (FAX: 309-677-2715). Hours: 8AM-5PM. Records go back to 1897. Degrees granted: Bachelors; Masters. Adverse incident record source: Student Judicial System, 309-677-2428.

Attendance and degree information available by phone, FAX, mail. Search requires name plus social security number, date of birth. Other helpful information: exact years of attendance. No fee for information.

Transcripts available by mail. Search requires name plus social security number, date of birth, signed release. Other helpful information: exact years of attendance. Fee is $4.00.

FAX copy of transcript only if emergency and prior arrangement.

Brainerd Community College, Registrar, 501 W College Dr, Brainerd, MN 56401, 218-828-2508 (FAX: 218-828-2710). Hours: 8AM-4:30PM. Records go back to 1958. Alumni records are maintained here also. Call 218-828-2525. Degrees granted: Associate.

Attendance information available by phone, FAX, mail. Search requires name plus signed release. Other helpful information: social security number, date of birth, approximate years of attendance. No fee for information.

Degree information available by phone, FAX, mail. Search requires name plus social security number. Other helpful information: date of birth, approximate years of attendance. No fee for information.

Transcripts available by written request only. Search requires name plus social security number, signed release. Other helpful information: date of birth, approximate years of attendance. No fee for transcripts.

Brandeis University, Registrar, Waltham, MA 02254-9110, 617-736-2010 (FAX: 617-736-3485). Hours: 9AM-5PM. Records go back to 1936. Alumni records are maintained here also. Call 617-736-4100. Degrees granted: Bachelors.

Attendance and degree information available by phone, FAX, mail. Search requires name plus social security number, signed release. No fee for information.

Transcripts available by mail. Search requires name plus social security number, signed release. First transcript is free. Additional ones are $2.00.

Brazosport College, Registrar, 500 College Dr, Lake Jackson, TX 77566, 409-265-6131 X221. Hours: 8AM-5PM. Records go back to 1947. Alumni records are maintained here at the same phone number. Degrees granted: Associate.

Attendance and degree information available by phone, mail. Search requires name plus social security number, exact years of attendance. No fee for information.

Transcripts available by mail. Search requires name plus social security number, exact years of attendance, signed release. No fee for transcripts.

Brenau University, Registrar, One Centennial Cir, Gainesville, GA 30501, 404-534-6203. Hours: 8:30AM-5PM. Records go back to 1800s. Degrees granted: Bachelors; Masters.

Attendance information available by mail. Search requires name only. Other helpful information: social security number. No fee for information.

Degree information available by mail. Search requires name plus signed release. Other helpful information: social security number. No fee for information.

Transcripts available by mail. Search requires name plus signed release. Other helpful information: social security number. Fee is $5.00. Expedited service available for $15.00.

Major credit cards accepted for payment.

Brescia College, Registrar, 717 Frederica St, Owensboro, KY 42301-3023, 505-685-3131. Degrees granted: Associate; Bachelors; Masters.

Attendance and degree information available by mail. Search requires name plus social security number, signed release. Other helpful information: date of birth, exact years of attendance. No fee for information.

Transcripts available by written request only. Search requires name plus social security number, signed release. Other helpful information: date of birth, exact years of attendance. Fee is $2.00.

Brevard College, Registrar, 400 N Broad St, Brevard, NC 28712-3306, 704-883-8292 (FAX: 704-884-3790). Hours: 8AM-4:30PM. Records go back to 1934. From 1986 records are on computer. Degrees granted: Associate. Adverse incident record source: Campus Life, 704-884-8258.

Attendance and degree information available by phone. Search requires name plus social security number, approximate years of attendance. No fee for information.

Transcripts available by FAX, mail. Search requires name plus social security number, approximate years of attendance, signed release. No fee for transcripts.

Brevard Community College, Registrar, 1519 Clearlake Rd, Cocoa, FL 32922, 407-632-1111 X3700. Hours: 8AM-4:30PM Summer; 8AM-5PM Fall. Records go back to 1962. Degrees granted: Associate.

Attendance and degree information available by phone, mail. Search requires name plus social security number, date of birth, approximate years of attendance, signed release. No fee for information.

Transcripts available by mail. Search requires name plus social security number, date of birth, approximate years of attendance, signed release. No fee for transcripts.

Brewton Parker College, Registrar, Hwy 280, Mount Vernon, GA 30445, 912-583-2241 (FAX: 912-583-4498). Hours: 8AM-5PM. Records go back to 1904. Degrees granted: Associate; Bachelors.

Attendance information available by phone, FAX, mail. Search requires name plus social security number, date of birth. Other helpful information: approximate years of attendance. No fee for information.

Degree information available by phone, FAX, mail. Search requires name plus social security number. Other helpful information: date of birth, approximate years of attendance. No fee for information.

Transcripts available by FAX, mail. Search requires name plus signed release. Other helpful information: social security number, date of birth, approximate years of attendance. Fee is $2.00. Expedited service available for $10.00.

Briar Cliff College, Registrar, 3033 Rebecca St, Sioux City, IA 51104, 712-279-5447 (FAX: 712-279-5410). Hours: 8AM-4:30PM. Records go back to founding date. Degrees granted: Associate; Bachelors. Adverse incident record source: Student Development, 712-279-5406: Security, 712-279-5464

Attendance and degree information available by phone, FAX, mail. Search requires name plus social security number, signed release. Other helpful information: date of birth, approximate years of attendance. No fee for information.

Transcripts available by FAX, mail. Search requires name plus social security number, signed release. Other helpful information: date of birth, approximate years of attendance. Fee is $3.00. Need maiden name.

Briarcliffe School, Inc., Registrar, 250 Crossways Park Dr, Woodbury, NY 11797-2015, 516-364-2055 X225 (FAX: 516-364-7127). Hours: 9AM-5PM. Records go back to 1966. Degrees granted: Associate.

Attendance and degree information available by phone, FAX, mail. Search requires name plus social security number, date of birth, approximate years of attendance, signed release. No fee for information.

Transcripts available by written request only. Search requires name plus social security number, date of birth, approximate years of attendance, signed release. Fee is $5.00.

Briarcliffe School, Inc., **(Branch Campus)**, Registrar, 10 Peninsula Blvd, Lynbrook, NY 11563, 516-596-1313. Records are not housed here. They are located at Briarcliffe School, Inc., Registrar, 250 Crossways Park Dr, Woodbury, NY 11797-2015.

Briarcliffe School, Inc., **(Branch Campus)**, Registrar, 10 Lake St, Patchogue, NY 11772, 516-654-5300. Records are not housed here. They are located at Briarcliffe School, Inc., Registrar, 250 Crossways Park Dr, Woodbury, NY 11797-2015.

Briarwood College, Registrar, 2279 Mt Vernon Rd, Southington, CT 06489, 203-628-4751. Alumni records are maintained here also. Call 203-628-4751. Degrees granted: Associate.

Attendance and degree information available by phone, FAX, mail. Search requires name only. No fee for information.

Transcripts available by FAX, mail. Search requires name plus signed release. Fee is $3.00. Expedited service available for $3.00.

Bridgewater College, Registrar, Bridgewater, VA 22812, 703-828-2501 (FAX: 703-828-5479). Hours: 8AM-Noon; 1-5PM. Records go back to 1920. Degrees granted: Bachelors.

Attendance and degree information available by phone, FAX, mail. Search requires name only. Other helpful information: social security number, date of birth, approximate years of attendance. No fee for information.

Transcripts available by FAX, mail. Search requires name plus social security number, date of birth, signed release. Other helpful information: approximate years of attendance. Fee is $2.00.

Bridgewater State College, Registrar, Bridgewater, MA 02325, 508-697-1200. Hours: 8AM-5PM. Records go back to 1840. Alumni records are maintained here also. Call 508-697-1200. Degrees granted: Bachelors; Masters.

Attendance and degree information available by phone, mail. Search requires name plus social security number, exact years of attendance. No fee for information.

Transcripts available by mail. Search requires name plus social security number, exact years of attendance, signed release. Fee is $2.00.

Brigham Young University, Records Dept B150 ASB, Provo, UT 84602, 801-378-2631.

Attendance and degree information available by phone, mail. Search requires name plus social security number, date of birth, approximate years of attendance. No fee for information.

Transcripts available by written request only. Search requires name plus social security number, date of birth, approximate years of attendance, signed release. Fee is $0.2.00.

Brigham Young University, (Hawaii), Registrar, Snow Administration Bldg, 55-220 Kulanui St, Laie, HI 96762, 808-293-3745 (FAX: 808-293-3745). Hours: 8AM-5PM. Records go back to 1955. Degrees granted: Associate; Bachelors; Professional Diploma.

Attendance information available by phone, FAX, mail. Search requires name plus social security number, signed release. Other helpful information: date of birth, exact years of attendance. No fee for information.

Degree information available by phone, FAX, mail. Search requires name plus signed release. Other helpful information: social security number, approximate years of attendance. No fee for information.

Transcripts available by phone, FAX, mail. Search requires name plus signed release. Fee is $2.00. Expedited service available for $5.00.

Written request only for transcripts sent to students.

Bristol Community College, Registrar, 777 Elsbree St, Fall River, MA 02720-7395, 508-678-2811 X240. Hours: 8AM-4:30PM. Records go back to 1965. Alumni records are maintained here also. Call 508-678-2811 X2169. Degrees granted: Associate.

Attendance and degree information available by phone, mail. Search requires name plus social security number, exact years of attendance, signed release. No fee for information.

Transcripts available by mail. Search requires name plus social security number, exact years of attendance, signed release. Fee is $1.00.

Bronx Community College, Registrar, W 181st St and University Ave, Bronx, NY 10453, 718-220-6935 (FAX: 718-220-6901). Hours: 9:15AM-4:45PM. Records go back to 1960. Degrees granted: Associate.

Attendance and degree information available by phone, mail. Search requires name plus social security number, date of birth, signed release. No fee for information.

Transcripts available by mail. Search requires name plus social security number, date of birth, signed release. Fee is $4.00.

Brookdale Community College, Registrar, 47 Throckmorton St, Freehold, NJ 07728, 908-224-2268 (FAX: 908-224-2240). Hours: 9AM-7PM M-Th; 9AM-5PM F; 9AM-1PM S. Records go back to 1970. Degrees granted: Associate.

Attendance and degree information available by mail. Search requires name plus social security number, signed release. No fee for information.

Transcripts available by mail. Search requires name plus social security number, signed release. Fee is $3.00. Expedited service available for $3.00.

Major credit cards accepted for payment.

Brookdale Community College, Registrar, Newman Springs Rd, Lincroft, NJ 07738, 908-224-2710 (FAX: 908-224-2242). Hours: 9AM-7PM M-Th; 9AM-5PM F; 9AM-Noon S. Records go back to 1969.

Attendance and degree information available by FAX, mail. Search requires name plus signed release. Other helpful information: social security number. No fee for information.

Transcripts available by FAX, mail. Search requires name plus signed release. Other helpful information: social security number. Fee is $3.00.

Major credit cards accepted for payment.

Brookdale Community College, (Asbury Park Learning Center), Registrar, Cookman St and Grand Ave, Asbury Park, NJ 07712, 908-842-1900. Records go back to founding date. Alumni records are maintained here at the same phone number. Degrees granted: Associate.

Attendance and degree information available by mail. Search requires name plus social security number, date of birth, exact years of attendance, signed release. No fee for information.

Transcripts available by written request only. Search requires name plus social security number, date of birth, exact years of attendance, signed release. Fee is $3.00.

Brookdale Community College, (Bayshore Learning Center), Registrar, 311 Laurel Ave, West Keansburg, NJ 07734, 908-842-1900. Records are not housed here. They are located at Brookdale Community College, (Asbury Park Learning Center), Registrar, Cookman St and Grand Ave, Asbury Park, NJ 07712.

Brookdale Community College, (Forth Monmouth Learning Center), Registrar, 918 Murphy Dr, Fort Monmouth, NJ 07703, 908-842-1900. Records are not housed here. They are located at Brookdale Community College, (Asbury Park Learning Center), Registrar, Cookman St and Grand Ave, Asbury Park, NJ 07712.

Brookdale Community College, (Long Branch Learning Center), Registrar, Third Ave and Broadway, Long Branch, NJ 07740, 908-842-1900. Records are not housed here. They are located at Brookdale Community College, (Asbury Park Learning Center), Registrar, Cookman St and Grand Ave, Asbury Park, NJ 07712.

Brookhaven College, Registrar, 3939 Valley View Lane, Farmers Branch, TX 75244-4997, 214-620-4700 (FAX: 214-620-4897). Hours: 8AM-4:30PM. Records go back to 1977. Alumni records are maintained here at the same phone number. Degrees granted: Associate.

Attendance and degree information available by FAX, mail. Search requires name plus social security number, exact years of attendance, signed release. No fee for information.

Transcripts available by FAX, mail. Search requires name plus social security number, exact years of attendance, signed release. No fee for transcripts.

Brooklyn College, Registrar, 2900 Bedford Ave, Brooklyn, NY 11210-2889, 718-951-5693. Hours: 10AM-4:30PM. Records go back to 1931. Alumni records are maintained here also. Call 718-951-5000 X5065. Degrees granted: Bachelors; Masters.

Attendance and degree information available by mail. Search requires name plus social security number, signed release. No fee for information.

Transcripts available by mail. Search requires name plus social security number, signed release. Fee is $4.00.

Brooklyn Law School, Registrar, 250 Joralemon St, Brooklyn, NY 11201, 718-780-7913 (FAX: 718-780-7555). Hours: 9AM-5PM M,W,Th,F; 8AM-6PM T. Records go back to 1901. Alumni records are maintained here also. Call 718-780-7966.

Attendance and degree information available by phone, FAX, mail. Search requires name plus social security number, date of birth, approximate years of attendance, signed release. No fee for information.

Transcripts available by mail. Search requires name plus social security number, date of birth, approximate years of attendance, signed release. First transcript free. Additional ones are $4.00 each.

Brooks College, Registrar, 4825 E Pacific Coast Hwy, Long Beach, CA 90804, 310-597-6611 (FAX: 310-597-7412). Hours: 8AM-5PM. Records go back to 1970. Degrees granted: Associate. Adverse incident record source: Registrar's Office, 310-597-6611.

Attendance and degree information available by FAX, mail. Search requires name plus social security number, exact years of attendance. No fee for information.

Transcripts available by mail. Search requires name plus social security number, exact years of attendance. Fee is $6.00.

Major credit cards accepted for payment.

Brooks Institute of Photography, Registrar, 801 Alston Rd, Santa Barbara, CA 93108, 805-966-3888 X229 (FAX: 805-564-1475). Hours: 8AM-5PM. Records go back to 1947. Alumni records are maintained here at the same phone number. Degrees granted: Bachelors.

Attendance and degree information available by phone, FAX, mail. Search requires name plus social security number, date of birth, exact years of attendance. No fee for information.

Transcripts available by FAX, mail. Search requires name plus social security number, date of birth, exact years of attendance, signed release. Fee is $4.00.

Broome Community College, Registrar, Upper Front St, PO Box 1017, Binghamton, NY 13902, 607-778-5527 (FAX: 607-778-5310). Hours: 9AM-5PM. Records go back to 1947. Alumni records are maintained here at the same phone number. Degrees granted: Associate.

Attendance and degree information available by phone, FAX, mail. Search requires name only. Other helpful information: social security number, date of birth, approximate years of attendance. No fee for information.

Transcripts available by mail. Search requires name plus signed release. Other helpful information: social security number, date of birth, approximate years of attendance. Fee is $5.00. Expedited service available for $5.00.

Major credit cards accepted for payment.

Broward Community College, Registrar, 225 E Las Olas Blvd, Fort Lauderdale, FL 33301, 305-761-7472 (FAX: 305-761-7466). Hours: 8AM-4PM. Records go back to 1951. Degrees granted: Associate.

Attendance and degree information available by phone, FAX, mail. Search requires name plus social security number, signed release. Other helpful information: approximate years of attendance. No fee for information.

Transcripts available by mail. Search requires name plus social security number, signed release. Other helpful information: approximate years of attendance. No fee for transcripts.

Brown Mackie College, Registrar, 126 S Santa Fe Ave, Salina, KS 67401, 913-825-5422 (FAX: 913-823-7448). Hours: 8AM-5PM. Records go back to 1950. Degrees granted: Associate.

Attendance information available by phone, FAX, mail. Search requires name only. Other helpful information: social security number, date of birth, approximate years of attendance. Fee is $2.00.

Degree information available by phone, FAX, mail. Search requires name plus social security number, approximate years of attendance. No fee for information.

Transcripts available by written request only. Search requires name plus social security number, date of birth, approximate years of attendance, signed release. Other helpful information: exact years of attendance. Fee is $2.00.

Brown University, Registrar, PO Box 1883, Providence, RI 02912, 401-863-1851. Hours: 8AM-4PM. Records go back to 1764. Alumni records are maintained here also. Call 401-863-3307. Degrees granted: Bachelors; Masters; Doctorate.

Attendance and degree information available by phone, mail. Search requires name plus exact years of attendance. No fee for information.

Transcripts available by mail. Search requires name plus exact years of attendance, signed release. Fee is $4.00.

Brunswick College, Registrar, Altama Ave at Fourth St, Brunswick, GA 31523, 912-264-7235. Hours: 8AM-5PM. Records go back to 1969. Alumni records are maintained here also. Call 912-262-3303. Degrees granted: Associate.

Attendance and degree information available by phone, mail. Search requires name plus social security number, exact years of attendance. No fee for information.

Transcripts available by mail. Search requires name plus social security number, exact years of attendance, signed release. Fee is $1.00.

Brunswick Community College, Registrar, PO Box 30, Supply, NC 28462-0030, 910-754-6900 X325 (FAX: 910-754-7805). Hours: 8AM-5PM. Records go back to 1979. Degrees granted: Associate.

Attendance and degree information available by phone, FAX, mail. Search requires name plus social security number. Other helpful information: date of birth, approximate years of attendance. No fee for information.

Transcripts available by mail. Search requires name plus social security number, signed release. Other helpful information: date of birth, approximate years of attendance. No fee for transcripts.

Bryan College, Registrar, Box 7000, Dayton, TN 37321-7000, 615-775-7237 (FAX: 615-775-7330). Hours: 8AM-5PM. Records go back to 1930s. Alumni records are maintained here also. Call 615-775-7312. Degrees granted: Associate; Bachelors.

Attendance and degree information available by phone, FAX, mail. Search requires name plus exact years of attendance. Other helpful information: social security number, approximate years of attendance. No fee for information.

Transcripts available by FAX, mail. Search requires name plus signed release. Other helpful information: social security number, date of birth, approximate years of attendance. Fee is $5.00.

Bryant & Stratton Business Institute, Registrar, 1259 Central Ave, Albany, NY 12205, 518-437-1802 X252 (FAX: 518-437-1048). Hours: 7:30AM-8PM. Records go back to 1800s. Alumni records are maintained here also. Call 518-437-1802 X229. Degrees granted: Associate.

Attendance and degree information available by phone, FAX, mail. Search requires name plus social security number. No fee for information.

Transcripts available by FAX, mail. Search requires name plus social security number, signed release. First transcript free. $5.00 for each additional one.

Bryant & Stratton Business Institute, Registrar, 1028 Main St, Buffalo, NY 14202, 716-884-9120 (FAX: 716-884-0091). Hours: 7:30AM-9PM. Records go back to 1932. Degrees granted: Associate.

Attendance and degree information available by phone, FAX, mail. Search requires name plus approximate years of attendance, signed release. Other helpful information: social security number. No fee for information.

Transcripts available by FAX, mail. Search requires name plus approximate years of attendance, signed release. Other helpful information: social security number. Fee is $5.00.

Bryant & Stratton Business Institute, Registrar, 12955 Snow Rd, Parma, OH 44130-1013, 216-265-3151 (FAX: 216-265-0325). Hours: 8AM-5PM. Records go back to 1852. Degrees granted: Associate.

Attendance and degree information available by mail. Search requires name plus social security number, exact years of attendance. No fee for information.

Transcripts available by mail. Search requires name plus social security number, exact years of attendance, signed release. Fee is $5.00.

Bryant & Stratton Business Institute, Registrar, 82 St Paul St, Rochester, NY 14604-1381, 716-325-6010 (FAX: 716-325-6805). Hours: 9:30AM-6PM. Records go back to 1973. Degrees granted: Associate.

Attendance and degree information available by phone, FAX, mail. Search requires name plus social security number, approximate years of attendance, signed release. No fee for information.

Transcripts available by mail. Search requires name plus social security number, approximate years of attendance, signed release. Fee is $5.00.

Bryant & Stratton Business Institute, Registrar, 953 James St, Syracuse, NY 13203-2502, 315-472-6603 (FAX: 315-474-4383). Hours: 8AM-7PM. Records go back to 1950. Alumni records are maintained here at the same phone number. Degrees granted: Associate.

Attendance and degree information available by phone, FAX, mail. Search requires name plus social security number, approximate years of attendance. No fee for information.

Transcripts available by FAX, mail. Search requires name plus social security number, approximate years of attendance, signed release. Other helpful information: date of birth. Fee is $5.00. Major credit cards accepted for payment.

Bryant & Stratton Business Institute, (Branch Campus), Registrar, 5775 S Bay Rd, Cicero, NY 13039, 315-452-1105 (FAX: 315-458-4536). Hours: 8AM-8PM. Records go back to 1983. Degrees granted: Associate.

Attendance and degree information available by phone, FAX, mail. Search requires name plus social security number, approximate years of attendance, signed release. No fee for information.

Transcripts available by mail. Search requires name plus social security number, approximate years of attendance, signed release. Fee is $5.00.

Bryant & Stratton Business Institute, (Branch Campus), Registrar, 1214 Abbott Rd, Lackawanna, NY 14218, 716-821-9331 X217 (FAX: 716-821-9343). Hours: 8AM-6PM M-Th; 9AM-5PM F. Records go back to 1988. Alumni records are maintained here also. Call 716-821-9331. Degrees granted: Associate.

Attendance and degree information available by phone, FAX, mail. Search requires name plus social security number, signed release. No fee for information.

Transcripts available by mail. Search requires name plus social security number, signed release. Fee is $3.00.

Bryant & Stratton Business Institute, (Branch Campus), Registrar, 1225 Jefferson Rd, Rochester, NY 14623, 716-292-5627 (FAX: 716-292-6015). Hours: 7:30AM-8PM M-Th; 7:30AM-5PM F, 9AM-1PM S. Records go back to 1985. Degrees granted: Associate.

Attendance and degree information available by phone, FAX, mail. Search requires name plus social security number, signed release. No fee for information.

Transcripts available by mail. Search requires name plus social security number, signed release. Fee is $5.00.

Bryant & Stratton Business Institute, (Branch Campus), Registrar, 200 Bryant and Stratton Way, Williamsville, NY 14221, 716-631-0260 X308 (FAX: 716-631-0273). Hours: 8AM-8:30PM. Records go back to 1988. Degrees granted: Associate.

Attendance and degree information available by FAX, mail. Search requires name plus social security number, approximate years of attendance, signed release. No fee for information.

Transcripts available by FAX, mail. Search requires name plus social security number, approximate years of attendance, signed release. Fee is $5.00.

Bryant & Stratton Business Institute, (Branch), Registrar, Sears Bldg 3rd Fl, 691 Richmond Rd, Richmond Heights, OH 44143, 216-461-3151. Records are not housed here. They are located at Bryant & Stratton Business Institute, Registrar, 12955 Snow Rd, Parma, OH 44130-1013.

Bryant College, Academic Records Office, 1150 Douglas Pike, Smithfield, RI 02917-1284, 401-232-6080 (FAX: 401-232-6065). Hours: 8AM-4:30PM. Degrees granted: Associate; Bachelors; Masters.

Attendance and degree information available by phone, FAX, mail. Search requires name plus date of birth, approximate years of attendance, signed release. Other helpful information: social security number. No fee for information.

Transcripts available by written request only. Search requires name plus date of birth, approximate years of attendance, signed release. Other helpful information: social security number. Fee is $5.00.

Bryn Mawr College, Registrar's Office, Bryn Mawr, PA 19010, 610-526-5141 (FAX: 610-526-7499). Hours: 9AM-5PM. Records go back to 1885. Alumni records are maintained here also. Call 610-526-5227. Degrees granted: Bachelors; Masters; Doctorate. Adverse incident record source: Security(Public Safety), 610-526-7302.

Attendance and degree information available by phone, FAX, mail. Search requires name plus social security number. No fee for information.

Transcripts available by mail. Search requires name plus social security number, signed release. Other helpful information: approximate years of attendance. Fee is $3.00.
Will not FAX back.

Bucknell University, Office of the Registrar, 102 Marts Hall, Lewisburg, PA 17837-2086, 717-524-1201 (FAX: 717-524-3922). Hours: 8:30AM-4:30PM. Records go back to 1846. Alumni records are maintained here also. Call 717-524-3223. Degrees granted: Bachelors; Masters. Adverse incident record source: Registrar, 717-524-1201.

Attendance information available by phone, mail. Search requires name only. Other helpful information: social security number, approximate years of attendance. No fee for information.

Degree information available by phone, mail. Search requires name only. Other helpful information: social security number, exact years of attendance. No fee for information.

Transcripts available by mail. Search requires name plus signed release. Other helpful information: social security number, exact years of attendance. Fee is $3.00. Expedited service available for $5.00.

FAX transcript copies are unofficial only.

Bucks County Community College, Registrar, Swamp Rd, Newtown, PA 18940, 215-968-8101. Hours: 7:45AM-4:30PM M-Th, 7:45AM-4PM F. Records go back to 1965. Alumni records are maintained here also. Call 215-968-8461. Degrees granted: Associate.

Attendance and degree information available by mail. Search requires name plus social security number, exact years of attendance. No fee for information.

Transcripts available by mail. Search requires name plus social security number, exact years of attendance, signed release. Fee is $1.00.

Buena Vista College, Registrar, 610 W Fourth St, Storm Lake, IA 50588, 712-749-2400. Hours: 8AM-5PM. Records go back to 1891. Degrees granted: Bachelors; Masters.

Attendance information available by phone, mail. Search requires name only. Other helpful information: social security number, date of birth, approximate years of attendance. No fee for information.

Degree information available by phone, mail. Search requires name only. Other helpful information: social security number, date of birth, approximate years of attendance. No fee for information.

Transcripts available by mail. Search requires name plus social security number, signed release. Other helpful information: date of birth, approximate years of attendance. Fee is $3.00.

Major credit cards accepted for payment.

Bunker Hill Community College, Registrar, 250 New Rutherford Ave, Boston, MA 02129, 617-228-2000 (FAX: 617-241-5335). Hours: 8AM-4:30PM. Records go back to 1973. Alumni records are maintained here also. Call 617-228-2000. Degrees granted: Associate.

Attendance and degree information available by phone, FAX, mail. Search requires name plus social security number, date of birth, exact years of attendance. No fee for information.

Transcripts available by FAX, mail. Search requires name plus social security number, date of birth, exact years of attendance, signed release. Fee is $2.00.

Burlington College, Registrar, 95 N Ave, Burlington, VT 05491-8477, 802-862-9616 (FAX: 802-658-0071). Hours: 9AM-5PM. Records go back to 1972. Degrees granted: Associate; Bachelors.

Attendance information available by phone, FAX, mail. Search requires name only. No fee for information.

Degree information available by phone, FAX, mail. Search requires name only. Other helpful information: social security number, date of birth. No fee for information.

Transcripts available by mail. Search requires name plus signed release. Other helpful information: social security number, date of birth. First transcript free. Additional ones are $5.00 each.

Burlington County College, Registrar, County Rte 530, Pemberton, NJ 08068-1599, 609-894-9311 (FAX: 609-894-0183). Records go back to founding date. Alumni records are maintained here also. Call 609-894-9311 X3311. Degrees granted: Associate.

Attendance and degree information available by FAX, mail. Search requires name plus social security number, approximate years of attendance, signed release. Other helpful information: exact years of attendance. No fee for information.

Transcripts available by written request only. Search requires name plus social security number, approximate years of attendance, signed release. Other helpful information: exact years of attendance. Fee is $2.00.

Butler County Community College, Registrar, College Dr, Oak Hills, PO Box 1203, Butler, PA 16003-1203, 412-287-8711 X331. Hours: 8AM-6:30PM M-Th; 8AM-4PM F. Records go back to 1965. Degrees granted: Associate.

Attendance information available by phone, mail. Search requires name plus social security number, signed release. Other helpful information: date of birth. No fee for information.

Degree information available by phone, mail. Search requires name plus social security number, signed release. Other helpful information: date of birth, approximate years of attendance. No fee for information.

Transcripts available by mail. Search requires name plus social security number, signed release. Other helpful information: date of birth, approximate years of attendance. Fee is $2.00. Expedited service available for $2.00.

Butler County Community College, Registrar, 901 S Haverhill Rd, El Dorado, KS 67042, 316-322-3124 (FAX: 316-322-3316). Hours: 8AM-5PM. Records go back to 1926. Alumni records are maintained here also. Call 316-322-3198. Degrees granted: Associate. Adverse incident record source: Dean of Students, 316-322-3297.

Attendance and degree information available by FAX, mail. Search requires name plus social security number, approximate years of attendance, signed release. No fee for information.

Transcripts available by FAX, mail. Search requires name plus social security number, approximate years of attendance, signed release. Fee is $3.00.

Butler University, Registrar, 4600 Sunset Ave, Indianapolis, IN 46208, 317-283-9203. Hours: 8:30AM-5PM. Records go back to 1900. Alumni records are maintained here also. Call 317-283-9900. Degrees granted: Bachelors; Masters. Adverse incident record source: Registrar, 317-283-9203.

Attendance and degree information available by phone, mail. Search requires name plus social security number, exact years of attendance. No fee for information.

Transcripts available by mail. Search requires name plus social security number, exact years of attendance, signed release. Fee is $5.00.

Information released if no hold on file.

Butte College, Registrar, 3536 Butte Campus Dr, Oroville, CA 95965, 916-895-2511. Hours: 8:30AM-4PM. Records go back to 1974. Degrees granted: Associate.

Attendance and degree information available by mail. Search requires name plus social security number, date of birth, exact years of attendance, signed release. No fee for information.

Transcripts available by mail. Search requires name plus social security number, date of birth, exact years of attendance, signed release. Fee is $3.00.

C

Cabrillo College, Registrar, 6500 Soquel Dr, Aptos, CA 95003, 408-479-6213 (FAX: 408-479-5782). Hours: 8AM-9PM M-Th, 8AM-5PM F. Records go back to 1959. Alumni records are maintained here also. Call 408-479-6100. Degrees granted: Associate. Adverse incident record source: Registrar, 408-479-6212.

Attendance information available by phone, FAX, mail. Search requires name plus social security number, signed release. Other helpful information: date of birth, approximate years of attendance. No fee for information.

Degree information available by phone, FAX, mail. Search requires name only. Other helpful information: social security number. No fee for information.

Transcripts available by written request only. Search requires name only. Fee is $3.00. Expedited service available for $10.00.

Credit cards accepted if total is 10.00 or more.

Cabrini College, Registrar's Office, 610 King of Prussia Rd, Radnor, PA 19087-3699, 610-902-8545 (FAX: 610-902-8309). Hours: 8AM-7PM M,T,W,Th; 8AM-5PM F. Degrees granted: Associate; Bachelors. Adverse incident record source: Dean of Students, 610-902-8406.

Attendance information available by phone, FAX, mail. Search requires name plus social security number, exact years of attendance. Other helpful information: date of birth, approximate years of attendance. No fee for information.

Degree information available by phone, FAX, mail. Search requires name plus social security number. Other helpful information: date of birth, approximate years of attendance. No fee for information.

Transcripts available by mail. Search requires name plus social security number, signed release. Other helpful information: date of birth, approximate years of attendance. Fee is $3.00.

Caldwell College, Registrar, 9 Ryerson Ave, Caldwell, NJ 07006-6195, 201-228-4424 (FAX: 201-403-1784). Hours: 9AM-4:30PM. Records go back to founding date. Degrees granted: Bachelors; Masters. Certification: EED, SNC.

Attendance information available by FAX, mail. Search requires name only. Other helpful information: social security number, date of birth, approximate years of attendance. No fee for information.

Degree information available by FAX, mail. Search requires name plus signed release. Other helpful information: social security number, date of birth, approximate years of attendance. No fee for information.

Transcripts available by FAX, mail. Search requires name plus signed release. Other helpful information: social security number, date of birth, approximate years of attendance. Fee is $3.00. Expedited service available for $5.00.

Caldwell Community College and Technical Institute, Registrar, PO Box 600, 2855 Hickory Blvd (Hudson 28638), Lenior, NC 28645, 704-726-2200 (FAX: 704-726-2216). Hours: 8AM-8PM M-Th, 8AM-5PM F. Records go back to 1960s. Degrees granted: Associate.

Attendance and degree information available by phone, FAX, mail. Search requires name plus social security number. No fee for information.

Transcripts available by FAX, mail. Search requires name plus social security number, exact years of attendance, signed release. No fee for transcripts.

California Baptist College, Registrar, 8432 Magnolia Ave, Riverside, CA 92504, 909-689-5771 X222 (FAX: 909-351-1808). Hours: 8AM-5PM. Degrees granted: Bachelors; Masters. Certification: Athletic Training; Church Business; Church Growth; Church Music; Computer (Bus. Applications, Programming); Public Adm. Adverse incident record source: Student Life, 909-689-5771 X217.

Attendance and degree information available by phone, FAX, mail. Search requires name only. Other helpful information: social security number, date of birth, approximate years of attendance. No fee for information.

Transcripts available by FAX, mail. Search requires name only. Other helpful information: social security number, date of birth, approximate years of attendance. Fee is $3.00.

Major credit cards accepted for payment.

California College for Health Sciences, Registrar, 222 W 24th St, National City, CA 91950-9998, 619-477-4800 (FAX: 619-477-4360). Hours: 8AM-5PM. Records go back to 1978. Degrees granted: Associate; Bachelors; Masters.

Attendance and degree information available by phone, FAX, mail. Search requires name plus social security number. No fee for information.

Transcripts available by mail. Search requires name plus social security number, signed release. Fee is $5.00.

California College of Arts and Crafts, Registrar, 5212 Broadway, Oakland, CA 94618, 501-597-3651. Hours: 8AM-4:30PM. Records go back to 1907. Alumni records are maintained here also. Call 510-597-3634.

Attendance and degree information available by phone, mail. Search requires name only. Other helpful information: date of birth, approximate years of attendance. No fee for information.

Transcripts available by mail. Search requires name plus signed release. Other helpful information: date of birth, approximate years of attendance. Fee is $3.00. Expedited service available for $11.75.

California College of Podiatric Medicine, Registrar, 1210 Scott St, San Francisco, CA 94115, 415-292-0414 (FAX: 415-292-0439). Hours: 9AM-5:30PM. Records go back to 1916. Alumni records are maintained here also. Call 415-292-0484. Degrees granted: Doctorate.

Attendance information available by phone, FAX, mail. Search requires name only. Other helpful information: social security number, date of birth, approximate years of attendance. No fee for information.

Degree information available by FAX, mail. Search requires name plus exact years of attendance, signed release. Other helpful information: social security number, date of birth, approximate years of attendance. No fee for information.

Transcripts available by FAX, mail. Search requires name plus exact years of attendance, signed release. Other helpful information: social security number, date of birth, approximate years of attendance. Fee is $5.00. Expedited service available for $14.50.

California Family Study Center, Registrar, 5433 Laurel Canyon Blvd, North Hollywood, CA 91607-2193, 818-509-5959 X252. Hours: 8AM-5PM. Records go back to 1971. Alumni records are maintained here also. Call 818-509-5959. Degrees granted: Masters. Adverse incident record source: Graduate Advisor, 818-509-5959.

Attendance and degree information available by phone, mail. Search requires name plus social security number, date of birth. No fee for information.

Transcripts available by mail. Search requires name plus social security number, date of birth, signed release. Fee is $4.00. Expedited service available for $15.00.

Major credit cards accepted for payment.

California Institute of Integral Studies, Registrar, 765 Ashbury St, San Francisco, CA 94117, 415-753-6100 X488. Hours: 10AM-12:30PM, 2-5PM. Degrees granted: Bachelors; Masters; Doctorate. Certification: ODT,EXA.

Attendance information available by phone, FAX, mail. Search requires name only. Other helpful information: social security number, date of birth, approximate years of attendance. No fee for information.

Degree information available by phone, FAX, mail. Search requires name plus social security number. Other helpful information: date of birth, approximate years of attendance. No fee for information.

Transcripts available by mail. Search requires name plus social security number, exact years of attendance, signed release. Other helpful information: approximate years of attendance. Fee is $3.00. Expedited service available for $12.00.

Major credit cards accepted for payment.

California Institute of Pennsylvania, Academic Records, 250 University, California, PA 15419-1934, 412-938-4434 (FAX: 412-938-4340). Hours: 8AM-4PM. Records go back to 1950. Alumni records are maintained here at the same phone number. Degrees granted: Associate; Bachelors; Masters; Registered Nurse Program. Adverse incident record source: Student Development, 412-938-4439: Public Safety, 412-938-4299

Attendance and degree information available by phone. Search requires name plus social security number, signed release. Other helpful information: approximate years of attendance. No fee for information.

Transcripts available by mail. Search requires name plus social security number, signed release. Other helpful information: exact years of attendance. Fee is $3.00.

California Institute of Technology, Registrar, 1201 E California Blvd, Pasadena, CA 91125, 818-395-6354 (FAX: 818-577-4215). Hours: 8AM-Noon, 1:00-5PM. Records go back to 1940. Alumni Records Office: 345 S Hill Ave, Pasadena, CA 91125. Degrees granted: Bachelors; Masters; Doctorate. Adverse incident record source: Undergraduate Dean's Office, 818-395-6351 : Graduate Dean's Office, 818-395-6346

Attendance and degree information available by phone, FAX, mail. Search requires name only. Other helpful information: social security number, date of birth, approximate years of attendance. No fee for information.

Transcripts available by mail. Search requires name plus social security number, date of birth, approximate years of attendance, signed release. Fee is $1.00.

California Institute of the Arts, Registrar, 24700 McBean Pkwy, Valencia, CA 91355, 805-253-7843 (FAX: 805-254-8352). Hours: 8:30AM-4PM. Records go back to 1930. Degrees granted: Bachelors; Masters.

Attendance and degree information available by phone, FAX, mail. Search requires name plus approximate years of attendance. Other helpful information: social security number, date of birth, exact years of attendance. No fee for information.

Transcripts available by FAX, mail. Search requires name plus approximate years of attendance, signed release. Other helpful information: social security number, date of birth, exact years of attendance. Fee is $2.00.

California Lutheran University, Registrar, 60 W Olsen Rd, Thousand Oaks, CA 91360, 805-493-3105. Hours: 8AM-4:30PM. Records go back to 1959. Alumni records are maintained here also. Call 805-493-3170. Degrees granted: Bachelors; Masters.

Attendance and degree information available by phone, mail. Search requires name plus social security number, date of birth, exact years of attendance. No fee for information.

Transcripts available by mail. Search requires name plus social security number, date of birth, exact years of attendance, signed release. Fee is $2.00.

California Maritime Academy, Registrar, 200 Maritime Academy Dr, PO Box 1392, Vallejo, CA 94590-0644, 707-648-4262 (FAX: 707-649-4773). Hours: 9AM-4:30PM. Records go back to 1920. Alumni records are maintained here also. Call 707-648-5386. Degrees granted: Bachelors.

Attendance and degree information available by phone, FAX, mail. Search requires name only. Other helpful information: approximate years of attendance. No fee for information.

Transcripts available by mail. Search requires name plus signed release. Other helpful information: approximate years of attendance. Fee is $4.00. Expedited service available for $15.00.

California Polytechnic State University, San Luis Obispo, Academic Records, San Luis Obispo, CA 93407, 805-756-6016 (FAX: 805-756-7237). Hours: 8AM-5PM. Records go back to 1901. Degrees granted: Bachelors; Masters. Adverse incident record source: Public Safety, 805-756-2281.

Attendance and degree information available by phone, mail. Search requires name only. Other helpful information: social security number, date of birth, approximate years of attendance. No fee for information.

Transcripts available by written request only. Search requires name plus signed release. Other helpful information: social security number, date of birth, approximate years of attendance. Fee is $4.00.

California School of Professional Psychology, Berkeley/Alameda, Registrar, 1005 Atlantic Ave, Alameda, CA 94501, 510-523-2300 (FAX: 510-521-3678). Hours: 9AM-5PM. Records go back to 1970. Degrees granted: Masters; Doctorate.

Attendance and degree information available by FAX, mail. Search requires name plus social security number, signed release. Other helpful information: date of birth, exact years of attendance. No fee for information.

Transcripts available by FAX, mail. Search requires name plus social security number, signed release. Other helpful information: date of birth, exact years of attendance. Fee is $3.00. Expedited service available for $5.00.

California School of Professional Psychology, Fresno, Registrar, 1350 M St, Fresno, CA 93721, 209-486-8420 (FAX: 209-486-0734). Hours: 8:30AM-4:30PM. Records go back to 1973. Alumni Records Office: 1000 S Fremont, Alhambra, CA 91803-1360. Degrees granted: Masters; Doctorate.

Attendance and degree information available by FAX, mail. Search requires name plus signed release. No fee for information.

Transcripts available by mail. Search requires name plus signed release. Fee is $3.00. Expedited service available for $5.00.

California School of Professional Psychology, Los Angeles, Registrar, 1000 S Fremont Ave, Alhambra, CA 91803-1360, 818-284-2777. Hours: 8:30AM-4PM. Records go back to 1969. Alumni records are maintained here at the same phone number. Degrees granted: Doctorate.

Attendance and degree information available by mail. Search requires name plus social security number, date of birth, exact years of attendance, signed release. No fee for information.

Transcripts available by mail. Search requires name plus social security number, date of birth, exact years of attendance, signed release. Fee is $3.00. Expedited service available for $5.00.

California School of Professional Psychology, San Diego, Registrar, 6212 Ferris Square, San Diego, CA 92121-3250, 619-452-1664 (FAX: 619-552-1974). Hours: 8:30AM-Noon, 2-4:30PM. Records go back 25 years. Alumni records are maintained here at the same phone number. Degrees granted: Masters; Doctorate. Certification: Doctoral Respecialization.

Attendance and degree information available by FAX, mail. Search requires name plus signed release. Other helpful information: social security number, date of birth, approximate years of attendance. No fee for information.

Transcripts available by mail. Search requires name plus signed release. Other helpful information: social security number, date of birth, approximate years of attendance. Fee is $3.00. Expedited service available for $5.00.

Requests must be accompanied by "release of info" form.

California State Polytechnic University, Pomona, Registrar, 3801 W Temple Ave, Pomona, CA 91768, 909-869-7659. Hours: 9AM-4PM. Degrees granted: Bachelors; Masters.

Attendance and degree information available by phone, mail. Search requires name plus social security number, date of birth, exact years of attendance. No fee for information.

Transcripts available by mail. Search requires name plus social security number, date of birth, exact years of attendance, signed release. Fee is $2.00.

California State University, Bakersfield, Registrar, 9001 Stockdale Hwy, Bakersfield, CA 93311-1099, 805-664-2147 (FAX: 805-664-3389). Hours: 8AM-5PM. Records go back to 1970. Alumni records are maintained here also. Call 805-664-3211. Degrees granted: Bachelors; Masters.

Attendance and degree information available by FAX, mail. Search requires name plus social security number, date of birth. Other helpful information: approximate years of attendance. No fee for information.

Transcripts available by written request only. Search requires name plus social security number, date of birth. Other helpful information: approximate years of attendance. First copy is $4.00; additional copies prepared at same time are $2.00 each.

Include a self addressed stamped envelope with mail request.

California State University, Chico, Admissions & Records, 180 - Meriam Library, Chico, CA 95929-0110, 916-898-5143 (FAX: 916-898-4359). Hours: 8AM-5PM. Records go back to 1927. Alumni records are maintained here also. Call 916-898-6472. Degrees granted: Bachelors; Masters.

Attendance and degree information available by phone, mail. Search requires name only. Other helpful information: social security number, date of birth, approximate years of attendance. No fee for information.

Transcripts available by mail. Search requires name plus signed release. Fee is $4.00. Expedited service available for $8.00.

California State University, Dominguez Hills, Registrar, 1000 E Victoria St, Carson, CA 90747, 310-516-3300 (FAX: 310-516-3622). Hours: 10AM-1PM, 3-6PM M-Th; 8AM-Noon F. Records go back to 1960. Alumni Records Office: Alumni Relations, 1000 E Victoria St, ERCG-521, Carson, CA 90747 310-516-4237. Degrees granted: Bachelors; Masters.

Attendance and degree information available by mail. Search requires name plus social security number, date of birth, exact years of attendance, signed release. Fee is $4.00.

Transcripts available by mail. Search requires name plus social security number, date of birth, exact years of attendance, signed release. Fee is $4.00. Expedited service available for $10.00.

Transcript requests can be made in person. Day time phone number needed. Credit cards may be used in person only.

California State University, Fresno, Registrar, 5150 N Maple Ave, Fresno, CA 93740-0057, 209-278-2328 (FAX: 209-278-4812). Hours: 8AM-5PM. Records go back to 1911. Degrees granted: Bachelors; Masters; Doctorate. Adverse incident record source: Dean of Students, 209-278-2541.

Attendance and degree information available by FAX, mail. Search requires name plus social security number, date of birth, signed release. Other helpful information: approximate years of attendance. Fee is $5.00. Expedited service available for $10.00.

Transcripts available by FAX, mail. Search requires name plus social security number, date of birth, signed release. Other helpful information: approximate years of attendance. Fee is $4.00. Expedited service available for $10.00.

Major credit cards accepted for payment.

California State University, Fullerton, Registrar, PO Box 34080, Fullerton, CA 92634, 714-773-2011. Degrees granted: Bachelors; Masters.

Attendance and degree information available by phone, FAX, mail. Search requires name only. Other helpful information: social security number, date of birth, approximate years of attendance. No fee for information.

Transcripts available by mail. Search requires name plus signed release. Other helpful information: social security number, date of birth, approximate years of attendance. Transcripts are $4.00 each. Written confirmation of degree and attendance are $10.00 each.

Require either SSN or DOB.

California State University, Hayward, Registrar, 25800 Carlos Bee Blvd, Hayward, CA 94542, 510-885-3075 (FAX: 510-885-3816). Hours: 8AM-5PM M-Th. Records go back to 1960. Degrees granted: Bachelors; Masters.

Attendance and degree information available by phone, FAX, mail. Search requires name plus social security number, date of birth, exact years of attendance. No fee for information.

Transcripts available by mail. Search requires name plus social security number, date of birth, exact years of attendance, signed release. Transcript fee is $4.00 for the first copy, and $2.00 each additional copy.

California State University, Long Beach, Records Transcripts, 1250 Bellflower Blvd, Long Beach, CA 90840, 310-985-5487. Degrees granted: Bachelors; Masters.

Attendance information available by phone, FAX, mail. Search requires name plus social security number, approximate years of attendance. Other helpful information: date of birth, exact years of attendance. No fee for information.

Degree information available by phone, FAX, mail. Search requires name plus approximate years of attendance. Other helpful information: social security number, date of birth, exact years of attendance. No fee for information.

Transcripts available by mail. Search requires name plus social security number, date of birth, approximate years of attendance, signed release. Other helpful information: exact years of attendance. Fee is $4.00. Expedited service available for $10.00.

California State University, Los Angeles, Registrar, 5151 State University Dr, Los Angeles, CA 90032, 213-343-3940 (FAX: 213-343-3840). Hours: 8AM-4:30PM. Records go back to 1965. Degrees granted: Bachelors; Masters; Doctorate.

Attendance and degree information available by phone, mail. Search requires name plus social security number, date of birth, exact years of attendance. No fee for information.

Transcripts available by mail. Search requires name plus social security number, date of birth, exact years of attendance, signed release. Transcript fee is $4.00, and $2.00 for each additional copy.

California State University, Northridge, Registrar, 18111 Nordhoff St, Northridge, CA 91330, 818-885-3776 (FAX: 818-885-3766). Hours: 8AM-5PM M; 10AM-7PM T&W; 8AM-5PM Th; 8AM-4PM F. Records go back 39 years. Degrees granted: Bachelors; Masters. Adverse incident record source: Campus Police, 818-885-2111.

Attendance information available by FAX, mail. Search requires name plus social security number. Other helpful information: date of birth, approximate years of attendance. No fee for information.

Degree information available by phone, FAX, mail. Search requires name plus social security number. Other helpful information: date of birth, approximate years of attendance. No fee for information.

Transcripts available by mail. Search requires name plus social security number, signed release. Other helpful information: date of birth, approximate years of attendance. Fee is $4.00.

Major credit cards accepted for payment.

California State University, Sacramento, Admissions & Records, 6000 J St, Sacramento, CA 95819-6048, 916-278-7111 (FAX: 916-278-5603). Hours: 10AM-2PM. Records go back to 1949. Alumni Records Office: 7750 College Town Dr #203, Sacramento, CA 95826. Degrees granted: Bachelors; Masters.

Attendance information available by phone, FAX, mail. Search requires name plus social security number, approximate years of attendance. No fee for information.

Degree information available by phone, FAX, mail. Search requires name plus social security number, exact years of attendance. Other helpful information: approximate years of attendance. No fee for information.

Transcripts available by mail. Search requires name plus social security number, signed release. Other helpful information: date of birth, approximate years of attendance. Fee is $4.00. Expedited service available for $10.00.

Confirm by phone only if permission is on file. FAX requires signed release. Credit cards are accepted for fees over $50.00.

California State University, San Bernardino, Registrar, 5500 State University Pkwy, San Bernardino, CA 92407-2397, 909-880-5200 (FAX: 909-880-7021). Hours: 8AM-6PM M-Th; 8AM-5PM F. Degrees granted: Bachelors; Masters.

Attendance and degree information available by phone, FAX, mail. Search requires name only. Other helpful information: social security number. Fee is $4.00.

Transcripts available by FAX, mail. Search requires name plus signed release. Other helpful information: social security number. Fee is $4.00. Expedited service available for $8.00.

California State University, San Marcos, Registrar, San Marcos, CA 92069, 619-750-4800 (FAX: 619-750-3285). Hours: 8AM-5PM. Records go back to 1990. Alumni records are maintained here also. Call 619-750-4970. Degrees granted: Bachelors; Masters; Teaching Credential. Adverse incident record source: Public Safety, 619-750-4562.

Attendance and degree information available by phone, FAX, mail. Search requires name only. Other helpful information: social security number, date of birth. No fee for information.

Transcripts available by mail. Search requires name plus social security number, signed release. Other helpful information: date of birth. Fee is $4.00. Expedited service available for $4.00.

Major credit cards accepted for payment.

California State University, Stanislaus, Registrar, 801 W Monte Vista Ave, Turlock, CA 95382, 209-667-3264 (FAX: 209-667-3788). Hours: 8AM-5PM. Records go back to 1960. Degrees granted: Bachelors; Masters. Adverse incident record source: Campus Police, 209-667-3114.

Attendance and degree information available by phone, FAX, mail. Search requires name only. Other helpful information: social security number. Fee is $5.00. Expedited service available for $10.00.

Transcripts available by mail. Search requires name plus signed release. Other helpful information: social security number, date of birth. Fee is $4.00. Expedited service available for $10.00.

Fee rate begins fall 1995. Major credit cards accepted for payment.

California Western School of Law, Registrar's Office, 225 Cedar St, San Diego, CA 92101, 619-525-1414 (FAX: 619-525-7092). Hours: 8AM-5PM. Records go back to 1962. Alumni records are maintained here also. Call 619-239-0391 X7644.

Attendance and degree information available by phone, FAX, mail. Search requires name plus social security number, signed release. Other helpful information: approximate years of attendance. No fee for information.

Transcripts available by phone, FAX, mail. Search requires name plus social security number, signed release. Other helpful information: approximate years of attendance. Fee is $3.00.

Calumet College of St. Joseph, Registrar's Office, 2400 New York Ave, Whiting, IN 46394, 219-473-4211 (FAX: 219-473-4259). Hours: 9AM-5PM. Records go back to 1951. Alumni records are maintained here also. Call 219-473-4326. Degrees granted: Associate; Bachelors.

Attendance and degree information available by phone, FAX, mail. Search requires name plus social security number, date of birth, exact years of attendance. No fee for information.

Transcripts available by FAX, mail. Search requires name plus social security number, date of birth, approximate years of attendance, signed release. Other helpful information: exact years of attendance. First transcript free. Additional ones are $3.00 each.

The Sourcebook of College and University Student Records

Major credit cards accepted for payment.

Calvary Bible College, Registrar, 15800 Calvary Rd, Kansas City, MO 64147-1341, 816-322-0110 (FAX: 816-331-4474). Hours: 8AM-4:30PM. Records go back to founding date. Degrees granted: Associate; Bachelors; Masters.

Attendance information available by phone, FAX, mail. Search requires name only. Other helpful information: social security number, date of birth, approximate years of attendance. No fee for information.

Degree information available by phone, FAX, mail. Search requires name plus exact years of attendance. Other helpful information: social security number, date of birth, approximate years of attendance. No fee for information. Expedite service available for $8.00.

Transcripts available by mail. Search requires name plus date of birth, exact years of attendance, signed release. Other helpful information: social security number, approximate years of attendance. Fee is $2.00. Expedited service available for $15.00.

Calvin College, Registrar, 3201 Burton St SE, Grand Rapids, MI 49546, 616-957-6155 (FAX: 616-957-8551). Hours: 8AM-5PM. Records go back to 1898. Alumni records are maintained here at the same phone number. Degrees granted: Bachelors.

Attendance and degree information available by phone, FAX, mail. Search requires name only. Other helpful information: social security number, date of birth, approximate years of attendance. No fee for information.

Transcripts available by written request only. Search requires name plus social security number, signed release. Other helpful information: date of birth, approximate years of attendance. Fee is $2.00.

Calvin Theological Seminary, Registrar, 3233 Burton St SE, Grand Rapids, MI 49546, 616-957-6027 (FAX: 616-957-8621). Hours: 8AM-5PM. Records go back to 1895. Alumni records are maintained here also. Call 616-957-6141. Degrees granted: Masters; PhD. Adverse incident record source: Alumni Office, 616-957-6141.

Attendance and degree information available by phone, FAX, mail. Search requires name plus approximate years of attendance, signed release. No fee for information.

Transcripts available by FAX, mail. Search requires name plus approximate years of attendance, signed release. Fee is $2.00.

Cambria-Rowe Business College, Registrar, 221 Central Ave, Johnstown, PA 15902, 814-536-5168 (FAX: 814-536-5160). Hours: 8AM-5PM. Records go back to 1897. Degrees granted: Associate. Adverse incident record source: Executive Director or President, 814-536-5168.

Attendance information available by phone, FAX, mail. Search requires name plus social security number. No fee for information.

Degree information available by phone, FAX, mail. Search requires name plus social security number, exact years of attendance. No fee for information.

Transcripts available by FAX, mail. Search requires name plus social security number, exact years of attendance, signed release. No fee for transcripts.

Available unless closed at student's request.

Cambria-Rowe Business College, **(Indiana)**, Registrar, 422 S 13th St, Indiana, PA 15701, 412-463-0222 (FAX: 412-463-7246). Hours: 8AM-5PM. Records go back 3 years. Degrees granted: Associate.

Attendance and degree information available by phone, FAX, mail. Search requires name plus social security number. Other helpful information: date of birth, approximate years of attendance. No fee for information.

Transcripts available by phone, FAX, mail. Search requires name plus social security number. Other helpful information: date of birth, approximate years of attendance. No fee for transcripts.

Cambridge College, Registrar, 1000 Massachusetts Ave #128, Cambridge, MA 02138, 617-868-1000 X101 (FAX: 617-349-3545). Hours: 9AM-9PM M-Th, 9AM-4PM F. Records go back to 1971. Alumni records are maintained here also. Call 617-868-1000 X131. Degrees granted: Bachelors; Masters.

Attendance and degree information available by phone, mail. Search requires name plus social security number, exact years of attendance. No fee for information.

Transcripts available by mail. Search requires name plus social security number, exact years of attendance, signed release. Fee is $3.00.

Major credit cards accepted for payment.

Camden County College, Registrar, PO Box 200, Blackwood, NJ 08012, 609-227-7200 X200. Hours: 8:30AM-8:30PM. Records go back to 1968. Alumni records are maintained here at the same phone number. Degrees granted: Associate.

Attendance and degree information available by FAX, mail. Search requires name plus social security number, signed release. Other helpful information: date of birth, approximate years of attendance. No fee for information.

Transcripts available by FAX, mail. Search requires name plus social security number, signed release. Other helpful information: date of birth, approximate years of attendance. Fee is $3.00.

Fee proposed as of July 1, 1995. Major credit cards accepted for payment.

Camden County College, **(Branch Campus)**, Registrar, 200 N Broadway, Camden, NJ 08102-1102, 609-338-1817. Records are not housed here. They are located at Camden County College, Registrar, PO Box 200, Blackwood, NJ 08012.

Cameron University, Registrar, 2800 Gore Blvd, Lawton, OK 73505, 405-581-2238. Hours: 8AM-5Pm. Records go back to 1920. Alumni records are maintained here also. Call 405-581-2988. Degrees granted: Associate; Bachelors; Masters. Adverse incident record source: Dean, 405-581-2209.

Attendance and degree information available by mail. Search requires name plus social security number, exact years of attendance. No fee for information.

Transcripts available by mail. Search requires name plus social security number, exact years of attendance, signed release. Fee is $3.00.

Campbell University, Registrar's Office, PO Box 367, Buies Creek, NC 27506, 910-893-1200 (FAX: 910-893-1424). Hours: 8:30AM-5PM. Records go back to 1836. Alumni Records Office: Alumni Association, PO Box 158, Buies Creek, NC 27506. Degrees granted: Bachelors; Masters; Doctorate.

Attendance information available by phone, FAX, mail. Search requires name plus social security number. No fee for information.

Degree Granting Institutions

Degree information available by phone, FAX, mail. Search requires name plus social security number, exact years of attendance. No fee for information.

Transcripts available by FAX, mail. Search requires name plus social security number, exact years of attendance, signed release. Fee is $5.00.

Need former names.

Campbellsville College, Director of Student Records, 200 W College St, Campbellsville, KY 42718-2799, 502-789-5233 (FAX: 502-789-5020). Hours: 8AM-5PM. Alumni records are maintained here also. Call 502-789-5211. Degrees granted: Associate; Bachelors; Masters. Adverse incident record source: Student Development, 502-789-5005.

Attendance and degree information available by phone, FAX, mail. Search requires name plus social security number. Other helpful information: date of birth, approximate years of attendance. No fee for information.

Transcripts available by mail. Search requires name plus social security number, signed release. Other helpful information: date of birth, approximate years of attendance. Fee is $3.00.

Canada College, Dottie Shiloh, 4200 Farm Hill Blvd, Redwood City, CA 94061, 415-306-3124 (FAX: 415-306-3475). Hours: 8AM-8:15PM M-Th; 8AM-4:30PM F. Records go back to 1968. Degrees granted: Associate.

Attendance information available by phone, FAX, mail. Search requires name plus social security number, approximate years of attendance, signed release. No fee for information.

Degree information available by phone, mail. Search requires name plus social security number, signed release. Other helpful information: approximate years of attendance. No fee for information.

Transcripts available by FAX, mail. Search requires name plus social security number, signed release. Other helpful information: approximate years of attendance. Fee is $3.00.

Major credit cards accepted for payment.

Canisius College, Registrar, 2001 Main St, Buffalo, NY 14208, 716-888-2990 (FAX: 716-888-2996). Hours: 8:30AM-7PM M-Th; 8:30AM-5PM F. Records go back to 1940. Alumni records are maintained here also. Call 716-888-2700. Degrees granted: Associate; Bachelors; Masters.

Attendance and degree information available by phone, mail. Search requires name plus social security number, approximate years of attendance. Other helpful information: exact years of attendance. No fee for information.

Transcripts available by mail. Search requires name plus social security number, approximate years of attendance, signed release. Other helpful information: exact years of attendance. No fee for transcripts.

Cape Cod Community College, Registrar, Rte 132, West Barnstable, MA 02668, 508-362-2131 X313. Hours: 8:30AM-4:30PM. Records go back to 1961. Alumni records are maintained here at the same phone number. Degrees granted: Associate. Adverse incident record source: Security, 508-362-2131.

Attendance and degree information available by phone, mail. Search requires name plus social security number, date of birth. No fee for information.

Transcripts available by mail. Search requires name plus social security number, date of birth, exact years of attendance, signed release. Fee is $1.00.

Cape Fear Community College, Registrar, 411 N Front St, Wilmington, NC 28401-3993, 910-343-0481 (FAX: 910-763-2279). Hours: 8AM-6PM M-Th, 8AM-5PM F. Records go back to 1967. Degrees granted: Associate. Adverse incident record source: Records & Registration, 910-343-0481.

Attendance information available by phone, FAX, mail. Search requires name plus social security number. No fee for information.

Degree information available by phone, FAX, mail. Search requires name plus social security number. Other helpful information: approximate years of attendance. No fee for information.

Transcripts available by FAX, mail. Search requires name plus social security number, signed release. Other helpful information: approximate years of attendance. No fee for transcripts.

Capital Community-Technical College, Registrar, 61 Woodland St, Hartford, CT 06105, 203-520-7828 (FAX: 203-520-7906). Hours: 8:30AM-5PM. Records go back to 1947. Degrees granted: Associate. Adverse incident record source: Security Office, 203-520-7813.

Attendance and degree information available by phone, FAX, mail. Search requires name plus signed notarized release. Other helpful information: social security number, approximate years of attendance. No fee for information.

Transcripts available by FAX, mail. Search requires name plus signed release. Other helpful information: social security number, approximate years of attendance. No fee for transcripts.

Capital Community-Technical College, (Flatbush), Registrar, 401 Flatbush Ave, Hartford, CT 06106, 203-520-7941 (FAX: 203-520-7906). Hours: 8:30AM-4:30PM. Alumni Records Office: Capital Community-Technical College Woodland, 61 Woodland Ct, Hartford, CT 06105. Degrees granted: Associate.

Attendance and degree information available by phone, FAX, mail. Search requires name plus social security number, exact years of attendance. No fee for information.

Transcripts available by FAX, mail. Search requires name plus social security number, exact years of attendance, signed release. No fee for transcripts.

Capital University, Registrar, 2199 E Main St, Columbus, OH 43209, 614-236-6150 (FAX: 614-236-6490). Hours: 8AM-4:30PM. Records go back to 1850. Alumni records are maintained here also. Call 614-236-6701. Degrees granted: Bachelors; Masters; JD. Adverse incident record source: Student Services, 614-236-6611.

Attendance and degree information available by phone, FAX, mail. Search requires name only. Other helpful information: social security number, date of birth, approximate years of attendance. No fee for information.

Transcripts available by mail. Search requires name plus signed release. Other helpful information: social security number, date of birth, approximate years of attendance. Fee is $2.00. Expedited service available for $5.00.

Capitol College, Registrar, 11301 Springfield Rd, Laurel, MD 20708, 301-953-0060 (FAX: 301-953-3876). Hours: 9AM-5PM M, 9AM-7PM T,W,Th, 9AM-3PM F. Records go back to 1964. Alumni records are maintained here at the same phone number. Degrees granted: Associate; Bachelors; Masters.

Attendance and degree information available by phone, FAX, mail. Search requires name plus social security number, exact years of attendance. No fee for information.

Transcripts available by mail. Search requires name plus social security number, exact years of attendance, signed release. Fee is $5.00.
Major credit cards accepted for payment.

Cardinal Stritch College, Registrar, 6801 N Yates Rd, Milwaukee, WI 53217, 414-352-5400. Hours: 8AM-5PM. Degrees granted: Bachelors; Masters.
Attendance and degree information available by mail. Search requires name plus social security number, date of birth, exact years of attendance. No fee for information.
Transcripts available by mail. Search requires name plus social security number, date of birth, exact years of attendance, signed release. Fee is $3.00.

Career College, (Branch), Registrar, 2400 SW 13th St, Gainesville, FL 32608, 904-335-4000 (FAX: 904-335-4303). Hours: 8AM-8PM. Records go back 7 years. Degrees granted: Associate.
Attendance information available by phone, mail. Search requires name plus social security number, approximate years of attendance, signed release. Other helpful information: date of birth. No fee for information.
Degree information available by FAX, mail. Search requires name plus social security number, approximate years of attendance, signed release. Other helpful information: date of birth. No fee for information.
Transcripts available by FAX, mail. Search requires name plus social security number, approximate years of attendance, signed release. Other helpful information: date of birth. No fee for transcripts.

CareerCom Junior College of Business, Registrar, 1102 S Virginia St, Hopkinsville, KY 42240, 502-886-1302 (FAX: 502-886-3544). Hours: 8AM-5PM. Records go back to 1984. Degrees granted: Associate.
Attendance and degree information available by phone, mail. Search requires name plus social security number, exact years of attendance. No fee for information.
Transcripts available by mail. Search requires name plus social security number, exact years of attendance, signed release. Fee is $3.00.

Caribbean Center for Advanced Studies, Registrar, Apartado 3711, Old San Juan Sta, San Juan, PR 00904-3711, 809-725-6500. Degrees granted: Bachelors; Masters; Doctorate.
Attendance information available by written request only. Search requires name plus social security number, signed release. No fee for information.
Degree information available by written request only. Search requires name plus social security number, signed release. Other helpful information: exact years of attendance. No fee for information.
Transcripts available by written request only. Search requires name plus signed release. Other helpful information: approximate years of attendance. No fee for transcripts.
Major credit cards accepted for payment.

Caribbean Center for Advanced Studies, (**Miami Institute of Psychology**), Registrar, 8180 NW 36th St 2nd Fl, Miami, FL 33166-6653, 305-593-1223 (FAX: 305-592-7930). Hours: 10AM-6PM. Records go back to 1980. Degrees granted: Bachelors; Masters; Doctorate.

Attendance and degree information available by FAX, mail. Search requires name plus approximate years of attendance, signed release. Other helpful information: social security number. No fee for information.
Transcripts available by FAX, mail. Search requires name plus signed release. Fee is $5.00.
Major credit cards accepted for payment.

Caribbean University, Registrar, PO Box 493, Rd 167km 21.2 Forest Hills, Bayamon, PR 00960-0493, 809-780-0070 (FAX: 809-785-0101). Hours: 8AM-5PM. Records go back to 1985. Degrees granted: Associate; Bachelors; Masters.
Attendance information available by mail. Search requires name plus social security number, signed release. No fee for information.
Degree information available by mail. Search requires name plus social security number, exact years of attendance, signed release. No fee for information.
Transcripts available by mail. Search requires name plus social security number, signed release. Other helpful information: approximate years of attendance. Fee is $2.00.
Major credit cards accepted for payment.

Carl Albert State College, Registrar, 1507 S McKenna, Poteau, OK 74953-5208, 918-647-1300 (FAX: 918-647-1201). Hours: 8AM-4:30PM. Records go back to 1934. Alumni records are maintained here also. Call 918-647-1213. Degrees granted: Associate. Adverse incident record source: Student Affairs, 918-647-1370.
Attendance and degree information available by phone, FAX, mail. Search requires name plus social security number, date of birth, exact years of attendance, signed release. No fee for information.
Transcripts available by mail. Search requires name plus social security number, date of birth, exact years of attendance, signed release. No fee for transcripts.

Carl Sandburg College, Registrar, 2232 S Lake Storey Rd, Galesburg, IL 61401, 309-344-2518 (FAX: 309-344-3291). Hours: 8AM-5PM. Records go back to 1967. Degrees granted: Associate.
Attendance and degree information available by phone, FAX, mail. Search requires name plus social security number. No fee for information.
Transcripts available by FAX, mail. Search requires name plus social security number, signed release. Fee is $2.00.

Carleton College, Registrar, One N College St, Northfield, MN 55057, 507-663-4289 (FAX: 507-663-5419). Hours: 8AM-5PM. Records go back to 1870. Pre-1953 are at school archives, 507-663-4270. Degrees granted: Bachelors.
Attendance and degree information available by phone, FAX, mail. Search requires name only. Other helpful information: social security number, date of birth, approximate years of attendance. No fee for information.
Transcripts available by FAX, mail. Search requires name plus signed release. Other helpful information: social security number, date of birth, approximate years of attendance. Fee is $2.00.
FAX requests must be followed by mail hard copy. Full name while attending required.

Carlow College, Registrar's Office, 3333 Fifth Ave, Pittsburgh, PA 15213-3165, 412-578-6084. Hours: 8AM-5PM. Records go back to 1929. Alumni records are maintained here also. Call 412-578-6087. Degrees granted: Bachelors; Masters.

Attendance and degree information available by phone, mail. Search requires name plus social security number, date of birth. No fee for information.

Transcripts available by mail. Search requires name plus social security number, exact years of attendance, signed release. Fee is $4.00.

Need former name.

Carnegie Mellon University, Registrar, 5000 Forbes Ave, Warner Hall 201, Pittsburgh, PA 15213, 412-268-2000 X2004 (FAX: 412-268-6651). Hours: 8:30AM-5PM. Records go back to 1920. Alumni records are maintained here also. Call 412-268-2063. Degrees granted: Bachelors; Masters; Doctorate. Adverse incident record source: Student Affairs, 412-268-2076.

Attendance and degree information available by phone, FAX, mail. Search requires name plus social security number, exact years of attendance. No fee for information.

Transcripts available by FAX, mail. Search requires name plus social security number, exact years of attendance, signed release. Fee is $4.00.

Major credit cards accepted for payment.

Carolina Regional College, Registrar, PO Box 4800, Carolina, PR 00984-4800, 809-257-0000.

Carroll College, Registrar, N Benton Ave, Helena, MT 59625, 406-447-5435 (FAX: 406-449-4533). Hours: 9AM-4PM. Alumni records are maintained here also. Call 406-447-4546. Degrees granted: Associate; Masters. Adverse incident record source: Student Affairs, 406-447-4531.

School will not confirm attendance or degree information. Search requires name plus exact years of attendance, signed release. Other helpful information: social security number, date of birth, approximate years of attendance. No fee for information.

Transcripts available by FAX, mail. Search requires name plus date of birth, exact years of attendance, signed release. Other helpful information: social security number, approximate years of attendance. Fee is $3.00.

Carroll College, Registrar, 100 N East Ave, Waukesha, WI 53186, 414-524-7119 (FAX: 414-524-7139). Hours: 8AM-4:30PM. Records go back to 1926. Records are available further back if necessary. Degrees granted: Bachelors; Masters.

Attendance and degree information available by phone, FAX, mail. Search requires name plus social security number. Other helpful information: date of birth, approximate years of attendance. No fee for information.

Transcripts available by written request only. Search requires name plus social security number, date of birth, signed release. Other helpful information: approximate years of attendance. Fee is $3.00.

Carson-Newman College, Registrar, Box 71985, Jefferson City, TN 37760, 615-471-3240 (FAX: 615-471-3502). Hours: 8:30AM-5PM. Records go back to 1930s. Alumni Records Office: Box 71988, Jefferson City, TN 37760, 615-471-3222. Degrees granted: Associate; Bachelors; Masters.

Attendance and degree information available by phone, FAX, mail. Search requires name only. Other helpful information: social security number, date of birth, approximate years of attendance. No fee for information.

Transcripts available by phone, FAX, mail. Search requires name plus signed release. Other helpful information: social security number, date of birth, approximate years of attendance. Fee is $3.00.

Carthage College, Registrar, 2001 Alford Dr, Kenosha, WI 53140, 414-551-8500 (FAX: 414-551-6208). Hours: 8AM-4:30PM. Degrees granted: Bachelors; Masters; Paralegal. Adverse incident record source: 414-551-8500.

Attendance and degree information available by phone, FAX, mail. Search requires name plus approximate years of attendance, signed release. Other helpful information: social security number, date of birth, exact years of attendance. No fee for information.

Transcripts available by written request only. Search requires name plus approximate years of attendance, signed release. Other helpful information: social security number, date of birth, exact years of attendance. No fee for transcripts.

Casco Bay College, Registrar, 477 Congress St, Portland, ME 04101-3483, 207-772-0196 (FAX: 207-772-0636). Hours: 8AM-5PM. Records go back to 1886. Degrees granted: Associate.

Attendance and degree information available by phone, FAX, mail. Search requires name plus social security number. No fee for information.

Transcripts available by mail. Search requires name plus social security number, exact years of attendance, signed release. First transcript is free. Additional ones are $5.00 each.

Case Western Reserve University, Registrar's Office, 10900 Euclid Ave, 223 Pardee Hall, Cleveland, OH 44106-7001, 216-368-4337. Hours: 9AM-4PM. Records go back 100 years. Degrees granted: Bachelors; Masters; Doctorate.

Attendance information available by FAX, mail. Search requires name plus social security number, approximate years of attendance. Other helpful information: date of birth. No fee for information.

Degree information available by FAX, mail. Search requires name plus social security number, approximate years of attendance. Other helpful information: date of birth, exact years of attendance. No fee for information.

Transcripts available by mail. Search requires name plus social security number, date of birth, approximate years of attendance, signed release. Fee is $2.00.

Casper College, Registrar, 125 College Dr, Casper, WY 82601, 307-268-2211 (FAX: 307-268-2611). Hours: 8AM-5PM. Records go back to 1945. Degrees granted: Associate. Adverse incident record source: Dean of Students, 307-268-2210.

Attendance and degree information available by phone, FAX, mail. Search requires name only. Other helpful information: social security number, date of birth, approximate years of attendance. No fee for information.

Transcripts available by FAX, mail. Search requires name plus signed release. Other helpful information: social security number, date of birth, approximate years of attendance. No fee for transcripts.

Castle College, Registrar, Searles Rd, Windham, NH 03087, 603-893-6111. Hours: 8AM-5PM. Records go back to 1965. Alumni records are maintained here at the same phone number. Degrees granted: Associate.

Attendance and degree information available by mail. Search requires name plus social security number, date of birth, exact years of attendance. Other helpful information: approximate years of attendance. No fee for information.

Transcripts available by written request only. Search requires name plus social security number, date of birth, exact years of attendance, signed release. Other helpful information: approximate years of attendance. No fee for transcripts.

Castleton State College, Registrar, Castleton, VT 05735, 802-468-5611 X274 (FAX: 802-468-5237). Hours: 8AM-4:30PM. Records go back to 1787. Alumni records are maintained here at the same phone number. Degrees granted: Bachelors; Masters.

Attendance and degree information available by mail. Search requires name plus social security number, exact years of attendance. No fee for information.

Transcripts available by mail. Search requires name plus social security number, exact years of attendance, signed release. Fee is $3.00.

Catawba College, Registrar, 2300 W Innes St, Salisbury, NC 28144, 704-637-4111 X411. Hours: 8:30AM-5PM. Alumni records are maintained here also. Call 704-637-4111. Degrees granted: Bachelors; Masters.

Attendance and degree information available by phone, mail. Search requires name plus social security number, date of birth, exact years of attendance. No fee for information.

Transcripts available by mail. Search requires name plus social security number, date of birth, exact years of attendance, signed release. Fee is $2.00.

Catawba Valley Community College, Student Records, 2550 Hwy 70 SE, Hickory, NC 28602, 704-327-7009 (FAX: 704-327-7000 X224). Hours: 8AM-9PM M-Th; 8AM-5PM F. Records go back to 1960. Degrees granted: Associate.

Attendance and degree information available by phone, FAX, mail. Search requires name plus social security number. Other helpful information: date of birth, approximate years of attendance. No fee for information.

Transcripts available by FAX, mail. Search requires name plus social security number, signed release. Other helpful information: date of birth, approximate years of attendance. No fee for transcripts.

Cateret Community College, Student Services, 3505 Arendell St, Morehead City, NC 28557, 919-247-4142 (FAX: 919-247-2514). Hours: 8AM-8AM M-Th; 8AM-3:30PM F. Records go back to 1963. Degrees granted: Associate.

Attendance and degree information available by phone, FAX, mail. Search requires name plus social security number. Other helpful information: date of birth, approximate years of attendance. No fee for information.

Transcripts available by FAX, mail. Search requires name plus social security number, signed release. Other helpful information: date of birth, approximate years of attendance. Fee is $1.00.

Catholic Theological Union, Registrar, 5401 S Cornell Ave, Chicago, IL 60615-5698, 313-753-5320. Hours: 8:30AM-4PM. Records go back to 1969. Degrees granted: Masters; Doctorate.

Attendance and degree information available by mail. Search requires name plus social security number, signed release. Other helpful information: exact years of attendance. No fee for information.

Transcripts available by mail. Search requires name plus social security number, signed release. Other helpful information: exact years of attendance. Fee is $5.00.

Catholic University of America, Registrar, 620 Michigan Ave NE, Washington, DC 20064, 202-319-5309. Hours: 9AM-5PM. Records go back 120+ years. Alumni records are maintained here at the same phone number. Degrees granted: Bachelors; Masters; Doctorate; Licentuate.

Attendance and degree information available by phone, mail. Search requires name plus signed release. Other helpful information: social security number, date of birth, approximate years of attendance. No fee for information.

Transcripts available by mail. Search requires name plus signed release. Other helpful information: social security number, date of birth, approximate years of attendance. No fee for transcripts.

Catonsville Community College, Registrar, 800 S Rolling Rd, Catonsville, MD 21228, 410-455-4380. Hours: 8AM-8PM M-Th; 8AM-4PM F. Records go back 35 years. Alumni records are maintained here also. Call 410-455-4944. Degrees granted: Associate. Adverse incident record source: 410-455-4352.

Attendance and degree information available by phone, mail. Search requires name plus social security number, approximate years of attendance, signed release. Other helpful information: date of birth, exact years of attendance. No fee for information.

Transcripts available by mail. Search requires name plus social security number, approximate years of attendance, signed release. Other helpful information: date of birth, exact years of attendance. No fee for transcripts.

Cayey University College, Registrar, Antonio R. Barcelo Ave, Cayey, PR 00633, 809-738-2161.

Cayuga County Community College, Registrar, 197 Franklin St, Auburn, NY 13021, 315-255-1743. Hours: 7:30AM-5PM. Records go back to 1954. Alumni records are maintained here also. Call 315-255-1743 X224. Degrees granted: Associate.

Attendance and degree information available by mail. Search requires name plus social security number, date of birth, signed release. No fee for information.

Transcripts available by mail. Search requires name plus social security number, date of birth, signed release. Fee is $2.00.

Cazenovia College, Registrar, Seminary St, Cazenovia, NY 13035, 315-655-9446 (FAX: 315-655-2190). Hours: 8:30AM-5PM. Records go back to 1900.

Attendance and degree information available by phone, FAX, mail. Search requires name only. Other helpful information: social security number, exact years of attendance. No fee for information.

Transcripts available by FAX, mail. Search requires name plus exact years of attendance, signed release. Other helpful information: social security number. Fee is $3.00.

Cecil Community College, Registrar, 1000 North East Rd, North East, MD 21901, 410-287-1004 (FAX: 410-287-1026). Hours: 8:30AM-4:30PM. Records go back to founding date. Alumni records are maintained here also. Call 410-287-1000. Degrees granted: Associate.

Attendance and degree information available by phone, FAX, mail. Search requires name plus social security number. Other helpful information: date of birth. No fee for information.

Transcripts available by mail. Search requires name plus social security number, signed release. No fee for transcripts.

Cecil's College, Registrar, 1567 Patton Ave, Asheville, NC 28806, 704-252-2486 (FAX: 704-252-8558). Hours: 9AM-6PM.

Records go back to 1930s. Degrees granted: Associate. Adverse incident record source: Records & Registration, 704-252-2486.

Attendance information available by phone, FAX, mail. Search requires name plus social security number. No fee for information.

Degree information available by phone, FAX, mail. Search requires name plus social security number, exact years of attendance. No fee for information.

Transcripts available by FAX, mail. Search requires name plus social security number, exact years of attendance, signed release. Fee is $2.00.

Cedar Crest College, Registrar, 100 College Dr, Allentown, PA 18104, 610-740-3765 (FAX: 610-740-3766). Hours: 8:30AM-4:30PM. Records go back to 1900s. Degrees granted: Bachelors.

Attendance and degree information available by phone, FAX, mail. Search requires name plus social security number, exact years of attendance. Other helpful information: date of birth. No fee for information.

Transcripts available by FAX. Search requires name plus social security number, approximate years of attendance, signed release. Other helpful information: date of birth, exact years of attendance. Fee is $3.00. Expedite fee is $15.00 to $20.00.

Major credit cards accepted for payment.

Cedar Valley College, Registrar, 3030 N Dallas Ave, Lancaster, TX 75134, 214-372-8200 (FAX: 214-372-8207). Hours: 8AM-4:30PM. Degrees granted: Associate.

Attendance and degree information available by phone, mail. Search requires name plus social security number. No fee for information.

Transcripts available by mail. Search requires name plus social security number, signed release. No fee for transcripts.

Cedarville College, Registrar, N Main St, Box 601, Cedarville, OH 45314-0601, 513-766-7710 (FAX: 513-766-7663). Hours: 8AM-5PM. Records go back to 1800s. Alumni records are maintained here also. Call 513-766-7858. Degrees granted: Associate; Bachelors.

Attendance information available by phone, FAX, mail. Search requires name only. Other helpful information: social security number, approximate years of attendance. No fee for information.

Degree information available by mail. Search requires name only. Other helpful information: social security number. No fee for information.

Transcripts available by FAX, mail. Search requires name plus signed release. Other helpful information: social security number. Fee is $3.00.

Centenary College, Registrar, 400 Jefferson St, Hackettstown, NJ 07840, 908-852-1400 (FAX: 908-852-3454). Hours: 8:30AM-6:45PM M-Th; 8:30AM-4:30PM F. Records go back to founding date. Alumni records are maintained here also. Call 908-852-1400. Degrees granted: Associate; Bachelors.

Attendance and degree information available by phone, FAX, mail. Search requires name plus exact years of attendance. Other helpful information: approximate years of attendance. No fee for information.

Transcripts available by written request only. Search requires name plus exact years of attendance, signed release. Other helpful information: approximate years of attendance. Fee is $3.00.

Centenary College of Louisiana, Registrar, PO Box 41188, Shreveport, LA 71134-1184, 318-869-5146 (FAX: 318-869-5026). Hours: 8AM-4:30PM. Records go back to 1920s. Degrees granted: Bachelors; Masters.

Attendance and degree information available by phone, mail. Search requires name plus social security number. Other helpful information: date of birth, approximate years of attendance. No fee for information.

Transcripts available by mail. Search requires name plus social security number, signed release. Other helpful information: date of birth, approximate years of attendance. Fee is $2.00. Expedited service available for $15.00.

Center for Creative Studies-College of Art and Design, Registrar, 201 E Kirby St, Detroit, MI 48202-4034, 313-872-3118 X226 (FAX: 313-872-8377). Hours: 8:30AM-4:30PM. Records go back to 1906. Alumni records are maintained here also. Call 313-872-3118 X278. Degrees granted: Bachelors. Adverse incident record source: Dean of Studen Affairs, 313-872-3118 X289.

Attendance and degree information available by phone, FAX, mail. Search requires name plus social security number, approximate years of attendance, signed release. No fee for information.

Transcripts available by mail. Search requires name plus social security number, approximate years of attendance, signed release. Fee is $2.00.

Center for Humanistic Studies, Registrar, 40 E Ferry Ave, Detroit, MI 48202, 313-875-7440 (FAX: 313-875-2610). Hours: 8:30AM-4PM. Records go back 15 years. Degrees granted: Masters. Adverse incident record source: WSU Police, 313-577-2222.

Attendance and degree information available by FAX, mail. Search requires name plus signed release. Other helpful information: social security number, date of birth, approximate years of attendance. No fee for information.

Transcripts available by mail. Search requires name plus signed release. Other helpful information: social security number, date of birth, approximate years of attendance. Fee is $6.00. Expedited service available for $6.00.

Central Alabama Community College, Registrar, 908 Cherokee Rd, PO Box 699, Alexander City, AL 35010, 205-234-6346 (FAX: 205-234-0384). Hours: 7:30AM-4:30PM. Records go back to 1965. Degrees granted: Associate. Special programs- Tech Records prior 1989 merger, 205-378-5570 X6420. Adverse incident record source: Assoc Dean of Students, 205-234-6346 X6510.

Attendance and degree information available by phone, FAX, mail. Search requires name only. Other helpful information: social security number, date of birth, approximate years of attendance. No fee for information.

Transcripts available by mail. Search requires name plus social security number, signed release. Other helpful information: date of birth, approximate years of attendance. No fee for transcripts.

Central Arizona College, Registrar, 8470 N Overfield Rd, Coolidge, AZ 85228, 520-426-4444 (FAX: 520-426-4234). Hours: 8AM-4:30PM. Records go back to 1969. Degrees granted: Associate.

Attendance and degree information available by phone, FAX, mail. Search requires name only. Other helpful information: social security number, date of birth, approximate years of attendance. No fee for information.

Transcripts available by mail. Search requires name plus social security number, signed release. Other helpful information: date of birth, approximate years of attendance. Fee is $4.00. Expedited service available for $19.00.

Major credit cards accepted for payment.

Central Baptist College, Registrar, 1501 College Ave, Conway, AR 72032, 501-329-6872 (FAX: 501-329-2941). Hours: 8AM-4:30PM. Records go back 30 years. Degrees granted: Associate; Bachelors.

Attendance and degree information available by phone, FAX, mail. Search requires name only. Other helpful information: social security number. No fee for information.

Transcripts available by mail. Search requires name plus signed release. Other helpful information: social security number. Fee is $3.00.

Central Baptist Theological Seminary, Registrar, 741 N 31st St, Kansas City, KS 66102-3964, 913-371-5313 (FAX: 913-371-8110). Hours: 8AM-4:30PM. Records go back to 1901. Alumni Records Office: 7215 NW Maple Lane, Kansas City, MO 64151. Degrees granted: Masters.

Attendance and degree information available by written request only. Search requires name plus signed release. Other helpful information: approximate years of attendance. No fee for information.

Transcripts available by written request only. Search requires name plus signed release. Other helpful information: approximate years of attendance. Fee is $3.00.

Central Carolina Community College, Registrar, 1105 Kelly Dr, Sanford, NC 27330, 919-775-5401 (FAX: 919-774-1500). Hours: 7:30AM-6PM M-Th; 7:30AM-3:30PM F. Records go back to 1962. Alumni records are maintained here at the same phone number.

Attendance and degree information available by phone, mail. Search requires name plus social security number. Other helpful information: approximate years of attendance. No fee for information.

Transcripts available by mail. Search requires name plus social security number, signed release. Other helpful information: approximate years of attendance. No fee for transcripts.

Include a self addressed stamped envelope with mail request. Fees for transcripts begin Fall 1995.

Central Carolina Technical College, Registrar, 506 N Guignard Dr, Sumter, SC 29150-2499, 803-778-1961 X430 (FAX: 800-221-8711). Records go back to 1963. Degrees granted: Associate.

Attendance and degree information available by phone, mail. Search requires name plus social security number, exact years of attendance. No fee for information.

Transcripts available by mail. Search requires name plus social security number, exact years of attendance, signed release. Fee is $2.00.

Central Christian College of the Bible, Registrar, 911 Urbandale Dr E, Moberly, MO 65270, 816-263-3900 (FAX: 816-263-3936). Hours: 8AM-Noon, 1-5PM. Records go back to 1957. Degrees granted: Associate; Bachelors.

Attendance information available by phone, FAX, mail. Search requires name plus signed release. Other helpful information: approximate years of attendance. No fee for information.

Degree information available by FAX, mail. Search requires name plus signed release. Fee is $3.00.

Transcripts available by FAX, mail. Search requires name plus signed release. Fee is $3.00.

Central College, Registrar, 1200 S Main St, McPherson, KS 67460, 316-241-0723 (FAX: 316-241-6032). Hours: 8AM-5PM. Records go back to 1914. Degrees granted: Associate; Bachelors. Adverse incident record source: Student Services, 316-241-0723.

Attendance information available by phone, FAX, mail. Search requires name plus social security number, date of birth, exact years of attendance. No fee for information.

Degree information available by phone, FAX, mail. Search requires name plus social security number, exact years of attendance, signed release. Other helpful information: date of birth. No fee for information.

Transcripts available by written request only. Search requires name plus social security number, exact years of attendance, signed release. Other helpful information: date of birth. Fee is $3.00. Expedited service available for $2.00.

Central College, Registrar, 812 University, Pella, IA 50219, 515-628-5267 (FAX: 515-628-5316). Hours: 8AM-5PM. Alumni records are maintained here also. Call 515-628-5281. Degrees granted: Bachelors.

Attendance and degree information available by phone, FAX, mail. Search requires name only. Other helpful information: social security number, date of birth, approximate years of attendance. No fee for information.

Transcripts available by FAX, mail. Search requires name plus signed release. Other helpful information: social security number, date of birth, approximate years of attendance. Fee is $3.00.

Major credit cards accepted for payment.

Central Community College, Registrar, PO Box 4903, Grand Island, NE 68802-4903, 308-384-5220. Alumni Records Office: 2727 W 2nd #211, Hastings, NE 68101, 402-462-4000.

Attendance and degree information available by mail. Search requires name plus social security number, approximate years of attendance. Other helpful information: date of birth, exact years of attendance. No fee for information.

Transcripts available by written request only. Search requires name plus social security number, approximate years of attendance, signed release. Other helpful information: date of birth, exact years of attendance. Fee is $2.00.

Central Connecticut State University, Registrar's Office, 1615 Stanley St, New Britain, CT 06050, 203-832-2244. Hours: 8AM-8:30PM. Degrees granted: Bachelors; Masters.

Attendance and degree information available by phone, mail. Search requires name plus social security number, approximate years of attendance. Other helpful information: date of birth. No fee for information.

Transcripts available by mail. Search requires name plus social security number, approximate years of attendance, signed release. Other helpful information: date of birth. Fee is $3.00.

Central Florida Community College, Registrar, PO Box 1388, Ocala, FL 34478, 904-237-2111 (FAX: 904-237-3747). Hours: 8AM-7PM M-Th, 8AM-4:30PM F. Records go back to 1957. Degrees granted: Associate.

Attendance and degree information available by FAX, mail. Search requires name plus social security number, exact years of attendance. No fee for information.

Transcripts available by FAX, mail. Search requires name plus social security number, exact years of attendance, signed release. Fee is $3.00.

Central Maine Medical Center School of Nursing, Registrar, Lewiston, ME 04240, 207-795-2858 (FAX: 207-795-2849). Hours: 8:30AM-5PM. Records go back to 1891. Degrees granted: Associate.

Attendance and degree information available by phone, FAX, mail. Search requires name only. Other helpful information: approximate years of attendance. No fee for information.

Transcripts available by written request only. Search requires name plus signed release. Other helpful information: approximate years of attendance. Fee is $2.00. Expedited service available for $2.00.

Central Maine Technical College, Registrar, 1250 Turner St, Auburn, ME 04210, 207-784-2385 (FAX: 207-777-7353). Hours: 8AM-4:30PM. Degrees granted: Associate.

School will not confirm attendance information. Search requires name plus social security number. Other helpful information: date of birth, approximate years of attendance. No fee for information.

Degree information available by phone. Search requires name plus social security number. Other helpful information: date of birth, approximate years of attendance. No fee for information.

Transcripts available by mail. Search requires name plus social security number, signed release. Other helpful information: date of birth, approximate years of attendance. Fee is $3.00. Expedited service available for $10.00.

Major credit cards accepted for payment.

Central Methodist College, Registrar, Fayette, MO 65248, 816-248-3391 X208 (FAX: 816-248-2622). Hours: 8AM-5PM. Records go back to 1900. Alumni records are maintained here also. Call 816-248-3391 X230. Degrees granted: Bachelors.

Attendance and degree information available by phone, FAX, mail. Search requires name plus social security number, approximate years of attendance, signed release. No fee for information.

Transcripts available by FAX, mail. Search requires name plus social security number, approximate years of attendance, signed release. Fee is $2.00.

Central Michigan University, Registrar, Mount Pleasant, MI 48859, 517-774-3261 (FAX: 517-774-3783). Hours: 8AM-5PM. Records go back to 1920. Alumni records are maintained here also. Call 517-774-3312. Degrees granted: Bachelors; Masters; Doctorate.

Attendance and degree information available by phone, FAX, mail. Search requires name only. Other helpful information: social security number, date of birth, approximate years of attendance. No fee for information.

Transcripts available by FAX, mail. Search requires name plus signed release. Other helpful information: social security number, date of birth, approximate years of attendance. No fee for transcripts. Expedited service available for $8.00.

Major credit cards accepted for payment.

Central Missouri State University, Registrar, Warrensburg, MO 64093, 816-543-4900 (FAX: 816-543-8400). Hours: 8AM-5PM. Records go back to 1871. Alumni records are maintained here also. Call 816-543-4025. Degrees granted: Associate; Bachelors; Masters; Education Specialist.

Attendance and degree information available by phone, mail. Search requires name only. Other helpful information: social security number, date of birth, approximate years of attendance. No fee for information.

Transcripts available by mail. Search requires name plus signed release. Other helpful information: social security number, date of birth, approximate years of attendance. Fee is $1.00.

Central Ohio Technical College, Registrar, 1179 University Dr, Newark, OH 43055-1767, 614-366-9208 X208 (FAX: 614-366-5047). Hours: 8AM-5PM. Records go back to 1971. Alumni records are maintained here at the same phone number. Degrees granted: Associate.

School will not confirm attendance information. Search requires name plus social security number, signed release. Other helpful information: date of birth, approximate years of attendance. No fee for information.

Degree information available by phone, FAX, mail. Search requires name plus social security number. Other helpful information: date of birth, approximate years of attendance. No fee for information.

Transcripts available by mail. Search requires name plus social security number, signed release. Other helpful information: date of birth, approximate years of attendance. Fee is $2.00. Expedited service available for $10.00.

Major credit cards accepted for payment.

Central Oregon Community College, Registrar, 2600 NW College Way, Bend, OR 97701, 503-383-7700 (FAX: 503-383-7506). Hours: 8AM-5PM. Records go back to 1949. Alumni records are maintained here at the same phone number. Degrees granted: Associate.

Attendance and degree information available by phone, FAX, mail. Search requires name only. No fee for information.

Transcripts available by FAX, mail. Search requires name plus social security number. Fee is $5.00.

FAX copies are 5.00 extra.

Central Pennsylvania Business School, Registrar, College Hill Rd, Summerdale, PA 17093-0309, 717-732-0702 X205 (FAX: 717-732-5254). Hours: 8AM-5PM. Records go back to 1960. Degrees granted: Associate.

Attendance and degree information available by phone, FAX, mail. Search requires name only. Other helpful information: social security number, approximate years of attendance. No fee for information.

Transcripts available by FAX, mail. Search requires name plus signed release. Other helpful information: social security number, approximate years of attendance. Fee is $2.00. Expedited service available for $2.00.

Central Piedmont Community College, Registrar, PO Box 35009, Charlotte, NC 28235, 704-342-6959 (FAX: 704-342-5933). Hours: 8AM-5PM. Records go back to 1965. Alumni records are maintained here also. Call 704-342-6666. Degrees granted: Associate. Adverse incident record source: Dean, 704-342-6888.

Attendance information available by phone, FAX, mail. Search requires name plus social security number. No fee for information.

Degree information available by phone, FAX, mail. Search requires name plus social security number, exact years of attendance. No fee for information.

Transcripts available by FAX, mail. Search requires name plus social security number, exact years of attendance, signed release. No fee for transcripts.

Central State University, Registrar, 1400 Brush Row Rd, Wilberforce, OH 45384, 513-376-6231 (FAX: 513-376-6530). Hours: 9AM-4PM. Records go back to 1947. Degrees granted: Associate; Bachelors; Masters. Adverse incident record source: Campus Police.

School will not confirm attendance information. Search requires name plus social security number, date of birth, exact years of attendance, signed release. No fee for information.

Degree information available by mail. Search requires name plus social security number, date of birth, exact years of attendance, signed release. No fee for information.

Transcripts available by phone. Search requires name plus social security number, date of birth, exact years of attendance, signed release. Fee is $3.00.

Central Technical Community College, Registrar, PO Box 1024, Hastings, NE 68902-1024, 402-463-9811. Hours: 9AM-5PM.

Attendance and degree information available by phone, FAX, mail. Search requires name plus approximate years of attendance. Other helpful information: social security number, date of birth, exact years of attendance. No fee for information.

Transcripts available by written request only. Search requires name plus exact years of attendance, signed release. Other helpful information: social security number, date of birth. No fee for transcripts.

Central Texas College, Registrar, PO Box 1800, Killeen, TX 76540-9990, 817-526-1308 (FAX: 817-526-1481). Hours: 8AM-5PM. Records go back to 1968. Degrees granted: Associate. Special programs- Hanau, German, 011-49-6181-95060: Camp Market, Korea, 011-82-32-523-5110.

Attendance and degree information available by phone, FAX, mail. Search requires name only. Other helpful information: social security number, date of birth, approximate years of attendance. No fee for information.

Transcripts available by FAX, mail. Search requires name plus social security number, signed release. Other helpful information: date of birth, approximate years of attendance. Fee is $3.00. Expedited service available for $5.00.

Major credit cards accepted for payment.

Central Virginia Community College, Registrar, 3506 Wards Rd, Lynchburg, VA 24502-2498, 804-386-4576 (FAX: 804-386-4681). Hours: 8:30AM-4:30PM. Records go back to 1967. Alumni records are maintained here also. Call 804-386-4535. Degrees granted: Associate.

Attendance and degree information available by phone, FAX, mail. Search requires name plus social security number. Other helpful information: date of birth, approximate years of attendance. No fee for information.

Transcripts available by FAX, mail. Search requires name plus social security number, signed release. Other helpful information: date of birth, approximate years of attendance. No fee for transcripts.

Central Washington University, Registrar, Mitchell Hall, 400 E 8th Ave, Ellensburg, WA 98926-7463, 509-963-3001 (FAX: 509-963-3022). Hours: 8AM-5PM. Records go back to 1890. Alumni records are maintained here also. Call 509-963-2752. Degrees granted: Bachelors; Masters.

Attendance and degree information available by phone, FAX, mail. Search requires name plus date of birth. Other helpful information: social security number, approximate years of attendance. No fee for information.

Transcripts available by FAX, mail. Search requires name plus date of birth, signed release. Other helpful information: social security number, approximate years of attendance. Fee is $5.00. Expedited service available for $10.00.

Major credit cards accepted for payment.

Central Wesleyan College, Registrar, PO Box 1020, 1 Wesleyan Dr, Central, SC 29630-1020, 803-639-2453 X325. Hours: 8AM-4:30PM. Alumni records are maintained here at the same phone number. Degrees granted: Bachelors; Masters.

Attendance and degree information available by phone, mail. Search requires name plus social security number. No fee for information.

Transcripts available by mail. Search requires name plus social security number, signed release. Fee is $3.00.

Need to provide ID number.

Central Wyoming College, Registrar, 2660 Peck Ave, Riverton, WY 82501, 307-856-9291 (FAX: 307-856-2264). Hours: 8AM-5PM. Records go back to 1966. Alumni records are maintained here at the same phone number. Degrees granted: Associate.

Attendance and degree information available by phone, FAX, mail. Search requires name plus social security number, date of birth, exact years of attendance, signed release. No fee for information.

Transcripts available by FAX, mail. Search requires name plus social security number, date of birth, exact years of attendance, signed release. Fee is $1.00.

Central Yeshiva Tomchei Tmimim-Lubavitch, Registrar, 841-853 Ocean Pkwy, Brooklyn, NY 11230, 718-859-2277. Hours: 9:30AM-5:30PM. Records go back to 1985. Alumni records are maintained here also. Call 718-859-2277. Degrees granted: Associate.

Attendance and degree information available by phone, mail. Search requires name plus social security number, date of birth, signed release. No fee for information.

Transcripts available by phone, mail. Search requires name plus social security number, date of birth, signed release. Fee is $5.00.

Centralia College, Registrar, 600 W Locust St, Centralia, WA 98531, 206-736-9391 X221. Hours: 8AM-4:30PM. Records go back to 1925. Alumni records are maintained here at the same phone number. Degrees granted: Associate.

Attendance and degree information available by phone, mail. Search requires name plus social security number, exact years of attendance. No fee for information.

Transcripts available by mail. Search requires name plus social security number, exact years of attendance, signed release. Fee is $2.00.

Centre College, Registrar, 600 W Walnut St, Danville, KY 40422, 606-238-5360 (FAX: 606-236-9610). Hours: 8:30AM-4:30PM. Records go back to 1900. Degrees granted: Bachelors. Adverse incident record source: Dean of Students, 606-238-5471.

Attendance and degree information available by phone, FAX, mail. Search requires name plus approximate years of attendance, signed release. Other helpful information: social security number, date of birth, exact years of attendance. No fee for information.

Transcripts available by mail. Search requires name plus social security number, date of birth, exact years of attendance, signed release. No fee for transcripts. Expedited service available for $5.00.

Centro de Estudios Avanzados de Puerto Rico y El Caribe, Registrar, Del Cristo St No 52, Box S 4467, San Juan, PR 00904, 809-723-4481.

Cerritos College, Registrar, 11110 Alondra Blvd, Norwalk, CA 90650, 310-860-2451 (FAX: 310-467-5005). Hours: 8AM-9PM M-Th, 8AM-4:30PM F. Records go back to 1955. Alumni records are maintained here also. Call 310-860-2451. Degrees granted: Associate.

Attendance and degree information available by phone, mail. Search requires name plus social security number, date of birth, exact years of attendance. No fee for information.

Transcripts available by mail. Search requires name plus social security number, date of birth, exact years of attendance, signed release. Fee is $2.00.

Cerro Coso Community College, Registrar, 3000 College Heights Blvd, Ridgecrest, CA 93555-7777, 619-375-5001 X357 (FAX: 619-375-4776). Hours: 8AM-7PM M-Th; 8AM-4PM F. Records go back to 1973. Alumni records are maintained here also. Call 619-375-5001 X230. Degrees granted: Associate. Adverse incident record source: Administrative Services.

Attendance and degree information available by phone, FAX, mail. Search requires name plus social security number. Other helpful information: date of birth, approximate years of attendance. No fee for information.

Transcripts available by FAX, mail. Search requires name plus social security number, signed release. Other helpful information: date of birth, approximate years of attendance. Fee is $5.00. Expedited service available for $7.50.

Major credit cards accepted for payment.

Chabot College, Registrar, 25555 Hesperian Blvd, Hayward, CA 94545, 510-786-6703. Hours: 8AM-7:30PM M-Th, 8AM-1PM F. Records go back to 1960. Alumni records are maintained here also. Call 510-786-6600. Degrees granted: Associate.

Attendance and degree information available by phone, mail. Search requires name plus social security number, exact years of attendance. No fee for information.

Transcripts available by mail. Search requires name plus social security number, exact years of attendance, signed release. Fee is $3.00.

Chadron State College, Director, Admissions & Records, 1000 Main St, Chadron, NE 69337, 308-432-6221 (FAX: 308-432-6229). Hours: 8AM-5PM. Records go back to 1911. Alumni records are maintained here also. Call 308-432-6362. Degrees granted: Bachelors; Masters. Adverse incident record source: Student Services, 308-432-6231.

Attendance and degree information available by phone, FAX, mail. Search requires name plus social security number. Other helpful information: date of birth, approximate years of attendance. No fee for information.

Transcripts available by FAX, mail. Search requires name plus social security number, signed release. Other helpful information: date of birth, approximate years of attendance. Fee is $2.00. Expedited service available for $10.00.

Chaffey College, Registrar, 5885 Have Ave, Rancho Cucamonga, CA 91701, 909-941-2100. Degrees granted: Associate.

Attendance and degree information available by mail. Search requires name plus social security number, date of birth, signed release. Other helpful information: exact years of attendance. No fee for information. Expedited service available for $10.00.

Transcripts available by mail. Search requires name plus social security number, date of birth, signed release. Other helpful information: exact years of attendance. First two are free. Expedited service available for $10.00.

Major credit cards accepted for payment.

Chaminade University of Honolulu, Registrar, 3140 Waialae Ave, Honolulu, HI 96816-1578, 808-735-4773 (FAX: 808-735-4777). Hours: 8AM-4PM. Records go back 40 years. Alumni Records Office: CUH-Alumni Association, 2636 Pamao Rd, Honolulu, HI 96822. Degrees granted: Associate; Bachelors; Masters.

Attendance information available by FAX, mail. Search requires name plus social security number, approximate years of attendance, signed release. Other helpful information: exact years of attendance. No fee for information.

Degree information available by phone, FAX, mail. Search requires name plus social security number. No fee for information.

Transcripts available by FAX, mail. Search requires name plus approximate years of attendance, signed release. Other helpful information: social security number, exact years of attendance. Fee is $10.00. Expedited service available for $12.00.

Major credit cards accepted for payment.

Champlain College, Registrar's Office, 163 S Willard St, Burlington, VT 05402-0670, 802-860-2715 (FAX: 802-860-2772). Hours: 8:30AM-5PM. Records go back to 1965. Degrees granted: Associate; Bachelors. Certification: Secretarial and Concentrated Study. Adverse incident record source: Security Office, 802-658-0800.

Attendance and degree information available by phone, FAX, mail. Search requires name plus approximate years of attendance. Other helpful information: social security number, exact years of attendance. No fee for information.

Transcripts available by FAX, mail. Search requires name plus social security number, approximate years of attendance, signed release. Other helpful information: exact years of attendance. Fee is $2.00. Expedited service available for $2.00.

Chandler-Gilbert Community College, Registrar, 2626 E Pecos Rd, Chandler, AZ 85225-2479, 602-732-7308 (FAX: 602-732-7099). Hours: 8:30AM-7PM. Records go back to 1987. Degrees granted: Associate. Adverse incident record source: Jose Garcia, 602-732-7280.

Attendance and degree information available by phone, FAX, mail. Search requires name plus signed release. Other helpful information: social security number, date of birth. No fee for information.

Transcripts available by FAX, mail. Search requires name plus signed release. Other helpful information: social security number, date of birth. Fee is $5.00.

Major credit cards accepted for payment.

Chaparral Career College, Registrar, 4585 E Speedway Blvd Ste 204, Tucson, AZ 85712, 520-327-6866 (FAX: 520-325-0105). Hours: 8AM-5PM. Records go back 23 years. Degrees granted: Associate.

Attendance and degree information available by phone, FAX, mail. Search requires name plus social security number, approximate years of attendance, signed release. Other helpful information: date of birth, exact years of attendance. No fee for information.

Transcripts available by FAX, mail. Search requires name plus social security number, approximate years of attendance, signed release. Other helpful information: date of birth, exact years of attendance. No fee for transcripts.

Major credit cards accepted for payment.

Chapman University, Registrar, 333 N Glassell St, Orange, CA 92666, 714-997-6701 (FAX: 714-997-6986). Hours: 8AM-4:30PM. Records go back to 1958. Degrees granted: Associate; Bachelors; Masters; Teaching Credential.

Attendance and degree information available by phone, mail. Search requires name plus social security number. Other helpful information: date of birth, approximate years of attendance. No fee for information.

Transcripts available by mail. Search requires name plus social security number, signed release. Other helpful information: date of birth, approximate years of attendance. Fee is $5.00. Expedited service available for $15.00.

Charles County Community College, Registrar, Mitchell Rd, PO Box 910, La Plata, MD 20646, 301-870-3008 (FAX: 301-934-5255). Hours: 8:30AM-4:30PM. Records go back to 1974. Degrees granted: Associate.

Attendance information available by phone, mail. Search requires name plus social security number, date of birth, approximate years of attendance. No fee for information.

Degree information available by phone, mail. Search requires name plus social security number, approximate years of attendance. Other helpful information: date of birth. No fee for information.

Transcripts available by written request only. Search requires name plus social security number, approximate years of attendance, signed release. Other helpful information: exact years of attendance. Fee is $3.00.

Charles R. Drew University of Medicine and Science, Registrar, 1621 E 120th St, Los Angeles, CA 90059, 213-563-4800 (FAX: 213-563-4957). Hours: 8AM-5PM. Records go back to 1966. Alumni records are maintained here at the same phone number. Degrees granted: Doctorate.

Attendance information available by phone, FAX, mail. Search requires name plus social security number. No fee for information.

Degree information available by FAX, mail. Search requires name plus social security number, exact years of attendance, signed release. No fee for information.

Transcripts available by FAX, mail. Search requires name plus social security number, exact years of attendance, signed release. Fee is $5.00.

Charles Stewart Mott Community College, Registrar, 1401 E Court St, Flint, MI 48503, 810-762-0221 (FAX: 810-762-0257). Hours: 7:30AM-7PM M, 8AM-4:30PM T-F. Records go back to 1945. Record on microfiche from 1945. Degrees granted: Associate.

Attendance and degree information available by phone, FAX, mail. Search requires name plus social security number, approximate years of attendance, signed release. No fee for information.

Transcripts available by mail. Search requires name plus social security number, approximate years of attendance, signed release. Fee is $2.00.

Charleston Southern University, Registrar, PO Box 10087, Charleston, SC 29411, 803-863-7000 (FAX: 803-863-8074). Alumni records are maintained here at the same phone number. Degrees granted: Bachelors; Masters.

Attendance and degree information available by phone, mail. Search requires name plus social security number, date of birth, exact years of attendance. No fee for information.

Transcripts available by mail. Search requires name plus social security number, date of birth, exact years of attendance, signed release. Fee is $3.00.

Charter Oak State College, Registrar, 66 Cedar St #301, Newington, CT 06111-2646, 203-666-4595 (FAX: 203-666-4852). Hours: 8:30AM-4:30PM. Records go back to 1974. Degrees granted: Associate; Bachelors.

Attendance and degree information available by phone, FAX, mail. Search requires name plus social security number, signed release. Other helpful information: date of birth. No fee for information.

Transcripts available by mail. Search requires name plus social security number, signed release. No fee for transcripts.

Chatfield College, Registrar, 20918 State Rte 251, St Martin, OH 45118, 513-875-3344 (FAX: 513-875-3912). Hours: 8AM-5PM. Records go back to 1968. Degrees granted: Associate.

Attendance and degree information available by phone, FAX, mail. Search requires name plus social security number, approximate years of attendance. Other helpful information: date of birth, exact years of attendance. No fee for information.

Transcripts available by FAX, mail. Search requires name plus social security number, approximate years of attendance, signed release. Other helpful information: date of birth, exact years of attendance. Fee is $2.00.

Former names needed.

Chatham College, Registrar's Office, Woodland Rd, Pittsburgh, PA 15232, 412-365-1121. Hours: 9AM-5PM. Records go back to 1920. Alumni records are maintained here also. Call 412-365-1255. Degrees granted: Bachelors; Masters.

Attendance information available by mail. Search requires name plus social security number, signed release. No fee for information.

Degree information available by phone, mail. Search requires name plus social security number, exact years of attendance. No fee for information.

Transcripts available by mail. Search requires name plus social security number, exact years of attendance, signed release. Fee is $3.00.

Chattahochee Technical Institute, Registrar, 980 S Cobb Dr, Marietta, GA 30060, 404-528-4545 (FAX: 404-528-4580). Hours: 7:30AM-7:30PM M-Th; 7:30AM-4PM F. Records go back 30 years. Degrees granted: Associate.

Attendance and degree information available by phone, FAX, mail. Search requires name plus social security number. Other helpful information: date of birth, approximate years of attendance. No fee for information.

School does not provide transcripts. Search requires name plus social security number, signed release. Other helpful information: date of birth, approximate years of attendance. Fee is $2.00.

Major credit cards accepted for payment.

Chattahoochee Valley State Community College, Registrar, 2602 College Dr, Phenix City, AL 36869, 334-291-

4928 (FAX: 334-291-4994). Hours: 8AM-5PM. Records go back to 1974. Degrees granted: Associate. Adverse incident record source: 205-291-4941.

Attendance and degree information available by FAX, mail. Search requires name plus social security number, exact years of attendance, signed release. Other helpful information: date of birth, approximate years of attendance. No fee for information.

Transcripts available by FAX, mail. Search requires name plus social security number, exact years of attendance, signed release. Other helpful information: date of birth, approximate years of attendance. No fee for transcripts.

Chattanooga State Technical Community College, Registrar, 4501 Amnicola Hwy, Chattanooga, TN 37406, 615-697-4404 (FAX: 615-697-4709). Hours: 7:30AM-5:30PM M-Th; 7:30AM-4:30PM F. Degrees granted: Associate.

Attendance and degree information available by phone, FAX, mail. Search requires name plus social security number, signed release. Other helpful information: date of birth, approximate years of attendance. No fee for information.

Transcripts available by written request only. Search requires name plus social security number, signed release. Other helpful information: date of birth, approximate years of attendance. No fee for transcripts.

Chemeketa Community College, Registrar, PO Box 14007, Salem, OR 97309, 503-399-5001 (FAX: 503-399-3918). Hours: 8AM-4:30PM. Records go back 10 years. Transcripts available from 1970 on. Degrees granted: Associate.

Attendance and degree information available by phone, FAX, mail. Search requires name plus social security number. Other helpful information: date of birth. No fee for information.

Transcripts available by FAX, mail. Search requires name plus social security number. Other helpful information: date of birth. Fee is $5.00.

Chesapeake College, Registrar, PO Box 8, Wye Mills, MD 21679, 410-228-4360 (FAX: 410-827-9466). Hours: 8AM-4PM. Records go back to 1965. Alumni records are maintained here also. Call 410-827-5808. Degrees granted: Associate.

Attendance and degree information available by phone, mail. Search requires name plus social security number, date of birth, exact years of attendance. No fee for information.

Transcripts available by mail. Search requires name plus social security number, date of birth, exact years of attendance, signed release. Fee is $2.00.

Chesterfield-Marlboro Technical College, Registrar, 1201 Chesterfield Hwy #9 W, PO Drawer 1007, Cheraw, SC 29520-1007, 803-921-6900 (FAX: 803-537-6148). Hours: 8AM-7PM M-Th; 8AM-1:30PM F. Records go back to 1969. Degrees granted: Associate.

Attendance and degree information available by phone, FAX, mail. Search requires name plus social security number. Other helpful information: date of birth, approximate years of attendance. No fee for information.

Transcripts available by FAX, mail. Search requires name plus social security number, signed release. Other helpful information: date of birth, approximate years of attendance. Fee is $2.00. Results available by FAX for $5.00.

Major credit cards accepted for payment.

Chestnut Hill College, Registrar's Office, 9601 Germantown Ave, Philadelphia, PA 19118-2695, 215-248-7005 (FAX: 215-248-7155). Hours: 8:30AM-4:30PM. Records go back to 1953. Alumni records are maintained here also. Call 215-248-7144. Degrees granted: Associate; Bachelors; Masters.

Attendance and degree information available by phone, FAX, mail. Search requires name plus social security number, approximate years of attendance. No fee for information.

Transcripts available by FAX, mail. Search requires name plus social security number, exact years of attendance, signed release. Fee is $3.00.

Need former name. Major credit cards accepted for payment.

Cheyney University of Pennsylvania, Registrar's Office, Cheyney and Creek Rds, Cheyney, PA 19319, 610-399-2225 (FAX: 610-399-2415). Hours: 8AM-5PM. Records go back to 1837. Alumni records are maintained here also. Call 610-399-2000. Degrees granted: Bachelors; Masters.

Attendance and degree information available by phone, FAX, mail. Search requires name plus social security number, exact years of attendance. No fee for information.

Transcripts available by mail. Search requires name plus social security number, exact years of attendance, signed release. Fee is $7.00.

Need to know when graduated and former names. Money orders only accepted.

Chicago College of Commerce, Registrar, 11 E Adams St, Chicago, IL 60603, 312-236-3312 (FAX: 312-236-0015). Hours: 9AM-5PM. Records go back 40 years. Degrees granted: Associate. Certification: Machine Shorthand, Legal Trans., Medical Trans.

Attendance and degree information available by phone. Search requires name only. Other helpful information: social security number, date of birth, approximate years of attendance. No fee for information.

Transcripts available by written request only. Search requires name plus social security number, signed release. Other helpful information: date of birth, approximate years of attendance. Fee is $3.00.

Chicago School of Professional Psychology, Registrar, 806 S Plymouth Ct, Chicago, IL 60605, 312-786-9443 (FAX: 312-786-9611). Hours: 9AM-5PM. Records go back to 1979. Degrees granted: Doctorate.

Attendance and degree information available by phone, FAX, mail. Search requires name plus social security number. No fee for information.

Transcripts available by FAX, mail. Search requires name plus social security number, exact years of attendance, signed release. Fee is $4.00.

Chicago State University, Registrar, 9501 S King Dr, Chicago, IL 60628, 312-995-2461 (FAX: 312-995-3618). Hours: 8:30AM-5PM M,T,W,F; 8:30AM-7PM Th. Records go back to 1905. Degrees granted: Bachelors; Masters. Adverse incident record source: 312-995-2111.

Attendance information available by FAX, mail. Search requires name plus social security number, signed release. Other helpful information: date of birth, approximate years of attendance. No fee for information.

Degree information available by phone, FAX, mail. Search requires name plus social security number. Other helpful information: date of birth, approximate years of attendance. No fee for information.

Transcripts available by mail. Search requires name plus social security number, approximate years of attendance, signed release. Other helpful information: date of birth. Fee is $2.00.

Chicago Theological Seminary, Registrar, 5757 S University Ave, Chicago, IL 60637, 312-752-5757 X227 (FAX: 312-752-5925). Hours: 8:30AM-4:30PM. Records go back 25 years. Degrees granted: Masters; Doctorate.

Attendance and degree information available by phone, FAX, mail. Search requires name plus exact years of attendance. Other helpful information: date of birth, approximate years of attendance. No fee for information.

Transcripts available by written request only. Search requires name plus exact years of attendance, signed release. Other helpful information: social security number, date of birth, approximate years of attendance. Fee is $3.00. Expedited service available for $3.00.

Chipola Junior College, Registrar, 3094 Indian Circle, Marianna, FL 32446-2053, 904-526-2761 (FAX: 904-526-4153). Hours: 7:30AM-4:30PM. Records go back to 1947. Degrees granted: Associate. Adverse incident record source: Marianna Police Dept, 904-526-3125.

Attendance and degree information available by phone, mail. Search requires name only. Other helpful information: social security number, date of birth, approximate years of attendance. No fee for information.

Transcripts available by mail. Search requires name plus signed release. Other helpful information: social security number, date of birth, approximate years of attendance. Fee is $1.00.

Chippewa Valley Technical College, Registrar, 620 W Clairemont Ave, Eau Claire, WI 54701, 715-833-6269 (FAX: 715-833-6470). Hours: 7:30AM-8:30PM. Records go back to 1940s. Alumni records are maintained here at the same phone number. Degrees granted: Associate.

Attendance information available by mail. Search requires name plus social security number, signed release. Other helpful information: exact years of attendance. No fee for information.

Degree information available by phone, FAX, mail. Search requires name plus signed release. Other helpful information: social security number, exact years of attendance. No fee for information.

Transcripts available by written request only. Search requires name plus signed release. Other helpful information: social security number, exact years of attendance. Fee is $1.00.

Chowan College, Registrar, PO Box 1848, Murfreesboro, NC 27855, 919-398-9101 (FAX: 919-398-1190). Hours: 8:30AM-5PM. Records go back 150 years. Degrees granted: Associate; Bachelors.

Attendance and degree information available by phone, FAX, mail. Search requires name plus social security number. Other helpful information: date of birth, exact years of attendance. No fee for information.

Transcripts available by mail. Search requires name plus social security number, signed release. Other helpful information: date of birth, exact years of attendance. Fee is $3.00.

Christ the King Seminary, Registrar, 711 Knox Rd, PO Box 607, East Aurora, NY 14052-0607, 716-652-8900 (FAX: 716-652-8903). Hours: 9AM-4PM. Records go back to 1950. Some records prior to 1974 destroyed. Degrees granted: Masters.

Attendance information available by phone, FAX, mail. Search requires name only. Other helpful information: social security number, date of birth, exact years of attendance. No fee for information.

Degree information available by phone, FAX, mail. Search requires name only. Other helpful information: social security number, date of birth. No fee for information.

Transcripts available by written request only. Search requires name plus social security number, date of birth, signed release. Other helpful information: approximate years of attendance. Fee is $5.00. Expedited service available for $5.00.

Christendom College, Registrar, 134 Christendon Dr, Front Royal, VA 22630, 703-636-2900 (FAX: 703-636-1655). Hours: 8:30AM-4:30PM. Records go back to 1977. Degrees granted: Associate; Bachelors.

Attendance and degree information available by phone, FAX, mail. Search requires name only. Other helpful information: social security number, date of birth, approximate years of attendance. No fee for information.

Transcripts available by mail. Search requires name plus signed release. Other helpful information: approximate years of attendance. Fee is $3.00. Expedited service available for $10.00.

Christian Brothers University, Registrar, 650 East Pkwy S, Memphis, TN 38104, 901-722-0239 (FAX: 901-722-0257). Hours: 8AM-4:30PM. Records go back to 1950s. Alumni records are maintained here at the same phone number. Degrees granted: Bachelors; Masters.

Attendance and degree information available by phone, FAX, mail. Search requires name plus approximate years of attendance. Other helpful information: social security number, date of birth, exact years of attendance. No fee for information.

Transcripts available by written request only. Search requires name plus approximate years of attendance, signed release. Other helpful information: social security number, date of birth, exact years of attendance. Fee is $2.00.

Christian Heritage College, Registrar, 2100 Greenfield Dr, El Cajon, CA 92019, 619-590-1784 (FAX: 619-440-0209). Hours: 8:30AM-3PM. Records go back to 19yr. Alumni records are maintained here also. Call 619-590-1750. Degrees granted: Bachelors.

Attendance and degree information available by phone, FAX, mail. Search requires name plus social security number. Other helpful information: date of birth, approximate years of attendance. No fee for information.

Transcripts available by mail. Search requires name plus social security number, signed release. Other helpful information: date of birth, approximate years of attendance. Fee is $2.00. Expedited service available for $5.00.

Christian Theological Seminary, Registrar, 1000 W 42nd St, Indianapolis, IN 46208-3301, 317-931-2382 (FAX: 317-923-1961). Hours: 8AM-4:30PM. Records go back to 1958. Alumni records are maintained here also. Call 317-924-1331. Degrees granted: Masters; Doctorate. Special programs- Advanced Studies, 317-924-1331.

Attendance and degree information available by phone, FAX, mail. Search requires name plus social security number, date of birth. Other helpful information: approximate years of attendance. No fee for information.

Transcripts available by FAX, mail. Search requires name plus social security number, date of birth, signed release. Other helpful information: approximate years of attendance. Fee is $10.00. Major credit cards accepted for payment.

Christopher Newport College, Registrar, 50 Shoe Lane, Newport News, VA 23606-2998, 804-594-7155 (FAX: 804-594-7713). Hours: 8AM-5PM. Records go back to 1971. Alumni records are maintained here also. Call 804-594-7712. Degrees granted: Bachelors.

Attendance and degree information available by phone, mail. Search requires name plus social security number. No fee for information.

Transcripts available by mail. Search requires name plus social security number, signed release. No fee for transcripts.

Chubb Institute-Keystone School, Registrar, 965 Baltimore Pike, Springfield, PA 19064, 610-543-1747 (FAX: 610-543-7479). Hours: 9AM-5PM. Records go back to 1950. Alumni records are maintained here also. Call 610-543-1747. Degrees granted: Associate. Adverse incident record source: Education Office, 610-543-1747.

Attendance and degree information available by phone, FAX, mail. Search requires name plus social security number, exact years of attendance. No fee for information.

Transcripts available by FAX, mail. Search requires name plus social security number, exact years of attendance, signed release. No fee for transcripts.

Church Divinity School of the Pacific, Registrar, 2451 Ridge Rd, Berkeley, CA 94709-1211, 510-204-0715 (FAX: 510-644-0712). Hours: 8AM-4PM. Alumni records are maintained here also. Call 510-204-0716. Degrees granted: Masters. Adverse incident record source: Security Officer.

Attendance information available by phone, FAX, mail. Search requires name only. No fee for information.

Degree information available by FAX, mail. Search requires name only. No fee for information.

Transcripts available by mail. Search requires name plus signed release. Fee is $5.00.

Church of God School of Theology, Registrar, PO Box 3330, 900 Walker St NE, Cleveland, TN 37311, 615-478-1131 X7725 (FAX: 615-478-7711). Hours: 8AM-5PM. Records go back to 1975. Degrees granted: Masters. Adverse incident record source: Student Services, 615-478-1131 X7933.

Attendance and degree information available by phone, FAX, mail. Search requires name plus signed release. Other helpful information: social security number, approximate years of attendance. No fee for information.

Transcripts available by FAX, mail. Search requires name plus signed release. Other helpful information: social security number, approximate years of attendance. Fee is $5.00. Major credit cards accepted for payment.

Churchman Business School, Registrar, 355 Spring Garden St, Easton, PA 18042, 610-258-5345 (FAX: 610-258-8086). Hours: 7:30AM-4PM. Records go back to 1911. Alumni records are maintained here at the same phone number. Degrees granted: Associate. Adverse incident record source: Administrator, 610-258-5345.

Attendance and degree information available by phone, FAX, mail. Search requires name plus social security number. No fee for information.

Transcripts available by FAX, mail. Search requires name plus social security number, exact years of attendance, signed release. First transcript is free. Additional ones are $4.00 each.

Cincinnati Bible College and Seminary, Registrar, 2700 Glenway Ave, Cincinnati, OH 45204, 513-244-8170 (FAX: 513-244-8140). Hours: 8:30AM-4:30PM. Alumni records are maintained here also. Call 513-244-8113. Degrees granted: Associate; Bachelors; Masters.

Attendance information available by phone, FAX, mail. Search requires name plus social security number, exact years of attendance. Other helpful information: date of birth, approximate years of attendance. No fee for information.

Degree information available by phone, FAX, mail. Search requires name plus social security number. Other helpful information: date of birth, approximate years of attendance. No fee for information.

Transcripts available by FAX, mail. Search requires name plus approximate years of attendance, signed release. Other helpful information: social security number, date of birth, exact years of attendance. Fee is $5.00.

Cincinnati College of Mortuary Science, Registrar, Cohen Ctr, 3860 Pacific Ave, Cincinnati, OH 45207-1033, 513-745-3631 (FAX: 513-745-1909). Hours: 8AM-4PM. Records go back 7 years. Degrees granted: Associate; Bachelors.

Attendance information available by written request only. Search requires name plus signed release. Other helpful information: social security number, approximate years of attendance. No fee for information.

Degree information available by phone, FAX, mail. Search requires name plus signed release. Other helpful information: social security number, approximate years of attendance. No fee for information.

Transcripts available by phone, FAX, mail. Search requires name plus signed release. Other helpful information: social security number, approximate years of attendance. Fee is $3.00.

Cincinnati State Technical & Community College, Registrar, 3520 Central Pkwy, Cincinnati, OH 45223, 513-569-1500 (FAX: 513-569-1495). Hours: 8AM-7PM M-Th, 8AM-5PM F. Records go back to 1968. Alumni records are maintained here at the same phone number. Degrees granted: Associate.

Attendance and degree information available by phone, FAX, mail. Search requires name plus social security number, signed release. Other helpful information: approximate years of attendance. No fee for information.

Transcripts available by written request only. Search requires name plus social security number, signed release. Other helpful information: approximate years of attendance. Fee is $3.00.

Circleville Bible College, Registrar, 1476 Lancaster Pike, PO Box 458, Circleville, OH 43113, 614-477-7729 (FAX: 614-477-7740). Hours: 8:30AM-4:30PM. Alumni records are maintained here also. Call 614-477-7760. Degrees granted: Associate; Bachelors.

Attendance information available by mail. Search requires name plus social security number, date of birth, signed release. Other helpful information: approximate years of attendance. Fee is $3.00. Expedited service available for $3.00.

Degree information available by written request only. Search requires name plus social security number, date of birth, signed release. Other helpful information: approximate years of attendance. Fee is $3.00. Expedite service available for $3.00.

Transcripts available by written request only. Search requires name plus social security number, date of birth, signed release. Other helpful information: approximate years of attendance. Fee is $3.00. Expedited service available for $3.00.

Cisco Junior College, Registrar, Rte 3 Box 3, Cisco, TX 76437, 817-442-2567 (FAX: 817-442-2546). Hours: 8AM-4PM. Records go back to 1920s. Degrees granted: Associate.

Attendance and degree information available by phone, FAX, mail. Search requires name plus social security number, date of birth, approximate years of attendance, signed release. Fee is $5.00.

Transcripts available by FAX, mail. Search requires name plus social security number, date of birth, approximate years of attendance, signed release. Fee is $5.00.

Citadel Military College of South Carolina, Registrar, Citadel Station 171 Moultrie St, Charleston, SC 29409, 803-953-1003 (FAX: 803-953-7630). Hours: 8AM-5PM. Records go back to 1842. Alumni records are maintained here also. Call 803-953-5000. Degrees granted: Bachelors; Masters.

Attendance and degree information available by phone, FAX, mail. Search requires name plus social security number, exact years of attendance. No fee for information.

Transcripts available by mail. Search requires name plus social security number, exact years of attendance, signed release. Fee is $3.00.

Citrus College, Registrar, 1000 W Foothill Blvd, Glendora, CA 91741-1899, 818-914-8511 (FAX: 818-335-3159). Hours: 8AM-9PM M-Th, 8AM-4:30PM F. Records go back to 1915. Alumni records are maintained here also. Call 818-963-0323. Degrees granted: Associate. Adverse incident record source: Dean of Students, 818-914-8534.

Attendance and degree information available by phone, FAX, mail. Search requires name plus social security number. No fee for information.

Transcripts available by FAX, mail. Search requires name plus social security number, exact years of attendance, signed release. Fee is $2.00. Expedited service available for $7.00.

Major credit cards accepted for payment.

City College, Registrar, Convent Ave at 138th St, New York, NY 10031, 212-650-7850 (FAX: 212-650-6108). Hours: 9AM-5PM M,Th,F; 9AM-6:30PM T,W. Records go back to 1910. Degrees granted: Bachelors; Masters. Special programs- BBA Degrees at Baruch College, 212-447-3000. Adverse incident record source: Dean of Students, 212-650-5426.

Attendance and degree information available by phone, FAX, mail. Search requires name plus social security number, approximate years of attendance. Other helpful information: date of birth, exact years of attendance. No fee for information.

Transcripts available by mail. Search requires name plus social security number, approximate years of attendance, signed release. Other helpful information: date of birth, exact years of attendance. Fee is $4.00.

Major credit cards accepted for payment.

City College of San Francisco, Registrar, 50 Phelan Ave, San Francisco, CA 94112, 415-239-3838 (FAX: 415-239-3936). Hours: 8AM-3PM M-Th; 8AM-Noon F. Records go back to 1935. Degrees granted: Associate.

Attendance information available by FAX, mail. Search requires name plus social security number, signed release. Other helpful information: date of birth. Fee is $5.00.

Degree information available by phone, FAX, mail. Search requires name plus social security number, date of birth, signed release. Other helpful information: approximate years of attendance. No fee for information.

Transcripts available by FAX, mail. Search requires name plus social security number, date of birth, approximate years of attendance, signed release. Other helpful information: exact years of attendance. Fee is $5.00.

City University, Registrar, 335 116th Ave SE, Bellevue, WA 98004, 800-426-5596 (FAX: 206-637-9689). Hours: 8AM-4:30PM. Degrees granted: Bachelors; Masters.

Attendance and degree information available by phone, FAX, mail. Search requires name plus social security number, exact years of attendance. No fee for information.

Transcripts available by FAX, mail. Search requires name plus social security number, exact years of attendance, signed release. Fee is $3.00.

Clackamas Community College, Registrar, 19600 S Molalla Ave, Oregon City, OR 97045, 503-657-6958 (FAX: 503-650-6654). Hours: 8AM-5PM. Records go back to 1966. Degrees granted: Associate.

Attendance information available by FAX, mail. Search requires name plus social security number, approximate years of attendance, signed release. No fee for information.

Degree information available by phone, FAX, mail. Search requires name plus social security number, approximate years of attendance, signed release. No fee for information.

Transcripts available by FAX, mail. Search requires name plus social security number, approximate years of attendance, signed release. Fee is $4.00.

Claflin College, Registrar, 700 College Ave NE, Orangeburg, SC 29115, 803-534-2710. Degrees granted: Bachelors. Adverse incident record source: Campus Security.

Attendance information available by phone, FAX, mail. Search requires name plus approximate years of attendance, signed release. Other helpful information: social security number. No fee for information.

Degree information available by phone, FAX, mail. Search requires name plus approximate years of attendance, signed release. Other helpful information: social security number. No fee for information.

Transcripts available by mail. Search requires name plus approximate years of attendance, signed release. Other helpful information: social security number. Fee is $4.00.

Claremont Graduate School, Registrar's Office, 170 E 10th St, Claremont, CA 91711, 909-621-8285 (FAX: 909-621-8390). Hours: 8:30AM-5PM. Records go back to 1925. Alumni records are maintained here also. Call 909-621-8204. Degrees granted: Masters; Doctorate.

Attendance information available by phone, FAX, mail. Search requires name plus social security number. Other helpful information: date of birth, approximate years of attendance. No fee for information.

Degree information available by phone, FAX, mail. Search requires name only. Other helpful information: social security number, date of birth, approximate years of attendance. No fee for information.

Transcripts available by written request only. Search requires name plus signed release. Other helpful information: social security number, date of birth, approximate years of attendance. Fee is $4.00. Expedited service available for $8.00.

Claremont McKenna College, (Bauer Center), Registrar, 500 E 9th St, Claremont, CA 91711-6400, 909-621-8101. Hours: 8AM-5PM. Records go back to 1946. Alumni Records Office: Alumni Association, 850 Columbia Ave, Claremont, CA 91711-6400. Degrees granted: Bachelors. Adverse incident record source: Registrar's Office, 909-621-8101 .

Attendance and degree information available by phone, mail. Search requires name plus social security number, exact years of attendance. No fee for information.

Transcripts available by mail. Search requires name plus social security number, exact years of attendance, signed release. Fee is $1.00. Expedited service available for $5.00.

Clarendon College, Registrar, PO Box 968, Clarendon, TX 79226, 806-874-3571 (FAX: 806-874-3201). Hours: 8AM-5PM. Records go back to 1925. Degrees granted: Associate. Adverse incident record source: Dean of Students.

Attendance and degree information available by phone, FAX, mail. Search requires name plus social security number, date of birth, signed release. Other helpful information: approximate years of attendance. No fee for information.

Transcripts available by written request only. Search requires name plus social security number, date of birth, signed release. Other helpful information: exact years of attendance. Fee is $2.00.

Clarion University of Pennsylvania, Registrar's Office, 122 Carrier Hall, Clarion, PA 16214, 814-226-2229. Hours: 8:30AM-4:30PM. Records go back to 1870. Alumni Records Office: Alumni Association, Clarion University of Pennsylvania, Alumni House, Clarion, PA 16214. Degrees granted: Associate; Bachelors; Masters. Adverse incident record source: Registrar, 814-226-2229.

Attendance information available by phone, mail. Search requires name plus social security number. No fee for information.

Degree information available by phone, mail. Search requires name plus social security number, exact years of attendance. No fee for information.

Transcripts available by mail. Search requires name plus social security number, exact years of attendance, signed release. Fee is $3.00.

Clarion University of Pennsylvania, (Venango), Registrar, W First St, Oil City, PA 16301, 814-676-6591. Records are not housed here. They are located at Clarion University of Pennsylvania, Registrar's Office, 122 Carrier Hall, Clarion, PA 16214.

Clark Atlanta University, Registrar, James P Brawley Dr at Fair St SW, Atlanta, GA 30314, 404-880-8759 (FAX: 404-880-6083). Hours: 8AM-4:30PM. Records go back to 1988. Alumni records are maintained here also. Call 404-880-8022. Degrees granted: Bachelors; Masters; Doctorate.

Attendance and degree information available by mail. Search requires name plus social security number, date of birth, exact years of attendance. No fee for information.

Transcripts available by mail. Search requires name plus social security number, date of birth, exact years of attendance, signed release. Fee is $3.00.

Clark College, Registrar, 1800 E McLoughlin Blvd, Vancouver, WA 98663, 206-699-0135 (FAX: 206-737-2008). Hours: 8AM-4:30PM. Alumni records are maintained here at the same phone number. Degrees granted: Associate.

Attendance and degree information available by phone, FAX, mail. Search requires name plus social security number, exact years of attendance. No fee for information.

Transcripts available by FAX, mail. Search requires name plus social security number, exact years of attendance, signed release. No fee for transcripts.

Clark State Community College, Registrar, 570 E Leffels Lane, PO Box 570, Springfield, OH 45505, 513-328-6014. Hours: 8AM-5PM. Records go back to 1962. Degrees granted: Associate.

Attendance and degree information available by phone, FAX, mail. Search requires name plus social security number. Other helpful information: approximate years of attendance. No fee for information.

Transcripts available by written request only. Search requires name plus social security number, signed release. Other helpful information: approximate years of attendance. Fee is $2.00.

Clark University, Registrar, Worcester, MA 01610-1477, 508-793-7426. Hours: 9AM-5PM. Records go back to 1900. Degrees granted: Bachelors; Masters; Doctorate. Special programs-Professional & Continuing Education, 508-793-7217.

Attendance and degree information available by phone, FAX, mail. Search requires name only. Other helpful information: social security number, date of birth, approximate years of attendance. No fee for information.

Transcripts available by mail. Search requires name plus signed release. Other helpful information: social security number, date of birth, approximate years of attendance. Fee is $3.00.

Clarke College, Registrar, 1550 Clarke Dr, Dubuque, IA 52001, 319-588-6314 (FAX: 319-588-6789). Hours: 8AM-4:30PM. Degrees granted: Associate; Bachelors; Masters.

Attendance information available by phone, FAX, mail. Search requires name only. Other helpful information: social security number, date of birth. No fee for information.

Degree information available by phone, FAX, mail. Search requires name only. Other helpful information: social security number. No fee for information.

Transcripts available by FAX, mail. Search requires name plus signed release. Other helpful information: social security number, date of birth. Fee is $2.00.

Clarkson College, Registrar, 101 S 42nd St, Omaha, NE 68131, 402-552-3041 (FAX: 402-552-6057). Hours: 8AM-5PM. Records go back to founding date. Degrees granted: Associate; Bachelors; Masters. Certification: Nurse Practitioner.

Attendance and degree information available by phone, FAX, mail. Search requires name plus social security number, approximate years of attendance. Other helpful information: date of birth, exact years of attendance. No fee for information.

Transcripts available by mail. Search requires name plus social security number, approximate years of attendance, signed release. Other helpful information: date of birth, exact years of attendance. Fee is $2.00. Expedited service available for $2.00.

Clarkson University, Registrar's Office, Box 5575, Potsdam, NY 13699-5575, 315-268-6451 (FAX: 315-268-6452). Hours: 8AM-4:30PM. Records go back to 1900. Alumni Records Office:

Box 5525, Potsdam, NY 13699-5575. Degrees granted: Bachelors; Masters; Doctorate.

Attendance and degree information available by phone, FAX, mail. Search requires name only. Other helpful information: social security number, date of birth, approximate years of attendance. No fee for information.

Transcripts available by FAX, mail. Search requires name plus signed release. Other helpful information: social security number, date of birth, approximate years of attendance. Fee is $4.00. Expedite fee is based on cost of service.'

Student number helpful.

Clatsop Community College, Registrar, 1653 Jerome Ave, Astoria, OR 97103, 503-325-0910 (FAX: 503-325-5738). Hours: 8AM-5PM. Records go back to 1958. Degrees granted: Associate.

Attendance and degree information available by phone, FAX, mail. Search requires name plus social security number, signed release. No fee for information.

Transcripts available by FAX, mail. Search requires name plus social security number, signed release. Fee is $2.00.

Clayton State College, Registrar, PO Box 285, Morrow, GA 30260, 404-961-3502 (FAX: 404-961-3700). Hours: 8AM-9PM M-Th; 8AM-4PM F; 8AM-Noon S. Records go back to 1969. Degrees granted: Associate; Bachelors.

Attendance and degree information available by FAX, mail. Search requires name plus social security number. Other helpful information: date of birth, approximate years of attendance. No fee for information.

Transcripts available by mail. Search requires name plus social security number, signed release. Other helpful information: date of birth, approximate years of attendance. No fee for transcripts.

Clear Creek Baptist Bible College, Registrar's Office, 300 Clear Creek Rd, Pineville, KY 40977, 606-377-3196 (FAX: 606-337-2372). Hours: 8AM-4:30PM. Records go back to 1926. Degrees granted: Associate; Bachelors. Adverse incident record source: Office of Student Life, 606-337-3196.

Attendance information available by FAX, mail. Search requires name plus signed release. Other helpful information: social security number, date of birth, approximate years of attendance. No fee for information.

Degree information available by FAX, mail. Search requires name plus signed release. Other helpful information: social security number, date of birth, approximate years of attendance. No fee for information.

Transcripts available by mail. Search requires name plus signed release. Other helpful information: social security number, date of birth, approximate years of attendance. Fee is $3.00.

Must prepay w/request

Clearwater Christian College, Registrar, 3400 Gulf-to-Bay Blvd, Clearwater, FL 34619, 813-726-1153 (FAX: 813-726-8597). Hours: 8AM-4:30PM. Records go back to 1966. Alumni records are maintained here at the same phone number. Degrees granted: Associate; Bachelors.

Attendance information available by phone, FAX, mail. Search requires name plus social security number, signed release. No fee for information.

Degree information available by FAX, mail. Search requires name plus social security number, signed release. No fee for information.

Transcripts available by FAX, mail. Search requires name plus social security number, signed release. Fee is $2.00. Expedited service available for $2.00.

Major credit cards accepted for payment.

Cleary College, Registrar, 2170 Washtenaw Ave, Ypsilanti, MI 48197, 313-483-4400 X3344 (FAX: 313-483-0090). Hours: 8AM-5PM. Records go back 112 years. Alumni records are maintained here also. Call 313-483-4400 X3354. Degrees granted: Associate; Bachelors.

Attendance and degree information available by FAX, mail. Search requires name plus social security number, date of birth, approximate years of attendance, signed release. No fee for information.

Transcripts available by mail. Search requires name plus social security number, date of birth, approximate years of attendance, signed release. Fee is $5.00.

Clemson University, Transcripts, 104 Sikes Hall, Clemson, SC 29634, 803-656-2174 (FAX: 803-656-0622). Hours: 8AM-4:30PM. Alumni Records Office: Box 345603, Clemson, SC 29634. Degrees granted: Bachelors; Masters; Doctorate.

Attendance and degree information available by phone, FAX, mail. Search requires name only. Other helpful information: social security number, exact years of attendance. No fee for information.

Transcripts available by FAX, mail. Search requires name plus signed release. Other helpful information: social security number, date of birth, approximate years of attendance. Fee is $5.00. Expedited service available for $15.50.

FAX request must be prepaid by credit card. Major credit cards accepted for payment.

Cleveland Chiropractic College, Registrar, 6401 Rockhill Rd, Kansas City, MO 64131, 816-333-8230 X232 (FAX: 816-361-0272). Hours: 8AM-5PM. Records go back to 1940. Alumni records are maintained here also. Call 816-333-8230. Degrees granted: Doctorate.

Attendance and degree information available by phone, FAX, mail. Search requires name plus social security number, signed release. No fee for information.

Transcripts available by FAX, mail. Search requires name plus social security number, signed release. No fee for transcripts.

Cleveland Chiropractic College, Registrar, 590 N Vermont Ave, Los Angeles, CA 90004, 213-660-6166 X58 (FAX: 213-660-3190). Hours: 7AM-3:30PM. Records go back to 1908. Adverse incident record source: Same as above.

Attendance information available by FAX, mail. Search requires name plus social security number, date of birth, signed release. Other helpful information: approximate years of attendance. No fee for information.

Degree information available by FAX, mail. Search requires name plus signed release. Other helpful information: social security number, date of birth, approximate years of attendance. No fee for information.

Transcripts available by written request only. Search requires name plus social security number, date of birth, signed release. Other helpful information: approximate years of attendance. Fee is $5.00. Usual fee is $5.00 or 10.00

Major credit cards accepted for payment.

Cleveland College of Jewish Studies, Registrar, 26500 Shaker Blvd, Beachwood, OH 44122, 216-464-4050 (FAX: 216-

464-5827). Hours: 8AM-4PM. Degrees granted: Bachelors; Masters.

Attendance and degree information available by phone, FAX, mail. Search requires name plus social security number. No fee for information.

Transcripts available by FAX, mail. Search requires name plus social security number, signed release. Fee is $3.00.

Cleveland Community College, Registrar, 137 S Post Rd, Shelby, NC 28150, 704-484-4099 (FAX: 704-484-4036). Hours: 8AM-4:30PM. Degrees granted: Associate.

Attendance and degree information available by phone, FAX, mail. Search requires name plus social security number, exact years of attendance. No fee for information.

Transcripts available by FAX, mail. Search requires name plus social security number, exact years of attendance, signed release. No fee for transcripts.

Need to provide maiden name and degrees granted.

Cleveland Institute of Art, Registrar, 11411 East Blvd, Cleveland, OH 44106, 216-421-7321 (FAX: 216-421-7333). Hours: 8:30AM-5PM. Records go back to 1882. Alumni records are maintained here also. Call 216-421-7412. Degrees granted: Bachelors. Adverse incident record source: Dean, 216-421-7428: Operations, 216-421-7314

Attendance and degree information available by phone, FAX, mail. Search requires name plus social security number, approximate years of attendance. No fee for information.

Transcripts available by FAX, mail. Search requires name plus social security number, approximate years of attendance. No fee for transcripts.

Cleveland Institute of Electronics, Inc., Registrar, 1776 E 17th St, Cleveland, OH 44114, 216-781-9400 (FAX: 216-781-0331). Hours: 8:30AM-4:45PM. Degrees granted: Associate.

Attendance and degree information available by phone, FAX, mail. Search requires name only. Other helpful information: social security number, approximate years of attendance. No fee for information.

Transcripts available by mail. Search requires name plus signed release. Other helpful information: social security number, approximate years of attendance. Fee is $10.00.

Major credit cards accepted for payment.

Cleveland Institute of Music, Registrar, 11021 East Blvd, Cleveland, OH 44106, 216-795-3203 (FAX: 216-791-1530). Hours: 9AM-5PM. Records go back to 1920. Alumni records are maintained here at the same phone number. Degrees granted: Bachelors; Masters; Doctorate.

Attendance information available by FAX, mail. Search requires name plus approximate years of attendance. Other helpful information: social security number, date of birth, exact years of attendance. No fee for information.

Degree information available by phone, FAX, mail. Search requires name plus approximate years of attendance. Other helpful information: social security number, date of birth, exact years of attendance. No fee for information.

Transcripts available by mail. Search requires name plus approximate years of attendance. Other helpful information: social security number, date of birth, exact years of attendance. Fee is $4.00.

Cleveland State Community College, Registrar, PO Box 3570, Cleveland, TN 37320-3570, 615-472-7141 X268 (FAX: 615-478-6255). Hours: 8AM-6PM M-Th, 8AM-4:30PM F. Records go back to 1967. Alumni records are maintained here at the same phone number. Degrees granted: Associate.

Attendance and degree information available by phone, mail. Search requires name plus social security number. No fee for information.

Transcripts available by mail. Search requires name plus social security number, signed release. No fee for transcripts.

Cleveland State University, Registrar, Euclid Ave at 24th St, Cleveland, OH 44115, 216-687-3700 (FAX: 216-687-5501). Hours: 8AM-6PM M-Th; 8AM-5PM F. Degrees granted: Bachelors; Masters; Doctorate.

Attendance and degree information available by phone, FAX, mail. Search requires name plus social security number, date of birth, signed release. Other helpful information: approximate years of attendance. No fee for information.

Transcripts available by FAX, mail. Search requires name plus social security number, date of birth, signed release. Other helpful information: approximate years of attendance. No fee for transcripts.

Clinch Valley College of the University of Virginia, Registrar, #1 College Ave, Wise, VA 24293, 703-328-0116 (FAX: 703-328-0115). Hours: 8AM-4:30PM. Records go back to 1954. Alumni records are maintained here at the same phone number. Degrees granted: Bachelors. Adverse incident record source: Dean of Students, 703-328-0214.

Attendance information available by phone, FAX, mail. Search requires name plus signed release. Other helpful information: social security number, date of birth, exact years of attendance. No fee for information.

Degree information available by phone, FAX, mail. Search requires name plus social security number, signed release. Other helpful information: date of birth, exact years of attendance. No fee for information.

Transcripts available by FAX, mail. Search requires name plus social security number, signed release. Other helpful information: date of birth, exact years of attendance. No fee for transcripts. Expedite fee is based on cost of service.'

Clinton Community College, Registrar, 1000 Lincoln Blvd, Clinton, IA 52732, 319-242-6841 (FAX: 319-242-7868). Hours: 7:30AM-5PM. Records go back 48 years. Alumni records are maintained here at the same phone number. Degrees granted: Associate.

School will not confirm attendance information. Search requires name only. Other helpful information: approximate years of attendance. No fee for information.

Degree information available by phone, FAX, mail. Search requires name plus social security number, signed release. Other helpful information: date of birth, approximate years of attendance. No fee for information.

Transcripts available by FAX, mail. Search requires name plus social security number, signed release. Other helpful information: date of birth, approximate years of attendance. Fee is $2.00.

Major credit cards accepted for payment.

Clinton Community College, Registrar, 136 Clifton Pt Dr, Plattsburgh, NY 12901, 518-562-4124 (FAX: 518-561-8621). Hours: 8AM-4PM. Records go back to 1976. Alumni records are maintained here also. Call 518-562-4195. Degrees granted: Associate. Adverse incident record source: Dean of Students, 518-562-4120.

Attendance and degree information available by phone, FAX, mail. Search requires name plus social security number, date of birth, approximate years of attendance, signed release. No fee for information.

Transcripts available by mail. Search requires name plus social security number, date of birth, approximate years of attendance, signed release. No fee for transcripts.

Cloud County Community College, Office of Student Records, 2221 Campus Dr, PO Box 1002, Concordia, KS 66901-1002, 913-243-1435 (FAX: 913-243-1043). Hours: 8AM-5PM. Records go back 27 years. Alumni records are maintained here also. Call 913-243-1435. Degrees granted: Associate.

Attendance information available by phone, FAX, mail. Search requires name plus social security number. Other helpful information: date of birth, approximate years of attendance. No fee for information.

Degree information available by phone, mail. Search requires name plus social security number. Other helpful information: date of birth, approximate years of attendance. No fee for information.

Transcripts available by mail. Search requires name plus social security number, signed release. Other helpful information: date of birth, approximate years of attendance. Fee is $3.00.

Major credit cards accepted for payment.

Clovis Community College, Registrar, 417 Schepps Blvd, Clovis, NM 88101, 505-769-4025. Hours: 8AM-4:30PM. Records go back to 1970. Degrees granted: Associate.

Attendance and degree information available by phone, mail. Search requires name plus social security number. No fee for information.

Transcripts available by mail. Search requires name plus social security number, signed release. No fee for transcripts.

Coahoma Community College, Registrar, 3240 Friars Point Rd, Clarksdale, MS 38614, 601-627-2571 (FAX: 601-627-2571). Hours: 8:30AM-4PM. Records go back to 1949. Degrees granted: Associate.

Attendance information available by mail. Search requires name plus social security number, date of birth, approximate years of attendance, signed release. No fee for information.

Degree information available by phone, FAX, mail. Search requires name plus social security number, approximate years of attendance. Other helpful information: date of birth. No fee for information.

Transcripts available by mail. Search requires name plus social security number, date of birth, approximate years of attendance, signed release. Fee is $3.00. Expedited service available for $9.00.

Coastal Carolina Community College, Registrar, 444 Western Blvd, Jacksonville, NC 28546-6877, 916-938-6252. Hours: 8AM-5PM. Records go back to 1967. Degrees granted: Associate.

Attendance and degree information available by phone, FAX, mail. Search requires name plus social security number. Other helpful information: date of birth, approximate years of attendance. No fee for information.

Transcripts available by FAX, mail. Search requires name plus social security number, signed release. Other helpful information: date of birth, approximate years of attendance. No fee for transcripts.

Coastal Carolina University, Registrar, PO Box 1954, Myrtle Beach, SC 29577, 803-349-2025 (FAX: 803-349-2909). Hours: 8AM-8PM. Records go back to 1993. Records prior to July 1, 1993 are housed at University of South Carolina. Degrees granted: Bachelors; Masters. Certification: Gerontology. Adverse incident record source: Campus Police, 803-349-2177.

Attendance and degree information available by phone, FAX, mail. Search requires name plus social security number, date of birth. Other helpful information: exact years of attendance. No fee for information.

Transcripts available by FAX, mail. Search requires name plus social security number, date of birth, signed release. Other helpful information: exact years of attendance. No fee for transcripts.

Major credit cards accepted for payment.

Coastline Community College, Registrar, 11460 Warner Ave, Fountain Valley, CA 92708, 714-241-6168 (FAX: 714-241-6288). Hours: 8AM-6:30PM M-Th, 8AM-2PM F. Records go back to 1976. Degrees granted: Associate.

Attendance and degree information available by phone, FAX, mail. Search requires name plus social security number, date of birth, exact years of attendance. No fee for information.

Transcripts available by FAX, mail. Search requires name plus social security number, date of birth, exact years of attendance, signed release. Fee is $3.00. Expedited service available for $5.00.

Cochise College, Registrar, 4190 Hwy 80, Douglas, AZ 85607-9724, 602-364-0241 (FAX: 602-364-0236). Hours: 8AM-4:30PM. Records go back to 1965. Degrees granted: Associate.

Attendance and degree information available by phone, FAX, mail. Search requires name plus social security number, exact years of attendance. No fee for information.

Transcripts available by mail. Search requires name plus social security number, exact years of attendance, signed release. Fee is $2.50.

Coe College, Registrar, Cedar Rapids, IA 52402, 319-399-8526 (FAX: 319-399-8748). Hours: 8AM-4:30PM. Records go back to 1885. Degrees granted: Bachelors; Masters.

Attendance and degree information available by phone, FAX, mail. Search requires name plus approximate years of attendance. Other helpful information: social security number, date of birth, exact years of attendance. No fee for information.

Transcripts available by written request only. Search requires name plus approximate years of attendance, signed release. Other helpful information: social security number, date of birth, exact years of attendance. Fee is $3.00. Expedited service available for $20.00.

Major credit cards accepted for payment.

Coffeyville Community College, Registrar, 400 W 11th, Coffeyville, KS 67337, 316-251-7700 X2021 (FAX: 316-252-7098). Hours: 8AM-5PM. Records go back to 1971. Alumni records are maintained here also. Call 316-251-7700 X2069. Degrees granted: Associate.

Attendance and degree information available by phone, mail. Search requires name plus social security number, signed release. Other helpful information: date of birth, approximate years of attendance. No fee for information.

Transcripts available by mail. Search requires name plus social security number, signed release. Other helpful information: date of birth, approximate years of attendance. Fee is $1.00. $5.00 for FAX is available.

Cogswell College North, Registrar, 10626 NE 37th Cir, Kirkland, WA 98033, 206-822-3137 (FAX: 206-822-1006). Hours: 9AM-6PM. Records go back to 1984. Degrees granted: Bachelors.

Attendance and degree information available by FAX, mail. Search requires name plus signed release. Other helpful information: social security number, approximate years of attendance. No fee for information.

Transcripts available by FAX, mail. Search requires name plus signed release. Other helpful information: social security number, approximate years of attendance. Fee is $10.00.

Major credit cards accepted for payment.

Cogswell Polytechnical College, Registrar, 1174 Bordeaux Dr, Sunnyvale, CA 94089-1299, 408-541-0100 X110 (FAX: 408-747-0764). Hours: 9AM-5:45PM. Records go back 40 years. Degrees granted: Associate; Bachelors.

Attendance and degree information available by phone, FAX, mail. Search requires name plus social security number, date of birth, exact years of attendance, signed release. Other helpful information: approximate years of attendance. No fee for information.

Transcripts available by FAX, mail. Search requires name plus social security number, date of birth, exact years of attendance, signed release. Other helpful information: approximate years of attendance. Fee is $10.00.

Major credit cards accepted for payment.

Coker College, Registrar, 300 E College Ave, Hartsville, SC 29550, 803-383-8022 (FAX: 803-383-8095). Degrees granted: Bachelors.

Attendance and degree information available by mail. Search requires name plus social security number, exact years of attendance. No fee for information.

Transcripts available by mail. Search requires name plus social security number, exact years of attendance, signed release. Fee is $3.00.

Colby College, Office of the Registrar, 4620 Mayflower Hill, Waterville, ME 04901-8846, 207-872-3199 (FAX: 207-872-3076). Hours: 8:30AM-4:30PM. Records go back to 1911. Degrees granted: Bachelors.

Attendance and degree information available by phone, FAX, mail. Search requires name plus social security number, date of birth, approximate years of attendance. No fee for information.

Transcripts available by FAX, mail. Search requires name plus social security number, date of birth, approximate years of attendance, signed release. Fee is $1.00. Expedited service available for $9.00.

Need class year, home address, maiden name.

Colby Community College, Registrar, 1255 S Range, Colby, KS 67701, 913-462-4675 (FAX: 913-462-4600). Hours: 8AM-5PM. Records go back to 1965. Alumni records are maintained here also. Call 913-462-3984. Degrees granted: Associate.

Attendance and degree information available by mail. Search requires name plus signed release. Other helpful information: social security number, date of birth, approximate years of attendance. Fee is $3.00.

Transcripts available by mail. Search requires name plus signed release. Other helpful information: social security number, date of birth, approximate years of attendance. Fee is $3.00.

Colby-Sawyer College, Registrar, 100 Main St, New London, NH 03257, 603-526-3673 (FAX: 603-526-2135). Hours: 8AM-5PM. Records go back to 1940. Alumni records are maintained here also. Call 603-526-3727. Degrees granted: Associate; Bachelors. Adverse incident record source: Student Development, 603-526-3755.

Attendance information available by phone, FAX, mail. Search requires name plus date of birth, approximate years of attendance. Other helpful information: social security number. No fee for information.

Degree information available by phone, FAX, mail. Search requires name plus date of birth. Other helpful information: social security number, approximate years of attendance. No fee for information.

Transcripts available by mail. Search requires name plus social security number, exact years of attendance, signed release. Other helpful information: date of birth, approximate years of attendance. Fee is $3.00.

Colegio Biblico Pentecostal, Registrar, Carretera 848 km 0.5, PO Box 901, St Just, PR 00978, 809-761-0640.

Colegio Universitario del Este, Registrar, PO Box 2010, Carolina, PR 00983-2010, 809-257-7373.

Coleman College, Registrar, 7380 Parkway Dr, La Mesa, CA 91942-1532, 619-475-3990 (FAX: 619-463-0162). Hours: 9AM-8PM M-Th. Records go back to 1963. Degrees granted: Associate; Bachelors; Masters.

Attendance and degree information available by phone, FAX, mail. Search requires name plus date of birth, signed release. Other helpful information: social security number, approximate years of attendance. No fee for information.

Transcripts available by FAX, mail. Search requires name plus date of birth, signed release. Other helpful information: social security number, approximate years of attendance. Fee is $3.00. Expedited service available for $5.00.

Colgate Rochester Divinity School/Bexley Hall/Crozer Theo. Sem., Registrar, 1100 S Goodman St, Rochester, NY 14620, 716-271-1320 X243 (FAX: 716-271-2166). Hours: 8AM-5PM. Records go back to 1817. Alumni records are maintained here at the same phone number. Degrees granted: Masters; Doctorate.

Attendance and degree information available by phone, FAX, mail. Search requires name plus signed release. Other helpful information: approximate years of attendance. No fee for information.

Transcripts available by mail. Search requires name plus signed release. Other helpful information: approximate years of attendance. Fee is $5.00. Expedited service available for $15.00.

Expedite fee is for unofficial FAX only.

Colgate University, Registrar, 13 Oak Dr, Hamilton, NY 13346, 315-824-7406 (FAX: 315-824-7125). Hours: 8AM-4:30PM. Degrees granted: Bachelors; Masters. Adverse incident record source: Dean of College, 315-824-7425.

Attendance and degree information available by phone, FAX, mail. Search requires name only. Other helpful information: social security number, date of birth, approximate years of attendance. No fee for information.

Transcripts available by FAX, mail. Search requires name plus signed release. Other helpful information: social security number,

date of birth, approximate years of attendance. No fee for transcripts. Expedited service available for $10.75.

College Misericordia, Registrar, 301 Lake St, Dallas, PA 18612-1098, 717-674-6756 (FAX: 717-675-2441). Hours: 8:30AM-4:30PM. Records go back to 1920s. Degrees granted: Associate; Bachelors; Masters.
  School will not confirm attendance information. Search requires name plus signed release. No fee for information.
  Degree information available by phone, FAX, mail. Search requires name plus approximate years of attendance. Other helpful information: social security number, date of birth. No fee for information.
  Transcripts available by mail. Search requires name plus approximate years of attendance, signed release. Other helpful information: social security number, date of birth. Fee is $5.00.
Need all names including maiden.

College for Lifelong Learning, Registrar, 125 N State St, Concord, NH 03301-6438, 603-228-3000. Records go back to 1972. Alumni records are maintained here also. Call 603-228-3000 X329. Degrees granted: Associate; Bachelors.
  Attendance and degree information available by phone, mail. Search requires name plus social security number, exact years of attendance. Other helpful information: date of birth, approximate years of attendance. No fee for information.
  Transcripts available by written request only. Search requires name plus social security number, exact years of attendance, signed release. Other helpful information: date of birth, approximate years of attendance. Fee is $3.00.

College of Aeronautics, Registrar, La Guardia Airport, Flushing, NY 11371, 718-429-6600 X146 (FAX: 718-429-0256). Hours: 9AM-5PM. Records go back to 1932. Alumni records are maintained here also. Call 718-429-6600 X189. Degrees granted: Associate; Bachelors.
  Attendance and degree information available by phone, FAX, mail. Search requires name plus social security number, approximate years of attendance, signed release. No fee for information.
  Transcripts available by FAX, mail. Search requires name plus social security number, approximate years of attendance, signed release. Fee is $5.00.

College of Alameda, Registrar, 555 Atlantic Ave, Alameda, CA 94501, 510-748-2228 (FAX: 510-769-6019). Hours: 9AM-7 M,T; 9AM-3PM W-F. Records go back to 1974. Alumni records are maintained here also. Call 510-522-7221. Degrees granted: Associate.
  Attendance and degree information available by phone, FAX, mail. Search requires name plus social security number, date of birth, exact years of attendance, signed release. No fee for information.
  Transcripts available by mail. Search requires name plus social security number, date of birth, exact years of attendance, signed release. First two transcripts are free. Additional ones are $1.00 each. Expedited service available for $2.00.
Information released by phone only if release on file.

College of Associated Arts, Registrar, 344 Summit Ave, St Paul, MN 55102-2199, 612-224-3416 (FAX: 612-224-8854). Degrees granted: Bachelors.
  Attendance information available by phone, FAX, mail. Search requires name plus social security number, date of birth, signed release. Other helpful information: approximate years of attendance. No fee for information.
  Degree information available by phone, FAX, mail. Search requires name plus social security number, date of birth. Other helpful information: approximate years of attendance. No fee for information.
  Transcripts available by mail. Search requires name plus social security number, date of birth, signed release. Other helpful information: approximate years of attendance. No fee for transcripts. Expedited service available for $2.00.

College of Charleston, Registrar's Office, 66 George St, Charleston, SC 29424, 803-953-5668 (FAX: 803-953-6560). Hours: 8:30AM-5PM. Alumni records are maintained here also. Call 803-953-5630. Degrees granted: Bachelors; Masters.
  Attendance information available by phone, FAX, mail. Search requires name plus social security number, approximate years of attendance. Other helpful information: date of birth, exact years of attendance. No fee for information.
  Degree information available by phone, FAX, mail. Search requires name plus social security number, approximate years of attendance. Other helpful information: date of birth, exact years of attendance. No fee for information.
  Transcripts available by FAX, mail. Search requires name plus social security number, approximate years of attendance, signed release. Other helpful information: date of birth, exact years of attendance. Fee is $5.00. Expedited service fee under consideration.
Major credit cards accepted for payment.

College of DuPage, Registrar, 22nd St and Lambert Rd, Glen Ellyn, IL 60137, 708-858-2800. Hours: 8:30AM-5PM. Records go back to 1967. Alumni records are maintained here also. Call 708-858-2800. Degrees granted: Associate.
  Attendance and degree information available by mail. Search requires name plus social security number, exact years of attendance, signed release. No fee for information.
  Transcripts available by mail. Search requires name plus social security number, exact years of attendance, signed release. First transcript is free. Additional ones are $2.00 each.

College of Eastern Utah, Registrar, 451 E 400 N, Price, UT 84501, 801-637-2120 X200 (FAX: 801-637-4102). Hours: 8AM-4:30PM. Degrees granted: Associate.
  Attendance and degree information available by phone, FAX, mail. Search requires name plus social security number, date of birth, exact years of attendance. No fee for information.
  Transcripts available by FAX, mail. Search requires name plus social security number, date of birth, exact years of attendance, signed release. Fee is $2.00.

College of Great Falls, Registrar, 1301 20th St S, Great Falls, MT 59405, 406-761-8210 X260. Hours: 8AM-5PM. Alumni records are maintained here also. Call 406-791-5292. Degrees granted: Associate; Bachelors; Masters.
  Attendance information available by mail. Search requires name plus approximate years of attendance, signed release. Other helpful information: social security number, exact years of attendance. No fee for information.
  Degree information available by mail. Search requires name plus approximate years of attendance, signed release. Other helpful information: social security number, date of birth, exact years of attendance. No fee for information.

Transcripts available by written request only. Search requires name plus approximate years of attendance, signed notarized release. Other helpful information: social security number, date of birth, exact years of attendance. Fee is $3.00.

College of Insurance, Registrar, 101 Murray St, New York, NY 10007, 212-962-4111 (FAX: 212-732-5669). Hours: 9AM-5:30PM M-Th; 9AM-5PM F. Records go back to 1901. Alumni records are maintained here also. Call 212-962-4111 X229. Degrees granted: Associate; Bachelors; Masters.
 Attendance and degree information available by FAX, mail. Search requires name plus date of birth, approximate years of attendance, signed release. Other helpful information: social security number, exact years of attendance. No fee for information.
 Transcripts available by FAX, mail. Search requires name plus date of birth, approximate years of attendance, signed release. Other helpful information: social security number, exact years of attendance. Fee is $4.00.

College of Lake County, Registrar, 19351 W Washington St, Grayslake, IL 60030, 708-223-6601 (FAX: 708-223-1017). Hours: 8AM-8PM M-Th; 8AM-4PM F. Records go back to 1969. Degrees granted: Associate.
 Attendance and degree information available by phone, mail. Search requires name plus social security number, date of birth. No fee for information.
 Transcripts available by mail. Search requires name plus social security number, date of birth, signed release. Fee is $1.00. Expedite fee is based on cost of service.'
Major credit cards accepted for payment.

College of Marin, Admissions, 1800 Ignacio Blvd, Novato, CA 94949, 415-883-2211. Hours: 9AM-3PM M-Th; 9AM-Noon F. Records go back to 1926. Degrees granted: Associate.
 School will not confirm attendance or degree information. Search requires name only. No fee for information.
 Transcripts available by written request only. Search requires name plus signed release. Other helpful information: social security number, date of birth, approximate years of attendance. Fee is $5.00. Expedited service available for $15.00.
Major credit cards accepted for payment.

College of Mount St. Joseph, Registrar's Office, 5701 Delhi Rd, Cincinnati, OH 45233, 513-244-4621 (FAX: 513-244-4222). Hours: 8:30AM-4:30PM. Records go back to 1920. Alumni records are maintained here also. Call 513-244-4425. Degrees granted: Associate; Bachelors; Masters.
 Attendance information available by phone, FAX, mail. Search requires name plus social security number, approximate years of attendance. Other helpful information: date of birth. No fee for information.
 Degree information available by phone, FAX, mail. Search requires name only. Other helpful information: social security number, date of birth, approximate years of attendance. No fee for information.
 Transcripts available by mail. Search requires name plus signed release. Other helpful information: social security number, date of birth, approximate years of attendance. Fee is $5.00. Expedited service available for $10.00.

College of Mount St. Vincent, Registrar, 6301 Riverdale Ave, Riverdale, NY 10471, 715-405-3254. Hours: 8:30AM-4:30PM. Records go back to 1913. Degrees granted: Associate; Bachelors; Masters.

School will not confirm attendance information. Search requires name only. Other helpful information: social security number. No fee for information.
 School will not confirm degree information. Search requires name plus exact years of attendance, signed release. Other helpful information: social security number, approximate years of attendance. No fee for information.
 Transcripts available by mail. Search requires name plus exact years of attendance, signed release. Other helpful information: social security number, approximate years of attendance. Fee is $5.00.
Major credit cards accepted for payment.

College of New Rochelle, Registrar, 29 Castle Pl, New Rochelle, NY 10805, 914-654-5214 (FAX: 914-654-5554). Hours: 9AM-6PM. Records go back to 1904. Degrees granted: Bachelors; Masters. Adverse incident record source: Security Dept.
 Attendance information available by phone, FAX, mail. Search requires name plus social security number, date of birth, approximate years of attendance, signed release. No fee for information.
 Degree information available by phone, FAX, mail. Search requires name plus social security number, date of birth, approximate years of attendance, signed release. No fee for information.
 Transcripts available by written request only. Search requires name plus social security number, date of birth, approximate years of attendance, signed release. Fee is $4.00.
Include a self addressed stamped envelope with mail request.

College of New Rochelle, **(Brooklyn Campus)**, Registrar, 1368 Fulton St, Brooklyn, NY 11216, 718-638-2500. Records are not housed here. They are located at College of New Rochelle, Registrar, 29 Castle Pl, New Rochelle, NY 10805.

College of New Rochelle, **(Co-op City Campus)**, Registrar, 950 Baychester Ave, Bronx, NY 10457, 212-320-0300. Records are not housed here. They are located at College of New Rochelle, Registrar, 29 Castle Pl, New Rochelle, NY 10805.

College of New Rochelle, **(DC 37 Campus)**, Registrar, 125 Barclay St, New York, NY 10007, 212-815-1710. Records are not housed here. They are located at College of New Rochelle, Registrar, 29 Castle Pl, New Rochelle, NY 10805.

College of New Rochelle, **(New York Theological Seminary Campus)**, Registrar, 5 W 29th St, New York, NY 10001, 212-689-6208. Records are not housed here. They are located at College of New Rochelle, Registrar, 29 Castle Pl, New Rochelle, NY 10805.

College of New Rochelle, **(Rosa Parks Campus)**, Registrar, 144 W 125th St, New York, NY 10024, 212-662-7500. Records are not housed here. They are located at College of New Rochelle, Registrar, 29 Castle Pl, New Rochelle, NY 10805.

College of New Rochelle, **(South Bronx Campus)**, Registrar, 332 E 149th St, Bronx, NY 10451, 212-665-1310. Records are not housed here. They are located at College of New Rochelle, Registrar, 29 Castle Pl, New Rochelle, NY 10805.

College of Notre Dame, Registrar's Office, 1500 Ralston Ave, Belmont, CA 94002, 415-508-3521 (FAX: 415-508-3736). Hours: 8:30AM-7PM M-Th; 8:30AM-4PM F. Alumni records are maintained here also. Call 415-508-3515. Degrees granted: Associate; Bachelors; Masters. Adverse incident record source: Head of Security, 415-508-5502.

Attendance and degree information available by phone, FAX, mail. Search requires name only. Other helpful information: social security number, date of birth, approximate years of attendance. No fee for information.

Transcripts available by mail. Search requires name plus signed release. Other helpful information: social security number, date of birth, approximate years of attendance. Fee is $3.00.

College of Notre Dame of Maryland, Registrar, 4701 N Charles St, Baltimore, MD 21210, 410-435-0100. Hours: 8AM-5PM. Records go back to 1895. Alumni records are maintained here also. Call 410-435-0100. Degrees granted: Bachelors; Masters.

Attendance and degree information available by phone, mail. Search requires name plus social security number, exact years of attendance. No fee for information.

Transcripts available by mail. Search requires name plus social security number, exact years of attendance, signed release. Fee is $10.00.

Major credit cards accepted for payment.

College of Oceaneering, Registrar, Los Angeles Harbor, 272 S Fries Ave, Wilmington, CA 90744, 310-834-2501 (FAX: 310-834-7132). Hours: 7:30AM-4:30PM. Records go back 20 years. Degrees granted: Associate.

Attendance information available by phone, FAX, mail. Search requires name plus social security number, signed release. Other helpful information: date of birth, approximate years of attendance. No fee for information.

Degree information available by phone, FAX, mail. Search requires name plus social security number. Other helpful information: date of birth, approximate years of attendance. No fee for information.

Transcripts available by FAX, mail. Search requires name plus social security number. Other helpful information: date of birth, approximate years of attendance. No fee for transcripts.

College of Osteopathic Medicine of the Pacific, Student Affairs Office, 309 E Second St, Pomona, CA 91766-1889, 909-469-5340 (FAX: 909-623-9623). Hours: 8:30AM-5PM. Records go back to 18yr. Alumni records are maintained here also. Call 909-469-5275. Degrees granted: Masters; Doctorate. Certification: P.A. Special programs- Rotations, 909-469-5260: Academic Affairs, 909-469-5267: Allied Health, 909-469-5378. Adverse incident record source: Deans' Office, 909-469-5267 .

Attendance and degree information available by phone, FAX, mail. Search requires name only. Other helpful information: social security number, approximate years of attendance. No fee for information.

Transcripts available by FAX, mail. Search requires name plus signed release. Other helpful information: social security number, approximate years of attendance. Fee is $2.00.

College of Our Lady of the Elms, Registrar, 291 Springfield St, Chicopee, MA 01013-2839, 413-594-2761 X236 (FAX: 413-592-4871). Hours: 8:30AM-4:30PM. Records go back to 1928. Degrees granted: Associate; Bachelors; Masters. Adverse incident record source: Peter Mascaro, 413-594-2761 X231.

Attendance information available by phone, FAX, mail. Search requires name plus date of birth, approximate years of attendance. Other helpful information: social security number. No fee for information.

Degree information available by phone, FAX, mail. Search requires name plus approximate years of attendance. Other helpful information: social security number. No fee for information.

Transcripts available by FAX, mail. Search requires name plus social security number, exact years of attendance, signed release. Other helpful information: date of birth, approximate years of attendance. Fee is $3.00.

College of San Mateo, Registrar, 1700 W Hillsdale Blvd, San Mateo, CA 94402, 415-574-6165. Hours: 8AM-4:30PM. Records go back to 1922. Alumni records are maintained here also. Call 415-574-6141. Degrees granted: Associate.

Attendance and degree information available by phone, mail. Search requires name plus social security number, date of birth. No fee for information.

Transcripts available by mail. Search requires name plus social security number, date of birth, exact years of attendance, signed release. Fee is $3.00.

College of Santa Fe, Registrar, 1600 St Michael's Dr, Santa Fe, NM 87501, 505-473-6317 (FAX: 505-473-6127). Hours: 8AM-5PM. Records go back to 1947. Alumni records are maintained here also. Call 505-473-6312. Degrees granted: Associate; Bachelors; Masters.

Attendance and degree information available by phone, FAX, mail. Search requires name plus approximate years of attendance. No fee for information. Include a stamped envelope.

Transcripts available by FAX, mail. Search requires name only. Other helpful information: approximate years of attendance. Fee is $3.00. Expedited service available for $5.00.

Major credit cards accepted for payment.

College of Southern Idaho, Registrar, 315 Falls Ave, PO Box 1238, Twin Falls, ID 83303-1238, 208-733-9554 (FAX: 208-736-3014). Hours: 8AM-7PM M-Th; 8AM-4:30PM F. Records go back to 1965. Degrees granted: Associate.

Attendance and degree information available by FAX, mail. Search requires name plus social security number, signed release. Other helpful information: date of birth, approximate years of attendance. No fee for information.

Transcripts available by FAX, mail. Search requires name plus social security number, signed release. Other helpful information: date of birth, approximate years of attendance. No fee for transcripts. $5.00 to FAX a transcript.

College of St. Benedict, Registrar, 37 S College Ave, St Joseph, MN 56374, 612-363-3396 (FAX: 612-363-2714). Records are not housed here. They are located at St. John's University, Registrar, Collegeville, MN 56321.

College of St. Catherine, Registrar, 2004 Randolph Ave, St Paul, MN 55105, 612-690-6531. Hours: 9AM-3:30PM. Records go back to 1905. Alumni records are maintained here also. Call 612-690-6000. Degrees granted: Bachelors. Adverse incident record source: Dean of Students, 612-690-6000.

Attendance and degree information available by phone, mail. Search requires name plus social security number, approximate years of attendance, signed release. No fee for information.

Transcripts available by mail. Search requires name plus social security number, approximate years of attendance, signed release. Fee is $3.00.

College of St. Catherine-Minneapolis, (St. Mary's), Records & Accounts, 601 25th Ave S, Minneapolis, MN 55454,

612-690-7777 (FAX: 612-690-7849). Hours: 10AM-6PM. Degrees granted: Associate; Masters.

Attendance information available by FAX, mail. Search requires name only. Other helpful information: social security number, approximate years of attendance. No fee for information.

Degree information available by phone, FAX, mail. Search requires name only. Other helpful information: social security number, approximate years of attendance. No fee for information.

Transcripts available by mail. Search requires name plus signed release. Other helpful information: social security number, approximate years of attendance. No fee for transcripts.

College of St. Elizabeth, Registrar, 2 Convent Rd, Morristown, NJ 07960-7989, 201-292-6300. Hours: 8AM-4:30PM. Records go back to founding date. Alumni records are maintained here also. Call 201-292-6300. Degrees granted: Associate; Bachelors; Masters.

Attendance and degree information available by phone, mail. Search requires name plus date of birth, exact years of attendance. Other helpful information: approximate years of attendance. No fee for information.

Transcripts available by written request only. Search requires name plus date of birth, exact years of attendance, signed release. Other helpful information: approximate years of attendance. Fee is $3.00.

College of St. Francis, Registrar, 500 N Wilcox St, Joliet, IL 60435, 815-740-3391 (FAX: 815-740-4285). Hours: 8AM-4:30PM. Records go back 60 years. Alumni records are maintained here at the same phone number. Degrees granted: Bachelors; Masters.

Attendance and degree information available by phone, FAX, mail. Search requires name only. Other helpful information: social security number, approximate years of attendance. No fee for information.

Transcripts available by FAX, mail. Search requires name plus signed release. Other helpful information: social security number, approximate years of attendance. Fee is $2.00. Expedited service available for $2.00.

College of St. Joseph, Registrar, Rutland, VT 05701, 802-773-5900 X241 (FAX: 802-773-5900 X258). Hours: 8:30AM-7:30PM. Records go back to 1964. Degrees granted: Associate; Bachelors; Masters. Adverse incident record source: Student Services.

Attendance and degree information available by phone, mail. Search requires name plus approximate years of attendance. Other helpful information: social security number, date of birth, exact years of attendance. No fee for information.

Transcripts available by phone, mail. Search requires name plus approximate years of attendance, signed release. Other helpful information: social security number, date of birth, exact years of attendance. Fee is $4.00. Expedited service available for $10.00. Phone requests for transcripts must be signed later.

College of St. Mary, Registrar, 1901 S 72nd St, Omaha, NE 68124, 402-399-2443. Hours: 9AM-5PM. Records go back to 1923. Degrees granted: Associate; Bachelors.

Attendance information available by phone, mail. Search requires name only. Other helpful information: social security number, date of birth. No fee for information.

Degree information available by phone, mail. Search requires name only. No fee for information.

Transcripts available by mail. Search requires name plus signed release. Other helpful information: social security number, date of birth. Fee is $2.00.

College of St. Rose, Registrar, 432 Western Ave, Albany, NY 12203, 518-454-5213 (FAX: 518-454-2100). Hours: 9:30AM-2:30PM, 3:30-6PM M-Th; 9:30AM-4:30PM F. Records go back to 1920. Degrees granted: Bachelors; Masters.

Attendance and degree information available by phone, FAX, mail. Search requires name plus social security number, approximate years of attendance. Other helpful information: date of birth, exact years of attendance. No fee for information.

Transcripts available by mail. Search requires name plus social security number, date of birth, approximate years of attendance, signed release. Other helpful information: exact years of attendance. Fee is $5.00. Expedited service available for $5.00. Major credit cards accepted for payment.

College of St. Scholastica, Registrar, 1200 Kenwood Ave, Duluth, MN 55811, 218-723-6039 (FAX: 218-723-6290). Hours: 8AM-4:30PM. Records go back to 1945. Alumni records are maintained here also. Call 218-723-6033 X6658. Degrees granted: Bachelors; Masters. Adverse incident record source: Dean, 218-723-6033 X6038.

Attendance and degree information available by phone, FAX, mail. Search requires name plus social security number, signed release. No fee for information.

Transcripts available by FAX, mail. Search requires name plus social security number, signed release. Fee is $3.00. Major credit cards accepted for payment.

College of Staten Island, Registrar, 2800 Victory Blvd, Staten Island, NY 10314, 718-982-2121. Hours: 9AM-5PM. Records go back to 1950. Alumni records are maintained here also. Call 718-982-2290. Degrees granted: Associate; Bachelors; Masters.

Attendance and degree information available by mail. Search requires name plus social security number, approximate years of attendance, signed release. No fee for information.

Transcripts available by mail. Search requires name plus social security number, approximate years of attendance, signed release. Fee is $4.00.

College of Staten Island, **(Sunnyside Campus)**, Registrar, 2800 Victory Blvd, Staten Island, NY 10314, 718-982-2120. Hours: 9AM-5PM. Records go back to 1956. Degrees granted: Associate; Bachelors; Masters.

Attendance and degree information available by mail. Search requires name plus social security number, signed release. Other helpful information: date of birth, approximate years of attendance. No fee for information.

Transcripts available by mail. Search requires name plus social security number, signed release. Other helpful information: date of birth, approximate years of attendance. Fee is $4.00.

College of West Virginia, Registrar, 609 S Kanawha St, Beckley, WV 25802, 304-253-7351 X35 (FAX: 304-253-0789). Records go back to 1933. Alumni records are maintained here at the same phone number. Degrees granted: Bachelors.

Attendance and degree information available by phone, mail. Search requires name plus social security number, date of birth, exact years of attendance. No fee for information.

Transcripts available by mail. Search requires name plus social security number, date of birth, exact years of attendance, signed release. Fee is $3.00.

College of William and Mary, Registrar, PO Box 8795, Williamsburg, VA 23187-8795, 804-221-2815 (FAX: 804-221-2799). Hours: 8AM-4:30PM. Records go back to 1693. Alumni records are maintained here also. Call 804-221-1842. Degrees granted: Bachelors; Masters; Doctorate.

Attendance and degree information available by phone, mail. Search requires name plus social security number, date of birth, exact years of attendance. No fee for information.

Transcripts available by mail. Search requires name plus social security number, date of birth, exact years of attendance, signed release. No fee for transcripts.

College of Wooster, Registrar, Wooster, OH 44691, 216-263-2366 (FAX: 216-263-2260). Hours: 8AM-4:30PM. Records go back to 1866. Alumni records are maintained here also. Call 216-263-2324. Degrees granted: Bachelors.

Attendance information available by phone, FAX, mail. Search requires name plus social security number, approximate years of attendance, signed release. No fee for information.

Degree information available by phone, FAX, mail. Search requires name plus social security number, approximate years of attendance. No fee for information.

Transcripts available by FAX, mail. Search requires name plus social security number, approximate years of attendance, signed release. Fee is $3.00.

College of the Albemarle, Registrar, PO Box 2327, Elizabeth City, NC 27906-2327, 919-335-0821 X252 (FAX: 919-335-2011). Hours: 8AM-4:30PM. Records go back to 1960. Degrees granted: Associate. Adverse incident record source: Records & Registration, 919-335-0821.

Attendance and degree information available by phone, FAX, mail. Search requires name plus social security number. No fee for information.

Transcripts available by mail. Search requires name plus social security number, exact years of attendance, signed release. No fee for transcripts.

Former names needed.

College of the Atlantic, Registrar, 105 Eden St, Bar Harbor, ME 04609, 207-288-5015 (FAX: 207-288-4126). Hours: 9AM-5PM. Records go back to 1972. Alumni records are maintained here at the same phone number. Degrees granted: Bachelors; Masters. Adverse incident record source: Registrar, 207-288-5015.

Attendance and degree information available by phone, FAX, mail. Search requires name plus exact years of attendance. No fee for information.

Transcripts available by FAX, mail. Search requires name plus social security number, exact years of attendance, signed release. Fee is $4.00.

Transcripts by student request only.

College of the Canyons, Admissions & Records Officd, 26455 N Rockwell Canyon Rd, Santa Clarita, CA 91355, 805-259-7900 (FAX: 805-259-8302). Hours: 9AM-7PM M-Th. Records go back to 1969. Degrees granted: Associate.

Attendance and degree information available by phone, FAX, mail. Search requires name plus social security number, date of birth, approximate years of attendance. No fee for information.

School does not provide transcripts. Search requires name plus social security number, date of birth, approximate years of attendance, signed release. First two transcripts free. Additional ones are $5.00 each. Expedited service available for $8.00.

College of the Desert, Registrar, 43-500 Monterey Ave, Palm Desert, CA 92260, 619-773-2518 (FAX: 619-776-0136). Hours: 8:30AM-7PM M-Th; 8:30AM-3PM F. Records go back to 1963. Degrees granted: Associate. Adverse incident record source: Administrative Support Services.

Attendance information available by written request only. Search requires name plus social security number, date of birth, signed release. Other helpful information: approximate years of attendance. No fee for information.

Degree information available by phone, FAX, mail. Search requires name plus social security number, date of birth, signed release. Other helpful information: approximate years of attendance. No fee for information.

Transcripts available by mail. Search requires name plus social security number, date of birth, signed release. Other helpful information: approximate years of attendance. Fee is $3.00. Expedited service available for $8.00.

College of the Holy Cross, Registrar, Worcester, MA 01610-2395, 508-793-2511 (FAX: 508-793-3790). Hours: 8:30AM-4:30PM. Records go back to 1907. Degrees granted: Bachelors.

Attendance and degree information available by phone, FAX, mail. Search requires name only. Other helpful information: social security number, approximate years of attendance. No fee for information.

Transcripts available by FAX, mail. Search requires name plus signed release. Other helpful information: social security number, approximate years of attendance. Fee is $3.00. Expedited service available for $5.00.

College of the Mainland, Admissions Office, 1200 Amburn Rd, Texas City, TX 77591, 409-938-1211 X263 (FAX: 409-938-1306). Hours: 8AM-5PM. Records go back to 1968. Degrees granted: Associate.

Attendance and degree information available by phone, FAX, mail. Search requires name plus social security number. Other helpful information: date of birth, approximate years of attendance. No fee for information.

Transcripts available by written request only. Search requires name plus social security number, signed release. Other helpful information: date of birth, approximate years of attendance. Fee is $1.00.

College of the Ozarks, Registrar, Point Lookout, MO 65726, 417-334-6411 (FAX: 417-335-2618). Hours: 8AM-Noon, 1-5PM, 4PM in summer. Records go back to 1960. Alumni records are maintained here also. Call 417-334-6411. Degrees granted: Bachelors.

Attendance and degree information available by phone, FAX, mail. Search requires name plus social security number, approximate years of attendance. Other helpful information: date of birth. No fee for information.

Transcripts available by written request only. Search requires name plus social security number, approximate years of attendance, signed release. Other helpful information: date of birth. Fee is $2.00.

College of the Redwoods, Dir, Admissions & Records, Attn: Transcripts, 7358 Tompkins Hill Rd, Eureka, CA 95501, 707-445-6717 (FAX: 707-445-6990). Hours: 8AM-7PM M-Th; 8AM-5PM F. Records go back to 1965. Alumni records are maintained here also. Call 707-445-6992. Degrees granted: Associate. Adverse incident record source: 707-445-6933.

Attendance and degree information available by written request only. Search requires name plus social security number, signed release. Other helpful information: date of birth, approximate years of attendance. No fee for information.

Transcripts available by written request only. Search requires name plus social security number, signed release. Other helpful information: date of birth, approximate years of attendance. First two transcripts free. Additional ones are $5.00 each.

College of the Sequoias, Registrar, 915 S Mooney Blvd, Visalia, CA 93277, 209-730-3775. Hours: 8:30AM-4PM. Records go back to 1922. Degrees granted: Associate.

Attendance and degree information available by mail. Search requires name plus social security number, date of birth, exact years of attendance. No fee for information.

Transcripts available by mail. Search requires name plus social security number, date of birth, exact years of attendance, signed release. Fee is $4.00.

College of the Siskiyous, Registrar, 800 College Ave, Weed, CA 96094, 916-938-5215 (FAX: 916-938-5367). Hours: 9AM-3PM. Records go back to 1937. Degrees granted: Associate.

Attendance and degree information available by FAX, mail. Search requires name plus date of birth, signed release. Other helpful information: social security number, exact years of attendance. No fee for information.

Transcripts available by FAX, mail. Search requires name plus date of birth, signed release. Other helpful information: social security number, exact years of attendance. Fee is $5.00. Expedited service available for $10.00.

College of the Southwest, Registrar, 6610 Lovington Hwy, Hobbs, NM 88240, 505-392-6561 (FAX: 505-392-6006). Hours: 8AM-5PM. Records go back to 1956. Degrees granted: Bachelors.

Attendance and degree information available by phone, FAX, mail. Search requires name only. Other helpful information: social security number, date of birth, approximate years of attendance. No fee for information.

Transcripts available by FAX, mail. Search requires name plus social security number, signed release. Other helpful information: date of birth, approximate years of attendance. Fee is $5.00. Expedited service available for $10.00.

Major credit cards accepted for payment.

Collin County Community College, Registrar, 2200 W University Dr, PO Box 8001, McKinney, TX 75070, 214-548-6744 (FAX: 214-548-6702). Hours: 8AM-5PM M,T,Th,F; 8AM-8PM W. Records go back to 1985. Degrees granted: Associate. Adverse incident record source: Dean of Students, 214-881-5790.

Attendance and degree information available by phone, FAX, mail. Search requires name plus social security number. Other helpful information: date of birth. No fee for information.

Transcripts available by written request only. Search requires name plus social security number, signed release. Other helpful information: date of birth. Fee is $2.00.

Major credit cards accepted for payment.

Colorado Christian University, Registrar, 180 S Garrison St, Lakewood, CO 80226, 303-238-5386 X140 (FAX: 303-274-7560). Hours: 8AM-5PM. Records go back to 1915. Alumni records are maintained here at the same phone number. Degrees granted: Associate; Bachelors; Masters. Certification: Education, LPC, Comp, OM.

Attendance and degree information available by phone, FAX, mail. Search requires name plus social security number, approximate years of attendance. No fee for information.

Transcripts available by FAX, mail. Search requires name plus social security number, approximate years of attendance, signed release. Fee is $5.00. Expedited service available for $7.00.

Student may request information be held confidential. FAX fee of $3.00 per page with two page minimum is available. Major credit cards accepted for payment.

Colorado College, Registrar, 14 E Cache la Pourde St, Colorado Springs, CO 80903, 719-389-6610 (FAX: 719-389-6931). Hours: 8:30AM-5PM. Records go back to 1895. Alumni records are maintained here also. Call 719-389-6000. Degrees granted: Bachelors; Masters.

Attendance and degree information available by phone, FAX, mail. Search requires name only. No fee for information.

Transcripts available by FAX, mail. Search requires name plus signed release. No fee for transcripts.

Colorado Institute of Art, Registrar, 200 E Ninth Ave, Denver, CO 80203-9947, 303-837-0825 (FAX: 303-860-8520). Hours: 7:30AM-5PM. Degrees granted: Associate.

Attendance information available by FAX, mail. Search requires name plus social security number, signed release. Other helpful information: approximate years of attendance. No fee for information.

Degree information available by phone, FAX, mail. Search requires name plus social security number, signed release. Other helpful information: approximate years of attendance. No fee for information.

Transcripts available by FAX, mail. Search requires name plus social security number, signed release. Other helpful information: approximate years of attendance. Fee is $2.00.

Major credit cards accepted for payment.

Colorado Mountain College, Registrar, Box 10001, 215 Ninth St, Glenwood Springs, CO 81602, 800-621-8559 (FAX: 970-928-8633). Hours: 8AM-5PM. Records go back to 1967. Second phone number is 970-945-8691. Alumni records are maintained here at the same phone number. Degrees granted: Associate.

Attendance and degree information available by FAX, mail. Search requires name plus approximate years of attendance. No fee for information.

Transcripts available by FAX, mail. Search requires name plus approximate years of attendance, signed release. Fee is $2.00.

Colorado Mountain College, **(Alpine)**, Registrar, 1370 Bob Adams Dr, Steamboat Springs, CO 80477, 303-879-3288. Records are not housed here. They are located at Colorado Mountain College, Registrar, Box 10001, 215 Ninth St, Glenwood Springs, CO 81602.

Colorado Mountain College, **(Roaring Fork)**, Registrar, 3000 County Rd 114, Glenwood Springs, CO 81601, 303-945-7841. Records are not housed here. They are located at Colorado

Mountain College, Registrar, Box 10001, 215 Ninth St, Glenwood Springs, CO 81602.

Colorado Mountain College, (Timberline), Registrar, 901 S Hwy 24, Leadville, CO 80461, 719-486-2015. Records are not housed here. They are located at Colorado Mountain College, Registrar, Box 10001, 215 Ninth St, Glenwood Springs, CO 81602.

Colorado Northwestern Community College, Registrar, 500 Kennedy Dr, Rangely, CO 81648, 970-675-3218 (FAX: 970-675-3343). Hours: 8AM-5PM. Records go back to 1960. Alumni records are maintained here also. Call 970-675-3346. Degrees granted: Associate. Adverse incident record source: Student Services, 970-675-3222.

Attendance and degree information available by phone, FAX, mail. Search requires name plus social security number, date of birth, approximate years of attendance. No fee for information.

Transcripts available by FAX, mail. Search requires name plus social security number, date of birth, approximate years of attendance, signed release. Fee is $2.00.

Colorado School of Mines, Registrar, 1500 Illinois St, Golden, CO 80401, 303-273-3200 (FAX: 303-273-3278). Hours: 8AM-5PM. Records go back to 1876. Alumni records are maintained here also. Call 303-273-3295. Degrees granted: Bachelors; Masters; PhD, Professional. Adverse incident record source: Dean of Students, 303-273-3350: Undergraduate, 303-273-3247

Attendance and degree information available by phone, FAX, mail. Search requires name plus social security number, signed release. Other helpful information: date of birth, approximate years of attendance. No fee for information.

Transcripts available by FAX, mail. Search requires name plus social security number, signed release. Other helpful information: date of birth, approximate years of attendance. Fee is $2.00.

Colorado State University, Records & Registration, Rm 200 Admin Annex, Fort Collins, CO 80523, 970-491-7148 (FAX: 970-491-2283). Hours: 7:45AM-4:45PM Winter; 7:30AM-4:30PM Summer. Records go back to 1875. Alumni Records Office: 645 S Shields St, Fort Collins, CO 80521. Degrees granted: Bachelors; Masters; Doctorate. Adverse incident record source: Judicial Affairs, 970-491-5312.

Attendance and degree information available by phone, FAX, mail. Search requires name only. Other helpful information: social security number, date of birth. No fee for information.

Transcripts available by mail. Search requires name plus signed release. Other helpful information: social security number, date of birth, approximate years of attendance. Fee is $5.00. Expedited service available for $10.00.

Colorado Technical College, Records, 4435 N Chestnut St, Colorado Springs, CO 80907, 719-598-0200 (FAX: 719-598-3740). Hours: 8AM-6PM. Records go back 70 years. Degrees granted: Associate; Bachelors; Masters; Doctorate.

Attendance information available by phone, FAX, mail. Search requires name plus social security number, signed release. Other helpful information: approximate years of attendance. No fee for information.

Degree information available by FAX, mail. Search requires name plus social security number, signed release. Other helpful information: approximate years of attendance. No fee for information.

Transcripts available by mail. Search requires name plus social security number, signed release. Other helpful information: approximate years of attendance. Fee is $10.00.

Columbia Basin College, Registrar, 2600 N 20th Ave, Pasco, WA 99302, 509-547-0511 (FAX: 509-546-0401). Hours: 7:30AM-4:30PM. Records go back to 1955. Degrees granted: Associate.

Attendance and degree information available by phone, FAX, mail. Search requires name plus social security number. Other helpful information: date of birth, exact years of attendance. No fee for information.

Transcripts available by FAX, mail. Search requires name plus social security number, signed release. Other helpful information: date of birth, exact years of attendance. Fee is $2.00.

Columbia College, Registrar, PO Box 8517, Carretera 183 KM 1.7, Caguas, PR 00762-8517, 809-743-4041.

Columbia College, Registrar, 600 S Michigan Ave, Chicago, IL 60605, 312-663-1600 (FAX: 312-663-5543). Hours: 9AM-5PM. Alumni Records Office: 624 S Michigan, Chicago, IL 60605. Degrees granted: Bachelors; Masters.

Attendance and degree information available by phone, FAX, mail. Search requires name only. Other helpful information: social security number, date of birth, approximate years of attendance. No fee for information.

Transcripts available by mail. Search requires name plus signed release. Other helpful information: social security number, date of birth, approximate years of attendance. Fee is $3.00.

Columbia College, Registrar, 1001 Rogers St, Columbia, MO 65216, 314-875-7504 (FAX: 314-875-8765). Hours: 8AM-5PM. Records go back to 1851. Degrees granted: Associate; Bachelors.

Attendance and degree information available by phone, FAX, mail. Search requires name only. Other helpful information: social security number, date of birth, approximate years of attendance. No fee for information.

Transcripts available by mail. Search requires name plus signed release. Other helpful information: social security number, date of birth, approximate years of attendance. Fee is $2.00.

Major credit cards accepted for payment.

Columbia College, Registrar, 1301 Columbia College Dr, Columbia, SC 29203, 803-786-3672 (FAX: 803-786-3771). Hours: 8:30AM-5PM. Degrees granted: Bachelors; Masters.

Attendance and degree information available by phone, FAX, mail. Search requires name plus social security number, approximate years of attendance. Other helpful information: date of birth, exact years of attendance. No fee for information.

Transcripts available by FAX, mail. Search requires name plus social security number, approximate years of attendance, signed release. Other helpful information: date of birth, exact years of attendance. Fee is $5.00. Expedited service available for $15.00.

Columbia College Hollywood, Registrar, 925 N La Brea Ave, Los Angeles, CA 90038-2392, 213-851-0550 (FAX: 213-851-6401). Hours: 8AM-4:30PM. Records go back to 1952. Degrees granted: Associate.

Attendance and degree information available by phone, FAX, mail. Search requires name plus social security number, exact years of attendance. No fee for information.

Transcripts available by mail. Search requires name plus social security number, exact years of attendance, signed release. Fee is $6.00.

Columbia College, Admissions and Records, 11600 Columbia College Dr, Sonora, CA 95370-8582, 209-533-5231 (FAX: 209-533-5104). Hours: 8AM-6:30PM M-Th; 8AM-4:30PM F. Records go back to 1968. Degrees granted: Associate. Certification: Vocational. Adverse incident record source: Student Services.

Attendance and degree information available by phone, FAX, mail. Search requires name only. Other helpful information: social security number, date of birth, approximate years of attendance. No fee for information.

Transcripts available by FAX, mail. Search requires name plus signed release. Other helpful information: social security number, date of birth, approximate years of attendance. Fee is $3.00. Expedited service available for $10.00.

Columbia College of Nursing, Registrar, 2121 E Newport Ave, Milwaukee, WI 53211, 414-961-3530. Hours: 8AM-4PM. Degrees granted: Associate.

Attendance and degree information available by phone, mail. Search requires name plus social security number. No fee for information.

Transcripts available by written request only. Search requires name plus social security number, signed release. Fee is $3.00.

Columbia College, (Branch Campus), Registrar, PO Box 3062, Yauco, PR 00698, 809-856-0845.

Columbia International University, Registrar, PO Box 3122, Columbia, SC 29203-3122, 803-754-4100 (FAX: 803-786-4209). Hours: 8AM-5PM. Records go back to 1927. Alumni records are maintained here also. Call 803-754-4100 X3004. Degrees granted: Associate; Bachelors; Masters; Doctorate.

Attendance and degree information available by phone, mail. Search requires name only. Other helpful information: social security number, date of birth, approximate years of attendance. No fee for information.

Transcripts available by FAX, mail. Search requires name plus social security number, date of birth, approximate years of attendance, signed release. Other helpful information: exact years of attendance. Fee is $3.00. Expedited service available for $5.00.

Columbia Junior College of Business, Registrar, PO Box 1196, 3810 Main St, Columbia, SC 29202, 803-799-9082 (FAX: 803-799-5009). Hours: 8AM-5:30PM. Records go back to 1935. Degrees granted: Associate.

Attendance and degree information available by phone, FAX, mail. Search requires name plus social security number, approximate years of attendance. Other helpful information: date of birth, exact years of attendance. No fee for information.

Transcripts available by mail. Search requires name plus social security number, approximate years of attendance, signed release. Other helpful information: date of birth, exact years of attendance. Fee is $2.00. Expedited service available for $5.00.

Columbia State Community College, Registrar, PO Box 1315, Hwy 412 W, Columbia, TN 38402-1315, 615-540-2545. Hours: 8AM-5PM. Records go back to 1966. Alumni records are maintained here also. Call 615-540-2514. Degrees granted: Associate.

Attendance and degree information available by phone, mail. Search requires name plus social security number. No fee for information.

Transcripts available by mail. Search requires name plus social security number, signed release. No fee for transcripts.

Columbia Theological Seminary, Registrar, PO Box 520, 701 Columbia Dr, Decatur, GA 30031, 404-378-8821 (FAX: 404-377-9696). Hours: 8:30AM-4:30PM. Degrees granted: Masters; Doctorate. Adverse incident record source: Business Office.

Attendance information available by FAX, mail. Search requires name plus signed release. Other helpful information: social security number, date of birth, approximate years of attendance. No fee for information.

Degree information available by phone, FAX, mail. Search requires name only. Other helpful information: social security number, date of birth, approximate years of attendance. No fee for information.

Transcripts available by FAX, mail. Search requires name plus signed release. Other helpful information: social security number, date of birth, approximate years of attendance. Fee is $2.00.

Columbia Union College, Registrar, 7600 Flower Ave, Takoma Park, MD 20912, 301-891-4119 (FAX: 301-891-4022). Hours: 9AM-Noon, 1-4PM M,T,Th; 9-11AM,1-4PM W; 9AM-Noon F. Records go back to 1904. Alumni records are maintained here also. Call 301-891-4132. Degrees granted: Associate; Masters.

Attendance and degree information available by FAX, mail. Search requires name plus social security number, approximate years of attendance, signed release. Other helpful information: date of birth, exact years of attendance. No fee for information. Expedited service available for $10.00.

Transcripts available by FAX, mail. Search requires name plus social security number, approximate years of attendance, signed release. Other helpful information: date of birth, exact years of attendance. No fee for transcripts. Expedited service available for $10.00.

Major credit cards accepted for payment.

Columbia University, Registrar, 116th St and Broadway, New York, NY 10027, 212-854-1458. Hours: 9AM-5PM. Records go back to 1754. Alumni records are maintained here at the same phone number. Degrees granted: Associate; Bachelors; Masters; Doctorate.

Attendance and degree information available by mail. Search requires name plus social security number, approximate years of attendance, signed release. No fee for information. Include a stamped envelope.

Transcripts available by mail. Search requires name plus social security number, approximate years of attendance, signed release. First transcript $5.00; $1.00 each additional one.

Columbia University Teachers College, Registrar, 525 W 120th St, New York, NY 10027, 212-678-4065 (FAX: 212-678-4048). Hours: 8AM-5PM. Records go back to 1898. Degrees granted: Masters; Doctorate.

Attendance and degree information available by phone, FAX, mail. Search requires name only. Other helpful information: social security number, date of birth, approximate years of attendance. No fee for information.

Transcripts available by mail. Search requires name plus signed release. Other helpful information: social security number, date of birth, approximate years of attendance. Fee is $5.00. Expedited service available for $6.00.

Columbia-Greene Community College, Registrar, 4400 Route 23, Hudson, NY 12534, 518-828-4181. Hours: 8AM-5PM. Records go back to 1969. Degrees granted: Associate.

Attendance and degree information available by phone, FAX, mail. Search requires name only. Other helpful information: social security number, date of birth, approximate years of attendance. No fee for information.

Transcripts available by FAX, mail. Search requires name plus social security number, signed release. Other helpful information: date of birth, approximate years of attendance. Fee is $3.00. Expedited service available for $3.00.

Major credit cards accepted for payment.

Columbus College, Registrar, 4225 University Ave, Columbus, GA 31907-5645, 706-568-2237 (FAX: 706-568-2462). Hours: 8AM-6PM F-Th; 8AM-5PM F. Records go back to 1937. Alumni records are maintained here also. Call 706-568-2280. Degrees granted: Associate; Bachelors; Masters. Certification: Comp Sci, Criminal Justice. E.D.S. Adverse incident record source: VP for Student Affairs, 706-568-2033.

Attendance and degree information available by phone, FAX, mail. Search requires name plus social security number, date of birth, signed release. Other helpful information: approximate years of attendance. No fee for information.

Transcripts available by FAX, mail. Search requires name plus social security number, date of birth, signed release. Other helpful information: approximate years of attendance. No fee for transcripts. $5.00 for FAX service.

Either SSN or DOB is necessary.

Columbus College of Art and Design, Registrar, 107 N Ninth St, Columbus, OH 43215, 614-224-9101 (FAX: 614-222-4040). Hours: 8:30AM-5PM. Records go back to 1960. Alumni records are maintained here at the same phone number. Degrees granted: Bachelors.

Attendance information available by mail. Search requires name plus social security number, approximate years of attendance. No fee for information.

Degree information available by mail. Search requires name only. No fee for information.

Transcripts available by mail. Search requires name only. Fee is $5.00.

Columbus Para-Professional Institute, Registrar, 1077 Lexington Ave, Columbus, OH 43201, 614-299-0200 (FAX: 614-299-1126). Hours: 8:30AM-6PM. Records go back to 1975.

Attendance and degree information available by FAX, mail. Search requires name plus social security number, date of birth, exact years of attendance, signed release. No fee for information.

Transcripts available by FAX, mail. Search requires name plus social security number, date of birth, exact years of attendance, signed release. First transcript is free. Additional ones are $7.00 each.

Columbus State Community College, Registrar, 550 E Spring St, PO Box 1609, Columbus, OH 43216-1609, 614-227-2643 (FAX: 614-227-5117). Hours: 8AM-7:30PM M-Th; 8AM-4:30PM F. Records go back to 1963. Degrees granted: Associate.

School will not confirm attendance or degree information. Search requires name only. Other helpful information: social security number, approximate years of attendance. No fee for information.

Transcripts available by FAX, mail. Search requires name plus social security number, signed release. Other helpful information: approximate years of attendance. Fee is $1.00. Expedited service available for $10.00.

Major credit cards accepted for payment.

Columbus Technical Institute, Registrar, 928 45th St, Columbus, GA 31904-6572, 706-649-1857 (FAX: 706-649-1885). Hours: 8AM-5PM. Records go back to 1961. Degrees granted: Associate.

Attendance and degree information available by phone, FAX, mail. Search requires name plus social security number. Other helpful information: date of birth, approximate years of attendance. No fee for information.

Transcripts available by FAX, mail. Search requires name plus social security number, signed release. Other helpful information: date of birth, approximate years of attendance. Fee is $2.00.

Major credit cards accepted for payment.

Commonwealth Business College, Registrar, 4200 W 81st Ave, Merrillville, IN 46410, 219-769-3321 (FAX: 219-738-1076). Hours: 8AM-5PM. Records go back 5 years. Degrees granted: Associate.

Attendance and degree information available by written request only. Search requires name plus social security number, signed release. Other helpful information: approximate years of attendance. Fee is $2.00.

Transcripts available by written request only. Search requires name plus social security number, signed release. Other helpful information: approximate years of attendance. Fee is $2.00.

Commonwealth Business College, (Branch), Registrar, 1527 47th Ave, Moline, IN 61265, 309-762-2100 (FAX: 309-762-2374). Hours: 8AM-9:30PM. Records go back 10 years.

Attendance information available by FAX, mail. Search requires name plus signed release. Other helpful information: social security number, date of birth, approximate years of attendance. No fee for information.

School will not confirm degree information. Search requires name only. No fee for information.

Transcripts available by phone, FAX, mail. Search requires name only. Other helpful information: social security number, date of birth, approximate years of attendance. No fee for transcripts.

Commonwealth Business College, (LaPorte), Registrar, 8895 N State Rte 39, La Porte, IN 46350, 219-362-3338 (FAX: 219-324-0112). Hours: 7:30AM-9:30PM M-Th; 8AM-5PM F. Records go back to founding date. Degrees granted: Associate. Adverse incident record source: Merrillville Campus, 219-769-3321.

Attendance information available by phone, mail. Search requires name plus social security number, approximate years of attendance, signed release. Other helpful information: date of birth. No fee for information.

Degree information available by phone, mail. Search requires name plus social security number. Other helpful information: date of birth, approximate years of attendance. No fee for information.

Transcripts available by phone, mail. Search requires name plus social security number, approximate years of attendance, signed release. Other helpful information: date of birth. No fee for transcripts.

Commonwealth College, Registrar, 301 Centre Pointe Drive, Virginia Beach, VA 23462, 804-499-7900 (FAX: 804-499-

9977). Hours: 8AM-5PM. Records go back to 1960s. Degrees granted: Associate.

Attendance information available by phone, FAX, mail. Search requires name plus social security number. Other helpful information: approximate years of attendance. No fee for information.

Degree information available by phone, FAX, mail. Search requires name plus social security number. Other helpful information: approximate years of attendance. No fee for information.

Transcripts available by mail. Search requires name plus social security number, signed release. Other helpful information: approximate years of attendance. Fee is $5.00. Expedited service available for $10.00.

Commonwealth College, **(Branch Campus)**, Registrar, 1120 W Mercury Blvd, Hampton, VA 23666-3309, 804-838-2122. Hours: 8AM-5PM. Records go back to 1981. Degrees granted: Associate.

Attendance and degree information available by FAX, mail. Search requires name plus social security number, signed release. No fee for information.

Transcripts available by written request only. Search requires name plus social security number, signed release. Fee is $5.00.

Commonwealth College, **(Branch Campus)**, Registrar, 300 Boush St, Norfolk, VA 23510-1216, 804-625-5891. Degrees granted: Associate.

Attendance and degree information available by phone, FAX, mail. Search requires name plus social security number, approximate years of attendance, signed release. Other helpful information: date of birth. No fee for information.

Transcripts available by FAX, mail. Search requires name plus social security number, approximate years of attendance, signed release. Other helpful information: date of birth. Fee is $5.00.

Commonwealth College, **(Branch Campus)**, Registrar, 5579 Portsmouth Blvd, Portsmouth, VA 23701, 804-484-2121. Hours: 8AM-5PM. Records go back to 1968. Degrees granted: Associate.

Attendance and degree information available by FAX, mail. Search requires name plus social security number, signed release. No fee for information.

Transcripts available by FAX, mail. Search requires name plus social security number, signed release. Fee is $5.00.

Commonwealth College, **(Branch Campus)**, Registrar, 8141 Hull St Rd, Richmond, VA 23235-6411, 804-745-2444. Hours: 8AM-5PM. Records go back to 1960s. Degrees granted: Associate.

Attendance and degree information available by FAX, mail. Search requires name plus social security number, signed release. No fee for information.

Transcripts available by written request only. Search requires name plus social security number, signed release. Fee is $5.00.

Commonwealth Institute of Funeral Service, Registrar, 415 Barren Springs Dr, Houston, TX 77090, 713-873-0262 (FAX: 713-873-5232). Hours: 8AM-4PM. Records go back to 1945. Degrees granted: Associate.

Attendance information available by phone. Search requires name only. Other helpful information: social security number, approximate years of attendance. No fee for information.

Degree information available by phone. Search requires name only. Other helpful information: approximate years of attendance. No fee for information.

Transcripts available by written request only. Search requires name plus signed release. Other helpful information: approximate years of attendance. Fee is $2.00.

Community College of Allegheny County, **(Allegheny)**, Registrar, 808 Ridge Ave, Byers Hall 211, Pittsburgh, PA 15212, 412-237-2525. Hours: 8AM-5PM. Records go back to 1966. Degrees granted: Associate.

Attendance and degree information available by mail. Search requires name plus social security number, signed release. No fee for information.

Transcripts available by mail. Search requires name plus social security number, exact years of attendance, signed release. No fee for transcripts.

Need to provide current address.

Community College of Allegheny County, **(Boyce)**, Registrar, 595 Beatty Rd, Monroeville, PA 15146, 412-325-6674 (FAX: 412-325-6797). Hours: 8:30AM-4:30PM. Records go back to 1966. Alumni records are maintained here also. Call 412-371-8651. Degrees granted: Associate.

Attendance and degree information available by phone, FAX, mail. Search requires name plus social security number. No fee for information.

Transcripts available by mail. Search requires name plus social security number, exact years of attendance, signed release. No fee for transcripts.

Community College of Allegheny County, **(North)**, Registrar, 8701 Perry Hwy, Pittsburgh, PA 15237, 412-369-3700. Hours: 8:30AM-4:30PM. Records go back to 1966. Alumni records are maintained here also. Call 412-366-7000. Degrees granted: Associate.

Attendance and degree information available by mail. Search requires name plus social security number, signed release. Other helpful information: exact years of attendance. No fee for information.

Transcripts available by mail. Search requires name plus social security number, exact years of attendance, signed release. Fee is $1.00.

Community College of Allegheny County, **(South)**, Registrar, 1750 Clairton Rd Rte 885, West Mifflin, PA 15122, 412-469-6202. Hours: 8:30AM-4:30PM. Records go back to 1960. Degrees granted: Associate.

Attendance information available by mail. Search requires name plus social security number, signed release. No fee for information.

Degree information available by mail. Search requires name plus social security number, exact years of attendance, signed release. No fee for information.

Transcripts available by mail. Search requires name plus social security number, exact years of attendance, signed release. Fee is $1.00.

Community College of Aurora, Registrar, 16000 E Centretech Pkwy, Aurora, CO 80011, 303-361-7411 (FAX: 303-361-7432). Hours: 9AM-6PM M-Th, 8AM-5PM F. Records go back to 1983. Degrees granted: Associate. Adverse incident record source: Dean of Students, 303-360-4752.

Attendance and degree information available by phone, FAX, mail. Search requires name plus social security number, approximate years of attendance. No fee for information.

Transcripts available by mail. Search requires name plus social security number, approximate years of attendance, signed release. Fee is $2.00.

Community College of Beaver County, Registrar, One Campus Dr, Monaca, PA 15061-2588, 412-775-8561. Hours: 8AM-4:30PM. Records go back to 1969. Alumni records are maintained here also. Call 412-775-8561. Degrees granted: Associate. Adverse incident record source: Campus Police, 412-775-8561.

Attendance information available by mail. Search requires name plus social security number, signed release. No fee for information.

Degree information available by mail. Search requires name plus social security number, exact years of attendance, signed release. No fee for information.

Transcripts available by mail. Search requires name plus social security number, exact years of attendance, signed release. Fee is $1.00.

Community College of Denver, Registrar, PO Box 173363, Denver, CO 80217-3363, 303-556-2430 (FAX: 303-446-2461). Hours: N/A. Records go back to 1969. Degrees granted: Associate. Adverse incident record source: Auraria Public Safety, 303-556-3271.

Attendance and degree information available by phone, FAX, mail. Search requires name plus social security number, signed release. Other helpful information: date of birth, approximate years of attendance. No fee for information.

Transcripts available by FAX, mail. Search requires name plus social security number, signed release. Other helpful information: date of birth, approximate years of attendance. Fee is $1.00. Expedited service available for $1.00.

Community College of Philadelphia, Registrar, 1700 Spring Garden St, Philadelphia, PA 19130-3991, 215-751-8261 (FAX: 215-751-8001). Hours: 9AM-4:45PM M-W, 9AM-3:45PM R. Records go back to 1964. Degrees granted: Associate.

Attendance information available by phone, FAX, mail. Search requires name plus signed release. Other helpful information: social security number, approximate years of attendance. No fee for information.

Degree information available by phone, FAX, mail. Search requires name plus social security number, signed release. Other helpful information: approximate years of attendance. No fee for information.

Transcripts available by mail. Search requires name plus social security number, signed release. Other helpful information: exact years of attendance. Fee is $2.00.

Community College of Rhode Island, Registrar, 400 East Ave, Warwick, RI 02886-1805, 401-825-2125. Hours: 8AM-5PM. Records go back to 1964. Alumni records are maintained here also. Call 401-825-2181. Degrees granted: Associate.

Attendance and degree information available by phone, mail. Search requires name plus social security number. No fee for information.

Transcripts available by mail. Search requires name plus social security number, signed release. Fee is $2.00.

Community College of Southern Nevada, Registrar, 3200 E Cheyenne Ave, North Las Vegas, NV 89030, 702-651-4060 (FAX: 702-643-1474). Hours: 8AM-6PM. Degrees granted: Associate.

Attendance information available by phone, mail. Search requires name plus social security number. No fee for information.

Degree information available by written request only. Search requires name plus social security number, signed release. No fee for information.

Transcripts available by written request only. Search requires name plus social security number, signed release. Fee is $2.00. Major credit cards accepted for payment.

Community College of Vermont, Registrar, Waterbury, VT 05676, 802-241-3535 (FAX: 802-241-3526). Hours: 8:30PM-4:30PM. Records go back to 1975. Degrees granted: Associate.

Attendance information available by phone, mail. Search requires name plus social security number, date of birth. No fee for information.

Degree information available by mail. Search requires name plus social security number, date of birth. No fee for information.

Transcripts available by written request only. Search requires name plus signed release. Fee is $5.00. Include a stamped envelope.

Community College of the Air Force, 882 TRSS/TSOR, 939 Missile Rd #1003, Sheppard AFB, TX 76311-2260, 817-676-6640 (FAX: 817-676-4025). Hours: 7AM-4PM. Records go back 30 years. Certification: Certificate of Training.

Attendance information available by mail. Search requires name plus social security number, exact years of attendance, signed release. No fee for information.

School will not confirm degree information. Search requires name only. No fee for information.

Transcripts available by mail. Search requires name plus social security number, exact years of attendance, signed release. No fee for transcripts.

Name at graduation date and graduation date also helpful.

Community College of the Air Force/RRR, Registrar, Simler Hall Ste 128, 130 W Maxwell Blvd, Maxwell Air Force Base, AL 36112-6613, 205-953-6436. Hours: 7AM-5PM. Records go back to 1976. Degrees granted: Associate. Adverse incident record source: Administrative Office, 205-953-6436.

Attendance and degree information available by phone, mail. Search requires name plus social security number, date of birth. No fee for information.

Transcripts available by mail. Search requires name plus social security number, date of birth, exact years of attendance, signed release. No fee for transcripts.

Community Hospital of Roanoke Valley College of Health Sciences, Registrar, PO Box 13186, Roanoke, VA 24016, 703-985-8206. Hours: 8AM-5PM. Records go back to 1982. Alumni records are maintained here also. Call 703-985-9031. Degrees granted: Associate.

Attendance and degree information available by phone, mail. Search requires name plus social security number, exact years of attendance. No fee for information.

Transcripts available by mail. Search requires name plus social security number, exact years of attendance, signed release. Fee is $2.00.

Compton Community College, Registrar, 1111 E Artesia Blvd, Compton, CA 90221, 310-637-2660 X2043 (FAX: 310-639-8260). Hours: 8AM-7PM M-W; 8AM-4:30PM Th-F. Records go back to 1929. Degrees granted: Associate. Adverse incident record source: Campus Police, 310-637-2660 X2790.

Attendance and degree information available by phone, FAX, mail. Search requires name plus date of birth. Other helpful information: social security number, approximate years of attendance. No fee for information.

Transcripts available by mail. Search requires name plus date of birth, signed release. Other helpful information: approximate years of attendance. Fee is $2.00. Expedited service available for $4.00.

Computer Tech, Registrar, 107 Sixth St, Pittsburgh, PA 15222, 412-391-4197 (FAX: 412-391-4224). Hours: 8AM-5PM. Records go back to 1967. Degrees granted: Associate.

Attendance and degree information available by phone, FAX, mail. Search requires name plus social security number, signed release. Other helpful information: date of birth, approximate years of attendance. Fee is $5.00.

Transcripts available by mail. Search requires name plus social security number, signed release. Other helpful information: date of birth, approximate years of attendance. Fee is $5.00.

Computer Tech, (Branch), Registrar, Country Club Rd Ext, Fairmont, WV 26554, 304-363-5100 (FAX: 304-366-9948). Hours: 8:30AM-6PM. Records go back to 1988. Degrees granted: Associate. Adverse incident record source: Registrar, 304-363-5100.

Attendance information available by phone, FAX, mail. Search requires name plus social security number. No fee for information.

Degree information available by phone, FAX, mail. Search requires name plus social security number, exact years of attendance. No fee for information.

Transcripts available by FAX, mail. Search requires name plus social security number, exact years of attendance, signed release. Fee is $5.00.

Conception Seminary College, Registrar, PO Box 502, Conception, MO 64433, 816-944-2218 (FAX: 816-944-2800). Hours: 8:30AM-3:30PM. Records go back 110 years. Alumni records are maintained here also. Call 816-944-2218. Degrees granted: Bachelors.

Attendance and degree information available by phone, FAX, mail. Search requires name plus signed release. No fee for information.

Transcripts available by FAX, mail. Search requires name plus signed release. Fee is $3.00.

Concord College, Registrar, PO Box 1000, Athens, WV 24712, 304-384-5237. Degrees granted: Bachelors.

Attendance and degree information available by phone, mail. Search requires name plus social security number, exact years of attendance. No fee for information.

Transcripts available by mail. Search requires name plus social security number, exact years of attendance, signed release. Fee is $3.00.

Concordia College, Registrar, 4090 Geddes Rd, Ann Arbor, MI 48105, 313-995-7324 (FAX: 313-995-4610). Hours: 8AM-4:30PM. Records go back to 1963. Alumni records are maintained here at the same phone number. Degrees granted: Associate; Bachelors. Certification: Teacher.

Attendance information available by phone, FAX, mail. Search requires name only. Other helpful information: social security number, date of birth, approximate years of attendance. No fee for information.

Degree information available by phone, FAX, mail. Search requires name only. Other helpful information: social security number, date of birth, approximate years of attendance. No fee for information.

Transcripts available by mail. Search requires name plus approximate years of attendance, signed release. Other helpful information: social security number, date of birth, exact years of attendance. No fee for transcripts.

Concordia College, Registrar, 171 White Plains Rd, Bronxville, NY 10708-1998, 914-337-9300 X2102 (FAX: 914-395-4500). Hours: 9AM-5PM. Records go back to 1881. Alumni records are maintained here also. Call 914-337-9300 X2167. Degrees granted: Associate; Masters.

Attendance and degree information available by phone, FAX, mail. Search requires name only. Other helpful information: social security number, date of birth, approximate years of attendance. No fee for information.

Transcripts available by FAX, mail. Search requires name plus date of birth, approximate years of attendance, signed release. Other helpful information: social security number, exact years of attendance. Fee is $2.00.

Concordia College, Registrar, 901 S 8th St, Moorhead, MN 56562, 218-299-3250. Hours: 8AM-5PM. Degrees granted: Bachelors. Adverse incident record source: Student Affairs, 218-299-3455.

Attendance and degree information available by phone, FAX, mail. Search requires name plus social security number. Other helpful information: date of birth, approximate years of attendance. No fee for information.

Transcripts available by written request only. Search requires name plus signed release. Other helpful information: social security number, date of birth, approximate years of attendance. Fee is $1.00. Expedited service available for $7.00.

Concordia College, Registrar, 2811 NE Holman St, Portland, OR 97211, 503-280-8510 (FAX: 503-280-8531). Hours: 8AM-6PM M-Th, 8AM-4:30PM F. Records go back to 1905. Alumni records are maintained here also. Call 503-225-4267. Degrees granted: Associate; Bachelors.

Attendance and degree information available by FAX, mail. Search requires name plus social security number, approximate years of attendance, signed release. No fee for information.

Transcripts available by FAX, mail. Search requires name plus social security number, approximate years of attendance, signed release. Fee is $5.00.

Concordia College, Registrar, 1804 Green St, PO Box 1329, Selma, AL 36701, 334-874-5700 (FAX: 334-874-5755). Hours: 8AM-4PM. Degrees granted: Associate; Bachelors. Adverse incident record source: Dean's Office, 334-874-5730.

Attendance information available by phone, FAX, mail. Search requires name only. No fee for information.

School will not confirm degree information. Search requires name only. No fee for information.

Transcripts available by mail. Search requires name plus approximate years of attendance, signed release. Other helpful information: social security number, date of birth. Fee is $5.00.

Concordia College, Registrar, 800 N Columbia Ave, Seward, NE 68434, 402-643-7230 (FAX: 402-643-4073). Hours: 8AM-5PM. Records go back to 1894. Degrees granted: Bachelors;

Masters. Certification: Lutheran Teacher Diploma. Adverse incident record source: Student Services, 402-643-7231.

Attendance and degree information available by phone, FAX, mail. Search requires name only. Other helpful information: social security number, approximate years of attendance. No fee for information.

Transcripts available by FAX, mail. Search requires name plus signed release. Other helpful information: social security number, approximate years of attendance. Fee is $3.00. Expedited service available for $16.00.

Major credit cards accepted for payment.

Concordia College, Registrar, 275 N Syndicate St, St Paul, MN 55104, 612-641-8223 (FAX: 612-659-0207). Hours: 8AM-4:30PM. Records go back 102 years. Alumni records are maintained here at the same phone number. Degrees granted: Associate; Bachelors; Masters.

Attendance and degree information available by phone, FAX, mail. Search requires name only. Other helpful information: social security number, date of birth, approximate years of attendance. No fee for information.

Transcripts available by phone, FAX, mail. Search requires name only. Other helpful information: social security number, date of birth, approximate years of attendance. Fee is $3.00. Expedited service available for $5.00.

Major credit cards accepted for payment.

Concordia Lutheran College, Registrar, 3400 I H 35 N, Austin, TX 78705, 512-452-7661 (FAX: 512-459-8517). Hours: 8AM-6PM M-Th; 8AM-5PM F. Records go back to 1926. Degrees granted: Associate; Bachelors. Adverse incident record source: Dean of Students, 512-452-7661.

Attendance and degree information available by phone, FAX, mail. Search requires name only. Other helpful information: social security number, date of birth, approximate years of attendance. No fee for information.

Transcripts available by written request only. Search requires name plus social security number, signed release. Other helpful information: date of birth, approximate years of attendance. Fee is $5.00. Expedited service available for $25.00.

Major credit cards accepted for payment.

Concordia Seminary, Registrar, 801 De Mun Ave, St Louis, MO 63105, 314-721-5934 (FAX: 314-721-5902). Hours: 8AM-Noon, 1-4:30PM. Records go back to 1926. Degrees granted: Masters; Doctorate.

Attendance and degree information available by phone, FAX, mail. Search requires name only. Other helpful information: approximate years of attendance. No fee for information.

Transcripts available by FAX, mail. Search requires name plus signed release. Other helpful information: social security number, approximate years of attendance. Fee is $3.00. Expedited service available for $3.00.

Concordia Theological Seminary, Registrar, 6600 N Clinton St, Fort Wayne, IN 46825-4996, 219-481-2153 (FAX: 219-481-2100). Hours: 8AM-4:30PM. Records go back to 1900. Alumni records are maintained here also. Call 219-481-2150. Degrees granted: Masters; Doctorate; First Professional.

Attendance and degree information available by phone, FAX, mail. Search requires name only. Other helpful information: social security number, date of birth, approximate years of attendance. No fee for information.

Transcripts available by FAX, mail. Search requires name plus signed release. Other helpful information: social security number, date of birth, approximate years of attendance. Fee is $4.00.

Concordia University, Registrar, 1530 Concordia W, Irvine, CA 92715-3299, 714-854-8002 (FAX: 714-854-6854). Hours: 8AM-4:30PM. Degrees granted: Bachelors; Masters. Certification: Lutheran Teaching; Director of Christian.

Attendance information available by phone, FAX, mail. Search requires name plus social security number. Other helpful information: date of birth, approximate years of attendance. No fee for information.

Degree information available by phone, FAX, mail. Search requires name plus social security number. Other helpful information: approximate years of attendance. No fee for information.

Transcripts available by mail. Search requires name plus social security number, signed release. Other helpful information: date of birth, approximate years of attendance. Fee is $5.00.

Mail requests with payment.

Concordia University, Registrar, 7400 Augusta St, River Forest, IL 60305, 708-383-7100 (FAX: 708-209-3176). Hours: 8AM-4:30PM. Records go back to 1913. Degrees granted: Bachelors; Masters. Certification: CAS.

Attendance and degree information available by phone, FAX, mail. Search requires name plus social security number, date of birth. Other helpful information: approximate years of attendance. No fee for information.

Transcripts available by written request only. Search requires name plus social security number, date of birth, signed release. Other helpful information: approximate years of attendance. Fee is $5.00. Expedite fee is $15.00; $18.00 by FAX; and $30.00 for overnight express.

Major credit cards accepted for payment.

Concordia University Wisconsin, Registrar, 12800 N Lake Shore Dr, Mequon, WI 53092, 414-243-4345 (FAX: 414-243-4351). Hours: 8AM-4:30PM. Records go back to 1800s. Degrees granted: Associate; Bachelors; Masters.

Attendance and degree information available by phone, FAX, mail. Search requires name only. Other helpful information: social security number, date of birth, approximate years of attendance. No fee for information.

Transcripts available by written request only. Search requires name plus signed release. Other helpful information: social security number, date of birth, approximate years of attendance. Fee is $3.00.

Connecticut College, Registrar, New London, CT 06320, 203-439-2068 (FAX: 203-439-5421). Hours: 8:30AM-5PM. Records go back to 1920. Alumni records are maintained here also. Call 203-439-2300. Degrees granted: Bachelors.

Attendance and degree information available by phone, FAX, mail. Search requires name plus exact years of attendance. No fee for information.

Transcripts available by phone, FAX, mail. Search requires name plus exact years of attendance, signed release. No fee for transcripts.

Connors State College, Registrar, Rte 1 Box 1000, Warner, OK 74469, 918-463-6241. Hours: 8AM-4:30PM. Records go back to 1927. Degrees granted: Associate. Adverse incident record source: Ed Hardeman, 918-463-6217.

Attendance and degree information available by phone, FAX, mail. Search requires name only. Other helpful information: social security number, date of birth, approximate years of attendance. No fee for information.

Transcripts available by written request only. Search requires name plus social security number, signed release. Other helpful information: date of birth, approximate years of attendance. Fee is $2.00.

Major credit cards accepted for payment.

Conservatory of Music of Puerto Rico, Registrar, PO Box 41227, Minillas Station, Santurce, PR 00940, 809-751-0160 (FAX: 809-767-4331). Hours: 8AM-4:30PM. Records go back to 1959. Degrees granted: Bachelors.

Attendance information available by phone, mail. Search requires name only. Other helpful information: social security number, approximate years of attendance. No fee for information.

Degree information available by mail. Search requires name only. Other helpful information: social security number, approximate years of attendance. No fee for information.

Transcripts available by FAX, mail. Search requires name plus signed release. Other helpful information: social security number, approximate years of attendance. Fee is $2.00. Expedited service available for $2.00.

Consolidated School of Business, Registrar, Stes I and J, 1817 Olde Homestead Lane, Lancaster, PA 17601, 717-394-6211 (FAX: 717-394-6213). Hours: 8AM-5PM. Records go back to 1986. Degrees granted: Associate.

Attendance and degree information available by FAX, mail. Search requires name plus social security number, exact years of attendance, signed release. No fee for information.

Transcripts available by FAX, mail. Search requires name plus social security number, exact years of attendance, signed release. No fee for transcripts.

Consolidated School of Business, Registrar, 1605 Clugston Rd, York, PA 17404, 717-764-9550 (FAX: 717-764-9469). Hours: 9AM-5:30PM. Records go back to 1976. Degrees granted: Associate.

Attendance and degree information available by FAX, mail. Search requires name plus social security number, exact years of attendance. No fee for information.

Transcripts available by mail. Search requires name plus social security number, exact years of attendance, signed release. Fee is $2.00.

Contra Costa College, Registrar, 2600 Mission Bell Dr, San Pablo, CA 94806, 510-235-7800 X382 (FAX: 510-236-6768). Hours: 8AM-4:30PM M-F; 5:30-8:30PM M-Th. Records go back to 1950. Degrees granted: Associate.

Attendance information available by phone, mail. Search requires name plus social security number, exact years of attendance. Other helpful information: approximate years of attendance. No fee for information.

Degree information available by phone, mail. Search requires name plus social security number. Other helpful information: approximate years of attendance. No fee for information.

Transcripts available by mail. Search requires name plus social security number, signed release. Other helpful information: date of birth, approximate years of attendance. Fee is $3.00. Expedited service available for $3.00.

Transcript request form in A&R office. Major credit cards accepted for payment.

Converse College, Registrar, 580 E Main St, Spartanburg, SC 29302-0006, 803-596-9094. Hours: 8:30AM-5PM. Records go back to 1800s. Degrees granted: Bachelors; Masters; EDS.

Attendance and degree information available by FAX, mail. Search requires name plus social security number, date of birth. Other helpful information: approximate years of attendance. No fee for information.

Transcripts available by mail. Search requires name plus social security number, date of birth, signed release. Other helpful information: approximate years of attendance. Fee is $5.00.

Major credit cards accepted for payment.

Conway School of Landscape Design, Registrar, Delabarre Ave, Conway, MA 01341, 413-369-4044. Hours: 8AM-5PM. Records go back to 1972. Degrees granted: Bachelors; Masters.

Attendance and degree information available by phone, mail. Search requires name plus exact years of attendance. No fee for information.

Transcripts available by mail. Search requires name plus social security number, exact years of attendance, signed release. Fee is $3.00.

Major credit cards accepted for payment.

Cooper Academy of Court Reporting, Registrar, 2247 Palm Beach Lakes Blvd Ste 110, West Palm Beach, FL 33401, 407-640-6999 (FAX: 407-686-8778). Hours: 8:30AM-5:30PM. Records go back 7 years.

Attendance and degree information available by phone, FAX, mail. Search requires name plus social security number. Other helpful information: approximate years of attendance. No fee for information.

Transcripts available by mail. Search requires name plus social security number, signed release. Other helpful information: approximate years of attendance. Fee is $2.00.

Cooper Union for the Advancement of Science and Art, Registrar, 30 Cooper Square, New York, NY 10003, 212-353-4124 (FAX: 212-353-4343). Hours: 9AM-4:30PM. Records go back to 1859. Degrees granted: Bachelors; Masters.

Attendance information available by phone, FAX, mail. Search requires name plus approximate years of attendance. Other helpful information: date of birth. No fee for information.

Degree information available by phone, FAX, mail. Search requires name plus approximate years of attendance. Other helpful information: date of birth, exact years of attendance. No fee for information.

Transcripts available by FAX, mail. Search requires name plus date of birth, signed release. Other helpful information: approximate years of attendance. No fee for transcripts.

Copiah-Lincoln Community College, Registrar, PO Box 457, Wesson, MS 39191, 601-643-8307. Hours: 8AM-4:30PM. Records go back to 1928.

Attendance and degree information available by phone, FAX, mail. Search requires name plus social security number, date of birth, approximate years of attendance, signed release. No fee for information.

Transcripts available by mail. Search requires name plus social security number, date of birth, approximate years of attendance, signed release. Fee is $2.00. Expedited service available for $0.

Coppin State College, Registrar, 500 W North Ave, Baltimore, MD 21216, 410-383-5550 (FAX: 410-225-7262). Hours:

8AM-5PM. Records go back to 1960s. Alumni records are maintained here also. Call 410-383-5960. Degrees granted: Bachelors; Masters.

Attendance information available by phone, FAX, mail. Search requires name plus social security number, signed release. Other helpful information: date of birth, approximate years of attendance. No fee for information.

Degree information available by FAX, mail. Search requires name plus social security number, signed release. Other helpful information: date of birth, approximate years of attendance. No fee for information.

Transcripts available by FAX, mail. Search requires name plus social security number, signed release. Other helpful information: date of birth, approximate years of attendance. No fee for transcripts. Expedited service available for $5.00.

Corcoran School of Art, Registrar, 500 17th St NW, Washington, DC 20006-4899, 202-638-0561 (FAX: 202-628-3186). Hours: 9AM-5PM. Records go back to 1965. Degrees granted: Bachelors.

Attendance information available by phone, FAX, mail. Search requires name plus approximate years of attendance, signed release. Other helpful information: social security number, date of birth, exact years of attendance. No fee for information.

Degree information available by phone, FAX, mail. Search requires name plus approximate years of attendance. Other helpful information: social security number, date of birth, exact years of attendance. No fee for information.

Transcripts available by phone, mail. Search requires name plus approximate years of attendance, signed release. Other helpful information: social security number, date of birth, exact years of attendance. Fee is $5.00.

Will confirm attendance only with "yes" or "no." 5.00 first copy, 2.00 subsequent copies. Major credit cards accepted for payment.

Cornell College, Registrar, 600 First St W, Mount Vernon, IA 52314, 319-895-4372 (FAX: 319-895-4492). Hours: 8AM-4:30PM. Records go back to 1853. Alumni records are maintained here also. Call 319-895-4204. Degrees granted: Bachelors.

Attendance and degree information available by phone, mail. Search requires name plus exact years of attendance. No fee for information.

Transcripts available by mail. Search requires name plus exact years of attendance, signed release. Fee is $2.00.

Cornell University, Registrar, 222 Day Hall, Ithaca, NY 14853, 607-255-4232 (FAX: 607-255-6262). Hours: 8AM-4:30PM; Open 9:30AM W. Records go back to 1885. Degrees granted: Bachelors; Masters; Doctorate. Special programs- M.D. at Cornell Univ. Medical College, 212-746-1056.

Attendance and degree information available by phone, FAX, mail. Search requires name only. Other helpful information: social security number, exact years of attendance. No fee for information.

Transcripts available by mail. Search requires name plus signed release. Other helpful information: social security number, date of birth, exact years of attendance. Fee is $2.00. Expedite service at cost of FedEx.

Cornerstone College and Grand Rapids Baptist College and Seminary, Registrar, 1001 E Beltline Ave NE, Grand Rapids, MI 49505, 616-285-9431. Hours: 8AM-4PM. Degrees granted: Associate; Bachelors; Masters; Doctorate.

Attendance and degree information available by phone, mail. Search requires name only. Other helpful information: social security number. No fee for information.

Transcripts available by mail. Search requires name only. Other helpful information: social security number. Fee is $3.00. Expedited service available for $6.00.

Corning Community College, Registrar, 1 Academic Dr, Corning, NY 14830-3297, 607-962-9230 (FAX: 607-962-9456). Hours: 8AM-5PM M-Th; 8AM-4PM F. Records go back to 1956. Alumni records are maintained here also. Call 607-962-9320. Degrees granted: Associate. Adverse incident record source: Dean of Students, 607-962-9264.

Attendance and degree information available by phone, FAX, mail. Search requires name plus social security number, approximate years of attendance, signed release. No fee for information.

Transcripts available by mail. Search requires name plus social security number, approximate years of attendance, signed release. Fee is $2.00.

Cornish College of the Arts, Registrar, 710 E Roy St, Seattle, WA 98102, 206-323-1400 (FAX: 206-720-1011). Hours: 9AM-4PM. Degrees granted: Bachelors. Certification: Acting.

Attendance and degree information available by phone, FAX, mail. Search requires name only. No fee for information.

Transcripts available by FAX, mail. Search requires name plus signed release. Other helpful information: social security number, date of birth, approximate years of attendance. Official transcript $5.00; unofficial $1.00.

Major credit cards accepted for payment.

Cosumnes River College, Admissions & Records, 8401 Center Pkwy, Sacramento, CA 95823, 916-688-7410 (FAX: 916-688-7467). Hours: 8AM-8PM M-Th; 8AM-5PM F. Records go back to 1970. Degrees granted: Associate.

Attendance information available by mail. Search requires name plus social security number, signed release. Other helpful information: date of birth. No fee for information.

Degree information available by mail. Search requires name plus signed release. No fee for information.

Transcripts available by mail. Search requires name plus social security number, date of birth, signed release. Fee is $2.00.

Cottey College, Registrar, 1000 W Austin St, Nevada, MO 64772, 417-667-8181 (FAX: 417-667-8103). Hours: 8AM-Noon, 1-5PM. Degrees granted: Associate.

Attendance and degree information available by phone, FAX, mail. Search requires name only. Other helpful information: social security number, date of birth, approximate years of attendance. No fee for information.

Transcripts available by FAX, mail. Search requires name plus signed release. Other helpful information: social security number, date of birth, approximate years of attendance. Fee is $2.00. Expedited service available for $5.00.

Any name changes helpful.

County College of Morris, Registrar, Rte 10 and Center Grove Rd, Randolph, NJ 07869, 201-328-5197. Hours: 8:30AM-4:30PM. Records go back to 1965. Degrees granted: Associate.

Attendance and degree information available by phone, FAX, mail. Search requires name plus social security number. No fee for information.

Transcripts available by mail. Search requires name plus social security number, signed release. Fee is $2.00.

Covenant College, Registrar, Scenic Hwy, Lookout Mountain, GA 30750, 706-820-1560 X1134 (FAX: 706-820-2165). Hours: 8AM-4:30PM. Records go back to 1955. Alumni records are maintained here also. Call 706-820-1560. Degrees granted: Associate; Bachelors; Masters. Adverse incident record source: Student Development, 706-820-1560.

Attendance and degree information available by phone, FAX, mail. Search requires name plus social security number. No fee for information.

Transcripts available by mail. Search requires name plus social security number, exact years of attendance, signed release. First transcript is free. Additional ones are $2.00 each.

Covenant Theological Seminary, Registrar, 12330 Conway Rd, St Louis, MO 63141, 314-434-4044 (FAX: 314-434-4819). Hours: 8AM-4:30PM. Records go back to 1956. Alumni records are maintained here at the same phone number. Degrees granted: Masters; Doctorate. Special programs- Extension Office, 314-434-4044.

Attendance and degree information available by phone, FAX, mail. Search requires name only. Other helpful information: social security number, date of birth, approximate years of attendance. No fee for information.

Transcripts available by mail. Search requires name plus signed release. Other helpful information: social security number, date of birth, approximate years of attendance. Fee is $3.00. Expedite fee is $3.00 plus shipping fees.

FAX request only if followed by mail request. Degree, maiden name if changed helpful.

Cowley County Community College, Registrar, 125 S Second St, PO Box 1147, Arkansas City, KS 67005, 316-442-0430 (FAX: 316-441-5350). Hours: 8AM-4:30PM. Records go back to 1922.

Attendance and degree information available by FAX, mail. Search requires name plus social security number, date of birth, signed release. Other helpful information: approximate years of attendance. No fee for information.

Transcripts available by FAX, mail. Search requires name plus social security number, date of birth, signed release. Other helpful information: approximate years of attendance. No fee for transcripts.

Crafton Hills College, Registrar, 11711 Sand Canyon Rd, Yucaipa, CA 92399, 909-389-3367 (FAX: 909-389-9141). Hours: 10AM-8AM M-Th; 10AM-4:30PM F. Records go back to 1972. Degrees granted: Associate.

Attendance and degree information available by phone, FAX, mail. Search requires name only. Other helpful information: social security number, date of birth, approximate years of attendance. No fee for information.

Transcripts available by FAX, mail. Search requires name plus signed release. Other helpful information: social security number, date of birth, approximate years of attendance. Fee is $3.00. Expedited service available for $5.00.

Major credit cards accepted for payment.

Cranbrook Academy of Art, Registrar, 1221 Woodward Ave, Bloomfield Hills, MI 48303, 810-645-3303 (FAX: 810-646-0046). Hours: 8:30AM-5PM. Records go back to 1932. Degrees granted: Masters.

Attendance and degree information available by phone, FAX, mail. Search requires name plus signed release. No fee for information.

Transcripts available by FAX, mail. Search requires name plus signed release. Fee is $2.00.

Creighton University, Registrar, 2500 California Plaza, Omaha, NE 68178, 402-280-2701 (FAX: 402-280-2527). Hours: 8:30AM-4:30PM. Records go back to 1878. Degrees granted: Associate; Bachelors; Masters; Doctorate.

Attendance and degree information available by FAX, mail. Search requires name only. Other helpful information: social security number, date of birth, approximate years of attendance. No fee for information.

Transcripts available by FAX, mail. Search requires name plus social security number, signed release. Other helpful information: date of birth, approximate years of attendance. $5.00 for first transcript; $1.00 each additional on same order.

Craven Community College, Registrar, 800 College Ct, New Bern, NC 28562, 919-638-7226 (FAX: 919-638-4232). Hours: 8AM-10PM M-Th, 8AM-5PM F. Records go back to 1968. Alumni records are maintained here also. Call 919-638-4131. Degrees granted: Associate.

Attendance and degree information available by phone, FAX, mail. Search requires name plus social security number, signed release. Other helpful information: date of birth, approximate years of attendance. No fee for information.

Transcripts available by FAX, mail. Search requires name plus social security number, signed release. Other helpful information: date of birth, approximate years of attendance. Fee is $1.00.

Crichton College, Registrar, PO Box 757830, Memphis, TN 38157-7830, 901-367-9800 (FAX: 901-367-3866). Hours: 8AM-5PM. Records go back to 1945. Degrees granted: Bachelors.

Attendance and degree information available by phone, FAX, mail. Search requires name plus social security number, exact years of attendance. No fee for information.

Transcripts available by FAX, mail. Search requires name plus social security number, exact years of attendance. Fee is $2.00.

Criswell College, Enrollment Services, 4010 Gaston Ave, Dallas, TX 75246, 214-821-5433 (FAX: 214-818-1310). Hours: 8AM-4:30PM. Records go back to 1970. Alumni records are maintained here at the same phone number. Degrees granted: Associate; Bachelors; Masters.

Attendance information available by FAX, mail. Search requires name plus social security number. Other helpful information: date of birth, approximate years of attendance. No fee for information.

Degree information available by FAX, mail. Search requires name plus social security number, date of birth, approximate years of attendance, signed release. No fee for information.

Transcripts available by FAX, mail. Search requires name plus social security number, date of birth, approximate years of attendance, signed release. Fee is $5.00.

Crowder College, Registrar, 6601 Laclede, Neosho, MO 64850, 417-451-3223 (FAX: 417-451-4280). Hours: 7:30AM-4:30PM. Records go back 30 years. Degrees granted: Associate.

Attendance and degree information available by phone, FAX, mail. Search requires name plus social security number, date of birth, signed release. Other helpful information: approximate years of attendance. Fee is $1.00.

Transcripts available by mail. Search requires name plus social security number, date of birth, signed release. Other helpful information: approximate years of attendance. Fee is $1.00.

Crown College, Registrar, 6425 County Rd 30, St Bonifacius, MN 55375, 612-446-4172 (FAX: 612-446-4149). Hours: 8AM-4:30PM. Degrees granted: Associate; Bachelors.

Attendance and degree information available by phone, FAX, mail. Search requires name only. No fee for information.

Transcripts available by phone, FAX, mail. Search requires name plus signed release. Other helpful information: social security number, approximate years of attendance. No fee for transcripts. Expedited service available for $10.00.

Cuesta College, Records Office Rm 3110, Hwy 1, San Luis Obispo, CA 93403, 805-546-3139 (FAX: 805-546-3904). Hours: 9AM-4PM M-Th; 9AM-3PM F. Records go back to 1965. Adverse incident record source: Dean of Students, 805-546-3130.

Attendance information available by phone, FAX, mail. Search requires name only. Other helpful information: social security number, approximate years of attendance. No fee for information.

Degree information available by phone, FAX, mail. Search requires name only. Other helpful information: social security number, exact years of attendance. No fee for information.

Transcripts available by FAX, mail. Search requires name plus signed release. Other helpful information: social security number, exact years of attendance. No fee for transcripts.

Major credit cards accepted for payment.

Culver-Stockton College, Registrar, Canton, MO 63435, 314-288-5221 (FAX: 314-288-3984). Hours: 8AM-Noon, 1-5PM. Records go back to 1853. Alumni records are maintained here at the same phone number. Degrees granted: Bachelors.

Attendance and degree information available by phone, FAX, mail. Search requires name plus social security number, date of birth. Other helpful information: approximate years of attendance. No fee for information.

Transcripts available by mail. Search requires name plus social security number, date of birth, signed release. Other helpful information: approximate years of attendance. Fee is $2.00. Add postage to expedite. Include a stamped envelope.

Cumberland College, Registrar, 6191 College Station, Williamsburg, KY 40769, 606-539-4316 (FAX: 606-539-4490). Hours: 8:30AM-5PM. Records go back to founding date. Transcripts permanent. Other records five years from last enrollment. Degrees granted: Bachelors; Masters.

Attendance and degree information available by phone, FAX, mail. Search requires name plus social security number, date of birth, signed release. Other helpful information: approximate years of attendance. No fee for information. Expedited service available for $10.00.

Transcripts available by mail. Search requires name plus social security number, date of birth, signed release. Other helpful information: approximate years of attendance. Fee is $3.00. Expedited service available for $10.00.

Cumberland County College, Registrar, College Dr, PO Box 517, Vineland, NJ 08360, 609-691-8600. Hours: 8AM-5:30PM. Records back to founding. Degrees granted: Associate.

Attendance and degree information available by phone, mail. Search requires name plus approximate years of attendance. Other helpful information: social security number, exact years of attendance. No fee for information.

Transcripts available by mail. Search requires name plus approximate years of attendance, signed release. Other helpful information: social security number, exact years of attendance. No fee for transcripts.

Cumberland University, Registrar, S Greenwood St, Lebanon, TN 37087-3554, 615-444-2562 (FAX: 615-444-2569). Hours: 8AM-4:30PM. Records go back to 1900. Alumni records are maintained here also. Call 615-444-2562 X238. Degrees granted: Associate; Bachelors; Masters.

Attendance and degree information available by phone, FAX, mail. Search requires name plus social security number. Other helpful information: approximate years of attendance. No fee for information.

Transcripts available by mail. Search requires name plus social security number, signed release. Other helpful information: date of birth, approximate years of attendance. Fee is $3.00.

Curry College, Registrar, Milton, MA 02186, 617-333-2348 (FAX: 617-333-6860). Hours: 8:30AM-4:30PM. Records go back to 1920. Alumni records are maintained here also. Call 617-333-2212. Degrees granted: Bachelors; Masters.

Attendance and degree information available by phone, FAX, mail. Search requires name plus social security number, signed release. No fee for information.

Transcripts available by mail. Search requires name plus social security number, signed release. First transcript free. Additional ones are $2.00 each.

Curtis Institute of Music, Registrar, 1726 Locust St, Philadelphia, PA 19103, 215-893-5252 (FAX: 215-893-9065). Hours: 9AM-5PM. Records go back to 1926. Alumni records are maintained here at the same phone number. Degrees granted: Bachelors; Masters. Adverse incident record source: Business Office, 215-893-5252.

Attendance information available by phone, FAX, mail. Search requires name plus social security number. No fee.

Degree information available by phone, FAX, mail. Search requires name plus social security number, exact years of attendance. No fee for information.

Transcripts available by mail. Search requires name plus social security number, signed release. Other helpful information: exact years of attendance. Fee is $5.00.

Cuyahoga Community College, **(Eastern)**, Registrar, 4250 Richmond Rd, Highland Hills, OH 44122, 216-987-2021 (FAX: 216-987-2214). Hours: 8:30AM-8PM M-Th; 8:30AM-5PM F; 11AM-1PM S. Records back to 1963. Degrees: Associate.

Attendance and degree information available by phone, mail. Search requires name plus date of birth. Other helpful information: social security number. No fee for information. Include a stamped envelope.

Transcripts available by mail. Search requires name plus date of birth, signed release. Other helpful information: social security number, approximate years of attendance. Fee is $1.00.

Cuyahoga Community College, **(Metropolitan)**, Registrar, 2900 Community College Ave, Cleveland, OH 44115, 216-987-4030 (FAX: 216-696-2567). Hours: 8:30AM-8PM. Records go back to 1969. Alumni Records Office: Cuyahoga Community College, 700 Carnegie Ave, Cleveland, OH 44115. Degrees granted: Associate. Adverse incident record source: Health Services, 216-987-4650.

Attendance and degree information available by phone, FAX, mail. Search requires name plus social security number, approximate years of attendance, signed notarized release. No fee.

Transcripts available by mail. Search requires name plus social security number, years of attendance, signed release. Fee is $1.00.

Cuyahoga Community College, **(Western)**, Admissions & Records, 11000 W Pleasant Valley Rd, Parma, OH 44130, 216-987-5150 (FAX: 216-987-5071). Hours: 8AM-8:30PM M-Th; 8AM-5PM F. Degrees granted: Associate.

Attendance and degree information available by phone, FAX, mail. Search requires name plus social security number, signed release. Other helpful information: date of birth, approximate years of attendance. No fee for information.

Transcripts available by mail. Search requires name plus social security number, signed release. Other helpful information: date of birth, approximate years of attendance. Fee is $1.00.

Cuyamaca College, Registrar, 2950 Jamacha Rd, El Cajon, CA 92019, 619-670-1980 (FAX: 619-670-7204). Hours: 8AM-7PM M-Th; 8AM-2PM F; 9AM-1PM S. Records go back to 1978. Alumni records are maintained here also. Call 619-670-1980. Degrees granted: Associate.

Attendance and degree information available by mail. Search requires name plus social security number, date of birth, signed release. Other helpful information: approximate years of attendance. Fee is $3.00. Expedited service available for $5.00.

Transcripts available by mail. Search requires name plus social security number, date of birth, signed release. Other helpful information: approximate years of attendance. Fee is $3.00. Expedited service available for $5.00.

Cypress College, Registrar, 9200 Valley View St, Cypress, CA 90630, 714-826-2220. Hours: 9AM-7PM M-Th. Records go back to 1966. Degrees granted: Associate.

Attendance and degree information available by phone, mail. Search requires name plus date of birth. Other helpful information: social security number, approximate years of attendance. Fee is $3.00. Expedited service available for $10.00.

Transcripts available by written request only. Search requires name plus signed release. Other helpful information: social security number, date of birth, approximate years of attendance. Fee is $3.00. Expedited service available for $10.00.

D

D'Youville College, Registrar, 320 Porter Ave, Buffalo, NY 14201, 716-881-7626 (FAX: 716-881-7740). Hours: 8:30AM-4:30PM. Records go back to 1908. Alumni Records Office: 631 Niagara St, Buffalo, NY 14201. Degrees granted: Bachelors; Masters.

Attendance and degree information available by phone, FAX, mail. Search requires name plus social security number, approximate years of attendance. Other helpful information: date of birth, exact years of attendance. No fee for information.

Transcripts available by FAX, mail. Search requires name plus social security number, approximate years of attendance, signed release. Other helpful information: date of birth, exact years of attendance. Fee is $5.00.

Major credit cards accepted for payment.

D-Q University, Registrar, PO Box 409, Davis, CA 95617-0409, 916-758-0470 (FAX: 916-758-4891). Hours: 8AM-4:30PM. Records go back to 1971. Alumni records are maintained here at the same phone number. Degrees granted: Associate.

Attendance and degree information available by mail. Search requires name plus social security number, date of birth. No fee for information.

Transcripts available by mail. Search requires name plus social security number, date of birth, exact years of attendance, signed release. Fee is $3.00.

Dabney S. Lancaster Community College, Registrar, PO Box 1000, Clifton Forge, VA 24422-1000, 703-862-4246 (FAX: 703-862-2398). Hours: 8AM-5PM. Records go back to 1967. Degrees granted: Associate.

Attendance and degree information available by phone. Search requires name only. No fee for information.

Transcripts available by mail. Search requires name plus social security number, signed release. No fee for transcripts.

Daemen College, Registrar, 4380 Main St, Amherst, NY 14226-3592, 716-839-8214 (FAX: 716-839-8516). Hours: 8:30AM-4:30PM. Records go back to 1947. Degrees granted: Bachelors; Masters. Adverse incident record source: Student Affairs, 716-839-8332.

Attendance and degree information available by FAX, mail. Search requires name plus social security number. Other helpful information: date of birth, approximate years of attendance. No fee for information.

Transcripts available by mail. Search requires name plus social security number, signed release. Other helpful information: date of birth, approximate years of attendance. Fee is $3.00.

Expedite: Express fees must be received in advance.

Dakota County Technical College, Registrar, 1300 145th St E, Rosemount, MN 55068, 612-423-8301 (FAX: 612-423-7028). Hours: 7AM-4PM. Records go back to 1972. Degrees granted: Associate.

Attendance and degree information available by phone, FAX, mail. Search requires name plus social security number. Other helpful information: date of birth, approximate years of attendance. No fee for information.

Transcripts available by phone, FAX, mail. Search requires name plus social security number, signed release. Other helpful information: date of birth, approximate years of attendance. Fee is $3.00. Expedited service available for $3.00.

Include a self addressed stamped envelope with mail request. Major credit cards accepted for payment.

Dakota State University, Registrar, 820 N Washington St, Madison, SD 57042, 605-256-5145 (FAX: 605-256-5020). Hours: 8AM-5PM. Records go back to 1881. Alumni records are maintained here also. Call 605-256-5122. Degrees granted: Associate; Bachelors.

Attendance and degree information available by phone, FAX, mail. Search requires name only. Other helpful information: social security number, date of birth, approximate years of attendance. No fee for information.

Transcripts available by FAX, mail. Search requires name plus signed release. Other helpful information: social security number, date of birth, approximate years of attendance. Fee is $5.00.

Major credit cards accepted for payment.

Dakota Wesleyan University, Registrar, 1200 W University, Campus Box 903, Mitchell, SD 57301, 605-995-2642 (FAX: 605-995-2643). Hours: 8AM-Noon, 1-5PM. Records go back to 1896. Also have records from Methodist School of Nursing. Alumni records are maintained here at the same phone number. Alumni Records Office: PO Box 908, Mitchell, SD 57301. Degrees granted: Associate; Bachelors; Masters. Adverse incident record source: Campus Life.

Attendance and degree information available by phone, FAX, mail. Search requires name only. Other helpful information: social security number, date of birth, approximate years of attendance. No fee for information.

Transcripts available by FAX, mail. Search requires name plus signed release. Other helpful information: social security number, date of birth, approximate years of attendance. Fee is $2.00. Expedited service available for $0.3.50.

Major credit cards accepted for payment.

Dallas Baptist University, Registrar, 3000 Mountain Creek Pkwy, Dallas, TX 75211-9299, 214-333-5334 (FAX: 214-333-5142). Hours: 8AM-6PM M-T; 8AM-5PM W-F. Records go back to 1965. Alumni records are maintained here also. Call 214-333-5601. Degrees granted: Associate; Bachelors; Masters; Police Adacemy.

Attendance and degree information available by phone, FAX, mail. Search requires name only. Other helpful information: approximate years of attendance. No fee for information.

Transcripts available by FAX, mail. Search requires name plus social security number, signed release. Other helpful information: approximate years of attendance. Fee is $5.00. Expedited service available for $11.00.

Major credit cards accepted for payment.

Dallas Christian College, Registrar, 2700 Christian Pkwy, Dallas, TX 75234, 214-241-3371 (FAX: 214-241-8021). Hours: 8AM-5PM. Records go back to 1950. Degrees granted: Associate; Bachelors.

Attendance information available by phone, FAX, mail. Search requires name plus signed release. Other helpful information: social security number, date of birth, approximate years of attendance. No fee for information.

Degree information available by phone, FAX, mail. Search requires name plus approximate years of attendance, signed release. Other helpful information: social security number, date of birth, exact years of attendance. No fee for information.

Transcripts available by phone, FAX, mail. Search requires name plus approximate years of attendance. Other helpful information: social security number, date of birth, exact years of attendance. Fee is $5.00.

Dallas Theological Seminary, Registrar, 3909 Swiss Ave, Dallas, TX 75204, 214-841-3608 (FAX: 214-841-3664). Hours: 8AM-4:30PM. Records go back to 1924. Alumni records are maintained here also. Call 214-841-3606.

Attendance information available by phone, FAX, mail. Search requires name only. Other helpful information: social security number. No fee for information. Expedited service available for $15.00.

Degree information available by phone, FAX, mail. Search requires name only. Other helpful information: social security number, approximate years of attendance. No fee for information. Expedite service available for $15.00.

Transcripts available by FAX, mail. Search requires name plus signed release. Other helpful information: social security number, approximate years of attendance. No fee for transcripts. Expedited service available for $15.00.

Major credit cards accepted for payment.

Dalton College, Registrar's Office, 213 N College Dr, Dalton, GA 30720, 706-272-4436 (FAX: 706-272-4588). Hours: 8AM-5PM. Records go back 27 years. Degrees granted: Associate.

Attendance information available by phone, FAX, mail. Search requires name plus social security number, date of birth, signed release. Other helpful information: approximate years of attendance. No fee for information.

Degree information available by written request only. Search requires name plus social security number, date of birth, signed release. Other helpful information: approximate years of attendance. No fee for information.

Transcripts available by written request only. Search requires name plus social security number, date of birth, signed release. Other helpful information: approximate years of attendance. Fee is $1.00.

Dana College, Registrar, 2848 College Dr, Blair, NE 68008, 402-426-7209 (FAX: 402-426-7386). Hours: 8AM-5PM. Records go back to 1930. Alumni records are maintained here also. Call 402-426-7235. Degrees granted: Bachelors.

Attendance and degree information available by phone, FAX, mail. Search requires name only. Other helpful information: social security number, date of birth, approximate years of attendance. No fee for information.

Transcripts available by mail. Search requires name plus signed release. Other helpful information: social security number, date of birth, approximate years of attendance. Fee is $3.00. Expedited service available for $5.00.

Will work with student via phone or FAX for emergencies.

Daniel Webster College, Registrar, Nashua, NH 03063, 603-577-6510 (FAX: 603-577-6001). Hours: 8:30AM-5PM. Records go back to 1965. Alumni records are maintained here also. Call 603-577-6626. Degrees granted: Associate; Bachelors. Adverse incident record source: Student Life, 603-577-6581: Security, 603-577-6529

Attendance information available by phone, FAX, mail. Search requires name only. Other helpful information: social security number, approximate years of attendance. No fee for information.

Degree information available by phone, FAX, mail. Search requires name only. Other helpful information: social security number. No fee for information.

Transcripts available by FAX, mail. Search requires name plus signed release. Other helpful information: social security number. Fee is $2.00.

Danville Area Community College, Registrar, 2000 E Main St, Danville, IL 61832, 217-443-8797 (FAX: 217-443-8560). Hours: 8AM-5PM Winter; 7:30AM-4PM Summer. Degrees granted: Associate.

Attendance and degree information available by phone, FAX, mail. Search requires name plus social security number. Other helpful information: date of birth, approximate years of attendance. No fee for information.

Transcripts available by mail. Search requires name plus social security number, signed release. Other helpful information: date of birth, approximate years of attendance. Fee is $2.00.

Major credit cards accepted for payment.

Danville Community College, Registrar, 1008 S Main St, Danville, VA 24541, 804-797-3553. Hours: 8AM-5PM. Records go back to 1968. Degrees granted: Associate.

Attendance and degree information available by phone, mail. Search requires name plus social security number, exact years of attendance. No fee for information.

Transcripts available by mail. Search requires name plus social security number, exact years of attendance, signed release. No fee for transcripts.

Darkei No'am Rabbinical College, Registrar, 2822 Ave J, Brooklyn, NY 11210, 718-338-6464 (FAX: 718-338-0622). Hours: 9AM-4PM. Records go back to 1978. Degrees granted: Bachelors.

Attendance and degree information available by FAX, mail. Search requires name plus social security number, signed release. No fee for information.

Transcripts available by FAX, mail. Search requires name plus social security number, signed release. Fee is $5.00.

Dartmouth College, Registrar, Hanover, NH 03755, 603-646-2246 (FAX: 603-646-1216). Hours: 8AM-4:30PM. Records go back to 1769. Alumni records are maintained here also. Call 603-646-3643. Degrees granted: Associate; Bachelors; Masters; Doctorate.

Attendance and degree information available by phone, FAX, mail. Search requires name plus social security number, exact years of attendance. Other helpful information: date of birth. No fee for information.

Transcripts available by written request only. Search requires name plus social security number, exact years of attendance, signed release. Other helpful information: date of birth. Fee is $2.00.

Darton College, Registrar, 2400 Gillionville Rd, Albany, GA 31707-3098, 912-430-6740 (FAX: 912-430-2926). Hours: 8AM-5PM. Records go back to 1965. Alumni records are maintained here also. Call 912-430-6000. Degrees granted: Associate.

Attendance and degree information available by phone, FAX, mail. Search requires name plus social security number. No fee for information.

Transcripts available by mail. Search requires name plus social security number, signed release. Other helpful information: exact years of attendance. Fee is $1.00.

Davenport College of Business, Registrar, 415 E Fulton St, Grand Rapids, MI 49503, 616-732-1210 (FAX: 616-732-1142). Hours: 8AM-6:30PM M-Th; 8AM-5PM F. Records go back to 1920. Degrees granted: Associate; Bachelors. Adverse incident record source: Student Services, 616-451-3511.

Attendance and degree information available by phone, FAX, mail. Search requires name plus date of birth. Other helpful information: social security number, approximate years of attendance. No fee for information.

Transcripts available by FAX, mail. Search requires name plus date of birth, signed release. Other helpful information: social security number, approximate years of attendance. Fee is $2.00. Expedited service available for $2.00.

Davenport College of Business, (Branch), Registrar, 7121 Grape Rd, Granger, IN 46530, 219-277-8447 (FAX: 219-272-2967). Hours: 8AM-5PM. Degrees granted: Associate.

Attendance and degree information available by phone, FAX, mail. Search requires name only. Other helpful information: social security number, approximate years of attendance. No fee for information.

Transcripts available by written request only. Search requires name plus social security number, signed release. Other helpful information: approximate years of attendance. Fee is $2.00.

Major credit cards accepted for payment.

Davenport College of Business, (Branch), Registrar, 643 Waverly Rd, Holland, MI 49423, 616-395-4610 (FAX: 616-395-4698). Hours: 8AM-6:30PM M-Th; 8AM-5PM F. Records go back to 1945. Alumni Records Office: 415 E Fulton, Grand Rapids, MI 49503. Degrees granted: Associate; Bachelors.

Attendance and degree information available by phone, FAX, mail. Search requires name plus social security number, exact years of attendance. No fee for information.

Transcripts available by FAX, mail. Search requires name plus social security number, exact years of attendance, signed release. Fee is $2.00.

Davenport College of Business, (Branch), Registrar, 4123 N Main St, Kalamazoo, MI 49006, 616-382-2835 (FAX: 616-382-3541). Hours: 8AM-6PM. Records go back to 1981. Degrees granted: Associate; Bachelors. Adverse incident record source: Human Resources, 616-382-2835.

Attendance and degree information available by phone, FAX, mail. Search requires name only. Other helpful information: social security number, date of birth, approximate years of attendance. No fee for information.

Transcripts available by FAX, mail. Search requires name plus signed release. Other helpful information: social security number, date of birth, approximate years of attendance. Fee is $2.00.

Davenport College of Business, (Branch), Registrar, 220 E Kalamazoo St, Lansing, MI 48933, 517-484-2600 (FAX: 517-484-9719). Hours: 8AM-7PM. Records go back 30 years. Alumni records are maintained here at the same phone number. Degrees granted: Associate; Bachelors.

Attendance information available by phone, FAX, mail. Search requires name only. Other helpful information: social security number, date of birth. No fee for information.

Degree information available by FAX, mail. Search requires name plus social security number, signed release. Other helpful information: date of birth. No fee for information.

Transcripts available by mail. Search requires name plus social security number, signed release. Other helpful information: date of birth. Fee is $2.00. Expedited service available for $2.00.

Davenport College of Business, (Branch), Registrar, 8200 Georgia St, Merrillville, IN 46410, 219-769-5556. Hours: 9AM-5PM M-Th, 8AM-4PM F. Records go back to 1987. Degrees granted: Associate.

Attendance and degree information available by phone, mail. Search requires name plus social security number, signed release. No fee for information.

Transcripts available by mail. Search requires name plus social security number, signed release. Fee is $2.00.

David Lipscomb University, Registrar, 3901 Granny White Pike, Nashville, TN 37204-3951, 615-269-1788 (FAX: 615-269-1808). Hours: 7:45AM-4:30PM. Degrees granted: Bachelors; Masters. Adverse incident record source: Dean of Students.

Attendance and degree information available by phone, FAX, mail. Search requires name only. Other helpful information: social security number, date of birth, approximate years of attendance. No fee for information.

Transcripts available by FAX, mail. Search requires name plus approximate years of attendance, signed release. Other helpful information: social security number, date of birth, exact years of attendance. Fee is $3.00. $5.00 FAX fee.

Davidson College, Registrar, PO Box 1719, Davidson, NC 28036, 704-892-2000 X227 (FAX: 704-892-2005). Hours: 8:30AM-5PM. Records go back to 1837. Alumni records are maintained here also. Call 704-892-2111. Degrees granted: Bachelors. Adverse incident record source: Public Safety, 704-892-2178.

Attendance and degree information available by phone, FAX, mail. Search requires name plus social security number. No fee for information.

Transcripts available by mail. Search requires name plus social security number, signed release. Other helpful information: approximate years of attendance. Fee is $3.00.

Student identification number is also requested.

Davidson County Community College, Student Records Office, PO Box 1287, Lexington, NC 27293-1287, 704-249-8186 (FAX: 704-249-0379). Hours: 8:30AM-5PM. Records go back 32 years. Degrees granted: Associate. Adverse incident record source: Student Development.

Attendance and degree information available by phone, FAX, mail. Search requires name only. Other helpful information: social security number, date of birth, approximate years of attendance. No fee for information.

Transcripts available by FAX, mail. Search requires name plus signed release. Other helpful information: social security number, date of birth, approximate years of attendance. Fee is $1.00.

Major credit cards accepted for payment.

Davis & Elkins College, Registrar, 100 Campus Dr, Elkins, WV 26241, 304-636-1900 (FAX: 304-636-8624). Hours: 8:30AM-5PM. Records go back to 1904. Degrees granted: Associate; Bachelors. Special programs- Practical Nursing, 304-636-3300.

Attendance information available by phone, FAX, mail. Search requires name only. Other helpful information: social security number. No fee for information.

Degree information available by phone, FAX, mail. Search requires name only. Other helpful information: social security number, date of birth. No fee for information.

Transcripts available by FAX. Search requires name plus signed release. Other helpful information: social security number, date of birth, exact years of attendance. Fee is $3.00.

Davis College, Registrar, 4747 Monroe St, Toledo, OH 43623, 419-473-2700 (FAX: 419-473-2472). Hours: 9AM-6PM. Records go back to 1945. Degrees granted: Associate.

Attendance and degree information available by phone, FAX, mail. Search requires name plus social security number, approximate years of attendance, signed release. No fee for information.

Transcripts available by FAX, mail. Search requires name only. Fee is $4.00.

Dawson Community College, Registrar, Glendive, MT 59330, 406-365-3396 (FAX: 406-365-8132). Hours: 8AM-4:30PM. Records go back to 1940. Alumni records are maintained here at the same phone number. Degrees granted: Associate.

Attendance information available by phone. Search requires name plus signed release. Other helpful information: social security number, date of birth. No fee for information.

Degree information available by phone. Search requires name only. Other helpful information: approximate years of attendance. No fee for information.

Transcripts available by written request only. Search requires name plus signed release. No fee for transcripts.

Daytona Beach Community College, Records Office, PO Box 2811, Daytona Beach, FL 32120-2811, 904-255-8131 (FAX: 904-254-4489). Hours: 8AM-7PM M-Th; 8AM-4:30PM F. Records go back to 1958. Alumni records are maintained here also. Call 904-255-8131 X3295. Degrees granted: Associate. Adverse incident record source: VP Student Development, 904-255-8131 X3797.

Attendance information available by FAX, mail. Search requires name plus social security number, signed release. Other helpful information: date of birth, approximate years of attendance. No fee for information.

Degree information available by phone, FAX, mail. Search requires name plus social security number, signed release. Other helpful information: date of birth, approximate years of attendance. No fee for information.

Transcripts available by mail. Search requires name plus social security number, signed release. Other helpful information: date of birth, approximate years of attendance. Fee is $2.00.

De Anza College, Registrar, 21250 Stevens Creek Blvd, Cupertino, CA 95014, 408-864-5300 (FAX: 408-864-8329). Hours: 8AM-7:30PM M-Th; 8AM-3PM F. Records go back to 1967. Degrees granted: Associate.

Attendance and degree information available by written request only. Search requires name plus social security number, signed release. Other helpful information: date of birth, approximate years of attendance. Fee is $3.00. Expedited service available for $7.50.

Transcripts available by written request only. Search requires name plus social security number, signed release. Other helpful information: date of birth, approximate years of attendance. Fee is $3.00. Expedited service available for $7.50.

Major credit cards accepted for payment.

De Sales School of Theology, Registrar, 721 Lawrence St NE, Washington, DC 20017, 202-269-9412 (FAX: 202-526-2720). Hours: 9AM-4PM. Records go back to 1985. Degrees granted: Masters. Adverse incident record source: Dean of Students, 202-269-9412.

Attendance and degree information available by phone, FAX, mail. Search requires name only. No fee for information.

Transcripts available by FAX, mail. Search requires name only. Fee is $5.00.

DeKalb College, Admissions & Records, 555 N Indian Creek Dr, Clarkston, GA 30021, 404-299-4566. Hours: 8AM-5PM M-Th; 8AM-4:30PM F. Records go back to 1964. Degrees granted: Associate.

Attendance and degree information available by phone, FAX, mail. Search requires name plus social security number, signed release. Other helpful information: date of birth, approximate years of attendance. No fee for information.

Transcripts available by mail. Search requires name plus social security number, signed release. Other helpful information: date of birth, approximate years of attendance. No fee for transcripts.

DeKalb Technical Institute, Registrar, 495 N Indian Creek Dr, Clarkston, GA 30021, 404-297-9522 X224 (FAX: 404-294-4234). Hours: 8AM-8PM. Records go back 32 years. Degrees granted: Associate.

Attendance and degree information available by phone, FAX, mail. Search requires name only. Other helpful information: social security number, date of birth, approximate years of attendance. No fee for information.

Transcripts available by mail. Search requires name plus social security number, signed release. Other helpful information: date of birth, approximate years of attendance. Fee is $5.00.

Major credit cards accepted for payment.

DePaul University, Registrar, 1 E Jackson Blvd, Chicago, IL 60604, 312-362-8610 (FAX: 312-362-5143). Hours: 8AM-6PM. Records go back to 1898. Alumni Records Office: 25 East Jackson Blvd, Chicago, IL 60604. Degrees granted: Bachelors; Masters; Doctorate. Adverse incident record source: Dean of Students, 312-362-5653.

Attendance and degree information available by phone, FAX, mail. Search requires name plus social security number. Other helpful information: date of birth, approximate years of attendance. No fee for information.

Transcripts available by mail. Search requires name plus social security number, signed release. Other helpful information: date of birth, approximate years of attendance. Fee is $5.00. Expedited service available for $8.00.

If student has restrict code (no info released), written release from student necessary.

DePauw University, Registrar, Greencastle, IN 46135, 317-658-4000 (FAX: 317-658-4139). Hours: 8AM-4:30PM. Records go back to 1837. Alumni records are maintained here also. Call 317-658-4208. Degrees granted: Bachelors.

Attendance and degree information available by phone, FAX, mail. Search requires name plus social security number, date of birth, exact years of attendance. No fee for information.

Transcripts available by mail. Search requires name plus social security number, date of birth, exact years of attendance, signed release. Fee is $2.00.

DeVry Institute of Technology, Phoenix, Registrar, 2149 W Dunlap Ave, Phoenix, AZ 85021, 602-870-9222 (FAX: 602-870-1209). Hours: 8AM-5PM. Records go back to 1967. Degrees granted: Associate; Bachelors.

Attendance and degree information available by phone, FAX, mail. Search requires name plus social security number, date of birth, approximate years of attendance. Other helpful information: exact years of attendance. No fee for information.

Transcripts available by FAX, mail. Search requires name plus social security number, date of birth, approximate years of attendance, signed release. Other helpful information: exact years of attendance. Fee is $2.00.

Major credit cards accepted for payment.

DeVry Institute of Technolgy, Kansas City, Registrar, 11224 Holmes Rd, Kansas City, MO 64131, 816-941-0430 (FAX: 816-941-0896). Hours: 8AM-5PM. Degrees granted: Associate; Bachelors.

Attendance and degree information available by phone, FAX, mail. Search requires name plus social security number, signed release. Other helpful information: date of birth, approximate years of attendance. No fee for information.

Transcripts available by mail. Search requires name plus social security number, signed release. Other helpful information: date of birth, approximate years of attendance. Fee is $2.00.

Major credit cards accepted for payment.

DeVry Institute of Technology, Registrar's Office, 901 Corporate Center Dr, Pomona, CA 91768, 909-622-9800. Hours: 8:30AM-4:30PM M,T,W,F; 8:30AM-8PM Th. Records go back to 1983. Alumni records are maintained here also. Call 909-622-9800. Degrees granted: Associate; Bachelors.

Attendance and degree information available by phone, mail. Search requires name plus social security number. No fee for information.

Transcripts available by mail. Search requires name plus social security number, exact years of attendance, signed release. Fee is $2.00.

Phone confirmation is given only if release on file.

DeVry Institute of Technology, Atlanta, Registrar, 250 N Arcadia Ave, Decatur, GA 30030, 404-292-7900 (FAX: 404-292-8117). Hours: 8:30PM 5PM M,W,F; 8:30PM-6PM T,Th. Records go back to 1971. Transcripts available for all years; other information for last five years only. Degrees granted: Associate; Bachelors.

Attendance and degree information available by phone, FAX, mail. Search requires name plus social security number. Other helpful information: approximate years of attendance. No fee for information.

Transcripts available by FAX, mail. Search requires name plus social security number, signed release. Other helpful information: approximate years of attendance. Fee is $2.00. Expedited service available for $10.00.

DeVry Institute of Technology, Chicago, Registrar, 3300 N Campbell Ave, Chicago, IL 60618, 312-929-8500 X2060 (FAX: 312-348-1780). Hours: 7:30AM-4:30PM M,T,F; 7:30AM-7:30PM W,Th. Records go back to 1948. Alumni Records Office: Alumni Association, DeVry Institute, One Tower Ln, Oakbrook Terrace, IL 60181. Degrees granted: Associate; Bachelors.

Attendance and degree information available by phone, FAX, mail. Search requires name plus social security number, exact years of attendance. No fee for information.

Transcripts available by FAX, mail. Search requires name plus social security number, exact years of attendance, signed release. First transcript free. Additional ones are $2.00 each.

DeVry Institute of Technology, Columbus, Registrar, 1350 Alum Creek Dr, Columbus, OH 43209, 708-571-7700 X4148 (FAX: 614-252-4108). Alumni records are maintained here at the same phone number. Degrees granted: Bachelors.

Attendance and degree information available by phone, mail. Search requires name plus social security number. No fee for information.

Transcripts available by mail. Search requires name plus social security number, signed release. Fee is $2.00.

Major credit cards accepted for payment.

DeVry Institute of Technology, Dallas, Registrar, 4801 Regent Blvd, Irving, TX 75063-2440, 214-929-6777 (FAX: 214-929-6778). Hours: 8AM-7PM M,T; 8AM-5PM W-F. Records go back to 1975. Degrees granted: Associate; Bachelors.

Attendance and degree information available by phone. Search requires name plus social security number. Other helpful information: date of birth, approximate years of attendance. No fee for information.

Transcripts available by mail. Search requires name plus social security number, signed release. Other helpful information: date of birth, approximate years of attendance. Fee is $2.00.

DeVry Institute of Technology, DuPage, Registrar, 1221 N Swift Rd, Addison, IL 60101-6106, 708-953-1300 (FAX: 708-953-1236). Hours: 8:30AM-7:30PM M-Th, 8:30AM-5PM F. Records go back to 1980. Alumni Records Office: Alumni Association, DeVry Institute, One Tower Ln, Oakbrook Terrace, IL 60181. Degrees granted: Associate; Bachelors.

Attendance and degree information available by phone, FAX, mail. Search requires name plus social security number, exact years of attendance. No fee for information.

Transcripts available by FAX, mail. Search requires name plus social security number, exact years of attendance, signed release. First transcript is free. Additional ones are $2.00 each.

DeVry Institutes, Registrar, One Tower Lane, Oak Brook Terrace, IL 60181, 708-571-7700. Hours: 8:30AM-7:30PM M-Th, 8:30AM-5PM F. Records go back to 1948. Alumni records are maintained here at the same phone number. Degrees granted: Associate; Bachelors.

Attendance and degree information available by phone, mail. Search requires name plus social security number, exact years of attendance. No fee for information.

Transcripts available by mail. Search requires name plus social security number, exact years of attendance, signed release. First transcript is free. Additional ones are $2.00 each.

DeVry Technical Institute, Registrar, 479 Green St, Woodbridge, NJ 07095, 908-634-3460 (FAX: 908-634-9455). Hours: 7AM-3:30PM. Records go back to 1985. Degrees granted: Associate.

Attendance and degree information available by phone, FAX, mail. Search requires name plus social security number, approximate years of attendance, signed release. No fee for information.

Transcripts available by mail. Search requires name plus social security number, approximate years of attendance, signed release. Fee is $2.00.

Deaconess College of Nursing, Registrar, 6150 Oakland Ave, St Louis, MO 63139, 314-768-3044 X31 (FAX: 314-768-5673). Hours: 8:30AM-4:30PM. Records go back 74+ years. Alumni records are maintained here also. Call 314-768-3807. Degrees granted: Associate; Bachelors. Adverse incident record source: Student Services, 314-768-3044.

Attendance information available by phone, FAX, mail. Search requires name only. Other helpful information: social security number, approximate years of attendance. No fee for information.

Degree information available by phone, FAX, mail. Search requires name plus exact years of attendance. Other helpful information: social security number, approximate years of attendance. No fee for information.

Transcripts available by FAX, mail. Search requires name plus signed release. Other helpful information: social security number, approximate years of attendance. Fee is $3.00.

Maiden name and married name helpful.

Dean College, Registrar, Franklin, MA 02038, 508-528-9100 (FAX: 508-520-6795). Hours: 8:30AM-4:30PM. Records go back to 1865. Alumni records are maintained here at the same phone number. Degrees granted: Associate.

Attendance and degree information available by phone, FAX, mail. Search requires name only. Other helpful information: social security number, date of birth, approximate years of attendance. No fee for information.

Transcripts available by FAX, mail. Search requires name plus signed release. Other helpful information: social security number, date of birth, approximate years of attendance. Fee is $2.00. Expedited service available for $5.00.

Dean Institute of Technology, Registrar, 1501 W Liberty Ave, Pittsburgh, PA 15226, 412-531-4433 (FAX: 412-531-4435). Hours: 7:45AM-4PM M-Th, 7:45AM-3PM F. Records go back to 1974. Degrees granted: Associate. Adverse incident record source: Registrar, 412-531-4433.

Attendance and degree information available by phone, FAX, mail. Search requires name plus social security number. No fee for information.

Transcripts available by FAX, mail. Search requires name plus social security number, exact years of attendance, signed release. Fee is $3.00.

Deep Springs College, Registrar, HC 72, Box 45001, Dyer, NV 89010-9803, 619-872-2000 (FAX: 619-872-4466). Hours: 8AM-5PM. Records go back to 1917. Alumni records are maintained here also. Call 619-872-2000. Degrees granted: Associate.

Attendance and degree information available by phone, mail. Search requires name plus exact years of attendance. No fee for information.

Transcripts available by phone, mail. Search requires name plus exact years of attendance. No fee for transcripts.

Defiance College, Registrar, 701 N Clinton St, Defiance, OH 43512, 419-783-2357 (FAX: 419-784-0426). Hours: 8AM-4:30PM. Records go back to 1906. Degrees granted: Associate; Bachelors; Masters.

Attendance and degree information available by phone, FAX, mail. Search requires name plus approximate years of attendance, signed release. Other helpful information: social security number, date of birth, exact years of attendance. No fee for information.

Transcripts available by written request only. Search requires name plus approximate years of attendance, signed release. Other helpful information: social security number, date of birth, exact years of attendance. Written request $3.00; FAX request $4.00; additional copies to same address $1.00.

Will not FAX transcript; request only. Major credit cards accepted for payment.

Del Mar College, Registrar, 101 Baldwin Blvd, Corpus Christi, TX 78404-3897, 512-886-1248 (FAX: 512-886-1595). Hours: 7:30AM-7:30PM M-Th; 7:30AM-Noon F. Records go back to 1935. Degrees granted: Associate.

Attendance and degree information available by phone, FAX, mail. Search requires name plus social security number. Other helpful information: date of birth, approximate years of attendance. No fee for information.

Transcripts available by FAX, mail. Search requires name plus social security number, signed release. Other helpful information: date of birth, approximate years of attendance. No fee for transcripts.

Delaware County Community College, Registrar, 901 S Media Line Rd, Media, PA 19063, 610-359-5336 (FAX: 610-359-5343). Hours: 9AM-9PM. Records go back to 1967. Degrees granted: Associate.

Attendance and degree information available by phone, FAX, mail. Search requires name only. Other helpful information: social security number. No fee for information.

Transcripts available by FAX, mail. Search requires name plus signed release. Other helpful information: social security number. No fee for transcripts.

Delaware State University, Records Department, 1200 N Dupont Hwy, Dover, DE 19901-1277, 302-739-4914 (FAX: 302-739-6279). Hours: 8:30AM-4:30PM. Records go back to founding date. Degrees granted: Bachelors; Masters. Adverse incident record source: Dr. Brevett, Registrar.

Attendance and degree information available by FAX, mail. Search requires name plus social security number, signed release. Other helpful information: date of birth, approximate years of attendance. No fee for information.

Transcripts available by mail. Search requires name plus social security number, signed release. Other helpful information: date of birth, approximate years of attendance. Fee is $2.00.

Delaware Technical & Community College, (Stanton/Willington), Registrar, 400 Stanton Christiana Rd, Newark, DE 19713, 302-454-3959 (FAX: 302-454-3184). Hours: 8:30AM-8PM m-Th. Records go back to 1968. Degrees granted: Associate.

Attendance and degree information available by phone, FAX, mail. Search requires name plus social security number. Other helpful information: date of birth. No fee for information.

Transcripts available by mail. Search requires name plus social security number, signed release. Other helpful information: date of birth. Fee is $2.00.

Delaware Technical & Community College, (Terry), Registrar, 1832 N Dupont Pkwy, Dover, DE 19901, 302-739-5225 (FAX: 302-739-6169). Hours: 8:30AM-7:30PM M-Th, 8:30AM-4PM F. Records go back to 1975. Alumni records are maintained here also. Call 302-739-5321. Degrees granted: Associate.

Attendance and degree information available by phone, FAX, mail. Search requires name plus social security number. Other helpful information: approximate years of attendance. No fee for information.

Transcripts available by mail. Search requires name plus social security number, signed release. Other helpful information: approximate years of attendance. Fee is $1.00.

Delaware Valley College of Science and Agriculture, Registrar's Officd, 700 E Butler Ave, Doylestown, PA 18901, 215-345-1500 X2378. Hours: 8:30AM-4:30PM. Records go back to 1896. Alumni records are maintained here also. Call 215-345-1500 X2424. Degrees granted: Associate; Bachelors. Adverse incident record source: Dean, 215-345-1500 X2215: Registrar, 215-345-1500 X2378

Attendance information available by phone, mail. Search requires name plus social security number. No fee for information.

Degree information available by phone, mail. Search requires name plus social security number, exact years of attendance. No fee for information.

Transcripts available by mail. Search requires name plus social security number, exact years of attendance, signed release. Fee is $4.00.

Deleware Technical & Community College, (Southern), Registrar, PO Box 610, Georgetown, DE 19947, 302-856-5400. Records are not housed here. They are located at Delaware Technical & Community College, (Terry), Registrar, 1832 N Dupont Pkwy, Dover, DE 19901.

Delgado Community College, Registrar, 501 City Park Ave, New Orleans, LA 70119, 504-483-4153 (FAX: 504-483-4090). Hours: 8:30AM-4:30PM. Records go back to 1924. Alumni records are maintained here also. Call 504-483-4400. Degrees granted: Associate.

Attendance and degree information available by phone, FAX, mail. Search requires name plus social security number, approximate years of attendance, signed release. No fee for information.

Transcripts available by mail. Search requires name plus social security number, approximate years of attendance, signed release. No fee for transcripts.

Delta College, Registrar, University Center, MI 48710, 517-686-9539. Hours: 8AM-7PM M,Th; 8AM-4:30PM T,W,F. Records go back to 1961. Degrees granted: Associate.

Attendance and degree information available by phone, FAX, mail. Search requires name only. Other helpful information: social security number, approximate years of attendance. No fee for information.

Transcripts available by FAX, mail. Search requires name plus signed release. Other helpful information: social security number, date of birth, approximate years of attendance. Fee is $5.00. Expedited service available for $10.00.

Major credit cards accepted for payment.

Delta Junior College, Registrar, 7290 Exchange Pl, Baton Rouge, LA 70806, 504-927-7780 (FAX: 504-927-9096). Hours: 8AM-5PM. Records go back to 1972. Degrees granted: Associate.

Attendance and degree information available by FAX, mail. Search requires name plus social security number, signed release. No fee for information.

Transcripts available by FAX, mail. Search requires name plus social security number, signed release. No fee for transcripts.

Delta Junior College, (Branch), Registrar, 100 Covington Ctr Ste 30, Covington, LA 70433, 504-892-5332.

Delta Junior College, (Delta College), Registrar, 3827 W Main St, Houma, LA 70360, 504-868-3075 (FAX: 504-868-4752). Records are not housed here. They are located at Delta Junior College, Registrar, 7290 Exchange Pl, Baton Rouge, LA 70806.

Delta School of Business and Technology, Registrar, 517 Broad St, Lake Charles, LA 70601, 318-439-5765 (FAX: 318-436-5151). Hours: 8AM-5PM. Degrees granted: Associate.

Attendance and degree information available by phone, FAX, mail. Search requires name plus social security number, approximate years of attendance. Other helpful information: date of birth, exact years of attendance. No fee for information.

Transcripts available by phone, FAX, mail. Search requires name plus social security number, approximate years of attendance, signed release. Other helpful information: date of birth, exact years of attendance. No fee for transcripts.

Delta State University, Registrar, Hwy 8 W, Cleveland, MS 38733, 601-846-4040 (FAX: 601-846-4016). Hours: 8AM-5PM. Records go back to 1924. Alumni records are maintained here also. Call 601-846-4705. Degrees granted: Bachelors; Masters; Doctorate. Adverse incident record source: Student Affairs, 601-846-4155.

Attendance and degree information available by phone, FAX, mail. Search requires name plus social security number, date of birth, approximate years of attendance, signed release. No fee for information.

Transcripts available by FAX, mail. Search requires name plus social security number, date of birth, approximate years of attendance, signed release. Fee is $4.00.

Denison University, Registrar, PO Box B, Granville, OH 43023, 614-587-6530 (FAX: 614-587-6417). Hours: 8:30AM-4:30PM. Records go back to 1940. Degrees granted: Bachelors. Special programs- Prior to 1940; Archives, 614-587-6399. Adverse incident record source: Student Affairs (active only), 614-587-6567.

Attendance and degree information available by phone, FAX, mail. Search requires name only. Other helpful information: social security number, date of birth, approximate years of attendance. No fee for information.

Transcripts available by FAX, mail. Search requires name only. Other helpful information: social security number, date of birth, approximate years of attendance. Fee is $2.00. Expedited service available for $5.00.

No specific requirement for SSN, DOB, years, but some combination required.

Denmark Technical College, Registrar, PO Box 327, Denmark, SC 29042, 803-793-3301 (FAX: 803-793-5942). Hours: 8:30AM-5PM. Degrees granted: Associate. Adverse incident record source: Dean of Students, 803-793-3301 X230: Public Safety, 803-793-3301 X273

Attendance information available by mail. Search requires name plus social security number, date of birth, approximate years of attendance, signed release. No fee for information.

School will not confirm degree information. Search requires name plus social security number, date of birth, approximate years of attendance, signed release. No fee for information.

Transcripts available by written request only. Search requires name plus social security number, date of birth, approximate years of attendance, signed release. Fee is $3.00.

Denver Business College, Registrar, 7350 N Broadway, Denver, CO 80221, 303-426-1000. Degrees granted: Associate.

Attendance and degree information available by FAX, mail. Search requires name plus signed release. Other helpful information: social security number, date of birth, approximate years of attendance. No fee for information.

Transcripts available by FAX, mail. Search requires name plus signed release. Other helpful information: social security number, date of birth, approximate years of attendance. Fee is $5.00.

Denver Business College, (Branch), Registrar, 419 South St #174, Honolulu, HI 96813, 808-942-1000 (FAX: 808-533-3064). Hours: 8AM-5PM. Records go back 86 years. Alumni records are maintained here at the same phone number. Degrees granted: Associate.

Attendance information available by phone, FAX, mail. Search requires name plus social security number, approximate years of attendance, signed release. Other helpful information: date of birth, exact years of attendance. Fee is $5.00.

Degree information available by FAX, mail. Search requires name plus social security number, approximate years of attendance, signed release. Other helpful information: date of birth, exact years of attendance. Fee is $5.00.

Transcripts available by mail. Search requires name plus social security number, approximate years of attendance, signed release. Other helpful information: date of birth, exact years of attendance. Fee is $5.00.

Denver Business College, (Branch), Registrar, 1550 S Alma School Rd #101, Mesa, AZ 85210, 602-834-1000 (FAX: 602-491-2970). Hours: 8AM-7PM. Records go back to 1987. Degrees granted: Associate.

Attendance information available by FAX, mail. Search requires name plus social security number, approximate years of attendance, signed release. No fee for information.

Degree information available by phone, FAX, mail. Search requires name plus social security number, approximate years of attendance, signed release. No fee for information.

Transcripts available by FAX, mail. Search requires name plus social security number, approximate years of attendance, signed release. First transcript is free; each additional 5.00.

Denver Conservative Baptist Seminary, Registrar, PO Box 10000, Denver, CO 80250-0100, 303-761-2482 (FAX: 303-761-8060). Hours: 8AM-4:30PM. Records go back to 1950. Alumni records are maintained here at the same phone number. Degrees granted: Masters; Doctorate.

Attendance and degree information available by phone, FAX, mail. Search requires name only. Other helpful information: social security number, date of birth, approximate years of attendance. No fee for information.

Transcripts available by FAX, mail. Search requires name plus signed release. Other helpful information: social security number, date of birth, approximate years of attendance. Fee is $2.00. Expedited service available for $5.00.

Additional cost for FAX.

Denver Institute of Technology, Registrar, 7350 N Broadway, Denver, CO 80221-3653, 303-426-1111 X362 (FAX: 303-426-1818). Hours: 7:30AM-7PM M-Th, 8AM-Noon F, Sat. Degrees granted: Associate; Bachelors.

Attendance and degree information available by phone, FAX, mail. Search requires name plus social security number, exact years of attendance, signed release. No fee for information.

Transcripts available by FAX, mail. Search requires name plus social security number, exact years of attendance, signed release. First transcript $5.00; each additional $1.00.

Denver Institute of Technology, (Health Careers Division), Registrar, 7350 N Broadway Annex HCD, Denver, CO 80221-3653, 303-650-5050. Records are not housed here. They are located at Denver Institute of Technology, Registrar, 7350 N Broadway, Denver, CO 80221-3653.

Denver Technical College, Registrar, 925 S Niagara St, Denver, CO 80224-1658, 303-329-3340 (FAX: 303-321-3412). Hours: 7AM-5PM. Records go back to 1986. Degrees granted: Associate; Bachelors; Masters.

Attendance and degree information available by phone, FAX, mail. Search requires name only. Other helpful information: social security number, approximate years of attendance. No fee for information.

Transcripts available by mail. Search requires name plus signed release. Other helpful information: social security number, approximate years of attendance. Fee is $2.00.

Denver Technical College at Colorado Springs, Registrar, 225 S Union Blvd, Colorado Springs, CO 80910-3138, 719-632-3000 X123 (FAX: 719-632-1909). Hours: 8AM-6PM M-Th, 8AM-Noon. Records go back to 1985. Degrees granted: Associate; Bachelors.

Attendance and degree information available by phone, FAX, mail. Search requires name plus social security number, signed release. Other helpful information: approximate years of attendance. No fee for information.

Transcripts available by mail. Search requires name plus social security number, signed release. Other helpful information: approximate years of attendance. Fee is $2.00.

Des Moines Area Community College, Student Records Bldg 1, 2006 S Ankeny Blvd, Ankeny, IA 50021, 515-964-6224 (FAX: 515-964-6391). Hours: 8AM-5PM Fall, Spring; 7:30AM-4PM Winter. Records go back to 1920. Degrees granted: Associate.

Attendance information available by phone, FAX, mail. Search requires name plus social security number. No fee for information.

Degree information available by phone, FAX, mail. Search requires name plus social security number. Other helpful information: approximate years of attendance. No fee for information.

Transcripts available by FAX, mail. Search requires name plus social security number, signed release. Other helpful information: date of birth, approximate years of attendance. Fee is $1.00. Expedite fee is $3.00 to $5.00.

Confirm attendance if currently enrolled. Written confirmation request if request is made by student. Institutions need not write for current term. Requests for multiple term enrollment verifications must be made in writing.

Design Institute of San Diego, Registrar, 8555 Commerce Ave, San Diego, CA 92121, 619-566-1200 (FAX: 619-566-2711). Hours: 8:30AM-4:30PM. Records go back to 1977. Alumni records are maintained here also. Call 619-566-1200. Degrees granted: Bachelors.

Attendance and degree information available by phone, FAX, mail. Search requires name plus social security number, signed release. No fee for information.

Transcripts available by FAX, mail. Search requires name plus social security number, signed release. Fee is $5.00.

Detroit College of Business, Registrar, 4801 Oakman Blvd, Dearborn, MI 48126, 313-581-4400 (FAX: 313-581-6822). Hours: 8AM-8PM M-Th; 8AM-4PM F. Records go back to 1962. Degrees granted: Associate; Bachelors.

Attendance and degree information available by phone, FAX, mail. Search requires name plus social security number, signed release. Other helpful information: date of birth. No fee for information.

Transcripts available by mail. Search requires name plus social security number, signed release. Other helpful information: date of birth. Fee is $2.00. Expedited service available for $5.00.

Major credit cards accepted for payment.

Detroit College of Law, Registrar, 130 E Elizabeth St, Detroit, MI 48201, 313-226-0153 (FAX: 313-226-0196). Hours: 9AM-6PM M,T; 9AM-4:30PM W,T. Files older than 3 years housed at Leonard Archives, 810-477-7007.

Attendance and degree information available by phone, FAX. Search requires name plus approximate years of attendance. Other helpful information: social security number. No fee for information.

Transcripts available by mail. Search requires name plus social security number, signed release. Fee is $3.00. Expedited service available for $5.00.

Diablo Valley College, Registrar, 321 Golf Club Rd, Pleasant Hill, CA 94523, 510-685-1230 X327 (FAX: 510-685-1551). Hours: 8AM-8PM M-Th; 8AM-4:30PM F. Records go back to 1949. Degrees granted: Associate.

Attendance information available by phone, FAX, mail. Search requires name plus date of birth, signed release. Other helpful information: social security number, approximate years of attendance. No fee for information.

Degree information available by phone, FAX, mail. Search requires name plus date of birth. Other helpful information: social security number, approximate years of attendance. No fee for information.

Transcripts available by FAX, mail. Search requires name plus social security number, date of birth, signed release. Other helpful information: approximate years of attendance. Fee is $3.00.

Major credit cards accepted for payment.

Dickinson College, Registrar, Carlisle, PA 17013, 717-245-1262 (FAX: 717-245-1534). Hours: 8AM-Noon, 1-4:30 PM. Records go back to 1783. Degrees granted: Bachelors.

Attendance and degree information available by phone, FAX, mail. Search requires name only. Other helpful information: social security number, date of birth, approximate years of attendance. No fee for information.

Transcripts available by FAX, mail. Search requires name plus signed release. Other helpful information: social security number, date of birth, approximate years of attendance. No fee for transcripts.

Major credit cards accepted for payment.

Dickinson School of Law, Registrar, 150 S College St, Carlisle, PA 17013, 717-240-5210. Hours: 8AM-5PM. Records go back to 1925. Alumni records are maintained here also. Call 717-240-5250. Degrees granted: Doctorate.

Attendance and degree information available by phone, mail. Search requires name plus social security number, exact years of attendance. No fee for information.

Transcripts available by mail. Search requires name plus social security number, exact years of attendance, signed release. First transcript is $5.00; each additional is $3.00.

Dickinson State University, Registrar, 291 Campus Dr, Dickinson, ND 58601, 701-277-2331 (FAX: 701-227-2006). Hours: 7:45AM-4:30PM. Records go back to 1918. Degrees granted: Associate; Masters. Certification: Truck Driving.

Attendance and degree information available by phone, FAX, mail. Search requires name only. Other helpful information: social security number, date of birth, approximate years of attendance. No fee for information. Expedited service available for $3.00.

Transcripts available by FAX, mail. Search requires name plus social security number, date of birth, signed release. Other helpful information: approximate years of attendance. No fee for transcripts. Expedited service available for $3.00.

Dillard University, Registrar, 2601 Gentilly Blvd, New Orleans, LA 70122, 504-286-4688. Hours: 8AM-5PM. Records go back to 1898. Alumni records are maintained here also. Call 504-286-4666. Degrees granted: Bachelors.

Attendance and degree information available by phone, mail. Search requires name plus social security number, approximate years of attendance. No fee for information.

Transcripts available by mail. Search requires name plus social security number, approximate years of attendance, signed release. Fee is $2.00.

District of Columbia School of Law, Registrar, 719 13th St NW, Washington, DC 20005, 202-727-3769 (FAX: 202-727-9608). Hours: 9AM-5:30PM. Records go back to 1991. Alumni records are maintained here at the same phone number. Degrees granted: Doctorate.

Attendance and degree information available by phone, FAX, mail. Search requires name plus exact years of attendance. Other helpful information: social security number, date of birth. No fee for information.

Transcripts available by mail. Search requires name plus exact years of attendance, signed release. Other helpful information: social security number, date of birth. Fee is $3.00. Expedited service available for $6.00.

Divine Word College, Registrar, S Center Ave, Epworth, IA 52045, 319-876-3353 X205. Hours: 9AM-5PM. Records go back to 1964. Alumni records are maintained here also. Call 319-876-3353. Degrees granted: Bachelors. Adverse incident record source: Registrar, 319-876-3353.

Attendance and degree information available by phone, mail. Search requires name plus social security number. No fee for information.

Transcripts available by mail. Search requires name plus social security number, signed release. Fee is $5.00.

Dixie College, Registrar, 225 S 700 E, St George, UT 84770, 801-673-4811 X348. Hours: 9AM-4:30PM. Records go back to 1911. Alumni records are maintained here at the same phone number. Degrees granted: Associate.

Attendance and degree information available by phone, mail. Search requires name plus social security number, exact years of attendance. No fee for information.

Transcripts available by mail. Search requires name plus social security number, exact years of attendance, signed release. Fee is $2.00.

Doane College, Registrar, 1014 Boswell Ave, Crete, NE 68333, 402-826-8251 (FAX: 402-826-8600). Hours: 8AM-Noon, 12:30-4:30PM. Records go back to 1975. Degrees granted: Bachelors; Masters.

Attendance and degree information available by phone, FAX, mail. Search requires name plus social security number. Other helpful information: approximate years of attendance. No fee for information. Expedited service available for $5.00.

Transcripts available by FAX, mail. Search requires name plus social security number, signed release. Other helpful information: approximate years of attendance. Fee is $3.00. Expedited service available for $20.00.

Major credit cards accepted for payment.

Dodge City Community College, Registrar, 2501 N 14th St, Dodge City, KS 67801, 316-225-1321 (FAX: 316-227-9277). Hours: 8AM-5PM. Records go back to 1934. Degrees granted: Associate. Certification: Vocational.

Attendance information available by phone, FAX, mail. Search requires name plus signed release. Other helpful information: social security number, approximate years of attendance. No fee for information.

Degree information available by FAX, mail. Search requires name only. Other helpful information: social security number, approximate years of attendance. No fee for information.

Transcripts available by FAX, mail. Search requires name plus social security number, signed release. Other helpful information: date of birth, approximate years of attendance. Fee is $2.00.

Major credit cards accepted for payment.

Dominican College of Blauvelt, Registrar, 470 Western Hwy, Orangeburg, NY 10962, 914-359-7800 (FAX: 914-359-2313). Hours: 8:30AM-5PM. Records go back to 1964. Degrees granted: Associate; Bachelors; Masters.

Attendance information available by phone, FAX, mail. Search requires name plus social security number, signed release. Other helpful information: approximate years of attendance. No fee for information.

Degree information available by phone, FAX, mail. Search requires name plus social security number, signed release. Other helpful information: approximate years of attendance. No fee for information.

Transcripts available by written request only. Search requires name plus social security number, signed release. Other helpful information: approximate years of attendance. Fee is $3.00.

Dominican College of San Rafael, Registrar, 50 Acacia St, San Rafael, CA 94901, 415-457-4440 X260. Hours: 9AM-5PM. Records go back to 1890. Alumni records are maintained here also. Call 415-457-4440. Degrees granted: Bachelors; Masters.

Attendance and degree information available by phone, mail. Search requires name plus social security number, exact years of attendance. No fee for information.

Transcripts available by mail. Search requires name plus social security number, exact years of attendance, signed release. Fee is $5.00.

Dominican House of Studies, Registrar, 487 Michigan Ave NE, Washington, DC 20017, 202-529-5300 (FAX: 202-636-4460). Hours: 9AM-4PM. Records go back to 1945. Degrees granted: M. Div; S.T.L.

Attendance and degree information available by written request only. Search requires name only. Other helpful information: approximate years of attendance. Fee is $3.00.

Transcripts available by written request only. Search requires name plus signed release. Other helpful information: approximate years of attendance. Fee is $3.00.

Dominican School of Philosophy and Theology, Registrar, 2401 Ridge Rd, Berkeley, CA 94709, 510-849-2030. Degrees granted: Bachelors; Masters. Certification: Theology.

Attendance and degree information available by mail. Search requires name plus approximate years of attendance, signed release. Other helpful information: date of birth, exact years of attendance. Fee is $3.00.

Transcripts available by mail. Search requires name plus approximate years of attendance, signed release. Other helpful information: date of birth, exact years of attendance. Fee is $3.00.

Don Bosco Technical Institute, Registrar, 1151 San Gabriel Blvd, Rosemead, CA 91770, 818-307-6522 (FAX: 818-280-9316). Hours: 8AM-3:30PM. Records go back to founding date. Alumni records are maintained here also. Call 818-307-6528. Degrees granted: Associate.

Attendance and degree information available by phone, FAX, mail. Search requires name only. Other helpful information: social security number, date of birth, approximate years of attendance. No fee for information.

Transcripts available by mail. Search requires name plus signed release. Other helpful information: social security number, date of birth, approximate years of attendance. Fee is $2.00.

Dona Ana Branch Community College, Registrar, Box 30001, Las Cruces, NM 88003, 505-646-3411 (FAX: 505-646-6330). Hours: 8AM-5PM. Records go back to 1970. Alumni records are maintained here also. Call 505-646-3616. Degrees granted: Associate.

Attendance and degree information available by phone, FAX, mail. Search requires name plus social security number, signed release. No fee for information.

Transcripts available by mail. Search requires name plus social security number, signed release. Fee is $3.00.

Donnelly College, Registrar, 608 N 18th St, Kansas City, KS 66102, 913-621-6070 X33 (FAX: 913-621-0354). Hours: 8:30AM-4:30PM. Alumni records are maintained here at the same phone number. Degrees granted: Associate.

Attendance and degree information available by phone, mail. Search requires name plus social security number, date of birth. No fee for information.

Transcripts available by phone, mail. Search requires name plus social security number, date of birth, signed release. Fee is $1.00.

Dordt College, Registrar, Sioux Center, IA 51250, 712-722-6030 (FAX: 712-722-4496). Hours: 8AM-Noon, 1-5PM. Records go back to 1955. Degrees granted: Associate; Bachelors; Masters. Adverse incident record source: Student Services.

Attendance and degree information available by phone, FAX, mail. Search requires name plus social security number. Other helpful information: date of birth, approximate years of attendance. No fee for information.

Transcripts available by FAX, mail. Search requires name plus social security number, date of birth, signed release. Other helpful information: approximate years of attendance. No fee for transcripts.

Douglas MacArthur State Technical College, Registrar, 1708 N Main St, Opp, AL 36467, 334-493-3573 X233 (FAX: 334-493-7003). Hours: 7:30AM-4:30PM. Records go back to 1965. Degrees granted: Associate.

Attendance and degree information available by phone, FAX, mail. Search requires name plus social security number. Other helpful information: date of birth, approximate years of attendance. No fee for information.

Transcripts available by phone, FAX, mail. Search requires name plus social security number. Other helpful information: date of birth, approximate years of attendance. No fee for transcripts.

Douglas School of Business, Registrar, 130 Seventh St, Monessen, PA 15062, 412-684-7644 (FAX: 412-684-7463). Hours: 8AM-5PM. Records go back to 1904. Degrees granted: Associate.

Attendance and degree information available by phone, FAX, mail. Search requires name plus exact years of attendance, signed release. Other helpful information: social security number, date of birth, approximate years of attendance. No fee for information.

Transcripts available by written request only. Search requires name plus signed release. Other helpful information: social security number, date of birth, approximate years of attendance. Fee is $2.00. Include a stamped envelope.

Major credit cards accepted for payment.

Dowling College, Registrar, Idle Hour Blvd, Oakdale, NY 11769-1999, 516-244-3250 (FAX: 516-589-6644). Hours: 8AM-8PM M-Th; 9AM-5PM F; 9AM-2PM S. Records go back to 1970. Alumni records are maintained here also. Call 516-244-3106. Degrees granted: Bachelors; Masters.

Attendance and degree information available by phone, FAX, mail. Search requires name plus social security number, signed release. No fee for information.

Transcripts available by mail. Search requires name plus social security number, signed release. Fee is $5.00.

Dr. William M. Scholl College of Podiatric Medicine, Registrar, 1001 N Dearborn St, Chicago, IL 60610, 312-280-2943 (FAX: 312-280-2495). Hours: 8:30AM-6PM. Records go back to 1916. Alumni records are maintained here also. Call 312-280-2880. Degrees granted: Bachelors; Doctorate.

Attendance and degree information available by phone, FAX, mail. Search requires name plus social security number, exact years of attendance. No fee for information.

Transcripts available by mail. Search requires name plus social security number, exact years of attendance, signed release. Fee is $2.00.

Drake University, Registrar, 25th St and University Ave, Des Moines, IA 50311, 515-271-3901 (FAX: 515-271-3977). Hours: 8AM-4:30PM. Records go back to 1881. Alumni Records Office: Alumni Development, Drake University, 1331 27th St, Des Moines, IA 50310. Degrees granted: Bachelors; Masters; Doctorate.

Attendance and degree information available by phone, FAX, mail. Search requires name plus social security number, date of birth, approximate years of attendance. Other helpful information: exact years of attendance. No fee for information.

Transcripts available by phone, FAX, mail. Search requires name plus social security number, approximate years of attendance. Other helpful information: date of birth, exact years of attendance. Fee is $5.00. Expedited service-$1.00 FAX; $9.00 Express.

Draughons Junior College, Registrar, 122 Commerce St, Montgomery, AL 36104, 334-263-1013 (FAX: 334-262-7326). Hours: 8AM-5PM. Records go back to 1950. Degrees granted: Associate.

Attendance and degree information available by phone, FAX, mail. Search requires name plus social security number. Other helpful information: approximate years of attendance. No fee for information.

Transcripts available by mail. Search requires name plus social security number, signed release. Other helpful information: approximate years of attendance. Fee is $5.00.

Major credit cards accepted for payment.

Draughons Junior College, Registrar, Plus Park at Pavilion Blvd, Nashville, TN 37217, 615-361-7555 (FAX: 615-367-2736). Hours: 8AM-6PM M-Th; 8AM-2PM F. Records go back to 1940s. Degrees granted: Associate.

Attendance and degree information available by phone, FAX, mail. Search requires name plus social security number, signed release. Other helpful information: date of birth, approximate years of attendance. No fee for information.

Transcripts available by mail. Search requires name plus social security number, approximate years of attendance, signed release. Other helpful information: date of birth. Fee is $2.00.

Draughons Junior College, (Branch Campus), Registrar, 2424 Airway Dr and Lovers Lane, Bowling Green, KY 42103, 502-843-6750. Hours: 8AM-5:30PM. Records go back to 1989. Degrees granted: Associate.

Attendance and degree information available by phone, mail. Search requires name plus social security number, exact years of attendance. No fee for information.

Transcripts available by mail. Search requires name plus social security number, exact years of attendance, signed release. No fee for transcripts.

Draughons Junior College, (Branch Campus), Registrar, 1860 Wilma Rudolph Blvd, Clarksville, TN 37040, 615-552-7600. Hours: 7:30AM-4:30PM. Records go back to 1954. Degrees granted: Associate.

Attendance and degree information available by phone, mail. Search requires name plus social security number, exact years of attendance. No fee for information.

Transcripts available by mail. Search requires name plus social security number, exact years of attendance, signed release. No fee for transcripts.

Drew University, Office of the Registrar, 36 Madison Ave, Madison, NJ 07940, 201-408-3025 (FAX: 201-408-3044). Hours: 9AM-5PM. Records go back to 1917. Alumni Records Office: 120 Madison Ave, Madison, NJ 07940. Degrees granted: Bachelors; Masters; Doctorate. Certification: Medical Humanities. Adverse incident record source: Office of Student Life, 201-408-3390.

Attendance and degree information available by phone, FAX, mail. Search requires name plus social security number. Other helpful information: date of birth, approximate years of attendance. No fee for information.

Transcripts available by written request only. Search requires name plus social security number, date of birth, approximate years of attendance, signed release. Fee is $5.00. Expedited service available for $10.00.

Transcripts requests by student only. Major credit cards accepted for payment.

Drexel University, Registrar, 32nd and Chestnut Sts, Philadelphia, PA 19104, 215-895-2300. Hours: 9AM-5PM. Records go back to 1891. Degrees granted: Bachelors; Masters; Doctorate.

Attendance information available by phone, FAX, mail. Search requires name only. Other helpful information: date of birth, approximate years of attendance. No fee for information.

Degree information available by phone, FAX, mail. Search requires name only. Other helpful information: social security number, date of birth, approximate years of attendance. No fee for information.

Transcripts available by mail. Search requires name plus social security number, approximate years of attendance, signed release. Other helpful information: date of birth, exact years of attendance. Fee is $2.00. Expedited service available for $5.00.

Drury College, Registrar, 900 N Benton Ave, Springfield, MO 65802, 417-873-7211. Hours: 8AM-8:30PM M-Th; 8AM-5PM F. Records go back 122 years. Degrees granted: Associate; Bachelors; Masters.

Attendance and degree information available by FAX, mail. Search requires name plus social security number, date of birth, approximate years of attendance, signed release. Other helpful information: exact years of attendance. No fee for information.

Transcripts available by FAX, mail. Search requires name plus social security number, date of birth, approximate years of attendance, signed release. Other helpful information: exact years of attendance. Fee is $5.00. Expedited service available for $12.00.

DuBois Business College, Registrar, One Beaver Dr, Du Bois, PA 15801, 814-371-6920 (FAX: 814-371-3974). Hours: 8:30AM-5PM. Records go back to 1960. Alumni records are maintained here also. Call 814-371-6920. Degrees granted: Associate. Adverse incident record source: Registrar, 814-371-6920.

Attendance information available by phone, FAX, mail. Search requires name plus social security number. No fee for information.

Degree information available by phone, FAX, mail. Search requires name plus social security number, signed release. No fee for information.

Transcripts available by FAX, mail. Search requires name plus social security number, exact years of attendance, signed release. Fee is $2.00.

Need former name.

Duff's Business Institute, Registrar, 110 Ninth St, Pittsburgh, PA 15222, 412-261-4530 (FAX: 412-261-4546). Hours: 8AM-4PM. Degrees granted: Associate.

Attendance information available by phone, FAX, mail. Search requires name plus social security number. Other helpful information: approximate years of attendance. No fee for information.

Degree information available by phone, FAX, mail. Search requires name plus social security number, approximate years of attendance. No fee for information.

Transcripts available by mail. Search requires name plus social security number, approximate years of attendance, signed release. Other helpful information: date of birth. Fee is $5.00. Expedited service available for $5.00.

Duke University, Registrar, PO Box 90054, Durham, NC 27708-0001, 919-684-2813 (FAX: 919-684-4500). Hours: 8AM-5PM. Records go back to 1938. Degrees granted: Bachelors; Masters; Doctorate. Adverse incident record source: Same as above.

Attendance and degree information available by phone, mail. Search requires name plus signed release. Other helpful information: social security number, date of birth, exact years of attendance. No fee for information.

Transcripts available by FAX, mail. Search requires name plus social security number, signed release. Other helpful information: date of birth. No fee for transcripts.

Duluth Technical School. Name changed to Lake Superior College as of July 1995.

Dundalk Community College, Registrar, 7200 Sollers Point Rd, Dundalk, MD 21222, 410-282-6700. Degrees granted: Associate.

Attendance and degree information available by phone, mail. Search requires name plus social security number, exact years of attendance. Other helpful information: approximate years of attendance. No fee for information.

Transcripts available by written request only. Search requires name plus social security number, exact years of attendance, signed release. Other helpful information: approximate years of attendance. No fee for transcripts.

Major credit cards accepted for payment.

Duquesne University, Registrar, 600 Forbes Ave, Pittsburgh, PA 15282, 412-396-6212. Hours: 8:30AM-4:30PM. Records go back to 1846. Alumni records are maintained here also. Call 412-396-6209. Degrees granted: Bachelors; Masters; Doctorate. Adverse incident record source: Registrar, 412-396-6212.

Attendance and degree information available by phone, mail. Search requires name plus social security number, date of birth, exact years of attendance. No fee for information.

Transcripts available by mail. Search requires name plus social security number, date of birth, exact years of attendance, signed release. Fee is $2.00.

Durham Technical Community College, Registrar, 1637 Lawson St, Durham, NC 27703, 919-598-9384 (FAX: 919-598-9183). Hours: 8AM-6PM M-Th; 8AM-5PM F. Records go back to 1960s. Practical Nursing records available from 1940's. Degrees granted: Associate.

Attendance and degree information available by phone, FAX, mail. Search requires name only. Other helpful information: social security number, date of birth, approximate years of attendance. No fee for information.

Transcripts available by FAX, mail. Search requires name plus signed release. Other helpful information: social security number, date of birth, approximate years of attendance. Fee is $1.00.

Dutchess Community College, Registrar, 53 Pendell Rd, Poughkeepsie, NY 12601-1595, 914-471-4500 X1500 (FAX: 914-431-8983). Hours: 8AM-5PM. Records go back to 1957. Alumni records are maintained here also. Call 914-471-4500. Degrees granted: Associate.

Attendance and degree information available by FAX, mail. Search requires name plus social security number, signed release. No fee for information.

Transcripts available by mail. Search requires name plus social security number, signed release. Fee is $3.00.

Dutchess Community College, (Branch Campus), Registrar, Martha Lawrence Ext Sit, Spackenhill Rd, Poughkeepsie,

The Sourcebook of College and University Student Records

NY 12603, 914-471-4500 X1500 (FAX: 914-471-4578). Hours: 8AM-9PM M-Th; 8AM-5PM F. Records go back to 1957. Degrees granted: Associate.

Attendance information available by FAX, mail. Search requires name plus social security number, signed release. No fee for information.

Degree information available by FAX, mail. Search requires name plus social security number, signed release. Other helpful information: approximate years of attendance. No fee for information.

Transcripts available by FAX, mail. Search requires name plus social security number, signed release. Other helpful information: approximate years of attendance. Fee is $1.00.

Dutchess Community College, (South Campus), Registrar, Hollowbrook Plaza, Wappingers Falls, NY 12590, 914-298-0755. Records are not housed here. They are located at Dutchess Community College, Registrar, 53 Pendell Rd, Poughkeepsie, NY 12601-1595.

Dyersburg State Community College, Admissions & Records, 1510 Lake Rd, Dyersburg, TN 38024, 901-286-3330 (FAX: 901-286-3333). Hours: 8AM-4:30PM. Records go back to 1969. Alumni records are maintained here also. Call 901-286-3247. Degrees granted: Associate.

Attendance and degree information available by phone, FAX, mail. Search requires name only. Other helpful information: social security number, date of birth, exact years of attendance. No fee for information.

Transcripts available by FAX, mail. Search requires name plus approximate years of attendance, signed release. Other helpful information: social security number, date of birth, exact years of attendance. No fee for transcripts.

Dyke College, Student Records, 112 Prospect Ave SE, Cleveland, OH 44115, 216-696-9000 X823 (FAX: 216-696-6430). Hours: 8:30AM-5PM. Records go back to 1848. Degrees granted: Associate; Bachelors.

Attendance and degree information available by phone, FAX, mail. Search requires name plus social security number, approximate years of attendance. Other helpful information: date of birth, exact years of attendance. No fee for information.

Transcripts available by mail. Search requires name plus social security number, approximate years of attendance, signed release. Other helpful information: date of birth, exact years of attendance. Fee is $2.00.

Major credit cards accepted for payment.

E

ETI Technical College, Registrar, 4300 Euclid Ave, Cleveland, OH 44103-9932, 216-431-4300 (FAX: 216-431-3198). Hours: 8AM-9PM. Records go back to 1940s. Degrees granted: Associate; Bachelors.

Attendance information available by phone, FAX, mail. Search requires name plus approximate years of attendance. No fee for information.

Degree information available by phone, FAX, mail. Search requires name plus social security number. Other helpful information: approximate years of attendance. No fee for information.

Transcripts available by FAX, mail. Search requires name plus social security number. Other helpful information: approximate years of attendance. Fee is $5.00.

Major credit cards accepted for payment.

ETI Technical College, Registrar, 1320 W Maple St NW, North Canton, OH 44720, 216-494-1214 (FAX: 216-494-8112). Hours: 9AM-5PM. Records go back to 1983. Degrees granted: Associate. Adverse incident record source: President, 216-494-1214.

Attendance and degree information available by phone, FAX, mail. Search requires name plus signed release. Other helpful information: social security number. No fee for information.

Transcripts available by FAX, mail. Search requires name plus signed release. Fee is $3.00.

ETI Technical College, (Niles), Registrar, 2076-86 Youngstown-Warren Rd, Niles, OH 44446-4398, 216-652-9916 X16 (FAX: 216-652-4399). Hours: 9AM-6PM. Records go back to 1989. Degrees granted: Associate.

Attendance and degree information available by phone, FAX, mail. Search requires name plus social security number, approximate years of attendance, signed release. No fee for information.

Transcripts available by phone, FAX, mail. Search requires name plus social security number. Fee is $7.00.

Earlham College, Registrar, National Rd W, Drawer 34, Richmond, IN 47374, 317-983-1515. Hours: 8AM-5PM. Records go back to 1847. Alumni Records Office: Drawer 193, Richmond, IN 47374 317-983-1313. Degrees granted: Bachelors; Masters.

Attendance and degree information available by phone, mail. Search requires name plus social security number, exact years of attendance. No fee for information.

Transcripts available by mail. Search requires name plus social security number, exact years of attendance, signed release. Fee is $2.00.

East Arkansas Community College, Registrar, 1700 Newcastle Rd, Forrest City, AR 72335-9598, 501-633-4480 (FAX: 501-633-7222). Hours: 8AM-8PM M-Th; 8AM-5PM F. Records go back to founding date. Degrees granted: Associate. Adverse incident record source: Carolyn Bowlin, 501-633-4480.

Attendance information available by phone, FAX, mail. Search requires name only. Other helpful information: social security number, date of birth, approximate years of attendance. No fee for information.

Degree information available by phone, FAX, mail. Search requires name only. Other helpful information: social security number, date of birth, approximate years of attendance. No fee for information.

Transcripts available by FAX, mail. Search requires name plus signed release. Other helpful information: social security number, date of birth, approximate years of attendance. Fee is $2.00.

East Carolina University, Registrar, E. Fifth St, Greenville, NC 27858-4353, 919-328-6524 (FAX: 919-325-4232). Hours: 8AM-5PM. Records go back to 1907. Alumni records are maintained here also. Call 919-328-6072. Degrees granted: Bachelors; Masters; Doctorate; Med. School. Special programs- Medical School, 919-816-2201. Adverse incident record source: Dean, 919-328-6824.

Attendance information available by phone, FAX, mail. Search requires name plus social security number. No fee for information.

Degree information available by phone, FAX, mail. Search requires name plus social security number, exact years of attendance. No fee for information.

Degree Granting Institutions

East Central College, Registrar, PO Box 529, Union, MO 63084, 314-583-5193 (FAX: 314-583-1897). Hours: 7:30AM-8PM. Records go back to founding date. Degrees granted: Associate.

Attendance and degree information available by phone, FAX, mail. Search requires name only. Other helpful information: social security number, date of birth. No fee for information.

Transcripts available by FAX, mail. Search requires name plus signed release. Other helpful information: social security number, date of birth. Fee is $2.00. Expedited service available for $2.00. Major credit cards accepted for payment.

East Central Community College, Registrar, PO Box 129, Decatur, MS 39327, 601-635-2111 X206 (FAX: 601-635-2150). Hours: 8AM-4:30PM. Records go back to 1928. Alumni records are maintained here also. Call 601-635-2111 X202. Degrees granted: Associate; Bachelors. Adverse incident record source: Dean of Students, 601-635-2111 X204.

Attendance and degree information available by phone, FAX, mail. Search requires name plus social security number, signed release. No fee for information.

Transcripts available by FAX, mail. Search requires name plus social security number, signed release. Fee is $2.00.

East Central University, Registrar, Ada, OK 74820, 405-332-8000 (FAX: 405-436-5495). Hours: 8AM-5PM. Records go back to 1907. Alumni records are maintained here also. Call 405-332-8000 X611. Degrees granted: Bachelors; Masters. Adverse incident record source: Student Services, 405-332-8000 X208.

Attendance information available by phone, FAX, mail. Search requires name plus social security number, approximate years of attendance. Other helpful information: date of birth. No fee for information.

Degree information available by phone, FAX, mail. Search requires name plus social security number. Other helpful information: date of birth, approximate years of attendance. No fee for information.

Transcripts available by FAX, mail. Search requires name plus social security number, signed release. Other helpful information: date of birth, approximate years of attendance. Fee is $2.00.

East Coast Bible College, Registrar, 6900 Wilkinson Blvd, Charlotte, NC 28214, 704-394-2307.

East Georgia College, Registrar, 13 College Circle, Swainsboro, GA 30401, 912-237-7831 (FAX: 912-237-5161). Hours: 8AM-5PM. Records go back to 1974. Degrees granted: Associate. Adverse incident record source: Student Affairs, 912-237-7831.

Attendance and degree information available by phone, FAX, mail. Search requires name plus social security number. No fee for information.

Transcripts available by mail. Search requires name plus social security number, signed release. No fee for transcripts.

East Los Angeles College, Registrar, 1301 Brooklyn Ave, Monterey Park, CA 91754, 213-265-8650. Hours: 8AM-5PM. Records go back to 1956. Alumni records are maintained here also. Call 213-265-8650. Degrees granted: Associate.

Attendance and degree information available by mail. Search requires name plus social security number, date of birth, exact years of attendance. Fee is $1.00.

Transcripts available by mail. Search requires name plus social security number, date of birth, exact years of attendance, signed release. Fee is $1.00.

East Mississippi Community College, Registrar, PO Box 158, Scooba, MS 39358, 601-476-8442 X219 (FAX: 601-476-4601). Hours: 8AM-4:30PM. Records go back to 1927. Degrees granted: Associate.

Attendance information available by phone, FAX, mail. Search requires name plus social security number, exact years of attendance. Other helpful information: date of birth. No fee for information.

Degree information available by phone, FAX, mail. Search requires name plus social security number, exact years of attendance. No fee for information.

Transcripts available by FAX, mail. Search requires name plus social security number, exact years of attendance, signed release. Other helpful information: date of birth. Fee is $3.00.

East Stroudsburg University of Pennsylvania, Registrar, 200 Prospect St, East Stroudsburg, PA 18301, 717-424-3148. Hours: 8AM-4:30PM. Records go back to 1890s. Alumni records are maintained here also. Call 714-424-3533. Degrees granted: Associate; Bachelors; Masters. Special programs- Graduate School, 717-424-3536. Adverse incident record source: Registrar, 717-424-3148.

Attendance and degree information available by phone, mail. Search requires name plus social security number, signed release. No fee for information.

Transcripts available by mail. Search requires name plus social security number, date of birth, exact years of attendance, signed release. Fee is $2.00.

East Tennessee State University, Registrar, PO Box 70561, Johnson City, TN 37614-0561, 615-929-4230 (FAX: 615-929-6604). Hours: 8AM-4:30PM. Records go back to 1911. Degrees granted: Associate; Bachelors; Masters; Doctorate. Certification: Respiratory Therapy, Surgican Technician, Dental Assistant. Adverse incident record source: Student Affairs.

Attendance and degree information available by phone, FAX, mail. Search requires name plus social security number. Other helpful information: approximate years of attendance. No fee for information.

Transcripts available by FAX, mail. Search requires name plus social security number, signed release. Other helpful information: approximate years of attendance. No fee for transcripts. FAX: $1.00 per page.

East Texas Baptist University, Registrar, 1209 N Grove Ave, Marshall, TX 75670-1498, 903-935-7963 (FAX: 903-938-1705). Hours: 8AM-4:30PM. Records go back to 1917. Degrees granted: Associate; Bachelors; Masters. Adverse incident record source: Student Affairs, 903-935-7963 X274.

Attendance and degree information available by phone, FAX, mail. Search requires name only. Other helpful information: social security number, date of birth, approximate years of attendance. No fee for information.

Transcripts available by mail. Search requires name plus social security number, date of birth, signed release. Other helpful information: approximate years of attendance. Fee is $2.00. Expedited service available for $12.00.

East Texas State University, Registrar, ETSU Station, Commerce, TX 75429-3011, 903-886-5448 (FAX: 903-886-5888). Hours: 8AM-5PM. Records go back to 1915. Degrees granted: Bachelors; Masters; Doctorate.

Attendance and degree information available by phone, FAX, mail. Search requires name only. Other helpful information: social security number, date of birth, approximate years of attendance. No fee for information.

Transcripts available by mail. Search requires name plus social security number, signed release. Other helpful information: date of birth, approximate years of attendance. No fee for transcripts.

East Texas State University at Texarkana, Admissions, ETSU-T, 2600 N Robison Rd, Texarkana, TX 75505, 903-838-6514 (FAX: 903-832-8890). Hours: 8AM-5PM. Records go back to 1923. Degrees granted: Bachelors; Masters.

Attendance and degree information available by phone, FAX, mail. Search requires name only. Other helpful information: social security number. No fee for information.

Transcripts available by mail. Search requires name plus social security number, signed release. Fee is $2.00.

East-West University, Registrar, 816 S Michigan Ave, Chicago, IL 60605, 312-934-0111 X16 (FAX: 312-939-0083). Hours: 8:30AM-5PM. Records go back to 1980. Degrees granted: Associate.

Attendance information available by phone, FAX. Search requires name plus social security number, signed release. No fee for information.

Degree information available by phone, FAX. Search requires name plus social security number, exact years of attendance, signed release. Other helpful information: date of birth, approximate years of attendance. No fee for information.

Transcripts available by FAX, mail. Search requires name plus social security number, date of birth, exact years of attendance, signed release. Other helpful information: approximate years of attendance. Fee is $3.00. Expedited service available for $6.00.

Eastern Arizona College, Records Office, Thatcher, AZ 85552-0769, 520-428-8250 (FAX: 520-428-8462). Hours: 9AM-4PM. Records go back to 1895. Alumni records are maintained here also. Call 520-428-8295. Degrees granted: Associate.

Attendance and degree information available by phone, FAX, mail. Search requires name plus social security number, date of birth, signed release. Other helpful information: approximate years of attendance. No fee for information.

Transcripts available by FAX, mail. Search requires name plus social security number, date of birth, signed release. Other helpful information: approximate years of attendance. Fee is $3.00.

Major credit cards accepted for payment.

Eastern Baptist Theological Seminary, Registrar, 6 Lancaster Ave, Wynnewood, PA 19096-3494, 610-645-9729 (FAX: 610-649-3834). Hours: 8:30AM-6:30PM. Records go back to 1925. Alumni records are maintained here also. Call 610-896-5000. Degrees granted: Masters. Certification: Christian Ministry.

Attendance information available by phone, FAX, mail. Search requires name plus approximate years of attendance. Other helpful information: social security number, exact years of attendance. No fee for information.

Degree information available by phone, FAX, mail. Search requires name only. Other helpful information: approximate years of attendance. No fee for information.

Transcripts available by written request only. Search requires name plus approximate years of attendance, signed release. Other helpful information: social security number, exact years of attendance. Fee is $5.00.

Eastern College, Registrar, 10 Fairview Dr, St Davids, PA 19087-3696, 610-341-5854 (FAX: 610-341-1707). Hours: 8AM-8PM. Records go back to 1952. Degrees granted: Associate; Bachelors; Masters. Adverse incident record source: Dean of Students, 610-341-5822.

Attendance and degree information available by phone, FAX, mail. Search requires name only. Other helpful information: social security number, approximate years of attendance. No fee for information.

Transcripts available by FAX, mail. Search requires name plus signed release. Other helpful information: social security number, approximate years of attendance. No fee for transcripts. Expedited service available for $5.00.

Eastern Connecticut State University, Registrar's Office, 83 Windham St, Willimantic, CT 06226-2295, 203-465-5224 (FAX: 203-465-4382). Hours: 8:30AM-4:30PM. Records go back to 1889. Degrees granted: Associate; Bachelors; Masters.

Attendance and degree information available by phone, FAX, mail. Search requires name plus social security number. Other helpful information: date of birth, approximate years of attendance. No fee for information.

Transcripts available by FAX, mail. Search requires name plus social security number, signed release. Other helpful information: date of birth, approximate years of attendance. Fee is $3.00.

Major credit cards accepted for payment.

Eastern Idaho Technical College, Registrar, 1600 S 2500 E, Idaho Falls, ID 83404, 208-524-3000 (FAX: 208-524-3007). Hours: 8AM-5PM. Records go back to 1971. Degrees granted: Associate.

Attendance and degree information available by phone, FAX, mail. Search requires name only. Other helpful information: social security number, date of birth, approximate years of attendance. No fee for information.

Transcripts available by mail. Search requires name plus signed release. Other helpful information: social security number, date of birth, approximate years of attendance. Fee is $2.00.

Eastern Illinois University, Registrar, 600 Lincoln Ave, Charleston, IL 61920, 217-581-3571 (FAX: 217-581-6452). Hours: 8AM-4PM. Records go back to 1895. Alumni records are maintained here also. Call 217-581-6616. Degrees granted: Bachelors; Masters. Adverse incident record source: Registrar, 217-581-3511.

Attendance and degree information available by phone, FAX, mail. Search requires name plus social security number, date of birth, exact years of attendance. No fee for information.

Transcripts available by FAX, mail. Search requires name plus social security number, date of birth, exact years of attendance, signed release. Fee is $4.00. Expedited service available for $0note.

Eastern Kentucky University, Records Office, Coates Box 28-A, Richmond, KY 40457-3101, 606-622-1102 (FAX: 606-622-6207). Hours: 8:30AM-4PM. Records go back to 1906. Degrees granted: Associate; Bachelors; Masters.

Attendance and degree information available by FAX, mail. Search requires name only. Other helpful information: social security number, date of birth. No fee for information.

Transcripts available by FAX, mail. Search requires name plus social security number, signed release. Other helpful information: date of birth, approximate years of attendance. No fee for transcripts. Expedite: Pay in advance for next day mail. Credit cards may be used over $10.00.

Major credit cards accepted for payment.

Eastern Maine Technical College, Registrar, 354 Hogan Rd, Bangor, ME 04401, 207-941-4625 (FAX: 207-941-4666). Hours: 9AM-4PM. Records go back 25 years. Degrees granted: Associate.

Attendance and degree information available by phone, FAX, mail. Search requires name plus social security number, date of birth. Other helpful information: approximate years of attendance. No fee for information.

Transcripts available by written request only. Search requires name plus social security number, date of birth, signed release. Other helpful information: approximate years of attendance. Fee is $3.00. Expedited service available for $10.00.

Need major.

Eastern Mennonite College and Seminary, Registrar, 1200 Park Rd, Harrisonburg, VA 22801-2462, 703-432-4110. Hours: 8AM-5PM. Records go back to 1917. Alumni records are maintained here also. Call 703-432-4206. Degrees granted: Bachelors; Masters; First Professional Degree.

Attendance and degree information available by phone, mail. Search requires name plus social security number, date of birth, exact years of attendance. No fee for information.

Transcripts available by mail. Search requires name plus social security number, date of birth, exact years of attendance, signed release. Fee is $2.00.

Eastern Michigan University, Registrar, Ypsilanti, MI 48197, 313-487-1849.

Attendance and degree information available by phone, mail. Search requires name plus social security number, signed release. Other helpful information: date of birth, approximate years of attendance. No fee for information.

Transcripts available by mail. Search requires name plus social security number, signed release. Other helpful information: date of birth, approximate years of attendance. Fee is $5.00. Expedited service available for $5.00.

Credit card may be used in person only.

Eastern Nazarene College, Registrar, 23 E Elm Ave, Quincy, MA 02170-2999, 617-745-3476/745-3477. Hours: 8AM-5PM. Alumni records are maintained here at the same phone number. Degrees granted: Bachelors; Masters.

Attendance and degree information available by phone, mail. Search requires name plus date of birth, exact years of attendance. No fee for information.

Transcripts available by mail. Search requires name plus date of birth, exact years of attendance, signed release. Fee is $3.00.

Eastern New Mexico University, Registrar, Portales, NM 88130, 505-562-2175 (FAX: 505-562-2566). Hours: 8AM-4PM. Records go back to 1950s. Degrees granted: Associate; Bachelors; Masters.

Attendance and degree information available by phone, mail. Search requires name plus social security number, signed release. Other helpful information: date of birth. No fee for information.

Transcripts available by FAX, mail. Search requires name plus social security number, signed release. Other helpful information: date of birth. No fee for transcripts.

Eastern New Mexico University-Roswell, Registrar, PO Box 6000, Roswell, NM 88202, 505-624-7145 (FAX: 505-624-7119). Hours: 8AM-5PM. Records go back to 1958. Degrees granted: Associate.

Attendance and degree information available by phone, FAX, mail. Search requires name plus social security number. Other helpful information: date of birth, approximate years of attendance. No fee for information.

Transcripts available by FAX, mail. Search requires name plus social security number, signed release. Other helpful information: date of birth, approximate years of attendance. No fee for transcripts.

Will accept FAX requests for transcripts, but will not send out by FAX.

Eastern Oklahoma State College, Registrar, 1301 W Main St, Wilburton, OK 74578, 918-465-2361 X346 (FAX: 918-465-2431). Hours: 7:30AM-4:30PM. Records go back to 1911. Degrees granted: Associate.

Attendance and degree information available by FAX, mail. Search requires name plus signed release. Other helpful information: social security number, approximate years of attendance. No fee for information.

Transcripts available by FAX, mail. Search requires name plus signed release. Other helpful information: social security number, approximate years of attendance. Fee is $2.00.

Eastern Oregon State College, Registrar, La Grande, OR 97850, 503-962-3519 (FAX: 503-962-3799). Hours: 8AM-5PM. Records go back to 1929. Alumni records are maintained here also. Call 503-962-3844. Degrees granted: Associate; Bachelors; MTE. Adverse incident record source: Security, 503-962-3350.

Attendance and degree information available by phone, FAX, mail. Search requires name plus social security number, approximate years of attendance. No fee for information.

Transcripts available by FAX, mail. Search requires name plus social security number, approximate years of attendance, signed release. First transcript $5.00; each additional $1.00.

Eastern Shore Community College, Registrar, Rte 1 Box 6, 29300 Lankford Hwy, Melfa, VA 23410, 804-787-5900 X15 (FAX: 804-787-5919). Hours: 8AM-5PM. Records go back to 1971. Alumni records are maintained here at the same phone number. Degrees granted: Associate.

Attendance and degree information available by phone, FAX, mail. Search requires name plus social security number, exact years of attendance. No fee for information.

Transcripts available by FAX, mail. Search requires name plus social security number, exact years of attendance, signed release. No fee for transcripts.

Eastern Virginia Medical School, Office of the Registrar, 721 Fairfax Ave #117, PO Box 1980, Norfolk, VA 23501-1980, 804-446-5244 (FAX: 804-446-5817). Hours: 8AM-4:30PM. Records go back to 1972. Degrees granted: Masters; Doctorate.

Attendance and degree information available by phone, mail. Search requires name plus social security number, signed release. Other helpful information: date of birth. No fee for information.

Transcripts available by mail. Search requires name plus social security number, signed release. No fee for transcripts.

Eastern Washington University, Registrar, MS 150, Cheney, WA 99004, 509-359-6202 (FAX: 509-359-6153). Hours: 8AM-5PM. Records go back to 1912. Alumni records are maintained here also. Call 509-359-6303. Degrees granted: Bachelors; Masters. Certification: Educ. Adverse incident record source: Campus Police, 509-359-6300.

School will not confirm attendance information. Search requires name plus signed release. Other helpful information: social security number, date of birth, approximate years of attendance. No fee for information.

Degree information available by phone. Search requires name plus signed release. Other helpful information: social security number, date of birth, approximate years of attendance. No fee for information.

Transcripts available by mail. Search requires name plus social security number, date of birth, signed release. Other helpful information: approximate years of attendance. Fee is $3.00.

Major credit cards accepted for payment.

Eastern Wyoming College, Registrar, 3200 W C St, Torrington, WY 82240, 307-532-8207 (FAX: 307-532-8222). Hours: 8AM-4:30PM. Degrees granted: Associate.

Attendance and degree information available by FAX, mail. Search requires name plus social security number, date of birth, signed release. Other helpful information: approximate years of attendance. No fee for information.

Transcripts available by phone, FAX. Search requires name plus social security number, date of birth, signed release. Other helpful information: approximate years of attendance. No fee for transcripts.

Eastfield College, Registrar, 3737 Motley Dr, Mesquite, TX 75150-2099, 214-324-7100. Hours: 8AM-5PM. Degrees granted: Associate.

Attendance and degree information available by mail. Search requires name plus social security number. No fee for information.

Transcripts available by mail. Search requires name plus social security number, signed release. No fee for transcripts.

Eckerd College, Registrar, 4200 54th Ave S, St Petersburg, FL 33711, 813-864-8217 (FAX: 813-864-8060). Hours: 8:30AM-5PM. Records go back to 1960. Alumni records are maintained here also. Call 813-864-8219. Degrees granted: Bachelors.

Attendance and degree information available by phone, FAX, mail. Search requires name only. No fee for information.

Transcripts available by FAX, mail. Search requires name only. Fee is $2.00.

Eden Theological Seminary, Registrar, 475 E Lockwood Ave, St Louis, MO 63119-3192, 314-961-3627 (FAX: 314-961-5738). Records go back to 1920s. Degrees granted: Masters; Doctorate.

Attendance and degree information available by phone, FAX, mail. Search requires name plus social security number, exact years of attendance, signed release. Other helpful information: approximate years of attendance. No fee for information.

Transcripts available by mail. Search requires name plus social security number, exact years of attendance, signed release. Other helpful information: approximate years of attendance. Fee is $5.00.

Edgecombe Community College, Registrar, 2009 W Wilson St, Tarboro, NC 27886, 919-823-5166. College was formerly Edgecombe Technical College.

Attendance and degree information available by phone, mail. Search requires name plus social security number, date of birth, approximate years of attendance. No fee for information.

Transcripts available by written request only. Search requires name plus social security number, date of birth, approximate years of attendance, signed release. Fee is $1.00.

Edgewood College, Registrar's Office, 855 Woodrow St, Madison, WI 53711, 608-257-4861. Hours: 8AM-4:30PM. Alumni records are maintained here at the same phone number. Degrees granted: Associate; Bachelors; Masters.

Attendance and degree information available by phone, FAX, mail. Search requires name only. Other helpful information: social security number, date of birth, approximate years of attendance. No fee for information.

Transcripts available by written request only. Search requires name plus signed release. Other helpful information: social security number, date of birth, approximate years of attendance. Fee is $2.00. Expedited service available for $10.00.

Edinboro University of Pennsylvania, Records & Registration, Edinboro, PA 16444, 814-732-2726 (FAX: 814-732-2680). Hours: 8AM-4:30PM. Records go back to 1900. Alumni records are maintained here also. Call 814-732-2715. Degrees granted: Associate; Bachelors; Masters. Adverse incident record source: Academic Affairs, 814-732-2825.

Attendance information available by phone, FAX, mail. Search requires name plus social security number. No fee for information.

Degree information available by phone, FAX, mail. Search requires name plus social security number, exact years of attendance. No fee for information.

Transcripts available by FAX, mail. Search requires name plus social security number, exact years of attendance, signed release. First transcript is free; $3.00 each additional.

Records released only if no privacy hold on file.

Edison Community College, Registrar, 8099 College Pkwy SW, PO Box 60210, Fort Myers, FL 33906-6210, 813-489-9317 (FAX: 813-489-9217). Hours: 8:30AM-4:30PM. Records go back to founding date. Degrees granted: Associate.

Attendance and degree information available by phone, mail. Search requires name plus social security number, exact years of attendance, signed release. Other helpful information: date of birth, approximate years of attendance. No fee for information.

Transcripts available by FAX, mail. Search requires name plus social security number, approximate years of attendance, signed release. Other helpful information: date of birth. No fee for transcripts.

Edison State Community College, Registrar, 1973 Edison Dr, Piqua, OH 45356, 513-778-8600 (FAX: 513-778-1920). Hours: 8AM-5PM. Records go back to 1973. Degrees granted: Associate.

Attendance and degree information available by phone, FAX, mail. Search requires name only. Other helpful information: social security number, date of birth. No fee for information.
Transcripts available by mail. Search requires name plus signed release. Other helpful information: date of birth. Fee is $2.00.
Major credit cards accepted for payment.

Edmonds Community College, Registrar, 20000 68th Ave W, Lynnwood, WA 98036, 206-771-7456 (FAX: 206-771-3366). Hours: 8AM-5PM. Degrees granted: Associate.
Attendance and degree information available by mail. Search requires name plus social security number, date of birth, exact years of attendance. No fee for information.
Transcripts available by mail. Search requires name plus social security number, date of birth, exact years of attendance, signed release. No fee for transcripts.

Edward Waters College, Registrar, 1658 Kings Rd, Jacksonville, FL 32209, 904-366-2710 (FAX: 904-366-2706). Hours: 8AM-5PM. Records go back to 1866. Degrees granted: Bachelors. Adverse incident record source: Student Affairs, 904-366-2514.
Attendance and degree information available by phone, FAX, mail. Search requires name plus social security number, signed release. No fee for information.
Transcripts available by mail. Search requires name plus social security number, signed release. Fee is $5.00.

El Camino College, Registrar, 16007 Crenshaw Blvd, Torrance, CA 90506, 310-660-3418 (FAX: 310-660-3818). Hours: 8AM-7:30PM. Records go back to 1945. Alumni records are maintained here also. Call 310-660-3500. Degrees granted: Associate. Adverse incident record source: Campus Security, 310-532-3670.
Attendance and degree information available by FAX, mail. Search requires name plus social security number, date of birth, exact years of attendance. No fee for information.
Transcripts available by mail. Search requires name plus social security number, date of birth, exact years of attendance, signed release. Fee is $2.00. Expedited service available for $5.00.

El Centro College, Registrar, Main and Lamar Sts, Callas, TX 75202-3604, 214-765-2311 (FAX: 214-746-2335). Hours: 8AM-7PM. Records go back to 1966. Degrees granted: Associate. Adverse incident record source: Student Services, 214-746-2017.
Attendance and degree information available by phone, FAX, mail. Search requires name plus social security number. Other helpful information: date of birth, approximate years of attendance. No fee for information.
Transcripts available by FAX, mail. Search requires name plus social security number, signed release. Other helpful information: date of birth, approximate years of attendance. No fee for transcripts.

El Paso Community College, Registrar, PO Box 20500, El Paso, TX 79998, 915-594-2300 (FAX: 915-594-2161). Hours: 8AM-5PM M-F; 8AM-Noon S. Records go back to 1970. Degrees granted: Associate.
Attendance and degree information available by phone, FAX, mail. Search requires name plus social security number, signed release. Other helpful information: date of birth, approximate years of attendance. No fee for information.
Transcripts available by FAX, mail. Search requires name plus social security number, signed release. Other helpful information: date of birth, approximate years of attendance. Fee is $2.00.

Major credit cards accepted for payment.

Elaine P. Nunez Community College, Registrar, 3700 LaFontaine St, Chalmette, LA 70043, 504-278-7350 (FAX: 504-278-7353). Hours: 8AM-7PM M,T,W; 8AM-4:30PM Th,F. Records go back 29 years. Also has records for former schools: St. Bernard Parish Community College, and Elain P. Nunez Technical Institute. Degrees granted: Associate. Adverse incident record source: VP Student Affairs, 504-278-7350.
Attendance information available by phone, FAX, mail. Search requires name plus social security number. Other helpful information: approximate years of attendance. No fee for information.
Degree information available by phone, FAX, mail. Search requires name only. Other helpful information: social security number, date of birth, approximate years of attendance. No fee for information.
Transcripts available by FAX, mail. Search requires name plus social security number, signed release. Other helpful information: date of birth, approximate years of attendance. Fee is $3.00. Expedited service available for $3.00.
Major credit cards accepted for payment.

Elaine P. Nunez Community College, (Branch), Registrar, PO Drawer 944, Port Sulphur, LA 70083, 504-564-2701. Records are not housed here. They are located at Nunez Community College, (Branch), Registrar, 901 Delery St, New Orleans, LA 70117.

Electronic Data Processing College, Registrar, PO Box 2303, Hato Rey, PR 00919, 809-765-3560 (FAX: 809-765-2650). Hours: 8AM-5PM. Degrees granted: Associate; Bachelors; Masters.
Attendance and degree information available by FAX, mail. Search requires name plus exact years of attendance, signed release. Other helpful information: approximate years of attendance. No fee for information.
Transcripts available by mail. Search requires name plus exact years of attendance, signed release. Other helpful information: approximate years of attendance. Fee is $3.00.

Electronic Data Processing College of PR, Inc., Registrar, PO Box 1674, San Sebastian, PR 00685, 809-896-2252 (FAX: 809-896-0066). Hours: 8AM-5PM. Records go back to 1978. Degrees granted: Associate.
Attendance and degree information available by mail. Search requires name plus social security number, signed release. Other helpful information: approximate years of attendance. No fee for information.
Transcripts available by mail. Search requires name plus social security number, signed release. Other helpful information: approximate years of attendance. Fee is $1.00.

Electronic Institutes, Registrar, 19 Jamesway Plaza, Middletown, PA 17057-4851, 717-944-2731 (FAX: 717-944-2734). Hours: 8AM-3PM. Records go back to 1959. Degrees granted: Associate.
Attendance and degree information available by phone, FAX, mail. Search requires name plus social security number. Other helpful information: approximate years of attendance. No fee for information.
Transcripts available by phone, FAX, mail. Search requires name plus social security number, signed release. Other helpful information: approximate years of attendance. No fee for transcripts.

Electronic Institutes, Registrar, 4634 Browns Hill Rd, Pittsburgh, PA 15217-2919, 412-521-8686 (FAX: 412-521-9277). Hours: 8AM-3:30PM. Records go back 30 years. Degrees granted: Associate.

Attendance and degree information available by phone, FAX, mail. Search requires name plus social security number, date of birth. Other helpful information: approximate years of attendance. No fee for information.

Transcripts available by FAX, mail. Search requires name plus social security number, date of birth, signed release. Other helpful information: approximate years of attendance. No fee for transcripts.

Elgin Community College, Registrar, 1700 Spartan Dr, Elgin, IL 60123, 708-697-1000 (FAX: 708-697-9209). Hours: 8AM-7PM. Records go back to 1949. Degrees granted: Associate.

Attendance and degree information available by FAX, mail. Search requires name plus social security number, signed release. Other helpful information: date of birth, approximate years of attendance. No fee for information.

Transcripts available by FAX, mail. Search requires name plus social security number, signed release. Other helpful information: date of birth, approximate years of attendance. Fee is $1.00.

Elizabeth City State University, Registrar, ECSU Box 790, Elizabeth City, NC 27909, 919-335-3400. Degrees granted: Bachelors.

Attendance and degree information available by phone, mail. Search requires name plus social security number, approximate years of attendance. No fee for information.

Transcripts available by written request only. Search requires name plus social security number, approximate years of attendance, signed release. Fee is $2.00.

Elizabethtown College, Registrar, One Alpha Dr, Elizabethtown, PA 17022-2298, 717-361-1409. Hours: 8:30AM-5PM. Records go back to 1940. Alumni records are maintained here also. Call 717-367-1151. Degrees granted: Bachelors.

Attendance and degree information available by phone, mail. Search requires name plus social security number, exact years of attendance. No fee for information.

Transcripts available by mail. Search requires name plus social security number, exact years of attendance, signed release. Fee is $2.00.

Elizabethtown Community College, Registrar, 600 College Street Rd, Elizabethtown, KY 42701, 502-769-1632. Hours: 8AM-5PM M-Th, 8AM-Noon F. Records go back to 1965. Degrees granted: Associate.

Attendance and degree information available by phone, mail. Search requires name plus social security number. Other helpful information: date of birth, approximate years of attendance. No fee for information.

Transcripts available by mail. Search requires name plus social security number, signed release. Other helpful information: date of birth, approximate years of attendance. Fee is $2.00. Expedited service available for $5.00.

Ellsworth Community College, Registrar, 1100 College Ave, Iowa Falls, IA 50126, 800-322-9235 X436 (FAX: 515-648-3128). Hours: 8AM-5PM. Records go back to 1940s. Alumni records are maintained here also. Call 800-322-9235 X247. Degrees granted: Associate.

Attendance and degree information available by phone, FAX, mail. Search requires name plus social security number, signed release. Other helpful information: date of birth, approximate years of attendance. No fee for information.

Transcripts available by written request only. Search requires name plus social security number, signed release. Other helpful information: exact years of attendance. Fee is $3.00.

Elmhurst College, Registration & Records, 190 Prospect St, Elmhurst, IL 60126-3296, 708-617-3052 (FAX: 708-617-3245). Hours: 8AM-9PM M-Th; 8AM-4PM F. Records go back to 1871. Degrees granted: Bachelors.

Attendance and degree information available by phone, FAX, mail. Search requires name only. Other helpful information: social security number, approximate years of attendance. No fee for information.

Transcripts available by FAX, mail. Search requires name plus signed release. Other helpful information: social security number, approximate years of attendance. Fee is $3.00. Expedited service available for $5.00.

Elmira College, Registrar, Park Place, Elmira, NY 14901, 607-735-1895 (FAX: 607-735-1758). Hours: 8:30AM-5PM. Records go back to 1855. Degrees granted: Associate; Bachelors; Masters.

Attendance and degree information available by phone, FAX, mail. Search requires name only. No fee for information.

Transcripts available by FAX, mail. Search requires name plus social security number, signed release. Other helpful information: approximate years of attendance. Fee is $3.00.

Elon College, Registrar, Campus Box 2106, Elon College, NC 27244, 919-584-2376.

Attendance and degree information available by phone, mail. Search requires name plus social security number. No fee for information.

Transcripts available by written request only. Search requires name plus social security number, signed release. Fee is $3.00.

Embry-Riddle Aeronautical University, Registrar, 600 S Clyde Morris Blvd, Daytona Beach, FL 32114-3900, 904-226-6030 (FAX: 904-226-7070). Hours: 8AM-5PM. Records go back to 1945. Alumni records are maintained here also. Call 904-226-6160. Degrees granted: Associate; Bachelors; Masters. Special programs- Aviation Maintenance Technology, 904-226-6779: Extended Campus, active records, 904-226-6910: Extended Campus, inactive records, 904-226-6920. Adverse incident record source: Office of Student Affairs, Daytona, 904-226-6326: Office of Student Affairs, Prescott, 602-776-3774

Attendance and degree information available by phone, FAX, mail. Search requires name plus social security number. Other helpful information: date of birth, approximate years of attendance. No fee for information.

Transcripts available by mail. Search requires name plus social security number, signed release. Other helpful information: date of birth, approximate years of attendance. Fee is $4.00. Expedite transcript: Student must prepay.

Embry-Riddle Aeronautical University, (Branch), Registrar, 3200 N Willow Creek Rd, Prescott, AZ 86301, 520-776-3808 (FAX: 520-776-3806). Hours: 8AM-5PM. Records go back to 18yr. Degrees granted: Associate; Bachelors; Masters. Adverse incident record source: Police Dept, 520-778-1444.

Attendance information available by phone, FAX, mail. Search requires name only. Other helpful information: social security number. No fee for information.

Degree information available by phone, FAX, mail. Search requires name only. Other helpful information: social security number, approximate years of attendance. No fee for information.

Transcripts available by FAX, mail. Search requires name plus signed release. Other helpful information: social security number, approximate years of attendance. Fee is $4.00.

Major credit cards accepted for payment.

Emerson College, Registrar, 100 Beacon St, Boston, MA 02116-1596, 617-578-8660 (FAX: 617-578-8619). Hours: 9AM-5PM. Records go back to 1965. Some records prior to 1965 stored on microfilm. Degrees granted: Bachelors; Masters.

Attendance and degree information available by phone, FAX, mail. Search requires name plus approximate years of attendance. Other helpful information: social security number, date of birth, exact years of attendance. No fee for information.

Transcripts available by mail. Search requires name plus approximate years of attendance, signed release. Other helpful information: social security number, date of birth, exact years of attendance. No fee for transcripts.

Emmanuel College, Registrar, 400 The Fenway, Boston, MA 02115, 617-735-9960 (FAX: 617-731-9877). Hours: 8:30AM-4:30PM. Records go back 75 years. Alumni records are maintained here at the same phone number. Degrees granted: Bachelors; Masters.

Attendance and degree information available by phone, FAX, mail. Search requires name plus social security number, signed release. No fee for information.

Transcripts available by mail. Search requires name plus social security number, signed release. Fee is $2.00.

Emmanuel College, Registrar, 212 Spring St, PO Box 129, Franklin Springs, GA 30639, 706-245-7226 (FAX: 706-245-4424). Hours: 8-11:30AM, 12:30-4PM. Records go back to 1919. Degrees granted: Associate; Bachelors.

Attendance and degree information available by phone, FAX, mail. Search requires name only. Other helpful information: social security number, date of birth, approximate years of attendance. No fee for information.

Transcripts available by FAX, mail. Search requires name plus signed release. Other helpful information: social security number, date of birth, approximate years of attendance. Fee is $2.00.

Emmanuel School of Religion, Registrar, One Walker Dr, Johnson City, TN 37601, 615-461-1520 (FAX: 615-461-1556). Hours: 8AM-5PM Winter; 8AM-4PM Summer. Degrees granted: Masters; Doctorate. Adverse incident record source: President's Office, 615-461-1510 .

Attendance and degree information available by phone, FAX, mail. Search requires name plus date of birth. Other helpful information: social security number, approximate years of attendance. No fee for information.

Transcripts available by phone, FAX, mail. Search requires name plus social security number, date of birth, signed release. Other helpful information: approximate years of attendance. Fee is $2.00.

Emmaus Bible College, Registrar, 2570 Asbury Rd, Dubuque, IA 52001, 319-588-8000 (FAX: 319-588-1216). Hours: 8AM-5PM. Records go back to 1945. Alumni records are maintained here also. Call 319-588-8000. Degrees granted: Associate; Bachelors.

Attendance and degree information available by phone, FAX, mail. Search requires name only. Other helpful information: social security number, date of birth, approximate years of attendance. No fee for information.

Transcripts available by mail. Search requires name plus signed release. Other helpful information: social security number, date of birth, approximate years of attendance. Fee is $2.00.

Emory University, Office of the Registrar, 100 Boisfeuillet Jones Center, Atlanta, GA 30322-1970, 404-727-6042. Hours: 8AM-4:30PM. Records go back to 1836. Alumni records are maintained here also. Call 404-727-6400. Degrees granted: Associate; Bachelors; Masters; Doctorate. Adverse incident record source: Registrar, 404-727-6042.

Attendance and degree information available by phone, mail. Search requires name only. Other helpful information: social security number, date of birth, approximate years of attendance. No fee for information.

Transcripts available by mail. Search requires name plus signed release. Other helpful information: social security number, date of birth, approximate years of attendance. Transcript fee ranges from $2.00 to $4.00.

Emory and Henry College, Registrar, PO Box 947, Emory, VA 24327, 703-944-4121 (FAX: 703-944-4438). Hours: 8AM-5PM. Records go back to 1902. Alumni records are maintained here at the same phone number. Degrees granted: Bachelors.

Attendance and degree information available by phone, mail. Search requires name plus social security number, exact years of attendance. No fee for information.

Transcripts available by mail. Search requires name plus social security number, exact years of attendance, signed release. Fee is $3.00.

Emperor's College of Traditional Oriental Medicine, Registrar, 1807-B Wilshire Blvd, Santa Monica, CA 90403, 310-453-8300 (FAX: 310-829-3838). Hours: 8AM-5PM. Records go back to 1982. Degrees granted: Masters.

Attendance and degree information available by mail. Search requires name plus social security number, date of birth, exact years of attendance, signed release. No fee for information.

Transcripts available by mail. Search requires name plus social security number, date of birth, exact years of attendance, signed release. No fee for transcripts.

Emperor's College of Traditional Oriental Medicine, (Branch), Registrar, 3625 W 6th St Ste 220, Los Angeles, CA 90020, 310-453-8300. Records are not housed here. They are located at Emperor's College of Traditional Oriental Medicine, Registrar, 1807-B Wilshire Blvd, Santa Monica, CA 90403.

Empire College, Registrar, 3033 Cleveland Ave Ste 102, Santa Rosa, CA 95403, 707-546-4000 (FAX: 707-546-4058). Hours: 8AM-5PM. Degrees granted: Associate; JD.

Attendance and degree information available by written request only. Search requires name plus social security number, date of birth, exact years of attendance, signed release. No fee for information.

Transcripts available by phone, FAX, mail. Search requires name plus date of birth, exact years of attendance, signed release. Other helpful information: social security number. No fee for transcripts.

Emporia State University, Registrar, 1200 Commercial St, Emporia, KS 66801, 316-341-5154 (FAX: 316-341-5073). Hours: 8AM-5PM; 7:30AM-4PM Summer. Records go back to 1900. Alumni Records Office: PO Box 4047, Emporia, KS 66801, 316-341-5440. Degrees granted: Bachelors; Masters; Doctorate. Adverse incident record source: 316-341-5337.

Attendance and degree information available by phone, FAX, mail. Search requires name only. Other helpful information: social security number, date of birth, approximate years of attendance. No fee for information.

Transcripts available by mail. Search requires name plus signed release. Other helpful information: social security number, date of birth, approximate years of attendance. Fee is $5.00.

Endicott College, Registrar, Beverly, MA 01915, 508-927-0585 X2065 (FAX: 508-927-0084). Hours: 9AM-5PM. Records go back to 1939. Degrees granted: Associate; Bachelors.

Attendance and degree information available by phone, FAX, mail. Search requires name plus exact years of attendance. Other helpful information: social security number. No fee for information.

Transcripts available by mail. Search requires name plus exact years of attendance, signed release. Other helpful information: social security number. Fee is $2.00.

Enterprise State Junior College, Registrar, 600 Plaza Dr, PO Box 1300, Enterprise, AL 36331, 334-347-2623 X233 (FAX: 334-347-1157). Hours: 7:45AM-4:30PM. Records go back to 1965. Degrees granted: Associate.

Attendance and degree information available by phone, FAX, mail. Search requires name plus social security number, date of birth. Other helpful information: approximate years of attendance. No fee for information.

Transcripts available by FAX, mail. Search requires name plus social security number, date of birth, signed release. Other helpful information: approximate years of attendance. No fee for transcripts.

Episcopal Divinity School, Registrar, 99 Brattle St, Cambridge, MA 02138, 617-868-3450 (FAX: 617-864-5385). Hours: 9AM-5PM. Degrees granted: Masters; Doctorate.

Attendance information available by phone, FAX, mail. Search requires name plus approximate years of attendance. No fee for information.

Degree information available by phone, FAX, mail. Search requires name plus approximate years of attendance. Other helpful information: exact years of attendance. No fee for information.

Transcripts available by mail. Search requires name plus approximate years of attendance, signed release. Other helpful information: exact years of attendance. Fee is $3.00. Expedited service available for $3.00.

Episcopal Theological Seminary of the Southwest, Registrar, PO Box 2247, Austin, TX 78768-2247, 512-472-4133 (FAX: 512-472-3098). Hours: 8:15AM-2PM. Records go back to 1955. Degrees granted: Masters.

Attendance and degree information available by phone, FAX, mail. Search requires name only. Other helpful information: social security number, approximate years of attendance. No fee for information.

Transcripts available by mail. Search requires name plus signed release. Other helpful information: social security number, approximate years of attendance. Fee is $2.00.

Erie Business Center, Registrar, 246 W Ninth St, Erie, PA 16501, 814-456-7504 (FAX: 814-456-4882). Hours: 8AM-5PM. Records go back to 1955. Alumni records are maintained here also. Call 814-456-7504. Degrees granted: Associate. Adverse incident record source: Registrar, 814-456-7504.

Attendance and degree information available by phone, FAX, mail. Search requires name plus social security number. No fee for information.

Transcripts available by FAX, mail. Search requires name plus social security number, signed release. Other helpful information: exact years of attendance. Fee is $3.00.

Major credit cards accepted for payment.

Erie Business Center, (Erie Business Center South), Registrar, 700 Moravia St, New Castle, PA 16101, 412-658-3595 (FAX: 412-658-3083). Hours: 9AM-5PM. Records go back to 1970. Degrees granted: Associate.

Attendance and degree information available by phone, mail. Search requires name plus social security number, exact years of attendance. No fee for information.

Transcripts available by mail. Search requires name plus social security number, exact years of attendance, signed release. Fee is $3.00.

Erie Community College City Campus, Registrar, 121 Ellicott St, Buffalo, NY 14203, 716-851-1166 (FAX: 716-851-1129). Hours: 8AM-6PM M,T; 8AM-4PM W-F. Records go back to 1971. Alumni Records Office: 4041 Southwestern Blvd, Orchard Park, NY 14127-2155. Degrees granted: Associate. Adverse incident record source: Dean of Students, 716-851-1120.

Attendance information available by phone, FAX, mail. Search requires name plus social security number. Other helpful information: date of birth, approximate years of attendance. No fee for information.

Degree information available by phone, FAX, mail. Search requires name plus social security number, signed release. Other helpful information: date of birth, approximate years of attendance. No fee for information.

Transcripts available by mail. Search requires name plus social security number, signed release. Other helpful information: date of birth, approximate years of attendance. Fee is $3.00. Expedited service available for $3.00.

FAX request for unofficial transcripts to be mailed. Major credit cards accepted for payment.

Erie Community College North (Amherst) Campus, Registrar, 6205 Main St, Williamsville, NY 14221, 716-851-1467 (FAX: 716-851-1429). Hours: 8AM-4PM M,Th,F; 8AM-6PM T,W. Records go back to 1950. Alumni records are maintained here also. Call 716-851-1002. Degrees granted: Associate.

Attendance and degree information available by phone, FAX, mail. Search requires name plus social security number, approximate years of attendance, signed release. No fee for information.

Transcripts available by mail. Search requires name plus social security number, approximate years of attendance, signed release. Fee is $3.00.

Erie Community College South Campus, Registrar, S-4041 Southwestern Blvd, Orchard Park, NY 14127-2199, 716-851-1166 (FAX: 716-851-1629). Hours: 8AM-4PM; 4-8PM W. Records go back to 1985. Alumni records are maintained here also. Call 716-851-1663. Degrees granted: Associate.

Attendance and degree information available by phone, FAX, mail. Search requires name plus social security number. Other

helpful information: approximate years of attendance. No fee for information.
Transcripts available by FAX, mail. Search requires name plus social security number, signed release. Other helpful information: approximate years of attendance. Fee is $3.00. Expedited service available for $8.00.
Major credit cards accepted for payment.

Erskine College Seminary, Registrar, 2 Washington St, Due West, SC 29639, 803-379-8773 (FAX: 803-379-8759). Hours: 8AM-5PM. Records go back to 1890s. Alumni records are maintained here also. Call 803-379-8881. Degrees granted: Bachelors; Masters; Doctorate. Certification: Theology.
Attendance information available by phone, FAX, mail. Search requires name plus signed release. No fee for information.
Degree information available by phone, FAX, mail. Search requires name only. No fee for information.
Transcripts available by mail. Search requires name plus signed release. Other helpful information: social security number, date of birth. Fee is $5.00. Expedite service at FedEx cost.

Essex Agricultural and Technical Institute, Registrar, 562 Maple St, Hathorne, MA 01937, 508-774-0050 X24. Hours: 8AM-4PM. Records go back to 1960. Degrees granted: Associate.
Attendance and degree information available by phone, mail. Search requires name plus approximate years of attendance, signed release. No fee for information.
Transcripts available by phone. Search requires name plus approximate years of attendance, signed release. Fee is $2.00.

Essex Community College, Registrar, 7201 Rossville Blvd, Baltimore, MD 21237, 410-780-6363 (FAX: 410-686-9503). Hours: 8:30AM-9PM M-Th; 9AM-4PM F. Records go back to 1957. Degrees granted: Associate.
Attendance information available by phone, FAX, mail. Search requires name plus social security number. Other helpful information: date of birth, approximate years of attendance. No fee for information.
Degree information available by mail. Search requires name plus social security number. Other helpful information: date of birth, approximate years of attendance. No fee for information.
Transcripts available by mail. Search requires name plus social security number, signed release. Other helpful information: date of birth, approximate years of attendance. No fee for transcripts.

Essex County College, Registrar, 303 University Ave, Newark, NJ 07102, 201-877-3111 (FAX: 201-623-6449). Hours: 8:30AM-7:30PM M-Th; 9AM-5PM F. Records go back to 1968. Degrees granted: Associate. Adverse incident record source: Security Office, 201-877-3131.
Attendance information available by phone, FAX, mail. Search requires name plus social security number, signed release. Other helpful information: approximate years of attendance. No fee for information.
Degree information available by phone, FAX, mail. Search requires name plus social security number, exact years of attendance, signed release. Other helpful information: approximate years of attendance. No fee for information.
Transcripts available by FAX, mail. Search requires name plus social security number, signed release. Other helpful information: date of birth, approximate years of attendance. Fee is $2.00. Expedited service available for $2.00.
Major credit cards accepted for payment.

Essex County College, (West Essex Branch Campus), Registrar, 730 Bloomfield Ave, West Caldwell, NJ 07006, 201-403-2560 (FAX: 201-228-6181). Hours: 8AM-4:30PM. Degrees granted: Associate.
Attendance and degree information available by mail. Search requires name plus social security number, exact years of attendance. No fee for information.
Transcripts available by mail. Search requires name plus social security number, exact years of attendance, signed release. Fee is $2.00.

Eugene Bible College, Registrar, 2155 Bailey Hill Rd, Eugene, OR 97405, 503-485-1780 (FAX: 503-485-5801). Hours: 8AM-5PM. Records go back 7 years. Degrees granted: Bachelors. Certification: Bible.
Attendance and degree information available by phone, FAX, mail. Search requires name plus approximate years of attendance. Other helpful information: social security number, exact years of attendance. No fee for information.
Transcripts available by phone, FAX, mail. Search requires name plus social security number, date of birth, approximate years of attendance, signed release. No fee for transcripts.

Eureka College, Registrar, 300 E College Ave, Eureka, IL 61530, 309-467-3721 (FAX: 309-467-6325). Hours: 8AM-5PM. Records go back to 1855. Alumni records are maintained here also. Call 309-467-6314. Degrees granted: Bachelors.
Attendance and degree information available by phone, FAX, mail. Search requires name plus social security number, exact years of attendance. No fee for information.
Transcripts available by FAX, mail. Search requires name plus social security number, exact years of attendance, signed release. Fee is $2.00. FAX fee 4.00.

Evangel College, Registrar, 1111 N Glenstone Ave, Springfield, MO 65802, 417-865-2811 X7431 (FAX: 417-865-9599). Hours: 8AM-4:30PM. Records go back to 1955. Alumni records are maintained here also. Call 417-865-2811 X7333. Degrees granted: Associate; Bachelors. Adverse incident record source: Student Development, 417-865-2811 X7316.
Attendance and degree information available by phone, FAX, mail. Search requires name plus social security number, signed release. No fee for information.
Transcripts available by FAX, mail. Search requires name plus social security number, signed release. Fee is $3.00.

Evangelical School of Theology, Registrar, 121 S College St, Myerstown, PA 17067, 717-866-5775. Hours: 8AM-4PM. Records go back to 1953. Alumni records are maintained here also. Call 717-866-5775. Degrees granted: Bachelors; Masters.
Attendance and degree information available by phone, mail. Search requires name plus social security number. No fee for information.
Transcripts available by mail. Search requires name plus social security number, signed release. Other helpful information: exact years of attendance. Fee is $2.00.

Evangelical Seminary of Puerto Rico, Registrar, 776 Ponce de Leon Ave, San Juan, PR 00925, 809-763-6084 (FAX: 809-751-0847). Hours: 7AM-4:30PM. Alumni records are maintained here at the same phone number. Degrees granted: Masters.
Attendance information available by mail. Search requires name plus social security number. No fee for information.

Degree information available by mail. Search requires name plus social security number. Other helpful information: approximate years of attendance. No fee for information.

Transcripts available by mail. Search requires name plus social security number. Fee is $25.00.

Everett Community College, Registrar, 801 Wetmore Ave, Everett, WA 98201-1327, 206-388-9206 (FAX: 206-388-9129). Hours: 9AM-5PM. Records go back to 1954. Degrees granted: Associate.

Attendance and degree information available by phone, FAX, mail. Search requires name plus social security number. Other helpful information: approximate years of attendance. No fee for information.

Transcripts available by FAX, mail. Search requires name plus social security number, signed release. Other helpful information: approximate years of attendance. Transcripts cost $5.00; unofficial student copies are free.

Major credit cards accepted for payment.

Evergreen State College, Registration & Records, Library 1100, Olympia, WA 98505, 360-866-6000 X6180 (FAX: 360-866-6680). Hours: 9AM-4PM. Records go back to founding date. Personal files are kept for 7 years after student leaves. Alumni records are maintained here also. Call 360-866-6000 X6551. Degrees granted: Bachelors; Masters. Adverse incident record source: Student Affairs.

Attendance and degree information available by phone, FAX, mail. Search requires name plus social security number, date of birth, signed release. Other helpful information: exact years of attendance. No fee for information.

Transcripts available by written request only. Search requires name plus social security number, date of birth, signed release. Other helpful information: exact years of attendance. Fee is $10.00.

Major credit cards accepted for payment.

Evergreen Valley College, Registrar, 3095 Yerba Buena Rd, San Jose, CA 95135, 408-270-6442 (FAX: 408-223-9351). Hours: 8AM-5PM. Records go back to 1975. Degrees granted: Associate.

Attendance information available by written request only. Search requires name plus social security number. Other helpful information: date of birth, exact years of attendance. No fee for information.

Degree information available by phone, FAX, mail. Search requires name plus social security number. Other helpful information: date of birth, exact years of attendance. No fee for information.

Transcripts available by FAX, mail. Search requires name plus social security number. Other helpful information: date of birth, exact years of attendance. Fee is $3.50. Expedited service available for $7.50.

Include a self addressed stamped envelope with mail request. Major credit cards accepted for payment.

F

Fairfield University, Registrar, Fairfield, CT 06430, 203-254-4000 (FAX: 203-254-4109). Alumni records are maintained here also. Call 203-254-4280. Degrees granted: Bachelors; Graduate, Nurse, Finance. Adverse incident record source: Dean's Office, 203-254-4000.

Attendance and degree information available by phone, FAX, mail. Search requires name plus social security number. Other helpful information: approximate years of attendance. No fee for information.

Transcripts available by FAX, mail. Search requires name plus social security number, signed release. Other helpful information: approximate years of attendance. Fee is $4.00.

Fairleigh Dickinson University, Registrar, 1000 River Rd, Teaneck, NJ 07666, 201-692-2218. Hours: 9AM-5PM. Records go back to 1952. Alumni records are maintained here also. Call 201-692-7013. Degrees granted: Bachelors; Masters; Ph.D.

Attendance information available by mail. Search requires name plus social security number, approximate years of attendance, signed release. No fee for information.

School will not confirm degree information. Search requires name plus social security number, approximate years of attendance, signed release. No fee for information.

Transcripts available by mail. Search requires name plus social security number, approximate years of attendance, signed release. Fee is $5.00.

Fairleigh Dickinson University, (Florham-Madison Campus), Offic of Enrollment Svcs, 285 Madison Ave, Madison, NJ 07940, 201-593-8600 (FAX: 201-593-8604). Hours: 9AM-5PM. Records go back to 1958. Degrees granted: Associate; Bachelors; Masters. Adverse incident record source: Madison & Teaneck Campuses.

Attendance and degree information available by phone, FAX, mail. Search requires name plus social security number, signed release. Other helpful information: date of birth, approximate years of attendance. Fee is $5.00.

Transcripts available by phone, FAX, mail. Search requires name plus social security number, signed release. Other helpful information: date of birth, approximate years of attendance. Fee is $5.00.

Fairleigh Dickinson University, (Rutherford Campus), Registrar, 223 Montrose Ave, Rutherford, NJ 07070, 201-460-5000. Transcripts are housed in Teaneck (see above). They will confirm attendance and degrees by phone or mail. Search requires name plus social security number and years attended.

Fairleigh Dickinson University, (Teaneck-Hackensack Campus), Registrar, University Plaza 3, Hackensack, NJ 07840, 201-692-9170. Records are not housed here. They are located at Fairleigh Dickinson University, Registrar, 1000 River Rd, Teaneck, NJ 07666.

Fairmont State College, Registrar, Locust Ave, Fairmont, WV 26554, 304-367-4141. Hours: 8AM-5PM. Alumni records are maintained here at the same phone number. Degrees granted: Bachelors.

Attendance and degree information available by phone, mail. Search requires name plus social security number. No fee for information.

Transcripts available by mail. Search requires name plus social security number, signed release. Fee is $3.00.

Faith Baptist Bible College and Theological Seminary, Registrar, 1900 NW Fourth St, Ankeny, IA 50021, 515-964-0601 X238 (FAX: 515-964-1638). Hours: 8AM-4:30PM. Records go back to founding date.

Attendance and degree information available by phone, FAX, mail. Search requires name only. Other helpful information: social security number, date of birth, approximate years of attendance. No fee for information.

Transcripts available by FAX, mail. Search requires name plus signed release. Other helpful information: social security number, date of birth, approximate years of attendance. No fee for transcripts.

Fashion Institute of Design and Merchandising, Registrar, 919 S Grand Ave, Los Angeles, CA 90015, 213-624-1200 (FAX: 213-624-4777). Hours: 8AM-5PM. Records go back to 1970. Alumni records are maintained here at the same phone number. Degrees granted: Associate. Adverse incident record source: Student Advisory, 213-624-1200.

Attendance and degree information available by phone, FAX, mail. Search requires name plus social security number, date of birth, signed release. No fee for information.

Transcripts available by mail. Search requires name plus social security number, date of birth, signed release. Fee is $3.00.

Fashion Institute of Design and Merchandising, **(Branch)**, Registrar, 3420 S Bristol St, Costa Mesa, CA 92626, 714-546-0930. Records are not housed here. They are located at Fashion Institute of Design and Merchandising, Registrar, 919 S Grand Ave, Los Angeles, CA 90015.

Fashion Institute of Design and Merchandising, **(Branch)**, Registrar, 1010 Second Ave Ste 200, San Diego, CA 92101, 619-235-4515 (FAX: 619-232-4322). Records are not housed here. They are located at Fashion Institute of Design and Merchandising, Registrar, 919 S Grand Ave, Los Angeles, CA 90015.

Fashion Institute of Design and Merchandising, **(Branch)**, Registrar, 55 Stockton St, San Francisco, CA 94108, 415-433-6691 (FAX: 415-296-7299). Degrees granted: Associate.

Attendance information available by phone, FAX, mail. Search requires name plus social security number, exact years of attendance, signed release. No fee for information.

Degree information available by phone, FAX, mail. Search requires name plus social security number, exact years of attendance. No fee for information.

Transcripts available by mail. Search requires name plus social security number, exact years of attendance, signed release. Fee is $3.00.

Major credit cards accepted for payment.

Fashion Institute of Technology, Registrar, Seventh Ave at 27th St, New York, NY 10001-5992, 212-760-7676. Hours: 10AM-4PM. Records go back to 1945. Alumni records are maintained here also. Call 212-760-7158. Degrees granted: Associate; Bachelors; Masters. Adverse incident record source: Dean of Students, 212-760-7681.

Attendance and degree information available by mail. Search requires name plus social security number. Other helpful information: date of birth, approximate years of attendance. No fee for information.

Transcripts available by mail. Search requires name plus social security number, signed release. Other helpful information: date of birth, approximate years of attendance. Fee is $5.00. Expedited service available for $10.00.

Faulkner University, Registrar, 5345 Atlanta Hwy, Montgomery, AL 36109-3398, 334-260-6241 (FAX: 334-260-6201). Hours: 8AM-5PM. Records go back to 1942. Alumni records are maintained here also. Call 334-260-6136. Degrees granted: Associate; Bachelors; JD. Adverse incident record source: Student Services, 334-260-6180.

Attendance and degree information available by phone, FAX, mail. Search requires name plus social security number, approximate years of attendance. Other helpful information: date of birth, exact years of attendance. No fee for information.

Transcripts available by mail. Search requires name plus social security number, approximate years of attendance, signed release. Other helpful information: date of birth. Fee is $3.00. Expedited service available for $3.00.

Fayetteville State University, Registrar, 1200 Murchison Rd, Fayetteville, NC 28302, 919-486-1185.

Attendance and degree information available by phone, mail. Search requires name plus social security number. No fee for information.

Transcripts available by written request only. Search requires name plus social security number, signed release. Fee is $3.00.

Fayetteville Technical Community College, Registrar, PO Box 35236, 2201 Hull Rd, Fayetteville, NC 28303, 919-678-8416 (FAX: 919-484-6600).

Attendance and degree information available by phone, FAX, mail. Search requires name plus social security number, approximate years of attendance. Other helpful information: exact years of attendance. No fee for information.

Transcripts available by written request only. Search requires name plus social security number, approximate years of attendance, signed release. Other helpful information: exact years of attendance. No fee for transcripts.

Feather River College, Registrar, PO Box 11110, Quincy, CA 95971, 916-283-0202 X285 (FAX: 916-283-3757). Hours: 8AM-5PM. Records go back to 1988. Degrees granted: Associate.

Attendance and degree information available by written request only. Search requires name plus social security number, date of birth, approximate years of attendance, signed release. Other helpful information: exact years of attendance. No fee for information.

Transcripts available by written request only. Search requires name plus social security number, date of birth, approximate years of attendance, signed release. Other helpful information: exact years of attendance. First two transcripts free; $2.00 each additional. Expedited service available for $5.00.

Felician College, Registrar, 262 S Main St, Lodi, NJ 07644, 201-778-1190 X6038 (FAX: 201-778-4111). Hours: 8:30AM-4:30PM MTF; 8:30AM-8PM WTh. Records go back to 1942. Degrees granted: Associate; Bachelors; Masters.

Attendance and degree information available by phone, FAX, mail. Search requires name plus social security number. Other helpful information: approximate years of attendance. No fee for information.

Transcripts available by FAX, mail. Search requires name plus social security number, signed release. Other helpful information: approximate years of attendance. Fee is $3.00. Expedited service available for $10.00.

Major credit cards accepted for payment.

Fergus Falls Community College, Registrar, 1414 College Way, Fergus Falls, MN 56537, 218-739-7500 (FAX: 218-739-7472). Hours: 8AM-5PM. Records go back to 1960. Degrees granted: Associate.

Attendance and degree information available by phone, FAX, mail. Search requires name plus social security number. Other helpful information: date of birth, approximate years of attendance. No fee for information.

Transcripts available by FAX, mail. Search requires name plus social security number, signed release. Other helpful information: date of birth. No fee for transcripts.

Ferris State University, Registrar's Office, 420 Oak St, Big Rapids, MI 49307, 616-592-2790 (FAX: 616-592-2978). Hours: 8AM-5PM. Records go back to 1895. Degrees granted: Associate; Bachelors; Masters; Doctorate. Adverse incident record source: Judicial Services, 616-592-3619.

Attendance and degree information available by phone, FAX, mail. Search requires name only. Other helpful information: social security number, date of birth, approximate years of attendance. No fee for information.

Transcripts available by FAX, mail. Search requires name plus signed release. Other helpful information: social security number, date of birth, approximate years of attendance. No fee for transcripts. Expedited service available for $5.00.

Phone request for transcripts only for student applying to another college. Major credit cards accepted for payment.

Ferrum College, Registrar, Ferrum, VA 24088, 703-365-4275. Hours: 8AM-5PM. Records go back to 1913. Alumni records are maintained here also. Call 703-365-4216. Degrees granted: Bachelors.

Attendance and degree information available by phone, mail. Search requires name plus social security number, exact years of attendance. No fee for information.

Transcripts available by mail. Search requires name plus social security number, exact years of attendance, signed release. Fee is $3.00.

Fielding Institute, Registrar, 2112 Santa Barbara St, Santa Barbara, CA 93105, 805-687-1099 (FAX: 805-687-9793). Hours: 9AM-5PM. Records go back to 1975. Degrees granted: Masters; Doctorate. Certification: Neurobehavioral Certificate Program.

Attendance and degree information available by phone, FAX, mail. Search requires name only. Other helpful information: social security number. No fee for information.

Transcripts available by FAX, mail. Search requires name plus signed release. Other helpful information: social security number. Fee is $5.00. Expedited service available for $20.00.

Major credit cards accepted for payment.

Finger Lakes Community College, Registrar, 4355 Lake Shore Dr, Canandaigua, NY 14424, 716-394-3500 X290 (FAX: 716-394-5005). Hours: 8:30AM-5PM. Records go back to 1968. Degrees granted: Associate.

Attendance and degree information available by phone, FAX, mail. Search requires name plus social security number. Other helpful information: date of birth, approximate years of attendance. No fee for information.

Transcripts available by written request only. Search requires name plus social security number, date of birth, signed release. Other helpful information: approximate years of attendance. Fee is $5.00.

Fisher College, Registrar, 118 Beacon St, Boston, MA 02116, 617-236-8826 (FAX: 617-236-8858). Hours: 8:30AM-4:30PM. Records go back to 1945. Alumni records are maintained here also. Call 617-262-3240. Degrees granted: Associate.

Attendance and degree information available by FAX, mail. Search requires name plus social security number, approximate years of attendance, signed release. No fee for information.

Transcripts available by mail. Search requires name plus social security number, approximate years of attendance, signed release. Fee is $3.00.

Fisk University, Registrar, 1000 17th Ave N, Nashville, TN 37208-3051, 615-239-8586. Hours: 9AM-5PM. Degrees granted: Bachelors; Masters.

Attendance and degree information available by written request only. Search requires name plus social security number, approximate years of attendance, signed release. Other helpful information: date of birth. No fee for information.

Transcripts available by written request only. Search requires name plus social security number, approximate years of attendance, signed release. Other helpful information: date of birth. Fee is $2.00.

Major credit cards accepted for payment.

Fitchburg State College, Registrar, 160 Pearl St, Fitchburg, MA 01420, 508-345-2151 X3138 (FAX: 508-665-3683). Hours: 8AM-5PM. Records go back to 1960. Degrees granted: Bachelors; Masters.

Attendance and degree information available by phone, FAX, mail. Search requires name plus approximate years of attendance. Other helpful information: social security number, date of birth, exact years of attendance. No fee for information.

Transcripts available by written request only. Search requires name plus approximate years of attendance, signed release. Other helpful information: social security number, date of birth, exact years of attendance. Fee is $1.00.

Five Towns College, Registrar, 305 N Service Rd, Dix Hills, NY 11746-6055, 516-424-7000. Hours: 8AM-6PM M-Th, 8AM-4PM F. Records go back to 1972. Alumni records are maintained here at the same phone number. Degrees granted: Associate; Bachelors.

Attendance and degree information available by phone, mail. Search requires name only. Other helpful information: social security number, date of birth, approximate years of attendance. No fee for information.

Transcripts available by written request only. Search requires name plus signed release. Other helpful information: social security number, date of birth, approximate years of attendance. Fee is $4.00.

Flagler Career Institute, Registrar, 3225 University Blvd S, Jacksonville, FL 32216-2736, 904-721-1622. Degrees granted: Associate.

Attendance information available by written request only. Search requires name plus social security number, date of birth, approximate years of attendance, signed release. Other helpful information: exact years of attendance. No fee for information.

Degree information available by written request only. Search requires name plus social security number, date of birth, approximate years of attendance, signed release. No fee for information. Include a stamped envelope.

Transcripts available by written request only. Search requires name plus social security number, date of birth, approximate years of attendance, signed release. Fee is $5.00. Include a stamped envelope.

Flagler College, Registrar, PO Box 1027, 74 King St, St Augustine, FL 32085-1027, 904-829-6481 (FAX: 904-826-0094). Hours: 8AM-Noon, 1-5PM. Records go back to 1968. Alumni records are maintained here at the same phone number. Degrees granted: Bachelors.

Attendance and degree information available by phone, FAX, mail. Search requires name only. Other helpful information: social security number. No fee for information.

Transcripts available by mail. Search requires name plus social security number, signed release. Other helpful information: exact years of attendance. Fee is $2.00.

Flathead Valley Community College, Registrar, 777 Grandview Dr, Kalispell, MT 59901, 406-756-3822 (FAX: 406-756-3965). Hours: 8AM-5PM. Records go back to 1967. Alumni records are maintained here also. Call 406-756-3962. Degrees granted: Associate. Certification: Clerical, Business Management, Accounting, Networking, Supervisory Management.

Attendance information available by phone, FAX, mail. Search requires name plus social security number. Other helpful information: date of birth, approximate years of attendance. No fee for information.

Degree information available by phone, FAX, mail. Search requires name plus social security number, signed release. Other helpful information: date of birth, approximate years of attendance. No fee for information.

Transcripts available by FAX, mail. Search requires name plus social security number, date of birth, signed release. Other helpful information: approximate years of attendance. First copy (per year) free; $2.00 additional copies per year. Expedite: $5.00 to FAX. Expedited service available for $5.00.

Major credit cards accepted for payment.

Florence-Darlington Technical College, Registrar, PO Box 100548, Florence, SC 29501-0548, 803-661-8090 (FAX: 803-661-8041). Hours: 8:30AM-8PM M-Th, 8:30AM-5PM F. Records go back to 1963. Alumni records are maintained here also. Call 803-661-8000. Degrees granted: Associate. Special programs- Continuing Education, 803-661-8126. Adverse incident record source: Security Guard House, 803-661-8210: Student Disciplinary Reports, 803-661-8150

Attendance and degree information available by phone, FAX, mail. Search requires name plus social security number, signed release. Other helpful information: date of birth, approximate years of attendance. No fee for information.

Transcripts available by FAX, mail. Search requires name plus social security number, signed release. Other helpful information: date of birth, approximate years of attendance. Fee is $2.00.

Information only if release in file.

Florida Agricultural and Mechanical University, Registrar, Foote Hilyer Admin Ctr #112, Tallahassee, FL 32307-3200, 904-599-3115 (FAX: 904-561-2428). Hours: 8AM-5PM. Records go back to 1887. Alumni records are maintained here also. Call 904-599-3861. Degrees granted: Associate; Bachelors; Masters; Doctorate. Adverse incident record source: Police, 904-599-3256: Ofc of Judicial Officer, 904-599-3541

Attendance and degree information available by phone, FAX, mail. Search requires name plus social security number. Other helpful information: date of birth, approximate years of attendance. No fee for information.

Transcripts available by FAX, mail. Search requires name plus social security number, signed release. Other helpful information: date of birth, approximate years of attendance. No fee for transcripts.

Florida Atlantic University, Registrar, 700 Glades Rd, PO Box 3091, Boca Raton, FL 33431-0991, 407-367-2711 (FAX: 407-367-2756). Hours: 8AM-5PM M-Th, 8AM-7PM F. Records go back to 1965. Alumni records are maintained here also. Call 407-367-3010. Degrees granted: Associate; Bachelors; Masters; Doctorate. Adverse incident record source: Dean of Students, 407-367-3546.

Attendance and degree information available by phone, FAX, mail. Search requires name plus social security number, approximate years of attendance, signed release. No fee for information.

Transcripts available by FAX, mail. Search requires name plus social security number, approximate years of attendance, signed release. Fee is $5.00.

No charge for unofficial transcripts.

Florida Baptist Theological College, Registrar, PO Box 1306, Graceville, FL 32440, 904-263-3261 (FAX: 904-263-7506). Hours: 8AM-4:30PM. Degrees granted: Associate; Bachelors.

Attendance and degree information available by phone, FAX, mail. Search requires name plus date of birth, exact years of attendance. Other helpful information: social security number, approximate years of attendance. No fee for information.

Transcripts available by written request only. Search requires name plus date of birth, approximate years of attendance, signed release. Other helpful information: social security number, exact years of attendance. Fee is $5.00.

Florida Bible College, Registrar, 1701 N Poinciana Blvd, Kissimmee, FL 34758, 407-933-4500 X213 (FAX: 407-933-4500 X206). Hours: 8:30AM-4:30PM. Records go back to 1962. Alumni records are maintained here at the same phone number. Degrees granted: Associate; Bachelors.

Attendance information available by phone. Search requires name only. No fee for information.

Degree information available by phone. Search requires name only. Other helpful information: social security number. No fee for information.

Transcripts available by FAX, mail. Search requires name plus signed release. Other helpful information: social security number. Fee is $3.00.

Florida Christian College, Registrar, 1011 Bill Beck Blvd, Kissimmee, FL 34744, 407-847-8966 (FAX: 407-847-8966 X375). Hours: 8:30AM-4:30PM. Records go back to 1976. Alumni records are maintained here at the same phone number. Degrees granted: Associate; Bachelors.

Attendance information available by phone, FAX, mail. Search requires name plus signed release. Other helpful information: date of birth, approximate years of attendance. No fee for information.

Degree information available by FAX. Search requires name plus signed release. Other helpful information: social security number, date of birth, approximate years of attendance. No fee for information.

Transcripts available by mail. Search requires name plus social security number, date of birth, signed release. Other helpful information: approximate years of attendance. Fee is $2.00.

Florida College, Registrar, 119 Glen Arven Ave, Temple Terrace, FL 33617, 813-988-5131 (FAX: 813-899-6772). Hours:

8AM-5PM. Records go back to 1945. Degrees granted: Associate. Certification: Biblical Studies.

Attendance and degree information available by phone, FAX, mail. Search requires name only. Other helpful information: social security number, date of birth, approximate years of attendance. No fee for information.

Transcripts available by phone, FAX, mail. Search requires name plus signed release. Other helpful information: social security number, date of birth, approximate years of attendance. Fee is $3.00. Expedited service available for $3.00.

Florida Community College at Jacksonville, Registrar, 501 W State St, Jacksonville, FL 32202, 904-632-3100 (FAX: 904-632-3109).

Attendance and degree information available by phone, FAX, mail. Search requires name plus social security number.

Transcripts available by written request only. Search requires name plus social security number, signed release.

Florida Computer & Business School, Registrar, 8300 Flagler St Ste 200, Miami, FL 33144, 305-553-6065 (FAX: 305-225-0128). Hours: 7:30AM-4:30PM. Records go back to 1982. Degrees granted: Associate.

Attendance and degree information available by FAX, mail. Search requires name plus social security number, date of birth, exact years of attendance, signed release. No fee for information.

Transcripts available by FAX, mail. Search requires name plus social security number, date of birth, exact years of attendance, signed release. Fee is $3.00.

Florida Institute of Technology, Registrar, 150 W University Blvd, Melbourne, FL 32901-6988, 407-768-8000 X8115 (FAX: 407-727-2419). Hours: 8AM-5PM. Records go back to 1990. Alumni records are maintained here also. Call 407-768-8000 X7190. Degrees granted: Associate; Bachelors; Masters; Doctorate.

Attendance and degree information available by phone, FAX, mail. Search requires name plus social security number, approximate years of attendance, signed release. No fee for information.

Transcripts available by FAX, mail. Search requires name plus social security number, approximate years of attendance, signed release. Fee is $5.00.

Florida International University, Registrar, University Park, Miami, FL 33199, 305-348-2383 (FAX: 305-348-2941). Hours: 8AM-7PM M-Th; 8AM-5PM F. Records go back 23 years. Degrees granted: Associate; Bachelors; Masters; Doctorate. Special programs- School of Hospitality Management, 305-948-4500: School of Journalism & Mass Communications, 305-940-5625: School of Nursing, 305-940-5915: School of Policy Management, 305-940-5890: School of Social Work, 305-940-5880: Continuing Education (non-credit), 305-940-5669. Adverse incident record source: Judicial Affairs, 305-348-3939: Public Safety, 305-348-2623

Attendance and degree information available by phone, FAX, mail. Search requires name plus social security number, signed release. Other helpful information: date of birth. No fee for information.

Transcripts available by mail. Search requires name plus social security number, signed release. Other helpful information: date of birth. Fee is $5.00.

Florida Keys Community College, Registrar, 5901 W College Rd, Key West, FL 33040, 305-296-9081 (FAX: 305-292-5155). Hours: 8:30AM-4PM. Records go back to 1965. Degrees granted: Associate.

Attendance and degree information available by phone, FAX, mail. Search requires name plus social security number. Other helpful information: date of birth. No fee for information.

Transcripts available by mail. Search requires name plus social security number, signed release. Other helpful information: date of birth. Fee is $2.00.

Major credit cards accepted for payment.

Florida Memorial College, Registrar, 15800 NW 42nd Ave, Miami, FL 33054, 305-626-3752 (FAX: 305-626-3669). Hours: 8AM-5PM. Records go back to 1879. Alumni records are maintained here also. Call 305-626-3657. Degrees granted: Bachelors. Adverse incident record source: Student Development, 305-626-1410.

Attendance information available by phone, FAX, mail. Search requires name plus social security number, date of birth, approximate years of attendance, signed release. No fee for information.

Degree information available by FAX, mail. Search requires name plus social security number, date of birth, approximate years of attendance, signed release. No fee for information.

Transcripts available by mail. Search requires name plus social security number, date of birth, approximate years of attendance, signed release. Fee is $10.00.

Florida Southern College, Registrar, 111 Lake Hollingsworth Dr, Lakeland, FL 33801, 813-680-4127 (FAX: 813-680-4565). Hours: 8AM-5PM. Records go back to 1915. Degrees granted: Bachelors; Masters. Special programs- Orlando Program, 407-855-1302: Charlotte-DeSoto Program, 813-494-7373. Adverse incident record source: Dean, 813-680-4206.

Attendance and degree information available by phone, FAX, mail. Search requires name plus social security number, approximate years of attendance. Other helpful information: date of birth, exact years of attendance. No fee for information.

Transcripts available by written request only. Search requires name plus social security number, approximate years of attendance, signed release. Other helpful information: date of birth, exact years of attendance. Fee is $2.00. FAX: $3.00 per page.

Florida State University, Registrar, Tallahassee, FL 32306-1011, 904-644-1050 (FAX: 904-644-0261). Hours: 8AM-5PM. Alumni Records Office: Alumni Office, Florida State University, 114 Longmire Bldg, Tallahassee, FL 32306-1052. Degrees granted: Associate; Bachelors; Masters; Doctorate.

Attendance and degree information available by phone, FAX, mail. Search requires name only. Other helpful information: social security number, date of birth, approximate years of attendance. No fee for information.

Transcripts available by FAX, mail. Search requires name plus signed release. Other helpful information: social security number, date of birth, approximate years of attendance. Fee is $5.00.

Signed release unless student has requested privacy. Unofficial transcripts are available at no charge.

Florida Technical College, Registrar, 8711 Lone Star Rd, Jacksonville, FL 32211, 904-724-2229 (FAX: 904-720-0920). Hours: 8AM-6PM. Records go back to 1984. Degrees granted: Associate. Adverse incident record source: Site Admin., 904-724-2229.

Attendance and degree information available by FAX, mail. Search requires name plus social security number, exact years of attendance, signed release. No fee for information.

Transcripts available by mail. Search requires name plus social security number, exact years of attendance, signed release. Fee is $5.00.

Floyd College, Registrar, PO Box 1864, Rome, GA 30162-1864, 706-802-5000. Hours: 8:30AM-5PM. Alumni records are maintained here at the same phone number. Degrees granted: Associate.

Attendance and degree information available by mail. Search requires name plus social security number, signed release. No fee for information.

Transcripts available by mail. Search requires name plus social security number, exact years of attendance, signed release. No fee for transcripts.

Fontbonne College, Registrar, 6800 Wydown Blvd, St Louis, MO 63105, 314-889-1421 (FAX: 314-889-1451). Hours: 8AM-4:30PM. Records go back to 1920. Degrees granted: Bachelors; Masters.

Attendance and degree information available by phone, FAX, mail. Search requires name plus social security number. Other helpful information: approximate years of attendance. No fee for information.

Transcripts available by FAX, mail. Search requires name plus social security number, signed release. Other helpful information: date of birth, approximate years of attendance. Fee is $2.00. Expedited service available for $5.00.

Foothill College, Registrar, 12345 El Monte Rd, Los Altos Hills, CA 94022, 415-949-7343 (FAX: 415-949-7375). Hours: 9AM-7:30PM M-Th, 9AM-4PM F. Records go back to 1958. Degrees granted: Associate. Adverse incident record source: Dean of Students, 415-949-7241.

Attendance and degree information available by phone, FAX, mail. Search requires name plus social security number, approximate years of attendance, signed release. No fee for information.

Transcripts available by FAX, mail. Search requires name plus social security number, approximate years of attendance, signed release. Fee is $3.00.

Fordham University, Registrar, E Fordham Rd, Bronx, NY 10458, 718-817-3901 (FAX: 718-367-9404). Hours: 9AM-4:45PM. Records go back to 1918. Alumni Records Office: 113 W 60th, New York, NY 10023. Degrees granted: Bachelors; Masters; Ph.D. Adverse incident record source: Dean of Students, 718-817-4731.

Attendance and degree information available by phone, FAX, mail. Search requires name plus social security number, approximate years of attendance, signed release. No fee for information.

Transcripts available by FAX, mail. Search requires name plus social security number, approximate years of attendance, signed release. Fee is $5.00.

Forest Institute of Professional Psychology, Registrar, 1322 S Campbell Ave, Springfield, MO 65807, 417-831-7902 (FAX: 417-831-6839). Hours: 8AM-5PM. Records go back to 1979. Degrees granted: Masters; Doctorate.

Attendance and degree information available by FAX, mail. Search requires name plus social security number, signed release. Other helpful information: date of birth, approximate years of attendance. No fee for information.

Transcripts available by FAX, mail. Search requires name plus social security number, signed release. Other helpful information: date of birth, approximate years of attendance. Fee is $5.00. Major credit cards accepted for payment.

Forrest Junior College, Registrar, 601 E River St, Anderson, SC 29624, 803-225-7653 (FAX: 803-261-7471). Hours: 8AM-9PM. Records go back to 1960. Degrees granted: Associate.

Attendance information available by phone, FAX, mail. Search requires name plus social security number, exact years of attendance. Other helpful information: approximate years of attendance. No fee for information.

Degree information available by phone, FAX, mail. Search requires name plus social security number, approximate years of attendance. No fee for information.

Transcripts available by phone, FAX, mail. Search requires name plus social security number, approximate years of attendance. Fee is $5.00. Expedited fees vary. Include stameped envelope.

Forsyth Technical Community College, Registrar, 2100 Silas Creek Pkwy, Winston-Salem, NC 27103, 919-723-0371.

Attendance and degree information available by written request only. Search requires name plus social security number, approximate years of attendance, signed release. No fee for information.

Transcripts available by written request only. Search requires name plus social security number, approximate years of attendance, signed release. No fee for transcripts.

Fort Belknap College, Registrar, PO Box 159, Harlem, MT 59526-0159, 406-353-2607 X20 (FAX: 406-353-2898). Hours: 8AM-5PM. Records go back to 1988. Degrees granted: Associate. Certification: Computer Applications.

Attendance and degree information available by phone, FAX, mail. Search requires name plus approximate years of attendance. No fee for information.

Transcripts available by mail. Search requires name plus date of birth, approximate years of attendance, signed release. No fee for transcripts.

Fort Berthold Community College, Registrar, PO Box 490, New Town, ND 58763, 701-627-3665 (FAX: 701-627-3609). Hours: 8AM-5PM. Records go back to 1978. Degrees granted: Associate.

Attendance and degree information available by phone, FAX, mail. Search requires name plus social security number, date of birth, signed release. No fee for information.

Transcripts available by phone, FAX, mail. Search requires name plus social security number, date of birth, signed release. Fee is $2.00.

Fort Hays State University, Registrar, 600 Park St, Hays, KS 67601, 913-628-4222 (FAX: 913-628-4046). Hours: 8AM-4:30PM. Records go back to 1902. Alumni records are maintained here also. Call 913-628-4430. Degrees granted: Associate; Bachelors; Masters.

Attendance and degree information available by phone, FAX, mail. Search requires name plus social security number, signed release. Other helpful information: date of birth, approximate years of attendance. No fee for information.

Transcripts available by mail. Search requires name plus social security number, date of birth, approximate years of attendance, signed release. Fee is $2.00.

Major credit cards accepted for payment.

The Sourcebook of College and University Student Records   **F**

Fort Lauderdale College, Registrar, 1040 Bayview Dr, Fort Lauderdale, FL 33304, 305-568-1600 (FAX: 305-568-2008). Hours: 8AM-8PM M-Th; 9AM-1PM F. Records go back to 1940. Degrees granted: Associate; Bachelors. Adverse incident record source: Academic Dean.
 Attendance information available by FAX, mail. Search requires name plus social security number, approximate years of attendance, signed release. Other helpful information: date of birth, exact years of attendance. No fee for information.
 Degree information available by phone, FAX, mail. Search requires name plus social security number, approximate years of attendance, signed release. Other helpful information: date of birth, exact years of attendance. No fee for information.
 Transcripts available by mail. Search requires name plus social security number, approximate years of attendance, signed release. Other helpful information: date of birth, exact years of attendance. Fee is $3.00.
 Major credit cards accepted for payment.

Fort Lewis College, Records Office, 108MSC, 1000 Rim Dr, Durango, CO 81301-3999, 303-247-7350. Hours: 9AM-Noon, 1-4PM. Records go back to 1925. Alumni records are maintained here also. Call 303-247-7427. Degrees granted: Associate; Bachelors. Adverse incident record source: Dean of Student Affairs, 303-247-7331.
 Attendance and degree information available by phone, mail. Search requires name plus social security number, date of birth, signed release. Other helpful information: approximate years of attendance. No fee for information.
 Transcripts available by written request only. Search requires name plus social security number, date of birth, exact years of attendance, signed release. Other helpful information: approximate years of attendance. Fee is $2.00.

Fort Peck Community College, Registrar, PO Box 398, Poplar, MT 59255, 406-768-5551 (FAX: 406-768-5552). Hours: 8AM-4:30PM. Records go back to 1980. Degrees granted: Associate.
 Attendance and degree information available by phone, FAX, mail. Search requires name only. Other helpful information: social security number, date of birth. No fee for information.
 Transcripts available by mail. Search requires name plus signed release. Other helpful information: social security number, date of birth, approximate years of attendance. Fee is $1.00.

Fort Scott Community College, Registrar, 2108 S Horton St, Fort Scott, KS 66701, 316-223-2700 (FAX: 316-223-6530). Hours: 7:30AM-5PM. Records go back to 1919. Degrees granted: Associate. Adverse incident record source: Dean of Students, 316-223-2700.
 Attendance and degree information available by written request only. Search requires name plus signed release. Other helpful information: social security number, date of birth, approximate years of attendance. No fee for information.
 Transcripts available by written request only. Search requires name plus signed release. Other helpful information: social security number, date of birth, approximate years of attendance. Fee is $2.00. Expedited service available for $10.00.

Fort Valley State College, Registrar, 1005 State College Dr, Fort Valley, GA 31030-3298, 912-825-6282. Hours: 8AM-5PM. Records go back to 1895. Alumni records are maintained here also. Call 912-825-6315. Degrees granted: Associate; Bachelors; Masters.
 Attendance and degree information available by phone, mail. Search requires name plus social security number. No fee for information.
 Transcripts available by mail. Search requires name plus social security number, signed release. Fee is $3.00.

Fox Valley Technical Institute, Registrar, 1825 N Bluemound Dr, PO Box 2277, Appleton, WI 54913-2277, 414-735-5712 (FAX: 414-735-4713). Hours: 8AM-8PM. Records go back to 1930s. Degrees granted: Associate.
 School will not confirm attendance or degree information. Search requires name only. Other helpful information: social security number, date of birth, approximate years of attendance. No fee for information.
 Transcripts available by FAX, mail. Search requires name plus signed release. Other helpful information: social security number, date of birth, approximate years of attendance. Fee is $1.00.

Framingham State College, Registrar, 100 State St, Framingham, MA 01701-9101, 508-626-4545. Hours: 8:30AM-4:30PM. Records go back to 1839. Degrees granted: Bachelors; Masters. Certification: Teachers Cert.
 Attendance and degree information available by phone, mail. Search requires name plus approximate years of attendance. Other helpful information: social security number, date of birth, exact years of attendance. No fee for information.
 Transcripts available by phone, mail. Search requires name plus approximate years of attendance, signed release. Other helpful information: social security number, date of birth, exact years of attendance. $2.00 for continuing education students; $1.00 for day students.
 Without release will only verify information requestor already has; will not correct information.

Francis Marion College, Registrar, PO Box 100547, Florence, SC 29501-0547, 803-661-1175. Records go back to 1970. Alumni records are maintained here also. Call 803-661-1228. Degrees granted: Bachelors; Masters.
 Attendance and degree information available by mail. Search requires name plus social security number. No fee for information.
 Transcripts available by mail. Search requires name plus social security number, signed release. Fee is $2.00.

Franciscan School of Theology, Registrar, 1712 Euclid Ave, Berkeley, CA 94709, 510-848-5232 (FAX: 510-549-9466). Hours: 8:30AM-12:30PM, 1:30-4:30pm. Records go back to founding date. Degrees granted: Masters.
 Attendance information available by written request only. Search requires name plus signed release. No fee for information.
 Degree information available by written request only. Search requires name plus signed release. Other helpful information: date of birth, approximate years of attendance. No fee for information.
 Transcripts available by written request only. Search requires name plus signed release. Other helpful information: date of birth, approximate years of attendance. Fee is $3.00. Expedited service available for $3.00.

Franciscan University of Steubenville, Registrar, University Blvd, Steubenville, OH 43952, 614-283-6207 (FAX: 614-283-6472). Hours: 8:30AM-4:30PM. Records go back to 1946. Alumni records are maintained here also. Call 614-283-3771 X6414. Degrees granted: Associate; Bachelors; Masters. Adverse incident record source: Dean, 614-283-6441.

Degree Granting Institutions

Attendance and degree information available by phone, FAX, mail. Search requires name plus social security number, approximate years of attendance. No fee for information.

Transcripts available by FAX, mail. Search requires name plus social security number, approximate years of attendance. Fee is $2.00.

Frank Lloyd Wright School of Architecture, Registrar, Taliesin West, Scottsdale, AZ 85261, 602-860-2700 (FAX: 602-391-4009). Hours: 9AM-4:30PM. Records go back to 1945. Degrees granted: Bachelors; Masters.

Attendance and degree information available by phone, FAX, mail. Search requires name plus exact years of attendance, signed release. Other helpful information: approximate years of attendance. No fee for information.

Transcripts available by phone, FAX, mail. Search requires name plus social security number, date of birth, exact years of attendance, signed release. Fee is $25.00. Expedite fee is based on cost of service. Include a stamped envelope.

Frank Phillips College, Registrar, PO Box 5118, Borger, TX 79008-5118, 806-274-5311 (FAX: 806-273-7642). Hours: 8-11:45AM, 1-4:30PM. Records go back to 1990. Degrees granted: Associate.

School will not confirm attendance or degree information. Search requires name plus social security number, signed release. Other helpful information: date of birth, exact years of attendance. No fee for information.

Transcripts available by FAX, mail. Search requires name plus social security number, signed release. Other helpful information: date of birth, exact years of attendance. Fee is $3.00.

Major credit cards accepted for payment.

Franklin & Marshall College, Registrar, PO Box 3003, Lancaster, PA 17604-3003, 717-291-4168 (FAX: 717-399-4413). Hours: 8:30AM-4:30PM. Records go back to 1853. Degrees granted: Bachelors.

Attendance and degree information available by phone, FAX, mail. Search requires name plus signed release. Other helpful information: social security number, date of birth, approximate years of attendance. No fee for information.

Transcripts available by FAX, mail. Search requires name plus signed release. Other helpful information: social security number, date of birth, approximate years of attendance. Transcript fee is $2.00 each up to 10, with no charge after 10.

Franklin College of Indiana, Registrar, 501 E Monroe St, Franklin, IN 46131, 317-738-8018. Hours: 8AM-5PM. Records go back to 1844. Alumni records are maintained here also. Call 317-738-1834. Degrees granted: Bachelors.

Attendance and degree information available by phone, mail. Search requires name plus social security number, date of birth. No fee for information.

Transcripts available by mail. Search requires name plus social security number, date of birth, exact years of attendance, signed release. Fee is $2.00.

Franklin Institute of Boston, Registrar, Boston, MA 02116, 617-423-4630 (FAX: 617-482-3706). Hours: 7:30AM-5PM. Records go back to 1908. Alumni records are maintained here at the same phone number. Degrees granted: Associate; Bachelors.

Attendance and degree information available by phone, FAX, mail. Search requires name plus approximate years of attendance, signed release. Other helpful information: social security number. No fee for information.

Transcripts available by mail. Search requires name plus approximate years of attendance, signed release. Other helpful information: social security number. Fee is $2.00.

Franklin Pierce College, Registrar, College Rd, Rindge, NH 03461, 603-899-4100 (FAX: 603-899-6448). Hours: 8AM-4PM. Records go back to founding date. Records on computer from 1980 on. Alumni records are maintained here also. Call 603-899-4100. Degrees granted: Associate; Bachelors.

Attendance and degree information available by phone, FAX, mail. Search requires name plus social security number, approximate years of attendance. Other helpful information: exact years of attendance. No fee for information.

Transcripts available by written request only. Search requires name plus social security number, approximate years of attendance, signed release. Other helpful information: exact years of attendance. Fee is $3.00.

Franklin Pierce Law Center, Registrar, 2 White St, Concord, NH 03301, 603-228-1541 X103 (FAX: 603-228-1074). Hours: 8AM-4:30PM. Records go back to founding date. Alumni records are maintained here also. Call 603-228-1541 X121. Degrees granted: Masters; Doctorate.

Attendance and degree information available by phone, FAX, mail. Search requires name only. Other helpful information: social security number, exact years of attendance. No fee for information.

Transcripts available by FAX, mail. Search requires name plus signed release. Other helpful information: social security number, exact years of attendance. Official transcripts cost $3.00 each; $1.00 for unofficial transcript. Expedited service available for $3.00.

Franklin University, Registrar, 201 S Grant Ave, Columbus, OH 43215-5399, 614-341-6242 (FAX: 614-224-0434). Hours: 8AM-6PM M-Th; 8AM-5PM F. Records go back to 1950. Alumni records are maintained here also. Call 614-341-6409. Degrees granted: Associate; Bachelors; Masters.

Attendance and degree information available by phone, FAX, mail. Search requires name plus social security number, approximate years of attendance, signed release. Other helpful information: date of birth, exact years of attendance. No fee for information. Expedited service available for $10.00.

Transcripts available by FAX, mail. Search requires name plus social security number, date of birth, approximate years of attendance, signed release. Other helpful information: exact years of attendance. No fee for transcripts. Expedited service available for $10.00.

Major credit cards accepted for payment.

Frederick Community College, Admissions/Registration Ofc, 7932 Oppossumtown Pike, Frederick, MD 21702, 301-846-2430 (FAX: 301-846-2498). Hours: 8:30AM-8PM M-Th; 8:30AM-4:30PM F. Records go back to 1957. Degrees granted: Associate. Adverse incident record source: Dean of Student Development.

Attendance and degree information available by phone, FAX, mail. Search requires name plus social security number. No fee for information.

Transcripts available by mail. Search requires name plus social security number, signed release. No fee for transcripts.

Free Will Baptist Bible College, Registrar, PO Box 50117, Nashville, TN 37205, 615-383-1340 (FAX: 615-269-6028). Hours: 8AM-4:30PM. Records go back to 1942. Alumni Records Office: 3606 West End Ave, Nashville, TN 37205. Degrees granted: Associate; Masters. Certification: Teacher Ed. Adverse incident record source: Dean of Students.

Attendance and degree information available by phone, FAX, mail. Search requires name plus social security number, date of birth, exact years of attendance, signed release. No fee for information.

Transcripts available by phone, FAX, mail. Search requires name plus social security number, date of birth, exact years of attendance, signed release. No fee for transcripts.

Freed-Hardeman University, Registrar, 158 E Main St, Henderson, TN 38340-2399, 901-989-6648 (FAX: 901-989-6775). Hours: 8AM-5PM. Records go back to 1900s. Degrees granted: Bachelors; Masters.

Attendance and degree information available by phone, FAX, mail. Search requires name only. Other helpful information: social security number, date of birth, approximate years of attendance. No fee for information.

Transcripts available by FAX, mail. Search requires name plus signed release. Other helpful information: social security number, date of birth, approximate years of attendance. Fee is $5.00. Expedited service available for $5.00.

Fresno City College, Registrar, 1101 E University Ave, Fresno, CA 93741, 209-442-4600 (FAX: 209-485-7304). Hours: 8AM-6:45PM M-Th; 8AM-5PM F; 7AM-3:30PM Summer. Records go back to 1948. Alumni Records Office: 1525 E Weldon Ave, Fresno, CA 93704. Degrees granted: Associate.

Attendance and degree information available by FAX, mail. Search requires name plus social security number, signed release. Other helpful information: date of birth, approximate years of attendance. No fee for information.

Transcripts available by FAX, mail. Search requires name plus social security number, signed release. Other helpful information: date of birth, approximate years of attendance. First two transcripts free; $2.00 each additional.

Fresno Pacific College, Registrar, 1717 S Chestnut Ave, Fresno, CA 93702, 209-453-2037 (FAX: 209-453-2007). Hours: 8AM-5PM. Records go back to 1965. Degrees granted: Associate; Bachelors; Masters; Teaching Credential. Special programs- Graduate Office, 209-453-2016: Center/Degree Completion, 209-453-2280. Adverse incident record source: Personnel Office, 209-453-2245: Safety & Security, 209-453-2298

Attendance and degree information available by phone. Search requires name only. No fee for information.

Transcripts available by FAX, mail. Search requires name plus social security number, date of birth, signed release. Other helpful information: approximate years of attendance. Fee is $5.00. Expedited service available for $10.00.

Major credit cards accepted for payment.

Friends University, Registrar, 2100 University Ave, Wichita, KS 67213, 316-261-5860 (FAX: 316-269-3538). Hours: 8AM-6PM M-Th; 8AM-5PM F. Records go back to 1900. Alumni records are maintained here also. Call 316-261-5802. Degrees granted: Associate; Bachelors; Masters.

Attendance and degree information available by phone, FAX, mail. Search requires name plus social security number. Other helpful information: date of birth, approximate years of attendance. No fee for information.

Transcripts available by FAX, mail. Search requires name plus social security number, approximate years of attendance, signed release. Other helpful information: date of birth, exact years of attendance. Fee is $3.00. Expedited service available for $5.00.

Major credit cards accepted for payment.

Front Range Community College, Registrar, 3645 W 112th Ave, Westminster, CO 80030, 303-466-8811 X313. Hours: 9AM-5PM M,Th; 9AM-7PM T,W; 9AM-Noon F. Records go back to 1970. Degrees granted: Associate. Adverse incident record source: Security, 303-466-8811 X403 info 5 yrs back: Current info, 303-466-8811 X313

Attendance and degree information available by mail. Search requires name plus social security number, signed release. No fee for information.

Transcripts available by mail. Search requires name plus social security number, signed release. Fee is $2.00.

Frontier Community College, Registrar, Frontier Dr, Fairfield, IL 62837, 618-842-3111. Records go back to 1973. Degrees granted: Associate.

Attendance and degree information available by written request only. Search requires name plus signed release. Other helpful information: social security number, date of birth. No fee for information.

Transcripts available by written request only. Search requires name plus signed release. Other helpful information: social security number, date of birth. Fee is $1.00.

Must use their specific release form. Credit card accepted in person only.

Frostburg State University, Registrar, Frostburg, MD 21532, 301-689-4346 (FAX: 301-689-4597). Hours: 8AM-4:30PM. Records go back to 1902. Degrees granted: Bachelors; Masters. Adverse incident record source: Student & Educational Services, 301-689-4311.

Attendance and degree information available by phone, FAX, mail. Search requires name plus social security number, approximate years of attendance. Other helpful information: date of birth. No fee for information.

Transcripts available by FAX, mail. Search requires name plus social security number, approximate years of attendance, signed release. Other helpful information: date of birth, exact years of attendance. No fee for transcripts. Expedited service available for $10.00.

Major credit cards accepted for payment.

Fugazzi College, Registrar, 406 Lafayette Ave, Lexington, KY 40502, 606-266-0401 (FAX: 606-266-2118). Hours: 9AM-5PM. Records go back 3 years. Degrees granted: Associate.

Attendance and degree information available by FAX, mail. Search requires name plus social security number, signed release. No fee for information.

Transcripts available by FAX, mail. Search requires name plus social security number, signed release. No fee for transcripts.

Fugazzi College, **(Branch)**, Registrar, 5042 Lindbar Dr, Nashville, TN 37211, 615-333-3344 (FAX: 615-333-3429). Hours: 8AM-5PM. Records go back 7 years. Degrees granted: Associate.

Attendance information available by phone, FAX, mail. Search requires name plus social security number, approximate years of attendance, signed release. No fee for information.

Degree information available by phone, FAX, mail. Search requires name only. No fee for information.

Transcripts available by FAX, mail. Search requires name only. Fee is $2.00.

Fuller Theological Seminary, Registrar, 135 N Oakland Ave, Pasadena, CA 91182, 818-584-5408. Hours: 8AM-5PM. Records go back to 1947. Alumni records are maintained here also. Call 818-584-5498. Degrees granted: Associate; Bachelors; Masters; Doctorate.

Attendance and degree information available by phone, mail. Search requires name plus social security number, date of birth, approximate years of attendance, signed release. No fee for information.

Transcripts available by mail. Search requires name plus social security number, date of birth, approximate years of attendance, signed release. Fee is $3.00.

Fullerton College, Admissions and Records, 321 E Chapman Ave, Fullerton, CA 92634-2095, 714-992-7568. Hours: 8AM-7PM M-Th; 8AM-3PM F. Records go back to 1913. Adverse incident record source: Student Affairs, 714-992-7248.

Attendance and degree information available by phone, mail. Search requires name plus date of birth, signed release. Other helpful information: social security number, approximate years of attendance. Fee is $3.00. Expedited service available for $13.00.

Transcripts available by mail. Search requires name plus date of birth, signed release. Other helpful information: social security number, approximate years of attendance. Fee is $3.00. Expedited service available for $13.00.

Fulton-Montgomery Community College, Registrar, Rte 67, Johnstown, NY 12095, 518-762-4651 X222 (FAX: 518-762-4334). Hours: 8AM-4PM. Records go back to 1964. Alumni records are maintained here at the same phone number. Degrees granted: Associate.

Attendance and degree information available by phone, FAX, mail. Search requires name plus social security number, signed release. Other helpful information: date of birth. Fee is $3.00.

Transcripts available by written request only. Search requires name plus social security number, signed release. Other helpful information: date of birth. Fee is $3.00.

Furman University, Registrar, 3300 Poinsett Hwy, Greenville, SC 29613, 803-294-2031 (FAX: 803-294-3551). Records go back to 1826. Alumni records are maintained here also. Call 803-294-2000. Degrees granted: Bachelors; Masters.

Attendance and degree information available by FAX, mail. Search requires name plus social security number, exact years of attendance. No fee for information.

Transcripts available by FAX, mail. Search requires name plus social security number, exact years of attendance, signed release. Fee is $2.00.

G

GMI Engineering and Management Institute, Registrar, 1700 W Third Ave, Flint, MI 48504, 810-762-7862 (FAX: 810-762-9836). Hours: 8AM-5PM. Records go back to 1919. Alumni records are maintained here also. Call 810-762-9883. Degrees granted: Bachelors; Masters. Adverse incident record source: Campus Safety, 810-762-9501.

Attendance information available by phone, FAX, mail. Search requires name plus social security number, date of birth. Other helpful information: approximate years of attendance. No fee for information.

Degree information available by phone, FAX, mail. Search requires name plus social security number. Other helpful information: date of birth, approximate years of attendance. No fee for information.

Transcripts available by FAX, mail. Search requires name plus social security number, signed release. Other helpful information: date of birth, approximate years of attendance. No fee for transcripts.

Gadsden State Community College, Registrar, PO Box 227, Gadsden, AL 35902-0227, 205-549-8261. Hours: 7:30AM-4PM. Records go back to 1925. Alumni records are maintained here also. Call 205-549-8224. Degrees granted: Associate. Adverse incident record source: Registrar, 205-549-8261.

Attendance and degree information available by phone, mail. Search requires name plus social security number, exact years of attendance, signed release. No fee for information.

Transcripts available by mail. Search requires name plus social security number, exact years of attendance, signed release. Fee is $3.00.

Major credit cards accepted for payment.

Gainesville College, Registrar, Mundy Mill Rd, PO Box 1358, Gainesville, GA 30503-1358, 404-535-6244 (FAX: 404-535-6359). Hours: 8AM-5PM. Records go back 27 years. Alumni records are maintained here also. Call 404-535-6248. Degrees granted: Associate.

Attendance and degree information available by phone, FAX, mail. Search requires name plus social security number, approximate years of attendance, signed release. No fee for information.

Transcripts available by FAX, mail. Search requires name plus social security number, approximate years of attendance, signed release. No fee for transcripts.

Gallaudet University, Registrar, 800 Florida Ave NE, Washington, DC 20002, 202-651-5393 (FAX: 202-651-5182). Hours: 8:30AM-4:30PM. Alumni records are maintained here also. Call 202-651-5060. Degrees granted: Associate; Bachelors; Masters; Doctorate. Adverse incident record source: Student Life, 202-651-5255.

Attendance and degree information available by phone, FAX, mail. Search requires name plus social security number, date of birth, signed release. No fee for information.

Transcripts available by FAX, mail. Search requires name plus social security number, date of birth, signed release. Fee is $5.00. Expedited service available for $10.00.

Major credit cards accepted for payment.

Galveston College, Registrar, 4015 Ave Q, Galveston, TX 77550, 409-763-6551. Hours: 8AM-4:30PM. Alumni records are maintained here at the same phone number. Degrees granted: Associate.

Attendance and degree information available by phone, mail. Search requires name plus social security number, signed release. No fee for information.

Transcripts available by mail. Search requires name plus social security number, signed release. No fee for transcripts.

Gannon University, Registrar's Officd, University Square, Erie, PA 16541, 814-871-7243 (FAX: 814-871-7338). Hours: 8AM-4:30PM. Records go back to 1930. Alumni records are maintained here also. Call 814-871-7473. Degrees granted: Associate; Bachelors; Masters. Adverse incident record source: Student Living, 814-871-7660.

Attendance information available by phone, FAX, mail. Search requires name plus social security number, date of birth. No fee for information.

Degree information available by phone, FAX, mail. Search requires name plus social security number, date of birth, exact years of attendance. No fee for information.

Transcripts available by FAX, mail. Search requires name plus social security number, date of birth, exact years of attendance, signed release. No fee for transcripts.

Garden City Community College, Registrar, 801 Campus Dr, Garden City, KS 67846, 316-276-7611 (FAX: 316-276-9573). Hours: 8AM-8PM M,Th; 8AM-4:30PM T,W,F. Records go back to 1919. Degrees granted: Associate. Adverse incident record source: Campus Police, 316-275-0005.

Attendance information available by phone, FAX. Search requires name plus signed release. Other helpful information: social security number, date of birth, approximate years of attendance. No fee for information.

Degree information available by phone, FAX, mail. Search requires name plus signed release. Other helpful information: social security number, date of birth, approximate years of attendance. No fee for information.

Transcripts available by written request only. Search requires name plus signed release. Other helpful information: social security number, date of birth, approximate years of attendance. Fee is $2.00.

Major credit cards accepted for payment.

Gardner-Webb University, Registrar, PO Box 997, Boiling Springs, NC 28017, 704-434-2361 X222.

Attendance and degree information available by phone, mail. Search requires name plus social security number.

Transcripts available by written request only. Search requires name plus social security number.

Garland County Community College, Registrar, PO Box 3470, Hot Springs, AR 71914-3450, 501-767-9371 (FAX: 501-767-6893). Hours: 8AM-4:30PM. Records go back to 1973. Degrees granted: Associate.

Attendance and degree information available by phone, FAX, mail. Search requires name plus social security number. Other helpful information: date of birth, approximate years of attendance. No fee for information.

Transcripts available by mail. Search requires name plus social security number, signed release. Other helpful information: date of birth, approximate years of attendance. Fee is $2.00.

Major credit cards accepted for payment.

Garrett Community College, Registrar, PO Box 151, Mosser Rd, McHenry, MD 21541, 301-387-3040 (FAX: 301-387-3055). Hours: 8:30AM-4:30PM. Records go back to 1971. Alumni records are maintained here also. Call 301-387-3056. Degrees granted: Associate.

Attendance and degree information available by phone, FAX, mail. Search requires name plus social security number. Other helpful information: approximate years of attendance. No fee for information.

Transcripts available by FAX, mail. Search requires name plus social security number, signed release. Other helpful information: date of birth, approximate years of attendance. Fee is $2.00.

Major credit cards accepted for payment.

Garrett-Evangelical Theological Seminary, Registrar, 2121 Sheridan Rd, Evanston, IL 60201, 708-866-3905 (FAX: 708-866-3957). Hours: 8:30AM-4:30PM. Records go back to 1892. Degrees granted: Masters; Doctorate.

Attendance and degree information available by phone, FAX, mail. Search requires name plus approximate years of attendance. Other helpful information: exact years of attendance. No fee for information.

Transcripts available by FAX, mail. Search requires name plus approximate years of attendance, signed release. Other helpful information: social security number, date of birth, exact years of attendance. Fee is $5.00.

Gaston College, Registrar, 201 Hwy 321 S, Dallas, NC 28034, 704-922-6200.

Gateway Community College, Registrar, 108 N 40th St, Phoenix, AZ 85034, 602-392-5189 (FAX: 602-392-5209). Hours: 8AM-7PM M-Th; 8AM-5PM F. Records go back to 1968. Degrees granted: Associate. Adverse incident record source: Security, 602-392-5020.

Attendance and degree information available by phone, FAX, mail. Search requires name only. Other helpful information: social security number, date of birth, approximate years of attendance. No fee for information.

Transcripts available by mail. Search requires name plus signed release. Other helpful information: social security number, date of birth, approximate years of attendance. Fee is $5.00.

Major credit cards accepted for payment.

Gateway Community-Technical College, Registrar, 60 Sargent Dr, New Haven, CT 06511, 203-789-7041 (FAX: 203-777-8415). Hours: 8:30AM-4:30PM. Records go back to founding date. Degrees granted: Associate. Adverse incident record source: Dean of Students, 203-789-7016.

Attendance information available by FAX, mail. Search requires name plus social security number, signed release. Other helpful information: date of birth, approximate years of attendance. No fee for information.

Degree information available by phone, FAX, mail. Search requires name plus social security number. Other helpful information: date of birth, approximate years of attendance. No fee for information.

Transcripts available by FAX, mail. Search requires name plus social security number, signed release. Other helpful information: date of birth, approximate years of attendance. No fee for transcripts.

Gateway Community-Technical College, **(North Haven)**, Registrar, 88 Bassett Rd, North Haven, CT 06473, 203-234-3300 (FAX: 203-234-3372). Hours: 8:30AM-4:30PM. Records go back to 1978. Alumni records are maintained here also. Call 203-234-3242. Degrees granted: Associate.

Attendance information available by phone, FAX, mail. Search requires name plus social security number. No fee for information.

Degree information available by phone, FAX, mail. Search requires name only. No fee for information.

Transcripts available by mail. Search requires name plus signed release. No fee for transcripts.

Gateway Technical College, Registrar, 3520 30th Ave, Kenosha, WI 53142, 414-656-6900. Degrees granted: Associate.

Attendance and degree information available by phone, mail. Search requires name plus social security number, exact years of attendance. No fee for information.

Transcripts available by mail. Search requires name plus social security number, exact years of attendance, signed release. Fee is $3.00.

Gavilan College, Admissions Office, 5055 Santa Teresa Blvd, Gilroy, CA 95020, 408-848-4735 (FAX: 408-848-4801). Hours: 8AM-5PM. Records go back to 1919. Degrees granted: Associate.

Attendance and degree information available by phone, FAX, mail. Search requires name plus social security number, signed release. Other helpful information: date of birth, approximate years of attendance. No fee for information. Expedited service available for $5.00.

Transcripts available by mail. Search requires name plus social security number, date of birth, signed release. Other helpful information: approximate years of attendance. Fee is $2.00. Expedited service available for $5.00.

Gem City College, Registrar, PO Box 179, 700 State St, Quincy, IL 62306, 217-222-0391 (FAX: 217-222-1559). Hours: 8AM-4:40PM. Records go back 125 years.

Attendance and degree information available by written request only. Search requires name plus social security number, date of birth, signed release. Other helpful information: approximate years of attendance. No fee for information.

Transcripts available by written request only. Search requires name plus social security number, date of birth, signed release. Other helpful information: approximate years of attendance. First transcript free; $5.00 each additional. Expedited service available for $15.00.

Major credit cards accepted for payment.

General Theological Seminary, Registrar, 175 Ninth Ave, New York, NY 10011-4977, 212-243-5150 (FAX: 212-727-3907). Hours: 8:30AM-5PM. Records go back to 1920. Degrees granted: Masters; Ph.D.

Attendance and degree information available by phone, FAX, mail. Search requires name plus social security number, approximate years of attendance, signed release. No fee for information.

Transcripts available by mail. Search requires name plus social security number, approximate years of attendance, signed release. Fee is $5.00.

Genesee Community College, Registrar, One College Rd, Batavia, NY 14020, 716-343-0055 X6218. Hours: 8AM-6:30PM M-Th; 8AM-4:30PM F; 8:30-10:30AM S. Records go back to 1967. Alumni records are maintained here also. Call 716-343-0055-X6262. Degrees granted: Associate.

Attendance and degree information available by mail. Search requires name plus social security number, approximate years of attendance, signed release. No fee for information.

Transcripts available by mail. Search requires name plus social security number, approximate years of attendance, signed release. Fee is $5.00.

Geneva College, Registrar, 3200 College Ave, Beaver Falls, PA 15010, 412-847-6600 (FAX: 412-847-6696). Hours: 8AM-4:30PM. Records go back to founding date. Alumni records are maintained here also. Call 412-847-6525. Degrees granted: Associate; Bachelors; Masters.

Attendance and degree information available by phone, FAX, mail. Search requires name only. Other helpful information: social security number, date of birth, approximate years of attendance. No fee for information.

Transcripts available by mail. Search requires name plus signed release. Other helpful information: social security number, date of birth, approximate years of attendance. Fee is $3.00.

George C. Wallace State Community College, Registrar, Route 6, Box 62, Dothan, AL 36303, 334-983-5321 X302 (FAX: 334-983-3600). Hours: 7:45AM-4:30PM. Records go back to 1949. Alumni records are maintained here at the same phone number. Degrees granted: Associate.

Attendance and degree information available by phone, FAX, mail. Search requires name plus social security number. No fee for information.

Transcripts available by mail. Search requires name plus social security number, date of birth, exact years of attendance, signed release. No fee for transcripts.

George Corley Wallace State Community College, Registrar, PO Drawer 1049, 3000 Range Line Rd, Selma, AL 36702-1049, 205-875-2634 X36 (FAX: 205-874-7116). Hours: 7:30AM-4:30PM M-Th, 7:30AM-3PM F. Records go back to 1965. Degrees granted: Associate.

Attendance and degree information available by phone, mail. Search requires name plus social security number, date of birth, exact years of attendance. No fee for information.

Transcripts available by mail. Search requires name plus social security number, date of birth, exact years of attendance, signed release. Fee is $2.00.

George Fox College, Registrar, Newberg, OR 97132, 503-538-8383 (FAX: 503-538-3867). Hours: 8AM-5PM. Alumni records are maintained here also. Call 503-538-8383. Degrees granted: Bachelors; Masters; Doctorate.

Attendance and degree information available by phone, FAX, mail. Search requires name plus social security number, date of birth, approximate years of attendance. Other helpful information: exact years of attendance. No fee for information.

Transcripts available by FAX, mail. Search requires name plus social security number, date of birth, approximate years of attendance, signed release. Other helpful information: exact years of attendance. Fee is $3.00. Expedited service available for $5.00.

George Mason University, Registrar, 4400 University Dr, Fairfax, VA 22030-4444, 703-993-2448. Hours: 8AM-5PM. Records go back to 1972. Alumni records are maintained here also. Call 703-993-8696. Degrees granted: Bachelors; Masters; Doctorate.

Attendance and degree information available by phone, mail. Search requires name plus social security number, exact years of attendance. No fee for information.

Transcripts available by mail. Search requires name plus social security number, exact years of attendance, signed release. No fee for transcripts.

George Washington University, Registrar, Washington, DC 20052, 202-994-6506 (FAX: 202-994-0709). Hours: 8:30AM-5:30PM. Records go back to 1820. Alumni records are maintained here also. Call 202-994-6435. Degrees granted: Associate; Bachelors; Masters; Doctorate. Adverse incident record source: Dean of Students, 202-994-6710.

Attendance and degree information available by phone, FAX, mail. Search requires name plus date of birth, exact years of attendance. No fee for information.

Transcripts available by mail. Search requires name plus date of birth, exact years of attendance, signed release. Fee is $3.00.

Georgetown College, Registrar, 400 E College St, Georgetown, KY 40324, 502-863-8024. Hours: 8AM-5PM. Records go back to 1900. Alumni records are maintained here also. Call 502-863-8041. Degrees granted: Bachelors; Masters.

Attendance and degree information available by phone, mail. Search requires name plus social security number, signed release. No fee for information.

Transcripts available by mail. Search requires name plus social security number, signed release. Fee is $3.00.

Georgetown University, Registrar, 37th and O Sts NW, Washington, DC 20057, 202-687-4020 (FAX: 202-687-3608). Hours: 9AM-5PM. Records go back to 1977. Alumni records are maintained here also. Call 202-687-1789. Degrees granted: Associate; Bachelors; Masters; Doctorate.

Attendance and degree information available by phone, FAX, mail. Search requires name plus social security number, approximate years of attendance, signed release. No fee for information.

Transcripts available by FAX, mail. Search requires name plus social security number, approximate years of attendance, signed release. Fee is $2.00.

Georgia College, Registrar, CPO Box 23, Milledgeville, GA 31061, 912-454-2772 (FAX: 912-453-1914). Hours: 8AM-6PM M-Th, 8AM-5PM F. Records go back to 1889. Alumni Records Office: CPO 98, Milledgeville, GA 31061 912-453-5400. Degrees granted: Bachelors; Masters. Adverse incident record source: Dept of Public Safety, 912-453-4400.

Attendance and degree information available by phone, FAX, mail. Search requires name plus social security number, approximate years of attendance, signed release. No fee for information.

Transcripts available by FAX, mail. Search requires name plus social security number, approximate years of attendance, signed release. Fee is $1.00.

Georgia Institute of Technology, Registrar, 225 North Ave NW, Atlanta, GA 30332-0315, 404-894-4151 (FAX: 404-853-0167). Hours: 8AM-4:30PM. Degrees granted: Bachelors; Masters; Doctorate.

Attendance and degree information available by phone, FAX, mail. Search requires name plus signed release. Other helpful information: social security number, date of birth, approximate years of attendance. No fee for information.

Transcripts available by FAX, mail. Search requires name plus signed release. Other helpful information: social security number,

date of birth, approximate years of attendance. No fee for transcripts.
Will take credit card for FedEx fee to expedite.

Georgia Military College, Registrar, 201 E Greene St, Milledgeville, GA 31061, 912-454-2684 (FAX: 912-454-2688). Hours: 8AM-5PM. Records go back to 1940. Alumni records are maintained here also. Call 912-454-2695. Degrees granted: Associate. Adverse incident record source: Commandant, 912-454-2710.
Attendance and degree information available by FAX, mail. Search requires name plus social security number, signed release. No fee for information.
Transcripts available by mail. Search requires name plus social security number, signed release. Fee is $3.00.

Georgia Southern University, Registrar, Landrum Box 8092, Statesboro, GA 30460-8033, 912-681-5826 (FAX: 912-681-0081). Hours: 8AM-5PM. Records go back to 1924. Alumni records are maintained here also. Call 912-681-5691. Degrees granted: Bachelors; Masters; Doctorate. Adverse incident record source: Judicial Affairs, 912-681-5409.
Attendance and degree information available by phone, FAX, mail. Search requires name plus social security number, approximate years of attendance, signed release. No fee for information.
Transcripts available by FAX, mail. Search requires name plus social security number, approximate years of attendance, signed release. No fee for transcripts.

Georgia Southwestern College, Registrar, 800 Wheatley St, Americus, GA 31709-4693, 912-928-1331 (FAX: 912-931-2059). Hours: 8AM-5PM. Records go back 70 years. Alumni records are maintained here also. Call 912-928-1373. Degrees granted: Associate; Bachelors; Masters.
Attendance and degree information available by phone, mail. Search requires name plus approximate years of attendance, signed release. Other helpful information: social security number, date of birth, exact years of attendance. No fee for information.
Transcripts available by phone, mail. Search requires name plus approximate years of attendance, signed release. Other helpful information: social security number, date of birth, exact years of attendance. Fee is $2.00.
Major credit cards accepted for payment.

Georgia State University, Student Service, PO Box 4017, Atlanta, GA 30302, 404-651-2383 (FAX: 404-651-1419). Hours: 8:30AM-5:15PM. Records go back to 1920. Degrees granted: Bachelors; Masters; Doctorate. Adverse incident record source: Dean of Students, 404-651-2200: Campus Police, 404-651-2100
Attendance information available by phone, FAX, mail. Search requires name plus social security number, date of birth. Other helpful information: approximate years of attendance. No fee for information.
Degree information available by phone, FAX, mail. Search requires name plus social security number. Other helpful information: date of birth, approximate years of attendance. No fee for information.
Transcripts available by phone, FAX, mail. Search requires name plus social security number, signed release. Other helpful information: date of birth, approximate years of attendance. Fee is $2.00.

Georgian Court College, Registrar's Office, Kingscote, Admin Bldg, Lakewood Ave & 7th St, Lakewood, NJ 08701-2697, 908-364-2200 X228 (FAX: 908-367-3920). Hours: 8:30AM-4PM. Records go back to 1908. Degrees granted: Bachelors; Masters. Adverse incident record source: Student Services, 908-364-2200 X315.
Attendance and degree information available by phone, mail. Search requires name plus approximate years of attendance, signed release. Other helpful information: social security number, date of birth. No fee for information.
Transcripts available by mail. Search requires name plus social security number, approximate years of attendance, signed release. Other helpful information: date of birth. Fee is $3.00.

Germanna Community College, Registrar, PO Box 339, Locust Grove, VA 22508, 703-423-1333 (FAX: 703-423-1009). Hours: 8AM-5PM. Records go back to 1970. Alumni records are maintained here at the same phone number. Degrees granted: Associate.
Attendance and degree information available by phone, FAX, mail. Search requires name plus social security number, signed release. No fee for information.
Transcripts available by FAX, mail. Search requires name plus social security number, signed release. No fee for transcripts.

Gettysburg College, Registrar, 300 N Washington St, Gettysburg, PA 17325-1486, 717-337-6240 (FAX: 717-337-6906). Hours: 8AM-5PM. Records go back to 1832. Alumni records are maintained here also. Call 717-337-6518. Degrees granted: Bachelors. Adverse incident record source: Academic Advising Files, 717-337-6579.
Attendance and degree information available by phone, FAX, mail. Search requires name plus exact years of attendance. No fee for information.
Transcripts available by FAX, mail. Search requires name plus social security number, exact years of attendance, signed release. No fee for transcripts.

Glen Oaks Community College, Registrar, 62249 Shimmel Rd, Centreville, MI 49032, 616-467-9945 (FAX: 616-467-4114). Hours: 8AM-4PM. Records go back to founding date. Degrees granted: Associate.
Attendance and degree information available by phone, FAX, mail. Search requires name only. Other helpful information: social security number, date of birth, approximate years of attendance. No fee for information.
Transcripts available by FAX, mail. Search requires name plus signed release. Other helpful information: social security number, date of birth, approximate years of attendance. Fee is $2.00.
Credit cards may be used in person only.

Glendale Community College, Registrar, 600 W Olive Ave, Glendale, AZ 85302, 602-435-3319. Hours: 8AM-7:30PM M-Th, 9AM-4PM F. Records go back to 1965. Alumni records are maintained here also. Call 602-435-3014. Degrees granted: Associate.
Attendance and degree information available by phone, mail. Search requires name plus social security number, date of birth, exact years of attendance, signed release. No fee for information.
Transcripts available by mail. Search requires name plus social security number, date of birth, exact years of attendance, signed release. Fee is $5.00.

Glendale Community College, Office of Admissions & Records, 1500 N Verdugo Rd, Glendale, CA 91208, 818-240-1000 (FAX: 818-549-9436). Hours: 8AM-8PM M-Th, 9AM-Noon

F. Records go back to 1927. Alumni records are maintained here also. Call 818-240-1000 X5126. Degrees granted: Associate.

Attendance and degree information available by FAX, mail. Search requires name plus social security number, date of birth, approximate years of attendance, signed release. Fee is $5.00. Expedited service available for $5.00.

Transcripts available by FAX, mail. Search requires name plus social security number, date of birth, approximate years of attendance, signed release. Fee is $5.00. Expedited service available for $5.00.

Glendale College ID number helpful.

Glenville State College, Registrar, 200 High St, Glenville, WV 26351, 304-462-4117 (FAX: 304-462-8619). Hours: 8AM-4PM. Records go back to 1820. Alumni records are maintained here also. Call 304-462-7361 X122. Degrees granted: Associate; Bachelors. Adverse incident record source: Campus Security, 304-462-7361 X322.

Attendance and degree information available by phone, FAX, mail. Search requires name plus social security number, signed release. Other helpful information: date of birth, approximate years of attendance. No fee for information.

Transcripts available by FAX, mail. Search requires name plus social security number, signed release. Other helpful information: date of birth, approximate years of attendance. Fee is $3.00.

Globe College of Business, Registrar, 175 Fifth St E Ste 201, Box 60, St Paul, MN 55101-2901, 612-224-4378 (FAX: 612-224-5684). Hours: 8AM-7:30PM M-Th; 8AM-4:30PM F. Degrees granted: Associate.

Attendance information available by phone. Search requires name plus social security number, date of birth, exact years of attendance, signed release. No fee for information.

Degree information available by phone. Search requires name plus social security number, date of birth, signed release. Other helpful information: exact years of attendance. No fee for information.

Transcripts available by written request only. Search requires name plus social security number, date of birth, exact years of attendance, signed release. Fee is $3.00.

Gloucester County College, Registrar, Tanyard Rd, Deptford Twp RR4, PO Box 203, Sewell, NJ 08080, 609-468-5000 X282 (FAX: 609-848-2507). Hours: 8:30AM-5PM. Records go back to 1968. Alumni records are maintained here also. Call 609-468-5000 X273. Degrees granted: Associate.

Attendance and degree information available by phone, mail. Search requires name plus social security number, approximate years of attendance. Other helpful information: date of birth, exact years of attendance. No fee for information.

Transcripts available by written request only. Search requires name plus social security number, approximate years of attendance, signed release. Other helpful information: date of birth, exact years of attendance. Fee is $2.00.

Major credit cards accepted for payment.

God's Bible College, Registrar, 1810 Young St, Cincinnati, OH 45210, 513-721-7944 X298 (FAX: 513-721-3971). Hours: 8AM-5PM. Records go back to 1900. Degrees granted: Bachelors.

Attendance information available by written request only. Search requires name plus approximate years of attendance, signed release. No fee for information.

Degree information available by phone, FAX, mail. Search requires name plus approximate years of attendance, signed release. No fee for information.

Transcripts available by FAX, mail. Search requires name plus approximate years of attendance, signed release. Fee is $5.00.

Goddard College, Registrar, Plainfield, VT 05667, 802-454-8311 X13 (FAX: 802-454-8017). Hours: 8AM-4:30PM. Records go back to 1938. Alumni records are maintained here at the same phone number. Degrees granted: Bachelors; Masters.

Attendance and degree information available by phone, mail. Search requires name only. No fee for information.

Transcripts available by mail. Search requires name plus signed release. First transcript is $25.00; each additional one is $10.00.

Gogebic Community College, Registrar, E-4946 Jackson Rd, Ironwood, MI 49938, 906-932-4231 X207 (FAX: 906-932-0868). Hours: 7:30AM-4:30PM. Records go back to 1932. Degrees granted: Associate.

Attendance and degree information available by phone, FAX, mail. Search requires name plus social security number, approximate years of attendance, signed release. No fee for information.

Transcripts available by FAX, mail. Search requires name plus social security number, approximate years of attendance, signed release. Fee is $3.00.

Golden Gate Baptist Theological Seminary, Registrar Box 97, 201 Seminary Dr, Mill Valley, CA 94941-3197, 415-388-808- X209 (FAX: 415-383-0723). Hours: 8:30AM-4:30PM. Records go back to founding date. Degrees granted: Masters; Doctorate.

Attendance and degree information available by phone, FAX, mail. Search requires name only. Other helpful information: social security number, date of birth, approximate years of attendance. No fee for information.

Transcripts available by mail. Search requires name plus signed release. Other helpful information: social security number, date of birth, approximate years of attendance. Fee is $5.00.

Major credit cards accepted for payment.

Golden Gate University, Records Office, 536 Mission St, San Francisco, CA 94105-2968, 415-442-7211 (FAX: 415-495-2671). Hours: 9AM-6:30PM M-Th; 9AM-5:30PM F. Records go back to 1900. Alumni Records Office: 562 Mission St, San Francisco, CA 94105-2968. Degrees granted: Associate; Bachelors; Masters; Doctorate. Adverse incident record source: Dean of Student Services, 415-442-7285.

Attendance and degree information available by phone, mail. Search requires name plus social security number, approximate years of attendance. Other helpful information: date of birth, exact years of attendance. No fee for information.

Transcripts available by mail. Search requires name plus social security number, approximate years of attendance, signed release. Other helpful information: date of birth, exact years of attendance. Fee is $7.00. Expedited service available for $15.00.

Major credit cards accepted for payment.

Golden West College, Registrar, 15744 Golden West St, PO Box 2710, Huntington Beach, CA 92647-0710, 714-895-8128 (FAX: 714-895-8960). Hours: 8AM-7PM M-Th; 8AM-3PM F. Records go back to 1966. Alumni records are maintained here also. Call 214-895-8315. Degrees granted: Associate. Special programs- Office of Instruction, 714-895-8134. Adverse incident record source: Safety/Security, 714-895-8924.

Attendance and degree information available by phone, FAX, mail. Search requires name only. Other helpful information: social security number, date of birth, approximate years of attendance. No fee for information.
Transcripts available by FAX, mail. Search requires name plus signed release. Other helpful information: social security number, date of birth, approximate years of attendance. Fee is $3.00. Expedited service available for $5.00.
Major credit cards accepted for payment.

Goldey-Beacom College, Registrar, 4701 Limestone Rd, Wilmington, DE 19808, 302-998-8814 (FAX: 302-998-8631). Hours: 8AM-5PM. Records go back to 1886. Alumni records are maintained here also. Call 302-998-8814. Degrees granted: Associate; Bachelors; Masters. Adverse incident record source: Student Affairs, 302-998-8814 X332.
Attendance and degree information available by FAX, mail. Search requires name plus social security number, date of birth, approximate years of attendance, signed release. No fee for information.
Transcripts available by phone, FAX, mail. Search requires name plus social security number, date of birth, approximate years of attendance, signed release. No fee for transcripts.
Major credit cards accepted for payment.

Gonzaga University, Registrar, Spokane, WA 99258, 509-328-4220 X3192 (FAX: 509-484-2818). Hours: 8AM-4:30PM. Records go back to 1887. Alumni records are maintained here at the same phone number. Degrees granted: Bachelors; Masters; Doctorate.
Attendance and degree information available by phone, FAX, mail. Search requires name plus social security number, date of birth, exact years of attendance. No fee for information.
Transcripts available by FAX, mail. Search requires name plus social security number, date of birth, exact years of attendance, signed release. Fee is $5.00.

Gordon College, Registrar, 419 College Dr, Barnesville, GA 30204, 404-358-5022 (FAX: 404-358-3031). Hours: 8AM-8PM M; 8AM-5PM T-F. Records go back to 1955. Degrees granted: Associate. Certification: Assoc of Applied Science Cooperative Degree Pgm. Adverse incident record source: Student Affairs, 404-358-5056.
Attendance and degree information available by phone, FAX, mail. Search requires name only. Other helpful information: social security number, date of birth, approximate years of attendance. No fee for information.
Transcripts available by FAX, mail. Search requires name plus signed release. Other helpful information: social security number, date of birth, approximate years of attendance. No fee for transcripts.

Gordon College, Registrar, Wenham, MA 01984, 508-927-2300 X4208 (FAX: 508-524-3724). Hours: 8AM-4:30PM. Alumni records are maintained here at the same phone number. Degrees granted: Bachelors. Adverse incident record source: Public Safety.
Attendance and degree information available by phone, FAX, mail. Search requires name only. Other helpful information: date of birth, approximate years of attendance. No fee for information.
Transcripts available by mail. Search requires name plus signed release. Other helpful information: date of birth, approximate years of attendance. Fee is $3.00. Expedited service available for $3.00.

Gordon-Conwell Theological Seminary, Registrar, 130 Essex St, South Hamilton, MA 01982, 508-468-5111 X380 (FAX: 508-468-6691). Hours: 9AM-4:30PM. Records go back to 1969. Degrees granted: Masters; Doctorate.
Attendance and degree information available by phone, FAX, mail. Search requires name only. Other helpful information: approximate years of attendance. No fee for information.
Transcripts available by written request only. Search requires name plus signed release. Fee is $5.00.

Goshen College, Registrar, 1700 S Main St, Goshen, IN 46526, 219-535-7517 (FAX: 219-535-7660). Hours: 8AM-5PM. Records go back to 1894. Alumni records are maintained here also. Call 219-535-7566. Degrees granted: Bachelors. Adverse incident record source: Student Development Office, 219-535-7539.
Attendance and degree information available by phone, FAX, mail. Search requires name plus date of birth. Other helpful information: social security number, approximate years of attendance. No fee for information.
Transcripts available by phone, FAX, mail. Search requires name plus date of birth, exact years of attendance, signed release. Other helpful information: social security number, approximate years of attendance. Fee is $2.00.
Phone may be used if caller can be verified as student.

Goucher College, Registrar, 1021 Dulaney Valley Rd, Baltimore, MD 21204, 410-337-6090 (FAX: 410-337-6123). Hours: 8:45AM-5PM. Records go back to 1885. Degrees granted: Bachelors; Masters.
Attendance and degree information available by phone, FAX, mail. Search requires name only. Other helpful information: social security number, date of birth, approximate years of attendance. No fee for information.
Transcripts available by mail. Search requires name plus signed release. Other helpful information: social security number, date of birth, approximate years of attendance. No fee for transcripts.

Governors State University, Registrar, University Park, IL 60466, 708-534-5000 X2148. Hours: 8AM-8PM M-Th, 8AM-5PM F. Records go back to 1971. Alumni records are maintained here also. Call 708-534-5000. Degrees granted: Bachelors; Masters.
Attendance and degree information available by phone, mail. Search requires name plus social security number, exact years of attendance. No fee for information.
Transcripts available by mail. Search requires name plus social security number, exact years of attendance, signed release. Fee is $2.00.

Grace Bible College, Registrar, 1011 Aldon St SW, PO Box 910, Grand Rapids, MI 49509-9990, 616-538-2330 (FAX: 616-538-0599). Hours: 8AM-4:30PM. Records go back to 1939. Alumni records are maintained here at the same phone number. Degrees granted: Associate; Bachelors.
Attendance and degree information available by phone, FAX, mail. Search requires name plus social security number. No fee for information.
Transcripts available by mail. Search requires name plus social security number, signed release. Fee is $2.00.

Grace College, Registrar, 200 Seminary Dr, Winona Lake, IN 46590, 219-372-5110. Hours: 8AM-4:30PM. Records go back to

1948. Degrees granted: Associate; Bachelors; Masters. Adverse incident record source: Jim Swanson, 219-372-5700.

Attendance and degree information available by phone, FAX. Search requires name plus signed notarized release. Other helpful information: social security number, date of birth. No fee for information.

Transcripts available by mail. Search requires name plus date of birth, signed release. Other helpful information: social security number. No fee for transcripts. Expedited service available for $15.00.

Major credit cards accepted for payment.

Grace Theological Seminary, Registrar, 200 Seminary Dr, Winona Lake, IN 46590, 219-372-5110 (FAX: 219-372-5114). Hours: 8AM-4:30PM. Records go back to 1937. Degrees granted: Masters; Doctorate. Adverse incident record source: Dave Plaster, 219-372-5104.

Attendance and degree information available by phone, FAX. Search requires name plus signed notarized release. Other helpful information: social security number, date of birth. No fee for information.

Transcripts available by mail. Search requires name plus date of birth, signed release. Other helpful information: social security number. No fee for transcripts. Expedited service available for $15.00.

Major credit cards accepted for payment.

Grace University, Registrar, Ninth and William, Omaha, NE 68108, 402-449-2811 (FAX: 402-341-9587). Hours: 8AM-Noon, 1-5PM. Records go back to 1943. Degrees granted: Associate; Masters.

Attendance information available by phone, FAX, mail. Search requires name only. Other helpful information: date of birth, approximate years of attendance. No fee for information.

Degree information available by phone, mail. Search requires name only. Other helpful information: social security number, date of birth, approximate years of attendance. No fee for information.

Transcripts available by written request only. Search requires name plus signed release. Other helpful information: social security number, date of birth, approximate years of attendance. First three transcripts free. Additional ones $3.00 each.

Graceland College, Registrar, Lamoni, IA 50140, 515-784-5220 (FAX: 515-784-5474). Hours: 8AM-5PM. Records go back to founding date. Alumni records are maintained here at the same phone number. Degrees granted: Bachelors; Masters.

Attendance and degree information available by phone, FAX, mail. Search requires name only. Other helpful information: social security number, date of birth, approximate years of attendance. No fee for information.

Transcripts available by phone, FAX, mail. Search requires name plus signed release. Other helpful information: social security number, date of birth, approximate years of attendance. Fee is $4.00.

Graduate School and University Center, Registrar, 33 W 42nd St, New York, NY 10036, 212-642-1600 (FAX: 212-642-2779). Hours: 9AM-5PM. Records go back to 1961. Alumni records are maintained here also. Call 212-642-2850. Degrees granted: Masters; Ph.D.

Attendance and degree information available by phone, FAX, mail. Search requires name plus social security number. No fee for information.

Transcripts available by mail. Search requires name plus social security number, signed release. Fee is $4.00.

Graduate Theological Union, Registrar, 2400 Ridge Rd, Berkeley, CA 94709, 510-649-2462 (FAX: 510-649-1730). Hours: 9AM-5PM. Records go back to 1962. Degrees granted: Masters; Doctorate.

Attendance and degree information available by phone, FAX, mail. Search requires name plus approximate years of attendance. Other helpful information: social security number, date of birth. No fee for information.

Transcripts available by FAX, mail. Search requires name plus approximate years of attendance, signed release. Other helpful information: social security number, date of birth. Fee is $3.00.

Current students: Can only state whether or not a student is attending if student has not requested privacy. Info on current students released only by separate written request from student.

Grambling State University, Registrar's Office, PO Box 589, Grambling, LA 71245, 318-274-2385 (FAX: 318-274-2777). Hours: 8MA-5PM. Records go back to 1930s. Alumni records are maintained here also. Call 318-274-2385. Degrees granted: Associate; Bachelors; Masters; Doctorate.

Attendance information available by phone, mail. Search requires name plus social security number, exact years of attendance. Other helpful information: date of birth, approximate years of attendance. No fee for information.

Degree information available by phone, mail. Search requires name plus social security number, signed release. Other helpful information: date of birth, approximate years of attendance. No fee for information.

Transcripts available by mail. Search requires name plus social security number, signed release. Other helpful information: date of birth, approximate years of attendance. No fee for transcripts.

Grand Canyon University, Registrar, 3300 W Camelback Rd, PO Box 11097, Phoenix, AZ 85061, 602-589-2850 (FAX: 602-589-2594). Hours: 8AM-5PM. Records go back to 1949. Alumni records are maintained here also. Call 602-249-3300. Degrees granted: Bachelors; Masters.

Attendance and degree information available by phone, FAX, mail. Search requires name plus social security number, date of birth, exact years of attendance. No fee for information.

Transcripts available by mail. Search requires name plus social security number, date of birth, exact years of attendance, signed release. Fee is $3.00.

Grand Rapids Community College, Registrar, 143 Bostwick St NE, Grand Rapids, MI 49503, 616-771-4120 (FAX: 616-771-4005). Hours: 7:30AM-5PM. Degrees granted: Associate. Adverse incident record source: Campus Safety, 616-771-4010.

Attendance and degree information available by FAX, mail. Search requires name plus social security number, date of birth, approximate years of attendance, signed release. Other helpful information: exact years of attendance. No fee for information.

Transcripts available by mail. Search requires name plus social security number, date of birth, approximate years of attendance, signed release. Other helpful information: exact years of attendance. Fee is $5.00.

Grand Valley State University, Registrar, One Campus Dr, Allendale, MI 49401, 616-895-3327 (FAX: 616-895-2000). Hours: 8AM-6PM M-Th; 8AM-5PM F. Degrees granted: Bachelors; Masters.

Attendance and degree information available by phone, FAX, mail. Search requires name plus signed release. Other helpful information: social security number, date of birth, approximate years of attendance. No fee for information.

Transcripts available by phone, FAX, mail. Search requires name plus signed release. Other helpful information: social security number, date of birth, approximate years of attendance. Fee is $4.00.

Major credit cards accepted for payment.

Grand View College, Registrar, 1200 Grandview Ave, Des Moines, IA 50316, 515-263-2818 (FAX: 515-263-6095). Hours: 8:15AM-4PM. Records go back to 1895. Alumni records are maintained here also. Call 515-263-2957. Degrees granted: Associate; Bachelors. Adverse incident record source: Dean of Students, 515-263-2885.

Attendance and degree information available by phone, FAX, mail. Search requires name only. Other helpful information: social security number, date of birth. No fee for information.

Transcripts available by FAX, mail. Search requires name plus signed release. Other helpful information: social security number, date of birth. Fee is $3.00.

Grantham College of Engineering, Registrar, 34641 Grantham College Rd, PO Box 5700, Slidell, LA 70469, 504-649-4191 (FAX: 504-649-4183). Hours: 9AM-5:30PM. Records go back to 1951. Degrees granted: Bachelors.

Attendance and degree information available by phone, FAX, mail. Search requires name plus signed release. No fee for information.

Transcripts available by mail. Search requires name plus signed release. Fee is $5.00.

Gratz College, Registrar, Old York Rd and Melrose Ave, Melrose Park, PA 19126, 215-635-7300. Hours: 9AM-5PM M-Th, 9AM-3PM F. Records go back to 1940. Alumni records are maintained here at the same phone number. Degrees granted: Bachelors; Masters.

Attendance and degree information available by mail. Search requires name plus exact years of attendance, signed release. No fee for information.

Transcripts available by mail. Search requires name plus social security number, exact years of attendance, signed release. Fee is $6.00.

Major credit cards accepted for payment.

Grays Harbor College, Records Office, 1620 Edward P. Smith Dr, Aberdeen, WA 98520, 360-538-4027 (FAX: 360-538-4299). Hours: 8AM-4:30PM. Records go back to 1930. Degrees granted: Associate.

Attendance and degree information available by phone, FAX, mail. Search requires name plus social security number, signed release. Other helpful information: date of birth, approximate years of attendance. No fee for information.

Transcripts available by FAX, mail. Search requires name plus social security number, signed release. Other helpful information: date of birth, approximate years of attendance. No fee for transcripts.

Grayson County College, Registrar, 6161 Grayson Dr, Denison, TX 75020, 903-463-8733 (FAX: 903-463-5284). Hours: 8AM-4:30PM. Degrees granted: Associate.

Attendance and degree information available by phone, FAX, mail. Search requires name plus social security number. No fee for information.

Transcripts available by FAX, mail. Search requires name plus social security number, signed release. Fee is $2.00. FAX fee is $5.00.

Major credit cards accepted for payment.

Great Lakes Christian College, Registrar, 6211 W Willow Hwy, Lansing, MI 48917, 517-321-0242. Hours: 8AM-5PM. Records go back to 1949. Degrees granted: Associate; Bachelors.

Attendance information available by FAX, mail. Search requires name plus social security number, date of birth, signed release. Other helpful information: exact years of attendance. No fee for information.

Degree information available by FAX, mail. Search requires name plus social security number, signed release. Other helpful information: date of birth, approximate years of attendance. No fee for information.

Transcripts available by FAX, mail. Search requires name plus social security number, exact years of attendance, signed release. Fee is $5.00.

Great Lakes Junior College, Registrar, 310 S Washington Ave, Saginaw, MI 48607, 517-755-3457 (FAX: 517-752-3453). Hours: 8AM-5PM. Records go back to 1957. Requests handled at last campus of attendance. Degrees granted: Associate.

Attendance and degree information available by phone, FAX, mail. Search requires name plus social security number. Other helpful information: date of birth, approximate years of attendance. No fee for information.

Transcripts available by written request only. Search requires name plus social security number, signed release. Other helpful information: date of birth, approximate years of attendance. No fee for transcripts.

Green Mountain College, Registrar, 16 College St, Poultney, VT 05764, 802-287-9313 X215. Hours: 8AM-4:30PM. Records go back to 1834. Alumni records are maintained here at the same phone number. Degrees granted: Bachelors.

Attendance and degree information available by phone, mail. Search requires name plus exact years of attendance. No fee for information.

Transcripts available by mail. Search requires name plus exact years of attendance, signed release. Fee is $2.00.

Green River Community College, Registrar, 12401 SE 320th St, Auburn, WA 98002, 206-833-9111 X248 (FAX: 206-939-5135). Hours: 8AM-5PM. Records go back to 1965. Degrees granted: Associate.

Attendance and degree information available by phone, FAX, mail. Search requires name plus social security number. No fee for information.

Transcripts available by FAX, mail. Search requires name plus social security number, signed release. No fee for transcripts.

Greenfield Community College, Registrar, One College Dr, Greenfield, MA 01301, 413-774-3131 (FAX: 413-773-5129). Hours: 8:30AM-5PM. Records go back to 1968. Degrees granted: Associate.

Attendance and degree information available by phone, FAX, mail. Search requires name plus social security number, date of birth. Other helpful information: approximate years of attendance. No fee for information.

Transcripts available by FAX, mail. Search requires name plus social security number, date of birth, signed release. Other helpful information: approximate years of attendance. Fee is $2.00.

Greensboro College, Registrar, PO Box 26050, 815 W Market St, Greensboro, NC 27420, 919-271-2207 (FAX: 919-271-2237).

Attendance and degree information available by phone, mail. Search requires name plus approximate years of attendance. No fee for information.

Transcripts available by written request only. Search requires name plus approximate years of attendance, signed release. Fee is $2.00.

Greenville College, Registrar, 315 E College Ave, Greenville, IL 62246, 618-664-1840 X216 (FAX: 618-664-1323). Hours: 8AM-4:30PM. Records go back to 1892. Alumni records are maintained here at the same phone number. Degrees granted: Bachelors. Adverse incident record source: Registrar, 618-664-1840 X216.

Attendance and degree information available by phone, FAX, mail. Search requires name plus social security number, exact years of attendance. No fee for information.

Transcripts available by FAX, mail. Search requires name plus social security number, exact years of attendance, signed release. Fee is $3.00.

Greenville Technical College, Registrar, PO Box 5616, Greenville, SC 29606, 803-250-8117 (FAX: 803-250-8535). Hours: 8AM-7PM M-Th; 8AM-1PM F. Records go back to 1963. Degrees granted: Associate. Adverse incident record source: Student Services, 803-250-8100.

Attendance information available by phone, FAX, mail. Search requires name plus social security number, signed release. Other helpful information: date of birth, approximate years of attendance. No fee for information.

Degree information available by phone, FAX, mail. Search requires name plus social security number. Other helpful information: date of birth, approximate years of attendance. No fee for information.

Transcripts available by FAX, mail. Search requires name plus social security number, approximate years of attendance, signed release. Other helpful information: date of birth, exact years of attendance. Fee is $3.00.

Grinnell College, Registrar, PO Box 805, Grinnell, IA 50112, 515-269-3450. Hours: 8AM-5PM. Records go back to 1846. Alumni records are maintained here also. Call 515-269-4801. Degrees granted: Bachelors.

Attendance and degree information available by phone, mail. Search requires name plus social security number. Other helpful information: exact years of attendance. No fee for information.

Transcripts available by mail. Search requires name plus social security number, exact years of attendance, signed release. Fee is $1.00. Fee for expedited service varies.

Major credit cards accepted for payment.

Grossmont College, Registrar, 8800 Grossmont College Dr, El Cajon, CA 92020, 619-465-1700. Hours: 8AM-7PM M-Th; 8AM-3PM F. Records go back 76 years. Alumni records are maintained here also. Call 619-465-1700 X169. Degrees granted: Associate.

Attendance and degree information available by mail. Search requires name plus signed release. Other helpful information: social security number, date of birth, approximate years of attendance. Fee is $3.00. Expedited service available for $5.00.

Transcripts available by mail. Search requires name plus signed release. Other helpful information: social security number, date of birth, approximate years of attendance. Fee is $3.00. Expedited service available for $5.00.

Grove City College, Registrar, 100 Campus Dr, Grove City, PA 16127-2104, 412-458-2172 (FAX: 412-458-3368). Hours: 8AM-Noon, 1-5PM. Records go back 100 years. Alumni records are maintained here also. Call 412-458-2300. Degrees granted: Bachelors; Masters.

Attendance and degree information available by phone, FAX, mail. Search requires name only. Other helpful information: social security number, date of birth, approximate years of attendance. No fee for information.

Transcripts available by mail. Search requires name plus signed release. Other helpful information: social security number, date of birth, approximate years of attendance. No fee for transcripts.

Guam Community College, Registrar, PO Box 23069, Guam Main Facility, Main Island, 96921, 761-734-4311.

Guilford College, Registrar, 5800 W Friendly Ave, Greensboro, NC 27410-4171, 910-316-2121 (FAX: 910-316-2948). Hours: 8:30PM-5PM. Records go back to 1837. Degrees granted: Bachelors.

Attendance and degree information available by phone, FAX, mail. Search requires name plus signed release. Other helpful information: social security number, date of birth, approximate years of attendance. No fee for information.

Transcripts available by FAX, mail. Search requires name plus signed release. Other helpful information: social security number, date of birth, approximate years of attendance. Fee is $3.00. Expedited service available for $6.00.

FAXed transcripts: $9.00.

Guilford Technical Community College, Registrar, PO Box 309, Jamestown, NC 27282, 910-454-1126 X2234 (FAX: 910-454-2510). Hours: 8AM-7PM M-Th, 8AM-5PM F. Records go back to 1966. Degrees granted: Associate. Adverse incident record source: Public Safety, 910-454-1126 X2398.

Attendance and degree information available by phone, FAX, mail. Search requires name plus social security number. No fee for information.

Transcripts available by FAX, mail. Search requires name plus social security number, signed release. Other helpful information: approximate years of attendance. Fee is $1.00.

Gulf Coast Community College, Admissions & Records, 5230 W US Hwy 98, Panama City, FL 32401-1041, 904-872-3892. Hours: 7:30AM-7:30PM M-Th; 7:30AM-4PM F. Records go back to 1960. Degrees granted: Associate; PSAV Certification.

Attendance and degree information available by phone, mail. Search requires name plus social security number, date of birth. Other helpful information: approximate years of attendance. No fee for information.

Transcripts available by mail. Search requires name plus social security number, date of birth, signed release. Other helpful information: approximate years of attendance. No fee for transcripts.

Gupton-Jones College of Funeral Service, Registrar, 5141 Snapfinger Woods Dr, Decatur, GA 30035-4022, 404-593-

2257 (FAX: 404-593-1891). Hours: 7:30AM-4PM. Records go back to 1970. Degrees granted: Associate.

Attendance information available by phone, mail. Search requires name only. Other helpful information: approximate years of attendance. No fee for information.

Degree information available by phone, mail. Search requires name plus signed release. Other helpful information: social security number, approximate years of attendance. No fee for information.

Transcripts available by mail. Search requires name plus signed release. Other helpful information: social security number, approximate years of attendance. Fee is $2.00.

Gustavus Adolphus College, Registrar, 800 W College Ave, St Peter, MN 56082, 507-933-7495 (FAX: 507-933-6270). Hours: 8AM-4PM. Records go back to 1860. Alumni records are maintained here also. Call 507-933-7552. Degrees granted: Bachelors. Adverse incident record source: Dean of Students, 507-933-7526.

Attendance and degree information available by phone, FAX, mail. Search requires name plus social security number, approximate years of attendance, signed release. No fee for information.

Transcripts available by FAX, mail. Search requires name plus social security number, approximate years of attendance, signed release. Fee is $2.00.

Gwinnett Technical Institute, Registrar, 1250 Atkinson Rd, PO Box 1505, Lawrenceville, GA 30246-1505, 404-962-7580 X121 (FAX: 404-962-7985). Hours: 8AM-6:30PM M-Th; 8AM-5PM F. Records go back 10 years. Degrees granted: Associate.

Attendance and degree information available by phone, FAX, mail. Search requires name plus social security number, signed release. Other helpful information: date of birth. No fee for information.

Transcripts available by FAX, mail. Search requires name plus social security number, signed release. Other helpful information: date of birth. Fee is $2.00. Expedited service available for $5.00.

Gwynedd-Mercy College, Registrar, Gwynedd Valley, PA 19437, 215-646-7300 (FAX: 215-641-5573). Hours: 8AM-4PM. Records go back 47 years. Alumni records are maintained here also. Call 215-646-7300 X178. Degrees granted: Associate; Bachelors; Masters.

Attendance and degree information available by phone, FAX, mail. Search requires name plus approximate years of attendance. Other helpful information: social security number, date of birth, exact years of attendance. No fee for information.

Transcripts available by FAX, mail. Search requires name plus approximate years of attendance, signed release. Other helpful information: social security number, date of birth, exact years of attendance. Fee is $3.00.

Major credit cards accepted for payment.

H

Hagerstown Business College, Registrar, 18618 Crestwood Dr, Hagerstown, MD 21742, 301-739-2670 X28 (FAX: 301-791-7661). Hours: 8AM-5PM. Records go back to 1958. Degrees granted: Associate.

Attendance and degree information available by FAX, mail. Search requires name only. Other helpful information: social security number, date of birth, approximate years of attendance. No fee for information.

Transcripts available by FAX, mail. Search requires name only. Other helpful information: social security number, date of birth, approximate years of attendance. Fee is $2.00.

Major credit cards accepted for payment.

Hagerstown Junior College, Registrar, 11400 Robinwood Dr, Hagerstown, MD 21742, 301-790-2800 X239 (FAX: 301-791-9165). Hours: 8AM-4PM. Records go back to 1946. Planning purge back 5-10 years. Alumni records are maintained here also. Call 301-790-2800 X346. Degrees granted: Associate.

Attendance and degree information available by phone, FAX, mail. Search requires name plus social security number, signed release. Other helpful information: date of birth, approximate years of attendance. No fee for information.

Transcripts available by phone, FAX, mail. Search requires name plus social security number, signed release. Other helpful information: date of birth, approximate years of attendance. Fee is $2.00.

Halifax Community College, Registrar, PO Drawer 809, Weldon, NC 27890, 919-536-7221 (FAX: 919-536-4144). Alumni records are maintained here also. Call 919-536-7289. Degrees granted: Associate.

Attendance and degree information available by phone, mail. Search requires name plus social security number, date of birth, approximate years of attendance, signed release. No fee for information.

Transcripts available by mail. Search requires name plus social security number, date of birth, approximate years of attendance, signed release. No fee for transcripts.

Hamilton College, Registrar, 198 College Hill Rd, Clinton, NY 13323, 315-859-4637 (FAX: 315-859-4632). Hours: 8:30AM-4:30PM. Records go back to 1810. Alumni records are maintained here also. Call 315-859-4412. Degrees granted: Bachelors. Adverse incident record source: Dean of Students, 315-859-4020.

Attendance and degree information available by phone, FAX, mail. Search requires name only. Other helpful information: approximate years of attendance. No fee for information.

Transcripts available by FAX, mail. Search requires name plus date of birth, exact years of attendance, signed release. Other helpful information: social security number, approximate years of attendance. Fee is $3.00. Expedited service available for $3.00.

Hamilton Technical College, Registrar, 1011 E 53rd St, Davenport, IA 52807-2616, 319-386-3570 (FAX: 319-386-6756). Hours: 8AM-6PM M-Th; 8AM-Noon F. Records go back to 1969. Degrees granted: Associate; Bachelors.

Attendance information available by phone, FAX, mail. Search requires name only. Other helpful information: social security number, date of birth, approximate years of attendance. No fee for information.

Degree information available by phone, FAX, mail. Search requires name only. Other helpful information: social security number, date of birth, approximate years of attendance. No fee for information.

Transcripts available by FAX, mail. Search requires name plus social security number, signed release. Other helpful information: date of birth, approximate years of attendance. Fee is $2.00.

Hamline University, Registrar, 1536 Hewitt Ave, St Paul, MN 55104, 612-641-2023 (FAX: 612-659-3043). Hours: 8AM-5PM. Records go back to 1864. Alumni records are maintained here also. Call 612-641-2015. Degrees granted: Bachelors; Masters. Adverse incident record source: Development Office, 612-641-2800.

Attendance and degree information available by phone, FAX, mail. Search requires name plus social security number, approximate years of attendance, signed release. No fee for information.

Transcripts available by mail. Search requires name plus social security number, approximate years of attendance, signed release. Fee is $4.00.

Hampden-Sydney College, Registrar's Office, Hampden-Sydney, VA 23943, 804-223-6274. Hours: 8:30AM-5PM. Degrees granted: Bachelors. Adverse incident record source: Dean of Students, 804-223-6164.

Attendance information available by phone, mail. Search requires name plus date of birth, approximate years of attendance, signed release. Other helpful information: social security number. No fee for information.

Degree information available by phone, mail. Search requires name plus signed release. Other helpful information: exact years of attendance. No fee for information.

Transcripts available by mail. Search requires name plus signed release. Other helpful information: social security number. Fee is $1.00.

Hampshire College, Central Records, Amherst, MA 01002, 413-582-5421 (FAX: 413-582-5584). Hours: 8:30AM-Noon, 1-4:30PM. Records go back to 1970. Alumni records are maintained here also. Call 413-582-5516. Degrees granted: Bachelors.

Attendance and degree information available by phone, FAX, mail. Search requires name only. Other helpful information: approximate years of attendance. No fee for information.

Transcripts available by FAX, mail. Search requires name plus signed release. Other helpful information: approximate years of attendance. No fee for transcripts.

Hampton University, Registrar, East Queen St, Hampton, VA 23668, 804-727-5323. Hours: 8AM-5PM. Records go back to 1868. Alumni records are maintained here also. Call 804-727-5485. Degrees granted: Bachelors; Masters; Doctorate.

Attendance and degree information available by mail. Search requires name plus social security number, exact years of attendance. No fee for information.

Transcripts available by mail. Search requires name plus social security number, exact years of attendance, signed release. Fee is $3.00.

Hannibal-LaGrange College, Registrar, 2800 Palmyra Rd, Hannibal, MO 63401, 314-221-3675 X207 (FAX: 314-221-6594). Hours: 8AM-5PM. Records go back 75 years. Degrees granted: Associate; Bachelors. Special programs- Admissions, 314-221-3675 X264: Business Office, 314-221-3675 X261: Financial Aid, 314-221-3675 X279. Adverse incident record source: Security, 314-221-3675 X273.

Attendance information available by phone, FAX, mail. Search requires name only. Other helpful information: approximate years of attendance. No fee for information.

Degree information available by phone, mail. Search requires name only. Other helpful information: social security number, date of birth, approximate years of attendance. No fee for information.

Transcripts available by mail. Search requires name plus social security number, signed release. Other helpful information: date of birth, approximate years of attendance. No fee for transcripts. Major credit cards accepted for payment.

Hanover College, Registrar, PO Box 108, Hanover, IN 47243-0108, 812-866-7051 (FAX: 812-866-2164). Hours: 8AM-5PM. Records go back to 1827. Alumni records are maintained here at the same phone number. Degrees granted: Bachelors. Adverse incident record source: Student Affairs, 812-866-7075.

Attendance and degree information available by phone, FAX, mail. Search requires name only. Other helpful information: social security number, approximate years of attendance. No fee for information.

Transcripts available by written request only. Search requires name plus signed release. Other helpful information: social security number, approximate years of attendance. Fee is $3.50. Expedited service available for $9.95.

Harcum College, Registrar, Morris and Montgomery Aves, Bryn Mawr, PA 19010, 610-526-6007. Hours: 9AM-5PM. Records go back 75 years. Alumni records are maintained here also. Call 610-526-6006. Degrees granted: Associate.

Attendance information available by phone, FAX, mail. Search requires name plus social security number, exact years of attendance. No fee for information.

Degree information available by phone, FAX, mail. Search requires name plus social security number. Other helpful information: approximate years of attendance. No fee for information.

Transcripts available by mail. Search requires name plus social security number, signed release. Other helpful information: approximate years of attendance. Fee is $2.00.

Need maiden name.

Hardin-Simmons University, Registrar, Sandefer Memorial Bldg, Box 16190, Abilene, TX 79698, 915-670-1200 (FAX: 915-670-1261). Hours: 9AM-5PM. Alumni Records Office: Box 15300, Abilene, TX 79698 915-670-1377. Degrees granted: Associate; Bachelors; Masters. Adverse incident record source: Campus Police, 915-670-1461.

Attendance and degree information available by phone, FAX, mail. Search requires name only. Other helpful information: social security number, approximate years of attendance. No fee for information.

Transcripts available by FAX, mail. Search requires name plus signed release. Other helpful information: social security number, approximate years of attendance. Fee is $5.00.

Major credit cards accepted for payment.

Harding University Graduate School of Religion, Registrar, 1000 Cherry Rd, Memphis, TN 38117, 901-761-1353 (FAX: 901-761-1358). Hours: 8AM-5PM. Records go back to 1958. Degrees granted: Masters; Doctorate.

Attendance and degree information available by phone, FAX, mail. Search requires name plus signed notarized release. Other helpful information: social security number, date of birth, exact years of attendance. No fee for information.

Transcripts available by phone, FAX, mail. Search requires name plus signed release. Other helpful information: social security number, date of birth, exact years of attendance. No fee for transcripts.

Transcript request must come from student.

Harding University, Registrar, Box 776, 900 E Center Ave, Searcy, AR 72149-0001, 501-279-4403 (FAX: 501-279-4388). Hours: 8AM-5PM. Alumni records are maintained here at the same phone number. Alumni Records Office: Box 768, Searcy, AR 72149-0001. Degrees granted: Associate; Bachelors; Masters. Adverse incident record source: Student Services.

Attendance and degree information available by phone, FAX, mail. Search requires name only. Other helpful information: social security number, date of birth, approximate years of attendance. No fee for information.

Transcripts available by FAX, mail. Search requires name plus social security number, signed release. Other helpful information: date of birth, approximate years of attendance. Fee is $5.00.

Harford Community College, Registrar, 401 Thomas Run Rd, Bel Air, MD 21015, 410-836-4222 (FAX: 410-836-4169). Hours: 8AM-7:30PM M-Th; 8AM-4:30PM F. Records go back to 1957. Degrees granted: Associate. Adverse incident record source: Campus Security, 410-836-4272.

Attendance information available by phone, FAX, mail. Search requires name plus social security number, approximate years of attendance. Other helpful information: date of birth, exact years of attendance. No fee for information.

Degree information available by phone, FAX, mail. Search requires name plus social security number, date of birth, approximate years of attendance. No fee for information.

Transcripts available by FAX, mail. Search requires name plus social security number, approximate years of attendance, signed release. Other helpful information: date of birth, exact years of attendance. No fee for transcripts.

Harold Washington College, Registrar, 30 E Lake St, Chicago, IL 60601, 312-553-6060 (FAX: 312-553-6077). Hours: 9AM-6PM. Records go back to 1962. Degrees granted: Associate.

Attendance and degree information available by phone, FAX, mail. Search requires name only. Other helpful information: social security number, date of birth, approximate years of attendance. No fee for information.

Transcripts available by FAX, mail. Search requires name plus signed release. Other helpful information: social security number, date of birth, approximate years of attendance. Fee is $5.00. Expedited service available for $10.00.

Harrington Institute of Interior Design, Registrar, 410 S Michigan Ave, Chicago, IL 60605-1496, 312-939-4975 (FAX: 312-939-8005). Hours: 8:30AM-5:00PM. Records go back 35 years. Degrees granted: Associate; Bachelors.

Attendance and degree information available by FAX, mail. Search requires name only. Other helpful information: approximate years of attendance. No fee for information.

Transcripts available by FAX, mail. Search requires name plus signed release. Other helpful information: approximate years of attendance. Fee is $3.00.

Major credit cards accepted for payment.

Harris-Stowe State College, Registrar, 3026 Laclede Ave, St Louis, MO 63103, 314-340-3600 (FAX: 314-340-3322). Hours: 8AM-10PM M-Th, 8AM-5PM F,Sat. Records go back to 1919. Alumni records are maintained here also. Call 314-340-3375. Degrees granted: Bachelors.

Attendance and degree information available by phone, FAX, mail. Search requires name plus social security number, date of birth, approximate years of attendance, signed release. No fee for information.

Transcripts available by mail. Search requires name plus social security number, date of birth, approximate years of attendance, signed release. Fee is $4.00.

Harrisburg Area Community College, Registrar, One HACC Dr, Harrisburg, PA 17110-2999, 717-780-2370 (FAX: 717-231-7674). Hours: 8AM-8PM M-Th; 8AM-5PM F; 9AM-1PM S. Records go back to 1964.

Attendance and degree information available by phone, FAX, mail. Search requires name only. Other helpful information: social security number, date of birth, approximate years of attendance. No fee for information.

Transcripts available by written request only. Search requires name plus social security number, date of birth, signed release. Other helpful information: approximate years of attendance. Fee is $3.00.

Harrisburg Area Community College, (Lancaster), Registrar, 1008 New Holland Ave, Lancaster, PA 17604, 717-293-5000. Hours: 9AM-7:30PM M,T; 9AM-5PM W,Th; 9AM-4:30PM F. Records go back to 1989. Alumni records are maintained here also. Call 717-780-2400. Degrees granted: Associate. Adverse incident record source: Dean, 717-295-2975.

Attendance and degree information available by phone, mail. Search requires name plus social security number, exact years of attendance. No fee for information.

Transcripts available by mail. Search requires name plus social security number, date of birth, exact years of attendance, signed release. Fee is $3.00.

Need to know degree. Major credit cards accepted for payment.

Harrisburg Area Community College, (Lebanon), Registrar, 735 Cumberland St, Lebanon, PA 17042, 717-270-4222. Hours: 7:30AM-8PM M-Th, 7:30AM-5PM F, 8AM-1PM Sat. Records go back to 1980. Alumni records are maintained here also. Call 717-780-2400. Degrees granted: Associate.

Attendance information available by phone, mail. Search requires name plus social security number. No fee for information.

Degree information available by mail. Search requires name plus social security number, exact years of attendance, signed release. No fee for information.

Transcripts available by phone, mail. Search requires name plus social security number, exact years of attendance, signed release. Fee is $3.00.

Major credit cards accepted for payment.

Harry M. Ayers State Technical College, Registrar, PO Box 1647, Anniston, AL 36202-1647, 205-835-5400. Hours: 7:30AM-4:30PM. Records go back to 1965. Degrees granted: Associate.

Attendance and degree information available by mail. Search requires name plus social security number. No fee for information.

Transcripts available by mail. Search requires name plus social security number, exact years of attendance, signed release. No fee for transcripts.

Harry S. Truman College, Registrar, 1145 W Wilson Ave, Chicago, IL 60640, 312-907-4769. Hours: 8:30AM-7PM M-Th, 8:30AM-3PM. Records go back to 1958. Alumni records are maintained here also. Call 312-907-4755. Degrees granted: Associate.

Attendance and degree information available by phone, mail. Search requires name plus social security number, exact years of attendance. No fee for information.

Transcripts available by mail. Search requires name plus social security number, exact years of attendance, signed release. First transcript free. Additional ones $5.00 each.

The Sourcebook of College and University Student Records

H

Hartford Graduate Center, Registrar, 275 Windsor St, Hartford, CT 06120, 203-548-2425 (FAX: 203-548-7823). Records are not housed here. They are located at Rensselaer Polytechnic Institute, Registrar, 110 Eighth St, Troy, NY 12180-3590.

Hartford Seminary, Registrar, 77 Sherman St, Hartford, CT 06105, 203-232-4451 (FAX: 203-236-8570). Hours: 8:30AM-4:30PM. Records go back to 1945. Degrees granted: Masters; Doctorate.

Attendance and degree information available by phone, FAX, mail. Search requires name plus approximate years of attendance. Other helpful information: social security number, date of birth, exact years of attendance. No fee for information.

Transcripts available by mail. Search requires name plus approximate years of attendance, signed release. Other helpful information: social security number, date of birth, exact years of attendance. Fee is $3.00.

Hartnell College, Registrar, 156 Homestead Ave, Salinas, CA 93901, 408-755-6711 (FAX: 408-759-6014). Hours: 8AM-7PM M-Th; 8AM-5PM F. Records go back to 1920. Degrees granted: Associate.

Attendance information available by written request only. Search requires name plus social security number, date of birth, approximate years of attendance, signed release. No fee for information.

Degree information available by phone, FAX, mail. Search requires name plus social security number, date of birth. Other helpful information: approximate years of attendance. No fee for information.

Transcripts available by FAX, mail. Search requires name plus social security number, date of birth, signed release. Other helpful information: approximate years of attendance. Fee is $4.00. Expedited service available for $10.00.

Major credit cards accepted for payment.

Hartwick College, Registrar, Oneonta, NY 13820, 607-431-4460 (FAX: 607-431-4460). Hours: 9AM-5PM. Alumni records are maintained here also. Call 607-431-4010. Degrees granted: Bachelors.

Attendance and degree information available by phone, FAX, mail. Search requires name only. Other helpful information: social security number, date of birth, approximate years of attendance. No fee for information.

Transcripts available by mail. Search requires name plus signed release. Other helpful information: social security number, date of birth, approximate years of attendance. Fee is $3.00. Expedited service available for $10.00.

Harvard University, (Faculty of Arts and Sciences), Office of the Registrar, Cambridge, MA 02138, 617-495-1543 (FAX: 617-495-0815). Hours: 9AM-5PM. Records go back to 1951. Earlier records are at Archives. Records for graduate schools other than arts and sciences are held separately. Call for information. Degrees granted: Bachelors; Masters; Doctorate.

Attendance and degree information available by phone, FAX, mail. Search requires name only. Other helpful information: date of birth, approximate years of attendance. No fee for information.

Transcripts available by written request only. Search requires name plus signed release. Other helpful information: date of birth, approximate years of attendance. Fee is $3.00.

Type of degree helpful.

Harvey Mudd College, Registrar, 301 E 12th St, Claremont, CA 91711, 909-621-8090 (FAX: 909-621-8494). Hours: 8AM-Noon, 1-5PM. Transcripts available since founding; other records for past 10 years. Degrees granted: Bachelors; Masters.

Attendance and degree information available by phone, FAX, mail. Search requires name plus signed release. Other helpful information: approximate years of attendance. No fee for information.

Transcripts available by written request only. Search requires name plus signed release. Other helpful information: approximate years of attendance. Fee is $2.00.

Haskell Indian Junior College, Registrar, 155 Indian Ave #1305, Lawrence, KS 66046-4800, 913-749-8454 (FAX: 913-749-8429). Hours: 9AM-4:30PM. Degrees granted: Associate.

Attendance and degree information available by phone, mail. Search requires name plus social security number. No fee for information.

Transcripts available by mail. Search requires name plus social security number, signed release. No fee for transcripts.

Hastings College, Registrar, 720 N Turner Ave, PO Box 269, Hastings, NE 68902-0269, 402-461-7306 (FAX: 402-463-3002). Hours: 8AM-Noon, 1-5PM. Records go back to 1883. Alumni records are maintained here also. Call 402-461-7433. Degrees granted: Bachelors.

Attendance information available by phone, FAX, mail. Search requires name plus social security number. Other helpful information: date of birth, approximate years of attendance. No fee for information.

Degree information available by phone, FAX, mail. Search requires name plus approximate years of attendance. Other helpful information: social security number, date of birth, exact years of attendance. No fee for information.

Transcripts available by mail. Search requires name plus social security number, date of birth, approximate years of attendance, signed release. Fee is $3.00.

Haverford College, Registrar, 370 Lancaster Ave, Haverford, PA 19041-1392, 610-896-1022 (FAX: 610-896-1224). Hours: 9AM-5PM Academic year; 8:30AM-4:30PM Summer. Records go back to 1883. Transcripts available to early 1900s. Alumni records are maintained here also. Call 610-896-1001. Degrees granted: Bachelors.

Attendance and degree information available by phone, FAX, mail. Search requires name only. Other helpful information: social security number, date of birth, approximate years of attendance. No fee for information.

Transcripts available by FAX, mail. Search requires name plus signed release. Other helpful information: social security number, date of birth, approximate years of attendance. Fee is $4.00.

Will take FAX requests, but will not FAX out.

Hawaii Community College, Registrar, 200 W Kauili, Hilo, HI 96720-4091, 808-933-3662 (FAX: 808-933-3692). Hours: 8AM-4:30PM. Records go back to 1992. Degrees granted: Associate.

Attendance and degree information available by phone, FAX, mail. Search requires name plus social security number. No fee for information.

Transcripts available by mail. Search requires name plus social security number. Fee is $1.00.

Degree Granting Institutions

Hawaii Pacific University, Registrar's Office, 1164 Bishop St #200, Honolulu, HI 96813, 808-544-0239 (FAX: 808-544-1163). Hours: 8AM-5PM. Records go back to 1965. Alumni Records Office: 1154 Fort St Mall #216, Honolulu, HI 96813. Degrees granted: Associate; Bachelors; Masters. Certification: T.E.S.L.Q.M. Adverse incident record source: Barbara Bonson, 808-544-9358.

Attendance information available by phone, FAX, mail. Search requires name plus approximate years of attendance. Other helpful information: social security number. No fee for information.

Degree information available by phone, FAX, mail. Search requires name only. Other helpful information: social security number. No fee for information.

Transcripts available by FAX, mail. Search requires name plus signed release. Other helpful information: social security number, approximate years of attendance. Fee is $5.00.

Major credit cards accepted for payment.

Hawkeye Community College, Registrar, 1501 E Orange Rd, Waterloo, IA 50704, 319-296-2320. Degrees granted: Associate.

Attendance and degree information available by phone, FAX, mail. Search requires name plus approximate years of attendance. Other helpful information: social security number, date of birth, exact years of attendance. No fee for information.

Transcripts available by FAX, mail. Search requires name plus approximate years of attendance, signed release. Other helpful information: social security number, date of birth, exact years of attendance. No fee for transcripts.

Haywood Community College, Registrar, Freedlander Dr, Clyde, NC 28721, 704-627-4507 (FAX: 704-627-4513). Hours: 8AM-7PM. Records go back to 1964. Degrees granted: Associate.

Attendance information available by mail. Search requires name plus date of birth. Other helpful information: social security number, approximate years of attendance. No fee for information.

Degree information available by phone, FAX, mail. Search requires name plus date of birth. Other helpful information: social security number, approximate years of attendance. No fee for information.

Transcripts available by FAX, mail. Search requires name plus date of birth, signed release. Other helpful information: social security number, approximate years of attendance. No fee for transcripts.

Hazard Community College, Registrar, One Community College Dr, Hazard, KY 41701, 606-436-5721 (FAX: 606-439-2988). Hours: 8AM-4:30PM. Records go back to 1989. Alumni Records Office: Alumni Association, 400 Rd St, Lexington, KY 40505. Degrees granted: Associate.

Attendance and degree information available by phone, FAX, mail. Search requires name plus social security number. No fee for information.

Transcripts available by FAX, mail. Search requires name plus social security number, signed release. Fee is $2.00.

Heald Business College-Concord, Registrar, 2150 John Glenn Dr Ste 100, Concord, CA 94520, 510-827-1300 (FAX: 510-827-1486). Hours: 7:30AM-6PM. Records go back to 1970. Degrees granted: Associate.

Attendance and degree information available by phone, FAX, mail. Search requires name plus social security number, approximate years of attendance. Other helpful information: date of birth, exact years of attendance. No fee for information.

Transcripts available by FAX, mail. Search requires name plus social security number, approximate years of attendance, signed release. Other helpful information: date of birth, exact years of attendance. Fee is $2.00.

Heald Business College-Fresno, Registrar, 255 W Bullard Ave, Fresno, CA 93704, 209-438-4222 (FAX: 209-438-6368). Hours: 8AM-7PM. Degrees granted: Associate.

Attendance and degree information available by phone, FAX, mail. Search requires name plus social security number, approximate years of attendance, signed release. No fee for information.

Transcripts available by FAX, mail. Search requires name plus social security number, approximate years of attendance, signed release. No fee for transcripts.

Heald Business College-Hayward, Registrar, 777 Southland Dr, Hayward, CA 94545, 510-784-7000 (FAX: 510-784-7050). Hours: 8AM-5PM. Records go back to 1863. Degrees granted: Associate.

Attendance and degree information available by phone, FAX, mail. Search requires name plus social security number. No fee for information.

Transcripts available by mail. Search requires name plus social security number, signed release. No fee for transcripts.

Heald Business College-Oakland, Registrar, 1000 Broadway, Ste 290, Oakland, CA 94607, 510-444-0201 (FAX: 510-839-2084). Hours: 8AM-6PM. Records go back to 1975. Degrees granted: Associate.

Attendance and degree information available by phone, FAX, mail. Search requires name plus social security number, approximate years of attendance, signed release. No fee for information.

Transcripts available by FAX, mail. Search requires name plus social security number, approximate years of attendance, signed release. Fee is $2.00.

Heald Business College-Sacramento, Registrar, 2910 Prospect Park Dr, Rancho Cordova, CA 95670, 916-638-1616 (FAX: 916-638-1580). Hours: 7:30AM-8PM. Records go back to 1950. Degrees granted: Associate. Adverse incident record source: Corporate Office, 415-864-5060.

Attendance and degree information available by phone, FAX, mail. Search requires name plus social security number, approximate years of attendance. No fee for information.

Transcripts available by FAX, mail. Search requires name plus social security number, approximate years of attendance. Fee is $2.00.

Heald Business College-Salinas, Registrar, 1333 Schilling Pl, PO Box 3167, Salinas, CA 93901, 408-757-1700 (FAX: 408-757-6393). Hours: 8AM-5PM. Records go back 4 years. Degrees granted: Associate.

Attendance information available by phone, FAX, mail. Search requires name only. Other helpful information: social security number, date of birth, approximate years of attendance. No fee for information.

Degree information available by phone, FAX, mail. Search requires name plus approximate years of attendance. Other helpful information: social security number, date of birth, exact years of attendance. No fee for information.

Transcripts available by phone, FAX, mail. Search requires name plus signed release. Other helpful information: social security number, date of birth, approximate years of attendance. No fee for transcripts.

Heald Business College-San Francisco, Registrar, 1453 Mission St, San Francisco, CA 94103, 415-673-5500 (FAX: 415-626-1404). Hours: 8AM-5PM. Records go back to 1965. Degrees granted: Associate.

Attendance information available by mail. Search requires name plus date of birth, signed release. Other helpful information: social security number, approximate years of attendance. Fee is $2.00.

Degree information available by phone, FAX, mail. Search requires name plus date of birth. Other helpful information: social security number, approximate years of attendance. Fee is $2.00.

Transcripts available by written request only. Search requires name plus social security number, date of birth, signed release. Other helpful information: approximate years of attendance. Fee is $2.00.

Major credit cards accepted for payment.

Heald Business College-San Jose, Registrar, 2665 N First St Ste 110, San Jose, CA 95134, 408-955-9555 (FAX: 408-955-9580). Hours: 8AM-5PM. Records go back to 1970. Degrees granted: Associate.

Attendance and degree information available by phone. Search requires name plus social security number, approximate years of attendance, signed release. No fee for information.

Transcripts available by FAX, mail. Search requires name plus social security number, approximate years of attendance, signed release. Fee is $5.00.

Heald Business College-Santa Rosa, Registrar, 2425 Mendocino Ave, Santa Rosa, CA 95403, 707-525-1300 (FAX: 707-527-0251). Hours: 9AM-4:30PM. Records go back to founding date. Degrees granted: Associate.

Attendance and degree information available by phone, FAX, mail. Search requires name plus social security number. Other helpful information: approximate years of attendance. No fee for information.

Transcripts available by phone, FAX, mail. Search requires name plus social security number. Other helpful information: approximate years of attendance. No fee for transcripts.

Heald Business College-Stockton, Registrar, 1605 E March Ln, Stockton, CA 95210, 209-477-1114 (FAX: 209-477-2739). Hours: 7:30AM-7PM. Records go back to 1863. Degrees granted: Associate.

Attendance and degree information available by FAX, mail. Search requires name plus social security number, signed release. No fee for information.

Transcripts available by FAX, mail. Search requires name plus social security number, exact years of attendance, signed release. No fee for transcripts.

Need to know what program.

Heald Institute of Technology-Hayward, Registrar, 24301 Southland Dr Ste 500, Hayward, CA 94545, 510-783-2100 (FAX: 510-783-3287). Hours: 8AM-4:30PM. Records go back to 1920. Degrees granted: Associate.

Attendance and degree information available by phone, FAX, mail. Search requires name plus social security number. No fee for information.

Transcripts available by FAX, mail. Search requires name plus social security number, signed release. No fee for transcripts.

Heald Institute of Technology-Martinez, Registrar, 2860 Howe Rd, Martinez, CA 94553, 510-228-9000 (FAX: 510-228-6991). Hours: 8AM-5PM. Records go back to 1985. Degrees granted: Associate.

Attendance and degree information available by phone, FAX, mail. Search requires name plus social security number, exact years of attendance. No fee for information.

Transcripts available by FAX, mail. Search requires name plus social security number, exact years of attendance, signed release. Transcript fee $5.00 for records prior to 1989; $3.00 after 1988.

Heald Institute of Technology-Sacramento, Registrar, 2910 Prospect Park Dr, Rancho Cordova, CA 95670, 916-638-1616 (FAX: 916-638-1580). Hours: 8AM-5PM. Records go back to 1868. Degrees granted: Associate.

Attendance and degree information available by FAX, mail. Search requires name plus social security number, exact years of attendance. No fee for information.

Transcripts available by FAX, mail. Search requires name plus social security number, exact years of attendance, signed release. Fee is $2.00.

Heald Institute of Technology-San Francisco, Registrar, 1453 Mission St, San Francisco, CA 94103, 415-673-5500 (FAX: 415-626-1404). Hours: 8AM-5PM. Records go back to 1863. Degrees granted: Associate.

Attendance and degree information available by phone, FAX, mail. Search requires name plus social security number, date of birth, exact years of attendance, signed release. No fee for information.

Transcripts available by FAX, mail. Search requires name plus social security number, date of birth, exact years of attendance, signed release. Fee is $2.00.

Confirmation given by phone only if release on file.

Heald Institute of Technology-San Jose, Registrar, 2665 N 1st St, San Jose, CA 95134, 408-955-9555 (FAX: 408-955-9580). Hours: 8AM-5PM. Records go back to 1863. Degrees granted: Associate.

Attendance and degree information available by FAX, mail. Search requires name plus social security number, signed release. No fee for information.

Transcripts available by FAX, mail. Search requires name plus social security number, signed release. No fee for transcripts.

Hebrew College, Registrar, 43 Hawes St, Brookline, MA 02156, 617-278-4944 (FAX: 617-734-9769). Hours: 9AM-5PM. Degrees granted: Bachelors; Masters.

Attendance and degree information available by phone, FAX, mail. Search requires name plus exact years of attendance, signed release. Other helpful information: social security number, date of birth. Fee is $3.00.

Transcripts available by phone, FAX, mail. Search requires name plus exact years of attendance, signed release. Other helpful information: social security number, date of birth. Fee is $3.00.

Hebrew Union College-Jewish Institute of Religion, Registrar, 3101 Clifton Ave, Cincinnati, OH 45220, 513-221-1875 (FAX: 513-221-0321). Records go back 90 years. Alumni records are maintained here at the same phone number. Degrees granted: Masters; Doctorate; M.Phil.

Attendance information available by phone, FAX, mail. Search requires name plus social security number. Other helpful information: approximate years of attendance. No fee for information.

Degree information available by phone, FAX, mail. Search requires name plus social security number. Other helpful information: approximate years of attendance. No fee for information.

Transcripts available by mail. Search requires name plus social security number, signed release. Other helpful information: date of birth, approximate years of attendance. Fee is $5.00.

Hebrew Union College-Jewish Institute of Religion, Registrar, 3077 University Ave, Los Angeles, CA 90007, 213-749-3424 (FAX: 213-747-6128). Hours: 8AM-5PM. Records go back to 1972. Alumni records are maintained here also. Call 213-749-3424. Degrees granted: Bachelors; Masters; Doctorate.

Attendance and degree information available by phone, FAX, mail. Search requires name only. Other helpful information: social security number, approximate years of attendance. Fee is $2.00.

Transcripts available by mail. Search requires name plus signed release. Other helpful information: social security number, approximate years of attendance. Fee is $2.00.

Fee to be increased soon.

Hebrew Union College-Jewish Institute of Religion, Registrar, One W Fourth St, New York, NY 10012, 212-674-5300 (FAX: 212-388-1720). Hours: 8:30AM-5:30PM. Alumni records are maintained here at the same phone number. Degrees granted: Masters; Doctorate. Special programs- Hebrew Union College, Cincinnati, 513-221-1875.

Attendance and degree information available by phone, FAX, mail. Search requires name plus approximate years of attendance. No fee for information.

Transcripts available by mail. Search requires name plus approximate years of attendance, signed release. Fee is $5.00.

Heidelberg College, Registrar, 310 E Market St, Tiffin, OH 44883, 419-448-2090 (FAX: 419-448-2124). Hours: 8AM-5PM. Alumni records are maintained here also. Call 419-448-2383. Degrees granted: Bachelors. Adverse incident record source: Student Services, 419-448-2058.

Attendance and degree information available by phone, FAX, mail. Search requires name plus exact years of attendance, signed release. No fee for information.

Transcripts available by FAX, mail. Search requires name plus exact years of attendance, signed release. First transcript is free. Additional ones are $3.00 each.

Helene Fuld School of Nursing, Registrar, 1879 Madison Ave, New York, NY 10035, 212-423-1000 X238 (FAX: 212-427-2453). Hours: 8AM-4PM. Records go back to 1946. Alumni records are maintained here also. Call 212-423-1000 X216. Degrees granted: Associate.

Attendance and degree information available by FAX, mail. Search requires name plus social security number, approximate years of attendance, signed release. No fee for information.

Transcripts available by FAX, mail. Search requires name plus social security number, approximate years of attendance, signed release. Fee is $4.00.

Hellenic College/Holy Cross Greek Orthodox School of Theology, Registrar, 50 Goddard Ave, Brookline, MA 02146, 617-731-3500 (FAX: 617-232-7819). Hours: 9AM-5PM. Records go back to 1937. Alumni records are maintained here at the same phone number. Degrees granted: Bachelors; Masters.

Attendance and degree information available by FAX, mail. Search requires name plus date of birth, approximate years of attendance, signed release. Other helpful information: social security number. No fee for information.

Transcripts available by FAX, mail. Search requires name plus date of birth, approximate years of attendance, signed release. Other helpful information: social security number. Fee is $2.00. Expedited service available for $2.00.

Include a self addressed stamped envelope with mail request.

Henderson Community College, Registrar, 2660 S Green St, Henderson, KY 42420, 502-827-1867 (FAX: 502-827-8635). Hours: 8AM-7PM M-Th; 8AM-5PM F. Records go back to 1960. Degrees granted: Associate.

Attendance and degree information available by phone, mail. Search requires name plus social security number. Other helpful information: date of birth. No fee for information.

Transcripts available by written request only. Search requires name plus social security number, date of birth, approximate years of attendance, signed release. Other helpful information: exact years of attendance. Fee is $2.00. Expedited service available for $5.00.

Henderson State University, Registrar, 1100 Henderson St, Arkadelphia, AR 71999-0001, 501-230-5135 (FAX: 501-230-5144). Hours: 8AM-5PM. Records go back to 1895. Alumni records are maintained here also. Call 501-230-5401. Degrees granted: Associate; Bachelors. Adverse incident record source: Security Office, 501-230-5098.

Attendance information available by FAX, mail. Search requires name plus social security number, date of birth, approximate years of attendance. No fee for information.

Degree information available by phone, FAX, mail. Search requires name plus social security number, date of birth, approximate years of attendance. No fee for information.

Transcripts available by FAX, mail. Search requires name plus social security number, date of birth, approximate years of attendance, signed release. Fee is $3.00.

Fee to receive FAX $1.00; to FAX back $1.00, plus $.50 per page.

Hendrix College, Registrar, 1601 Harkrider St, Conway, AR 72032-3080, 501-450-1226 (FAX: 501-450-1200). Hours: 8AM-5PM. Records go back 110 years. Alumni records are maintained here also. Call 501-450-1223. Degrees granted: Bachelors.

Attendance and degree information available by phone, FAX, mail. Search requires name plus signed release. Other helpful information: social security number, date of birth, approximate years of attendance. Fee is $2.00.

Transcripts available by FAX, mail. Search requires name plus signed release. Other helpful information: social security number, date of birth, approximate years of attendance. Fee is $2.00.

Major credit cards accepted for payment.

Henry Ford Community College, Registrar, 5101 Evergreen Rd, Dearborn, MI 48128, 313-845-6403 (FAX: 313-845-6464). Hours: 8AM-7:30PM M-Th; 8AM-4:30PM F. Degrees granted: Associate.

Attendance and degree information available by phone, FAX, mail. Search requires name plus social security number, date of birth. Other helpful information: approximate years of attendance. No fee for information.

Transcripts available by mail. Search requires name plus social security number, date of birth, signed release. Other helpful information: approximate years of attendance. Fee is $3.00.

Herbert H. Lehman College, Registrar, 250 Bedford Park Blvd W, Bronx, NY 10468, 718-960-8613. Hours: 9AM-5PM. Records go back to 1970. Alumni records are maintained here also. Call 718-960-8044. Degrees granted: Bachelors; Masters.

Attendance and degree information available by mail. Search requires name plus social security number, approximate years of attendance, signed release. No fee for information.

Transcripts available by mail. Search requires name plus social security number, approximate years of attendance, signed release. Fee is $4.00.

Heritage College, Registrar, 3240 Fort Rd, Toppenish, WA 98948, 509-865-2244 X1605 (FAX: 509-865-4469). Hours: 8AM-4:30PM. Records go back to 1982. Degrees granted: Bachelors; Masters.

Attendance and degree information available by phone, FAX, mail. Search requires name plus social security number, date of birth. No fee for information.

Transcripts available by FAX, mail. Search requires name plus social security number, date of birth, signed release. Fee is $5.00.

Herkimer County Community College, Registrar, Reservoir Rd, Herkimer, NY 13350, 315-866-0300 X280 (FAX: 315-866-7253). Hours: 8AM-4PM. Records go back to 1968. Degrees granted: Associate. Adverse incident record source: Dean of Students, 315-866-0300 X276: Safety Office, 315-866-0300 X336

Attendance and degree information available by phone, FAX, mail. Search requires name only. Other helpful information: social security number, approximate years of attendance. No fee for information.

Transcripts available by phone, FAX, mail. Search requires name plus signed release. Other helpful information: social security number, approximate years of attendance. Fee is $5.00.

Major credit cards accepted for payment.

Herman M. Finch University of Health Sciences, (The Chicago Medical School), Registrar, 3333 Green Bay Rd, North Chicago, IL 60046, 708-578-3228 (FAX: 708-578-3284). Hours: 8:30AM-4:30PM. Alumni Records Office: AMOCCO Bldg, North Chicago, IL 60046. Degrees granted: Bachelors; Masters; Doctorate.

Attendance information available by phone, FAX, mail. Search requires name only. Other helpful information: social security number, date of birth, approximate years of attendance. No fee for information.

Degree information available by phone, FAX, mail. Search requires name only. Other helpful information: social security number, date of birth, approximate years of attendance. No fee for information.

Transcripts available by mail. Search requires name plus social security number, date of birth, signed release. Other helpful information: approximate years of attendance. Fee is $3.00.

Hesser College, Registrar, 3 Sundial Ave, Manchester, NH 03103, 603-668-6660. Records go back to 1915. Degrees granted: Associate.

Attendance and degree information available by phone, FAX, mail. Search requires name plus social security number, signed release. Other helpful information: date of birth, approximate years of attendance. No fee for information.

Transcripts available by phone, FAX, mail. Search requires name plus social security number, signed release. Other helpful information: date of birth, approximate years of attendance. Fee is $5.00. Expedited service available for $10.00.

Major credit cards accepted for payment.

Hesston College, Registrar, PO Box 3000, Hesston, KS 67062, 316-327-8231 (FAX: 316-327-8300). Hours: 8AM-5PM. Records go back to 1909. Degrees granted: Associate.

Attendance and degree information available by phone, FAX, mail. Search requires name plus social security number, approximate years of attendance. Other helpful information: exact years of attendance. No fee for information.

Transcripts available by FAX, mail. Search requires name plus signed release. Other helpful information: social security number, approximate years of attendance. Fee is $3.00. Expedited service available for $2.00.

Hibbing Community College, Records Office, 1515 E 25th St, Hibbing, MN 55746, 218-262-6700 (FAX: 218-262-6717). Hours: 8AM-4:30PM. Records go back to 1916. Degrees granted: Associate. Adverse incident record source: Administration Office.

Attendance and degree information available by phone, mail. Search requires name plus social security number, signed release. Other helpful information: date of birth. No fee for information.

Transcripts available by mail. Search requires name plus social security number, signed release. Other helpful information: date of birth. No fee for transcripts.

Hickey School, Registrar, 940 W Port Plaza, St Louis, MO 63146, 314-434-2212 (FAX: 314-434-1974). Hours: 7:30AM-5PM. Records go back to 1933. Degrees granted: Associate.

Attendance and degree information available by phone, FAX, mail. Search requires name plus exact years of attendance. Other helpful information: social security number, approximate years of attendance. No fee for information.

Transcripts available by FAX, mail. Search requires name plus exact years of attendance, signed release. Other helpful information: social security number, approximate years of attendance. Fee is $5.00.

High Point University, Registrar, University Station, Montlieu Ave, High Point, NC 27262-3598, 910-841-9131 (FAX: 910-841-5723). Hours: 8:30AM-5PM; 4:30 in Summer. Records go back to 1924. Alumni records are maintained here also. Call 910-841-9135. Degrees granted: Bachelors; Masters. Adverse incident record source: Dean Evans, 910-841-9026.

Attendance and degree information available by phone, FAX, mail. Search requires name only. Other helpful information: approximate years of attendance. No fee for information.

Transcripts available by FAX, mail. Search requires name plus approximate years of attendance, signed release. Fee is $2.00. Expedited service available for $2.00.

FAX only under special circumstances. DOB not released.

Highland Community College, Registrar, 2998 Pearl City Rd, Freeport, IL 61032, 815-235-6121 (FAX: 815-235-6130). Hours: 8AM-5PM. Records go back to 1962. Alumni records are maintained here also. Call 815-235-6121 X205. Degrees granted: Associate.

Attendance and degree information available by phone, FAX, mail. Search requires name plus signed notarized release. Other

helpful information: approximate years of attendance. No fee for information.
Transcripts available by FAX, mail. Search requires name plus signed release. Other helpful information: approximate years of attendance. Fee is $2.00. Expedited service available for $2.00.
Major credit cards accepted for payment.

Highland Community College, Registrar, PO Box 68, Highland, KS 66035, 913-442-6025 (FAX: 913-442-6100). Hours: 8:30AM-4:30PM. Degrees granted: Associate.
Attendance and degree information available by phone, mail. Search requires name plus social security number. Other helpful information: date of birth, approximate years of attendance. No fee for information.
Transcripts available by mail. Search requires name plus social security number, signed release. Other helpful information: date of birth, approximate years of attendance. Fee is $2.00.
Major credit cards accepted for payment.

Highland Park Community College, Registrar, Glendale Ave at Third St, Highland Park, MI 48203, 313-252-0475 X240 (FAX: 313-252-0425). Hours: 8AM-4:30PM. Records go back to 1920. Degrees granted: Associate.
Attendance and degree information available by FAX, mail. Search requires name plus social security number, date of birth, approximate years of attendance, signed release. Other helpful information: exact years of attendance. No fee for information.
Transcripts available by FAX, mail. Search requires name plus social security number, date of birth, approximate years of attendance, signed release. Other helpful information: exact years of attendance. Fee is $2.00.
Major credit cards accepted for payment.

Highline Community College, Registrar, PO Box 98000, Des Moines, WA 98198-9800, 206-878-3710 X559. Hours: 8AM-4:30PM. Records go back to 1961. Alumni records are maintained here at the same phone number. Degrees granted: Associate.
Attendance and degree information available by mail. Search requires name plus social security number, date of birth, exact years of attendance, signed release. No fee for information.
Transcripts available by mail. Search requires name plus social security number, date of birth, exact years of attendance, signed release. No fee for transcripts.

Hilbert College, Registrar, 5200 S Park Ave, Hamburg, NY 14075-1597, 716-649-7900 (FAX: 716-649-0702). Hours: 8:30AM-5PM. Records go back to 1957. Degrees granted: Associate; Bachelors.
Attendance and degree information available by phone, FAX, mail. Search requires name plus social security number. Other helpful information: date of birth, approximate years of attendance. No fee for information.
Transcripts available by written request only. Search requires name plus social security number, signed release. Other helpful information: date of birth, approximate years of attendance. Fee is $3.00. Expedited service available for $3.00.

Hill College, Registrar, PO Box 619, Hillsboro, TX 76645, 817-582-2555 (FAX: 817-582-7591). Hours: 8AM-4PM. Records go back to 1923. Degrees granted: Associate. Adverse incident record source: Dean, 817-582-2555.
School will not confirm attendance information. Search requires name only. No fee for information.

Degree information available by phone, FAX, mail. Search requires name plus social security number. Other helpful information: approximate years of attendance. No fee for information.
School does not provide transcripts. Search requires name plus social security number, signed release. Other helpful information: approximate years of attendance. Fee is $2.00.

Hillsborough Community College, HCC Admissions Office, PO Box 5096, Tampa, FL 33631-3127, 813-253-7004. Hours: 8AM-4:30PM. Records go back 26 years. Degrees granted: Associate. Adverse incident record source: Campuses: Dale Mabry, 253-7280; Ybor City, 253-7680: Brandon, 253-7880; Plant City, 757-2102
Attendance and degree information available by phone, FAX, mail. Search requires name plus social security number. Other helpful information: approximate years of attendance. No fee for information.
Transcripts available by mail. Search requires name plus social security number, signed release. Other helpful information: approximate years of attendance. Fee is $5.00.
Name when in attendance.

Hillsdale College, Registrar, 33 E College Ave, Hillsdale, MI 49242, 517-437-7341 (FAX: 517-437-0190). Hours: 8:30AM-5PM Fall; 8AM-4PM Summer. Records go back to 1877. Alumni records are maintained here also. Call 517-437-7341 X2461. Degrees granted: Bachelors.
Attendance information available by phone, FAX, mail. Search requires name plus approximate years of attendance, signed release. No fee for information.
Degree information available by phone, FAX, mail. Search requires name plus signed release. No fee for information.
Transcripts available by phone, FAX, mail. Search requires name plus signed release. Fee is $1.00.

Hinds Community College, Admissions & Records, Raymond, MS 39154, 601-857-3211 (FAX: 601-857-3539). Hours: 8AM-4:30PM. Records go back to 1940s. Degrees granted: Associate.
Attendance and degree information available by phone, FAX, mail. Search requires name plus social security number, date of birth, approximate years of attendance, signed release. No fee for information.
Transcripts available by written request only. Search requires name plus social security number, date of birth, approximate years of attendance, signed release. Fee is $2.00.

Hiram College, Registrar, Hiram, OH 44234, 216-569-5210 (FAX: 216-569-5211). Hours: 8:30AM-5PM. Alumni records are maintained here also. Call 216-569-5283. Degrees granted: Bachelors.
Attendance and degree information available by phone, FAX, mail. Search requires name plus social security number. No fee for information.
Transcripts available by FAX. Search requires name plus social security number. No fee for transcripts.

Hiwassee College, Registrar, HC Box 646, 225 Hiwassee College Dr, Madisonville, TN 37354, 615-442-2001 X215. Hours: 8AM-5PM. Records go back to 1849. Alumni records are maintained here also. Call 615-442-2091. Degrees granted: Associate.
Attendance and degree information available by phone, mail. Search requires name plus social security number. No fee for information.

Transcripts available by mail. Search requires name plus social security number, signed release. Fee is $2.00.

Hobart & William Smith College, Registrar, Geneva, NY 14456, 315-781-3651 (FAX: 315-781-3920). Hours: 9AM-4PM. Records go back to 1908. Alumni records are maintained here also. Call 315-781-3700. Degrees granted: Bachelors.
 Attendance and degree information available by phone, FAX, mail. Search requires name plus social security number, approximate years of attendance, signed release. No fee for information.
 Transcripts available by mail. Search requires name plus social security number, approximate years of attendance, signed release. Fee is $5.00.

Hobe Sound Bible College, Registrar, PO Box 1065, 11298 SE Gomez Ave, Hobe Sound, FL 33455, 407-546-5554 (FAX: 407-545-1422). Hours: 8AM-5PM. Records go back to founding date. Degrees granted: Associate; Bachelors.
 Attendance information available by phone, FAX, mail. Search requires name plus approximate years of attendance. No fee for information.
 Degree information available by phone, FAX, mail. Search requires name only. Other helpful information: date of birth, approximate years of attendance. No fee for information.
 Transcripts available by phone, FAX, mail. Search requires name only. Other helpful information: date of birth, approximate years of attendance. Fee is $2.00.

Hocking Technical College, Registrar, 3301 Hocking Pkwy, Nelsonville, OH 45764, 614-753-3591 (FAX: 614-753-2586). Hours: 8AM-5:30PM M-Th, 8AM-4:30PM F. Records go back to 1968. Alumni records are maintained here at the same phone number. Degrees granted: Associate; LPN.
 Attendance and degree information available by phone, FAX, mail. Search requires name plus social security number, approximate years of attendance. No fee for information.
 Transcripts available by FAX, mail. Search requires name plus social security number, approximate years of attendance. First transcript $2.00; $1.00 each additional.

Hofstra University, Office of Financial and Academic Records, Room 126, Hempstead, NY 11550, 516-463-6691 (FAX: 516-560-7660). Hours: 8AM-4:30PM. Alumni records are maintained here at the same phone number. Degrees granted: Bachelors; Masters; Doctorate.
 Attendance and degree information available by FAX, mail. Search requires name plus social security number, exact years of attendance. No fee for information.
 Transcripts available by FAX, mail. Search requires name plus social security number, exact years of attendance, signed release. No fee for transcripts.

Hollins College, Registrar, PO Box 9688, Roanoke, VA 24020, 703-362-6311 (FAX: 703-362-6642). Hours: 8:30AM-4:30PM. Degrees granted: Bachelors; Masters.
 Attendance information available by phone, FAX, mail. Search requires name plus social security number. Other helpful information: approximate years of attendance. No fee for information.
 Degree information available by phone, FAX, mail. Search requires name plus social security number. Other helpful information: date of birth, approximate years of attendance. No fee for information.
 Transcripts available by FAX, mail. Search requires name plus social security number, signed release. Other helpful information: date of birth, approximate years of attendance. Fee is $4.00. Major credit cards accepted for payment.

Holmes Community College, Registrar, PO Box 369, Goodman, MS 39079, 601-472-2312 X23 (FAX: 601-472-9852). Hours: 8AM-3PM. Records go back to 1925. Alumni records are maintained here also. Call 601-472-2312 X53. Degrees granted: Associate. Adverse incident record source: Dean of Students, 601-472-2312 X25.
 Attendance and degree information available by phone, FAX, mail. Search requires name plus social security number, approximate years of attendance, signed release. No fee for information.
 Transcripts available by FAX, mail. Search requires name plus social security number, approximate years of attendance, signed release. Fee is $2.00.

Holy Apostles College and Seminary, Registrar, Cromwell, CT 06416, 203-632-3033 (FAX: 203-632-0176). Hours: 9AM-5PM. Records go back to 1953. Degrees granted: Bachelors; Masters; M. Div.
 Attendance and degree information available by phone, FAX, mail. Search requires name plus approximate years of attendance, signed release. Other helpful information: social security number, date of birth. Fee is $5.00.
 Transcripts available by phone, FAX, mail. Search requires name plus approximate years of attendance, signed release. Other helpful information: social security number, date of birth. Fee is $5.00.
 Major credit cards accepted for payment.

Holy Cross College, Registrar, Box 308, Notre Dame, IN 46556, 219-233-6813 (FAX: 219-233-7427). Hours: 8AM-5PM. Records go back to 1966. Alumni records are maintained here at the same phone number. Degrees granted: Associate.
 Attendance and degree information available by phone, FAX, mail. Search requires name only. Other helpful information: social security number, approximate years of attendance. No fee for information.
 Transcripts available by FAX, mail. Search requires name plus social security number, signed release. Other helpful information: date of birth, approximate years of attendance. Fee is $2.00.
 Expedited service is available.

Holy Family College, Registrar's Office, Grant and Frankford Aves, Philadelphia, PA 19114-2094, 215-637-4851 (FAX: 215-281-9067). Hours: 8AM-7:30PM M-Th, 8AM-4:30PM F, 8:30AM-12:30PM Sat. Records go back to 1950. Alumni records are maintained here also. Call 215-637-7700. Degrees granted: Associate; Bachelors. Adverse incident record source: Dean, 215-637-3971.
 Attendance information available by phone, mail. Search requires name plus social security number. No fee for information.
 Degree information available by phone, mail. Search requires name plus social security number, exact years of attendance. No fee for information.
 Transcripts available by mail. Search requires name plus social security number, exact years of attendance, signed release. Fee is $2.00.

Holy Names College, Registrar, 3500 Mountain Blvd, Oakland, CA 94619-9989, 510-436-1133 (FAX: 510-436-1199). Hours: 9:30AM-3:30PM M,T,Th,F; 11AM-7PM F. Records go back to 1868. Alumni records are maintained here also. Call 510-436-1240. Degrees granted: Bachelors; Masters.

Attendance information available by phone, FAX, mail. Search requires name plus social security number, approximate years of attendance. No fee for information.

Degree information available by phone, FAX, mail. Search requires name plus approximate years of attendance. Other helpful information: social security number, date of birth. No fee for information.

Transcripts available by FAX, mail. Search requires name plus social security number, approximate years of attendance, signed release. Other helpful information: date of birth. Fee is $5.00. Expedited service available for $5.00.

Major credit cards accepted for payment.

Holyoke Community College, Registrar, 303 Homestead Ave, Holyoke, MA 01040, 413-552-2751. Hours: 9AM-4:30PM. Records go back to 1956. Alumni records are maintained here also. Call 413-552-2253. Degrees granted: Associate.

Attendance and degree information available by mail. Search requires name plus social security number, approximate years of attendance, signed release. No fee for information.

Transcripts available by mail. Search requires name plus social security number, approximate years of attendance, signed release. Fee is $3.00.

Home Study International, Registrar, 12501 Old Columbia Pike, PO Box 4437, Silver Spring, MD 20914, 301-680-6570. Hours: 8:30AM-4:30PM M-Th, 8:30-11:30AM F. Records go back to 1954. Degrees granted: Associate.

Attendance and degree information available by phone, mail. Search requires name plus social security number, date of birth, exact years of attendance. No fee for information.

Transcripts available by mail. Search requires name plus social security number, date of birth, exact years of attendance, signed release. Fee is $5.00.

Home Study International, (Griggs University), Registrar, 12501 Old Columbia Pike, PO Box 4437, Silver Spring, MD 20914, 301-680-6570 (FAX: 301-680-6577). Hours: 8:30AM-5PM. Alumni records are maintained here at the same phone number. Degrees granted: Associate; Bachelors.

Attendance and degree information available by written request only. Search requires name plus approximate years of attendance, signed release. Other helpful information: social security number, date of birth, exact years of attendance. No fee for information. Expedited service available for $12.00.

Transcripts available by written request only. Search requires name plus approximate years of attendance, signed release. Other helpful information: social security number, date of birth, exact years of attendance. Fee is $3.00. Expedited service available for $12.00.

Major credit cards accepted for payment.

Honolulu Community College, Registrar, 874 Dillingham Blvd, Honolulu, HI 96817, 808-845-9120 (FAX: 808-845-9183). Hours: 7:45AM-4:30PM. Records go back 30 years. Degrees granted: Associate.

Attendance and degree information available by phone, mail. Search requires name only. No fee for information.

Transcripts available by written request only. Search requires name plus social security number, signed release. Other helpful information: date of birth, approximate years of attendance. Fee is $1.00.

Hood College, Registrar, 401 Rosemont Ave, Frederick, MD 21701, 301-696-3616 (FAX: 301-696-3597). Hours: 8AM-5PM. Records go back to 1893. Degrees granted: Bachelors; Masters.

Attendance and degree information available by phone, FAX, mail. Search requires name plus social security number. Other helpful information: approximate years of attendance. No fee for information.

Transcripts available by mail. Search requires name plus social security number, exact years of attendance, signed release. Other helpful information: approximate years of attendance. Fee is $3.00. Expedited service available for $10.00.

Hope College, Registrar, 141 E 12th St, PO Box 9000, Holland, MI 49422-9000, 616-395-7760 (FAX: 616-395-7680). Hours: 8AM-5PM. Alumni records are maintained here also. Call 616-395-7860. Degrees granted: Bachelors.

Attendance and degree information available by phone, mail. Search requires name plus social security number, approximate years of attendance. Other helpful information: date of birth, exact years of attendance. No fee for information.

Transcripts available by mail. Search requires name plus social security number, approximate years of attendance, signed release. Other helpful information: date of birth, exact years of attendance. Fee is $3.00. Expedite: $3.00 plus express mail fee.

Hopkinsville Community College, Registrar, PO Box 2100, Hopkinsville, KY 42241-2100, 502-886-3921 (FAX: 502-886-0237). Hours: 8AM-4:30PM. Records go back 30 years. Degrees granted: Associate.

Attendance and degree information available by phone, mail. Search requires name plus social security number. Other helpful information: approximate years of attendance. No fee for information.

Transcripts available by written request only. Search requires name plus social security number, signed release. Other helpful information: approximate years of attendance. Fee is $2.00. Expedited service available for $5.00.

Horry-Georgetown Technical College, Registrar, PO Box 1966, Conway, SC 29526, 803-347-3186 (FAX: 803-347-2962). Hours: 8AM-8:30PM M-Th; 8AM-4:30PM F. Records go back to 1966. Degrees granted: Associate.

Attendance and degree information available by phone, FAX, mail. Search requires name plus social security number, date of birth, approximate years of attendance. No fee for information.

Transcripts available by mail. Search requires name plus social security number, date of birth, approximate years of attendance, signed release. Fee is $2.00.

Major credit cards accepted for payment.

Hostos Community College, Registrar, 475 Grand Concourse, Bronx, NY 10451, 718-518-6771 (FAX: 718-518-6548). Hours: 11AM-7PM. Records go back to 1970. Alumni records are maintained here also. Call 718-518-4306. Degrees granted: Associate.

Attendance and degree information available by phone, FAX, mail. Search requires name plus social security number, signed release. No fee for information.

Transcripts available by FAX, mail. Search requires name plus social security number, signed release. Fee is $4.00.

Houghton College, Registrar, Houghton, NY 14744, 716-567-9257 (FAX: 716-567-9572). Hours: 8AM-5PM. Records go back to 1883. Alumni records are maintained here also. Call 716-567-9353. Degrees granted: Bachelors.

Attendance and degree information available by phone, FAX, mail. Search requires name plus social security number, approximate years of attendance, signed release. No fee for information.

Transcripts available by mail. Search requires name plus social security number, approximate years of attendance, signed release. Fee is $3.00.

Houghton College, (Buffalo Suburban Campus), Registrar, 910 Union Rd, West Seneca, NY 14224, 716-674-6363. Records are not housed here. They are located at Houghton College, Registrar, Houghton, NY 14744.

Housatonic Community-Technical College, Registrar, 510 Barnum Ave, Bridgeport, CT 06608, 203-579-6400 (FAX: 203-579-6993). Hours: 8AM-4:30PM. Records go back to 1966. Degrees granted: Associate.

Attendance and degree information available by phone, FAX, mail. Search requires name only. Other helpful information: social security number, date of birth, approximate years of attendance. No fee for information.

Transcripts available by FAX, mail. Search requires name plus signed release. Other helpful information: social security number. No fee for transcripts.

A student may request no release.

Houston Baptist University, Registrar, 7502 Fondren Rd, Houston, TX 77074-3298, 713-774-7661. Degrees granted: Bachelors; Masters.

Attendance and degree information available by mail. Search requires name plus social security number, signed release. Other helpful information: date of birth, exact years of attendance. Fee is $3.00.

Transcripts available by mail. Search requires name plus social security number, signed release. Other helpful information: date of birth, exact years of attendance. Fee is $3.00.

Houston Community College, Registrar, PO Box 7819, Houston, TX 77270-7849, 713-868-0763 (FAX: 713-869-5743). Hours: 8AM-4:30PM. Records go back to 1971. Degrees granted: Associate.

Attendance and degree information available by mail. Search requires name plus social security number, signed release. Other helpful information: approximate years of attendance. No fee for information.

Transcripts available by mail. Search requires name plus social security number, signed release. Other helpful information: date of birth, approximate years of attendance. No fee for transcripts.

Copies of transcript available by phone request only from another school. Major credit cards accepted for payment.

Houston Community College System, Registrar, PO Box 7849, Houston, TX 77270, 713-868-0763 (FAX: 713-869-5743). Hours: 8AM-4:30PM. Records go back to 1971. Degrees granted: Associate.

Attendance and degree information available by FAX, mail. Search requires name plus social security number, date of birth, signed release. Other helpful information: approximate years of attendance. No fee for information. Expedited service available for $15.00.

Transcripts available by FAX, mail. Search requires name plus social security number, date of birth, signed release. Other helpful information: approximate years of attendance. No fee for transcripts. Expedited service available for $15.00.

Major credit cards accepted for payment.

Houston Community College, (Central College), Registrar, 1300 Holman Ave, PO Box 7849, Houston, TX 77004, 713-868-0763. Hours: 8AM-5PM. Alumni records are maintained here at the same phone number. Degrees granted: Associate.

Attendance and degree information available by mail. Search requires name plus social security number, exact years of attendance, signed release. No fee for information.

Transcripts available by mail. Search requires name plus social security number, exact years of attendance, signed release. Fee is $3.00.

Houston Community College, (College Without Walls), Registrar, 4310 Dunlavy St, Houston, TX 77270, 713-868-0795. Records are not housed here. They are located at Houston Community College, (Central College), Registrar, 1300 Holman Ave, PO Box 7849, Houston, TX 77004.

Houston Community College, (Northeast College), Registrar, 4638 Airline Dr, PO Box 7849, Houston, TX 77270-7849, 713-694-5384. Records are not housed here. They are located at Houston Community College, (Central College), Registrar, 1300 Holman Ave, PO Box 7849, Houston, TX 77004.

Houston Community College, (Southeast College), Registrar, 6815 Rustic St, Houston, TX 77012, 713-641-2725. Records are not housed here. They are located at Houston Community College, (Central College), Registrar, 1300 Holman Ave, PO Box 7849, Houston, TX 77004.

Houston Community College, (Southwest College), Registrar, 5407 Gulfton St, Houston, TX 77081, 713-661-4589. Records are not housed here. They are located at Houston Community College, (Central College), Registrar, 1300 Holman Ave, PO Box 7849, Houston, TX 77004.

Houston Graduate School of Theology, Registrar, 6910 Fannin St Ste 207, Houston, TX 77030-2805, 713-791-9505. Hours: 8AM-4PM. Records go back to 1986. Alumni records are maintained here at the same phone number. Degrees granted: Masters; Doctorate.

Attendance and degree information available by phone, mail. Search requires name plus social security number, exact years of attendance. No fee for information.

Transcripts available by mail. Search requires name plus social security number, exact years of attendance, signed release. First transcript is free. Additional ones are $2.00 each.

Howard College, Admissions Office, 1001 Birdwell Lane, Big Spring, TX 79720, 915-264-5000 (FAX: 915-264-5082). Hours: 8AM-6PM M-Th; 8AM-3PM F. Records go back to 1945. Alumni records are maintained here also. Call 915-264-5000. Degrees granted: Associate.

Attendance and degree information available by mail. Search requires name plus signed release. Other helpful information: social security number, date of birth, approximate years of attendance. No fee for information.

Transcripts available by mail. Search requires name plus signed release. Other helpful information: social security number, date of birth, approximate years of attendance. Fee is $2.00.

Major credit cards accepted for payment.

Howard Community College, Registrar, 10901 Little Patuxent Pkwy, Columbia, MD 21044, 410-992-4800 (FAX: 410-715-2426). Hours: 8:30AM-5PM. Records go back to 1970. Alumni records are maintained here at the same phone number. Degrees granted: Associate.

Attendance and degree information available by phone, FAX, mail. Search requires name plus social security number, exact years of attendance. No fee for information.

Transcripts available by FAX, mail. Search requires name plus social security number, exact years of attendance, signed release. No fee for transcripts.

Howard Payne University, Registrar, 1000 Fisk Ave, Brownwood, TX 76801, 915-649-8011 (FAX: 915-649-8901). Hours: 8AM-5PM. Records go back to 1889.

Attendance and degree information available by phone, FAX, mail. Search requires name plus social security number, date of birth. Other helpful information: approximate years of attendance. No fee for information.

Transcripts available by mail. Search requires name plus social security number, date of birth, signed release. Other helpful information: approximate years of attendance. Fee is $3.00. FAX: $.85 per page.

Major credit cards accepted for payment.

Howard University, Registrar, 2400 Sixth St NW, Washington, DC 20059, 202-806-2712 (FAX: 202-806-4466). Hours: 8AM-5PM. Degrees granted: Bachelors; Masters; Doctorate.

Attendance information available by phone, FAX, mail. Search requires name only. Other helpful information: social security number, date of birth, exact years of attendance. No fee for information.

Degree information available by phone, FAX, mail. Search requires name only. Other helpful information: social security number, date of birth, approximate years of attendance. No fee for information.

Transcripts available by mail. Search requires name plus signed release. Other helpful information: social security number, date of birth, approximate years of attendance. Fee is $5.00.

Hudson County Community College, Registrar, 901 Bergen Ave, Jersey City, NJ 07306, 201-714-2138 (FAX: 201-656-8961). Hours: 9AM-6PM M-Th; 9AM-5PM F. Records go back to 1974. Alumni records are maintained here also. Call 201-714-2228. Degrees granted: Associate.

Attendance and degree information available by mail. Search requires name plus social security number, approximate years of attendance, signed release. No fee for information.

Transcripts available by mail. Search requires name plus social security number, approximate years of attendance, signed release. Fee is $3.00.

Hudson Valley Community College, Registrar, 80 Vandenburgh Ave, Troy, NY 12180, 518-270-1569 (FAX: 518-270-1576). Hours: 8AM-5PM. Records go back to 1988. Alumni records are maintained here also. Call 518-270-7556. Degrees granted: Associate. Adverse incident record source: Public Safety, 518-270-7210.

Attendance information available by phone, mail. Search requires name plus social security number, signed release. Other helpful information: date of birth, approximate years of attendance. No fee for information.

Degree information available by phone, mail. Search requires name plus social security number, date of birth, exact years of attendance, signed release. No fee for information.

Transcripts available by mail. Search requires name plus social security number, date of birth, signed release. Other helpful information: approximate years of attendance. Fee is $3.00.

Huertas Junior College, Registrar, PO Box 8429, Caguas, PR 00626, 809-743-2156 (FAX: 809-743-0203). Hours: 8AM-4PM. Degrees granted: Associate.

School will not confirm attendance or degree information. Search requires name plus social security number, date of birth, signed release. Other helpful information: exact years of attendance. No fee for information.

Transcripts available by written request only. Search requires name plus social security number, date of birth, signed release. Other helpful information: exact years of attendance. Fee is $2.00. Major credit cards accepted for payment.

Humacao Community College, Registrar, 101-103 Cruz Ortiz Stella, Box 8948, Humacao, PR 00661, 809-850-0055 (FAX: 809-257-8865). Hours: 8AM-5PM. Degrees granted.

Attendance and degree information available by written request only. Search requires name plus social security number, exact years of attendance, signed release. Other helpful information: approximate years of attendance. No fee for information.

Transcripts available by written request only. Search requires name plus social security number, exact years of attendance, signed release. Other helpful information: approximate years of attendance. Fee is $3.00.

Humacao Community College, **(Branch Campus)**, Registrar, PO Box 1185, Gerrido Morales #52, Fajardo, PR 00648, 809-863-5210.

Humacao University College, Registrar, CUH Sta Rd 908 Bo. Tejas, Humacao, PR 00791, 809-850-9314 (FAX: 809-850-9383). Hours: 8AM-Noon, 1-4:30PM. Records go back to 1962. Degrees granted: Associate; Bachelors. Adverse incident record source: Student Affairs, 809-850-9328.

Attendance information available by mail. Search requires name plus social security number, signed release. Other helpful information: approximate years of attendance. Fee is $1.00.

Degree information available by mail. Search requires name plus social security number, signed release. Fee is $1.00.

Transcripts available by mail. Search requires name plus social security number, signed release. Other helpful information: approximate years of attendance. Fee is $1.00.

Humboldt State University, Registrar, Arcata, CA 95521, 707-826-4402 (FAX: 707-826-6194). Hours: 9AM-4PM. Records go back to 1922. Alumni records are maintained here also. Call 707-826-5101. Degrees granted: Bachelors; Masters. Adverse incident record source: Registrar, 707-826-4402.

Attendance and degree information available by FAX, mail. Search requires name plus social security number, signed release. No fee for information.

Transcripts available by FAX, mail. Search requires name plus social security number, signed release. Fee is $4.00.

Humphrey's College, Registrar, 6650 Inglewood St, Stockton, CA 95207, 209-478-0800. Hours: 7:30AM-8:30PM M-Th, 8AM-5PM F. Records go back to 1896. Alumni records are maintained here at the same phone number. Degrees granted: Bachelors.

Attendance and degree information available by mail. Search requires name plus social security number, date of birth, exact years of attendance, signed release. No fee for information.

Transcripts available by mail. Search requires name plus social security number, date of birth, exact years of attendance, signed release. Fee is $2.00.

Hunter College, Registrar, 695 Park Ave, New York, NY 10021, 212-772-4500. Hours: 10AM-6PM. Records go back to 1906. Alumni records are maintained here also. Call 212-772-4087. Degrees granted: Bachelors; Masters.

Attendance and degree information available by mail. Search requires name plus social security number, date of birth, approximate years of attendance, signed release. No fee for information.

Transcripts available by mail. Search requires name plus social security number, date of birth, approximate years of attendance, signed release. No fee for transcripts.

Huntingdon College, Registrar, 1500 E Fairview Ave, Montgomery, AL 36106-2148, 334-265-0511 (FAX: 334-264-2951). Hours: 8AM-5PM Sept.-May, 7:30AM-4:30PM June-Aug. Records go back to 1900s. Alumni records are maintained here at the same phone number. Degrees granted: Associate; Bachelors.

Attendance and degree information available by phone, FAX, mail. Search requires name plus signed release. Other helpful information: social security number, date of birth, approximate years of attendance. No fee for information.

Transcripts available by mail. Search requires name plus signed release. Other helpful information: social security number, date of birth, approximate years of attendance. Fee is $3.00.

Huntington College, Registrar, 2303 College Ave, Huntington, IN 46750, 219-356-6000 (FAX: 219-356-9448). Hours: 8AM-5PM. Records go back to 1897. Degrees granted: Associate; Bachelors; Masters.

Attendance and degree information available by phone, FAX, mail. Search requires name plus approximate years of attendance. Other helpful information: social security number, date of birth, exact years of attendance. No fee for information.

Transcripts available by FAX, mail. Search requires name plus approximate years of attendance, signed release. Other helpful information: social security number, date of birth, exact years of attendance. No fee for transcripts.

Name(s) attended and alternate names helpful. Major credit cards accepted for payment.

Huntington Junior College, Registrar, 900 Fifth Ave, Huntington, WV 25701, 304-697-7550 (FAX: 304-697-7554). Degrees granted: Associate.

Attendance and degree information available by phone, mail. Search requires name plus social security number, exact years of attendance, signed release. No fee for information.

Transcripts available by mail. Search requires name plus social security number, exact years of attendance, signed release. No fee for transcripts.

Huron University, Registrar, 333 Ninth St SW, Huron, SD 57350, 605-352-8721. Hours: 8AM-5PM. Records go back to 1883. Degrees granted: Associate; Bachelors; Masters.

Attendance and degree information available by phone, FAX, mail. Search requires name only. Other helpful information: social security number, date of birth, approximate years of attendance. No fee for information.

Transcripts available by FAX, mail. Search requires name plus signed release. Other helpful information: social security number, date of birth, approximate years of attendance. Fee is $5.00.

Major credit cards accepted for payment.

Hussian School of Art, Registrar, 1118 Market St, Philadelphia, PA 19107-3679, 215-981-0900 (FAX: 215-864-9115). Hours: 9AM-3PM. Records go back 50 years. Degrees granted: Associate.

Attendance and degree information available by FAX, mail. Search requires name plus signed release. Other helpful information: social security number, date of birth, approximate years of attendance. No fee for information.

Transcripts available by FAX, mail. Search requires name plus signed release. Other helpful information: social security number, date of birth, approximate years of attendance. Fee is $3.00.

Major credit cards accepted for payment.

Husson College, Registrar, Bangor, ME 04401, 207-941-7000. Hours: 7:30AM-4:30PM. Records go back to 1920s. Degrees granted: Associate; Bachelors; Masters.

Attendance information available by phone, mail. Search requires name plus social security number, signed release. Other helpful information: date of birth, approximate years of attendance. No fee for information.

Degree information available by phone, mail. Search requires name plus social security number. Other helpful information: date of birth, approximate years of attendance. No fee for information.

Transcripts available by written request only. Search requires name plus social security number, signed release. Other helpful information: date of birth, approximate years of attendance. Fee is $3.00.

Huston-Tillotson College, Registrar, 900 Chicon St, Austin, TX 78702, 512-505-3082 (FAX: 512-505-3190). Hours: 8:30AM-5:30PM. Degrees granted: Bachelors.

Attendance information available by phone, FAX, mail. Search requires name plus signed release. Other helpful information: social security number, date of birth, approximate years of attendance. No fee for information.

Degree information available by phone, FAX, mail. Search requires name only. Other helpful information: approximate years of attendance. No fee for information.

Transcripts available by written request only. Search requires name plus signed release. Other helpful information: social security number, date of birth, approximate years of attendance. Fee is $3.00.

Hutchinson Community College, Registrar, 1300 N Plum St, Hutchinson, KS 67501, 316-665-3520 (FAX: 316-665-3310). Hours: 8AM-5PM. Records go back to 1928. Degrees granted: Associate.

Attendance information available by mail. Search requires name plus social security number, approximate years of attendance, signed release. Other helpful information: date of birth, exact years of attendance. No fee for information.

Degree information available by phone, FAX, mail. Search requires name plus social security number, approximate years of attendance. Other helpful information: date of birth, exact years of attendance. No fee for information.

Transcripts available by mail. Search requires name plus social security number, approximate years of attendance, signed release.

Other helpful information: date of birth, exact years of attendance. Fee is $2.00.
Major credit cards accepted for payment.

Hutchinson-Willmar Regional Technical College, Registrar, PO Box 1097, Willmar, MN 56201, 612-235-5114 (FAX: 612-231-7677). Hours: 8AM-4:30PM. Records go back to 1961. Alumni records are maintained here also. Call 612-231-2935. Degrees granted: Associate. Special programs- Student Services, 612-231-2915. Adverse incident record source: Student Affairs, 612-231-2915.

Attendance and degree information available by phone, FAX, mail. Search requires name plus social security number, signed release. No fee for information.

Transcripts available by FAX, mail. Search requires name plus social security number, signed release. Fee is $1.00.

I

ICI University, Registrar, 6300 N Belt Line Rd, Irving, TX 75063, 214-751-1111 (FAX: 214-714-8185). Hours: 8AM-4:30PM. Degrees granted: Associate; Bachelors; Masters.

Attendance information available by written request only. Search requires name plus date of birth, signed release. Other helpful information: approximate years of attendance. No fee for information.

Degree information available by written request only. Search requires name plus date of birth. Other helpful information: approximate years of attendance. No fee for information.

Transcripts available by written request only. Search requires name plus approximate years of attendance, signed release. Other helpful information: date of birth. Fee is $2.00.

ICM School of Business, Registrar, 10 Wood St, Pittsburgh, PA 15222, 412-261-2647 (FAX: 412-261-6491). Hours: 8AM-4:30PM. Records go back to 1960. Degrees granted: Associate. Adverse incident record source: Registrar, 412-261-2647.

Attendance and degree information available by phone, FAX, mail. Search requires name plus social security number, exact years of attendance. No fee for information.

Transcripts available by mail. Search requires name plus social security number, exact years of attendance, signed release. Fee is $5.00.

ITT Technical Institute, Registrar, 2201 Arlington Downs Rd, Arlington, TX 76011-6319, 817-640-7100. Hours: 8AM-5PM. Records go back to 1963. Alumni Records Office: 9511 Angola Ct, Indianapolis, IN 46268. Degrees granted: Associate.

Attendance and degree information available by mail. Search requires name plus social security number, date of birth, exact years of attendance. No fee for information.

Transcripts available by mail. Search requires name plus social security number, date of birth, exact years of attendance, signed release. Fee is $4.00.

ITT Technical Institute, Registrar, 2121 S Blackhawk St, Aurora, CO 80014-1416, 303-695-1913 (FAX: 303-751-5603). Hours: 8AM-5PM. Records go back 7 years. Degrees granted: Associate; Bachelors.

ITT Technical Institute, Registrar, 950 Lusk St, Boise, ID 83706-2831, 208-344-8376 (FAX: 208-345-0056). Hours: 8AM-5PM. Records go back to 1968. Alumni Records Office: Alumni Association, ITT Technical Institute, 9511 Angola Ct, Indianapolis, IN 46268. Degrees granted: Associate.

Attendance and degree information available by phone, FAX, mail. Search requires name plus social security number, exact years of attendance, signed release. No fee for information.

Transcripts available by mail. Search requires name plus social security number, exact years of attendance, signed release. No fee for transcripts.

ITT Technical Institute, Registrar, 7100 Knott Ave Plaza, Buena Park, CA 90620-1374, 714-535-3700 (FAX: 714-535-1802). Hours: 8AM-5PM. Records go back to 1983. Alumni Records Office: ITT Technical Institute, 9511 Angola Ct, Indianapolis, IN 46268. Degrees granted: Associate.

Attendance and degree information available by phone, FAX, mail. Search requires name plus social security number. No fee for information.

Transcripts available by mail. Search requires name plus social security number, signed release. No fee for transcripts.

ITT Technical Institute, Registrar, 2035 E 223rd St, Carson, CA 90810-1698, 310-835-5595 (FAX: 310-835-8986). Hours: 8AM-5PM M-W,F; 11AM-8PM Th. Records go back to 1989. Alumni Records Office: ITT Technical Institute, 9511 Angola Ct, Indianapolis, IN 46268. Degrees granted: Associate.

Attendance and degree information available by phone, FAX, mail. Search requires name plus social security number, exact years of attendance. No fee for information.

Transcripts available by phone, FAX, mail. Search requires name plus social security number, exact years of attendance. No fee for transcripts.

ITT Technical Institute, Registrar, 3325 Stop Eight Rd, Dayton, OH 45414-9915, 513-454-2267 (FAX: 513-454-2278). Hours: 8AM-5PM. Records go back to 1948. Degrees granted: Associate.

Attendance and degree information available by phone, mail. Search requires name plus approximate years of attendance, signed release. Other helpful information: exact years of attendance. No fee for information.

Transcripts available by phone, mail. Search requires name plus approximate years of attendance, signed release. Other helpful information: exact years of attendance. No fee for transcripts.

ITT Technical Institute, Registrar, 13505 Lakefront Dr, Earth City, MO 63045-1416, 314-298-7800. Hours: 9AM-5PM. Records go back to 1936. Degrees granted: Associate; Bachelors.

Attendance and degree information available by phone, mail. Search requires name plus social security number. Other helpful information: approximate years of attendance. No fee for information.

Transcripts available by mail. Search requires name plus social security number, signed release. Other helpful information: approximate years of attendance. No fee for transcripts.

ITT Technical Institute, Registrar, 5115 Oak Grove Rd, Evansville, IN 47715-2340, 812-479-1441 (FAX: 812-479-1460). Hours: 8AM-5PM. Evansville information only at this location. Degrees granted: Associate.

Attendance information available by mail. Search requires name plus social security number, signed release. Other helpful information: date of birth. No fee for information.

Degree information available by phone, mail. Search requires name plus social security number, signed release. Other helpful information: date of birth. No fee for information.

Transcripts available by mail. Search requires name plus social security number, signed release. Other helpful information: date of birth. No fee for transcripts.

ITT Technical Institute, Registrar, 4919 Coldwater Rd, Fort Wayne, IN 46825-5532, 219-484-4107 X209. Hours: 8AM-5PM. Records go back to 1968. Degrees granted: Associate.

Attendance and degree information available by phone, mail. Search requires name plus social security number. No fee for information.

Transcripts available by mail. Search requires name plus social security number, signed release. Fee is $1.00.

ITT Technical Institute, Registrar, 1671 Worcester Rd, Framingham, MA 01701-9465, 508-879-6266 (FAX: 508-879-9745). Hours: 8AM-5PM. Records go back 5 years. Degrees granted: Associate.

Attendance and degree information available by phone, FAX, mail. Search requires name plus social security number, date of birth, signed release. No fee for information.

Transcripts available by phone, FAX, mail. Search requires name plus social security number, date of birth, signed release. No fee for transcripts.

ITT Technical Institute, Registrar, 1640 Eastgate Dr, Garland, TX 75041-5585, 214-279-0500 (FAX: 214-613-4523). Hours: 8AM-5PM. Records go back to 1990. Degrees granted: Associate.

Attendance and degree information available by phone, FAX, mail. Search requires name plus signed release. Other helpful information: social security number, approximate years of attendance. No fee for information.

Transcripts available by phone, FAX, mail. Search requires name plus signed release. Other helpful information: social security number, approximate years of attendance. No fee for transcripts.

ITT Technical Institute, Registrar, 6300 W Layton Ave, Greenfield, WI 53220-4612, 414-282-9797. Hours: 8AM-4PM. Records go back to 1970S. Alumni Records Office: 9511 Angola Ct, Indianapolis, IN 46268. Degrees granted: Associate.

Attendance and degree information available by phone, mail. Search requires name plus social security number, exact years of attendance. No fee for information.

Transcripts available by written request only. Search requires name plus social security number, exact years of attendance, signed release. No fee for transcripts.

ITT Technical Institute, Education Department, One Marcus Dr Ste 402, Greenville, SC 29615, 803-288-0777 (FAX: 803-297-0930). Hours: 8AM-5PM. Degrees granted: Associate.

Attendance and degree information available by mail. Search requires name plus signed release. Other helpful information: approximate years of attendance. No fee for information.

Transcripts available by mail. Search requires name plus signed release. Other helpful information: approximate years of attendance. No fee for transcripts.

ITT Technical Institute, Registrar, 9421 W Sam Houston Pkwy, Houston, TX 77099-1849, 713-952-2294. Hours: 8AM-5PM. Records go back to 1970. Alumni Records Office: 9511 Angola Ct, Indianapolis, IN 46268. Degrees granted: Associate.

Attendance and degree information available by mail. Search requires name plus social security number, date of birth, exact years of attendance. No fee for information.

Transcripts available by mail. Search requires name plus social security number, date of birth, exact years of attendance, signed release. Fee is $4.00.

ITT Technical Institute, Registrar, 9511 Angola Ct, Indianapolis, IN 46268-1119, 317-875-8640 X249 (FAX: 317-875-8641). Hours: 8AM-5PM. Records go back to 1968. Degrees granted: Associate.

Attendance and degree information available by phone, mail. Search requires name plus exact years of attendance. No fee for information.

Transcripts available by mail. Search requires name plus exact years of attendance, signed release. No fee for transcripts.

ITT Technical Institute, Registrar, 10208 Technology Dr, Knoxville, TN 37932, 615-671-2800. Hours: 8AM-5PM. Records go back to 1988. Alumni Records Office: ITT Technical Institute, 9511 Angola Ct, Indianapolis, IN 46268. Degrees granted: Associate.

Attendance and degree information available by mail. Search requires name plus social security number, date of birth, exact years of attendance. No fee for information.

Transcripts available by mail. Search requires name plus social security number, date of birth, exact years of attendance, signed release. No fee for transcripts.

ITT Technical Institute, Registrar, 2600 Lake Lucien Dr, Maitland, FL 32751-9754, 407-660-2900 (FAX: 407-660-2566). Records go back 6 years. Degrees granted: Associate; Bachelors.

Attendance and degree information available by FAX, mail. Search requires name only. Other helpful information: approximate years of attendance. No fee for information.

Transcripts available by FAX, mail. Search requires name plus signed release. Other helpful information: approximate years of attendance. No fee for transcripts.

Requests must have student's signature.

ITT Technical Institute, Registrar, 920 W LeVoy Dr, Murray, UT 84123-2500, 801-263-3313. Hours: 8AM-5PM. Records go back to 1970s. Alumni Records Office: 9511 Angola Ct, Indianapolis, IN 46286. Degrees granted: Associate.

Attendance and degree information available by phone, mail. Search requires name plus social security number. No fee for information.

Transcripts available by written request only. Search requires name plus social security number, signed release. No fee for transcripts.

ITT Technical Institute, Registrar, 441 Donelson Pike, Nashville, TN 37214-8029, 615-889-8700 (FAX: 615-872-7209). Hours: 8AM-5PM. Records go back to 1985. Alumni records are maintained here also. Call 317-594-4274. Degrees granted: Associate; Bachelors.

Attendance information available by written request only. Search requires name plus social security number, date of birth, approximate years of attendance, signed release. No fee for information.

Degree information available by phone, mail. Search requires name plus social security number, date of birth, approximate years of attendance, signed release. No fee for information.

Transcripts available by written request only. Search requires name plus social security number, date of birth, approximate years of attendance, signed release. No fee for transcripts.

ITT Technical Institute, Registrar, 4837 E McDowell Rd, Phoenix, AZ 85008-4292, 602-252-2331. Hours: 7AM-4PM. Records go back to 1985. Alumni Records Office: Alumni Association, 5975 Castle Creek Pkwy N Dr, Indianapolis, IN 46250. Degrees granted: Associate.
Attendance and degree information available by phone, FAX, mail. Search requires name plus social security number, exact years of attendance. No fee for information.
Transcripts available by mail. Search requires name plus social security number, exact years of attendance, signed release. No fee for transcripts.

ITT Technical Institute, Registrar, 6035 NE 78th Ct, Portland, OR 97218-2854, 503-255-6500 (FAX: 503-255-6135). Records go back to 1979. Alumni records are maintained here at the same phone number. Degrees granted: Bachelors.
Attendance and degree information available by phone, FAX, mail. Search requires name plus social security number, exact years of attendance. No fee for information.
Transcripts available by FAX, mail. Search requires name plus social security number, exact years of attendance, signed release. Fee is $3.00.
Major credit cards accepted for payment.

ITT Technical Institute, Registrar, 9700 Goethe Rd, Sacramento, CA 95827-5281, 916-366-3900 (FAX: 916-366-9225). Hours: 8AM-5PM. Records go back to 1984. Degrees granted: Associate; Bachelors.
Attendance and degree information available by phone, FAX, mail. Search requires name only. No fee for information.
Transcripts available by phone, FAX, mail. Search requires name only. No fee for transcripts.

ITT Technical Institute, Registrar, 4242 Piedras Dr E Ste 100, San Antonio, TX 78228-1414, 210-737-1881. Hours: 8AM-5PM. Records go back to 1970s. Alumni Records Office: 9511 Angola Ct, Indianapolis, IN 46268. Degrees granted: Associate.
Attendance and degree information available by phone, mail. Search requires name plus social security number. No fee for information.
Transcripts available by written request only. Search requires name plus social security number, signed release. No fee for transcripts.

ITT Technical Institute, Registrar, 630 E Brier Dr Ste 150, San Bernardino, CA 92408-2800, 909-889-3800 (FAX: 909-888-6970). Hours: 8AM-5PM. Records go back to 1907. Alumni Records Office: ITT Technical Institute, 9511 Angola Ct, Indianapolis, IN 46268. Degrees granted: Associate; Bachelors.
Attendance information available by mail. Search requires name plus approximate years of attendance, signed release. No fee for information.
Degree information available by phone, mail. Search requires name plus approximate years of attendance, signed release. No fee for information.
Transcripts available by mail. Search requires name plus signed release. Other helpful information: approximate years of attendance. No fee for transcripts.

ITT Technical Institute, Registrar, 9680 Granite Ridge Dr, San Diego, CA 92123-2662, 619-571-8500 (FAX: 619-571-1277). Hours: 7AM-6PM. Records go back to 1980. Alumni Records Office: ITT Technical Institute, 9511 Angola Ct, Indianapolis, IN 46268. Degrees granted: Associate; Bachelors.
Attendance and degree information available by phone, FAX, mail. Search requires name plus social security number. No fee for information.
Transcripts available by FAX, mail. Search requires name plus social security number, exact years of attendance, signed release. Fee is $5.00.

ITT Technical Institute, Registrar, 12720 Gateway Dr Ste 100, Seattle, WA 98168-3333, 206-244-3300 (FAX: 206-246-7635). Hours: 8AM-8PM. Records go back to 1969. Degrees granted: Associate; Bachelors.
Attendance information available by phone, FAX, mail. Search requires name plus approximate years of attendance. Other helpful information: social security number, date of birth. No fee for information.
Degree information available by FAX, mail. Search requires name plus approximate years of attendance, signed release. Other helpful information: social security number, date of birth. No fee for information.
Transcripts available by mail. Search requires name plus approximate years of attendance, signed release. Other helpful information: social security number, date of birth. No fee for transcripts.

ITT Technical Institute, Registrar, N 1050 Argonne Rd, Spokane, WA 99212-2610, 509-926-2900. Hours: 8AM-5PM. Records go back to 1985. Alumni Records Office: 9511 Angola Ct, Indianapolis, IN 46268. Degrees granted: Associate.
Attendance and degree information available by phone, mail. Search requires name plus social security number, date of birth, exact years of attendance. No fee for information.
Transcripts available by mail. Search requires name plus social security number, date of birth, exact years of attendance, signed release. Fee is $3.00.

ITT Technical Institute, Registrar, 4809 Memorial Hwy, Tampa, FL 33634-7350, 813-885-2244 (FAX: 813-888-6078). Hours: 8AM-5PM. Records go back 12 years. Degrees granted: Associate; Bachelors.
Attendance and degree information available by phone, FAX, mail. Search requires name plus social security number. Other helpful information: date of birth, approximate years of attendance. No fee for information.
Transcripts available by FAX, mail. Search requires name plus social security number, signed release. Other helpful information: date of birth, approximate years of attendance. No fee for transcripts.

ITT Technical Institute, Registrar, 1840 E Benson Hwy, Tucson, AZ 85714-1770, 602-294-2944. Hours: 8AM-10PM. Records go back to 1980. Degrees granted: Associate.
Attendance information available by phone, mail. Search requires name plus social security number. No fee for information.
Degree information available by phone, mail. Search requires name plus social security number, exact years of attendance. No fee for information.
Transcripts available by mail. Search requires name plus social security number, exact years of attendance, signed release. Fee is $5.00.

ITT Technical Institute, Registrar, 6723 Van Nuys Blvd, Van Nuys, CA 91405-4620, 818-989-1177 (FAX: 818-989-2093). Hours: 8AM-5PM. Records go back to 1985. Alumni Records Office: ITT Technical Institute, 9511 Angola Ct, Indianapolis, IN 46268. Degrees granted: Associate.
   Attendance and degree information available by phone, FAX, mail. Search requires name plus social security number. No fee for information.
   Transcripts available by mail. Search requires name plus social security number, signed release. No fee for transcripts.

ITT Technical Institute, Registrar, 1530 W Cameron Ave, West Covina, CA 91790-2767, 818-960-8681 (FAX: 818-337-5271). Hours: 8AM-5PM. Records go back to 1982. Alumni Records Office: ITT Technical Institute, 9511 Angola Ct, Indianapolis, IN 46268. Degrees granted: Associate; Bachelors.
   Attendance and degree information available by phone, FAX, mail. Search requires name plus social security number. No fee for information.
   Transcripts available by FAX, mail. Search requires name plus social security number, signed release. No fee for transcripts.

ITT Technical Institute, Registrar, 655 Wick Ave, Youngstown, OH 44502, 216-747-5555 (FAX: 216-747-7718). Hours: 8AM-10PM. Records go back to 1968. Degrees granted: Associate.
   Attendance and degree information available by phone, FAX, mail. Search requires name plus approximate years of attendance, signed release. No fee for information.
   Transcripts available by phone, FAX, mail. Search requires name plus approximate years of attendance, signed release. Fee is $2.00.

ITT Technical Institute, (Branch of Tucson, AZ), Registrar, 5100 Masthead NE, Albuquerque, NM 87109-4366, 505-828-1114 (FAX: 505-828-1849). Hours: 8AM-5PM. Records go back 89 years. Degrees granted: Associate.
   Attendance information available by phone, FAX, mail. Search requires name only. Other helpful information: social security number, date of birth, approximate years of attendance. No fee for information.
   Degree information available by phone, FAX, mail. Search requires name only. Other helpful information: social security number, date of birth, approximate years of attendance. No fee for information.
   Transcripts available by FAX, mail. Search requires name plus social security number, date of birth, signed release. Other helpful information: approximate years of attendance. No fee for transcripts.

ITT Technical Institute, (Branch of Indianapolis, IN), Registrar, 1821 Rutherford Lane, Austin, TX 78754-5101, 512-467-6800 (FAX: 512-467-6677). Hours: 8AM-6PM. Alumni Records Office: 6330 Hwy 290E, S150, Austin, TX 78723-9975. Degrees granted: Associate.
   Attendance and degree information available by phone, FAX, mail. Search requires name plus social security number, date of birth, signed release. Other helpful information: approximate years of attendance. No fee for information.
   Transcripts available by phone, FAX, mail. Search requires name plus social security number, date of birth, signed release. Other helpful information: approximate years of attendance. No fee for transcripts.

ITT Technical Institute, (Branch of Fort Wayne, IN), Registrar, 3401 S University Dr, Fort Lauderdale, FL 33328, 305-476-9300 (FAX: 305-476-6889). Hours: 8AM-5PM. Alumni records are maintained here at the same phone number. Degrees granted: Associate.
   Attendance information available by phone, FAX, mail. Search requires name plus signed release. Other helpful information: social security number, date of birth, approximate years of attendance. No fee for information.
   Degree information available by FAX, mail. Search requires name plus signed release. Other helpful information: social security number, date of birth, approximate years of attendance. No fee for information.
   Transcripts available by FAX, mail. Search requires name plus signed release. Other helpful information: social security number, date of birth, approximate years of attendance. No fee for transcripts.

ITT Technical Institute, (Branch of Indianapolis, IN), Director of Education, 375 W Higgins Rd, Hoffman Estates, IL 60195, 708-519-9300 X20 (FAX: 708-519-0153). Hours: 8AM-5PM. Records go back to 1986. Alumni records are maintained here at the same phone number. Degrees granted: Associate; Bachelors.
   Attendance and degree information available by FAX, mail. Search requires name plus signed release. Other helpful information: approximate years of attendance. No fee for information.
   Transcripts available by FAX, mail. Search requires name plus signed release. Other helpful information: approximate years of attendance. No fee for transcripts.
   Need ITT student number.

ITT Technical Institute, (Branch of Indianapolis, IN), Registrar, 15621 Blue Ash Dr Ste 160, Houston, TX 77090-5818, 713-873-0512 (FAX: 713-873-0518). Hours: 8AM-4:30PM. Records go back to 1970. Alumni Records Office: ITT Technical Institute, 9511 Angola Ct, Indianapolis, IN 46268. Degrees granted: Associate.
   Attendance and degree information available by phone, FAX, mail. Search requires name plus social security number, exact years of attendance. No fee for information.
   Transcripts available by mail. Search requires name plus social security number, exact years of attendance, signed release. Fee is $3.00.

ITT Technical Institute, (Branch of Tampa, FL), Registrar, 6600 Youngerman Cir #10, Jacksonville, FL 32244, 904-573-9100 (FAX: 904-573-0512). Hours: 8AM-5PM. Records go back to 1991. Alumni Records Office: ITT Technical Institute, 9511 Angola Ct, Indianapolis, IN 46268. Degrees granted: Associate.
   Attendance and degree information available by phone, mail. Search requires name plus social security number. No fee for information.
   Transcripts available by mail. Search requires name plus social security number, signed release. No fee for transcripts.

ITT Technical Institute, (Branch of Evansville, IN), Registrar, 10509 Timberwood Cir, Louisville, KY 40223, 502-527-7424 (FAX: 502-327-7624). Hours: 8AM-10PM. Records go back to 1993. Started in June 1993. Alumni Records Office: PO Box 50466, Indianapolis, IN 46250-0466. Degrees granted: Associate.
   Attendance and degree information available by phone, FAX, mail. Search requires name plus approximate years of attendance,

signed release. Other helpful information: social security number, date of birth, exact years of attendance. No fee for information.

Transcripts available by mail. Search requires name plus approximate years of attendance, signed release. Other helpful information: social security number, date of birth, exact years of attendance. No fee for transcripts.

ITT Technical Institute, **(Branch of Evansville, IN)**, Registrar, 863 Glenrock Rd, Norfolk, VA 23502, 804-466-1260 (FAX: 804-466-7630). Hours: 8AM-5PM. Records go back to 1988. Alumni Records Office: ITT Technical Institute, 9511 Angola Ct, Indianapolis, IN 46268. Degrees granted: Associate; Bachelors.

Attendance and degree information available by phone, mail. Search requires name plus social security number, date of birth, exact years of attendance. No fee for information.

Transcripts available by mail. Search requires name plus social security number, date of birth, exact years of attendance, signed release. Fee is $4.00.

ITT Technical Institute, **(Branch of Earth City, MO)**, Registrar, 9814 M St, Omaha, NE 68127-2056, 402-331-2900 (FAX: 402-331-9495). Hours: 7:30AM-5PM. Records go back to 1990. Degrees granted: Associate.

Attendance information available by phone. Search requires name plus approximate years of attendance, signed release. No fee for information.

Degree information available by FAX, mail. Search requires name plus approximate years of attendance, signed release. No fee for information.

Transcripts available by FAX, mail. Search requires name plus approximate years of attendance, signed release. No fee for transcripts.

ITT Technical Institute, **(Branch of Youngstown, OH)**, Registrar, 8 Parkway Ctr, Pittsburgh, PA 15220, 412-937-9150. Hours: 8AM-6PM. Records go back to 1992. Degrees granted: Associate.

Attendance and degree information available by mail. Search requires name plus social security number, date of birth, exact years of attendance, signed release. No fee for information.

Transcripts available by mail. Search requires name plus social security number, date of birth, exact years of attendance, signed release. No fee for transcripts.

ITT Technical Institute, **(Branch of Fort Wayne, IN)**, Registrar, 1225 E Big Beaver Rd, Troy, MI 48083-1905, 810-524-1800 (FAX: 810-528-2218). Hours: 8AM-5PM. Records go back to 1963. Alumni Records Office: ITT Technical Institute, 9511 Angola Ct, Indianapolis, IN 46268. Degrees granted: Associate.

Attendance and degree information available by phone, FAX, mail. Search requires name plus social security number, exact years of attendance. No fee for information.

Transcripts available by mail. Search requires name plus social security number, exact years of attendance, signed release. Fee is $5.00.

Idaho State University, Registration & Records, PO Box 8196, Pocatello, ID 83209, 208-236-2661 (FAX: 208-236-4231). Hours: 8AM-5PM. Records go back to 1901. Alumni records are maintained here at the same phone number. Alumni Records Office: PO Box 8033, Pocatello, ID 83209. Degrees granted: Associate; Bachelors; Masters; Doctorate. Adverse incident record source: Public Safety & Security, 208-236-2515.

Attendance and degree information available by phone, FAX, mail. Search requires name only. Other helpful information: social security number, date of birth, approximate years of attendance. No fee for information.

Transcripts available by FAX, mail. Search requires name plus social security number, date of birth, signed release. Other helpful information: approximate years of attendance. Fee is $3.00.

Iliff School of Theology, Registrar, 2201 S University Blvd, Denver, CO 80210, 303-744-1287 X227 (FAX: 303-777-3387). Hours: 8AM-4:30PM. Records go back to 1892. Alumni records are maintained here also. Call 303-744-127 X285. Degrees granted: Masters.

Attendance information available by phone, FAX, mail. Search requires name plus social security number, signed release. No fee for information.

Degree information available by phone, FAX, mail. Search requires name plus social security number. No fee for information.

Transcripts available by FAX, mail. Search requires name plus social security number, signed release. No fee for transcripts.

Illinois Benedictine College, Registrar, 5700 College Rd, Lisle, IL 60532, 708-960-1500 (FAX: 708-960-1126). Hours: 8AM-6:30PM M-Th; 8AM-4PM F. Records go back 95 years. Alumni records are maintained here at the same phone number. Degrees granted: Bachelors; Masters. Certification: IFM.

Attendance and degree information available by phone, FAX, mail. Search requires name only. Other helpful information: social security number, date of birth, approximate years of attendance. No fee for information.

Transcripts available by FAX. Search requires name plus signed release. Other helpful information: social security number, date of birth, approximate years of attendance. No fee for transcripts. Expedited service available for $5.00.

Illinois Central College, Registrar L-211, One College Dr, East Peoria, IL 61635, 309-694-5235 (FAX: 309-694-5450). Hours: 8AM-4:30PM. Degrees granted: Associate. Adverse incident record source: Student Services, 309-694-5784.

Attendance and degree information available by phone, mail. Search requires name plus social security number. Other helpful information: date of birth, approximate years of attendance. No fee for information.

Transcripts available by mail. Search requires name plus social security number, signed release. Other helpful information: date of birth, approximate years of attendance. Fee is $2.00. $10.00 minimum on credit cards. Major credit cards accepted for payment.

Illinois College, Registrar, 1101 W College Ave, Jacksonville, IL 62650, 217-245-3013 (FAX: 217-245-3034). Hours: 8:30AM-4:30PM. Records go back to 1829.

Attendance and degree information available by phone, FAX, mail. Search requires name only. Other helpful information: social security number, date of birth, approximate years of attendance. No fee for information.

Transcripts available by FAX, mail. Search requires name plus signed release. Other helpful information: social security number, date of birth, approximate years of attendance. No fee for transcripts.

Signature required for transcript.

Illinois College of Optometry, Registrar, 3241 S Michigan Ave, Chicago, IL 60616, 312-225-1700 (FAX: 312-225-

3405). Hours: 8:30AM-5PM. Alumni records are maintained here also. Call 312-225-1700 X612. Degrees granted: Bachelors; Doctorate.

Attendance and degree information available by phone, FAX, mail. Search requires name only. Other helpful information: social security number, date of birth, approximate years of attendance. No fee for information.

Transcripts available by FAX, mail. Search requires name plus social security number, date of birth, approximate years of attendance, signed release. Other helpful information: exact years of attendance. Fee is $10.00.

Major credit cards accepted for payment.

Illinois Institute of Technology, Registrar, 3300 S Federal St, Chicago, IL 60616, 312-567-3310 (FAX: 312-567-3313). Hours: 8:30AM-5PM. Records go back to 1890. Degrees granted: Bachelors; Masters; Doctorate.

Attendance and degree information available by phone, FAX, mail. Search requires name plus social security number, exact years of attendance. Other helpful information: date of birth, approximate years of attendance. No fee for information.

Transcripts available by mail. Search requires name plus social security number, exact years of attendance, signed release. Other helpful information: date of birth, approximate years of attendance. Fee is $5.00.

Illinois State University, Registrar, Normal, IL 61790-1000, 309-438-2188/438-2181. Hours: 8AM-4:30PM. Records go back to 1857. Alumni Records Office: Campus Box 3100, Normal, IL 61790-1000 309-438-2586. Degrees granted: Bachelors; Masters; Doctorate. Adverse incident record source: Registrar, 309-438-2586.

Attendance and degree information available by phone, mail. Search requires name plus social security number, exact years of attendance. No fee for information.

Transcripts available by mail. Search requires name plus social security number, exact years of attendance, signed release. Fee is $6.00.

Illinois Valley Community College, Registrar, 815 N Orlando Smith Ave, Oglesby, IL 61348-9691, 815-224-2720. Degrees granted: Associate. Adverse incident record source: Student Development, 815-224-2720 X435.

Attendance and degree information available by phone, FAX, mail. Search requires name plus signed release. Other helpful information: social security number, date of birth, approximate years of attendance. No fee for information.

Transcripts available by FAX, mail. Search requires name plus signed release. Other helpful information: social security number, date of birth, approximate years of attendance. Fee is $2.00.

Illinois Wesleyan University, Registrar, PO Box 2900, Bloomington, IL 61702, 309-556-3161 (FAX: 309-556-3411). Hours: 8AM-5PM. Records go back to 1850. Degrees granted: Bachelors. Adverse incident record source: Dean of Students, 309-556-3111.

Attendance and degree information available by phone, FAX, mail. Search requires name plus approximate years of attendance. Other helpful information: social security number. No fee for information.

Transcripts available by FAX, mail. Search requires name plus approximate years of attendance, signed release. Other helpful information: social security number. Fee is $3.00.

Immaculata College, Registrar, Immaculata, PA 19345, 610-647-4400 X3009 (FAX: 610-251-1668). Hours: 8:30AM-4:30PM. Records go back to 1925. Degrees granted: Associate; Bachelors; Masters; Doctorate.

Attendance and degree information available by phone, FAX, mail. Search requires name plus social security number, approximate years of attendance. Other helpful information: date of birth, exact years of attendance. No fee for information.

Transcripts available by FAX, mail. Search requires name plus social security number, date of birth, approximate years of attendance, signed release. Fee is $3.00. Expedited service available for $5.00.

Immaculate Conception Seminary, Registrar, 400 S Orange Ave, South Orange, NJ 07079, 201-761-9238. Hours: 9AM-5PM. Records go back to 1945. Degrees granted: Masters.

Attendance and degree information available by mail. Search requires name plus social security number, signed release. No fee for information.

Transcripts available by mail. Search requires name plus social security number, signed release. Fee is $3.00.

Imperial Valley College, Registrar, PO Box 158, Imperial, CA 92251, 619-352-8320. Degrees granted: Associate.

Attendance and degree information available by phone, mail. Search requires name plus social security number. Other helpful information: date of birth, approximate years of attendance. No fee for information.

Transcripts available by mail. Search requires name plus social security number, signed release. Other helpful information: date of birth, approximate years of attendance. Fee is $2.00.

Incarnate Word College, Registrar, 4301 Broadway, San Antonio, TX 78209, 210-829-6006 (FAX: 210-829-3922). Hours: 8AM-5PM. Records go back to 1910. Alumni records are maintained here also. Call 210-829-6104. Degrees granted: Bachelors; Masters.

Attendance and degree information available by phone, FAX, mail. Search requires name only. Other helpful information: social security number, date of birth, approximate years of attendance. No fee for information.

Transcripts available by FAX, mail. Search requires name plus signed release. Other helpful information: social security number, date of birth, approximate years of attendance. Fee is $3.00. Expedited service available for $3.00.

Independence Community College, Registrar, College Ave and Brookside Dr, Independence, KS 67301, 316-331-4100 (FAX: 316-331-0946). Hours: 8AM-5PM. Records go back to 1925. Degrees granted: Associate. Adverse incident record source: Student Services, 316-331-4100.

Attendance and degree information available by mail. Search requires name plus social security number, date of birth, approximate years of attendance, signed release. No fee for information.

Transcripts available by mail. Search requires name plus social security number, date of birth, approximate years of attendance, signed release. Fee is $3.00.

Indian Hills Community College, Registrar, 525 Grandview Ave, Ottumwa, IA 52501, 515-683-5151 (FAX: 515-683-5184). Hours: 8:30AM-4:30PM. Records go back to 1966. Degrees granted: Associate.

Attendance and degree information available by phone, FAX, mail. Search requires name plus social security number. No fee for information.
Transcripts available by FAX, mail. Search requires name plus social security number, signed release. No fee for transcripts.

Indian Hills Community College, **(Centerville)**, Registrar, Centerville, IA 52544, 515-856-2143 (FAX: 515-856-5527). Hours: 8AM-4PM. Degrees granted: Associate.
Attendance and degree information available by phone, FAX, mail. Search requires name plus social security number. No fee for information.
Transcripts available by mail. Search requires name plus social security number, signed release. No fee for transcripts.

Indian River Community College, Registrar, 3209 Virginia Ave, Fort Pierce, FL 34981-5599, 407-462-4766. Hours: 8AM-5PM. Records go back to 1960. Alumni records are maintained here also. Call 407-462-4706. Degrees granted: Associate. Adverse incident record source: Dean of Students, 407-462-4706.
Attendance and degree information available by mail. Search requires name plus social security number, signed release. Other helpful information: date of birth, approximate years of attendance. No fee for information.
Transcripts available by mail. Search requires name plus social security number, signed release. Other helpful information: date of birth, approximate years of attendance. No fee for transcripts.
Major credit cards accepted for payment.

Indiana Business College, Registrar, 802 N Meridian St, Indianapolis, IN 46204, 317-264-5656 (FAX: 317-634-0471). Hours: 7:30AM-7:30PM. Records go back to 1902.
Attendance and degree information available by phone, FAX, mail. Search requires name only. Other helpful information: social security number, approximate years of attendance. No fee for information.
Transcripts available by written request only. Search requires name plus social security number, signed release. Other helpful information: approximate years of attendance. Fee is $3.00.

Indiana Business College, **(Branch)**, Registrar, Applegate Business Park, 1320 E 53rd St Ste 106, Anderson, IN 46103, 317-644-7514 (FAX: 317-644-5724). Hours: 7:30AM-5PM. Records go back to 1902. Degrees granted: Associate.
Attendance information available by mail. Search requires name plus social security number, date of birth, signed release. Other helpful information: approximate years of attendance. No fee for information.
Degree information available by phone, FAX, mail. Search requires name plus social security number, date of birth. Other helpful information: approximate years of attendance. No fee for information.
Transcripts available by FAX, mail. Search requires name plus social security number, date of birth, signed release. Other helpful information: approximate years of attendance. Fee is $3.00.
Major credit cards accepted for payment.

Indiana Business College, **(Branch)**, Registrar, 3550 Two Mile House Rd, PO Box 1906, Columbus, IN 47201, 812-342-1000 (FAX: 812-342-1058). Hours: 7:30AM-9PM M-Th; 7:30AM-4:30PM F. Records go back 9+ years. Degrees granted: Associate.
Attendance and degree information available by phone, FAX, mail. Search requires name plus approximate years of attendance. Other helpful information: social security number. No fee for information.
Transcripts available by mail. Search requires name plus approximate years of attendance, signed release. Other helpful information: social security number. Fee is $3.00.
Major credit cards accepted for payment.

Indiana Business College, **(Branch)**, Registrar, 4601 Theater Dr, Evansville, IN 47715, 812-476-6000 (FAX: 812-471-8576). Hours: 8AM-5PM. Records go back to 1993. Degrees granted: Associate.
Attendance and degree information available by phone, FAX, mail. Search requires name plus social security number, date of birth, exact years of attendance. No fee for information.
Transcripts available by FAX, mail. Search requires name plus social security number, date of birth, exact years of attendance, signed release. Fee is $3.00.

Indiana Business College, **(Branch)**, Registrar, 5460 Victory Dr Ste 100, Indianapolis, IN 46203, 317-783-5100. Hours: 8AM-6PM. Records go back to 1993. Degrees granted: Associate.
Attendance and degree information available by phone, mail. Search requires name plus social security number, signed release. No fee for information.
Transcripts available by mail. Search requires name plus social security number, signed release. No fee for transcripts.

Indiana Business College, **(Branch)**, Registrar, 1170 S Creasy Lane, Lafayette, IN 47905, 317-447-9550 (FAX: 317-447-0868). Hours: 8AM-5PM. Records go back to 1907. Degrees granted: Associate.
Attendance and degree information available by phone, FAX, mail. Search requires name plus social security number, date of birth, exact years of attendance. No fee for information.
Transcripts available by FAX, mail. Search requires name plus social security number, date of birth, exact years of attendance, signed release. Fee is $3.00.

Indiana Business College, **(Branch)**, Registrar, 830 N Miller Ave, Marion, IN 46952, 317-662-7497 (FAX: 317-651-9421). Hours: 8AM-5PM. Records go back to 1902. Degrees granted: Associate.
Attendance and degree information available by FAX, mail. Search requires name plus social security number, signed release. No fee for information.
Transcripts available by FAX, mail. Search requires name plus social security number, signed release. Fee is $3.00.

Indiana Business College, **(Branch)**, Registrar, 1809 N Walnut St, Muncie, IN 47303, 317-288-8681. Hours: 8AM-5PM. Records go back to 1902. Degrees granted: Associate.
Attendance and degree information available by mail. Search requires name plus social security number, exact years of attendance, signed release. No fee for information.
Transcripts available by mail. Search requires name plus social security number, exact years of attendance, signed release. Fee is $3.00.

Indiana Business College, **(Branch)**, Registrar, 3175 S Third St, Terre Haute, IN 47802, 812-232-4458 (FAX: 812-234-2361). Hours: 7:30AM-5PM. Records go back 15 years. Degrees granted: Associate. Adverse incident record source: Main Campus, 317-264-5656.

Attendance and degree information available by phone, FAX, mail. Search requires name plus social security number. No fee for information.
Transcripts available by written request only. Search requires name plus social security number, signed release. Fee is $3.00. Expedited service available for $5.00.
Transcripts may be FAXed or mailed with written request.

Indiana Business College, (Branch), Registrar, 1431 Willow St, Vincennes, IN 47591, 812-882-2550 (FAX: 812-882-2270). Hours: 8AM-4PM. Records go back to 1922. Degrees granted: Associate. Adverse incident record source: Director's office .
Attendance information available by phone, FAX, mail. Search requires name plus social security number, approximate years of attendance. Other helpful information: exact years of attendance. No fee for information.
Degree information available by phone, FAX, mail. Search requires name plus social security number, approximate years of attendance. No fee for information.
Transcripts available by phone, FAX, mail. Search requires name plus social security number, approximate years of attendance. Fee is $3.00.
Major credit cards accepted for payment.

Indiana Institute of Technology, Registrar, 1600 E Washington Blvd, Fort Wayne, IN 46803, 219-422-5561. Hours: 8:30AM-5PM. Degrees granted: Associate; Bachelors.
Attendance and degree information available by phone, FAX, mail. Search requires name only. Other helpful information: date of birth, approximate years of attendance. No fee for information.
Transcripts available by FAX, mail. Search requires name plus signed release. Other helpful information: date of birth, approximate years of attendance. Fee is $5.00.
FAX request for transcript to be followed by written request. Major credit cards accepted for payment.

Indiana State University, Registrar, 200 N 7th St, Terre Haute, IN 47809, 812-237-2020 (FAX: 812-237-8039). Hours: 8AM-4:30PM. Records go back to 1865. Alumni records are maintained here also. Call 812-237-2020 X3707. Degrees granted: Bachelors; Masters. Adverse incident record source: Registrar, 812-237-2020.
Attendance and degree information available by phone, FAX, mail. Search requires name plus social security number, exact years of attendance. No fee for information.
Transcripts available by FAX, mail. Search requires name plus social security number, exact years of attendance, signed release. Fee is $2.00.

Indiana University East, Student Records, 116 Whitewater Hall, Richmond, IN 47374, 317-973-8270. Hours: 8AM-7:30PM M-Th; 8AM-5PM F. Degrees granted: Associate; Bachelors.
Attendance and degree information available by phone. Search requires name only. Other helpful information: social security number. No fee for information.
Transcripts available by written request only. Search requires name plus signed release. Other helpful information: social security number. Fee is $6.00.
Major credit cards accepted for payment.

Indiana University Northwest, Registrar, 3400 Broadway, Gary, IN 46408-1197, 219-980-6815 (FAX: 219-981-4200). Hours: 8AM-6PM M,Th; 8AM-5PM T,W,F. Records go back to 1966. Alumni records are maintained here also. Call 219-980-6768. Degrees granted: Associate; Bachelors; Masters; PBC.
Attendance and degree information available by phone, FAX, mail. Search requires name only. Other helpful information: social security number, exact years of attendance. No fee for information.
Transcripts available by FAX, mail. Search requires name plus signed release. Other helpful information: social security number, exact years of attendance. Fee is $6.00. Expedited service available for $6.00.
FAX available for requests only, not results. Major credit cards accepted for payment.

Indiana University Southeast, LB100, Registrar, 4201 Grant Line Rd, New Albany, IN 47150, 812-941-2240 (FAX: 812-941-2493). Hours: 8AM-5PM. Records go back to 1941. Alumni records are maintained here at the same phone number. Degrees granted: Associate; Bachelors; Masters; Doctorate.
Attendance and degree information available by phone, mail. Search requires name plus social security number. Other helpful information: date of birth, approximate years of attendance. No fee for information.
Transcripts available by mail. Search requires name plus social security number, signed release. Other helpful information: date of birth, approximate years of attendance. Fee is $6.00.
Major credit cards accepted for payment.

Indiana University at Bloomington, Registrar, Franklin Hall Room 100, Bloomington, IN 47405, 812-855-0121. Hours: 9AM-4PM. Records go back to 1820. Alumni Records Office: Alumni Association, Indiana University, Fountain Square Ste 219, Bloomington, IN 47404. Degrees granted: Bachelors; Masters; Doctorate.
Attendance and degree information available by phone, mail. Search requires name plus social security number, exact years of attendance. No fee for information.
Transcripts available by mail. Search requires name plus social security number, exact years of attendance, signed release. Fee is $6.00.
Major credit cards accepted for payment.

Indiana University at Kokomo, Registrar, PO Box 9003, Kokomo, IN 46904-9003, 317-455-9514 (FAX: 317-455-9475). Hours: 8AM-5PM. Records go back to 1965. Alumni records are maintained here also. Call 317-455-9411. Degrees granted: Bachelors; Masters.
Attendance and degree information available by phone, mail. Search requires name plus social security number. No fee for information.
Transcripts available by mail. Search requires name plus social security number, exact years of attendance, signed release. Fee is $6.00.
Major credit cards accepted for payment.

Indiana University at South Bend, Registrar, 1700 Mishawaka Ave, PO Box 7111, South Bend, IN 46634, 219-237-4451 (FAX: 219-237-4834). Hours: 8AM-5PM. Records go back to 1965. Alumni records are maintained here also. Call 219-237-4111. Degrees granted: Bachelors; Masters.
Attendance and degree information available by phone, FAX, mail. Search requires name plus social security number, exact years of attendance. No fee for information.

Transcripts available by mail. Search requires name plus social security number, exact years of attendance, signed release. Fee is $6.00.

Indiana University of Pennsylvania, Registrar's Office, 68 Sutton Hall, Indiana, PA 15705, 412-357-2217. Hours: 8AM-4:30PM. Records go back to 1940. Alumni records are maintained here also. Call 412-357-7942. Degrees granted: Bachelors; Masters; Doctorate.

Attendance information available by phone, mail. Search requires name plus social security number. No fee for information.

Degree information available by phone, mail. Search requires name plus social security number, exact years of attendance. No fee for information.

Transcripts available by mail. Search requires name plus social security number, exact years of attendance, signed release. Fee is $3.00.

Indiana University of Pennsylvania, **(Armstrong County)**, Registrar, Kittanning, PA 16201, 412-543-1078. Records are not housed here. They are located at Indiana University of Pennsylvania, Registrar's Office, 68 Sutton Hall, Indiana, PA 15705.

Indiana University of Pennsylvania, **(Punxsutawney)**, Registrar, Punxsutawney, PA 15767, 814-938-6711. Records are not housed here. They are located at Indiana University of Pennsylvania, Registrar's Office, 68 Sutton Hall, Indiana, PA 15705.

Indiana University-Purdue University at Fort Wayne, Registrar, 2101 Coliseum Blvd E, Fort Wayne, IN 46805, 219-481-6815 (FAX: 219-481-6880). Hours: 8AM-5PM. Records go back to founding date. Alumni records are maintained here at the same phone number. Degrees granted: Associate; Bachelors; Masters.

Attendance and degree information available by phone, FAX, mail. Search requires name plus social security number. Other helpful information: date of birth, approximate years of attendance. No fee for information.

Transcripts available by mail. Search requires name plus social security number, signed release. Other helpful information: date of birth, approximate years of attendance. Fee is $6.00. Expedited service available for $6.00.

Indiana University-Purdue University at Indianapolis, Registrar, 425 University Blvd, Indianapolis, IN 46202, 317-274-1501 (FAX: 317-278-2240). Hours: 8AM-7PM M-Th, 8AM-5PM. Records go back to 1965. Alumni records are maintained here also. Call 317-274-8828. Degrees granted: Associate; Bachelors; Masters; Doctorate.

Attendance and degree information available by phone, FAX, mail. Search requires name plus social security number. No fee for information.

Transcripts available by FAX, mail. Search requires name plus social security number, exact years of attendance, signed release. Fee is $6.00.

Indiana Vocational Tech. College-Columbus/Bloomington Tech. Inst., Registrar, 4475 Central Ave, Columbus, IN 47203, 812-372-9925 X130 (FAX: 812-372-9925 X121). Hours: 8AM-7:30PM M-Th, 8AM-5PM F. Records go back to 1968. Degrees granted: Associate.

Attendance and degree information available by phone, FAX, mail. Search requires name plus social security number. No fee for information.

Transcripts available by FAX, mail. Search requires name plus social security number, date of birth, exact years of attendance, signed release. No fee for transcripts.

Indiana Vocational Tech. College-Eastcentral Technical Institute, Registrar, 4301 S Cowan Rd, PO Box 3100, Muncie, IN 47307, 317-289-2291 (FAX: 317-289-2291 X502). Hours: 8AM-5PM. Records go back to 1969. Degrees granted: Associate. Certification: Technical.

Attendance information available by FAX, mail. Search requires name plus social security number, signed release. Other helpful information: date of birth, approximate years of attendance. No fee for information.

Degree information available by phone, FAX, mail. Search requires name plus social security number, signed release. Other helpful information: date of birth, approximate years of attendance. No fee for information.

Transcripts available by FAX, mail. Search requires name plus social security number, signed release. Other helpful information: date of birth, approximate years of attendance. No fee for transcripts.

Must have release form.

Indiana Wesleyan University, Registrar, 4201 S Washington St, Marion, IN 46953, 317-677-2131 (FAX: 317-677-2809). Hours: 8AM-5PM. Records go back to 1920. Alumni records are maintained here also. Call 317-677-2110. Degrees granted: Bachelors; Masters. Adverse incident record source: Registrar, 317-677-2131.

Attendance and degree information available by phone, FAX, mail. Search requires name plus exact years of attendance. No fee for information.

Transcripts available by FAX, mail. Search requires name plus exact years of attendance, signed release. Fee is $2.00.

Institute for Christian Studies, Registrar, 1909 University Ave at 20th St, Austin, TX 78705, 512-476-2772 (FAX: 512-476-3919). Hours: 8AM-5PM. Records go back to 1977. Degrees granted: Bachelors; Masters.

Attendance information available by phone, FAX, mail. Search requires name only. Other helpful information: date of birth, approximate years of attendance. Fee is $2.00.

Degree information available by phone, FAX, mail. Search requires name only. Other helpful information: social security number, date of birth, approximate years of attendance. Fee is $2.00.

Transcripts available by mail. Search requires name plus signed release. Other helpful information: social security number, date of birth, approximate years of attendance. Fee is $2.00.

Institute of American Indian and Alaskan Native Culture and Arts, Registrar, St. Michael's Dr, Box 20007, Santa Fe, NM 87504, 505-988-6440. Degrees granted: Associate.

Attendance and degree information available by phone, FAX, mail. Search requires name plus date of birth, exact years of attendance, signed release. Other helpful information: social security number, approximate years of attendance. No fee for information.

Transcripts available by FAX, mail. Search requires name plus date of birth, exact years of attendance, signed release. Other helpful information: social security number, approximate years of attendance. No fee for transcripts.

Institute of Electronic Technology, Registrar, PO Box 8252, 509 s 30th St, Paducah, KY 42002-8252, 502-444-9676 (FAX: 502-441-7202). Hours: 8:30AM-5PM. Records go back to 1976. Degrees granted: Associate.

Attendance and degree information available by phone, FAX, mail. Search requires name plus social security number, approximate years of attendance, signed release. No fee for information.

Transcripts available by FAX, mail. Search requires name plus social security number, approximate years of attendance, signed release. No fee for transcripts.

Institute of Electronic Technology, **(Lexington Electronics Institute)**, Registrar, 3340 Holwyn Rd, Lexington, KY 40503-9938, 606-223-9608 (FAX: 606-223-3310). Hours: 8AM-5PM. Records go back to 1989. Degrees granted: Associate. Special programs- Financial Aid, 606-223-9608.

Attendance and degree information available by phone, FAX, mail. Search requires name plus social security number, approximate years of attendance, signed release. No fee for information.

Transcripts available by mail. Search requires name plus social security number, approximate years of attendance, signed release. Fee is $3.00.

Institute of Paper Science and Technology, Registrar, 500 10th St NW, Atlanta, GA 30318, 404-853-9556 (FAX: 404-853-9510). Hours: 8AM-5PM. Records go back to 1929. Alumni records are maintained here also. Call 404-853-9800. Degrees granted: Masters; PhD.

Attendance and degree information available by phone, FAX, mail. Search requires name plus social security number. No fee for information.

Transcripts available by phone, FAX, mail. Search requires name plus social security number, signed release. No fee for transcripts.

Institute of Textile Technology, Registrar, PO Box 391, Charlottesville, VA 22902, 804-296-5511. Hours: 8AM-4:30PM. Records go back to 1971. Degrees granted: Associate.

Attendance and degree information available by phone, mail. Search requires name plus social security number, approximate years of attendance. No fee for information.

Transcripts available by written request only. Search requires name plus social security number, approximate years of attendance, signed release. No fee for transcripts.

Instituto Comercial de Puerto Rico Junior College, Registrar, 558 Munoz Rivera Ave, PO Box 304, Hato Rey, PR 00919, 809-763-1010 (FAX: 809-763-7249). Hours: 7AM-4PM. Degrees granted: Associate.

Attendance and degree information available by mail. Search requires name plus social security number, approximate years of attendance, signed release. No fee for information.

Transcripts available by mail. Search requires name plus social security number, approximate years of attendance, signed release. Fee is $2.00.

Instituto Comercial de Puerto Rico Junior College, **(Arecibo Campus)**, Registrar, Rd 2 KM 80.4, San Daniel Box 1606, Arecibo, PR 00612-1606, 809-890-6000 (FAX: 809-878-7150). Hours: 8AM-5PM. Records go back to 18yrs. Degrees granted: Associate.

Attendance and degree information available by mail. Search requires name plus social security number, exact years of attendance, signed release. Other helpful information: approximate years of attendance. Fee is $2.00.

Transcripts available by mail. Search requires name plus social security number, exact years of attendance, signed release. Other helpful information: approximate years of attendance. Fee is $2.00.

Include a self addressed stamped envelope with mail request.

Instituto Comercial de Puerto Rico Junior College, **(Mayaguez Campus)**, Registrar, PO Box 1108, Mayaguez, PR 00708-1108, 809-832-2250.

Inter American University of Puerto Rico Aguadilla Campus, Registrar, Cal Box 20000, Aguadilla, PR 00605, 809-891-0925 (FAX: 809-882-3020). Hours: 8AM-5PM. Degrees granted: Associate; Bachelors.

Attendance and degree information available by mail. Search requires name plus social security number, signed release. Other helpful information: exact years of attendance. Fee is $2.00.

Transcripts available by mail. Search requires name plus social security number, signed release. Other helpful information: exact years of attendance. Fee is $2.00.

Include a self addressed stamped envelope with mail request.

Inter American University of Puerto Rico Arecibo Campus, Registrar, Call Box UI, Arecibo, PR 00613, 809-878-5475.

Inter American University of Puerto Rico Barranquitas Campus, Registrar, PO Box 517, Barranquitas, PR 00794, 809-857-3600 X2152 (FAX: 809-857-2244). Hours: 8AM-Noon, 1-5PM. Degrees granted: Associate; Bachelors.

Attendance and degree information available by written request only. Search requires name plus social security number, signed release. Other helpful information: date of birth, approximate years of attendance. No fee for information.

Transcripts available by written request only. Search requires name plus social security number, signed release. Other helpful information: date of birth, approximate years of attendance. Fee is $2.00.

Inter American University of Puerto Rico Bayamon Campus, Registrar, Rd 174 Minnillas Industrial Park, Bayamon, PR 00959, 809-780-4040 (FAX: 809-740-4020). Hours: 8AM-5PM. Records go back to 1984. Degrees granted: Associate.

Attendance and degree information available by FAX, mail. Search requires name plus social security number, date of birth, approximate years of attendance, signed release. No fee for information.

Transcripts available by mail. Search requires name plus social security number, date of birth, approximate years of attendance, signed release. Fee is $2.00.

Inter American University of Puerto Rico Guayama Campus, Registrar, CAll Box 10004, Guayama, PR 00785, 809-864-2222 (FAX: 809-864-3232). Hours: 8AM-5PM. Records go back to 1987. Degrees granted: Associate; Bachelors. Certification: Medical Records.

Attendance and degree information available by mail. Search requires name plus social security number, signed release. Other helpful information: date of birth, approximate years of attendance. No fee for information.

Transcripts available by mail. Search requires name plus social security number, signed release. Other helpful information: date of birth, approximate years of attendance. Fee is $2.00.

Major credit cards accepted for payment.

Inter American University of Puerto Rico Metropolitan Campus, Registrar, PO Box 1293, Hato Rey, PR 00919-1293, 809-250-1912 (FAX: 809-250-0782). Hours: 8AM-5PM. Records go back to 1962. Degrees granted: Associate; Bachelors; Masters; Doctorate.

Attendance and degree information available by written request only. Search requires name plus social security number, signed release. Other helpful information: approximate years of attendance. No fee for information.

Transcripts available by written request only. Search requires name plus social security number, signed release. Other helpful information: approximate years of attendance. Fee is $2.00.

Major credit cards accepted for payment.

Inter American University of Puerto Rico Ponce Campus, Registrar, Mercedita, PR 00715, 809-840-9090.

Inter American University of Puerto Rico San German Campus, Bursar's Office, PO Box 5100, San German, PR 00683, 809-892-5725 (FAX: 809-892-6350). Hours: 8AM-5PM. Records go back to 1912. Degrees granted: Associate; Bachelors; Masters.

Attendance information available by FAX, mail. Search requires name plus social security number, approximate years of attendance, signed release. No fee for information.

Degree information available by FAX, mail. Search requires name plus social security number, signed release. Other helpful information: approximate years of attendance. No fee for information.

Transcripts available by mail. Search requires name plus social security number, signed release. Other helpful information: approximate years of attendance. Fee is $2.00. Expedited service available for $2.00.

Inter American University of Puerto Rico School of Law, Registrar's Office, PO Box 70351, Fernandez Juncos Sta, San Juan, PR 00910-8351, 809-751-1912 (FAX: 809-751-2975). Hours: 8AM-5PM. Alumni records are maintained here also. Call 809-751-1912/751-2039.

Attendance and degree information available by mail. Search requires name plus social security number, signed release. Other helpful information: approximate years of attendance. No fee for information.

Transcripts available by mail. Search requires name plus social security number, signed release. Other helpful information: approximate years of attendance. Fee is $2.00.

Major credit cards accepted for payment.

Inter American University of Puerto Rico School of Optometry, Registrar, 118 Eleanor Roosevelt St, Hato Rey, PR 00919, 809-754-6690.

Inter American University of Puerto Rico, (Fajardo Campus), Registrar's Office, Call Box 70003, Fajardo, PR 00738-7003, 809-863-2390 (FAX: 809-860-3470). Hours: 8AM-7PM M-Th; 8AM-5PM F; 8AM-Noon S. Records go back to 1960. Alumni records are maintained here also. Call 809-863-2390 X2254. Degrees granted: Associate; Masters. Special programs- Transfer Programs, 809-250-1912. Adverse incident record source: Local Police, 809-863-2020.

Attendance and degree information available by written request only. Search requires name plus social security number, signed release. Other helpful information: date of birth, approximate years of attendance. No fee for information.

Transcripts available by written request only. Search requires name plus social security number, signed release. Other helpful information: date of birth, approximate years of attendance. Fee is $2.00.

Major credit cards accepted for payment.

Interboro Institute, Registrar, 450 W 56th St, New York, NY 10019, 212-399-0091 (FAX: 212-765-5772). Hours: 9AM-5PM. Records go back to 1945. Degrees granted: Associate.

Attendance and degree information available by FAX, mail. Search requires name plus social security number, approximate years of attendance, signed release. No fee for information.

Transcripts available by mail. Search requires name plus social security number, approximate years of attendance, signed release. Fee is $5.00.

Interdenominational Theological Center, Registrar, 671 Beckwith St SW, Atlanta, GA 30314, 404-527-7708 (FAX: 404-527-0901). Hours: 9AM-5PM. Degrees granted: Masters; Doctorate.

Attendance and degree information available by phone, FAX, mail. Search requires name plus social security number, approximate years of attendance. Other helpful information: date of birth, exact years of attendance. No fee for information.

Transcripts available by written request only. Search requires name plus social security number, date of birth, signed release. Fee is $2.00.

Interior Designers Institute, Registrar, 1061 Camelback Rd, Newport Beach, CA 92660, 714-675-4451. Hours: 8AM-5PM. Records go back to 1961. Degrees granted: Associate; Bachelors.

Attendance and degree information available by mail. Search requires name plus exact years of attendance, signed release. No fee for information.

Transcripts available by mail. Search requires name plus exact years of attendance, signed release. Fee is $10.00.

Major credit cards accepted for payment.

International Academy of Merchandising and Design, Registrar, One N State St #400, Chicago, IL 60602, 312-541-3910 (FAX: 312-541--3929). Hours: 8AM-5PM. Records go back to 1979. Degrees granted: Associate; Bachelors.

Attendance and degree information available by phone, FAX, mail. Search requires name only. Other helpful information: social security number, approximate years of attendance. No fee for information.

Transcripts available by FAX, mail. Search requires name plus social security number, signed release. Other helpful information: approximate years of attendance. Fee is $5.00. Expedited service available for $5.00.

International Academy of Merchandising and Design, Registrar, 211 S Hoover St, Tampa, FL 33609-9785, 813-881-0007 X235 (FAX: 813-881-0008). Hours: 8AM-4:30PM. Records go back to 1985. Degrees granted: Associate.

Attendance and degree information available by phone, FAX, mail. Search requires name plus social security number, exact years of attendance. No fee for information.

Transcripts available by mail. Search requires name plus social security number, exact years of attendance, signed release. Fee is $4.00.

International Bible College, Registrar, 3625 Helton Dr, PO Box IBC, Florence, AL 35630, 205-766-6610 (FAX: 205-760-0981). Hours: 8AM-4:30PM. Records go back to 1971. Alumni Records Office: Alumni President, PO Box 716, Haleyville, AL 35565. Degrees granted: Associate; Bachelors.

Attendance and degree information available by phone, FAX, mail. Search requires name plus social security number, signed release. Other helpful information: date of birth, approximate years of attendance. No fee for information.

Transcripts available by written request only. Search requires name plus social security number, signed release. Other helpful information: date of birth, approximate years of attendance. Fee is $3.00.

International Business College, Registrar, 3811 Illinois Rd, Fort Wayne, IN 46804, 219-432-8702 (FAX: 219-436-1896). Hours: 8:30AM-9PM M-Th; 8:30AM-5PM F. Records go back to 1918. Degrees granted: Associate.

Attendance information available by phone, FAX, mail. Search requires name plus social security number, exact years of attendance. No fee for information.

Degree information available by phone, FAX, mail. Search requires name plus social security number, date of birth, approximate years of attendance. No fee for information.

Transcripts available by written request only. Search requires name plus social security number, date of birth, approximate years of attendance, signed release. Fee is $5.00.

Need major, maiden name.

International Business College, Registrar, 7205 Shadeland Station, Indianapolis, IN 46256, 317-841-6400 (FAX: 317-841-6419). Hours: 8AM-4:30PM. Records go back 10 years. Degrees granted: Associate.

Attendance information available by written request only. Search requires name plus date of birth, signed release. Other helpful information: social security number, approximate years of attendance. No fee for information.

Degree information available by phone, FAX, mail. Search requires name plus date of birth. Other helpful information: social security number, approximate years of attendance. No fee for information.

Transcripts available by mail. Search requires name plus date of birth, signed release. Other helpful information: social security number, approximate years of attendance. Fee is $5.00. Expedited service available for $5.00.

Major credit cards accepted for payment.

International Business College, Registrar, PO Box 8245, San Juan, PR 00910, 809-725-8718.

International College, Registrar, 2654 E Tamiami Trail, Naples, FL 33962-5790, 813-774-4700 (FAX: 813-774-4593). Hours: 9AM-6:30PM. Records go back to founding date. Degrees granted: Associate; Bachelors.

Attendance information available by phone, FAX, mail. Search requires name only. Other helpful information: exact years of attendance. No fee for information.

Degree information available by phone, FAX, mail. Search requires name only. No fee for information.

Transcripts available by phone, FAX, mail. Search requires name plus signed notarized release. Fee is $3.00.

Major credit cards accepted for payment.

International College of Broadcasting, Registrar, 6 S Smithville Rd, Dayton, OH 45431-1833, 513-258-8251 (FAX: 513-258-8714). Hours: 8AM-8PM. Records go back 63 years. Degrees granted: Associate.

Attendance information available by phone, FAX, mail. Search requires name plus signed release. Other helpful information: social security number, date of birth, exact years of attendance. No fee for information.

Degree information available by phone, FAX. Search requires name plus signed release. Other helpful information: social security number, date of birth, exact years of attendance. No fee for information.

Transcripts available by phone, FAX, mail. Search requires name plus signed release. Other helpful information: social security number, date of birth, exact years of attendance. No fee for transcripts.

Major credit cards accepted for payment.

International College of Business & Technology, **(Branch Campus)**, Registrar, Plaza San Alfonso 2nd Fl, Caguas, PR 00627, 809-746-3777.

International College of Business & Technology, **(Branch Campus)**, Registrar, Junacao Shopping Ctr, Font Martelo St, Junacao, PR 00971, 809-850-0055.

International College, **(Branch)**, Registrar, 8695 College Pkwy Ste 217, Fort Myers, FL 33919, 813-482-0019 (FAX: 813-482-1714). Records are not housed here. They are located at International College, Registrar, 2654 E Tamiami Trail, Naples, FL 33962-5790.

International Fine Arts College, Registrar, 1737 N Bayshore Dr, Miami, FL 33132, 305-373-4684 (FAX: 305-374-7946). Hours: 7AM-6PM. Records go back 25 years. Degrees granted: Associate.

Attendance and degree information available by phone, FAX, mail. Search requires name plus social security number. Other helpful information: date of birth, approximate years of attendance. No fee for information.

Transcripts available by FAX, mail. Search requires name plus social security number, signed release. Other helpful information: date of birth, approximate years of attendance. Fee is $10.00.

Major credit cards accepted for payment.

International Institute of Chinese Medicine, Registrar, PO Box 4991, Santa Fe, NM 87502-4991, 505-473-5233 (FAX: 505-471-5551). Hours: 9AM-5PM. Records go back to 1985. Degrees granted: Masters.

Attendance and degree information available by phone, FAX, mail. Search requires name plus approximate years of attendance, signed release. Other helpful information: social security number, date of birth. Fee is $5.00.

Transcripts available by FAX, mail. Search requires name plus approximate years of attendance, signed release. Other helpful information: social security number, date of birth. Fee is $5.00.

Inver Hills Community College, Registrar, 2500 E 80th St, Inver Grove Heights, MN 55076, 612-450-8405 (FAX: 612-

450-8677). Hours: 7:30AM-4:30PM. Records go back to 1970. Degrees granted: Associate. Certification: Vocational.

Attendance and degree information available by phone, FAX, mail. Search requires name only. Other helpful information: social security number. No fee for information.

Transcripts available by FAX, mail. Search requires name plus signed release. Other helpful information: social security number. No fee for transcripts.

Iona College, Registrar, 715 North Ave, New Rochelle, NY 10801-1890, 914-633-2508 (FAX: 914-633-2182). Hours: 9AM-5PM. Records go back to 1941. Alumni Records Office: 115 Beechmont Dr, New Rochelle, NY 10801. Degrees granted: Associate; Bachelors; Masters.

Attendance and degree information available by phone, mail. Search requires name plus approximate years of attendance, signed release. Other helpful information: social security number, date of birth, exact years of attendance. No fee for information.

Transcripts available by written request only. Search requires name plus social security number, signed release. Other helpful information: date of birth, approximate years of attendance. Fee is $3.00. Expedited service available for $5.00.

Major credit cards accepted for payment.

Iona College, (Manhattan Campus), Registrar, 425 W 33rd St, New York, NY 10001, 212-630-0270. Records are not housed here. They are located at Iona College, Registrar, 715 North Ave, New Rochelle, NY 10801-1890.

Iona College, (Rockland Campus), Registrar, One Dutch Hill Rd, Orangeburg, NY 10962, 914-359-2252. Records are not housed here. They are located at Iona College, Registrar, 715 North Ave, New Rochelle, NY 10801-1890.

Iona College, (Yonkers Campus), Registrar, 1061 N Broadway, Yonkers, NY 10701, 914-378-8000. Records are not housed here. They are located at Iona College, Registrar, 715 North Ave, New Rochelle, NY 10801-1890.

Iowa Central Community College, Registrar, 330 Ave M, Fort Dodge, IA 50501, 515-576-7201 X2409 (FAX: 515-576-7206). Hours: 8AM-5PM M-Th, 8AM-4:30PM F. Records go back to 1966. Degrees granted: Associate.

Attendance and degree information available by phone, mail. Search requires name plus social security number, exact years of attendance, signed release. No fee for information.

Transcripts available by mail. Search requires name plus social security number, exact years of attendance, signed release. First transcript is free. Additional ones are $5.00 each.

Phone confirmation given if release in file.

Iowa Lakes Community College, (Emmetsburg Campus), Registrar, 3200 College Dr, Emmetsburg, IA 50536, 712-852-3554 (FAX: 712-852-2152). Hours: 8AM-5PM. Records go back to 1928. Degrees granted: Associate.

Attendance and degree information available by phone, FAX, mail. Search requires name only. Other helpful information: social security number, date of birth, approximate years of attendance. No fee for information.

Transcripts available by FAX, mail. Search requires name plus signed release. Other helpful information: social security number, date of birth, approximate years of attendance. Fee is $2.00. Expedited service available for $8.00.

Major credit cards accepted for payment.

Iowa Lakes Community College, (Estherville), Registrar, 19 S 7th St, Estherville, IA 51334, 712-362-2604 (FAX: 712-362-7649). Hours: 8AM-5PM. Records go back to 1928. Degrees granted: Associate.

Attendance and degree information available by phone, FAX, mail. Search requires name only. Other helpful information: social security number, date of birth, approximate years of attendance. No fee for information.

Transcripts available by FAX, mail. Search requires name plus signed release. Other helpful information: social security number, date of birth, approximate years of attendance. Fee is $2.00. Expedited service available for $8.00.

Major credit cards accepted for payment.

Iowa State University, Office of the Registrar, 214 Alumni Hall, Ames, IA 50011, 515-294-1840 (FAX: 515-294-1088). Hours: 8AM-5PM. Records go back to 1858. Alumni Records Office: Alumni Suite, Memorial Union, Ames, IA 50011 515-294-6525. Degrees granted: Bachelors; Masters; Doctorate.

Attendance and degree information available by phone, FAX, mail. Search requires name only. Other helpful information: social security number, approximate years of attendance. No fee for information.

Transcripts available by phone, mail. Search requires name plus social security number, signed release. Other helpful information: date of birth, approximate years of attendance. Fee is $3.00. Expedited service available for $2.00.

Iowa Wesleyan College, Registrar, 601 N Main St, Mount Pleasant, IA 52641, 319-385-6225 (FAX: 319-385-6296). Hours: 8AM-Noon, 1-5PM. Records go back to founding date. Degrees granted: Bachelors. Adverse incident record source: 319-385-6256.

Attendance and degree information available by phone, FAX, mail. Search requires name only. Other helpful information: social security number, date of birth, approximate years of attendance. No fee for information.

Transcripts available by FAX, mail. Search requires name plus signed release. Other helpful information: social security number, date of birth, approximate years of attendance. Fee is $2.00.

Iowa Western Community College, Registrar, 2700 College Rd, Council Bluffs, IA 51501, 712-325-3200. Degrees granted: Associate.

Attendance and degree information available by phone, FAX, mail. Search requires name plus social security number, signed release. Other helpful information: date of birth, approximate years of attendance. No fee for information.

Transcripts available by written request only. Search requires name plus social security number, signed release. Other helpful information: date of birth, approximate years of attendance. Fee is $1.00.

Include a self addressed stamped envelope with mail request.

Irvine Valley College, Admissions & Records, Transcript Unit, 5500 Irvine Center Dr, Irvine, CA 92720, 714-559-3461 (FAX: 714-559-3443). Hours: 9AM-7PM M-Th; 9AM-3PM F. Records go back to 1969. Alumni records are maintained here also. Call 714-559-3216. Degrees granted: Associate.

Attendance information available by FAX, mail. Search requires name plus date of birth, exact years of attendance, signed release. Other helpful information: social security number, approximate years of attendance. Fee is $3.00. Expedited service available for $8.00.

Degree information available by FAX, mail. Search requires name plus date of birth, signed release. Other helpful information: social security number. Fee is $3.00. Expedite service available for $8.00.

Transcripts available by FAX, mail. Search requires name plus date of birth, signed release. Other helpful information: social security number. Fee is $3.00. Expedited service available for $8.00.

Major credit cards accepted for payment.

Isothermal Community College, Registrar, PO Box 804, Spindale, NC 28160, 704-286-3636 X267 (FAX: 704-286-8109). Hours: 8AM-9PM M-Th; 8AM-4:30PM. Alumni records are maintained here also. Call 704-286-3636 X261. Degrees granted: Associate. Adverse incident record source: Dean of Students, 704-286-3636 X267.

Attendance and degree information available by phone, FAX, mail. Search requires name plus social security number, approximate years of attendance. Other helpful information: date of birth, exact years of attendance. No fee for information.

Transcripts available by written request only. Search requires name plus social security number, approximate years of attendance, signed release. Other helpful information: date of birth, exact years of attendance. No fee for transcripts.

Itasca Community College, Registrar, 1851 E Hwy 169, Grand Rapids, MN 55744, 218-327-4468 (FAX: 218-327-4350). Hours: 8AM-4:30PM. Records go back to 1926. Degrees granted: Associate.

Attendance and degree information available by FAX, mail. Search requires name plus social security number, signed release. Other helpful information: date of birth, approximate years of attendance. No fee for information.

Transcripts available by FAX, mail. Search requires name plus social security number, signed release. Other helpful information: date of birth, approximate years of attendance. No fee for transcripts.

Itawamba Community College, Registrar, 602 W Hill St, Fulton, MS 38843-1099, 601-862-3101 X234 (FAX: 601-862-9540). Hours: 8AM-4PM. Records go back to 1948. Alumni records are maintained here also. Call 601-862-3101 X225. Degrees granted: Associate. Adverse incident record source: Security, 601-862-3101 X201.

Attendance and degree information available by phone, FAX, mail. Search requires name plus social security number, signed release. No fee for information.

Transcripts available by mail. Search requires name plus social security number, signed release. Fee is $2.00.

Ithaca College, Office of the Registrar, Transcript Requests, 228 Job Hall, Ithaca, NY 14850-7014, 607-274-3127 (FAX: 607-274-1366). Hours: 8AM-5PM. Records go back to 1892. Degrees granted: Bachelors; Masters. Adverse incident record source: Campus Safety, 607-274-3333.

Attendance and degree information available by phone, FAX, mail. Search requires name only. Other helpful information: social security number, date of birth, approximate years of attendance. No fee for information.

Transcripts available by FAX, mail. Search requires name plus social security number, signed release. Other helpful information: date of birth, approximate years of attendance. Fee is $2.00.

Ivy Tech State College, Registrar, One W 26th St, PO Box 1763, Indianapolis, IN 46206-1763, 317-921-4745 (FAX: 317-921-4753). Hours: 8AM-6PM M-Th, 9AM-5PM F. Records go back to 1968. Alumni records are maintained here also. Call 317-921-4882. Degrees granted: Associate.

Attendance and degree information available by phone, FAX, mail. Search requires name plus social security number, date of birth, exact years of attendance. No fee for information.

Transcripts available by FAX, mail. Search requires name plus social security number, date of birth, exact years of attendance, signed release. No fee for transcripts.

Ivy Tech State College-Kokomo Technical Institute, Registrar, 1815 E Morgan St, Kokomo, IN 46901, 317-459-0561 (FAX: 317-454-5111). Hours: 7:30AM-5:30PM. Degrees granted: Associate. Adverse incident record source: Security Office, 317-459-0561.

Attendance and degree information available by written request only. Search requires name plus social security number. Other helpful information: approximate years of attendance. No fee for information.

Transcripts available by written request only. Search requires name plus social security number, signed release. Other helpful information: approximate years of attendance. No fee for transcripts.

Ivy Tech State College-Lafayette Technical Inst., Registrar, 3208 Ross Rd, PO Box 6299, Lafayette, IN 47903, 317-477-9119 (FAX: 317-477-9214). Hours: 8AM-5PM. Records go back 25 years. Alumni records are maintained here also. Call 317-477-9193. Degrees granted: Associate. Adverse incident record source: Jim Javanovic, 317-477-9117.

Attendance and degree information available by phone, FAX, mail. Search requires name plus approximate years of attendance. Other helpful information: social security number, date of birth. No fee for information.

Transcripts available by FAX, mail. Search requires name plus social security number, approximate years of attendance, signed release. Other helpful information: date of birth. No fee for transcripts.

Ivy Tech State College-Northcentral Technical Inst., Registrar, 1534 W Sample St, South Bend, IN 46619, 219-289-7001 X326 (FAX: 219-236-7172). Hours: 8AM-6PM M-F; 8AM-Noon S. Records go back to founding date. Degrees granted: Associate. Adverse incident record source: Director of Students, 219-289-7001 X 354.

Attendance information available by phone, FAX, mail. Search requires name plus social security number, signed release. Other helpful information: approximate years of attendance. No fee for information.

Degree information available by FAX, mail. Search requires name plus social security number, signed release. Other helpful information: approximate years of attendance. No fee for information.

Transcripts available by FAX, mail. Search requires name plus social security number, signed release. Other helpful information: approximate years of attendance. No fee for transcripts.

Ivy Tech State College-Northeast Technical Inst., Registrar, 3800 N Anthony Blvd, Fort Wayne, IN 46805, 219-480-4255 (FAX: 219-480-4177). Hours: 8AM-5PM. Records go back 26 years. Degrees granted: Associate.

Attendance and degree information available by phone, FAX, mail. Search requires name plus social security number. Other helpful information: date of birth, approximate years of attendance. No fee for information.

Transcripts available by written request only. Search requires name plus social security number, signed release. Other helpful information: date of birth, approximate years of attendance. No fee for transcripts.

Ivy Tech State College-Northwest Technical Inst., Registrar, 1440 E 35th Ave, Gary, IN 46409, 219-981-1111 X272. Hours: 8AM-5PM. Records go back to 1963. Degrees granted: Associate.

Attendance and degree information available by phone, mail. Search requires name plus social security number, date of birth. No fee for information.

Transcripts available by mail. Search requires name plus social security number, date of birth, signed release. No fee for transcripts.

Ivy Tech State College-Northwest Technical Inst., **(Branch)**, Registrar, 1440 E 35th Ave, Gary, IN 46409, 219-981-1111 X272. Hours: 8AM-5PM. Records go back to 1969. Degrees granted: Associate.

Attendance information available by phone, mail. Search requires name plus social security number, date of birth. No fee for information.

Degree information available by phone, mail. Search requires name plus social security number, date of birth. Other helpful information: exact years of attendance. No fee for information.

Transcripts available by mail. Search requires name plus social security number, date of birth, exact years of attendance, signed release. No fee for transcripts.

Ivy Tech State College-Southcentral Tech. Inst., Registrar, 8204 Hwy 311 W, Sellersburg, IN 47172, 812-246-3301 X4139 (FAX: 812-246-9905). Hours: 9AM-6PM M-Th; 8AM-5PM F. Records go back to founding date. Alumni records are maintained here also. Call 812-246-3301 X4129. Degrees granted: Associate.

Attendance information available by written request only. Search requires name plus social security number, signed release. Other helpful information: date of birth, approximate years of attendance. No fee for information.

Degree information available by phone, FAX, mail. Search requires name plus social security number. Other helpful information: date of birth, approximate years of attendance. No fee for information.

Transcripts available by mail. Search requires name plus social security number, date of birth, approximate years of attendance, signed release. Other helpful information: exact years of attendance. No fee for transcripts.

Ivy Tech State College-Southeast Tech. Inst., Registrar, 590 Ivy Tech Dr, Madison, IN 47250, 812-265-2580 X4130 (FAX: 812-265-4028). Hours: 8AM-5PM. Records go back to 1971. Degrees granted: Associate. Certification: Technical. Adverse incident record source: Same as above.

Attendance and degree information available by phone, FAX, mail. Search requires name only. Other helpful information: social security number, date of birth, exact years of attendance. No fee for information.

Transcripts available by FAX, mail. Search requires name plus signed release. Other helpful information: social security number, date of birth, exact years of attendance. No fee for transcripts. Major credit cards accepted for payment.

Ivy Tech State College-Southwest Tech. Inst., Registrar, 3501 First Ave, Evansville, IN 47710, 812-429-1433 (FAX: 812-429-9834). Hours: 8AM-6PM. Degrees granted: Associate. Certification: TC. Adverse incident record source: Director of Facilities, 812-429-1488.

Attendance and degree information available by phone, FAX, mail. Search requires name plus social security number. Other helpful information: date of birth, approximate years of attendance. No fee for information.

Transcripts available by FAX, mail. Search requires name plus social security number, signed release. Other helpful information: date of birth, approximate years of attendance. No fee for transcripts.

Ivy Tech State College-Wabash Valley Tech. Inst., Registrar, 7999 US Hwy 41, Terre Haute, IN 47802, 812-299-1121 (FAX: 812-299-5723). Hours: 8AM-8PM M-Th; 8AM-4:45PM F. Degrees granted: Associate. Adverse incident record source: Records/Registration.

Attendance information available by mail. Search requires name plus social security number, signed release. Other helpful information: date of birth, approximate years of attendance. No fee for information.

Degree information available by FAX, mail. Search requires name plus social security number, signed release. Other helpful information: date of birth, approximate years of attendance. No fee for information.

Transcripts available by FAX, mail. Search requires name plus social security number, signed release. Other helpful information: approximate years of attendance. No fee for transcripts. Major credit cards accepted for payment.

Ivy Tech State College-Whitewater Tech. Inst., Registrar, 2325 Chester Blvd, Richmond, IN 47374, 317-966-2656 (FAX: 317-962-8741). Hours: 8AM-5PM. Records go back to 1968. Degrees granted: Associate. Certification: Technical.

Attendance and degree information available by FAX, mail. Search requires name plus social security number, date of birth, approximate years of attendance, signed release. Other helpful information: exact years of attendance. No fee for information.

Transcripts available by FAX, mail. Search requires name plus social security number, date of birth, approximate years of attendance, signed release. Other helpful information: exact years of attendance. No fee for transcripts.

J

J. F. Drake State Technical College, Registrar, 3421 Meridian St, Huntsville, AL 35811, 205-539-8161 X110 (FAX: 205-539-6439). Hours: 7:30AM-4PM. Records go back to 1961. Alumni records are maintained here also. Call 205-539-8161. Degrees granted: Associate.

Attendance and degree information available by phone, mail. Search requires name plus social security number, exact years of attendance. No fee for information.

Transcripts available by mail. Search requires name plus social security number, exact years of attendance, signed release. Fee is $2.00.

J. Sargeant Reynolds Community College, Registrar, PO Box 85622, Richmond, VA 23285-5622, 804-371-3029 (FAX: 804-371-3631). Hours: 8:15AM-5PM. Records go back to founding date. Degrees granted: Associate.

Attendance and degree information available by phone, FAX, mail. Search requires name plus social security number. Other helpful information: date of birth. No fee for information.

Transcripts available by mail. Search requires name plus social security number, signed release. Other helpful information: date of birth. No fee for transcripts.

Jackson Community College, Registrar, 2111 Emmons Rd, Jackson, MI 49201, 517-787-0800 (FAX: 517-789-1631). Hours: 8AM-5PM. Records go back to 1928. Alumni records are maintained here also. Call 517-787-0800. Degrees granted: Associate.

Attendance and degree information available by phone, FAX, mail. Search requires name plus social security number, signed release. No fee for information.

Transcripts available by FAX, mail. Search requires name plus social security number, signed release. No fee for transcripts.

Jackson State Community College, Records Office, 2046 North Pkwy, Jackson, TN 38301-3797, 901-425-2654 (FAX: 901-425-2647). Hours: 8AM-4:30PM. Records go back to 1967. Degrees granted: Associate.

Attendance and degree information available by phone, FAX, mail. Search requires name plus social security number. Other helpful information: approximate years of attendance. No fee for information.

Transcripts available by mail. Search requires name plus social security number, signed release. Other helpful information: approximate years of attendance. No fee for transcripts.

Jackson State University, Registrar, 1400 J R Lynch St, Jackson, MS 39217, 601-968-2300 (FAX: 601-968-2399). Hours: 8AM-5PM. Records go back to 1900s. Degrees granted: Bachelors; Masters; Doctorate.

Attendance and degree information available by phone, FAX, mail. Search requires name only. Other helpful information: social security number, date of birth, approximate years of attendance. No fee for information.

Transcripts available by phone, mail. Search requires name only. Other helpful information: social security number, date of birth, approximate years of attendance. Fee is $5.00.

Major credit cards accepted for payment.

Jacksonville College, Registrar, 105 B.J. Albritton Dr, Jacksonville, TX 75766-4759, 903-589-2801 (FAX: 903-586-0743). Hours: 8AM-5PM. Records go back to 1899. Alumni records are maintained here also. Call 903-586-2518. Degrees granted: Associate.

Attendance and degree information available by phone, FAX, mail. Search requires name only. Other helpful information: social security number, approximate years of attendance. No fee for information.

Transcripts available by written request only. Search requires name plus signed release. Other helpful information: social security number, approximate years of attendance. Fee is $3.00. Expedited service available for $3.00.

Major credit cards accepted for payment.

Jacksonville State University, Registrar, 700 N Pelham Rd, Jacksonville, AL 36265-9982, 205-782-5400. Hours: 8AM-4:30PM. Records go back to founding date. Alumni records are maintained here also. Call 205-782-5404. Degrees granted: Bachelors; Masters; Educational Specialists.

Attendance and degree information available by phone, mail. Search requires name only. Other helpful information: social security number, date of birth, approximate years of attendance. No fee for information.

Transcripts available by mail. Search requires name plus signed release. Other helpful information: social security number, date of birth, approximate years of attendance. Fee is $5.00.

Major credit cards accepted for payment.

Jacksonville University, Registrar, 2800 University Blvd N, Jacksonville, FL 32211, 904-745-7090 (FAX: 904-745-7086). Hours: 8:30AM-5PM. Records go back to 1930. Alumni records are maintained here also. Call 904-745-7201. Degrees granted: Bachelors; Masters. Adverse incident record source: Dean of Students, 904-745-7070: Security, 904-744-3950 X2213

Attendance and degree information available by phone, FAX, mail. Search requires name only. Other helpful information: social security number, date of birth, approximate years of attendance. No fee for information.

Transcripts available by FAX, mail. Search requires name plus signed release. Other helpful information: social security number, date of birth, approximate years of attendance. Fee is $2.00. Expedited service available for $4.00.

Major credit cards accepted for payment.

James H. Faulkner State Community College, Registrar, 1900 Hwy 31 S, Bay Minette, AL 36507, 205-937-9581 X311. Hours: 8AM-5PM. Records go back to 1965. Degrees granted: Associate.

Attendance and degree information available by phone, mail. Search requires name only. Other helpful information: social security number. No fee for information.

Transcripts available by mail. Search requires name plus social security number, signed release. No fee for transcripts.

James Madison University, Registrar, Harrisonburg, VA 22807, 703-568-6281. Hours: 8AM-4:30PM. Records go back to 1908. Alumni records are maintained here also. Call 703-568-3628. Degrees granted: Bachelors; Masters.

Attendance and degree information available by phone, mail. Search requires name plus social security number. No fee for information.

Transcripts available by mail. Search requires name plus social security number, signed release. No fee for transcripts.

James Sprunt Community College, Registrar, PO Box 398, Kenansville, NC 28349-0398, 910-296-2400. Degrees granted: Associate.

Attendance and degree information available by phone, FAX, mail. Search requires name plus social security number, date of birth. Other helpful information: approximate years of attendance. No fee for information.

Transcripts available by FAX, mail. Search requires name plus social security number, date of birth, signed release. Other helpful information: approximate years of attendance. No fee for transcripts.

Jamestown Business College, Registrar, PO Box 429, Fairmont Ave, Jamestown, NY 14702-0429, 716-664-5100 (FAX: 716-664-3144). Hours: 8AM-5PM. Records go back to 1920. Degrees granted: Associate.

Attendance and degree information available by phone, FAX, mail. Search requires name plus social security number, signed release. Other helpful information: approximate years of attendance. No fee for information.

Transcripts available by FAX, mail. Search requires name plus social security number, signed release. Other helpful information: approximate years of attendance. No fee for transcripts.

Jamestown College, Registrar, 600 College Ln, Jamestown, ND 58405, 701-252-3467 (FAX: 701-253-4318). Hours: 8AM-5PM. Records go back to 1920. Alumni records are maintained here also. Call 701-252-3467 X2557. Degrees granted: Bachelors.

Attendance information available by phone, FAX, mail. Search requires name only. Other helpful information: social security number, date of birth, approximate years of attendance. No fee for information.

Degree information available by phone, FAX, mail. Search requires name plus signed release. Other helpful information: social security number, date of birth, approximate years of attendance. No fee for information.

Transcripts available by mail. Search requires name plus signed release. Other helpful information: social security number, date of birth, approximate years of attendance. Fee is $3.00. Expedited service available for $12.00.

Jamestown Community College, Academic Transcripts, 525 Falconer St, Jamestown, NY 14701, 716-665-5220 X332 (FAX: 716-665-4115). Hours: 8:30AM-5PM. Records go back to 1950. Degrees granted: Associate. Special programs- Financial Aid Transcripts: Financial Aids Office, 716-665-5220.

Attendance and degree information available by phone, FAX, mail. Search requires name plus social security number, approximate years of attendance. Other helpful information: date of birth. No fee for information.

Transcripts available by written request only. Search requires name plus social security number, approximate years of attendance, signed release. Other helpful information: date of birth. Fee is $3.00.

Need any other last names student had. Major credit cards accepted for payment.

Jamestown Community College, **(Cattaraugus County Campus)**, Registrar, 244 N Union St, Olean, NY 14760, 716-665-5220 X332 (FAX: 716-665-4115). Hours: 8:30AM-4:30PM. Records go back to 1950. Degrees granted: Associate.

Attendance and degree information available by phone, FAX, mail. Search requires name plus social security number, date of birth. Other helpful information: approximate years of attendance. No fee for information.

Transcripts available by FAX, mail. Search requires name plus social security number, date of birth, signed release. Other helpful information: approximate years of attendance. Fee is $3.00.

Major credit cards accepted for payment.

Jarvis Christian College, Registrar, PO Drawer G, Hawkins, TX 75765-9989, 903-769-5738 (FAX: 903-769-4842). Hours: 8AM-5PM. Records go back to 1914. Degrees granted: Bachelors.

Attendance and degree information available by phone, FAX, mail. Search requires name plus social security number. Other helpful information: approximate years of attendance. No fee for information.

Transcripts available by mail. Search requires name plus social security number, signed release. Other helpful information: approximate years of attendance. Fee is $3.00.

Jefferson College, Registrar, 1000 Viking Dr, Hillsboro, MO 63050, 314-789-3951 (FAX: 314-789-5103). Hours: 8AM-4:30PM. Records go back to 1964. Degrees granted: Associate. Adverse incident record source: Dean, 314-789-3951 X200.

Attendance information available by phone, FAX, mail. Search requires name plus approximate years of attendance. Other helpful information: social security number, exact years of attendance. No fee for information.

Degree information available by phone, FAX, mail. Search requires name only. Other helpful information: social security number, approximate years of attendance. No fee for information.

Transcripts available by FAX, mail. Search requires name plus signed release. Other helpful information: social security number, approximate years of attendance. Fee is $3.00. Expedited service available for $5.00.

Jefferson Community College, Registrar, 109 E Broadway, Louisville, KY 40202, 502-584-0181 X2128. Hours: 8AM-5PM M-Th, 8AM-4:30PM. Records go back to 1968. Degrees granted: Associate.

Attendance and degree information available by phone, mail. Search requires name plus social security number, signed release. No fee for information.

Transcripts available by mail. Search requires name plus social security number, signed release. Fee is $2.00.

Jefferson Community College, Registrar, Outer Coffeen St, Watertown, NY 13601, 315-786-2417 (FAX: 315-786-0158). Hours: 9AM-5PM. Records go back to 1961. Alumni records are maintained here also. Call 315-786-2327. Degrees granted: Associate. Adverse incident record source: Security, 315-786-2359.

Attendance and degree information available by phone, FAX, mail. Search requires name plus social security number. Other helpful information: date of birth, approximate years of attendance. No fee for information.

Transcripts available by mail. Search requires name plus social security number, signed release. Other helpful information: date of birth, approximate years of attendance. Fee is $5.00. Expedite: $5.00 FAX, $10.00 overnight mail. Credit card minimum $15.00.

Major credit cards accepted for payment.

Jefferson Davis Community College, Registrar's Office, 220 Alco Dr, Brewton, AL 36426, 205-867-4832 X45 (FAX: 205-867-7399). Hours: 7:30AM-4:30PM. Records go back to 1965. Degrees granted: Associate. Adverse incident record source: Registrar, 205-867-4832.

Attendance and degree information available by mail. Search requires name plus social security number, signed release. No fee for information.

Transcripts available by mail. Search requires name plus social security number, exact years of attendance, signed release. No fee for transcripts.

Jefferson State Community College, Registrar, 2601 Carson Rd, Birmingham, AL 35215-3098, 205-853-1200 X1272. Hours: 8AM-4:30PM. Records go back to 1965. Degrees granted: Associate. Adverse incident record source: Security Office, 205-856-6093.

Attendance and degree information available by mail. Search requires name plus social security number, signed release. No fee for information.

Transcripts available by mail. Search requires name plus social security number, exact years of attendance, signed release. No fee for transcripts.

Jefferson Technical College, Registrar, 4000 Sunset Blvd, Steubenville, OH 43952, 614-264-5591 (FAX: 614-264-1338). Hours: 8AM-7:30PM. Records go back 27 years. Degrees granted: Associate.

Attendance and degree information available by phone, FAX, mail. Search requires name plus social security number. No fee for information.

Transcripts available by FAX, mail. Search requires name plus social security number, signed release. Fee is $2.00.

Major credit cards accepted for payment.

Jersey City State College, Registrar, 2039 Kennedy Blvd, Jersey City, NJ 07305, 201-200-3336 (FAX: 201-200-2044). Hours: 8:30AM-4:30PM. Records go back to 1993. Alumni records are maintained here also. Call 201-200-3196. Degrees granted: Bachelors.

Attendance and degree information available by phone, FAX, mail. Search requires name plus social security number, signed release. No fee for information.

Transcripts available by mail. Search requires name plus social security number, signed release. Fee is $2.00.

Jesuit School of Theology at Berkeley, Registrar, 1735 LeRoy Ave, Berkeley, CA 94709-1193, 510-841-8804 (FAX: 510-841-8536). Hours: 8:30AM-5PM. Records go back to 1969. Degrees granted: Masters; Doctorate.

Attendance and degree information available by phone, FAX, mail. Search requires name plus approximate years of attendance. Other helpful information: social security number, date of birth. No fee for information.

Transcripts available by FAX, mail. Search requires name plus approximate years of attendance, signed release. Other helpful information: social security number, date of birth. Fee is $3.00.

Applies only to graduated or withdrawn students. Current attendance can be confirmed only, and then if student did not request privacy.

Jewish Theological Seminary of America, Registrar, 3080 Broadway, New York, NY 10027, 212-678-8007 (FAX: 212-678-8947). Hours: 9AM-5PM. Records go back to 1885. Degrees granted: Bachelors; Masters; Doctorate; Rabbamic Ordination.

Attendance information available by phone, FAX, mail. Search requires name plus social security number, date of birth, exact years of attendance, signed release. No fee for information.

Degree information available by FAX, mail. Search requires name plus social security number, date of birth, exact years of attendance, signed release. No fee for information.

Transcripts available by mail. Search requires name plus social security number, date of birth, exact years of attendance, signed release. First copy $5.00; $2.00 each additional. Expedited service available for $3.00.

John A. Gupton College, Registrar, 1616 Church St, Nashville, TN 37203, 615-327-3927 (FAX: 615-321-4518). Hours: 8:30AM-4:30PM. Records go back to 1946. Degrees granted: Associate.

Attendance and degree information available by phone, FAX, mail. Search requires name only. No fee for information.

Transcripts available by mail. Search requires name plus signed release. Other helpful information: social security number, date of birth, approximate years of attendance. Fee is $5.00.

John A. Logan College, Registrar, Carterville, IL 62918, 618-985-3741 X221 (FAX: 618-985-2248). Hours: 8AM-8PM M-Th; 8AM-4:30PM F. Records go back to 1967. Degrees granted: Associate.

Attendance and degree information available by phone, FAX, mail. Search requires name plus social security number, signed release. Other helpful information: date of birth, approximate years of attendance. No fee for information.

Transcripts available by FAX, mail. Search requires name plus social security number, signed release. Other helpful information: date of birth, approximate years of attendance. No fee for transcripts.

John Brown University, Registrar, Siloam Springs, AR 72761, 501-524-7103 (FAX: 501-524-9548). Hours: 7:30AM-5PM. Records go back to 1919.

Attendance and degree information available by phone, FAX, mail. Search requires name plus approximate years of attendance. Other helpful information: social security number, date of birth, exact years of attendance. No fee for information.

Transcripts available by FAX, mail. Search requires name plus social security number, date of birth, approximate years of attendance, signed release. Other helpful information: exact years of attendance. Fee is $2.00. Expedited service available for $2.00.

John C. Calhoun State Community College, Registrar, PO Box 23216, Decatur, AL 35609-2216, 205-306-2601 (FAX: 205-306-2885). Hours: 8AM-8PM M-Th; 8AM-4PM F. Records go back to 1950. Degrees granted: Associate.

Attendance and degree information available by mail. Search requires name plus social security number, signed release. Other helpful information: date of birth, approximate years of attendance. No fee for information.

Transcripts available by mail. Search requires name plus social security number, signed release. Other helpful information: date of birth, approximate years of attendance. No fee for transcripts.

John Carroll University, Registrar, 20700 N Park Blvd, University Heights, OH 44118, 216-397-4291 (FAX: 216-397-3049). Hours: 8:30AM-5PM. Records go back to 1886. Alumni records are maintained here also. Call 216-397-4322. Degrees granted: Bachelors; Masters. Adverse incident record source: Dean, 216-397-4401.

Attendance and degree information available by phone, FAX, mail. Search requires name plus social security number, date of birth, approximate years of attendance, signed release. No fee for information.

Transcripts available by FAX, mail. Search requires name plus social security number, date of birth, approximate years of attendance, signed release. Fee is $3.00.

John F. Kennedy University, Registrar, 12 Altarinda Rd, Orinda, CA 94563, 510-254-0200 (FAX: 510-254-6949). Hours: 10AM-6PM. Records go back to 1964. Degrees granted: Bachelors; Masters.

Attendance and degree information available by phone, FAX, mail. Search requires name only. Other helpful information: social security number, approximate years of attendance. No fee for information.

Transcripts available by written request only. Search requires name plus approximate years of attendance, signed release. Other helpful information: social security number, exact years of attendance. Fee is $3.00. Expedited service available for $8.00.

John Jay College of Criminal Justice, Registrar, 445 W 59th St Room 4113, New York, NY 10019, 212-237-8878. Hours: 9AM-5PM. Records go back to 1965. Degrees granted: Bachelors.

Attendance and degree information available by phone, mail. Search requires name plus social security number, date of birth, exact years of attendance. No fee for information.

Transcripts available by mail. Search requires name plus social security number, date of birth, exact years of attendance, signed release. Fee is $4.00.

John M. Patterson State Technical College, Registrar, 3920 Troy Hwy, Montgomery, AL 36116, 334-284-9356 (FAX: 334-284-9357). Hours: 8AM-6:30PM M-Th, 8AM-4PM F. Records go back to 1962. Degrees granted: Associate.

Attendance and degree information available by phone, FAX, mail. Search requires name plus social security number, approximate years of attendance. Other helpful information: date of birth, exact years of attendance. No fee for information.

Transcripts available by mail. Search requires name plus social security number, approximate years of attendance, signed release. Other helpful information: date of birth, exact years of attendance. No fee for transcripts.

Major credit cards accepted for payment.

John Marshall Law School, Registrar, 315 S Plymouth Ct, Chicago, IL 60604, 312-427-2737 X466. Hours: 9AM-5:30PM. Records go back to 1898. Alumni records are maintained here also. Call 312-427-2737. Degrees granted: Masters; Doctorate.

Attendance and degree information available by phone, mail. Search requires name plus social security number, exact years of attendance. No fee for information.

Transcripts available by mail. Search requires name plus social security number, exact years of attendance, signed release. Fee is $5.00.

John Tyler Community College, Admissions & Records, 13101 Jefferson Davis Hwy, Chester, VA 23831-5399, 804-796-4151 (FAX: 804-796-4163). Hours: 7:40AM-7PM M-Th; 7:45AM-5PM F. Records go back to 1967. Degrees granted: Associate.

Attendance and degree information available by phone, mail. Search requires name plus social security number. Other helpful information: date of birth, approximate years of attendance. No fee for information.

Transcripts available by mail. Search requires name plus social security number, signed release. Other helpful information: date of birth, approximate years of attendance. Fee is $1.00.

John Wesley College, Registrar, 2314 N Centennial St, High Point, NC 27265, 910-889-2262 (FAX: 910-889-2261). Hours: 8AM-5PM. Alumni records are maintained here also. Call 910-889-2262. Degrees granted: Associate; Bachelors. Certification: Christian Workers.

Attendance and degree information available by phone, FAX, mail. Search requires name plus social security number, date of birth, signed release. Other helpful information: approximate years of attendance. No fee for information.

Transcripts available by mail. Search requires name plus social security number, date of birth, signed release. Other helpful information: approximate years of attendance. Fee is $3.00.

Major credit cards accepted for payment.

John Wood Community College, Registrar, 150 S 48th St, Quincy, IL 62301, 217-224-6500 (FAX: 217-224-4208). Hours: 8AM-5PM. Degrees granted: Associate; Vocational.

Attendance and degree information available by FAX, mail. Search requires name plus social security number. Other helpful information: date of birth, approximate years of attendance. No fee for information.

Transcripts available by FAX, mail. Search requires name plus social security number, signed release. Other helpful information: date of birth, approximate years of attendance. Fee is $2.00. Expedited service available for $2.00.

FAX: $2.00. Major credit cards accepted for payment.

Johns Hopkins University, Registrar, 75 Garland Hall, 3400 N Charles St, Baltimore, MD 21218-2688, 410-516-8600 (FAX: 410-516-6477). Hours: 8:30AM-5PM. Records go back to 1879. Degrees granted: Associate; Bachelors; Masters; Doctorate.

Attendance and degree information available by phone, FAX, mail. Search requires name plus social security number, signed release. Other helpful information: date of birth, approximate years of attendance. No fee for information.

Transcripts available by mail. Search requires name plus social security number, signed release. Other helpful information: date of birth, approximate years of attendance. No fee for transcripts. Expedited service available for $10.00.

Johns Hopkins University, **(Columbia Center)**, Registrar, 6740 Alexander Bell Dr, Columbia, MD 21046, 410-516-8499 (FAX: 410-516-6477). Hours: 8:30AM-4:30PM. Records go back to 1880. Alumni Records Office: 3400 N Charles St, Baltimore, MD 21218. Degrees granted: Associate; Bachelors; Masters; Doctorate. Special programs- Medicine, 410-955-3080: Hygiene, 410-955-7540.

Attendance and degree information available by phone, FAX, mail. Search requires name plus social security number, exact years of attendance. No fee for information.

Transcripts available by mail. Search requires name plus social security number, exact years of attendance, signed release. No fee for transcripts.

Johns Hopkins University, **(Peabody Institute of the Johns Hopkins University)**, Registrar, One E Mount Vernon Pl, Baltimore, MD 21202, 410-659-8266 (FAX: 410-659-8129). Hours: 8:30AM-5PM. Records go back to 1932. Alumni records are maintained here also. Call 410-659-8176. Degrees granted: Bachelors; Masters; Doctorate; Artist Diploma. Adverse incident record source: Local Police, 410-396-2525.

Attendance and degree information available by phone, mail. Search requires name plus approximate years of attendance, signed release. Other helpful information: date of birth. No fee for information.

Transcripts available by mail. Search requires name plus approximate years of attendance, signed release. Other helpful information: social security number, date of birth. Fee is $3.00.

Johns Hopkins University, **(School of Advanced International Studies)**, Registrar, 1740 Massachusetts Ave NW, Washington, DC 20036, 202-663-5708 (FAX: 202-663-5615). Hours: 9AM-4:45PM. Records go back to 1943. Alumni records are maintained here at the same phone number. Degrees granted: Masters; Doctorate.

Attendance and degree information available by phone, FAX, mail. Search requires name plus social security number, approximate years of attendance. No fee for information.

Transcripts available by phone, FAX, mail. Search requires name plus social security number, approximate years of attendance, signed release. Fee is $3.00.

Johnson & Wales University, Registrar, 8 Abbott Park Pl, Providence, RI 02903, 401-598-1000 (FAX: 401-598-2837). Hours: 8:30AM-4:30PM. Records go back to 1952. Inactive records: "Dept of Inactive Records," same address. Degrees granted: Associate; Bachelors; Masters. Adverse incident record source: Student Affairs, 401-598-1109.

Attendance and degree information available by FAX, mail. Search requires name plus signed release. Other helpful information: social security number, date of birth, approximate years of attendance. No fee for information.

Transcripts available by mail. Search requires name plus signed release. Other helpful information: social security number, date of birth, approximate years of attendance. Fee is $2.00. Expedited service available for $15.00.

Major credit cards accepted for payment.

Johnson & Wales University, (Branch Campus), Registrar, 701 E Bay St, BTC Box 1409, Charleston, SC 29403, 803-727-3032. Hours: 8:30AM-4:30PM. Records go back to 1984. Alumni Records Office: 8 Abbott Park Pl, Providence, RI 02903. Degrees granted: Associate; Bachelors.

Attendance and degree information available by phone, mail. Search requires name plus social security number, exact years of attendance. No fee for information.

Transcripts available by mail. Search requires name plus social security number, exact years of attendance, signed release. Fee is $2.00.

Johnson & Wales University, (Branch Campus), Registrar, 2428 Almeda Ave Stes 316-318, Norfolk, VA 23513, 804-853-3508. Hours: 8:30AM-4:30PM. Records go back to 1987. Alumni Records Office: 8 Abbott Park Pl, Providence, RI 02903. Degrees granted: Associate.

Attendance and degree information available by phone, mail. Search requires name plus social security number, exact years of attendance. No fee for information.

Transcripts available by mail. Search requires name plus social security number, exact years of attendance, signed release. Fee is $2.00.

Johnson & Wales University, (Branch Campus), Registrar, 1701 NE 127th St, North Miami, FL 33261, 305-892-7038 (FAX: 305-892-7019). Hours: 8:30AM-4:30PM. Records go back to 1991. Degrees granted: Associate. Adverse incident record source: Chris Magnan, 305-892-7006.

Attendance information available by phone, FAX, mail. Search requires name only. Other helpful information: social security number. No fee for information.

Degree information available by phone, FAX, mail. Search requires name only. Other helpful information: social security number. No fee for information.

Transcripts available by mail. Search requires name plus signed release. Other helpful information: social security number. Fee is $2.00.

Johnson & Wales University, (Branch Campus), Registrar, 616 W Lionshead Cir, Vail, CO 81657, 303-476-2993. Hours: 8AM-5PM. Records go back to 1993. Alumni Records Office: 8 Abbott Park Pl, Providence, RI 02903. Degrees granted: Associate.

Attendance and degree information available by phone, mail. Search requires name plus social security number, exact years of attendance. No fee for information.

Transcripts available by mail. Search requires name plus social security number, exact years of attendance, signed release. Fee is $2.00.

Johnson Bible College, Registrar, 7900 Johnson Dr, Knoxville, TN 37998, 615-579-2302 (FAX: 615-579-2337). Hours: 8AM-5PM. Records go back to 1893. Alumni records are maintained here also. Call 615-579-2353. Degrees granted: Associate; Bachelors; Masters.

Attendance and degree information available by phone, mail. Search requires name only. No fee for information.

Transcripts available by mail. Search requires name plus signed release. Fee is $2.00. Expedited service available for $5.00.

Johnson C. Smith University, Registrar, 100 Beatties Ford Rd, Charlotte, NC 28216, 704-378-1013. Hours: 8:15AM-5:15PM. Adverse incident record source: Mrs. Treva Norman, 704-378-1039.

Attendance information available by phone, FAX, mail. Search requires name only. Other helpful information: social security number, approximate years of attendance. No fee for information.

Degree information available by phone, FAX, mail. Search requires name only. Other helpful information: approximate years of attendance. No fee for information.

Transcripts available by mail. Search requires name plus signed release. Other helpful information: approximate years of attendance. Fee is $4.00.

Johnson County Community College, Records Office, 12345 College Blvd, Overland Park, KS 66210-1299, 913-469-8500. Hours: 8AM-5PM. Records go back 25 years. Degrees granted: Associate. Adverse incident record source: Security, 913-469-8500.

Attendance information available by phone, mail. Search requires name plus social security number, approximate years of attendance, signed release. Other helpful information: date of birth, exact years of attendance. No fee for information.

Degree information available by phone, mail. Search requires name plus social security number, signed release. Other helpful information: date of birth, approximate years of attendance. No fee for information.

Transcripts available by mail. Search requires name plus social security number, signed release. Other helpful information: date of birth, approximate years of attendance. Fee is $2.00.

Johnson State College, Registrar, Johnson, VT 05656, 802-635-2356 X229 (FAX: 802-635-2069). Hours: 8AM-5PM. Records go back to 1828. Alumni records are maintained here at the same phone number. Degrees granted: Bachelors; Masters.

Attendance and degree information available by phone, FAX, mail. Search requires name plus social security number, exact years of attendance. No fee for information.

Transcripts available by mail. Search requires name plus social security number, exact years of attendance, signed release. Fee is $5.00.

Johnson Technical Institute, Registrar, 3427 N Main Ave, Scranton, PA 18508-1495, 717-342-6404. Hours: 8AM-5PM. Records go back to 1920. Alumni records are maintained here also. Call 717-342-6404 X51. Degrees granted: Associate. Adverse incident record source: President, 717-342-6404 X12.

Attendance and degree information available by mail. Search requires name plus social security number, exact years of attendance, signed release. No fee for information.

Transcripts available by mail. Search requires name plus social security number, exact years of attendance, signed release. Fee is $2.00.

Johnson Technical Institute, **(Branch)**, Registrar, 200 Shady Lane, Philipsburg, PA 16866, 814-342-5680. Records are not housed here. They are located at Johnson Technical Institute, Registrar, 3427 N Main Ave, Scranton, PA 18508-1495.

Johnston Community College, Registrar, PO Box 2350, Smithfield, NC 27577, 919-934-3051 (FAX: 919-934-2823). Hours: 8AM-9PM M-Th; 8AM-5PM F. Records go back 25 years. Degrees granted: Associate.

Attendance and degree information available by phone, FAX, mail. Search requires name plus social security number. Other helpful information: date of birth, approximate years of attendance. No fee for information.

Transcripts available by FAX, mail. Search requires name plus social security number, signed release. Other helpful information: date of birth, approximate years of attendance. Fee is $1.00.

Joint Military Intelligence College, Registrar, Defense Intelligence Analysis Ctr, Washington, DC 20340-5485, 202-373-3344. Degrees granted: Masters.

Attendance information available by phone, FAX, mail. Search requires name plus social security number, exact years of attendance, signed release. Other helpful information: date of birth, approximate years of attendance. No fee for information.

Degree information available by phone, FAX, mail. Search requires name plus social security number, signed release. Other helpful information: date of birth. No fee for information.

Transcripts available by mail. Search requires name plus social security number, signed release. Other helpful information: date of birth. No fee for transcripts.

Joliet Junior College, JJC-Transcript Request, 1215 Houbolt Ave, Joliet, IL 60436-9352, 815-729-9020 X2242. Hours: 7:30AM-4PM. Records go back to 1910. Alumni records are maintained here also. Call 815-729-6620. Degrees granted: Associate. Special programs- Nursing Dept holds limited records for 5 years. Adverse incident record source: Current, Campus Police, 815-729-9020 X2234: Older records, Student Services, 815-729-9020 X2308

Attendance and degree information available by phone, mail. Search requires name plus social security number, approximate years of attendance. Other helpful information: date of birth. No fee for information.

Transcripts available by mail. Search requires name plus social security number, approximate years of attendance, signed release. Other helpful information: date of birth. Fee is $3.00.

Jones College, Registrar, 5353 Alrington Expy, Jacksonville, FL 32211-5588, 904-743-1122 (FAX: 904-743-1122). Hours: 8AM-5PM. Alumni records are maintained here at the same phone number. Degrees granted: Associate; Bachelors.

Attendance and degree information available by FAX, mail. Search requires name plus social security number, signed release. Other helpful information: date of birth, approximate years of attendance. No fee for information.

Transcripts available by FAX, mail. Search requires name plus social security number, signed release. Other helpful information: date of birth, approximate years of attendance. Fee is $2.00.

Jones College, **(Branch)**, Registrar, 5975 Sunset Dr Ste 100, South Miami, FL 33143, 904-743-1122. Records are not housed here. They are located at Jones College, Registrar, 5353 Alrington Expy, Jacksonville, FL 32211-5588.

Jones County Junior College, Registrar, 900 Court St, Ellisville, MS 39437, 601-477-4036 (FAX: 601-477-4017). Hours: 8AM-4:30PM. Records go back to 1911.

Attendance and degree information available by phone, FAX, mail. Search requires name plus social security number, signed release. Other helpful information: date of birth, approximate years of attendance. No fee for information.

Transcripts available by mail. Search requires name plus social security number, signed release. Other helpful information: date of birth, approximate years of attendance. Fee is $1.00.

Judge Advocate General's School, Registrar, 600 Massie Rd, Charlottesville, VA 22903-1781, 804-972-6310. Hours: 8AM-4:30PM. Alumni records are maintained here at the same phone number. Degrees granted: Bachelors; Masters.

Attendance and degree information available by phone, mail. Search requires name plus social security number. No fee for information.

Transcripts available by written request only. Search requires name plus social security number, signed release. Fee is $2.00.

Judson College, Registrar, 1151 N State St, Elgin, IL 60123, 708-695-2500 X2210 (FAX: 708-695-4410). Hours: 8AM-5PM. Records go back to 1963. Alumni records are maintained here also. Call 708-695-2500. Degrees granted: Bachelors.

Attendance and degree information available by phone, FAX, mail. Search requires name plus social security number, date of birth, exact years of attendance. No fee for information.

Transcripts available by mail. Search requires name plus social security number, date of birth, exact years of attendance, signed release. No fee for transcripts.

Judson College, Registrar, PO Box 120, Marion, AL 36756, 334-683-5129 (FAX: 334-683-5147). Hours: 8AM-5PM. Records go back to founding date. Degrees granted: Bachelors. Certification: Teacher.

Attendance and degree information available by FAX, mail. Search requires name plus approximate years of attendance, signed release. Other helpful information: social security number, date of birth, exact years of attendance. No fee for information.

Transcripts available by FAX, mail. Search requires name plus approximate years of attendance, signed release. Other helpful information: social security number, date of birth, exact years of attendance. Fee is $5.00.

Julliard School, Registrar, 60 Lincoln Center Plaza, New York, NY 10023-6590, 212-799-5000 (FAX: 212-724-0263). Hours: 9AM-5PM. Records go back to 1905. Alumni records are maintained here also. Call 212-799-5000 X344. Degrees granted: Bachelors; Masters; Doctorate.

Attendance and degree information available by FAX, mail. Search requires name only. No fee for information.

Transcripts available by FAX, mail. Search requires name only. Fee is $5.00.

Juniata College, Registrar, 1700 Moore St, Huntingdon, PA 16652, 814-643-4310 X270 (FAX: 814-643-6034). Hours: 8:30AM-5PM. Records go back to 1932. Alumni records are maintained here also. Call 814-643-4310. Degrees granted: Bachelors.

Attendance and degree information available by phone, FAX, mail. Search requires name plus social security number, exact years of attendance. No fee for information.

Transcripts available by FAX, mail. Search requires name plus social security number, exact years of attendance, signed release. No fee for transcripts.

K

KD Studio, Registrar, 2600 Stemmons Fwy #117, Dallas, TX 75207, 214-638-0484. Hours: 8AM-5PM. Records go back to 1979. Degrees granted: Associate.

Attendance and degree information available by mail. Search requires name plus social security number. No fee for information.

Transcripts available by written request only. Search requires name plus social security number, signed release. No fee for transcripts.

Kalamazoo College, Registrar, 1200 Academy St, Kalamazoo, MI 49007, 616-337-7204 (FAX: 616-337-7252). Hours: 8AM-5PM. Records go back to 1833. Degrees granted: Bachelors.

Attendance and degree information available by phone, FAX, mail. Search requires name plus social security number. Other helpful information: date of birth, approximate years of attendance. No fee for information.

Transcripts available by mail. Search requires name plus signed release. Other helpful information: social security number, date of birth, approximate years of attendance. Fee is $3.00. Expedited service available for $3.00.

Major credit cards accepted for payment.

Kalamazoo Valley Community College, Registrar, PO Box 4070, Kalamazoo, MI 49003-4070, 616-372-5281. Hours: 8AM-4:30PM M,T,Th,F; 8AM-7PM W. Records go back to 1969. Degrees granted: Associate.

Attendance and degree information available by phone, mail. Search requires name plus social security number, signed release. No fee for information.

Transcripts available by mail. Search requires name plus social security number, signed release. Fee is $1.00.

Kankakee Community College, Registrar, PO Box 888, Kankakee, IL 60901, 815-933-0246 (FAX: 815-933-0217). Hours: 8AM-5PM. Records go back to 1968. Alumni records are maintained here also. Call 815-933-0345. Degrees granted: Associate.

Attendance and degree information available by phone, FAX, mail. Search requires name plus social security number. No fee for information.

Transcripts available by mail. Search requires name plus social security number, exact years of attendance, signed release. Fee is $2.00. Expedited service available for $5.00.

Kansai Gaidai Hawaii College, Registrar, 5257 Kalanianaole Hwy, Honolulu, HI 96821, 808-377-5402 (FAX: 808-373-4754). Hours: 8AM-5PM. Records go back to 1948. Alumni records are maintained here at the same phone number. Degrees granted: Bachelors.

Attendance and degree information available by phone, mail. Search requires name plus social security number, exact years of attendance. No fee for information.

Transcripts available by mail. Search requires name plus social security number, exact years of attendance, signed release. Fee is $5.00.

Kansas City Art Institute, Registrar, 4415 Warwick Blvd, Kansas City, MO 64111-1874, 816-561-4852 X244 (FAX: 816-561-6404). Hours: 8:30AM-5PM. Records go back to 1930.

Alumni records are maintained here also. Call 816-561-4852. Degrees granted: Bachelors.

Attendance and degree information available by phone, FAX, mail. Search requires name only. Other helpful information: social security number, date of birth, approximate years of attendance. No fee for information.

Transcripts available by written request only. Search requires name plus signed release. Other helpful information: social security number, date of birth, approximate years of attendance. Official transcripts $2.00; student copies $.50. For expedited service pay mail fee. Official transcripts $2.00; student copies $.50. For expedited service pay mail fee.

Kansas City Kansas Community College, Registrar, 7250 State Ave, Kansas City, KS 66112, 913-334-1100 (FAX: 913-596-9609). Hours: 7:30AM-4:30PM. Records go back to founding date. Alumni records are maintained here also. Call 913-334-1100 X632. Degrees granted: Associate.

Attendance and degree information available by phone, FAX, mail. Search requires name plus social security number, signed release. Other helpful information: date of birth, approximate years of attendance. No fee for information.

Transcripts available by written request only. Search requires name plus social security number, signed release. Other helpful information: date of birth, approximate years of attendance. No fee for transcripts.

Major credit cards accepted for payment.

Kansas Newman College, Registrar, 3100 McCormick Ave, Wichita, KS 67213, 316-942-4291 X121 (FAX: 316-942-4483). Hours: 8AM-6:30PM M-Th; 8AM-5PM F; 7:30-10:30AM S. Degrees granted: Associate; Bachelors; Masters.

Attendance and degree information available by phone, FAX, mail. Search requires name plus social security number. No fee for information.

Transcripts available by FAX, mail. Search requires name plus social security number, signed release. Other helpful information: approximate years of attendance. Fee is $3.00.

Kansas State University, Registrar's Office, 118 Anderson Hall, Manhattan, KS 66506-0114, 913-532-6254 (FAX: 913-532-6393). Hours: 8AM-Noon, 1-5PM. Records go back to 1863. Alumni Records Office: 2323 Anderson Ave, Manhattan, KS 66502. Degrees granted: Associate; Bachelors; Masters; Doctorate.

Attendance and degree information available by phone, FAX, mail. Search requires name only. Other helpful information: social security number, date of birth, approximate years of attendance. No fee for information. Expedited service available for $3.00.

Transcripts available by FAX, mail. Search requires name plus signed release. Other helpful information: social security number, date of birth, approximate years of attendance. Fee is $3.00. Expedited service available for $3.00.

Major credit cards accepted for payment.

Kansas State University, (Salina College of Technology), Registrar, 2409 Scanlan Ave, Salina, KS 67401-8196, 913-826-2607 (FAX: 913-826-2936). Hours: 8AM-5PM. Records go back to 1965. Alumni records are maintained here also. Call 913-826-2632. Degrees granted: Associate; Bachelors.

Attendance and degree information available by phone, FAX, mail. Search requires name plus social security number, approximate years of attendance, signed release. No fee for information.

Transcripts available by FAX, mail. Search requires name plus social security number, approximate years of attendance, signed release. Fee is $3.00. Expedited service available for $10.00.

Kansas Wesleyan University, Registrar, 100 E Clafin, Salina, KS 67401, 913-827-5541 (FAX: 913-827-0927). Hours: 8:15AM-Noon, 1-5PM. Records go back to 1890s. Degrees granted: Associate; Bachelors; Masters. Certification: Education.

Attendance and degree information available by phone, FAX, mail. Search requires name plus social security number. Other helpful information: approximate years of attendance. No fee for information.

Transcripts available by FAX, mail. Search requires name plus social security number, signed release. Other helpful information: approximate years of attendance. Fee is $3.00. Expedited service available for $3.00.

Kapiolani Community College, Registrar, 4303 Diamond Head Rd, Honolulu, HI 96816, 808-734-9532. Hours: 8AM-4:30PM. Records go back to 1960. Degrees granted: Associate.

Attendance and degree information available by phone, mail. Search requires name plus social security number. Other helpful information: date of birth, approximate years of attendance. No fee for information.

Transcripts available by mail. Search requires name plus social security number, signed release. Other helpful information: date of birth, approximate years of attendance. Fee is $1.00.

Restrictions apply to phone confirmation. Fees under review.

Kaskaskia College, Registrar, 27210 College Rd, Centralia, IL 62801, 618-532-1981 X241 (FAX: 618-532-1990). Hours: 7:30AM-3:30PM. Records go back to 1965. Alumni records are maintained here also. Call 618-532-1981. Degrees granted: Associate.

Attendance and degree information available by phone, FAX, mail. Search requires name plus social security number. Other helpful information: date of birth, approximate years of attendance. No fee for information.

Transcripts available by mail. Search requires name plus social security number, signed release. Other helpful information: date of birth, approximate years of attendance. Fee is $2.00.

Katharine Gibbs School, Registrar, 126 Newbury St, Boston, MA 02116, 617-578-7100 (FAX: 617-262-6210). Hours: 8AM-5PM. Degrees granted: Associate.

Attendance information available by phone, FAX, mail. Search requires name only. Other helpful information: social security number, approximate years of attendance. No fee for information.

Degree information available by FAX, mail. Search requires name only. Other helpful information: social security number, approximate years of attendance. No fee for information.

Transcripts available by mail. Search requires name plus social security number, signed release. Other helpful information: approximate years of attendance. Fee is $5.00.

Katharine Gibbs School, Registrar, 142 East Ave, Norwalk, CT 06851, 203-838-4173 (FAX: 203-899-0788). Hours: 7:30AM-5PM. Degrees granted: Associate.

Attendance and degree information available by phone, mail. Search requires name plus approximate years of attendance. Other helpful information: social security number, exact years of attendance. No fee for information.

Transcripts available by written request only. Search requires name plus approximate years of attendance. Other helpful information: social security number, exact years of attendance. Fee is $3.00.

Katharine Gibbs School, Registrar, 178 Butler Ave, Providence, RI 02906, 401-861-1420 (FAX: 401-421-6230). Hours: 9AM-5PM. Records go back to 1911. Degrees granted.

Attendance and degree information available by phone, FAX, mail. Search requires name plus social security number, exact years of attendance. Other helpful information: date of birth, approximate years of attendance. No fee for information.

Transcripts available by FAX, mail. Search requires name plus social security number, exact years of attendance, signed release. Other helpful information: date of birth, approximate years of attendance. Fee is $5.00.

Katherine Gibbs School, Registrar, 535 Broad Hollow Rd, Melville, NY 11747, 516-293-2460 (FAX: 516-293-1276). Hours: 9AM-10PM. Records go back to 1915. Alumni records are maintained here also. Call 516-293-1024. Degrees granted: Associate.

Attendance and degree information available by phone, FAX, mail. Search requires name plus social security number, signed release. No fee for information.

Transcripts available by mail. Search requires name plus social security number, signed release. Fee is $5.00.

Katherine Gibbs School, Registrar, 33 Plymount St, Montclair, NJ 07042, 201-744-2010 (FAX: 201-744-2298). Hours: 8AM-10PM. Records go back to 1960. Alumni Records Office: 717 5th Ave, New York, NY 10022. Degrees granted: Associate.

Attendance and degree information available by FAX, mail. Search requires name plus social security number, approximate years of attendance, signed release. No fee for information.

Transcripts available by FAX, mail. Search requires name plus social security number, approximate years of attendance, signed release. Fee is $5.00.

Katherine Gibbs School, Registrar, 200 Park Ave, New York, NY 10166, 212-973-4954 (FAX: 212-338-9606). Hours: 8:30AM-8:30PM. Records go back to 1918. Alumni records are maintained here also. Call 212-745-9480. Degrees granted: Associate.

Attendance and degree information available by FAX, mail. Search requires name plus social security number, approximate years of attendance, signed release. No fee for information.

Transcripts available by FAX, mail. Search requires name plus social security number, approximate years of attendance, signed release. Fee is $5.00.

Major credit cards accepted for payment.

Katherine Gibbs School, (Branch Campus), Registrar, 80 Kingsbridge Rd, Piscataway, NJ 08854, 908-885-1580 (FAX: 908-885-1235). Alumni records are maintained here at the same phone number. Degrees granted: Associate.

Attendance and degree information available by FAX, mail. Search requires name plus social security number, exact years of attendance, signed release. No fee for information.

Transcripts available by FAX, mail. Search requires name plus social security number, exact years of attendance, signed release. Fee is $5.00.

Kauai Community College, Registrar, 3-1901 Kaumualii Hwy, Lihue, HI 96766, 808-245-8226 (FAX: 808-246-6377). Hours: 8AM-4:30PM. Records go back to 1952. Alumni records are maintained here also. Call 808-245-8271. Degrees granted: Associate.

Attendance and degree information available by phone, mail. Search requires name plus social security number, signed release. Other helpful information: date of birth, approximate years of attendance. No fee for information.

Transcripts available by mail. Search requires name plus social security number, signed release. Other helpful information: date of birth, approximate years of attendance. Fee is $1.00.

Kean College of New Jersey, Registrar, 1000 Morris Ave, Union, NJ 07083, 908-527-2445 (FAX: 908-527-0423). Hours: 8:30AM-4:30PM. Records go back to 1960. Alumni records are maintained here also. Call 908-527-2526. Degrees granted: Bachelors; Masters. Adverse incident record source: Dean of Students, 908-527-2190.

Attendance and degree information available by phone, FAX, mail. Search requires name plus social security number, signed release. No fee for information.

Transcripts available by FAX, mail. Search requires name plus social security number, signed release. Fee is $5.00.

Keene State College, Registrar, 229 Main St, Keene, NH 03431, 603-358-2321. Hours: 9AM-4:30PM. Records go back to 1909. Degrees granted: Associate; Bachelors; Masters.

Attendance and degree information available by phone, mail. Search requires name plus social security number. Other helpful information: date of birth, approximate years of attendance. No fee for information.

Transcripts available by mail. Search requires name plus social security number, signed release. Other helpful information: date of birth, approximate years of attendance. Fee is $2.00. Expedited service available for $12.00.

Kehilath Yakov Rabbinical Seminary, Registrar, 206 Wilson St, Brooklyn, NY 11211, 718-963-3940 (FAX: 718-387-8586). Hours: 9AM-5:30PM. Degrees granted: Bachelors.

Attendance and degree information available by FAX, mail. Search requires name plus social security number, approximate years of attendance, signed release. No fee for information.

Transcripts available by FAX, mail. Search requires name plus social security number, approximate years of attendance, signed release. No fee for transcripts.

Keiser College, Registrar, 1500 NW 49th St, Fort Lauderdale, FL 33309-3779, 305-776-4456. Hours: 8AM-5PM M-Th, 8AM-Noon F. Records go back to 1979. Degrees granted: Associate. Adverse incident record source: Registrar, 305-776-4456.

Attendance and degree information available by mail. Search requires name plus social security number, exact years of attendance, signed release. No fee for information.

Transcripts available by mail. Search requires name plus social security number, exact years of attendance, signed release. Fee is $5.00.

Keiser College, (Branch), Registrar, 701 S Babcock St, Melbourne, FL 32901-1461, 407-255-2255. Hours: 7:30AM-8PM. Records go back to 1977.

Attendance and degree information available by mail. Search requires name plus social security number, exact years of attendance, signed release. No fee for information.

Transcripts available by mail. Search requires name plus social security number, exact years of attendance, signed release. First transcript is free. Additional ones are $5.00 each.

Keiser College, (Branch), Registrar, 1605 E Plaza Dr, Tallahassee, FL 32308, 904-942-9494 (FAX: 904-942-9497). Alumni records are maintained here at the same phone number. Degrees granted: Associate.

Attendance information available by mail. Search requires name only. Other helpful information: approximate years of attendance. No fee for information.

Degree information available by FAX, mail. Search requires name plus social security number, signed release. Other helpful information: date of birth, approximate years of attendance. No fee for information.

Transcripts available by FAX, mail. Search requires name plus social security number, signed release. Other helpful information: date of birth, approximate years of attendance. Fee is $5.00. Major credit cards accepted for payment.

Keller Graduate School of Management, Registrar, 10 S Riverside Plaza, Chicago, IL 60606, 312-454-0880 (FAX: 312-454-6103). Hours: 9AM-6PM M-Th, 9AM-5PM F. Records go back to 1972. Alumni records are maintained here at the same phone number. Degrees granted: Masters. Adverse incident record source: Registrar, 708-574-1960.

Attendance and degree information available by phone, mail. Search requires name plus social security number, exact years of attendance. No fee for information.

Transcripts available by mail. Search requires name plus social security number, exact years of attendance, signed release. Fee is $2.00.

Keller Graduate School of Management, (East Valley Center), Registrar, 1201 S Alma School Rd Ste 5450, Mesa, AZ 85210, 602-827-1511. Records are not housed here. They are located at Keller Graduate School of Management, (Phoenix/Northwest Center), Registrar, 2149 W Dunlap Ave, Phoenix, AZ 85021.

Keller Graduate School of Management, (Kansas City Downtown), Registrar, City Center Square, 1100 Main St, Kansas City, MO 64105-2112, 816-221-1300. Records are not housed here. They are located at Keller Graduate School of Management, Registrar, 10 S Riverside Plaza, Chicago, IL 60606.

Keller Graduate School of Management, (Kansas City South), Registrar, 11224 Holmes Rd, Kansas City, MO 64131, 816-941-2224. Records are not housed here. They are located at Keller Graduate School of Management, Registrar, 10 S Riverside Plaza, Chicago, IL 60606.

Keller Graduate School of Management, (Milwaukee Center), Registrar, 100 E Wisconsin Ave #2550, Milwaukee, WI 53202, 414-278-7677. Records are not housed here. They are located at Keller Graduate School of Management, Registrar, 10 S Riverside Plaza, Chicago, IL 60606.

Keller Graduate School of Management, (North Suburban Center), Registrar, Tri State Intl Office Ctr, Bldg 25 Ste 13, Lincolnshire, IL 60069-4460, 708-940-7768. Records are not housed here. They are located at Keller Graduate School of Management, Registrar, 10 S Riverside Plaza, Chicago, IL 60606.

Keller Graduate School of Management, (Northwest Suburban Center), Registrar, 1051 Perimeter Dr, Schaumburg, IL 60173-5009, 708-574-1960. Hours: 9AM-6PM M-Th, 9AM-5PM F. Records go back to 1971. Degrees granted: Masters.

Attendance and degree information available by phone, mail. Search requires name plus social security number, exact years of attendance. No fee for information.

Transcripts available by mail. Search requires name plus social security number, exact years of attendance, signed release. Fee is $2.00.

Keller Graduate School of Management, **(Phoenix/Northwest Center)**, Registrar, 2149 W Dunlap Ave, Phoenix, AZ 85021, 602-870-0117. Hours: 8:30AM-8PM M-Th, 8:30AM-5PM, Sat by appointment. Records go back to 1973. Alumni records are maintained here also. Call 602-870-0117. Degrees granted: Masters. Adverse incident record source: Registrar, 602-870-0117.

Attendance and degree information available by phone, mail. Search requires name plus social security number, exact years of attendance. No fee for information.

Transcripts available by mail. Search requires name plus social security number, exact years of attendance, signed release. Fee is $2.00.

Keller Graduate School of Management, **(South Suburban Center)**, Registrar, 15255 S 94th Ave, Orland Park, IL 60462-3823, 708-460-9580. Records are not housed here. They are located at Keller Graduate School of Management, Registrar, 10 S Riverside Plaza, Chicago, IL 60606.

Keller Graduate School of Management, **(Waukesha Center)**, Registrar, 20935 Swenson Dr, Waukesha, WI 53186, 414-798-9889. Records are not housed here. They are located at Keller Graduate School of Management, Registrar, 10 S Riverside Plaza, Chicago, IL 60606.

Keller Graduate School of Management, **(West Suburban Center)**, Registrar, 1101 31st St, Downers Grove, IL 60515-5515, 708-969-6624. Records are not housed here. They are located at Keller Graduate School of Management, Registrar, 10 S Riverside Plaza, Chicago, IL 60606.

Kellogg Community College, Registrar, 450 North Ave, Battle Creek, MI 49017-3397, 616-965-3931 X2612. Hours: 9AM-7PM M-Th, 9AM-4:30PM F. Records go back to 1956. Degrees granted: Associate.

Attendance and degree information available by phone, mail. Search requires name plus social security number, date of birth, approximate years of attendance, signed release. No fee for information.

Transcripts available by mail. Search requires name plus social security number, date of birth, approximate years of attendance, signed release. Fee is $3.00.

Kelsey-Jenney College, Registrar, 201 "A" St, San Diego, CA 92101, 619-549-5070 (FAX: 619-549-2027). Hours: 7:30AM-9:40PM. Records go back to 1960. Degrees granted: Associate.

Attendance and degree information available by FAX, mail. Search requires name plus social security number, approximate years of attendance, signed release. Other helpful information: date of birth, exact years of attendance. No fee for information.

Transcripts available by FAX, mail. Search requires name plus social security number, approximate years of attendance, signed release. Other helpful information: date of birth, exact years of attendance. Fee is $3.00.

FAX and mail request by student only.

Kemper Military School and College, Registrar, 701 Third St, Boonville, MO 65233, 816-882-5623 (FAX: 816-882-3332). Hours: 7:30AM-5PM. Records go back 70 years. Alumni records are maintained here at the same phone number. Degrees granted: Associate.

Attendance and degree information available by phone, FAX, mail. Search requires name plus exact years of attendance, signed release. Other helpful information: social security number, date of birth, approximate years of attendance. No fee for information.

Transcripts available by mail. Search requires name plus exact years of attendance, signed release. Other helpful information: social security number, date of birth, approximate years of attendance. Fee is $5.00.

Kenai Peninsula College, Registrar, 34820 College Dr, Soldotna, AK 99669, 907-262-0300 (FAX: 907-262-9280). Records are not housed here. They are located at University of Alaska Anchorage, Records Dept., 3211 Providence Dr, Anchorage, AK 99508-8038.

Kendall College, Registrar, 2408 Orrington Ave, Evanston, IL 60201, 708-866-1325 (FAX: 708-866-6842). Hours: 8AM-4:30PM. Records go back to 1960. Alumni records are maintained here at the same phone number. Degrees granted: Associate; Bachelors.

Attendance and degree information available by phone, mail. Search requires name plus social security number, exact years of attendance. Other helpful information: date of birth, approximate years of attendance. No fee for information.

Transcripts available by mail. Search requires name plus social security number, exact years of attendance, signed release. Other helpful information: date of birth, approximate years of attendance. Fee is $3.00.

Major credit cards accepted for payment.

Kendall College of Art and Design, Registrar, 111 Division Ave N, Grand Rapids, MI 49503, 616-451-2787 (FAX: 616-451-9867). Hours: 8AM-5PM. Records go back to founding date. Degrees granted: Bachelors.

Attendance and degree information available by written request only. Search requires name plus social security number, date of birth, exact years of attendance. No fee for information.

Transcripts available by mail. Search requires name plus social security number, date of birth, exact years of attendance, signed release. Fee is $5.00.

Major credit cards accepted for payment.

Kennebec Valley Technical College, Registrar's Office, 92 Western Ave, Fairfield, ME 04937-1367, 207-453-9762 (FAX: 207-453-5010). Hours: 9AM-Noon, 1-4PM. Records go back to founding date. Degrees granted: Associate.

Attendance information available by phone, FAX, mail. Search requires name plus social security number, approximate years of attendance, signed release. Other helpful information: date of birth, exact years of attendance. No fee for information.

Degree information available by phone, FAX, mail. Search requires name plus social security number, approximate years of attendance, signed release. Other helpful information: date of birth. No fee for information.

Transcripts available by written request only. Search requires name plus social security number, approximate years of attendance, signed release. Other helpful information: date of birth, exact years of attendance. Fee is $3.00. Expedited service available for $10.00.

Major credit cards accepted for payment.

Kennedy-King College, Registrar, 6800 S Wentworth Ave, Chicago, IL 60621, 312-602-5062 (FAX: 312-602-5247). Hours: 8:30AM-7PM M-Th, 8:30AM-5PM F. Degrees granted: Associate. Adverse incident record source: Security Office, 312-602-5149.

Attendance and degree information available by FAX, mail. Search requires name plus social security number, date of birth, exact years of attendance, signed release. Other helpful information: approximate years of attendance. No fee for information.

Transcripts available by FAX, mail. Search requires name plus social security number, date of birth, exact years of attendance, signed release. Other helpful information: approximate years of attendance. Fee is $5.00. Expedited service available for $10.00. Major credit cards accepted for payment.

Kennesaw State College, Registrar, PO Box 444, Marietta, GA 30061, 404-423-6200 (FAX: 404-423-6541) Hours: 8AM-7PM M-Th; 8AM-5PM F. Records go back to 1964. Degrees granted: Associate; Bachelors; Masters. Adverse incident record source: 404-423-6666.

Attendance and degree information available by phone, FAX, mail. Search requires name plus social security number, signed release. Other helpful information: date of birth, approximate years of attendance. No fee for information.

Transcripts available by FAX, mail. Search requires name plus social security number, signed release. Other helpful information: date of birth, approximate years of attendance. No fee for transcripts.

Kenrick-Glennon Seminary, Registrar, 5200 Glennon Dr, St Louis, MO 63119-4399, 314-644-0266 (FAX: 314-644-3079). Hours: 8AM-3:30PM. Degrees granted: Masters.

Attendance and degree information available by phone, FAX, mail. Search requires name only. Other helpful information: approximate years of attendance. No fee for information.

Transcripts available by FAX, mail. Search requires name plus signed release. Other helpful information: approximate years of attendance. Fee is $5.00.

Kent State University, Registrar, PO Box 5190, Kent, OH 44242, 216-672-3131 (FAX: 216-672-4836). Hours: 8AM-5PM. Records go back 75 years. Alumni records are maintained here also. Call 216-672-5368. Degrees granted: Associate; Bachelors; Masters; Doctorate. Adverse incident record source: Student Conduct, 216-672-4054.

Attendance and degree information available by phone, FAX, mail. Search requires name only. Other helpful information: social security number, date of birth, approximate years of attendance. No fee for information.

Transcripts available by FAX, mail. Search requires name plus social security number, signed release. Other helpful information: date of birth, approximate years of attendance. No fee for transcripts.

Kent State University, (Ashtabula), Registrar, Ms. Bates, 3325 W 13th St, Ashtabula, OH 44004, 216-964-4216 (FAX: 216-964-4269). Hours: 8AM-5PM. Records go back to 1921. Degrees granted: Associate; Bachelors.

Attendance information available by phone, FAX, mail. Search requires name plus social security number, date of birth, signed release. Other helpful information: approximate years of attendance. No fee for information.

Degree information available by mail. Search requires name plus social security number, date of birth, signed release. Other helpful information: approximate years of attendance. No fee for information.

Transcripts available by FAX, mail. Search requires name plus social security number, date of birth, signed release. Other helpful information: approximate years of attendance. No fee for transcripts.

Kent State University, (East Liverpool), Registrar, 400 E Fourth St, East Liverpool, OH 43920, 216-385-3805 (FAX: 216-385-3857). Hours: 8AM-8PM M-Th, 8AM-5PM F. Records go back to 1963. Alumni records are maintained here at the same phone number. Degrees granted: Associate.

Attendance and degree information available by phone, FAX, mail. Search requires name plus social security number, approximate years of attendance, signed release. No fee for information.

Transcripts available by FAX, mail. Search requires name plus social security number, approximate years of attendance, signed release. No fee for transcripts.

Kent State University, (Geuaga), Registrar, 14111 Claridon-Troy Rd, Burton Township, OH 44021, 216-834-4187 (FAX: 216-834-8846). Hours: 8AM-8PM M-Th, 8AM-5PM F, 8AM-2PM Sat. Records go back to 1960. Degrees granted: Associate.

Attendance and degree information available by FAX, mail. Search requires name plus social security number, approximate years of attendance, signed release. No fee for information.

Transcripts available by FAX, mail. Search requires name plus social security number, approximate years of attendance, signed release. No fee for transcripts.

Kent State University, (Salem), Registrar, 2491 State Rte 45 S, Salem, OH 44460, 216-332-0361 (FAX: 216-332-9256). Hours: 9AM-8PM M, 9AM-6PM T-Th, 9AM-4:30PM F. Records go back to 1965. Degrees granted: Associate; Bachelors.

Attendance and degree information available by phone, FAX, mail. Search requires name plus social security number, approximate years of attendance. No fee for information.

Transcripts available by FAX, mail. Search requires name plus social security number, approximate years of attendance, signed release. No fee for transcripts.

Kent State University, (Stark), Registrar, 6000 Frank Ave NW, Canton, OH 44720, 216-499-9600 (FAX: 216-494-6121). Hours: 8AM-7:30PM M-Th, 8AM-5PM F. Records go back to 1950. Degrees granted: Associate; Bachelors. Adverse incident record source: Business, 216-499-9600 X231.

Attendance and degree information available by phone, FAX, mail. Search requires name plus social security number, approximate years of attendance, signed release. No fee for information.

Transcripts available by FAX, mail. Search requires name plus social security number, signed release. No fee for transcripts.

Kent State University, (Trumbull), Registrar, 4314 Mahoning Ave NW, Warren, OH 44483, 216-847-0571 (FAX: 216-847-6172). Hours: 8AM-6PM M-Th, 8AM-5PM F, 9AM-1PM Sat. Records go back to 1960. Degrees granted: Associate.

Attendance information available by phone, FAX, mail. Search requires name plus social security number, approximate years of attendance. No fee for information.

Degree information available by phone, FAX, mail. Search requires name plus social security number. No fee for information.

Transcripts available by mail. Search requires name plus social security number, signed release. No fee for transcripts.

Kent State University, **(Tuscarawas)**, Registrar, 330 University Dr NE, New Philadelphia, OH 44663-9447, 216-339-3391 (FAX: 216-339-3321). Hours: 8AM-8PM M-Th; 8AM-5PM F and when not in session. Records go back to 1962. Degrees granted: Associate. Adverse incident record source: Same as above.

Attendance and degree information available by phone, FAX, mail. Search requires name plus social security number. Other helpful information: date of birth, approximate years of attendance. No fee for information.

Transcripts available by mail. Search requires name plus social security number, signed release. Other helpful information: date of birth, approximate years of attendance. No fee for transcripts.

Kentucky Christian College, Registrar, 100 Academic Pkwy, Grayson, KY 41143-2205, 606-474-3212 (FAX: 606-474-3154). Hours: 8:30AM-4:30PM. Records go back to founding date. Degrees granted: Associate; Bachelors.

Attendance and degree information available by phone, FAX, mail. Search requires name only. Other helpful information: social security number, date of birth, approximate years of attendance. No fee for information.

Transcripts available by FAX, mail. Search requires name plus signed release. Other helpful information: social security number, date of birth, approximate years of attendance. Fee is $2.00.

Kentucky College of Business, Registrar, 628 E Main St, Lexington, KY 40508, 606-253-0621 (FAX: 606-233-3054). Hours: 8AM-4:30PM. Records go back to 1941. Degrees granted: Associate.

Attendance and degree information available by phone, FAX, mail. Search requires name plus social security number, date of birth, exact years of attendance. No fee for information.

Transcripts available by mail. Search requires name plus social security number, date of birth, exact years of attendance, signed release. Fee is $6.00.

Kentucky College of Business, **(Branch)**, Registrar, 115 E Lexington Ave, Danville, KY 40422, 606-236-6991 (FAX: 703-986-0559). Records are not housed here. They are located at National Business College, Registrar, PO Box 6400, Roanoke, VA 24017.

Kentucky College of Business, **(Branch)**, Registrar, 7627 Tanners Lane, Florence, KY 41042, 606-525-6510. Records are not housed here. They are located at National Business College, Registrar, PO Box 6400, Roanoke, VA 24017.

Kentucky College of Business, **(Branch)**, Registrar, 3950 Dixie Hwy, Louisville, KY 40216, 502-447-7665. Records are not housed here. They are located at National Business College, Registrar, PO Box 6400, Roanoke, VA 24017.

Kentucky College of Business, **(Branch)**, Registrar, 198 S Mayo Trail, Pikeville, KY 41501, 606-432-5477. Records are not housed here. They are located at National Business College, Registrar, PO Box 6400, Roanoke, VA 24017.

Kentucky College of Business, **(Branch)**, Registrar, 139 Killarney Lane, Richmond, KY 40475, 606-623-8956. Records go back 7 years. Degrees granted: Associate.

Attendance information available by phone, mail. Search requires name plus social security number. Other helpful information: approximate years of attendance. No fee for information.

Degree information available by phone, FAX, mail. Search requires name plus social security number, approximate years of attendance. Other helpful information: date of birth. No fee for information.

Transcripts available by written request only. Search requires name plus social security number, date of birth, approximate years of attendance, signed release. Fee is $5.00.

Kentucky State University, Registrar, E Main St, Frankfort, KY 40601, 502-227-6340 (FAX: 502-227-6239). Hours: 8AM-4:30PM. Degrees granted: Associate; Bachelors; Masters.

Attendance information available by phone, FAX, mail. Search requires name plus social security number, exact years of attendance. No fee for information.

Degree information available by phone, FAX. Search requires name plus signed release. Other helpful information: social security number, date of birth, approximate years of attendance. No fee for information.

Transcripts available by FAX. Search requires name plus signed release. Other helpful information: social security number, date of birth, approximate years of attendance. Fee is $3.00.

Kentucky Wesleyan College, Registrar, 3000 Frederica St, PO Box 1039, Owensboro, KY 42302-1039, 502-926-3111 (FAX: 502-926-3196). Hours: 8AM-5PM. Records go back to 1900. Degrees granted: Associate; Bachelors. Adverse incident record source: Student Life, 502-926-3111.

Attendance and degree information available by phone, FAX, mail. Search requires name only. Other helpful information: social security number, date of birth, approximate years of attendance. No fee for information.

Transcripts available by mail. Search requires name plus signed release. Other helpful information: social security number, date of birth, approximate years of attendance. Fee is $3.00. Expedited service available for $3.00.

Any possible name changes helpful.

Kenyon College, Registrar, Gambier, OH 43022-9623, 614-427-5121 (FAX: 614-427-4610). Hours: 8:30AM-4:30PM. Records go back to 1930. Alumni records are maintained here also. Call 614-427-5147. Degrees granted: Bachelors.

Attendance information available by FAX, mail. Search requires name plus date of birth, signed release. Other helpful information: social security number, approximate years of attendance. No fee for information.

Degree information available by FAX, mail. Search requires name plus social security number, date of birth, signed release. Other helpful information: approximate years of attendance. No fee for information.

Transcripts available by FAX, mail. Search requires name plus social security number, date of birth, approximate years of attendance, signed release. Fee is $3.00.

Kettering College of Medical Arts, Registrar, 3737 Southern Blvd, Kettering, OH 45429, 513-296-7289 (FAX: 513-296-4238). Hours: 9AM-4PM M,Th; 10AM-6PM T; 9AM-Noon F. Records go back to 1967. Alumni Records Office: Alumni Association, 3535 Southern Blvd, Kettering, OH 45429. Degrees granted: Associate.

Attendance and degree information available by phone, FAX, mail. Search requires name plus social security number, exact years of attendance. No fee for information.

Transcripts available by written request only. Search requires name plus signed release. Other helpful information: social security number. Fee is $5.00.

They do emergency transcripts if signature FAXed with hard copy to follow.

Keuka College, Registrar, Keuka Park, NY 14478, 315-536-5204 (FAX: 315-536-5216). Hours: 8:30AM-4:30PM. Degrees granted: Bachelors.

Attendance and degree information available by phone, FAX, mail. Search requires name only. Other helpful information: social security number, approximate years of attendance. No fee for information.

Transcripts available by mail. Search requires name plus signed release. Other helpful information: social security number, approximate years of attendance. Fee is $5.00. Expedited service available for $5.00.

Expedite: include prepaid envelope.

Keystone Junior College, Registrar, PO Box 50, La Plume, PA 18440-0200, 717-945-5141 X2301. Hours: 9AM-5PM. Records go back to 1868. Alumni records are maintained here also. Call 717-945-5141. Degrees granted: Associate.

Attendance and degree information available by phone, mail. Search requires name plus social security number, exact years of attendance. No fee for information.

Transcripts available by mail. Search requires name plus social security number, exact years of attendance, signed release. Fee is $3.00.

Kilgore College, Registrar, 1100 Broadway, Kilgore, TX 75662-3299, 903-984-8531 (FAX: 903-983-8607). Hours: 8AM-4:30PM. Degrees granted: Associate.

Attendance and degree information available by phone, FAX, mail. Search requires name plus social security number, date of birth, exact years of attendance. No fee for information.

Transcripts available by FAX, mail. Search requires name plus social security number, date of birth, exact years of attendance, signed release. No fee for transcripts.

Kilian Community College, Registrar, 224 S Phillips Ave, Sioux Falls, SD 57102, 605-336-1711 (FAX: 605-336-2606). Hours: 8AM-5PM. Records go back to 1977. Degrees granted: Associate.

Attendance and degree information available by phone, FAX, mail. Search requires name plus signed release. Other helpful information: social security number, date of birth, approximate years of attendance. Fee is $2.00.

Transcripts available by mail. Search requires name plus social security number, signed release. Other helpful information: date of birth, approximate years of attendance. Fee is $2.00.

King College, Registrar, 1350 King College Rd, Bristol, TN 37620, 615-652-4739 (FAX: 615-968-4456). Hours: 8AM-5PM. Records go back to 1800s. Alumni records are maintained here also. Call 615-652-4717. Degrees granted: Bachelors.

Attendance and degree information available by phone, FAX, mail. Search requires name only. No fee for information.

Transcripts available by mail. Search requires name only. No fee for transcripts.

King's College, Registrar, Lodge Rd, Briarcliff Manor, NY 10510, 914-941-7200 (FAX: 914-941-9460). Hours: 8:30AM-5PM. Records go back to 1976. Degrees granted: Associate; Bachelors. Certification: Teacher.

Attendance and degree information available by phone, FAX, mail. Search requires name plus social security number, date of birth, approximate years of attendance. No fee for information.

Transcripts available by mail. Search requires name plus social security number, approximate years of attendance, signed release. Other helpful information: date of birth. Fee is $5.00. Expedited service available for $11.50.

King's College, Registrar, 133 N River St, Wilkes-Barre, PA 18711, 717-826-5870. Hours: 8:30AM-4:30PM. Records go back to 1946. Alumni records are maintained here also. Call 717-826-5900. Degrees granted: Bachelors. Adverse incident record source: Registrar, 717-826-5870.

Attendance and degree information available by phone, mail. Search requires name plus social security number, date of birth, exact years of attendance, signed release. No fee for information.

Transcripts available by mail. Search requires name plus social security number, date of birth, exact years of attendance, signed release. Fee is $5.00.

Kings River Community College, Registrar, 995 N Reed Ave, Reedley, CA 93654, 209-638-3641. Hours: 8AM-4PM. Records go back to 1926. Degrees granted: Associate. Adverse incident record source: Dean of Students: Campus Police

Attendance information available by phone, mail. Search requires name plus social security number. Other helpful information: date of birth, approximate years of attendance. No fee for information.

Degree information available by phone, mail. Search requires name plus social security number. Other helpful information: date of birth, approximate years of attendance. No fee for information.

Transcripts available by mail. Search requires name plus social security number, signed release. Other helpful information: date of birth, approximate years of attendance. Fee is $2.00. Expedited service available for $2.00.

Kingsborough Community College, Registrar, 2001 Oriental Blvd, Manhattan Beach, Brooklyn, NY 11235, 718-368-5000. Hours: 9AM-4:45PM. Records go back to 1960. Alumni records are maintained here at the same phone number. Degrees granted: Associate.

Attendance and degree information available by mail. Search requires name plus social security number, approximate years of attendance, signed release. No fee for information.

Transcripts available by mail. Search requires name plus social security number, approximate years of attendance, signed release. Fee is $4.00.

Kingwood College, Registrar, 20000 Kingwood Dr, Kingwood, TX 77339, 713-359-1600. Hours: 8AM-4PM. Records go back to 1960s. Alumni records are maintained here at the same phone number. Degrees granted: Associate.

Attendance and degree information available by phone, mail. Search requires name plus social security number. Other helpful information: approximate years of attendance. No fee for information.

Transcripts available by written request only. Search requires name plus social security number, signed release. Other helpful information: approximate years of attendance. No fee for transcripts.

Kirksville College of Osteopathic Medicine, Registrar, 800 W Jefferson Ave, Kirksville, MO 63501, 816-626-2356 (FAX: 816-626-2815). Hours: 8AM-5PM. Records go back to 1892. Degrees granted: Doctorate.

Attendance and degree information available by phone, FAX, mail. Search requires name only. Other helpful information: social security number, approximate years of attendance. No fee for information.

Transcripts available by FAX, mail. Search requires name plus signed release. Other helpful information: social security number, approximate years of attendance. Fee is $2.00.

Kirkwood Community College, Office of the Registrar, 6301 Kirkwood Blvd SW, PO Box 2068, Cedar Rapids, IA 52406-2068, 319-398-5603 (FAX: 319-398-4928). Hours: 8AM-6PM M-Th; 8AM-5PM F. Records go back to 1966. Alumni records are maintained here at the same phone number. Degrees granted: Associate. Special programs- Community Relation (noncredit), 319-398-5412: Truck Driving, 319-398-5690: Skills Center, 319-398-5455: GED/HS Completion, 319-366-0142.

Attendance and degree information available by phone, FAX, mail. Search requires name plus social security number, date of birth. Other helpful information: approximate years of attendance. No fee for information.

Transcripts available by phone, FAX, mail. Search requires name plus social security number, date of birth, signed release. Other helpful information: approximate years of attendance. No fee for transcripts.

Student only may phone for transcript. Major credit cards accepted for payment.

Kirtland Community College, Registrar, 10775 N St Helen Rd, Roscommon, MI 48653, 517-275-5121 X248 (FAX: 517-275-8210). Hours: 8AM-4:30PM. Alumni records are maintained here also. Call 517-275-5121 X259. Degrees granted: Associate.

Attendance and degree information available by FAX, mail. Search requires name plus social security number, signed release. No fee for information.

Transcripts available by mail. Search requires name plus social security number, signed release. Fee is $3.00.

Major credit cards accepted for payment.

Kishwaukee College, Admissions, Registration & Records, 21193 Malta Rd, Malta, IL 60150, 815-825-2086 X218 (FAX: 815-825-2086 X579). Hours: 7:30AM-7PM M-Th; 7:30AM-5PM F. Records go back 27 years. Degrees granted: Associate; GED.

Attendance information available by phone, FAX, mail. Search requires name only. Other helpful information: social security number, date of birth, approximate years of attendance. No fee for information.

Degree information available by phone, FAX, mail. Search requires name only. Other helpful information: social security number, date of birth, approximate years of attendance. No fee for information.

Transcripts available by FAX, mail. Search requires name plus signed release. Other helpful information: social security number, date of birth, approximate years of attendance. Fee is $3.00.

Need previous name. Major credit cards accepted for payment.

Knowledge Systems Institute, Registrar, 3420 Main St, Skokie, IL 60076, 708-679-3135. Hours: 10:30AM-6:30PM. Records go back to 1989. Degrees granted: Masters. Adverse incident record source: Registrar, 708-679-3135.

Attendance and degree information available by mail. Search requires name plus social security number, exact years of attendance, signed release. No fee for information.

Transcripts available by mail. Search requires name plus social security number, exact years of attendance, signed release. Fee is $3.00.

Knox College, Registrar, Galesburg, IL 61401, 309-343-0112 X205. Hours: 8AM-4:30PM. Records go back to 1837. Degrees granted: Bachelors.

Attendance and degree information available by phone, mail. Search requires name plus exact years of attendance. No fee for information.

Transcripts available by mail. Search requires name plus exact years of attendance, signed release. Fee is $3.00.

Knoxville Business College, Registrar, 720 N Fifth Ave, Knoxville, TN 37917, 615-524-3043 X45. Hours: 8AM-5PM. Records go back to 1882. Degrees granted: Associate.

Attendance and degree information available by phone, mail. Search requires name plus social security number, date of birth, exact years of attendance. No fee for information.

Transcripts available by mail. Search requires name plus social security number, date of birth, exact years of attendance, signed release. No fee for transcripts.

Knoxville College, **(Morristown)**, Registrar, 901 College St, Knoxville, TN 37921, 615-524-6577 X510 (FAX: 615-524-6686). Hours: 8AM-5PM. Records go back to 1875. Degrees granted: Bachelors. Adverse incident record source: Dean of Students, 615-524-6551.

Attendance and degree information available by phone, mail. Search requires name plus social security number, date of birth, exact years of attendance. No fee for information.

Transcripts available by mail. Search requires name plus social security number, date of birth, exact years of attendance, signed release. Fee is $3.00.

Kodiak College, Registrar, 117 Benny Benson Dr, Kodiak, AK 99615, 907-486-4161 X44 (FAX: 907-486-4166). Hours: 8AM-5PM. Records go back to 1970. Degrees granted: Associate.

Attendance and degree information available by phone, FAX, mail. Search requires name plus social security number, exact years of attendance, signed release. No fee for information.

Transcripts available by mail. Search requires name plus social security number, exact years of attendance, signed release. Fee is $4.00.

Kutztown University of Pennslyvania, Registrar,s Office, Kutztown, PA 19530, 610-683-4485. Hours: 8AM-4:30PM. Records go back to 1867. Alumni records are maintained here also. Call 610-683-4110. Degrees granted: Bachelors; Masters. Adverse incident record source: Public Safety, 610-683-4002.

Attendance and degree information available by phone, mail. Search requires name plus social security number, exact years of attendance. No fee for information.

Transcripts available by mail. Search requires name plus social security number, exact years of attendance, signed release. Transcript $2.00 or $4.00.

L

L.I.F.E Bible College, Registrar, 1100 Covina Blvd, San Dimas, CA 91773, 909-599-5433 X304 (FAX: 909-599-6690). Hours: 8AM-5PM. Records go back to 1930. Degrees granted: Associate; Bachelors.

Attendance and degree information available by phone, FAX, mail. Search requires name plus social security number, date of birth, approximate years of attendance, signed release. No fee for information.

Transcripts available by mail. Search requires name plus social security number, date of birth, approximate years of attendance, signed release. First transcript is free. Additional ones are $3.00 each.

LDS Business College, Registrar, 411 E S Temple St, Salt Lake City, UT 84111, 801-524-8140 (FAX: 801-524-1900). Hours: 8AM-5PM. Records go back to 1932. Prior records in archives. Degrees granted: Associate.

Attendance and degree information available by phone, FAX, mail. Search requires name plus approximate years of attendance. Other helpful information: social security number, date of birth. No fee for information.

Transcripts available by FAX, mail. Search requires name plus social security number, date of birth, approximate years of attendance, signed release. Fee is $2.00. Expedited service available for $2.00.

Major credit cards accepted for payment.

La Guardia Community College, Registrar, 31-10 Thomson Ave, Long Island City, NY 11101, 718-482-7232. Hours: 9:30AM-5PM M,T; 2-8PM W; 9:30AM-8PM Th; Closed F. Alumni records are maintained here also. Call 718-482-5054. Degrees granted: Associate.

Attendance and degree information available by written request only. Search requires name plus social security number, signed release. Other helpful information: date of birth, approximate years of attendance. No fee for information.

Transcripts available by written request only. Search requires name plus social security number, signed release. Other helpful information: date of birth, approximate years of attendance. Fee is $4.00.

La Montana Regional College, Registrar, Call Box 2500, Utuado, PR 00641, 809-894-2828.

La Roche College, Registrar, 9000 Babcock Blvd, Pittsburgh, PA 15237, 412-367-9248. Hours: 8:30AM-6:30PM M, 8:30AM-4:30PM T-Th. Records go back to 1963. Alumni records are maintained here also. Call 412-367-9300 X140. Degrees granted: Bachelors; Masters. Adverse incident record source: Dean, 412-367-9300 X147.

Attendance and degree information available by phone, mail. Search requires name plus social security number, approximate years of attendance. No fee for information.

Transcripts available by mail. Search requires name plus social security number, approximate years of attendance, signed release. Fee is $3.00.

La Salle University, Registrar, 1900 W Olney Ave, Philadelphia, PA 19141, 215-951-1020. Hours: 8:30AM-4:30PM. Records go back to 1863. Degrees granted: Associate; Bachelors; Masters.

Attendance and degree information available by phone, mail. Search requires name plus social security number, date of birth, approximate years of attendance. Other helpful information: exact years of attendance. No fee for information.

Transcripts available by mail. Search requires name plus social security number, date of birth, approximate years of attendance, signed release. Other helpful information: exact years of attendance. Fee is $2.00. Expedited service available for $2.00. $10.00 for FedEx.

La Sierra University, Registrar, 4700 Pierce St, Riverside, CA 92515, 909-785-2006 (FAX: 909-785-2447). Hours: 8:30AM-4:30PM M-Th; 8:30AM-Noon F. Records go back to 1922. Alumni records are maintained here at the same phone number. Degrees granted: Associate; Bachelors; Masters; Doctorate. Adverse incident record source: Student Life.

Attendance and degree information available by FAX, mail. Search requires name plus signed release. Other helpful information: social security number, date of birth, approximate years of attendance. No fee for information.

Transcripts available by FAX, mail. Search requires name plus signed release. Other helpful information: social security number, date of birth, approximate years of attendance. Fee is $4.00. Expedited service available for $8.00.

Major credit cards accepted for payment.

LaGrange College, Registrar, 601 Broad St, Lagrange, GA 30240-2999, 706-812-7237 (FAX: 706-884-6567). Hours: 8:15AM-5PM. Records go back 100 years. Degrees granted: Associate; Bachelors; Masters.

Attendance and degree information available by phone, FAX, mail. Search requires name only. Other helpful information: social security number, date of birth, approximate years of attendance. No fee for information.

Transcripts available by FAX, mail. Search requires name plus signed release. Other helpful information: social security number, date of birth, approximate years of attendance. No fee for transcripts.

Labette Community College, Registrar, 200 S 14th St, Parsons, KS 67357, 316-421-6700 X68 (FAX: 316-421-0180). Hours: 8AM-8PM M-Th, 8AM-4:30PM F. Records go back to 1923. Alumni records are maintained here also. Call 316-421-0180 X40. Degrees granted: Associate. Adverse incident record source: Dean of Instructors, 316-421-6700 X24.

Attendance information available by phone, FAX, mail. Search requires name plus social security number, approximate years of attendance, signed release. No fee for information.

Degree information available by FAX, mail. Search requires name plus social security number, approximate years of attendance, signed release. No fee for information.

Transcripts available by FAX, mail. Search requires name plus social security number, approximate years of attendance, signed release. Fee is $1.00.

Laboratory Institute of Merchandising, Registrar, 12 E 53rd St, New York, NY 10022, 212-752-1530 (FAX: 212-832-6708). Hours: 9AM-4:30PM. Records go back to 1939. Alumni records are maintained here at the same phone number. Degrees granted: Associate; Bachelors.

Attendance and degree information available by phone, FAX, mail. Search requires name plus approximate years of attendance. Other helpful information: social security number, date of birth. No fee for information.

Transcripts available by mail. Search requires name plus approximate years of attendance, signed release. Other helpful information: social security number, date of birth. Fee is $5.00. Maiden name needed if applicable.

Laboure College, Registrar, 2120 Dorchester Ave, Boston, MA 02124, 617-296-8300 X4025. Hours: 8AM-4:30PM. Alumni records are maintained here also. Call 617-296-8300 X4030. Degrees granted: Associate.

Attendance and degree information available by phone, mail. Search requires name plus approximate years of attendance. Other helpful information: social security number, exact years of attendance. No fee for information.

Transcripts available by mail. Search requires name plus approximate years of attendance, signed release. Other helpful information: social security number, exact years of attendance. No fee for transcripts.

LacCourte Oreilles Ojibwa Community College, Registrar, Rte 2 Box 2357, Hayward, WI 54843, 715-634-4790 (FAX: 715-634-5049). Hours: 8AM-4:30PM. Records go back to 1981. Degrees granted: Associate.

Attendance and degree information available by phone. Search requires name plus social security number, approximate years of attendance, signed release. Fee is $10.00. Expedited service available for $15.00.

Transcripts available by written request only. Search requires name plus social security number, approximate years of attendance, signed release. Fee is $10.00. Expedited service available for $15.00.

Lackawanna Senior College, Registrar's Office, 901 Prospect Ave, Scranton, PA 18505, 717-961-7840 (FAX: 717-961-7858). Hours: 9AM-6PM M,Th; 9AM-5PM T,W; 9AM-4:30PM F. Records go back to 1900s. Alumni records are maintained here also. Call 717-961-7829. Degrees granted: Associate.

Attendance and degree information available by FAX, mail. Search requires name plus social security number, signed release. Other helpful information: date of birth, approximate years of attendance. No fee for information.

Transcripts available by FAX, mail. Search requires name plus social security number, signed release. Other helpful information: date of birth, approximate years of attendance. Fee is $3.00. Major credit cards accepted for payment.

Lafayette College, Registrar, High St, Easton, PA 18042, 610-250-5090 (FAX: 610-250-9850). Hours: 8:45AM-5PM Fall-Spring hours; 8:15AM-4:30PM Summer hours. Records go back to 1800. Alumni records are maintained here also. Call 610-250-5040. Degrees granted: Bachelors. Adverse incident record source: Dean, 610-250-5080.

Attendance and degree information available by phone, FAX, mail. Search requires name plus social security number, approximate years of attendance, signed release. No fee for information.

Transcripts available by FAX, mail. Search requires name plus social security number, approximate years of attendance, signed release. Fee is $1.00.

Lake Area Vocational-Technical Institute, Registrar, 230 11th St NE, Watertown, SD 57201, 605-886-5872 (FAX: 605-886-2824). Hours: 8AM-5PM. Records go back to 1965. Degrees granted: Associate.

Attendance and degree information available by phone, FAX, mail. Search requires name only. Other helpful information: social security number, approximate years of attendance. No fee for information.

Transcripts available by mail. Search requires name plus signed release. Other helpful information: social security number, approximate years of attendance. Fee is $4.00.

Lake City Community College, Registrar, Rte 3 Box 7, Lake City, FL 32055, 904-752-1822 (FAX: 904-755-1521). Hours: 8AM-4:30PM. Records go back 32 years.

Attendance information available by phone, mail. Search requires name plus social security number, exact years of attendance, signed release. Other helpful information: date of birth, approximate years of attendance. No fee for information.

Degree information available by mail. Search requires name plus social security number, exact years of attendance, signed release. Other helpful information: date of birth, approximate years of attendance. No fee for information.

Transcripts available by mail. Search requires name plus social security number, exact years of attendance, signed release. Other helpful information: date of birth, approximate years of attendance. Fee is $5.00.

Lake Erie College, Registrar, 391 W Washington St, Painesville, OH 44077, 216-639-7825 (FAX: 216-352-3533). Hours: 8AM-5PM M-F; 8AM-7PM T. Records go back to 1856. Alumni records are maintained here also. Call 216-639-7831. Degrees granted: Bachelors; Masters.

Attendance information available by phone, FAX, mail. Search requires name plus social security number, approximate years of attendance. No fee for information.

Degree information available by phone, FAX, mail. Search requires name plus social security number. Other helpful information: approximate years of attendance. No fee for information.

Transcripts available by mail. Search requires name plus social security number, approximate years of attendance, signed release. Other helpful information: date of birth. Fee is $2.00.

Lake Erie College of Osteopathic Medicine, Registrar, 1858 W Grandview Blvd, Erie, PA 16509, 814-866-8115 (FAX: 814-864-8699). Hours: 8AM-4:30PM. Records go back to 1993. Degrees granted: Doctorate.

Attendance and degree information available by phone, FAX, mail. Search requires name plus social security number. No fee for information.

Transcripts available by mail. Search requires name plus social security number. Fee is $5.00.

Lake Forest College, Registrar, 555 N Sheridan Rd, Lake Forest, IL 60045, 708-735-5025 (FAX: 708-735-6292). Hours: 8:30AM-5PM. Records go back to 1860. Alumni records are maintained here also. Call 708-735-6016. Degrees granted: Bachelors; Masters. Adverse incident record source: Dean of Students, 708-735-5200.

Attendance and degree information available by phone, FAX, mail. Search requires name plus exact years of attendance. No fee for information.

Transcripts available by FAX, mail. Search requires name plus exact years of attendance, signed release. Other helpful information: social security number. Fee is $2.00.

Lake Forest Graduate School of Management, Registrar, 240 N Sheridan Rd, Lake Forest, IL 60045, 708-234-5005 (FAX: 708-295-3656). Hours: 8:30AM-4:30PM. Records go back to 1960. Degrees granted: Masters.

Attendance and degree information available by phone, FAX, mail. Search requires name plus social security number, date of birth. Other helpful information: approximate years of attendance. No fee for information.

Transcripts available by mail. Search requires name plus social security number, date of birth, signed release. Other helpful information: approximate years of attendance. Fee is $2.00. Expedited service available for $2.00.

Major credit cards accepted for payment.

Lake Land College, Registrar, 5001 Lake Land Blvd, Mattoon, IL 61938, 217-234-5378. Hours: 7:30AM-6:30PM M-Th, 7:30AM-5PM F. Records go back to 1970. Alumni records are maintained here also. Call 217-234-5253. Degrees granted: Associate.

Attendance and degree information available by phone, mail. Search requires name plus social security number, date of birth, exact years of attendance. No fee for information.

Transcripts available by FAX, mail. Search requires name plus social security number, date of birth, exact years of attendance, signed release. Fee is $2.00.

FAX fee $10.00.

Lake Michigan College, Registrar, 2755 E Napier St, Benton Harbor, MI 49022, 616-927-8614. Hours: 8AM-5PM. Degrees granted: Associate.

Attendance and degree information available by phone, FAX, mail. Search requires name plus social security number. Other helpful information: date of birth, approximate years of attendance. No fee for information.

Transcripts available by mail. Search requires name plus social security number, signed release. Other helpful information: date of birth, approximate years of attendance. Fee is $3.00.

Major credit cards accepted for payment.

Lake Superior College, Office of Student Records, 2101 Trinity Rd, Duluth, MN 55811-3399, 218-722-2801 (FAX: 218-722-2899). Hours: 8AM-4PM. Records go back 40 years. Known as Duluth Technical College before July 1995.

Attendance and degree information available by phone, FAX, mail. Search requires name only. Other helpful information: social security number, date of birth, approximate years of attendance. Fee is $3.00.

Transcripts available by mail. Search requires name plus social security number, date of birth, signed release. Other helpful information: approximate years of attendance. Fee is $3.00.

Lake Superior State University, Registrar, 1000 College Dr, Sault Ste. Marie, MI 49783, 906-635-2683 (FAX: 906-635-2111). Hours: 8AM-5PM. Records go back to 1946. Alumni records are maintained here also. Call 906-635-2831. Degrees granted: Associate; Bachelors; Masters. Adverse incident record source: Security, 906-635-2210: Student Services, 906-635-2684

Attendance and degree information available by phone, FAX, mail. Search requires name plus social security number. Other helpful information: date of birth, approximate years of attendance. No fee for information.

Transcripts available by FAX, mail. Search requires name plus social security number, signed release. Other helpful information: date of birth, approximate years of attendance. Fee is $5.00. Expedited service available for $5.00.

Lake Tahoe Community College, Registrar, One College Dr, South Lake Tahoe, CA 96150, 916-541-4660 X211 (FAX: 916-541-7852). Hours: 8AM-5PM. Records go back to 1976. Alumni records are maintained here also. Call 916-541-4660. Degrees granted: Associate.

Attendance and degree information available by phone, FAX, mail. Search requires name plus social security number, date of birth, exact years of attendance, signed release. No fee for information.

Transcripts available by FAX, mail. Search requires name plus social security number, date of birth, exact years of attendance, signed release. No fee for transcripts.

Confirmation given if release on file.

Lake Washington Technical College, Registrar, 11605 132nd Ave NE, Kirkland, WA 98034, 206-828-5600. Hours: 8AM-4:30PM. Records go back to 1949. Degrees granted: Associate.

Attendance and degree information available by phone, mail. Search requires name plus social security number, exact years of attendance. No fee for information.

Transcripts available by mail. Search requires name plus social security number, exact years of attendance, signed release. Fee is $2.00.

Need to know program of study.

Lake-Sumter Community College, Registrar, 9501 US Hwy 441, Leesburg, FL 34788-8751, 904-365-3572 (FAX: 904-365-3501). Hours: 8AM-9PM M-Th, 8AM-4:30PM F. Records go back to 1962. Alumni records are maintained here also. Call 904-787-3747. Degrees granted: Associate.

Attendance and degree information available by phone, mail. Search requires name plus social security number, date of birth, exact years of attendance, signed release. No fee for information.

Transcripts available by mail. Search requires name plus social security number, date of birth, exact years of attendance, signed release. No fee for transcripts.

Lakeland College, Registrar, PO Box 359, Sheboygan, WI 53082-0359, 414-565-1216 (FAX: 414-565-1206). Hours: 8AM-4:30PM. Records go back to 1920. Alumni records are maintained here at the same phone number. Degrees granted: Bachelors; Masters. Adverse incident record source: Student Affairs, 414-565-1248.

Attendance information available by phone, FAX, mail. Search requires name only. Other helpful information: date of birth, approximate years of attendance. No fee for information.

Degree information available by phone, FAX, mail. Search requires name plus exact years of attendance. Other helpful information: social security number, date of birth. No fee for information.

Transcripts available by mail. Search requires name plus approximate years of attendance, signed release. Other helpful information: social security number, date of birth, exact years of attendance. No fee for transcripts.

Need college ID#.

Lakeland Community College, Registrar, 7700 Clocktower Dr, Mentor, OH 44060, 216-953-7100 (FAX: 216-975-4330). Hours: 7:30AM-8:30PM M-Th, 7:30AM-5PM F, 8:30AM-12:30PM Sat. Records go back to 1967. Degrees granted: Associate. Adverse incident record source: Security Office, 216-953-7246.

Attendance and degree information available by phone, FAX, mail. Search requires name plus social security number, signed release. No fee for information.

Transcripts available by mail. Search requires name plus social security number, signed release. Fee is $1.00.

Lakeshore Technical College, Registrar/Records, 1290 North Ave, Cleveland, WI 53015, 414-458-4183 X115 (FAX: 414-693-3561). Hours: 7:30AM-3:45PM. Records go back to 1940. Degrees granted: Associate.

Attendance and degree information available by FAX, mail. Search requires name plus social security number, date of birth, approximate years of attendance, signed release. No fee for information.

Transcripts available by FAX, mail. Search requires name plus social security number, date of birth, approximate years of attendance, signed release. Other helpful information: exact years of attendance. Fee is $3.00.

Major credit cards accepted for payment.

Lakewood Community College, Registrar, 3401 Century Ave, White Bear Lake, MN 55110, 612-779-3298. Hours: 8AM-4PM. Records go back 26 years. Alumni records are maintained here also. Call 612-779-3338. Degrees granted: Associate.

Attendance and degree information available by phone, mail. Search requires name plus social security number, date of birth. Other helpful information: approximate years of attendance. No fee for information.

Transcripts available by mail. Search requires name plus social security number, date of birth, signed release. Fee is $2.00. Expedited service available for $7.00.

Previous names needed. Major credit cards accepted for payment.

Lamar Community College, Registrar, 2401 S Main St, Lamar, CO 81052, 719-336-2248 X125 (FAX: 719-336-2448). Hours: 8AM-5PM. Records go back to 1937. Alumni Records Office: 2401 S Main St, Lamar, CO 81052. Degrees granted: Associate.

Attendance and degree information available by phone, FAX, mail. Search requires name plus exact years of attendance. Other helpful information: social security number. No fee for information.

Transcripts available by FAX, mail. Search requires name plus exact years of attendance, signed release. Other helpful information: social security number. Fee is $2.00.

Phone requests only for records since 1987. Major credit cards accepted for payment.

Lamar University at Beaumont, Registrar, 4400 Martin Luther King, Jr. Pkwy Blvd, Beaumont, TX 77710, 409-880-8365 (FAX: 409-880-8463). Records go back to 1923. Alumni records are maintained here at the same phone number. Degrees granted: Bachelors; Masters; Doctorate.

Attendance and degree information available by phone, mail. Search requires name plus social security number, date of birth. No fee for information.

Transcripts available by mail. Search requires name plus social security number, date of birth, signed release. Fee is $2.00.

Lamar University at Orange, Registrar, 410 W Front St, Orange, TX 77630, 409-883-7750. Hours: 8AM-4:30PM. Degrees granted: Associate.

Attendance and degree information available by phone, mail. Search requires name plus social security number. No fee for information.

Transcripts available by written request only. Search requires name plus social security number, signed release. Fee is $2.00.

Lamar University at Port Arthur, Registrar, PO Box 310, Port Arthur, TX 77641-0310, 409-983-4921 (FAX: 409-984-6000). Hours: 8AM-5PM M,T,W,F; 8AM-6PM W. Records go back to 1975. Degrees granted: Associate.

Attendance information available by phone, FAX, mail. Search requires name plus social security number, approximate years of attendance. Other helpful information: date of birth. No fee for information.

Degree information available by phone, FAX, mail. Search requires name plus social security number, approximate years of attendance, signed release. Other helpful information: date of birth. No fee for information.

Transcripts available by written request only. Search requires name plus social security number, date of birth, approximate years of attendance, signed release. Fee is $2.00.

Major credit cards accepted for payment.

Lambuth University, Registrar, 705 Lambuth Blvd, Jackson, TN 38301, 901-425-3207 (FAX: 901-423-1990). Hours: 8:30AM-Noon, 1-4:30PM. Records go back to 1920s. Alumni records are maintained here also. Call 901-425-3354. Degrees granted: Bachelors. Adverse incident record source: Student Life, 901-425-3211.

Attendance and degree information available by phone, FAX, mail. Search requires name only. Other helpful information: social security number, date of birth, approximate years of attendance. No fee for information.

Transcripts available by FAX, mail. Search requires name plus signed release. Other helpful information: social security number, date of birth, approximate years of attendance. Fee is $2.00. Expedited service available for $5.00.

Degree helpful.

Lamson Business College, Registrar, 6367 E Tanque Verde Rd Ste 100, Tucson, AZ 85715, 602-327-6851. Hours: 8AM-5PM. Records go back to 1960. Degrees granted: Associate. Adverse incident record source: Registrar's Office, 602-327-6851.

Attendance and degree information available by phone, mail. Search requires name plus social security number, date of birth, exact years of attendance. No fee for information.

Transcripts available by mail. Search requires name plus social security number, date of birth, exact years of attendance, signed release. Fee is $2.00.

Lancaster Bible College, Registrar, 901 Eden Rd, Lancaster, PA 17601, 717-569-7071 (FAX: 717-560-8211). Hours: 8AM-4PM. Records go back 66 years. Degrees granted: Associate; Bachelors; Masters.

Attendance and degree information available by phone, mail. Search requires name plus exact years of attendance. Other helpful information: date of birth, approximate years of attendance. Fee is $2.00.

Transcripts available by phone, mail. Search requires name plus exact years of attendance. Other helpful information: date of birth, approximate years of attendance. Fee is $2.00.

Major credit cards accepted for payment.

Lancaster Theological Seminary, Registrar, 555 W James St, Lancaster, PA 17603-2897, 717-290-8718 (FAX: 717-393-4254). Hours: 8AM-5PM. Records go back to 1900s. Alumni records are maintained here also. Call 717-290-8729. Degrees granted: Masters; Doctorate.

Attendance and degree information available by FAX, mail. Search requires name plus social security number, exact years of attendance, signed release. No fee for information.

Transcripts available by FAX, mail. Search requires name plus social security number, exact years of attendance, signed release. Fee is $2.00.

Lander University, Registrar, 320 Stanley Ave, Greenwood, SC 29649-2099, 803-229-8398 (FAX: 803-229-8890). Hours: 8AM-5PM. Records go back to 1872. Alumni records are maintained here also. Call 803-229-8351. Degrees granted: Bachelors; Masters.

Attendance and degree information available by phone, FAX, mail. Search requires name plus social security number, exact years of attendance. No fee for information.

Transcripts available by FAX, mail. Search requires name plus social security number, exact years of attendance, signed release. Fee is $5.00.

Landmark College, Registrar, Putney, VT 05346, 802-387-4767. Hours: 8AM-4:30PM. Degrees granted: Associate.

Attendance and degree information available by phone, mail. Search requires name plus social security number. Other helpful information: approximate years of attendance. No fee for information.

Transcripts available by written request only. Search requires name plus social security number. Other helpful information: approximate years of attendance. Fee is $3.00.

Lane College, Registrar, 545 Lane Ave, Jackson, TN 38301-4598, 901-426-7600. Hours: 8AM-5PM. Records go back to 1882. Alumni records are maintained here also. Call 901-426-7523. Degrees granted: Bachelors.

Attendance and degree information available by phone, mail. Search requires name plus social security number, exact years of attendance. No fee for information.

Transcripts available by mail. Search requires name plus social security number, exact years of attendance, signed release. Fee is $2.00.

Lane Community College, Registrar, 4000 E 30th Ave, Eugene, OR 97405, 503-726-2213 (FAX: 503-744-3995). Hours: 8AM-4:45PM M,T,W,F; 9AM-4:45PM Th. Records go back to 1964. Degrees granted: Associate. Adverse incident record source: Student Services, 503-741-3075: Security, 503-747-4501 X2558

Attendance and degree information available by phone, FAX, mail. Search requires name only. Other helpful information: social security number, approximate years of attendance. No fee for information.

Transcripts available by mail. Search requires name plus social security number, signed release. Other helpful information: approximate years of attendance. First transcript is $3.00, each additional is $2.00.

Laney College, Registrar, 900 Fallon St, Oakland, CA 94607, 510-464-3122. Hours: 9AM-7PM M-T, 9AM-3PM W-F. Records go back to 1940. Degrees granted: Associate.

Attendance and degree information available by mail. Search requires name plus social security number, date of birth, exact years of attendance, signed release. No fee for information.

Transcripts available by mail. Search requires name plus social security number, date of birth, exact years of attendance, signed release. First two transcripts are free. Additional ones are $1.00 each.

Langston University, Registrar, PO Box 907, Langston, OK 73050-0907, 405-466-3225 (FAX: 405-466-3381). Hours: 8AM-5PM. Records go back to 1910. Alumni records are maintained here also. Call 405-466-3201 X2999. Degrees granted: Associate; Bachelors; Masters. Adverse incident record source: Student Affairs, 405-466-3444.

Attendance and degree information available by phone, FAX, mail. Search requires name plus social security number. No fee for information.

Transcripts available by mail. Search requires name plus social security number, approximate years of attendance, signed release. Fee is $2.00.

Lansdale School of Business, Registrar, 201 Church Rd, North Wales, PA 19454, 215-699-5700 (FAX: 215-699-8770). Hours: 8AM-10PM. Records go back to 1950. Degrees granted: Associate. Adverse incident record source: President, 215-699-5700.

Attendance and degree information available by phone, FAX, mail. Search requires name only. No fee for information.

Transcripts available by FAX, mail. Search requires name plus signed release. Fee is $2.00.

Lansing Community College, 26 Office of Registrar, PO Box 40010, Lansing, MI 48901-7210, 517-483-1266 (FAX: 517-483-9795). Hours: 8AM-5PM M-F; 8AM-8AM Th. Records go back to 1957. Degrees granted: Associate.

Attendance and degree information available by FAX, mail. Search requires name plus signed release. Other helpful information: social security number, date of birth, approximate years of attendance. No fee for information.

Transcripts available by FAX, mail. Search requires name plus signed release. Other helpful information: social security number, date of birth, approximate years of attendance. Fee is $2.00.

Laramie County Community College, Registrar, 1400 E College Dr, Cheyenne, WY 82007, 307-778-5222. Hours: 8AM-5PM. Records go back to 1968. Alumni records are maintained here also. Call 307-778-1213. Degrees granted: Associate.

Attendance and degree information available by mail. Search requires name plus social security number, exact years of attendance, signed release. No fee for information.

Transcripts available by mail. Search requires name plus social security number, exact years of attendance, signed release. No fee for transcripts.

Laredo Community College, Registrar, W End Washington St, Laredo, TX 78040-4395, 210-721-5109 (FAX: 210-721-5493). Hours: 8AM-4:30PM. Degrees granted: Associate.

Attendance and degree information available by phone, mail. Search requires name plus social security number, date of birth. No fee for information.

Transcripts available by mail. Search requires name plus social security number, date of birth, signed release. Fee is $2.00.

Las Positas College, Admissions & Records, 3033 Collier Canyon Rd, Livermore, CA 94550, 510-373-4647 (FAX: 510-606-6437). Hours: 9AM-7:30PM M-Th, 9AM-5PM F. Records go back to 1960. Degrees granted: Associate.

Attendance information available by FAX, mail. Search requires name plus social security number, signed release. No fee for information.

Degree information available by FAX, mail. Search requires name plus social security number, exact years of attendance, signed release. No fee for information.

Transcripts available by FAX, mail. Search requires name plus social security number, exact years of attendance, signed release. First two transcripts are free. Additional ones are $1.00 each.

Lasell College, Registrar, Newton, MA 02166, 617-243-2133 (FAX: 617-243-2326). Hours: 8:30PM-4:30PM. Degrees granted: Associate; Bachelors.

Attendance and degree information available by phone, FAX, mail. Search requires name plus approximate years of attendance. No fee for information.

Transcripts available by written request only. Search requires name plus approximate years of attendance, signed release. Fee is $2.00.

Lassen College, Registrar, PO Box 3000, Susanville, CA 96130, 916-257-6181 (FAX: 916-257-8964). Hours: 8AM-4:30PM. Records go back to 1927. Degrees granted: Associate.

Attendance and degree information available by phone, FAX, mail. Search requires name plus social security number, date of birth, exact years of attendance. No fee for information.

Transcripts available by mail. Search requires name plus social security number, date of birth, exact years of attendance, signed release. Fee is $3.00. Expedited service available for $5.00.

Laurel Business Institute, Registrar, 11-15 Penn St, Uniontown, PA 15401, 412-439-4900. Hours: 8AM-5PM. Degrees granted: Associate.

Attendance and degree information available by written request only. Search requires name plus social security number, date of birth, approximate years of attendance, signed release. No fee for information.

Transcripts available by written request only. Search requires name plus social security number, date of birth, approximate years of attendance, signed release. No fee for transcripts.

Lawrence Technological University, Registrar, 21000 W Ten Mile Rd, Southfield, MI 48075, 810-204-3100 (FAX: 810-204-3727). Hours: 7:30AM-8PM M-Th; 7:30AM-5PM F. Records go back to 1932. Degrees granted: Associate; Bachelors; Masters.

Attendance and degree information available by phone, FAX, mail. Search requires name only. Other helpful information: social security number, date of birth, approximate years of attendance. No fee for information.

Transcripts available by mail. Search requires name plus signed release. Other helpful information: social security number, date of birth, approximate years of attendance. Fee is $3.00. Expedited service available for $5.00.

Lawrence University, Registrar, PO Box 599, Appleton, WI 54912, 414-832-6578 (FAX: 414-832-6606). Hours: 8AM-Noon, 1-5PM. Records go back to 1920. Degrees granted: Bachelors. Adverse incident record source: Dean of Students, 414-832-6530.

Attendance and degree information available by phone, FAX, mail. Search requires name plus approximate years of attendance. Other helpful information: social security number, date of birth, exact years of attendance. No fee for information.

Transcripts available by written request only. Search requires name plus approximate years of attendance, signed release. Other helpful information: social security number, date of birth, exact years of attendance. Fee is $2.00.

Lawson State Community College, Registrar, 3060 Wilson Rd SW, Birmingham, AL 35221, 205-929-6309 (FAX: 205-929-6316). Hours: 8AM-5PM. Degrees granted: Associate. Adverse incident record source: Security, 205-925-2515 X235.

Attendance and degree information available by phone, FAX, mail. Search requires name plus social security number, date of birth, signed release. Other helpful information: approximate years of attendance. No fee for information.

Transcripts available by phone, mail. Search requires name plus social security number, date of birth, exact years of attendance, signed release. Other helpful information: approximate years of attendance. Fee is $3.00.

LeMoyne College, Registrar, Le Moyne Heights, Syracuse, NY 13214, 315-445-4100 (FAX: 315-445-4540). Degrees granted: Bachelors; Masters.

Attendance and degree information available by phone, FAX, mail. Search requires name plus date of birth, signed release. Other helpful information: social security number, approximate years of attendance. Fee is $3.00.

Transcripts available by mail. Search requires name plus date of birth, signed release. Other helpful information: social security number, approximate years of attendance. Fee is $3.00.

LeMoyne-Owen College, Registrar, 807 Walker Ave, Memphis, TN 38126, 901-942-7392 (FAX: 901-942-7810). Hours: 8AM-6PM. Records go back to 1915. Degrees granted: Bachelors; Masters. Adverse incident record source: Student Affairs.

Attendance and degree information available by phone, FAX, mail. Search requires name plus social security number, approximate years of attendance, signed release. Other helpful information: date of birth, exact years of attendance. No fee for information.

Transcripts available by FAX, mail. Search requires name plus social security number, approximate years of attendance, signed release. Other helpful information: date of birth, exact years of attendance. Fee is $2.00. Expedited service available for $10.00.

LeTourneau University, Registrar, PO Box 7001, Longview, TX 75607, 903-753-0231 (FAX: 903-237-2732). Hours: 8AM-5PM. Records go back to 1946. Degrees granted: Associate; Bachelors; Masters.

Attendance and degree information available by phone, FAX, mail. Search requires name only. Other helpful information: social security number, date of birth, approximate years of attendance. No fee for information.

Transcripts available by mail. Search requires name plus signed release. Other helpful information: social security number, date of birth, approximate years of attendance. Fee is $5.00. Expedited service available for $25.00.

Lebanon Valley College, Registrar, 101 N College Ave, Annville, PA 17003-0501, 717-867-6215 (FAX: 717-867-6018). Hours: 8AM-4:30PM. Records go back to 1883. Degrees granted: Associate; Bachelors; Masters. Adverse incident record source: Security Office, 717-867-6111.

Attendance and degree information available by phone, FAX, mail. Search requires name plus social security number. Other helpful information: date of birth, approximate years of attendance. No fee for information.

Transcripts available by FAX, mail. Search requires name plus social security number, signed release. Other helpful information:

date of birth, approximate years of attendance. Fee is $2.00. Expedited service available for $18.00.

Lee College, Admissions & Records, PO Box 818, Baytown, TX 77520-0818, 713-425-6393 (FAX: 713-425-6831). Hours: 7:30AM-7:30PM M,Th; 7:30AM-5PM T,W; 7:30AM-12:30PM F. Records go back to 1934. Degrees granted: Associate. Special programs- Administrative Services, 713-425-6348.

Attendance and degree information available by phone, mail. Search requires name plus signed release. Other helpful information: social security number, date of birth, approximate years of attendance. No fee for information.

Transcripts available by phone, mail. Search requires name plus signed release. Other helpful information: social security number, date of birth, approximate years of attendance. No fee for transcripts.

Phone request for transcripts only if being sent to another college/university.

Lee College, Registrar, PO Box 3450, Cleveland, TN 37320-3450, 615-478-7319 (FAX: 615-478-7075). Hours: 9AM-Noon; 1-5PM. Records go back to 1947. Degrees granted: Bachelors; Masters.

Attendance and degree information available by FAX, mail. Search requires name plus social security number, signed release. Other helpful information: date of birth, exact years of attendance. No fee for information.

Transcripts available by FAX, mail. Search requires name plus social security number, signed release. Other helpful information: date of birth. Fee is $3.00. Expedited service available for $5.00.

Lees College, Registrar, 601 Jefferson Ave, Jackson, KY 41339, 606-666-7521 (FAX: 606-666-8910). Hours: 8AM-5PM. Records go back to 1900s. Degrees granted: Associate.

Attendance information available by mail. Search requires name plus signed release. Other helpful information: social security number, date of birth, approximate years of attendance. No fee for information.

Degree information available by mail. Search requires name plus social security number, signed release. Other helpful information: date of birth, approximate years of attendance. No fee for information.

Transcripts available by mail. Search requires name plus social security number, signed release. Other helpful information: date of birth, approximate years of attendance. Fee is $3.00.

Major credit cards accepted for payment.

Lees-McRae College, Registrar, PO Box 128, Banner Elk, NC 28604, 704-898-8738 (FAX: 704-898-8814). Hours: 8:30AM-4:30PM. Records go back to 1932. Degrees granted: Bachelors. Adverse incident record source: Student Development, 704-898-5241 X8211.

Attendance and degree information available by phone, FAX, mail. Search requires name plus exact years of attendance. Other helpful information: approximate years of attendance. No fee for information.

Transcripts available by FAX, mail. Search requires name plus signed release. Fee is $2.00.

Leeward Community College, Registrar, 96-045 Ala Ike, Pearl City, HI 96782, 808-455-0219 (FAX: 808-455-0471). Hours: 7:45AM-4:30PM. Records go back to 1968. Degrees granted: Associate.

Attendance and degree information available by phone, FAX, mail. Search requires name plus social security number, approximate years of attendance, signed release. Other helpful information: date of birth. No fee for information.

Transcripts available by phone, mail. Search requires name plus social security number, approximate years of attendance, signed release. Other helpful information: date of birth. Fee is $1.00.

Legal Career Institute, (Branch), Registrar, 7289 Garden Rd Ste 204, Riviera Beach, FL 33404, 305-848-2223. Records are not housed here. They are located at Atlantic Coast Institute, Registrar, 5225 W Broward Blvd, Fort Lauderdale, FL 33317.

Lehigh Carbon Community College, Registrar, 4525 Education Park Dr, Schnecksville, PA 18078-2598, 610-799-1174 (FAX: 610-799-1527). Hours: 8AM-9PM. Records go back to 1968. Alumni records are maintained here also. Call 610-799-2121. Degrees granted: Associate. Adverse incident record source: Security, 610-799-1169.

Attendance and degree information available by phone, mail. Search requires name only. Other helpful information: social security number, date of birth, approximate years of attendance. No fee for information.

Transcripts available by mail. Search requires name plus signed release. Other helpful information: social security number, date of birth, approximate years of attendance. Fee is $2.00. Expedited service available for $5.00.

Major credit cards accepted for payment.

Lehigh University, Registrar, 27 Memorial Dr W, Bethlehem, PA 18015, 610-758-3200 (FAX: 610-758-3198). Hours: 8:15AM-4:45PM. Records go back to 1860. Alumni records are maintained here also. Call 610-758-3183. Degrees granted: Bachelors; Masters; PhD. Adverse incident record source: Dean, 610-758-4159.

Attendance and degree information available by phone, FAX, mail. Search requires name plus social security number, exact years of attendance. No fee for information.

Transcripts available by FAX, mail. Search requires name plus social security number, exact years of attendance, signed release. No fee for transcripts.

Lenoir Community College, Registrar, PO Box 188, Kinston, NC 28501, 919-527-6223 X306 (FAX: 919-527-1199). Hours: 8AM-5PM M-Th, 8AM-4PM F. Records go back to 1960s. Alumni records are maintained here at the same phone number. Degrees granted: Associate.

Attendance information available by phone, FAX, mail. Search requires name plus social security number. No fee for information.

Degree information available by phone, FAX, mail. Search requires name plus social security number, exact years of attendance. No fee for information.

Transcripts available by FAX, mail. Search requires name plus social security number, exact years of attendance, signed release. No fee for transcripts.

Lenoir-Rhyne College, Registrar, Seventh Ave and Eighth St NE, Hickory, NC 28603, 704-328-7278 (FAX: 704-328-7368). Hours: 8:30AM-5PM. Records go back to 1940s. Alumni records are maintained here at the same phone number. Degrees granted: Bachelors; Masters. Adverse incident record source: Dean, 704-328-7246.

Attendance information available by phone, FAX, mail. Search requires name plus social security number. No fee for information.

Degree information available by phone, FAX, mail. Search requires name plus social security number, exact years of attendance. No fee for information.

Transcripts available by FAX, mail. Search requires name plus social security number, exact years of attendance, signed release. Fee is $3.00.

Lesley College, Registrar, 29 Everett St, Cambridge, MA 02138-2790, 617-349-8740. Hours: 9AM-7PM M-Th, 9AM-5PM F. Records go back to 1909. Alumni records are maintained here also. Call 617-349-8622. Degrees granted: Bachelors; Masters.

Attendance and degree information available by mail. Search requires name plus social security number, signed release. No fee for information.

Transcripts available by mail. Search requires name plus social security number, signed release. Fee is $5.00.

Lewis College of Business, Registrar, 17370 Meyers Rd, Detroit, MI 48235, 313-862-6300 X233. Hours: 9AM-6PM Fall, 8AM-5:15PM Summer. Records go back to 1939. Alumni records are maintained here also. Call 313-862-6300 X217. Degrees granted: Associate. Adverse incident record source: Business Office, 313-862-6300 X262.

Attendance and degree information available by mail. Search requires name plus social security number, approximate years of attendance, signed release. No fee for information.

Transcripts available by mail. Search requires name plus social security number, approximate years of attendance, signed release. Fee is $3.00.

Lewis University, Registrar, Ret 53, Romeoville, IL 60441, 815-838-0500 X217. Hours: 8:30AM-5PM. Records go back to 1932. Alumni records are maintained here also. Call 815-838-0500 X244. Degrees granted: Bachelors; Masters.

Attendance and degree information available by phone, mail. Search requires name plus social security number, exact years of attendance. No fee for information.

Transcripts available by mail. Search requires name plus social security number, exact years of attendance, signed release. Fee is $5.00.

Lewis and Clark College, Registrar, 0615 SW Palatine Hill Rd, Portland, OR 97219, 503-768-7334 (FAX: 503-768-7333). Hours: 8AM-4:30PM. Alumni records are maintained here also. Call 503-768-7950. Degrees granted: Bachelors; Masters. Adverse incident record source: Dean of Students, 503-768-7115.

Attendance and degree information available by phone, FAX, mail. Search requires name only. Other helpful information: social security number, approximate years of attendance. No fee for information.

Transcripts available by FAX, mail. Search requires name plus social security number, date of birth, approximate years of attendance, signed release. Fee is $5.00.

Lewis and Clark Community College, Registrar, 5800 Godfrey Rd, Godfrey, IL 62035, 618-466-3411 X5112 (FAX: 618-467-2210). Hours: 8AM-4PM M,Th,F; 8AM-7PM T,W. Records go back to 1970. Degrees granted: Associate.

Attendance and degree information available by phone, FAX, mail. Search requires name plus social security number. Other helpful information: date of birth. No fee for information.

Transcripts available by FAX, mail. Search requires name plus social security number, signed release. Other helpful information: date of birth. No fee for transcripts.

Lewis-Clark State College, Registrar, 500 8th Ave, Lewiston, ID 83501, 208-799-2223 (FAX: 208-746-7354). Hours: 8AM-5PM. Records go back to 1893. Alumni records are maintained here also. Call 208-799-2216. Degrees granted: Bachelors.

Attendance information available by mail. Search requires name plus social security number. No fee for information.

Degree information available by phone, FAX, mail. Search requires name plus social security number. No fee for information.

Transcripts available by mail. Search requires name plus social security number, signed release. Fee is $3.00.

Lexington Community College, Registrar, Oswald Bldg, Cooper Dr, Lexington, KY 40506-0235, 606-257-4460 (FAX: 606-257-4339). Hours: 8AM-7:30PM M-Th, 8AM-4:30PM. Records go back to 1965. Degrees granted: Associate.

Attendance and degree information available by phone, FAX, mail. Search requires name plus social security number, signed release. No fee for information.

Transcripts available by mail. Search requires name plus social security number, signed release. Fee is $2.00.

Lexington Institute of Hospitality Careers, Registrar, 10840 S Western Ave, Chicago, IL 60643, 312-779-3800. Hours: 8:45AM-4PM. Records go back to 1976. Degrees granted: Associate.

Attendance and degree information available by mail. Search requires name plus social security number, exact years of attendance, signed release. No fee for information.

Transcripts available by mail. Search requires name plus social security number, exact years of attendance, signed release. Fee is $5.00.

Lexington Theological Seminary, Registrar, 631 S Limestone St, Lexington, KY 40508, 606-252-0361 (FAX: 606-281-6042). Hours: 8AM-4:45PM. Records go back to 1865. Alumni records are maintained here also. Call 606-252-0361. Degrees granted: Masters.

Attendance and degree information available by FAX, mail. Search requires name plus social security number. No fee for information.

Transcripts available by FAX, mail. Search requires name plus social security number. Fee is $3.00.

Liberty University, Registrar, PO Box 20000, Lynchburg, VA 24506-8001, 804-582-2397 (FAX: 804-582-2187). Hours: 8:30AM-4PM. Records go back to 1971. Alumni records are maintained here also. Call 804-582-2834. Degrees granted: Associate; Bachelors; Masters; Doctorate.

Attendance and degree information available by phone, FAX, mail. Search requires name plus social security number. Other helpful information: date of birth, approximate years of attendance. No fee for information.

Transcripts available by FAX, mail. Search requires name plus social security number, signed release. Other helpful information: date of birth, approximate years of attendance. Fee is $2.00. Expedited service available for $8.50.

Major credit cards accepted for payment.

Life Chiropractic College-West, Registrar, 2005 Via Barrett, San Lorenzo, CA 94580, 510-276-9013 (FAX: 510-276-

4893). Hours: 8AM-5PM. Records go back to 17yr. Degrees granted: Doctorate. Adverse incident record source: Dean of Students, 510-276-9013 X251.

Attendance and degree information available by FAX, mail. Search requires name plus signed release. No fee for information.

Transcripts available by FAX, mail. Search requires name plus signed release. Fee is $5.00.

Life College, Registrar, 1269 Barclay Cir, Marietta, GA 30060, 404-424-0554 (FAX: 404-429-1512). Hours: 8AM-5PM. Records go back to 1977. Alumni records are maintained here also. Call 404-424-0554 X298. Degrees granted: Bachelors; Masters; Doctorate.

Attendance information available by mail. Search requires name plus signed release. Other helpful information: social security number, exact years of attendance. No fee for information.

Degree information available by mail. Search requires name plus signed release. Other helpful information: social security number. No fee for information.

Transcripts available by mail. Search requires name plus signed release. Other helpful information: social security number. Fee is $5.00.

Major credit cards accepted for payment.

Lima Technical College, Registrar, 4240 Campus Dr, Lima, OH 45804, 419-221-1112 X319 (FAX: 419-221-0450). Hours: 8AM-5PM. Records go back to 1974. Degrees granted: Associate. Adverse incident record source: Security, 419-221-1112 X499.

Attendance information available by FAX, mail. Search requires name plus social security number. No fee for information.

Degree information available by phone, FAX, mail. Search requires name plus social security number. No fee for information.

Transcripts available by phone, FAX, mail. Search requires name plus social security number. No fee for transcripts.

Limestone College, Registrar, 1115 College Dr, Gaffney, SC 29340, 803-489-7151 (FAX: 803-487-8706). Hours: 8:30AM-5PM. Records go back to 1895. Alumni records are maintained here also. Call 803-489-7151 X604. Degrees granted: Associate; Bachelors.

Attendance and degree information available by phone, FAX, mail. Search requires name only. Other helpful information: social security number, date of birth, approximate years of attendance. No fee for information.

Transcripts available by written request only. Search requires name plus signed release. Other helpful information: social security number, date of birth, approximate years of attendance. Fee is $3.00. Expedited service available for $3.00.

Lincoln Christian College and Seminary, Registrar, 100 Campus View Dr, Lincoln, IL 62656, 217-732-3168 X2244 (FAX: 217-732-5914). Hours: 7:30AM-4:30PM. Records go back 50 years. Degrees granted: Associate; Bachelors; Masters.

Attendance and degree information available by phone, FAX, mail. Search requires name only. Other helpful information: approximate years of attendance. No fee for information.

Transcripts available by FAX, mail. Search requires name plus signed release. Other helpful information: approximate years of attendance. Fee is $3.00.

Lincoln College, Registrar, 300 Keokuk St, Lincoln, IL 62656, 217-732-3155 (FAX: 217-732-8859). Hours: 8AM-5PM. Records go back to 1800s. Alumni records are maintained here also. Call 217-732-3155 X215. Degrees granted: Associate.

Attendance and degree information available by FAX, mail. Search requires name plus social security number, date of birth, signed release. Other helpful information: approximate years of attendance. No fee for information.

Transcripts available by FAX, mail. Search requires name plus social security number, date of birth, signed release. Other helpful information: approximate years of attendance. Fee is $2.00.

Lincoln Land Community College, Admissions and Records, Shepherd Rd, Springfield, IL 62794-9256, 217-786-2200 (FAX: 217-786-2492). Hours: 8AM-5PM. Degrees granted: Associate. Adverse incident record source: Enrollment Services, 217-786-2212.

Attendance and degree information available by phone. Search requires name only. Other helpful information: social security number, date of birth, approximate years of attendance. No fee for information.

Transcripts available by phone, mail. Search requires name plus signed release. Other helpful information: social security number, date of birth, approximate years of attendance. No fee for transcripts.

You may FAX requests, but they will not FAX back.

Lincoln Memorial University, Registrar, Cumberland Gap Pkwy, Harrogate, TN 37752-0901, 615-869-6387 (FAX: 615-869-4825). Hours: 8AM-4PM. Records go back to 1915. Degrees granted: Associate; Bachelors; Masters; Ed.S.

Attendance and degree information available by phone, FAX, mail. Search requires name plus social security number. Other helpful information: date of birth, exact years of attendance. No fee for information.

Transcripts available by mail. Search requires name plus social security number, signed release. Other helpful information: date of birth, exact years of attendance. Fee is $4.00.

Lincoln School of Commerce, Registrar, PO Box 82826, 1821 K St, Lincoln, NE 68501-2826, 402-474-5315. Hours: 8AM-10PM. Records go back to 1885. Degrees granted: Associate.

Attendance and degree information available by phone, FAX, mail. Search requires name plus social security number, exact years of attendance, signed release. Other helpful information: approximate years of attendance. No fee for information.

Transcripts available by FAX, mail. Search requires name plus social security number, signed release. Other helpful information: approximate years of attendance. No fee for transcripts.

Lincoln Trail College, Registrar, 11220 State Hwy 1, Robinson, IL 62454-5707, 618-544-8657 X1137 (FAX: 618-544-9384). Hours: 8AM-5PM. Records go back 25 years. Degrees granted: Associate.

Attendance and degree information available by phone, FAX, mail. Search requires name plus social security number, signed release. Other helpful information: date of birth, approximate years of attendance. No fee for information.

Transcripts available by mail. Search requires name plus social security number, signed release. Other helpful information: date of birth, approximate years of attendance. Fee is $2.00.

Major credit cards accepted for payment.

Lincoln University, Registrar, 820 Chestnut St, Jefferson City, MO 65102-0029, 314-681-5011. Hours: 8AM-5PM. Records go back to 1912. Alumni records are maintained here also. Call

314-681-5570. Degrees granted: Associate; Bachelors; Masters. Adverse incident record source: Public Safety, PO Box 29, Jefferson City, MO 65102-0029.

Attendance and degree information available by phone, mail. Search requires name only. Other helpful information: social security number, date of birth, approximate years of attendance. No fee for information.

Transcripts available by mail. Search requires name plus signed release. Other helpful information: social security number, date of birth, approximate years of attendance. Fee is $3.00.

Lincoln University, Registrar, Lincoln University, PA 19352-0999, 610-932-3283 (FAX: 610-932-7659). Hours: 8AM-5PM. Records go back to 1930. Degrees granted: Bachelors; Masters.

Attendance and degree information available by phone, FAX, mail. Search requires name plus social security number, signed release. Other helpful information: approximate years of attendance. No fee for information.

Transcripts available by FAX, mail. Search requires name plus social security number, signed release. Other helpful information: approximate years of attendance. Fee is $5.00.

Lincoln University, Registrar, 281 Masonic Ave, San Francisco, CA 94118, 415-221-1212 (FAX: 415-387-9730). Hours: 9AM-5PM. Records go back to 1926. Degrees granted: Bachelors; Masters.

Attendance and degree information available by phone, FAX, mail. Search requires name plus date of birth, approximate years of attendance. Other helpful information: exact years of attendance. No fee for information.

Transcripts available by written request only. Search requires name plus date of birth, approximate years of attendance, signed release. Other helpful information: exact years of attendance. Fee is $5.00.

Major credit cards accepted for payment.

Lindenwood College, Registrar, 209 S Kingshighway Blvd, St Charles, MO 63301, 314-949-4954. Hours: 8AM-6PM M-Th, 8AM-5PM F. Records go back to 1827. Alumni records are maintained here also. Call 314-949-4906. Degrees granted: Bachelors; Masters. Adverse incident record source: Dean, 314-949-4984.

Attendance and degree information available by mail. Search requires name plus social security number, date of birth, approximate years of attendance, signed release. No fee for information.

Transcripts available by mail. Search requires name plus social security number, date of birth, approximate years of attendance, signed release. Fee is $5.00.

Lindsey Wilson College, Registrar, 210 Lindsey Wilson St, Columbia, KY 42728, 502-384-2126 X8024 (FAX: 502-384-8200). Hours: 7:30AM-4:30PM. Alumni records are maintained here also. Call 502-384-8400. Degrees granted: Associate; Bachelors; Masters. Adverse incident record source: Dean of Students, 502-384-2126 X8036.

Attendance and degree information available by phone, FAX, mail. Search requires name plus social security number. Other helpful information: date of birth, approximate years of attendance. No fee for information.

Transcripts available by mail. Search requires name plus signed release. Other helpful information: social security number, date of birth, approximate years of attendance. Fee is $3.00.

Linfield College, Office of the Registrar, Unit D - 900 SW Baker, McMinnville, OR 97128, 503-434-2200 (FAX: 503-434-2215). Hours: 8AM-5PM. Records go back to 1847. Alumni records are maintained here also. Call 503-434-2200. Degrees granted: Bachelors; Masters.

Attendance information available by phone, FAX, mail. Search requires name plus social security number. Other helpful information: approximate years of attendance. No fee for information.

Degree information available by phone, FAX, mail. Search requires name plus social security number, exact years of attendance. No fee for information.

Transcripts available by mail. Search requires name plus social security number, exact years of attendance, signed release. No fee for transcripts.

Need former names.

Linn-Benton Community College, Registrar, 6500 SW Pacific Blvd, Albany, OR 97321, 503-967-8801 (FAX: 503-928-6352). Hours: 8:30AM-4:30PM. Records go back to 1967. Degrees granted: Associate. Adverse incident record source: Dean, 503-917-4999.

Attendance and degree information available by phone, FAX, mail. Search requires name plus social security number. No fee for information.

Transcripts available by FAX, mail. Search requires name plus social security number, signed release. Other helpful information: exact years of attendance. Fee is $5.00.

Major credit cards accepted for payment.

Little Big Horn College, Registrar, PO Box 370, Crow Agency, MT 59022, 406-638-7212 (FAX: 406-638-7213). Hours: 8AM-5PM. Records go back to 1984. Degrees granted.

Attendance and degree information available by mail. Search requires name only. No fee for information.

Transcripts available by mail. Search requires name plus signed release. Other helpful information: social security number, date of birth. No fee for transcripts.

Little Hoop Community College, Registrar, PO Box 269, Fort Totten, ND 58335, 701-766-4077 (FAX: 701-766-4077). Hours: 8AM-4:30PM. Records go back to 1974. Degrees granted: Associate; Vocational.

Attendance and degree information available by FAX, mail. Search requires name plus social security number, approximate years of attendance, signed release. No fee for information.

Transcripts available by FAX, mail. Search requires name plus social security number, approximate years of attendance, signed release. Fee is $1.00.

Livingston University, Registrar, 205 N Washington St, Livingston, AL 35470, 205-652-9661 (FAX: 205-652-4065). Hours: 8AM-5PM. Records go back 83 years. Degrees granted: Associate; Bachelors; Masters.

Attendance and degree information available by phone, FAX, mail. Search requires name plus social security number. Other helpful information: date of birth, approximate years of attendance. No fee for information.

Transcripts available by written request only. Search requires name plus social security number, signed release. Other helpful information: date of birth, approximate years of attendance. Fee is $3.00. Expedited service available for $12.00.

Livingstone College, Registrar, 701 W Monroe St, Salisbury, NC 28144, 704-638-5523 (FAX: 704-638-5636). Hours:

8AM-5PM. Degrees granted: Bachelors; Masters. Adverse incident record source: Dean.

Attendance and degree information available by phone, FAX, mail. Search requires name plus social security number, date of birth, exact years of attendance, signed release. Other helpful information: approximate years of attendance. Fee is $3.00.

Transcripts available by mail. Search requires name plus social security number, date of birth, exact years of attendance, signed release. Other helpful information: approximate years of attendance. Fee is $3.00.

Major credit cards accepted for payment.

Lock Haven University, Student Records, Sullivan Hall 207, Lock Haven, PA 17745, 717-893-2006 (FAX: 717-893-2432). Hours: 8AM-4PM. Records go back to 1935. Alumni records are maintained here also. Call 717-893-2021. Degrees granted: Associate; Bachelors; Masters. Certification: Teacher Education.

Attendance and degree information available by phone, FAX, mail. Search requires name plus social security number. Other helpful information: date of birth, approximate years of attendance. No fee for information.

Transcripts available by written request only. Search requires name plus social security number, date of birth, approximate years of attendance, signed release. Fee is $2.00.

Logan College of Chiropractic, Registrar, 1851 Schoettler Rd, PO Box 1065, Chesterfield, MO 63006-1065, 314-227-2100 (FAX: 314-227-9338). Hours: 7AM-4:30PM. Records go back to 1939. Degrees granted: Bachelors; Doctorate.

Attendance and degree information available by phone, FAX, mail. Search requires name plus approximate years of attendance. Other helpful information: social security number. No fee for information.

Transcripts available by FAX, mail. Search requires name plus approximate years of attendance, signed release. Other helpful information: social security number. Fee is $5.00.

Major credit cards accepted for payment.

Loma Linda University, Office of University Records, Loma Linda, CA 92350, 909-824-4508 (FAX: 909-824-4879). Hours: 8:30AM-4PM M,T; 9AM-4PM W; 9AM-6PM Th; 8:30AM-2PM F. Records go back to founding date. Degrees granted: Associate; Bachelors; Masters; Doctorate.

Attendance and degree information available by FAX, mail. Search requires name plus social security number, signed release. Other helpful information: date of birth, approximate years of attendance. No fee for information.

Transcripts available by FAX, mail. Search requires name plus social security number, signed release. Other helpful information: date of birth, approximate years of attendance. Fee is $2.00. Expedited service available for $5.00.

Major credit cards accepted for payment.

Lon Morris College, Registrar, 800 College Ave, Jacksonville, TX 75766, 903-589-4005 (FAX: 903-586-8562). Alumni records are maintained here at the same phone number. Degrees granted: Associate.

Attendance and degree information available by mail. Search requires name plus social security number, exact years of attendance. No fee for information.

Transcripts available by mail. Search requires name plus social security number, exact years of attendance, signed release. Fee is $5.00.

Long Beach City College, Registrar, 4901 E Carson St, Long Beach, CA 90808, 310-420-4139 (FAX: 310-420-4118). Hours: 8AM-7PM M-Th, 8AM-4:30PM F. Records go back to 1927. Alumni records are maintained here also. Call 310-420-4203. Degrees granted: Associate. Adverse incident record source: Dean of Students, 310-420-4155.

Attendance and degree information available by phone, mail. Search requires name plus social security number, date of birth, approximate years of attendance, signed release. Fee is $3.00.

School does not provide transcripts. Search requires name plus social security number, date of birth, approximate years of attendance, signed release. Fee is $3.00.

Long Island University, Registrar, Northern Blvd, Brookville, NY 11548, 516-299-2756 (FAX: 516-299-2721). Hours: 9AM-5PM M,W,Th,F; 9AM-8PM T. Records go back to 1954. Degrees granted: Associate; Bachelors; Masters; Doctorate.

Attendance and degree information available by phone, FAX, mail. Search requires name plus social security number. Other helpful information: date of birth, approximate years of attendance. No fee for information.

Transcripts available by FAX, mail. Search requires name plus social security number, signed release. Other helpful information: date of birth, approximate years of attendance. Fee is $5.00.

Major credit cards accepted for payment.

Long Island University, Registrar, 555 Broadway, Dobbs Ferry, NY 10522, 914-674-7445 (FAX: 914-674-7269). Hours: 9:30AM-7PM. Records go back to 1975. Degrees granted: Masters.

Attendance and degree information available by FAX, mail. Search requires name plus social security number, signed release. Other helpful information: date of birth, approximate years of attendance. No fee for information.

Transcripts available by mail. Search requires name plus social security number, signed release. Other helpful information: date of birth, approximate years of attendance. Fee is $3.00. Expedited service available for $3.00.

Credit cards may be used for fees over $50.00.

Long Island University, (Brentwood Campus), Registrar, Second Ave, Brentwood, NY 11717, 516-299-2756. Hours: 9AM-5PM M,W,Th,F; 9AM-8PM T. Records go back to 1954.

Attendance and degree information available by phone, FAX, mail. Search requires name plus social security number. Other helpful information: date of birth, approximate years of attendance. No fee for information.

Transcripts available by mail. Search requires name plus social security number, signed release. Other helpful information: date of birth, approximate years of attendance. Fee is $5.00.

Major credit cards accepted for payment.

Long Island University, (Brooklyn Campus), Registrar, University Plaza, Brooklyn, NY 11201, 718-488-1000. Degrees granted: Associate.

Attendance information available by mail. Search requires name plus social security number, approximate years of attendance, signed release. Other helpful information: date of birth. No fee for information.

Degree information available by mail. Search requires name plus social security number, date of birth, approximate years of attendance, signed release. No fee for information.

Transcripts available by mail. Search requires name plus social security number, date of birth, approximate years of attendance, signed release. Fee is $5.00.
Major credit cards accepted for payment.

Long Island University, **(C.W. Post Campus)**, Registrar, Brookville, NY 11548, 516-299-2755 (FAX: 516-299-2721). Hours: 9AM-5PM M,W,Th,F; 9AM-8PM T. Records go back to 1954. Alumni records are maintained here also. Call 516-299-2263.
Attendance and degree information available by phone, mail. Search requires name plus social security number. Other helpful information: date of birth, approximate years of attendance. No fee for information.
Transcripts available by mail. Search requires name plus social security number, signed release. Other helpful information: date of birth, approximate years of attendance. Fee is $5.00.

Long Island University, **(Rockland Campus)**, Registrar, Rte 340, Orangeburg, NY 10962, 914-359-7200 (FAX: 914-359-7248). Hours: 8AM-8PM M-Th; 9AM-5PM F. Records go back to 1990. Degrees granted: Masters. Certification: Adv. Business. Special programs- Graduate Records at C W Post, 516-299-2755.
Attendance and degree information available by phone, FAX, mail. Search requires name plus social security number, date of birth, signed release. Other helpful information: approximate years of attendance. No fee for information.
Transcripts available by mail. Search requires name plus social security number, date of birth, signed release. Other helpful information: approximate years of attendance. Fee is $5.00.
Major credit cards accepted for payment.

Longview Community College, Registrar, 500 Longview Rd, Lee's Summit, MO 64081, 816-672-2244 (FAX: 816-672-2040). Hours: 8AM-6PM. Records go back to 1969. Degrees granted: Associate.
Attendance and degree information available by phone, FAX, mail. Search requires name plus social security number. Other helpful information: date of birth, approximate years of attendance. No fee for information.
Transcripts available by mail. Search requires name plus date of birth, signed release. Other helpful information: social security number, approximate years of attendance. Fee is $2.00.

Longwood College, Registrar, 201 High St, Farmville, VA 23909, 804-395-2095 (FAX: 804-395-2252). Hours: 8:15AM-5PM. Records go back to 1884. Alumni records are maintained here also. Call 804-395-2044. Degrees granted: Bachelors; Masters. Adverse incident record source: Campus Police, 804-395-2612.
Attendance information available by phone, FAX, mail. Search requires name plus social security number, approximate years of attendance, signed notarized release. Other helpful information: date of birth. No fee for information.
Degree information available by mail. Search requires name plus social security number, date of birth, approximate years of attendance, signed release. No fee for information.
Transcripts available by mail. Search requires name plus social security number, date of birth, approximate years of attendance, signed release. Fee is $3.00. Expedited service available for $3.00.

Lorain County Community College, Admissions & Records, 1005 N Abbe Rd, Elyria, OH 44035, 800-995-5222 (FAX: 216-365-6519). Hours: 8:30AM-7:30PM M-Th; 8:30AM-4:30PM F. Records go back to 1965. Degrees granted: Associate. Adverse incident record source: Student Life, 800-995-5222 X7646: Campus Services, 800-995-5222 X7530
Attendance and degree information available by phone, FAX, mail. Search requires name plus social security number, date of birth. Other helpful information: approximate years of attendance. No fee for information.
Transcripts available by FAX, mail. Search requires name plus social security number, date of birth, signed release. Other helpful information: approximate years of attendance. Fee is $2.00.
Major credit cards accepted for payment.

Loras College, Registrar, 1450 Alta Vista, Dubuque, IA 52004, 319-588-7106 (FAX: 319-588-7964). Hours: 8AM-4:30PM. Records go back to 1839. Alumni records are maintained here also. Call 319-588-7170. Degrees granted: Bachelors; Masters.
Attendance and degree information available by phone, FAX, mail. Search requires name plus social security number, exact years of attendance. No fee for information.
Transcripts available by mail. Search requires name plus social security number, exact years of attendance. Fee is $3.00. Expedited service available for $5.00.

Lord Fairfax Community College, Registrar, PO Box 47, Middletown, VA 22645, 703-869-1120 X126 (FAX: 703-869-7881). Hours: 8AM-5PM. Records go back to 1970. Alumni records are maintained here at the same phone number. Degrees granted: Associate.
Attendance and degree information available by mail. Search requires name plus social security number, signed release. No fee for information.
Transcripts available by mail. Search requires name plus social security number, signed release. No fee for transcripts.

Los Angeles City College, Registrar, 855 N Vermont Ave, Los Angeles, CA 90029, 213-953-4448 (FAX: 213-953-4536). Hours: 9AM-7PM. Records go back to 1990. Alumni records are maintained here also. Call 213-953-4415. Degrees granted: Associate. Adverse incident record source: Campus Police, 213-953-4311.
Attendance and degree information available by phone, FAX, mail. Search requires name plus social security number, approximate years of attendance, signed release. No fee for information.
Transcripts available by phone, FAX, mail. Search requires name plus social security number, approximate years of attendance, signed release. Fee is $1.00.

Los Angeles College of Chiropractic, Registrar, 16200 E Amber Valley Dr, Whittier, CA 90604, 310-902-3380 (FAX: 310-947-5724). Hours: 8AM-5PM. Records go back to 1911. Alumni records are maintained here also. Call 310-947-8755. Degrees granted: Bachelors; Doctorate. Adverse incident record source: Academic Dean, 310-947-8755 X313.
Attendance and degree information available by written request only. Search requires name plus social security number, date of birth, approximate years of attendance, signed release. Fee is $10.00. Expedited service available for $15.00.
Transcripts available by written request only. Search requires name plus social security number, date of birth, approximate years of attendance, signed release. Fee is $20.00. Expedited service available for $15.00.

Los Angeles Harbor College, Registrar, 1111 Figueroa Pl, Wilmington, CA 90744, 310-522-8216 (FAX: 310-834-1882). Hours: 9AM-7PM M-Th; 9AM-3PM F. Records go back to 1949.

Attendance and degree information available by mail. Search requires name plus social security number, date of birth, exact years of attendance, signed release. Other helpful information: approximate years of attendance. Fee is $1.00. Expedited service available for $5.00.

Transcripts available by mail. Search requires name plus social security number, date of birth, exact years of attendance, signed release. Other helpful information: approximate years of attendance. Fee is $1.00. Expedited service available for $5.00.

Los Angeles Mission College, Registrar, 13356 Eldridge Ave, Sylmar, CA 91342-3245, 818-364-7663 (FAX: 818-364-7755). Hours: 9AM-7PM. Records go back to 1975. Degrees granted: Associate.

Attendance and degree information available by FAX, mail. Search requires name plus social security number, date of birth, approximate years of attendance, signed release. No fee for information.

Transcripts available by FAX, mail. Search requires name plus social security number, date of birth, approximate years of attendance, signed release. Fee is $1.00.

Los Angeles Pierce College, Registrar, 6201 Winnetka Ave, Woodland Hills, CA 91371, 818-347-5553 (FAX: 818-710-9844). Hours: 8:30AM-8:30PM M-Th, 8:30AM-4PM F. Records go back to 1940. Alumni records are maintained here at the same phone number. Degrees granted: Associate. Adverse incident record source: Academic, 818-347-6448.

Attendance and degree information available by phone, FAX, mail. Search requires name plus social security number, approximate years of attendance, signed release. No fee for information.

Transcripts available by mail. Search requires name plus social security number, approximate years of attendance, signed release. Fee is $1.00.

Los Angeles Southwest College, Admission Office, 1600 W Imperial Hwy, Los Angeles, CA 90047, 213-241-5320 (FAX: 213-241-5325). Hours: 8:30AM-8PM M-Th; 8:30AM-3PM F. Records go back to 1967. Degrees granted: Associate. Adverse incident record source: Campus Police, 213-241-5311.

Attendance information available by FAX, mail. Search requires name plus social security number, date of birth, signed release. Other helpful information: approximate years of attendance. Fee is $1.00. Expedited service available for $5.00.

Degree information available by mail. Search requires name plus date of birth, signed release. Other helpful information: social security number, approximate years of attendance. No fee for information.

Transcripts available by mail. Search requires name plus social security number, date of birth, signed release. Other helpful information: approximate years of attendance. Fee is $1.00. Expedited service available for $5.00.

Los Angeles Trade-Technical College, Registrar, 400 W Washington Blvd, Los Angeles, CA 90015, 213-744-9420 (FAX: 213-744-9425). Hours: 8:30AM-8PM M-Th; 8:30AM-4PM F. Records go back to 1949. Degrees granted: Associate.

Attendance information available by FAX, mail. Search requires name plus social security number, approximate years of attendance, signed release. Other helpful information: date of birth, exact years of attendance. First two transcripts/verifications free. Additional ones are $1.00 each.

Degree information available by FAX, mail. Search requires name plus social security number, signed release. Other helpful information: date of birth, approximate years of attendance. First two transcripts/verifications free. Additional ones are $1.00 each.

Transcripts available by mail. Search requires name plus social security number, date of birth, signed release. Other helpful information: approximate years of attendance. First two transcripts/verifications free. Additional ones are $1.00 each. Expedited service available for $5.00.

Los Angeles Valley College, Registrar, 5800 Fulton Ave, Van Nuys, CA 91401, 818-781-1200 X255 (FAX: 818-781-4672). Hours: 8:30AM-8:30PM M-Th, 8:30AM-4PM F. Records go back to 1940. Degrees granted: Associate.

Attendance information available by mail. Search requires name plus social security number, date of birth, approximate years of attendance, signed release. Fee is $1.00.

Degree information available by FAX, mail. Search requires name plus social security number, date of birth, approximate years of attendance, signed release. Fee is $1.00.

Transcripts available by FAX, mail. Search requires name plus social security number, date of birth, approximate years of attendance, signed release. Fee is $1.00.

Los Medanos College, Registrar, 2700 E Leland Rd, Pittsburg, CA 94565, 510-439-2181 (FAX: 510-427-1599). Hours: 9AM-8PM M-Th; 9AM-3PM F. Records go back to 1974. Degrees granted: Associate.

Attendance and degree information available by phone, FAX, mail. Search requires name only. Other helpful information: social security number, date of birth. No fee for information.

Transcripts available by FAX, mail. Search requires name plus social security number, signed release. Other helpful information: date of birth, approximate years of attendance. First two transcripts are free. Additioonal ones are $3.00 each.

Major credit cards accepted for payment.

Louisburg College, Registrar Office, 501 N Main St, Louisburg, NC 27549, 919-496-2521 (FAX: 919-496-1788). Hours: 8:30AM-5PM. Records go back to 1900s. Alumni records are maintained here at the same phone number. Degrees granted: Associate. Adverse incident record source: Student Affairs, 919-496-2521 X235.

Attendance information available by phone, FAX, mail. Search requires name plus social security number. No fee for information.

Degree information available by phone, FAX, mail. Search requires name plus social security number, exact years of attendance. No fee for information.

Transcripts available by FAX, mail. Search requires name plus social security number, exact years of attendance, signed release. Fee is $3.00.

Major credit cards accepted for payment.

Louise Salinger Academy of Fashion, Registrar, 101 Jessie St, San Francisco, CA 94105-3593, 415-974-6666 (FAX: 415-982-0113). Hours: 9AM-5PM. Records go back to 1939. Degrees granted: Associate; Bachelors.

Attendance information available by written request only. Search requires name plus social security number, approximate years of attendance, signed release. Other helpful information: date of birth. No fee for information.

Degree information available by written request only. Search requires name plus approximate years of attendance, signed release. Other helpful information: social security number, date of birth. No fee for information.

Transcripts available by written request only. Search requires name plus social security number, approximate years of attendance, signed release. Other helpful information: date of birth. Fee is $5.00.

Louisiana College, Registrar, 1140 College Dr, Pineville, LA 71359, 318-487-7222 (FAX: 318-487-7191). Hours: 8AM-4:30PM. Records go back to 1990. Alumni records are maintained here also. Call 318-487-7301. Degrees granted: Associate; Bachelors; Masters.

Attendance and degree information available by phone, FAX, mail. Search requires name plus social security number, approximate years of attendance, signed release. No fee for information.

Transcripts available by FAX, mail. Search requires name plus social security number, approximate years of attendance, signed release. No fee for transcripts.

Louisiana State University Medical Center, Registrar, 433 Bolivar St, New Orleans, LA 70112, 504-568-4829. Hours: 8AM-4:30PM. Records go back to 1979. Alumni records are maintained here also. Call 504-568-4894. Degrees granted: Associate; Bachelors; Masters; Doctorate; Ph.

Attendance and degree information available by phone, mail. Search requires name plus social security number, date of birth, approximate years of attendance, signed release. No fee for information.

Transcripts available by mail. Search requires name plus social security number, date of birth, approximate years of attendance, signed release. Fee is $2.00.

Louisiana State University and Agricultural & Mechanical College, Office of Records & Registration, 112 Thomas Boyd Hall, Baton Rouge, LA 70803, 504-388-1686 (FAX: 504-388-5991). Hours: 8:30AM-5PM. Alumni records are maintained here at the same phone number. Degrees granted: Bachelors.

Attendance and degree information available by phone, mail. Search requires name plus social security number, exact years of attendance. No fee for information.

Transcripts available by FAX, mail. Search requires name plus social security number, exact years of attendance, signed release. No fee for transcripts.

Louisiana State University at Alexandria, Registrar, 8100 Hwy 71 S, Alexandria, LA 71302, 318-473-6541 (FAX: 318-473-6418). Hours: 8AM-4:30PM. Records go back to 1960. Degrees granted: Associate.

Attendance information available by phone, FAX, mail. Search requires name only. Other helpful information: social security number, approximate years of attendance. No fee for information.

Degree information available by phone, FAX, mail. Search requires name only. Other helpful information: social security number, date of birth, approximate years of attendance. No fee for information.

Transcripts available by FAX, mail. Search requires name plus signed release. Other helpful information: social security number, approximate years of attendance. First five transcripts are free. Additional ones are $5.00 each.

Louisiana State University at Eunice, Registrar, PO Box 1129, Eunice, LA 70535, 318-457-7311 (FAX: 318-546-6620). Hours: 8AM-4:30PM. Records go back to 1967. Degrees granted: Associate.

Attendance and degree information available by FAX, mail. Search requires name plus social security number. Other helpful information: date of birth, approximate years of attendance. No fee for information.

Transcripts available by FAX, mail. Search requires name plus social security number, signed release. Other helpful information: date of birth, approximate years of attendance. No fee for transcripts.

Louisiana State University at Shreveport, Registrar, One University Pl, Shreveport, LA 71115, 318-797-5061. Hours: 8AM-5PM. Records go back to 1957. Alumni records are maintained here also. Call 318-797-5202. Degrees granted: Bachelors; Masters. Adverse incident record source: Student Affairs, 318-797-5116.

Attendance and degree information available by phone, mail. Search requires name plus social security number, date of birth, approximate years of attendance, signed release. No fee for information.

Transcripts available by mail. Search requires name plus social security number, date of birth, approximate years of attendance, signed release. Fee is $4.00.

Louisiana Tech University, Registrar, PO Box 3155 Tech Station, Ruston, LA 71272, 318-257-2176 (FAX: 318-257-4041). Hours: 8AM-5PM. Degrees granted: Associate; Bachelors; Masters; Doctorate. Adverse incident record source: 318-257-4018.

Attendance and degree information available by phone, FAX, mail. Search requires name only. Other helpful information: social security number, date of birth, approximate years of attendance. No fee for information.

Transcripts available by FAX, mail. Search requires name plus social security number, signed release. Other helpful information: date of birth, approximate years of attendance. No fee for transcripts.

FAX must be followed by a written request.

Louisville Presbyterian Theological Seminary, Registrar, 1044 Alta Vista Rd, Louisville, KY 40205, 502-895-3411 (FAX: 502-895-1096). Hours: 8:30AM-5PM. Records go back to 1920. Degrees granted: Masters; Doctorate.

Attendance and degree information available by phone, FAX, mail. Search requires name plus approximate years of attendance, signed release. Other helpful information: social security number, date of birth, exact years of attendance. No fee for information.

Transcripts available by written request only. Search requires name plus approximate years of attendance, signed release. Other helpful information: social security number, date of birth, exact years of attendance. Fee is $5.00.

Louisville Technical Institute, Registrar, 3901 Atkinson Dr, Louisville, KY 40218-4528, 502-456-6509 (FAX: 502-456-2341). Degrees granted: Associate.

Attendance and degree information available by phone, FAX, mail. Search requires name plus social security number, approximate years of attendance. No fee for information.

Transcripts available by FAX, mail. Search requires name plus social security number, approximate years of attendance, signed release. Fee is $5.00.

Lourdes College, Registrar, 6832 Convent Blvd, Sylvania, OH 43560, 419-885-4917 X207 (FAX: 419-882-3987). Hours: 8:30AM-6PM M-Th, 8:30AM-4:30PM, 9AM-1PM Sat. Alumni records are maintained here at the same phone number. Degrees granted: Bachelors. Adverse incident record source: Student Services, 419-885-4917 X200.

Attendance information available by FAX, mail. Search requires name plus social security number, date of birth, approximate years of attendance, signed release. No fee for information.

Degree information available by phone, FAX, mail. Search requires name plus social security number, date of birth, approximate years of attendance, signed release. No fee for information.

Transcripts available by FAX, mail. Search requires name plus social security number, date of birth, approximate years of attendance, signed release. First transcript is free. Additional ones are $3.00 each.

Lower Columbia College, Registrar, PO Box 3010, 1600 Maple St, Longview, WA 98632-0310, 206-577-2303 (FAX: 206-577-3400). Hours: 8AM-4:30PM. Records go back to 1934. Alumni records are maintained here at the same phone number. Degrees granted: Associate.

Attendance and degree information available by phone, mail. Search requires name plus social security number, signed release. No fee for information.

Transcripts available by mail. Search requires name plus social security number, signed release. Fee is $3.00.

Lowthian College, Registrar, 825 2nd Ave S, Minneapolis, MN 55402, 612-332-3361. Hours: 9AM-5PM. Records go back to 1965. Alumni records are maintained here also. Call 612-332-3361. Degrees granted: Associate.

Attendance and degree information available by phone, mail. Search requires name plus approximate years of attendance. No fee for information.

Transcripts available by mail. Search requires name plus approximate years of attendance, signed release. Fee is $3.00.

Loyola College in Maryland, Registrar, Records Office MH 121, 4501 N Charles St, Baltimore, MD 21210-2699, 410-617-2504 (FAX: 410-617-5031). Hours: 7AM-7:45PM M-Th; 7AM-3PM F. Records go back to 1900. Degrees granted: Bachelors; Masters; Doctorate. Certification: 30 credit beyond the Masters.

Attendance information available by phone, FAX, mail. Search requires name plus social security number, approximate years of attendance, signed release. Other helpful information: date of birth. No fee for information.

Degree information available by phone, FAX, mail. Search requires name plus social security number, exact years of attendance, signed release. Other helpful information: date of birth, approximate years of attendance. No fee for information.

Transcripts available by phone, FAX, mail. Search requires name plus social security number, approximate years of attendance, signed release. Other helpful information: date of birth, exact years of attendance. Fee is $3.00.

FAX available only in emergency situations.

Loyola Marymount University, Registrar, Loyola Blvd at W 80th St, Los Angeles, CA 90045, 310-338-2740 (FAX: 310-338-4466). Hours: 8AM-5PM. Degrees granted: Bachelors; Masters.

Attendance and degree information available by phone, FAX, mail. Search requires name only. Other helpful information: social security number, date of birth, approximate years of attendance. No fee for information.

Transcripts available by FAX, mail. Search requires name plus signed release. Other helpful information: social security number, date of birth, approximate years of attendance. No fee for transcripts. Expedited service available for $10.00.

Loyola University, Registrar, 6363 St. Charles Ave, New Orleans, LA 70118, 504-865-3237 (FAX: 504-865-3110). Hours: 8:30AM-4:45PM. Records go back to 1920. Alumni records are maintained here at the same phone number. Degrees granted: Bachelors; Masters; Law School. Adverse incident record source: Public Safety, 504-865-3434.

Attendance and degree information available by phone, FAX, mail. Search requires name plus social security number, signed release. No fee for information.

Transcripts available by FAX, mail. Search requires name plus social security number, signed release. Fee is $2.00.

Loyola University of Chicago, Registrar, 820 N Michigan Ave, Chicago, IL 60611, 312-915-7221 (FAX: 312-915-6448). Hours: 8:30AM-5PM. Records go back to founding date. Alumni Records Office: 6525 N Sheridan Rd, Chicago, IL 60626. Degrees granted: Bachelors; Masters; Doctorate. Special programs- Stritch School of Medicine, 708-216-3222.

Attendance and degree information available by phone, FAX, mail. Search requires name plus social security number, approximate years of attendance. Other helpful information: date of birth, exact years of attendance. No fee for information.

Transcripts available by FAX, mail. Search requires name plus social security number, approximate years of attendance, signed release. Other helpful information: date of birth, exact years of attendance. Fee is $3.00.

College and major also helpful.

Lubbock Christian University, Registrar, 5601 19th St, Lubbock, TX 79407-2099, 806-796-8800 X226 (FAX: 806-796-8917). Records go back to 1957. Alumni records are maintained here also. Call 806-796-8800 X244. Degrees granted: Bachelors.

Attendance and degree information available by phone, FAX, mail. Search requires name plus social security number, exact years of attendance. No fee for information.

Transcripts available by FAX, mail. Search requires name plus social security number, exact years of attendance, signed release. Fee is $3.00.

Luna Vocational Technical Institute, Registrar, PO Drawer K, Las Vegas, NM 87701, 505-454-2548 (FAX: 505-454-2518). Hours: 8AM-4:30PM. Records go back to 1970. Degrees granted: Associate. Adverse incident record source: Student Services, 505-454-2554.

Attendance and degree information available by phone, FAX, mail. Search requires name plus social security number, approximate years of attendance, signed release. No fee for information.

Transcripts available by mail. Search requires name plus social security number, approximate years of attendance, signed release. First transcript free, $1.00 each additional.

Lurleen B. Wallace State Junior College, Registrar, PO Box 1418, Andalusia, AL 36420, 334-222-6591 X273 (FAX: 334-222-6567). Hours: 8AM-5PM. Records go back to 1969. Degrees granted: Associate.

Attendance and degree information available by phone, mail. Search requires name only. Other helpful information: social security number, date of birth, approximate years of attendance. No fee for information.

Transcripts available by mail. Search requires name plus social security number, signed release. Other helpful information: approximate years of attendance. Fee is $1.00.

Luther College, Registrar's Office, 700 College Dr, Decorah, IA 52101-1045, 319-387-1167 (FAX: 319-387-2158). Hours: 8AM-5PM. Degrees granted: Bachelors.

Attendance and degree information available by phone, FAX, mail. Search requires name plus social security number. Other helpful information: date of birth, approximate years of attendance. No fee for information. Expedite fee: $9.00 to $11.00.

Transcripts available by FAX, mail. Search requires name plus social security number, signed release. Other helpful information: date of birth, approximate years of attendance. Fee is $4.00. Expedite fee: $9.00 to $11.00.

Luther Seminary, Registrar, 2481 Como Ave, St Paul, MN 55108, 612-641-3473. Hours: 8:30-10AM, 10:40-Noon, 1-3:30PM Closed for Chapel. Records go back to 1869. Alumni records are maintained here also. Call 612-641-3451. Degrees granted: Masters. Adverse incident record source: Dean of Students, 612-641-3229.

Attendance and degree information available by phone, mail. Search requires name plus social security number, approximate years of attendance, signed release. No fee for information.

Transcripts available by mail. Search requires name plus social security number, approximate years of attendance, signed release. Fee is $3.00.

Lutheran Bible Institute of Seattle, Registrar, 4221 228th Ave SE, Issaquah, WA 98027, 206-392-0400 (FAX: 206-392-0404). Hours: 8AM-5PM. Records go back to 1945. Degrees granted: Associate; Bachelors.

Attendance and degree information available by phone, FAX, mail. Search requires name only. Other helpful information: approximate years of attendance. No fee for information.

Transcripts available by FAX, mail. Search requires name plus signed release. Other helpful information: approximate years of attendance. Fee is $3.00.

Lutheran College of Health Professions, Registrar, 3024 Fairfield Ave, Fort Wayne, IN 46807, 219-458-2453 (FAX: 219-458-3077). Hours: 8AM-4:30PM. Records go back to 1904. Degrees granted: Associate; Bachelors.

Attendance and degree information available by written request only. Search requires name plus social security number, approximate years of attendance, signed release. Other helpful information: date of birth, exact years of attendance. No fee for information.

Transcripts available by written request only. Search requires name plus social security number, date of birth, approximate years of attendance, signed release. Other helpful information: exact years of attendance. Fee is $3.00.

Lutheran School of Theology at Chicago, Registrar, 1100 E 55th St, Chicago, IL 60615-5199, 312-753-0700 (FAX: 312-753-0782). Hours: 8:30AM-4:30PM. Records go back to 1940. Degrees granted: Masters; Doctorate. Certification: Theology.

Attendance information available by phone, mail. Search requires name plus social security number, signed release. Other helpful information: date of birth, approximate years of attendance. No fee for information.

Degree information available by phone, FAX, mail. Search requires name plus social security number, signed release. Other helpful information: date of birth, approximate years of attendance. No fee for information.

Transcripts available by mail. Search requires name plus social security number, signed release. Other helpful information: date of birth, approximate years of attendance. Fee is $2.00. Expedited service available for $2.00.

Lutheran Theological Seminary at Gettysburg, Registrar, 61 NW Confederate Ave, Gettysburg, PA 17325-1795, 717-334-6286 X201 (FAX: 717-334-3469). Hours: 8:30AM-4:30PM. Records go back to 1930. Alumni records are maintained here also. Call 717-334-3469 X210. Degrees granted: Masters; STM. Adverse incident record source: Dean, 717-334-3469 X202.

Attendance and degree information available by FAX, mail. Search requires name plus approximate years of attendance. No fee for information.

Transcripts available by mail. Search requires name plus approximate years of attendance, signed release. Fee is $3.00.

Lutheran Theological Seminary at Philadelphia, Registrar, 7301 Germantown Ave, Philadelphia, PA 19119, 215-248-4616 (FAX: 215-248-4577). Hours: 9AM-4:30PM; Summer hours 8:30AM-4PM. Records go back to 1864. Alumni records are maintained here also. Call 215-248-4616.

Attendance and degree information available by phone, FAX, mail. Search requires name plus social security number, approximate years of attendance. No fee for information.

Transcripts available by FAX, mail. Search requires name plus social security number, approximate years of attendance, signed release. Fee is $2.00.

Lutheran Theological Southern Seminary, Registrar, 4201 N Main St, Columbia, SC 29203, 803-786-5150 X210. Hours: 8:30AM-4:30PM. Alumni records are maintained here at the same phone number. Degrees granted: Bachelors; Masters.

Attendance and degree information available by phone, mail. Search requires name plus social security number, exact years of attendance. No fee for information.

Transcripts available by mail. Search requires name plus social security number, exact years of attendance, signed release. Fee is $2.00.

Luzerne County Community College, Registrar, 1333 S Prospect St, Nanticoke, PA 18634, 717-829-7340 (FAX: 717-735-6130). Hours: 8AM-5PM. Records go back to 1968. Alumni records are maintained here also. Call 717-829-7387. Degrees granted: Associate. Adverse incident record source: Dean, 717-829-7344.

Attendance and degree information available by phone, mail. Search requires name plus social security number, exact years of attendance. No fee for information.

Transcripts available by mail. Search requires name plus social security number, exact years of attendance, signed release. First transcript is free. Additional ones are $2.00 each.

Need address and phone number.

Lycoming College, Registrar's Office, 700 College Pl, Williamsport, PA 17701, 717-321-4045 (FAX: 717-321-4337). Hours: 8AM-4:30PM. Records go back to 1812. Alumni records are maintained here also. Call 717-321-4025. Degrees granted:

Bachelors. Adverse incident record source: Student Affairs, 717-321-4039.

Attendance and degree information available by phone, FAX, mail. Search requires name plus social security number, exact years of attendance. No fee for information.

Transcripts available by FAX, mail. Search requires name plus social security number, exact years of attendance, signed release. Fee is $3.00.

Need date of graduation.

Lynchburg College, Registrar, 1501 Lakeside Dr, Lynchburg, VA 24501-3199, 804-522-8100 X218 (FAX: 804-522-0658). Hours: 8AM-5PM. Records go back to 1903. Alumni records are maintained here at the same phone number. Degrees granted: Bachelors; Masters.

Attendance and degree information available by phone, mail. Search requires name plus social security number. No fee for information.

Transcripts available by mail. Search requires name plus social security number, signed release. Fee is $3.00.

Lyndon State College, Registrar, Vail Hill, Lyndonville, VT 05851, 802-626-9371 X194. Hours: 8AM-4:30PM. Records go back to 1911. Alumni records are maintained here at the same phone number. Degrees granted: Bachelors; Masters.

Attendance and degree information available by phone, mail. Search requires name plus social security number, exact years of attendance. No fee for information.

Transcripts available by mail. Search requires name plus social security number, exact years of attendance, signed release. Fee is $5.00.

Lynn University, Registrar, 3601 N Military Tr, Boca Raton, FL 33431, 407-994-0770 X177 (FAX: 407-241-3552). Hours: 9AM-6PM M-Th; 9AM-5PM F. Records go back 30 years. Alumni records are maintained here also. Call 407-994-0770 X238. Degrees granted: Associate; Bachelors; Masters.

Attendance and degree information available by phone, FAX, mail. Search requires name only. Other helpful information: social security number, date of birth, approximate years of attendance. No fee for information.

Transcripts available by FAX, mail. Search requires name plus social security number, approximate years of attendance, signed release. Other helpful information: date of birth, exact years of attendance. Fee is $3.00.

Major credit cards accepted for payment.

Lyon College, Office of the Registrar, PO Box 2317, 2300 Highland Rd, Batesville, AR 72503, 501-698-4204 (FAX: 501-698-4622). Hours: 8AM-5PM. Alumni records are maintained here also. Call 501-698-4238. Degrees granted: Bachelors. Special programs- National Testing Information, 501-698-4311. Adverse incident record source: Dean of Students, 501-698-4314.

Attendance and degree information available by phone, FAX, mail. Search requires name only. Other helpful information: social security number, date of birth, approximate years of attendance. No fee for information.

Transcripts available by mail. Search requires name plus signed release. Other helpful information: social security number, date of birth, approximate years of attendance. Fee is $3.00. Expedited service available for $15.00.

M

MGH Institute of Health Professions, Registrar, 101 Merrimac St, Boston, MA 02114-4719, 617-726-3140 (FAX: 617-726-8010). Hours: 8:30AM-5PM. Records go back 80 years. Degrees granted: Masters. Certification: NP,PT.

Attendance and degree information available by phone, FAX, mail. Search requires name only. Other helpful information: social security number. No fee for information.

Transcripts available by FAX, mail. Search requires name plus approximate years of attendance, signed release. Other helpful information: social security number, exact years of attendance. Fee is $4.00. Expedited service available for $4.00.

MTI Business College, Registrar, 1140 Euclid Ave, Cleveland, OH 44115, 216-621-8228 (FAX: 216-621-6488). Hours: 7:30AM-5:30PM. Records go back to 1961. Degrees granted: Associate.

Attendance and degree information available by phone, FAX, mail. Search requires name plus approximate years of attendance. Other helpful information: social security number, date of birth, exact years of attendance. No fee for information.

Transcripts available by phone, FAX, mail. Search requires name plus social security number, approximate years of attendance. Other helpful information: date of birth, exact years of attendance. Fee is $10.00.

MacCormac Junior College, Registrar, 506 S Wabash Ave, Chicago, IL 60605-1667, 312-922-1884. Hours: 8AM-5PM. Degrees granted: Associate.

Attendance and degree information available by phone, FAX, mail. Search requires name only. Other helpful information: social security number. No fee for information.

Transcripts available by mail. Search requires name plus signed release. Other helpful information: social security number. Fee is $3.00. Expedited service available for $5.00.

MacMurray College, Records and Registration, 477 E College Ave, Jacksonville, IL 62650, 217-479-7912 (FAX: 217-245-0405). Hours: 8AM-4:30PM. Records go back to founding date. Alumni records are maintained here also. Call 217-479-7024. Degrees granted: Associate; Bachelors.

Attendance and degree information available by phone, mail. Search requires name only. Other helpful information: approximate years of attendance. No fee for information.

Transcripts available by FAX, mail. Search requires name plus social security number, date of birth, approximate years of attendance, signed release. Fee is $3.00. Expedited service available for $3.00.

Credit cards may be used in emergency only.

Macalester College, Registrar, 1600 Grand Ave, St Paul, MN 55105, 612-696-6200 (FAX: 612-696-6600). Hours: 8AM-4:30PM. Records go back to 1940. Alumni records are maintained here also. Call 612-696-6295. Degrees granted: Bachelors. Adverse incident record source: Dean of Students, 612-696-6220.

Attendance and degree information available by phone, FAX, mail. Search requires name plus social security number, date of birth, signed release. No fee for information.

Transcripts available by FAX, mail. Search requires name plus social security number, date of birth, signed release. Fee is $3.00.

The Sourcebook of College and University Student Records

Macomb Community College, Registrar, 14500 E Twelve Mile Rd, Warren, MI 48093, 810-445-7225 (FAX: 810-445-7140). Hours: 8AM-7:15PM M,T; 8AM-4:30PM W,Th,F. Records go back 40 years. Degrees granted: Associate. Adverse incident record source: Campus Police, 810-445-7135.
 Attendance and degree information available by phone, FAX, mail. Search requires name plus social security number. Other helpful information: date of birth, approximate years of attendance. No fee for information.
 Transcripts available by written request only. Search requires name plus social security number, signed release. Other helpful information: date of birth, approximate years of attendance. No fee for transcripts.

Macon College, Registrar, 100 College Station Dr, Macon, GA 31297, 912-471-2855 (FAX: 912-471-5343). Hours: 8AM-6PM M-Th; 8AM-4:30PM F. Records go back to 1968. Alumni records are maintained here also. Call 912-471-2732. Degrees granted: Associate. Adverse incident record source: Student Affairs, 912-471-2732.
 Attendance and degree information available by phone, FAX, mail. Search requires name plus social security number. Other helpful information: date of birth, approximate years of attendance. No fee for information.
 Transcripts available by FAX, mail. Search requires name plus social security number, signed release. Other helpful information: approximate years of attendance. No fee for transcripts.

Madison Area Technical College, Registrar, 3350 Anderson St, Madison, WI 53704, 608-246-6210 (FAX: 608-246-6880). Degrees granted: Associate.
 Attendance and degree information available by phone, mail. Search requires name plus social security number, exact years of attendance. No fee for information.
 Transcripts available by mail. Search requires name plus social security number, exact years of attendance, signed release. No fee for transcripts.

Madison Junior College of Business, Registrar, 31 S Henry St, Madison, WI 53703, 608-251-6522 (FAX: 608-251-6590). Hours: 7AM-4PM. Records go back to 1905. Degrees granted: Associate.
 Attendance and degree information available by phone, FAX, mail. Search requires name plus signed release. Other helpful information: date of birth, approximate years of attendance. No fee for information.
 Transcripts available by FAX, mail. Search requires name plus signed release. Other helpful information: date of birth, approximate years of attendance. Fee is $2.00.
 Major credit cards accepted for payment.

Madisonville Community College, Registrar, 2000 College Dr, Madisonville, KY 42431, 502-821-2250 (FAX: 502-821-1555). Hours: 8AM-4:30PM. Degrees granted: Associate.
 Attendance and degree information available by phone, FAX, mail. Search requires name plus social security number, signed release. Other helpful information: date of birth, approximate years of attendance. No fee for information.
 Transcripts available by mail. Search requires name plus social security number, signed release. Other helpful information: date of birth, approximate years of attendance. Fee is $2.00. Expedited service available for $5.00.

Madonna University, Registrar, 36600 Schoolcraft Rd, Livonia, MI 48150, 313-591-5038 (FAX: 313-591-0156). Hours: 8AM-5PM. Records go back to 1947. Degrees granted: Associate; Bachelors; Masters.
 Attendance information available by written request only. Search requires name plus signed release. Other helpful information: social security number, approximate years of attendance. No fee for information.
 Degree information available by phone, FAX, mail. Search requires name only. Other helpful information: social security number, approximate years of attendance. No fee for information.
 Transcripts available by written request only. Search requires name plus signed release. Other helpful information: social security number, approximate years of attendance. Fee is $5.00. Expedited service available for $7.00.

Magnolia Bible College, Registrar, PO Box 1109, Kosciusko, MS 39090, 601-289-2896 (FAX: 601-289-1850). Hours: 8AM-4:30PM. Records go back to 1976. Alumni records are maintained here also. Call 601-289-2896. Degrees granted: Bachelors. Adverse incident record source: Dean of Students.
 Attendance and degree information available by phone, FAX, mail. Search requires name only. Other helpful information: social security number, date of birth, approximate years of attendance. Fee is $1.00.
 Transcripts available by mail. Search requires name plus signed release. Other helpful information: social security number, date of birth, approximate years of attendance. Fee is $2.00.
 Major credit cards accepted for payment.

Maharishi International University, Registrar, 1000 N Fourth St DB 1104, Fairfield, IA 52557, 515-472-1144 (FAX: 515-472-1106). Hours: 10AM-4PM. Records go back to 1971. Degrees granted: Associate; Bachelors; Masters; Doctorate.
 Attendance and degree information available by phone, FAX, mail. Search requires name only. Other helpful information: social security number, date of birth, exact years of attendance. No fee for information.
 Transcripts available by FAX, mail. Search requires name plus signed release. Other helpful information: social security number, date of birth, exact years of attendance. Fee is $3.00.

Maine College of Art, Registrar, 97 Spring St, Portland, ME 04101, 207-775-3052 (FAX: 207-772-5069). Hours: 9AM-5PM. Records go back to 1882. Alumni records are maintained here at the same phone number. Degrees granted: Bachelors.
 Attendance and degree information available by mail. Search requires name plus social security number, date of birth, exact years of attendance. No fee for information.
 Transcripts available by mail. Search requires name plus social security number, date of birth, exact years of attendance, signed release. No fee for transcripts.

Maine Maritime Academy, Registrar, Castine, ME 04420, 207-326-4311 X426. Hours: 7:30AM-4PM. Records go back to 1941. Alumni records are maintained here at the same phone number. Degrees granted: Bachelors; Masters.
 Attendance and degree information available by phone, mail. Search requires name plus social security number, exact years of attendance. No fee for information.
 Transcripts available by mail. Search requires name plus social security number, exact years of attendance, signed release. Fee is $2.00.

Degree Granting Institutions

Malcolm X College, Registrar, 1900 W Van Buren St, Chicago, IL 60612, 312-850-7098 (FAX: 312-850-7092). Hours: 8:30AM-6PM. Records go back 30 years. Degrees granted: Associate.

Attendance and degree information available by phone, FAX, mail. Search requires name plus social security number, signed release. Other helpful information: date of birth, approximate years of attendance. No fee for information.

Transcripts available by FAX, mail. Search requires name plus social security number, signed release. Other helpful information: date of birth, approximate years of attendance. Fee is $5.00. Expedited service available for $10.00.

Major credit cards accepted for payment.

Malone College, Registrar, 515 25th St NW, Canton, OH 44709, 216-471-8129 (FAX: 216-454-6977). Hours: 8AM-5PM. Records go back to 1892. Alumni records are maintained here also. Call 216-471-8237. Degrees granted: Bachelors; Masters.

Attendance and degree information available by phone, FAX, mail. Search requires name plus social security number, date of birth, signed release. No fee for information.

Transcripts available by FAX, mail. Search requires name plus social security number, date of birth, signed release. Fee is $2.00.

Manatee Community College, Registrar, 5840 26th St W, Bradenton, FL 34207, 813-755-1511 X4231 (FAX: 813-755-1511 X4331). Hours: 8AM-4:30PM. Records go back to 1958. Alumni records are maintained here also. Call 813-755-1511 X4389. Degrees granted: Associate.

Attendance and degree information available by FAX. Search requires name plus social security number, signed release. Other helpful information: date of birth, approximate years of attendance. No fee for information.

Transcripts available by FAX. Search requires name plus social security number, signed release. Other helpful information: date of birth, approximate years of attendance. No fee for transcripts.

Manchester College, Registrar, 604 College Ave, North Manchester, IN 46962, 219-982-5234 (FAX: 219-982-6868). Hours: 8AM-Noon,1-5PM. Records go back to 1800s. Degrees granted: Associate; Bachelors; MACCTY.

Attendance and degree information available by phone, FAX, mail. Search requires name plus signed release. Other helpful information: date of birth, approximate years of attendance. No fee for information.

Transcripts available by FAX, mail. Search requires name plus signed release. Other helpful information: date of birth, approximate years of attendance. No fee for transcripts.

Manchester Community-Technical College, Registrar, PO Box 1046, Manchester, CT 06045-1046, 203-647-6147 (FAX: 203-647-6297). Hours: 8AM-4:30PM. Records go back to 1963. Alumni records are maintained here also. Call 203-647-6137. Degrees granted: Associate.

Attendance and degree information available by phone, FAX, mail. Search requires name plus social security number. Other helpful information: date of birth. No fee for information.

Transcripts available by mail. Search requires name plus social security number, signed release. Other helpful information: date of birth. No fee for transcripts.

Manhattan Christian College, Registrar, 1415 Anderson Ave, Manhattan, KS 66502, 913-539-3571 (FAX: 913-539-0832). Hours: 8AM-5PM. Records go back to 1927.

Attendance and degree information available by phone, FAX, mail. Search requires name plus social security number, approximate years of attendance. No fee for information.

Transcripts available by FAX, mail. Search requires name plus social security number, approximate years of attendance, signed release. Other helpful information: date of birth, exact years of attendance. Fee is $2.00. Expedite: $5.00 FAX, $9.00 overnight.

Manhattan College, Registrar, Manhattan College Pkwy, Riverdale, NY 10471, 718-920-0312 (FAX: 718-920-0457). Hours: 9AM-4:30PM. Records go back to 1800. Degrees granted: Associate; Bachelors; Masters. Adverse incident record source: Dean of Students, 718-920-0246.

Attendance and degree information available by phone, FAX, mail. Search requires name plus approximate years of attendance. Other helpful information: social security number, date of birth. No fee for information.

Transcripts available by mail. Search requires name plus approximate years of attendance, signed release. Other helpful information: social security number, date of birth. Fee is $5.00. Expedite: $2.90 to $10.75.

Manhattan School of Music, Registrar, 120 Claremont Ave, New York, NY 10027, 212-749-2802. Hours: 9AM-5PM. Records go back to 1918. Alumni records are maintained here also. Call 212-749-2802 X502. Degrees granted: Bachelors; Masters; Doctorate.

Attendance and degree information available by mail. Search requires name plus social security number, date of birth, approximate years of attendance, signed release. No fee for information.

Transcripts available by mail. Search requires name plus social security number, date of birth, approximate years of attendance, signed release. Fee is $5.00.

Manhattanville College, Registrar, 2900 Purchase St, Purchase, NY 10577, 914-694-2200. Hours: 9AM-5PM. Records go back to 1914. Alumni records are maintained here also. Call 914-694-2200 X202. Degrees granted: Bachelors; Masters.

Attendance and degree information available by phone, mail. Search requires name plus social security number, approximate years of attendance, signed release. No fee for information.

Transcripts available by mail. Search requires name plus social security number, approximate years of attendance, signed release. Fee is $5.00.

Mankato State University, Registrar's Office, MSU 15, PO Box 8400, Mankato, MN 56002-8400, 507-389-6266 (FAX: 507-389-5917). Hours: 8AM-5PM. Records go back to 1876. Alumni records are maintained here also. Call 507-389-1515. Degrees granted: Associate; Bachelors; Masters.

Attendance and degree information available by phone, FAX, mail. Search requires name plus social security number. Other helpful information: date of birth, approximate years of attendance. No fee for information. Include a stamped envelope.

Transcripts available by mail. Search requires name plus social security number, signed release. Fee is $2.00.

Major credit cards accepted for payment.

Manor Junior College, Registrar, 700 Fox Chase Rd, Jenkintown, PA 19046, 215-885-2360 X51. Hours: 9AM-5PM. Records go back 48 years. Degrees granted: Associate.

Attendance and degree information available by phone, mail. Search requires name plus social security number, date of birth, exact years of attendance. Other helpful information: approximate years of attendance. No fee for information.

Transcripts available by written request only. Search requires name plus social security number, date of birth, approximate years of attendance, signed release. Other helpful information: exact years of attendance. Fee is $2.00. Expedited service available for $2.00.

Mansfield University of Pennsylvania, Registrar's Office, 112 S Hall, Mansfield, PA 16933, 717-662-4202 (FAX: 717-662-4112). Hours: 8AM-4:15PM. Records go back to 1950. Degrees granted: Bachelors; Masters.

Attendance and degree information available by phone, FAX, mail. Search requires name plus social security number. No fee for information.

Transcripts available by mail. Search requires name plus social security number, exact years of attendance, signed release. No fee for transcripts.

Maple Woods Community College, Registrar, 2601 NE Barry Rd, Kansas City, MO 64156, 816-437-3100 (FAX: 816-437-3049). Hours: 8AM-7PM M-Th; 8AM-4:30PM F. Records go back to 1969. Degrees granted: Associate.

Attendance and degree information available by phone, FAX, mail. Search requires name only. Other helpful information: social security number, date of birth. No fee for information.

Transcripts available by mail. Search requires name plus signed release. Other helpful information: social security number, date of birth. Fee is $2.00.

Marantha Baptist Bible College, Registrar, PO Box 438, 745 W Main St, Watertown, WI 53094, 414-261-9300 X363. Hours: 8AM-5PM. Records go back to 1968. Degrees granted: Associate; Bachelors; Masters. Certification: P.C.T.

Attendance and degree information available by phone, FAX, mail. Search requires name only. Other helpful information: approximate years of attendance. No fee for information.

Transcripts available by FAX, mail. Search requires name plus signed release. Other helpful information: approximate years of attendance. Fee is $3.00.

Major credit cards accepted for payment.

Maria College of Albany, Registrar, Rm 100, 700 New Scotland Ave, Albany, NY 12208-1798, 518-438-3111 X24 (FAX: 518-438-7170). Hours: 8:30AM-4PM. Records go back to 1963. Degrees granted: Associate. Adverse incident record source: 518-438-3111 X28.

Attendance and degree information available by phone, FAX, mail. Search requires name plus signed release. Other helpful information: social security number, date of birth, approximate years of attendance. No fee for information.

Transcripts available by FAX, mail. Search requires name plus signed release. Other helpful information: social security number, date of birth, approximate years of attendance. Fee is $3.00.

Major credit cards accepted for payment.

Marian College, Registrar, 3200 Cold Spring Rd, Indianapolis, IN 46222, 317-929-0213 (FAX: 317-929-0263). Hours: 8AM-4:30PM. Records go back to 1851. Alumni records are maintained here also. Call 317-929-0227. Degrees granted: Bachelors. Adverse incident record source: Dean of Students, 317-929-0123.

Attendance and degree information available by mail. Search requires name plus social security number, date of birth. No fee for information.

Transcripts available by mail. Search requires name plus social security number, date of birth, signed release. Fee is $2.00.

Marian College of Fond du Lac, Registrar, 45 S National Ave, Fond Du Lac, WI 54935, 414-923-7618. Hours: 8AM-6PM M-Th; 8AM-4:30PM F. Degrees granted: Bachelors; Masters.

Attendance and degree information available by phone, FAX, mail. Search requires name plus social security number, date of birth, approximate years of attendance. Other helpful information: exact years of attendance. No fee for information.

Transcripts available by FAX, mail. Search requires name plus social security number, date of birth, approximate years of attendance, signed release. Other helpful information: exact years of attendance. Fee is $2.00. Expedited service available for $5.00.

Major credit cards accepted for payment.

Marian Court College, Registrar, 35 Little's Point Rd, Swampscott, MA 01907, 617-595-6768 (FAX: 617-595-3560). Hours: 9AM-4PM. Degrees granted: Associate.

Attendance and degree information available by phone, FAX, mail. Search requires name plus exact years of attendance. Other helpful information: social security number. No fee for information.

Transcripts available by mail. Search requires name plus exact years of attendance, signed release. Other helpful information: social security number. Fee is $2.00.

Marietta College, Registrar, Marietta, OH 45750, 614-376-4728 (FAX: 614-376-4896). Hours: 8:30AM-5PM. Degrees granted: Associate; Bachelors; Masters. Adverse incident record source: Dean of Students, 614-376-4736.

Attendance and degree information available by phone, FAX, mail. Search requires name plus social security number. Other helpful information: date of birth, approximate years of attendance. No fee for information.

Transcripts available by FAX, mail. Search requires name plus social security number, signed release. Other helpful information: date of birth, approximate years of attendance. Fee is $3.00.

Major credit cards accepted for payment.

Marion Military Institute, Registrar, 1101 Washington St, Marion, AL 36756, 334-683-2304 X334 (FAX: 334-683-2380). Hours: 8AM-4PM. Records go back to 1920. Degrees granted: Associate. Adverse incident record source: Commandant Office, 334-683-2321 or 2322.

Attendance and degree information available by phone, FAX, mail. Search requires name plus date of birth, signed release. Other helpful information: exact years of attendance. Fee is $5.00.

Transcripts available by written request only. Search requires name plus date of birth, signed release. Other helpful information: exact years of attendance. Fee is $5.00.

Marion Technical College, Student Records, 1467 Mt Vernon Ave, Marion, OH 43302-5694, 614-389-4636 (FAX: 614-389-6136). Hours: 8AM-6PM. Records go back to 1971. Degrees granted: Associate. Adverse incident record source: President's Office, 614-389-4636

Attendance information available by FAX, mail. Search requires name plus signed release. Other helpful information: social security number, date of birth, approximate years of attendance. No fee for information.

Degree information available by phone, FAX, mail. Search requires name only. Other helpful information: social security num-

ber, date of birth, approximate years of attendance. No fee for information.
Transcripts available by FAX, mail. Search requires name plus signed release. Other helpful information: social security number, date of birth, approximate years of attendance. Fee is $2.00. Expedited service available for $2.00.
Major credit cards accepted for payment.

Marist College, Registrar, 290 North Rd, Poughkeepsie, NY 12601, 914-575-2250. Hours: 8AM-5PM. Records go back to 1945. Alumni records are maintained here at the same phone number. Degrees granted: Bachelors; Masters. Adverse incident record source: Dean of Students, 914-575-3000.
Attendance and degree information available by mail. Search requires name plus social security number, approximate years of attendance, signed release. No fee for information.
Transcripts available by mail. Search requires name plus social security number, approximate years of attendance, signed release. Fee is $3.00.

Marlboro College, Registrar, Marlboro, VT 05344, 802-257-4333 X233. Hours: 8AM-4:30PM. Records go back to 1946. Alumni records are maintained here at the same phone number. Degrees granted: Bachelors.
Attendance and degree information available by phone, mail. Search requires name only. No fee for information.
Transcripts available by mail. Search requires name plus signed release. No fee for transcripts.

Marquette University, Registrar, 1217 W Wisconsin Ave, PO Box 1881, Milwaukee, WI 53201, 414-288-6326 (FAX: 414-288-3300). Hours: 8AM-5PM. Records go back to 1881. Alumni Records Office: 1212 W Wisconsin Ave, Milwaukee, WI 53201 414-288-7443. Degrees granted: Bachelors; Masters; Doctorate.
Attendance and degree information available by phone, mail. Search requires name plus social security number, date of birth, exact years of attendance, signed release. No fee for information.
Transcripts available b. Search requires name plus social security number, date of birth, exact years of attendance, signed release. Fee is $3.00.

Mars Hill College, Registrar, Marshall St, Mars Hill, NC 28754, 704-689-1151 (FAX: 704-689-1478). Hours: 8AM-4:30PM. Alumni records are maintained here also. Call 704-689-1102. Degrees granted: Bachelors.
Attendance information available by phone, FAX. Search requires name plus approximate years of attendance. Other helpful information: social security number, exact years of attendance. No fee for information.
Degree information available by phone, FAX. Search requires name only. No fee for information.
Transcripts available by mail. Search requires name plus signed release. Other helpful information: social security number, date of birth, approximate years of attendance. Fee is $3.00. Expedite fee is based on cost of service.'

Marshall University, Registrar, Huntington, WV 25701, 304-696-6410 (FAX: 304-696-2252). Hours: 8AM-4:30PM. Alumni records are maintained here at the same phone number. Degrees granted: Bachelors; Masters; First Professional Degree.
Attendance and degree information available by FAX, mail. Search requires name plus social security number, exact years of attendance. No fee for information.
Transcripts available by FAX, mail. Search requires name plus social security number, exact years of attendance, signed release. Fee is $5.00.

Marshalltown Community College, Registrar's Office, 3700 S Center, Marshalltown, IA 50158, 515-752-7106 (FAX: 515-752-8149). Hours: 8AM-4:30PM. Records go back to 1957. Alumni records are maintained here at the same phone number. Degrees granted: Associate.
Attendance information available by phone. Search requires name plus social security number. Other helpful information: date of birth, approximate years of attendance. No fee for information.
Degree information available by phone, FAX, mail. Search requires name plus social security number. Other helpful information: date of birth, approximate years of attendance. No fee for information.
Transcripts available by FAX, mail. Search requires name plus social security number, date of birth, signed release. Other helpful information: approximate years of attendance. Fee is $3.00.

Martin Community College, Registrar, 1161 Kuhukee Park Rd, Williamston, NC 27892-9988, 919-792-1521 (FAX: 919-792-4425). Hours: 8AM-4:30PM. Records go back to 1968. Degrees granted: Associate.
Attendance and degree information available by phone, FAX, mail. Search requires name only. Other helpful information: social security number, date of birth, approximate years of attendance. No fee for information.
Transcripts available by FAX, mail. Search requires name plus signed release. Other helpful information: social security number, date of birth, approximate years of attendance. No fee for transcripts.
Former names needed.

Martin Luther College, Registrar, 1995 Luther Ct, New Ulm, MN 56073, 507-354-8221 (FAX: 507-354-8225). Hours: 8AM-4:30PM. Records go back to 1884. Degrees granted: Bachelors.
Attendance and degree information available by phone, FAX, mail. Search requires name only. Other helpful information: social security number, date of birth, approximate years of attendance. No fee for information.
Transcripts available by mail. Search requires name plus signed release. Other helpful information: social security number, date of birth, approximate years of attendance. Fee is $2.00.

Martin Methodist College, Registrar, 433 W Madison St, Pulaski, TN 38478, 915-363-9809 (FAX: 915-363-9818). Hours: 8AM-4:30PM. Records go back to 1870. Alumni records are maintained here also. Call 615-363-7456. Degrees granted: Bachelors.
Attendance and degree information available by phone, mail. Search requires name plus social security number, exact years of attendance. No fee for information.
Transcripts available by mail. Search requires name plus social security number, exact years of attendance, signed release. Fee is $3.00.

Martin University, Registrar, 2171 Avondale Pl, PO Box 18567, Indianapolis, IN 46218, 317-543-3249 (FAX: 317-543-3257). Hours: 8AM-4:30PM. Records go back to 1977. Alumni records are maintained here also. Call 317-543-4822. Degrees granted: Bachelors; Masters.

Attendance and degree information available by phone, mail. Search requires name plus social security number, date of birth, signed release. No fee for information.

Transcripts available by mail. Search requires name plus social security number, date of birth, signed release. Fee is $5.00.

Signed release can be in the file. Major credit cards accepted for payment.

Mary Baldwin College, Registrar, Frederick and New St, Staunton, VA 24401, 703-887-7071 (FAX: 703-886-5561). Hours: 8AM-5PM. Records go back to 1842. Alumni records are maintained here also. Call 703-887-7007. Degrees granted: Bachelors; Masters.

Attendance and degree information available by phone, mail. Search requires name only. No fee for information.

Transcripts available by mail. Search requires name plus signed release. Fee is $4.00.

Mary Holmes College, Registrar, PO Box 1257, Hwy 50 W, West Point, MS 39773, 601-494-6820 (FAX: 601-494-1881). Hours: 8AM-5PM. Records go back 50 years. Degrees granted: Associate.

Attendance information available by phone, FAX, mail. Search requires name plus social security number, exact years of attendance. Other helpful information: date of birth, approximate years of attendance. No fee for information.

Degree information available by phone, FAX, mail. Search requires name plus social security number, exact years of attendance. Other helpful information: approximate years of attendance. No fee for information.

Transcripts available by FAX, mail. Search requires name plus social security number, exact years of attendance, signed release. Other helpful information: date of birth, approximate years of attendance. No fee for transcripts.

Mary Washington College, Registrar, 1301 College Ave, Fredericksburg, VA 22401-5358, 703-654-1063. Hours: 8AM-5PM. Records go back to 1911. Alumni records are maintained here also. Call 703-899-4648. Degrees granted: Bachelors; Masters. Certification: Education.

Attendance and degree information available by phone, mail. Search requires name plus social security number. Other helpful information: date of birth, approximate years of attendance. No fee for information.

Transcripts available by mail. Search requires name plus social security number, signed release. Other helpful information: date of birth, approximate years of attendance. No fee for transcripts. Overnight service must be prepaid.

Marygrove College, Registrar, 8425 W McNichols Rd, Detroit, MI 48221, 313-862-8000 X400. Hours: 9AM-5PM M; 9AM-6PM T,W; 9AM-5PM Th; 9AM-1PM F. Records go back to 1950. Alumni records are maintained here also. Call 313-862-8000 X568. Degrees granted: Associate; Bachelors; Masters. Adverse incident record source: Student Affairs, 313-862-2000 X273 or X277.

Attendance and degree information available by phone, mail. Search requires name plus social security number, signed release. No fee for information.

Transcripts available by mail. Search requires name plus social security number, signed release. Fee is $3.00.

Maryland College of Art and Design, Registrar, 10500 Georgia Ave, Silver Spring, MD 20902, 301-649-4454 (FAX: 301-649-2940). Hours: 8AM-5PM. Records go back 10 years. Degrees granted: Associate.

Attendance and degree information available by FAX, mail. Search requires name plus social security number, exact years of attendance, signed release. Other helpful information: approximate years of attendance. No fee for information.

Transcripts available by FAX, mail. Search requires name plus social security number, exact years of attendance, signed release. Other helpful information: approximate years of attendance. Fee is $3.50. Expedited service available for $3.50.

Major credit cards accepted for payment.

Maryland Institute College of Art, Registrar, 1300 W Mt Royal Ave, Baltimore, MD 21217, 410-225-2236. Hours: 8:30AM-4PM. Alumni records are maintained here also. Call 410-225-2339. Degrees granted: Bachelors; Masters.

Attendance and degree information available by phone, mail. Search requires name only. Other helpful information: social security number, date of birth, approximate years of attendance. No fee for information.

Transcripts available by mail. Search requires name plus social security number, signed release. Other helpful information: date of birth, approximate years of attendance. Fee is $2.00. Full name, any former names helpful.

Marylhurst College, Registrar, PO Box 621, Marylhurst, OR 97036, 503-636-8141 X319 (FAX: 503-636-9526). Hours: 8AM-5PM. Records go back to 1893. Degrees granted: Bachelors; Masters.

Attendance information available by phone, FAX, mail. Search requires name plus signed release. Other helpful information: social security number, approximate years of attendance. No fee for information.

Degree information available by phone, FAX, mail. Search requires name only. Other helpful information: social security number, approximate years of attendance. No fee for information.

Transcripts available by FAX, mail. Search requires name plus signed release. Other helpful information: social security number, approximate years of attendance. First transcript is $6.00; each additional at same time is $2.00.

Major credit cards accepted for payment.

Marymount College, Registrar, 30800 Palos Verdes Dr E, Rancho Palos Verdes, CA 90274-6299, 310-377-5501 X214 (FAX: 310-377-6223). Hours: 8AM-5PM. Records go back to 1972. Degrees granted: Associate. Adverse incident record source: Ofc of Student Development, 310-377-5501 X254.

Attendance and degree information available by phone, FAX, mail. Search requires name plus approximate years of attendance. Other helpful information: social security number, date of birth, exact years of attendance. No fee for information.

Transcripts available by FAX, mail. Search requires name plus approximate years of attendance, signed release. Other helpful information: social security number, date of birth, exact years of attendance. Fee is $4.00. Expedited service available for $10.00.

Major credit cards accepted for payment.

Marymount College, Registrar, 100 Marymount Ave, Tarrytown, NY 10591-3796, 914-332-8211. Hours: 9AM-5PM. Degrees granted: Bachelors.

Attendance and degree information available by phone, mail. Search requires name only. Other helpful information: social security number, date of birth, approximate years of attendance. No fee for information.

Transcripts available by mail. Search requires name plus signed release. Other helpful information: social security number, date of birth, approximate years of attendance. Fee is $3.00.

Marymount Manhattan College, Registrar, 221 E 71st St, New York, NY 10021, 212-517-0400 (FAX: 212-517-0413). Hours: 8AM-4:30PM. Degrees granted: Bachelors. Special programs- Continuing Education, 212-517-0564.

Attendance and degree information available by phone, FAX, mail. Search requires name plus approximate years of attendance. Other helpful information: social security number, date of birth, exact years of attendance. No fee for information.

Transcripts available by mail. Search requires name plus approximate years of attendance, signed release. Other helpful information: social security number, date of birth, exact years of attendance. Fee is $5.00. Expedited service available for $15.00. Major credit cards accepted for payment.

Marymount University, Registrar, 2807 N Glebe Rd, Arlington, VA 22207, 703-284-1520. Hours: 8AM-6PM F-Th; 8AM-5PM F. Records go back to 1950. Alumni records are maintained here also. Call 703-284-1541. Degrees granted: Associate; Bachelors; Masters.

Attendance information available by phone, FAX, mail. Search requires name plus signed release. Other helpful information: social security number, date of birth, approximate years of attendance. No fee for information.

Degree information available by phone, FAX, mail. Search requires name only. Other helpful information: social security number, date of birth, approximate years of attendance. No fee for information.

Transcripts available by FAX, mail. Search requires name plus signed release. Other helpful information: social security number, date of birth, approximate years of attendance. No fee for transcripts.

Maryville College, Registrar, 502 E Lamar Alexander Pkwy, Maryville, TN 37801, 615-981-8212 (FAX: 615-981-8010). Hours: 8AM-5PM. Records go back to 1819. Alumni records are maintained here also. Call 615-981-8200. Degrees granted: Bachelors.

Attendance and degree information available by phone, FAX, mail. Search requires name plus social security number, exact years of attendance. No fee for information.

Transcripts available by mail. Search requires name plus social security number, exact years of attendance, signed release. Fee is $2.00.

Maryville University of St. Louis, Registrar, 13550 Conway Rd, St Louis, MO 63141, 314-529-9370 (FAX: 314-529-9925). Hours: 8AM-5PM. Records go back 70 years. Degrees granted: Bachelors; Masters.

Attendance and degree information available by FAX, mail. Search requires name plus social security number. Other helpful information: date of birth, approximate years of attendance. No fee for information.

Transcripts available by FAX, mail. Search requires name plus social security number, signed release. Other helpful information: date of birth, approximate years of attendance. Fee is $3.00. Expedited service available for $3.00.

Marywood College, Registrar, 2300 Adams Ave, Scranton, PA 18509, 717-348-6280 X482 (FAX: 717-341-0748). Hours: 8:30AM-6PM M-Th, 8:30AM-4:30PM F. Records go back to 1915. Alumni records are maintained here also. Call 717-348-6206. Degrees granted: Bachelors; Masters.

Attendance and degree information available by FAX, mail. Search requires name plus social security number, signed release. No fee for information.

Transcripts available by mail. Search requires name plus social security number, signed release. Other helpful information: exact years of attendance. Fee is $4.00.

Massachusetts Bay Community College, Registrar, 50 Oakland St, Wellesley Hills, MA 02181-5399, 617-237-1100 X172. Hours: 8AM-4:45PM. Records go back to 1961. Alumni records are maintained here at the same phone number. Degrees granted: Associate.

Attendance and degree information available by mail. Search requires name plus social security number, approximate years of attendance, signed release. No fee for information.

Transcripts available by mail. Search requires name plus social security number, approximate years of attendance, signed release. First transcript is free. Additional ones are $5.00 each.

Massachusetts College of Art, Registrar, 621 Huntington Ave, Boston, MA 02115, 617-232-1555 x243 (FAX: 617-566-4034). Hours: 9AM-5PM. Alumni records are maintained here also. Call 617-232-1555 X258. Degrees granted: Bachelors; Masters. Certification: Design Teaching.

Attendance and degree information available by FAX, mail. Search requires name plus social security number, signed release. Other helpful information: date of birth, exact years of attendance. No fee for information.

Transcripts available by FAX, mail. Search requires name plus social security number, signed release. Other helpful information: date of birth, exact years of attendance. Fee is $2.00.

Massachusetts College of Pharmacy and Allied Health Services, Registrar, 179 Longwood Ave, Boston, MA 02115, 617-732-2855. Hours: 8:30AM-4:30PM. Records go back to 1915. Degrees granted: Associate; Bachelors; Masters; Doctorate. Special programs- Continuing Education, 617-732-2961.

Attendance and degree information available by phone, mail. Search requires name only. Other helpful information: approximate years of attendance. No fee for information.

Transcripts available by mail. Search requires name plus signed release. Other helpful information: social security number, date of birth, approximate years of attendance. Fee is $3.00.

Massachusetts Institute of Technology, Registrar's Office, E19-335, 77 Massachusetts Ave, Cambridge, MA 02139, 617-253-4784 (FAX: 617-253-7459). Hours: 9AM-5PM. Records go back to 1800s. Alumni records are maintained here at the same phone number. Degrees granted: Bachelors; Masters; Doctorate.

Attendance information available by phone, FAX, mail. Search requires name only. Other helpful information: social security number, approximate years of attendance. No fee for information.

Degree information available by phone, FAX, mail. Search requires name only. Other helpful information: social security number, date of birth, approximate years of attendance. No fee for information.

Transcripts available by FAX, mail. Search requires name plus signed release. Other helpful information: social security number, date of birth, approximate years of attendance. Fee is $2.00. Major credit cards accepted for payment.

The Sourcebook of College and University Student Records

Massachusetts Maritime Academy, Registrar, Academy Dr, Buzzards Bay, MA 02532, 508-830-5036 (FAX: 508-830-5018). Hours: 8AM-4:30PM. Records go back 100 years. Alumni Records Office: PO Box 1910, Boston, MA 02210. Degrees granted: Bachelors. Adverse incident record source: Commandant's Office, 508-830-5047.

Attendance and degree information available by phone, FAX, mail. Search requires name plus social security number. Other helpful information: date of birth, approximate years of attendance. No fee for information.

Transcripts available by FAX, mail. Search requires name plus social security number, signed release. Other helpful information: approximate years of attendance. Fee is $2.50. Expedited service available for $2.50.

Major credit cards accepted for payment.

Massachusetts School of Professional Psychology, Registrar, 221 Rivermore St, Boston, MA 02132, 617-327-6777 (FAX: 617-327-4447). Hours: 9AM-5PM. Records go back to 1984. Degrees granted: Doctorate.

Attendance and degree information available by phone, FAX, mail. Search requires name only. Other helpful information: social security number, date of birth, approximate years of attendance. No fee for information.

Transcripts available by mail. Search requires name plus signed release. Other helpful information: social security number, date of birth, approximate years of attendance. Fee is $2.00.

Massasoit Community College, Registrar, One Massasoit Blvd, Brockton, MA 02402, 508-588-9100 (FAX: 508-427-1255). Hours: 8AM-5PM. Records go back to 1966. Alumni records are maintained here also. Call 508-588-9100 X1431. Degrees granted: Associate.

Attendance and degree information available by phone, FAX, mail. Search requires name plus social security number, approximate years of attendance, signed release. No fee for information.

Transcripts available by phone, FAX, mail. Search requires name plus social security number, approximate years of attendance, signed release. Fee is $1.00.

Massey College of Business & Technology, Registrar, 3355 Lenox Rd Ste 100, Atlanta, GA 30326, 404-816-4533 (FAX: 404-816-5576). Hours: 7:30AM-6PM. Records go back to 1979. Degrees granted: Associate. Special programs- Before 1979: Atlanta Art Institute, 404-266-2662.

Attendance and degree information available by phone, FAX, mail. Search requires name plus social security number, approximate years of attendance, signed release. Other helpful information: date of birth. No fee for information.

Transcripts available by phone, FAX, mail. Search requires name plus social security number, approximate years of attendance, signed release. Other helpful information: date of birth. Official transcripts are $3.00 each. Personal transcript copies are $2.00.

Massey College of Business & Technology, (**Massey Institute**), Registrar, 3355 Lenox Rd Ste 100, Atlanta, GA 30326, 404-816-4533 (FAX: 404-816-5576). Hours: 7:30AM-6PM. Records go back to 1979. Degrees granted: Associate.

Attendance and degree information available by phone, FAX, mail. Search requires name plus social security number, exact years of attendance, signed release. Other helpful information: approximate years of attendance. No fee for information.

Transcripts available by FAX, mail. Search requires name plus social security number, exact years of attendance, signed release. Other helpful information: approximate years of attendance. Fee is $3.00.

Master's College, Registrar' Office #42, 21726 Placerita Canyon Rd, Santa Clara, CA 91321-1200, 805-259-3540 X311 (FAX: 805-288-1037). Hours: 8:30AM-5PM. Records go back to 1927. Degrees granted: Bachelors. Adverse incident record source: Campus Security, 805-259-3540 X344.

Attendance and degree information available by phone, FAX, mail. Search requires name only. Other helpful information: social security number, date of birth, approximate years of attendance. No fee for information.

Transcripts available by FAX, mail. Search requires name plus signed release. Other helpful information: social security number, date of birth, approximate years of attendance. Fee is $3.00. Expedited service available for $13.00.

Major credit cards accepted for payment.

Mater Dei College, Registrar, Rural Rte 2 Box 45, Ogdensburg, NY 13669-1034, 315-393-5930 (FAX: 315-393-5930 X440). Hours: 8AM-5PM. Records go back to 1960. Alumni records are maintained here at the same phone number. Degrees granted: Associate.

Attendance and degree information available by mail. Search requires name plus social security number, date of birth, signed release. Other helpful information: exact years of attendance. No fee for information.

Transcripts available by mail. Search requires name plus social security number, date of birth, signed release. Other helpful information: exact years of attendance. Fee is $2.00.

Mayland Community College, Registrar, PO Box 547, Spruce Pine, NC 28777, 704-765-7351 (FAX: 704-765-0728). Hours: 8AM-5PM. Records go back to 1972. Degrees granted: Associate.

Attendance and degree information available by FAX, mail. Search requires name plus social security number, signed release. Other helpful information: date of birth, approximate years of attendance. No fee for information.

Transcripts available by FAX, mail. Search requires name plus social security number, signed release. Other helpful information: date of birth, approximate years of attendance. No fee for transcripts.

Mayo Graduate School, Registrar, 200 First St SW, Rochester, MN 55905, 507-284-2220 (FAX: 507-284-0532). Hours: 8AM-5PM. Records go back to 1940. Alumni records are maintained here also. Call 507-284-2317.

Attendance and degree information available by FAX, mail. Search requires name plus social security number, date of birth, approximate years of attendance, signed release. No fee for information.

Transcripts available by mail. Search requires name plus social security number, date of birth, approximate years of attendance, signed release. Fee is $15.00.

Maysville Community College, Registrar, 1755 US 68, Maysville, KY 41056, 606-759-7141 X225 (FAX: 606-759-7176). Hours: 8AM-4:30PM. Records go back to 1968. Degrees granted: Associate.

Attendance and degree information available by phone, FAX, mail. Search requires name plus social security number, signed release. Other helpful information: approximate years of attendance. No fee for information.

Degree Granting Institutions

Transcripts available by FAX, mail. Search requires name plus social security number, signed release. Other helpful information: approximate years of attendance. Fee is $2.00.

Mayville State University, Registrar, 330 Third St NE, Mayville, ND 58257, 701-786-4774 (FAX: 701-786-4748). Hours: 8AM-Noon, 12:30-4:30PM. Records go back to 1889. Alumni records are maintained here also. Call 701-786-4854. Degrees granted: Associate; Bachelors. Adverse incident record source: Student Services, 701-786-4842.

Attendance and degree information available by phone, FAX, mail. Search requires name plus social security number, date of birth. Other helpful information: approximate years of attendance. No fee for information.

Transcripts available by phone, FAX, mail. Search requires name plus social security number, date of birth, signed release. Other helpful information: approximate years of attendance. Fee is $2.00.

McCann School of Business, Registrar, Main and Pine Sts, Mahanoy City, PA 17948, 717-773-1820 (FAX: 717-773-0483). Hours: 8AM-5PM. Records go back to 1897. Alumni records are maintained here at the same phone number. Degrees granted: Associate; Paralegal.

Attendance and degree information available by phone, FAX, mail. Search requires name plus social security number, date of birth, exact years of attendance. No fee for information.

Transcripts available by mail. Search requires name plus social security number, date of birth, exact years of attendance, signed release. Fee is $5.00.

McCann School of Business, (Branch), Registrar, 2004 Wyoming Ave, Wyoming, PA 18644, 717-287-4400. Hours: 8:30AM-4:30PM. Records go back to 1932. Alumni records are maintained here at the same phone number. Degrees granted: Associate.

Attendance and degree information available by phone, mail. Search requires name plus social security number, date of birth, exact years of attendance. No fee for information.

Transcripts available by mail. Search requires name plus social security number, date of birth, exact years of attendance, signed release. Fee is $5.00.

McCarrie Schools of Health Sciences and Technology Inc., Registrar, 512-520 S Broad St, Philadelphia, PA 19146-1613, 215-545-7772. Hours: 8AM-4PM. Records go back to 1917. Degrees granted: Associate.

Attendance and degree information available by mail. Search requires name plus social security number, exact years of attendance, signed release. No fee for information.

Transcripts available by mail. Search requires name plus social security number, exact years of attendance, signed release. Fee is $2.00.

McCook Community College, Registrar, 1205 E Third St, McCook, NE 69001, 800-658-4348. Hours: 8AM-5:30PM M-Th; 8AM-4PM F. Records go back to 1926. Alumni records are maintained here at the same phone number. Degrees granted: Associate.

Attendance and degree information available by phone, mail. Search requires name plus social security number, date of birth, exact years of attendance. No fee for information.

Transcripts available by mail. Search requires name plus social security number, date of birth, exact years of attendance, signed release. Fee is $2.00.

McCormick Theological Seminary, Registrar, 5555 S Woodlawn Ave, Chicago, IL 60637, 312-947-6285 (FAX: 312-947-0376). Hours: 8:30AM-4:30PM. Records go back to 1918. Alumni records are maintained here also. Call 312-947-6262. Degrees granted: Masters; Doctorate.

Attendance and degree information available by phone, FAX, mail. Search requires name only. Other helpful information: approximate years of attendance. No fee for information.

Transcripts available by mail. Search requires name plus signed release. Other helpful information: approximate years of attendance. Fee is $2.00. Expedited service available for $0.

McDowell Technical Community College, Registrar, Rte 1 Box 170, Marion, NC 28752, 704-652-6021 X401 (FAX: 704-652-1014). Hours: 9AM-8:30PM T,Th; 8AM-4PM M,W,F. Records go back to 1964. Degrees granted: Associate.

Attendance information available by phone, FAX, mail. Search requires name plus social security number. No fee for information.

Degree information available by phone, FAX, mail. Search requires name plus social security number, exact years of attendance. No fee for information.

Transcripts available by FAX, mail. Search requires name plus social security number, exact years of attendance, signed release. No fee for transcripts.

FAX copies of transcripts for emergency only.

McHenry County College, Registrar, 8900 US Hwy 14, Crystal Lake, IL 60012-2794, 815-455-3700 (FAX: 815-455-3766). Hours: 8AM-7:30PM M-Th; 8AM-4PM F. Records go back to 1967. Degrees granted: Associate.

Attendance and degree information available by phone, FAX, mail. Search requires name only. Other helpful information: social security number, date of birth.

Transcripts available by FAX, mail. Search requires name plus signed release. Other helpful information: social security number, date of birth.

Major credit cards accepted for payment.

McIntosh College, Registrar, 23 Cataract Ave, Dover, NH 03820, 603-742-1234 (FAX: 603-742-7292). Hours: 7:30AM-10:30PM. Records go back to 1920. Degrees granted: Associate.

Attendance and degree information available by mail. Search requires name plus social security number, date of birth, signed release. Other helpful information: approximate years of attendance. Fee is $2.00.

Transcripts available by written request only. Search requires name plus social security number, date of birth, signed release. Other helpful information: approximate years of attendance. Fee is $2.00.

McKendree College, Registrar, 701 College Rd, Lebanon, IL 62254, 618-537-6818 (FAX: 618-537-6259). Hours: 8AM-5PM. Records go back to 1928. Alumni records are maintained here also. Call 618-537-4481. Degrees granted: Associate; Bachelors.

Attendance and degree information available by phone, FAX, mail. Search requires name only. Other helpful information: social security number, approximate years of attendance. No fee for information.

Transcripts available by mail. Search requires name plus signed release. Other helpful information: social security number, approximate years of attendance. Fee is $3.00. Expedited service available for $6.00.

McLennan Community College, Registrar, 1400 College Dr, Waco, TX 78708, 817-750-3507 (FAX: 817-750-3753). Hours: 8AM-8PM M-Th; 8AM-5PM F. Records go back to 1966. Degrees granted: Associate. Adverse incident record source: Local Police, 817-750-7500.

Attendance and degree information available by FAX, mail. Search requires name plus social security number, approximate years of attendance, signed release. Other helpful information: date of birth. No fee for information.

Transcripts available by mail. Search requires name plus social security number, approximate years of attendance, signed release. Other helpful information: date of birth. Fee is $3.00.

McMurry University, Registrar, PO Box 338, McMurry Station, Abilene, TX 79697, 915-691-6400 (FAX: 915-691-6599). Hours: 8AM-5PM. Records go back to 1923. Alumni Records Office: PO Box 938, Abilene, TX 79697 915-691-6387. Degrees granted: Associate; Bachelors.

Attendance and degree information available by phone. Search requires name plus social security number, signed release. Other helpful information: approximate years of attendance. No fee for information.

Transcripts available by written request only. Search requires name plus social security number, signed release. Other helpful information: approximate years of attendance. Fee is $3.00. Expedite: $3.00 plus overnight fee if applicable.

Need full name & past names. Major credit cards accepted for payment.

McNeese State University, Registrar, 4100 Ryan St, Lake Charles, LA 70609, 318-475-5356 (FAX: 318-475-5189). Hours: 7:45AM-4:30PM. Records go back to 1939. Degrees granted: Associate; Bachelors; Masters.

Attendance and degree information available by phone, FAX, mail. Search requires name plus social security number, date of birth, approximate years of attendance, signed release. No fee for information.

Transcripts available by FAX, mail. Search requires name plus social security number, date of birth, approximate years of attendance, signed release. First five transcripts are free. Additional ones are $2.00 each.

McPherson College, Registrar, 1600 E Euclid, PO Box 1402, McPherson, KS 67460, 316-241-0731 (FAX: 316-241-8443). Hours: 8AM-5PM. Records go back to 1934. Degrees granted: Bachelors. Certification: Education.

Attendance and degree information available by phone, FAX, mail. Search requires name only. Other helpful information: social security number, date of birth, approximate years of attendance. No fee for information.

Transcripts available by FAX, mail. Search requires name plus signed release. Other helpful information: social security number, date of birth, approximate years of attendance. Fee is $3.00. Expedited service available for $5.00.

Meadville/Lombard Theological School, Registrar, 5701 S Woodlawn Ave, Chicago, IL 60637, 312-753-3282. Hours: 9AM-5PM. Records go back to 1935. Alumni records are maintained here also. Call 312-753-3195. Degrees granted: Masters; Doctorate.

Attendance and degree information available by mail. Search requires name plus social security number, exact years of attendance, signed release. No fee for information.

Transcripts available by mail. Search requires name plus social security number, exact years of attendance, signed release. Fee is $4.00.

Medaille College, Registrar, 18 Agassiz Circle, Buffalo, NY 14214, 716-884-3281 (FAX: 716-884-0291). Hours: 8AM-8:15PM M,T; 8AM-6PM W,Th; 8AM-4PM F. Records go back to 1937. Alumni records are maintained here also. Call 716-884-3281 X208. Degrees granted: Associate; Bachelors.

Attendance and degree information available by phone, FAX, mail. Search requires name plus social security number, approximate years of attendance, signed release. No fee for information.

Transcripts available by mail. Search requires name plus social security number, approximate years of attendance, signed release. Fee is $2.00.

Medcenter One College of Nursing, Registrar, 512 N Seventh St, Bismarck, ND 58501, 701-224-6271 (FAX: 701-224-6967). Hours: 8AM-4:30PM. Records go back to 1909. Alumni records are maintained here also. Call 701-224-6283. Degrees granted: Bachelors.

Attendance and degree information available by phone, FAX, mail. Search requires name plus date of birth, approximate years of attendance. Other helpful information: social security number, exact years of attendance. No fee for information.

Transcripts available by FAX, mail. Search requires name plus social security number, date of birth, approximate years of attendance, signed release. Other helpful information: exact years of attendance. Fee is $3.00.

Medgar Evers College, Registrar's Office, 1150 Carroll St RC-101, Brooklyn, NY 11225, 718-270-6079 (FAX: 718-270-6496). Hours: 9AM-7PM M,Th; 9AM-2PM W; 9AM-5PM T; 10AM-5PM F. Records go back to 1975. Degrees granted: Associate; Bachelors.

Attendance and degree information available by FAX, mail. Search requires name plus social security number, date of birth, exact years of attendance, signed release. Other helpful information: approximate years of attendance. No fee for information.

Transcripts available by written request only. Search requires name plus social security number, date of birth, exact years of attendance, signed release. Other helpful information: approximate years of attendance. No fee for transcripts.

Median School of Allied Health Careers, Registrar, 125 Seventh St, Pittsburgh, PA 15222-3400, 412-391-7021 (FAX: 412-232-4348). Hours: 8AM-4:30PM. Records go back to 1970. Degrees granted: Associate.

Attendance and degree information available by phone, FAX, mail. Search requires name plus exact years of attendance. Other helpful information: social security number. No fee for information.

Transcripts available by written request only. Search requires name plus social security number, exact years of attendance, signed release. Diploma/Assoc. Degree copy $2.00; original $10.00.

Medical College of Georgia, Registrar, 1120 15th St, Augusta, GA 30912, 706-721-2201 (FAX: 706-721-0186). Hours:

8AM-5PM. Records go back to 1828. Alumni records are maintained here at the same phone number. Degrees granted: Associate; Bachelors; Masters; Doctorate. Adverse incident record source: Public Safety, 706-721-2911.

Attendance information available by phone, FAX, mail. Search requires name plus social security number. No fee for information.

Degree information available by phone, FAX, mail. Search requires name plus social security number. Other helpful information: date of birth, approximate years of attendance. No fee for information.

Transcripts available by FAX. Search requires name plus social security number, signed release. Other helpful information: date of birth, approximate years of attendance. No fee for transcripts. Major required.

Medical College of Ohio at Toledo, Registrar, Caller Svc No. 10008, Toledo, OH 43699, 419-381-4172 (FAX: 419-381-1008). Hours: 8:30AM-5PM. Records go back to 1955. Alumni records are maintained here at the same phone number. Degrees granted: Masters; Doctorate. Adverse incident record source: Written Management, 419-381-4172.

Attendance and degree information available by phone, FAX, mail. Search requires name plus social security number, date of birth, approximate years of attendance, signed release. Other helpful information: exact years of attendance. No fee for information.

Transcripts available by mail. Search requires name plus social security number, date of birth, approximate years of attendance, signed release. Other helpful information: exact years of attendance. Fee is $5.00.

Medical College of Pennsylvania and Hahnemann University, Registrar's Office, 2900 Queen Lane, Philadelphia, PA 19129, 215-842-6000. Hours: 8AM-5PM. Alumni records are maintained here at the same phone number. Degrees granted: Doctorate.

Attendance information available by phone, mail. Search requires name plus social security number. No fee for information.

Degree information available by phone, mail. Search requires name plus social security number, exact years of attendance. No fee for information.

Transcripts available by mail. Search requires name plus social security number, exact years of attendance, signed release. Fee is $5.00.

Medical College of Wisconsin, Registrar, 8701 Watertown Plank Rd, Milwaukee, WI 53226, 414-456-8296. Hours: 8AM-5PM. Alumni records are maintained here at the same phone number. Degrees granted: Bachelors; Masters; Doctorate.

Attendance and degree information available by phone, mail. Search requires name plus exact years of attendance. No fee for information.

Transcripts available by mail. Search requires name plus exact years of attendance, signed release. Transcript fee $1.00 for current student, and $3.00 for alumni.

Medical University of South Carolina, Registrar, 171 Ashley Ave, Charleston, SC 29425, 803-792-3281 (FAX: 803-792-3764). Hours: 8AM-5PM. Records go back 50 years. Alumni records are maintained here also. Call 803-792-7979. Degrees granted: Bachelors; Masters; Doctorate.

Attendance information available by phone, FAX, mail. Search requires name plus social security number. Other helpful information: date of birth, approximate years of attendance. No fee for information.

Degree information available by written request only. Search requires name plus social security number, signed release. Other helpful information: date of birth, approximate years of attendance. No fee for information.

Transcripts available by written request only. Search requires name plus social security number, signed release. Other helpful information: date of birth, approximate years of attendance. Fee is $4.00.

Meharry Medical College, Registrar, 1005 D.B. Todd Blvd, Nashville, TN 37208, 615-327-6223 (FAX: 615-327-6540). Hours: 8:30AM-5PM. Records go back to 1897. Alumni records are maintained here also. Call 615-327-6266. Degrees granted: Doctorate.

Attendance and degree information available by phone, mail. Search requires name plus social security number. No fee for information.

Transcripts available by mail. Search requires name plus social security number, signed release. Transcript fee $2.00 for graduate students, and $5.00 for undergraduate students. Each additional transcript is $2.00.

Memphis College of Art, Registrar, 1930 Poplar Ave, Overton Park, Memphis, TN 38112-2764, 901-726-4085 X29 (FAX: 901-726-9371). Hours: 8AM-5PM. Records go back to 1936. Alumni records are maintained here at the same phone number. Degrees granted: Bachelors; Masters.

Attendance and degree information available by mail. Search requires name plus social security number, exact years of attendance, signed release. No fee for information.

Transcripts available by mail. Search requires name plus social security number, exact years of attendance, signed release. No fee for transcripts.

Memphis Theological Seminary, Registrar, 168 East Pkwy S, Memphis, TN 38104, 901-458-8232 (FAX: 901-452-4051). Degrees granted: Masters; Doctorate.

Attendance and degree information available by phone, FAX, mail. Search requires name plus approximate years of attendance. Other helpful information: social security number, date of birth, exact years of attendance. No fee for information.

Transcripts available by FAX, mail. Search requires name plus signed release. Other helpful information: social security number, date of birth, approximate years of attendance. Fee is $3.00. Major credit cards accepted for payment.

Mendocino College, Registrar, PO Box 3000, Ukiah, CA 95482, 707-468-3103 (FAX: 707-468-3120). Hours: 8AM-5PM. Records go back to 1973. Degrees granted: Associate. Adverse incident record source: Student Services, 707-468-3105.

Attendance and degree information available by phone, FAX, mail. Search requires name plus social security number, date of birth. Other helpful information: approximate years of attendance. No fee for information.

Transcripts available by mail. Search requires name plus social security number, date of birth, signed release. Other helpful information: approximate years of attendance. Fee is $2.00. Expedited service available for $5.00.

Menlo College, Office of the Registrar, 1000 El Camino Real, Atherton, CA 94027-4185, 415-688-3764 (FAX: 415-324-2347). Hours: 9AM-5PM. Records go back to 1930. Alumni Records

Office: c/o External Relations, 1000 El Camino Real, Atherton, CA 94027-4185. Degrees granted: Associate; Bachelors. Adverse incident record source: Office of Student Life, 415-688-3751; Security & Facilities, 415-688-3714

Attendance and degree information available by phone, mail. Search requires name only. No fee for information.

Transcripts available by FAX, mail. Search requires name plus social security number, date of birth, approximate years of attendance, signed release. Other helpful information: exact years of attendance. Fee is $5.00-10. Expedited service available for $20.00-4.

Include all legal names & AKA's.

Mennonite Brethren Biblical Seminary, Registrar, 4824 E Butler Ave, Fresno, CA 93727-5097, 209-452-1723 (FAX: 209-251-7212). Hours: 8AM-5PM. Records go back to 1955. Degrees granted: Masters.

Attendance information available by phone, FAX, mail. Search requires name plus social security number, exact years of attendance. Other helpful information: approximate years of attendance. No fee for information.

Degree information available by phone, FAX, mail. Search requires name plus social security number, approximate years of attendance, signed release. Other helpful information: date of birth, exact years of attendance. No fee for information.

Transcripts available by FAX, mail. Search requires name plus social security number, approximate years of attendance, signed release. Other helpful information: date of birth, exact years of attendance. Fee is $4.00.

Mennonite College of Nursing, Registrar, 804 N East St, Bloomington, IL 61701, 309-829-0715 (FAX: 309-829-0765). Hours: 8AM-4:30PM. Records go back to 1919. Degrees granted: Bachelors.

Attendance and degree information available by phone, FAX, mail. Search requires name only. Other helpful information: social security number, date of birth, approximate years of attendance. No fee for information.

Transcripts available by FAX, mail. Search requires name plus signed release. Other helpful information: social security number, date of birth, approximate years of attendance. Fee is $2.00.

Merced College, Registrar, 3600 M St, Merced, CA 95340, 209-384-6188 (FAX: 209-384-6339). Hours: 8AM-5PM. Records go back to 1965. Degrees granted: Associate. Adverse incident record source: Dean's Office, 209-384-6191.

Attendance and degree information available by phone, FAX, mail. Search requires name plus social security number, signed release. No fee for information.

Transcripts available by mail. Search requires name plus social security number, signed release. Fee is $3.00. Expedited service available for $10.00.

Mercer County Community College, Registrar, 1200 Old Trenton Rd, Box B, Trenton, NJ 08690-0182, 609-586-4800 (FAX: 609-586-6944). Hours: 8AM-7PM M-Th; 8AM-5PM F. Records go back to founding date.

Attendance and degree information available by FAX, mail. Search requires name plus social security number, date of birth, signed release. Other helpful information: approximate years of attendance. No fee for information.

Transcripts available by FAX, mail. Search requires name plus social security number, date of birth, signed release. Other helpful information: approximate years of attendance. Fee is $5.00.

Major credit cards accepted for payment.

Mercer County Community College, (James Kerney Campus), Registrar, N Broad and Academy Sts, Trenton, NJ 08690, 609-586-4800. Records are not housed here. They are located at Mercer County Community College, Registrar, 1200 Old Trenton Rd, Box B, Trenton, NJ 08690-0182.

Mercer University, Registrar, 1400 Coleman Ave, Macon, GA 31207, 912-752-2683 (FAX: 912-752-2455). Hours: 8:30AM-5PM. Records go back to 1833. Alumni records are maintained here also. Call 912-752-2715. Degrees granted: Masters.

Attendance information available by FAX, mail. Search requires name plus social security number, approximate years of attendance. No fee for information.

Degree information available by phone, FAX, mail. Search requires name plus social security number, approximate years of attendance. No fee for information.

Transcripts available by mail. Search requires name plus social security number, approximate years of attendance, signed release. Fee is $2.00.

Mercy College, Registrar, 555 Broadway, Dobbs Ferry, NY 10522, 914-674-7265 (FAX: 914-693-9455). Hours: 9AM-7PM M-Th; 9AM-5PM F; 9AM-12:30PM S. Records go back to 1950s. Alumni records are maintained here also. Call 914-674-7314.

Attendance and degree information available by phone, FAX, mail. Search requires name plus approximate years of attendance, signed release. Other helpful information: social security number, date of birth. No fee for information.

Transcripts available by mail. Search requires name plus approximate years of attendance, signed release. Other helpful information: social security number, date of birth. Student copy $2.00; official $4.00.

Mercy College, (Bronx Campus), Registrar, 50 Antin Place, Bronx, NY 10462, 212-798-8952. Records are not housed here. They are located at Mercy College, Registrar, 555 Broadway, Dobbs Ferry, NY 10522.

Mercy College, (White Plains Campus), Registrar, Martine Ave and S Broadway, White Plains, NY 10601, 914-948-3666. Records are not housed here. They are located at Mercy College, Registrar, 555 Broadway, Dobbs Ferry, NY 10522.

Mercy College, (Yorktown Campus), Registrar, 2651 Stang Blvd, Yorktown Heights, NY 10598, 914-245-6100. Records are not housed here. They are located at Mercy College, Registrar, 555 Broadway, Dobbs Ferry, NY 10522.

Mercyhurst College, Registrar, 501 E 38th St, Erie, PA 16546, 814-824-2250 (FAX: 814-824-2438). Hours: 8AM-4:30PM. Records go back to 1926. Alumni records are maintained here also. Call 814-824-2538. Degrees granted: Bachelors; Masters.

Attendance and degree information available by phone, mail. Search requires name plus social security number, signed release. No fee for information.

Transcripts available by mail. Search requires name plus social security number, exact years of attendance, signed release. Fee is $2.00.

Meredith College, Registrar, 3800 Hillsborough St, Raleigh, NC 27607-5298, 919-829-8593. Hours: 8AM-5PM. Records go back to 1900s. Alumni records are maintained here also. Call 919-829-8391. Degrees granted: Bachelors; Masters. Special programs- Graduate Dept., 919-829-8353.

Attendance and degree information available by mail. Search requires name plus social security number. No fee for information.

Transcripts available by mail. Search requires name plus social security number, exact years of attendance, signed release. Fee is $2.00.

To confirm attendance or degree, request must be on letterhead and explanation must be provided.

Meridian Community College, Registrar, 910 Hwy 19 N, Meridian, MS 39307, 601-484-8636 (FAX: 601-484-8607). Hours: 8AM-4:30PM M-Th; 8AM-3:30PM F. Records go back to 1937. Degrees granted: Associate. Adverse incident record source: 601-484-8622.

Attendance and degree information available by phone, FAX, mail. Search requires name plus social security number, date of birth, signed release. Other helpful information: approximate years of attendance. No fee for information.

Transcripts available by written request only. Search requires name plus social security number, date of birth, signed release. Other helpful information: approximate years of attendance. Fee is $2.00. Expedited service available for $12.00.

Transcripts are given only to students.

Merrimack College, Registrar, North Andover, MA 01845, 508-837-5000 X4125. Hours: 8:30AM-4:30PM. Records go back to 1947. Alumni records are maintained here also. Call 508-837-5000 X5440. Degrees granted: Bachelors.

Attendance and degree information available by phone, mail. Search requires name plus approximate years of attendance, signed release. No fee for information.

Transcripts available by mail. Search requires name plus approximate years of attendance, signed release. Fee is $2.00.

Merritt College, Registrar, 12500 Campus Dr, Oakland, CA 94619, 510-436-2475 (FAX: 510-436-2512). Hours: 8AM-7PM M-T, 8AM-3PM W-F. Records go back to 1953. Degrees granted: Associate.

Attendance and degree information available by FAX, mail. Search requires name plus social security number, signed release. No fee for information.

Transcripts available by FAX, mail. Search requires name plus social security number, signed release. No fee for transcripts.

Mesa Community College, Registrar, 1833 W Southern Ave, Mesa, AZ 85202, 602-461-7659 (FAX: 602-471-7805). Hours: 8AM-8PM M-Th. Records go back to 1965. Degrees granted: Associate. Adverse incident record source: Public Safety, 602-461-7000.

Attendance and degree information available by FAX, mail. Search requires name plus social security number, signed release. Other helpful information: date of birth. No fee for information.

Transcripts available by FAX, mail. Search requires name plus social security number, signed release. Other helpful information: date of birth. Fee is $5.00.
Major credit cards accepted for payment.

Mesa State College, Registrar, PO Box 2647, Grand Junction, CO 81502, 970-248-1641 (FAX: 970-248-1131). Hours: 8AM-5PM. Records go back to 1928. Degrees granted: Associate; Bachelors. Adverse incident record source: Disciplinary Officer: Mesa State College

Attendance information available by phone, FAX, mail. Search requires name plus social security number, approximate years of attendance. Other helpful information: date of birth. No fee for information.

Degree information available by phone, FAX, mail. Search requires name plus social security number, approximate years of attendance. Other helpful information: date of birth. No fee for information.

Transcripts available by FAX, mail. Search requires name plus social security number, approximate years of attendance, signed release. Other helpful information: date of birth. Fee is $3.00. Expedited service available for $10.75.

Need copy of driver's license with FAX requests. Major credit cards accepted for payment.

Mesabi Community College, Registrar, 1001 Chestnut West, Virginia, MN 55792, 218-749-7762 (FAX: 218-749-0318). Hours: 8AM-4:30PM. Records go back to 1900. Alumni records are maintained here also. Call 800-657-3860. Degrees granted: Associate.

Attendance and degree information available by phone, FAX, mail. Search requires name plus social security number, approximate years of attendance, signed release. No fee for information.

Transcripts available by FAX, mail. Search requires name plus social security number, approximate years of attendance, signed release. No fee for transcripts.

Mesivta Tifereth Jerusalem of America, Registrar, 141 E Broadway, New York, NY 10002, 212-964-3830 (FAX: 212-349-5213). Hours: 9AM-5PM. Records go back to 1937. Alumni records are maintained here at the same phone number.

Attendance and degree information available by FAX, mail. Search requires name plus social security number, approximate years of attendance, signed release. No fee for information.

Transcripts available by mail. Search requires name plus approximate years of attendance, signed release. Other helpful information: social security number. Fee is $1.00.

Mesivta Torah Vodaath Rabbinical Seminary, Registrar, 425 E 9th St, Brooklyn, NY 11218, 718-941-8000 (FAX: 718-941-8032). Hours: 8AM-4PM.

Attendance and degree information available by mail. Search requires name plus social security number, date of birth, exact years of attendance. No fee for information.

Transcripts available by mail. Search requires name plus social security number, date of birth, exact years of attendance, signed release. No fee for transcripts.

Mesivta of Eastern Parkway Rabbinical Seminary, Registrar, 510 Dahill Rd, Brooklyn, NY 11218, 718-438-1002. Hours: 8AM-4PM.

Attendance and degree information available by written request only. Search requires name plus exact years of attendance, signed release. Other helpful information: social security number, date of birth. No fee for information.

Transcripts available by written request only. Search requires name plus exact years of attendance, signed release. Other helpful information: social security number, date of birth. No fee for transcripts.

Messiah College, Registrar, Grantham, PA 17027, 717-691-6074 (FAX: 717-691-6025). Hours: 8AM-Noon, 1-5PM. Records go back to founding date. Alumni records are maintained here also. Call 717-691-6019.

Attendance and degree information available by phone, FAX. Search requires name plus social security number, date of birth, approximate years of attendance, signed release. No fee for information.

School does not provide transcripts. Search requires name plus social security number, date of birth, approximate years of attendance, signed release. Fee is $2.00. Expedited service available for $7.00.

Messiah College, (City), Registrar, 2026 N Broad St, Philadelphia, PA 19121, 717-691-6074 (FAX: 717-691-6025). Records are not housed here. They are located at Messiah College, Registrar, Grantham, PA 17027.

Methodist College, Registrar, 5400 Ramsey St, Fayetteville, NC 28311-1420, 910-630-7036 (FAX: 910-630-7119). Hours: 8AM-5PM. Records go back to 1963. Alumni records are maintained here also. Call 910-630-7170. Degrees granted: Associate; Bachelors. Adverse incident record source: Security Office, 910-630-7149.

Attendance information available by phone, FAX, mail. Search requires name plus social security number. No fee for information.

Degree information available by phone, FAX, mail. Search requires name plus social security number, exact years of attendance. No fee for information.

Transcripts available by FAX, mail. Search requires name plus social security number, exact years of attendance, signed release. Fee is $5.00.

Former names needed.

Methodist Theological School in Ohio, Registrar, PO Box 1204, 3081 Columbus Pike, Delaware, OH 43015-0931, 614-362-3344 (FAX: 614-362-3135). Hours: 8:30AM-4:30PM. Records go back to 1960. Alumni records are maintained here also. Call 614-363-1146. Degrees granted: Masters. Adverse incident record source: Dean, 614-363-1146.

Attendance and degree information available by FAX, mail. Search requires name plus social security number, exact years of attendance, signed release. No fee for information.

Transcripts available by FAX, mail. Search requires name plus social security number, exact years of attendance, signed release. No fee for transcripts.

Metropolitan Community College, Registrar, PO Box 3777, Omaha, NE 68103, 402-449-8400.

Attendance and degree information available by phone, FAX, mail. Search requires name plus social security number. Other helpful information: date of birth, approximate years of attendance. No fee for information.

Transcripts available by written request only. Search requires name plus social security number, signed release. Other helpful information: date of birth, approximate years of attendance. No fee for transcripts.

Metropolitan State College of Denver, Registrar, PO Box 173362, Denver, CO 80217-3362, 303-556-3989 (FAX: 303-556-3999). Hours: 8AM-5:30PM Summer; 7:30AM-6:30PM M-Th, 8AM-5PM F Fall. Records go back to 1963. Alumni records are maintained here also. Call 303-556-8320.

Attendance information available by FAX, mail. Search requires name plus social security number, approximate years of attendance, signed release. No fee for information.

Degree information available by phone, FAX, mail. Search requires name plus social security number, approximate years of attendance, signed release. No fee for information.

Transcripts available by FAX, mail. Search requires name plus social security number, approximate years of attendance, signed release. No fee for transcripts.

Metropolitan State University, Registrar, 700 E 7th St, St Paul, MN 55106-5000, 612-772-7772 (FAX: 612-772-7738). Hours: 8AM-5PM. Records go back to 1970. Alumni records are maintained here also. Call 612-772-7800. Degrees granted: Bachelors; Masters.

Attendance and degree information available by phone, FAX, mail. Search requires name plus social security number, signed release. No fee for information.

Transcripts available by FAX, mail. Search requires name plus social security number, signed release. Fee is $2.00.

Miami University, Office of the Registrar, Oxford, OH 45056, 513-529-2026 (FAX: 513-529-7255). Hours: 8AM-5PM. Records go back to 1826. Degrees granted: Associate; Bachelors; Masters; Doctorate. Adverse incident record source: Student Affairs, 513-529-1417.

Attendance and degree information available by phone, FAX, mail. Search requires name only. Other helpful information: social security number, date of birth, approximate years of attendance. No fee for information.

Transcripts available by mail. Search requires name plus signed release. Other helpful information: social security number, date of birth, approximate years of attendance. No fee for transcripts. Expedited service available for $10.00.

Miami University, (Hamilton), Registrar, 1601 Peck Blvd, Hamilton, OH 45011, 513-863-8833 (FAX: 513-863-1655). Records are not housed here. They are located at Miami University, Office of the Registrar, Oxford, OH 45056.

Miami University, (Middletown), Recrods & Registration, 4200 E University Blvd, Middletown, OH 45042, 513-424-4444 (FAX: 513-424-4632). Hours: 9AM-5PM. Records go back to 1976. Degrees granted: Associate.

Attendance and degree information available by mail. Search requires name plus social security number. Other helpful information: date of birth, approximate years of attendance. No fee for information.

Transcripts available by mail. Search requires name plus social security number, signed release. Other helpful information: date of birth, approximate years of attendance. No fee for transcripts.

Miami-Dade Community College, Registrar, 300 NE Second Ave, Miami, FL 33132, 305-237-3336. Hours: 8AM-4:30PM. Records go back to 1959. Alumni records are maintained here also. Call 305-237-4000. Degrees granted: Associate. Adverse incident record source: Campus Security, 305-237-4000.

Attendance and degree information available by phone, mail. Search requires name plus social security number. No fee for information.

Transcripts available by mail. Search requires name plus social security number, signed release. No fee for transcripts.

Miami-Jacobs College, Registrar, PO Box 1433, 400 E Second St, Dayton, OH 45402, 513-461-5174 (FAX: 513-461-5174). Hours: 8AM-4:30PM. Records go back to 1960. Degrees granted: Associate. Adverse incident record source: Finance, 513-461-5174 X156.

Attendance information available by FAX, mail. Search requires name plus social security number, exact years of attendance, signed release. No fee for information.

Degree information available by FAX, mail. Search requires name only. No fee for information.

Transcripts available by FAX, mail. Search requires name only. Fee is $3.00.

Michiana College, Registrar, 1030 E Jefferson Blvd, South Bend, IN 46617, 219-237-0774. Records go back to 1882. Degrees granted: Associate.

Attendance and degree information available by mail. Search requires name plus social security number, approximate years of attendance, signed release. Other helpful information: date of birth. Fee is $5.00.

Transcripts available by mail. Search requires name plus social security number, approximate years of attendance, signed release. Other helpful information: date of birth. Fee is $5.00.

Michiana College, (Branch), Registrar, 4807 Illinois Rd, Fort Wayne, IN 46804, 219-436-2738. Hours: 8AM-5:30PM. Records go back to 1993. Degrees granted: Associate.

Attendance and degree information available by phone, mail. Search requires name plus social security number. No fee for information.

Transcripts available by mail. Search requires name plus social security number, signed release. Fee is $5.00.

Michigan Christian College, Registrar, 800 W Avon Rd, Rochester Hills, MI 48307, 810-650-6035 (FAX: 810-650-6060). Hours: 8:30AM-5PM. Records go back to 1959. Alumni records are maintained here also. Call 810-650-6013. Degrees granted: Associate; Bachelors.

Attendance and degree information available by phone, FAX, mail. Search requires name only. Other helpful information: social security number, date of birth, approximate years of attendance. No fee for information.

Transcripts available by FAX, mail. Search requires name plus social security number, signed release. Other helpful information: date of birth, approximate years of attendance. Fee is $3.00.

Michigan State University, Registrar, 50 Administration Bldg, East Lansing, MI 48824, 517-355-3300 (FAX: 517-432-1649). Hours: 8AM-6PM M-Th; 8AM-5PM F. Records go back to 1855. Alumni records are maintained here also. Call 517-355-8314. Degrees granted: Bachelors; Masters; Doctorate. Certification: 2 year Agricultural Tech. Adverse incident record source: Student Affairs, 517-355-2264.

Attendance and degree information available by phone, FAX, mail. Search requires name only. Other helpful information: social security number, date of birth, approximate years of attendance. No fee for information.

Transcripts available by phone, FAX, mail. Search requires name plus signed release. Other helpful information: social security number, date of birth, approximate years of attendance. Fee is $5.00.

Major credit cards accepted for payment.

Michigan Technological University, Registrar, 1400 Townsend Dr, Houghton, MI 49931, 906-487-2319 (FAX: 906-487-3343). Hours: 8AM-5PM. Records go back to 1887. Degrees granted: Associate; Bachelors; Masters; Doctorate.

Attendance information available by phone, FAX, mail. Search requires name only. Other helpful information: social security number, approximate years of attendance. No fee for information.

Degree information available by phone, FAX, mail. Search requires name only. Other helpful information: social security number, approximate years of attendance. No fee for information.

Transcripts available by mail. Search requires name plus signed release. Other helpful information: social security number, approximate years of attendance. Fee is $3.00.

Need major & last year of attendance. Major credit cards accepted for payment.

Mid Michigan Community College, Registrar, 1375 S Clare Ave, Harrison, MI 48625, 517-386-6658 (FAX: 517-386-9088). Hours: 8AM-6:30PM M-Th; 8AM-4:30PM F. Records go back to 1968. Degrees granted: Associate.

Attendance and degree information available by phone, FAX, mail. Search requires name only. Other helpful information: social security number, date of birth, approximate years of attendance. No fee for information.

Transcripts available by FAX, mail. Search requires name plus signed release. Other helpful information: social security number, date of birth, approximate years of attendance. Fee is $2.00. $10.00 FAX fee.

Major credit cards accepted for payment.

Mid-America Baptist Theological Seminary, Registrar's Office, 1255 Poplar Ave, Memphis, TN 38104, 901-726-9171 (FAX: 901-726-6791). Hours: 8AM-4:30PM. Records go back to 1971. Alumni records are maintained here at the same phone number. Degrees granted: Associate; Masters; Doctorate.

Attendance information available by phone, FAX, mail. Search requires name only. Other helpful information: social security number, date of birth, exact years of attendance. No fee for information.

Degree information available by phone, FAX, mail. Search requires name only. Other helpful information: social security number, date of birth, approximate years of attendance. No fee for information.

Transcripts available by mail. Search requires name plus signed release. Other helpful information: social security number, date of birth. Fee is $5.00.

Mid-America Bible College, Registrar, 3500 SW 119th St, Oklahoma City, OK 73170-9797, 405-691-3800 (FAX: 405-692-3165). Hours: 8:30AM-4PM. Records go back 40 years. Degrees granted: Associate; Bachelors.

Attendance and degree information available by phone, FAX, mail. Search requires name only. Other helpful information: social security number, approximate years of attendance. No fee for information.

Transcripts available by FAX, mail. Search requires name plus social security number, signed release. Other helpful information: date of birth, approximate years of attendance. Fee is $2.00. FAX copy is unofficial copy.

Mid-America College of Funeral Service, Registrar, 3111 Hamburg Pike, Jeffersonville, IN 47130, 812-288-8878 (FAX: 812-288-5942). Hours: 7:30AM-4PM. Records go back to 1920. Degrees granted: Associate.

Attendance and degree information available by phone, FAX, mail. Search requires name plus approximate years of attendance. Other helpful information: social security number, date of birth, exact years of attendance. No fee for information.

Transcripts available by mail. Search requires name plus approximate years of attendance, signed release. Other helpful information: social security number, date of birth, exact years of attendance. Fee is $2.00.

Mid-Continent Baptist Bible College, Registrar, PO Box 7010, Mayfield, KY 42066, 502-247-8521 (FAX: 502-247-7681). Records go back to 1949. Degrees granted: Bachelors.

Attendance information available by FAX. Search requires name plus social security number, date of birth, signed release. Other helpful information: approximate years of attendance. No fee for information.

Degree information available by written request only. Search requires name plus social security number, date of birth, signed release. Other helpful information: approximate years of attendance. No fee for information.

Transcripts available by written request only. Search requires name plus social security number, date of birth, signed release. Other helpful information: approximate years of attendance. Fee is $3.00.

Mid-Plains Community College, Registrar's Office, 1101 Halligan Dr, North Platte, NE 69101, 308-532-8740 (FAX: 308-532-8494). Hours: 8AM-5PM. Records go back to 1965. Degrees granted: Associate.

Attendance and degree information available by phone, FAX, mail. Search requires name plus social security number. Other helpful information: date of birth, approximate years of attendance. No fee for information.

Transcripts available by FAX, mail. Search requires name plus social security number, approximate years of attendance, signed release. Other helpful information: date of birth, exact years of attendance. Fee is $2.00.

Mid-State College, Registrar, 88 Hardscrabble Rd, Auburn, ME 04210, 207-783-1478 (FAX: 207-783-1477). Hours: 8AM-4PM. Records go back 10 years. Degrees granted: Associate.

Attendance and degree information available by written request only. Search requires name plus social security number, date of birth, signed release. No fee for information.

Transcripts available by written request only. Search requires name plus social security number, date of birth, signed release. Fee is $3.00. Expedited service available for $3.00.

Mid-State College, **(Branch)**, Registrar, 218 Water St, Augusta, ME 04430, 207-623-3962. Hours: 8AM-8PM M-Th, 8AM-4PM. Records go back to 1950. Alumni records are maintained here at the same phone number. Degrees granted: Associate.

Attendance and degree information available by mail. Search requires name plus social security number, signed release. No fee for information.

Transcripts available by mail. Search requires name plus social security number, signed release. Fee is $3.00.

Mid-State Technical College, Registrar, 500 32nd St N, Wisconsin Rapids, WI 54494, 715-422-5502 (FAX: 715-422-5345). Hours: 7:30AM-4:30PM. Records go back to 1967. Degrees granted: Associate.

Attendance and degree information available by phone, FAX, mail. Search requires name plus social security number. No fee for information.

Transcripts available by written request only. Search requires name plus social security number, signed release. No fee for transcripts.

Major credit cards accepted for payment.

MidAmerica Nazarene College, Registrar, 2030 E College Wy, Olathe, KS 66062-1899, 913-782-3750 (FAX: 913-791-3290). Hours: 8AM-5PM. Records go back to founding date. Degrees granted: Associate; Bachelors; Masters.

Attendance and degree information available by phone, FAX, mail. Search requires name plus social security number. Other helpful information: date of birth, approximate years of attendance. No fee for information.

Transcripts available by written request only. Search requires name plus social security number, signed release. Other helpful information: date of birth, approximate years of attendance. Fee is $2.00.

Middle Georgia College, Registrar, 1100 Second St SE, Cochran, GA 31014, 912-934-3036 (FAX: 912-934-3049). Hours: 8AM-5PM. Records go back to 1884. Alumni records are maintained here also. Call 912-934-3301. Degrees granted: Associate. Adverse incident record source: Student Affairs, 912-934-3027.

Attendance and degree information available by phone, FAX, mail. Search requires name plus social security number, approximate years of attendance, signed release. No fee for information.

Transcripts available by mail. Search requires name plus social security number, approximate years of attendance, signed release. Fee is $3.00.

Middle Tennessee State University, Registrar, Murfreesboro, TN 37132, 615-898-2600. Hours: 8AM-4:30PM. Records go back to 1926. Alumni records are maintained here also. Call 615-898-2922. Degrees granted: Bachelors; Masters; Doctorate.

Attendance and degree information available by phone, mail. Search requires name plus social security number, date of birth. No fee for information.

Transcripts available by mail. Search requires name plus social security number, date of birth, signed release. No fee for transcripts.

Middlebury College, Registrar, Old Chapel Bldg, Middlebury, VT 05753, 802-388-3711 X5389 (FAX: 802-388-9646). Hours: 8AM-5PM. Records go back to 1800. Alumni records are maintained here at the same phone number. Degrees granted: Bachelors; Masters; Doctorate.

Attendance and degree information available by phone, FAX, mail. Search requires name plus social security number. No fee for information.

Transcripts available by FAX, mail. Search requires name plus social security number, signed release. Fee is $2.00.

Middlesex Community College, Registrar, Springs Rd, Bedford, MA 01730, 617-280-3614. Hours: 8:30AM-9:30PM M-Th, 8:30AM-5PM F, 8:30-11:30AM Sat. Records go back to 1970. Alumni records are maintained here also. Call 617-280-3523. Degrees granted: Associate.

Attendance and degree information available by phone, mail. Search requires name plus social security number, approximate years of attendance, signed release. No fee for information.

School does not provide transcripts. Search requires name plus social security number, approximate years of attendance, signed release. Fee is $2.00.

Middlesex Community College, (Lowell), Registrar, Kearney Square, Lowell, MA 01852, 508-656-3200. Records are not housed here. They are located at Middlesex Community College, Registrar, Springs Rd, Bedford, MA 01730.

Middlesex Community-Technical College, Registrar, 100 Training Hill Rd, Middletown, CT 06457, 203-343-5720 (FAX: 203-344-7488). Hours: 8:30AM-4:30PM. Records go back to 1966. Degrees granted: Associate.
Attendance and degree information available by phone, FAX, mail. Search requires name only. Other helpful information: social security number, approximate years of attendance. No fee for information.
Transcripts available by mail. Search requires name plus social security number, signed release. Other helpful information: approximate years of attendance. No fee for transcripts.

Middlesex County College, Registrar's Office, 155 Mill Rd, PO Box 3050, Edison, NJ 08818-3050, 908-548-6000. Alumni records are maintained here also. Call 908-906-2564. Degrees granted: Associate. Special programs- Liberal Arts, 908-906-2528: Business Tech, 908-906-2502: Engineering & Science, 908-906-2501: Health Tech, 908-906-2533: Open College, 908-906-2533. Adverse incident record source: Student Services, 908-906-2514.
Attendance and degree information available by phone, FAX, mail. Search requires name plus social security number, signed release. Other helpful information: date of birth, approximate years of attendance. No fee for information.
Transcripts available by phone, mail. Search requires name plus signed release. Other helpful information: social security number, date of birth, approximate years of attendance. Fee is $3.00.
Will FAX in special cases.

Midland College, Registrar, 3600 N Garfield St, Midland, TX 79705, 915-685-4508 (FAX: 915-685-4714). Hours: 8AM-4:30PM. Degrees granted: Associate.
Attendance and degree information available by phone, mail. Search requires name plus social security number, exact years of attendance. No fee for information.
Transcripts available by mail. Search requires name plus social security number, exact years of attendance, signed release. No fee for transcripts.

Midland Lutheran College, Registrar, 900 Clarkson St, Fremont, NE 68025, 402-721-5480 X6220 (FAX: 402-721-0250). Hours: 8AM-4:30PM. Records go back to 1883. Degrees granted: Associate; Bachelors. Adverse incident record source: Student Services.
Attendance information available by phone, FAX, mail. Search requires name plus approximate years of attendance. Other helpful information: social security number, date of birth, exact years of attendance. No fee for information.
Degree information available by phone, FAX, mail. Search requires name only. Other helpful information: social security number, date of birth, approximate years of attendance. No fee for information.
Transcripts available by mail. Search requires name plus approximate years of attendance, signed release. Other helpful information: social security number, date of birth, exact years of attendance. Fee is $5.00. Expedited service available for $5.00.
Major credit cards accepted for payment.

Midlands Technical College, Registrar, PO Box 2408, Columbia, SC 29202, 803-738-7703 (FAX: 803-738-7880). Hours: 8AM-6:30PM M-Th; 8AM-4:30PM F. Records go back to 1905. Alumni records are maintained here also. Call 803-732-5333. Degrees granted: Associate. Adverse incident record source: SDS, 803-738-7699.
Attendance and degree information available by phone, FAX, mail. Search requires name plus social security number. Other helpful information: date of birth, approximate years of attendance. No fee for information.
Transcripts available by FAX, mail. Search requires name plus social security number, signed release. Other helpful information: date of birth, approximate years of attendance. Fee is $2.00.

Midstate College, Registrar, 244 SW Jefferson St, Peoria, IL 61602, 304-673-6365 (FAX: 309-673-5814). Hours: 8AM-4:30PM. Records go back to 1950s. Degrees granted: Associate.
Attendance and degree information available by phone, FAX, mail. Search requires name plus social security number, signed release. Other helpful information: date of birth, approximate years of attendance. No fee for information.
Transcripts available by mail. Search requires name plus social security number, signed release. Other helpful information: date of birth, approximate years of attendance. Fee is $3.00. Expedited service available for $3.00.
Major credit cards accepted for payment.

Midway College, Starks Hall/101, Registrar, 512 E Stephens St, Midway, KY 40347-1120, 606-846-5350 (FAX: 606-846-5349). Hours: 8AM-5PM. Records go back 148 years. Degrees granted: Associate; Bachelors.
Attendance and degree information available by phone, FAX, mail. Search requires name only. Other helpful information: social security number, date of birth, approximate years of attendance. No fee for information.
Transcripts available by mail. Search requires name plus signed release. Other helpful information: social security number, date of birth, approximate years of attendance. Fee is $2.00. Expedited service available for $4.00.
Major credit cards accepted for payment.

Midwestern Baptist Theological Seminary, Registrar, 5001 N Oak St Trafficway, Kansas City, MO 64118, 816-453-4600 (FAX: 816-455-3528). Hours: 8AM-4:30PM. Records go back to 1958. Degrees granted: Associate; Masters; Doctorate.
Attendance and degree information available by phone, FAX, mail. Search requires name only. Other helpful information: social security number, date of birth, approximate years of attendance. No fee for information.
Transcripts available by FAX, mail. Search requires name plus signed release. Other helpful information: social security number, date of birth, approximate years of attendance. Fee is $3.00. Expedite fee is $3.00 plus overnight fee.

Midwestern State University, Registrar & Admissions, 3410 Taft Blvd, Wichita Falls, TX 76308-2099, 817-689-4321 (FAX: 817-689-4042). Hours: 8AM-5PM. Records go back to 1922. Alumni records are maintained here also. Call 817-689-4121. Degrees granted: Associate; Bachelors; Masters. Certification: Teacher Cert. Adverse incident record source: Dean of Students, 817-689-4291.

Attendance and degree information available by phone, mail. Search requires name plus social security number. Other helpful information: date of birth, approximate years of attendance. No fee for information.

Transcripts available by mail. Search requires name plus social security number, signed release. Other helpful information: date of birth, approximate years of attendance. Fee is $3.00. Expedite fee is $3.00 plus express mail fees.

Nee to know any last names used.

Midwestern University, Registrar, 555 31st St, Downers Grove, IL 60515, 708-515-6074 (FAX: 708-515-7140). Hours: 8AM-5PM. Records go back 75 years. Degrees granted: Bachelors; Masters; Doctorate. Adverse incident record source: Student Affairs, 708-515-6470.

Attendance and degree information available by phone, FAX, mail. Search requires name only. Other helpful information: social security number, date of birth, approximate years of attendance. No fee for information.

Transcripts available by FAX, mail. Search requires name plus signed release. Other helpful information: social security number, date of birth, approximate years of attendance. Fee is $5.00.

Miles College, Registrar, PO Box 3800, Birmingham, AL 35208, 205-923-2771 X276 (FAX: 205-923-9292). Hours: 8AM-5PM. Records go back to 1905. Alumni records are maintained here also. Call 205-923-2771 X291. Degrees granted: Bachelors.

Attendance and degree information available by phone, FAX, mail. Search requires name plus social security number, exact years of attendance. No fee for information.

Transcripts available by phone, FAX, mail. Search requires name plus social security number, exact years of attendance, signed release. Fee is $5.00.

Miles Community College, Registrar, Miles City, MT 59301, 406-232-3031 (FAX: 406-232-5705). Hours: 7:30AM-5PM. Records go back to 1939. Degrees granted: Associate. Adverse incident record source: Dean of Student Services.

Attendance and degree information available by phone, FAX, mail. Search requires name only. Other helpful information: social security number, date of birth, approximate years of attendance. No fee for information. Expedited service available for $10.00.

Transcripts available by phone, FAX, mail. Search requires name plus signed release. Other helpful information: social security number, date of birth, approximate years of attendance. Fee is $2.00. Expedited service available for $12.00.

Millersville University of Pennsylvania, Registrar, PO Box 1002, Millersville, PA 17551-1002, 717-872-3035 (FAX: 717-871-2022). Hours: 9AM-5PM. Alumni records are maintained here also. Call 717-872-3352. Degrees granted: Associate; Bachelors; Masters.

Attendance information available by phone, FAX, mail. Search requires name plus signed release. Other helpful information: social security number, date of birth, approximate years of attendance. No fee for information.

Degree information available by phone, FAX, mail. Search requires name only. Other helpful information: social security number, date of birth, approximate years of attendance. No fee for information.

Transcripts available by written request only. Search requires name plus social security number, signed release. Other helpful information: date of birth, approximate years of attendance. No fee for transcripts.

Milligan College, Registrar, PO Box 52, Milligan College, TN 37682, 615-461-8788 (FAX: 615-461-8716). Hours: 8AM-Noon, 1-5PM. Records go back to 1913. Degrees granted: Associate; Bachelors; Masters. Adverse incident record source: Student Development, 615-461-8760.

Attendance information available by phone, FAX, mail. Search requires name plus social security number, date of birth, exact years of attendance. Other helpful information: approximate years of attendance. No fee for information.

Degree information available by phone, FAX, mail. Search requires name only. Other helpful information: social security number, date of birth, approximate years of attendance. No fee for information.

Transcripts available by FAX, mail. Search requires name plus signed release. Other helpful information: social security number, date of birth, approximate years of attendance. Fee is $2.00.

Millikin University, Registrar, 1184 W Main St, Decatur, IL 62522, 217-424-6217 (FAX: 217-424-3993). Hours: 8AM-5PM. Records go back to 1903. Alumni records are maintained here also. Call 217-424-6384. Degrees granted: Bachelors. Adverse incident record source: Student Development, 217-424-6240.

Attendance and degree information available by phone, FAX, mail. Search requires name plus social security number, date of birth, approximate years of attendance. No fee for information.

Transcripts available by written request only. Search requires name plus social security number, date of birth, approximate years of attendance, signed release. No fee for transcripts.

Mills College, Registrar, Oakland, CA 94613, 510-430-2083 (FAX: 510-430-3314). Hours: 9AM-4PM. Records go back to 1871. Degrees granted: Bachelors; Masters. Certification: Post Bac.

Attendance information available by phone, FAX, mail. Search requires name plus exact years of attendance, signed release. Other helpful information: social security number, date of birth, approximate years of attendance. No fee for information.

Degree information available by phone, FAX, mail. Search requires name plus exact years of attendance, signed release. Other helpful information: date of birth, approximate years of attendance. No fee for information.

Transcripts available by mail. Search requires name plus social security number, signed release. Other helpful information: date of birth, approximate years of attendance. Fee is $3.00.

Millsaps College, Office of Records, PO Box 150110, Jackson, MS 39210, 601-974-1120 (FAX: 601-974-1114). Hours: 8AM-4:30PM. Records go back to 1890. Degrees granted: Bachelors; Masters.

Attendance and degree information available by phone, mail. Search requires name plus social security number. Other helpful information: date of birth, approximate years of attendance. No fee for information.

Transcripts available by mail. Search requires name plus social security number, date of birth, signed release. Other helpful information: approximate years of attendance. Fee is $5.00.

Milwaukee Area Technical College, Registrar, 700 W State St, Milwaukee, WI 53233, 414-297-7017 (FAX: 414-297-6371). Hours: 7:45AM-4:15PM. Records go back to 1920. Degrees granted: Associate.

Attendance information available by phone, FAX, mail. Search requires name plus social security number, signed release. Other helpful information: date of birth, approximate years of attendance. Fee is $3.00. Expedited service available for $5.00.

Degree information available by phone, FAX, mail. Search requires name plus social security number, exact years of attendance, signed release. Other helpful information: date of birth, approximate years of attendance. Fee is $15.00.

Transcripts available by mail. Search requires name plus social security number, exact years of attendance, signed release. Other helpful information: date of birth, approximate years of attendance. Fee is $3.00. Expedited service available for $5.00.

Major credit cards accepted for payment.

Milwaukee Institute of Art and Design, Registrar, 273 E Erie St, Milwaukee, WI 53202, 414-276-7889 (FAX: 414-291-8077). Hours: 8AM-4:30PM. Records go back to 1974. Alumni records are maintained here also. Call 414-276-7889. Degrees granted: Bachelors.

Attendance and degree information available by phone, FAX, mail. Search requires name plus social security number, date of birth, approximate years of attendance. Other helpful information: exact years of attendance. No fee for information.

Transcripts available by FAX, mail. Search requires name plus social security number, date of birth, approximate years of attendance, signed release. Other helpful information: exact years of attendance. Fee is $3.00.

Milwaukee School of Engineering, Registrar, 1025 N Broadway, Milwaukee, WI 53202-3109, 414-277-7220. Alumni records are maintained here at the same phone number. Degrees granted: Associate; Bachelors; Masters.

Attendance and degree information available by phone, FAX, mail. Search requires name only. Other helpful information: social security number, approximate years of attendance. No fee for information.

Transcripts available by phone, FAX, mail. Search requires name plus signed release. Other helpful information: social security number, approximate years of attendance. Fee is $5.00.

Mineral Area College, Registrar, PO Box 1000, Hwy 67 and 32, Park Hills, MO 63601, 314-431-4593 (FAX: 314-431-2321). Hours: 8AM-4PM. Records go back to 1922. Degrees granted: Associate.

Attendance and degree information available by phone, mail. Search requires name plus social security number. Other helpful information: date of birth, approximate years of attendance. No fee for information.

Transcripts available by mail. Search requires name plus social security number, signed release. Other helpful information: date of birth, approximate years of attendance. Fee is $2.00.

Minneapolis College of Art and Design, Registrar, 2501 Stevens Ave S, Minneapolis, MN 55404, 612-874-3727 (FAX: 612-874-3704). Hours: 8:30AM-5PM. Records go back to 1912. Alumni records are maintained here also. Call 612-874-3792. Degrees granted: Bachelors; Masters.

Attendance and degree information available by phone, FAX, mail. Search requires name plus social security number, date of birth, signed release. No fee for information.

Transcripts available by mail. Search requires name plus social security number, date of birth, signed release. Fee is $5.00.

Minneapols Community College, Records & Admissions, 1501 Hennepin Ave, Minneapolis, MN 55403, 612-341-7006 (FAX: 612-341-7075). Hours: 8:30AM-4:30PM. Records go back to 1968. Degrees granted: Associate.

Attendance and degree information available by phone, FAX, mail. Search requires name only. Other helpful information: social security number, date of birth. No fee for information.

Transcripts available by written request only. Search requires name plus signed release. Other helpful information: social security number, date of birth. No fee for transcripts.

Minnesota Bible College, Registrar, 920 Mayowood Rd SW, Rochester, MN 55902, 507-288-4563 (FAX: 507-288-9046). Hours: 8AM-4:30PM. Records go back 50 years. Degrees granted: Associate; Bachelors.

Attendance information available by phone, FAX, mail. Search requires name only. Other helpful information: date of birth, approximate years of attendance. No fee for information.

Degree information available by written request only. Search requires name plus signed release. No fee for information.

Transcripts available by written request only. Search requires name plus signed release. Fee is $2.00.

Minot State University, Registrar, Minot, ND 58701, 701-857-3340 (FAX: 701-839-6933). Hours: 7:30AM-4:30PM. Records go back to 1913. Alumni records are maintained here also. Call 701-857-3234. Degrees granted: Associate; Bachelors; Masters.

Attendance information available by phone, FAX, mail. Search requires name only. Other helpful information: social security number, date of birth, approximate years of attendance. No fee for information.

Degree information available by phone, FAX, mail. Search requires name only. Other helpful information: social security number, date of birth, approximate years of attendance. No fee for information.

Transcripts available by mail. Search requires name plus signed release. Other helpful information: social security number, date of birth, approximate years of attendance. Fee is $2.00.

Mira Costa College, Registrar, One Barnard Dr, Oceanside, CA 92056, 619-757-2121 (FAX: 619-721-8760). Hours: 8AM-7PM M-Th; 8AM-4:30PM F. Records go back to 1937. Alumni records are maintained here also. Call 619-757-2121 X259. Degrees granted: Associate. Adverse incident record source: Dick Robertson, 619-757-2121 X295.

Attendance information available by mail. Search requires name plus social security number, date of birth, approximate years of attendance, signed release. No fee for information.

Degree information available by mail. Search requires name plus social security number, date of birth, approximate years of attendance, signed release. Other helpful information: exact years of attendance. No fee for information.

Transcripts available by mail. Search requires name plus social security number, date of birth, approximate years of attendance, signed release. Other helpful information: exact years of attendance. Fee is $2.00.

Mirrer Yeshiva Central Institute, Registrar, 1791 S Ocean Pkwy, Brooklyn, NY 11223, 718-645-0536 (FAX: 718-645-9251). Hours: 8AM-4:30PM.

Attendance and degree information available by FAX, mail. Search requires name plus social security number, exact years of attendance, signed release. No fee for information.

Transcripts available by mail. Search requires name plus social security number, exact years of attendance, signed release. Fee is $25.00.
Major credit cards accepted for payment.

Miss Wade's Fashion Merchandising College, Registrar, PO Box 586343, Dallas Apparel Mart Ste M5120, Dallas, TX 75258, 214-637-3520 (FAX: 214-637-0827). Hours: 8AM-4:30PM. Degrees granted: Associate.

Attendance and degree information available by phone, FAX, mail. Search requires name plus social security number, exact years of attendance. No fee for information.

Transcripts available by FAX, mail. Search requires name plus social security number, exact years of attendance, signed release. Fee is $5.00.

Mission College, Registrar, 3000 Mission College Blvd, Santa Clara, CA 95054, 408-988-2200 (FAX: 408-980-8980). Hours: 9:30AM-6:30PM M-Th, 9:30AM-1PM F. Degrees granted: Associate.

Attendance and degree information available by phone, FAX, mail. Search requires name plus social security number, date of birth, approximate years of attendance, signed release. No fee for information.

Transcripts available by mail. Search requires name plus social security number, date of birth, approximate years of attendance, signed release. Fee is $4.00.

Mississippi College, Registrar, PO Box 4186, Clinton, MS 39058, 601-925-3210 (FAX: 601-925-3804). Hours: 8AM-4:30PM. Records go back to 1826. Degrees granted: Bachelors; Masters.

Attendance and degree information available by phone, FAX, mail. Search requires name plus social security number, date of birth. Other helpful information: approximate years of attendance. No fee for information.

Transcripts available by mail. Search requires name plus social security number, date of birth, signed release. Other helpful information: approximate years of attendance. Fee is $5.00.

Mississippi County Community College, Registrar, PO Drawer 1109, Blytheville, AR 72316, 501-762-1020 (FAX: 501-763-3704). Hours: 8AM-4:30PM. Records go back to 1975. Degrees granted: Associate.

Attendance and degree information available by FAX, mail. Search requires name plus social security number. Other helpful information: approximate years of attendance. No fee for information.

Transcripts available by FAX, mail. Search requires name plus social security number, signed release. Other helpful information: approximate years of attendance. No fee for transcripts.

Mississippi Delta Community College, Registrar, PO Box 668, Moorhead, MS 38761, 601-246-6306 (FAX: 601-246-6321). Hours: 8AM-4PM Summer, 8AM-4:30PM Fall. Records go back to 1940. Alumni records are maintained here also. Call 601-246-6457. Degrees granted: Associate. Certification: Vocational. Adverse incident record source: Dean of Students, 601-246-6444.

Attendance information available by phone, FAX, mail. Search requires name plus social security number, date of birth, approximate years of attendance, signed release. No fee for information.

Degree information available by FAX, mail. Search requires name plus social security number, date of birth, approximate years of attendance, signed release. No fee for information.

Transcripts available by mail. Search requires name plus social security number, date of birth, approximate years of attendance, signed release. Fee is $2.00.

Mississippi Gulf Coast Community College, Registrar, PO Box 67, Perkinston, MS 39573, 601-928-5211 (FAX: 601-928-6359). Hours: 8AM-4:30PM. Records go back to 1912. Degrees granted: Associate. Adverse incident record source: Student Services, 601-928-5211.

Attendance and degree information available by phone, FAX, mail. Search requires name plus social security number, exact years of attendance, signed release. Other helpful information: date of birth, approximate years of attendance. No fee for information. Expedited service available for $5.00.

Transcripts available by FAX, mail. Search requires name plus social security number, exact years of attendance, signed release. Other helpful information: date of birth, approximate years of attendance. Fee is $2.00. Expedited service available for $00,5.00.

Mississippi State University, Registrar's Office, 112 Allen Hall, PO Box 5268, Mississippi State, MS 39762, 601-325-1843 (FAX: 601-325-1846). Hours: 8AM-5PM. Records go back to 1878. Degrees granted: Bachelors; Masters; Doctorate.

Attendance and degree information available by phone, FAX. Search requires name plus social security number, date of birth. Other helpful information: approximate years of attendance. No fee for information.

Transcripts available by FAX, mail. Search requires name plus social security number, date of birth, signed release. Other helpful information: approximate years of attendance. Fee is $4.00. $10.00 for FAXed transcript.

Mississippi University for Women, Registrar, PO Box W-1605, Columbus, MS 39701, 601-329-7131 (FAX: 601-329-7297). Hours: 8AM-5PM. Records go back to 1884. Alumni records are maintained here at the same phone number. Alumni Records Office: PO Box W-10, Columbus, MS 39701. Degrees granted: Associate; Bachelors; Masters. Adverse incident record source: Security, 601-329-7436.

Attendance and degree information available by phone, FAX, mail. Search requires name plus social security number, approximate years of attendance. Other helpful information: date of birth, exact years of attendance. No fee for information. Include a stamped envelope.

Transcripts available by mail. Search requires name plus social security number, date of birth, approximate years of attendance, signed release. Other helpful information: exact years of attendance. Transcripts $1.00 in person and $3.00 by mail. Expedited service available for $3.00.

Mississippi Valley State University, Registrar, 14000 Hwy 82 W, Itta Bena, MS 38941, 601-254-3325. Hours: 8AM-5PM M,T,W,Th; 8AM-4PM F. Records go back to founding date. Alumni records are maintained here also. Call 601-254-3576. Degrees granted: Bachelors; Masters. Adverse incident record source: Student Services, 601-254-3636.

Attendance information available by written request only. Search requires name plus social security number, signed release. Other helpful information: date of birth, approximate years of attendance. No fee for information.

School will not confirm degree information. Search requires name plus signed release. Other helpful information: date of birth, approximate years of attendance. No fee for information.

Transcripts available by written request only. Search requires name plus social security number, signed release. Other helpful information: date of birth, approximate years of attendance. Fee is $4.00.

Change of name since leaving school helpful.

Missouri Baptist College, Records Office, One College Park Dr, St Louis, MO 63141, 314-434-1115 X2233 (FAX: 314-434-1115 X2233). Hours: 8AM-4:30PM. Records go back to 1968. Degrees granted: Associate; Bachelors.

Attendance and degree information available by phone, FAX, mail. Search requires name plus social security number. Other helpful information: date of birth, approximate years of attendance. No fee for information.

Transcripts available by FAX, mail. Search requires name plus social security number, signed release. Other helpful information: date of birth, approximate years of attendance. First copy free. $5.00 each additional. Expedite: Pay overnight fee

FAX request must be paid by credit card. Major credit cards accepted for payment.

Missouri Southern State College, Registrar, 3950 Newman Rd, Joplin, MO 64801, 417-625-9340 (FAX: 417-625-3117). Hours: 8AM-5PM. Records go back to 1938. Alumni records are maintained here at the same phone number. Degrees granted: Associate; Bachelors. Adverse incident record source: Dean of Students.

Attendance and degree information available by FAX, mail. Search requires name plus social security number, signed release. Other helpful information: date of birth, approximate years of attendance. No fee for information.

Transcripts available by FAX, mail. Search requires name plus social security number, signed release. Other helpful information: date of birth, approximate years of attendance. Fee is $1.00.

Missouri Valley College, Registrar, 500 E College Dr, Marshall, MO 65340, 816-886-6924 (FAX: 816-886-9818). Hours: 9AM-5PM. Records go back to 1890. Degrees granted: Associate; Bachelors.

Attendance and degree information available by phone, FAX, mail. Search requires name only. Other helpful information: social security number, date of birth, approximate years of attendance. No fee for information.

Transcripts available by mail. Search requires name plus social security number, signed release. Other helpful information: date of birth, approximate years of attendance. Fee is $4.00. Expedited service available for $4.00.

Major credit cards accepted for payment.

Missouri Western State College, Registrar, 4525 Downs Dr, St Joseph, MO 64507, 816-271-4228. Hours: 8AM-4:30PM. Records go back to 1915. Alumni records are maintained here also. Call 816-271-4253. Degrees granted: Associate; Bachelors. Adverse incident record source: Dean of Students, 816-271-4432.

Attendance and degree information available by phone, mail. Search requires name plus social security number. Other helpful information: date of birth. No fee for information.

Transcripts available by mail. Search requires name plus social security number, signed release. Other helpful information: date of birth. Fee is $2.00.

Mitchell College, Registrar, New London, CT 06320, 203-443-2811 (FAX: 203-437-0632). Hours: 8:30AM-4:30PM. Degrees granted: Associate.

Attendance information available by FAX, mail. Search requires name only. Other helpful information: social security number, date of birth, approximate years of attendance. No fee for information.

Degree information available by FAX, mail. Search requires name only. Other helpful information: social security number, date of birth, approximate years of attendance. No fee for information.

Transcripts available by FAX, mail. Search requires name plus social security number, signed release. Other helpful information: date of birth, approximate years of attendance. Fee is $3.00.

Mitchell Community College, Registrar, 500 W Broad St, Statesville, NC 28677, 704-878-3246 (FAX: 704-878-0872). Hours: 8AM-5PM. Records go back to 1930. Degrees granted: Associate.

Attendance and degree information available by phone, FAX, mail. Search requires name plus social security number, signed release. Other helpful information: date of birth, approximate years of attendance. No fee for information.

Transcripts available by mail. Search requires name plus social security number, signed release. Other helpful information: date of birth, approximate years of attendance. No fee for transcripts.

Mitchell Technical Institute, Registrar, 821 N Capital St, Mitchell, SD 57301, 605-995-3024. Hours: 8AM-5PM. Records go back to 1968. Degrees granted: Associate.

Attendance and degree information available by mail. Search requires name plus social security number, exact years of attendance, signed release. No fee for information.

Transcripts available by mail. Search requires name plus social security number, exact years of attendance, signed release. Fee is $2.00.

Need to know program of study.

Moberly Area Community College, Student Services, College and Rollins Sts, Moberly, MO 65270, 816-263-4110 (FAX: 816-263-6448). Hours: 8AM-10PM M-Th; 8AM-8PM F. Records go back to 1927. Degrees granted: Associate. Certification: LPN.

Attendance and degree information available by phone, FAX, mail. Search requires name only. Other helpful information: social security number, date of birth, approximate years of attendance. No fee for information.

Transcripts available by FAX, mail. Search requires name plus signed release. Other helpful information: social security number, date of birth, approximate years of attendance. Fee is $1.00.

Major credit cards accepted for payment.

Modesto Junior College, Registrar, 435 College Ave, Modesto, CA 95350, 209-575-6470 (FAX: 209-575-6666). Hours: 8AM-5PM. Records go back to 1921. Degrees granted: Associate.

Attendance information available by phone, FAX, mail. Search requires name plus social security number, exact years of attendance, signed release. Other helpful information: date of birth, approximate years of attendance. No fee for information.

Degree information available by mail. Search requires name plus social security number, exact years of attendance, signed release. Other helpful information: date of birth, approximate years of attendance. No fee for information.

Transcripts available by mail. Search requires name plus social security number, exact years of attendance, signed release. Other helpful information: date of birth, approximate years of attendance. First two transcripts free. Additional ones are $3.00. Expedited service available for $10.00.

Mohave Community College, Registrar, 1971 Jagerson Ave, Kingman, AZ 86401, 520-757-0847 (FAX: 520-757-0808). Hours: 8AM-5PM. Records go back to 1971. Degrees granted: Associate.

Attendance and degree information available by phone, FAX, mail. Search requires name plus social security number, signed release. Other helpful information: date of birth, approximate years of attendance. No fee for information.

Transcripts available by FAX, mail. Search requires name plus social security number, signed release. Other helpful information: date of birth, approximate years of attendance. Fee is $2.00.

Mohawk Valley Community College, Registrar, 1101 Sherman Dr, Utica, NY 13501, 315-792-5336 (FAX: 315-792-5698). Hours: 8AM-8:30PM M-Th; 8AM-4:30PM F. Records go back to 1988. Alumni records are maintained here also. Call 314-792-5340. Degrees granted: Associate.

Attendance and degree information available by phone, FAX, mail. Search requires name plus social security number, date of birth, exact years of attendance, signed release. No fee for information.

Transcripts available by mail. Search requires name plus social security number, date of birth, exact years of attendance, signed release. Fee is $3.00.

Mohawk Valley Community College, **(Branch Campus)**, Registrar, Floyd Ave, Rome, NY 13440, 315-792-5494. Hours: 8:30AM-4:30PM. Records go back to 1900s. Degrees granted: Associate.

Attendance information available by phone, FAX, mail. Search requires name plus social security number. Other helpful information: date of birth, approximate years of attendance. No fee for information.

Degree information available by phone, FAX, mail. Search requires name plus social security number. Other helpful information: date of birth, approximate years of attendance. No fee for information.

Transcripts available by FAX, mail. Search requires name plus social security number, signed release. Other helpful information: date of birth, approximate years of attendance. Fee is $3.00.

Major credit cards accepted for payment.

Molloy College, Registrar, PO Box 5002, Rockville Centre, NY 11571-5002, 516-678-5000 X229. Alumni records are maintained here also. Call 516-678-5000 X218. Degrees granted: Associate; Bachelors; Masters.

Attendance and degree information available by phone, mail. Search requires name plus social security number, exact years of attendance. Other helpful information: date of birth, approximate years of attendance. No fee for information.

Transcripts available by mail. Search requires name plus social security number, signed release. Other helpful information: date of birth, approximate years of attendance. Fee is $5.00.

Monmouth College, Registrar, 700 E Broadway, Monmouth, IL 61462, 309-457-2326 (FAX: 309-457-2141). Hours: 8AM-Noon, 1-4:30PM. Records go back to 1920s. Alumni records are maintained here also. Call 309-457-2336. Degrees granted: Bachelors. Adverse incident record source: Dean of Students.

Attendance and degree information available by phone, FAX, mail. Search requires name only. Other helpful information: social security number, date of birth, approximate years of attendance. No fee for information.

Transcripts available by mail. Search requires name plus signed release. Other helpful information: social security number, date of birth, approximate years of attendance. Fee is $3.00.

Monmouth University, Registrar, Norwood and Cedar Aves, West Long Branch, NJ 07764-1898, 908-571-3477 (FAX: 908-571-7510). Hours: 9AM-5PM. Records go back to 1933. Degrees granted: Associate; Bachelors; Masters.

Attendance and degree information available by FAX, mail. Search requires name plus social security number. Other helpful information: date of birth, approximate years of attendance. No fee for information.

Transcripts available by mail. Search requires name plus social security number, signed release. Other helpful information: date of birth, approximate years of attendance. Fee is $5.00.

Monroe College, Registrar, 29 E Fordham Rd, Bronx, NY 10468, 718-933-6700 X230 (FAX: 718-220-3032). Hours: 8:30AM-7:30PM M-Th; 8:30AM-2PM F. Records go back to 1960. Alumni records are maintained here also. Call 718-933-6700 X310. Degrees granted: Associate.

Attendance and degree information available by phone, FAX, mail. Search requires name plus social security number, approximate years of attendance, signed release. No fee for information.

Transcripts available by mail. Search requires name plus social security number, approximate years of attendance, signed release. Fee is $3.00.

Monroe College, **(New Rochelle Campus)**, Registrar, 434 Main St, New Rochelle, NY 10801, 914-632-5400 (FAX: 914-632-5462). Hours: 8:30AM-7:30PM. Records go back to 1983. Degrees granted: Associate.

Attendance information available by written request only. Search requires name plus social security number, approximate years of attendance, signed release. Other helpful information: date of birth. No fee for information.

Degree information available by written request only. Search requires name plus social security number, approximate years of attendance, signed release. No fee for information.

Transcripts available by written request only. Search requires name plus social security number, approximate years of attendance, signed release. Fee is $3.00.

Major credit cards accepted for payment.

Monroe Community College, Registrar, 1000 E Henrietta Rd, Rochester, NY 14623, 716-292-2300 (FAX: 716-292-3850). Hours: 8AM-4:30PM. Records go back to 1961. Alumni records are maintained here also. Call 716-292-2000.

Attendance and degree information available by phone, FAX, mail. Search requires name plus social security number. Other helpful information: date of birth, approximate years of attendance. No fee for information.

Transcripts available by mail. Search requires name plus social security number, signed release. Other helpful information: date of birth, approximate years of attendance. Fee is $3.00.

Major credit cards accepted for payment.

Monroe County Community College, Registrar, 1555 S Raisinville Rd, Monroe, MI 48161, 313-242-7300 (FAX: 313-242-9711). Hours: 8AM-4:30PM. Records go back to founding date. Alumni records are maintained here also. Call 313-242-7300 X375. Degrees granted: Associate.

Attendance and degree information available by phone, FAX, mail. Search requires name plus social security number. Other helpful information: date of birth, approximate years of attendance. No fee for information.

Transcripts available by mail. Search requires name plus social security number, date of birth, signed release. Other helpful information: approximate years of attendance. Fee is $2.00.

Major credit cards accepted for payment.

Montana College of Technology of the University of Montana, Registrar, 115 N Roberts St, Helena, MT 59620, 406-444-6800. Hours: 8:30AM-5PM. Records go back to 1939.

Attendance and degree information available by phone, mail. Search requires name only. Other helpful information: date of birth, approximate years of attendance. No fee for information.

School does not provide transcripts. Search requires name only. No fee for transcripts.

Montana State University College of Technology-Great Falls, Registrar, 2100 16th Ave S, Great Falls, MT 59405, 406-771-1240 (FAX: 406-453-6769). Hours: 8AM-5PM. Records go back to 1969. Degrees granted: Associate.

Attendance and degree information available by phone, mail. Search requires name plus social security number, date of birth, exact years of attendance. No fee for information.

Transcripts available by mail. Search requires name plus social security number, date of birth, exact years of attendance, signed release. No fee for transcripts.

Montana State University-Billings, Registrar, 1500 N 30th, Billings, MT 59101, 406-657-2303 (FAX: 406-657-2302). Hours: 8AM-5PM. Records go back to 1927. Alumni records are maintained here also. Call 406-657-2244. Degrees granted: Associate; Bachelors; Masters. Special programs- Vocational, 406-656-4445 X120.

Attendance and degree information available by phone, FAX, mail. Search requires name plus social security number, date of birth. Other helpful information: approximate years of attendance. No fee for information.

Transcripts available by written request only. Search requires name plus social security number, date of birth, signed release. Other helpful information: approximate years of attendance. Fee is $3.00.

Major credit cards accepted for payment.

Montana State University-Bozeman, Registrar, Bozeman, MT 59717, 406-994-0211. Alumni Records Office: Alumni & Development, MSU Bozeman, 1501 S 11th, Bozeman, MT 59717. Degrees granted: Bachelors; Masters; Doctorate.

Attendance and degree information available by phone, mail. Search requires name plus social security number. Other helpful information: date of birth, approximate years of attendance. No fee for information.

Transcripts available by written request only. Search requires name plus social security number, signed release. Other helpful information: date of birth, approximate years of attendance. No fee for transcripts.

Montana Tech of the University of Montana, Registrar, 1300 W Park St, Butte, MT 59701-8997, 406-496-4256 (FAX: 406-496-4710). Hours: 8AM-4:30PM. Records go back to 1900. Alumni records are maintained here also. Call 406-496-4278. Degrees granted: Associate; Bachelors; Masters.

Attendance information available by phone, FAX, mail. Search requires name plus approximate years of attendance. Other helpful information: social security number, exact years of attendance. No fee for information.

Degree information available by phone, FAX, mail. Search requires name plus social security number, date of birth, approximate years of attendance. Other helpful information: exact years of attendance. No fee for information.

Transcripts available by FAX, mail. Search requires name plus social security number, date of birth, exact years of attendance, signed release. Fee is $3.00.

Major credit cards accepted for payment.

Montana Tech of the University of Montana-Division of Technology, Registrar, Basin Creek Rd, Butte, MT 59701, 406-494-2910 (FAX: 406-494-2977). Hours: 7:30AM-5PM. Records go back to 1969. Degrees granted: Associate.

Attendance and degree information available by phone, FAX, mail. Search requires name only. Other helpful information: social security number, date of birth, approximate years of attendance. No fee for information.

Transcripts available by FAX, mail. Search requires name plus signed release. Other helpful information: social security number, date of birth, approximate years of attendance. Fee is $2.00. Expedited service available for $2.00.

Major credit cards accepted for payment.

Montay College, Registrar, 3750 W Peterson Ave, Chicago, IL 60659, 312-539-1919 (FAX: 312-539-1913). Hours: 8AM-4PM. Records go back 30 years. Degrees granted: Associate.

Attendance and degree information available by FAX, mail. Search requires name plus approximate years of attendance, signed release. Other helpful information: social security number, date of birth, exact years of attendance. No fee for information.

Transcripts available by mail. Search requires name plus signed release. Other helpful information: social security number, date of birth, exact years of attendance. Fee is $3.00. Expedited service available for $10.00.

Montcalm Community College, Registrar, 2800 College Dr SW, Sidney, MI 48885, 517-328-1230 (FAX: 517-328-2950). Hours: 8AM-4:30PM. Records go back to founding date. Degrees granted: Associate.

Attendance and degree information available by phone, FAX, mail. Search requires name only. Other helpful information: social security number, date of birth, approximate years of attendance. No fee for information.

Transcripts available by written request only. Search requires name plus signed release. Other helpful information: social security number, date of birth, approximate years of attendance. Fee is $1.00.

Montclair State College, Registrar, Valley Rd and Normal Ave, Upper Montclair, NJ 07043-1624, 201-655-4376. Hours: 8:30AM-4:30PM. Records go back to 1950. Alumni records are maintained here also. Call 201-655-4141. Degrees granted: Bachelors; Masters. Adverse incident record source: Dean of Students, 201-655-4118.

Attendance and degree information available by phone, mail. Search requires name plus social security number, date of birth, approximate years of attendance, signed release. No fee for information.
Transcripts available by mail. Search requires name plus social security number, date of birth, approximate years of attendance, signed release. Fee is $3.00.

Monterey Institute of International Studies, Registrar, 425 Van Buren, Monterey, CA 93940, 408-647-4121 (FAX: 408-647-4199). Hours: 8:30AM-5PM. Records go back to 1959. Alumni records are maintained here also. Call 408-647-4130. Degrees granted: Bachelors; Masters.
Attendance and degree information available by phone, FAX, mail. Search requires name only. Other helpful information: date of birth, approximate years of attendance. No fee for information.
Transcripts available by written request only. Search requires name plus signed release. Other helpful information: date of birth, approximate years of attendance. Fee is $3.00. Expedited service available for $10.00.
Major credit cards accepted for payment.

Monterey Peninsula College, Admissions & Records, 980 Fremont St, Monterey, CA 93940, 408-646-4002 (FAX: 408-655-2627). Hours: 8AM-6:30PM M-Th; 8AM-2:30PM F. Records go back to 1947. Degrees granted: Associate. Adverse incident record source: Campus Security, 408-646-4099.
Attendance and degree information available by phone, FAX, mail. Search requires name only. Other helpful information: social security number, date of birth, approximate years of attendance. Fee is $2.00. Expedited service available for $2.00.
Transcripts available by FAX, mail. Search requires name plus signed release. Other helpful information: social security number, date of birth, approximate years of attendance. Fee is $4.00. Expedited service available for $10.00.

Montgomery College-Germantown Campus, Registrar, Attn: Cashier, 20200 Observation Dr, Germantown, MD 20876, 301-353-7821 (FAX: 301-353-7815). Hours: 8:30AM-6:30PM M-Th; 8:30AM-5PM F. Records go back 49 years. Degrees granted: Associate.
Attendance information available by mail. Search requires name plus signed release. Other helpful information: social security number, date of birth, approximate years of attendance. Fee is $5.00.
Degree information available by mail. Search requires name plus exact years of attendance, signed release. Other helpful information: social security number, date of birth, approximate years of attendance. No fee for information.
Transcripts available by mail. Search requires name plus social security number, signed release. Other helpful information: date of birth, approximate years of attendance. Fee is $5.00.

Montgomery College-Rockville Campus, Registrar, 51 Mannakee St, Rockville, MD 20850, 301-279-5046 (FAX: 301-279-5037). Records are not housed here. They are located at Montgomery College-Germantown Campus, Registrar, Attn: Cashier, 20200 Observation Dr, Germantown, MD 20876.

Montgomery College-Takoma Park Campus, Registrar, Takoma Ave and Fenton St, Takoma Park, MD 20912, 301-650-1500 (FAX: 301-650-1497). Hours: 8:30AM-6:30PM M-Th; 8:30AM-4:30PM F. Records go back to 1945. Degrees granted: Associate. Adverse incident record source: Student Services, 301-650-1469.
Attendance and degree information available by mail. Search requires name only. Other helpful information: social security number, date of birth, approximate years of attendance. Fee is $10.00.
Transcripts available by written request only. Search requires name plus signed release. Other helpful information: social security number, date of birth, approximate years of attendance. Fee is $10.00.
Major credit cards accepted for payment.

Montgomery Community College, Registrar, PO Box 787, Troy, NC 27371, 910-576-6222 X239. Hours: 8AM-5PM M-Th; 8AM-3PM F. Records go back to 1967. Degrees granted: Associate.
Attendance and degree information available by written request only. Search requires name plus social security number, approximate years of attendance, signed release. Other helpful information: date of birth, exact years of attendance. No fee for information.
Transcripts available by written request only. Search requires name plus social security number, approximate years of attendance, signed release. Other helpful information: date of birth, exact years of attendance. First three transcripts are free. Additional ones are $1.00 each.

Montgomery County Community College, Office of Admissions, PO Box 400, Blue Bell, PA 19422-0796, 215-641-6551 (FAX: 215-641-6681). Hours: 8:30AM-7PM M-Th; 8:30AM-5PM F. Records go back 30 years. Alumni records are maintained here also. Call 215-641-6359. Degrees granted: Associate.
Attendance and degree information available by FAX, mail. Search requires name plus signed release. Other helpful information: social security number, date of birth, approximate years of attendance. No fee for information.
Transcripts available by mail. Search requires name plus signed release. Other helpful information: social security number, date of birth, approximate years of attendance. Fee is $3.00. Expedited service available for $3.00.

Montreat-Anderson College, Registrar, PO Box 1267, Montreat, NC 28757, 704-669-8011 X3731 (FAX: 704-669-9554). Hours: 8AM-4:30PM. Records go back to 1916. Alumni records are maintained here also. Call 704-669-8011 X3703. Degrees granted: Associate. Adverse incident record source: Student Development, 704-669-8011 X3632.
Attendance and degree information available by phone, FAX, mail. Search requires name only. Other helpful information: social security number, date of birth, approximate years of attendance. No fee for information.
Transcripts available by FAX, mail. Search requires name plus signed release. Other helpful information: social security number, date of birth, approximate years of attendance. Fee is $2.00. Expedited service available for $5.00.

Montserrat College of Art, Registrar, 23 Exxex St, Beverly, MA 01915, 508-922-8222 (FAX: 508-922-4268). Hours: 9AM-4PM. Records go back 25 years. Alumni records are maintained here also. Call 508-922-8222. Degrees granted: Bachelors.
Attendance and degree information available by FAX, mail. Search requires name plus social security number, exact years of

attendance, signed release. Other helpful information: approximate years of attendance. No fee for information.

Transcripts available by FAX, mail. Search requires name plus social security number, approximate years of attendance, signed release. Fee is $4.00.

Major credit cards accepted for payment.

Moody Bible Institute, Registrar, 820 N La Salle Dr, Chicago, IL 60610, 312-329-4261 (FAX: 312-329-4328). Hours: 8AM-5PM. Records go back to 1885. Alumni records are maintained here also. Call 312-329-4412. Degrees granted: Masters.

Attendance and degree information available by phone, FAX, mail. Search requires name plus social security number, exact years of attendance. No fee for information.

Transcripts available by FAX, mail. Search requires name plus social security number, exact years of attendance, signed release. Fee is $2.00.

Moore College of Art and Design, Registrar, The Parkway at 20th St, Philadelphia, PA 19103, 215-568-4515 (FAX: 215-568-8017). Hours: 9AM-5PM. Records go back to 1844. Alumni records are maintained here at the same phone number. Degrees granted: Bachelors.

Attendance and degree information available by phone, FAX, mail. Search requires name plus social security number, exact years of attendance, signed release. No fee for information.

Transcripts available by FAX, mail. Search requires name plus social security number, exact years of attendance, signed release. Fee is $5.00.

Major credit cards accepted for payment.

Moorhead State University, Registrar, 1104 7th Ave S, Moorhead, MN 56563, 218-236-2565 (FAX: 218-236-2168). Hours: 8AM-4:30PM. Records go back 107 years. Alumni records are maintained here also. Call 218-236-3265. Degrees granted: Associate; Bachelors; Masters. Adverse incident record source: Student Services, 218-236-2171.

Attendance information available by phone, FAX, mail. Search requires name plus social security number, date of birth. Other helpful information: approximate years of attendance. No fee for information.

Degree information available by phone, FAX, mail. Search requires name plus social security number. Other helpful information: date of birth, approximate years of attendance. No fee for information.

Transcripts available by FAX, mail. Search requires name plus social security number, signed release. Other helpful information: date of birth, approximate years of attendance. No fee for transcripts. Expedited service available for $5.00.

Moorpark College, Registrar, 7075 Campus Rd, Moorpark, CA 93021, 805-378-1429 (FAX: 805-378-1583). Hours: 7:30AM-7PM M-Th; 7:30AM-5PM F. Records go back to 1967. Degrees granted: Associate.

Attendance and degree information available by FAX, mail. Search requires name plus social security number, date of birth, signed release. Other helpful information: approximate years of attendance. Fee is $3.00. Expedited service available for $5.00.

Transcripts available by FAX, mail. Search requires name plus social security number, date of birth, signed release. Other helpful information: approximate years of attendance. Fee is $3.00. Expedited service available for $5.00.

Moraine Park Technical College, Registrar, PO Box 1940, 235 N National Ave, Fond Du Lac, WI 54936-1940, 414-924-3308 (FAX: 414-924-3421). Degrees granted: Associate.

Attendance and degree information available by phone, mail. Search requires name plus social security number, date of birth. Other helpful information: approximate years of attendance. No fee for information.

Transcripts available by mail. Search requires name plus social security number, date of birth, signed release. Other helpful information: approximate years of attendance. Fee is $3.00.

Major credit cards accepted for payment.

Moraine Valley Community College, Registrar, 10900 S 88th Ave, Palos Hills, IL 60465, 708-974-5346 (FAX: 708-974-0974). Hours: 8:30AM-7:30PM M,T; 8:30AM-5PM W-F. Records go back 27 years. Degrees granted: Associate. Adverse incident record source: Public Safety, 708-974-5500.

Attendance information available by phone, mail. Search requires name plus social security number, date of birth, signed release. Other helpful information: approximate years of attendance. No fee for information.

Degree information available by phone, mail. Search requires name plus social security number, date of birth, signed release. Other helpful information: approximate years of attendance. No fee for information.

Transcripts available by mail. Search requires name plus social security number, date of birth, signed release. Other helpful information: approximate years of attendance. Fee is $3.00. Expedited service available for $6.00.

Major credit cards accepted for payment.

Moravian College, Registrar, 1200 Main St, Bethlehem, PA 18018, 610-861-1350. Hours: 8AM-4:30PM. Records go back to 1742. Alumni records are maintained here also. Call 610-861-1366. Degrees granted: Bachelors; Masters. Adverse incident record source: Campus Security, 610-861-1421: Dean, 610-861-1503

Attendance information available by phone, mail. Search requires name plus social security number. No fee for information.

Degree information available by phone, mail. Search requires name plus social security number, exact years of attendance. No fee for information.

Transcripts available by mail. Search requires name plus social security number, exact years of attendance, signed release. Fee is $3.00.

Morehead State University, Registrar, University Blvd, Morehead, KY 40351, 606-783-2221 (FAX: 606-783-5038). Hours: 8AM-4:30PM. Records go back to 1923. Alumni records are maintained here also. Call 606-783-2221 X2080. Degrees granted: Bachelors; Masters.

Attendance and degree information available by mail. Search requires name plus social security number, date of birth, exact years of attendance. No fee for information.

Transcripts available by mail. Search requires name plus social security number, date of birth, exact years of attendance, signed release. Fee is $2.00.

Morehouse College, Registrar, 830 Westview Dr SW, Atlanta, GA 30314, 404-215-2641 (FAX: 404-215-2711). Hours: 9AM-5PM. Records go back to 1870. Alumni records are maintained here also. Call 404-215-2707. Degrees granted: Bachelors.

Attendance and degree information available by phone, FAX, mail. Search requires name only. Other helpful information: social

security number, approximate years of attendance. No fee for information.
 Transcripts available by phone, FAX, mail. Search requires name plus signed notarized release. Other helpful information: social security number, approximate years of attendance. Fee is $3.00. Expedite fee is based on cost of service.'

Morehouse School of Medicine, Office of Admissions, 720 Westview Dr SW, Atlanta, GA 30310-1495, 404-752-1652 (FAX: 404-752-1512). Hours: 9AM-5PM. Records go back to 1978. Degrees granted: Doctorate.
 Attendance information available by phone, FAX, mail. Search requires name plus social security number, date of birth, approximate years of attendance, signed release. Fee is $2.00.
 Degree information available by phone, FAX, mail. Search requires name plus social security number, date of birth, exact years of attendance, signed release. Other helpful information: approximate years of attendance. Fee is $2.00.
 Transcripts available by mail. Search requires name plus social security number, date of birth, exact years of attendance, signed release. Other helpful information: approximate years of attendance. Fee is $2.00.

Morgan Community College, Registrar, 17800 Rd 20, Fort Morgan, CO 80701, 303-867-3081 (FAX: 303-867-6608). Hours: 8AM-5PM. Records go back to 1971. Degrees granted: Associate.
 Attendance and degree information available by phone, FAX, mail. Search requires name plus social security number. Other helpful information: date of birth, approximate years of attendance. No fee for information.
 Transcripts available by FAX, mail. Search requires name plus social security number, date of birth, signed release. Other helpful information: approximate years of attendance. No fee for transcripts.

Morgan State University, Registrar, Hillen Rd and Cold Spring Lane, Baltimore, MD 21239, 410-319-3300 (FAX: 410-319-3259). Hours: 8AM-5PM. Records go back 80 years. Degrees granted: Bachelors; Masters; Doctorate. Adverse incident record source: MSU Police, 410-319-3103.
 Attendance and degree information available by phone, FAX, mail. Search requires name plus social security number. Other helpful information: date of birth, approximate years of attendance. No fee for information.
 Transcripts available by mail. Search requires name plus social security number, signed release. Other helpful information: date of birth, approximate years of attendance. Fee is $2.00. Expedited service available for $5.00.

Morningside College, Registrar, 1501 Morningside Ave, Sioux City, IA 51106, 712-274-5110 (FAX: 712-274-5101). Hours: 8AM-5PM. Records go back to 1894. Alumni records are maintained here also. Call 712-274-5107. Degrees granted: Bachelors; Masters.
 Attendance and degree information available by phone, FAX, mail. Search requires name plus social security number, exact years of attendance. No fee for information.
 Transcripts available by mail. Search requires name plus social security number, exact years of attendance, signed release. Fee is $3.00.
 Major credit cards accepted for payment.

Morris Brown College, Registrar, 643 Martin Luther King, Jr. Dr NW, Atlanta, GA 30314, 404-220-0145 (FAX: 404-659-4315). Hours: 9AM-5PM. Degrees granted: Bachelors. Adverse incident record source: Student Affairs, 404-220-0300.
 Attendance and degree information available by phone, FAX. Search requires name plus social security number, exact years of attendance. Other helpful information: date of birth, approximate years of attendance. No fee for information.
 Transcripts available by written request only. Search requires name plus social security number, exact years of attendance, signed release. Other helpful information: date of birth, approximate years of attendance. Fee is $2.00.

Morris College, Registrar, 100 W College St, Sumter, SC 29150-3599, 803-775-9371 X225 (FAX: 803-773-3687). Alumni records are maintained here at the same phone number. Degrees granted: Bachelors.
 Attendance and degree information available by FAX, mail. Search requires name plus social security number, exact years of attendance. No fee for information.
 Transcripts available by mail. Search requires name plus social security number, exact years of attendance, signed release. Fee is $3.00.

Morrison College-Reno, Records Dept, 140 Washington St, Reno, NV 89503, 702-323-4145 (FAX: 702-323-8495). Hours: 8:30AM-7:30PM M-Th; 8AM-5PM F. Records go back to 1960. Alumni records are maintained here at the same phone number. Degrees granted: Associate; Bachelors. Adverse incident record source: Same as above.
 Attendance and degree information available by phone, FAX, mail. Search requires name plus approximate years of attendance, signed release. Other helpful information: social security number, exact years of attendance. No fee for information.
 Transcripts available by FAX, mail. Search requires name plus approximate years of attendance, signed release. Other helpful information: social security number, date of birth, exact years of attendance. Fee is $3.00.
 Major credit cards accepted for payment.

Morrison Institute of Technology, Registrar, 701 Portland Ave, Morrison, IL 61270-0410, 815-772-7218 (FAX: 815-772-7584). Hours: 8AM-4:30PM. Records go back to 1973. Alumni records are maintained here at the same phone number. Degrees granted: Associate.
 Attendance and degree information available by phone, mail. Search requires name plus social security number. No fee for information.
 Transcripts available by mail. Search requires name plus social security number, signed release. Fee is $2.00.

Morton College, Registrar, 3801 S Central Ave, Cicero, IL 60650, 708-656-8000 (FAX: 708-656-9592). Hours: 9AM-8PM M-Th, 9AM-4PM F. Records go back to 1925. Degrees granted: Associate.
 Attendance information available by FAX, mail. Search requires name plus social security number, date of birth, signed release. Other helpful information: approximate years of attendance. No fee for information.
 Degree information available by phone, FAX, mail. Search requires name plus social security number, date of birth. Other helpful information: approximate years of attendance. No fee for information.

Transcripts available by mail. Search requires name plus social security number, date of birth, signed release. Other helpful information: approximate years of attendance. Fee is $2.00.

Motlow State Community College, Admissions & Records, PO Box 88100, Tullahoma, TN 37388-8100, 615-393-1500 (FAX: 615-393-1681). Hours: 8AM-4:30PM. Records go back to 1969. Degrees granted: Associate.

Attendance information available by phone, FAX, mail. Search requires name plus social security number. Other helpful information: date of birth, approximate years of attendance. No fee for information.

Degree information available by phone, FAX, mail. Search requires name plus social security number, signed release. Other helpful information: date of birth, approximate years of attendance. No fee for information.

Transcripts available by FAX, mail. Search requires name plus social security number, signed release. Other helpful information: date of birth, approximate years of attendance. No fee for transcripts.

Mount Aloysius College, Registration & Records, 7373 Admiral Peary Hwy, Cresson, PA 16630, 814-886-6343. Hours: 8:30AM-4:30PM. Records go back to 1939. Alumni records are maintained here also. Call 814-886-6408. Degrees granted: Associate; Bachelors. Adverse incident record source: Dean, 814-886-6472.

Attendance and degree information available by phone, mail. Search requires name plus social security number. No fee for information.

Transcripts available by mail. Search requires name plus social security number, exact years of attendance, signed release. Fee is $2.00.

Mount Angel Seminary, Records & Registration, St. Benedict, OR 97373, 503-845-3951 (FAX: 503-845-3126). Hours: 8AM-5PM. Records go back to 1900s. Alumni records are maintained here at the same phone number. Degrees granted: Bachelors; Masters.

Attendance information available by phone, FAX, mail. Search requires name plus social security number. No fee for information.

Degree information available by mail. Search requires name plus social security number, exact years of attendance, signed release. No fee for information.

Transcripts available by mail. Search requires name plus social security number, exact years of attendance, signed release. Fee is $5.00.

Mount Holyoke College, Registrar, South Hadley, MA 01075, 413-538-2025. Hours: 8:30AM-5PM. Records go back to 1898. Alumni records are maintained here also. Call 413-538-2300. Degrees granted: Bachelors; Masters.

Attendance information available by phone, mail. Search requires name only. Other helpful information: social security number, date of birth, approximate years of attendance. No fee for information.

Degree information available by phone, mail. Search requires name only. Other helpful information: social security number, date of birth, approximate years of attendance. No fee for information.

Transcripts available by mail. Search requires name plus signed release. Other helpful information: social security number, date of birth, approximate years of attendance. No fee for transcripts.

Mount Hood Community College, Admissions Office, 26000 SE Stark St, Gresham, OR 97030, 503-667-6422 (FAX: 503-667-7388). Hours: 8:30AM-7:30PM M-Th, 8:30AM-4:30PM F. Records go back to 1965. Alumni records are maintained here at the same phone number. Degrees granted: Associate.

Attendance information available by phone, FAX, mail. Search requires name plus social security number. No fee for information.

Degree information available by phone, FAX, mail. Search requires name plus social security number, exact years of attendance. No fee for information.

Transcripts available by mail. Search requires name plus social security number, exact years of attendance, signed release. Fee is $3.00.

Mount Ida College, Registrar, 777 Dedham St, Newton Centre, MA 02159, 617-925-4500 (FAX: 617-928-4760). Hours: 8AM-4:30PM. Records go back to 1899. Degrees granted: Associate; Bachelors.

Attendance and degree information available by FAX, mail. Search requires name only. Other helpful information: social security number, date of birth, approximate years of attendance. No fee for information.

Transcripts available by FAX, mail. Search requires name plus signed release. Other helpful information: social security number, date of birth, approximate years of attendance. Fee is $2.00.

Grahm Junior College-Bryant & Stratton records require a one time $20.00 fee.

Mount Marty College, Registrar, 1105 W Eighth St, Yankton, SD 57078, 605-668-1515 (FAX: 605-668-1357). Hours: 8AM-5PM. Records go back to 1936. Alumni records are maintained here also. Call 605-668-1526. Degrees granted: Associate; Bachelors; Masters. Certification: Secretarial.

Attendance and degree information available by phone, FAX, mail. Search requires name plus social security number, date of birth. Other helpful information: approximate years of attendance. No fee for information.

Transcripts available by FAX, mail. Search requires name plus social security number, date of birth, signed release. Other helpful information: approximate years of attendance. Fee is $2.00.

Mount Mary College, Registrar, 2900 N Menomonee River Pkwy, Milwaukee, WI 53222, 414-258-4810 X281 (FAX: 414-256-1224). Hours: 8AM-4:30PM. Records go back to 1915. Alumni records are maintained here also. Call 414-258-4810. Degrees granted: Bachelors; Masters.

Attendance and degree information available by phone, FAX, mail. Search requires name plus social security number. Other helpful information: date of birth, approximate years of attendance. No fee for information.

Transcripts available by written request only. Search requires name plus social security number, signed release. Other helpful information: date of birth, approximate years of attendance. Fee is $4.00. Expedited service available for $8.00.

Mount Mercy College, Registrar, 1330 Elmhurst Dr NE, Cedar Rapids, IA 52402, 319-363-8213 (FAX: 319-363-5270). Hours: 8:30AM-5PM. Records go back to 1928. Alumni records are maintained here also. Call 319-363-8213. Degrees granted: Bachelors.

Attendance and degree information available by phone, mail. Search requires name plus social security number, date of birth. No fee for information.

Transcripts available by mail. Search requires name plus social security number, date of birth, signed release. Fee is $5.00.

Mount Olive College, Registrar, 634 Henderson St, Mount Olive, NC 28365, 919-658-7165 X3019 (FAX: 919-658-8934). Hours: 8AM-5PM. Records go back to 1951. Alumni records are maintained here also. Call 919-658-2502. Degrees granted: Associate. Adverse incident record source: Dean, 919-658-7167.

Attendance information available by phone, mail. Search requires name plus social security number. No fee for information.

Degree information available by phone, mail. Search requires name plus social security number. Other helpful information: approximate years of attendance. No fee for information.

Transcripts available by FAX, mail. Search requires name plus social security number, exact years of attendance, signed release. Transcript fee is $5.00 for alumni; $2.00 if currently enrolled.

Mount San Jacinto College, Registrar, 1499 N State St, San Jacinto, CA 92583, 909-654-8011 X1410 (FAX: 909-654-6738). Hours: 8AM-8PM M-Th, 8AM-4:30PM F. Records go back to 1963. Degrees granted: Associate.

Attendance information available by mail. Search requires name plus social security number, exact years of attendance, signed release. Other helpful information: date of birth, approximate years of attendance. No fee for information.

Degree information available by mail. Search requires name plus social security number, exact years of attendance, signed release. No fee for information.

Transcripts available by mail. Search requires name plus social security number, exact years of attendance, signed release. Fee is $3.00.

Include a self addressed stamped envelope with mail request. Major credit cards accepted for payment.

Mount Senario College, Registrar, 1500 W College Ave, Ladysmith, WI 54848, 715-532-5511 X120 (FAX: 715-532-7690). Hours: 8AM-4:30PM. Records go back to 1964. Alumni records are maintained here also. Call 715-532-5511 X107. Degrees granted: Associate; Bachelors. Special programs- Outreach Department, 715-532-5511 X189.

Attendance and degree information available by phone, FAX, mail. Search requires name plus social security number. Other helpful information: approximate years of attendance. No fee for information.

Transcripts available by FAX, mail. Search requires name plus social security number, signed release. Other helpful information: approximate years of attendance. Fee is $5.00. Expedited service available for $10.00.
FAX: $15.00.

Mount Sinai School of Medicine, Registrar, One Gustave L Levy Pl, New York, NY 10029, 212-241-6691 (FAX: 212-369-6013). Records go back to 1972. Alumni records are maintained here at the same phone number. Degrees granted: Bachelors; Masters; First Professional Degree.

Attendance and degree information available by phone, mail. Search requires name plus social security number, date of birth, exact years of attendance. No fee for information.

Transcripts available by mail. Search requires name plus social security number, date of birth, exact years of attendance, signed release. Fee is $2.00.

Major credit cards accepted for payment.

Mount St. Clare College, Registrar, 400 N Bluff Blvd, Clinton, IA 52732, 319-242-4023 (FAX: 319-242-2003). Hours: 7:30AM-4:30PM. Degrees granted: Associate; Bachelors. Adverse incident record source: Student Life, 319-242-4023.

Attendance and degree information available by phone, FAX, mail. Search requires name only. Other helpful information: social security number, date of birth, approximate years of attendance. No fee for information.

Transcripts available by FAX, mail. Search requires name plus signed release. Other helpful information: social security number, date of birth, approximate years of attendance. Fee is $2.00.

Mount St. Mary College, Registrar, 330 Powell Ave, Newburgh, NY 12550, 914-569-3258 (FAX: 914-562-6762). Hours: 8AM-5PM. Records go back to 1935. Alumni records are maintained here also. Call 914-569-3217. Degrees granted: Bachelors; Masters. Adverse incident record source: Dean of Students, 914-569-3114.

Attendance and degree information available by phone, FAX, mail. Search requires name only. Other helpful information: social security number, date of birth, approximate years of attendance. No fee for information.

Transcripts available by FAX, mail. Search requires name plus signed release. Other helpful information: social security number, date of birth, approximate years of attendance. Fee is $3.00. Expedite: $3.00 plus cost of service.

Mount St. Mary's College, Registrar, 12001 Chalon Rd, Los Angeles, CA 90049, 310-471-9560 (FAX: 310-471-9566). Hours: 8:30AM-4:30PM. Records go back to 1925. Degrees granted: Associate; Bachelors; Masters.

Attendance and degree information available by phone, FAX, mail. Search requires name plus exact years of attendance. Other helpful information: social security number, date of birth, approximate years of attendance. Fee is $5.00.

Transcripts available by FAX, mail. Search requires name plus exact years of attendance. Other helpful information: social security number, date of birth, approximate years of attendance. Fee is $5.00.

Mount St. Mary's College and Seminary, Registrar, Emmitsburg, MD 21727, 301-447-5215 (FAX: 301-447-5755). Hours: 9AM-Noon, 1-5PM. Records go back to 1808. Alumni records are maintained here also. Call 301-447-5362. Degrees granted: Bachelors; Masters.

Attendance and degree information available by phone, FAX, mail. Search requires name only. Other helpful information: social security number, date of birth, approximate years of attendance. No fee for information.

Transcripts available by mail. Search requires name plus signed release. Other helpful information: social security number, date of birth, approximate years of attendance. Fee is $3.00. Expedited service available for $3.00.

Major credit cards accepted for payment.

Mount St. Mary's College, (Doheny), Registrar, 10 Chester Pl, Los Angeles, CA 90007, 213-746-045- X2200. Hours: 8:30AM-4PM. Records go back to founding date. Alumni Records Office: 12001 Chalon, Los Angeles, CA 90049. Degrees granted: Associate; Bachelors; Masters.

Attendance and degree information available by mail. Search requires name plus social security number, date of birth, signed release. Other helpful information: approximate years of attendance. No fee for information.

Transcripts available by mail. Search requires name plus social security number, date of birth, signed release. Other helpful information: approximate years of attendance. Fee is $5.00. Expedited service available for $5.00.

Mount Union College, Registrar, 1972 Clark Ave, Alliance, OH 44601, 216-823-6018 (FAX: 216-823-3457). Hours: 8AM-5PM. Records go back to 1800s. Degrees granted: Bachelors.
Attendance and degree information available by phone, FAX, mail. Search requires name only. Other helpful information: social security number, date of birth, approximate years of attendance. No fee for information.
Transcripts available by FAX, mail. Search requires name plus signed release. Other helpful information: social security number, date of birth, approximate years of attendance. Fee is $3.00.
Transcript info/request applies to student only.

Mount Vernon College, Registrar, 2100 Foxhall Rd NW, Washington, DC 20007, 202-625-4527 (FAX: 202-338-1089). Hours: 9AM-5PM. Alumni records are maintained here also. Call 202-625-4685. Degrees granted: Associate; Bachelors; Masters.
Attendance information available by phone, FAX, mail. Search requires name plus social security number, approximate years of attendance. Other helpful information: date of birth. No fee for information.
Degree information available by phone, FAX, mail. Search requires name plus social security number, approximate years of attendance. Other helpful information: date of birth, exact years of attendance. No fee for information.
Transcripts available by FAX, mail. Search requires name plus social security number, approximate years of attendance, signed release. Other helpful information: date of birth. Up to 7 transcripts free per semester.

Mount Vernon Nazarene College, Registrar, 800 Martinsburg Rd, Mount Vernon, OH 43050, 614-397-6862. Hours: 8AM-4:30PM. Records go back to 1968. Degrees granted: Associate; Bachelors; Masters.
Attendance information available by written request only. Search requires name plus signed release. No fee for information.
Degree information available by FAX. Search requires name plus signed release. No fee for information.
Transcripts available by written request only. Search requires name plus signed release. Fee is $3.00. Expedited service available for $5.00.

Mount Wachusett Community College, Registrar, 444 Green St, Gardner, MA 01440, 508-632-6600 (FAX: 508-632-6155). Hours: 8AM-5PM. Records go back to 1980. Degrees granted: Associate.
School will not confirm attendance information. Search requires name only. No fee for information.
Degree information available by written request only. Search requires name plus social security number, exact years of attendance, signed release. Other helpful information: approximate years of attendance. No fee for information.
Transcripts available by written request only. Search requires name plus social security number, exact years of attendance, signed release. Other helpful information: approximate years of attendance. Fee is $3.00.
Include a stamped self addressed envelope.

Mountain Empire Community College, Registrar, PO Drawer 700, Big Stone Gap, VA 24219, 703-523-2400 X209 (FAX: 703-523-2400 X323). Hours: 8AM-4:30PM. Records go back to 1972. Alumni records are maintained here at the same phone number. Degrees granted: Associate.
Attendance and degree information available by phone, FAX, mail. Search requires name plus social security number. No fee for information.
Transcripts available by FAX, mail. Search requires name plus social security number, signed release. No fee for transcripts.

Mountain State College, Registrar, Spring at 16th St, Parkersburg, WV 26101, 304-485-5487. Hours: 8AM-5PM. Records go back to 1888. Degrees granted: Associate.
Attendance and degree information available by phone, mail. Search requires name plus social security number, date of birth, exact years of attendance. No fee for information.
Transcripts available by mail. Search requires name plus social security number, date of birth, exact years of attendance, signed release. Fee is $5.00.
Major credit cards accepted for payment.

Mountain View College, Registrar, 4849 W Illinois Ave, Dallas, TX 75211-6599, 214-333-8600 (FAX: 214-333-8570). Hours: 8AM-8PM M-Th; 8AM-5PM F. Records go back to 1965. Degrees granted: Associate.
Attendance information available by FAX, mail. Search requires name only. Other helpful information: social security number. No fee for information.
Degree information available by FAX, mail. Search requires name plus social security number. No fee for information.
Transcripts available by FAX, mail. Search requires name plus social security number, signed release. No fee for transcripts.

Mt. San Antonio College, Director, Admissions & Records, 1100 N Grand Ave, Walnut, CA 91789, 909-594-5611 X4419 (FAX: 909-468-3932). Hours: 8AM-8PM M-Th, 8AM-4:30PM F. Records go back 49 years. Degrees granted: Associate.
Attendance and degree information available by phone, FAX, mail. Search requires name plus social security number, date of birth, signed release. Other helpful information: approximate years of attendance. Fee is $2.00.
Transcripts available by mail. Search requires name plus social security number, date of birth, signed release. Other helpful information: approximate years of attendance. Fee is $2.00.

Muhlenberg College, Registrar, 2400 Chew St, Allentown, PA 18104, 610-821-3190 (FAX: 610-821-3234). Hours: 8AM-5PM. Records go back to 1900s. Alumni records are maintained here also. Call 610-821-3305. Degrees granted: Bachelors. Adverse incident record source: Dean, 610-821-3182.
Attendance and degree information available by phone, FAX, mail. Search requires name plus social security number, exact years of attendance. No fee for information.
Transcripts available by FAX, mail. Search requires name plus social security number, exact years of attendance, signed release. Transcript fee 2.00, walkins 8.00. FAX fee 10.00 but unofficial transcript.

Multnomah Bible College, Registrar, 8435 NE Glisan St, Portland, OR 97220, 503-255-0332 X372 (FAX: 503-254-1268). Hours: 8AM-5PM. Records go back to 1936. Alumni records are maintained here at the same phone number. Degrees granted: Bachelors; Masters.

Attendance information available by phone, FAX, mail. Search requires name plus social security number. No fee for information.

Degree information available by phone, FAX, mail. Search requires name plus social security number, exact years of attendance. No fee for information.

Transcripts available by FAX, mail. Search requires name plus social security number, exact years of attendance, signed release. Fee is $3.00.

Murray State College, Registrar, 1100 S Murray, Tishomingo, OK 73460, 405-371-2371 X108 (FAX: 405-371-9844). Hours: 8AM-4:30PM. Alumni records are maintained here at the same phone number. Degrees granted: Associate.

Attendance and degree information available by phone, mail. Search requires name plus social security number, date of birth, exact years of attendance. No fee for information.

Transcripts available by mail. Search requires name plus social security number, date of birth, exact years of attendance, signed release. Fee is $2.00.

Murray State University, Registrar, PO Box 9, Murray, KY 42071-0009, 502-762-3753 (FAX: 502-762-3050). Hours: 8:30AM-4:30PM. Records go back to 1923. Alumni records are maintained here also. Call 502-762-3011. Degrees granted: Associate; Bachelors; Masters. Adverse incident record source: Security, 502-762-2222.

Attendance and degree information available by phone, FAX, mail. Search requires name plus social security number, approximate years of attendance, signed release. No fee for information.

Transcripts available by mail. Search requires name plus social security number, approximate years of attendance, signed release. Fee is $2.00.

Muscatine Community College, Registrar, 152 Colorado St, Muscatine, IA 52761, 319-263-8250 (FAX: 319-264-8341). Hours: 8AM-5PM. Records go back to 1929. Alumni records are maintained here at the same phone number. Degrees granted: Associate.

Attendance and degree information available by FAX, mail. Search requires name plus social security number, signed release. Other helpful information: date of birth, approximate years of attendance. No fee for information.

Transcripts available by FAX, mail. Search requires name plus social security number, signed release. Other helpful information: date of birth, approximate years of attendance. No fee for transcripts.

Muskegon Community College, Registrar, 221 S Quarterline Rd, Muskegon, MI 49442, 616-777-0364 (FAX: 616-777-0334). Hours: 8AM-4:30PM. Records go back 60 years. Degrees granted: Associate.

Attendance information available by phone, FAX, mail. Search requires name only. Other helpful information: social security number, date of birth, approximate years of attendance. No fee for information. Expedited service available for $5.00.

Degree information available by mail. Search requires name plus signed release. Other helpful information: social security number, date of birth, approximate years of attendance. No fee for information. Expedite service available for $5.00.

Transcripts available by written request only. Search requires name plus signed release. Other helpful information: social security number, date of birth, approximate years of attendance. Fee is $2.00. Expedited service available for $5.00.

Major credit cards accepted for payment.

Muskingum Area Technical College, Registrar, 1555 Newark Rd, Zanesville, OH 43701, 614-454-2501 (FAX: 614-454-0035). Hours: 8AM-5PM. Records go back 25 years. Degrees granted: Associate.

Attendance information available by FAX, mail. Search requires name plus signed release. Other helpful information: social security number, date of birth, approximate years of attendance. No fee for information.

Degree information available by phone, FAX, mail. Search requires name only. Other helpful information: social security number, date of birth, approximate years of attendance. No fee for information.

Transcripts available by FAX, mail. Search requires name plus signed release. Other helpful information: social security number, date of birth, approximate years of attendance. Fee is $2.00.

Major credit cards accepted for payment.

Muskingum College, Registrar, New Concord, OH 43762, 614-826-8164. Hours: 8AM-Noon, 1-5PM. Records go back to 1904. Alumni records are maintained here at the same phone number. Degrees granted: Bachelors; Masters.

Attendance and degree information available by phone, mail. Search requires name plus approximate years of attendance. Other helpful information: social security number, date of birth, exact years of attendance. No fee for information.

Transcripts available by mail. Search requires name plus approximate years of attendance, signed release. Other helpful information: social security number, date of birth, exact years of attendance. Fee is $3.00.

N

NAES College, Registrar, 2838 W Peterson Ave, Chicago, IL 60659, 312-761-5000 (FAX: 312-761-3808). Hours: 9AM-5PM. Records go back to 1977. Alumni records are maintained here also. Call 312-761-5000. Degrees granted: Bachelors.

Attendance and degree information available by phone, FAX, mail. Search requires name plus social security number. No fee for information.

Transcripts available by FAX, mail. Search requires name plus social security number, exact years of attendance, signed release. First transcript fee. Additional ones are $5.00 each.

Napa Valley College, Registrar, 2277 Napa-Vallejo Hwy, Napa, CA 94558, 707-253-3000 (FAX: 707-253-3064). Hours: 7:30AM-8PM M-Th; 7:30AM-5PM F. Records go back to 1942. Degrees granted: Associate.

Attendance and degree information available by mail. Search requires name plus social security number, date of birth, exact years of attendance. No fee for information.

Transcripts available by mail. Search requires name plus social security number, date of birth, exact years of attendance, signed release. Fee is $2.00.

Major credit cards accepted for payment.

Naropa Institute, Registrar, 2130 Arapahoe Ave, Boulder, CO 80302, 303-546-3500 (FAX: 303-546-3536). Hours: 9AM-3PM M-Th. Records go back to 1974. Degrees granted: Bachelors; Masters. Adverse incident record source: Student Services, 303-546-3562.

Attendance and degree information available by phone, FAX, mail. Search requires name plus social security number. No fee for information.

Transcripts available by FAX, mail. Search requires name plus social security number, date of birth, exact years of attendance, signed release. Fee is $5.00. Expedited service available for $20.00.

Major credit cards accepted for payment.

Nash Community College, Registrar, PO Box 7488, Rocky Mount, NC 27804-0488, 919-443-4011 (FAX: 919-443-0828). Hours: 8AM-5PM M-Th; 8AM-4PM F. Records go back to 1968. Degrees granted: Associate.

Attendance and degree information available by phone, FAX, mail. Search requires name plus social security number. Other helpful information: date of birth, approximate years of attendance. No fee for information.

Transcripts available by mail. Search requires name plus social security number, signed release. Other helpful information: date of birth, approximate years of attendance. Fee is $1.00. Expedited service available for $1.00.

Nashotah House, Registrar, 2777 Mission Rd, Nashotah, WI 53058-9793, 414-646-3371 (FAX: 414-646-2215). Hours: 8:30AM-4:30PM. Degrees granted: Masters; Anglican Studies.

Attendance information available by phone. Search requires name only. Other helpful information: exact years of attendance. No fee for information.

Degree information available by phone, mail. Search requires name only. Other helpful information: exact years of attendance. No fee for information.

Transcripts available by written request only. Search requires name plus exact years of attendance, signed release. Other helpful information: date of birth. No fee for transcripts.

Nashville State Technical Institute, Registrar, 120 White Bridge Rd, Nashville, TN 37209-4515, 615-353-3210 (FAX: 615-353-3202). Hours: 8AM-4:30PM. Records go back to 1970. Degrees granted: Associate.

Attendance and degree information available by phone, FAX, mail. Search requires name plus social security number. No fee for information.

Transcripts available by FAX, mail. Search requires name plus social security number, signed release. No fee for transcripts.

Nassau Community College, Registrar, One Education Dr, Garden City, NY 11530, 516-572-7205 (FAX: 516-572-7130). Hours: 8AM-9PM M-Th; 8AM-4:30PM F. Records go back to 1959. Alumni records are maintained here at the same phone number. Degrees granted: Associate.

Attendance information available by phone, FAX, mail. Search requires name plus social security number, signed release. No fee for information.

Degree information available by FAX, mail. Search requires name plus social security number, signed release. No fee for information.

Transcripts available by mail. Search requires name plus social security number, signed release. Fee is $3.00.

National Business College, Registrar, PO Box 6400, Roanoke, VA 24017, 800-666-6221 (FAX: 504-389-5239). Records are not housed here. They are located at National Business College, (Corporate Office), Registrar, Transcripts, 1813 E Main St, Salem, VA 24153.

National Business College, **(Branch Campus)**, Registrar, 100 Logan St, Bluefield, VA 24605, 703-326-3621. Records are not housed here. They are located at National Business College, (Corporate Office), Registrar, Transcripts, 1813 E Main St, Salem, VA 24153.

National Business College, **(Branch Campus)**, Registrar, 300A Piedmont Ave, Bristol, VA 24201, 703-669-5333. Records are not housed here. They are located at National Business College, (Corporate Office), Registrar, Transcripts, 1813 E Main St, Salem, VA 24153.

National Business College, **(Branch Campus)**, Registrar, 1819 Emmet St, Charlottesville, VA 22903, 804-295-0136. Records are not housed here. They are located at National Business College, (Corporate Office), Registrar, Transcripts, 1813 E Main St, Salem, VA 24153.

National Business College, **(Branch Campus)**, Registrar, 734 Main St, Danville, VA 24541, 804-793-6822. Records are not housed here. They are located at National Business College, (Corporate Office), Registrar, Transcripts, 1813 E Main St, Salem, VA 24153.

National Business College, **(Branch Campus)**, Registrar, 51-B Burgess Rd, Harrisonburg, VA 22801, 703-432-0943. Records are not housed here. They are located at National Business College, (Corporate Office), Registrar, Transcripts, 1813 E Main St, Salem, VA 24153.

National Business College, **(Branch Campus)**, Registrar, 104 Candlewood Ct, Lynchburg, VA 24502, 804-239-3500. Records are not housed here. They are located at National Business College, (Corporate Office), Registrar, Transcripts, 1813 E Main St, Salem, VA 24153.

National Business College, **(Corporate Office)**, Registrar, Transcripts, 1813 E Main St, Salem, VA 24153, 800-666-6221.

Attendance and degree information available by phone, FAX, mail. Search requires name plus social security number. Other helpful information: approximate years of attendance. No fee for information.

Transcripts available by written request only. Search requires name plus social security number, signed release. Other helpful information: approximate years of attendance. Fee is $2.00.

National College, Registrar's Office, PO Box 1780, Rapid City, SD 57701, 605-394-4907 (FAX: 605-394-4871). Hours: 8AM-5PM. Records go back to 1950s. Degrees granted: Associate; Bachelors.

Attendance and degree information available by phone, FAX, mail. Search requires name only. Other helpful information: social security number, date of birth, approximate years of attendance. No fee for information.

Transcripts available by mail. Search requires name plus signed release. Other helpful information: social security number, date of birth, approximate years of attendance. Fee is $5.00.

FAX transcripts to campus locations only.

National College of Business & Technology, Registrar, PO Box 2036, Bayamon, PR 00621, 809-780-5134.

National College of Business & Technology, **(Branch Campus)**, Registrar, Ave Gonzalo Marin Ste 109, Arecibo, PR 00612, 809-879-5044.

National College of Chiropractic, Registrar, 200 E Roosevelt Rd, Lombard, IL 60148, 708-889-6548 (FAX: 708-889-6554). Hours: 8:30AM-5PM. Records go back to 1945. Alumni records are maintained here also. Call 708-629-9664. Degrees granted: Bachelors; Doctorate. Adverse incident record source: Registrar, 708-889-6548.

Attendance and degree information available by phone, FAX, mail. Search requires name plus social security number, exact years of attendance. No fee for information.

Transcripts available by FAX, mail. Search requires name plus social security number, exact years of attendance, signed release. Fee is $5.00.

National Education Center Thompson Campus, Registrar, 5650 Derry St, Harrisburg, PA 17111-4112, 717-564-8710 (FAX: 717-564-3779). Hours: 8:30AM-4:30PM. Records go back to 1918. Degrees granted: Associate.

Attendance and degree information available by mail. Search requires name plus exact years of attendance. No fee for information.

Transcripts available by mail. Search requires name plus exact years of attendance, signed release. Fee is $5.00.

National Education Center Thompson Campus, **(Branch)**, Registrar, University City Science Ctr, 3440 Market St, Philadelphia, PA 19104, 215-387-1530 (FAX: 215-387-9006). Degrees granted: Associate.

Attendance and degree information available by mail. Search requires name plus social security number, exact years of attendance. No fee for information.

Transcripts available by mail. Search requires name plus social security number, exact years of attendance, signed release. Fee is $5.00.

National Education Center, **(Brydan)**, Registrar, 3505 N Harg Ave, Rosemead, CA 91770, 818-573-5470 X171 (FAX: 818-280-4011). Hours: 9AM-5PM. Records go back to 1970. Degrees granted: Associate.

Attendance and degree information available by FAX, mail. Search requires name plus social security number, approximate years of attendance, signed release. No fee for information.

Transcripts available by FAX, mail. Search requires name plus social security number, approximate years of attendance, signed release. No fee for transcripts.

National Education Center, **(Skadron)**, Registrar, 825 E Hospitality Lane, San Bernardino, CA 92408, 909-885-3896 (FAX: 909-885-2396). Hours: 7:30AM-5PM. Records go back to 1970. Degrees granted: Associate.

Attendance and degree information available by phone, FAX, mail. Search requires name plus social security number, approximate years of attendance, signed release. No fee for information.

Transcripts available by mail. Search requires name plus social security number, approximate years of attendance, signed release. First transcript $5.00, each additional $1.00.

National Technological University, Registrar, 700 Centre Ave, Fort Collins, CO 80526, 970-495-6403 (FAX: 970-498-0601). Hours: 8AM-5PM. Records go back to 1984. Alumni records are maintained here at the same phone number. Degrees granted: Masters.

Attendance and degree information available by FAX, mail. Search requires name plus social security number, signed release. No fee for information.

Transcripts available by FAX, mail. Search requires name plus social security number, signed release. No fee for transcripts.

National Theatre Conservatory, Registrar, 1050 13th St, Denver, CO 80204, 303-446-4855 (FAX: 303-821-2117). Hours: 8AM-5PM. Records go back to 1985. Alumni records are maintained here also. Call 303-446-4855. Degrees granted: Masters.

Attendance and degree information available by FAX, mail. Search requires name plus social security number, approximate years of attendance. No fee for information.

Transcripts available by FAX, mail. Search requires name plus social security number, approximate years of attendance, signed release. No fee for transcripts.

National University, Registrar, 4025 Camino del Rio S Ste 200, San Diego, CA 92108, 619-563-7360 (FAX: 619-563-7397). Hours: 8AM-5:30PM. Records go back to founding date. Degrees granted: Associate; Bachelors; Masters.

Attendance information available by phone, FAX, mail. Search requires name plus social security number, signed release. Other helpful information: date of birth, exact years of attendance. No fee for information.

Degree information available by phone, FAX, mail. Search requires name plus social security number. Other helpful information: date of birth, exact years of attendance. No fee for information.

Transcripts available by FAX, mail. Search requires name plus social security number, date of birth, signed release. Other helpful information: exact years of attendance. Fee is $4.00. Major credit cards accepted for payment.

National-Louis University, Transcript Department, 1000 Capitol Dr, Wheeling, IL 60090, 708-475-1100. Hours: 8:30AM-4:30PM. Records go back to 1886. Degrees granted: Bachelors; Masters; Doctorate.

Attendance and degree information available by phone, mail. Search requires name plus social security number. Other helpful information: approximate years of attendance. No fee for information. Include a stamped envelope.

Transcripts available by mail. Search requires name plus social security number, signed release. Other helpful information: approximate years of attendance. Fee is $3.00. Expedited service available for $10.00.

Naugatuck Valley Community-Technical College, Registrar, 750 Chase Pkwy, Waterbury, CT 06708, 203-575-8012 (FAX: 203-596-8766). Hours: 8:30AM-4:30PM. Records go back 30 years. Alumni records are maintained here also. Call 203-596-8751. Degrees granted: Associate.

Attendance and degree information available by phone, FAX, mail. Search requires name only. Other helpful information: social security number, date of birth, approximate years of attendance. No fee for information.

Transcripts available by FAX, mail. Search requires name plus signed release. Other helpful information: social security number, date of birth, approximate years of attendance. No fee for transcripts.

Navajo Community College, Records/Admissions Officer, Tsaile, AZ 86556, 602-724-3311 X110 (FAX: 602-624-3349). Hours: 8AM-5PM. Records go back 5 years. Degrees granted: Associate. Adverse incident record source: Security Office, 602-724-3220.

Attendance and degree information available by written request only. Search requires name plus social security number, exact years of attendance, signed release. No fee for information.

Transcripts available by written request only. Search requires name plus social security number, exact years of attendance, signed release. Fee is $2.00. Expedited service available for $2.00.

Naval Postgraduate School, Registration & Scheduling, Code 61, 589 Dyer Rd, Monterey, CA 93943-5133, 408-656-2591 (FAX: 408-656-2891). Hours: 8AM-4:30PM. Records go back to 1948. Degrees granted: Masters; Doctorate. Certification: Aviation Safety.

Attendance and degree information available by phone, FAX, mail. Search requires name plus social security number. Other helpful information: approximate years of attendance. No fee for information.

Transcripts available by FAX, mail. Search requires name plus social security number. Other helpful information: approximate years of attendance. Fee is $3.00. Expedited service available for $10.00.

Include a self addressed stamped envelope with mail request.

Naval War College, Registrar, 686 Cushing Rd, Newport, RI 02841-5010, 401-841-6597 (FAX: 401-841-3084). Hours: 7:30AM-4PM. Records go back to 1884. Alumni records are maintained here at the same phone number. Degrees granted: Masters. Special programs- CCE, 401-841-2134.

Attendance and degree information available by phone, FAX, mail. Search requires name plus social security number, exact years of attendance. Other helpful information: date of birth, approximate years of attendance. No fee for information.

Transcripts available by mail. Search requires name plus social security number, exact years of attendance, signed release. Other helpful information: date of birth, approximate years of attendance. No fee for transcripts.

Navarro College, Registrar, 3200 W Seventh Ave, Corsicana, TX 75110, 903-874-6501. Degrees granted: Associate.

Attendance and degree information available by written request only. Search requires name plus social security number, signed release. No fee for information.

Transcripts available by written request only. Search requires name plus social security number, signed release. No fee for transcripts.

Nazarene Bible College, Registrar, PO Box 15749, 1111 Chapman Dr, Colorado Springs, CO 80916, 719-596-5110 (FAX: 719-550-9437). Hours: 8AM-4:30PM. Records go back 28 years. Degrees granted: Associate.

Attendance and degree information available by phone, FAX, mail. Search requires name plus social security number, signed release. Other helpful information: date of birth, approximate years of attendance. No fee for information.

Transcripts available by FAX, mail. Search requires name plus social security number, signed release. Other helpful information: date of birth, approximate years of attendance. Fee is $5.00. Expedited service available for $5.75.

Nazarene Bible College, (Emmanuel Bible College), Registrar, 1605 E Elizabeth St, Pasadena, CA 91104, 818-791-2575 (FAX: 818-398-2424). Hours: 8AM-5PM. Records go back 13 years.

Attendance and degree information available by FAX, mail. Search requires name plus social security number, date of birth, approximate years of attendance, signed release. No fee for information.

Transcripts available by FAX, mail. Search requires name plus social security number, date of birth, approximate years of attendance, signed release. No fee for transcripts.

Nazarene Bible College, (Instituto Teologico Nazareno), Registrar, 1539 E Howard St, Pasadena, CA 91104, 619-221-2200 (FAX: 619-221-2579). Hours: 8AM-4:30PM. Records go back to 1902. Alumni records are maintained here also. Call 619-221-2586. Degrees granted: Bachelors; Masters. Adverse incident record source: Student Development, 619-221-2255.

Attendance and degree information available by phone, FAX, mail. Search requires name plus signed release. No fee for information.

Transcripts available by phone, FAX, mail. Search requires name plus signed release. No fee for transcripts.

Nazarene Bible College, (Nazarene Indian Bible College), Registrar, 2315 Markham Rd SW, Albuquerque, NM 87105, 505-877-0240 (FAX: 505-877-6214). Hours: 8AM-5PM Fall; 9AM-4:30PM Summer. Records go back to 1955. Degrees granted: Associate; Bachelors. Adverse incident record source: Bookkeeper, 505-877-0240.

Attendance and degree information available by phone, FAX, mail. Search requires name only. No fee for information.

Transcripts available by FAX, mail. Search requires name plus signed release. Fee is $2.00.

Nazarene Theological Seminary, Registrar, 1700 E Meyer Blvd, Kansas City, MO 64131, 816-333-6254 (FAX: 816-333-6271). Hours: 8AM-4:30PM. Records go back to 1945. Alumni records are maintained here also. Call 816-333-6254. Degrees granted: Masters; Doctorate.

Attendance and degree information available by phone, FAX, mail. Search requires name plus exact years of attendance. Other helpful information: social security number, date of birth, approximate years of attendance. No fee for information.

Transcripts available by FAX, mail. Search requires name plus signed release. Other helpful information: social security number, date of birth, approximate years of attendance. No fee for transcripts.

Nazareth College of Rochester, Registrar, 4245 East Ave, Rochester, NY 14618-3790, 716-586-2525 X408 (FAX: 716-586-2452). Hours: 8:30AM-5PM. Records go back to 1924. Degrees granted: Bachelors; Masters.

Attendance information available by phone, FAX, mail. Search requires name plus approximate years of attendance. Other helpful information: social security number. No fee for information.

Degree information available by phone, FAX, mail. Search requires name plus approximate years of attendance. Other helpful information: social security number, date of birth, exact years of attendance. No fee for information.

Transcripts available by mail. Search requires name plus social security number, date of birth, approximate years of attendance, signed release. Other helpful information: exact years of attendance. Fee is $5.00. Expedited service available for $10.00.

Nebraska Christian College, Registrar, 1800 Syracuse St, Norfolk, NE 68701, 402-371-5960. Alumni records are maintained here at the same phone number. Degrees granted: Bachelors.

Attendance and degree information available by phone, FAX, mail. Search requires name only. Other helpful information: approximate years of attendance. No fee for information.

Transcripts available by written request only. Search requires name plus signed release. Other helpful information: approximate years of attendance. No fee for transcripts.

Nebraska College of Business, Registrar, 3636 California St, Omaha, NE 68131, 402-553-8500. Hours: 9AM-6PM. Records go back to 1940s. Degrees granted: Associate.

Attendance and degree information available by phone, FAX, mail. Search requires name plus social security number, approximate years of attendance, signed release. Other helpful information: date of birth, exact years of attendance. No fee for information.

Transcripts available by phone, FAX, mail. Search requires name plus social security number, approximate years of attendance, signed release. Other helpful information: date of birth, exact years of attendance. No fee for transcripts.

Nebraska College of Technical Agriculture, Registrar, Curtis, NE 69025, 308-367-4124. Hours: 8AM-5PM. Records go back to 1967. Alumni records are maintained here also. Call 308-367-4124. Degrees granted: Associate.

Attendance and degree information available by phone, mail. Search requires name plus social security number, exact years of attendance. No fee for information.

Transcripts available by mail. Search requires name plus social security number, exact years of attendance, signed release. Fee is $4.00.

Nebraska Indian Community College, Registrar, PO Box 752, Winnebago, NE 68071, 402-878-2414 (FAX: 402-878-2522). Hours: 8AM-5PM. Records go back to 1980. Alumni records are maintained here at the same phone number. Degrees granted: Associate. Adverse incident record source: Student Services.

School will not confirm attendance or degree information. Search requires name plus approximate years of attendance, signed release. Other helpful information: social security number, date of birth, exact years of attendance. No fee for information.

Transcripts available by FAX, mail. Search requires name plus signed release. Other helpful information: social security number, date of birth, approximate years of attendance. Fee is $2.00.

Nebraska Methodist College of Nursing and Allied Health, Registrar, 8501 W Dodge Rd, Omaha, NE 68114, 402-390-4879. Alumni records are maintained here also. Call 402-354-4952. Degrees granted: Associate; Bachelors.

Attendance information available by written request only. Search requires name plus signed release. Other helpful information: social security number, approximate years of attendance. No fee for information.

Degree information available by phone, FAX, mail. Search requires name only. Other helpful information: social security number, approximate years of attendance. No fee for information.

Transcripts available by FAX, mail. Search requires name plus signed release. Other helpful information: social security number, date of birth, approximate years of attendance. Fee is $5.00.

Nebraska Wesleyan University, Registrar, 5000 St Paul Ave, Lincoln, NE 68504, 402-465-2242 (FAX: 402-465-2179). Hours: 8AM-5PM. Records go back to 1887. Alumni records are maintained here also. Call 402-465-2316. Degrees granted: Bachelors. Adverse incident record source: Student Affairs.

Attendance and degree information available by phone, FAX, mail. Search requires name only. Other helpful information: social security number, date of birth, approximate years of attendance. No fee for information.

Transcripts available by mail. Search requires name plus signed release. Other helpful information: social security number, date of birth, approximate years of attendance. Fee is $3.00.

Neosho County Community College, Registrar, 1000 S Allen, Chanute, KS 66720, 316-431-2820 (FAX: 316-431-0082). Hours: 8AM-5PM. Records go back 15 years. Degrees granted: Associate.

Attendance and degree information available by phone, FAX, mail. Search requires name plus social security number, exact years of attendance, signed release. No fee for information.

Transcripts available by written request only. Search requires name plus social security number, exact years of attendance, signed release. Fee is $2.00.

Include a self addressed stamped envelope with mail request.

Ner Israel Rabbinical College, Registrar, 400 Mount Wilson Lane, Baltimore, MD 21208, 410-487-7200 X234 (FAX: 410-

484-3060). Hours: 1-6PM. Records go back to 1933. Degrees granted: Bachelors; Masters; Doctorate.

Attendance and degree information available by phone, FAX, mail. Search requires name only. No fee for information.

Transcripts available by FAX, mail. Search requires name only. No fee for transcripts.

Nettleton Junior College, Registrar, 100 S Spring Ave, Sioux Falls, SD 57104, 605-336-1837 (FAX: 605-336-7626). Hours: 8AM-9:30PM. Records go back to 1919. Alumni records are maintained here also. Call 605-336-1837. Degrees granted: Associate.

Attendance and degree information available by phone, FAX, mail. Search requires name plus approximate years of attendance. Other helpful information: social security number, date of birth, exact years of attendance. No fee for information.

Transcripts available by FAX, mail. Search requires name plus approximate years of attendance, signed release. Other helpful information: social security number, date of birth, exact years of attendance. Fee is $2.00.

Neumann College, Registrar, Concord Rd, Aston, PA 19014, 610-459-0905 X5522. Hours: 9AM-5PM. Records go back to 1965. Alumni records are maintained here also. Call 610-459-0905. Degrees granted: Associate; Bachelors; Masters. Adverse incident record source: Registrar, 610-459-0905 X5522.

Attendance and degree information available by phone, mail. Search requires name plus social security number, exact years of attendance. No fee for information.

Transcripts available by mail. Search requires name plus social security number, exact years of attendance, signed release. Fee is $3.00.

New Brunswick Theological Seminary, Registrar, 17 Seminary Pl, New Brusnwick, NJ 08901-1196, 908-247-5241 (FAX: 908-249-5412). Hours: 8:30AM-4PM. Records go back to 1920s. Alumni records are maintained here also. Call 908-247-5241.

Attendance and degree information available by phone, FAX, mail. Search requires name plus approximate years of attendance. Other helpful information: social security number, date of birth. No fee for information.

Transcripts available by FAX, mail. Search requires name plus approximate years of attendance, signed release. Other helpful information: social security number, date of birth. Fee is $3.50.

Major credit cards accepted for payment.

New College of California, Registrar, 50 Fell St, San Francisco, CA 94102, 415-6226-1694. Hours: 8AM-4:30PM. Records go back to 1972. Alumni records are maintained here at the same phone number. Degrees granted: Bachelors; Masters.

Attendance and degree information available by phone, mail. Search requires name plus social security number, signed release. No fee for information.

Transcripts available by mail. Search requires name plus social security number, exact years of attendance, signed release. Fee is $2.00.

New England Banking Institute, Registrar, One Lincoln Plaza, 89 South St, Boston, MA 02111, 617-951-2350 (FAX: 617-951-2533). Hours: 8:30AM-4:30PM. Records go back to 1970. Alumni records are maintained here at the same phone number. Degrees granted: Associate.

Attendance and degree information available by phone, FAX, mail. Search requires name plus social security number, signed release. No fee for information.

Transcripts available by mail. Search requires name plus social security number, signed release. Fee is $3.00.

New England College, Registrar, Henniker, NH 03242-0788, 603-428-2203 (FAX: 603-428-2266). Hours: 8:30AM-4:30PM. Records go back to 1947.

Attendance and degree information available by phone, mail. Search requires name only. Other helpful information: social security number, approximate years of attendance. No fee for information.

Transcripts available by FAX, mail. Search requires name plus signed release. Other helpful information: social security number, approximate years of attendance. Fee is $5.00. Expedited service available for $10.00.

Major credit cards accepted for payment.

New England College of Optometry, Registrar, 424 Beacon St, Boston, MA 02115, 617-236-6272 (FAX: 617-424-9202). Hours: 9AM-4PM. Records go back to 1900. Alumni records are maintained here also. Call 617-236-6285. Degrees granted: Bachelors; Doctorate.

Attendance information available by phone, mail. Search requires name plus social security number, date of birth, signed release. Other helpful information: approximate years of attendance. No fee for information.

Degree information available by phone, FAX, mail. Search requires name plus social security number, date of birth, signed release. Other helpful information: approximate years of attendance. No fee for information.

Transcripts available by mail. Search requires name plus social security number, date of birth, approximate years of attendance, signed release. Fee is $3.00. Expedited service available for $10.00.

Major credit cards accepted for payment.

New England Conservatory of Music, Registrar, 290 Huntington Ave, Boston, MA 02115, 617-262-1120 (FAX: 617-272-0500). Hours: 9AM-5PM. Records go back to 1900. Degrees granted: Bachelors; Masters; Doctorate; Graduate, Artist Diploma.

Attendance and degree information available by phone, FAX, mail. Search requires name only. Other helpful information: approximate years of attendance. No fee for information.

Transcripts available by FAX, mail. Search requires name plus signed release. Other helpful information: approximate years of attendance. Fee is $5.00.

New England Institute of Technology, Registrar, 2500 Post Rd, Warwick, RI 02886-2251, 401-739-5000 (FAX: 401-738-5122). Hours: 8:30AM-5:30PM. Records go back to 1985. Degrees granted: Associate; Bachelors.

Attendance and degree information available by phone, FAX, mail. Search requires name plus approximate years of attendance. Other helpful information: social security number, date of birth, exact years of attendance. No fee for information.

Transcripts available by written request only. Search requires name plus social security number, approximate years of attendance, signed release. Other helpful information: date of birth, exact years of attendance. Fee is $2.00.

New England School of Law, Registrar, 154 Stuart St, Boston, MA 02116, 617-422-7215 (FAX: 617-422-7200). Hours:

9AM-5PM. Alumni records are maintained here also. Call 617-422-7203. Degrees granted: Doctorate; J.D.

Attendance and degree information available by phone, FAX, mail. Search requires name plus social security number. Other helpful information: approximate years of attendance. No fee for information.

Transcripts available by mail. Search requires name plus social security number, approximate years of attendance, signed release. Other helpful information: exact years of attendance. Fee is $3.00.

New Hampshire College, Registrar, 2500 N River Rd, Manchester, NH 03106-1045, 603-668-2211 (FAX: 603-645-9665). Hours: 8AM-4:30PM. Degrees granted: Associate; Bachelors; Masters.

Attendance and degree information available by phone, FAX, mail. Search requires name plus social security number. Other helpful information: date of birth, approximate years of attendance. No fee for information.

Transcripts available by mail. Search requires name plus social security number, signed release. Other helpful information: date of birth, approximate years of attendance. Fee is $3.00.

Major credit cards accepted for payment.

New Hampshire Technical College, Registrar, One College Dr, Claremont, NH 03743-9707, 603-542-7744 (FAX: 603-543-1844). Hours: 8AM-4:30PM. Records go back to 1968. Degrees granted: Associate.

Attendance and degree information available by FAX, mail. Search requires name only. Other helpful information: social security number, date of birth, approximate years of attendance. No fee for information.

Transcripts available by FAX, mail. Search requires name only. Other helpful information: social security number, date of birth, approximate years of attendance. Students allowed 2 free transcripts, then $3.00 each. FAX back costs $5.00.

New Hampshire Technical College at Berlin, Registrar, 2020 Riverside Dr, Berlin, NH 03570, 603-572-1113. Hours: 8AM-4:30PM. Records go back to founding date. Degrees granted: Associate.

Attendance and degree information available by phone, mail. Search requires name plus social security number, approximate years of attendance. Other helpful information: exact years of attendance. No fee for information.

Transcripts available by mail. Search requires name plus social security number, approximate years of attendance, signed release. Other helpful information: exact years of attendance. Fee is $3.00.

New Hampshire Technical College at Laconia, Registrar, Prescott Hill Rte 106, Laconia, NH 03246, 603-524-3207. Hours: 8AM-4:30PM. Records go back to founding date. Degrees granted: Associate.

Attendance and degree information available by phone, mail. Search requires name plus social security number, approximate years of attendance. Other helpful information: exact years of attendance. No fee for information.

Transcripts available by written request only. Search requires name plus social security number, approximate years of attendance, signed release. Other helpful information: exact years of attendance. Fee is $2.00.

New Hampshire Technical College at Manchester, Registrar, 1066 Front St, Manchester, NH 03102, 603-668-6706 (FAX: 603-668-5354). Hours: 8AM-4PM. Records go back to 1984. Degrees granted: Associate.

Attendance information available by FAX, mail. Search requires name plus social security number. Other helpful information: approximate years of attendance. No fee for information.

Degree information available by phone, FAX, mail. Search requires name plus social security number. Other helpful information: approximate years of attendance. No fee for information.

Transcripts available by FAX, mail. Search requires name plus social security number, signed release. Other helpful information: approximate years of attendance. Fee is $3.00.

New Hampshire Technical College at Nashua, Registrar, 505 Amerst St, PO Box 2052, Nashua, NH 03061-2052, 603-882-6923. Hours: 8AM-4:30PM. Records go back to founding date. Degrees granted: Associate.

Attendance and degree information available by phone, mail. Search requires name plus social security number, approximate years of attendance. Other helpful information: exact years of attendance. No fee for information.

Transcripts available by mail. Search requires name plus social security number, approximate years of attendance, signed release. Other helpful information: exact years of attendance. Fee is $2.00.

New Hampshire Technical College at Stratham, Registrar, PO Box 365, Stratham, NH 03885, 603-772-1194. Hours: 8AM-4:30PM. Records go back to founding date.

Attendance and degree information available by phone, mail. Search requires name plus social security number, approximate years of attendance. Other helpful information: exact years of attendance. No fee for information.

Transcripts available by written request only. Search requires name plus social security number, approximate years of attendance, signed release. Other helpful information: exact years of attendance. Fee is $3.00.

New Hampshire Technical Institute, Registrar, 11 Institute Dr, Concord, NH 03301-7412, 603-225-1800. Hours: 8AM-4:30PM. Records go back to founding date. Degrees granted: Associate.

Attendance and degree information available by phone, mail. Search requires name plus social security number, approximate years of attendance. Other helpful information: exact years of attendance. No fee for information.

Transcripts available by written request only. Search requires name plus social security number, approximate years of attendance, signed release. Other helpful information: exact years of attendance. Fee is $3.00.

New Jersey Institute of Technology, Registrar, University Heights, Newark, NJ 07102-9938, 201-596-3239 (FAX: 201-802-1854). Hours: 8:30AM-4:30PM. Records go back to 1919. Alumni records are maintained here at the same phone number. Degrees granted: Bachelors; Masters; Doctorate. Adverse incident record source: Campus Police, 201-596-3111.

Attendance and degree information available by phone, FAX, mail. Search requires name plus social security number, date of birth, approximate years of attendance, signed release. Other helpful information: exact years of attendance. No fee for information.

Transcripts available by FAX, mail. Search requires name plus social security number, approximate years of attendance, signed release. Other helpful information: date of birth, exact years of attendance. Fee is $3.00. Expedited service available for $20.00.

Major credit cards accepted for payment.

New Kensington Commercial School, Registrar, 945 Greensburg Rd, New Kensington, PA 15068, 412-339-7542 (FAX: 412-339-2950). Hours: 8AM-5PM. Records go back 50 years. Degrees granted: Associate.

Attendance information available by mail. Search requires name plus social security number, approximate years of attendance, signed release. Other helpful information: exact years of attendance. No fee for information.

Degree information available by phone, FAX, mail. Search requires name plus social security number, signed release. Other helpful information: approximate years of attendance. No fee for information.

Transcripts available by mail. Search requires name plus social security number, signed release. Other helpful information: approximate years of attendance. Fee is $2.00.

New Mexico Highlands University, Registrar, National Ave, Las Vegas, NM 87701, 505-454-3424 (FAX: 505-454-3552). Hours: 8AM-5PM. Degrees granted: Associate; Bachelors; Masters.

Attendance and degree information available by phone, FAX, mail. Search requires name plus social security number. Other helpful information: date of birth, approximate years of attendance. No fee for information.

Transcripts available by FAX, mail. Search requires name plus social security number, signed release. Other helpful information: date of birth, approximate years of attendance. Fee is $2.00. Expedited service available for $10.00.

New Mexico Institute of Mining and Technology, Registrar, Socorro, NM 87801, 505-835-5133 (FAX: 505-835-6511). Hours: 8AM-5PM. Records go back to 1889. Degrees granted: Associate; Bachelors; Masters; Doctorate. Adverse incident record source: Campus Police, 505-835-5434.

Attendance information available by phone, mail. Search requires name plus social security number, signed release. No fee for information.

Degree information available by phone, mail. Search requires name plus signed release. Other helpful information: social security number, approximate years of attendance. No fee for information.

Transcripts available by phone, FAX, mail. Search requires name plus signed release. Fee is $2.00. Expedited service available for $5.00.

Major credit cards accepted for payment.

New Mexico Junior College, Registrar, 5317 Lovington Hwy, Hobbs, NM 88240, 505-392-5113 (FAX: 505-392-2526). Hours: 8AM-5PM. Records go back to 1967. Degrees granted: Associate.

Attendance information available by phone, FAX, mail. Search requires name plus social security number. Other helpful information: date of birth. No fee for information.

Degree information available by FAX, mail. Search requires name plus social security number. Other helpful information: date of birth. No fee for information.

Transcripts available by mail. Search requires name plus social security number, signed release. Other helpful information: date of birth. Fee is $2.00. Expedited service available for $10.00.

New Mexico Military Institute, Registrar, 100 W College Blvd, Roswell, NM 88201, 505-624-8070 (FAX: 505-624-8058). Hours: 7:30AM-4:30PM. Records go back to 1885. Degrees granted: Associate.

Attendance and degree information available by phone, FAX, mail. Search requires name only. Other helpful information: social security number, date of birth, approximate years of attendance. No fee for information.

Transcripts available by mail. Search requires name plus signed release. Other helpful information: social security number, date of birth, approximate years of attendance. Fee is $1.00.

Use credit card for transcript only.

New Mexico State University, Registrar, Box 30001, Las Cruces, NM 88003, 505-646-3411 (FAX: 505-646-6330). Hours: 8AM-5PM. Degrees granted: Associate; Bachelors; Masters; Doctorate.

Attendance information available by phone, FAX, mail. Search requires name plus social security number, signed release. No fee for information.

Degree information available by phone, FAX, mail. Search requires name plus social security number. Other helpful information: approximate years of attendance. No fee for information.

Transcripts available by mail. Search requires name plus social security number, signed release. Other helpful information: date of birth, exact years of attendance. Fee is $3.00. Expedited service available for $9.50.

New Mexico State University at Alamogordo, Registrar, PO Box 477, Alamogordo, NM 88311-0477, 505-439-3600. Records are not housed here. They are located at Dona Ana Branch Community College, Registrar, Box 30001, Las Cruces, NM 88003.

New Mexico State University at Carlsbad, Registrar, 1500 University Dr, Carlsbad, NM 88220, 505-885-8831 (FAX: 505-885-4951). Hours: 8AM-5PM. Records go back to 1950. Degrees granted: Associate.

Attendance information available by phone, FAX, mail. Search requires name plus social security number, exact years of attendance, signed release. Other helpful information: date of birth, approximate years of attendance. No fee for information.

Degree information available by phone, FAX, mail. Search requires name plus social security number, exact years of attendance, signed release. No fee for information.

Transcripts available by FAX, mail. Search requires name plus social security number, exact years of attendance, signed release. Fee is $3.00.

New Mexico State University at Grants, Registrar, 1500 3rd St, Grants, NM 87020, 505-287-7981 (FAX: 505-287-2329). Records are not housed here. They are located at New Mexico State University, Registrar, Box 30001, Las Cruces, NM 88003.

New Orleans Baptist Theological Seminary, Registrar, 3939 Gentilly Blvd, New Orleans, LA 70126, 504-282-4455 X3337 (FAX: 504-286-3591). Hours: 8AM-5PM. Records go back 77 years. Alumni records are maintained here at the same phone number. Degrees granted: Associate; Bachelors; Masters.

Attendance and degree information available by phone, FAX, mail. Search requires name plus social security number, signed release. No fee for information.

Transcripts available by mail. Search requires name plus social security number, signed release. Fee is $5.00.

New River Community College, Registrar, PO Drawer 1127, Dublin, VA 24084, 703-674-3603. Hours: 8AM-5PM. Records go back to 1969. Alumni records are maintained here also. Call 703-674-3600. Degrees granted: Associate.

Attendance and degree information available by phone, mail. Search requires name plus social security number. No fee for information.

Transcripts available by mail. Search requires name plus social security number, signed release. No fee for transcripts.

New School for Social Research, Registrar, 66 W 12th St, New York, NY 10011, 212-229-5600 (FAX: 212-229-5359). Hours: 7:30AM-4:30PM. Records go back to 1919. Alumni records are maintained here also. Call 212-229-5662. Degrees granted: Bachelors; Masters; Doctorate.

Attendance and degree information available by phone, FAX, mail. Search requires name only. Other helpful information: social security number, date of birth, approximate years of attendance. No fee for information.

Transcripts available by mail. Search requires name plus signed release. Other helpful information: social security number, date of birth, approximate years of attendance. Fee is $4.00. Expedited service available for $8.00.

New School for Social Research, (Parsons School of Design), Registrar, 66 Fifth Ave, New York, NY 10011, 212-229-8950 (FAX: 212-229-8974). Hours: 9AM-6PM. Records go back to 1800s. Alumni records are maintained here also. Call 212-229-5662. Degrees granted: Bachelors; Masters.

Attendance and degree information available by phone, FAX, mail. Search requires name plus social security number, approximate years of attendance, signed release. No fee for information.

Transcripts available by mail. Search requires name plus social security number, approximate years of attendance, signed release. Fee is $4.00.

New York Chiropractic College, Registrar, 2360 State Rte 89, Seneca Falls, NY 13148-0800, 315-568-3000. Degrees granted: Doctorate.

Attendance information available by phone, FAX, mail. Search requires name only. Other helpful information: social security number, date of birth, approximate years of attendance. No fee for information.

Degree information available by phone, FAX, mail. Search requires name only. Other helpful information: social security number, date of birth, approximate years of attendance. No fee for information.

Transcripts available by mail. Search requires name plus signed release. Other helpful information: social security number, date of birth, approximate years of attendance. Fee is $5.00. Expedited service available for $10.00.

New York City Technical College, Registrar, 300 Jay St, Brooklyn, NY 11201, 718-260-5800 (FAX: 718-260-5198). Hours: 9:30AM-6:30PM M,W,Th; 9:30AM-4:30PM T,F. Records go back to 1940. Alumni records are maintained here also. Call 718-260-5402. Degrees granted: Associate; Bachelors.

Attendance and degree information available by FAX, mail. Search requires name plus social security number, date of birth, approximate years of attendance, signed release. No fee for information.

Transcripts available by mail. Search requires name plus social security number, date of birth, approximate years of attendance, signed release. Fee is $4.00.

New York College of Podiatric Medicine, Registrar, 53 E 124th St, New York, NY 10035, 212-410-8054 (FAX: 212-722-4918). Hours: 9AM-5PM. Records go back to 1911. Alumni records are maintained here at the same phone number. Degrees granted: Doctorate.

Attendance and degree information available by FAX, mail. Search requires name plus social security number, signed release. No fee for information.

Transcripts available by mail. Search requires name plus social security number, signed release. Fee is $5.00.

New York Institute of Technology, Registrar, 268 Wheatley Rd, Old Westbury, NY 11568-1036, 516-686-7580. Hours: 9AM-5PM. Records go back to 1955. Alumni records are maintained here also. Call 516-626-7632. Degrees granted: Associate; Bachelors; Masters; D.O.

Attendance and degree information available by phone, FAX, mail. Search requires name plus social security number. Other helpful information: date of birth, approximate years of attendance. No fee for information.

Transcripts available by written request only. Search requires name plus social security number, signed release. Other helpful information: date of birth, approximate years of attendance. Fee is $5.00.

New York Institute of Technology, (Central Islip Campus), Registrar, 211 Carleton Ave, Central Islip, NY 11722, 516-686-7580. Records are not housed here. They are located at New York Institute of Technology, Registrar, 268 Wheatley Rd, Old Westbury, NY 11568-1036.

New York Institute of Technology, (Manhattan Campus), Registrar, 1855 Broadway, New York, NY 10023, 212-261-1600 (FAX: 212-261-1646). Records are not housed here. They are located at New York Institute of Technology, Registrar, 268 Wheatley Rd, Old Westbury, NY 11568-1036.

New York Medical College, Registrar, Sunshine Cottage, Admin Bldg, Valhalla, NY 10595, 914-993-4495 (FAX: 914-993-4613). Hours: 9AM-5PM. Records go back to 1920. Alumni records are maintained here also. Call 914-993-4555. Degrees granted: Masters; Doctorate; Ph.D.

Attendance and degree information available by phone, FAX, mail. Search requires name plus social security number, signed release. No fee for information.

Transcripts available by mail. Search requires name plus social security number, signed release. Fee is $5.00.

New York School of Interior Design, Registrar, 170 E 70th St, New York, NY 10021-5110, 212-472-1500 (FAX: 212-472-3800). Hours: 9AM-5PM. Records go back to founding date. Degrees granted: Associate; Bachelors.

Attendance information available by phone, FAX, mail. Search requires name plus social security number, date of birth, signed release. Other helpful information: approximate years of attendance. No fee for information.

Degree information available by phone, FAX, mail. Search requires name plus social security number, date of birth, signed release. Other helpful information: approximate years of attendance. No fee for information.

Transcripts available by FAX, mail. Search requires name plus social security number, date of birth, signed release. Other helpful information: approximate years of attendance. Fee is $5.00. Expedited service available for $5.00. Include stamped envelope.

Major credit cards accepted for payment.

New York School of Law, Registrar, 57 Worth St, New York, NY 10013, 212-431-3200 (FAX: 212-343-2137). Hours: 9AM-7PM M-Th; 9AM-5PM F. Records go back to 1895. Alumni records are maintained here also. Call 212-431-2800. Degrees granted: Doctorate.

Attendance and degree information available by phone, FAX, mail. Search requires name plus social security number, signed release. No fee for information.

Transcripts available by mail. Search requires name plus social security number, signed release. Fee is $2.00.

New York Theological Seminary, Registrar, 5 W 29th St, New York, NY 10001-4599, 212-532-4012 (FAX: 212-684-0757). Hours: 9AM-5PM. Records go back to 1906. Degrees granted: Masters; Doctorate.

Attendance information available by FAX. Search requires name plus social security number, signed release. Other helpful information: date of birth, approximate years of attendance. No fee for information.

Degree information available by FAX. Search requires name plus social security number, date of birth, exact years of attendance, signed release. Other helpful information: approximate years of attendance. Fee is $5.00. Expedite service available for $5.00.

Transcripts available by written request only. Search requires name plus social security number, date of birth, exact years of attendance, signed release. Other helpful information: approximate years of attendance. Fee is $5.00. Expedited service available for $5.00.

New York University, Registrar, PO Box 910, New York, NY 10276-0910, 212-998-4250 (FAX: 212-995-4587). Hours: 9AM-5PM. Records go back to 1913. Alumni records are maintained here also. Call 212-998-6965. Degrees granted: Bachelors; Masters; Doctorate; Ph.D.

Attendance and degree information available by phone, FAX, mail. Search requires name plus social security number, signed release. No fee for information.

Transcripts available by mail. Search requires name plus social security number, signed release. Fee is $3.00.

Newberry College, Registrar, 2100 College St, Newberry, SC 29108, 803-321-5124 (FAX: 803-321-5627). Hours: 8AM-4:30PM. Alumni records are maintained here also. Call 803-321-5143. Degrees granted: Bachelors.

Attendance and degree information available by phone, FAX, mail. Search requires name only. Other helpful information: approximate years of attendance. No fee for information.

Transcripts available by FAX, mail. Search requires name plus signed release. Other helpful information: approximate years of attendance. Fee is $5.00. Expedited service available for $0.note.

Newbury College, Registrar, 129 Fisher Ave, Brookline, MA 02146, 617-730-7112 (FAX: 617-730-7095). Hours: 9AM-5PM. Degrees granted: Associate; Bachelors.

Attendance and degree information available by phone, FAX, mail. Search requires name plus social security number, approximate years of attendance. Other helpful information: exact years of attendance. No fee for information.

Transcripts available by mail. Search requires name plus social security number, approximate years of attendance, signed release. Other helpful information: date of birth. Fee is $4.00. Expedited service available for $15.00.

Niagara County Community College, Registrar, 3111 Saunders Settlement Rd, Sanborn, NY 14132, 716-731-3271 (FAX: 716-731-4053). Hours: 8AM-5PM. Records go back to 1968. Degrees granted: Associate. Adverse incident record source: Academic Affairs, 716-731-3271 X172.

Attendance and degree information available by phone, FAX, mail. Search requires name only. Other helpful information: social security number, date of birth, approximate years of attendance. No fee for information.

Transcripts available by mail. Search requires name plus signed release. Other helpful information: social security number, date of birth, approximate years of attendance. Fee is $3.00.

Niagara University, Registrar, Niagara University, NY 14109, 716-286-8727 (FAX: 716-286-8733). Hours: 9AM-5PM. Records go back to 1856. Degrees granted: Bachelors; Masters. Adverse incident record source: Student Affairs, 716-286-8566.

Attendance and degree information available by phone, FAX, mail. Search requires name plus social security number, date of birth, approximate years of attendance, signed release. No fee for information.

Transcripts available by mail. Search requires name plus social security number, date of birth, approximate years of attendance, signed release. Fee is $3.00.

Nicholls State University, Office of Records, PO Box 2059, Thibodaux, LA 70310, 504-448-4153 (FAX: 504-448-4929). Hours: 8AM-4:30PM. Records go back to 1948. Alumni Records Office: PO Box 2158, Thibodaux, LA 70310. Degrees granted: Associate; Bachelors; Masters.

Attendance information available by mail. Search requires name plus social security number, date of birth, signed release. Other helpful information: approximate years of attendance. No fee for information.

Degree information available by phone, mail. Search requires name plus social security number, date of birth, signed release. Other helpful information: approximate years of attendance. No fee for information.

Transcripts available by mail. Search requires name plus social security number, date of birth, signed release. Other helpful information: approximate years of attendance. Fee is $2.00.

Major credit cards accepted for payment.

Nichols College, Office of the Registrar, PO Box 5000, Dudley, MA 01571-5000, 508-943-1560. Hours: 8:30AM-4:30PM. Records go back to 1930s. Degrees granted: Associate; Bachelors; Masters.

Attendance information available by phone, mail. Search requires name plus social security number, date of birth. No fee for information.

Degree information available by phone, mail. Search requires name only. No fee for information.

Transcripts available by mail. Search requires name plus social security number, date of birth, signed release. Fee is $2.00.

Nicolet Area Technical College, Registrar, Box 518, Rhinelander, WI 54501, 715-365-4410 (FAX: 715-365-4445). Hours: 8AM-4:30PM. Records go back to 1968. Degrees granted: Associate.

Attendance and degree information available by phone, FAX, mail. Search requires name plus social security number, date of birth. No fee for information.

Transcripts available by FAX, mail. Search requires name plus social security number, date of birth, signed release. No fee for transcripts.

Norfolk State University, Registrar, 2401 Corprew Ave, Norfolk, VA 23504, 804-683-8610 (FAX: 804-683-8907). Hours: 8AM-4:30PM. Records go back to 1935. Alumni records are maintained here also. Call 804-683-8670. Degrees granted: Bachelors; Masters.

Attendance and degree information available by FAX, mail. Search requires name plus social security number, exact years of attendance. No fee for information.

Transcripts available by FAX, mail. Search requires name plus social security number, exact years of attendance, signed release. Fee is $5.00.

Normandale Community College, Registrar, 9700 France Ave S, Bloomington, MN 55431, 612-832-6314 (FAX: 612-832-6571). Hours: 8AM-9PM. Records go back to 1968. Degrees granted: Associate.

Attendance and degree information available by phone, FAX, mail. Search requires name plus social security number, date of birth, signed release. No fee for information.

Transcripts available by FAX, mail. Search requires name plus social security number, date of birth, signed release. No fee for transcripts.

North Adams State College, Registrar, North Adams, MA 01247, 413-662-4611 (FAX: 413-662-5580). Hours: 8:30AM-4:45PM. Records go back to 1908. Degrees granted: Bachelors; Masters.

Attendance and degree information available by phone, FAX, mail. Search requires name plus social security number, approximate years of attendance. Other helpful information: date of birth, exact years of attendance. No fee for information.

Transcripts available by FAX, mail. Search requires name plus social security number, date of birth, approximate years of attendance, signed release. Other helpful information: exact years of attendance. Fee is $1.00.

College helpful.

North American Baptist Seminary, Registrar, 1525 S Grange Ave, Sioux Falls, SD 57105-1599, 605-336-6588 (FAX: 605-335-9090). Hours: 8AM-4:30PM. Degrees granted: Masters; Doctorate.

Attendance and degree information available by phone, FAX, mail. Search requires name only. Other helpful information: approximate years of attendance. No fee for information.

Transcripts available by mail. Search requires name plus signed release. Other helpful information: approximate years of attendance. Fee is $2.00.

North Arkansas Community/Technical College, Registrar, Pioneer Ridge, Harrison, AR 72601, 501-743-3000 (FAX: 501-743-3577). Hours: 8AM-5PM. Records go back to 1974. Degrees granted: Associate.

Attendance and degree information available by phone, FAX, mail. Search requires name plus social security number. Other helpful information: date of birth, approximate years of attendance. No fee for information.

Transcripts available by mail. Search requires name plus social security number, signed release. Other helpful information: date of birth, approximate years of attendance. No fee for transcripts.

North Carolina Agricultural and Technical State University, Office of the Registrar, Dowdy Bldg, 1601 E Market St, Greensboro, NC 27411, 910-334-7595 (FAX: 910-334-7013). Hours: 8AM-5PM M,Th,F; 8AM-7PM T,W. Records go back to 1930. Alumni records are maintained here also. Call 910-334-7583. Degrees granted: Bachelors; Masters; Doctorate. Adverse incident record source: University Police, 910-334-7675.

Attendance and degree information available by phone, FAX, mail. Search requires name only. Other helpful information: social security number, approximate years of attendance. No fee for information.

Transcripts available by mail. Search requires name plus signed release. Other helpful information: social security number, approximate years of attendance. Fee is $2.00. Expedite: Student furnishes pre-paid overnight or FedEx envelope.

North Carolina Central University, Registrar, 1801 Fayetteville St, Durham, NC 27707, 919-560-6262 (FAX: 919-560-5012). Hours: 8AM-5PM. Alumni records are maintained here also. Call 919-560-6363. Degrees granted: Bachelors; Masters. Adverse incident record source: Student Life, 919-560-6490.

School will not confirm attendance information. Search requires name only. Other helpful information: social security number, date of birth, approximate years of attendance. No fee for information.

Degree information available by phone, mail. Search requires name plus social security number, exact years of attendance, signed release. Other helpful information: date of birth. No fee for information.

Transcripts available by written request only. Search requires name plus social security number, exact years of attendance, signed release. Other helpful information: date of birth. Fee is $2.00.

Major credit cards accepted for payment.

North Carolina School of the Arts, Registrar, 200 Waughtown St, PO Box 12189, Winston-Salem, NC 27117-2189, 910-770-3294. Hours: 8:30AM-5PM. Records go back to 1965. Alumni records are maintained here also. Call 910-770-3332. Degrees granted: Bachelors; Masters.

Attendance information available by phone, mail. Search requires name plus social security number. No fee for information.

Degree information available by phone, mail. Search requires name plus social security number, exact years of attendance. No fee for information.

Transcripts available by mail. Search requires name plus social security number, exact years of attendance, signed release. Fee is $3.00.

North Carolina State University, Registrar, PO Box 7313, Raleigh, NC 27695-7313, 919-515-2572 (FAX: 919-515-2376). Hours: 8AM-5PM. Degrees granted: Bachelors; Masters; Doctorate.

Attendance and degree information available by phone, FAX, mail. Search requires name plus social security number, signed release. Other helpful information: date of birth, approximate years of attendance. No fee for information.

Transcripts available by FAX, mail. Search requires name plus social security number, signed release. Other helpful information: date of birth, approximate years of attendance. Fee is $5.00.

North Carolina Wesleyan College, Registrar, 3400 N Wesleyan Blvd, Rocky Mount, NC 27804, 919-985-5124 (FAX: 919-977-3701). Hours: 8AM-5PM. Records go back to 1960.

Alumni records are maintained here also. Call 919-985-5145. Degrees granted: Bachelors.

Attendance and degree information available by phone, FAX, mail. Search requires name only. Other helpful information: social security number, approximate years of attendance. No fee for information.

Transcripts available by mail. Search requires name plus signed release. Other helpful information: social security number, approximate years of attendance. Fee is $3.00. Expedited service available for $3.00.

North Central Bible College, Registrar, 910 Elliot Ave S, Minneapolis, MN 55404, 612-343-4409 (FAX: 612-343-4778). Hours: 8AM-4:30PM. Records go back to 1930. Degrees granted: Associate; Bachelors. Special programs- Carlson Institute Correspondence Course Dept, 612-343-4430. Adverse incident record source: Security Office, 612-343-4444.

Attendance and degree information available by phone, FAX, mail. Search requires name plus approximate years of attendance. Other helpful information: social security number, exact years of attendance. No fee for information.

Transcripts available by FAX, mail. Search requires name plus approximate years of attendance, signed release. Other helpful information: social security number, exact years of attendance. Fee is $4.00. Expedited service available for $6.00.

North Central College, Registrar, 30 N Brainerd St, PO Box 3063, Naperville, IL 60566-7063, 708-420-3430. Hours: 8AM-4PM. Degrees granted: Bachelors; Masters. Adverse incident record source: Dispute Resolution Program.

Attendance and degree information available by phone, mail. Search requires name plus approximate years of attendance. Other helpful information: social security number, date of birth. No fee for information.

Transcripts available by phone, mail. Search requires name plus approximate years of attendance, signed release. Other helpful information: social security number, date of birth. Fee is $3.00. Expedited service available for $5.00.

North Central Michigan College, Registrar, 1515 Howard St, Petoskey, MI 49770, 616-348-6605 (FAX: 616-348-6672). Hours: 8:30AM-5PM. Records go back to 1958. Degrees granted: Associate. Adverse incident record source: Business Office, 616-348-6602.

Attendance and degree information available by phone, FAX, mail. Search requires name plus social security number, approximate years of attendance, signed release. No fee for information.

Transcripts available by FAX, mail. Search requires name plus social security number, approximate years of attendance, signed release. No fee for transcripts.

North Central Missouri College, Registrar, 1301 Main St, Trenton, MO 64683, 816-359-3032. Hours: 8AM-4PM. Records go back to 1925. Degrees granted: Associate.

School will not confirm attendance information. Search requires name only. No fee for information.

Degree information available by mail. Search requires name plus social security number. Other helpful information: approximate years of attendance. No fee for information.

Transcripts available by written request only. Search requires name plus social security number, approximate years of attendance, signed release. Other helpful information: date of birth, exact years of attendance. Fee is $1.00.

Major credit cards accepted for payment.

North Central Technical College, Registrar, PO Box 698, Mansfield, OH 44901-0698, 419-755-4837 (FAX: 419-755-4750). Hours: 8:30AM-7:45PM M-Th; 8:30AM-4:30PM F. Records go back 30 years. Degrees granted: Associate.

Attendance and degree information available by phone, FAX, mail. Search requires name plus social security number. Other helpful information: date of birth, approximate years of attendance. No fee for information.

Transcripts available by mail. Search requires name plus social security number, approximate years of attendance, signed release. Other helpful information: date of birth, exact years of attendance. Fee is $2.00.

North Central Technical College, Registrar, 1000 Campus Dr, Wausau, WI 54401, 715-675-3331 (FAX: 715-675-9776). Hours: 8AM-6PM M-Th, 8AM-4:30PM F. Records go back to 1912. Alumni records are maintained here at the same phone number. Degrees granted: Associate.

Attendance and degree information available by phone, mail. Search requires name plus social security number, exact years of attendance. No fee for information.

Transcripts available by mail. Search requires name plus social security number, exact years of attendance, signed release. No fee for transcripts.

North Central Texas College, Registrar, 1525 W California St, Gainesville, TX 76240, 817-668-4222 (FAX: 817-668-6049). Hours: 8AM-8PM in session. Records go back to 1924. Degrees granted: Associate. Adverse incident record source: Gainesville Police, 817-668-7777.

Attendance and degree information available by phone, FAX, mail. Search requires name only. Other helpful information: social security number, approximate years of attendance. No fee for information.

Transcripts available by mail. Search requires name plus signed release. Other helpful information: social security number, approximate years of attendance. Fee is $2.00. Expedited service available for $10.00.

North Country Community College, Registrar, 20 Winona Ave, PO Box 89, Saranac Lake, NY 12983, 518-891-2915. Degrees granted: Associate.

Attendance and degree information available by phone, FAX, mail. Search requires name plus signed release. Other helpful information: social security number. No fee for information.

Transcripts available by FAX, mail. Search requires name plus social security number, signed release. Other helpful information: date of birth, approximate years of attendance. Fee is $2.00.

North Country Community College, Registrar, PO Box 89, Saranac Lake, NY 12983, 518-891-2915 X245 (FAX: 518-891-2915 X214). Hours: 8:30AM-4:30PM. Records go back to 1968. Alumni records are maintained here also. Call 518-891-2915 X224. Degrees granted: Associate. Adverse incident record source: Dean of Admissions, 518-891-2915 X204.

Attendance and degree information available by phone, FAX, mail. Search requires name plus social security number, signed release. No fee for information.

Transcripts available by mail. Search requires name plus social security number, signed release. Fee is $2.00.

North Country Community College, (Branch Campus), Registrar, College Ave, Malone, NY 12953, 518-891-2915 (FAX:

518-891-2915 X214). Hours: 8:30PM-4:30PM. Records go back to 1968. Degrees granted: Associate.

Attendance information available by phone, FAX, mail. Search requires name plus social security number. No fee for information.

Degree information available by phone, FAX, mail. Search requires name only. Other helpful information: social security number, date of birth, approximate years of attendance. No fee for information.

Transcripts available by mail. Search requires name plus signed release. Other helpful information: social security number, date of birth, approximate years of attendance. Fee is $2.00.

North Dakota State College of Science, Registrar, 800 N Sixth St, Wahpeton, ND 58076, 800-342-4325 X2203 (FAX: 701-671-2145). Hours: 7:45AM-4:45PM. Records go back to 1903. Degrees granted: Associate.

Attendance and degree information available by FAX, mail. Search requires name plus social security number, date of birth, approximate years of attendance, signed release. No fee for information.

Transcripts available by FAX, mail. Search requires name plus social security number, date of birth, approximate years of attendance, signed release. No fee for transcripts.

Include a self addressed stamped envelope with mail request. FAX fee $5.00.

North Dakota State University (Bottineau), Registrar, First St and Simrall Blvd, Bottineau, ND 58318, 701-228-5487 (FAX: 701-228-5499). Hours: 8AM-5PM. Records go back to 1906. Alumni records are maintained here also. Call 701-228-5435.

Attendance and degree information available by phone, FAX. Search requires name plus social security number, date of birth, approximate years of attendance, signed release. No fee for information.

Transcripts available by phone, FAX. Search requires name plus social security number, date of birth, approximate years of attendance, signed release. No fee for transcripts.

North Dakota State University, Office of the Registrar, PO Box 5196, Fargo, ND 58105, 701-231-8295 (FAX: 701-231-8959). Hours: 8AM-5PM Sep-May; 7:30AM-4PM Jun-Aug. Records go back to 1896. Alumni Records Office: PO Box 5144, Fargo, ND 58105. Degrees granted: Bachelors; Masters; Doctorate. Adverse incident record source: Student Affairs.

Attendance and degree information available by phone, FAX, mail. Search requires name only. Other helpful information: social security number, date of birth, approximate years of attendance. No fee for information.

Transcripts available by FAX, mail. Search requires name plus signed release. Other helpful information: social security number, date of birth, approximate years of attendance. Fee is $2.00.

Copies of transcript to student can be requested by phone. College, major helpful.

North Florida Junior College, Registrar, 100 Turner Davis Dr, Madison, FL 32340, 904-973-2288 X151 (FAX: 904-973-2288). Hours: 8AM-4:30PM. Records go back to 1958. Degrees granted: Associate.

Attendance and degree information available by phone, FAX, mail. Search requires name plus social security number, date of birth. Other helpful information: approximate years of attendance. No fee for information.

Transcripts available by FAX, mail. Search requires name plus social security number, date of birth, signed release. Other helpful information: approximate years of attendance. Fee is $1.00. Expedited service available for $1.00.

North Georgia College, Registrar, College Ave, Dahlonega, GA 30597, 706-846-1753. Hours: 7:30AM-4:30PM. Records go back to 1873. Degrees granted: Associate; Bachelors; Masters.

Attendance information available by phone, FAX, mail. Search requires name plus social security number. Other helpful information: exact years of attendance. No fee for information.

Degree information available by phone, FAX, mail. Search requires name plus social security number. Other helpful information: approximate years of attendance. No fee for information.

Transcripts available by FAX, mail. Search requires name plus social security number, signed release. Other helpful information: approximate years of attendance. Fee is $2.00. Expedited service available for $10.00.

FAX request must be prepaid by credit card. Major credit cards accepted for payment.

North Greenville College, Records Office, PO Box 1892, Tigerville, SC 29688, 803-977-7009 (FAX: 803-977-7021). Hours: 8:30AM-5PM M-Th; 8:30AM-Noon F. Records go back to founding date. Degrees granted: Associate; Bachelors.

Attendance information available by phone. Search requires name plus social security number, signed release. Other helpful information: date of birth, approximate years of attendance. No fee for information.

School will not confirm degree information. Search requires name plus social security number, signed release. Other helpful information: date of birth, approximate years of attendance. No fee for information.

Transcripts available by written request only. Search requires name plus social security number, signed release. Other helpful information: date of birth, approximate years of attendance. Fee is $5.00.

North Harris Montgomery Community College, Registrar, 250 N Sam Houston Pkwy E, Houston, TX 77060, 713-591-3573 (FAX: 713-591-9301). Hours: 8AM-5PM. Records go back to 1975. Degrees granted: Associate.

Attendance information available by phone, FAX, mail. Search requires name plus social security number. Other helpful information: date of birth, approximate years of attendance. No fee for information.

Degree information available by phone, FAX, mail. Search requires name plus social security number. Other helpful information: date of birth, approximate years of attendance. No fee for information.

Transcripts available by phone, mail. Search requires name plus signed release. Other helpful information: social security number, date of birth, approximate years of attendance. No fee for transcripts.

Transcript requests by student only.

North Hennepin Community College, Registrar, 7411 85th Ave N, Brooklyn Park, MN 55445, 612-424-0719 (FAX: 612-424-0929). Hours: 8AM-7PM M-Th, 8AM-4:30PM F. Records go back to 1966. Degrees granted: Associate.

Attendance and degree information available by phone, FAX, mail. Search requires name only. Other helpful information: social security number, date of birth, approximate years of attendance. No fee for information.

Transcripts available by FAX, mail. Search requires name plus signed release. Other helpful information: social security number, date of birth, approximate years of attendance. No fee for transcripts.

North Idaho College, Registrar, Coeur D' Alene, ID 83814, 208-769-3320 (FAX: 208-769-3292). Hours: 7:30AM-5PM M-Th; 7:30AM-2:30PM F. Records go back to 1933. Degrees granted: Associate.
 Attendance information available by FAX, mail. Search requires name only. Other helpful information: social security number, date of birth, approximate years of attendance. No fee for information.
 Degree information available by phone, FAX, mail. Search requires name only. Other helpful information: social security number, date of birth, approximate years of attendance. No fee for information.
 Transcripts available by FAX, mail. Search requires name plus signed release. Other helpful information: social security number, date of birth, approximate years of attendance. Fee is $2.00.

North Iowa Area Community College, Registrar, 500 College Dr, Mason City, IA 50401, 515-421-4205 (FAX: 515-423-1711). Hours: 7:45AM-4:15PM. Records go back to 1918. Degrees granted: Associate.
 Attendance and degree information available by phone, FAX, mail. Search requires name plus social security number, exact years of attendance, signed release. Other helpful information: date of birth, approximate years of attendance. No fee for information. Include stamped envelope.
 Transcripts available by FAX, mail. Search requires name plus social security number, exact years of attendance, signed release. Other helpful information: date of birth, approximate years of attendance. Fee is $2.00.
 Major credit cards accepted for payment.

North Lake College, Registrar, 5001 N MacArthur Blvd, Irving, TX 75038-3899, 214-659-5220. Hours: 8AM-8PM M-Th; 8AM-4:30PM F. Records go back to 1977. Degrees granted: Associate.
 Attendance and degree information available by mail. Search requires name plus social security number. No fee for information.
 Transcripts available by mail. Search requires name plus social security number, signed release. No fee for transcripts.

North Park College and Theological Seminary, Registrar, 3225 W Foster Ave, Chicago, IL 60625-4895, 312-244-5560 (FAX: 312-583-0858). Hours: 8AM-4:30PM. Records go back to 1886. Alumni records are maintained here also. Call 312-244-5754. Degrees granted: Bachelors; Masters. Certification: Teacher.
 Attendance information available by phone, FAX, mail. Search requires name plus social security number, date of birth. Other helpful information: approximate years of attendance. No fee for information.
 Degree information available by phone, FAX, mail. Search requires name plus social security number, date of birth, approximate years of attendance. No fee for information.
 Transcripts available by FAX, mail. Search requires name plus social security number, date of birth, approximate years of attendance, signed release. Fee is $5.00. Expedited service available for $20.00.

North Seattle Community College, Registrar, 9600 College Way N, Seattle, WA 98103, 206-527-3669. Hours: 8AM-4:30PM. Records go back to 1970. Alumni records are maintained here also. Call 206-527-3604. Degrees granted: Associate.
 Attendance and degree information available by phone, mail. Search requires name plus social security number. No fee for information.
 Transcripts available by mail. Search requires name plus social security number, signed release. Fee is $1.00.

North Shore Community College, Registrar, One Ferncroft Rd, Danvers, MA 01923-4093, 508-762-4000 (FAX: 508-762-4021). Hours: 8AM-4PM. Records go back to 1965. Degrees granted: Associate.
 Attendance and degree information available by phone, FAX, mail. Search requires name plus social security number, approximate years of attendance. Other helpful information: date of birth, exact years of attendance. No fee for information.
 Transcripts available by mail. Search requires name plus social security number, approximate years of attendance, signed release. Other helpful information: date of birth, exact years of attendance. Fee is $1.00.

Northampton County Area Community College, Registrar, 3835 Green Pond Rd, Bethlehem, PA 18017, 610-861-5494 (FAX: 610-861-5551). Hours: 8AM-7PM M-Th, 8AM-4PM F; Summer closed on Friday. Records go back to 1967. Alumni records are maintained here also. Call 610-861-5453. Degrees granted: Associate.
 Attendance and degree information available by phone, FAX, mail. Search requires name plus social security number. No fee for information.
 Transcripts available by FAX, mail. Search requires name plus social security number, signed release. Fee is $2.00.

Northeast Alabama State Community College, Registrar, PO Box 159, Hwy 35, Rainsville, AL 35986, 205-638-4418 X238. Hours: 8AM-4:30PM. Records go back to 1965. Degrees granted: Associate. Adverse incident record source: Admissions, 205-638-4418 X222.
 Attendance and degree information available by mail. Search requires name plus social security number, signed release. No fee for information.
 Transcripts available by mail. Search requires name plus social security number, signed release. No fee for transcripts.

Northeast Community College, Registrar, 801 E Benjamin Ave, PO Box 469, Norfolk, NE 68702-0469, 402-644-0415. Hours: 8AM-5PM. Records go back to 1928. Alumni records are maintained here also. Call 402-644-0463. Degrees granted: Associate.
 Attendance and degree information available by mail. Search requires name plus social security number, signed release. Other helpful information: approximate years of attendance. No fee for information.
 Transcripts available by mail. Search requires name plus social security number, signed release. Other helpful information: approximate years of attendance. Fee is $1.00.

Northeast Institute of Education, Registrar, PO Box 470, 314 Adams Ave, Scranton, PA 18501-0470, 717-346-6666. Hours: 8AM-5PM. Records go back to 1936. Alumni records are maintained here at the same phone number. Degrees granted: Bachelors; Masters.

Attendance and degree information available by phone, mail. Search requires name plus social security number, exact years of attendance. No fee for information.

Transcripts available by mail. Search requires name plus social security number, exact years of attendance, signed release. Fee is $4.00.

Northeast Institute of Education, (Branch), Registrar, Fountain Ct Rte 611 Box 574, Bartonsville, PA 18321, 717-629-5555. Records are not housed here. They are located at Northeast Institute of Education, Registrar, PO Box 470, 314 Adams Ave, Scranton, PA 18501-0470.

Northeast Iowa Community College, Registrar, Box 400 Hwy 150, Calmar, IA 52132, 319-562-3263 X233 (FAX: 319-562-3719). Hours: 7:30AM-4PM. Records go back to 1967. Alumni records are maintained here also. Call 319-562-3263 X300. Degrees granted: Associate.

Attendance and degree information available by phone, FAX, mail. Search requires name plus social security number, signed release. No fee for information.

Transcripts available by mail. Search requires name plus social security number, signed release. Fee is $2.00.

Northeast Louisiana University, Registrar, 700 University Ave, Monroe, LA 71209, 318-342-5262 (FAX: 318-342-5274). Hours: 8AM-4:30PM. Records go back 64 years. Degrees granted: Associate; Bachelors; Masters; Doctorate. Adverse incident record source: Student Life, 318-342-5230.

Attendance and degree information available by phone, FAX, mail. Search requires name plus social security number, date of birth. Other helpful information: approximate years of attendance. No fee for information.

Transcripts available by mail. Search requires name plus social security number, signed release. Other helpful information: approximate years of attendance. No fee for transcripts.

Northeast Metro Technical College, Registrar, 3300 Century Ave N, White Bear Lake, MN 55110, 612-779-5827 (FAX: 612-779-5779). Hours: 7:30AM-4PM. Records go back to 1971. Degrees granted: Associate.

Attendance information available by phone, FAX, mail. Search requires name plus social security number, approximate years of attendance. Other helpful information: exact years of attendance. No fee for information.

Degree information available by phone, FAX, mail. Search requires name plus social security number. Other helpful information: approximate years of attendance. No fee for information.

Transcripts available by phone, FAX, mail. Search requires name plus social security number, signed release. Other helpful information: approximate years of attendance. Fee is $2.00.

Northeast Mississippi Community College, Registrar, Cunningham Blvd, Booneville, MS 38829, 601-728-7751 (FAX: 601-728-1165). Hours: 8AM-4:30PM. Records go back to 1948. Alumni records are maintained here also. Call 601-720-7300. Degrees granted: Associate.

Attendance and degree information available by phone, FAX, mail. Search requires name plus social security number, approximate years of attendance, signed release. No fee for information.

Transcripts available by mail. Search requires name plus social security number, approximate years of attendance, signed release. First transcript is free. Additional ones are $2.00 each.

Northeast Missouri State University, Registrar, Kirksville, MO 63501, 816-785-4143 (FAX: 816-785-4181). Hours: 8AM-5PM. Records go back to 1867. Degrees granted: Bachelors; Masters.

Attendance and degree information available by phone, FAX. Search requires name plus social security number, approximate years of attendance. Other helpful information: date of birth. No fee for information.

Transcripts available by FAX, mail. Search requires name plus social security number, approximate years of attendance, signed release. Other helpful information: date of birth. Fee is $2.00. Expedited service available for $2.00.

Degree & major helpful. Major credit cards accepted for payment.

Northeast State Technical Community College, Registrar, PO Box 246, 2425 Hwy 75, Blountville, TN 37617-0246, 615-323-3191. Degrees granted: Associate.

Attendance and degree information available by phone, FAX, mail. Search requires name plus social security number. Other helpful information: date of birth, approximate years of attendance. No fee for information.

Transcripts available by mail. Search requires name plus social security number, signed release. Other helpful information: date of birth, approximate years of attendance. No fee for transcripts.

Northeast Texas Community College, Registrar, PO Drawer 1307, Mount Pleasant, TX 75456-1307, 903-572-1911 (FAX: 903-572-6712). Hours: 8AM-6PM M-Th; 8AM-Noon F. Records go back to 1985. Degrees granted: Associate.

Attendance and degree information available by phone, FAX, mail. Search requires name only. No fee for information.

Transcripts available by FAX, mail. Search requires name plus signed release. Fee is $2.00.

Major credit cards accepted for payment.

Northeast Wisconsin Technical College, Registrar, PO Box 19042, 2740 W Mason St, Green Bay, WI 54307, 414-498-5579 (FAX: 414-498-6242). Hours: 8AM-5PM. Records go back to 1913. Alumni records are maintained here also. Call 414-498-5426. Degrees granted: Associate.

Attendance and degree information available by phone, mail. Search requires name plus social security number. No fee for information.

Transcripts available by mail. Search requires name plus social security number, signed release. No fee for transcripts.

Northeastern Illinois University, Admissions and Records, 5500 N St Louis Ave, Chicago, IL 60625, 312-583-4050 (FAX: 312-794-6246). Hours: 8:30AM-4:30PM. Records go back to 1962. Alumni Records Office: 5350 St Louis Ave, Chicago, IL 60625. Degrees granted: Bachelors; Masters. Adverse incident record source: Dean of Students, 312-583-4050 X 3167.

Attendance and degree information available by phone, FAX, mail. Search requires name only. Other helpful information: social security number, approximate years of attendance. No fee for information.

Transcripts available by FAX, mail. Search requires name plus signed release. Other helpful information: social security number, approximate years of attendance. Fee is $10.00.

Northeastern Junior College, NJC Records Office, 100 College Dr, Sterling, CO 80751, 970-522-6600 X767 (FAX: 970-

522-4945). Hours: 8AM-4:30PM. Records go back 7 years. Degrees granted: Associate.

Attendance and degree information available by written request only. Search requires name plus social security number, date of birth, signed release. Other helpful information: approximate years of attendance. No fee for information.

Transcripts available by written request only. Search requires name plus social security number, date of birth, signed release. Other helpful information: approximate years of attendance. Fee is $5.00. Expedited service available for $9.00.

Northeastern Ohio Universities College of Medicine, Registrar, 4209 State Rte 44, PO Box 95, Rootstown, OH 44272-0095, 216-325-2511 (FAX: 216-325-0522). Hours: 7:30AM-5PM. Records go back to 1977. Alumni records are maintained here at the same phone number.

Attendance and degree information available by phone, FAX, mail. Search requires name only. Other helpful information: exact years of attendance. No fee for information.

Transcripts available by FAX, mail. Search requires name plus signed release. Other helpful information: social security number. Fee is $2.00. Expedited service available for $5.00.

Northeastern Oklahoma A&M College, Registrar, 200 I St NE, Miami, OK 74354, 918-542-8441 (FAX: 918-542-9759). Hours: 8AM-4:30PM. Records go back to 1940s. Alumni records are maintained here also. Call 918-542-8441 X385. Degrees granted: Associate.

Attendance and degree information available by phone, mail. Search requires name plus social security number, date of birth. Other helpful information: approximate years of attendance. No fee for information.

Transcripts available by mail. Search requires name plus social security number, date of birth, signed release. Other helpful information: approximate years of attendance. Fee is $2.00.

Northeastern State University, Registrar, Tahlequah, OK 74464, 918-456-5511 X2200. Hours: 8AM-Noon, 1-5PM. Degrees granted: Bachelors; Masters.

Attendance and degree information available by mail. Search requires name plus social security number, date of birth. Other helpful information: approximate years of attendance. No fee for information.

Transcripts available by mail. Search requires name plus social security number, date of birth, signed release. Other helpful information: approximate years of attendance. No fee for transcripts.

Northeastern University, Transcripts Office, 117 Hayden Hall, 360 Huntington Ave, Boston, MA 02115, 617-373-5411 (FAX: 617-373-5351). Hours: 8:30AM-4:30PM. Records go back to 1945. Degrees granted: Associate; Bachelors; Masters; Doctorate.

Attendance and degree information available by phone, mail. Search requires name plus social security number, approximate years of attendance, signed release. Other helpful information: date of birth, exact years of attendance. No fee for information.

Transcripts available by mail. Search requires name plus social security number, approximate years of attendance, signed release. Other helpful information: date of birth, exact years of attendance. Fee is $2.00. Expedited service available for $11.00.

Northern Arizona University, Registrar, Box 4103, Flagstaff, AZ 86011-4092, 602-523-2108. Hours: 8AM-5PM Fall/Spring; 7:30AM-4:30PM Summer. Records go back to 1900.

Degrees granted: Bachelors; Masters; Doctorate. Adverse incident record source: Campus Safety & Security, 602-523-3611.

Attendance information available by phone, mail. Search requires name plus social security number, approximate years of attendance, signed release. Other helpful information: date of birth. No fee for information.

Degree information available by mail. Search requires name plus social security number, approximate years of attendance, signed release. Other helpful information: date of birth, exact years of attendance. No fee for information.

Transcripts available by mail. Search requires name plus social security number, date of birth, approximate years of attendance, signed release. Other helpful information: exact years of attendance. Fee is $5.00. Expedited service available for $5.00.

Major credit cards accepted for payment.

Northern Baptist Theological Seminary, Registrar, 660 E Butterfield Rd, Lombard, IL 60148, 708-620-2105 (FAX: 708-620-2194). Hours: 8:30AM-4:30PM. Degrees granted: Masters; Doctorate.

Attendance and degree information available by written request only. Search requires name plus signed release. Other helpful information: social security number, date of birth, approximate years of attendance. No fee for information.

Transcripts available by written request only. Search requires name plus signed release. Other helpful information: social security number, date of birth, approximate years of attendance. Fee is $5.00.

Northern Essex Community College, Registrar, 100 Elliott Way, Haverhill, MA 01830-2399, 508-374-3700 (FAX: 508-374-3729). Hours: 8AM-8PM M-Th; 8AM-4PM F. Records go back to founding date. Degrees granted: Associate.

Attendance information available by phone, mail. Search requires name plus social security number, date of birth, signed release. Other helpful information: approximate years of attendance. Fee is $1.00. Expedited service available for $1.00.

Degree information available by phone, FAX, mail. Search requires name plus social security number, date of birth, signed release. Other helpful information: approximate years of attendance. Fee is $1.00. Expedite service available for $1.00.

Transcripts available by written request only. Search requires name plus social security number, date of birth, signed release. Other helpful information: approximate years of attendance. Fee is $1.00. Expedited service available for $1.00.

Major credit cards accepted for payment.

Northern Illinois University, Office of Registration & Records, Altgeld Hall Rm 212, De Kalb, IL 60115, 815-743-0689 (FAX: 815-743-0149). Hours: 8AM-4:30PM. Records go back to 1899. Alumni records are maintained here also. Call 815-753-1452. Degrees granted: Bachelors; Masters; Doctorate.

Attendance and degree information available by phone, FAX, mail. Search requires name plus social security number. Other helpful information: date of birth, approximate years of attendance. Fee is $3.50.

Transcripts available by FAX, mail. Search requires name plus social security number, signed release. Other helpful information: date of birth, approximate years of attendance. Fee is $5.00.

Northern Kentucky University, Office of Registrar, Service Center LAC 301, Highland Heights, KY 41099-7011, 606-572-5556. Hours: 8:15AM-6:15PM M-Th; 8:15AM-4:30PM F. Records go back to 1970. Alumni records are maintained here

The Sourcebook of College and University Student Records

also. Call 606-572-5486. Degrees granted: Associate; Bachelors; Masters. Adverse incident record source: Dean of Students, 606-572-5500.

Attendance and degree information available by phone, mail. Search requires name plus social security number. Other helpful information: approximate years of attendance. No fee for information.

Transcripts available by FAX, mail. Search requires name plus social security number, signed release. No fee for transcripts.

Northern Maine Technical College, Registrar, 33 Edgemont Dr, Presque Isle, ME 04769, 207-768-2791 (FAX: 207-768-2831). Hours: 8AM-5PM. Records go back to founding date. Graduate and Withdrawal files - 5 years. Alumni records are maintained here also. Call 207-768-2808. Degrees granted: Associate.

Attendance and degree information available by phone, FAX, mail. Search requires name only. Other helpful information: social security number, approximate years of attendance. No fee for information.

Transcripts available by FAX, mail. Search requires name plus signed release. Other helpful information: social security number, approximate years of attendance. Fee is $2.00. Expedited service available for $25.00.

Major credit cards accepted for payment.

Northern Michigan University, Records Office, 301 Cohodas Bldg, 1401 Presque isle Ave, Marquette, MI 49855-5323, 906-227-2278 (FAX: 906-227-2231). Hours: 8AM-5PM. Alumni records are maintained here at the same phone number. Degrees granted: Associate; Bachelors; Masters. Adverse incident record source: Dean of Students, 906-227-1700.

Attendance and degree information available by phone, mail. Search requires name plus social security number. Other helpful information: date of birth, approximate years of attendance. No fee for information.

Transcripts available by FAX, mail. Search requires name plus social security number, signed release. Other helpful information: date of birth, approximate years of attendance. Fee is $4.00. Expedited service available for $10.00.

FAX requests must contain picture ID, signature and prepayment of unstated fee via Mastercard or Visa. Credit card: $10.00 minimum.

Northern Montana College, Registrar, PO Box 7751, Havre, MT 59501, 406-265-3700. Records go back to founding date. Alumni records are maintained here also. Call 406-265-3791. Degrees granted: Bachelors; Masters.

Attendance and degree information available by phone, mail. Search requires name plus social security number, date of birth. Other helpful information: approximate years of attendance. No fee for information.

Transcripts available by written request only. Search requires name plus social security number, date of birth, exact years of attendance, signed release. Other helpful information: approximate years of attendance. No fee for transcripts.

Northern Nevada Community College, Registrar, 901 Elm St, Elko, NV 89801, 702-753-2272 (FAX: 702-753-2311). Hours: 8AM-5PM. Records go back to 1969. Degrees granted: Associate.

Attendance information available by phone, FAX, mail. Search requires name plus social security number. No fee for information.

School will not confirm degree information. Search requires name plus social security number, signed release. No fee for information.

Transcripts available by mail. Search requires name plus social security number, signed release. Fee is $2.00. Expedited service available for $3.00.

Northern New Mexico Community College, Registrar, 1002 N Onate St, Espanola, NM 87532, 505-747-2112 (FAX: 505-747-2180). Hours: 8AM-5PM M,W,Th; 8AM-6PM T,F. Records go back to 1970. Degrees granted: Associate.

Attendance and degree information available by FAX, mail. Search requires name plus social security number, date of birth, approximate years of attendance, signed release. No fee for information.

Transcripts available by mail. Search requires name plus social security number, date of birth, approximate years of attendance, signed release. Fee is $2.00.

Northern Oklahoma College, Registrar, PO Box 310, 1220 E Grand Ave, Tonkawa, OK 74653-0310, 405-628-2581 (FAX: 405-628-5260). Hours: 8AM-5PM. Degrees granted: Associate.

Attendance and degree information available by mail. Search requires name plus social security number, date of birth. No fee for information.

Transcripts available by mail. Search requires name plus social security number, date of birth, signed release. Fee is $1.00.

Northern State University, Registrar, 1200 S Jay St, Aberdeen, SD 57401, 605-626-2012. Hours: 8AM-5PM; 7:30AM-4:30PM Summer. Records go back to 1902. Alumni records are maintained here at the same phone number. Degrees granted: Associate; Bachelors; Masters. Adverse incident record source: Student Affairs, 605-626-2530.

Attendance and degree information available by phone, FAX, mail. Search requires name plus signed release. Other helpful information: social security number, date of birth, approximate years of attendance. No fee for information.

Transcripts available by FAX, mail. Search requires name plus signed release. Other helpful information: social security number, date of birth, approximate years of attendance. Fee is $4.00. Expedited service available for $6.00.

Northern Virginia Community College, (Alexandria Campus), Registrar, 3001 N Beauregard St, Alexandria, VA 22311, 703-845-6200. Hours: 8AM-5:30PM. Records go back to 1970s. Degrees granted: Associate.

Attendance and degree information available by phone, mail. Search requires name plus social security number. No fee for information.

Transcripts available by written request only. Search requires name plus social security number, signed release. No fee for transcripts.

Northern Virginia Community College, (Annandale Campus), Registrar, 8333 Little River Tpke, Annandale, VA 22003, 703-323-3328 (FAX: 703-323-3367). Hours: 9AM-6PM M-Th, 9AM-4PM F. Records go back to 1965. Alumni records are maintained here also. Call 703-323-3747. Degrees granted: Associate.

Attendance and degree information available by phone, mail. Search requires name plus social security number. No fee for information.

Degree Granting Institutions

Transcripts available by mail. Search requires name plus social security number, signed release. No fee for transcripts.

Northern Virginia Community College, (Loudon Campus), Registrar, 1000 Harry Flood Byrd Hwy, Sterling, VA 22170, 703-450-2500. Hours: 8AM-5:30PM. Records go back to 1974. Alumni records are maintained here also. Call 703-323-2364. Degrees granted: Associate.

Attendance and degree information available by phone, mail. Search requires name plus social security number. No fee for information.

Transcripts available by written request only. Search requires name plus social security number, signed release. No fee for transcripts.

Northern Virginia Community College, (Manassas Campus), Registrar, 6901 Sudley Rd, Manassas, VA 22110, 703-257-6600. Hours: 8AM-5:30PM. Records go back to 1970s. Degrees granted: Associate.

Attendance and degree information available by phone, mail. Search requires name plus social security number. No fee for information.

Transcripts available by written request only. Search requires name plus social security number, signed release. No fee for transcripts.

Northern Virginia Community College, (Woodbridge Campus), Registrar, 15200 Neabsco Mills Rd, Woodbridge, VA 22191, 703-878-5700. Hours: 8AM-5PM. Records go back to 1970s. Degrees granted: Associate.

Attendance and degree information available by phone, mail. Search requires name plus social security number. No fee for information.

Transcripts available by written request only. Search requires name plus social security number, signed release. No fee for transcripts.

Northern Wyoming Community College District, (Gillette Campus), Registrar, 720 W 8th St, Gillette, WY 82716, 307-686-0254 X403 (FAX: 307-687-7141). Hours: 8AM-5PM. Degrees granted: Associate.

Attendance and degree information available by phone, FAX, mail. Search requires name plus social security number, date of birth. Other helpful information: approximate years of attendance. No fee for information.

Transcripts available by phone, FAX, mail. Search requires name plus social security number, date of birth. Other helpful information: approximate years of attendance. Fee is $1.00.

Major credit cards accepted for payment.

Northland College, Registrar, 1411 Ellis Ave, Ashland, WI 54806, 715-682-1227 (FAX: 715-682-1308). Hours: 8AM-Noon, 1-4PM. Records go back to 1892. Alumni records are maintained here also. Call 715-682-1497. Degrees granted: Bachelors.

Attendance and degree information available by phone, mail. Search requires name plus social security number, date of birth. Other helpful information: approximate years of attendance. No fee for information.

Transcripts available by written request only. Search requires name plus social security number, date of birth, signed release. Other helpful information: approximate years of attendance. Fee is $4.00. Expedited service available for $14.00.

Major credit cards accepted for payment.

Northland Community College, Registrar, Hwy 1 E, Thief River Falls, MN 56701, 218-681-0701 (FAX: 218-681-0724). Hours: 8AM-4:30PM. Records go back to 1965. Degrees granted: Associate.

Attendance and degree information available by phone, FAX, mail. Search requires name plus social security number, date of birth. No fee for information.

Transcripts available by phone, FAX, mail. Search requires name plus social security number, date of birth, signed release. No fee for transcripts.

Northland Pioneer College, Registrar, 103 First Ave at Hope Dr, PO Box 610, Holbrook, AZ 86025, 520-524-1993 (FAX: 520-524-1997). Hours: 8AM-5PM. Records go back to 1975. Degrees granted: Associate. Certification: CAS.

Attendance and degree information available by FAX, mail. Search requires name plus social security number, signed release. Other helpful information: approximate years of attendance. No fee for information.

Transcripts available by FAX, mail. Search requires name plus social security number, signed release. Other helpful information: date of birth, approximate years of attendance. Fee is $3.00.

Major credit cards accepted for payment.

Northwest Arkansas Community College, Registrar, PO Box 1408, Bentonville, AR 72712, 501-636-7202 (FAX: 501-636-7036). Hours: 8AM-5:30PM. Records go back to 1990. Degrees granted: Associate. Special programs- Nursing, 501-631-9762. Adverse incident record source: Student Services.

Attendance and degree information available by FAX, mail. Search requires name only. Other helpful information: social security number. No fee for information.

Transcripts available by mail. Search requires name plus social security number, signed release. Other helpful information: approximate years of attendance. Fee is $2.00.

Major credit cards accepted for payment.

Northwest Christian College, Registrar, 828 E 11th Ave, Eugene, OR 97401, 503-343-1641 X15 (FAX: 503-343-9159). Hours: 8AM-5PM. Records go back to 1895. Alumni records are maintained here also. Call 503-343-1641. Adverse incident record source: Registrar, 503-343-1641.

Attendance information available by phone, FAX, mail. Search requires name plus social security number. No fee for information.

Degree information available by phone, FAX, mail. Search requires name plus social security number, exact years of attendance. No fee for information.

Transcripts available by FAX, mail. Search requires name plus social security number, exact years of attendance, signed release. Fee is $6.00.

Major credit cards accepted for payment.

Northwest College, Registrar, 231 W Sixth St, Powell, WY 82435, 307-754-3149 (FAX: 307-754-6700). Hours: 8AM-5PM. Records go back to 1946. Degrees granted: Associate.

Attendance information available by phone, FAX, mail. Search requires name plus social security number, date of birth, approximate years of attendance. No fee for information.

Degree information available by phone, FAX, mail. Search requires name plus social security number, date of birth, approximate years of attendance. No fee for information.

Transcripts available by mail. Search requires name plus social security number, date of birth, approximate years of attendance. Fee is $1.00.

Northwest College of the Assemblies of God, Registrar, PO Box 579, Kirkland, WA 98083, 206-822-8266 X5230 (FAX: 206-827-0148). Hours: 8AM-4:30PM. Records go back to 1934. Alumni records are maintained here also. Call 206-889-5206. Degrees granted: Bachelors.

Attendance and degree information available by phone, FAX, mail. Search requires name plus social security number, exact years of attendance. No fee for information.

Transcripts available by mail. Search requires name plus social security number, exact years of attendance, signed release. Fee is $3.00.

Northwest Indian College, Registrar, 2522 Kwina Rd, Bellingham, WA 98226, 206-676-2772. Hours: 8AM-4:30PM. Records go back to 1948. Degrees granted: Associate; Bachelors.

Attendance and degree information available by phone, mail. Search requires name plus social security number, exact years of attendance. No fee for information.

Transcripts available by mail. Search requires name plus social security number, exact years of attendance, signed release. Fee is $3.00.

Northwest Institute of Acupuncture and Oriental Medicine, Registrar, 1307 N 45th St, Seattle, WA 98103, 206-633-2419 (FAX: 206-633-5578). Hours: 9AM-6PM M-Th. Records go back to 1981. Degrees granted: Masters.

Attendance and degree information available by phone, FAX, mail. Search requires name only. Other helpful information: date of birth, approximate years of attendance. No fee for information.

Transcripts available by mail. Search requires name plus signed release. Other helpful information: social security number, date of birth, approximate years of attendance. Fee is $3.00.

Major credit cards accepted for payment.

Northwest Iowa Community College, Registrar, 603 W Park St, Sheldon, IA 51201, 712-324-5061 X115 (FAX: 712-324-4136). Hours: 8AM-4:30PM. Records go back to 1967. Alumni records are maintained here also. Call 712-324-5061 X110. Degrees granted: Associate. Adverse incident record source: Dean, 712-324-5061 X122.

Attendance and degree information available by phone, FAX, mail. Search requires name plus social security number, approximate years of attendance, signed release. No fee for information.

Transcripts available by FAX, mail. Search requires name plus social security number, approximate years of attendance, signed release. Fee is $2.00.

Northwest Mississippi Community College, Registrar, 510 N Panola, Senatobia, MS 38668, 601-562-3219 (FAX: 601-562-3221). Hours: 8AM-4:30PM. Records go back to 1900. Alumni records are maintained here also. Call 602-562-3222. Degrees granted: Associate.

Attendance information available by mail. Search requires name plus social security number, approximate years of attendance, signed release. Other helpful information: date of birth. No fee for information.

Degree information available by phone, FAX, mail. Search requires name plus social security number, approximate years of attendance. Other helpful information: date of birth. No fee for information.

Transcripts available by written request only. Search requires name plus social security number, approximate years of attendance, signed release. Other helpful information: date of birth. Fee is $2.00.

Northwest Missouri State University, Registrar, 800 University Dr, Maryville, MO 64468-6001, 816-562-1151 (FAX: 816-562-1993). Hours: 8AM-5PM. Degrees granted: Bachelors; Masters. Adverse incident record source: Dean of Students, 816-562-1154.

Attendance and degree information available by phone, FAX, mail. Search requires name plus social security number. Other helpful information: date of birth, approximate years of attendance. No fee for information.

Transcripts available by FAX, mail. Search requires name plus social security number, signed release. Other helpful information: date of birth, approximate years of attendance. Fee is $3.00.

Northwest Nazarene College, Office of the Registrar, Dewey at Holly Sts, Nampa, ID 83686, 208-467-8541 (FAX: 208-467-1098). Hours: 8AM-5PM. Records go back to 1913. Degrees granted: Associate; Bachelors; Masters.

Attendance and degree information available by phone, FAX, mail. Search requires name only. Other helpful information: social security number, date of birth, approximate years of attendance. No fee for information.

Transcripts available by FAX, mail. Search requires name plus signed release. Other helpful information: social security number, date of birth, approximate years of attendance. No fee for transcripts.

Northwest Shoals Community College, Registrar, PO Box 2545, George Wallace Blvd, Muscle Shoals, AL 35662, 205-331-5200 (FAX: 205-331-5366). Hours: 7:30AM-4PM. Records go back to 1963. Degrees granted: Associate. Special programs- Some records at Phil Campbell, AL, 205-3.

Attendance and degree information available by FAX, mail. Search requires name plus social security number, approximate years of attendance, signed release. Other helpful information: date of birth. No fee for information.

Transcripts available by mail. Search requires name plus social security number, approximate years of attendance, signed release. Other helpful information: date of birth. No fee for transcripts.

Major credit cards accepted for payment.

Northwest Technical College, Registrar, 22-600 State Rte 34, Archbold, OH 43502, 419-267-5511 (FAX: 419-267-2688). Hours: 8AM-4PM. Records go back to 1965. Degrees granted: Associate.

Attendance information available by phone, FAX, mail. Search requires name plus social security number. No fee for information.

Degree information available by mail. Search requires name plus social security number. No fee for information.

Transcripts available by mail. Search requires name plus social security number. Fee is $2.00.

Northwest Technical College, Registrar, Hwy 200 N, PO Box 111, East Grand Forks, MN 56721, 218-773-3441 (FAX: 218-773-4502). Hours: 8AM-5PM. Records go back to 1972. Degrees granted: Associate.

Attendance information available by phone, FAX, mail. Search requires name plus social security number, signed release. Other

helpful information: date of birth, approximate years of attendance. No fee for information.

Degree information available by phone, FAX, mail. Search requires name plus social security number, date of birth, signed release. Other helpful information: approximate years of attendance. No fee for information.

Transcripts available by FAX, mail. Search requires name plus social security number, date of birth, signed release. Other helpful information: approximate years of attendance. No fee for transcripts.

Northwest Technical College-Moorhead, Registrar, 1900 28th Ave S, Moorhead, MN 56560, 218-299-6593 (FAX: 218-236-0342). Hours: 9AM-4PM. Records go back to 1970. Degrees granted: Associate. Adverse incident record source: Dean of Students, 218-299-6503.

Attendance and degree information available by phone, FAX, mail. Search requires name plus social security number, signed release. No fee for information.

Transcripts available by FAX, mail. Search requires name plus social security number, signed release. No fee for transcripts.

Northwest Technical Institute, Registrar, 11995 Singletree Lane, Eden Prairie, MN 55344-5351, 612-944-0080 (FAX: 612-944-9274). Hours: 8AM-5PM. Records go back 38 years. Degrees granted: Associate.

Attendance and degree information available by phone, FAX, mail. Search requires name plus signed release. No fee for information.

Transcripts available by phone, FAX, mail. Search requires name plus signed release. No fee for transcripts.

Northwestern Business College, Registrar, 4829 N Lipps Ave, Chicago, IL 60630, 312-777-4220 (FAX: 312-777-2861). Hours: 8AM-4PM. Alumni records are maintained here at the same phone number. Degrees granted: Associate.

Attendance and degree information available by FAX, mail. Search requires name plus social security number, date of birth, approximate years of attendance, signed release. No fee for information.

Transcripts available by mail. Search requires name plus social security number, date of birth, approximate years of attendance, signed release. First transcript is free. Additional ones are $3.00 each.

Northwestern Business College, (Southwestern), Registrar, 8020 W 87th St, Hickory Hills, IL 60457, 708-430-0990 (FAX: 708-430-0995). Hours: 8AM-8PM. Records go back to founding date.

Attendance and degree information available by phone, mail. Search requires name plus social security number, date of birth, signed release. Other helpful information: approximate years of attendance. No fee for information.

Transcripts available by FAX, mail. Search requires name plus social security number, date of birth, signed release. Other helpful information: approximate years of attendance. Fee is $3.00.

Northwestern College, Registrar, 1441 N Cable Rd, Lima, OH 45805, 419-998-3141 (FAX: 419-229-6926). Hours: 7:30AM-4:30PM. Records go back to 1925. Degrees granted: Associate.

Attendance and degree information available by phone, FAX, mail. Search requires name only. Other helpful information: social security number, approximate years of attendance. No fee for information.

Transcripts available by FAX, mail. Search requires name plus signed release. Other helpful information: social security number, approximate years of attendance. Fee is $3.00. Expedited service available for $3.00.

Major credit cards accepted for payment.

Northwestern College, Registrar, 101 7th SW, Orange City, IA 51041, 712-737-7145 (FAX: 712-737-7117). Hours: 8AM-5PM. Records go back to 1888. Alumni records are maintained here also. Call 712-737-7106. Degrees granted: Associate; Bachelors; Masters. Adverse incident record source: Student Affairs, 712-737-7200.

Attendance and degree information available by phone, FAX, mail. Search requires name plus social security number, approximate years of attendance, signed release. No fee for information.

Transcripts available by FAX, mail. Search requires name plus social security number, approximate years of attendance, signed release. Fee is $2.00.

Northwestern College, Registrar, 3003 N Snelling Ave, St Paul, MN 55113, 612-631-5248 (FAX: 612-631-5124). Hours: 8:15AM-4PM. Records go back to 1900. Degrees granted: Associate; Bachelors. Certification: Biblical Arts.

Attendance information available by phone, FAX, mail. Search requires name plus social security number, approximate years of attendance. Other helpful information: date of birth, exact years of attendance. No fee for information.

Degree information available by phone, FAX, mail. Search requires name plus approximate years of attendance. Other helpful information: social security number, exact years of attendance. No fee for information.

Transcripts available by FAX, mail. Search requires name plus social security number, signed release. Other helpful information: date of birth, approximate years of attendance. Fee is $1.00.

Northwestern College, Registrar, 1300 Western Ave, Watertown, WI 53094, 414-261-4352 (FAX: 414-262-8118). Records are not housed here. They are located at Martin Luther College, Registrar, 1995 Luther Ct, New Ulm, MN 56073.

Northwestern College of Chiropractic, Registrar, 2501 W 84th St, Bloomington, MN 55431-1599, 612-888-4777 (FAX: 612-888-6713). Hours: 8AM-4:30PM. Records go back to 1941. Alumni records are maintained here at the same phone number. Degrees granted: Bachelors; First Professional.

Attendance and degree information available by phone, FAX, mail. Search requires name plus social security number, date of birth, signed release. Other helpful information: approximate years of attendance. No fee for information.

Transcripts available by FAX, mail. Search requires name plus social security number, date of birth, signed release. Other helpful information: approximate years of attendance. Fee is $10.00.

Need student ID number.

Northwestern Connecticut Community-Technical College, Registrar, Park Place E, Winsted, CT 06098, 203-738-6314 (FAX: 203-379-4465). Hours: 8:30AM-4:30PM. Records go back to 1965. Alumni records are maintained here also. Call 203-738-6349. Degrees granted: Associate.

Attendance information available by FAX, mail. Search requires name plus social security number, approximate years of attendance, signed release. No fee for information.

Degree information available by phone, FAX, mail. Search requires name plus social security number, approximate years of attendance, signed release. No fee for information.

Transcripts available by FAX, mail. Search requires name plus social security number, approximate years of attendance, signed release. No fee for transcripts.

Northwestern Michigan College, Records Office, 1701 E Front St, Traverse City, MI 49686-3061, 616-922-1047 (FAX: 616-922-1570). Hours: 8AM-5PM. Records go back to 1951. Degrees granted: Associate. Adverse incident record source: Student Services, 616-922-1031.

Attendance and degree information available by phone, FAX, mail. Search requires name only. Other helpful information: social security number, approximate years of attendance. No fee for information.

Transcripts available by FAX, mail. Search requires name plus social security number, signed release. Other helpful information: approximate years of attendance. Fee is $2.00.

FAX request for transcript must include credit card number and expiration date. Major credit cards accepted for payment.

Northwestern Oklahoma State University, Registrar, 709 Oklahoma Blvd, Alva, OK 73717, 405-327-8553 (FAX: 405-327-1881). Hours: 8AM-5PM. Records go back to 1897. Degrees granted: Bachelors; Masters. Adverse incident record source: Dean of Students, 405-327-8414: Alva Police, 405-327-2121

Attendance and degree information available by phone, FAX, mail. Search requires name only. Other helpful information: social security number, date of birth, approximate years of attendance. No fee for information.

Transcripts available by FAX, mail. Search requires name plus signed release. Other helpful information: social security number, date of birth, approximate years of attendance. Fee is $2.00.

Northwestern State University, Registrar, College Ave, Natchitoches, LA 71497, 318-357-6171 (FAX: 318-357-5823). Hours: 8AM-4:30PM. Records go back to 1885. Alumni records are maintained here at the same phone number. Degrees granted: Associate; Bachelors; Masters; Doctorate. Certification: Teacher.

Attendance information available by phone, FAX, mail. Search requires name only. Other helpful information: social security number, date of birth, approximate years of attendance. No fee for information.

Degree information available by phone, FAX, mail. Search requires name plus exact years of attendance. Other helpful information: social security number, date of birth, approximate years of attendance. No fee for information.

Transcripts available by mail. Search requires name plus exact years of attendance, signed release. Other helpful information: social security number, date of birth, approximate years of attendance. No fee for transcripts.

Northwestern University, Registrar, 633 Clark St, Evanston, IL 60208, 708-491-5234 (FAX: 708-491-8458). Hours: 8:30AM-5PM. Records go back to 1882. Alumni Records Office: Alumni Agency, 1800 Sheridan Rd, Evanston, IL 60208. Degrees granted: Bachelors; Masters; Doctorate. Adverse incident record source: Student Affairs, 708-491-8430.

Attendance and degree information available by phone, FAX, mail. Search requires name only. Other helpful information: social security number, date of birth, approximate years of attendance. No fee for information.

Transcripts available by FAX, mail. Search requires name plus signed release. Other helpful information: social security number, date of birth, approximate years of attendance. Fee is $3.00. Expedited service available for $7.00.

Northwood University, Registrar, 3225 Cook Rd, Midland, MI 48640, 517-837-4216 (FAX: 517-832-9590). Hours: 8:30AM-5PM. Records go back to 1959. Degrees granted: Associate; Bachelors; Masters. Adverse incident record source: Dean of Students, 517-837-4398.

Attendance and degree information available by phone, FAX, mail. Search requires name plus social security number. Other helpful information: date of birth, approximate years of attendance. No fee for information.

Transcripts available by mail. Search requires name plus social security number, signed release. Other helpful information: date of birth, approximate years of attendance. Fee is $2.00.

Northwood University, (Branch), Registrar, 1114 W FM 1382, PO Box 58, Cedar Hill, TX 75104, 214-291-1541 (FAX: 214-291-3824). Hours: 8AM-5PM. Records go back to 1946. Alumni records are maintained here at the same phone number. Degrees granted: Associate; Bachelors.

Attendance and degree information available by phone, mail. Search requires name plus social security number. No fee for information.

Transcripts available by mail. Search requires name plus social security number, signed release. Fee is $2.00.

Northwood University, (Branch), Registrar, 2600 N Military Trail, West Palm Beach, FL 33409, 407-478-5500 (FAX: 407-640-3328). Hours: 9AM-5PM. Records go back 10 years. Degrees granted: Associate; Bachelors.

Attendance information available by phone, mail. Search requires name plus social security number, signed release. Other helpful information: approximate years of attendance. No fee for information.

Degree information available by phone, mail. Search requires name plus social security number, approximate years of attendance, signed release. No fee for information.

Transcripts available by mail. Search requires name plus social security number, approximate years of attendance, signed release. Fee is $2.00.

Norwalk Community-Technical College, Registrar, 188 Richards Ave, Norwalk, CT 06854, 203-857-7035 (FAX: 203-857-7012). Hours: 9AM-6:30PM M-Th; 9AM-4PM F. Records go back to 1960.

Attendance and degree information available by FAX, mail. Search requires name plus social security number, signed release. Other helpful information: date of birth, approximate years of attendance. No fee for information.

Transcripts available by mail. Search requires name plus social security number, signed release. Other helpful information: date of birth, approximate years of attendance. No fee for transcripts.

Norwich University, Registrar, Northfield, VT 05663, 802-485-2035 (FAX: 802-485-2042). Hours: 8AM-4:30PM. Alumni records are maintained here at the same phone number. Degrees granted: Associate; Bachelors; Masters. Special programs-Graduate Programs & Adult Degree BA, 802-828-8725.

Attendance and degree information available by phone, FAX, mail. Search requires name plus date of birth. Other helpful information: social security number, approximate years of attendance. No fee for information. Expedited service available for $2.50.

Transcripts available by mail. Search requires name plus social security number, date of birth, signed release. Other helpful information: approximate years of attendance. Fee: $4.00 to $7.00. Expedited service available for $10.00.

Notre Dame College, Registrar, 2321 Elm St, Manchester, NH 03104-2299, 603-669-4298 (FAX: 603-644-8316). Hours: 8AM-5PM. Records go back to 1950. Alumni records are maintained here also. Call 603-669-4298. Degrees granted: Associate; Bachelors; Masters. Certification: Early Childhood Paralegal.

Attendance and degree information available by FAX, mail. Search requires name plus signed release. Other helpful information: social security number, date of birth, approximate years of attendance. No fee for information.

Transcripts available by FAX, mail. Search requires name plus signed release. Other helpful information: social security number, date of birth, approximate years of attendance. Fee is $3.00.

Notre Dame College, Registrar, 4545 College Rd, South Euclid, OH 44121, 216-381-1680 X243 (FAX: 216-381-3802). Hours: 8:30AM-4:30PM. Records go back to 1922. Alumni records are maintained here at the same phone number. Degrees granted: Associate; Bachelors; Masters. Certification: Bus. Admin., Gerontology. Adverse incident record source: Geri Cahill, 216-381-1680 X204.

Attendance and degree information available by phone, mail. Search requires name only. Other helpful information: social security number, approximate years of attendance. No fee for information.

Transcripts available by phone, mail. Search requires name plus signed release. Other helpful information: social security number, approximate years of attendance. Fee is $4.00.

Notre Dame Seminary Graduate School of Theology, Registrar, 2901 S Carrollton Ave, New Orleans, LA 70118, 504-866-7426. Hours: 8AM-4PM. Records go back to 1950. Degrees granted: Masters.

Attendance information available by mail. Search requires name plus signed release. Other helpful information: social security number. No fee for information.

Degree information available by written request only. Search requires name plus signed release. Other helpful information: social security number. No fee for information.

Transcripts available by mail. Search requires name plus signed release. Other helpful information: social security number. Fee is $2.00.

Nova University, Registrar, 3301 College Ave, Fort Lauderdale, FL 33314, 305-475-7300 (FAX: 305-475-7621). Hours: 8:30AM-7PM M-Th, 8:30AM-6PM F. Records go back to 1967. Alumni records are maintained here at the same phone number. Degrees granted: Bachelors; Masters; Doctorate. Adverse incident record source: Registrar, 305-475-7300.

Attendance and degree information available by FAX, mail. Search requires name plus social security number. No fee for information.

Transcripts available by mail. Search requires name plus social security number, signed release. Fee is $5.00.

Nunez Community College, (Branch), Registrar, 901 Delery St, New Orleans, LA 70117, 504-278-7440 X222 (FAX: 504-278-7353). Hours: 8AM-7PM M-W 8AM-4:30PM Th,F. Records go back to 1970. Degrees granted: Associate.

Attendance and degree information available by phone, FAX, mail. Search requires name plus social security number, signed release. Other helpful information: approximate years of attendance. No fee for information.

Transcripts available by FAX, mail. Search requires name plus social security number, signed release. Other helpful information: approximate years of attendance. First transcript is free. Additional ones are $3.00 each.

Nyack College, Registrar, One South Blvd, Nyack, NY 10960-3698, 914-358-1710 X121 (FAX: 914-353-6429). Hours: 8:30AM-4:30PM M,T,Th,F; 8AM-Noon W. Records go back to 1910. Alumni records are maintained here also. Call 914-358-1710 X361. Degrees granted: Associate; Bachelors. Special programs- Adult Degree Completion, 914-358-1710 X572. Adverse incident record source: Student Development, 914-358-1710.

Attendance and degree information available by phone, FAX, mail. Search requires name only. Other helpful information: social security number, approximate years of attendance. No fee for information.

Transcripts available by FAX, mail. Search requires name plus social security number, approximate years of attendance, signed release. Other helpful information: exact years of attendance. Fee is $5.00. Expedited service available for $3.00.

O

O'More College of Design, Registrar, 423 S Margin St, PO Box 908, Franklin, TN 37065, 615-794-4254 (FAX: 615-790-1662). Hours: 8AM-4:30PM. Records go back to 1970. Alumni records are maintained here at the same phone number. Degrees granted: Bachelors.

Attendance and degree information available by phone, mail. Search requires name plus exact years of attendance. No fee for information.

Transcripts available by mail. Search requires name plus exact years of attendance, signed release. Fee is $2.00.

Oak Hills Bible College, Registrar, 1600 Oak Hills Rd SW, Bemidji, MN 56601, 218-751-8670w (FAX: 218-751-8825). Hours: 8AM-5PM. Records go back to 1940s. Degrees granted: Associate; Bachelors. Certification: 1 year Bible.

Attendance information available by phone, FAX, mail. Search requires name plus date of birth, signed release. Other helpful information: social security number, approximate years of attendance. No fee for information.

Degree information available by phone, FAX, mail. Search requires name plus date of birth, signed release. Other helpful information: social security number, approximate years of attendance. No fee for information.

Transcripts available by mail. Search requires name plus date of birth, signed release. Other helpful information: social security number, approximate years of attendance. No fee for transcripts. Include a self addressed stamped envelope with mail request.

Oakland City College, Registrar, 143 N Lucretia St, Oakland City, IN 47660, 812-749-1238 (FAX: 812-749-1233). Hours: 8AM-Noon, 1-4:30PM. Alumni records are maintained here also. Call 812-749-1223. Degrees granted: Associate; Bachelors; Masters.

Attendance and degree information available by phone, FAX, mail. Search requires name only. Other helpful information: social security number, date of birth, approximate years of attendance. No fee for information.

Transcripts available by FAX, mail. Search requires name plus signed release. Other helpful information: social security number, date of birth, approximate years of attendance. Fee is $2.00. Expedited service available for $5.00.

$5.00 for FAX.

Oakland Community College, Registrar, 2480 Opdyke Rd, Bloomfield Hills, MI 48304-2266, 810-540-1548 (FAX: 810-540-1841). Hours: 8AM-8PM M-Th, 8AM-5PM F. Records go back to 1960. Alumni records are maintained here also. Call 810-540-1803. Degrees granted: Associate. Adverse incident record source: Records Office, 810-540-1500.

Attendance and degree information available by phone, FAX, mail. Search requires name plus social security number, signed release. No fee for information.

Transcripts available by mail. Search requires name plus social security number, signed release. Fee is $2.00.

Oakland Community College, **(Auburn Hills)**, Registrar, 2480 Pldyke Rd, Bloomfield Hills, MI 48304, 810-540-1589 (FAX: 810-540-1841). Hours: 8:30AM-5PM. Records go back to 1965. Degrees granted: Associate.

Attendance and degree information available by phone, FAX, mail. Search requires name plus signed release. Other helpful information: social security number, approximate years of attendance. No fee for information.

Transcripts available by mail. Search requires name plus signed release. Other helpful information: social security number, approximate years of attendance. Fee is $2.00. Expedited service available for $11.00.

Oakland Community College, **(Highland Lakes)**, Registrar, 7350 Cooley Lake Rd, Waterford, MI 48327-4187, 313-540-1500. Records are not housed here. They are located at Oakland Community College, Registrar, 2480 Opdyke Rd, Bloomfield Hills, MI 48304-2266.

Oakland Community College, **(Orchard Ridge)**, Registrar, 27055 Orchard Lake Rd, Farmington Hills, MI 48334, 810-540-1548 (FAX: 810-540-1841). Records are not housed here. They are located at Oakland Community College, Registrar, 2480 Opdyke Rd, Bloomfield Hills, MI 48304-2266.

Oakland Community College, **(Southfield)**, Attn Records, 2480 Opdyke Rd, Bloomfield Hills, MI 48304-2266, 810-540-1548 (FAX: 810-548-1841). Hours: 8:30AM-5PM. Records go back to 1965. Alumni records are maintained here also. Call 810-258-4417. Degrees granted: Associate.

Attendance and degree information available by written request only. Search requires name plus social security number, signed release. Other helpful information: date of birth, approximate years of attendance. No fee for information.

Transcripts available by mail. Search requires name plus social security number, signed release. Other helpful information: date of birth, approximate years of attendance. Fee is $2.00. Expedited service available for $2.00.

Release forms required for confirmations.

Oakland University, Academic Records Office, 102 O'Dowd Hall, Rochester, MI 48309-4401, 810-370-3452 (FAX: 810-370-3461). Hours: 8AM-5PM M,T,Th,F; 8AM-6:30PM W. Records go back to 1959. Alumni Records Office: John Dodge House, Rochester, MI 48309-4401, 810-370-2158. Degrees granted: Bachelors; Masters; Doctorate. Special programs- Continuing Education, 810-370-3120. Adverse incident record source: Dean of Students, 810-370-3352: OU Police, 810-370-3331

Attendance and degree information available by phone, FAX, mail. Search requires name only. Other helpful information: social security number, date of birth, approximate years of attendance. No fee for information.

Transcripts available by FAX, mail. Search requires name plus signed release. Other helpful information: social security number, date of birth, approximate years of attendance. Fee is $5.00. Expedited service available for $10.00.

Oakton Community College, Registrar, 1600 E Golf Rd, Des Plaines, IL 60016, 708-635-1991 (FAX: 708-635-1706). Hours: 8:30AM-8PM M-Th, 8:30AM-5PM F, 9AM-Noon Sat Fall;8:30AM-8PM M-Th Summer. Records go back to 1970. Degrees granted: Associate. Adverse incident record source: Public Safety, 708-635-1880.

Attendance and degree information available by phone, FAX, mail. Search requires name plus social security number, signed release. No fee for information.

Transcripts available by FAX, mail. Search requires name plus social security number, signed release. No fee for transcripts.

Oakwood College, Registrar, Oakwood Rd NW, Huntsville, AL 35896, 205-726-7346 (FAX: 205-726-7199). Hours: 9AM-4PM M-Th, 9AM-Noon F. Records go back to 1896. Alumni records are maintained here also. Call 205-726-7039. Degrees granted: Associate; Bachelors. Adverse incident record source: Student Affairs, 205-726-7400 X7400.

Attendance and degree information available by phone, FAX, mail. Search requires name plus social security number, date of birth. No fee for information.

Transcripts available by FAX, mail. Search requires name plus social security number, date of birth, signed release. Transcripts are $2.00 for official copy or $1.00 for unofficial copy.

Oberlin College, Registrar, Oberlin, OH 44074, 216-775-8450 (FAX: 216-775-8800). Hours: 8AM-4:30PM. Records go back to 1985. Alumni records are maintained here also. Call 216-775-8692. Degrees granted: Bachelors; Masters; Performance Diploma. Special programs- Student Health Office, 216-775-1651. Adverse incident record source: Student Support, 216-775-8464.

Attendance and degree information available by phone, FAX, mail. Search requires name plus approximate years of attendance, signed release. No fee for information.

Transcripts available by mail. Search requires name plus approximate years of attendance, signed release. Fee is $4.00.

Oblate College, Registrar, 391 Michigan Ave NE, Washington, DC 20017-1587, 202-529-6544. Hours: 9AM-3PM. Records go back to 1950. Degrees granted: Bachelors; Masters. Adverse incident record source: Dean, 202-529-6544.

Attendance information available by phone, mail. Search requires name plus signed release. No fee for information.

Degree information available by mail. Search requires name plus signed release. No fee for information.

Transcripts available by mail. Search requires name plus signed release. Fee is $5.00.

Oblate School of Theology, Registrar, 285 Oblate Dr, San Antonio, TX 78216-6693, 210-341-1366 X212. Hours: 8AM-Noon, 1-3PM. Records go back to 1930s. Degrees granted: Masters; Doctorate.

Attendance and degree information available by mail. Search requires name plus social security number, date of birth, signed release. Other helpful information: approximate years of attendance. Fee is $3.00.

Transcripts available by mail. Search requires name plus social security number, date of birth, signed release. Other helpful information: approximate years of attendance. Fee is $3.00.

Occidental College, Registrar, 1600 Campus Rd, Los Angeles, CA 90041-3314, 213-259-2686 (FAX: 213-259-2958). Hours: 8AM-5PM. Records go back to 1887. Degrees granted: Bachelors; Masters.

Attendance and degree information available by phone, FAX, mail. Search requires name only. Other helpful information: social security number, date of birth, approximate years of attendance. No fee for information.

Transcripts available by mail. Search requires name plus signed release. Other helpful information: social security number, date of birth, exact years of attendance. No fee for transcripts.

Ocean County College, Admissions & Records, College Dr/PO Box 2001, Toms River, NJ 08754-2001, 9083-255-0304. Hours: 8AM-9PM M-Th; 8AM-5PM F. Records go back to founding date. Alumni records are maintained here also. Call 908-255-0400. Degrees granted: Associate.

Attendance and degree information available by mail. Search requires name plus social security number, signed release. Other helpful information: date of birth, approximate years of attendance. No fee for information.

Transcripts available by mail. Search requires name plus social security number, signed release. Other helpful information: date of birth, approximate years of attendance. Fee is $3.00.

Odessa College, Registrar, 201 W University Blvd, Odessa, TX 79764, 915-335-6404 (FAX: 915-335-6303). Hours: 8AM-4:30PM. Degrees granted: Associate.

Attendance and degree information available by FAX, mail. Search requires name plus social security number, date of birth, exact years of attendance, signed release. No fee for information.

Transcripts available by FAX, mail. Search requires name plus social security number, date of birth, exact years of attendance, signed release. Fee is $1.00.

Oglala Lakota College, Registrar, PO Box 490, Kyle, SD 57752, 605-455-2321 X236 (FAX: 605-455-2787). Hours: 8:30AM-5PM. Records go back to 1978. Degrees granted: Associate; Bachelors; Masters.

Attendance information available by phone, FAX, mail. Search requires name plus social security number, signed release. Other helpful information: approximate years of attendance. No fee for information.

Degree information available by phone, mail. Search requires name plus social security number, signed release. Other helpful information: approximate years of attendance. No fee for information.

Transcripts available by FAX, mail. Search requires name plus social security number, signed release. Other helpful information: approximate years of attendance. Fee is $2.00.

Oglethorpe University, Registrar, 4484 Peachtree Rd NE, Atlanta, GA 30319-2797, 404-364-8315 (FAX: 404-364-8500). Hours: 8:30AM-5PM. Records go back to 1916. Degrees granted: Bachelors; Masters. Certification: Teacher Cert.

Attendance and degree information available by phone, FAX, mail. Search requires name plus date of birth. Other helpful information: social security number, approximate years of attendance. No fee for information.

Transcripts available by mail. Search requires name plus signed release. Other helpful information: social security number, approximate years of attendance. Fee is $2.00.

Ohio College of Podiatric Medicine, Student Records, 10515 Carnegie Ave, Cleveland, OH 44106, 216-231-3300 X348 (FAX: 216-231-1005). Hours: 9AM-4PM. Records go back to 1917. Degrees granted: Doctorate.

Attendance and degree information available by phone, FAX, mail. Search requires name plus approximate years of attendance. Other helpful information: social security number, exact years of attendance. No fee for information.

Transcripts available by FAX, mail. Search requires name plus approximate years of attendance. Other helpful information: social security number, exact years of attendance. Fee is $2.00.

Ohio Dominican College, Registrar's Office, 1216 Sunbury Rd, Columbus, OH 43219, 614-251-4650 (FAX: 614-252-0776). Hours: 8AM-4:30PM. Records go back to 1911. Degrees granted: Associate; Bachelors.

School will not confirm attendance information. Search requires name plus signed release. Other helpful information: social security number, date of birth, approximate years of attendance. No fee for information.

Degree information available by phone, FAX, mail. Search requires name only. Other helpful information: social security number, date of birth, approximate years of attendance. No fee for information.

Transcripts available by written request only. Search requires name plus approximate years of attendance, signed release. Other helpful information: social security number, date of birth, exact years of attendance. Fee is $3.00. Expedited service available for $10.00.

Major credit cards accepted for payment.

Ohio Northern University, Registrar, 525 S Main St, Ada, OH 45810, 419-772-2024. Hours: 8AM-5PM. Records go back to 1871. Alumni records are maintained here also. Call 419-772-2038. Degrees granted: Bachelors; Parm D, TD.

Attendance and degree information available by phone, mail. Search requires name plus social security number. Other helpful information: date of birth, approximate years of attendance. No fee for information.

Transcripts available by mail. Search requires name plus social security number, signed release. Other helpful information: date of birth, approximate years of attendance. Fee is $4.00. Expedited service available for $8.00.

Ohio State University, Registrar, 190 N Oval Dr, Columbus, OH 43210, 614-292-8500 (FAX: 614-292-2363). Hours: 9:30AM-5PM M,T,Th,F; 9:30AM-6PM W. Records go back to 1873. Alumni Records Office: Alumni House, 567 Fawcett Center, 2400 Olintangy Rd, Columbus, OH 43201. Degrees granted: Bachelors; Masters; Doctorate; Medical.

The Sourcebook of College and University Student Records

Attendance information available by phone, FAX, mail. Search requires name plus social security number, exact years of attendance. No fee for information.

Degree information available by phone, FAX, mail. Search requires name plus social security number. No fee for information.

Transcripts available by FAX, mail. Search requires name plus social security number, date of birth, approximate years of attendance, signed release. Fee is $5.00. Expedited service available for $10.00. Include a stamped envelope.

Ohio State University, (Agricultural Technical Institute), Registrar, 1328 Dover Rd, Wooster, OH 44691, 216-264-3911. Records are not housed here. They are located at Ohio State University, Registrar, 190 N Oval Dr, Columbus, OH 43210.

Ohio State University, (Lima), Registrar, 4240 Campus Dr, Lima, OH 45804, 419-221-1641. Records are not housed here. They are located at Ohio State University, Registrar, 190 N Oval Dr, Columbus, OH 43210.

Ohio State University, (Mansfield), Registrar, 1680 University Dr, Mansfield, OH 44906, 419-755-4011. Records are not housed here. They are located at Ohio State University, Registrar, 190 N Oval Dr, Columbus, OH 43210.

Ohio State University, (Marion), Registrar, 1465 Mount Vernon Ave, Marion, OH 43302, 614-389-2361. Records are not housed here. They are located at Ohio State University, Registrar, 190 N Oval Dr, Columbus, OH 43210.

Ohio State University, (Newark), Registrar, University Dr, Newark, OH 43055, 614-366-3321. Records are not housed here. They are located at Ohio State University, Registrar, 190 N Oval Dr, Columbus, OH 43210.

Ohio University, Registrar, Athens, OH 45701, 614-593-4180 (FAX: 614-593-4184). Hours: 8AM-5PM. Records go back to 1893. Alumni records are maintained here also. Call 614-593-4300. Degrees granted: Associate; Bachelors; Masters; PhD. Adverse incident record source: Legal Affairs, 614-593-2626.

Attendance and degree information available by phone, FAX, mail. Search requires name plus social security number, date of birth, approximate years of attendance, signed release. No fee for information.

Transcripts available by mail. Search requires name plus social security number, date of birth, approximate years of attendance, signed release. Fee is $2.00.

Major credit cards accepted for payment.

Ohio University, (Chillicothe), Student Records, Chillicothe, OH 45601, 614-774-7240 (FAX: 614-774-7214). Records are not housed here. They are located at Ohio University, Registrar, Athens, OH 45701.

Ohio University, (Eastern), Registrar, St Clairsville, OH 43950, 614-695-1720. Records are not housed here. They are located at Ohio University, Registrar, Athens, OH 45701.

Ohio University, (Lancaster), Registrar, 1570 Granville Pike, Lancaster, OH 43130, 614-654-6711. Records are not housed here. They are located at Ohio University, Registrar, Athens, OH 45701.

Ohio University, (Southern), Registrar, 1804 Liberty Ave, Ironton, OH 45638, 614-533-4600 (FAX: 614-533-4632). Hours: 9AM-6PM.

Attendance and degree information available by phone, FAX, mail. Search requires name plus social security number, date of birth, approximate years of attendance, signed release. No fee for information.

Transcripts available by mail. Search requires name plus social security number, date of birth, approximate years of attendance, signed release. No fee for transcripts.

Ohio University, (Zanesville), Registrar, Zanesville, OH 43701, 614-453-0762 (FAX: 614-453-6161). Records are not housed here. They are located at Ohio University, Registrar, Athens, OH 45701.

Ohio Valley Business College, Registrar, PO Box 7000, 500 Maryland Ave, East Liverpool, OH 43920, 216-385-1070 (FAX: 216-385-4606). Hours: 8AM-4PM. Records go back 75 years. Degrees granted: Associate. Special programs- Administration, 216-385-1070.

Attendance and degree information available by mail. Search requires name plus social security number. No fee for information.

Transcripts available by FAX, mail. Search requires name plus social security number. Fee is $1.00.

Ohio Valley College, Registrar, 4501 College Pkwy, Parkersburg, WV 26101, 304-485-7384 (FAX: 304-485-3106). Hours: 8AM-5PM. Records go back to 1960. Alumni records are maintained here also. Call 304-485-7384. Degrees granted: Associate; Bachelors. Special programs- NCJC records at King of Prussia, 610-337-7328. Adverse incident record source: Student Services, 304-485-7384: Parkersburg Police, 304-424-8444

Attendance and degree information available by phone, FAX, mail. Search requires name only. Other helpful information: social security number, date of birth, approximate years of attendance. No fee for information.

Transcripts available by FAX, mail. Search requires name plus signed release. Other helpful information: social security number, approximate years of attendance. Fee is $5.00.

Ohio Wesleyan University, Registrar, 61 S Sanusky St, Delaware, OH 43015, 614-368-3201 (FAX: 614-368-3299). Hours: 8:30AM-Noon, 1-5PM. Records go back 50 years. Degrees granted: Bachelors.

Attendance and degree information available by phone, FAX, mail. Search requires name only. Other helpful information: social security number, date of birth, approximate years of attendance. No fee for information.

Transcripts available by FAX, mail. Search requires name plus signed release. Other helpful information: social security number, date of birth, approximate years of attendance. No fee for transcripts.

Ohlone College, Admissions & Records, 43600 Mission Blvd, Fremont, CA 94539, 510-659-6100 (FAX: 510-659-6057). Hours: 9AM-8PM M-Th; 9AM-4PM F. Records go back 26 years. Degrees granted: Associate.

Attendance and degree information available by FAX, mail. Search requires name plus signed release. No fee for information.

Transcripts available by FAX, mail. Search requires name plus social security number, date of birth, signed release. Other helpful information: approximate years of attendance. Fee is $4.00. Expedited service available for $10.00.

Ohr Hameir Theological Seminary, Registrar, Furnace Woods Rd, PO Box 2130, Peekskill, NY 10566, 914-736-1500 (FAX: 914-736-1055). Hours: 8AM-4:30PM.

Attendance and degree information available by phone, mail. Search requires name plus social security number, exact years of attendance. No fee for information.

Transcripts available by mail. Search requires name plus social security number, exact years of attendance, signed release. No fee for transcripts.

Ohr Somayach Institutions, Registrar, 244 Route 306, PO Box 334, Monsey, NY 10952, 914-425-1370 (FAX: 914-425-8865). Records go back to 1985. Alumni Records Office: 115 S Gate Dr, Spring Valley, NY 10977. Degrees granted: Associate; Bachelors.

Attendance and degree information available by phone, mail. Search requires name plus social security number, date of birth, exact years of attendance. No fee for information.

Transcripts available by mail. Search requires name plus social security number, date of birth, exact years of attendance, signed release. Fee is $50.00. Expedited service available for $25.00.

Okaloosa-Walton Community College, Registrar, 100 College Blvd, Niceville, FL 32578, 904-678-5111. Degrees granted: Associate.

Attendance and degree information available by mail. Search requires name plus social security number, signed release. Other helpful information: date of birth, approximate years of attendance. No fee for information.

Transcripts available by mail. Search requires name plus social security number, signed release. Other helpful information: date of birth, approximate years of attendance. No fee for transcripts.

Oklahoma Baptist University, Registrar, OBU Box 61173, Shawnee, OK 74801, 405-878-2023 (FAX: 405-878-2046). Hours: 8AM-5PM. Records go back to 1910. Alumni Records Office: OBU Box 61275, Shawnee, OK 74801 405-878-2706. Degrees granted: Associate; Bachelors; Masters. Adverse incident record source: Dean of Students, 405-878-4206.

Attendance and degree information available by phone, FAX, mail. Search requires name plus social security number, date of birth. Other helpful information: approximate years of attendance. No fee for information.

Transcripts available by FAX, mail. Search requires name plus social security number, date of birth, signed release. Other helpful information: approximate years of attendance. No fee for transcripts.

FAX: $1.00 incoming, $0.50 outgoing.

Oklahoma Christian University of Science and Arts, Registrar, PO Box 11000, Oklahoma City, OK 73136, 405-425-5200 (FAX: 405-425-5208). Hours: 8AM-5PM. Records go back 45 years. Alumni records are maintained here also. Call 405-425-5120. Degrees granted: Bachelors; Masters. Adverse incident record source: Student Development, 405-425-5220.

Attendance and degree information available by phone, FAX, mail. Search requires name only. Other helpful information: social security number, date of birth, approximate years of attendance. No fee for information.

Transcripts available by FAX, mail. Search requires name plus signed release. Other helpful information: social security number, date of birth, approximate years of attendance. Fee is $2.00. Expedited service available for $5.00.

FAX: $5.00.

Oklahoma City Community College, Registrar, 7777 S May Ave, Oklahoma City, OK 73159, 405-682-7512 (FAX: 405-682-7521). Hours: 8AM-8PM M; 8AM-6PM T,W; 11:30AM-6PM Th; 8AM-5PM F. Records go back to 1990. Alumni records are maintained here also. Call 405-682-7523. Degrees granted: Associate. Adverse incident record source: Dean, 405-682-7590.

Attendance and degree information available by phone, FAX, mail. Search requires name plus social security number, approximate years of attendance, signed release. No fee for information.

Transcripts available by phone, FAX, mail. Search requires name plus social security number, date of birth, approximate years of attendance, signed release. No fee for transcripts.

Oklahoma City University, Registrar, 2501 N Blackwelder Ave, Oklahoma City, OK 73106, 405-521-5296 (FAX: 405-521-5029). Hours: 8AM-6PM M, 8AM-5PM T-F. Records go back to 1901. Alumni records are maintained here at the same phone number. Degrees granted: Bachelors; Masters.

Attendance information available by mail. Search requires name plus social security number, signed release. Other helpful information: date of birth. No fee for information.

Degree information available by phone, FAX, mail. Search requires name plus social security number, signed release. Other helpful information: date of birth. No fee for information.

Transcripts available by mail. Search requires name plus social security number, signed release. Other helpful information: date of birth. Fee is $6.00.

Oklahoma Junior College, Registrar, 2901 N Classen Ste 100, Oklahoma City, OK 73106, 405-524-3400 (FAX: 405-524-3165). Hours: 8AM-7PM. Records go back to 1985. Degrees granted: Associate.

Attendance and degree information available by phone, FAX, mail. Search requires name plus social security number, signed release. Other helpful information: approximate years of attendance. No fee for information.

Transcripts available by FAX, mail. Search requires name plus social security number, signed release. Other helpful information: approximate years of attendance. Fee is $2.00.

Oklahoma Panhandle State University, Registrar, Box 430, Goodwell, OK 73939, 405-349-2611 X223 (FAX: 405-349-2302). Hours: 8AM-4:30PM. Records go back to 1921. Alumni records are maintained here also. Call 405-349-2611. Degrees granted: Associate; Bachelors.

Attendance information available by phone, FAX, mail. Search requires name plus social security number. Other helpful information: date of birth, approximate years of attendance. No fee for information.

Degree information available by phone, FAX, mail. Search requires name only. Other helpful information: social security number, date of birth, approximate years of attendance. No fee for information.

Transcripts available by FAX, mail. Search requires name plus social security number, signed release. Other helpful information: date of birth. No fee for transcripts.

Oklahoma State University (Oklahoma City), Registrar, 900 N Portland Ave, Oklahoma City, OK 73107, 405-945-3291 (FAX: 405-945-3277). Hours: 8AM-6PM. Records go back to 1961. Alumni records are maintained here also. Call 405-945-8618. Degrees granted: Associate.

Attendance and degree information available by phone, FAX, mail. Search requires name plus social security number, date of birth, approximate years of attendance. No fee for information.

Transcripts available by FAX, mail. Search requires name plus social security number, date of birth, approximate years of attendance, signed release. Fee is $2.00.

Oklahoma State University (Okmulgee), Registrar, 1801 E Fourth St, Okmulgee, OK 74447, 918-756-6211 (FAX: 918-756-4157). Hours: 7:30AM-4:30PM. Alumni records are maintained here also. Call 918-756-6211. Degrees granted: Associate. Adverse incident record source: Student Services, 918-756-6211 X364.

Attendance information available by phone, FAX. Search requires name plus social security number, approximate years of attendance, signed release. No fee for information.

Degree information available by FAX, mail. Search requires name plus social security number, approximate years of attendance, signed release. No fee for information.

Transcripts available by FAX, mail. Search requires name plus social security number, approximate years of attendance, signed release. Transcripts $3.00 to $4.00; over four ordered at one time $1.00 each.

Oklahoma State University College of Osteopathic Medicine, Registrar, 1111 W 17th St, Tulsa, OK 74107, 800-677-1972 (FAX: 918-561-8243). Hours: 8AM-5PM. Records go back to 1977. Alumni records are maintained here also. Call 918-582-1972.

Attendance and degree information available by phone, FAX, mail. Search requires name plus social security number, approximate years of attendance, signed release. No fee for information.

Transcripts available by FAX, mail. Search requires name plus social security number, approximate years of attendance, signed release. Fee is $1.00.

Oklahoma State University, Registrar's Office, 103 Whitehurst, Stillwater, OK 74078, 405-744-6888 (FAX: 405-744-8426). Hours: 8AM-5PM. Records go back to 1900. Alumni Records Office: 212 Student Union, Stillwater, OK 74078 405-744-5368. Degrees granted: Bachelors; Masters; Doctorate. Adverse incident record source: Student Conduct Officer: University Counseling

Attendance and degree information available by phone, FAX, mail. Search requires name plus social security number, approximate years of attendance. Other helpful information: date of birth, exact years of attendance. No fee for information.

Transcripts available by FAX, mail. Search requires name plus social security number, approximate years of attendance, signed release. Other helpful information: date of birth, exact years of attendance. Fee is $3.00. Expedited service available for $9.00. Prepayment required. Additional fee for FAX. Major credit cards accepted for payment.

Old Dominion University, Registrar, 5215 Hampton Blvd, Norfolk, VA 23529, 804-683-4425 (FAX: 804-683-5357). Hours: 8AM-5PM. Records go back to 1930. Alumni records are maintained here also. Call 804-683-3097. Degrees granted: Bachelors; Masters; Doctorate.

Attendance and degree information available by phone, mail. Search requires name plus social security number, date of birth, exact years of attendance. No fee for information.

Transcripts available by mail. Search requires name plus social security number, date of birth, exact years of attendance, signed release. Fee is $5.00.

Olean Business Institute, Registrar, 301 N Union St, Olean, NY 14760, 716-372-7978 (FAX: 716-372-2120). Hours: 8AM-5PM. Records go back to 1960. Degrees granted: Associate.

Attendance information available by phone, FAX, mail. Search requires name plus social security number, approximate years of attendance. No fee for information.

Degree information available by phone, FAX, mail. Search requires name plus social security number, approximate years of attendance, signed release. No fee for information.

Transcripts available by phone, FAX, mail. Search requires name plus social security number, approximate years of attendance, signed release. Fee is $3.00.

Major credit cards accepted for payment.

Olive-Harvey College, Registrar, 10001 S Woodlawn Ave, Chicago, IL 60628, 312-291-6346 (FAX: 312-291-6304). Hours: 8AM-7PM. Records go back to 1961. Degrees granted: Associate. Adverse incident record source: Security, 312-291-6348.

Attendance information available by phone, FAX, mail. Search requires name plus social security number, approximate years of attendance, signed release. Other helpful information: date of birth, exact years of attendance. No fee for information.

Degree information available by FAX, mail. Search requires name plus social security number, approximate years of attendance, signed release. Other helpful information: date of birth, exact years of attendance. No fee for information.

Transcripts available by written request only. Search requires name plus social security number, approximate years of attendance, signed release. Other helpful information: date of birth, exact years of attendance. No fee for transcripts. Expedited service available for $10.00.

Major credit cards accepted for payment.

Olivet College, Registrar, Olivet, MI 49076, 616-749-7637 (FAX: 616-749-7178). Hours: 8:30AM-Noon, 1-5PM. Degrees granted: Bachelors. Adverse incident record source: Asst Dean of Students, 616-749-7116.

Attendance information available by phone, FAX, mail. Search requires name only. Other helpful information: social security number, approximate years of attendance. No fee for information.

Degree information available by phone, FAX, mail. Search requires name only. Other helpful information: social security number, date of birth, approximate years of attendance. No fee for information.

Transcripts available by mail. Search requires name plus exact years of attendance, signed release. Other helpful information: social security number, date of birth, approximate years of attendance. Fee is $2.00.

Olivet Nazarene University, Registrar, Kankakee, IL 60901, 815-939-5201 (FAX: 815-935-4992). Hours: 8AM-5PM. Records go back to 1907. Alumni records are maintained here also. Call 815-939-5258. Degrees granted: Associate; Bachelors; Masters.

Attendance and degree information available by phone, FAX, mail. Search requires name only. Other helpful information: social security number, date of birth, approximate years of attendance. No fee for information.

Transcripts available by FAX, mail. Search requires name plus signed release. Other helpful information: social security number,

date of birth, approximate years of attendance. No fee for transcripts. Expedited service available for $5.00.

Olney Central College, Registrar, 305 N West St, Olney, IL 62450, 618-395-4351 X2230 (FAX: 618-392-3293). Hours: 8AM-5PM Fall, 7:30AM-4PM Summer. Records go back to 1963. Alumni records are maintained here also. Call 618-395-4351 X2226. Degrees granted: Associate; Vocational.

Attendance and degree information available by phone, FAX, mail. Search requires name plus social security number, approximate years of attendance, signed release. No fee for information.

Transcripts available by FAX, mail. Search requires name plus social security number, approximate years of attendance, signed release. Fee is $2.00.

Olympic College, Registrar, 1600 Chester Ave, Bremerton, WA 98337, 206-474-4544 (FAX: 206-792-2135). Hours: 8AM-4:30PM. Degrees granted: Associate.

Attendance and degree information available by FAX, mail. Search requires name plus social security number, date of birth, signed release. No fee for information.

Transcripts available by FAX, mail. Search requires name plus social security number, date of birth, signed release. Fee is $2.00.

Onondaga Community College, Registration Office, Syracuse, NY 13215, 315-469-2357 (FAX: 315-469-6775). Hours: 8:30AM-4:30PM. Alumni records are maintained here at the same phone number. Degrees granted: Associate. Adverse incident record source: Campus Security, 315-469-2357 X2478.

Attendance and degree information available by phone, FAX, mail. Search requires name plus social security number. No fee for information.

Transcripts available by mail. Search requires name plus social security number, signed release. Fee is $5.00.

Oral Roberts University, Registrar, 7777 S Lewis Ave, Tulsa, OK 74171, 918-495-6549. Hours: 8AM-4:30PM. Records go back to 1960. Alumni records are maintained here also. Call 918-495-6627. Degrees granted: Bachelors; Masters; Doctorate.

Attendance and degree information available by phone, mail. Search requires name plus social security number, signed release. No fee for information.

Transcripts available by mail. Search requires name plus social security number, signed release. No fee for transcripts.

Orange Coast College, Student Records, 2701 Fairview Rd, PO Box 5005, Costa Mesa, CA 92628, 714-432-5771. Hours: 8:00AM-7PM M-Th; 8AM-3PM F. Degrees granted: Associate.

Attendance and degree information available by phone, mail. Search requires name only. Other helpful information: social security number, date of birth, approximate years of attendance. Fee is $3.00. Expedited service available for $5.00.

Transcripts available by mail. Search requires name only. Other helpful information: social security number, date of birth, approximate years of attendance. Fee is $3.00. Expedited service available for $5.00.

Orange County Community College, Registrar, 115 South St, Middletown, NY 10940, 914-343-1121 (FAX: 914-342-8662). Hours: 9AM-8PM M-Th;9AM-4:30PM F. Records go back to founding date. Alumni records are maintained here also. Call 914-344-6222. Degrees granted: Associate. Adverse incident record source: Campus Security, 914-341-4932.

Attendance information available by phone, FAX, mail. Search requires name plus social security number. Other helpful information: date of birth, approximate years of attendance. No fee for information.

Degree information available by phone, mail. Search requires name plus social security number. Other helpful information: date of birth, approximate years of attendance. No fee for information.

Transcripts available by mail. Search requires name plus social security number, date of birth, exact years of attendance, signed release. Fee is $3.00.

Walk-in transcripts available.

Orangeburg-Calhoun Technical College, Registrar, 3250 St Matthews Rd, Orangeburg, SC 29115, 803-536-0311 (FAX: 803-535-1388). Hours: 8:30AM-5PM. Records go back to 1968. Degrees granted: Associate. Adverse incident record source: Campus Security, 803-535-1336.

Attendance information available by phone, FAX, mail. Search requires name plus social security number, approximate years of attendance, signed release. Other helpful information: date of birth. No fee for information.

Degree information available by FAX, mail. Search requires name plus social security number, approximate years of attendance, signed release. Other helpful information: date of birth. No fee for information.

Transcripts available by FAX, mail. Search requires name plus social security number, approximate years of attendance, signed release. Other helpful information: date of birth. Fee is $3.00.

Prefer written requests. Major credit cards accepted for payment.

Oregon College of Oriental Medicine, Registrar, 10525 Cherry Blossom Dr, Portland, OR 97216, 503-253-3443. Hours: 9AM-5PM. Records go back to 1983. Degrees granted: Masters.

Attendance information available by phone, mail. Search requires name plus social security number. No fee for information.

Degree information available by phone, mail. Search requires name plus social security number, exact years of attendance. No fee for information.

Transcripts available by mail. Search requires name plus social security number, exact years of attendance, signed release. First transcript free; $5.00 per additional one.

Major credit cards accepted for payment.

Oregon Graduate Institute of Science and Technology, Registrar, PO Box 91000, 20000 NW Walker Rd, Portland, OR 97291-1000, 503-690-1121 (FAX: 503-690-1029). Hours: 8AM-5PM. Records go back to 1965. Degrees granted: Masters; Doctorate. Adverse incident record source: Registration, 503-690-1121.

Attendance information available by phone, mail. Search requires name plus social security number. No fee for information.

Degree information available by phone, mail. Search requires name plus social security number. Other helpful information: exact years of attendance. No fee for information.

Transcripts available by mail. Search requires name plus social security number, exact years of attendance, signed release. Fee is $4.00.

Major credit cards accepted for payment.

Oregon Health Sciences University, Registrar's Office L109A, 3181 SW SamJacksonPark Rd, Portland, OR 97201, 503-494-7800 (FAX: 503-494-4629). Hours: 7:30AM-4PM. Degrees granted: Bachelors; Masters; Ph.D.,DMD,MD. Special programs-School of Dentistry, 503-494-8825.

Attendance and degree information available by phone, FAX, mail. Search requires name only. Other helpful information: approximate years of attendance. No fee for information.

Transcripts available by mail. Search requires name plus signed release. Other helpful information: approximate years of attendance. Fee is $5.00.

Oregon Institute of Technology, Registrar, Klamath Falls, OR 97601-8801, 503-885-1300 (FAX: 503-885-1115). Hours: 8AM-5PM. Records go back to 1947. Alumni records are maintained here also. Call 503-885-1130. Degrees granted: Associate; Bachelors; Masters. Adverse incident record source: Security, 503-885-1111.

Attendance and degree information available by phone, FAX, mail. Search requires name plus date of birth. Other helpful information: social security number, approximate years of attendance. No fee for information.

Transcripts available by mail. Search requires name plus social security number, signed release. Other helpful information: date of birth, approximate years of attendance. Fee is $5.00.

Major credit cards accepted for payment.

Oregon Polytechnic Institute, Registrar, 900 SE Sandy Blvd, Portland, OR 97214, 503-234-9333 (FAX: 503-233-0195). Hours: 8AM-5PM. Records go back 49 years. Degrees granted: Associate.

School will not confirm attendance information. Search requires name plus approximate years of attendance, signed release. Other helpful information: social security number, exact years of attendance. No fee for information.

Degree information available by phone, FAX, mail. Search requires name plus approximate years of attendance, signed release. Other helpful information: social security number, exact years of attendance. No fee for information.

Transcripts available by mail. Search requires name plus approximate years of attendance, signed release. Other helpful information: social security number, exact years of attendance. Fee is $3.00.

Oregon State University, Registrar, Corvallis, OR 97331, 503-737-4331 (FAX: 503-737-2482). Hours: 8AM-5PM. Records go back to 1868. Alumni records are maintained here also. Call 503-737-2351. Degrees granted: Bachelors; Masters; Doctorate.

Attendance and degree information available by phone, FAX, mail. Search requires name only. Other helpful information: social security number. Fee is $3.00.

Transcripts available by FAX, mail. Search requires name plus signed release. Other helpful information: social security number. Fee is $3.00.

Orlando College, Registrar, 5421 Diplomat Cir, Orlando, FL 32810, 407-628-5870 (FAX: 407-628-1344). Hours: 10AM-7PM M-W; 8:30AM-7PM Th; 8:30AM-5PM F. Records go back 40 years. Degrees granted: Associate; Bachelors; Masters. Adverse incident record source: Dean's Office.

Attendance information available by phone, FAX, mail. Search requires name plus social security number. Other helpful information: approximate years of attendance. No fee for information.

Degree information available by phone, FAX, mail. Search requires name plus social security number. Other helpful information: approximate years of attendance. No fee for information.

Transcripts available by FAX, mail. Search requires name plus social security number, signed release. Other helpful information: approximate years of attendance. Fee is $2.00.

Orlando College, (Branch), Registrar, 2411 Sand Lake Rd, Orlando, FL 32809, 407-851-2525 (FAX: 407-851-1477). Hours: 9AM-7:30PM M-Th; 9AM-5PM F. Records go back 5 years. Degrees granted: Associate; Bachelors; Masters. Special programs- Prior to 1989, 407-628-5870.

School will not confirm attendance information. Search requires name only. No fee for information.

Degree information available by phone, mail. Search requires name plus social security number, signed release. Other helpful information: date of birth, approximate years of attendance. Fee is $2.00.

Transcripts available by written request only. Search requires name plus social security number, signed release. Other helpful information: date of birth, approximate years of attendance. Fee is $2.00.

Otero Junior College, Registrar, 1802 Colorado Ave, La Junta, CO 81050, 719-384-6833 (FAX: 719-384-6800). Hours: 7:30AM-9PM M-Th, 7:30AM-5PM F. Records go back to 1942. Degrees granted: Associate.

Attendance and degree information available by phone, FAX, mail. Search requires name plus social security number, approximate years of attendance, signed release. No fee for information.

Transcripts available by mail. Search requires name plus social security number, approximate years of attendance, signed release. Fee is $1.00.

Otis College of Art and Design, Office of Registration & Records, 2401 Wilshire Blvd, Los Angeles, CA 90057, 213-251-0510. Hours: 8:30AM-5PM. Records go back to 1950. Alumni records are maintained here also. Call 213-251-0522. Degrees granted: Bachelors; Masters. Adverse incident record source: Dean of Students, 213-251-0540.

Attendance information available by mail. Search requires name plus signed release. Other helpful information: social security number, date of birth, approximate years of attendance. No fee for information.

Degree information available by phone, mail. Search requires name plus signed release. Other helpful information: social security number, date of birth, approximate years of attendance. No fee for information.

Transcripts available by phone, mail. Search requires name plus date of birth, signed release. Other helpful information: social security number, approximate years of attendance. Fee is $5.00. Expedited service available for $25.00.

Major credit cards accepted for payment.

Ottawa University, Registrar, 1001 S Cedar #5, Ottawa, KS 66067-3399, 913-242-5200 X5582 (FAX: 913-242-7429). Hours: 8AM-Noon, 1-5PM. Alumni Records Office: 1001 S Cedar #16, Ottawa, KS 66067-3399 800-755-5200. Degrees granted: Bachelors; Masters.

Attendance and degree information available by phone, FAX, mail. Search requires name plus social security number. Other helpful information: date of birth, approximate years of attendance. No fee for information.

Transcripts available by FAX, mail. Search requires name plus social security number, signed release. Other helpful information: date of birth, approximate years of attendance. Fee is $3.00.

Major credit cards accepted for payment.

Otterbein College, Registrar, Westerville, OH 43081, 614-823-1350 (FAX: 614-823-1315). Hours: 8:30AM-5PM. Records go back to 1847. Alumni records are maintained here also. Call 614-823-1400. Degrees granted: Bachelors; Masters.

Attendance information available by phone, FAX, mail. Search requires name plus exact years of attendance. Other helpful information: social security number. No fee for information.

Degree information available by phone, FAX, mail. Search requires name only. Other helpful information: social security number. No fee for information.

Transcripts available by mail. Search requires name plus signed release. Other helpful information: social security number. Fee is $5.00.

Ouachita Baptist University, Registrar, OBU Box 3757, Arkadelphia, AR 71998-0001, 501-245-5578 (FAX: 501-245-5500). Hours: 8AM-5PM. Records go back to 1940s. Alumni records are maintained here at the same phone number. Alumni Records Office: Box 3762, Arkadelphia, AR 71998-0001. Degrees granted: Bachelors. Adverse incident record source: Dean of Students.

Attendance and degree information available by phone, FAX, mail. Search requires name only. Other helpful information: social security number, date of birth, exact years of attendance. No fee for information.

Transcripts available by FAX, mail. Search requires name plus signed release. Other helpful information: date of birth, exact years of attendance. Fee is $3.00.

Our Lady of Holy Cross College, Registrar, 4123 Woodland Dr, New Orleans, LA 70131, 504-394-7744. Hours: 8:30AM-5PM. Records go back to founding date. Degrees granted: Associate; Bachelors; Masters.

Attendance information available by phone, FAX, mail. Search requires name plus social security number, signed release. Other helpful information: approximate years of attendance. No fee for information.

Degree information available by written request only. Search requires name plus social security number, signed release. Other helpful information: date of birth, approximate years of attendance. No fee for information.

Transcripts available by written request only. Search requires name plus signed release. Other helpful information: social security number, date of birth, approximate years of attendance. Fee is $5.00.

Our Lady of the Lake University, Registrar, 411 SW 24th St, San Antonio, TX 78207-4689, 210-434-6711 X316 (FAX: 210-436-2314). Degrees granted: Bachelors; Masters; Doctorate.

Attendance and degree information available by phone, FAX, mail. Search requires name only. Other helpful information: social security number, date of birth, approximate years of attendance. No fee for information.

Transcripts available by FAX, mail. Search requires name plus signed release. Other helpful information: social security number, date of birth, approximate years of attendance. No fee for transcripts.

Owens Community College, Registrar, PO Box 10000, 30335 Oregon Rd, Toledo, OH 43699, 419-661-7323. Hours: 8AM-7:30PM M,Th; 8AM-5PM T,W; 8AM-4:30PM F. Records go back to 1965. Degrees granted: Associate.

Attendance information available by mail. Search requires name plus approximate years of attendance. Other helpful information: social security number, date of birth, exact years of attendance. No fee for information.

Degree information available by phone, FAX, mail. Search requires name plus approximate years of attendance. Other helpful information: social security number, date of birth, exact years of attendance. No fee for information.

Transcripts available by FAX, mail. Search requires name plus approximate years of attendance, signed release. Other helpful information: social security number, date of birth, exact years of attendance. Fee is $2.00.

Major credit cards accepted for payment.

Owens Community College, (Branch), Registrar, 300 Davis St, Findlay, OH 45840, 419-423-6827 (FAX: 419-423-0246). Hours: 8AM-5PM. Records go back 7 years. Degrees granted: Associate. Special programs- Toledo Campus, 419-661-7220.

Attendance information available by phone, FAX, mail. Search requires name plus social security number, approximate years of attendance, signed release. No fee for information.

Degree information available by FAX, mail. Search requires name plus social security number, approximate years of attendance, signed release. No fee for information.

Transcripts available by FAX, mail. Search requires name plus social security number, approximate years of attendance, signed release. Fee is $2.00.

Owensboro Community College, Registrar, 4800 New Hartford Rd, Owensboro, KY 42303, 502-686-4400 (FAX: 502-686-4496). Hours: 8AM-4:30PM. Records go back to 1986. Degrees granted: Associate.

Attendance and degree information available by FAX, mail. Search requires name plus social security number, signed release. Other helpful information: approximate years of attendance. No fee for information.

Transcripts available by FAX, mail. Search requires name plus social security number, signed release. Other helpful information: approximate years of attendance. Fee is $2.00. Expedited service available for $5.00.

Owensboro Junior College of Business, Registrar, 1515 E 18th St, Owensboro, KY 42303, 502-926-4040 X25. Hours: 7:30AM-4:30PM. Records go back to 1963. Degrees granted: Associate.

Attendance and degree information available by phone, mail. Search requires name plus social security number, exact years of attendance. No fee for information.

Transcripts available by mail. Search requires name plus social security number, exact years of attendance, signed release. Fee is $5.00.

Oxnard College, Registrar, 4000 S Rose Ave, Oxnard, CA 93033, 805-986-5810 (FAX: 805-986-5806). Hours: 8AM-5PM. Records go back to 1975. Alumni records are maintained here also. Call 805-986-5808. Degrees granted: Associate.

Attendance and degree information available by phone, FAX, mail. Search requires name plus social security number. No fee for information.

Transcripts available by mail. Search requires name plus social security number, signed release. Fee is $3.00.

Major credit cards accepted for payment.

Ozark Christian College, Registrar's Office, 1111 N Main St, Joplin, MO 64801, 417-624-2518 (FAX: 417-624-0090).

Hours: 8AM-5PM. Records go back to 1942. Alumni records are maintained here at the same phone number. Degrees granted: Associate; Bachelors.

Attendance and degree information available by phone, FAX, mail. Search requires name only. Other helpful information: social security number, date of birth, approximate years of attendance. No fee for information.

Transcripts available by FAX, mail. Search requires name plus signed release. Other helpful information: social security number, date of birth, approximate years of attendance. Fee is $2.00. Expedited service available for $10.00.

Ozarks Technical Community College, Registrar, 1417 N Jefferson Ave, Springfield, MO 65802, 417-895-7195 (FAX: 417-895-7161). Hours: 8AM-4:30PM. Records go back 30 years. Degrees granted: Associate.

Attendance and degree information available by mail. Search requires name plus social security number, approximate years of attendance, signed release. Other helpful information: date of birth, exact years of attendance. No fee for information.

Transcripts available by mail. Search requires name plus social security number, approximate years of attendance, signed release. Other helpful information: date of birth, exact years of attendance. Fee is $3.00.

Major credit cards accepted for payment.

P

Pace Institute, Registrar, 606 Court St, Reading, PA 19601, 610-375-1212 (FAX: 610-375-1924). Hours: 10AM-5PM two days, 7AM-3PM three days. This varies. Records go back to 1977. Degrees granted: Associate.

Attendance and degree information available by phone, FAX, mail. Search requires name plus social security number, approximate years of attendance. No fee for information.

Transcripts available by FAX, mail. Search requires name plus social security number, approximate years of attendance, signed release. No fee for transcripts.

Pace University, Registrar, One Pace Plaza, New York, NY 10038, 212-356-1315 (FAX: 212-356-1643). Hours: 9AM-5PM. Records go back to 1905. Degrees granted: Associate; Bachelors; Masters; Doctorate.

Attendance and degree information available by phone, FAX, mail. Search requires name plus social security number, exact years of attendance, signed release. Other helpful information: date of birth, approximate years of attendance. No fee for information.

Transcripts available by FAX, mail. Search requires name plus social security number, exact years of attendance, signed release. Other helpful information: date of birth, approximate years of attendance. No fee for transcripts.

Pace University, **(Pleasantville/Briarcliff)**, Registrar, 861 Bedford Rd, Pleasantville, NY 10570, 914-773-3200 (FAX: 914-773-3851). Hours: 9AM-5PM. Records go back to 1960s. Alumni records are maintained here at the same phone number. Degrees granted: Associate; Bachelors; Masters. Certification: Teaching. Adverse incident record source: Security, 914-773-3830.

Attendance and degree information available by phone, FAX, mail. Search requires name plus social security number. No fee for information.

Transcripts available by mail. Search requires name plus social security number, signed release. Other helpful information: approximate years of attendance. First transcript is free; $5.00 each additional.

Pace University, **(White Plains)**, Registrar, 78 N Broadway, White Plains, NY 10603, 914-422-4213 (FAX: 914-422-4248). Records are not housed here. They are located at Pace University, (Pleasantville/Briarcliff), Registrar, 861 Bedford Rd, Pleasantville, NY 10570.

Pacific Christian College, Registrar, 2500 E Nutwood Ave, Fullerton, CA 92631, 714-879-3901 X256 (FAX: 714-526-0231). Hours: 8AM-5PM. Records go back to 1928. Degrees granted: Associate; Bachelors; Masters.

Attendance information available by phone, FAX, mail. Search requires name plus date of birth. Other helpful information: social security number, approximate years of attendance. No fee for information.

Degree information available by phone, FAX, mail. Search requires name only. Other helpful information: social security number, date of birth, approximate years of attendance. No fee for information.

Transcripts available by FAX, mail. Search requires name plus social security number, signed release. Other helpful information: approximate years of attendance. No fee for transcripts.

Major credit cards accepted for payment.

Pacific College of Oriental Medicine, Registrar, 7445 Mission Valley Rd Ste 105, San Diego, CA 92108-4408, 619-574-6909 (FAX: 619-574-6641). Hours: 9AM-5PM. Records go back to 1986. Degrees granted: Masters.

Attendance and degree information available by phone, FAX, mail. Search requires name plus social security number, signed release. No fee for information.

Transcripts available by mail. Search requires name plus social security number, signed release. Fee is $5.00.

Pacific College of Oriental Medicine, **(Branch)**, Registrar, 915 Broadway 3rd Fl, New York, NY 10010, 212-982-3456 (FAX: 212-982-6514). Hours: 9AM-5:30PM M-Th, 9AM-5PM F. Records go back to 1993. Degrees granted: Masters.

Attendance information available by FAX, mail. Search requires name plus social security number, date of birth, signed release. Other helpful information: approximate years of attendance. No fee for information.

Degree information available by written request only. Search requires name plus social security number, date of birth, signed release. Other helpful information: approximate years of attendance. No fee for information.

Transcripts available by written request only. Search requires name plus social security number, date of birth, signed release. Other helpful information: approximate years of attendance. Fee is $5.00.

Include a self addressed stamped envelope with mail request. Major credit cards accepted for payment.

Pacific Graduate School of Psychology, Registrar, 935 E Meadow Dr, Palo Alto, CA 94306, 415-843-2405 (FAX: 415-493-6147). Hours: 9:30AM-5:30PM. Records go back to 1975. Alumni records are maintained here also. Call 415-843-3403. Degrees granted: Doctorate.

Attendance and degree information available by phone, FAX, mail. Search requires name plus social security number, approximate years of attendance, signed release. No fee for information.

Transcripts available by mail. Search requires name plus social security number, approximate years of attendance, signed release. Fee is $3.00.

Pacific Lutheran Theological Seminary, Registrar, 2700 Marin Ave, Berkeley, CA 94708-5264, 510-524-5264. Hours: 8AM-4:30PM. Records go back to 1950. Alumni records are maintained here at the same phone number. Degrees granted: Masters. Adverse incident record source: Business Office, 510-524-5264.

Attendance and degree information available by mail. Search requires name plus date of birth, signed release. No fee for information.

Transcripts available by mail. Search requires name plus date of birth, signed release. Fee is $3.00.

Pacific Lutheran University, Registrar's Office, Tacoma, WA 98447, 206-535-7136 (FAX: 206-535-8320). Hours: 8AM-6PM M-Th; 8AM-5PM F. Degrees granted: Masters; Doctorate. Certification: Teaching. Adverse incident record source: Student Life, 206-535-7191.

Attendance and degree information available by phone, FAX, mail. Search requires name plus social security number. Other helpful information: approximate years of attendance. No fee for information.

Transcripts available by FAX, mail. Search requires name plus social security number, approximate years of attendance, signed release. Fee is $5.00.

Major credit cards accepted for payment.

Pacific Northwest College of Art, Registrar, 1219 SW Park Ave, Portland, OR 97205, 503-226-4391 (FAX: 503-226-4842). Hours: 9AM-5PM. Records go back to 1911. Degrees granted: Bachelors.

Attendance and degree information available by phone, FAX, mail. Search requires name only. Other helpful information: social security number, date of birth, approximate years of attendance. No fee for information.

Transcripts available by mail. Search requires name plus signed release. Other helpful information: social security number, date of birth, approximate years of attendance. First transcript is $5.00; each additional $1.00.

Pacific Oaks College, Registrar, 5 Westmoreland Pl, Pasadena, CA 91103, 818-397-1342 (FAX: 818-577-6144). Hours: 8:30AM-4:30PM. Records go back to 1959. Alumni records are maintained here also. Call 818-397-1314. Degrees granted: Bachelors; Masters. Certification: Post-Grad. Special programs-Extension Division, 818-397-1375.

Attendance information available by phone, FAX, mail. Search requires name only. Other helpful information: social security number, date of birth, approximate years of attendance. No fee for information.

Degree information available by phone, FAX, mail. Search requires name plus approximate years of attendance. Other helpful information: social security number, date of birth, exact years of attendance. No fee for information.

Transcripts available by mail. Search requires name plus social security number, date of birth, approximate years of attendance, signed release. Other helpful information: exact years of attendance. Fee is $10.00. Expedited service available for $20.00.

Major credit cards accepted for payment.

Pacific School of Religion, Registrar, 1798 Scenic Ave, Berkeley, CA 94709, 510-848-0528 (FAX: 510-845-8948). Hours: 8:30AM-5PM. Degrees granted: Masters; Doctorate.

Attendance and degree information available by phone, FAX, mail. Search requires name only. No fee for information.

Transcripts available by FAX, mail. Search requires name plus signed release. Fee is $3.00.

Pacific Union College, Records Office, Angwin, CA 94508-9707, 707-965-6673 (FAX: 707-965-6432). Hours: 8:30AM-4:30PM M-Th; 8:30AM-Noon F. Alumni records are maintained here also. Call 707-965-6306. Degrees granted: Associate; Bachelors; Masters.

Attendance and degree information available by phone, FAX, mail. Search requires name only. Other helpful information: social security number, date of birth, approximate years of attendance. No fee for information.

Transcripts available by phone, FAX, mail. Search requires name plus social security number. Other helpful information: date of birth, approximate years of attendance. Fee is $3.00.

Pacific University, Registrar, 2043 College Way, Forest Grove, OR 97116, 503-359-2234 (FAX: 503-359-2242). Hours: 8AM-5PM. Records go back to 1900s. Alumni records are maintained here also. Call 503-359-6151 X2206. Degrees granted: Bachelors; Masters; Doctorate. Adverse incident record source: Records & Regristration, 503-359-2234.

Attendance information available by phone, FAX, mail. Search requires name plus social security number. No fee for information.

Degree information available by phone, FAX, mail. Search requires name plus social security number, exact years of attendance. No fee for information.

Transcripts available by FAX, mail. Search requires name plus social security number, exact years of attendance, signed release. Fee is $2.00.

Minimum credit card charge $10.

Paducah Community College, Registrar, PO Box 7380, Paducah, KY 42002-7380, 502-554-9200 (FAX: 502-554-6302). Hours: 8AM-5PM. Records go back to 1968. Degrees granted: Associate.

Attendance and degree information available by written request only. Search requires name plus social security number, approximate years of attendance, signed release. No fee for information.

Transcripts available by written request only. Search requires name plus social security number, approximate years of attendance, signed release. Fee is $2.00. Expedited service available for $5.00.

Paier College of Art, Registrar, 20 Gorham Ave, Hamden, CT 06154, 203-287-3032 (FAX: 203-287-3021). Hours: 9AM-4PM. Records go back to 1950. Alumni records are maintained here also. Call 203-287-3036. Degrees granted: Associate; Bachelors. Adverse incident record source: President, 203-287-3054.

Attendance and degree information available by phone, FAX, mail. Search requires name plus social security number. No fee for information.

Transcripts available by mail. Search requires name plus social security number, signed release. Fee is $2.00.

Paine College, Registrar, 1235 15th St, Augusta, GA 30901-3182, 706-821-8311 (FAX: 706-821-8293). Hours: 9AM-5PM. Records go back to 1920. Alumni records are maintained here also. Call 706-821-8247. Degrees granted: Bachelors. Adverse incident record source: Dean of Students, 706-821-8302.

Attendance and degree information available by phone, FAX, mail. Search requires name plus social security number, exact years of attendance, signed release. No fee for information.

Transcripts available by mail. Search requires name plus social security number, exact years of attendance, signed release. Fee is $3.00.

Palm Beach Atlantic College, Registrar, 901 S Flagler Dr, PO Box 24708, West Palm Beach, FL 33416-4708, 407-835-4347 (FAX: 407-835-4349). Hours: 8AM-7PM M-Th, 8MA-5PM F, 9AM-1PM Sat. Records go back to 1968. Alumni records are maintained here also. Call 407-650-7700. Degrees granted: Bachelors; Masters.

Attendance and degree information available by mail. Search requires name plus social security number, signed release. No fee for information.

Transcripts available by mail. Search requires name plus social security number, signed release. Fee is $5.00.

Palm Beach Community College, Registrar, 4200 Congress Ave, Lake Worth, FL 33461-4796, 407-439-8284 (FAX: 407-439-8255). Hours: 9AM-7PM M-Th. Records go back to 1933. Alumni records are maintained here also. Call 407-439-8072. Degrees granted: Associate.

Attendance and degree information available by phone, mail. Search requires name plus social security number. No fee for information.

Transcripts available by mail. Search requires name plus social security number, signed release. Fee is $3.00.

Palmer College of Chiropractic, Registrar, 1000 Brady St, Davenport, IA 52803, 319-326-9862 (FAX: 319-327-0181). Hours: 8AM-4:30PM. Degrees granted: Associate; Bachelors; Masters; Doctorate; C.T. Adverse incident record source: Student Affairs, 319-326-9643.

Attendance information available by phone, mail. Search requires name plus social security number. Other helpful information: date of birth, approximate years of attendance. No fee for information.

Degree information available by phone, mail. Search requires name plus signed release. Other helpful information: social security number, approximate years of attendance. No fee for information. Include a stamped envelope.

Transcripts available by mail. Search requires name plus social security number, signed release. Other helpful information: date of birth, approximate years of attendance. Fee is $5.00.

Palmer College of Chiropractic-West, Registrar, 90 E Tasman Dr, San Jose, CA 95134, 408-944-6099 (FAX: 408-944-6017). Hours: 8AM-4:30PM. Records go back to 1981. Alumni records are maintained here also. Call 408-944-6043. Degrees granted: Doctorate.

Attendance and degree information available by phone, mail. Search requires name plus exact years of attendance, signed release. Other helpful information: social security number, approximate years of attendance. No fee for information.

Transcripts available by phone, mail. Search requires name plus exact years of attendance, signed release. Other helpful information: social security number, approximate years of attendance. Fee is $5.00.

Palo Alto College, Registrar, 1400 W Villaret Blvd, San Antonio, TX 78224-2499, 512-921-5000. Hours: 8AM-5PM. Degrees granted: Associate.

Attendance and degree information available by phone, mail. Search requires name plus social security number. No fee for information.

Transcripts available by written request only. Search requires name plus social security number, signed release. No fee for transcripts.

Palo Verde College, Registrar, 811 W Chanslorway, Blythe, CA 92225, 619-922-6168 (FAX: 619-922-0230). Hours: 8AM-5PM. Degrees granted: Associate. Adverse incident record source: Business Services.

Attendance and degree information available by mail. Search requires name plus social security number, date of birth, signed release. Other helpful information: approximate years of attendance. No fee for information.

Transcripts available by mail. Search requires name plus social security number, date of birth, signed release. Other helpful information: approximate years of attendance. Fee is $2.00. Expedited service available for $5.00.

Palomar College, Registrar, 1140 W Mission Rd, San Marcos, CA 92069, 619-744-1150 X2169 (FAX: 619-744-2932). Hours: 7:30AM-7PM M-Th; 7:30AM-2PM F. Degrees granted: Associate. Adverse incident record source: Student Activities.

Attendance and degree information available by phone, FAX, mail. Search requires name plus social security number. Other helpful information: date of birth, approximate years of attendance. No fee for information.

Transcripts available by mail. Search requires name plus social security number, date of birth, signed release. Other helpful information: approximate years of attendance. Fee is $3.00. Expedited service available for $5.00.

Pamlico Community College, Registrar, PO Box 185, Hwy 306 S, Grantsboro, NC 28529, 919-249-1851. Hours: 7:30AM-10PM. Records go back to 1962. Alumni records are maintained here at the same phone number. Degrees granted: Associate.

Attendance and degree information available by mail. Search requires name plus social security number. Other helpful information: date of birth, approximate years of attendance. Fee is $3.00. Expedited service available for $3.00.

Transcripts available by mail. Search requires name plus social security number, signed release. Fee is $3.00. Expedited service available for $3.00.

Panola College, Registrar, 1109 W Panola St, Carthage, TX 75633, 903-693-2038 (FAX: 903-693-5588). Hours: 8AM-4:30PM. Degrees granted: Associate.

Attendance and degree information available by phone, FAX, mail. Search requires name plus social security number, exact years of attendance. Other helpful information: date of birth. No fee for information.

Transcripts available by mail. Search requires name plus social security number, signed release. Other helpful information: exact years of attendance. Fee is $2.00. Expedited service available for $2.00.

Paradise Valley Community College, Registrar, 18401 N 32nd St, Phoenix, AZ 85032, 602-493-2610 (FAX: 602-493-2983). Hours: 8AM-7PM M-Th; 8AM-5PM F. Records go back to

1987. Degrees granted: Associate. Adverse incident record source: Security Office, 602-493-2650.

School will not confirm attendance information.

Degree information available by written request only. Search requires name plus signed release. Other helpful information: social security number, exact years of attendance. No fee for information.

Transcripts available by FAX, mail. Search requires name plus signed release. Other helpful information: social security number, exact years of attendance. Fee is $5.00.

Major credit cards accepted for payment.

Paralegal Institute, Inc., Registrar, 3602 W Thomas Rd Ste 9, PO Drawer 11408, Phoenix, AZ 85061-1408, 602-272-1855 (FAX: 602-269-0793). Hours: 8AM-5PM. Records go back to 1975. Degrees granted: Associate.

Attendance and degree information available by phone, FAX, mail. Search requires name plus social security number. No fee for information.

Transcripts available by mail. Search requires name plus social security number, date of birth, exact years of attendance, signed release. Fee is $10.00.

Student ID number needed. Major credit cards accepted for payment.

Paris Junior College, Records Office, 2400 Clarksville St, Paris, TX 75460, 903-784-9212 (FAX: 903-784-9309). Hours: 8AM-5PM. Records go back to 1924. Alumni records are maintained here also. Call 903-785-9574. Degrees granted: Associate. Adverse incident record source: Student Life, 903-784-9402.

Attendance and degree information available by phone, FAX, mail. Search requires name plus social security number. Other helpful information: date of birth, approximate years of attendance. No fee for information.

Transcripts available by FAX, mail. Search requires name plus social security number, signed release. Other helpful information: date of birth, approximate years of attendance. Fee is $2.00. Expedited service available for $2.00.

Park College, Registrar, 8700 River Park Dr, Parkville, MO 64152, 816-741-2000 X272 (FAX: 816-746-6423). Hours: 8AM-4:30PM. Records go back to 1936. Alumni records are maintained here also. Call 816-714-2000 X211. Degrees granted: Bachelors; Masters. Adverse incident record source: Personnel, 816-741-2000 X386.

Attendance and degree information available by phone, FAX, mail. Search requires name plus social security number, approximate years of attendance. No fee for information.

Transcripts available by mail. Search requires name plus social security number, approximate years of attendance. Fee is $4.00.

Include a self addressed stamped envelope with mail request.

Parker College of Chiropractic, Registrar, 2500 Walnut Hill Lane, Dallas, TX 75229-5668, 214-438-6932 (FAX: 214-352-8425). Hours: 8AM-5PM.

Attendance and degree information available by phone, FAX, mail. Search requires name plus social security number. No fee for information.

Transcripts available by FAX, mail. Search requires name plus social security number, signed release. Fee is $5.00.

Parkland College, Registrar, 2400 W Bradley Ave, Champaign, IL 61821, 217-351-9625 (FAX: 217-351-7640). Hours: 7:30AM-8PM M-Th; 7:30AM-5PM F; 9AM-Noon S. Records go back to 1966. Degrees granted: Associate.

Attendance and degree information available by phone, FAX, mail. Search requires name plus social security number, approximate years of attendance. Other helpful information: date of birth. No fee for information.

Transcripts available by FAX, mail. Search requires name plus social security number, date of birth, approximate years of attendance, signed release. Fee is $2.00. Expedited service available for $3.00.

Parks College, Registrar, 1023 Tijeras Ave NW, Albuquerque, NM 87102, 505-843-7500 (FAX: 505-242-1986). Hours: 8AM-6PM. Records go back to 1895. Degrees granted: Associate.

Attendance and degree information available by phone, mail. Search requires name plus social security number, date of birth, exact years of attendance. No fee for information.

Transcripts available by written request only. Search requires name plus social security number, date of birth, exact years of attendance, signed release. No fee for transcripts.

Parks College, **(Branch Campus)**, Registrar, 6922 E Broadway, Tucson, AZ 85710, 520-886-7979 (FAX: 520-886-2395). Hours: 8AM-5PM M-Th; 8AM-3PM F. Records go back to 1987. Degrees granted: Associate.

Attendance and degree information available by FAX, mail. Search requires name plus social security number, approximate years of attendance, signed release. No fee for information.

Transcripts available by mail. Search requires name plus social security number, approximate years of attendance, signed release. Fee is $5.00.

Parks Junior College, Registrar, 9065 Grant St, Denver, CO 80229, 303-457-2757 (FAX: 303-457-4030). Hours: 10:30AM-7:30PM. Records go back to 1970. Degrees granted: Associate.

Attendance information available by phone, FAX, mail. Search requires name plus social security number, exact years of attendance, signed release. Other helpful information: date of birth. No fee for information.

Degree information available by mail. Search requires name plus social security number, approximate years of attendance, signed release. Other helpful information: date of birth, exact years of attendance. No fee for information.

Transcripts available by mail. Search requires name plus social security number, date of birth, exact years of attendance, signed release. Fee is $2.00.

Parks Junior College, **(Branch)**, Registrar, 6 Abilene St, Aurora, CO 80011, 303-367-2757 (FAX: 303-461-9706). Hours: 7AM-6PM. Records go back to 1895. Degrees granted: Associate.

Attendance and degree information available by FAX, mail. Search requires name plus social security number, approximate years of attendance. No fee for information.

Transcripts available by mail. Search requires name plus social security number, approximate years of attendance. Fee is $2.00.

Pasadena City College, Records Office, 1570 E Colorado Blvd, Pasadena, CA 91106, 818-585-7475. Hours: 8AM-7:30PM. Records go back to 1945. Alumni records are maintained here at the same phone number. Degrees granted: Associate. Special programs- Financial Aid, 818-585-7401. Adverse incident record source: Safety Office, 818-585-7484.

Attendance and degree information available by mail. Search requires name plus social security number, date of birth, approximate years of attendance, signed release. Other helpful information: exact years of attendance. Fee is $3.00. Expedited service available for $6.00.

Transcripts available by mail. Search requires name plus social security number, date of birth, approximate years of attendance, signed release. Other helpful information: exact years of attendance. Fee is $3.00. Expedited service available for $6.00.

Pasco-Hernando Community College, Registrar, 36727 Blanton Rd, Dade City, FL 33525-7599, 813-847-2727. Hours: 8AM-4:30PM. Records go back to 1972. Degrees granted: Associate.

Attendance and degree information available by phone, FAX, mail. Search requires name plus social security number. No fee for information.

Transcripts available by written request only. Search requires name plus social security number, signed release. No fee for transcripts.

Passiac County Community College, Registrar, One College Blvd, Paterson, NJ 07505-1179, 201-684-6400 (FAX: 201-684-6778). Hours: 9AM-7PM M-Th; 9AM-5PM F. Records go back to 1971. Alumni records are maintained here also. Call 201-684-5656. Degrees granted: Associate.

Attendance information available by FAX, mail. Search requires name plus social security number, signed release. No fee for information.

Degree information available by phone, FAX, mail. Search requires name plus social security number, signed release. No fee for information.

Transcripts available by FAX, mail. Search requires name plus social security number, signed release. Fee is $2.00.

Patten College, Registrar, 2433 Coolidge Ave, Oakland, CA 94601, 510-533-8300 X220. Hours: 9AM-5PM. Records go back 7 years. Alumni records are maintained here also. Call 510-533-8300 X255. Degrees granted: Bachelors.

Attendance and degree information available by mail. Search requires name plus social security number, date of birth, approximate years of attendance, signed release. No fee for information.

Transcripts available by mail. Search requires name plus social security number, date of birth, approximate years of attendance, signed release. Fee is $5.00.

Paul D. Camp Community College, Registrar, 100 N College Dr, PO Box 737, Franklin, VA 23851-0737, 804-569-6722 (FAX: 804-569-6795). Hours: 8AM-4:30PM. Records go back to 1970. Degrees granted: Associate.

Attendance information available by written request only. Search requires name plus approximate years of attendance, signed release. Other helpful information: social security number. No fee for information.

Degree information available by written request only. Search requires name plus signed release. Other helpful information: social security number, approximate years of attendance. No fee for information.

Transcripts available by written request only. Search requires name plus signed release. Other helpful information: social security number, approximate years of attendance. No fee for transcripts.

Paul Quinn College, Registrar, 3837 Simpson Stuart Rd, PO Box 411238, Dallas, TX 75241, 214-302-3540/302-3526. Hours: 8AM-4:30PM. Alumni records are maintained here at the same phone number. Degrees granted: Bachelors.

Attendance and degree information available by phone, mail. Search requires name plus social security number, exact years of attendance. No fee for information.

Transcripts available by mail. Search requires name plus social security number, exact years of attendance, signed release. Fee is $5.00.

Paul Smith's College, Registrar, Paul Smiths, NY 12970, 518-327-6231 (FAX: 518-327-6161). Hours: 8AM-5PM. Records go back to 1937. Alumni records are maintained here at the same phone number. Degrees granted: Associate. Certification: Baking. Adverse incident record source: Student Affairs, 518-327-6222.

Attendance and degree information available by phone, FAX, mail. Search requires name only. No fee for information.

Transcripts available by FAX. Search requires name plus signed release. Fee is $2.00. Expedited service available for $2.00.

Major credit cards accepted for payment.

Peace College, Registrar, 15 E Peace St, Raleigh, NC 27604, 919-508-2250 (FAX: 919-508-2326). Hours: 8:15AM-4:45PM. Records go back to 1900. Alumni records are maintained here also. Call 919-508-2000. Degrees granted: Associate. Adverse incident record source: Business Office, 919-508-2000.

Attendance information available by phone, FAX, mail. Search requires name only. Other helpful information: social security number, approximate years of attendance. No fee for information.

Degree information available by phone, FAX. Search requires name only. Other helpful information: social security number, approximate years of attendance. No fee for information.

Transcripts available by mail. Search requires name plus signed release. Other helpful information: social security number, date of birth, approximate years of attendance. Fee is $2.00.

Pearl River Community College, Registrar, 101 Hwy 11 N, Poplarville, MS 39470-2298, 601-795-6801 (FAX: 601-795-1129). Hours: 8AM-4PM. Records go back to 1909. Degrees granted: Associate.

Attendance information available by mail. Search requires name plus social security number, signed release. Other helpful information: exact years of attendance. No fee for information.

Degree information available by written request only. Search requires name plus social security number, signed release. Other helpful information: exact years of attendance. No fee for information.

Transcripts available by written request only. Search requires name plus social security number, signed release. Other helpful information: exact years of attendance. Fee is $1.00.

Pellissippi State Technical Community College, Registrar, 10915 Hardin Valley Rd, PO Box 22990, Knoxville, TN 37933-0990, 615-694-6632 (FAX: 615-694-6435). Degrees granted: Associate.

Attendance and degree information available by phone, FAX, mail. Search requires name only. Other helpful information: social security number. No fee for information.

Transcripts available by mail. Search requires name plus signed release. Other helpful information: social security number. No fee for transcripts.

Attendance confirmation only for lending agencies.

Pembroke State University, Registrar, One University Dr, Pembroke, NC 28372, 910-521-6303 (FAX: 910-521-6548). Hours: 8AM-5PM. Records go back to 1900s. Degrees granted: Masters. Adverse incident record source: Student Affairs.

Attendance and degree information available by phone, FAX, mail. Search requires name plus social security number. Other helpful information: approximate years of attendance. No fee for information.

Transcripts available by FAX, mail. Search requires name plus social security number, signed release. Other helpful information: approximate years of attendance. Fee is $3.00. Expedited service available for $5.00.

Peninsula College, Registrar, 1502 E Lauridsen Blvd, Port Angeles, WA 98362, 360-452-9277 (FAX: 360-457-8100). Hours: 8AM-5PM. Degrees granted: Associate.

Attendance and degree information available by phone, FAX, mail. Search requires name plus social security number. Other helpful information: approximate years of attendance. No fee for information.

Transcripts available by mail. Search requires name plus social security number, signed release. Other helpful information: approximate years of attendance. Fee is $2.00.

Major credit cards accepted for payment.

Penn Technical Institute, Registrar, 110 Ninth St, Pittsburgh, PA 15222-3618, 412-355-0455. Hours: 8AM-5PM T,Th,F; 5-9PM M,W. Records go back 47 years. Degrees granted: Associate. Adverse incident record source: Director, 412-355-0455.

Attendance and degree information available by phone, mail. Search requires name plus social security number, approximate years of attendance. No fee for information.

Transcripts available by mail. Search requires name plus social security number, approximate years of attendance, signed release. No fee for transcripts.

Penn Valley Community College, Registrar, 3201 SW Trafficway, Kansas City, MO 64111, 816-759-4100 (FAX: 816-759-4478). Hours: 8AM-4:30PM Fall; 7AM-5:30PM M-Th Summer. Records go back to 1919. Degrees granted: Associate.

Attendance and degree information available by phone, FAX, mail. Search requires name plus social security number, signed release. No fee for information.

Transcripts available by mail. Search requires name plus social security number, signed release. Fee is $2.00.

Pennco Tech, Registrar, 3815 Otter St, Bristol, PA 19007-3696, 215-824-3200 X42 (FAX: 215-785-1945). Hours: 8AM-4:30PM. Records go back to 1970. Degrees granted: Associate.

Attendance and degree information available by FAX, mail. Search requires name plus social security number, approximate years of attendance, signed release. No fee for information.

Transcripts available by FAX, mail. Search requires name plus social security number, approximate years of attendance, signed release. Fee is $5.00.

Pennsylvania Academy of the Fine Arts, Registrar, 118 N Broad St, Philadelphia, PA 19102, 215-972-7600 X3501 (FAX: 215-569-0153). Hours: 9AM-5PM. Records go back to 1806. Alumni records are maintained here at the same phone number. Adverse incident record source: School Office, 215-972-7623 X3215.

Attendance and degree information available by phone, FAX, mail. Search requires name plus approximate years of attendance. No fee for information.

Transcripts available by mail. Search requires name plus approximate years of attendance, signed release. Fee is $3.00.

Pennsylvania Business Institute, Registrar, 81 Robinson St, Pottstown, PA 19464, 610-326-6150 (FAX: 610-326-4142). Hours: 8AM-5PM. Records go back to 1986. Degrees granted: Associate.

Attendance and degree information available by FAX, mail. Search requires name plus signed release. Other helpful information: social security number, approximate years of attendance. No fee for information.

Transcripts available by FAX, mail. Search requires name plus signed release. Other helpful information: social security number, approximate years of attendance. Fee is $2.00. No transcript fee for graduates.

Pennsylvania Business Institute, (Branch), Registrar, One Angelini Ave, Nesquehoning, PA 18240, 800-220-7241 (FAX: 717-326-4142). Records are not housed here. They are located at Pennsylvania Business Institute, Registrar, 81 Robinson St, Pottstown, PA 19464.

Pennsylvania College of Optometry, Registrar, 1200 W Godfrey Ave, Philadelphia, PA 19141, 215-276-6260. Hours: 8:30AM-4:30PM. Records go back to 1919. Degrees granted: Bachelors; Masters; Doctorate.

Attendance information available by phone, mail. Search requires name only. No fee for information.

Degree information available by phone, mail. Search requires name plus exact years of attendance. Other helpful information: social security number, date of birth, approximate years of attendance. No fee for information.

Transcripts available by FAX, mail. Search requires name plus social security number, signed release. Other helpful information: approximate years of attendance. Fee is $2.00.

Pennsylvania College of Podiatric Medicine, Registrar, 8th and Race Sts, Philadelphia, PA 19107, 215-625-5444 (FAX: 215-627-2815). Hours: 8:30AM-5PM. Alumni records are maintained here also. Call 215-625-5411. Degrees granted: Doctorate.

Attendance information available by FAX, mail. Search requires name plus social security number, approximate years of attendance, signed release. No fee for information.

Degree information available by mail. Search requires name plus social security number, approximate years of attendance, signed release. No fee for information.

Transcripts available by mail. Search requires name plus social security number, approximate years of attendance, signed release. Transcripts are $5.00; for current students $1.00.

Pennsylvania College of Technology, Registrar, 1 College Ave, Williamsport, PA 17701, 717-327-4772 (FAX: 717-321-5536). Hours: 8AM-4:30PM Summer hours 7:30AM-5:30PM M-W, 7:30AM-5PM Th. Records go back to 1963. Alumni records are maintained here at the same phone number. Degrees granted: Associate; Bachelors. Adverse incident record source: Security, 717-321-5527.

Attendance and degree information available by phone, FAX, mail. Search requires name plus social security number, approximate years of attendance, signed release. No fee for information.

Transcripts available by mail. Search requires name plus social security number, approximate years of attendance, signed release. No fee for transcripts.

Pennsylvania College of Technology, Registrar, One College Ave, Williamsport, PA 17701, 717-326-3761. Degrees granted: Bachelors. Adverse incident record source: Campus Police.
 Attendance and degree information available by phone, FAX, mail. Search requires name only. Other helpful information: social security number, date of birth, approximate years of attendance. No fee for information.
 Transcripts available by mail. Search requires name plus signed release. Other helpful information: social security number, date of birth, approximate years of attendance. No fee for transcripts.

Pennsylvania Institute of Technology, Registrar, 800 Manchester Ave, Media, PA 19063, 610-892-1525 (FAX: 610-892-1510). Hours: 8AM-8PM. Records go back to 1950. Degrees granted: Associate.
 Attendance and degree information available by phone. Search requires name plus signed release. Other helpful information: social security number. No fee for information.
 Transcripts available by FAX, mail. Search requires name plus signed release. Other helpful information: social security number. No fee for transcripts.

Pennsylvania State University, Registrar, 112 Shields Bldg, University Park, PA 16802, 814-865-6357 (FAX: 814-865-6359). Hours: 8AM-5PM. Records go back to 1800s. Alumni Records Office: Alumni Association, The Pennsylvania State University, 101 Old Main, University Park, PA 16802. Degrees granted: Associate; Bachelors; Masters; Doctorate. Adverse incident record source: Conduct Standards & Judicial Affairs, 814-863-0342.
 Attendance and degree information available by phone, FAX, mail. Search requires name plus social security number, approximate years of attendance, signed release. No fee for information.
 Transcripts available by FAX, mail. Search requires name plus social security number, approximate years of attendance, signed release. Fee is $4.00.
 Major credit cards accepted for payment.

Pennsylvania State University, **(Allentown)**, Registrar, 6090 Mohr Lane, Fogelsville, PA 18051, 215-285-4811.
 Attendance and degree information available by phone, FAX, mail. Search requires name plus social security number, approximate years of attendance.
 Transcripts available from main campus in University Park (see above).

Pennsylvania State University, **(Altoona)**, Registrar, Ivyside Park, Altoona, PA 16001-3760, 814-949-5000.
 Attendance and degree information available by phone, FAX, mail. Search requires name plus social security number, approximate years of attendance.
 Transcripts available from main campus in University Park (see above).

Pennsylvania State University, **(Beaver)**, Registrar, Brodhead Rd, Monaca, PA 15061, 412-773-3500.
 Attendance and degree information available by phone, FAX, mail. Search requires name plus social security number, approximate years of attendance.

Transcripts available from main campus in University Park (see above).

Pennsylvania State University, **(Berks)**, Registrar, Tulpehocken Rd, Reading, PA 19610, 215-320-4800.
 Attendance and degree information available by phone, FAX, mail. Search requires name plus social security number, approximate years of attendance.
 Transcripts available from main campus in University Park (see above).

Pennsylvania State University, **(Delaware County)**, Registrar, 25 Yearsley Mill Rd, Media, PA 19063, 215-565-3300.
 Attendance and degree information available by phone, FAX, mail. Search requires name plus social security number, approximate years of attendance.
 Transcripts available from main campus in University Park (see above).

Pennsylvania State University, **(DuBois)**, Registrar, College Pl, Du Bois, PA 15801, 814-375-4700.
 Attendance and degree information available by phone, FAX, mail. Search requires name plus social security number, approximate years of attendance.
 Transcripts available from main campus in University Park (see above).

Pennsylvania State University, **(Erie-Behrend College)**, Registrar, Station Rd, Erie, PA 16563, 814-898-6000. Alumni records are maintained here also. Call 814-898-6159. Degrees granted: Associate; Bachelors; Masters. Adverse incident record source: Student Affairs, 814-898-6111.
 Attendance and degree information available by phone, FAX, mail. Search requires name plus social security number, approximate years of attendance.
 Transcripts available from main campus in University Park (see above).

Pennsylvania State University, **(Fayette)**, Registrar, PO Box 519, Rte 119 N, Uniontown, PA 15401, 412-430-4100.
 Attendance and degree information available by phone, FAX, mail. Search requires name plus social security number, approximate years of attendance.
 Transcripts available from main campus in University Park (see above).

Pennsylvania State University, **(Great Valley Graduate Center)**, Registrar, 30 E Swedesford Rd, Malvern, PA 19355, 215-889-1300.
 Attendance and degree information available by phone, FAX, mail. Search requires name plus social security number, approximate years of attendance.
 Transcripts available from main campus in University Park (see above).

Pennsylvania State University, **(Harrisburg-Capital College)**, Registrar, Rte 230, Middletown, PA 17057, 717-948-6020 (FAX: 717-948-6325). Hours: 8AM-6PM M,Th; 8AM-5PM T,W,F. Alumni records are maintained here at the same phone number. Degrees granted: Associate; Bachelors; Masters; Doctorate.
 Attendance and degree information available by phone, FAX, mail. Search requires name plus social security number, approximate years of attendance.

Transcripts available from main campus in University Park (see above).

Pennsylvania State University, (Hazleton), Registrar, Highacres, Hazleton, PA 18201, 717-450-3000.

Attendance and degree information available by phone, FAX, mail. Search requires name plus social security number, approximate years of attendance.

Transcripts available from main campus in University Park (see above).

Pennsylvania State University, (Hershey Medical Center), Registrar, 500 University Dr, Hershey, PA 17033, 717-531-8521.

Attendance and degree information available by phone, FAX, mail. Search requires name plus social security number, approximate years of attendance.

Transcripts available from main campus in University Park (see above).

Pennsylvania State University, (McKeesport Campus), Registrar's Office, University Dr, McKeesport, PA 15132, 412-678-9170 (FAX: 412-675-9278). Alumni Records Office: 105 Old Main, McKeesport, PA 15132. Degrees granted: Associate.

Attendance and degree information available by phone, FAX, mail. Search requires name plus social security number, approximate years of attendance. No fee for information.

Transcripts available from main campus in University Park (see above).

Pennsylvania State University, (Mont Alto Campus), Registrar, Campus Dr, Mont Alto, PA 17237, 717-749-6000.

Attendance and degree information available by phone, FAX, mail. Search requires name plus social security number, approximate years of attendance.

Transcripts available from main campus in University Park (see above).

Pennsylvania State University, (New Kensington Campus), Registrar, 3550 Seventh Street Rd, New Kensington, PA 15068, 412-339-5466 (FAX: 412-339-5434).

Attendance and degree information available by phone, FAX, mail. Search requires name plus social security number, approximate years of attendance.

Transcripts available from main campus in University Park (see above).

Pennsylvania State University, (Ogontz Campus), Registrar, 1600 Woodland Rd, Abington, PA 19001, 215-881-7332 (FAX: 215-881-7317). Hours: 8AM-5PM. Records go back to 1983. Alumni Records Office: The Pennsylvania State University, 105 Old Main, University Park, PA 16802. Degrees granted: Associate; Bachelors. Adverse incident record source: Abington Twp Police, 215-885-4450.

Attendance and degree information available by phone, FAX, mail. Search requires name plus social security number, approximate years of attendance. No fee for information.

Transcripts available from main campus in University Park (see above).

Pennsylvania State University, (Schuylkill Campus), Registrar, 200 University Dr, Schuylkill Haven, PA 17972, 717-385-6000.

Attendance and degree information available by phone, FAX, mail. Search requires name plus social security number, approximate years of attendance.

Transcripts available from main campus in University Park (see above).

Pennsylvania State University, (Shenango Campus), Registrar, 147 Shenango Ave, Sharon, PA 16146, 412-983-5860.

Attendance and degree information available by phone, FAX, mail. Search requires name plus social security number, approximate years of attendance.

Transcripts available from main campus in University Park (see above).

Pennsylvania State University, (Wilkes-Barre Campus), Registrar, PO Box PSU, Lehman, PA 18627, 717-675-2171.

Attendance and degree information available by phone, FAX, mail. Search requires name plus social security number, approximate years of attendance.

Transcripts available from main campus in University Park (see above).

Pennsylvania State University, (Worthington-Scranton Campus), Registrar, 120 Ridge View Dr, Dunmore, PA 18512, 717-963-4757.

Attendance and degree information available by phone, FAX, mail. Search requires name plus social security number, approximate years of attendance.

Transcripts available from main campus in University Park (see above).

Pennsylvania State University, (York Campus), Registrar, 1031 Edgecomb Ave, York, PA 17403, 717-771-4057 (FAX: 717-771-4062). Hours: 8AM-5PM. Records go back to 1984. Degrees granted: Associate.

Attendance and degree information available by phone, FAX, mail. Search requires name plus social security number, approximate years of attendance. No fee for information.

Transcripts available from main campus in University Park (see above).

Pensacola Junior College, Registrar, 1000 College Blvd, Pensacola, FL 32504, 904-484-1600 (FAX: 904-484-1689). Hours: 7:30AM-4PM. Records go back to 1948. Degrees granted: Associate. Adverse incident record source: Adverse Info: Student Life: Incident Reports: Public Safety

Attendance and degree information available by phone, FAX, mail. Search requires name plus social security number, date of birth, approximate years of attendance. Other helpful information: exact years of attendance. No fee for information.

Transcripts available by FAX, mail. Search requires name plus social security number, date of birth, approximate years of attendance, signed release. Other helpful information: exact years of attendance. No fee for transcripts.

Pepperdine University, Registrar, 24255 Pacific Coast Hwy, Malibu, CA 90263, 310-456-4542 (FAX: 310-456-4358). Hours: 8AM-5PM. Records go back to 1937. Alumni records are maintained here also. Call 310-456-4248. Degrees granted: Bachelors; Masters; Doctorate.

Attendance and degree information available by phone, FAX, mail. Search requires name plus social security number, date of birth, approximate years of attendance, signed release. No fee for information.

Transcripts available by mail. Search requires name plus social security number, date of birth, approximate years of attendance, signed release. Fee is $4.00.

Peru State College, Registrar, Peru, NE 68421, 402-872-2239. Hours: 8:30AM-4:30PM. Records go back to founding date. Alumni Records Office: PO Box 10, Peru, NE 68421. Degrees granted: Associate; Bachelors; Masters.

Attendance and degree information available by phone, mail. Search requires name plus social security number. Other helpful information: date of birth, approximate years of attendance. No fee for information.

Transcripts available by written request only. Search requires name plus social security number, signed release. Other helpful information: date of birth, approximate years of attendance. Fee is $3.00.

Pfeiffer College, Registrar, PO Box 960, Misenheimer, NC 28109-0960, 704-463-1360 X2056 (FAX: 704-463-1363). Hours: 8AM-Noon, 1-5PM. Records go back to 1955. Degrees granted: Bachelors; Masters.

Attendance and degree information available by phone, FAX, mail. Search requires name only. Other helpful information: social security number, date of birth, approximate years of attendance. No fee for information.

Transcripts available by written request only. Search requires name plus signed release. Other helpful information: social security number, date of birth, approximate years of attendance. Fee is $2.00. Expedited service available for $10.00.

Philadelphia College of Bible, Records Office, 200 Manor Ave, Langhorne, PA 19047-2990, 215-752-5800 (FAX: 215-752-5812). Hours: 8AM-7:30PM. Records go back to 1913. Alumni records are maintained here at the same phone number. Degrees granted: Associate; Bachelors; Masters. Adverse incident record source: Student Development.

Attendance and degree information available by phone, FAX, mail. Search requires name only. Other helpful information: social security number, date of birth, approximate years of attendance. No fee for information.

Transcripts available by FAX, mail. Search requires name plus signed release. Other helpful information: social security number, date of birth, approximate years of attendance. Fee is $2.00. Expedite: $5.00 to $10.00

Philadelphia College of Osteopathic Medicine, Registrar, 4150 City Ave, Philadelphia, PA 19131, 215-871-6100. Alumni records are maintained here also. Call 215-871-6100.

Attendance and degree information available by phone, mail. Search requires name plus social security number, exact years of attendance. No fee for information.

Transcripts available by mail. Search requires name plus social security number, exact years of attendance, signed release. No fee for transcripts.

Philadelphia College of Pharmacy and Science, Registrar, 600 S 43rd St, Philadelphia, PA 19104-4495, 215-596-8813 (FAX: 215-895-1177). Records go back to 1821. Alumni records are maintained here also. Call 215-596-8856. Degrees granted: Bachelors; Masters; Doctorate.

Attendance and degree information available by phone, mail. Search requires name plus social security number. No fee for information.

Transcripts available by mail. Search requires name plus social security number, signed release. Fee is $2.00.

Philadelphia College of Textiles and Science, Registrar, 4201 Henry Ave, Philadelphia, PA 19144, 215-951-2700 (FAX: 215-951-2615). Hours: 8AM-4:30PM. Records go back to 1884. Alumni records are maintained here also. Call 215-951-2710. Degrees granted: Bachelors; Masters.

Attendance and degree information available by mail. Search requires name plus social security number, exact years of attendance. No fee for information.

Transcripts available by mail. Search requires name plus social security number, exact years of attendance, signed release. No fee for transcripts.

Philander Smith College, Registrar, 812 W 13th St, Little Rock, AR 72202, 501-370-5220 (FAX: 501-370-5278). Hours: 8:30AM-5PM. Records go back to founding date.

Attendance information available by FAX, mail. Search requires name plus social security number, signed release. Other helpful information: date of birth, approximate years of attendance. No fee for information.

Degree information available by FAX, mail. Search requires name plus social security number, signed release. Other helpful information: date of birth. No fee for information.

Transcripts available by written request only. Search requires name plus social security number, signed release. Other helpful information: date of birth. Fee is $2.00.

Phillips Beth Israel School of Nursing, Registrar, 310 E 22nd St, New York, NY 10010, 212-614-6108 (FAX: 212-614-6109). Hours: 8AM-4:30PM. Records go back to 1904. Alumni records are maintained here at the same phone number.

Attendance and degree information available by FAX, mail. Search requires name plus social security number, approximate years of attendance, signed release. Other helpful information: date of birth. No fee for information.

Transcripts available by FAX, mail. Search requires name plus social security number, approximate years of attendance, signed release. Other helpful information: date of birth. Fee is $5.00. Expedited service available for $5.00.

Phillips College Inland Empire Campus, Registrar, 4300 Central Ave, Riverside, CA 92506, 909-787-9300 (FAX: 909-787-9452). Hours: 9AM-5PM. Records go back 21 years. Degrees granted: Associate.

Attendance and degree information available by FAX, mail. Search requires name plus social security number, signed release. Other helpful information: approximate years of attendance. No fee for information.

Transcripts available by mail. Search requires name plus social security number, signed release. Other helpful information: approximate years of attendance. Fee is $5.00.

Phillips County Community College, Registrar, Box 785, Helena, AR 72342, 501-338-6474 (FAX: 501-338-7542). Hours: 8AM-4:30PM. Records go back to 1966. Degrees granted: Associate.

Attendance information available by phone, FAX, mail. Search requires name plus social security number, signed release. Other helpful information: date of birth, approximate years of attendance. No fee for information.

Degree information available by written request only. Search requires name plus social security number, signed release. Other

helpful information: date of birth, approximate years of attendance. No fee for information.

Transcripts available by FAX, mail. Search requires name plus social security number, signed release. Other helpful information: date of birth, approximate years of attendance. No fee for transcripts. Expedited service available for $4.00.

Phillips Graduate Seminary, Registrar, 102 University Dr, PO Box 2335 University Station, Enid, OK 73702, 405-548-2239 (FAX: 405-237-7686). Records are not housed here. They are located at Phillips University, Registrar, 100 S University Ave, Enid, OK 73701.

Phillips Junior College Condie Campus, Registrar, One W Campbell Ave, Campbell, CA 95008, 408-866-6666 (FAX: 408-866-5542). Hours: 9AM-12:30PM M-Th. Records go back to 1979. Degrees granted: Associate.

Attendance information available by written request only. Search requires name plus social security number, approximate years of attendance, signed release. No fee for information.

Degree information available by phone, FAX, mail. Search requires name plus social security number, signed release. Other helpful information: approximate years of attendance. No fee for information.

Transcripts available by mail. Search requires name plus social security number, signed release. Other helpful information: exact years of attendance. Fee is $3.00. Expedited service available for $15.00.

Major credit cards accepted for payment.

Phillips Junior College Fresno Campus, Registrar, 2048 N Fine Ave, Fresno, CA 93727, 209-453-1000 (FAX: 209-453-1747). Hours: 8AM-8PM. Records go back 89 years. Degrees granted: Associate. Special programs- National College, 800-843-8892.

Attendance and degree information available by phone, FAX, mail. Search requires name plus social security number, signed release. Other helpful information: date of birth, exact years of attendance. No fee for information.

Transcripts available by mail. Search requires name plus social security number, signed release. Other helpful information: date of birth, exact years of attendance. Fee is $3.00.

Phillips Junior College, Registrar, 2680 Insurance Center Dr, Jackson, MS 39216, 601-362-6341 (FAX: 601-366-9407). Hours: 8AM-4:30PM. Records go back to 1973. Degrees granted: Associate.

Attendance and degree information available by FAX, mail. Search requires name plus social security number, exact years of attendance, signed release. No fee for information.

Transcripts available by FAX, mail. Search requires name plus social security number, exact years of attendance, signed release. Fee is $2.00.

Phillips Junior College, Registrar, 2401 N Harbor City Blvd, Melbourne, FL 32935, 407-254-6459 (FAX: 407-255-2017). Hours: 8AM-5PM. Records go back to 1972. Degrees granted: Associate; Bachelors.

Attendance and degree information available by written request only. Search requires name plus social security number, signed release. Other helpful information: date of birth, approximate years of attendance. No fee for information.

Transcripts available by written request only. Search requires name plus social security number, signed release. Other helpful information: date of birth, approximate years of attendance. Fee is $2.00. Expedited service available for $2.00.

Phillips Junior College, Registrar, 3446 Demetropolis Rd, Mobile, AL 36693, 334-666-9696 (FAX: 334-666-9761). Hours: 10AM-7PM. Records go back to 1989. Degrees granted: Associate.

Attendance information available by written request only. Search requires name plus social security number. Other helpful information: approximate years of attendance. No fee for information.

Degree information available by written request only. Search requires name plus social security number, signed release. Other helpful information: approximate years of attendance. No fee for information.

Transcripts available by written request only. Search requires name plus social security number, signed release. Other helpful information: approximate years of attendance. Fee is $3.00.

Phillips Junior College, Registrar, 822 S Clearview Pkwy, New Orleans, LA 70123, 504-734-0123 X351 (FAX: 504-734-1667). Hours: 9AM-6PM M-Th, 9AM-4PM F. Records go back to 1976. Degrees granted: Associate.

Attendance and degree information available by phone, FAX, mail. Search requires name plus social security number, exact years of attendance, signed release. No fee for information.

Transcripts available by FAX, mail. Search requires name plus social security number, exact years of attendance, signed release. First transcript free; two additional at $2.00 each.

Phillips Junior College, Registrar, 3098 Highland Dr, Salt Lake City, UT 84106, 801-485-0221 (FAX: 801-485-0057). Degrees granted: Associate.

Attendance and degree information available by phone, FAX, mail. Search requires name plus social security number, exact years of attendance. No fee for information.

Transcripts available by FAX, mail. Search requires name plus social security number, exact years of attendance, signed release. Fee is $3.00.

Phillips Junior College, Registrar, 1010 W Sunshine St, Springfield, MO 65807, 417-864-7220 (FAX: 417-864-5697). Hours: 8AM-6PM. Records go back to 1989. Degrees granted: Associate.

Attendance and degree information available by phone, FAX, mail. Search requires name plus social security number, approximate years of attendance, signed release. Other helpful information: date of birth, exact years of attendance. No fee for information.

Transcripts available by mail. Search requires name plus social security number, approximate years of attendance, signed release. Other helpful information: date of birth, exact years of attendance. Fee is $3.00.

Phillips Junior College, Registrar, 15400 Sherman Way, Ste 250`, Van Nuys, CA 91406, 818-895-2220 X115 (FAX: 818-895-5282). Hours: 8AM-6:30PM M-Th, 8AM-5PM F. Records go back to 1989. Degrees granted: Associate.

Attendance and degree information available by FAX, mail. Search requires name plus social security number. No fee for information.

Transcripts available by FAX, mail. Search requires name plus social security number. Fee is $3.00.

The Sourcebook of College and University Student Records **P**

Phillips Junior College at Birmingham, Registrar, 115 Office Par Dr, Mountain Brook, AL 35223, 205-879-5100 (FAX: 205-871-4881). Hours: 8AM-5PM. Records go back to 1975. Degrees granted: Associate.

Attendance and degree information available by FAX, mail. Search requires name plus social security number, approximate years of attendance. No fee for information.

Transcripts available by FAX, mail. Search requires name plus social security number, approximate years of attendance, signed release. Fee is $2.00.

Phillips Junior College at Birmingham, (Phillips Junior College), Registrar, 4900 Corporate Dr NW Ste E, Huntsville, AL 35805, 205-430-3377 (FAX: 205-430-3411). Hours: 8AM-6PM M-Th; 8AM-Noon F. Records go back 84 years. Degrees granted: Associate.

Attendance and degree information available by phone, FAX, mail. Search requires name plus signed release. Other helpful information: social security number, date of birth, approximate years of attendance. No fee for information.

Transcripts available by FAX, mail. Search requires name plus signed release. Other helpful information: social security number, date of birth, approximate years of attendance. Fee is $3.00.

Phillips Junior College of Las Vegas, Registrar, 3320 E Flamingo Rd Ste 30, Las Vegas, NV 89121-4306, 702-434-0486 (FAX: 702-434-8601). Hours: 7AM-4PM. Records go back to founding date. Degrees granted: Associate.

Attendance and degree information available by FAX, mail. Search requires name plus social security number, signed release. Other helpful information: approximate years of attendance. No fee for information.

Transcripts available by FAX, mail. Search requires name plus social security number, signed release. Other helpful information: approximate years of attendance. No fee for transcripts.

Phillips Junior College, (Branch), Registrar, One Civic Plaza Ste 110, Carson, CA 90745-2264, 310-518-2600 (FAX: 310-518-3652). Hours: 9AM-5PM. Records go back to 1988. Degrees granted: Associate.

Attendance and degree information available by phone, FAX, mail. Search requires name plus social security number, date of birth, approximate years of attendance, signed release. No fee for information.

Transcripts available by phone, FAX, mail. Search requires name plus social security number, date of birth, approximate years of attendance, signed release. Fee is $2.00.

Phillips Junior College, (Branch), Registrar, 1491 S Nova Rd, Daytona Beach, FL 32114, 904-255-1707 (FAX: 904-239-0995). Hours: 9AM-8PM M-Th; 9AM-4PM F. Records go back 7 years. Degrees granted: Associate. Adverse incident record source: In house, periodical crime reports, security.

Attendance and degree information available by FAX, mail. Search requires name plus signed release. Other helpful information: social security number, approximate years of attendance. No fee for information.

Transcripts available by FAX, mail. Search requires name plus signed release. Other helpful information: social security number, approximate years of attendance. Fee is $2.00.

Phillips University, Registrar, 100 S University Ave, Enid, OK 73701, 405-548-2272 (FAX: 405-237-1607). Hours: 8:30AM-4PM. Records go back to 1906f. Alumni records are maintained here also. Call 405-548-2293. Degrees granted: Bachelors; Masters.

Attendance and degree information available by phone, FAX, mail. Search requires name plus social security number, approximate years of attendance, signed release. No fee for information.

Transcripts available by FAX, mail. Search requires name plus social security number, approximate years of attendance, signed release. Fee is $4.00.

Phoenix College, Registrar, 1202 W Thomas Rd, Phoenix, AZ 85013, 602-285-7500 (FAX: 602-285-7813). Hours: 7:30AM-7:30PM M-Th; 7:30AM-4:30PM F. Records go back to 1920. Degrees granted: Associate. Certification: Fire Science.

Attendance and degree information available by phone, FAX, mail. Search requires name plus social security number, date of birth, signed release. Other helpful information: approximate years of attendance. No fee for information.

Transcripts available by FAX, mail. Search requires name plus social security number, date of birth, signed release. Other helpful information: approximate years of attendance. Fee is $5.00.

Major credit cards accepted for payment.

Piedmont Bible College, Registrar, 716 Franklin St, Winston-Salem, NC 27101, 910-725-8344 (FAX: 910-725-5522). Hours: 8AM-5PM. Records go back to 1947. Alumni records are maintained here at the same phone number. Degrees granted: Associate; Bachelors; Masters.

Attendance and degree information available by phone, mail. Search requires name only. No fee for information.

Transcripts available by mail. Search requires name only. Fee is $3.00.

Piedmont College, Registrar, PO Box 10, Demorest, GA 30535, 706-778-3000 (FAX: 706-776-2811). Hours: 8AM-5PM. Records go back to 1897. Degrees granted: Bachelors; Masters.

Attendance and degree information available by phone, FAX, mail. Search requires name plus social security number. Other helpful information: approximate years of attendance. No fee for information.

Transcripts available by mail. Search requires name plus social security number, signed release. Other helpful information: approximate years of attendance. Fee is $2.00. Expedited service available for $5.00.

Piedmont Community College, Registrar, PO Box 1197, Roxboro, NC 27573, 910-599-1181 (FAX: 910-597-3817). Hours: 8AM-5PM. Records go back to 1970.

Attendance and degree information available by phone, FAX, mail. Search requires name only. Other helpful information: social security number, approximate years of attendance. No fee for information.

Transcripts available by FAX, mail. Search requires name plus signed release. Other helpful information: social security number, approximate years of attendance. Fee is $3.00.

Major credit cards accepted for payment.

Piedmont Technical College, Student Records, Emerald Rd, Greenwood, SC 29648, 803-941-8364 (FAX: 803-941-8566). Hours: 8AM-8:30PM M-Th; 8AM-5PM F. Records go back to 1966. Degrees granted: Associate. Adverse incident record source: Student Development, 803-941-8358.

Attendance and degree information available by phone, FAX, mail. Search requires name plus social security number. Other

Degree Granting Institutions

helpful information: approximate years of attendance. No fee for information.

Transcripts available by FAX, mail. Search requires name plus social security number, signed release. Other helpful information: approximate years of attendance. Transcript fee: $2.00 issued, $3.00 mailed. Expedite: $5.00 FAX. Expedited service available for $5.00.

Major credit cards accepted for payment.

Piedmont Virginia Community College, Registrar, Rte 6 Box 1, Charlottesville, VA 22902, 804-977-3900. Degrees granted: Associate.

Attendance and degree information available by phone, mail. Search requires name plus social security number, signed release. Other helpful information: date of birth. No fee for information.

Transcripts available by mail. Search requires name plus social security number, signed release. Other helpful information: date of birth. Fee is $1.00.

Pierce College, Transcripts/Records, 9401 Farwest Dr SW, Tacoma, WA 98498, 206-964-6500. Degrees granted: Associate. Adverse incident record source: Dean of Students.

Attendance and degree information available by phone, FAX, mail. Search requires name plus social security number. Other helpful information: date of birth, approximate years of attendance. No fee for information.

Transcripts available by FAX, mail. Search requires name plus social security number, signed release. Other helpful information: date of birth, approximate years of attendance. No fee for transcripts.

Pierce Junior College, Registrar, 1420 Pine St, Philadelphia, PA 19102, 215-545-6400 (FAX: 215-546-5996). Hours: 8:30AM-5PM. Records go back to 1940s. Alumni records are maintained here also. Call 215-545-6400. Degrees granted: Associate. Certification: Proficency.

Attendance and degree information available by phone, FAX, mail. Search requires name plus social security number, approximate years of attendance, signed release. Other helpful information: date of birth. No fee for information.

Transcripts available by written request only. Search requires name plus social security number, approximate years of attendance, signed release. Other helpful information: date of birth. Fee is $3.00.

Major credit cards accepted for payment.

Pikes Peak Community College, Records Office, Box 8, 5675 S Academy Blvd, Colorado Springs, CO 80906, 719-540-7116 (FAX: 719-540-7614). Hours: 8AM-8PM M,T; 8AM-5PM W-F. Records go back to 1969. Degrees granted: Associate. Adverse incident record source: Public Safety, 719-540-7111.

Attendance and degree information available by phone, mail. Search requires name plus social security number. Other helpful information: date of birth, approximate years of attendance. No fee for information.

Transcripts available by mail. Search requires name plus social security number, signed release. Other helpful information: date of birth, approximate years of attendance. Fee is $1.00. Expedited service available for $5.00.

Pikeville College, Registrar, 214 Sycamore St, Pikeville, KY 41501, 606-432-9369 (FAX: 606-432-9328). Hours: 8:30AM-5PM. Records go back 60 years. Alumni records are maintained here also. Call 606-432-9326. Degrees granted: Associate; Bachelors.

Attendance and degree information available by phone, FAX, mail. Search requires name plus social security number, date of birth, signed release. Other helpful information: approximate years of attendance. No fee for information.

Transcripts available by mail. Search requires name plus social security number, date of birth, signed release. Other helpful information: approximate years of attendance. Fee is $3.00. Expedited service available for $5.00.

Major credit cards accepted for payment.

Pima County Community College District, Registrar, 4907 E Broadway Blvd, Tucson, AZ 85709-1010, 520-748-4640 (FAX: 520-748-4790). Hours: 8:15AM-4:45PM. Records go back to 1969. Alumni Records Office: Alumni Association, Pima County Community College, 4905 E Broadway Blvd, Tucson, AZ 85709. Degrees granted: Associate; Basic, Advanced & Technical. Special programs- Associate, 520-748-4903: Advanced & Technical, 520-478-4961. Adverse incident record source: Department of Public Safety, 520-748-2692.

Attendance and degree information available by phone, FAX, mail. Search requires name plus social security number. Other helpful information: date of birth, approximate years of attendance. No fee for information.

Transcripts available by mail. Search requires name plus social security number, signed release. Other helpful information: date of birth, approximate years of attendance. Fee is $2.00. Expedited service available for $11.00.

Pima Medical Institute, Registrar, 1627 Eastlake Ave E, Seattle, WA 98102, 206-322-6100 (FAX: 206-324-1985). Hours: 7:30AM-6PM. Records go back to 1990. Degrees granted: Associate.

Attendance and degree information available by phone, FAX, mail. Search requires name plus social security number, approximate years of attendance, signed release. No fee for information.

Transcripts available by FAX, mail. Search requires name plus social security number, approximate years of attendance, signed release. Fee is $2.00. Expedited service available for $2.00.

Pima Medical Institute, Registrar, 3350 E Grant Rd, Tucson, AZ 85716, 602-326-1600. Hours: 7:15AM-8:30PM M-Th, 8AM-5PM F. Records go back to 1972. Alumni records are maintained here also. Call 602-326-1600. Degrees granted: Associate.

Attendance and degree information available by phone, FAX, mail. Search requires name plus social security number, date of birth, exact years of attendance. No fee for information.

Transcripts available by mail. Search requires name plus social security number, date of birth, exact years of attendance, signed release. Fee is $2.00.

Pima Medical Institute, (Branch), Registrar, 2201 San Pedro Dr NE Bldg 3 Ste 100, Albuquerque, NM 87110, 505-881-1234.

Pima Medical Institute, (Branch), Registrar, 1701 W 72nd Ave #130, Denver, CO 80221, 303-426-1800 (FAX: 303-430-4048). Hours: 8AM-5PM. Records go back to 1989. Degrees granted: Associate.

Attendance information available by phone, FAX, mail. Search requires name plus social security number, date of birth. No fee for information.

Degree information available by phone, FAX, mail. Search requires name plus social security number. No fee for information.

Transcripts available by phone, FAX, mail. Search requires name plus social security number, signed release. No fee for transcripts.

Pima Medical Institute, (Branch), Registrar, 957 S Dobson Rd, Mesa, AZ 85202, 602-345-777. Hours: 8AM-5PM. Records go back to 1970. Degrees granted: Associate.

School will not confirm attendance information. Search requires name only. No fee for information.

Degree information available by phone, mail. Search requires name plus social security number, exact years of attendance. No fee for information.

Transcripts available by mail. Search requires name plus social security number, exact years of attendance, signed release. No fee for transcripts.

Pine Manor College, Registrar, 400 Heath St, Chestnut Hill, MA 02167, 617-731-7135 (FAX: 617-731-7199). Hours: 9AM-5PM. Records go back to 1917. Alumni records are maintained here also. Call 617-731-7132. Degrees granted: Associate; Bachelors; Masters; MED.

Attendance and degree information available by phone, FAX, mail. Search requires name plus social security number, approximate years of attendance, signed release. No fee for information.

Transcripts available by mail. Search requires name plus social security number, approximate years of attendance, signed release. Fee is $5.00.

Pitt Community College, Registrar, PO Drawer 7007, Greenville, NC 27835-7007, 919-321-4232 (FAX: 919-321-4401). Hours: 8AM-5PM. Records go back to 1963. Degrees granted: Associate.

Attendance and degree information available by FAX, mail. Search requires name plus social security number. Other helpful information: date of birth, approximate years of attendance. No fee for information.

Transcripts available by FAX, mail. Search requires name plus social security number, signed release. Other helpful information: date of birth, approximate years of attendance. Fee is $1.00.

Pittsburg State University, Registrar, 1701 S Broadway, Pittsburg, KS 66762, 316-235-4206 (FAX: 316-235-4015). Hours: 8AM-4:30PM. Records go back to 1903. Degrees granted: Associate; Bachelors; Masters.

Attendance and degree information available by phone, FAX, mail. Search requires name only. Other helpful information: social security number, date of birth, approximate years of attendance. No fee for information.

Transcripts available by phone, FAX, mail. Search requires name only. Other helpful information: social security number, date of birth, approximate years of attendance. Fee is $3.00. Expedited service available for $3.00.

Major credit cards accepted for payment.

Pittsburgh Institute of Aeronautics, Registrar, PO Box 10897, Pittsburgh, PA 15236-0897, 412-462-9011 (FAX: 412-466-0513). Hours: 8AM-4:30PM. Records go back to 1930s. Degrees granted: Associate.

Attendance and degree information available by phone, FAX, mail. Search requires name plus social security number, exact years of attendance. No fee for information.

Transcripts available by FAX, mail. Search requires name plus social security number, exact years of attendance, signed release. Fee is $2.00.

Major credit cards accepted for payment.

Pittsburgh Institute of Mortuary Science, Registrar, 5808 Baum blvd, Pittsburgh, PA 15206, 412-362-8500. Hours: 8AM-4PM. Records go back to 1939. Degrees granted: Associate; Bachelors.

Attendance and degree information available by phone, mail. Search requires name plus social security number, date of birth, exact years of attendance. No fee for information.

Transcripts available by mail. Search requires name plus social security number, date of birth, exact years of attendance, signed release. Fee is $3.00.

Pittsburgh Technical Institute, Registrar, 635 Smithfield St, Pittsburgh, PA 15222-2560, 412-741-1011 (FAX: 412-471-9014). Hours: 7AM-6PM. Records go back to 1970s. Degrees granted: Associate.

Attendance and degree information available by phone, FAX, mail. Search requires name only. Other helpful information: social security number, date of birth, approximate years of attendance. No fee for information.

Transcripts available by phone, FAX, mail. Search requires name only. Other helpful information: social security number, date of birth, approximate years of attendance. No fee for transcripts.

Pittsburgh Theological Seminary, Registrar, 616 N Highland Ave, Pittsburgh, PA 15206, 412-362-5610 (FAX: 412-363-3260). Hours: 8:30AM-4:30PM. Records go back to 1910. Degrees granted: Masters; Doctorate.

Attendance and degree information available by phone, FAX, mail. Search requires name plus approximate years of attendance. No fee for information.

Transcripts available by mail. Search requires name plus approximate years of attendance, signed release. Fee is $4.00.

Pitzer College, Registrar, 1050 N Mills Ave, Claremont, CA 91711-6110, 909-621-8000 X3036. Hours: 8AM-5PM. Records go back to 1963. Alumni records are maintained here also. Call 909-621-8000 X8130. Degrees granted: Bachelors.

Attendance and degree information available by phone, FAX, mail. Search requires name plus approximate years of attendance. Other helpful information: social security number, date of birth. No fee for information.

Transcripts available by mail. Search requires name plus social security number, approximate years of attendance, signed release. Fee is $2.00. Expedited service available for $5.00.

Plaza Business Institute, Registrar, 74-09 37th Ave, Jackson Heights, NY 11372, 718-779-1430 (FAX: 718-779-7423). Hours: 8AM-8:30PM M,T,Th;8AM-5PM W,F. Records go back to 1970s. Degrees granted: Associate.

Attendance and degree information available by mail. Search requires name plus social security number, approximate years of attendance, signed release. Fee is $10.00.

Transcripts available by mail. Search requires name plus social security number, approximate years of attendance, signed release. Fee is $10.00.

Plymouth State College, Registrar, Plymouth, NH 03264, 603-535-2345. Hours: 8AM-4:30PM. Records go back to 1900.

Alumni records are maintained here also. Call 603-535-2218. Degrees granted: Associate; Bachelors; Masters.

Attendance and degree information available by phone, mail. Search requires name plus social security number. Other helpful information: date of birth, approximate years of attendance. No fee for information.

Transcripts available by mail. Search requires name plus social security number, signed release. Other helpful information: date of birth, approximate years of attendance. Fee is $3.00.

Point Loma Nazarene College, Registrar, 3900 Lomaland Dr, San Diego, CA 92106, 619-221-2286 (FAX: 619-221-2579). Hours: 8AM-4:30PM. Records go back to 1902. Degrees granted: Bachelors; Masters; EDS.

Attendance and degree information available by mail. Search requires name plus date of birth, approximate years of attendance, signed release. Other helpful information: social security number, exact years of attendance. No fee for information.

Transcripts available by mail. Search requires name plus date of birth, approximate years of attendance, signed release. Other helpful information: social security number, exact years of attendance. Fee is $4.00.

Point Park College, Registrar, 201 Wood St, Pittsburgh, PA 15222, 412-392-3861 (FAX: 412-391-1980). Hours: 8:30AM-4:30PM. Records go back to 1960. Alumni records are maintained here also. Call 412-392-3816. Degrees granted: Associate; Bachelors; Masters. Adverse incident record source: Security, 412-392-3960.

Attendance and degree information available by phone, FAX, mail. Search requires name only. Other helpful information: social security number, date of birth, approximate years of attendance. No fee for information.

Transcripts available by mail. Search requires name plus signed release. Other helpful information: social security number, date of birth, approximate years of attendance. Fee is $3.00.

Polk Community College, Registrar, 999 Ave H NE, Winter Haven, FL 33881-4299, 813-297-1002 (FAX: 813-297-1006). Hours: 8AM-5PM. Records go back 30 years. Degrees granted: Associate. Certification: EMT & Paramedic.

Attendance information available by FAX, mail. Search requires name plus approximate years of attendance, signed release. Other helpful information: social security number, date of birth, exact years of attendance. No fee for information.

Degree information available by phone, FAX, mail. Search requires name plus approximate years of attendance, signed release. Other helpful information: social security number, date of birth, exact years of attendance. No fee for information.

Transcripts available by FAX, mail. Search requires name plus approximate years of attendance, signed release. Other helpful information: social security number, date of birth, exact years of attendance. No fee for transcripts. Student pays FedEx fee.

Polytechnic University, Office of the Registrar, 6 MetroTech Ctr, Brooklyn, NY 11201, 718-260-3486 (FAX: 718-260-3136). Hours: 9AM-6PM M,Th; 9AM-5PM T,W,F. Records go back to founding date. Alumni records are maintained here also. Call 718-260-3486 X3188. Degrees granted: Bachelors; Masters; Doctorate.

Attendance information available by phone, FAX, mail. Search requires name plus exact years of attendance. Other helpful information: social security number, date of birth, approximate years of attendance. No fee for information.

Degree information available by phone, FAX, mail. Search requires name only. Other helpful information: social security number, date of birth, approximate years of attendance. No fee for information.

Transcripts available by FAX, mail. Search requires name plus social security number, approximate years of attendance, signed release. Other helpful information: date of birth, exact years of attendance. Fee is $5.00. Expedited service available for $5.00. Major credit cards accepted for payment.

Polytechnic University, **(Long Island Center)**, Office of the Registrar, Rte 100, Farmingdale, NY 11735, 516-755-4400. Records are not housed here. They are located at Polytechnic University, Office of the Registrar, 6 MetroTech Ctr, Brooklyn, NY 11201.

Polytechnic University, **(Westchester Graduate Center)**, Registrar, 36 Saw Mill River Rd, Hawthorne, NY 10532, 718-260-3900 (FAX: 718-260-3136). Records are not housed here. They are located at Polytechnic University, Office of the Registrar, 6 MetroTech Ctr, Brooklyn, NY 11201.

Pomona College, Registrar, 550 N College Ave, Claremont, CA 91711, 909-621-8147 (FAX: 909-621-8403). Hours: 8AM-5PM. Records go back to 1887. Alumni records are maintained here also. Call 909-621-8110. Degrees granted: Bachelors. Adverse incident record source: Student Affairs, 909-621-8131 X2250.

Attendance and degree information available by phone, FAX, mail. Search requires name plus date of birth, approximate years of attendance, signed release. No fee for information.

Transcripts available by mail. Search requires name plus date of birth, approximate years of attendance, signed release. Fee is $2.00.

Ponce School of Medicine, Registrar, Box 7004, Ponce, PR 00732, 809-840-2575 X246 (FAX: 809-259-1931). Hours: 8AM-4:30PM. Records go back to 1981. Degrees granted: Doctorate; Ph.D; Biomedical Science.

Attendance information available by phone, FAX, mail. Search requires name plus social security number, date of birth, exact years of attendance, signed release. Fee is $2.00.

Degree information available by FAX, mail. Search requires name plus social security number, date of birth, exact years of attendance, signed release. Fee is $2.00.

Transcripts available by written request only. Search requires name plus social security number, date of birth, exact years of attendance, signed release. Fee is $2.50.

Include a stamped envelope.

Ponce Technological University College, Registrar, Box 7186, Ponce, PR 00732, 809-844-2318. Hours: 8AM-4:30PM. Records go back to 1970. Degrees granted: Associate; Bachelors.

Attendance information available by mail. Search requires name plus signed release. Other helpful information: social security number, date of birth. Fee is $1.00.

Degree information available by mail. Search requires name plus signed release. Other helpful information: social security number. Fee is $1.00.

Transcripts available by mail. Search requires name plus signed release. Other helpful information: social security number, date of birth. Fee is $1.00.

Transcript request with money orders only.

Pontifical Catholic University of Puerto Rico, Registrar, Las Americas Ave Sta 6, Ponce, PR 00732, 809-841-2000.

Pontifical Catholic University of Puerto Rico, (Arecibo Branch Campus), Registrar, PO Box 495, Arecibo, PR 00613, 809-881-1212.

Pontifical Catholic University of Puerto Rico, (Guayama Branch Campus), Registrar, PO Box 809, Guayama, PR 00654, 809-864-0550.

Pontifical Catholic University of Puerto Rico, (Mayaguez Branch Campus), Registrar, PO Box 1326, Mayaguez, PR 00709, 809-834-5151.

Pontifical College Josephinum, Registrar, 7625 N High St, Columbus, OH 43235, 614-885-5585 (FAX: 614-885-2307). Hours: 8AM-5:30PM. Alumni records are maintained here at the same phone number. Degrees granted: Bachelors; Masters.

Attendance and degree information available by phone, mail. Search requires name plus social security number, date of birth. No fee for information.

Transcripts available by mail. Search requires name plus social security number, date of birth, signed release. Fee is $2.00.

Pope John XXIII National Seminary, Registrar, 558 South Ave, Weston, MA 02193-2699, 617-899-5500 (FAX: 617-899-9057). Hours: 9AM-4:30PM. Records go back to 1962. Alumni records are maintained here at the same phone number. Degrees granted: Masters.

Attendance information available by mail. Search requires name plus signed release. No fee for information.

Degree information available by phone, FAX, mail. Search requires name plus signed release. No fee for information.

Transcripts available by mail. Search requires name plus signed release. Fee is $5.00.

Porterville College, Registrar, 100 E College Ave, Porterville, CA 93257, 209-781-3130 X220 (FAX: 209-784-4779). Hours: 8AM-7PM M-Th; 8AM-4:30PM F. Records go back to 1927. Degrees granted: Associate.

Attendance information available by phone, FAX, mail. Search requires name only. Other helpful information: social security number, date of birth, approximate years of attendance. No fee for information.

Degree information available by FAX, mail. Search requires name plus signed release. Other helpful information: social security number, date of birth, approximate years of attendance. No fee for information.

Transcripts available by FAX, mail. Search requires name plus signed release. Other helpful information: social security number, date of birth, approximate years of attendance. Fee is $2.00. Expedited service available for $5.00.

$5.00 charge for FAX.

Portland Community College, Student Records, PO Box 19000, Portland, OR 97219-0990, 503-414-2401 (FAX: 503-226-1536). Hours: 8AM-5PM. Degrees granted: Associate; GEO, High School Completion.

Attendance and degree information available by FAX, mail. Search requires name plus social security number, signed release. Other helpful information: date of birth, approximate years of attendance. No fee for information.

Transcripts available by mail. Search requires name plus social security number, signed release. Other helpful information: date of birth, approximate years of attendance. Fee is $3.00.

Include a self addressed stamped envelope with mail request.

Portland State University, Registrar, PO Box 1389, Portland, OR 97207-1389, 503-725-3435 (FAX: 503-725-5525). Hours: 8AM-5PM. Records go back to 1955. Alumni Records Office: Alumni Association, PO Box 751, Portland, OR 97207. Degrees granted: Bachelors; Masters; Doctorate.

Attendance and degree information available by phone, mail. Search requires name plus social security number, exact years of attendance. No fee for information.

Transcripts available by mail. Search requires name plus social security number, exact years of attendance, signed release. Fee is $5.00.

Records released if no holds on records. Transcripts require current address, identification numbers. Need to know if person has graduated, deadline if any, and former names.

Potomac State College of West Virginia University, Registrar, Fort Ave, Keyser, WV 26726, 304-788-6800 (FAX: 304-788-6940). Hours: 8AM-4:30PM. Records go back to 1901. Alumni records are maintained here at the same phone number. Degrees granted: Associate.

Attendance and degree information available by phone, mail. Search requires name plus social security number, exact years of attendance. No fee for information.

Transcripts available by mail. Search requires name plus social security number, exact years of attendance, signed release. Fee is $3.00.

Prairie State College, Registrar, 202 S Halsted St, Chicago Heights, IL 60411, 708-709-3514 (FAX: 708-755-2587). Hours: 8AM-4:30PM. Records go back to 1958. Alumni records are maintained here also. Call 708-709-3734. Degrees granted: Associate. Adverse incident record source: Information Office.

Attendance and degree information available by phone, FAX, mail. Search requires name plus social security number. Other helpful information: date of birth, approximate years of attendance. No fee for information.

Transcripts available by FAX, mail. Search requires name plus social security number, signed release. Other helpful information: date of birth, approximate years of attendance. Fee is $2.00. Expedited service available for $4.00.

Prairie View A&M University, Registrar, PO Box 519, Prairie View, TX 77446, 409-857-2025 (FAX: 409-857-2699). Hours: 8AM-5PM. Records go back to 1930s. Degrees granted: Bachelors; Masters.

Attendance and degree information available by phone, FAX, mail. Search requires name plus social security number. Other helpful information: date of birth, approximate years of attendance. No fee for information.

Transcripts available by phone, FAX, mail. Search requires name plus social security number, date of birth, signed release. Other helpful information: approximate years of attendance. Fee is $3.00.

Major credit cards accepted for payment.

Pratt Community College, Registrar, 348 NE SR61, Pratt, KS 67124, 316-672-5641 (FAX: 316-672-5288). Hours: 8AM-5PM. Alumni records are maintained here at the same phone number. Degrees granted: Associate.

Attendance and degree information available by phone, FAX, mail. Search requires name plus social security number. Other helpful information: date of birth, approximate years of attendance. No fee for information.

Transcripts available by mail. Search requires name plus social security number, signed release. Other helpful information: date of birth, approximate years of attendance. Fee is $3.00.

Pratt Institute, Registrar, 200 Willoughby Ave, Brooklyn, NY 11205, 718-636-3534 (FAX: 718-636-3548). Hours: 9AM-5PM. Records go back to 1887. Confirming from 1986 on is quick; before 1986 research must be done. Degrees granted: Associate; Bachelors; Masters.

Attendance and degree information available by phone, FAX, mail. Search requires name plus signed release. Other helpful information: social security number, date of birth, approximate years of attendance. No fee for information.

Transcripts available by written request only. Search requires name plus signed release. Fee is $5.00. Expedited service available for $10.00.

Major credit cards accepted for payment.

Presbyterian College, Registrar, S Broad St, PO Box 975, Clinton, SC 29325, 803-833-8224 (FAX: 803-833-8481). Hours: 9AM-5PM. Alumni records are maintained here also. Call 803-833-8211. Degrees granted: Bachelors. Adverse incident record source: Public Safety, 803-833-8301.

Attendance and degree information available by phone, FAX, mail. Search requires name only. Other helpful information: social security number, date of birth, approximate years of attendance. No fee for information.

Transcripts available by mail. Search requires name plus social security number, signed release. Other helpful information: date of birth, approximate years of attendance. Fee is $5.00.

Presbyterian School of Christian Education, Registrar, 1205 Palmyra Ave, Richmond, VA 23227, 804-254-8054. Hours: 9AM-5PM. Records go back to 1915. Alumni records are maintained here at the same phone number. Degrees granted: Masters; Doctorate; Ed. S.

Attendance information available by phone, FAX. Search requires name plus signed release. Other helpful information: approximate years of attendance. No fee for information. Expedite fee is based on cost of service.

Degree information available by phone, FAX, mail. Search requires name only. Other helpful information: approximate years of attendance. No fee for information. Expedite fee is based on cost of service.'

Transcripts available by FAX, mail. Search requires name plus signed release. Other helpful information: approximate years of attendance. Fee is $5.00. Expedite fee is based on cost of service.'

Prescott College, Registrar, 220 Grove Ave, Prescott, AZ 86301, 520-776-5162 (FAX: 520-776-5137). Hours: 8AM-5PM. Records go back to 1929. Alumni records are maintained here also. Call 520-776-5223. Degrees granted: Bachelors; Masters.

Attendance and degree information available by phone, FAX, mail. Search requires name plus social security number. No fee for information.

Transcripts available by written request only. Search requires name plus social security number, exact years of attendance, signed release. Fee is $4.00. Expedited service available for $4.00.

Major credit cards accepted for payment.

Presentation College, Registrar, 1500 N Main St, Aberdeen, SD 57401, 605-229-8426. Hours: 8AM-5PM. Alumni records are maintained here also. Call 605-229-8442. Degrees granted: Associate; Bachelors.

Attendance and degree information available by phone, FAX, mail. Search requires name only. Other helpful information: social security number, approximate years of attendance. No fee for information.

Transcripts available by mail. Search requires name plus signed release. Other helpful information: social security number, approximate years of attendance. Fee is $2.00.

Prestonsburg Community College, Registrar, One Bert T. Combs Dr, Prestonsburg, KY 41653, 606-886-3863 X224 (FAX: 606-886-6943). Hours: 8AM-4:30PM. Records go back to 1964. Degrees granted: Associate.

Attendance and degree information available by phone, FAX, mail. Search requires name plus social security number. Other helpful information: date of birth. No fee for information.

Transcripts available by FAX, mail. Search requires name plus social security number, signed release. Other helpful information: date of birth, exact years of attendance. Fee is $2.00. Expedited service available for $5.00.

Prince George's Community College, Registrar, 301 Largo Rd, Largo, MD 20772, 301-322-0801 (FAX: 301-808-0960). Hours: 8:30AM-7:30PM. Records go back to 1958.

Attendance and degree information available by phone, FAX, mail. Search requires name plus social security number. Other helpful information: approximate years of attendance. No fee for information.

Transcripts available by mail. Search requires name plus social security number, approximate years of attendance, signed release. Other helpful information: exact years of attendance. Fee is $3.00.

Prince George's Community College, **(Branch)**, Registrar, Andrews AFB Degree Center, Patrick Ave Bldg 3611, Andrews Air Force Base, MD 20331, 301-322-0778. Records are not housed here. They are located at Prince George's Community College, Registrar, 301 Largo Rd, Largo, MD 20772.

Prince William Sound Community College, Registrar, PO Box 97, Valdez, AK 99686, 907-835-2697 (FAX: 907-835-2593). Hours: 8AM-5:30PM. Records go back to 1980. Alumni records are maintained here at the same phone number. Degrees granted: Associate; Bachelors. Adverse incident record source: Police, 907-835-4560.

Attendance and degree information available by phone, FAX, mail. Search requires name only. Other helpful information: social security number, date of birth, approximate years of attendance. No fee for information.

Transcripts available by FAX, mail. Search requires name plus social security number, signed release. Other helpful information: date of birth, approximate years of attendance. Fee is $4.00. Expedited service available for $4.00.

Major credit cards accepted for payment.

Princeton Theological Seminary, Registrar, 64 Mercer St CN 821, Princeton, NJ 08542-0803, 609-497-7820. Hours: 8:30AM-4:30PM. Records go back to 1920. Alumni records are maintained here at the same phone number. Degrees granted: Masters; Ph.D.

Attendance and degree information available by phone, mail. Search requires name plus social security number. No fee for information.

Transcripts available by mail. Search requires name plus social security number, signed release. Fee is $2.00.

Princeton University, Office of the Registrar, Box 70, Princeton, NJ 08542, 609-258-6191 (FAX: 609-258-6328). Hours: 8:45AM-5PM. Records go back to 1909. Degrees granted: Bachelors; Masters; Doctorate.

Attendance and degree information available by phone, FAX, mail. Search requires name plus signed release. Other helpful information: social security number, approximate years of attendance. No fee for information.

Transcripts available by FAX, mail. Search requires name plus signed release. Other helpful information: social security number, approximate years of attendance. Fee is $3.00.

FAX request for transcript with follow up mail of original request. DOB illegal to give out in NJ.

Principia College, Registrar, Elsah, IL 62028, 618-374-5100 (FAX: 618-374-5122). Hours: 8AM-4PM. Alumni Records Office: 13202 Clayton Rd, St Louis, MO 63131-1099. Degrees granted: Bachelors.

Attendance and degree information available by phone, FAX, mail. Search requires name only. Other helpful information: approximate years of attendance. No fee for information.

Transcripts available by FAX, mail. Search requires name plus signed release. Other helpful information: approximate years of attendance. No fee for transcripts.

Prospect Hall School of Business, Registrar, 2620 Hollywood Blvd, Hollywood, FL 33020, 305-923-8100. Hours: 8AM-1PM. Records go back to 1973. Degrees granted: Associate.

Attendance and degree information available by written request only. Search requires name plus approximate years of attendance, signed release. Other helpful information: social security number, date of birth. Fee is $3.00.

Transcripts available by written request only. Search requires name plus approximate years of attendance, signed release. Other helpful information: social security number, date of birth. Fee is $3.00.

Protestant Episcopal Theological Seminary in Virginia, Registrar, 3737 Seminary Rd, Alexandria, VA 22304, 703-370-6600 (FAX: 703-370-6234). Hours: 8:45AM-4:45PM. Records go back to 1985. Alumni records are maintained here also. Call 703-370-6600 X1712. Degrees granted: Masters; Doctorate.

Attendance and degree information available by phone, FAX, mail. Search requires name only. Other helpful information: date of birth, approximate years of attendance. No fee for information.

Transcripts available by FAX, mail. Search requires name plus social security number, signed release. Other helpful information: date of birth, approximate years of attendance. Fee is $2.00. Expedited service available for $2.00.

Providence College, Registrar, Providence, RI 02918, 401-865-2366. Hours: 8AM-5PM. Records go back to 1919. Alumni records are maintained here also. Call 401-865-2414. Degrees granted: Bachelors; Masters; Doctorate.

Attendance and degree information available by phone, mail. Search requires name plus social security number, exact years of attendance. No fee for information.

Transcripts available by mail. Search requires name plus social security number, exact years of attendance, signed release. Fee is $2.00.

Pueblo College of Business and Technology, Registrar, 330 Lake Ave, Pueblo, CO 81004, 719-545-3100. Hours: 7:30AM-4:30PM. Records go back to 1983. Degrees granted: Associate.

Attendance and degree information available by phone, mail. Search requires name plus social security number. No fee for information.

Transcripts available by mail. Search requires name plus social security number, signed release. First transcript is free; $2.00 each additional.

Pueblo Community College, Registrar, 900 W Orman Ave, Pueblo, CO 81004, 719-549-3016 (FAX: 719-543-7566). Hours: 8AM-5PM. Records go back to 1979. Degrees granted: Associate. Special programs- 6/1974 & Previous, U of CO, 719-549-2261. Adverse incident record source: PCC Security, 719-549-3291.

Attendance and degree information available by phone, FAX, mail. Search requires name plus social security number, signed release. Other helpful information: date of birth, approximate years of attendance. No fee for information.

Transcripts available by mail. Search requires name plus social security number, signed release. Other helpful information: date of birth, approximate years of attendance. Fee is $2.00. Expedite fee is based on cost of service.

Major credit cards accepted for payment.

Puget Sound Christian College, Registrar, 410 Fourth Ave N, Edmonds, WA 98020, 206-775-8686 (FAX: 206-775-8688). Hours: 7:30AM-4:30PM. Records go back to 1950. Alumni records are maintained here at the same phone number.

Attendance and degree information available by phone, FAX, mail. Search requires name only. Other helpful information: social security number. No fee for information.

Transcripts available by mail. Search requires name plus signed release. Other helpful information: social security number. Fee is $5.00.

Major credit cards accepted for payment.

Pulaski Technical College, Registrar, 3000 W Scenic Rd, North Little Rock, AR 72118-3399, 501-771-1000 (FAX: 501-771-2844). Hours: 8AM-5PM. Records go back to 1900. Degrees granted: Associate.

Attendance and degree information available by FAX, mail. Search requires name plus social security number, approximate years of attendance, signed release. Other helpful information: date of birth. Fee is $2.00.

Transcripts available by FAX, mail. Search requires name plus social security number, approximate years of attendance, signed release. Other helpful information: date of birth. Fee is $2.00.

Purdue University Calumet, Registrar, Hammond, IN 46323, 219-989-2993. Records are not housed here. They are located at Purdue University, Office of the Registrar, 1095 Houde Hall Rm55, West Lafayette, IN 47907-1095.

Purdue University North Central, Registrar, 1401 S US Hwy 421, Westville, IN 46391, 219-785-5200. Records go back 15 years. Degrees granted: Associate; Bachelors; Masters.

Attendance and degree information available by phone, FAX, mail. Search requires name only. Other helpful information: approximate years of attendance. No fee for information.

Transcripts available by FAX, mail. Search requires name plus signed release. Other helpful information: approximate years of attendance. No fee for transcripts.

Purdue University, Office of the Registrar, 1095 Houde Hall Rm55, West Lafayette, IN 47907-1095, 317-494-6153. Hours: 8:30AM-5PM. Records go back to 1875. Phone number for transcripts is 317-494-6151. Alumni records are maintained here also. Call 317-494-5189. Degrees granted: Associate; Bachelors; Masters; Doctorate.

Attendance and degree information available by phone, FAX, mail. Search requires name only. Other helpful information: social security number, date of birth, approximate years of attendance. No fee for information.

Transcripts available by FAX, mail. Search requires name plus signed release. Other helpful information: social security number, date of birth, approximate years of attendance. No fee for transcripts.

Expedite: FedEx only. Major credit cards accepted for payment.

Q

Queen of the Holy Rosary College, Registrar, PO Box 3908, Mission San Jose, CA 94539, 510-657-2468. Hours: 8AM-4PM. Records go back to 1930. Degrees granted: Associate.

Attendance and degree information available by mail. Search requires name plus social security number, date of birth, exact years of attendance. Fee is $3.00.

Transcripts available by mail. Search requires name plus social security number, date of birth, exact years of attendance. Fee is $3.00.

Queens College, Registrar, 1900 Selwyn Ave, Charlotte, NC 28274, 704-337-2200 (FAX: 704-337-2218). Hours: 8:30AM-6PM M-Th, 8:30AM-3PM F. Records go back to 1900. Alumni records are maintained here also. Call 704-337-2214. Degrees granted: Bachelors; MBA, MED, MAT. Adverse incident record source: Student Development, 704-327-2226.

Attendance and degree information available by phone, FAX, mail. Search requires name plus social security number, date of birth, approximate years of attendance. No fee for information.

Transcripts available by phone, FAX, mail. Search requires name plus social security number, date of birth, approximate years of attendance. Fee is $5.00.

Include a self addressed stamped envelope with mail request.

Queens College, Transcript & Records Dept, Jefferson Hall Rm 100, 65-30 Kissena Blvd, Flushing, NY 11367, 718-997-4400. Hours: 8AM-5PM. Records go back 50 years. Alumni records are maintained here also. Call 718-997-3930. Degrees granted: Bachelors; Masters. Adverse incident record source: Dean of Students, 718-997-5500: Incident reports: Security, 718-997-5412

Attendance and degree information available by mail. Search requires name plus social security number, date of birth, exact years of attendance, signed release. No fee for information.

Transcripts available by mail. Search requires name plus social security number, date of birth, exact years of attendance, signed release. Fee is $4.00.

Credit cards in person only.

Queensborough Community College, Registrar, 222-05 56th Ave, Bayside, NY 11364-1497, 718-631-6212 (FAX: 718-281-5041). Hours: 9AM-5PM. Records go back to 1962. Alumni records are maintained here also. Call 718-631-6391. Degrees granted: Associate. Adverse incident record source: Dean, 718-631-6351.

Attendance and degree information available by FAX, mail. Search requires name plus social security number, signed release. No fee for information.

Transcripts available by FAX, mail. Search requires name plus social security number, signed release. Fee is $4.00.

Quincy College, Registrar, 34 Coddington St, Quincy, MA 02169, 617-984-1601 (FAX: 617-984-1789). Hours: 8AM-5PM. Records go back to 1958. Degrees granted: Associate.

Attendance information available by phone, FAX. Search requires name plus social security number, signed release. No fee for information.

Degree information available by mail. Search requires name plus social security number, signed release. No fee for information.

Transcripts available by mail. Search requires name plus social security number, signed release. Fee is $3.00.

Quincy University, Registrar, 1800 College Ave, Quincy, IL 62301, 217-228-5280. Hours: 8AM-5PM. Records go back to founding date. Degrees granted: Bachelors; Masters.

Attendance and degree information available by phone, mail. Search requires name only. Other helpful information: social security number, date of birth, approximate years of attendance. No fee for information.

Transcripts available by mail. Search requires name plus social security number, date of birth, signed release. Other helpful information: approximate years of attendance. Fee is $3.00.

Quinebaug Valley Community-Technical College, Records Office, 742 Upper Maple St, Danielson, CT 06239, 203-774-1130 (FAX: 203-774-7768). Hours: 8:30AM-4:30PM. Records go back to 1972. Degrees granted: Associate.

Attendance and degree information available by phone, FAX, mail. Search requires name plus social security number, date of birth. Other helpful information: approximate years of attendance. No fee for information.

Transcripts available by written request only. Search requires name plus social security number, date of birth, signed release. Other helpful information: approximate years of attendance. No fee for transcripts.

Quinnipiac College, Registrar, Hamden, CT 06518-0569, 203-281-8695 (FAX: 203-248-4703). Hours: 8AM-6PM M-Th, 8AM-4PM F. Records go back to 1970. Alumni records are maintained here also. Call 203-281-8667. Degrees granted: Bachelors; Masters.

Attendance and degree information available by phone, FAX, mail. Search requires name plus social security number. No fee for information.

Transcripts available by mail. Search requires name plus social security number. Fee is $2.00.

Quinsigamond Community College, Registrar, 670 W Boylston St, Worcester, MA 01606, 508-853-2300 (FAX: 508-852-6943). Hours: 8AM-4:30PM. Records go back to 1965. Alumni records are maintained here also. Call 508-853-2300 X4281. Degrees granted: Associate.

Attendance and degree information available by phone, FAX, mail. Search requires name plus social security number. Other helpful information: date of birth, approximate years of attendance. No fee for information.

Transcripts available by mail. Search requires name plus social security number, signed release. Other helpful information: date of birth, approximate years of attendance. Fee is $1.00. Expedited service available for $1.00.

R

Rabbinical Academy Mesivta Rabbi Chaim Berlin, Registrar, 1605 Coney Island Ave, Brooklyn, NY 11230, 718-377-0777 (FAX: 718-338-5578).

Attendance and degree information available by mail. Search requires name plus social security number, exact years of attendance. No fee for information.

Transcripts available by mail. Search requires name plus social security number, exact years of attendance, signed release. Fee is $15.00.

Rabbinical College Beth Shraga, Registrar, 28 Saddle River Rd, Monsey, NY 10952, 914-356-1980 (FAX: 914-425-2604). Degrees granted: Bachelors.

Attendance and degree information available by phone, mail. Search requires name plus social security number, date of birth, exact years of attendance. No fee for information.

Transcripts available by mail. Search requires name plus social security number, date of birth, exact years of attendance, signed release. No fee for transcripts.

Rabbinical College Bobover Yeshiva B'nei Zion, Registrar, 1577 48th St, Brooklyn, NY 11219, 718-438-2018. Hours: 9AM-5PM. Alumni records are maintained here at the same phone number.

Attendance and degree information available by mail. Search requires name plus social security number. No fee for information.

Transcripts available by mail. Search requires name plus social security number, signed release. Other helpful information: approximate years of attendance. No fee for transcripts.

Rabbinical College Ch'san Sofer, Registrar, 1876 50th St, Brooklyn, NY 11204, 718-236-1171 (FAX: 718-236-1119).

Attendance and degree information available by mail. Search requires name plus social security number, exact years of attendance. No fee for information.

Transcripts available by mail. Search requires name plus social security number, exact years of attendance, signed release. No fee for transcripts.

Rabbinical College of America, Registrar, 226 Sussex Ave, Morristown, NJ 07960, 201-267-9404 (FAX: 201-267-5208). Hours: 9AM-5PM. Records go back to 1965. Degrees granted: Bachelors.

Attendance information available by phone, FAX, mail. Search requires name plus approximate years of attendance. No fee for information.

Degree information available by FAX, mail. Search requires name plus approximate years of attendance. No fee for information.

Transcripts available by mail. Search requires name plus approximate years of attendance, signed release. Fee is $5.00.

Rabbinical College of Long Island, Registrar, 201 Magnolia Blvd, Long Beach, NY 11561, 516-431-7304 (FAX: 516-431-8662). Hours: 9AM-5PM. Records go back to 1970s. Alumni records are maintained here at the same phone number.

Attendance and degree information available by phone, FAX, mail. Search requires name plus social security number. No fee for information.

Transcripts available by phone, FAX, mail. Search requires name plus social security number. No fee for transcripts.

Rabbinical College of Telshe, Registrar, 28400 Euclid Ave, Wickliffe, OH 44092, 216-943-5300 (FAX: 216-943-5303). Hours: 8AM-5PM. Degrees granted: Doctorate.

Attendance and degree information available by mail. Search requires name plus social security number, date of birth, exact years of attendance. No fee for information.

Transcripts available by mail. Search requires name plus social security number, date of birth, exact years of attendance, signed release. Fee is $3.00.

Need date of graduation.

Rabbinical Seminary Adas Yereim, Registrar, 185 Wilson St, Brooklyn, NY 11211, 718-388-1751 (FAX: 718-388-3531). Hours: 9:30AM-5:30PM. Records go back to 1990.

Attendance information available by phone, FAX, mail. Search requires name plus social security number, signed release. No fee for information.

Degree information available by phone, FAX, mail. Search requires name plus social security number, signed release. Other helpful information: approximate years of attendance. No fee for information.

Transcripts available by FAX, mail. Search requires name plus social security number, approximate years of attendance, signed release. Other helpful information: exact years of attendance. No fee for transcripts.

If a signed release is on file, party may call or FAX to obtain information.

Rabbinical Seminary M'kor Chaim, Registrar, 1571 55th St, Brooklyn, NY 11219, 718-851-0183 (FAX: 718-853-2967).

Attendance and degree information available by phone, mail. Search requires name plus social security number, date of birth. No fee for information.

Transcripts available by mail. Search requires name plus social security number, date of birth, exact years of attendance, signed release. No fee for transcripts.

Rabbinical Seminary of America, Registrar, 92-15 69th Ave, Forest Hills, NY 11375, 718-268-4700 (FAX: 718-268-4684).

Attendance and degree information available by mail. Search requires name only. No fee for information.

Transcripts available by mail. Search requires name plus signed release. No fee for transcripts.

Radcliffe College, Registrar, 10 Garden St, Cambridge, MA 02138, 617-495-1543 (FAX: 617-495-0815). Hours: 9AM-5PM. Records go back to 1964. Alumni records are maintained here also. Call 617-495-8641. Degrees granted: Bachelors; Masters; PhD.

Attendance and degree information available by phone, FAX, mail. Search requires name plus signed release. No fee for information.

Transcripts available by mail. Search requires name plus signed release. First transcript $3.00, each additional $2.00.

Radford University, Registrar, PO Box 6904, Radford, VA 24142, 703-831-5271 (FAX: 703-831-5138). Hours: 8AM-5PM. Records go back to 1910. Alumni records are maintained here also. Call 703-831-5248. Degrees granted: Bachelors; Masters.

Attendance and degree information available by phone, mail. Search requires name plus social security number. No fee for information.

Transcripts available by mail. Search requires name plus social security number, signed release. No fee for transcripts.

Rainy River Community College, Registrar, 1501 Hwy 71, International Falls, MN 56649, 218-285-2207 (FAX: 218-285-2239). Hours: 8AM-4:30PM. Records go back to 1967. Degrees granted: Associate. Adverse incident record source: Student Development.

Attendance and degree information available by phone, FAX, mail. Search requires name plus signed release. Other helpful information: social security number, date of birth. No fee for information.

Transcripts available by FAX, mail. Search requires name plus signed release. Other helpful information: social security number, date of birth. No fee for transcripts.

Major credit cards accepted for payment.

Ramapo College of New Jersey, Registrar, 505 Ramapo Valley Rd, Mahwah, NJ 07430-1680, 201-529-7700. Hours: 8:30AM-4:30PM. Records go back to 1971. Degrees granted: Bachelors; Masters. Adverse incident record source: Dean of Students, 201-529-7700 X7457.

Attendance information available by phone, FAX. Search requires name plus social security number. Other helpful information: date of birth, approximate years of attendance. No fee for information.

Degree information available by phone. Search requires name plus social security number. Other helpful information: date of birth, approximate years of attendance. No fee for information.

Transcripts available by written request only. Search requires name plus social security number, signed release. Other helpful information: date of birth, approximate years of attendance. Fee is $5.00. Unofficial transcripts are free.

Ramirez College of Business and Technology, Registrar, PO Box 8074, Santurce, PR 00910, 809-763-3120 (FAX: 809-763-7038). Hours: 8AM-9:30PM. Records go back to founding date. Degrees granted: Associate.

Attendance and degree information available by phone, mail. Search requires name plus social security number. Other helpful information: approximate years of attendance. No fee for information.

Transcripts available by mail. Search requires name plus social security number, signed release. Other helpful information: approximate years of attendance. Fee is $3.00.

Rancho Santiago Community College, Registrar, 1530 W 17th St, Santa Ana, CA 92706, 714-564-6000 (FAX: 714-564-6379). Hours: 8AM-9PM. Degrees granted: Associate.

Attendance information available by written request only. Search requires name plus date of birth, signed release. Other helpful information: social security number, approximate years of attendance. Fee is $2.00.

Degree information available by phone, FAX, mail. Search requires name plus date of birth. Other helpful information: social security number, approximate years of attendance. Fee is $2.00.

Transcripts available by FAX, mail. Search requires name plus social security number, date of birth, exact years of attendance, signed release. Other helpful information: approximate years of attendance. Fee is $3.00. Expedited service available for $8.00.

Rand Graduate School of Policy Studies, Registrar, 1700 Main St, PO Box 2138, Santa Monica, CA 90407-2138, 310-393-0411 X1690 (FAX: 310-451-6978). Hours: 8AM-5PM. Records go back to 1948. Alumni records are maintained here at the same phone number. Degrees granted: Doctorate.

Attendance and degree information available by phone, FAX, mail. Search requires name plus exact years of attendance. No fee for information.

Transcripts available by mail. Search requires name plus social security number, exact years of attendance, signed release. No fee for transcripts.

Randolph Community College, Registrar, PO Box 1009, Asheboro, NC 27204-1009, 910-629-1471 (FAX: 910-629-4695).

Hours: 8AM-5PM. Records go back to 1963. Degrees granted: Associate.

Attendance and degree information available by phone, FAX, mail. Search requires name plus social security number. Other helpful information: date of birth, approximate years of attendance. No fee for information.

Transcripts available by mail. Search requires name plus social security number, signed release. Other helpful information: date of birth, approximate years of attendance. No fee for transcripts.

Randolph-Macon College, Registrar, PO Box 5005, Ashland, VA 23005-5505, 804-752-7227 (FAX: 804-752-7231). Hours: 8:30AM-4:30PM. Records go back to 1875. Alumni records are maintained here also. Call 804-752-7222. Degrees granted: Bachelors.

Attendance and degree information available by phone, FAX, mail. Search requires name plus social security number, exact years of attendance. Other helpful information: approximate years of attendance. No fee for information.

Transcripts available by mail. Search requires name plus social security number, exact years of attendance, signed release. Other helpful information: approximate years of attendance. Fee is $2.00. Expedited service available for $4.00.

Randolph-Macon Woman's College, Registrar, 2500 Rivermont Ave, Lynchburg, VA 24503-1526, 804-947-8143. Hours: 9AM-5PM. Records go back to founding date. Alumni records are maintained here also. Call 804-947-8102. Degrees granted: Bachelors.

Attendance and degree information available by phone, mail. Search requires name plus approximate years of attendance. Other helpful information: social security number, date of birth, exact years of attendance. No fee for information.

Transcripts available by mail. Search requires name plus approximate years of attendance, signed release. Other helpful information: social security number, date of birth, exact years of attendance. Fee is $3.00. Expedite: $5.00 plus overnight charges.

Range Technical College, Registrar, 2900 E Beltline, Hibbing, MN 55746, 218-262-7212 (FAX: 218-262-7222). Hours: 7:30AM-4:30PM. Records go back to 1965. Degrees granted: Associate.

Attendance and degree information available by phone, FAX, mail. Search requires name plus social security number, signed release. No fee for information.

Transcripts available by mail. Search requires name plus social security number, signed release. Fee is $3.00.

Ranger College, Registrar, College Cir, Ranger, TX 76470-3298, 817-647-3234. Degrees granted: Associate.

Attendance and degree information available by phone, FAX, mail. Search requires name only. Other helpful information: social security number, date of birth, approximate years of attendance. No fee for information.

Transcripts available by FAX, mail. Search requires name plus signed release. Other helpful information: social security number, date of birth, approximate years of attendance. Fee is $3.00.

Ranken Technical College, Registrar, 4431 Finney Ave, St Louis, MO 63113, 314-371-0236 X1180 (FAX: 314-371-0241). Hours: 7:30AM-6:30PM M,T,Th; 7:30AM-4PM W,F. Records go back to 1909. Alumni records are maintained here also. Call 314-371-0236 X1650. Degrees granted: Associate.

Attendance and degree information available by phone, FAX, mail. Search requires name plus social security number, approximate years of attendance, signed release. No fee for information.

Transcripts available by mail. Search requires name plus social security number, approximate years of attendance, signed release. Fee is $3.00.

Rappahannock Community College, Registrar, PO Box 287, Glenns, VA 23149, 804-758-6700 (FAX: 804-758-3852). Hours: 8AM-5PM. Records go back to 1970. Alumni records are maintained here at the same phone number. Degrees granted: Associate.

Attendance and degree information available by phone, FAX, mail. Search requires name plus social security number, exact years of attendance. No fee for information.

Transcripts available by FAX, mail. Search requires name plus social security number, exact years of attendance, signed release. Fee is $1.00.

Raritan Valley Community College, Registrar's Office, PO Box 3300, Rt 28 and Lamington Rd, Somerville, NJ 08876, 908-526-1200 (FAX: 908-231-8811). Hours: 8:30AM-4:30PM. Records go back to 1970. Degrees granted: Associate. Adverse incident record source: Student Affairs, 908-526-1200.

Attendance and degree information available by phone, FAX, mail. Search requires name plus social security number, signed release. Other helpful information: approximate years of attendance. No fee for information.

Transcripts available by FAX, mail. Search requires name plus social security number, signed release. Other helpful information: date of birth, approximate years of attendance. Fee is $5.00.

Major credit cards accepted for payment.

Rasmussen Business College, Registrar, 3500 Federal Dr, Eagan, MN 55122, 612-687-9000 (FAX: 612-687-0507). Hours: 7AM-10PM. Records go back to 1975. Degrees granted: Associate.

Attendance and degree information available by phone, FAX, mail. Search requires name plus social security number, approximate years of attendance, signed release. No fee for information.

Transcripts available by FAX, mail. Search requires name plus social security number, approximate years of attendance, signed release. No fee for transcripts.

Rasmussen Business College, Registrar, 501 Holly Ln, Mankato, MN 56001, 507-625-6556 (FAX: 507-625-6557). Hours: 8AM-9:30PM. Records go back to 1983. Degrees granted: Associate.

Attendance information available by phone, FAX, mail. Search requires name plus social security number. Other helpful information: approximate years of attendance. No fee for information.

Degree information available by phone, mail. Search requires name plus social security number. Other helpful information: approximate years of attendance. No fee for information.

Transcripts available by FAX, mail. Search requires name plus social security number, signed release. Other helpful information: date of birth, approximate years of attendance. Fee is $1.00.

Rasmussen Business College, Registrar, 12450 Wayzata Blvd Ste 315, Minnetonka, MN 55305-9845, 612-545-2000 (FAX: 612-545-7038). Hours: 8AM-9PM. Records go back to 1966. Degrees granted: Associate.

Attendance and degree information available by phone, FAX, mail. Search requires name plus social security number, approximate years of attendance, signed release. No fee for information.

Transcripts available by FAX, mail. Search requires name plus social security number, approximate years of attendance, signed release. No fee for transcripts.

Ray College of Design, Registrar, 350 N Orleans St #136, Chicago, IL 60654-3532, 312-280-3500 (FAX: 312-280-3528). Hours: 9AM-4PM. Records go back to 1960s. Degrees granted: Associate; Bachelors.

Attendance information available by written request only. Search requires name plus social security number, approximate years of attendance, signed release. Other helpful information: exact years of attendance. No fee for information.

Degree information available by mail. Search requires name plus social security number. Other helpful information: approximate years of attendance. No fee for information.

Transcripts available by written request only. Search requires name plus social security number, signed release. Other helpful information: approximate years of attendance. Fee is $3.00.

Major credit cards accepted for payment.

Ray College of Design, **(Branch)**, Registrar, 1051 Perimeter Dr, Schaumburg, IL 60173-5070, 708-619-3450 (FAX: 708-619-3064). Hours: 8:30AM-4:30PM. Records go back 12 years. Records go back 12 years for branch campus. Degrees granted: Associate; Bachelors. Special programs- Ray College of Design, Chicago, 312-280-3500.

Attendance information available by mail. Search requires name plus social security number, signed release. Other helpful information: date of birth, approximate years of attendance. No fee for information.

Degree information available by phone, FAX, mail. Search requires name plus social security number, approximate years of attendance, signed release. Other helpful information: date of birth. No fee for information.

Transcripts available by mail. Search requires name plus social security number, approximate years of attendance, signed release. Other helpful information: date of birth. Fee is $3.00.

Major credit cards accepted for payment.

Reading Area Community College, Registrar, PO Box 1706, 10 S 2nd St, Reading, PA 19603-1706, 610-372-4721 X224 (FAX: 610-375-8255). Hours: 8AM-5PM. Records go back to 1971. Alumni records are maintained here at the same phone number. Degrees granted: Associate.

Attendance and degree information available by phone, mail. Search requires name plus social security number. No fee for information.

Transcripts available by mail. Search requires name plus social security number, signed release. Fee is $2.00.

Reconstructionist Rabbinical College, Registrar, Greenwood Ave and Church Rd, Wyncote, PA 19095, 215-576-0800 (FAX: 215-576-6143). Hours: 9AM-4PM. Records go back to 1970. Degrees granted: Masters; Doctorate; Rabbi.

Attendance and degree information available by phone, FAX, mail. Search requires name only. Other helpful information: approximate years of attendance. No fee for information.

Transcripts available by mail. Search requires name plus signed release. Other helpful information: approximate years of attendance. Fee is $2.00.

Include a self addressed stamped envelope with mail request.

Red Rocks Community College, Registrar, 13300 W Sixth Ave, Lakewood, CO 80401-5398, 303-988-6160 (FAX: 303-988-6191). Hours: 8AM-7PM M-Th, 9AM-5PM F. Records go back to 1969. Degrees granted: Associate. Adverse incident record source: Security, 303-988-6160.

Attendance and degree information available by phone, FAX, mail. Search requires name plus social security number, exact years of attendance. No fee for information.

Transcripts available by mail. Search requires name plus social security number, exact years of attendance, signed release. No fee for transcripts.

Information released if no holds on file.

Redlands Community College, Registrar, 1300 S Country Club Rd, El Reno, OK 73036-0370, 405-262-2552 (FAX: 405-262-7960). Hours: 8AM-5PM. Records go back to 1938. Alumni records are maintained here at the same phone number. Degrees granted: Associate.

Attendance and degree information available by phone, FAX, mail. Search requires name only. Other helpful information: social security number, date of birth, approximate years of attendance. No fee for information.

Transcripts available by written request only. Search requires name plus social security number, date of birth, signed release. Other helpful information: approximate years of attendance. Fee is $2.00. Expedited service available for $2.00.

Reed College, Registrar, 3203 SE Woodstock Blvd, Portland, OR 97202, 503-771-1112 X7793. Hours: 10AM-5PM. Records go back to 1930. Second phone number is 503-777-7293. Alumni records are maintained here also. Call 503-771-7589. Degrees granted: Bachelors; Masters.

Attendance and degree information available by phone, mail. Search requires name plus social security number, exact years of attendance, signed release. No fee for information.

Transcripts available by mail. Search requires name plus social security number, exact years of attendance, signed release. Fee is $3.00. Expedited service available for $5.00.

Information available over the phone if release in file. Need deadline if any, Reed ID#, former names needed. Signed release can be in file for phone use.

Reformed Bible College, Registrar, 3333 E Beltline Ave NE, Grand Rapids, MI 49505, 616-363-2050 (FAX: 616-363-9771). Hours: 8AM-5PM. Records go back to 1940. Degrees granted: Associate.

Attendance and degree information available by phone, FAX, mail. Search requires name only. No fee for information.

Transcripts available by FAX, mail. Search requires name plus social security number, date of birth. Other helpful information: approximate years of attendance. Fee is $2.00.

Major credit cards accepted for payment.

Reformed Theological Seminary, Registrar, 5422 Clinton Blvd, Jackson, MS 39209, 601-922-4988 X236 (FAX: 601-922-1153). Hours: 8AM-5PM. Records go back to 1966. Degrees granted: Masters; Doctorate.

Attendance and degree information available by phone, FAX, mail. Search requires name only. Other helpful information: social security number, approximate years of attendance. No fee for information.

Transcripts available by mail. Search requires name plus signed release. Other helpful information: social security number, approximate years of attendance. Fee is $3.00. Expedited service available for $3.00.

Regent University, Registrar, 1000 Centerville Tpke, Virginia Beach, VA 23464, 804-579-4094 (FAX: 804-575-5317). Hours: 8AM-5PM. Records go back to 1977. Alumni records are maintained here also. Call 804-579-4461. Degrees granted: Bachelors; Masters; Doctorate.

Attendance and degree information available by phone, FAX, mail. Search requires name plus social security number. No fee for information.

Transcripts available by FAX, mail. Search requires name plus signed release. No fee for transcripts.

Regents College of the University of the State of New York, Registrar, 7 Columbia Cir, Albany, NY 12203-5159, 518-464-8500 (FAX: 518-464-8777). Hours: 9AM-5PM. Records go back to 1970s. Alumni records are maintained here at the same phone number. Degrees granted: Bachelors.

Attendance and degree information available by phone, FAX, mail. Search requires name plus social security number. No fee for information.

Transcripts available by FAX, mail. Search requires name plus social security number, signed release. Other helpful information: approximate years of attendance. Fee is $7.00.

Major credit cards accepted for payment.

Regis College, Registrar, Weston, MA 02193, 617-873-1820 (FAX: 617-899-4725). Hours: 9AM-4:30PM Winter; 8AM-5PM Summer. Records go back to 1927. Degrees granted: Bachelors; Masters.

Attendance and degree information available by phone, FAX, mail. Search requires name plus approximate years of attendance. Other helpful information: social security number, date of birth, exact years of attendance. No fee for information.

Transcripts available by FAX, mail. Search requires name plus approximate years of attendance, signed release. Other helpful information: social security number, date of birth, exact years of attendance. Fee is $3.00.

Regis University, Registrar, 3333 Regis Blvd, Denver, CO 80221-1099, 303-458-4114 (FAX: 303-964-5536). Hours: 8:30AM-5PM. Records go back to 1877. Degrees granted: Associate; Bachelors; Masters. Certification: Teacher. Adverse incident record source: Student Life Office: Probation/suspension posted to transcript

Attendance and degree information available by phone, FAX, mail. Search requires name plus social security number, date of birth. Other helpful information: approximate years of attendance. No fee for information.

Transcripts available by FAX, mail. Search requires name plus social security number, date of birth, exact years of attendance, signed release. Other helpful information: approximate years of attendance. Fee is $5.00. Expedited service available for $6.00.

Major credit cards accepted for payment.

Reid State Technical College, Registrar, I-65 at Hwy 83, Evergreen, AL 36401, 334-578-1313 X106 (FAX: 334-578-5345). Hours: 7AM-4PM. Records go back to 1963. Degrees granted: Associate. Adverse incident record source: Dean of Students, 334-578-1313.

Attendance and degree information available by phone, FAX, mail. Search requires name only. Other helpful information: social

security number, date of birth, approximate years of attendance. No fee for information. Expedited service available for $5.00.

Transcripts available by mail. Search requires name plus signed release. Other helpful information: social security number, date of birth, approximate years of attendance. No fee for transcripts. Expedited service available for $5.00.

Major credit cards accepted for payment.

Reinhardt College, Registrar, PO Box 128, Waleska, GA 30183, 404-720-5534 (FAX: 404-720-5602). Hours: 8:30AM-5PM. Degrees granted: Associate; Bachelors. Adverse incident record source: Student Development, 404-720-5537.

Attendance information available by phone, FAX, mail. Search requires name plus social security number, date of birth, signed release. Other helpful information: approximate years of attendance. No fee for information.

Degree information available by phone, FAX, mail. Search requires name plus social security number. Other helpful information: date of birth, approximate years of attendance. No fee for information.

Transcripts available by FAX, mail. Search requires name plus social security number, signed release. Other helpful information: date of birth, approximate years of attendance. Fee is $2.00.

Remington College, Registrar, 303 Rue Louis XIV, Lafayette, LA 70508, 318-981-4010 (FAX: 318-981-4098). Hours: 7:30AM-7PM. Records go back 5 years. Formerly known as Southern Technical College. Degrees granted: Associate.

Attendance information available by phone, FAX, mail. Search requires name plus social security number, approximate years of attendance, signed release. Other helpful information: exact years of attendance. No fee for information.

Degree information available by phone, FAX, mail. Search requires name plus social security number, approximate years of attendance. Other helpful information: exact years of attendance. No fee for information.

Transcripts available by phone, FAX, mail. Search requires name plus social security number, approximate years of attendance, signed release. Other helpful information: exact years of attendance. Fee is $3.00.

Rend Lake College, Registrar, Rural Rte 1, Ina, IL 62846, 618-437-5321 (FAX: 618-437-5677). Hours: 8AM-4:30PM M-Th; 8AM-4PM F. Records go back 40 years. Degrees granted: Associate.

Attendance information available by phone, FAX, mail. Search requires name plus social security number. Other helpful information: date of birth, approximate years of attendance. No fee for information.

Degree information available by phone, FAX, mail. Search requires name only. No fee for information.

Transcripts available by FAX, mail. Search requires name plus social security number, signed release. Other helpful information: date of birth, approximate years of attendance. No fee for transcripts.

Rensselaer Polytechnic Institute, Registrar, 110 Eighth St, Troy, NY 12180-3590, 518-276-6231 (FAX: 518-276-6180). Hours: 8:30AM-5PM Fall & Spring; 8AM-4:30PM Summer. Records go back to 1900s. Alumni records are maintained here also. Call 518-276-6205. Degrees granted: Bachelors; Masters; Doctorate. Special programs- Hartford Graduate Center, 275 Windsor St, Hartford, CT 06120. Adverse incident record source: Dean of Students.

Attendance and degree information available by phone, FAX, mail. Search requires name plus social security number, exact years of attendance, signed release. Other helpful information: date of birth, approximate years of attendance. No fee for information. Expedited service available for $10.75.

Transcripts available by FAX, mail. Search requires name plus social security number, exact years of attendance, signed release. Other helpful information: date of birth, approximate years of attendance. No fee for transcripts. Expedited service available for $10.75.

Renton Technical College, Registrar, 3000 Fourth St NE, Renton, WA 98056, 206-235-2352. Degrees granted: Associate.

Attendance and degree information available by FAX, mail. Search requires name plus social security number, date of birth, approximate years of attendance, signed release. Other helpful information: exact years of attendance. Fee is $3.00.

Transcripts available by FAX, mail. Search requires name plus social security number, date of birth, approximate years of attendance, signed release. Other helpful information: exact years of attendance. Fee is $3.00.

Major credit cards accepted for payment.

Research College of Nursing, Registrar, 2316 E Meyer Blvd, Kansas City, MO 64132, 816-926-4057 (FAX: 816-926-4588). Records are not housed here. They are located at Rockhurst College, Registrar, 1100 Rockhurst Rd, Kansas City, MO 64110.

Rhode Island College, Registrar, Providence, RI 02908, 401-456-8212. Hours: 8AM-4:30PM. Records go back to 1854. Degrees granted: Bachelors; Masters; Doctorate; CAGS.

Attendance and degree information available by written request only. Search requires name plus signed release. No fee for information.

Transcripts available by written request only. Search requires name plus signed release. Fee is $2.00.

Rhode Island School of Design, Registrar, 2 College St, Providence, RI 02903, 401-454-6151. Hours: 8:30AM-4:30PM. Records go back to 1930s. Alumni records are maintained here also. Call 401-454-6620. Degrees granted: Bachelors; Masters.

Attendance and degree information available by phone, FAX, mail. Search requires name only. Other helpful information: social security number, date of birth, approximate years of attendance. No fee for information. Include a stamped envelope.

Transcripts available by mail. Search requires name plus signed release. Other helpful information: social security number, date of birth, approximate years of attendance. No fee for transcripts.

Major credit cards accepted for payment.

Rhodes College, Registrar, 2000 North Pkwy, Memphis, TN 38112, 901-726-3885 (FAX: 901-726-3576). Hours: 8:30AM-3:30PM. Records go back to 1848. Degrees granted: Bachelors; Masters.

Attendance and degree information available by phone, FAX, mail. Search requires name only. Other helpful information: social security number, date of birth, approximate years of attendance. No fee for information.

Transcripts available by FAX. Search requires name plus signed release. Other helpful information: social security number, date of birth, approximate years of attendance. Fee is $2.00.

Major credit cards accepted for payment.

Rice University, Office of the Registrar, 6100 Main St, Houston, TX 77005-1892, 713-527-4999 (FAX: 713-285-5323). Hours: 8:30PM-5PM. Records go back to 1916. Degrees granted: Bachelors; Masters; Doctorate. Adverse incident record source: Dean of Students.

Attendance and degree information available by phone, FAX, mail. Search requires name only. Other helpful information: social security number, date of birth, approximate years of attendance. No fee for information.

Transcripts available by FAX, mail. Search requires name plus signed release. Other helpful information: social security number, date of birth, approximate years of attendance. Fee is $3.00. Long distance FAXes: $3.00 in Texas; $5.00 in USA; $10.00 outside US.

Rich Mountain Community College, Registrar, 1100 Bush St, Mena, AR 71953, 501-394-5012 (FAX: 501-394-2828). Hours: 8AM-4:30PM. Records go back to 1976. Degrees granted: Associate. Adverse incident record source: Registrar's Office

Attendance and degree information available by FAX, mail. Search requires name plus signed release. Other helpful information: social security number, date of birth, approximate years of attendance. No fee for information.

Transcripts available by FAX, mail. Search requires name plus signed release. Other helpful information: social security number, date of birth, approximate years of attendance. Fee is $1.00.

Richard Bland College, Registrar, 11301 Johnson Rd, Petersburg, VA 23805, 804-862-6206 (FAX: 804-862-6189). Hours: 8AM-5PM. Alumni records are maintained here also. Call 804-862-6215. Degrees granted: Associate.

Attendance and degree information available by phone, FAX, mail. Search requires name plus social security number, exact years of attendance. Other helpful information: date of birth. No fee for information.

Transcripts available by FAX, mail. Search requires name plus social security number, signed release. Other helpful information: date of birth, approximate years of attendance. No fee for transcripts.

Richard J. Daley College, Registrar, 7500 S PUlaski Rd, Chicago, IL 60652, 312-838-7600 (FAX: 312-838-7605). Hours: 8AM-7PM. Records go back to 1960. Degrees granted: Associate.

Attendance and degree information available by phone, FAX, mail. Search requires name plus social security number, exact years of attendance, signed release. No fee for information.

Transcripts available by mail. Search requires name plus social security number, exact years of attendance, signed release. Fee is $5.00.

Richland College, Registrar, 12800 Abrams Rd, Dallas, TX 75243-2199, 214-238-6104 (FAX: 214-238-6149). Hours: 8:30AM-7PM M-Th; 8:30AM-5PM F. Records go back to 1972. Degrees granted: Associate. Adverse incident record source: 214-238-6911.

School will not confirm attendance or degree information. Search requires name plus social security number, signed release. No fee for information.

Transcripts available by phone, FAX, mail. Search requires name plus social security number. No fee for transcripts.

Transcript requests must be made by student.

Richland Community College, Registrar, One College Park, Decatur, IL 62521, 217-875-7200 (FAX: 217-875-6965). Hours: 8AM-8PM M-Th; 8AM-5PM F. Records go back to 1972. Degrees granted: Associate.

Attendance and degree information available by phone, FAX, mail. Search requires name plus social security number, date of birth. Other helpful information: approximate years of attendance. No fee for information.

Transcripts available by written request only. Search requires name plus social security number, date of birth, signed release. Other helpful information: approximate years of attendance. Fee is $2.00. Expedited service available for $5.00.

Major credit cards accepted for payment.

Richmond Community College, Registrar, PO Box 1189, Hamlet, NC 28345, 910-582-7107. Hours: 8AM-5PM. Records go back 30 years. Degrees granted: Associate.

Attendance and degree information available by phone, FAX, mail. Search requires name plus social security number, approximate years of attendance, signed release. Other helpful information: date of birth, exact years of attendance. No fee for information.

Transcripts available by mail. Search requires name plus social security number, approximate years of attendance, signed release. Other helpful information: date of birth, exact years of attendance. No fee for transcripts.

Ricks College, Transcripts, Rexburg, ID 83460-4125, 208-356-1011 (FAX: 208-356-1035). Hours: 8AM-5PM. Records go back to 1888. Degrees granted: Associate. Adverse incident record source: Dean of Students, 208-356-1120.

Attendance and degree information available by phone, FAX, mail. Search requires name plus signed release. Other helpful information: social security number, date of birth, approximate years of attendance. No fee for information.

Transcripts available by FAX, mail. Search requires name plus signed release. Other helpful information: social security number, date of birth, approximate years of attendance. Fee is $2.00. Expedited service available for $2.00.

Major credit cards accepted for payment.

Rider College, Registrar, 2083 Lawrenceville Rd, Lawrenceville, NJ 08648-3099, 609-895-5065 (FAX: 609-895-5447). Hours: 8:30AM-5PM. Records go back to 1925. Alumni records are maintained here also. Call 609-895-5340. Degrees granted: Bachelors; Masters. Adverse incident record source: Dean of Students, 609-895-5103.

Attendance information available by FAX, mail. Search requires name plus social security number, date of birth, approximate years of attendance, signed release. No fee for information.

Degree information available by phone, FAX, mail. Search requires name plus social security number, date of birth, approximate years of attendance, signed release. No fee for information.

Transcripts available by mail. Search requires name plus social security number, date of birth, approximate years of attendance, signed release. No fee for transcripts.

Rider College, **(Westminster Choir College)**, Registrar, 101 Walnut Lane, Princeton, NJ 08540, 609-921-7100 X294 (FAX: 609-921-8829). Hours: 8:30AM-5PM. Records go back to 1920. Degrees granted: Bachelors; Masters.

Attendance and degree information available by phone, FAX, mail. Search requires name plus signed release. No fee for information.

Transcripts available by mail. Search requires name plus signed release. Fee is $3.00.

Ringling School of Art and Design, Registrar, 2700 N Tamiami Tr, Sarasota, FL 34234, 813-351-4614 (FAX: 813-359-7517). Hours: 8:30AM-4:30PM. Records go back to 1931. Degrees granted: Bachelors. Adverse incident record source: Security RSAD.

Attendance information available by FAX, mail. Search requires name only. Other helpful information: social security number, date of birth, approximate years of attendance. No fee for information.

Degree information available by FAX, mail. Search requires name plus social security number, date of birth, approximate years of attendance, signed release. No fee for information.

Transcripts available by FAX, mail. Search requires name plus social security number, date of birth, signed release. Other helpful information: approximate years of attendance. No fee for transcripts.

Major credit cards accepted for payment.

Rio Hondo College, Registrar, 3600 Workman Mill Rd, Whittier, CA 90608, 310-692-0921 X3153 (FAX: 310-692-8318). Hours: 8AM-8PM M-Th, 8AM-4PM F. Records go back to 1963. Alumni records are maintained here also. Call 310-692-0921 X3445. Degrees granted: Associate.

Attendance and degree information available by phone, FAX, mail. Search requires name plus social security number, date of birth, signed release. No fee for information.

Transcripts available by FAX, mail. Search requires name plus social security number, date of birth, signed release. Fee is $3.00.

Rio Salado Community College, Registrar, 640 N First Ave, Phoenix, AZ 85003, 602-223-4001 (FAX: 602-223-4331). Hours: 8:15AM-5:45PM M-Th; 8:15AM-4:45PM F. Records go back to 1978. Alumni records are maintained here also. Call 602-223-4230. Degrees granted: Associate.

Attendance information available by FAX, mail. Search requires name plus signed release. Other helpful information: social security number. No fee for information.

Degree information available by mail. Search requires name plus signed release. Other helpful information: social security number. Fee is $5.00.

Transcripts available by FAX, mail. Search requires name plus signed release. Other helpful information: social security number. Fee is $5,00.

Major credit cards accepted for payment.

Ripon College, Registrar, PO Box 248, 300 Seward St, Ripon, WI 54971, 414-748-8119 (FAX: 414-748-9262). Hours: 8AM-5PM. Records go back to 1851. Alumni records are maintained here also. Call 414-748-8126. Degrees granted: Bachelors.

Attendance and degree information available by phone, mail. Search requires name plus exact years of attendance. No fee for information.

Transcripts available by mail. Search requires name plus exact years of attendance, signed release. Fee is $2.00.

Riverside Community College, Registrar, 4800 Magnolia Ave, Riverside, CA 92506-1299, 909-222-8000 (FAX: 909-222-8028). Hours: 7:30AM-7PM. Records go back to founding date. Degrees granted: Associate. Adverse incident record source: Safety & Security.

Attendance information available by FAX, mail. Search requires name plus date of birth, approximate years of attendance, signed release. Other helpful information: social security number. No fee for information. Include a stamped envelope.

Degree information available by phone, FAX, mail. Search requires name only. Other helpful information: social security number, date of birth, approximate years of attendance. No fee for information.

Transcripts available by mail. Search requires name plus social security number, date of birth, signed release. Fee is $3.00. Expedited service available for $5.00.

Rivier College, Registrar, 420 S Main St, Nashua, NH 03060-5086, 603-888-1311. Hours: 8AM-5PM. Records go back to 1937. Alumni records are maintained here also. Call 603-888-1311 X8522. Degrees granted: Associate; Bachelors; Masters.

Attendance and degree information available by phone, mail. Search requires name plus social security number, approximate years of attendance. Other helpful information: exact years of attendance. No fee for information.

Transcripts available by written request only. Search requires name plus social security number, approximate years of attendance, signed release. Other helpful information: exact years of attendance. Fee is $3.00.

Roane State Community College, Registrar, Rte 8 Box 69, Patton Lane, Harriman, TN 37748, 615-882-4523 (FAX: 615-882-4562). Hours: 8:30AM-5PM. Records go back to 1971. Degrees granted: Associate.

Attendance and degree information available by phone, FAX, mail. Search requires name plus social security number. No fee for information.

Transcripts available by FAX, mail. Search requires name plus social security number, signed release. No fee for transcripts.

Roanoke Bible College, Registrar, 714 First St, Elizabeth City, NC 27909, 919-338-5191 (FAX: 919-338-0801). Hours: 9AM-5PM. Records go back to 1948. Degrees granted: Associate; Bachelors.

Attendance and degree information available by phone, FAX, mail. Search requires name plus social security number, date of birth, signed release. Other helpful information: approximate years of attendance. No fee for information.

Transcripts available by FAX, mail. Search requires name plus social security number, date of birth, signed release. Other helpful information: approximate years of attendance. Fee is $5.00. Expedited service available for $2.00.

Include a self addressed stamped envelope with mail request.

Roanoke College, Registrar, 221 College Lane, Salem, VA 24153-3794, 703-375-2210 (FAX: 703-375-2213). Hours: 8AM-4:30PM. Degrees granted: Bachelors. Adverse incident record source: Campus Safety, 703-375-2310.

Attendance and degree information available by phone, FAX, mail. Search requires name plus social security number, date of birth, approximate years of attendance. Other helpful information: exact years of attendance. No fee for information.

Transcripts available by FAX, mail. Search requires name plus social security number, date of birth, approximate years of attendance, signed release. Other helpful information: exact years of attendance. Fee is $2.00. Expedite fee is based on cost of service.'

Roanoke-Chowan Community College, Registrar, Rte 2 Box 46-A, Ahoskie, NC 27910, 919-332-5921 (FAX: 919-332-2210). Hours: 8:15AM-5PM. Records go back to 1967. Adverse incident record source: Jack Henderson, 919-332-5921 X243.

Attendance and degree information available by phone, FAX, mail. Search requires name plus social security number. Other

helpful information: date of birth, approximate years of attendance. No fee for information.

Transcripts available by mail. Search requires name plus social security number, signed release. Other helpful information: date of birth, approximate years of attendance. Fee is $1.00.

Major credit cards accepted for payment.

Robert Morris College, Registrar, 180 N LaSalle St, Chicago, IL 60601, 312-836-4807 (FAX: 312-836-4853). Hours: 8:30AM-5PM. Records go back to 1950. Alumni records are maintained here also. Call 312-836-5469. Degrees granted: Associate; Bachelors.

Attendance and degree information available by phone, FAX, mail. Search requires name plus social security number, exact years of attendance, signed release. No fee for information.

Transcripts available by FAX, mail. Search requires name plus social security number, exact years of attendance, signed release. No fee for transcripts.

Robert Morris College, Director Student Records, Narrows Run Rd, Coraopolis, PA 15108, 412-262-8274. Hours: 8AM-9PM. Records go back to 1940s. Alumni records are maintained here also. Call 412-262-8481. Degrees granted: Associate; Bachelors; Masters. Adverse incident record source: Campus Police, 412-262-8352.

Attendance and degree information available by phone, mail. Search requires name only. Other helpful information: social security number, approximate years of attendance. No fee for information.

Transcripts available by written request only. Search requires name plus signed release. Other helpful information: social security number, approximate years of attendance. Fee is $2.00.

College, major helpful.

Robert Morris College, **(Pittsburgh College)**, Registrar, Coraopolis, PA 15108, 412-227-6800. Hours: 8AM-5PM. Records go back to 1962. Alumni records are maintained here at the same phone number. Degrees granted: Associate; Bachelors; Masters.

Attendance and degree information available by phone, mail. Search requires name plus social security number, date of birth, exact years of attendance. No fee for information.

Transcripts available by mail. Search requires name plus social security number, date of birth, exact years of attendance, signed release. Fee is $2.00.

Roberts Wesleyan College, Registrar, 2301 Westside Dr, Rochester, NY 14624-1997, 716-594-6220 (FAX: 716-594-6371). Hours: 8AM-5PM. Degrees granted: Associate; Bachelors; Masters. Special programs- MHR, OM, M.Ed, M.S.W., 716-594-6455.

Attendance and degree information available by phone, FAX. Search requires name plus social security number, exact years of attendance. Other helpful information: date of birth, approximate years of attendance. No fee for information.

Transcripts available by written request only. Search requires name plus social security number, exact years of attendance, signed release. Other helpful information: date of birth, approximate years of attendance. Fee is $5.00. Expedited service available for $5.00.

Robeson Community College, Registrar, PO Box 1420, Lumberton, NC 28359, 910-738-7101. Degrees granted: Associate; Vocational Diploma.

Attendance and degree information available by mail. Search requires name plus social security number, signed release. Other helpful information: date of birth, approximate years of attendance. No fee for information.

Transcripts available by mail. Search requires name plus social security number, signed release. Other helpful information: date of birth, approximate years of attendance. Fee is $1.00.

Rochester Business Institute, Registrar, 1850 Ridge Rd E, Rochester, NY 14622, 716-266-0430 (FAX: 716-266-8243). Hours: 8AM-6PM M-Th, 8AM-5PM F. Records go back to 1920. Degrees granted: Associate.

Attendance and degree information available by phone, FAX, mail. Search requires name plus social security number, signed release. No fee for information.

Transcripts available by mail. Search requires name plus social security number, approximate years of attendance, signed release. Fee is $5.00.

Written permission needed unless sponsoring agency or student. Major credit cards accepted for payment.

Rochester Community College, Admissions & Records, 851 30th Ave SE, Rochester, MN 55904-4999, 507-285-7265 (FAX: 507-285-7496). Hours: 8AM-8PM M-Th; 8AM-4:30PM F. Records go back to 1915. Degrees granted: Associate.

Attendance information available by phone, FAX, mail. Search requires name plus social security number, date of birth, exact years of attendance. No fee for information. Include a stamped envelope.

Degree information available by phone, FAX, mail. Search requires name plus social security number. Other helpful information: date of birth, approximate years of attendance. No fee for information.

Transcripts available by FAX, mail. Search requires name plus social security number, date of birth, signed release. Other helpful information: approximate years of attendance. No fee for transcripts.

Rochester Institute of Technology, Office of the Registrar, George Eastman Bldg, 27 Lomb Memorial Dr, Rochester, NY 14623-5603, 716-475-2885 (FAX: 716-475-7005). Hours: 8:30AM-4:30PM. Records go back to 1800s. Degrees granted: Associate; Bachelors; Masters; Doctorate.

Attendance and degree information available by phone, FAX, mail. Search requires name plus signed release. Other helpful information: social security number, date of birth, approximate years of attendance. No fee for information.

Transcripts available by FAX, mail. Search requires name plus signed release. Other helpful information: social security number, date of birth, approximate years of attendance. Fee is $4.00.

Major credit cards accepted for payment.

Rock Valley College, Registrar, 3301 N Mulford Rd, Rockford, IL 61114, 815-654-4306 (FAX: 815-654-5568). Hours: 8AM-5PM. Records go back to 1965. Alumni records are maintained here also. Call 815-654-4277. Degrees granted: Associate. Adverse incident record source: Dean of Students, 815-654-4270.

Attendance and degree information available by phone, FAX, mail. Search requires name plus social security number. Other helpful information: date of birth, exact years of attendance. No fee for information.

Transcripts available by mail. Search requires name plus social security number, signed release. Other helpful information: approximate years of attendance. No fee for transcripts.

Rockford Business College, Registrar, 730 N Church St, Rockford, IL 61103, 815-965-8616 (FAX: 815-965-0360). Hours: 8AM-9PM. Records go back to 1950s. Degrees granted: Associate. Adverse incident record source: Financial Aide, 815-965-8616.

Attendance information available by phone, FAX, mail. Search requires name plus social security number, approximate years of attendance, signed release. Other helpful information: exact years of attendance. No fee for information.

Degree information available by phone, FAX, mail. Search requires name plus approximate years of attendance, signed release. Other helpful information: social security number, exact years of attendance. No fee for information.

Transcripts available by mail. Search requires name plus social security number, approximate years of attendance, signed release. Other helpful information: exact years of attendance. Fee is $5.00. Expedited service available for $7.00.

Must have authorization from student to release information. Major credit cards accepted for payment.

Rockford College, Registrar, 5050 E State St, Rockford, IL 61108, 815-226-4070 (FAX: 815-226-4119). Hours: 8AM-5PM. Records go back to 1925. Alumni records are maintained here also. Call 815-226-4080. Degrees granted: Bachelors; Masters.

Attendance information available by phone, FAX, mail. Search requires name plus social security number, signed release. Other helpful information: approximate years of attendance. No fee for information.

Degree information available by phone, FAX, mail. Search requires name plus social security number. Other helpful information: approximate years of attendance. No fee for information.

Transcripts available by mail. Search requires name plus social security number, signed release. Other helpful information: approximate years of attendance. Fee is $3.00.

Rockhurst College, Registrar, 1100 Rockhurst Rd, Kansas City, MO 64110, 816-926-4057 (FAX: 816-926-4588). Hours: 8AM-6PM M-Th, 8AM-4:30PM F. Records go back to 1910. Degrees granted: Bachelors; Masters. Adverse incident record source: Rockhurst Security, 816-926-4000.

Attendance and degree information available by phone, FAX, mail. Search requires name only. Other helpful information: social security number, date of birth, approximate years of attendance. No fee for information.

Transcripts available by FAX, mail. Search requires name plus signed release. Other helpful information: social security number, date of birth, approximate years of attendance. No fee for transcripts. Expedited service available for $5.00.

Major credit cards accepted for payment.

Rockingham Community College, Registrar, PO Box 38, Wentworth, NC 27375-0038, 910-342-4261 X118 (FAX: 910-349-9986). Hours: 8AM-5PM. Records go back to 1966. Degrees granted: Associate.

Attendance and degree information available by phone, FAX, mail. Search requires name plus signed release. Other helpful information: social security number, date of birth. No fee for information.

Transcripts available by FAX, mail. Search requires name plus signed release. Other helpful information: social security number, date of birth. No fee for transcripts.

Rockland Community College, Registrar, 145 College Rd, Suffern, NY 10901, 914-574-4328 (FAX: 914-574-4499). Hours: 8AM-8PM M-Th, 9AM-5PM. Records go back to 1959. Alumni Records Office: Rockland Community College, 145 College Rd, Rm 6206, Suffern, NY 10901. Degrees granted: Associate. Adverse incident record source: Dean, 914-574-4207.

Attendance and degree information available by FAX, mail. Search requires name plus social security number, approximate years of attendance, signed release. No fee for information.

Transcripts available by FAX, mail. Search requires name plus social security number, approximate years of attendance, signed release. Fee is $3.00.

Rockland Community College, (Haverstraw Learning Center), Registrar, 36-39 Main St, Haverstraw, NY 10927, 914-942-0624. Records are not housed here. They are located at Rockland Community College, Registrar, 145 College Rd, Suffern, NY 10901.

Rockland Community College, (Nyack Learning Center), Registrar, 92-94 Main St, Nyack, NY 10960, 914-358-9392. Records are not housed here. They are located at Rockland Community College, Registrar, 145 College Rd, Suffern, NY 10901.

Rockland Community College, (Spring Valley Learning Center), Registrar, 185 N Main St, Spring Valley, NY 10977, 914-352-5535. Records are not housed here. They are located at Rockland Community College, Registrar, 145 College Rd, Suffern, NY 10901.

Rocky Mountain College, Registrar, 1511 Poly Dr, Billings, MT 59102, 406-657-1030 (FAX: 406-259-9251). Hours: 8AM-Noon, 1-4:30PM. Records go back to 1900. Alumni records are maintained here also. Call 406-657-1009. Degrees granted: Associate; Bachelors.

Attendance information available by phone, FAX, mail. Search requires name only. Other helpful information: social security number. No fee for information.

Degree information available by phone, FAX, mail. Search requires name only. Other helpful information: social security number, approximate years of attendance. No fee for information.

Transcripts available by FAX, mail. Search requires name plus approximate years of attendance, signed release. Other helpful information: social security number. Fee is $5.00. Expedited service available for $5.00.

Rocky Mountain College of Art and Design, Registrar, 6875 E Evans Ave, Denver, CO 80224-2359, 303-753-6046 (FAX: 303-759-4970). Hours: 8AM-4:30PM. Records go back to 1963. Alumni records are maintained here also. Call 800-888-2787. Degrees granted: Bachelors.

Attendance and degree information available by phone, FAX, mail. Search requires name plus social security number, exact years of attendance. No fee for information.

Transcripts available by mail. Search requires name plus social security number, exact years of attendance, signed release. Fee is $3.00.

Roger Williams University, Registrar, One Old Ferry Rd, Bristol, RI 02809-2921, 401-253-3033 (FAX: 401-254-3450). Hours: 8AM-5PM. Records go back to 1948. Degrees granted: Associate; Bachelors.

Attendance and degree information available by phone, FAX, mail. Search requires name plus approximate years of attendance, signed release. Other helpful information: social security number, date of birth, exact years of attendance. No fee for information.

Transcripts available by mail. Search requires name plus approximate years of attendance, signed release. Other helpful information: social security number, date of birth, exact years of attendance. Fee is $3.00.

Rogers State College, Registrar, Will Rogers and College Hill, Claremore, OK 74017, 918-343-7540 (FAX: 918-343-7595). Hours: 8AM-5PM. Alumni records are maintained here also. Call 918-343-7769. Degrees granted: Associate.

Attendance and degree information available by phone, FAX, mail. Search requires name plus social security number. Other helpful information: date of birth, approximate years of attendance. No fee for information.

Transcripts available by written request only. Search requires name plus social security number, approximate years of attendance, signed release. Other helpful information: date of birth, exact years of attendance. No fee for transcripts.

Rogue Community College, Student Records, 3345 Redwood Hwy, Grants Pass, OR 97527, 503-471-3500 (FAX: 503-471-3588). Hours: 9AM-4PM. Records go back to 1971. Degrees granted: Associate. Adverse incident record source: In student file.

Attendance information available by phone, FAX, mail. Search requires name plus exact years of attendance. Other helpful information: social security number, date of birth. No fee for information.

Degree information available by phone, FAX, mail. Search requires name only. Other helpful information: social security number, date of birth, approximate years of attendance. No fee for information.

Transcripts available by FAX, mail. Search requires name plus signed release. Other helpful information: social security number, date of birth, approximate years of attendance. Fee is $2.00.

Rollins College, Registrar, 1000 Holt Ave, Winter Park, FL 32789-4499, 407-646-2144 (FAX: 407-646-1576). Hours: 8:30AM-5PM. Records go back to 1895. Alumni records are maintained here also. Call 407-646-2266. Degrees granted: Associate; Bachelors; Masters. Adverse incident record source: Safety, 407-646-2401.

Attendance and degree information available by phone, FAX, mail. Search requires name plus social security number, exact years of attendance. No fee for information.

Transcripts available by FAX, mail. Search requires name plus social security number, exact years of attendance, signed release. Fee is $3.00.

Roosevelt University, Registrar, 430 S Michigan Ave, Chicago, IL 60605, 312-341-3526 (FAX: 312-341-3660). Hours: 9AM-6PM M,T; 9AM-5PM W,Th; 9AM-3PM F. Records go back to 1945. Degrees granted: Bachelors; Masters; Doctorate. Adverse incident record source: Student Affairs, 312-341-3540.

Attendance and degree information available by phone, FAX, mail. Search requires name plus social security number. Other helpful information: date of birth, approximate years of attendance. No fee for information.

Transcripts available by FAX, mail. Search requires name plus social security number, signed release. Other helpful information: date of birth, approximate years of attendance. No fee for transcripts.

Rosary College, Registrar, 7900 W Division St, River Forest, IL 60305, 708-366-2490. Degrees granted: Bachelors; Masters.

Attendance and degree information available by phone, mail. Search requires name only. Other helpful information: social security number, date of birth, approximate years of attendance. No fee for information.

Transcripts available by mail. Search requires name plus signed release. Other helpful information: social security number, date of birth, approximate years of attendance. Fee is $5.00.

Rose State College, Registrar, 6420 SE 15th St, Midwest City, OK 73110, 405-733-7308. Hours: 8AM-8PM M-Th, 8AM-6PMF. Records go back to 1971. Alumni records are maintained here also. Call 405-736-0313. Degrees granted: Associate.

Attendance and degree information available by phone, mail. Search requires name plus social security number. No fee for information.

Transcripts available by mail. Search requires name plus social security number, exact years of attendance, signed release. Fee is $2.00.

Need to know degree.

Rose-Hulman Institute of Technology, Registrar, 5500 Wabash Ave, Terre Haute, IN 47803, 812-877-1511 X298 (FAX: 812-877-8141). Hours: 8AM-5PM. Records go back to 1874. Alumni records are maintained here also. Call 812-877-8359. Degrees granted: Bachelors; Masters.

Attendance and degree information available by phone, FAX, mail. Search requires name only. Other helpful information: date of birth, approximate years of attendance. No fee for information. Include a stamped envelope.

Transcripts available by FAX, mail. Search requires name plus signed release. Other helpful information: approximate years of attendance. Fee is $2.00. Exedite: actual postage.

Rosemont College, Registrar, 1400 Montgomery Ave, Rosemont, PA 19010-1699, 610-527-0200 X2306. Hours: 8AM-5PM. Alumni records are maintained here at the same phone number. Degrees granted: Bachelors; Masters.

Attendance and degree information available by phone, mail. Search requires name plus social security number. No fee for information.

Transcripts available by mail. Search requires name plus social security number, signed release. Fee is $4.00.

Rowan College of New Jersey, Registrar, 201 Mullica Hill Rd, Glassboro, NJ 08028-1701, 609-256-4350 (FAX: 609-256-4929). Hours: 8AM-4:30PM. Records go back to 1980. Alumni records are maintained here also. Call 609-256-4131. Degrees granted: Bachelors; Masters. Adverse incident record source: Dean of Students, 609-256-4040.

Attendance and degree information available by phone, FAX, mail. Search requires name plus social security number, signed release. No fee for information.

Transcripts available by mail. Search requires name plus social security number, signed release. Fee is $5.00.

Rowan College of New Jersey, (Camden Campus), Registrar, One Broadway, Camden, NJ 08102, 609-757-2857. Records are not housed here. They are located at Rowan College of New Jersey, Registrar, 201 Mullica Hill Rd, Glassboro, NJ 08028-1701.

Rowan-Cabarrus Community College, Registrar, PO Box 1595, Salisbury, NC 28145, 704-637-0760. Degrees granted: Associate.

Attendance and degree information available by phone, FAX, mail. Search requires name plus social security number. Other helpful information: date of birth, approximate years of attendance. No fee for information.

Transcripts available by FAX. Search requires name plus social security number, signed release. Other helpful information: date of birth, approximate years of attendance. First five transcripts free; $1.00 each additional.

FAX requires written request.

Roxbury Community College, Registrar, 1234 Columbus Ave, Roxbury Crossing, MA 02120-3400, 617-427-0060 (FAX: 617-541-5351). Hours: 8:30AM-4:30PM. Records go back 15 years. Degrees granted: Associate.

Attendance and degree information available by FAX, mail. Search requires name plus social security number, date of birth, approximate years of attendance, signed release. No fee for information.

Transcripts available by FAX, mail. Search requires name plus social security number, date of birth, approximate years of attendance, signed release. Fee is $1.00.

Include a self addressed stamped envelope with mail request.

Rush University, Registrar, 1653 W Congress Pkwy, Chicago, IL 60612, 312-942-5681 (FAX: 312-942-6219). Hours: 8AM-5PM. Alumni records are maintained here also. Call 312-942-7165. Degrees granted: Doctorate; PhD.

Attendance information available by phone, FAX, mail. Search requires name plus social security number, approximate years of attendance, signed release. No fee for information.

Degree information available by mail. Search requires name plus social security number, approximate years of attendance, signed release. No fee for information.

Transcripts available by mail. Search requires name plus social security number, approximate years of attendance, signed release. No fee for transcripts.

Rust College, Registrar, 150 E Rust Ave, Holly Springs, MS 38635, 601-252-8000 X4057 (FAX: 601-252-8000 X6107). Hours: 8AM-5PM. Records go back to 1957. Alumni records are maintained here also. Call 601-252-8000 X4015. Degrees granted: Associate; Bachelors.

Attendance and degree information available by phone, FAX, mail. Search requires name plus social security number, signed release. No fee for information.

Transcripts available by FAX, mail. Search requires name plus social security number, signed release. Fee is $1.50.

Rutgers, The State University of New Jersey Camden Campus, Registrar, 311 N Fifth St, Camden, NJ 08102, 609-225-6053 (FAX: 609-225-6453). Hours: 8:30AM-4:30PM. Records go back to founding date. Alumni Records Office: Capehart Bldg, Camden, NJ 08102 609-225-6028. Degrees granted: Bachelors; Masters; School of Law J.D. . Adverse incident record source: Student Affairs, Brunswick, NJ, 908-932-9090.

Attendance and degree information available by phone, FAX, mail. Search requires name plus social security number. Other helpful information: date of birth, approximate years of attendance. No fee for information.

Transcripts available by FAX, mail. Search requires name plus social security number, date of birth, signed release. Other helpful information: approximate years of attendance. Fee is $3.00. FAX: Domestic $5.00; Foreign $10.00. Priority Mail $3.20.

Mail or FAX preferred. Attendance available via computer tapes to lending and loan service organizations. Names at time of enrollment helpful.

Rutgers, The State University of New Jersey New Brunswick Campus, Registrar, Old Queens Bldg, New Brunswick, NJ 08903, 908-932-1766. Degrees granted: Bachelors; Masters; Doctorate.

Attendance information available by FAX, mail. Search requires name plus social security number, signed release. Other helpful information: approximate years of attendance. No fee for information.

Degree information available by phone, FAX, mail. Search requires name plus social security number, signed release. Other helpful information: approximate years of attendance. No fee for information.

Transcripts available by FAX, mail. Search requires name plus social security number, signed release. Other helpful information: approximate years of attendance. Fee is $3.00.

Rutgers, The State University of New Jersey Newark Campus, Registrar, 15 Washington St, Newark, NJ 07102, 201-648-5324 (FAX: 201-648-1357). Hours: 8:30AM-4:30PM. Records go back to 1940. Alumni records are maintained here also. Call 201-648-5242. Degrees granted: Bachelors; Masters.

Attendance and degree information available by phone, FAX, mail. Search requires name plus social security number, approximate years of attendance, signed release. No fee for information.

Transcripts available by FAX, mail. Search requires name plus social security number, approximate years of attendance, signed release. Fee is $3.00.

S

Sacramento City College, Registrar, 3835 Freeport Blvd, Sacramento, CA 95822, 916-558-2351 (FAX: 916-558-2190). Hours: 7:30AM-8PM M-Th; 7:30AM-4:30PM F. Records go back to 1916. Degrees granted: Associate.

Attendance information available by phone, mail. Search requires name plus social security number, date of birth, signed release. Other helpful information: approximate years of attendance. No fee for information.

Degree information available by mail. Search requires name plus social security number, date of birth, signed release. Other helpful information: approximate years of attendance. No fee for information.

Transcripts available by mail. Search requires name plus social security number, date of birth, signed release. Other helpful information: approximate years of attendance. Fee is $2.00. Expedited service available for $10.00.

Sacred Heart Major Seminary, Registrar, 2701 Chicago Blvd, Detroit, MI 48206, 313-883-8500 (FAX: 313-868-6440). Hours: 8:30AM-4:30PM. Degrees granted: Associate; Bachelors; Masters.

Attendance information available by phone, FAX, mail. Search requires name plus social security number, date of birth, signed release. Other helpful information: approximate years of attendance. No fee for information.

Degree information available by phone, FAX, mail. Search requires name plus social security number, date of birth, exact years of attendance, signed release. No fee for information.

Transcripts available by FAX, mail. Search requires name plus social security number, date of birth, signed release. Other helpful information: approximate years of attendance. Fee is $5.00. Expedited service available for $5.00.

Sacred Heart School of Theology, Registrar, PO Box 429, 7335 S Hwy 100, Hales Corners, WI 53130-0429, 414-425-8300 X7228. Hours: 8AM-5PM. Records go back to 1968. Alumni records are maintained here at the same phone number. Degrees granted: Bachelors; Masters; First Professional Degree.

Attendance and degree information available by mail. Search requires name only. No fee for information.

Transcripts available by mail. Search requires name plus signed release. Fee is $3.00.

Sacred Heart University, Registrar, 5151 Park Ave, Fairfield, CT 06432, 203-371-7890 (FAX: 203-365-7509). Hours: 8AM-8PM M-Th, 8AM-4PM F. Records go back to 1963. Alumni records are maintained here also. Call 203-371-7861. Degrees granted: Associate; Bachelors; Masters. Adverse incident record source: Dean of Students, 203-371-7918.

Attendance and degree information available by phone, FAX, mail. Search requires name only. Other helpful information: social security number, date of birth, approximate years of attendance. No fee for information.

Transcripts available by written request only. Search requires name plus signed release. Other helpful information: social security number, date of birth, approximate years of attendance. Fee is $5.00.

Major credit cards accepted for payment.

Saddleback College, Office of Admissions & Records, 28000 Marguerite Pkwy, Mission Viejo, CA 92692, 714-582-4555. Hours: 8AM-5PM. Records go back to 1968. Degrees granted: Associate. Adverse incident record source: VP Student Service, 714-582-4566.

Attendance information available by phone, FAX, mail. Search requires name plus date of birth, signed release. Other helpful information: social security number, approximate years of attendance. No fee for information.

Degree information available by mail. Search requires name plus date of birth, signed release. Other helpful information: social security number, approximate years of attendance. Fee is $3.00. Expedite service available for $5.00.

Transcripts available by mail. Search requires name plus date of birth, signed release. Other helpful information: social security number, approximate years of attendance. Fee is $3.00. Expedited service available for $5.00.

Need student ID number. Credit cards in person only.

Sage Colleges, Registrar, 45 Ferry St, Troy, NY 12180, 518-270-2205 (FAX: 518-270-2460). Hours: 8:30AM-5PM. Records go back to 1917. Alumni records are maintained here also. Call 518-270-2242. Degrees granted: Associate; Bachelors; Masters. Special programs- Associate Level, 518-270-2000. Adverse incident record source: Russell Sage College, 518-270-2000.

Attendance and degree information available by phone, FAX, mail. Search requires name plus social security number, approximate years of attendance. Other helpful information: exact years of attendance. No fee for information.

Transcripts available by FAX, mail. Search requires name plus social security number, approximate years of attendance, signed release. Other helpful information: exact years of attendance. Fee is $3.00.

Former names needed. Major credit cards accepted for payment.

Sage Colleges, (Sage Junior College of Albany), Registrar, 140 New Scotland Ave, Albany, NY 12208, 518-445-1715. Hours: 8:30AM-5PM; 8:30AM-4:30PM Summer. Records go back to 1957. Degrees granted: Associate. Certification: Legal Studies, Computer Science.

Attendance information available by phone, mail. Search requires name plus social security number, exact years of attendance. Other helpful information: date of birth, approximate years of attendance. No fee for information.

Degree information available by phone, mail. Search requires name plus social security number. Other helpful information: date of birth, approximate years of attendance. No fee for information.

Transcripts available by mail. Search requires name plus signed release. Other helpful information: social security number, date of birth, approximate years of attendance. Fee is $3.00.

Five working days to process transcripts.

Saginaw Valley State University, Registrar, 7400 Bay Rd, University Center, MI 48710, 517-790-4347. Hours: 8AM-4:30PM. Records go back to 1964. Alumni records are maintained here also. Call 517-790-7075. Degrees granted: Bachelors; Masters.

Attendance information available by mail. Search requires name only. Other helpful information: social security number, date of birth, approximate years of attendance. No fee for information.

Degree information available by mail. Search requires name only. Other helpful information: social security number, date of birth, approximate years of attendance. No fee for information.

Transcripts available by mail. Search requires name plus signed release. Other helpful information: social security number, date of birth, approximate years of attendance. Fee is $4.00.

Major credit cards accepted for payment.

Saint Joseph's College, Registrar's Office, PO Box 929, Rensselaer, IN 47978, 219-866-6161 (FAX: 219-866-6100). Hours: 8AM-Noon, 1-4:30PM. Records go back to 1891. Alumni Records Office: PO Box 870, Rensselaer, IN 47978. Degrees granted: Associate; Bachelors; Masters. Certification: Music.

Attendance information available by phone, FAX, mail. Search requires name only. Other helpful information: social security number, approximate years of attendance. No fee for information.

Degree information available by phone, FAX, mail. Search requires name only. Other helpful information: social security number, date of birth, approximate years of attendance. No fee for information.

Transcripts available by FAX, mail. Search requires name plus social security number, date of birth, signed release. Other helpful information: approximate years of attendance. Fee is $3.00. Expedited service available for $5.00.

Saint Mary's College, Registrar, Notre Dame, IN 46556, 219-284-4560 (FAX: 219-284-4716). Hours: 8AM-Noon, 1-4:30PM. Records go back to 1900. Alumni Records Office: Alumnae Relations, LeMans Hall, Notre Dame, IN 46556. Degrees granted: Bachelors.

Attendance and degree information available by phone, FAX, mail. Search requires name only. Other helpful information: social security number, date of birth, approximate years of attendance. No fee for information.

Transcripts available by FAX, mail. Search requires name plus signed release. Other helpful information: social security number,

date of birth, approximate years of attendance. Fee is $2.00. Expedite fee varies.

Saint Mary's College of California, Office of the Registrar, PO Box 4748, Moraga, CA 94575-4748, 510-631-4214 (FAX: 510-376-8339). Hours: 8:30AM-4:30PM. Alumni Records Office: Alumni Association, Saint Mary's College of California, PO Box 3400, Moraga, CA 94575-3400. Degrees granted: Associate; Bachelors; Masters.

Attendance and degree information available by phone, FAX, mail. Search requires name only. Other helpful information: social security number, date of birth, approximate years of attendance. No fee for information.

Transcripts available by FAX, mail. Search requires name plus signed release. Other helpful information: social security number, date of birth, approximate years of attendance. Fee is $3.00. Expedited service available for $13.00.

Credit cards accepted over $13.00.

Salem College, Registrar, Salem Station, PO Box 10548, Winston-Salem, NC 27180, 910-721-2618 (FAX: 910-917-5432). Hours: 8:30AM-5PM. Records go back to 1925. Degrees granted: Bachelors; Masters.

Attendance and degree information available by phone, FAX, mail. Search requires name only. Other helpful information: social security number, date of birth, approximate years of attendance. No fee for information.

Transcripts available by mail. Search requires name plus signed release. Other helpful information: social security number, date of birth, approximate years of attendance. Fee is $2.00.

Salem Community College, Registrar, 460 Hollywood Ave, Carneys Point, NJ 08069, 609-299-2100 (FAX: 609-299-9193). Hours: 8:30AM-7:30PM M-Th; 8:30AM-4:30PM F. Records go back to 1972. Alumni records are maintained here at the same phone number. Degrees granted: Associate.

Attendance and degree information available by mail. Search requires name plus social security number, signed release. Other helpful information: date of birth. No fee for information.

Transcripts available by mail. Search requires name plus social security number, signed release. Other helpful information: date of birth. Fee is $3.00. Expedited service available for $5.00.

Salem State College, Registrar, 352 Lafayette St, Salem, MA 01970-4589, 508-741-6091. Hours: 8:30AM-5PM. Records go back to 1915. Alumni records are maintained here also. Call 508-741-6605. Degrees granted: Bachelors. Adverse incident record source: Campus Police: Judicial Affairs

Attendance and degree information available by mail. Search requires name plus social security number, approximate years of attendance, signed release. Other helpful information: date of birth. No fee for information.

Transcripts available by mail. Search requires name plus social security number, approximate years of attendance, signed release. Other helpful information: date of birth. Fee is $2.00.

Salem-Teikyo University, Registrar, 223 W Main St, Salem, WV 26426, 304-782-5297. Records go back to 1888. Degrees granted: Bachelors; Masters.

Attendance and degree information available by phone, mail. Search requires name plus social security number, date of birth, exact years of attendance. No fee for information.

Transcripts available by mail. Search requires name plus social security number, date of birth, exact years of attendance, signed release. Fee is $5.00.

Salisbury State University, Registrar, Salisbury, MD 21801, 410-543-6150 (FAX: 410-548-5979). Hours: 8AM-5PM. Records go back to 1926. Alumni records are maintained here also. Call 410-543-6042. Degrees granted: Bachelors; Masters. Adverse incident record source: Dean of Students, 410-543-6080.

Attendance information available by phone, FAX, mail. Search requires name plus social security number, signed release. No fee for information.

Degree information available by phone, FAX, mail. Search requires name plus social security number, date of birth, approximate years of attendance. No fee for information.

Transcripts available by FAX, mail. Search requires name plus social security number, date of birth, approximate years of attendance, signed release. No fee for transcripts.

Salish Kootenai College, Registrar, PO Box 117, Pablo, MT 59855, 406-675-4800 (FAX: 406-675-4801). Alumni records are maintained here at the same phone number. Degrees granted: Associate; Bachelors.

Attendance and degree information available by phone, FAX, mail. Search requires name plus social security number, date of birth. Other helpful information: approximate years of attendance. No fee for information.

Transcripts available by written request only. Search requires name plus social security number, date of birth, signed release. Other helpful information: exact years of attendance. Fee is $2.00.

Salt Lake Community College, Registrar's Office, PO Box 30808, Salt Lake City, UT 84130, 801-957-4298 (FAX: 801-957-4958). Hours: 8AM-8PM M-Th; 8AM-4:30PM F. Records go back to 1948. Alumni records are maintained here also. Call 801-957-4555. Degrees granted: Associate. Adverse incident record source: Security Office, 801-957-4270.

Attendance and degree information available by phone, FAX, mail. Search requires name plus social security number. Other helpful information: date of birth, approximate years of attendance. No fee for information.

Transcripts available by written request only. Search requires name plus social security number, signed release. Other helpful information: date of birth, approximate years of attendance. Fee is $2.00. Expedited service available for $2.00.

Salvation Army School for Officers' Training, Registrar, 30840 Hawthorne Blvd, Rancho Palos Verdes, CA 90275, 310-544-6467 (FAX: 310-265-6506). Hours: 8:15AM-4:15PM. Records go back to 1900s. Degrees granted: Associate.

Attendance and degree information available by phone, FAX, mail. Search requires name plus approximate years of attendance, signed release. No fee for information.

Transcripts available by FAX, mail. Search requires name plus approximate years of attendance, signed release. Fee is $2.00.

Salve Regina University, Registrar, 100 Ochre Point Ave, Newport, RI 02840-4192, 401-847-6650. Hours: 8AM-5PM. Records go back to 1947. Alumni records are maintained here also. Call 401-847-6650. Degrees granted: Associate; Bachelors; Masters; Doctorate. Adverse incident record source: Dean of Students, 401-847-6650.

Attendance and degree information available by phone, mail. Search requires name plus approximate years of attendance. Other helpful information: social security number, date of birth, exact years of attendance. No fee for information.

Transcripts available by mail. Search requires name plus signed release. Other helpful information: social security number, date of birth, approximate years of attendance. Fee is $5.00. Expedited service available for $10.00.

Sam Houston State University, Registrar, PO Box 2029, Huntsville, TX 77341, 409-294-1035 (FAX: 409-294-1097). Hours: 8AM-5PM. Records go back to 1800s. Alumni records are maintained here also. Call 409-294-1841. Degrees granted: Bachelors; Masters; Doctorate. Certification: Teacher.

Attendance and degree information available by phone, FAX, mail. Search requires name plus social security number, signed release. Other helpful information: date of birth, approximate years of attendance. No fee for information.

Transcripts available by mail. Search requires name plus social security number, signed release. Other helpful information: date of birth, approximate years of attendance. Fee is $3.00.

Samford University, Registrar, 800 Lakeshore Dr, Birmingham, AL 35229, 205-870-2911 (FAX: 205-870-2908). Hours: 7:30AM-5PM. Records go back to 1887. Degrees granted: Associate; Bachelors; Masters; Doctorate.

Attendance and degree information available by phone, FAX, mail. Search requires name plus social security number. No fee for information.

Transcripts available by mail. Search requires name plus social security number, signed release. Other helpful information: date of birth, approximate years of attendance. Fee is $5.00.

Major credit cards accepted for payment.

Sampson Community College, Registrar, PO Drawer 318, Clinton, NC 28328, 910-592-8081. Degrees granted: Associate.

Attendance and degree information available by phone, FAX, mail. Search requires name plus social security number. Other helpful information: date of birth, approximate years of attendance. No fee for information.

Transcripts available by FAX, mail. Search requires name plus social security number, signed release. Other helpful information: date of birth, approximate years of attendance. No fee for transcripts.

Samra University of Oriental Medicine, Registrar, 600 St Paul Ave, Los Angeles, CA 90017, 213-482-8448 (FAX: 213-842-9020). Hours: 10:30AM-6:30PM. Degrees granted: Masters.

Attendance and degree information available by written request only. Search requires name plus social security number, date of birth, signed release. Other helpful information: approximate years of attendance. Fee is $5.00.

Transcripts available by written request only. Search requires name plus social security number, date of birth, approximate years of attendance, signed release. Fee is $5.00.

Major credit cards accepted for payment.

Samuel Merritt College, Registrar, 370 Hawthorne Ave, Oakland, CA 94609, 510-869-6131 (FAX: 510-869-6525). Hours: 8AM-5PM. Records go back to 1909. Alumni records are maintained here also. Call 510-869-6618. Degrees granted: Bachelors; Masters.

Attendance and degree information available by phone, FAX, mail. Search requires name plus approximate years of attendance, signed release. Other helpful information: social security number, date of birth. No fee for information.

Transcripts available by mail. Search requires name plus approximate years of attendance, signed release. Other helpful information: social security number, date of birth. Fee is $3.00. Expedited service available for $10.00.

San Antonio College, Registrar, 1300 San Pedro Ave, San Antonio, TX 78212-4299, 210-733-2000. Hours: 8AM-4:30PM. Records go back to 1960s. Degrees granted: Associate.

Attendance and degree information available by phone, mail. Search requires name plus social security number. Other helpful information: approximate years of attendance. No fee for information.

Transcripts available by written request only. Search requires name plus social security number, signed release. Other helpful information: approximate years of attendance. Fee is $2.00.

San Bernardino Valley College, Registrar, 701 S Mt Vernon Ave, San Bernardino, CA 92410, 909-888-6511 (FAX: 909-889-4988). Hours: 8AM-7PM. Records go back to 1926. Degrees granted: Associate.

Attendance information available by written request only. Search requires name plus social security number, approximate years of attendance, signed release. Other helpful information: date of birth, exact years of attendance. No fee for information.

Degree information available by phone, FAX, mail. Search requires name plus social security number, approximate years of attendance. Other helpful information: date of birth, exact years of attendance. No fee for information.

Transcripts available by FAX, mail. Search requires name plus social security number, approximate years of attendance, signed release. Other helpful information: date of birth, exact years of attendance. Fee is $3.00. Expedited service available for $8.00.

Major credit cards accepted for payment.

San Diego City College, Registrar, 1313 Twelfth Ave, San Diego, CA 92101, 619-230-2472 (FAX: 619-230-2135). Hours: 8AM-7:30PM. Records go back to 1950. Degrees granted: Associate.

Attendance and degree information available by FAX, mail. Search requires name plus social security number, date of birth, approximate years of attendance, signed release. No fee for information.

Transcripts available by FAX, mail. Search requires name plus social security number, date of birth, approximate years of attendance, signed release. Fee is $5.00.

San Diego Mesa College, Registrar, 7250 Mesa College Dr, San Diego, CA 92111, 619-627-2805 (FAX: 619-627-2808). Hours: 8AM-6PM M-Th, 8AM-3:30PM F. Records go back to 1964. Degrees granted: Associate.

Attendance information available by phone, FAX, mail. Search requires name plus social security number, date of birth, signed release. No fee for information.

Degree information available by phone, FAX, mail. Search requires name only. No fee for information.

Transcripts available by mail. Search requires name only. Fee is $5.00.

San Diego Miramar College, Registrar, 10440 Black Mountain Rd, San Diego, CA 92126, 619-584-6931 (FAX: 619-584-6946). Hours: 8AM-5PM M-Th; 8AM-3PM F. Records go back to 1946. Degrees granted: Associate. Special programs-

Continuing Education, 619-527-5280: Law Enforcement Academy, 619-536-7320. Adverse incident record source: Campus Police, 619-230-2910.

Attendance and degree information available by FAX, mail. Search requires name plus social security number, date of birth, signed release. Other helpful information: approximate years of attendance. No fee for information.

Transcripts available by FAX, mail. Search requires name plus social security number, date of birth, signed release. Other helpful information: approximate years of attendance. Fee is $5.00.

San Diego State University, Registrar, 5500 Campanile Dr, San Diego, CA 92182-7455, 619-594-6871 (FAX: 619-594-4902). Hours: 8AM-4:30PM. Records go back to 1890. Alumni records are maintained here also. Call 619-594-ALUM. Degrees granted: Bachelors; Masters; Doctorate. Special programs- College of Extended Studies, 619-594-5821. Adverse incident record source: Judicial Procedures, 619-594-4437: Public Safety, 619-594-1991

Attendance and degree information available by phone, FAX, mail. Search requires name only. Other helpful information: social security number, date of birth, approximate years of attendance. No fee for information.

Transcripts available by mail. Search requires name plus social security number, date of birth, signed release. Other helpful information: approximate years of attendance. Fee is $4.00.

E-Mail coming soon. Major credit cards accepted for payment.

San Francisco Art Institute, Registrar, 800 Chestnut St, San Francisco, CA 94133, 415-749-4535 (FAX: 415-749-4590). Hours: 9AM-5PM. Records go back to 1930s. Alumni records are maintained here also. Call 415-749-5842. Degrees granted: Bachelors; Masters.

Attendance and degree information available by phone, FAX, mail. Search requires name plus social security number, approximate years of attendance, signed release. No fee for information.

Transcripts available by mail. Search requires name plus social security number, approximate years of attendance, signed release. Fee is $5.00.

San Francisco College of Mortuary Science, Registrar, 1598 Dolores St, San Francisco, CA 94110, 415-824-1313 (FAX: 415-824-1390). Hours: 8AM-4:30PM. Records go back to 1965. Alumni records are maintained here at the same phone number. Degrees granted: Associate.

Attendance and degree information available by FAX, mail. Search requires name plus social security number, signed release. No fee for information.

Transcripts available by mail. Search requires name plus social security number, signed release. Fee is $6.00.

San Francisco Conservatory of Music, Registrar, 1201 Ortega St, San Francisco, CA 94122, 415-759-3431 (FAX: 415-759-3499). Hours: 9AM-5PM. Records go back 40 years. Degrees granted: Bachelors; Masters.

Attendance and degree information available by phone, FAX, mail. Search requires name plus date of birth, signed release. Other helpful information: social security number, approximate years of attendance. No fee for information.

Transcripts available by phone, FAX, mail. Search requires name plus date of birth, signed release. Other helpful information: social security number, approximate years of attendance. Fee is $3.00.

Major credit cards accepted for payment.

San Francisco State University, Registrar, 1600 Holloway Ave, San Francisco, CA 94132, 415-338-2077. Hours: 8:30AM-5PM. Records go back to 1960. Alumni records are maintained here also. Call 415-338-2217. Degrees granted: Bachelors; Masters.

Attendance and degree information available by phone, mail. Search requires name plus social security number, approximate years of attendance, signed release. No fee for information.

Transcripts available by mail. Search requires name plus social security number, approximate years of attendance, signed release. Fee is $4.00.

San Francisco Theological Seminary, Registrar, 2 Kensington Rd, San Anselmo, CA 94960, 415-258-6553 (FAX: 415-454-2493). Hours: 9AM-5PM. Records go back to 1900. Degrees granted: Bachelors; Masters; Doctorate. Certification: Spir. Direction. Adverse incident record source: Facilities, 415-258-6606.

Attendance and degree information available by phone, FAX, mail. Search requires name only. Other helpful information: approximate years of attendance. No fee for information.

Transcripts available by mail. Search requires name plus signed release. Other helpful information: approximate years of attendance. Fee is $5.00. Expedited service available for $5.00.

Degree program helpful.

San Jacinto College, Registrar, 8060 Spencer Hwy, Pasadena, TX 77505, 713-476-1844. Hours: 8AM-4:30PM. Degrees granted: Associate.

Attendance and degree information available by phone, mail. Search requires name plus social security number. No fee for information.

Transcripts available by mail. Search requires name plus social security number, signed release. No fee for transcripts.

San Joaquin College of Law, Registrar, 3385 E Shields Ave, Fresno, CA 93726, 209-225-4953 (FAX: 209-225-4322). Hours: 9AM-5PM. Records go back to 1974. Alumni records are maintained here at the same phone number. Degrees granted: Masters; Doctorate.

Attendance information available by phone, FAX, mail. Search requires name plus social security number. Other helpful information: date of birth, approximate years of attendance. No fee for information.

Degree information available by FAX, mail. Search requires name plus social security number, signed release. Other helpful information: date of birth, approximate years of attendance. No fee for information.

Transcripts available by phone, FAX, mail. Search requires name plus social security number, signed release. Other helpful information: date of birth, approximate years of attendance. Fee is $2.00. Expedited service available for $10.00.

San Joaquin Delta College, Registrar, 5151 Pacific Ave, Stockton, CA 95207, 209-474-5636. Hours: 8AM-5PM M-Th. Records go back to 1963. Degrees granted: Associate.

Attendance and degree information available by phone, mail. Search requires name plus social security number, date of birth, exact years of attendance. No fee for information.

Transcripts available by mail. Search requires name plus social security number, date of birth, exact years of attendance, signed release. Other helpful information: approximate years of attendance. Fee is $4.00.

San Jose Christian College, Registrar, PO Box 1090, 790 S 12th St, San Jose, CA 95112, 408-293-9058 (FAX: 408-293-7352). Hours: 8AM-4:30PM. Records go back to 1939. Degrees granted: Associate; Bachelors. Certification: Bible Counseling.

Attendance and degree information available by phone, FAX, mail. Search requires name plus approximate years of attendance. No fee for information.

Transcripts available by FAX, mail. Search requires name plus social security number, date of birth, approximate years of attendance, signed release. Fee is $3.00. Expedited service available for $10.00.

San Jose City College, Registrar, 2100 Moorpark Ave, San Jose, CA 95128, 408-298-2181 (FAX: 408-298-1935). Hours: 8AM-7PM M-Th; 9AM-5PM F. Degrees granted: Associate.

Attendance and degree information available by phone, FAX, mail. Search requires name plus social security number, date of birth. Other helpful information: approximate years of attendance. Fee is $2.00.

Transcripts available by written request only. Search requires name plus social security number, date of birth, signed release. Other helpful information: approximate years of attendance. Fee is $2.00.3. Expedited service available for $7.50.

Major credit cards accepted for payment.

San Jose State University, Registrar, One Washington Square, San Jose, CA 95192, 408-924-2000 (FAX: 408-924-2050). Hours: 9AM-4PM. Records go back to 1917. Alumni records are maintained here also. Call 408-924-6515. Degrees granted: Bachelors.

Attendance and degree information available by phone, FAX, mail. Search requires name plus social security number, date of birth, signed release. No fee for information.

Transcripts available by mail. Search requires name plus social security number, date of birth, signed release. Fee is $4.00.

San Juan College, Records Office, 4601 College Blvd, Farmington, NM 87402, 505-599-0320 (FAX: 505-599-0500). Hours: 8AM-5PM. Records go back to 1972. Degrees granted: Associate.

Attendance and degree information available by mail. Search requires name plus social security number, signed release. Other helpful information: date of birth, approximate years of attendance. No fee for information.

Transcripts available by mail. Search requires name plus social security number, signed release. Other helpful information: date of birth, approximate years of attendance. Fee is $2.00. Expedited service available for $10.00.

Sandhills Community College, Registrar, 2200 Airport Rd, Pinehurst, NC 28374, 910-695-3739 (FAX: 910-695-1823). Hours: 8AM-4:30PM. Records go back to 1963. Degrees granted: Associate.

Attendance and degree information available by phone, mail. Search requires name plus social security number, approximate years of attendance, signed release. No fee for information.

Transcripts available by mail. Search requires name plus social security number, approximate years of attendance, signed release. Fee is $1.00.

Sanford-Brown Business College, Registrar, 12006 Manchester Rd, Des Peres, MO 63131, 314-822-7100 (FAX: 314-822-4017). Hours: 9AM-6PM. Records go back to 1987.

Attendance and degree information available by FAX, mail. Search requires name plus social security number, signed release. Other helpful information: approximate years of attendance. No fee for information.

Transcripts available by FAX, mail. Search requires name plus social security number, signed release. Other helpful information: approximate years of attendance. No fee for transcripts.

Sanford-Brown Business College, (Branch), Registrar, 355 Brooks Dr, Hazelwood, MO 63042, 314-731-5200. Hours: 7AM-7PM M-Th, 7AM-4PM F. Records go back to 1985. Degrees granted: Associate.

Attendance and degree information available by phone, mail. Search requires name plus social security number, exact years of attendance. No fee for information.

Transcripts available by mail. Search requires name plus social security number, exact years of attendance, signed release. Fee is $3.00.

Sanford-Brown Business College, (Branch), Registrar, 2702 Rockcreek Pkwy Ste 300, North Kansas City, MO 64117, 816-472-7400 (FAX: 816-472-0688). Degrees granted: Associate.

Attendance and degree information available by mail. Search requires name plus signed release. Other helpful information: social security number, approximate years of attendance. No fee for information.

Transcripts available by mail. Search requires name plus social security number, signed release. Other helpful information: approximate years of attendance. Fee is $2.00.

Sanford-Brown Business College, (Branch), Registrar, 3555 Franks Dr, St Charles, MO 63301, 314-949-2620 (FAX: 314-949-5081). Hours: 8AM-4PM. Degrees granted: Associate.

Attendance and degree information available by phone, FAX, mail. Search requires name plus social security number, date of birth, exact years of attendance, signed release. No fee for information.

Transcripts available by phone, FAX, mail. Search requires name plus social security number, date of birth, exact years of attendance, signed release. First transcript is free; $4.00 each additional. Expedited service available for $4.00.

Sangamon State University, Registrar, Springfield, IL 62794-9243, 217-786-6709 (FAX: 217-786-7280). Hours: 8:30AM-5PM. Records go back to 1970. Degrees granted: Bachelors; Masters.

Attendance and degree information available by phone, FAX, mail. Search requires name only. Other helpful information: social security number, date of birth, approximate years of attendance. No fee for information.

Transcripts available by FAX, mail. Search requires name plus signed release. Other helpful information: social security number, date of birth, approximate years of attendance. Fee is $2.00.

Santa Barbara City College, Registrar, 721 Cliff Dr, Santa Barbara, CA 93109, 805-965-0581 (FAX: 805-963-7222). Hours: 8AM-7:30PM M-Th; 8AM-4:15PM F. Degrees granted: Associate. Adverse incident record source: Campus Security, 805-965-0581 X2264: Dean of Students, 805-965-0581 X2278

Attendance information available by written request only. Search requires name plus social security number, signed release. Other helpful information: date of birth, approximate years of attendance. No fee for information.

Degree information available by phone, FAX, mail. Search requires name plus social security number, approximate years of attendance. Other helpful information: exact years of attendance. No fee for information.

Transcripts available by FAX, mail. Search requires name plus social security number, approximate years of attendance, signed release. Other helpful information: exact years of attendance. Fee is $3.00. Expedited service available for $5.00.

Santa Clara University, Registrar, Santa Clara, CA 95053, 408-554-4999 (FAX: 408-554-6926). Hours: 8AM-5PM. Records go back to 1800s. Alumni records are maintained here also. Call 405-554-6800. Degrees granted: Bachelors; Masters; PhD.

Attendance and degree information available by phone, FAX, mail. Search requires name plus social security number, date of birth, approximate years of attendance, signed release. No fee for information.

Transcripts available by FAX, mail. Search requires name plus social security number, date of birth, approximate years of attendance, signed release. Fee is $3.00.

Santa Fe Community College, Registrar, 3000 NW 83rd St, Gainesville, FL 32606, 904-395-5457 (FAX: 904-395-5922). Hours: 8AM-4:30PM. Degrees granted: Associate; Bachelors.

Attendance information available by phone. Search requires name plus social security number. Other helpful information: date of birth, approximate years of attendance. No fee for information.

Degree information available by written request only. Search requires name plus social security number. Other helpful information: date of birth, approximate years of attendance. No fee for information.

Transcripts available by FAX, mail. Search requires name plus social security number. Other helpful information: date of birth, approximate years of attendance. No fee for transcripts.

Santa Monica College, Admissions & Records, 1900 Pico Blvd, Santa Monica, CA 90405, 310-452-9382 (FAX: 310-399-1730). Hours: 8AM-5PM M-Th. Degrees granted: Associate.

Attendance and degree information available by mail. Search requires name plus date of birth, signed release. Other helpful information: social security number, approximate years of attendance. Fee is $3.00.

Transcripts available by mail. Search requires name plus date of birth, signed release. Other helpful information: social security number, approximate years of attendance. Fee is $3.00. Expedite $10.00 in person only.

Santa Rosa Junior College, Admissions & Records, Transcripts, 1501 Mendocino Ave, Santa Rosa, CA 95401, 707-527-4513 (FAX: 707-527-4798). Hours: 8AM-5PM. Records go back to 1917. Alumni records are maintained here also. Call 707-527-4733. Degrees granted: Associate.

Attendance and degree information available by FAX, mail. Search requires name plus social security number, signed release. Other helpful information: date of birth, approximate years of attendance. No fee for information.

Transcripts available by phone, FAX, mail. Search requires name plus social security number, signed release. Other helpful information: date of birth, approximate years of attendance. Fee is $1.00. Expedited service available for $1.00.

Sante Fe Community College, Registrar, PO Box 4187, Santa Fe, NM 87502-4187, 505-471-8200 (FAX: 505-438-1237). Hours: 8AM-5PM. Records go back 13 years. Degrees granted: Associate. Adverse incident record source: Dean of Student Affairs, 505-471-8200.

Attendance and degree information available by mail. Search requires name plus social security number, signed release. Other helpful information: date of birth, exact years of attendance. No fee for information.

Transcripts available by mail. Search requires name plus social security number, signed release. Other helpful information: date of birth, exact years of attendance. Fee is $1.00.

Sarah Lawrence College, Registrar, One Meadway, Bronxville, NY 10708, 914-395-2301. Hours: 9AM-5PM. Records go back to 1928. Alumni records are maintained here at the same phone number. Degrees granted: Bachelors; Masters. Adverse incident record source: Dean, 914-395-2250.

Attendance and degree information available by phone, mail. Search requires name plus social security number. No fee for information.

Transcripts available by mail. Search requires name plus social security number, signed release. Other helpful information: approximate years of attendance. Fee is $6.00.

Sauk Valley Community College, Registrar, 173 Illinois Rte 2, Dixon, IL 61021, 815-288-5511 (FAX: 815-288-3190). Hours: 8AM-4:30PM. Records go back to 1965. Alumni records are maintained here at the same phone number. Degrees granted: Associate.

Attendance information available by phone, FAX, mail. Search requires name plus social security number, approximate years of attendance. Other helpful information: date of birth, exact years of attendance. No fee for information.

Degree information available by phone, FAX, mail. Search requires name plus social security number. No fee for information.

Transcripts available by mail. Search requires name plus social security number, approximate years of attendance, signed release. Other helpful information: exact years of attendance. Fee is $3.00. Major credit cards accepted for payment.

Savannah College of Art and Design, Registrar, 201 W Charlton St, Savannah, GA 31401, 912-238-2400. Hours: 9AM-5PM. Records go back to 1979. Alumni records are maintained here also. Call 912-238-2400. Degrees granted: Bachelors.

Attendance and degree information available by mail. Search requires name plus social security number. No fee for information.

Transcripts available by mail. Search requires name plus social security number, exact years of attendance, signed release. Fee is $10.00.

Savannah State College, Registrar, State College Branch, PO Box 20479, Savannah, GA 31404, 912-356-2212. Hours: 8AM-5PM. Records go back to 1931. Alumni records are maintained here also. Call 912-356-2427. Degrees granted: Bachelors; Masters. Adverse incident record source: 912-356-2194.

Attendance information available by phone, mail. Search requires name plus social security number, date of birth, signed release. Other helpful information: approximate years of attendance. No fee for information.

Degree information available by phone, FAX, mail. Search requires name plus social security number, date of birth, signed release. Other helpful information: approximate years of attendance. No fee for information.

Transcripts available by mail. Search requires name plus social security number, date of birth, approximate years of attendance, signed release. Fee is $4.00. Expedited service available for $4.00.

Savannah Technical Institute, Registrar, 5717 White Bluff Rd, Savannah, GA 31499, 912-351-4494 (FAX: 912-352-4362). Hours: 8AM-6PM M-Th, 8AM-4PM F. Records go back to 1960. Alumni records are maintained here also. Call 912-351-4450. Degrees granted: Associate.

Attendance information available by phone, FAX, mail. Search requires name plus social security number, date of birth, approximate years of attendance, signed release. Other helpful information: exact years of attendance. No fee for information.

Degree information available by FAX, mail. Search requires name only. No fee for information.

Transcripts available by mail. Search requires name only. Fee is $1.00.

Sawyer College, Inc., Registrar, 6040 Hohman Ave, Hammond, IN 46320, 219-931-0436 (FAX: 219-933-1239). Hours: 8AM-5PM. Records go back to 1990. Degrees granted: Associate.

Attendance and degree information available by FAX, mail. Search requires name plus social security number, exact years of attendance, signed release. No fee for information.

Transcripts available by mail. Search requires name plus social security number, exact years of attendance, signed release. Fee is $2.00.

Sawyer College, Inc., **(Branch)**, Registrar, 3803 E Lincoln Hwy, Merrillville, IN 46410, 219-736-0436 (FAX: 219-942-3762). Hours: 8AM-5PM. Records go back to 1985. Degrees granted: Associate.

Attendance and degree information available by mail. Search requires name plus social security number, exact years of attendance, signed release. No fee for information.

Transcripts available by mail. Search requires name plus social security number, exact years of attendance, signed release. Fee is $5.00.

Sawyer School, Registrar, 717 Liberty Ave, Pittsburgh, PA 15222, 412-261-5700 (FAX: 412-261-5039). Hours: 8AM-5PM. Records go back to 1956. Degrees granted: Associate.

Attendance and degree information available by phone, mail. Search requires name plus social security number, exact years of attendance. No fee for information.

Transcripts available by mail. Search requires name plus social security number, exact years of attendance, signed release. Fee is $4.00.

Saybrook Institute Graduate School & Research Center, Registrar, 450 Pacific Ave 3rd Flr, San Francisco, CA 94133, 415-433-9200 (FAX: 415-433-9271). Hours: 8:30AM-4:30pm. Records go back to 1971.

Attendance information available by FAX, mail. Search requires name plus social security number, exact years of attendance, signed release. No fee for information.

Degree information available by phone, FAX, mail. Search requires name only. Other helpful information: approximate years of attendance. No fee for information.

Transcripts available by FAX, mail. Search requires name plus signed release. Other helpful information: approximate years of attendance. Fee is $4.00.

Major credit cards accepted for payment.

Schenectady County Community College, Registrar, 78 Washington Ave, Schenectady, NY 12305, 518-346-6211 (FAX: 518-346-0379). Hours: 8:30AM-7:30PM M-Th, 8:30AM-4:30PM F. Records go back to 1970s. Alumni records are maintained here at the same phone number. Degrees granted: Associate.

Attendance and degree information available by FAX, mail. Search requires name plus social security number, signed release. Other helpful information: approximate years of attendance. No fee for information.

Transcripts available by FAX, mail. Search requires name plus social security number, signed release. Other helpful information: approximate years of attendance. Fee is $2.00.

School for International Training, Registrar, PO Box 676, Brattleboro, VT 05301, 802-257-7751 (FAX: 802-258-3248). Hours: 8AM-5PM. Records go back to 1964. Alumni records are maintained here at the same phone number. Degrees granted: Bachelors; Masters.

Attendance and degree information available by phone, mail. Search requires name only. No fee for information.

Transcripts available by mail. Search requires name plus signed release. Fee is $3.00.

Need to know program of study.

School of Theology at Claremont, Registrar, 1325 N College Ave, Claremont, CA 91711-3199, 909-626-3521 (FAX: 909-626-7062). Hours: 9AM-Noon, 1-5PM. Records go back to 1965. Degrees granted: Masters; Doctorate.

Attendance information available by phone, FAX, mail. Search requires name only. Other helpful information: social security number, date of birth, approximate years of attendance. No fee for information.

Degree information available by phone, FAX, mail. Search requires name only. Other helpful information: social security number. No fee for information.

Transcripts available by written request only. Search requires name plus signed release. Other helpful information: approximate years of attendance. Fee is $5.00.

School of Visual Arts, Registrar, 209 E 23rd St, New York, NY 10010, 212-679-7350 (FAX: 212-725-3587). Hours: 8AM-5:45PM. Records go back to 1940s. Alumni records are maintained here also. Call 212-592-2300. Degrees granted: Bachelors; Masters.

Attendance and degree information available by phone, FAX, mail. Search requires name plus social security number. Other helpful information: approximate years of attendance. No fee for information.

Transcripts available by FAX, mail. Search requires name plus social security number, signed release. Other helpful information: approximate years of attendance. Transcript fee $10.00 official; $5.00 unofficial.

School of the Art Institute of Chicago, Registrar, 37 S Wabash Ave, Chicago, IL 60603, 312-899-5117 (FAX: 312-263-0141). Hours: 8:30AM-4:30PM. Records go back to 1900. Alumni records are maintained here also. Call 312-899-5217. Degrees granted: Bachelors; Masters; Post Graduate.

Attendance and degree information available by phone, FAX, mail. Search requires name plus social security number, date of birth, approximate years of attendance, signed release. No fee for information.

Transcripts available by mail. Search requires name plus social security number, date of birth, approximate years of attendance, signed release. Fee is $3.00.

School of the Museum of Fine Arts, Boston, Registrar, 230 The Fenway, Boston, MA 02115-9975, 617-369-3621 (FAX: 617-424-6271). Hours: 9AM-5PM. Records go back to 1930. Alumni records are maintained here also. Call 617-369-3897. Degrees granted: Bachelors; Masters.

Attendance information available by phone, FAX, mail. Search requires name plus social security number, exact years of attendance. Other helpful information: date of birth. No fee for information.

Degree information available by phone, FAX, mail. Search requires name plus social security number, approximate years of attendance. Other helpful information: date of birth, exact years of attendance. No fee for information.

Transcripts available by written request only. Search requires name plus social security number, date of birth, approximate years of attendance, signed release. Fee is $4.00. Expedited service available for $10.00.

Schoolcraft College, Registrar, 18600 Haggerty Rd, Livonia, MI 48152, 313-462-4430 (FAX: 313-462-4506). Hours: 8AM-6PM M-Th; 8AM-4:30PM F. Records go back to 1964. Degrees granted: Associate. Adverse incident record source: VP for Student Services, 313-462-4400.

Attendance and degree information available by phone, FAX, mail. Search requires name plus social security number. Other helpful information: date of birth. No fee for information.

Transcripts available by mail. Search requires name plus social security number, signed release. No fee for transcripts. Expedite: $15.00 plus overnight delivery.

Schreiner College, Registrar, 2100 Memorial Blvd, Kerrville, TX 78028, 210-896-5411 X224 (FAX: 210-896-3232). Hours: 8AM-5PM. Records go back to 1923. Alumni records are maintained here also. Call 210-896-5411 X200. Degrees granted: Associate; Bachelors. Certification: Voc. Nursing.

Attendance and degree information available by phone, FAX, mail. Search requires name plus social security number. Other helpful information: date of birth, approximate years of attendance. No fee for information.

Transcripts available by written request only. Search requires name plus social security number, signed release. Other helpful information: date of birth. Fee is $5.00.

Schuylkill Business Institute, Registrar, 2400 W End Ave, Pottsville, PA 17901, 717-622-4835. Hours: 8AM-5PM. Records go back to 1977. Degrees granted: Associate.

Attendance and degree information available by phone, mail. Search requires name plus social security number, exact years of attendance. No fee for information.

Transcripts available by mail. Search requires name plus social security number, exact years of attendance, signed release. No fee for transcripts.

Scott Community College, Registrar, 500 Belmont Rd, Bettendorf, IA 52722, 319-359-7531 (FAX: 319-359-0519). Hours: 7:30AM-5:30PM M-Th; 7:30AM-4:30PM F. Degrees granted: Associate. Adverse incident record source: Dean of Students, 315-359-7531 X225.

Attendance information available by mail. Search requires name only. No fee for information.

Degree information available by phone, FAX, mail. Search requires name plus social security number. Other helpful information: date of birth, approximate years of attendance. No fee for information.

Transcripts available by FAX, mail. Search requires name plus social security number, signed release. Other helpful information: date of birth, approximate years of attendance. No fee for transcripts.

Scottsdale Community College, Registrar, 9000 E Chaparral Rd, Scottsdale, AZ 85250, 602-423-6000 (FAX: 602-423-6200). Hours: 8AM-7PM M-Th, 8AM-4PM F. Records go back 20 years. Degrees granted: Associate.

Attendance information available by phone, FAX, mail. Search requires name only. Other helpful information: social security number, date of birth, approximate years of attendance. No fee for information.

Degree information available by phone, FAX, mail. Search requires name plus signed release. Other helpful information: social security number, date of birth, approximate years of attendance. No fee for information.

Transcripts available by FAX, mail. Search requires name plus social security number, date of birth, signed release. Other helpful information: approximate years of attendance. Fee is $5.00.

Major credit cards accepted for payment.

Scripps College, Registrar, 1030 N Columbia Ave, Claremont, CA 91711, 909-621-8273 (FAX: 909-621-8323). Hours: 9AM-Noon, 1-4PM. Records go back to 1926. Alumni records are maintained here at the same phone number. Degrees granted: Bachelors. Certification: Post-Bac Pre-Med.

Attendance and degree information available by phone, mail. Search requires name only. Other helpful information: social security number, date of birth, approximate years of attendance. No fee for information.

Transcripts available by mail. Search requires name plus signed release. Other helpful information: social security number, date of birth, approximate years of attendance. Fee is $3.00.

Scripps Research Institute, Registrar, 10666 N Torrey Pines Rd, La Jolla, CA 92037, 619-554-8469 (FAX: 619-554-6602). Hours: 8:30AM-5PM. Records go back to 1989.

Attendance and degree information available by phone, FAX, mail. Search requires name plus social security number, date of birth, approximate years of attendance, signed release. No fee for information.

Transcripts available by mail. Search requires name plus social security number, date of birth, approximate years of attendance, signed release. No fee for transcripts.

Seabury-Western Theological Seminary, Registrar, 2122 Sheridan Rd, Evanston, IL 60201, 708-328-9300 (FAX: 708-328-9624). Hours: 8:30AM-5PM; 9AM-4PM Jun-Aug. Records go back 65 years. Alumni records are maintained here at the same phone number. Degrees granted: Masters; Doctorate.

Attendance and degree information available by phone, FAX, mail. Search requires name plus date of birth, approximate years of attendance. Other helpful information: social security number, exact years of attendance. No fee for information.

Transcripts available by mail. Search requires name plus date of birth, approximate years of attendance. Other helpful information: social security number. Fee is $2.00.

Seattle Central Community College, Registrar, 1701 Broadway, Seattle, WA 98122, 206-587-6918 (FAX: 206-587-3805). Hours: 8AM-5PM. Degrees granted: Associate.

Attendance and degree information available by mail. Search requires name plus social security number, date of birth, exact years of attendance. No fee for information.

Transcripts available by mail. Search requires name plus social security number, date of birth, exact years of attendance, signed release. Fee is $3.00.

Seattle Pacific University, Registrations & Records, 3307 Third Ave W, Seattle, WA 98119, 206-281-2034 (FAX: 206-281-2669). Hours: 8:30AM-5PM. Records go back to 1892. Degrees granted: Bachelors; Masters; Doctorate.

Attendance and degree information available by phone, FAX, mail. Search requires name plus social security number. Other helpful information: date of birth, approximate years of attendance. No fee for information.

Transcripts available by FAX, mail. Search requires name plus social security number, approximate years of attendance, signed release. Other helpful information: date of birth. Fee is $3.00. Expedited service available for $25.00.

Major credit cards accepted for payment.

Seattle University, Registrar, 12th Ave and E Columbia St, Seattle, WA 98122, 206-296-5850 (FAX: 206-296-2443). Hours: 8AM-4:30PM. Records go back to 1897. Alumni records are maintained here also. Call 206-296-6127. Degrees granted: Bachelors; Masters; Doctorate.

Attendance and degree information available by phone, mail. Search requires name plus social security number, date of birth, exact years of attendance. No fee for information.

Transcripts available by mail. Search requires name plus social security number, date of birth, exact years of attendance, signed release. No fee for transcripts.

Selma University, Admissions & Records, Director, 1501 Lapsley St, Selma, AL 36701, 334-872-2533 (FAX: 334-872-7746). Hours: 8:30AM-4PM. Records go back to 1892. Degrees granted: Associate; Bachelors.

Attendance information available by mail. Search requires name plus social security number, approximate years of attendance, signed release. Other helpful information: exact years of attendance. Fee is $2.00. Expedited service available for $2.00.

Degree information available by mail. Search requires name plus social security number, date of birth, approximate years of attendance, signed release. Fee is $2.00. Expedite service available for $2.00.

Transcripts available by mail. Search requires name plus social security number, date of birth, approximate years of attendance, signed release. Fee is $2.00. Expedited service available for $2.00.

Include a self addressed stamped envelope with mail request.

Seminary of the Immaculate Conception, Registrar, 440 W Neck Rd, Huntington, NY 11743, 516-423-0483 (FAX: 516-423-2346). Hours: 8:30AM-4:30PM. Records go back 60 years. Degrees granted: Masters; Doctorate.

Attendance and degree information available by written request only. Search requires name plus social security number, date of birth, exact years of attendance, signed release. No fee for information.

Transcripts available by written request only. Search requires name plus social security number, date of birth, exact years of attendance, signed release. No fee for transcripts.

Seminole Community College, Registrar, 100 Weldon Blvd, Sanford, FL 32773-6199, 407-328-2025 (FAX: 407-328-2029). Hours: 8:30AM-7:30PM M-Th; 8:30AM-4PM F. Records go back to 1966. Degrees granted: Associate.

Attendance information available by phone, FAX, mail. Search requires name plus social security number, date of birth. Other helpful information: approximate years of attendance. No fee for information.

Degree information available by FAX, mail. Search requires name plus social security number, date of birth, signed release. Other helpful information: approximate years of attendance. No fee for information.

Transcripts available by FAX, mail. Search requires name plus social security number, date of birth, signed release. Other helpful information: approximate years of attendance. No fee for transcripts.

Seminole Junior College, Registrar, PO Box 351, Seminole, OK 74868-0351, 405-382-9950 X248 (FAX: 405-382-3122). Hours: 8AM-5PM. Records go back to 1970. Degrees granted: Associate.

Attendance and degree information available by phone, FAX, mail. Search requires name plus social security number, approximate years of attendance. Other helpful information: exact years of attendance. No fee for information.

Transcripts available by mail. Search requires name plus social security number, approximate years of attendance, signed release. Other helpful information: exact years of attendance. Fee is $2.00.

Major credit cards accepted for payment.

Seton Hall University, Registrar, 400 S Orange Ave, South Orange, NJ 07079, 201-761-9374. Hours: 8:45AM-4:45PM. Degrees granted: Bachelors; Masters; Doctorate.

Attendance and degree information available by phone, mail. Search requires name plus social security number, signed release. Other helpful information: approximate years of attendance. No fee for information.

Transcripts available by mail. Search requires name plus social security number, signed release. Other helpful information: approximate years of attendance. No fee for transcripts.

Seton Hall University, (School of Law), Registrar, One Newark Ctr, Newark, NJ 07102-5210, 201-642-8162 (FAX: 201-642-8734). Hours: 8:30AM-6PM. Records go back to 1930. Alumni records are maintained here also. Call 201-642-8711. Degrees granted: Doctorate.

Attendance and degree information available by phone, FAX, mail. Search requires name plus social security number, approximate years of attendance. No fee for information.

Transcripts available by mail. Search requires name plus social security number, approximate years of attendance, signed release. Fee is $2.50.

Seton Hill College, Registrar, Greensburg, PA 15601, 412-838-4218 (FAX: 412-830-4611). Hours: 8AM-6PM M-Th; 8AM-4PM F. Records go back to 1920. Alumni records are maintained here also. Call 412-838-4226. Degrees granted: Bachelors; Masters.

Attendance and degree information available by phone, FAX, mail. Search requires name only. Other helpful information: social

security number, date of birth, approximate years of attendance. Fee is $2.00.

Transcripts available by mail. Search requires name plus signed release. Other helpful information: social security number, date of birth, approximate years of attendance. Fee is $2.00.

Seward County Community College, Registrar, 1801 N Kansas St, Box 1137, Liberal, KS 67901, 316-629-2616 (FAX: 316-629-2725). Hours: 7:45AM-4:45PM. Records go back to founding date. Alumni records are maintained here also. Call 316-629-2664. Degrees granted: Associate.

Attendance and degree information available by phone. Search requires name plus social security number, approximate years of attendance, signed release. Other helpful information: date of birth, exact years of attendance. No fee for information.

Transcripts available by written request only. Search requires name plus social security number, approximate years of attendance, signed release. Other helpful information: date of birth, exact years of attendance. Fee is $3.00.

Major credit cards accepted for payment.

Sh'or Yoshuv Rabbinical College, Registrar, 1526 Central Ave, Far Rockaway, NY 11691, 718-327-7444 (FAX: 718-237-6303). Hours: 9AM-5PM. Records go back 5 years. Degrees granted: Bachelors.

Attendance and degree information available by phone, FAX, mail. Search requires name only. Other helpful information: social security number, date of birth, approximate years of attendance. No fee for information.

Transcripts available by FAX, mail. Search requires name only. Other helpful information: social security number, date of birth, approximate years of attendance. No fee for transcripts.

Shasta College, Registrar, PO Box 496006, Redding, CA 96049, 916-225-4841 (FAX: 916-225-4995). Hours: 8AM-8PM M-Th, 8AM-5PM F Summer: 8AM-8PM M-Th, 8AM-4:30PM F. Records go back to 1950s. Degrees granted: Associate. Adverse incident record source: VP Student Personnel Services, 916-2225-4711.

Attendance and degree information available by FAX, mail. Search requires name plus social security number, date of birth, approximate years of attendance, signed release. No fee for information.

Transcripts available by FAX, mail. Search requires name plus social security number, date of birth, approximate years of attendance, signed release. Fee is $3.00.

Shaw University, Registrar, 118 E South St, Raleigh, NC 27601, 919-546-8415. Hours: 8AM-5PM. Records go back to 1930. Alumni records are maintained here also. Call 919-546-8270. Degrees granted: Bachelors. Adverse incident record source: Dean of Students, 919-546-8270.

Attendance and degree information available by phone, mail. Search requires name plus social security number, approximate years of attendance, signed release. No fee for information.

Transcripts available by mail. Search requires name plus social security number, approximate years of attendance, signed release. Fee is $4.00.

Shawnee Community College, Registrar, Rural Rte 1 Box 53, Ullin, IL 62992-9725, 618-634-2242 (FAX: 618-634-9028). Hours: 8AM-4PM. Records go back to 1969. Degrees granted: Associate.

Attendance and degree information available by phone, FAX, mail. Search requires name plus social security number, date of birth. Other helpful information: approximate years of attendance. No fee for information.

Transcripts available by FAX, mail. Search requires name plus social security number, date of birth, signed release. Other helpful information: approximate years of attendance. Fee is $2.00. Expedited service available for $2.00.

Shawnee State University, Registrar, 940 Second St, Portsmouth, OH 45662, 614-355-2262 (FAX: 614-355-2593). Hours: 7AM-6PM M-Th, 7AM-5PM F. Records go back to 1970. Alumni records are maintained here also. Call 614-355-2257. Degrees granted: Associate; Bachelors.

Attendance and degree information available by phone, FAX, mail. Search requires name plus social security number, signed release. No fee for information.

Transcripts available by mail. Search requires name plus social security number, signed release. Fee is $3.00. Expedited service available for $10.00.

Shelby State Community College, Registrar, PO Box 40568, Memphis, TN 38174-0568, 901-544-5668 (FAX: 901-544-5520). Hours: 8AM-7PM. Degrees granted: Associate. Adverse incident record source: 901-544-5555.

Attendance information available by phone, FAX, mail. Search requires name plus social security number, signed release. Other helpful information: date of birth, approximate years of attendance. No fee for information.

Degree information available by phone, FAX, mail. Search requires name plus social security number. Other helpful information: date of birth, approximate years of attendance. No fee for information.

Transcripts available by mail. Search requires name plus social security number, signed release. Other helpful information: date of birth, approximate years of attendance. No fee for transcripts.

Sheldon Jackson College, Registrar, 801 Lincoln, Sitka, AK 99835, 907-747-5216 (FAX: 907-747-5212). Hours: 8AM-Noon, 1-5PM. Records go back to 1898. Degrees granted: Associate; Bachelors.

Attendance and degree information available by phone, FAX, mail. Search requires name only. Other helpful information: social security number, approximate years of attendance. No fee for information.

Transcripts available by FAX, mail. Search requires name plus signed release. Other helpful information: social security number, approximate years of attendance. Fee is $3.00. Expedited service available for $5.00.

Must prepay for FAX. Major credit cards accepted for payment.

Shelton State Community College, Registrar, 202 Skyland Blvd, Tuscaloosa, AL 35405, 205-391-2214 (FAX: 205-759-2495). Hours: 8AM-5PM. Records go back to 1950. Alumni records are maintained here also. Call 205-391-2221. Degrees granted: Associate.

Attendance and degree information available by phone, FAX, mail. Search requires name plus social security number, approximate years of attendance. No fee for information.

Transcripts available by mail. Search requires name plus social security number, approximate years of attendance, signed release. First transcript is free; $3.00 each additional.

Shenandoah University, Registrar, 1460 University Dr, Winchester, VA 22601, 703-665-4536 (FAX: 703-665-5446). Hours: 9AM-5PM. Records go back to 1930. Degrees granted: Associate; Bachelors; Masters.

Attendance and degree information available by phone, FAX, mail. Search requires name only. Other helpful information: social security number, date of birth, exact years of attendance. No fee for information.

Transcripts available by FAX, mail. Search requires name plus social security number, date of birth, approximate years of attendance, signed release. Other helpful information: exact years of attendance. Fee is $3.00.

Shenango Valley School of Business, Registrar, 335 Boyd Dr, Sharon, PA 16146, 412-983-0700 (FAX: 412-983-8355). Hours: 8:30AM-4:30PM. Records go back to 1985. Degrees granted: Associate.

Attendance and degree information available by written request only. Search requires name plus social security number, exact years of attendance, signed release. Fee is $5.

Transcripts available by written request only. Search requires name plus social security number, exact years of attendance, signed release. Fee is $5.00,5. Expedited service available for $5.00.

Include a self addressed stamped envelope with mail request.

Shenango Valley School of Business, (Branch Campus), Registrar, RD 1 Schoolhouse Rd, Pulaski, PA 16143, 412-654-1976. Hours: 8AM-4PM. Records go back to 1977. Alumni records are maintained here at the same phone number. Degrees granted: Associate.

Attendance and degree information available by phone, mail. Search requires name plus social security number, exact years of attendance. No fee for information.

Transcripts available by mail. Search requires name plus social security number, exact years of attendance, signed release. Fee is $5.00.

Shenango Valley School of Business, (Branch Campus), Registrar, 124 W Spring St, Titusville, PA 16354, 814-827-9567. Hours: 8AM-4PM. Records go back to 1955. Alumni records are maintained here at the same phone number. Degrees granted: Associate.

Attendance and degree information available by phone, mail. Search requires name plus social security number, exact years of attendance. No fee for information.

Transcripts available by mail. Search requires name plus social security number, exact years of attendance, signed release. Fee is $5.00.

Shepherd College, Registrar, Shepherdstown, WV 25443, 304-876-5463 (FAX: 304-876-5136). Hours: 8AM-4:30PM. Records go back to 1871. Alumni records are maintained here also. Call 304-876-5157. Degrees granted: Associate; Bachelors.

Attendance and degree information available by phone, FAX, mail. Search requires name plus social security number. Other helpful information: date of birth, approximate years of attendance. No fee for information.

Transcripts available by FAX, mail. Search requires name plus social security number, approximate years of attendance, signed release. Other helpful information: date of birth. Fee is $3.00. Expedited service available for $10.00.

Sheridan College, Registrar, PO Box 1500, Sheridan, WY 82801, 307-674-6446 (FAX: 307-674-7205). Hours: 8AM-5PM. Records go back to 1948. Alumni records are maintained here also. Call 307-674-6446. Degrees granted: Associate. Adverse incident record source: Campus Police, 307-674-6446.

Attendance information available by phone, FAX, mail. Search requires name plus social security number, date of birth. Other helpful information: approximate years of attendance. No fee for information.

Degree information available by phone, FAX, mail. Search requires name plus social security number. Other helpful information: approximate years of attendance. No fee for information.

Transcripts available by phone, FAX, mail. Search requires name plus social security number, date of birth, signed release. Other helpful information: approximate years of attendance. Fee is $1.00. Expedite: $1.00 to $10.00.

Transcript request to student in writing. To third party, student can request by phone, FAX or mail. Students can request no directory information.

Sherman College of Straight Chiropractic, Registrar, 2020 Springfield Rd, PO Box 1452, Spartanburg, SC 29304, 803-578-8770 (FAX: 803-599-7145). Hours: 8AM-4:30PM. Degrees granted: Doctorate.

Attendance and degree information available by phone, FAX, mail. Search requires name plus signed release. Other helpful information: social security number, date of birth, approximate years of attendance. No fee for information.

Transcripts available by mail. Search requires name plus signed release. Other helpful information: social security number, date of birth, approximate years of attendance. Fee is $5.00.

Shimer College, Registrar, PO Box A500, 438 N Sheridan Rd, Waukegan, IL 60079, 708-249-7183 (FAX: 708-249-7171). Hours: 9AM-5PM. Records go back to 1853. Alumni records are maintained here also. Call 708-249-7191. Degrees granted: Bachelors. Special programs- Academic, 708-623-8400.

Attendance and degree information available by phone, FAX, mail. Search requires name plus signed release. No fee for information.

Transcripts available by mail. Search requires name plus signed release. First transcript $5.00; each additional $3.00. Unofficial transcripts $2.00.

Shippensburg University of Pennsylvania, Registrar, Shippensburg, PA 17257, 717-532-1381 (FAX: 717-532-1388). Hours: 8AM-4:30PM. Alumni records are maintained here also. Call 717-532-1381 X1218. Degrees granted: Bachelors; Masters.

Attendance and degree information available by phone, mail. Search requires name plus social security number, exact years of attendance. No fee for information.

Transcripts available by mail. Search requires name plus social security number, exact years of attendance, signed release. Fee is $3.00.

Shoreline Community College, Records Office, 16101 Greenwood Ave N, Seattle, WA 98133, 206-546-5623 (FAX: 206-546-5826). Hours: 8AM-4:30PM. Records go back to 1964. Call 206-546-4614 for transcripts. Degrees granted: Associate.

Attendance and degree information available by phone, FAX, mail. Search requires name only. Other helpful information: social security number, date of birth, approximate years of attendance. No fee for information.

Transcripts available by FAX, mail. Search requires name plus date of birth, signed release. Other helpful information: social security number, approximate years of attendance. Fee is $2.00.
FAX must be prepaid with Mastercard or Visa. Major credit cards accepted for payment.

Shorter College, Registrar, 604 Locust St, North Little Rock, AR 72114, 501-374-6305 (FAX: 501-374-9333). Hours: 8:30AM-5pm. Degrees granted: Associate.
Attendance information available by phone, FAX, mail. Search requires name plus social security number, date of birth, signed release. Other helpful information: approximate years of attendance. No fee for information.
Degree information available by mail. Search requires name plus social security number, date of birth, signed release. Other helpful information: approximate years of attendance. No fee for information.
Transcripts available by mail. Search requires name plus social security number, date of birth, signed release. Other helpful information: approximate years of attendance. Fee is $2.00.

Shorter College, Registrar, 315 Shorter Ave, Rome, GA 30165-4298, 706-291-2121 X206 (FAX: 706-236-1515). Hours: 8AM-5PM. Records go back to 1911. Alumni records are maintained here also. Call 706-291-2121 X242. Degrees granted: Bachelors. Special programs- School of Prof. Programs, Marietta, GA, 404-989-5671.
Attendance and degree information available by phone, FAX, mail. Search requires name only. Other helpful information: social security number, approximate years of attendance. No fee for information.
Transcripts available by FAX, mail. Search requires name plus signed release. Other helpful information: social security number, approximate years of attendance. Fee is $1.00. Expedited service available for $5.00.

Siena College, Registrar, 515 Loudon Rd, Loudonville, NY 12211-1462, 518-783-2310 (FAX: 518-786-5060). Hours: 8:30AM-4:30PM. Records go back to 1950s. Alumni records are maintained here also. Call 518-783-2430. Degrees granted: Bachelors. Adverse incident record source: Student Affairs, 518-783-2328.
Attendance and degree information available by phone, FAX, mail. Search requires name plus social security number. No fee for information.
Transcripts available by mail. Search requires name plus social security number, exact years of attendance, signed release. Other helpful information: approximate years of attendance. Fee is $2.00.
If student has suppressed information, written consent needed. Major credit cards accepted for payment.

Siena Heights College, Registrar, 1247 E Siena Heights Dr, Adrian, MI 49221, 517-263-0731 X236 (FAX: 517-265-3380). Hours: 8AM-5PM. Records go back to 1919. Alumni records are maintained here also. Call 517-263-0731 X215. Degrees granted: Associate; Bachelors; Masters. Adverse incident record source: Campus Security, 517-263-0731 X250.
Attendance and degree information available by phone, FAX, mail. Search requires name plus social security number, date of birth. Other helpful information: approximate years of attendance. No fee for information.
Transcripts available by written request only. Search requires name plus social security number, date of birth, signed release. Other helpful information: approximate years of attendance. Fee is $2.00. Expedited service available for $3.00.

Sierra College, Assistant Dean, 5000 Rocklin Rd, Rocklin, CA 95677, 916-781-0430 (FAX: 916-781-0403). Hours: 7:30AM-7:30PM M-Th; 7:30AM-3PM F. Records go back 59 years. Alumni records are maintained here also. Call 916-773-5659. Degrees granted: Associate. Adverse incident record source: Campus Police, 916-781-0570.
Attendance and degree information available by phone, FAX, mail. Search requires name plus signed release. Other helpful information: social security number, date of birth, approximate years of attendance. No fee for information.
Transcripts available by FAX, mail. Search requires name plus signed release. Other helpful information: social security number, date of birth, approximate years of attendance. Fee is $2.00.
Major credit cards accepted for payment.

Sierra Nevada College, Registrar, PO Box 4269, Incline Village, NV 89450-4269, 702-831-1314 (FAX: 702-831-1347). Hours: 8AM-5PM. Records go back to 1989. Degrees granted: Bachelors.
Attendance and degree information available by phone, FAX, mail. Search requires name only. Other helpful information: social security number, date of birth, approximate years of attendance. No fee for information.
Transcripts available by FAX, mail. Search requires name plus social security number, date of birth, approximate years of attendance, signed release. Other helpful information: exact years of attendance. Fee is $3.00.

Silver Lake College, Registrar, 2406 S Alverno Rd, Manitowoc, WI 54220, 414-684-6691 (FAX: 414-684-7082). Hours: 8AM-4:30PM. Records go back to 1930s. Alumni records are maintained here at the same phone number. Degrees granted: Associate; Bachelors; Masters.
Attendance and degree information available by phone, FAX, mail. Search requires name only. Other helpful information: social security number, date of birth, approximate years of attendance. No fee for information.
Transcripts available by written request only. Search requires name plus signed release. Other helpful information: social security number, date of birth, approximate years of attendance. Fee is $2.00. Expedite: $2.00 plus mail cost.

Simmons College, Registrar, 300 The Fenway, Boston, MA 02115, 617-521-2107 (FAX: 617-521-3199). Hours: 8AM-4:30PM M,T,Th,F; 8AM-6PM W. Records go back to 1905. Degrees granted: Bachelors; Masters; Doctorate.
Attendance information available by phone, FAX, mail. Search requires name plus approximate years of attendance. Other helpful information: social security number. No fee for information.
Degree information available by phone, FAX, mail. Search requires name plus approximate years of attendance. Other helpful information: social security number, date of birth. No fee for information.
Transcripts available by FAX, mail. Search requires name plus social security number, date of birth, approximate years of attendance, signed release. Fee is $3.00. Expedited service available for $3.00.

Simmons Institute of Funeral Service, Registrar, 1828 South Ave, Syracuse, NY 13207, 315-475-5142 (FAX: 315-475-3817). Hours: 8AM-3PM M-F, 8AM-Noon Sat. Records go back to 1950s. Alumni records are maintained here at the same phone number. Adverse incident record source: Records & Registration, 315-475-5142.

Attendance information available by phone, FAX, mail. Search requires name plus social security number. No fee for information.

Degree information available by phone, FAX, mail. Search requires name plus social security number. Other helpful information: exact years of attendance. No fee for information.

Transcripts available by mail. Search requires name plus social security number, signed release. Fee is $5.00.

Simon's Rock College of Bard, Registrar, Great Barrington, MA 01230-9702, 413-528-7201 (FAX: 413-528-7365). Hours: 9AM-5PM. Records go back to 1966. Degrees granted: Associate; Bachelors. Adverse incident record source: Dean, 413-528-7245.

Attendance and degree information available by phone, FAX, mail. Search requires name only. Other helpful information: date of birth, approximate years of attendance. No fee for information. Include a stamped envelope.

Transcripts available by mail. Search requires name plus approximate years of attendance, signed release. Other helpful information: exact years of attendance. Fee is $5.00. Expedite: $20.00 FedEx fee.

Simpson College, Registrar, 701 N C St, Indianola, IA 50125, 515-961-1642 (FAX: 515-961-1498). Hours: 8AM-4:30PM. Alumni records are maintained here also. Call 515-961-1547. Degrees granted: Bachelors. Adverse incident record source: Security, 515-961-7111.

Attendance and degree information available by phone, FAX, mail. Search requires name only. Other helpful information: social security number, date of birth, approximate years of attendance. No fee for information.

Transcripts available by FAX. Search requires name plus signed release. Other helpful information: social security number, date of birth, approximate years of attendance. Fee is $2.00. Expedited service available for $2.00.

Simpson College, Registrar, 2211 College View Dr, Redding, CA 96003, 916-224-5600 X2111 (FAX: 916-224-5608). Hours: 8AM-6PM. Records go back to 1921. Alumni records are maintained here also. Call 916-224-5600 X2503. Degrees granted: Associate; Bachelors; Masters.

Attendance and degree information available by phone, FAX, mail. Search requires name plus social security number, date of birth, approximate years of attendance, signed release. No fee for information.

Transcripts available by mail. Search requires name plus social security number, date of birth, approximate years of attendance, signed release. Fee is $3.00.

Sinclair Community College, Registrar, 444 W Third St, Dayton, OH 45402, 513-226-2736. Hours: 8AM-7PM M-Th; 8AM-5PM F. Alumni records are maintained here also. Call 513-226-3030. Degrees granted: Associate. Adverse incident record source: Student Activities, 513-226-2509.

Attendance and degree information available by phone, mail. Search requires name plus social security number. Other helpful information: approximate years of attendance. No fee for information.

Transcripts available by mail. Search requires name plus social security number, signed release. Other helpful information: approximate years of attendance. Fee is $2.00.

Sinte Gleska University, Registrar, PO Box 490, Rosebud, SD 57570, 605-747-2263 (FAX: 605-747-2098). Hours: 9AM-5PM. Records go back to 1972. Degrees granted: Associate; Bachelors; Masters.

Attendance and degree information available by phone, FAX, mail. Search requires name plus social security number. Other helpful information: date of birth, exact years of attendance. No fee for information.

Transcripts available by mail. Search requires name plus social security number, signed release. Other helpful information: date of birth, exact years of attendance. Fee is $3.00.

Student request for all applications.

Sisseton-Wahpeton Community College, Registrar, PO Box 689 Old Agency, Agency Village, SD 57262, 605-698-3966. Hours: 8AM-5PM. Records go back to 1979. Degrees granted: Associate.

Attendance and degree information available by phone, mail. Search requires name plus social security number, exact years of attendance. No fee for information.

Transcripts available by mail. Search requires name plus social security number, exact years of attendance, signed release. Fee is $2.00.

Skagit Valley College, Registrar, 2405 College Way, Mount Vernon, WA 98273, 206-428-1261/428-1155 (FAX: 206-428-1612). Hours: 8AM-4:30PM. Records go back to 1926. Degrees granted: Associate.

Attendance and degree information available by FAX, mail. Search requires name plus social security number, signed release. No fee for information.

Transcripts available by FAX, mail. Search requires name plus social security number, signed release. Fee is $1.00.

Skidmore College, Registrar, 815 N Broadway, Saratoga Springs, NY 12866-1632, 518-584-5000 X2210 (FAX: 518-584-7963). Hours: 8AM-4:30PM. Records go back to 1912. Degrees granted: Bachelors; Masters. Special programs- UWW, 518-584-5000 X2294: MALS, 518-584-5000 X2274. Adverse incident record source: Dean of Studies, 518-584-5000 X2203.

Attendance and degree information available by phone, mail. Search requires name plus exact years of attendance. Other helpful information: social security number, date of birth, approximate years of attendance. No fee for information.

Transcripts available by mail. Search requires name plus exact years of attendance, signed release. Other helpful information: social security number, date of birth, approximate years of attendance. Fee is $5.00. Expedited service available for $10.00.

FAX for emergency only. Former name, if appropriate, needed.

Skyline College, Admissions & Records Office, 3300 College Dr, San Bruno, CA 94066, 415-738-4252. Hours: 8AM-10PM M-Th, 8AM-4:30PM F, 8AM-Noon Sat. Records go back to 1969. Degrees granted: Associate. Adverse incident record source: Campus Security, 415-738-4199 (day), 415-738-4256 (eve.).

Attendance information available by mail. Search requires name plus social security number, approximate years of attendance, signed release. Fee is $1.00.

Degree information available by phone, mail. Search requires name plus social security number, approximate years of attendance, signed release. Fee is $1.00.

Transcripts available by mail. Search requires name plus social security number, approximate years of attendance, signed release. First two transcripts are free; $3.00 each additional.

Only current attendance and degree issued confirmed by phone.

Slippery Rock University of Pennsylvania, Academic Records, Slippery Rock, PA 16057, 412-738-2020 (FAX: 412-738-2936). Hours: 8AM-4:30PM. Records go back to 1890s. Alumni records are maintained here also. Call 412-738-2018. Degrees granted: Bachelors; Masters.

Attendance and degree information available by phone, FAX, mail. Search requires name plus social security number. Other helpful information: date of birth, approximate years of attendance. No fee for information.

Transcripts available by FAX, mail. Search requires name plus social security number, signed release. Other helpful information: date of birth, approximate years of attendance. Fee is $3.00. Expedited service available for $10.00.

Major credit cards accepted for payment.

Smith College, Registrar, Northampton, MA 01063, 413-584-2700 X2550 (FAX: 413-585-2557). Hours: 8AM-4:30PM. Records go back to 1800s. Alumni records are maintained here also. Call 413-584-2700. Degrees granted: Bachelors; Masters. Adverse incident record source: Dean, 413-584-2700.

Attendance and degree information available by phone, FAX, mail. Search requires name plus social security number, date of birth, approximate years of attendance, signed release. No fee for information.

Transcripts available by FAX, mail. Search requires name plus social security number, date of birth, approximate years of attendance, signed release. Fee is $3.00.

Snead State Community College, Registrar, PO Drawer D, 200 N Walnut St, Boaz, AL 35957, 205-593-5120 X207 (FAX: 205-593-7180). Hours: 7:30AM-4PM. Records go back to 1934. Alumni records are maintained here also. Call 205-593-5120. Degrees granted: Associate.

Attendance information available by phone, FAX, mail. Search requires name plus social security number. Other helpful information: date of birth, exact years of attendance. No fee for information.

Degree information available by mail. Search requires name plus social security number. Other helpful information: date of birth, exact years of attendance. No fee for information.

Transcripts available by mail. Search requires name plus social security number, signed release. Other helpful information: date of birth, exact years of attendance. No fee for transcripts.

Snow College, Registrar, Ephraim, UT 84627, 801-283-4021 (FAX: 801-283-6874). Hours: 9AM-4PM. Records go back to 1888. Degrees granted: Associate.

Attendance and degree information available by phone, FAX, mail. Search requires name only. Other helpful information: social security number, date of birth, approximate years of attendance. No fee for information.

Transcripts available by written request only. Search requires name plus social security number, signed release. Other helpful information: date of birth, approximate years of attendance. Fee is $2.00. Expedited service available for $3.00.

Major credit cards accepted for payment.

Sojourner-Douglass College, Registrar, 500 N Caroline St, Baltimore, MD 21205, 410-276-0306 X39. Hours: 8AM-4:30PM. Records go back to 1980. Alumni records are maintained here also. Call 410-276-0306. Degrees granted: Bachelors.

Attendance and degree information available by mail. Search requires name plus social security number, exact years of attendance. No fee for information.

Transcripts available by mail. Search requires name plus social security number, exact years of attendance, signed release. Fee is $3.00.

Solano Community College, Admissions & Records, 4000 Suisun Valley Rd, Suisun, CA 94585, 707-864-7171. Hours: 8AM-8:30PM M-Th; 8AM-3PM F. Records go back to 1960. Degrees granted: Associate. Adverse incident record source: Campus Police, 707-864-7000.

Attendance and degree information available by mail. Search requires name plus social security number, signed release. Other helpful information: date of birth, approximate years of attendance. No fee for information.

Transcripts available by mail. Search requires name plus social security number, signed release. Other helpful information: date of birth, approximate years of attendance. Fee is $2.00. Expedited service available for $7.50.

Major credit cards accepted for payment.

Somerset Community College, Registrar, 808 Monticello Rd, Somerset, KY 42501, 606-679-8501 (FAX: 606-679-5139). Hours: 8AM-5PM. Records go back to 1965. Degrees granted: Associate.

Attendance and degree information available by phone, FAX, mail. Search requires name plus social security number, approximate years of attendance. Other helpful information: date of birth, exact years of attendance. No fee for information.

Transcripts available by FAX, mail. Search requires name plus social security number, approximate years of attendance, signed release. Other helpful information: date of birth, exact years of attendance. Fee is $2.00. Expedite: $5.00 to $8.00.

Sonoma State University, Registrar, 1801 E Cotati Ave, Rohnert Park, CA 94928, 707-664-2778 (FAX: 707-664-2060). Hours: 8AM-4:30PM. Records go back to 1960. Alumni records are maintained here also. Call 707-664-2426. Degrees granted: Bachelors.

Attendance and degree information available by phone, FAX, mail. Search requires name plus social security number, approximate years of attendance, signed release. No fee for information.

Transcripts available by mail. Search requires name plus social security number, approximate years of attendance, signed release. Fee is $4.00.

South Arkansas Community College, Registrar, PO Box 7010, El Dorado, AR 71731-7010, 501-862-8131 (FAX: 501-864-7122). Hours: 8AM-5PM. Records go back to 1975. Alumni records are maintained here also. Call 501-862-8131. Degrees granted: Associate. Adverse incident record source: Student Affairs, 501-862-8131.

Attendance and degree information available by phone, FAX, mail. Search requires name plus social security number. No fee for information.

Transcripts available by FAX, mail. Search requires name plus social security number, signed release. No fee for transcripts.

South Baylo University, Registrar, 1126 N Brookhurst St, Anaheim, CA 92801, 714-533-1495 (FAX: 714-533-1640). Hours: 10AM-6PM. Records go back to 1982. Degrees granted: Masters.

Attendance and degree information available by phone, FAX, mail. Search requires name plus social security number, signed release. No fee for information.

Transcripts available by phone, FAX, mail. Search requires name plus social security number, signed release. No fee for transcripts.

South Baylo University, (Branch), Registrar, 1543 W Olympic Blvd, Los Angeles, CA 90015, 213-738-1974. Records are not housed here. They are located at South Baylo University, Registrar, 1126 N Brookhurst St, Anaheim, CA 92801.

South Carolina State University, Registrar, 300 College Ave NE, PO Box 1627, Orangeburg, SC 29117, 803-536-7185 (FAX: 803-536-8990). Hours: 8AM-5PM. Records go back to 1896. Alumni records are maintained here also. Call 803-536-8946. Degrees granted: Bachelors; Masters; Doctorate.

Attendance and degree information available by phone, mail. Search requires name plus social security number, date of birth, exact years of attendance. No fee for information.

Transcripts available by mail. Search requires name plus social security number, date of birth, exact years of attendance, signed release. Fee is $3.00.

South College, Registrar's Office, 709 Mall Blvd, Savannah, GA 31406, 912-651-8100 (FAX: 912-356-1409). Hours: 8:30AM-5PM. Records go back to 1977. Degrees granted: Associate.

Attendance and degree information available by phone, FAX, mail. Search requires name plus approximate years of attendance. Other helpful information: social security number, date of birth, exact years of attendance. No fee for information.

Transcripts available by FAX, mail. Search requires name plus approximate years of attendance, signed release. Other helpful information: social security number, date of birth, exact years of attendance. Fee is $5.00.

South College, Registrar, 1760 N Congress Ave, West Palm Beach, FL 33409, 407-697-9200 (FAX: 407-697-9944). Hours: 8AM-5PM. Records go back to 1986. Degrees granted: Associate.

Attendance and degree information available by mail. Search requires name plus social security number, date of birth, exact years of attendance. No fee for information.

Transcripts available by mail. Search requires name plus social security number, date of birth, exact years of attendance, signed release. Fee is $2.00.

South Dakota School of Mines and Technology, Registrar, 501 E St. Joseph St, Rapid City, SD 57701, 605-394-2414 (FAX: 605-394-6131). Hours: 7:30AM-4:30PM. Records go back 3-10 years. Degrees granted: Bachelors; Masters; Doctorate. Adverse incident record source: Dean of Students.

Attendance and degree information available by phone, FAX, mail. Search requires name plus signed release. Other helpful information: social security number, date of birth. No fee for information.

Transcripts available by FAX, mail. Search requires name plus signed release. Other helpful information: social security number, date of birth. Fee is $5.00. Expedited service available for $5.00.

South Dakota State University, Registrar, Box 2201 University Station, Brookings, SD 57007, 605-688-4121 (FAX: 605-688-6384). Hours: 8AM-5PM. Records go back to 1881. Degrees granted: Associate; Bachelors; Masters; Doctorate.

Attendance and degree information available by phone, FAX, mail. Search requires name plus social security number. Other helpful information: date of birth, approximate years of attendance. No fee for information.

Transcripts available by FAX, mail. Search requires name plus social security number, signed release. Other helpful information: date of birth, approximate years of attendance. Fee is $5.00. Expedited service available for $5.00.

Major credit cards accepted for payment.

South Florida Community College, Registrar, 600 W College Dr, Avon Park, FL 33825, 813-453-6661. Degrees granted: Associate. Adverse incident record source: Student Services, 813-453-6661 X104.

Attendance and degree information available by FAX, mail. Search requires name plus signed release. Other helpful information: social security number, approximate years of attendance. No fee for information.

Transcripts available by phone, FAX, mail. Search requires name plus signed release. Other helpful information: social security number, approximate years of attendance. No fee for transcripts.

Phone request limited to Florida colleges and universities, and from student.

South Georgia College, Registrar, 100 W College Park Dr, Douglas, GA 31533-5098, 912-383-4200 (FAX: 912-383-4392). Hours: 8AM-5PM. Records go back 90 years. Alumni records are maintained here at the same phone number. Degrees granted: Associate. Adverse incident record source: Robert Bidwell, 912-383-4281.

Attendance and degree information available by phone, FAX, mail. Search requires name only. Other helpful information: social security number, date of birth, approximate years of attendance. No fee for information.

Transcripts available by FAX, mail. Search requires name plus signed release. Other helpful information: social security number, date of birth, approximate years of attendance. Fee is $1.00. Expedited service available for $10.00.

South Hills Business School, Registrar, 480 Waupelani Dr, State College, PA 16801-4516, 814-324-7755. Hours: 8AM-5PM. Records go back to 1966. Degrees granted: Associate.

Attendance and degree information available by mail. Search requires name plus social security number, exact years of attendance, signed release. No fee for information.

Transcripts available by mail. Search requires name plus social security number, exact years of attendance, signed release. First five transcripts are free; $2.00 each additional.

Need to know name of program.

South Mountain Community College, Admissions & Records, 7050 S 24th St, Phoenix, AZ 85040, 602-243-8000 (FAX: 602-243-8199).

Attendance and degree information available by mail. Search requires name plus social security number, signed release. Other helpful information: date of birth, exact years of attendance. No fee for information.

Transcripts available by mail. Search requires name plus social security number, signed release. Other helpful information: date of birth, exact years of attendance. Fee is $5.00.

Major credit cards accepted for payment.

South Plains College, Registrar, 1401 College Ave, Levelland, TX 79336, 806-894-9611 X345 (FAX: 806-894-5274). Hours: 8AM-4PM. Alumni records are maintained here also. Call 806-894-9611 X217. Degrees granted: Associate.

Attendance and degree information available by phone, FAX, mail. Search requires name plus social security number. Other helpful information: approximate years of attendance. No fee for information.

Transcripts available by written request only. Search requires name plus social security number, signed release. Other helpful information: approximate years of attendance. Fee is $2.00. Expedited service available for $10.00.

South Puget Sound Community College, Registrar, 2011 Mottman Rd SW, Olympia, WA 98512, 360-754-7711 X243 (FAX: 360-586-6054). Hours: 8AM-5PM. Records go back to 1965. Degrees granted: Associate.

Attendance and degree information available by phone, FAX, mail. Search requires name plus social security number, date of birth. Other helpful information: approximate years of attendance. No fee for information.

Transcripts available by FAX, mail. Search requires name plus social security number, date of birth, signed release. Other helpful information: approximate years of attendance. No fee for transcripts.

South Seattle Community College, Records, 6000 16th Ave SW, Seattle, WA 98106, 206-764-5399 (FAX: 206-764-7947). Hours: 7:30AM-5PM. Records go back to 1975. Degrees granted: Associate.

Attendance and degree information available by phone, FAX, mail. Search requires name plus social security number. Other helpful information: date of birth, approximate years of attendance. No fee for information.

Transcripts available by written request only. Search requires name plus social security number, signed release. Other helpful information: date of birth, approximate years of attendance. Fee is $3.00.

Major credit cards accepted for payment.

South Suburban College of Cook County, Registrar, 15800 S State St, South Holland, IL 60473, 708-596-2000 (FAX: 708-210-5746). Hours: 8AM-4:30PM. Alumni records are maintained here also. Call 708-596-2000 X456. Degrees granted: Associate.

Attendance information available by phone, mail. Search requires name plus social security number, date of birth. Other helpful information: approximate years of attendance. No fee for information.

Degree information available by phone, mail. Search requires name plus social security number. Other helpful information: date of birth, approximate years of attendance. No fee for information.

Transcripts available by mail. Search requires name plus social security number, date of birth, signed release. Other helpful information: approximate years of attendance. Fee is $5.00.

South Texas College of Law, Registrar, 1303 San Jacinto St, Houston, TX 77002-7000, 713-659-8040 X63. Hours: 8AM-5PM. Alumni records are maintained here at the same phone number.

Attendance and degree information available by mail. Search requires name plus social security number, exact years of attendance, signed release. No fee for information.

Transcripts available by mail. Search requires name plus social security number, exact years of attendance, signed release. No fee for transcripts.

Southampton College of Long Island University, Registrar Office, 239 Montauk Hwy, Southampton, NY 11968, 516-283-4000 X8325 (FAX: 516-283-4081). Hours: 8AM-5PM. Records go back to 1963. Alumni records are maintained here also. Call 516-283-4000 X8347. Degrees granted: Bachelors; Masters.

Attendance and degree information available by phone, FAX, mail. Search requires name plus social security number. Other helpful information: date of birth, approximate years of attendance. No fee for information.

Transcripts available by FAX, mail. Search requires name plus social security number, signed release. Other helpful information: date of birth, approximate years of attendance. Fee is $5.00. Expedited service available for $10.75.

Major credit cards accepted for payment.

Southeast Community College, Registrar, 700 College Rd, Cumberland, KY 40823, 606-589-2145. Hours: 8:30AM-4:30PM. Records go back 61 years. Degrees granted: Associate.

Attendance and degree information available by phone, mail. Search requires name plus social security number, signed release. Other helpful information: approximate years of attendance. No fee for information.

Transcripts available by mail. Search requires name plus social security number, signed release. Other helpful information: approximate years of attendance. Fee is $2.00. Expedited service available for $5.00.

Southeast Community College, Registrar, 8800 O St, Lincoln, NE 68520, 402-437-2609 (FAX: 402-437-2404). Hours: 8AM-8:30PM M-Th; 8AM-5PM F. Records go back to 1970. Degrees granted: Associate. Adverse incident record source: Corrections Division, 402-479-6144.

Attendance and degree information available by phone, FAX, mail. Search requires name only. Other helpful information: social security number, date of birth, approximate years of attendance. No fee for information.

Transcripts available by FAX, mail. Search requires name plus signed release. Other helpful information: social security number, date of birth, approximate years of attendance. No fee for transcripts.

Southeast Missouri State University, Registrar, One University Plaza, Cape Girardeau, MO 63701, 314-651-2250 (FAX: 314-651-5155). Hours: 8AM-5PM. Records go back 75 years. Degrees granted: Associate; Bachelors; Masters.

Attendance and degree information available by phone, FAX, mail. Search requires name plus social security number. Other helpful information: date of birth, approximate years of attendance. No fee for information. Expedited service available for $2.00.

Transcripts available by FAX, mail. Search requires name plus social security number, signed release. Other helpful information: date of birth, approximate years of attendance. Fee is $3.00. Expedited service available for $5.00.

Southeast Technical Institute, Registrar, 2301 Career Pl, Sioux Falls, SD 57107, 605-381-7624. Degrees granted: Associate.

School will not confirm attendance or degree information. Search requires name plus signed release. Other helpful information: social security number, date of birth. No fee for information.

Transcripts available by FAX, mail. Search requires name plus signed release. Other helpful information: social security number, date of birth. Fee is $2.00. Expedited service available for $2.00. Major credit cards accepted for payment.

Southeastern Academy, Inc., Registrar, 233 Academy Dr, PO Box 421768, Kissimmee, FL 32742, 407-847-4444 (FAX: 407-847-8793). Hours: 8:30AM-5PM. Records go back to 1975. Adverse incident record source: Dean of Students, 407-847-4444 X391.

Attendance and degree information available by phone, FAX, mail. Search requires name plus social security number, exact years of attendance. No fee for information.

Transcripts available by phone, FAX, mail. Search requires name plus social security number, exact years of attendance. Fee is $5.00.

Southeastern Academy, Inc., (Peoples College of Independent Studies), Registrar, 233 Academy Dr, PO BOx 421768, Kissimmee, FL 34742-1768, 407-847-4444. Records are not housed here. They are located at Southeastern Academy, Inc., Registrar, 233 Academy Dr, PO Box 421768, Kissimmee, FL 32742.

Southeastern Baptist College, Registrar, 4229 Hwy 15 N, Laurel, MS 39440, 601-426-6346. Hours: 8AM-4:30PM. Records go back to 1948. Degrees granted: Associate; Bachelors.

Attendance and degree information available by phone, FAX, mail. Search requires name only. Other helpful information: social security number, date of birth, approximate years of attendance. No fee for information.

Transcripts available by FAX. Search requires name plus signed release. Other helpful information: social security number, date of birth, approximate years of attendance. Fee is $2.00. Expedited service available for $10.00.

Southeastern Baptist Theological Seminary, Registrar, PO Box 1889, Wake Forest, NC 27588-1889, 919-556-3101 X215 (FAX: 919-556-0998). Hours: 8AM-4:30PM. Records go back 42 years. Degrees granted: Associate; Bachelors; Masters; Doctorate.

Attendance and degree information available by phone, FAX, mail. Search requires name plus approximate years of attendance. Other helpful information: social security number, exact years of attendance. No fee for information.

Transcripts available by FAX, mail. Search requires name plus approximate years of attendance, signed release. Other helpful information: social security number, exact years of attendance. Fee is $2.00. Expedited service available for $5.00.

Southeastern Bible College, Registrar, 3001 Hwy 28 E, Birmingham, AL 35243, 205-970-9208 (FAX: 205-970-9207). Hours: 8AM-4:30PM. Records go back to 1940. Alumni records are maintained here at the same phone number. Degrees granted: Associate; Bachelors; Masters. Adverse incident record source: Dean of Students, 205-969-0880.

Attendance and degree information available by FAX, mail. Search requires name only. No fee for information.

Transcripts available by mail. Search requires name plus signed release. Fee is $2.00.

Southeastern Business College, Registrar, 1855 Western Ave, Chillicothe, OH 45601, 614-774-6300 (FAX: 614-774-6317). Hours: 8:30AM-10PM. Records go back to 1985. Degrees granted: Associate.

Attendance and degree information available by phone, FAX, mail. Search requires name plus social security number, exact years of attendance, signed release. No fee for information.

Transcripts available by FAX, mail. Search requires name plus social security number, exact years of attendance, signed release. No fee for transcripts.

Southeastern Business College, Registrar, 529 Jackson Pike Ste 312, Gallipolis, OH 45631, 614-446-4367. Records are not housed here. They are located at Southeastern Business College, Registrar, 1855 Western Ave, Chillicothe, OH 45601.

Southeastern Business College, Registrar, 1907 N Ridge Rd, Lorain, OH 44055, 216-277-0021 (FAX: 216-277-7989). Hours: 8:30AM-5PM. Records go back to 1971. Degrees granted: Associate.

Attendance and degree information available by phone, FAX, mail. Search requires name plus social security number. Other helpful information: approximate years of attendance. No fee for information.

Transcripts available by phone, FAX, mail. Search requires name plus social security number, signed release. Other helpful information: approximate years of attendance. No fee for transcripts. Major credit cards accepted for payment.

Southeastern Business College, (Branch), Registrar, 420 E Main St, Jackson, OH 45640, 614-286-1554. Records are not housed here. They are located at Southeastern Business College, Registrar, 1855 Western Ave, Chillicothe, OH 45601.

Southeastern Business College, (Branch), Registrar, 1522 Sheridan Dr, Lancaster, OH 43130, 614-687-6126. Records are not housed here. They are located at Southeastern Business College, Registrar, 1855 Western Ave, Chillicothe, OH 45601.

Southeastern Business College, (Branch), Registrar, 3879 Rhodes Ave, New Boston, OH 45662, 614-456-4124 (FAX: 614-456-5163). Hours: 8:30AM-5PM. Records go back 15 years. Also have some (not all) records from Portsmouth Interstate Business College from 1940's. Degrees granted: Associate.

Attendance and degree information available by phone, FAX, mail. Search requires name plus approximate years of attendance. Other helpful information: social security number, date of birth, exact years of attendance. No fee for information.

Transcripts available by mail. Search requires name plus approximate years of attendance, signed release. Other helpful information: social security number, date of birth, exact years of attendance. No fee for transcripts.

Southeastern Business College, (Branch), Registrar, 4020 Milan Rd, Sandusky, OH 44870, 419-627-8345. Records are not housed here. They are located at Southeastern Business College, Registrar, 1855 Western Ave, Chillicothe, OH 45601.

Southeastern College of the Assemblies of God, Registrar, 1000 Longfellow Blvd, Lakeland, FL 33801, 813-665-4404 (FAX: 813-666-8103). Hours: 8AM-4:30PM. Records go back to 1935. Alumni records are maintained here at the same phone number. Degrees granted: Bachelors.

Attendance and degree information available by phone, FAX, mail. Search requires name only. Other helpful information: social security number, date of birth, approximate years of attendance. No fee for information.

Transcripts available by FAX, mail. Search requires name plus signed release. Other helpful information: social security number, date of birth, approximate years of attendance. Fee is $5.00. Expedited service available for $5.00.

Major credit cards accepted for payment.

Southeastern Community College, Registrar, Drawer F, West Burlington, IA 52655, 319-752-2731 X133 (FAX: 319-752-4957). Hours: 8AM-4:30PM. Records go back to founding date. Degrees granted: Associate.

Attendance information available by phone, FAX, mail. Search requires name only. Other helpful information: social security number, date of birth. No fee for information.

Degree information available by phone, FAX, mail. Search requires name only. No fee for information.

Transcripts available by FAX, mail. Search requires name plus signed release. Other helpful information: social security number, date of birth, approximate years of attendance. No fee for transcripts.

Major credit cards accepted for payment.

Southeastern Community College, Registrar, PO Box 151, Whiteville, NC 28472, 910-642-5658 X248 (FAX: 910-642-5658). Hours: 8:30AM-5PM. Records go back to 1965. Degrees granted: Associate.

Attendance and degree information available by FAX, mail. Search requires name plus social security number, date of birth, signed release. Other helpful information: approximate years of attendance. No fee for information.

Transcripts available by FAX, mail. Search requires name plus social security number, date of birth, signed release. Other helpful information: approximate years of attendance. No fee for transcripts.

Southeastern Louisiana University, Registrar, PO Box 784 University Station, Hammond, LA 70402, 504-549-2062 (FAX: 504-549-5632). Hours: 7:45AM-4:30PM. Records go back to 1925. Alumni records are maintained here also. Call 504-549-2150. Degrees granted: Masters. Adverse incident record source: Dean of Students, 504-549-2212.

Attendance and degree information available by phone, FAX, mail. Search requires name plus social security number, approximate years of attendance, signed release. No fee for information.

Transcripts available by FAX, mail. Search requires name plus social security number, approximate years of attendance, signed release. No fee for transcripts.

Southeastern Oklahoma State University, Registrar, PO Box 4139, Durant, OK 74701-0609, 405-924-0121 (FAX: 405-920-7472). Hours: 8AM-5PM. Records go back to 1915. Degrees granted: Bachelors; Masters. Adverse incident record source: Student Affairs.

Attendance and degree information available by phone, FAX, mail. Search requires name plus signed release. Other helpful information: social security number, date of birth, approximate years of attendance. No fee for information.

Transcripts available by FAX, mail. Search requires name plus signed release. Other helpful information: social security number, date of birth, approximate years of attendance. No fee for transcripts.

Major credit cards accepted for payment.

Southeastern University, Registrar, 501 Eye St SW, Washington, DC 20024, 202-488-8162 X264 (FAX: 202-488-8093). Hours: 10AM-7PM. Records go back to 1990. Alumni records are maintained here also. Call 202-488-8162 X251. Degrees granted: Bachelors; Masters.

Attendance and degree information available by phone, FAX, mail. Search requires name plus social security number, date of birth, approximate years of attendance, signed release. No fee for information.

Transcripts available by FAX, mail. Search requires name plus social security number, date of birth, approximate years of attendance, signed release. Fee is $5.00.

Southeastern University of the Health Sciences, Registrar, 1750 NE 168th St, North Miami Beach, FL 33162, 305-949-4000 X1115 (FAX: 305-957-1630). Hours: 7:30AM-5PM. Records go back to 1979. Alumni records are maintained here also. Call 305-949-4000 X1308. Degrees granted: Bachelors; Masters; Doctorate; Physician Asst., Occupational Therapy Cert. . Adverse incident record source: VP Student Affairs, 305-949-4000.

Attendance and degree information available by phone, FAX, mail. Search requires name plus social security number. No fee for information.

Transcripts available by FAX, mail. Search requires name plus social security number, exact years of attendance, signed release. Fee is $1.00.

Southern Arkansas University, Registrar, SAU Box 1402, Magnolia, AR 71753, 501-235-4031 (FAX: 501-235-5001). Hours: 8AM-5PM. Degrees granted: Associate; Bachelors; Masters.

Attendance and degree information available by phone, mail. Search requires name plus social security number. Other helpful information: date of birth, approximate years of attendance. No fee for information.

Transcripts available by written request only. Search requires name plus social security number, signed release. Other helpful information: date of birth, approximate years of attendance. Fee is $4.00. Expedited service available for $6.00.

Southern Arkansas University Tech, Registrar, SAU Tech Station, Camden, AR 71701, 501-574-4500 (FAX: 501-574-4520). Hours: 8AM-5:30PM. Alumni records are maintained here at the same phone number. Degrees granted: Associate. Adverse incident record source: Student Affairs, 501-574-4500.

Attendance information available by phone, FAX, mail. Search requires name plus social security number, approximate years of attendance. No fee for information.

Degree information available by mail. Search requires name plus social security number, approximate years of attendance. No fee for information.

Transcripts available by mail. Search requires name plus social security number, approximate years of attendance, signed release. Fee is $2.00.

Southern Baptist Theological Seminary, Registrar, 2825 Lexington Rd, Louisville, KY 40280, 502-897-4209 (FAX: 502-899-1781). Hours: 8AM-4:30PM. Records go back to 1859. Degrees granted: Associate; Masters; Doctorate.

Attendance and degree information available by phone, mail. Search requires name plus social security number. Other helpful information: date of birth, approximate years of attendance. No fee for information.

Transcripts available by mail. Search requires name plus social security number, approximate years of attendance, signed release. Other helpful information: date of birth, exact years of attendance. Fee is $10.00. Expedited service available for $5.00.

Southern California College, Registrar, 55 Fair Dr, Costa Mesa, CA 92626, 714-556-3610 (FAX: 714-668-6194). Hours: 8AM-4:30PM. Records go back to 1920. Alumni records are maintained here at the same phone number. Degrees granted: Bachelors; Masters.

Attendance and degree information available by phone, FAX, mail. Search requires name plus social security number. Other helpful information: date of birth, approximate years of attendance. No fee for information.

Transcripts available by FAX, mail. Search requires name plus signed release. Other helpful information: social security number, date of birth, approximate years of attendance. Fee is $4.00. Expedited service available for $10.00.

Southern California College of Optometry, Registrar, 2575 Yorba Linda Blvd, Fullerton, CA 92631-1699, 714-449-7445 (FAX: 714-879-9834). Hours: 8AM-5PM. Records go back 90 years. Alumni records are maintained here also. Call 714-449-7461. Degrees granted: Doctorate.

Attendance information available by phone, FAX, mail. Search requires name only. Other helpful information: social security number, date of birth, approximate years of attendance. No fee for information.

Degree information available by phone, FAX, mail. Search requires name only. Other helpful information: social security number, approximate years of attendance. No fee for information.

Transcripts available by mail. Search requires name plus signed release. Other helpful information: social security number, approximate years of attendance. Fee is $5.00.

Major credit cards accepted for payment.

Southern Christian University, Registrar, 1200 Taylor Rd, Montgomery, AL 36117-3553, 334-277-2277 (FAX: 334-271-0002). Hours: 9AM-5PM. Alumni records are maintained here at the same phone number. Degrees granted: Bachelors; Masters; Doctorate.

Attendance and degree information available by phone, FAX, mail. Search requires name plus social security number, date of birth, signed release. Other helpful information: approximate years of attendance. Fee is $10.00.

Transcripts available by mail. Search requires name plus social security number, date of birth, signed release. Other helpful information: approximate years of attendance. Fee is $10.00.

Major credit cards accepted for payment.

Southern College, Registrar, 5600 Lake Underhill Rd, Orlando, FL 32807, 407-273-1000 (FAX: 407-273-0492). Hours: 8AM-5PM. Records go back to 1968. Degrees granted: Associate.

Attendance information available by FAX, mail. Search requires name plus social security number, signed release. Other helpful information: date of birth, approximate years of attendance. No fee for information.

Degree information available by phone, FAX, mail. Search requires name plus social security number. Other helpful information: date of birth, approximate years of attendance. No fee for information.

Transcripts available by FAX, mail. Search requires name plus social security number, signed release. Other helpful information: date of birth, approximate years of attendance. Fee is $1.00.

Southern College of Optometry, Registrar, 1245 Madison Ave, Memphis, TN 38104, 901-722-3228 (FAX: 901-722-3279). Hours: 8:30AM-4:30PM. Records go back to 1932. Degrees granted: Doctorate.

Attendance and degree information available by phone, FAX, mail. Search requires name plus social security number, exact years of attendance. Other helpful information: date of birth, approximate years of attendance. No fee for information.

Transcripts available by FAX, mail. Search requires name plus social security number, exact years of attendance, signed release. Other helpful information: date of birth, approximate years of attendance. No fee for transcripts.

Southern College of Seventh-Day Adventists, Registrar, PO Box 370, Collegedale, TN 37315-0370, 615-238-2111 (FAX: 615-238-3003). Hours: 8AM-Noon, 1-5PM. Records go back to 1892. Degrees granted: Associate; Bachelors. Certification: Auto Body & Auto Mechanics.

Attendance and degree information available by phone, FAX, mail. Search requires name plus social security number. Other helpful information: date of birth, approximate years of attendance. No fee for information.

Transcripts available by FAX, mail. Search requires name plus signed release. Other helpful information: social security number, date of birth, approximate years of attendance. No fee for transcripts. Expedited service available for $5.00.

Southern College of Technology, Registrar, 100 S Marietta Pkwy, Marietta, GA 30060-2896, 404-528-7267 (FAX: 404-528-7292). Hours: 9AM-7PM M-Th; 9AM-5PM F. Records go back to 1948. Degrees granted: Associate; Bachelors; Masters. Adverse incident record source: Student Affairs, 404-528-7225.

Attendance and degree information available by phone, FAX, mail. Search requires name only. Other helpful information: social security number, approximate years of attendance. No fee for information.

Transcripts available by FAX, mail. Search requires name plus social security number, signed release. Other helpful information: approximate years of attendance. No fee for transcripts.

Southern Connecticut State University, Registrar, New Haven, CT 06505-0901, 203-392-5300 (FAX: 203-392-5320). Hours: 8:30AM-4:30PM. Alumni Records Office: 501 Crescent St, New Haven, CT 06515. Degrees granted: Associate; Bachelors; Masters.

Attendance information available by FAX, mail. Search requires name plus social security number, date of birth, approximate years of attendance, signed release. Other helpful information: exact years of attendance. No fee for information.

Degree information available by FAX, mail. Search requires name plus social security number, date of birth, signed release. Other helpful information: exact years of attendance. No fee for information.

Transcripts available by FAX, mail. Search requires name plus social security number, date of birth, signed release. Other helpful information: approximate years of attendance. Fee is $3.00. Expedited service available for $3.00.

Major credit cards accepted for payment.

Southern Illinois University at Carbondale, Admissions & Records, Carbondale, IL 62901, 618-453-4381 (FAX: 618-453-3250). Hours: 8AM-4:30PM. Degrees granted: Associate; Bachelors; Masters; Doctorate. Adverse incident record source: Campus Police, 618-453-2381.

Attendance and degree information available by phone, FAX, mail. Search requires name plus social security number, date of birth. Other helpful information: approximate years of attendance. No fee for information.

Transcripts available by written request only. Search requires name plus social security number, date of birth, signed release. Other helpful information: approximate years of attendance. Fee is $2.00. Expedite fees vary.

Major credit cards accepted for payment.

Southern Illinois University at Edwardsville, Admissions & Records, Campus Box 1047, Edwardsville, IL 62026, 618-692-2080 (FAX: 618-692-2081). Hours: 8AM-8PM M-Th, 8AM-4:30PM F, 8AM-2PM Sat. Records go back to 1957. Alumni records are maintained here at the same phone number. Degrees granted: Bachelors; Masters.

Attendance information available by phone, FAX, mail. Search requires name plus social security number, exact years of attendance, signed release. Other helpful information: date of birth, approximate years of attendance. No fee for information.

Degree information available by phone, FAX, mail. Search requires name plus social security number, signed release. No fee for information.

Transcripts available by mail. Search requires name plus social security number, signed release. Other helpful information: approximate years of attendance. First transcript 1.00, each additional 2.00.

Southern Maine Technical College, Registrar, Fort Road, South Portland, ME 04106, 207-767-9538 (FAX: 207-767-9671). Hours: 8AM-5PM. Records go back to 1948. Alumni records are maintained here also. Call 207-767-9507. Degrees granted: Associate.

Attendance information available by phone, FAX, mail. Search requires name plus social security number. Other helpful information: date of birth, approximate years of attendance. No fee for information.

Degree information available by phone, FAX, mail. Search requires name plus social security number. Other helpful information: approximate years of attendance. No fee for information.

Transcripts available by mail. Search requires name plus social security number, signed release. Other helpful information: approximate years of attendance. Fee is $5.00. Expedited service available for $7.00.

Major credit cards accepted for payment.

Southern Methodist University, Registrar, PO Box 750276, Dallas, TX 75275-0276, 214-768-2045 (FAX: 214-768-2507). Hours: 8:30AM-5PM. Records go back to 1913. Degrees granted: Bachelors; Masters; Doctorate. Adverse incident record source: Student Life, 214-768-4564: DPS, 214-768-2490

Attendance and degree information available by phone, mail. Search requires name plus social security number, approximate years of attendance. Other helpful information: date of birth, exact years of attendance. No fee for information.

Transcripts available by phone, FAX, mail. Search requires name plus social security number, date of birth, approximate years of attendance, signed release. Other helpful information: exact years of attendance. Fee is $5.00.

Major credit cards accepted for payment.

Southern Nazarene University, Registrar's Office, 6729 NW 39th Expwy, Bethany, OK 73008, 405-491-6386 (FAX: 405-491-6381). Hours: 8AM-5PM. Records go back to 1900s. Alumni records are maintained here also. Call 405-491-6312. Degrees granted: Bachelors; Masters. Adverse incident record source: Student Development, 405-491-6336.

Attendance and degree information available by phone, FAX, mail. Search requires name plus social security number. No fee for information.

Transcripts available by FAX, mail. Search requires name plus social security number, exact years of attendance, signed release. Fee is $3.00.

Requester must be employer or bank. Major credit cards accepted for payment.

Southern Ohio College, Registrar, 1055 Laidlaw Ave, Cincinnati, OH 45237, 513-242-3791 (FAX: 513-242-4774). Hours: 9AM-5:30PM. Degrees granted: Associate.

Attendance and degree information available by phone, FAX, mail. Search requires name plus social security number, approximate years of attendance. No fee for information.

Transcripts available by FAX, mail. Search requires name plus social security number, approximate years of attendance, signed release. Fee is $4.00.

Major credit cards accepted for payment.

Southern Ohio College, (Branch), Registrar, 2791 Mogadore Rd, Akron, OH 44312, 216-733-8766 X51 (FAX: 216-733-5853). Hours: 8AM-5PM T,Th,F; 8AM-6:30PM M,W. Records go back to 1975. Degrees granted: Associate.

Attendance and degree information available by phone, FAX, mail. Search requires name plus social security number. No fee for information.

Transcripts available by FAX, mail. Search requires name plus social security number, signed release. Fee is $5.00.

Southern Ohio College, (Branch), Registrar, 4641 Bach Lane, Fairfield, OH 45014, 513-829-7100 (FAX: 513-829-0809). Hours: 9AM-5PM. Records go back 15 years.

Attendance and degree information available by FAX, mail. Search requires name plus social security number. Other helpful information: date of birth, exact years of attendance. No fee for information.

Transcripts available by written request only. Search requires name plus social security number, signed release. Other helpful information: date of birth, exact years of attendance. Fee is $4.00.

Southern Ohio College, (Northern Kentucky), Registrar, 309 Buttermilk Pike, Fort Mitchell, KY 41017, 606-341-5627 (FAX: 606-341-6483). Hours: 9AM-6PM. Records go back to founding date. Degrees granted: Associate.

Attendance information available by FAX, mail. Search requires name plus social security number. Other helpful information: date of birth, approximate years of attendance. No fee for information.

Degree information available by FAX, mail. Search requires name plus social security number. Other helpful information: date of birth, approximate years of attendance. No fee for information.

Transcripts available by FAX, mail. Search requires name plus social security number, signed release. Other helpful information: date of birth, approximate years of attendance. Fee is $4.00. Expedited service available for $4.00.

Major credit cards accepted for payment.

Southern Oregon State College, Registrar, 1250 Siskiyou Blvd, Ashland, OR 97520, 503-552-6600 (FAX: 503-552-6329). Hours: 8AM-5PM. Records go back to 1920. Alumni records are maintained here also. Call 503-552-6361. Degrees granted: Associate; Bachelors; Masters. Certification: Education Accounting.

Attendance and degree information available by phone, FAX, mail. Search requires name plus social security number, signed release. Other helpful information: date of birth, approximate years of attendance. No fee for information.

Transcripts available by mail. Search requires name plus social security number, signed release. Other helpful information: date of birth, approximate years of attendance. Fee is $5.00.

Major credit cards accepted for payment.

Southern State Community College, Registrar, 200 Hobart Dr, Hillsboro, OH 45133, 513-393-3431 (FAX: 513-393-9370). Hours: 8AM-5PM. Records go back 20 years. Alumni records are maintained here at the same phone number. Degrees granted: Associate.

Attendance and degree information available by phone, FAX, mail. Search requires name only. Other helpful information: social security number. No fee for information.

Transcripts available by written request only. Search requires name plus social security number, signed release. No fee for transcripts.

Southern Union State Community College, Registrar, PO Box 1000, Wadley, AL 36276, 205-395-2211 (FAX: 205-395-2215). Hours: 7:30AM-4:30PM. Records go back to 1922. Alumni records are maintained here also. Call 205-745-6437. Degrees granted: Associate. Adverse incident record source: Dean, 205-395-2211.

Attendance and degree information available by phone, FAX, mail. Search requires name plus social security number, date of birth. Other helpful information: approximate years of attendance. No fee for information.

Transcripts available by written request only. Search requires name plus social security number, date of birth, signed release. Other helpful information: approximate years of attendance. Fee is $3.00.

Southern University & Agricultural & Mech. College at Baton Rouge, Registrar, Southern Branch PO Box 9454, Baton Rouge, LA 70813, 504-771-5050 (FAX: 504-771-5064). Hours: 8AM-5PM. Records go back to 1920s. Degrees granted: Associate; Bachelors; Masters; Doctorate.

Attendance information available by phone, FAX, mail. Search requires name plus social security number, exact years of attendance. Other helpful information: date of birth, approximate years of attendance. No fee for information.

Degree information available by phone, FAX, mail. Search requires name plus social security number, approximate years of attendance, signed release. Other helpful information: date of birth. No fee for information.

Transcripts available by FAX, mail. Search requires name plus social security number, exact years of attendance, signed release. Other helpful information: date of birth, approximate years of attendance. Fee is $2.00. Expedited service available for $2.00.

Southern University at New Orleans, Registrar, 6400 Press Dr, New Orleans, LA 70126, 504-286-5175 (FAX: 504-286-5131). Hours: 8AM-5PM. Records go back to 1967. Alumni records are maintained here also. Call 504-286-5341. Degrees granted: Masters.

Attendance and degree information available by phone, FAX, mail. Search requires name plus social security number, signed release. No fee for information.

Transcripts available by mail. Search requires name plus social security number, signed release. Fee is $2.00.

Southern University/Shreveport Bossier, Registrar, 3050 Martin Luther King, Jr. Dr, Shreveport, LA 71107, 318-674-3343. Hours: 8AM-5PM. Records go back to 1967. Degrees granted: Associate.

Attendance and degree information available by phone, mail. Search requires name plus social security number. No fee for information.

Transcripts available by mail. Search requires name plus social security number, exact years of attendance, signed release. Fee is $1.00.

Southern Utah University, Registrar, 351 W Center, Cedar City, UT 84720, 801-586-7715 (FAX: 801-865-8223). Hours: 8AM-5PM. Records go back to 1896. Alumni records are maintained here at the same phone number. Degrees granted: Bachelors; Masters.

Attendance and degree information available by phone, mail. Search requires name plus social security number, date of birth, exact years of attendance. No fee for information.

Transcripts available by mail. Search requires name plus social security number, date of birth, exact years of attendance, signed release. Fee is $2.00.

Southern Vermont College, Registrar, Monument View Rd, Bennington, VT 05201, 802-442-5427 X228 (FAX: 802-442-5529). Hours: 8AM-4:30PM. Records go back to 1926. Alumni records are maintained here at the same phone number. Degrees granted: Bachelors.

Attendance and degree information available by phone, mail. Search requires name plus social security number, exact years of attendance. No fee for information.

Transcripts available by mail. Search requires name plus social security number, exact years of attendance, signed release. Fee is $5.00.

Southern Virginia College, Registrar, One College Hill Dr, Buena Vista, VA 24416, 703-261-8400. Hours: 8AM-4PM. Records go back to 1950S. Alumni records are maintained here at the same phone number. Degrees granted: Associate.

Attendance and degree information available by phone, mail. Search requires name plus social security number. Other helpful information: approximate years of attendance. No fee for information.

Transcripts available by written request only. Search requires name plus social security number, approximate years of attendance, signed release. No fee for transcripts.

Southern West Virginia Community College, Registrar, PO Box 2900, Logan, WV 25601-2900, 304-792-4300 (FAX: 304-792-4399). Hours: 8AM-5PM. Degrees granted: Associate.

Attendance and degree information available by phone, FAX, mail. Search requires name plus social security number, exact years of attendance. No fee for information.

Transcripts available by mail. Search requires name plus social security number, exact years of attendance, signed release. Fee is $3.00.

Southestern Illinois College, Registrar, 3575 College Rd, Harrisburg, IL 62946, 618-252-6376 (FAX: 618-252-6376). Hours: 8AM-4:30PM. Records go back to 1960. Degrees granted: Associate. Special programs- Incarcerated Students: Vienna Corr Cen, 618-658-2211.

Attendance and degree information available by phone, FAX, mail. Search requires name only. Other helpful information: social security number, date of birth, approximate years of attendance. No fee for information.

Transcripts available by FAX, mail. Search requires name plus social security number, signed release. Other helpful information: date of birth, approximate years of attendance. Fee is $1.00.

Southside Virginia Community College, Admissions & Records, 109 Campus Dr, Alberta, VA 23821, 804-949-1014 (FAX: 804-949-7863). Hours: 8AM-4:30PM. Records go back to 1970. Degrees granted: Associate.

Attendance and degree information available by phone, FAX, mail. Search requires name plus social security number. Other helpful information: date of birth, approximate years of attendance. No fee for information.

Transcripts available by mail. Search requires name plus social security number, signed release. Other helpful information: date of birth, approximate years of attendance. No fee for transcripts.

Southwest Acupuncture College, Registrar, 325 Paseo De Peralta #500, Santa Fe, NM 87501, 505-988-3538 (FAX: 505-988-5438). Hours: 9AM-5PM. Records go back to 1981. Degrees granted: Masters.

Attendance information available by phone, FAX, mail. Search requires name plus social security number, approximate years of attendance. Other helpful information: date of birth, exact years of attendance. Fee is $7.00. Expedited service available for $17.00.

Degree information available by phone, FAX, mail. Search requires name plus social security number, approximate years of attendance. Other helpful information: date of birth, exact years of attendance. Fee is $7.00. Expedite service available for $17.00.

Transcripts available by FAX, mail. Search requires name plus social security number, approximate years of attendance, signed release. Other helpful information: date of birth, exact years of attendance. Fee is $7.00. Expedited service available for $17.00.

Southwest Acupuncture College, **(Branch Campus)**, Registrar, 4308 Carlisle Blvd NE Ste 205, Albuquerque, NM 87107, 505-888-8898. Records are not housed here. They are located at Southwest Acupuncture College, Registrar, 325 Paseo De Peralta #500, Santa Fe, NM 87501.

Southwest Baptist University, Registrar, 1601 S Springfield St, Bolivar, MO 65613, 417-326-1605 (FAX: 417-326-1514). Hours: 8AM-5PM. Degrees granted: Associate; Bachelors; Masters.

Attendance and degree information available by phone, FAX, mail. Search requires name only. Other helpful information: social security number, date of birth, approximate years of attendance. No fee for information.

Transcripts available by mail. Search requires name plus signed release. Other helpful information: social security number, date of birth, approximate years of attendance. Fee is $3.00. Expedited service available for $5.00.

Major credit cards accepted for payment.

Southwest Florida College of Business, Registrar, 1685 Medical Lane Ste 200, Fort Myers, FL 33907, 813-939-4766 (FAX: 813-936-4040). Hours: 8AM-7PM. Records go back to 1983. Degrees granted: Associate.

Attendance and degree information available by phone, FAX, mail. Search requires name only. Other helpful information: social security number, date of birth. No fee for information.

Transcripts available by written request only. Search requires name plus signed release. Other helpful information: social security number, date of birth. Fee is $2.00. Expedited service available for $2.00.

Major credit cards accepted for payment.

Southwest Mississippi Community College, Registrar, Summit, MS 39666, 601-276-2001 (FAX: 601-276-3888). Hours: 8AM-4:30PM. Records go back to 1932. Degrees granted: Associate.

Attendance and degree information available by FAX, mail. Search requires name only. Other helpful information: social security number, date of birth, approximate years of attendance. No fee for information.

Transcripts available by mail. Search requires name plus signed release. Other helpful information: social security number, date of birth, approximate years of attendance. Fee is $2.00. Expedited service available for $10.00.

Southwest Missouri State University, Registrar, 901 S National Ave, Springfield, MO 65804, 417-836-5519. Hours: 9AM-5PM. Records go back to 1908. 1908-1982 on microfilm; 1982 forward on computer. Alumni records are maintained here also. Call 417-836-5654. Degrees granted: Bachelors; Masters. Adverse incident record source: Police.

Attendance and degree information available by phone, mail. Search requires name plus social security number, date of birth. No fee for information.

Transcripts available by written request only. Search requires name plus social security number, date of birth, signed release. Fee is $3.00. $6.00 FAX fee; 17.00 express mail fee.

Southwest State University, Registrar, 1501 State St, Marshall, MN 56258, 507-537-6206 (FAX: 507-537-7154). Hours: 8:30AM-4:30PM. Records go back to 1967. Degrees granted: Associate; Bachelors; Masters.

Attendance and degree information available by phone, FAX, mail. Search requires name plus social security number. Other helpful information: approximate years of attendance. No fee for information.

Transcripts available by phone, FAX, mail. Search requires name plus social security number. Other helpful information: approximate years of attendance. No fee for transcripts.

Southwest Texas Junior College, Registrar, 2401 Garner Field Rd, Uvalde, TX 78801-6297, 210-278-4401 (FAX: 210-278-1610). Hours: 8AM-6PM M-Th; 8AM-5PM F. Records go back to 1945. Degrees granted: Associate.

Attendance and degree information available by phone, FAX, mail. Search requires name only. Other helpful information: social security number, date of birth, approximate years of attendance. No fee for information.

Transcripts available by FAX, mail. Search requires name plus social security number, signed release. Other helpful information: date of birth, approximate years of attendance. Fee is $3.00.

Southwest Texas State University, Registrar, 601 University Dr, San Marcos, TX 78666-4616, 512-245-2728 (FAX: 512-245-8126). Hours: 8AM-5PM. Records go back to 1900s.

Degrees granted: Associate; Bachelors; Masters. Adverse incident record source: 512-245-2890.

Attendance and degree information available by phone, FAX, mail. Search requires name plus social security number, signed release. Other helpful information: date of birth, approximate years of attendance. No fee for information.

Transcripts available by phone, FAX, mail. Search requires name plus social security number, signed release. Other helpful information: date of birth, approximate years of attendance. Fee is $5.00.

Major credit cards accepted for payment.

Southwest Virginia Community College, Registrar, PO Box SVCC, Richlands, VA 24641, 703-964-2555 X294 (FAX: 703-964-9307). Hours: 8AM-4:30PM. Records go back to 1968. Alumni records are maintained here at the same phone number. Degrees granted: Associate.

Attendance and degree information available by phone, mail. Search requires name plus social security number. No fee for information.

Transcripts available by mail. Search requires name plus social security number, signed release. No fee for transcripts.

Southwest Wisconsin Technical College, Registrar, 1800 Bronson Blvd, Fennimore, WI 53809, 608-822-3262 (FAX: 608-822-6019). Hours: 7:30AM-4PM. Records go back to 1969. Degrees granted: Associate. Adverse incident record source: 608-822-3262.

Attendance and degree information available by phone, FAX, mail. Search requires name only. Other helpful information: social security number, date of birth, approximate years of attendance. No fee for information.

Transcripts available by written request only. Search requires name plus signed release. Other helpful information: social security number, date of birth, approximate years of attendance. Fee is $2.00.

Majors helpful.

Southwestern Adventist College, Registrar, PO Box 567, Keene, TX 76059, 817-645-3921 X221 (FAX: 817-556-4744). Hours: 8AM-4:30PM. Degrees granted: Bachelors; Masters.

Attendance and degree information available by phone, FAX, mail. Search requires name plus social security number, date of birth. No fee for information.

Transcripts available by FAX, mail. Search requires name plus social security number, date of birth, signed release. Fee is $2.00.

Southwestern Assemblies of God University, Registrar, 1200 Sycarmore St, Waxahachie, TX 75165, 214-937-4010 X142 (FAX: 214-923-0488). Hours: 8AM-5PM. Records go back to 1930s. Degrees granted: Associate; Bachelors. Adverse incident record source: Business Office, 214-937-4010 X104.

Attendance and degree information available by phone, FAX, mail. Search requires name only. Other helpful information: social security number, date of birth, approximate years of attendance. No fee for information.

Transcripts available by mail. Search requires name plus social security number, signed release. Other helpful information: date of birth, approximate years of attendance. Fee is $5.00. Expedited service available for $10.00.

Southwestern Baptist Theological Seminary, Registrar, PO Box 22000, Fort Worth, TX 76122, 817-923-1921 X2000 (FAX: 817-923-1921 X2119). Hours: 8AM-Noon, 1-5PM. Records go back to 1908. Alumni records are maintained here also. Call 817-923-1921 X2380. Degrees granted: Masters; Doctorate.

Attendance and degree information available by phone, FAX, mail. Search requires name only. Other helpful information: social security number, date of birth, approximate years of attendance. No fee for information.

Transcripts available by mail. Search requires name plus social security number, signed release. Other helpful information: date of birth, approximate years of attendance. Fee is $5.00. Expedited service available for $25.00.

Southwestern Christian College, Registrar, PO Box 10, Terrell, TX 75160, 214-524-3341 X128 (FAX: 214-563-7133). Hours: 8AM-5PM. Records go back to 1950. Degrees granted: Associate; Bachelors.

Attendance and degree information available by phone, FAX, mail. Search requires name plus social security number, date of birth, approximate years of attendance. No fee for information.

Transcripts available by phone, FAX, mail. Search requires name plus social security number, date of birth, approximate years of attendance, signed release. Fee is $2.00.

Major credit cards accepted for payment.

Southwestern College Business, Registrar, 2929 S Dixie Hwy, Crestview Hills, KY 41017, 606-341-6633. Hours: 9AM-7PM M-Th; 9AM-1PM F. Degrees granted: Associate.

Attendance and degree information available by phone, mail. Search requires name plus social security number, approximate years of attendance, signed release. Other helpful information: date of birth, exact years of attendance. Fee is $2.00.

Transcripts available by phone, mail. Search requires name plus social security number, approximate years of attendance, signed release. Other helpful information: date of birth, exact years of attendance. Fee is $2.00.

Southwestern College, Admissions Center, 900 Otay Lakes Rd, Chula Vista, CA 91910, 619-482-6550 (FAX: 619-482-6413). Hours: 7:30AM-8PM M-Th; 7:30AM-5PM F. Records go back to 196yr. Degrees granted: Associate. Adverse incident record source: Student Activities, 619-421-6700 X5432.

School will not confirm attendance information. Search requires name plus signed release. Other helpful information: social security number, date of birth, approximate years of attendance. No fee for information.

School will not confirm degree information. Search requires name only. No fee for information.

Transcripts available by FAX, mail. Search requires name plus signed release. Other helpful information: social security number, date of birth, approximate years of attendance. No fee for transcripts.

Major credit cards accepted for payment.

Southwestern College, Registrar, 2625 E Cactus Rd, Phoenix, AZ 85032, 602-992-6101 (FAX: 602-404-2159). Hours: 8:30AM-4:30PM. Records go back to 1960. Degrees granted: Associate; Bachelors.

Attendance and degree information available by phone, FAX, mail. Search requires name only. Other helpful information: social security number, date of birth, approximate years of attendance. No fee for information.

Transcripts available by mail. Search requires name plus signed release. Other helpful information: social security number, date of birth, approximate years of attendance. Fee is $2.00. Expedited service available for $5.00.

Southwestern College, Registrar, 100 College St, Winfield, KS 67156, 316-221-8268 (FAX: 316-221-8224). Hours: 8AM-Noon, 1-5PM. Records go back to 1886. Degrees granted: Bachelors; Masters.

Attendance and degree information available by phone, FAX, mail. Search requires name only. Other helpful information: social security number, date of birth, approximate years of attendance. No fee for information.

Transcripts available by FAX, mail. Search requires name plus signed release. Other helpful information: social security number, date of birth, approximate years of attendance. Fee is $3.00. Expedited service available for $10.00.

Major credit cards accepted for payment.

Southwestern College of Business, Registrar, 9910 Princeton-Glendale Rd, Cincinnati, OH 45246, 513-874-0432 (FAX: 513-874-0123). Hours: 9AM-7PM. Records go back to 1977. Degrees granted: Associate. Adverse incident record source: Director, 513-874-0432.

Attendance and degree information available by FAX, mail. Search requires name plus social security number, exact years of attendance, signed release. No fee for information.

Transcripts available by FAX, mail. Search requires name plus social security number, exact years of attendance, signed release. Fee is $2.00.

Southwestern College of Business, Registrar, 225 W First St, Dayton, OH 45402, 513-224-0061 X14. Hours: 9AM-7PM M-Th, 9AM-1PM F. Records go back 20 years. Degrees granted: Associate. Special programs- Corporate Office, 513-874-0432.

Attendance information available by phone, mail. Search requires name plus social security number, approximate years of attendance. Other helpful information: exact years of attendance. No fee for information.

Degree information available by phone, mail. Search requires name plus social security number, approximate years of attendance. Other helpful information: date of birth, exact years of attendance. No fee for information.

Transcripts available by phone, mail. Search requires name plus social security number, date of birth, approximate years of attendance. Other helpful information: exact years of attendance. No fee for transcripts.

Southwestern College of Business, (Branch), Registrar, 717 Race St, Cincinnati, OH 45202, 513-874-0432. Hours: 8AM-7PM. Records go back to 1977. Degrees granted: Associate.

Attendance and degree information available by mail. Search requires name plus date of birth, signed release. Other helpful information: social security number, approximate years of attendance. Fee is $2.00. Expedited service available for $4.00.

Transcripts available by mail. Search requires name plus date of birth, signed release. Other helpful information: social security number, approximate years of attendance. Fee is $2.00. Expedited service available for $4.00.

Southwestern College of Business, (Branch), Registrar, 631 S Briel Blvd, Middletown, OH 45044, 513-423-3346 (FAX: 513-874-0123). Hours: 8:30AM-6:30PM M-Th, 9AM-1PM F. Records go back to 1979. Degrees granted: Associate.

Attendance and degree information available by phone, FAX, mail. Search requires name plus social security number, approximate years of attendance, signed release. No fee for information.

Transcripts available by FAX, mail. Search requires name plus social security number, approximate years of attendance, signed release. First transcript is free; $2.00 each additional.

Southwestern College of Christian Ministries, Registrar, PO Box 340, Bethany, OK 73008, 405-789-7661 X3423 (FAX: 405-789-7661 X3432). Hours: 8:30AM-4:30PM. Records go back to 1946. Alumni records are maintained here at the same phone number. Degrees granted: Associate; Bachelors; Masters.

Attendance and degree information available by phone, FAX, mail. Search requires name plus social security number. Other helpful information: date of birth, approximate years of attendance. No fee for information.

Transcripts available by FAX, mail. Search requires name plus social security number, date of birth, signed release. Other helpful information: approximate years of attendance. Fee is $5.00.

Southwestern Community College, Registrar, 1501 Townline St, Creston, IA 50801, 515-782-7081 (FAX: 515-782-3312). Hours: 8AM-4:30PM. Records go back to 1932. Degrees granted: Associate.

Attendance and degree information available by phone, FAX, mail. Search requires name only. Other helpful information: social security number, date of birth, approximate years of attendance. No fee for information.

Transcripts available by FAX, mail. Search requires name plus signed release. Other helpful information: social security number, date of birth, approximate years of attendance. Fee is $3.00. Expedite: $10.00 to $15.00 depending on service.

Southwestern Community College, Registrar, 275 Webster Rd, Sylva, NC 28779, 704-586-4091 X219 (FAX: 704-586-3129). Hours: 8AM-5PM. Records go back to 1964. Alumni records are maintained here at the same phone number. Degrees granted: Associate.

Attendance and degree information available by FAX, mail. Search requires name plus social security number, date of birth, signed release. No fee for information.

Transcripts available by FAX, mail. Search requires name only. No fee for transcripts.

Southwestern Indian Polytechnic Institute, Registrar, 9169 Coors Rd NW, Box 10146, Albuquerque, NM 87184, 505-897-5346 (FAX: 505-897-5343). Hours: 8AM-4:30PM. Records go back to 1971. Degrees granted: Associate.

Attendance information available by phone, FAX, mail. Search requires name only. No fee for information.

Degree information available by written request only. Search requires name plus social security number, exact years of attendance, signed release. No fee for information.

Transcripts available by written request only. Search requires name plus social security number, exact years of attendance, signed release. Fee is $2.00. Expedited service available for $2.00.

Southwestern Michigan College, Registrar, 58900 Cherry Grove Rd, Dowagiac, MI 49047-9793, 616-782-5113 (FAX: 616-782-8414). Hours: 8AM-8PM M-Th; 8AM-5PM F. Records go back to 1966. Alumni records are maintained here also. Call 616-782-5113. Degrees granted: Associate.

Attendance and degree information available by phone, FAX, mail. Search requires name only. Other helpful information: social security number, date of birth, approximate years of attendance. No fee for information.

Transcripts available by FAX, mail. Search requires name plus signed release. Other helpful information: social security number, date of birth, approximate years of attendance. No fee for transcripts.

Southwestern Oklahoma State University, Registrar, 100 Campus Dr, Weatherford, OK 73096, 405-772-6611 (FAX: 405-774-3795). Hours: 8AM-5PM. Records go back to 1918. Alumni records are maintained here also. Call 405-774-3267. Degrees granted: Associate; Bachelors; Masters. Special programs- Associate, 405-928-5533. Adverse incident record source: Public Safety, 405-774-3785.

Attendance information available by phone, FAX, mail. Search requires name plus social security number. No fee for information.

Degree information available by phone, FAX, mail. Search requires name plus social security number, approximate years of attendance. Other helpful information: exact years of attendance. No fee for information.

Transcripts available by FAX, mail. Search requires name plus social security number, date of birth, exact years of attendance, signed release. Fee is $1.00.

Southwestern Oklahoma State University, (Sayre), Registrar, 409 E Mississippi, Sayre, OK 73662, 405-928-5533 (FAX: 405-928-5533). Hours: 8AM-5PM. Records go back to 1938. Degrees granted: Associate. Adverse incident record source: Registrar, 405-928-5533.

Attendance and degree information available by phone, FAX, mail. Search requires name plus social security number. No fee for information.

Transcripts available by FAX, mail. Search requires name plus social security number, exact years of attendance, signed release. Fee is $1.00.

Southwestern Oregon Community College, Registrar, 1988 Newmark, Coos Bay, OR 97420, 503-888-2525 (FAX: 503-888-7247). Hours: 8AM-5PM. Records go back to 1962. Adverse incident record source: Dean, 503-888-7416.

Attendance information available by phone, mail. Search requires name plus social security number, date of birth. No fee for information.

Degree information available by mail. Search requires name plus social security number, date of birth, exact years of attendance, signed release. No fee for information.

Transcripts available by mail. Search requires name plus social security number, date of birth, exact years of attendance, signed release. Fee is $5.00.

Major credit cards accepted for payment.

Southwestern Technical College, Registrar, 1593 11th Ave, Granite Falls, MN 56241, 612-564-4511 (FAX: 612-564-2318). Hours: 8AM-4:30PM. Records go back to 1965.

Attendance and degree information available by FAX, mail. Search requires name plus social security number, approximate years of attendance, signed release. Other helpful information: exact years of attendance. No fee for information.

Transcripts available by phone, FAX, mail. Search requires name plus social security number, approximate years of attendance, signed release. Other helpful information: exact years of attendance. No fee for transcripts.

Southwestern University, Registrar, University Ave at Maple St, Georgetown, TX 78627, 512-363-1952 (FAX: 512-863-5788). Hours: 8AM-Noon, 1-5PM. Records go back to 1840s. Degrees granted: Bachelors.

Attendance and degree information available by phone, FAX, mail. Search requires name only. Other helpful information: social security number, date of birth, approximate years of attendance. No fee for information.

Transcripts available by FAX, mail. Search requires name plus signed release. Other helpful information: social security number, date of birth, approximate years of attendance. Fee is $2.00. Expedited service available for $2.00.

FAX transcript followed by original in mail. FAX: $2.00 per page.

Southwestern University School of Law, Registrar, 675 S Westmoreland Ave, Los Angeles, CA 90005, 213-638-6710.

Attendance and degree information available by mail. Search requires name plus social security number. No fee for information.

Transcripts available by mail. Search requires name plus social security number, signed release. Fee is $5.00.

Spalding University, Registrar's Office, 851 S Fourth St, Louisville, KY 40203, 502-585-7110 (FAX: 502-585-7158). Hours: 8AM-5PM. Records go back to 1920. Alumni records are maintained here at the same phone number. Degrees granted: Associate; Bachelors; Masters; Doctorate.

Attendance and degree information available by phone, FAX, mail. Search requires name only. Other helpful information: social security number, date of birth, approximate years of attendance. No fee for information.

Transcripts available by mail. Search requires name plus social security number, date of birth, signed release. Other helpful information: approximate years of attendance. Fee is $4.00.

Sparks State Technical College, Registrar, PO Drawer 580, Hwy 432 S, Eufaula, AL 36072-0580, 334-687-3543 (FAX: 334-687-0255). Hours: 8AM-5PM. Records go back to 1963. Alumni records are maintained here at the same phone number. Degrees granted: Associate.

Attendance and degree information available by phone, mail. Search requires name plus social security number, exact years of attendance. No fee for information.

Transcripts available by mail. Search requires name plus social security number, exact years of attendance, signed release. No fee for transcripts.

Spartanburg Methodist College, Registrar, 1200 Textile Rd, Spartanburg, SC 29301-0009, 803-587-4232 (FAX: 803-574-6919). Hours: 8AM-5PM. Records go back to 1911. Degrees granted: Associate.

Attendance and degree information available by phone, FAX, mail. Search requires name plus exact years of attendance. Other helpful information: social security number, approximate years of attendance. No fee for information.

Transcripts available by FAX, mail. Search requires name plus exact years of attendance, signed release. Other helpful information: social security number, approximate years of attendance. Fee is $3.00. Expedited service available for $3.00.

Spartanburg Technical College, Registrar, PO Drawer 4386, Spartanburg, SC 29305-4386, 803-591-3686 (FAX: 803-591-3642). Hours: 8AM-6:30PM M,T; 8AM-5PM W,Th; 8AM-1:30PM F. Records go back to 1962. Degrees granted: Associate.

Attendance and degree information available by phone, FAX, mail. Search requires name plus social security number. Other helpful information: approximate years of attendance. No fee for information.

Transcripts available by FAX, mail. Search requires name plus social security number, signed release. Other helpful information: date of birth, approximate years of attendance. Fee is $5.00. Expedited service available for $5.00.

Spelman College, Registrar, 350 Spelman La SW, Atlanta, GA 30314-4399, 404-223-1424 (FAX: 404-223-1449). Hours: 9AM-5PM. Records go back to 1881. Alumni records are maintained here also. Call 404-223-1427. Degrees granted: Bachelors. Adverse incident record source: Student Affairs, 404-223-1469.

Attendance and degree information available by phone, FAX, mail. Search requires name plus social security number, exact years of attendance, signed release. No fee for information.

Transcripts available by mail. Search requires name plus social security number, exact years of attendance, signed release. Fee is $3.00.

Spencer College, Registrar, PO Box 5065, 217 W Fifth St, Spencer, IA 51301, 800-383-7290.

Spencer School of Business, Registrar, PO Box 399, 410 W Second St, Grand Island, NE 68802, 308-382-8044 (FAX: 308-382-5072). Hours: 7:30AM-5PM. Records go back to 1983. See alternate location before 1983. Degrees granted: Associate.

Attendance and degree information available by phone, FAX, mail. Search requires name plus social security number, approximate years of attendance, signed notarized release. No fee for information.

Transcripts available by phone, FAX, mail. Search requires name plus social security number, approximate years of attendance, signed notarized release. Fee is $2.00. Expedited service available for $1.00.

Spertus Institute of Jewish Studies, Registrar, 618 S Michigan Ave, Chicago, IL 60605, 312-922-9012 (FAX: 312-922-6406). Hours: 9AM-5PM. Records go back to 1924. Degrees granted: Masters; Doctorate.

Attendance and degree information available by phone, FAX, mail. Search requires name only. Other helpful information: exact years of attendance. No fee for information.

Transcripts available by FAX. Search requires name plus signed release. Other helpful information: exact years of attendance. Fee is $2.00. Expedited service available for $0.

Spokane Community College, Registrar, 1810 N Greene St MS2150, Spokane, WA 99207-5399, 509-533-7011 (FAX: 509-533-8839). Hours: 7:30AM-4:30PM. Records go back to 1970. Degrees granted: Associate; AAS.

Attendance and degree information available by phone, FAX, mail. Search requires name plus social security number, signed release. Other helpful information: approximate years of attendance. No fee for information.

Transcripts available by FAX, mail. Search requires name plus social security number, signed release. Other helpful information: approximate years of attendance. No fee for transcripts.

Follow up FAX request with written request.

Spokane Falls Community College, Registrar, W 3410 Fort George Wright Dr, Spokane, WA 99204, 509-533-3518 (FAX: 509-533-3237). Hours: 8AM-4:30PM. Degrees granted: Associate.

Attendance and degree information available by phone, mail. Search requires name plus social security number. No fee for information.

Transcripts available by mail. Search requires name plus social security number, signed release. No fee for transcripts.

Spoon River College, Records Dept, 23235 N Co 22, Canton, IL 61520, 309-647-4645 (FAX: 309-647-6498). Hours: 8AM-5PM. Records go back to 1959. Degrees granted: Associate.

Attendance and degree information available by phone, FAX, mail. Search requires name plus social security number. Other helpful information: date of birth, approximate years of attendance. No fee for information.

Transcripts available by FAX, mail. Search requires name plus social security number, signed release. Other helpful information: date of birth, approximate years of attendance. Fee is $2.00. Expedited service available for $2.00.

Major credit cards accepted for payment.

Spring Arbor College, Registrar, Spring Arbor, MI 49283, 517-750-6520 (FAX: 517-750-6534). Hours: 8AM-5PM. Records go back to 1938. Alumni records are maintained here also. Call 517-750-6398. Degrees granted: Associate; Bachelors; Masters.

Attendance information available by phone, FAX, mail. Search requires name plus social security number, date of birth, approximate years of attendance. No fee for information.

Degree information available by phone, FAX, mail. Search requires name plus social security number, date of birth, approximate years of attendance. Other helpful information: exact years of attendance. No fee for information.

Transcripts available by mail. Search requires name plus signed release. Other helpful information: social security number, date of birth, approximate years of attendance. Transcript fee is $4.00, unofficial copy $2.00.

Spring Hill College, Registrar, 4000 Dauphin St, Mobile, AL 36608, 334-380-2240 (FAX: 334-460-2192). Hours: 8AM-5PM. Records go back to 1900. Alumni records are maintained here also. Call 334-380-2280. Degrees granted: Associate; Bachelors.

Attendance and degree information available by phone, FAX, mail. Search requires name plus social security number, date of birth, approximate years of attendance, signed release. No fee for information.

Transcripts available by mail. Search requires name plus social security number, date of birth, approximate years of attendance, signed release. Fee is $4.00.

Springfield College, Registrar's Office, 263 Alden St, Springfield, MA 01109-3797, 413-748-3149 (FAX: 413-748-3764). Hours: 8:30AM-4:15PM. Records go back to 1885. Degrees granted: Bachelors; Masters; Doctorate.

Attendance and degree information available by phone, FAX, mail. Search requires name only. Other helpful information: social security number, approximate years of attendance. No fee for information.

Transcripts available by FAX, mail. Search requires name plus signed release. Other helpful information: social security number, approximate years of attendance. Fee is $3.00. Expedited service available for $3.00.

FAX only accepted from students.

Springfield College in Illinois, Registrar, 1500 N Fifth St, Springfield, IL 62702, 217-525-1420 X213. Hours: 8AM-4:30PM Fall; 7:30AM-4PM M-Th Summer. Records go back to 1929. Alumni records are maintained here also. Call 217-525-1420 X228. Degrees granted: Associate.

Attendance and degree information available by mail. Search requires name plus social security number, exact years of attendance, signed release. No fee for information.

Transcripts available by mail. Search requires name plus social security number, exact years of attendance, signed release. Fee is $2.00.

Springfield Technical Community College, Registrar, One Armory Square, Springfield, MA 01105, 413-781-7822 X3879 (FAX: 413-739-5066). Hours: 8AM-4PM. Records go back to 1984. Alumni records are maintained here also. Call 413-781-7822 X3873. Degrees granted: Associate. Adverse incident record source: Dean of Students, 413-781-7822 X3454.

Attendance and degree information available by phone, FAX, mail. Search requires name plus social security number, approximate years of attendance, signed release. No fee for information.

Transcripts available by mail. Search requires name plus social security number, approximate years of attendance, signed release. Fee is $3.00.

St. Ambrose University, Registrar, 518 W Locust St, Davenport, IA 52803, 319-383-8747 (FAX: 319-383-8791). Hours: 9AM-4PM. Records go back to 1908. Alumni records are maintained here also. Call 319-383-8944. Degrees granted: Bachelors; Masters. Adverse incident record source: Dean of Students, 319-383-8822.

Attendance and degree information available by phone, FAX, mail. Search requires name plus date of birth. Other helpful information: social security number, approximate years of attendance. No fee for information.

Transcripts available by FAX, mail. Search requires name plus date of birth, approximate years of attendance, signed release. Other helpful information: social security number, exact years of attendance. Fee is $2.00. Expedite fee is based on cost of service.'

Phone: Directory & Loan information only. Will not FAX transcripts.

St. Andrews Presbyterian College, Registrar, 1700 Dogwood Mile, Laurinburg, NC 28352, 910-277-5221. Hours: 8:30AM-5PM. Records go back to 1961. Alumni records are maintained here also. Call 910-277-5668. Degrees granted: Bachelors.

Attendance and degree information available by mail. Search requires name plus exact years of attendance, signed release. Other helpful information: social security number, date of birth. No fee for information.

Transcripts available by mail. Search requires name plus exact years of attendance, signed release. Other helpful information: social security number, date of birth. No fee for transcripts.

St. Anselm College, Registrar, Manchester, NH 03102-1310, 603-641-7000. Hours: 8AM-4PM. Records go back to 1800s. Alumni records are maintained here also. Call 603-641-7220. Degrees granted: Associate; Bachelors.

Attendance and degree information available by phone, mail. Search requires name plus social security number, date of birth, approximate years of attendance. Other helpful information: exact years of attendance. No fee for information.

Transcripts available by written request only. Search requires name plus social security number, date of birth, approximate years of attendance, signed release. Other helpful information: exact years of attendance. Fee is $3.00.

St. Augustine College, Registrar, 1333 W Argyle St, Chicago, IL 60640, 312-878-8756 (FAX: 312-878-9032). Hours: 9AM-8PM. Records go back to 1981. Degrees granted: Associate. Adverse incident record source: Student Affairs, 312-878-8756.

Attendance and degree information available by phone, FAX, mail. Search requires name plus social security number, signed release. No fee for information.

Transcripts available by FAX, mail. Search requires name plus social security number, signed release. Fee is $3.00.

For 24 hour service fee is $5.00.

St. Augustine's College, Registrar, 1315 Oakwood Ave, Raleigh, NC 27610-2298, 919-516-4199 (FAX: 919-516-4415). Hours: 9AM-5PM. Records go back to 1920. Alumni records are maintained here also. Call 919-516-4023. Degrees granted: Bachelors. Adverse incident record source: Public Safety, 919-516-4220 or 919-516-4640.

Attendance and degree information available by phone, FAX, mail. Search requires name plus social security number, approximate years of attendance, signed release. Other helpful information: date of birth. No fee for information.

Transcripts available by mail. Search requires name plus social security number, approximate years of attendance, signed release. Other helpful information: date of birth. Fee is $5.00.

St. Bernard's Institute, Registrar, 1100 S Goodman St, Rochester, NY 14620, 716-271-3657 (FAX: 716-271-2045). Hours: 8:30AM-4:30PM. Records go back to 1893. Alumni records are maintained here at the same phone number. Degrees granted: Bachelors; Masters.

Attendance and degree information available by phone, FAX, mail. Search requires name plus social security number. Other helpful information: approximate years of attendance. No fee for information.

Transcripts available by FAX, mail. Search requires name plus social security number, signed release. Other helpful information: approximate years of attendance. Fee is $7.50.

Address helpful.

St. Bonaventure University, Registrar, Rte 417, St Bonaventure, NY 14778, 716-375-2020 (FAX: 716-375-2135). Hours: 8:30AM-4:30PM. Records go back to 1920s. Alumni records are maintained here also. Call 716-375-2375. Degrees granted: Masters.

Attendance and degree information available by phone, FAX, mail. Search requires name only. Other helpful information: social security number, date of birth, approximate years of attendance. No fee for information.

Transcripts available by mail. Search requires name plus approximate years of attendance, signed release. Other helpful information: social security number, date of birth, exact years of attendance. Fee is $5.00. Expedited service available for $15.00.

St. Catharine College, Registrar, 2735 Bardstown Rd, St Catharine, KY 40061, 606-336-5082 (FAX: 606-336-5031). Hours: 8AM-5PM. Alumni records are maintained here at the same phone number. Degrees granted: Associate.

Attendance and degree information available by phone, FAX, mail. Search requires name plus social security number, approximate years of attendance. Other helpful information: date of birth, exact years of attendance. No fee for information.

Transcripts available by FAX, mail. Search requires name plus social security number, approximate years of attendance, signed release. Other helpful information: date of birth, exact years of attendance. Fee is $5.00.

FAXed transcript requests must be followed up with original by mail.

St. Charles Borromeo Seminary, Registrar, 1000 E Wynnewood Rd, Wynnewood, PA 19096-3099, 610-667-3394. Hours: 8AM-5PM. Degrees granted: Bachelors; Masters.

Attendance and degree information available by phone, mail. Search requires name plus social security number, date of birth, exact years of attendance. No fee for information.

Transcripts available by mail. Search requires name plus social security number, date of birth, exact years of attendance, signed release. Fee is $3.00.

St. Charles County Community College, Attn: Records, 4601 Mid Rivers Mall Dr, St Peters, MO 63376, 314-922-8237 (FAX: 314-922-8236). Hours: 8AM-7PM M-Th; 8AM-4:30PM F. Records go back to 1987. Alumni records are maintained here also. Call 314-922-8473. Degrees granted: Associate.

Attendance and degree information available by phone, FAX, mail. Search requires name plus social security number. Other helpful information: approximate years of attendance. No fee for information.

Transcripts available by FAX, mail. Search requires name plus social security number, signed release. Other helpful information: approximate years of attendance. Fee is $3.00. Expedited service available for $6.00.

Major credit cards accepted for payment.

St. Clair County Community College, Registrar, 323 Erie St, PO Box 5015, Port Huron, MI 48061-5015, 810-984-3881. Hours: 8AM-4:30PM. Records go back to 1923. Alumni records are maintained here also. Call 810-984-3881. Degrees granted: Associate.

Attendance and degree information available by mail. Search requires name plus social security number, date of birth, approximate years of attendance, signed release. No fee for information.

Transcripts available by mail. Search requires name plus social security number, date of birth, approximate years of attendance, signed release. Fee is $3.00.

St. Cloud State University, Registrar, 740 Fourth Ave S, St Cloud, MN 56301-4498, 612-255-2111. Hours: 8AM-4:30PM. Degrees granted: Associate; Bachelors; Masters.

Attendance information available by mail. Search requires name plus signed release. Other helpful information: social security number. No fee for information.

Degree information available by phone, FAX, mail. Search requires name only. Other helpful information: social security number. No fee for information.

Transcripts available by written request only. Search requires name plus signed release. Other helpful information: social security number. Fee is $2.00.

St. Cloud Technical College, Registrar, 1540 Northway Dr, St Cloud, MN 56303, 612-654-5075 (FAX: 612-654-5981). Hours: 7:30AM-5PM M-Th; 7:30AM-4PM F. Degrees granted: Associate.

Attendance and degree information available by phone, FAX, mail. Search requires name plus social security number, approximate years of attendance. Other helpful information: date of birth, exact years of attendance. No fee for information.

Transcripts available by written request only. Search requires name plus social security number, approximate years of attendance, signed release. Other helpful information: date of birth, exact years of attendance. Fee is $3.00. Expedited service available for $5.00.

Major credit cards accepted for payment.

St. Edward's University, Registrar, 3001 S Congress Ave, Austin, TX 78704, 512-448-8750 (FAX: 512-448-8492). Records go back to 1885. Alumni records are maintained here also. Call 512-448-8512. Degrees granted: Bachelors; Masters.

Attendance and degree information available by phone, FAX, mail. Search requires name plus exact years of attendance. No fee for information.

Transcripts available by FAX, mail. Search requires name plus exact years of attendance, signed release. No fee for transcripts.

St. Francis College, Registrar, 180 Remsen St, Brooklyn, NY 11201, 718-522-2300 X242 (FAX: 718-522-1274). Hours: 9AM-5PM. Records go back to 1930. Alumni records are maintained here also. Call 718-522-2300 X362. Degrees granted: Associate; Bachelors. Adverse incident record source: E. Boyd, 718-522-2300 X275.

Attendance and degree information available by FAX, mail. Search requires name plus signed release. Other helpful information: social security number, date of birth, approximate years of attendance. No fee for information.

Transcripts available by mail. Search requires name plus signed release. Other helpful information: social security number, date of birth, approximate years of attendance. Fee is $5.00. Expedited service available for $25.00.

St. Francis College, Registrar, 2701 Spring St, Fort Wayne, IN 46808, 219-434-3252 (FAX: 219-434-3183). Hours: 8:30AM-Noon,12:30-5PM. Records go back to founding date. Degrees granted: Associate; Bachelors; Masters.

Attendance and degree information available by phone, FAX, mail. Search requires name plus social security number. Other helpful information: approximate years of attendance. No fee for information.

Transcripts available by FAX, mail. Search requires name plus signed release. Other helpful information: social security number, approximate years of attendance. Fee is $2.00. Expedited service available for $2.00.

St. Francis College, Office of the Registrar, PO Box 600, Loretto, PA 15940, 814-472-3009. Hours: 9AM-Noon, 12:30-4:30PM. Records go back to 1895. Alumni records are maintained here also. Call 814-472-3015. Degrees granted: Associate; Bachelors; Masters.

Attendance and degree information available by phone, FAX, mail. Search requires name plus social security number. Other helpful information: date of birth, approximate years of attendance. No fee for information.

Transcripts available by mail. Search requires name plus social security number, date of birth, approximate years of attendance, signed release. Other helpful information: exact years of attendance. Fee is $3.00. Expedite: $3.00 plus extra postage.

St. Francis Medical Center College of Nursing, Registrar, 511 NE Greenleaf St, Peoria, IL 61603, 309-655-2596 (FAX: 309-655-3648). Hours: 7AM-3:30PM. School of Nursing from 1956; College of Nursing from 1988. Alumni records are maintained here also. Call 309-655-4125. Degrees granted: Bachelors.

School will not confirm attendance or degree information. Search requires name plus social security number. Other helpful information: approximate years of attendance. No fee for information.

Transcripts available by phone, mail. Search requires name plus social security number, signed release. Other helpful information: approximate years of attendance. Fee is $3.00.

May inquire initially by phone but must receive written request.

St. Francis Seminary, Registrar, 3257 S Lake Dr, St Francis, WI 53235, 414-747-6450 (FAX: 414-747-6442). Hours: 8AM-5PM. Records go back to 1845. Alumni records are maintained here at the same phone number. Degrees granted: Bachelors; Masters.

Attendance and degree information available by phone, mail. Search requires name only. No fee for information.

Transcripts available by mail. Search requires name plus signed release. Fee is $4.00.

St. Gregory's College, Registrar, 1900 W MacArthur, Shawnee, OK 74801, 405-878-5433 (FAX: 405-878-5198). Hours: 8AM-4:30PM. Records go back to 1920. Alumni records are maintained here also. Call 405-878-5100. Degrees granted: Associate. Adverse incident record source: Dean, 405-878-5400.

Attendance information available by phone, FAX, mail. Search requires name plus social security number. No fee for information.

Degree information available by FAX, mail. Search requires name plus social security number, exact years of attendance, signed release. No fee for information.

Transcripts available by mail. Search requires name plus social security number, exact years of attendance, signed release. Fee is $2.00.

St. Hyacinth College and Seminary, Registrar, Granby, MA 01033, 413-467-7191 X509 (FAX: 413-467-9609). Hours: 8:30AM-4:30PM. Records go back to 1957. Degrees granted: Associate; Bachelors.

Attendance and degree information available by FAX, mail. Search requires name plus social security number, signed release. No fee for information.

Transcripts available by mail. Search requires name plus social security number, signed release. Fee is $3.00.

St. John Fisher College, Registrar, 3690 East Ave, Rochester, NY 14618, 716-385-8015 (FAX: 716-385-8129). Hours: 8:30AM-4:30PM. Records go back to 1951. Degrees granted: Bachelors; Masters. Certification: ACCT. Special programs- Academic Dean, 716-385-8116. Adverse incident record source: Protective Services, 716-385-8025.

Attendance and degree information available by phone, FAX, mail. Search requires name only. Other helpful information: social security number, approximate years of attendance. No fee for information.

Transcripts available by FAX, mail. Search requires name plus signed release. Other helpful information: social security number, approximate years of attendance. Fee is $5.00.

Major credit cards accepted for payment.

St. John Vianney College Seminary, Registrar, 2900 SW 87th Ave, Miami, FL 33165, 305-223-4561. Hours: 8AM-5PM. Records go back to 1959. Alumni records are maintained here at the same phone number. Degrees granted: Bachelors.

Attendance and degree information available by mail. Search requires name plus social security number, signed release. No fee for information.

Transcripts available by mail. Search requires name plus social security number, signed release. Fee is $2.00.

St. John's College, Registrar, 60 College Ave, PO Box 2800, Annapolis, MD 21404, 410-626-2513 (FAX: 410-626-0789). Hours: 8:30AM-Noon. Degrees granted: Bachelors; Masters.

Attendance and degree information available by FAX, mail. Search requires name plus signed release. Other helpful information: social security number, exact years of attendance. No fee for information.

Transcripts available by FAX, mail. Search requires name plus signed release. Other helpful information: social security number, exact years of attendance. Fee is $2.00.

Major credit cards accepted for payment.

St. John's College, Registrar, Santa Fe, NM 87501-4599, 505-984-6075 (FAX: 505-984-6003). Hours: 9AM-5PM. Records go back to 1964. Degrees granted: Bachelors; Masters.

Attendance and degree information available by phone, FAX, mail. Search requires name only. Other helpful information: social security number, date of birth, approximate years of attendance. No fee for information.

Transcripts available by mail. Search requires name plus signed release. Other helpful information: social security number, date of birth, approximate years of attendance. Fee is $2.00.

Credit cards over $10.00.

St. John's Seminary, Registrar, 127 Lake St, Brighton, MA 02135, 617-254-2610 (FAX: 617-787-2336). Hours: 9-11:30AM, 1-3PM. Records go back to 1900. Degrees granted: Masters.

Attendance and degree information available by mail. Search requires name plus approximate years of attendance, signed release. Other helpful information: social security number, date of birth. No fee for information.

Transcripts available by mail. Search requires name plus approximate years of attendance, signed release. Other helpful information: social security number, date of birth. Fee is $5.00.

St. John's Seminary, Registrar, 5012 Seminary Rd, Camarillo, CA 93012-2598, 805-482-2755 (FAX: 805-484-4074). Hours: 8AM-4:30PM. Records go back to 1939. Degrees granted: Masters.

Attendance and degree information available by phone, FAX, mail. Search requires name plus social security number, date of birth. Other helpful information: approximate years of attendance. No fee for information.

Transcripts available by mail. Search requires name plus social security number, date of birth, signed release. Other helpful information: approximate years of attendance. Fee is $5.00. Expedite fee varies.

St. John's Seminary College, Registrar, 5118 E Seminary Rd, Camarillo, CA 93012-2599, 805-482-2755 X202 (FAX: 805-987-5097). Hours: 8AM-4PM. Alumni Records Office: 1531 W Ninth St, Los Angeles, CA 90015. Degrees granted: Bachelors.

Attendance and degree information available by mail. Search requires name plus social security number, date of birth, signed release. Other helpful information: approximate years of attendance. No fee for information.

Transcripts available by written request only. Search requires name plus social security number, date of birth, signed release. Other helpful information: approximate years of attendance. Fee is $2.00.

St. John's University, Registrar, Collegeville, MN 56321, 612-363-3395 (FAX: 612-363-2714). Hours: 8AM-4:30PM. Records go back 139 years. Alumni records are maintained here also. Call 612-363-2591. Degrees granted: Bachelors; Masters.

Attendance and degree information available by phone, mail. Search requires name only. Other helpful information: social security number, date of birth, approximate years of attendance. No fee for information.

Transcripts available by FAX, mail. Search requires name plus signed release. Other helpful information: social security number, date of birth, approximate years of attendance. Fee is $2.00.

St. John's University, Registrar, 8000 Utopia Pkwy, Jamaica, NY 11439, 718-990-1487. Hours: 8:30AM-7:30PM M, 8:30AM-4:30PM T-Th, 8:30AM-3PM. Alumni records are maintained here also. Call 718-990-6232. Degrees granted: Associate; Bachelors; Masters; Doctorate. Adverse incident record source: Student Life, 718-990-6256.

Attendance and degree information available by phone, mail. Search requires name plus social security number. No fee for information.

Transcripts available by mail. Search requires name plus social security number, approximate years of attendance, signed release. Fee is $3.00.

Type of degree needed.

St. John's University, (Branch), Registrar, 300 Howard Ave, Staten Island, NY 10301, 718-390-4545. Records are not housed here. They are located at St. John's University, Registrar, 8000 Utopia Pkwy, Jamaica, NY 11439.

St. Johns River Community College, Registrar, 5001 St Johns Ave, Palatka, FL 32177-3897, 904-328-1571 X133. Hours: 8AM-5PM. Records go back to 1958. Degrees granted: Associate.

Attendance and degree information available by mail. Search requires name plus social security number, date of birth, signed release. Other helpful information: approximate years of attendance. No fee for information.

Transcripts available by mail. Search requires name plus social security number, date of birth, signed release. Other helpful information: approximate years of attendance. Fee is $3.00.

Major credit cards accepted for payment.

St. Joseph College, Registrar, 1678 Asylum Ave, West Hartford, CT 06117, 203-232-4571 (FAX: 203-231-8396). Hours: 8:30AM-4:30PM. Records go back 63 years. Alumni records are maintained here at the same phone number. Degrees granted: Bachelors; Masters. Certification: rt:Six year.

Attendance and degree information available by phone, FAX, mail. Search requires name only. Other helpful information: approximate years of attendance. No fee for information.

Transcripts available by mail. Search requires name plus approximate years of attendance, signed release. Other helpful information: date of birth. Fee is $4.00.

St. Joseph College of Nursing, Registrar, 290 N Springfield Ave, Joliet, IL 60435, 815-741-7143 (FAX: 815-741-7131). Hours: 8AM-4PM. Records go back to 1922. Degrees granted: Bachelors.

Attendance and degree information available by phone, FAX, mail. Search requires name plus social security number, approximate years of attendance. Other helpful information: date of birth. No fee for information.

Transcripts available by written request only. Search requires name plus social security number, approximate years of attendance, signed release. Other helpful information: date of birth. Fee is $3.00. Expedited service available for $3.00.

St. Joseph Seminary College, Registrar, St Benedict, LA 70457, 504-892-1800 (FAX: 504-892-3723). Hours: 8AM-5PM. Records go back to 1891. Degrees granted: Bachelors.

Attendance and degree information available by phone, FAX, mail. Search requires name plus social security number. Other helpful information: date of birth. No fee for information. Include a stamped envelope.

Transcripts available by FAX, mail. Search requires name plus social security number, date of birth, signed release. Other helpful information: approximate years of attendance. Fee is $2.00. Expedited service available for $2.00.

St. Joseph's College, Registrar, 245 Clinton Ave, Brooklyn, NY 11205-3688, 718-636-6813 (FAX: 718-398-4936). Hours: 9AM-5PM. Records go back 75 years. Degrees granted: Bachelors.

Attendance and degree information available by mail. Search requires name plus social security number. Other helpful information: date of birth, approximate years of attendance. No fee for information.

Transcripts available by mail. Search requires name plus social security number, signed release. Other helpful information: date of birth, approximate years of attendance. Fee is $3.00. Expedited service available for $3.00.

Major credit cards accepted for payment.

St. Joseph's College, Registrar, Windham, ME 04062, 207-892-6766 (FAX: 207-893-7861). Hours: 8:30AM-4:30PM. Records go back to founding date. Degrees granted: Bachelors; Masters.

Attendance and degree information available by phone, FAX, mail. Search requires name only. Other helpful information: social security number, date of birth. No fee for information. Expedited service available for $10.00.

Transcripts available by FAX, mail. Search requires name plus signed release. Other helpful information: social security number, date of birth, approximate years of attendance. Fee is $3.00. Expedited service available for $10.00.

Major credit cards accepted for payment.

St. Joseph's College, (Suffolk), Registrar, 155 Roe Blvd, Patchogue, NY 11772, 516-447-3239 (FAX: 516-654-1782). Hours: 8:30AM-5PM. Records go back to 1920s. Alumni records are maintained here also. Call 516-447-3215. Degrees granted: Bachelors; Masters. Special programs- Graduate Files, 718-636-6800.

Attendance information available by phone, FAX, mail. Search requires name plus social security number. No fee for information.

Degree information available by phone, FAX, mail. Search requires name plus social security number, approximate years of

The Sourcebook of College and University Student Records

attendance. Other helpful information: exact years of attendance. No fee for information.

Transcripts available by FAX, mail. Search requires name plus social security number, signed release. Other helpful information: approximate years of attendance. Fee is $3.00.

Major credit cards accepted for payment.

St. Joseph's Seminary, Registrar, 201 Seminary Ave, Yonkers, NY 10704, 914-968-6200 (FAX: 914-968-7912). Hours: 9AM-5PM. Records go back to 1896. Alumni records are maintained here at the same phone number. Degrees granted: Masters; M.Div.

Attendance information available by phone, FAX, mail. Search requires name plus social security number. No fee for information.

Degree information available by phone, FAX, mail. Search requires name plus social security number, exact years of attendance. No fee for information.

Transcripts available by FAX, mail. Search requires name plus social security number, exact years of attendance, signed release. Fee is $2.00.

Major credit cards accepted for payment.

St. Joseph's University, Registrar, 5600 City Line Ave, Philadelphia, PA 19131, 610-660-1010 (FAX: 610-660-1019). Alumni records are maintained here at the same phone number. Degrees granted: Bachelors; Masters.

Attendance and degree information available by phone, mail. Search requires name plus social security number, exact years of attendance. No fee for information.

Transcripts available by mail. Search requires name plus social security number, exact years of attendance, signed release. Fee is $2.00.

St. Lawrence University, Registrar, 23 Ramona Dr, Canton, NY 13617, 315-379-5267 (FAX: 315-379-5502). Hours: 8AM-4:30PM. Records go back to 1856. Alumni records are maintained here at the same phone number. Degrees granted: Bachelors; Masters. Adverse incident record source: Security Dept, 315-379-5555.

Attendance and degree information available by phone, FAX, mail. Search requires name plus social security number. No fee for information.

Transcripts available by mail. Search requires name plus social security number, approximate years of attendance, signed release. Fee is $3.50.

St. Leo College, Registrar, PO Box 2278, Saint Leo, FL 33574, 904-588-8234 (FAX: 904-588-8390). Hours: 8AM-5PM. Records go back to 1920. Alumni Records Office: Alumni/Parent Relation, PO Box 2227, Saint Leo, FL 33574. Adverse incident record source: Student Affairs, 904-588-8992.

Attendance and degree information available by phone, FAX, mail. Search requires name plus social security number, date of birth, signed release. Other helpful information: approximate years of attendance. No fee for information.

Transcripts available by FAX, mail. Search requires name plus social security number, signed release. Other helpful information: date of birth, approximate years of attendance. Fee is $5.00.

St. Louis Christian College, Registrar, 1360 Grandview Dr, Florissant, MO 63033, 314-837-6777 (FAX: 314-837-8291). Hours: 8AM-5PM. Records go back to 1956. Alumni records are maintained here at the same phone number. Degrees granted: Associate; Bachelors. Adverse incident record source: Dean of Students.

Attendance and degree information available by phone, FAX, mail. Search requires name only. Other helpful information: social security number, approximate years of attendance. No fee for information.

Transcripts available by written request only. Search requires name plus signed release. Other helpful information: social security number, approximate years of attendance. Fee is $2.00.

St. Louis College of Pharmacy, Registrar, 4588 Parkview Pl, St Louis, MO 63110, 314-367-8700 X1064 (FAX: 314-367-2784). Hours: 8:30AM-5PM. Records go back 70 years. Alumni records are maintained here also. Call 314-367-4217. Degrees granted: Bachelors; Masters; Pharm. D.

Attendance and degree information available by phone, FAX, mail. Search requires name only. Other helpful information: social security number, date of birth, approximate years of attendance. No fee for information.

Transcripts available by mail. Search requires name plus signed release. Other helpful information: social security number, date of birth, approximate years of attendance. Fee is $5.00.

St. Louis Community College, Central Records, 5600 Oakland Ave, St Louis, MO 63110, 314-644-9100 (FAX: 314-644-9752).

Attendance and degree information available by phone, FAX, mail. Search requires name plus signed release. Other helpful information: social security number, date of birth. No fee for information.

Transcripts available by mail. Search requires name plus social security number, signed release. Other helpful information: date of birth. Fee is $2.00.

St. Louis Community College at Florissant Valley, Registrar, 3400 Pershall Rd, St Louis, MO 63135, 314-595-4244. Hours: 8AM-8PM M-Th, 8AM-4:30PM F. Records go back to 1962. Alumni records are maintained here also. Call 314-595-4556. Degrees granted: Associate. Adverse incident record source: President, 314-595-4208.

Attendance and degree information available by phone, mail. Search requires name plus social security number, date of birth, signed release. No fee for information.

Transcripts available by mail. Search requires name plus social security number, date of birth, signed release. Fee is $2.00.

St. Louis Community College at Meramec, Registrar, 11333 Big Bend Blvd, Kirkwood, MO 63122, 314-984-7601 (FAX: 314-984-7117). Hours: 7:30AM-9PM M-Th, 7:30AM-5PM F. Records go back to 1973. Alumni records are maintained here also. Call 314-984-7641. Degrees granted: Associate.

Attendance and degree information available by phone, FAX, mail. Search requires name plus social security number, date of birth, approximate years of attendance, signed release. No fee for information.

Transcripts available by mail. Search requires name plus social security number, date of birth, approximate years of attendance, signed release. Fee is $2.00.

St. Louis University, Registrar, 221 N Grand Blvd, St Louis, MO 63103, 314-977-2269. Hours: 8:30AM-5PM. Records go back 85 years. Alumni records are maintained here also. Call 314-977-2308. Degrees granted: Associate; Bachelors; Masters; Doctorate. Adverse incident record source: Public Safety, 214-977-3877.

Degree Granting Institutions

Attendance and degree information available by phone, mail. Search requires name plus social security number, date of birth, approximate years of attendance. Other helpful information: exact years of attendance. No fee for information.

Transcripts available by FAX, mail. Search requires name plus social security number, date of birth, approximate years of attendance, signed release. Other helpful information: exact years of attendance. Fee is $3.00. Expedited service available for $10.00. Credit cards available soon.

St. Louis University, (Parks College), Registrar, Falling Springs Rd, Cahokia, IL 62206, 618-337-7575 (FAX: 618-332-6802). Hours: 8AM-4:30PM. Records go back to 1927. Alumni Records Office: 221 N Grand Dubourg Hall 318, St Louis, MO 63103. Degrees granted: Bachelors. Adverse incident record source: Risk Management, 314-977-3952.

Attendance and degree information available by phone, FAX, mail. Search requires name plus social security number, approximate years of attendance. Other helpful information: date of birth. No fee for information.

Transcripts available by FAX. Search requires name plus social security number, approximate years of attendance, signed release. Other helpful information: date of birth, exact years of attendance. Fee is $3.00. Expedited service available for $3.00.

St. Martin's College, Registrar, Lacey, WA 98503, 360-438-4356. Hours: 8AM-6PM. Records go back to 1920. Alumni records are maintained here also. Call 360-438-4366. Degrees granted: Associate; Bachelors; Masters.

Attendance and degree information available by phone, FAX, mail. Search requires name plus social security number. Other helpful information: date of birth, approximate years of attendance. No fee for information.

Transcripts available by FAX, mail. Search requires name plus social security number, signed release. Other helpful information: date of birth, approximate years of attendance. No fee for transcripts.

St. Mary College, Registrar, 4100 S 4th St Trafficway, Leavenworth, KS 66048-5082, 913-682-5151 (FAX: 913-758-6140). Hours: 8AM-4:30PM. Records go back to 1928.

Attendance and degree information available by phone, FAX, mail. Search requires name plus social security number, date of birth. Other helpful information: approximate years of attendance. No fee for information.

Transcripts available by written request only. Search requires name plus social security number, date of birth, signed release. Other helpful information: approximate years of attendance. Transcript fee is $3.00 for inactive students; $1.00 currently enrolled.

St. Mary Seminary, Registrar, 28700 Euclid Ave, Wickliffe, OH 44092-2585, 216-943-7667 (FAX: 216-943-7577). Hours: 8AM-4PM. Records go back 20 years. Degrees granted: Masters.

Attendance information available by mail. Search requires name plus signed release. Other helpful information: social security number, date of birth, approximate years of attendance. No fee for information.

Degree information available by phone, FAX, mail. Search requires name plus signed release. Other helpful information: social security number, date of birth, approximate years of attendance. No fee for information.

Transcripts available by mail. Search requires name plus signed release. Other helpful information: social security number, date of birth, approximate years of attendance. Fee is $3.00.

St. Mary's College, Registrar, 3535 Indian Trail, Orchard Lake, MI 48324, 810-683-0522 (FAX: 810-683-0433). Hours: 9AM-5PM. Degrees granted: Bachelors.

Attendance and degree information available by phone, FAX, mail. Search requires name plus social security number. Other helpful information: date of birth. No fee for information.

Transcripts available by FAX, mail. Search requires name plus social security number, signed release. Fee is $3.00.

Major credit cards accepted for payment.

St. Mary's College, Registrar, 900 Hillsborough St, Raleigh, NC 27603-1689, 919-839-4009 (FAX: 919-832-4831). Hours: 8:30AM-4:30PM. Records go back to 1852. Alumni records are maintained here also. Call 919-839-4101. Degrees granted: Associate. Adverse incident record source: Dean, 919-839-4015.

Attendance and degree information available by phone, FAX, mail. Search requires name plus social security number, date of birth, exact years of attendance, signed release. No fee for information.

Transcripts available by FAX, mail. Search requires name plus social security number, date of birth, exact years of attendance, signed release. Fee is $2.00.

St. Mary's College of Maryland, Registrar, St. Mary's City, MD 20686, 301-862-0336 (FAX: 301-862-0995). Hours: 8AM-5PM. Records go back to 1924. Alumni records are maintained here also. Call 301-862-0280. Degrees granted: Bachelors. Adverse incident record source: Dean of Students, 301-862-0208.

Attendance and degree information available by phone, FAX, mail. Search requires name plus social security number, exact years of attendance. No fee for information.

Transcripts available by mail. Search requires name plus social security number, exact years of attendance, signed release. No fee for transcripts.

St. Mary's Seminary and University, Registrar, 5400 Roland Ave, Baltimore, MD 21210, 410-323-3200 (FAX: 410-323-3554). Hours: 8:30AM-4:30PM. Alumni records are maintained here also. Call 410-323-3200 X74. Degrees granted: Bachelors; Masters.

Attendance and degree information available by phone, FAX, mail. Search requires name plus social security number, date of birth, signed release. Other helpful information: approximate years of attendance. No fee for information.

Transcripts available by FAX, mail. Search requires name plus social security number, date of birth, signed release. Other helpful information: approximate years of attendance. Fee is $5.00. Expedited service available for $5.00.

Written authorization from student needed to release transcript.

St. Mary's University, Registrar, One Camino Santa Maria, San Antonio, TX 78228-8576, 210-436-3701 (FAX: 210-431-2217). Hours: 8AM-5PM Winter; 8AM-4PM Summer. Records go back to 1930. Alumni records are maintained here also. Call 210-436-3325. Degrees granted: Bachelors; Masters; Doctorate; JD. Special programs- Continuing Studies, 210-436-3321. Adverse incident record source: Dean of Students, 210-436-3714.

Attendance and degree information available by phone, FAX, mail. Search requires name only. Other helpful information: social security number, approximate years of attendance. No fee for information.

Transcripts available by FAX, mail. Search requires name plus signed release. Other helpful information: social security number,

date of birth, approximate years of attendance. Fee is $3.00. Expedited service available for $5.00.

St. Mary's University of Minnesota, Registrar, 700 Terrace Heights, Winona, MN 55987-1399, 507-457-1428. Hours: 7:30AM-4PM Summer, 7:30AM-4:30PM Fall. Records go back to 1912. Alumni records are maintained here also. Call 507-457-1499. Degrees granted: Bachelors; Masters. Adverse incident record source: Dean of Students, 507-457-1403.

Attendance and degree information available by phone, mail. Search requires name plus approximate years of attendance, signed release. Other helpful information: social security number. No fee for information.

Transcripts available by mail. Search requires name plus approximate years of attendance, signed release. Other helpful information: social security number. Fee is $2.00.

St. Mary-Of-The-Woods College, Registrar, St. Mary-of-the-Woods, IN 47876, 812-535-5269 (FAX: 812-535-4613). Hours: 8:30AM-Noon, 1-4:30PM. Records go back to 1898. Alumni records are maintained here also. Call 812-535-5211. Degrees granted: Associate; Bachelors; Masters. Certification: Gerontology. Adverse incident record source: Le Fer Hall, 812-535-5216.

Attendance and degree information available by phone, FAX, mail. Search requires name only. Other helpful information: approximate years of attendance. No fee for information.

Transcripts available by mail. Search requires name plus signed release. Other helpful information: approximate years of attendance. Fee is $5.00.

Major credit cards accepted for payment.

St. Meinrad College, Registrar, St Meinrad, IN 47577, 812-357-6525 (FAX: 812-357-6964). Hours: 8AM-4:30PM. Records go back to 1880. Degrees granted: Bachelors. Adverse incident record source: Physical Facilities.

Attendance and degree information available by phone, FAX, mail. Search requires name only. Other helpful information: social security number, date of birth, approximate years of attendance. No fee for information.

Transcripts available by FAX, mail. Search requires name plus signed release. Other helpful information: social security number, date of birth, approximate years of attendance. Fee is $2.00. Expedited service available for $2.00.

Major credit cards accepted for payment.

St. Meinrad School of Theology, Registrar, St Meinrad, IN 47577, 812-357-6525 (FAX: 812-357-6964). Hours: 8AM-4:30PM. Records go back to 1880. Degrees granted: Masters. Adverse incident record source: Physical Facilities, 812-357-6593.

Attendance and degree information available by phone, FAX, mail. Search requires name only. Other helpful information: social security number, date of birth, approximate years of attendance. No fee for information.

Transcripts available by FAX, mail. Search requires name plus signed release. Other helpful information: social security number, date of birth, approximate years of attendance. Fee is $2.00. Expedited service available for $2.00.

St. Michael's College, Registrar, Winooski Park, Colchester, VT 05439, 802-654-2571 (FAX: 802-655-3680). Hours: 8AM-4PM. Records go back to 1901. Alumni records are maintained here also. Call 802-654-2527. Degrees granted: Bachelors; Masters; Doctorate.

Attendance and degree information available by phone, FAX, mail. Search requires name plus date of birth, approximate years of attendance. Other helpful information: social security number, exact years of attendance. No fee for information.

Transcripts available by FAX, mail. Search requires name plus date of birth, approximate years of attendance, signed release. Other helpful information: social security number, exact years of attendance. Fee is $2.00. Expedited service available for $5.00.

St. Norbert College, Registrar, 100 Grant St, De Pere, WI 54115-2099, 414-337-3216 (FAX: 414-337-4033). Hours: 8AM-Noon, 1-4:30PM. Records go back to 1902. Alumni records are maintained here also. Call 414-337-3022. Degrees granted: Bachelors; Masters.

Attendance and degree information available by phone, mail. Search requires name only. Other helpful information: social security number. No fee for information.

Transcripts available by mail. Search requires name plus signed release. Other helpful information: social security number. Fee is $3.00.

St. Olaf College, Registrar, 1520 St Olaf Ave, Northfield, MN 55057, 507-646-3014. Hours: 8AM-5PM. Records go back to 1874. Alumni records are maintained here also. Call 507-646-3028. Degrees granted: Bachelors. Special programs- Continuing Education, 507-646-3066.

Attendance and degree information available by phone, mail. Search requires name plus date of birth, signed release. Other helpful information: social security number, approximate years of attendance. No fee for information.

Transcripts available by mail. Search requires name plus date of birth, signed release. Other helpful information: social security number, approximate years of attendance. Fee is $2.00.

St. Patrick's Seminary, Registrar, 320 Middlefield Rd, Menlo Park, CA 94025, 415-325-5621 (FAX: 415-322-0997). Hours: 9AM-Noon, 1-4PM. Records go back 100 years. Alumni records are maintained here at the same phone number. Degrees granted: Masters.

Attendance and degree information available by phone, FAX, mail. Search requires name plus social security number, date of birth. Other helpful information: approximate years of attendance. No fee for information.

Transcripts available by mail. Search requires name plus social security number, date of birth, exact years of attendance, signed release. Fee is $5.00. Expedited service available for $5.00.

St. Paul School of Theology, Registrar, 5123 Truman Rd, Kansas City, MO 64127, 816-483-9600 (FAX: 816-483-9605). Hours: 8AM-4:30PM. Records go back to 1962. Alumni records are maintained here also. Call 816-483-9600. Degrees granted: Doctorate.

Attendance and degree information available by phone, FAX, mail. Search requires name plus social security number, approximate years of attendance, signed release. No fee for information.

School does not provide transcripts. Search requires name plus social security number, approximate years of attendance, signed release. Fee is $5.00.

St. Paul Technical College, Registrar, 235 Marshall Ave, St Paul, MN 55102, 612-221-1300 (FAX: 612-221-1416). Hours: 7:30AM-4PM. Records go back to 1919. Degrees granted: Associate.

Attendance and degree information available by phone, FAX, mail. Search requires name only. Other helpful information: social security number, date of birth, approximate years of attendance. No fee for information.

Transcripts available by mail. Search requires name plus social security number, signed release. Other helpful information: date of birth, approximate years of attendance. Fee is $2.00. Expedited service available for $6.00.

Major credit cards accepted for payment.

St. Paul's College, Registrar, 406 Winsor Ave, Lawrenceville, VA 23868, 804-848-4356. Hours: 8AM-5PM. Records go back to 1888. Alumni records are maintained here at the same phone number. Degrees granted: Bachelors.

Attendance and degree information available by phone, mail. Search requires name plus social security number. No fee for information.

Transcripts available by mail. Search requires name plus social security number, signed release. Fee is $3.00.

St. Peter's College, Registrar, 2641 Kennedy Blvd, Jersey City, NJ 07306, 201-915-9035 (FAX: 201-915-9038). Hours: 9AM-8PM M-Th; 9AM-5PM F. Records go back to 1916. Alumni records are maintained here also. Call 201-915-9204. Degrees granted: Associate; Bachelors; Masters.

Attendance and degree information available by phone, FAX, mail. Search requires name plus social security number, signed release. No fee for information.

Transcripts available by FAX, mail. Search requires name plus social security number, signed release. Fee is $2.00.

St. Peter's College, (Englewood Cliffs Campus), Registrar, Hudson Terrace, Englewood Cliffs, NJ 07632, 201-568-7730. Records are not housed here. They are located at St. Peter's College, Registrar, 2641 Kennedy Blvd, Jersey City, NJ 07306.

St. Petersburg Junior College, Registrar, PO Box 13489, St Petersburg, FL 33733-3489, 813-341-3600 (FAX: 813-341-4792). Hours: 8AM-7PM M-Th, 8AM-5:30PM F. Records go back to 1928. Alumni records are maintained here at the same phone number. Degrees granted: Associate. Adverse incident record source: Dean of Students, 813-341-3600.

Attendance and degree information available by phone, FAX, mail. Search requires name plus social security number, date of birth, exact years of attendance. No fee for information.

Transcripts available by FAX, mail. Search requires name plus social security number, date of birth, exact years of attendance, signed release. No fee for transcripts.

St. Philip's College, Registrar, 2111 Nevada St, San Antonio, TX 78203, 210-531-3296. Hours: 8AM-4PM. Degrees granted: Associate.

Attendance and degree information available by mail. Search requires name plus social security number, signed release. No fee for information.

Transcripts available by mail. Search requires name plus social security number, signed release. No fee for transcripts.

St. Thomas Aquinas College, Records Office, 125 Rte 340, Sparkill, NY 10976, 914-398-4300. Hours: 8:30AM-5PM. Records go back to 1958. Degrees granted: Associate; Bachelors; Masters. Special programs- Continuing Education (HS), 914-398-4200.

Attendance and degree information available by phone, mail. Search requires name plus social security number. Other helpful information: approximate years of attendance. No fee for information.

Transcripts available by mail. Search requires name plus social security number, signed release. Other helpful information: approximate years of attendance. Fee is $5.00. Expedited service available for $15.00.

St. Thomas Theological Seminary, Registrar, 1300 S Steele St, Denver, CO 80210-2599, 303-722-4687. School closed as of 6/30/95. Housing of records undetermined at press time.

St. Thomas University, Registrar, 16400 NW 32nd Ave, Miami, FL 33054, 305-628-6537. Hours: 9AM-5PM M-Th, 9AM-6:30PM F. Records go back to 1961. Alumni records are maintained here also. Call 305-628-6641. Degrees granted: Bachelors; Masters.

Attendance and degree information available by phone, mail. Search requires name plus social security number. No fee for information.

Transcripts available by mail. Search requires name plus social security number, signed release. Fee is $3.00. Expedited service available for $9.00.

Major credit cards accepted for payment.

St. Vincent College and Seminary, Registrar, Frazier Purchase Rd, Latrobe, PA 15650, 412-537-4559 (FAX: 412-537-4554). Hours: 9AM-4PM. Records go back to 1871. Degrees granted: Bachelors; Masters. Adverse incident record source: Dean of Students, 412-537-4564.

Attendance and degree information available by phone, FAX, mail. Search requires name only. Other helpful information: social security number, date of birth, approximate years of attendance. No fee for information.

Transcripts available by mail. Search requires name plus signed release. Other helpful information: social security number, date of birth, approximate years of attendance. Fee is $3.00. Expedite: add mail expenses.

St. Vincent de Paul Regional Seminary, Registrar, 10701 S Military Tr, Boynton Beach, FL 33436-4899, 407-732-4424 (FAX: 407-737-2205). Hours: 9AM-4PM. Records go back to founding date. Degrees granted: Masters.

Attendance and degree information available by phone, FAX, mail. Search requires name only. Other helpful information: social security number, approximate years of attendance. No fee for information.

Transcripts available by mail. Search requires name plus signed release. Other helpful information: social security number, approximate years of attendance. Fee is $3.00.

St. Vladimir's Orthodox Theological Seminary, Registrar, 575 Scarsdale Rd, Crestwood, NY 10707, 914-337-4566 (FAX: 914-961-4507). Hours: 9AM-3PM. Degrees granted: Masters; Doctorate.

Attendance and degree information available by phone, FAX, mail. Search requires name plus approximate years of attendance. Other helpful information: exact years of attendance. No fee for information. Include a stamped envelope.

Transcripts available by written request only. Search requires name plus signed release. Other helpful information: approximate years of attendance. Fee is $3.00.

St. Xavier University, Office of the Registrar, 3700 W 103rd St, Chicago, IL 60655, 312-298-3501 (FAX: 312-298-3508). Hours: 8:30AM-7PM. Records go back to 1925. Alumni records are maintained here also. Call 312-298-3318. Degrees granted: Bachelors; Masters. Adverse incident record source: Dean of Students.

Attendance and degree information available by phone, mail. Search requires name plus social security number, approximate years of attendance, signed release. Other helpful information: date of birth. No fee for information.

Transcripts available by mail. Search requires name plus social security number, date of birth, signed release. Other helpful information: approximate years of attendance. Fee is $3.00. Expedited service available for $6.00.

Standing Rock College, Registrar, HC1 Box 4, Fort Yates, ND 58538, 701-854-3861 (FAX: 701-854-3403). Hours: 8AM-4:30PM. Records go back 25 years. Alumni records are maintained here at the same phone number. Degrees granted: Associate.

Attendance and degree information available by FAX, mail. Search requires name plus social security number, date of birth, approximate years of attendance, signed release. No fee for information.

Transcripts available by FAX, mail. Search requires name plus social security number, date of birth, approximate years of attendance, signed release. Transcripts are $2.00 after the first.

Stanford University, Transcripts & Registration, Old Union Bldg, Stanford, CA 94305, 415-723-2086 (FAX: 415-725-7248). Hours: 9AM-Noon, 1-5PM. Records go back to 1891. Alumni records are maintained here also. Call 415-723-2021. Degrees granted: Bachelors; Masters; Doctorate. Adverse incident record source: Campus Police, 415-723-9633.

Attendance and degree information available by phone, FAX, mail. Search requires name only. No fee for information.

Transcripts available by mail. Search requires name plus date of birth, approximate years of attendance, signed release. No fee for transcripts.

Stanly Community College, Registrar, 141 College Dr, Albemarle, NC 28001, 704-982-0121 X237 (FAX: 704-982-0819). Hours: 8AM-5PM. Records go back 72 years. Degrees granted: Associate.

Attendance and degree information available by phone, FAX, mail. Search requires name only. Other helpful information: social security number, approximate years of attendance. No fee for information.

Transcripts available by FAX, mail. Search requires name plus social security number, signed release. Other helpful information: approximate years of attendance. No fee for transcripts.

Stark Technical College, Registrar, 6200 Frank Ave NW, Canton, OH 44720, 216-966-5460 (FAX: 216-497-6313). Hours: 8AM-8PM. Records go back 63 years. Degrees granted: Associate.

Attendance and degree information available by FAX, mail. Search requires name plus social security number, signed release. No fee for information.

Transcripts available by FAX, mail. Search requires name plus social security number, signed release. Fee is $2.00.

Major credit cards accepted for payment.

Starr King School for the Ministry, Registrar, 2441 LeConte Ave, Berkeley, CA 94709, 510-845-6232 (FAX: 510-845-6273). Hours: 9AM-5PM. Records go back to 1900s. Alumni records are maintained here at the same phone number. Degrees granted: Masters.

Attendance and degree information available by phone, FAX, mail. Search requires name only. No fee for information.

Transcripts available by phone, FAX, mail. Search requires name only. Fee is $3.00.

State Community College of East St. Louis, Registrar, 601 James R Thompson Blvd, East St Louis, IL 62201, 618-583-2609 (FAX: 618-583-2661). Hours: 8:30AM-5PM. Records go back to 1969. Alumni records are maintained here also. Call 618-583-2575. Degrees granted: Associate. Adverse incident record source: Campus Police, 618-583-2525.

Attendance and degree information available by FAX, mail. Search requires name plus social security number, signed release. No fee for information.

Transcripts available by FAX, mail. Search requires name plus social security number, signed release. Fee is $2.00.

State Fair Community College, Registrar, 3201 W 16th St, Sedalia, MO 65301, 816-530-5800 X296 (FAX: 816-530-5820). Hours: 8AM-7PM M-Th, 8AM-4PM F. Records go back to 1968. Alumni records are maintained here also. Call 816-530-5800 X250. Degrees granted: Associate. Adverse incident record source: Dean of Students, 816-530-5800.

Attendance and degree information available by phone, FAX, mail. Search requires name plus social security number. No fee for information.

Transcripts available by FAX, mail. Search requires name plus social security number, signed release. No fee for transcripts. FAX fee $3.00.

State Technical Institute at Memphis, Records Office, 5983 Macon Cove, Memphis, TN 38134-7693, 901-383-4190 (FAX: 901-383-4473). Hours: 8AM-7PM M-Th; 8AM-4:30PM F. Records go back to 1976. Degrees granted: Associate.

Attendance information available by phone, FAX, mail. Search requires name plus social security number. Other helpful information: date of birth, approximate years of attendance. No fee for information.

Degree information available by phone, FAX, mail. Search requires name plus social security number. Other helpful information: date of birth, approximate years of attendance. No fee for information.

Transcripts available by FAX, mail. Search requires name plus social security number, signed release. Other helpful information: date of birth, approximate years of attendance. First five transcripts free; $1.00 each additional.

Major credit cards accepted for payment.

State University College at Brockport, Registrar, 350 New Campus Dr, Brockport, NY 14420, 716-395-2211. Hours: 8AM-5PM. Records go back to 1940s. Alumni records are maintained here also. Call 716-395-5124. Degrees granted: Bachelors; Masters. Certification: rt:ADV Study.

Attendance and degree information available by phone, mail. Search requires name plus social security number. No fee for information.

Transcripts available by mail. Search requires name plus social security number, exact years of attendance, signed release. Fee is $5.00.

Return address and phone number required, as well as degree and former name.

State University College at Buffalo, Registrar, 1300 Elmwood Ave, Buffalo, NY 14222, 716-878-4811 (FAX: 716-878-3159). Hours: 8:15AM-4:30PM. Alumni records are maintained here also. Call 716-878-6001. Degrees granted: Bachelors; Masters.

Attendance information available by phone, FAX, mail. Search requires name plus signed release. Other helpful information: social security number, approximate years of attendance. No fee for information.

Degree information available by phone, FAX, mail. Search requires name only. Other helpful information: social security number, approximate years of attendance. No fee for information.

Transcripts available by mail. Search requires name plus social security number, signed release. Other helpful information: approximate years of attendance. Fee is $5.00.

Major credit cards accepted for payment.

State University College at Cortland, Registrar, PO Box 2000, Cortland, NY 13045, 607-753-4701 (FAX: 607-753-5989). Hours: 8:30AM-4PM. Records go back to 1867. Alumni records are maintained here also. Call 607-753-2516. Degrees granted: Bachelors; Masters. Certification: CAS.

Attendance and degree information available by phone, FAX, mail. Search requires name only. Other helpful information: social security number, date of birth, approximate years of attendance. No fee for information.

Transcripts available by FAX, mail. Search requires name plus signed release. Other helpful information: social security number, date of birth, approximate years of attendance. Fee is $5.00. Expedited service available for $10.00.

Major credit cards accepted for payment.

State University College at Fredonia, Registrar, Fredonia, NY 14063, 716-673-3171. Hours: 9AM-5PM. Records go back to 1900s. Alumni records are maintained here also. Call 716-673-3553. Degrees granted: Bachelors; Masters.

Attendance and degree information available by phone, mail. Search requires name plus social security number, exact years of attendance. No fee for information.

Transcripts available by mail. Search requires name plus social security number, exact years of attendance, signed release. Fee is $5.00.

State University College at Geneseo, Records Office, Erwin 102, 1 College Circle, Geneseo, NY 14454, 716-245-5566 (FAX: 716-245-5005). Hours: 8AM-4:15PM. Records go back to 1800s. Degrees granted: Bachelors; Masters. Adverse incident record source: Student Services.

Attendance and degree information available by phone, FAX, mail. Search requires name only. Other helpful information: social security number, approximate years of attendance. No fee for information.

Transcripts available by mail. Search requires name plus social security number, signed release. Other helpful information: approximate years of attendance. Fee is $5.00. Expedited service available for $5.00.

Major credit cards accepted for payment.

State University College at Old Westbury, Registrar, PO Box 210, Old Westbury, NY 11568, 516-876-3055. Hours: 9AM-4:45PM. Records go back to 20+yr. Degrees granted: Bachelors.

Attendance and degree information available by phone, mail. Search requires name plus social security number, signed release. No fee for information.

Transcripts available by phone, mail. Search requires name plus social security number, signed release. Fee is $5.00.

State University College at Oneonta, Registrar, Oneonta, NY 13820-4015, 607-436-2531 (FAX: 607-436-3103). Hours: 7:30AM-4:30PM. Degrees granted: Bachelors; Masters. Adverse incident record source: Dean of Students, 607-436-2513.

Attendance and degree information available by phone, FAX, mail. Search requires name plus social security number. Other helpful information: approximate years of attendance. No fee for information.

Transcripts available by FAX, mail. Search requires name plus social security number, signed release. Other helpful information: date of birth, approximate years of attendance. Fee is $5.00.

State University College at Oswego, Registrar, Oswego, NY 13126, 315-341-2171. Hours: 8AM-5PM. Records go back to 1940. Degrees granted: Bachelors; Masters.

Attendance and degree information available by phone, mail. Search requires name plus social security number, exact years of attendance. No fee for information.

Transcripts available by mail. Search requires name plus social security number, exact years of attendance, signed release. Fee is $5.00.

State University College at Plattsburgh, Registrar, Plattsburgh, NY 12901, 518-564-2100 (FAX: 518-564-2079). Hours: 9AM-4PM. Records go back to 1890s. Alumni records are maintained here also. Call 518-564-2090. Degrees granted: Bachelors; Masters. Adverse incident record source: Student Affairs, 518-564-2280.

Attendance and degree information available by phone, FAX, mail. Search requires name plus social security number. Other helpful information: date of birth. No fee for information.

Transcripts available by mail. Search requires name plus social security number, exact years of attendance, signed release. Other helpful information: date of birth. Fee is $5.00.

Financial obligation must be fulfilled before information released. Need former names.

State University College at Potsdam, Registrar, Pierrepont Ave, Potsdam, NY 13676, 315-267-2154 (FAX: 315-267-2157). Hours: 8AM-4:30PM. Records go back to 1880s. Alumni records are maintained here also. Call 315-267-2120. Degrees granted: Bachelors; Masters. Adverse incident record source: Dean, 315-267-2117.

Attendance and degree information available by phone, mail. Search requires name plus social security number. No fee for information.

Transcripts available by FAX, mail. Search requires name plus social security number, signed release. Other helpful information: exact years of attendance. Fee is $5.00.

State University College at Purchase, Registrar, 735 Anderson Hill Rd, Purchase, NY 10577-1400, 914-251-6360 (FAX: 914-251-6373). Hours: 8:30AM-5PM. Records go back to 1970. Alumni records are maintained here also. Call 914-251-6054. Degrees granted: Bachelors; Masters. Adverse incident record source: Statistics Div, 914-251-6018.

Attendance and degree information available by phone, FAX, mail. Search requires name plus social security number. No fee for information.

Transcripts available by mail. Search requires name plus social security number, signed release. Other helpful information: exact years of attendance. Fee is $5.00.

Former names needed.

State University of New York College at Farmingdale, Office of the Registrar, Greenley Hall, Melville Rd, Farmingdale, NY 11735-1021, 516-420-2776 (FAX: 516-420-2257). Hours: 8:30AM-8PM M-Th; 8:30AM-4:30PM F. Records go back to 1965. Degrees granted: Associate; Bachelors.

Attendance and degree information available by phone, mail. Search requires name plus social security number. Other helpful information: date of birth, approximate years of attendance. No fee for information.

Transcripts available by mail. Search requires name plus social security number, signed release. Other helpful information: date of birth, approximate years of attendance. Fee is $5.00.

State University of New York College of Ag and Tech at Cobleskill, Registrar, Cobleskill, NY 12043, 518-234-5521 (FAX: 518-234-5333). Hours: 8AM-4:15PM. Records go back to 1930s. Alumni records are maintained here also. Call 518-234-5628. Degrees granted: Associate; Masters. Adverse incident record source: Public Safety.

Attendance and degree information available by phone, FAX, mail. Search requires name plus social security number, approximate years of attendance, signed release. Other helpful information: date of birth. No fee for information.

Transcripts available by FAX, mail. Search requires name plus social security number, approximate years of attendance, signed release. Other helpful information: date of birth. Fee is $5.00.

Major credit cards accepted for payment.

State University of New York College of Ag and Tech/Morrisville, Registrar, Morrisville, NY 13408, 315-684-6066 (FAX: 315-684-6421). Hours: 8AM-5PM. Records go back to 1920s. Alumni records are maintained here also. Call 315-684-6030. Degrees granted: Associate. Adverse incident record source: Dean, 315-684-6070.

Attendance and degree information available by phone, FAX, mail. Search requires name plus social security number. Other helpful information: approximate years of attendance. No fee for information.

Transcripts available by FAX, mail. Search requires name plus social security number, approximate years of attendance, signed release. Other helpful information: exact years of attendance. Fee is $5.00.

Major credit cards accepted for payment.

State University of New York College of Technology at Alfred, Registrar, Huntington Bldg, Alfred, NY 14802, 607-587-4796 (FAX: 607-587-3294). Hours: 8AM-4PM. Records go back to 1911. Alumni records are maintained here also. Call 607-587-4260. Degrees granted: Associate; Bachelors. Adverse incident record source: Student Affairs, 607-587-3247.

Attendance and degree information available by phone, FAX, mail. Search requires name plus social security number. No fee for information.

Transcripts available by FAX, mail. Search requires name plus social security number, approximate years of attendance, signed release. Other helpful information: exact years of attendance. Fee is $5.00.

Major credit cards accepted for payment.

State University of New York College of Technology at Alfred, **(Branch)**, Registrar, Alfred, NY 14802, 607-587-3105 (FAX: 607-587-3294). Hours: 8AM-4PM. Records go back to 1940s. Alumni records are maintained here also. Call 607-587-4260. Degrees granted: Associate; Bachelors. Adverse incident record source: Student Affairs, 607-587-3247.

Attendance and degree information available by phone, FAX, mail. Search requires name plus social security number. No fee for information.

Transcripts available by FAX, mail. Search requires name plus social security number, approximate years of attendance, signed release. Other helpful information: exact years of attendance. Fee is $5.00.

Major credit cards accepted for payment.

State University of New York College of Technology at Canton, Registrar, Cornell Dr, Canton, NY 13617, 315-386-7042 (FAX: 315-386-7930). Hours: 8AM-5PM Winter; 8AM-4PM Summer. Records go back to 1906. Alumni records are maintained here also. Call 315-386-7127. Degrees granted: Associate. Adverse incident record source: Dean of Students, 315-386-7120.

Attendance and degree information available by phone, mail. Search requires name plus social security number. Other helpful information: date of birth, approximate years of attendance. No fee for information.

Transcripts available by mail. Search requires name plus social security number, signed release. Other helpful information: date of birth, approximate years of attendance. Fee is $5.00. Expedited service available for $6.75.

Major credit cards accepted for payment.

State University of New York College of Technology at Delhi, Office of Records & Registration, 117 Bush Hall, Delhi, NY 13753, 607-746-4562. Hours: 8AM-5PM. Records go back to 1968. Alumni records are maintained here also. Call 607-746-4603. Degrees granted: Associate. Adverse incident record source: Student Affairs, 607-746-4440.

Attendance and degree information available by mail. Search requires name plus social security number, signed release. Other helpful information: approximate years of attendance. No fee for information.

Transcripts available by mail. Search requires name plus social security number, signed release. Other helpful information: date of birth, approximate years of attendance. Fee is $5.00.

Major credit cards accepted for payment.

State University of New York Empire State College, Registrar, Two Union Ave, Saratoga Springs, NY 12866, 518-587-2100 X209 (FAX: 518-587-5404). Hours: 8:30AM-4:30PM. Degrees granted: Associate; Bachelors; Masters.

Attendance and degree information available by phone, FAX, mail. Search requires name plus social security number. No fee for information.

Transcripts available by mail. Search requires name plus social security number, signed release. Fee is $5.00.

State University of New York Empire State College, **(Genessee Valley Regional Center)**, Registrar, 8 Prince St,

Rochester, NY 14607, 716-244-3641. Records are not housed here. They are located at State University of New York Empire State College, Registrar, Two Union Ave, Saratoga Springs, NY 12866.

State University of New York Empire State College, (Hudson Valley Regional Center), Registrar, 200 N Central Ave, Hartsdale, NY 10530, 914-948-6206. Records are not housed here. They are located at State University of New York Empire State College, Registrar, Two Union Ave, Saratoga Springs, NY 12866.

State University of New York Empire State College, (Long Island Regional Center), Registrar, Trainor House, PO Box 130, Old Westbury, NY 11568, 516-997-4700. Records are not housed here. They are located at State University of New York Empire State College, Registrar, Two Union Ave, Saratoga Springs, NY 12866.

State University of New York Empire State College, (Metropolitan Regional Center), Registrar, 666 Broadway, New York, NY 10012, 212-598-0640. Records are not housed here. They are located at State University of New York Empire State College, Registrar, Two Union Ave, Saratoga Springs, NY 12866.

State University of New York Empire State College, (Niagara Frontier Regional Center), Registrar, 564 Franklin St, Buffalo, NY 14202, 716-886-8020. Records are not housed here. They are located at State University of New York Empire State College, Registrar, Two Union Ave, Saratoga Springs, NY 12866.

State University of New York Empire State College, (Northeast Center), Registrar, 845 Central Ave, Albany, NY 12206, 518-485-5964. Records are not housed here. They are located at State University of New York Empire State College, Registrar, Two Union Ave, Saratoga Springs, NY 12866.

State University of New York Health Science Center at Brooklyn, Registrar, 450 Clarkson Ave, Brooklyn, NY 11203, 718-270-1875 (FAX: 718-270-7592). Hours: 10AM-6PM. Alumni records are maintained here at the same phone number. Degrees granted: Bachelors; Masters; Doctorate.

Attendance information available by phone, FAX, mail. Search requires name plus social security number. No fee for information.

Degree information available by phone, FAX, mail. Search requires name plus social security number. Other helpful information: approximate years of attendance. No fee for information.

Transcripts available by mail. Search requires name plus social security number, exact years of attendance, signed release. Fee is $5.00.

State University of New York Health Science Center at Syracuse, Registrar, 155 Elizabeth Blackwell St, Syracuse, NY 13210, 315-464-4604 (FAX: 315-464-8867). Hours: 8:30AM-4:40PM. Records go back to 1902. Alumni records are maintained here also. Call 315-464-4361. Degrees granted: Associate; Bachelors; Masters; Doctorate. Special programs- College of Medicine Alumni, 315-464-4361: Health Related Professions Alumni, 315-464-4416.

Attendance and degree information available by phone, FAX, mail. Search requires name only. Other helpful information: social security number, date of birth, approximate years of attendance. No fee for information.

Transcripts available by FAX, mail. Search requires name plus social security number, signed release. Other helpful information: date of birth, approximate years of attendance. Fee is $5.00.

State University of New York Institute of Technology / Utica/Rome, Registrar, PO Box 3050, Utica, NY 13504-3050, 315-792-7265 (FAX: 315-792-7804). Hours: 8AM-5PM. Records go back to 1966. Degrees granted: Bachelors; Masters.

Attendance and degree information available by phone, FAX, mail. Search requires name plus social security number. Other helpful information: date of birth, approximate years of attendance. No fee for information.

Transcripts available by FAX, mail. Search requires name plus social security number, signed release. Other helpful information: date of birth, approximate years of attendance. Fee is $5.00. Major credit cards accepted for payment.

State University of New York Maritime College, Registrar, Fort Schuyler, Throggs Neck, NY 10465, 718-409-7266 (FAX: 718-409-7392). Hours: 8:30AM-4:30PM. Records go back 118 years. Alumni Records Office: Alumni Association, SUNY Maritime College, 6 Pennyfield Ave, Bronx, NY 10465. Degrees granted: Bachelors; Masters. Adverse incident record source: Public Safety, 718-409-7310: Regimental Office, 718-409-7451

Attendance and degree information available by phone, FAX, mail. Search requires name plus approximate years of attendance. No fee for information.

Transcripts available by FAX, mail. Search requires name plus approximate years of attendance, signed release. Fee is $5.00.

State University of New York Maritime College, (Stenotype Academy), Registrar, 15 Park Row #4FL, New York, NY 10038, 212-962-0002 (FAX: 212-608-8210). Hours: 8AM-7PM M-Th, 8AM-4PM F. Records go back to 1970s. Degrees granted: Associate.

Attendance and degree information available by phone, FAX, mail. Search requires name plus social security number. Other helpful information: approximate years of attendance. No fee for information.

Transcripts available by FAX, mail. Search requires name plus social security number, signed release. Other helpful information: approximate years of attendance. Fee is $3.00.

Need address.

State University of New York at Albany, Registrar, 1400 Washington Ave, Albany, NY 12222, 518-442-5530. Hours: 9AM-5PM. Alumni records are maintained here at the same phone number. Degrees granted: Bachelors; Masters; Doctorate.

Attendance and degree information available by mail. Search requires name plus social security number, exact years of attendance, signed release. No fee for information.

Transcripts available by mail. Search requires name plus social security number, exact years of attendance, signed release. Fee is $5.00.

Need former names.

State University of New York at Binghamton, Registrar, PO Box 6000, Binghamton, NY 13902-6000, 607-777-6872 (FAX: 607-777-6515). Hours: 9:30AM-4PM. Records go back to 1950s. Alumni records are maintained here also. Call 607-777-2431. Degrees granted: Bachelors; Masters; Doctorate.

Attendance and degree information available by phone, FAX, mail. Search requires name plus social security number. No fee for information.

Transcripts available by mail. Search requires name plus social security number, signed release. Other helpful information: date of birth, approximate years of attendance. Fee is $5.00.

State University of New York at Buffalo, Registrar, 1300 Elmwood Ave, Buffalo, NY 14222, 716-878-4811 (FAX: 716-878-3159). Hours: 8:15AM-5PM. Records go back to 1920s. Alumni records are maintained here also. Call 716-878-6001. Degrees granted: Bachelors; Masters. Adverse incident record source: Public Safety, 716-878-6333.

Attendance and degree information available by phone, FAX, mail. Search requires name plus social security number, exact years of attendance. No fee for information.

Transcripts available by mail. Search requires name plus social security number, exact years of attendance, signed release. Fee is $5.00.

State University of New York at New Paltz, Records & Registration, 75 S Manheim Blvd, New Paltz, NY 12561, 914-257-3100 (FAX: 914-257-3009). Hours: 8:30AM-4:30PM. Alumni records are maintained here also. Call 914-257-3230. Degrees granted: Bachelors; Masters.

Attendance information available by FAX, mail. Search requires name plus approximate years of attendance, signed release. Other helpful information: social security number, date of birth, exact years of attendance. No fee for information.

Degree information available by phone, FAX, mail. Search requires name plus approximate years of attendance, signed release. Other helpful information: social security number, date of birth, exact years of attendance. No fee for information.

Transcripts available by FAX, mail. Search requires name plus approximate years of attendance, signed release. Other helpful information: social security number, date of birth, exact years of attendance. Fee is $5.00.

State University of New York at Stony Brook, Registrar Office, Stony Brook, NY 11794-1101, 516-632-6885 (FAX: 516-632-9685). Hours: 8:40AM-4PM. Records go back to 1961. Alumni records are maintained here also. Call 516-632-6330. Degrees granted: Bachelors; Masters; Doctorate. Adverse incident record source: Student Affairs, 516-632-6700.

Attendance and degree information available by phone, FAX, mail. Search requires name plus social security number. No fee for information.

Transcripts available by FAX, mail. Search requires name plus social security number, signed release. Other helpful information: approximate years of attendance. Fee is $5.00.

Major credit cards accepted for payment.

State University of New York, (College of Environmental Science and Forestry), Registrar, Syracuse, NY 13210, 315-470-6655 (FAX: 315-470-6933). Hours: 8AM-4:30PM. Records go back to 1912. Alumni records are maintained here also. Call 315-470-6632. Degrees granted: Associate; Bachelors; Masters; Doctorate. Adverse incident record source: Student Affairs, 315-470-6658.

Attendance and degree information available by phone, FAX, mail. Search requires name plus social security number. Other helpful information: approximate years of attendance. No fee for information.

Transcripts available by mail. Search requires name plus social security number, signed release. Other helpful information: approximate years of attendance. Fee is $5.00.

State University of New York, (College of Optometry at New York City), Registrar, 100 E 24th St, Manhattan, NY 10010, 212-780-4900. Hours: 8AM-5PM. Records go back to 1945. Alumni records are maintained here at the same phone number. Degrees granted: Masters; Doctorate; O.D.

Attendance information available by mail. Search requires name plus social security number, approximate years of attendance, signed release. No fee for information.

Degree information available by mail. Search requires name plus social security number, exact years of attendance, signed release. No fee for information.

Transcripts available by mail. Search requires name plus social security number, date of birth, exact years of attendance, signed release. Fee is $5.00. Expedited service available for $5.00.

Stautzenberger College (Central), Registrar, 5355 Southwyck Blvd, Toledo, OH 43614, 419-866-0261 (FAX: 419-867-9821). Hours: 8AM-10PM M-Th, 9AM-5PM F. Degrees granted: Associate.

Attendance and degree information available by phone, FAX, mail. Search requires name plus social security number, approximate years of attendance, signed release. No fee for information.

Transcripts available by phone, FAX, mail. Search requires name plus social security number, approximate years of attendance, signed release. Fee is $5.00.

Stautzenberger College (Findlay), Registrar, 1637 Tiffin Ave, Findlay, OH 45840, 419-423-2211. Hours: 8AM-5PM. Degrees granted: Associate.

Attendance information available by mail. Search requires name plus social security number, date of birth, approximate years of attendance, signed release. Other helpful information: exact years of attendance. No fee for information.

Degree information available by phone, FAX, mail. Search requires name plus social security number, date of birth, exact years of attendance, signed release. Other helpful information: approximate years of attendance. No fee for information.

Transcripts available by mail. Search requires name plus social security number, date of birth, exact years of attendance, signed release. Other helpful information: approximate years of attendance. Fee is $3.00.

Include a self addressed stamped envelope with mail request.

Stephen F. Austin State University, Office of the Registrar, SFA PO Box 13050, Nacogdoches, TX 75962, 409-468-2501 (FAX: 409-468-2261). Hours: 8AM-5PM. Records go back to 1923. Alumni Records Office: SFA PO Box 6096, Nacogdoches, TX 75962 409-468-3407. Degrees granted: Bachelors; Masters; Doctorate. Adverse incident record source: Student Development, 409-468-2703.

Attendance information available by phone, mail. Search requires name plus social security number. Other helpful information: approximate years of attendance. No fee for information.

Degree information available by phone, mail. Search requires name plus social security number. No fee for information.

Transcripts available by phone, mail. Search requires name plus social security number, signed release. Other helpful information: date of birth, approximate years of attendance. Fee is $2.00. Expedited service available for $4.00.

Major credit cards accepted for payment.

Stephens College, Registrar, Columbia, MO 65215, 314-876-7277 (FAX: 314-876-7248). Hours: 8AM-Noon, 1-5PM. Records go back to 1900. Alumni records are maintained here at the same phone number. Degrees granted: Associate; Bachelors.

Attendance and degree information available by phone, FAX, mail. Search requires name only. Other helpful information: social security number, date of birth, approximate years of attendance. No fee for information.

Transcripts available by mail. Search requires name plus social security number, date of birth, exact years of attendance, signed release. Other helpful information: approximate years of attendance. Fee is $5.00. Expedited service available for $15.00.

Sterling College, Registrar, Craftsbury Common, VT 05827, 802-586-7711 (FAX: 802-586-2596). Hours: 9AM-5PM. Records go back to 1958. Degrees granted: Associate.

Attendance and degree information available by phone, FAX, mail. Search requires name only. Other helpful information: social security number, date of birth, approximate years of attendance. No fee for information.

Transcripts available by phone, FAX, mail. Search requires name only. Other helpful information: social security number, date of birth, approximate years of attendance. Fee is $3.00.

Sterling College, Registrar, Sterling, KS 67579, 316-278-4280 (FAX: 316-278-3690). Hours: 8AM-5PM. Records go back to 1887. Alumni records are maintained here also. Call 316-278-4329. Degrees granted: Bachelors. Adverse incident record source: Student Affairs, 316-278-4222.

Attendance and degree information available by phone, FAX, mail. Search requires name plus signed release. Other helpful information: social security number, approximate years of attendance. No fee for information.

Transcripts available by FAX, mail. Search requires name plus signed release. Other helpful information: social security number, approximate years of attendance. Fee is $2.00.

Stetson University, Registrar, 421 N Woodland Blvd, Deland, FL 32720, 904-822-7140 (FAX: 904-822-7146). Hours: 8AM-4:30PM. Degrees granted: Bachelors; Masters; EDS. Adverse incident record source: Campus Life, 904-822-7201.

Attendance and degree information available by phone, mail. Search requires name only. Other helpful information: social security number, date of birth, approximate years of attendance. No fee for information.

Transcripts available by mail. Search requires name plus social security number, signed release. Other helpful information: date of birth, approximate years of attendance. Fee is $2.00.

Stevens College of Business, Registrar, 2168 Washington Blvd, Ogden, UT 84401-1467, 801-394-7791. Hours: 8AM-5PM. Records go back to 1965. Degrees granted: Associate.

Attendance and degree information available by phone, mail. Search requires name plus social security number. No fee for information.

Transcripts available by written request only. Search requires name plus social security number, signed release. No fee for transcripts.

Stevens Institute of Technology, Registrar, Castle Point on the Hudson, Hoboken, NJ 07030, 201-216-5210 (FAX: 201-216-8030). Hours: 8AM-5PM. Records go back to 1870. Alumni records are maintained here also. Call 201-216-5163. Degrees granted: Bachelors; Masters; Doctorate.

Attendance and degree information available by phone, FAX, mail. Search requires name plus social security number, approximate years of attendance. Other helpful information: date of birth, exact years of attendance. No fee for information.

Transcripts available by mail. Search requires name plus social security number, approximate years of attendance, signed release. Other helpful information: date of birth, exact years of attendance. Fee is $3.00.

Stevens-Henager College of Business, (Branch Campus), Registrar, 25 E 1700 S, Provo, UT 84606-6157, 801-375-5455 (FAX: 801-375-9836). Records are not housed here. They are located at Stevens College of Business, Registrar, 2168 Washington Blvd, Ogden, UT 84401-1467.

Stillman College, Registrar, PO Drawer 1430, Tuscaloosa, AL 35403, 205-349-4240 X347 (FAX: 205-349-4252). Hours: 8AM-5PM. Degrees granted: Bachelors.

Attendance information available by phone, FAX, mail. Search requires name plus social security number, date of birth, exact years of attendance, signed release. No fee for information. Expedited service available for $5.00.

Degree information available by phone, mail. Search requires name plus social security number, date of birth, exact years of attendance, signed release. No fee for information. Expedite service available for $5.00.

Transcripts available by mail. Search requires name plus social security number, date of birth, exact years of attendance, signed release. Fee is $5.00. Expedited service available for $10.00.

Confirmation of degree not given if student in default or in debt to college.

Stockton College of New Jersey, Registrar, Jimmy Leeds Rd, Pomona, NJ 80240, 906-652-1776.

Stockton State College, Registrar, Jimmy Leeds Rd, Pomona, NJ 08240, 609-652-4235. Hours: 8:30AM-4:30PM. Records go back to 1975. Alumni records are maintained here also. Call 609-652-4468.

Attendance and degree information available by phone, mail. Search requires name plus social security number. No fee for information.

Transcripts available by mail. Search requires name plus social security number, signed release. Fee is $2.00.

Stone Child Community College, Registrar, RR 1 Box 1082, Box Elder, MT 59521-9796, 406-395-4313 (FAX: 406-395-4836). Hours: 8AM-4:30PM. Records go back to 1990. Degrees granted: Associate. Adverse incident record source: Local Police, 406-395-4513.

Attendance information available by mail. Search requires name plus social security number. No fee for information.

Degree information available by phone, mail. Search requires name plus social security number, date of birth, signed release. No fee for information.

Transcripts available by mail. Search requires name plus social security number, signed release. Other helpful information: approximate years of attendance. Fee is $2.00.

Stonehill College, Registrar, North Easton, MA 02357, 508-230-1315 (FAX: 508-230-1434). Hours: 8AM-4:30PM. Records go back to 1952. Alumni records are maintained here also. Call 508-230-1343. Degrees granted: Bachelors. Adverse incident record source: Student Affairs, 508-230-1290.

Attendance information available by phone, FAX, mail. Search requires name plus approximate years of attendance, signed release. No fee for information.

Degree information available by phone, FAX, mail. Search requires name plus signed release. No fee for information.

Transcripts available by FAX, mail. Search requires name plus signed release. Fee is $2.00.

Stratton College, Registrar, 1300 N Jackson St, Milwaukee, WI 53202-2608, 414-276-5200 X6. Hours: 8AM-5PM. Records go back to 1863. Alumni records are maintained here at the same phone number. Degrees granted: Associate.

Attendance and degree information available by phone, mail. Search requires name plus social security number, exact years of attendance. No fee for information.

Transcripts available by mail. Search requires name plus social security number, exact years of attendance, signed release. Fee is $5.00.

Strayer College, Registrar, 1025 15th St NW, Washington, DC 20005, 703-892-5100 (FAX: 703-769-2610). Hours: 9AM-6PM. Records go back to 1920s. Degrees granted: Associate; Bachelors; Masters.

Attendance and degree information available by phone, FAX, mail. Search requires name plus social security number, signed release. Other helpful information: date of birth, approximate years of attendance. No fee for information.

Transcripts available by mail. Search requires name plus social security number, signed release. Other helpful information: date of birth, approximate years of attendance. Fee is $5.00.

Major credit cards accepted for payment.

Sue Bennett College, Registrar, 151 College St, London, KY 40741, 606-846-2238 (FAX: 606-864-2238 X1198). Hours: 8AM-4:30PM. Records go back to 1900. Alumni records are maintained here also. Call 606-864-2238 X1125. Degrees granted: Associate; Bachelors.

Attendance and degree information available by FAX, mail. Search requires name plus signed release. Other helpful information: social security number, date of birth. No fee for information.

Transcripts available by FAX, mail. Search requires name plus signed release. Other helpful information: social security number, date of birth. Fee is $5.00.

Suffolk Community College, **(Ammerman)**, Registrar, 533 College Rd, Selden, NY 11784, 516-451-4008 (FAX: 516-451-4015). Hours: 9AM-8PM M-Th, 9AM-5PM F. Alumni records are maintained here also. Call 516-732-7979. Degrees granted: Associate.

Attendance information available by phone, FAX, mail. Search requires name plus social security number, signed release. No fee for information.

Degree information available by FAX, mail. Search requires name plus social security number, signed release. No fee for information.

Transcripts available by phone, FAX, mail. Search requires name plus social security number, signed release. Fee is $5.00.

Suffolk Community College, **(Eastern)**, Registrar, Speonk-Riverhead Rd, Riverhead, NY 11901, 516-548-2500. Records are not housed here. They are located at Suffolk Community College, (Ammerman), Registrar, 533 College Rd, Selden, NY 11784.

Suffolk Community College, **(Western)**, Registrar, Crooked Hill Rd, Brentwood, NY 11717, 516-434-6750. Records are not housed here. They are located at Suffolk Community College, (Ammerman), Registrar, 533 College Rd, Selden, NY 11784.

Suffolk University, Registrar, 8 Ashburton Pl, Beacon Hill, Boston, MA 02108, 617-573-8430 (FAX: 617-573-8703). Hours: 8AM-7PM M-Th, 8AM-4:45PM F. Records go back to 1985. Alumni records are maintained here also. Call 617-573-8443. Degrees granted: Associate; Bachelors; Masters; PhD.

Attendance and degree information available by phone, FAX, mail. Search requires name plus social security number, approximate years of attendance, signed release. No fee for information.

Transcripts available by FAX, mail. Search requires name plus social security number, approximate years of attendance, signed release. Fee is $2.00.

Sul Ross State University, Admissions & Records, Box C-2, Alpine, TX 79832, 915-837-8050 (FAX: 915-837-8431). Hours: 8AM-5PM. Records go back to 1924. Alumni Records Office: Box C-187, Alpine, TX 79832 915-837-8059. Degrees granted: Associate; Bachelors; Masters. Adverse incident record source: Public Safety, 915-837-8100.

Attendance and degree information available by phone, FAX, mail. Search requires name only. Other helpful information: social security number, date of birth, approximate years of attendance. No fee for information.

Transcripts available by mail. Search requires name plus signed release. Other helpful information: social security number, date of birth, approximate years of attendance. Fee is $3.00.

Sul Ross State University, **(Branch Campus)**, Registrar, Uvalde Ctr, Uvalde, TX 78801, 512-278-3339. Hours: 8AM-5PM. Alumni records are maintained here at the same phone number. Degrees granted: Bachelors; Masters.

Attendance and degree information available by phone, mail. Search requires name plus social security number. No fee for information.

Transcripts available by written request only. Search requires name plus social security number, signed release. No fee for transcripts.

Sullivan College, Registrar, 3101 Bardstown Rd, Louisville, KY 40205, 502-456-6504 (FAX: 502-454-4880). Hours: 7:30AM-8PM M-Th; 7:30AM-4:30PM F; 8AM-2PM S. Records go back to 1960s. Degrees granted: Associate; Bachelors.

Attendance and degree information available by phone, FAX, mail. Search requires name plus social security number, approximate years of attendance. Other helpful information: exact years of attendance. No fee for information.

Transcripts available by mail. Search requires name plus social security number, approximate years of attendance, signed release. Other helpful information: exact years of attendance. Fee is $5.00.

Sullivan College, **(Branch)**, Registrar, 2659 Regency Rd, Lexington, KY 40503, 606-276-4357. Records are not housed here. They are located at Sullivan College, Registrar, 3101 Bardstown Rd, Louisville, KY 40205.

Sullivan County Community College, Registrar, PO Box 4002, Loch Sheldrake, NY 12759, 914-434-5750 (FAX: 914-434-4806). Degrees granted: Associate.

Attendance and degree information available by phone, FAX, mail. Search requires name only. Other helpful information: social security number, date of birth. No fee for information.

Transcripts available by FAX, mail. Search requires name plus signed release. Other helpful information: social security number, date of birth. Fee is $3.00.

Major credit cards accepted for payment.

Suomi College, Registrar, 601 Quincy St, Hancock, MI 49930, 906-487-7272 (FAX: 906-487-7509). Hours: 8AM-4:30PM. Records go back to 1896. Alumni records are maintained here also. Call 906-487-7367. Degrees granted: Associate. Adverse incident record source: Dean of Students, 906-487-7370.

Attendance and degree information available by phone, FAX, mail. Search requires name plus social security number, date of birth, approximate years of attendance, signed release. No fee for information.

Transcripts available by FAX, mail. Search requires name plus social security number, date of birth, approximate years of attendance, signed release. Fee is $3.00.

Surry Community College, Dept of Student Services, PO Box 304, Dobson, NC 27017, 910-386-8121 (FAX: 910-386-8951). Hours: 8AM-8PM. Records go back to 1965. Alumni records are maintained here at the same phone number. Degrees granted: Associate.

Attendance and degree information available by phone, FAX, mail. Search requires name plus social security number, approximate years of attendance, signed release. Other helpful information: exact years of attendance. No fee for information.

Transcripts available by written request only. Search requires name plus social security number, signed release. No fee for transcripts.

Susquehanna University, Office of the Registrar, Selinsgrove, PA 17870, 717-372-4109 (FAX: 717-372-2722). Hours: 8:15AM-Noon, 1-4:30PM. Records go back to 1950. Alumni records are maintained here also. Call 717-372-4115. Degrees granted: Bachelors.

Attendance and degree information available by phone, FAX, mail. Search requires name only. Other helpful information: social security number, approximate years of attendance. No fee for information.

Transcripts available by FAX, mail. Search requires name plus social security number, signed release. Other helpful information: approximate years of attendance. Fee is $3.00. Expedited service available for $3.00.

Sussex County Community College, Registrar, College Hill, Newton, NJ 07860, 201-300-2215 (FAX: 201-579-5226). Hours: 8AM-8PM M-Th; 8AM-5PM F. Records go back to 1982. Degrees granted: Associate. Adverse incident record source: Dean of Students.

Attendance information available by phone, mail. Search requires name only. No fee for information.

Degree information available by phone, mail. Search requires name only. Other helpful information: approximate years of attendance. No fee for information.

Transcripts available by FAX, mail. Search requires name plus signed release. Other helpful information: social security number, date of birth. No fee for transcripts.

Swarthmore College, Registrar, 500 College Ave, Swarthmore, PA 19081, 215-328-8000. Degrees granted: Bachelors; Masters.

Attendance information available by phone, mail. Search requires name plus approximate years of attendance. Other helpful information: exact years of attendance. No fee for information.

Degree information available by phone, mail. Search requires name plus approximate years of attendance. No fee for information.

Transcripts available by mail. Search requires name plus exact years of attendance, signed release. Fee is $5.00.

Sweet Briar College, Registrar, Sweet Briar, VA 24595, 804-381-6179. Hours: 8AM-5PM. Records go back to 1901. Alumni records are maintained here also. Call 804-381-6131. Degrees granted: Bachelors.

Attendance and degree information available by phone, mail. Search requires name plus social security number, exact years of attendance. No fee for information.

Transcripts available by mail. Search requires name plus social security number, exact years of attendance, signed release. Fee is $3.00.

Syracuse University, Registrar, Syracuse, NY 13244, 315-443-1870. Hours: 8:30AM-5PM. Alumni records are maintained here also. Call 315-443-3514. Degrees granted: Bachelors. Adverse incident record source: Student Affairs, 315-443-4263.

Attendance information available by phone, mail. Search requires name plus approximate years of attendance. Other helpful information: social security number. No fee for information.

Degree information available by phone, mail. Search requires name plus social security number, approximate years of attendance, signed release. No fee for information.

Transcripts available by mail. Search requires name plus social security number, approximate years of attendance, signed release. Other helpful information: exact years of attendance. Fee is $3.00.

T

Tabor College, Registrar, 400 S Jefferson St, Hillsboro, KS 67063, 316-947-3121 (FAX: 316-947-2607). Hours: 8AM-5PM. Degrees granted: Associate; Bachelors.
 Attendance and degree information available by phone, FAX, mail. Search requires name only. Other helpful information: social security number, date of birth, approximate years of attendance. No fee for information.
 Transcripts available by FAX, mail. Search requires name plus signed release. Other helpful information: social security number, date of birth, approximate years of attendance. Fee is $2.00.

Tacoma Community College, Registrar, 5900 S 12th St, Tacoma, WA 98465, 206-566-5036. Hours: 8AM-4:30PM. Alumni records are maintained here at the same phone number. Degrees granted: Associate.
 Attendance and degree information available by mail. Search requires name plus social security number, date of birth, exact years of attendance. No fee for information.
 Transcripts available by mail. Search requires name plus social security number, date of birth, exact years of attendance, signed release. Fee is $2.00.

Taft College, Registrar, 29 Emmons Park Dr, Taft, CA 93268, 805-763-4282 (FAX: 805-763-1038). Hours: 8AM-5PM. Records go back to 1922. Degrees granted: Associate.
 Attendance and degree information available by phone, FAX. Search requires name plus social security number, date of birth, approximate years of attendance, signed release. No fee for information.
 Transcripts available by FAX, mail. Search requires name plus social security number, date of birth, approximate years of attendance, signed release. Fee is $1.00. Expedited service available for $5.00.

Tai Hsuan Foundation College of Acupuncture and Herbal Medicine, Registrar, 2600 S King St #206, Honolulu, HI 96826, 808-947-4788 (FAX: 808-947-1152). Hours: 9AM-5PM. Degrees granted: Masters; Doctorate.
 Attendance and degree information available by phone, FAX. Search requires name plus signed release. Other helpful information: social security number, date of birth, approximate years of attendance. No fee for information.
 Transcripts available by phone, FAX, mail. Search requires name plus signed release. Other helpful information: social security number, date of birth, approximate years of attendance. Fee is $15.00.
 Major credit cards accepted for payment.

Talladega College, Registrar, 627 W Battle St, Talladega, AL 35160, 205-761-6219 (FAX: 205-362-2268). Hours: 8AM-5PM. Records go back to 1867. Alumni records are maintained here also. Call 205-362-0206. Degrees granted: Bachelors. Adverse incident record source: Student Activities, 205-362-0206.
 Attendance and degree information available by phone, FAX, mail. Search requires name plus social security number, approximate years of attendance. No fee for information.
 Transcripts available by mail. Search requires name plus social security number, approximate years of attendance, signed release. Fee is $5.00.

Tallahassee Community College, Registrar, 444 Appleyard Dr, Tallahassee, FL 32304-2895, 904-921-2269 (FAX: 904-921-0563). Hours: 8AM-7PM M-Th; 8AM-5PM F. Records go back to 1966. Degrees granted: Associate.
 Attendance and degree information available by phone, FAX, mail. Search requires name only. Other helpful information: social security number. No fee for information.
 Transcripts available by FAX, mail. Search requires name plus signed release. Other helpful information: social security number. No fee for transcripts.

Talmudic College of Florida, Registrar, 1910 Alton Rd, Miami Beach, FL 33139-1507, 305-534-7050 (FAX: 305-534-8444). Hours: 9AM-5:30PM. Degrees granted: Bachelors; Masters; Doctorate; 1st Talmudic Degree.
 Attendance and degree information available by phone, FAX, mail. Search requires name plus social security number, date of birth. Other helpful information: approximate years of attendance. No fee for information.
 Transcripts available by mail. Search requires name plus social security number, date of birth, exact years of attendance, signed release. No fee for transcripts.

Talmudical Academy of New Jersey, Registrar, Rte 524, Adelphia, NJ 07710, 908-431-1600 (FAX: 908-431-3951). Hours: 9AM-5PM. Records go back to 1971. Alumni records are maintained here at the same phone number. Degrees granted: Bachelors.
 Attendance and degree information available by FAX, mail. Search requires name plus social security number, date of birth, signed release. No fee for information.
 Transcripts available by FAX, mail. Search requires name plus social security number, date of birth, signed release. No fee for transcripts.

Talmudical Seminary Oholei Torah, Registrar, 667 Eastern Pkwy, Brooklyn, NY 11213, 718-774-5050. Hours: 9:30AM-5PM. Records go back to 1985.
 Attendance and degree information available by mail. Search requires name plus social security number, approximate years of attendance, signed release. No fee for information.
 Transcripts available by mail. Search requires name plus social security number, approximate years of attendance, signed release. No fee for transcripts.

Talmudical Yeshiva of Philadelphia, Registrar, 6063 Drexel Rd, Philadelphia, PA 19131, 215-477-1000 (FAX: 215-477-5065). Hours: 8AM-5PM.
 Attendance and degree information available by phone, mail. Search requires name plus social security number. No fee for information.
 Transcripts available by mail. Search requires name plus social security number, signed release. No fee for transcripts.

Tampa College, Registrar, 13900 US Hwy 19 N, Clearwater, FL 34624, 813-530-9495 (FAX: 813-524-8017). Hours: 8AM-8PM. Records go back to 1989. Degrees granted: Associate; Bachelors; Masters.
 Attendance information available by mail. Search requires name plus social security number, date of birth, signed release. Other helpful information: approximate years of attendance. No fee for information.
 Degree information available by phone, FAX, mail. Search requires name plus social security number, date of birth, signed

release. Other helpful information: approximate years of attendance. No fee for information.
 Transcripts available by mail. Search requires name plus social security number, date of birth, signed release. Other helpful information: approximate years of attendance. Fee is $3.00.

Tampa College, Registrar, 3319 W Hillsborough Ave, Tampa, FL 33614, 813-879-6000. Records go back to founding date. Degrees granted: Associate; Bachelors; Masters.
 Attendance and degree information available by mail. Search requires name plus social security number, date of birth, signed release. Other helpful information: exact years of attendance. No fee for information.
 Transcripts available by mail. Search requires name plus social security number, date of birth, signed release. Other helpful information: exact years of attendance. Fee is $3.00.
 Include a self addressed stamped envelope with mail request.

Tampa College, **(Branch)**, Registrar, 1200 US Hwy 98 S, Lakeland, FL 33801, 813-686-1444 (FAX: 813-682-1077). Hours: 7:30AM-5PM. Degrees granted: Associate; Bachelors; Masters. Adverse incident record source: Lakeland Police, 813-499-6936.
 Attendance information available by FAX, mail. Search requires name plus social security number, signed release. Other helpful information: date of birth, approximate years of attendance. No fee for information.
 Degree information available by phone, FAX, mail. Search requires name plus social security number, signed release. Other helpful information: date of birth, approximate years of attendance. No fee for information.
 Transcripts available by FAX, mail. Search requires name plus social security number, signed release. Other helpful information: date of birth, approximate years of attendance. Fee is $3.00.

Tampa College, **(Branch)**, Registrar, Sabal Business Ctr, 3924 Coconut Palm Dr, Tampa, FL 33619, 813-621-0041 (FAX: 813-623-5769). Hours: 8:30AM-8PM. Records go back 6 years. Degrees granted: Associate; Bachelors; Masters.
 Attendance and degree information available by phone, FAX, mail. Search requires name plus social security number, approximate years of attendance, signed release. No fee for information.
 Transcripts available by written request only. Search requires name plus social security number, approximate years of attendance, signed release. Fee is $3.00.

Tarleton State University, Registrar, 1297 W Washington St, Tarleton Station, Stephenville, TX 76402, 817-968-9121 (FAX: 817-968-9389). Hours: 8AM-5PM. Degrees granted: Associate; Bachelors; Masters.
 Attendance and degree information available by phone, FAX, mail. Search requires name plus social security number, signed release. Other helpful information: date of birth, approximate years of attendance. No fee for information.
 Transcripts available by mail. Search requires name plus social security number, signed release. Other helpful information: date of birth, approximate years of attendance. Fee is $3.00.
 xTranscripts available by phone with credit card payment. Major credit cards accepted for payment.

Tarrant County Junior College, Dir, Admissions & Records, 1500 Houston St, Fort Worth, TX 76102-6599, 817-882-5291 (FAX: 817-882-5278). Hours: 8AM-5PM. Records go back to 1967. Degrees granted: Associate.
 Attendance and degree information available by FAX, mail. Search requires name plus social security number, signed release. Other helpful information: date of birth. No fee for information.
 Transcripts available by FAX, mail. Search requires name plus social security number, signed release. Other helpful information: date of birth. Fee is $3.00. Expedited service available for $6.00. Major credit cards accepted for payment.

Tarrant County Junior College, **(Northeast Campus)**, Registrar, 828 Harwood Rd, Hurst, TX 76054, 817-788-6965 (FAX: 817-788-6988). Hours: 8AM-7PM M-Th; 8AM-5PM F. Records go back to 1967. Degrees granted: Associate.
 Attendance and degree information available by phone, FAX, mail. Search requires name plus social security number, signed release. Other helpful information: date of birth, approximate years of attendance. No fee for information.
 Transcripts available by mail. Search requires name plus social security number, date of birth, signed release. Other helpful information: approximate years of attendance. Fee is $3.00. Major credit cards accepted for payment.

Tarrant County Junior College, **(Northwest Campus)**, Registrar, 4801 Marine Creek Pkwy, Fort Worth, TX 76179, 817-232-2900. Hours: 8AM-5PM. Records go back to 1976. Degrees granted: Associate.
 Attendance and degree information available by phone, mail. Search requires name plus social security number. No fee for information.
 Transcripts available by written request only. Search requires name plus social security number, signed release. Fee varies.

Tarrant County Junior College, **(South Campus)**, Registrar, 5301 Campus Dr, Fort Worth, TX 76119, 817-531-4501. Hours: 8AM-5PM. Records go back to 1970s. Degrees granted: Associate.
 Attendance and degree information available by phone, mail. Search requires name plus social security number. No fee for information.
 Transcripts available by written request only. Search requires name plus social security number, signed release. Fee varies.

Taylor Business Institute, Registrar, 36 S State St Ste 800, Chicago, IL 60603, 312-236-6400 X32 (FAX: 312-853-0390). Hours: 8:30AM-6PM. Records go back to 1975. Degrees granted: Associate.
 Attendance information available by phone, FAX, mail. Search requires name only. No fee for information.
 Degree information available by FAX, mail. Search requires name only. No fee for information.
 Transcripts available by FAX, mail. Search requires name only. First transcript is free; $2.00 each additional.

Taylor Business Institute, Registrar, One Penn Plaza, Concourse Level, New York, NY 10019-0118, 212-279-0510. Hours: 9AM-5PM. Records go back to 1970. Degrees granted: Associate.
 Attendance and degree information available by mail. Search requires name plus social security number, date of birth, exact years of attendance, signed release. No fee for information.
 Transcripts available by mail. Search requires name plus social security number, date of birth, exact years of attendance, signed release. Fee is $4.00.

Taylor University, Registrar, 500 W Reade Ave, Upland, IN 46989, 317-998-5330/998-5193 (FAX: 317-998-4910). Hours: 8AM-4:30PM. Records go back to 1846. Alumni records are maintained here also. Call 317-998-5115. Degrees granted: Associate; Bachelors.

Attendance information available by phone, FAX, mail. Search requires name plus social security number, approximate years of attendance. Other helpful information: exact years of attendance. No fee for information. Expedited service available for $10.00.

Degree information available by phone, FAX, mail. Search requires name plus social security number, approximate years of attendance. Other helpful information: date of birth, exact years of attendance. No fee for information. Expedite service available for $10.00.

Transcripts available by mail. Search requires name plus social security number, approximate years of attendance, signed release. Other helpful information: date of birth, exact years of attendance. Fee is $4.00. Expedited service available for $10.00.

Taylor University, (Fort Wayne), Registrar, 1025 W Rudisill Blvd, Fort Wayne, IN 46807, 219-456-2211 (FAX: 219-456-2119). Hours: 8AM-5pM. Records go back to 1890. Alumni records are maintained here also. Call 219-456-2211 X3331. Degrees granted: Associate; Bachelors. Adverse incident record source: Student Affairs, 219-456-2211 X3314.

Attendance and degree information available by phone, FAX, mail. Search requires name plus social security number, exact years of attendance. No fee for information.

Transcripts available by FAX, mail. Search requires name plus social security number, exact years of attendance, signed release. No fee for transcripts.

Technical Career Institute, Registrar, 320 W 31st St, New York, NY 10001, 212-594-4000 X270 (FAX: 212-629-3937). Hours: 8:45AM-6:45PM M, 8:45AM-4:45PM W-F. Records go back to 1940. Degrees granted: Associate.

Attendance and degree information available by FAX, mail. Search requires name plus social security number, date of birth, approximate years of attendance, signed release. No fee for information.

Transcripts available by FAX, mail. Search requires name plus social security number, date of birth, approximate years of attendance, signed release. Fee is $3.00.

Include a self addressed stamped envelope with mail request.

Technical College of the Lowcountry, Registrar, 921 S Ribaut Rd, PO Box 1288, Beaufort, SC 29902, 803-525-8210 (FAX: 803-525-8285). Hours: 8:30AM-5PM. Records go back to 1988. Degrees granted: Associate.

Attendance information available by phone, mail. Search requires name plus social security number. Other helpful information: date of birth, approximate years of attendance. No fee for information.

Degree information available by phone. Search requires name only. Other helpful information: social security number. No fee for information.

Transcripts available by written request only. Search requires name plus social security number, signed release. Other helpful information: date of birth, exact years of attendance. No fee for transcripts.

Technological College of the Municipality of San Juan, Registrar, Jose Oliver St, Industrial Park, Hato Rey, PR 00918, 809-250-7111 X271. Hours: 8AM-4PM. Records go back to 1972. Degrees granted: Associate.

Attendance and degree information available by mail. Search requires name plus social security number, signed release. Other helpful information: approximate years of attendance. No fee for information.

Transcripts available by mail. Search requires name plus social security number, signed release. Other helpful information: approximate years of attendance. No fee for transcripts. Expedited service available for $1.00.

Teikyo Marycrest University, Registrar, 1607 W 12th St, Davenport, IA 52804, 319-326-9216 (FAX: 319-326-9250). Hours: 8AM-5PM. Records go back to 1939. Degrees granted: Associate; Bachelors; Masters.

Attendance and degree information available by phone, FAX, mail. Search requires name only. Other helpful information: social security number, date of birth, approximate years of attendance. No fee for information.

Transcripts available by FAX, mail. Search requires name plus signed release. Other helpful information: social security number, date of birth, approximate years of attendance. Fee is $5.00.

Major credit cards accepted for payment.

Teikyo Post University, Registrar, 800 Country Club Rd, Waterbury, CT 06708, 203-596-4619 (FAX: 203-575-9691). Hours: 8AM-8PM M-Th; 8AM-5PM F. Records go back to 1950s. Alumni records are maintained here also. Call 203-546-4605. Degrees granted: Associate; Masters.

Attendance and degree information available by mail. Search requires name plus signed release. Other helpful information: social security number, approximate years of attendance. No fee for information.

Transcripts available by mail. Search requires name plus signed release. Other helpful information: social security number, approximate years of attendance. Fee is $5.00. Expedited service available for $5.00.

Teikyo Westmar University, Registrar, 1002 Third Ave SE, Le Mars, IA 51031, 712-546-2006 (FAX: 712-546-2020). Hours: 8AM-Noon, 1-5PM. Degrees granted: Bachelors. Adverse incident record source: Student Affairs, 712-546-2090.

Attendance and degree information available by phone, FAX, mail. Search requires name only. Other helpful information: social security number, date of birth, approximate years of attendance. No fee for information.

Transcripts available by mail. Search requires name plus signed release. Other helpful information: social security number, date of birth, approximate years of attendance. Fee is $3.00. Expedited service available for $3.00.

Major credit cards accepted for payment.

Telshe Yeshiva-Chicago, Registrar, 3535 W Foster Ave, Chicago, IL 60625, 312-463-7738 (FAX: 312-463-2849). Hours: 8AM-5PM. Records go back to 1960. Degrees granted: Masters.

Attendance and degree information available by mail. Search requires name plus social security number. No fee for information.

Transcripts available by mail. Search requires name plus social security number, signed release. No fee for transcripts.

Temple Junior College, Registrar, 2600 S First St, Temple, TX 76504-7435, 817-773-9961 (FAX: 817-773-5265). Hours: 8AM-4:30PM. Degrees granted: Associate.

Attendance and degree information available by phone, mail. Search requires name plus social security number, exact years of attendance. No fee for information.

Transcripts available by mail. Search requires name plus social security number, exact years of attendance, signed release. Fee is $3.00.

Temple University, Registrar, Broad and Montgomery Sts, Philadelphia, PA 19122, 215-787-1131. Degrees granted: Bachelors; Masters; Doctorate.

Attendance and degree information available by phone, mail. Search requires name plus social security number, exact years of attendance. No fee for information.

Transcripts available by mail. Search requires name plus social security number, exact years of attendance, signed release. Fee is $3.00.

Major credit cards accepted for payment.

Tennessee State University, Registrar's Office, 3500 John Merritt Blvd, Nashville, TN 37209-1561, 615-963-5131 (FAX: 615-963-5108). Hours: 8AM-4:30pm. Records go back to 1912. Alumni records are maintained here also. Call 615-963-5880. Degrees granted: Associate; Bachelors; Masters; Doctorate.

Attendance and degree information available by phone, mail. Search requires name plus social security number, approximate years of attendance, signed release. Other helpful information: date of birth, exact years of attendance. No fee for information.

Transcripts available by mail. Search requires name plus social security number, approximate years of attendance, signed release. Other helpful information: date of birth, exact years of attendance. Fee is $1.00.

Tennessee Technological University, Registrar, Office of Records, Box 5097, Cookeville, TN 38505, 615-372-3317 (FAX: 615-372-6111). Hours: 8AM-4:30PM. Records go back to 1915. Alumni Records Office: Box 5157, Cookeville, TN 38505 615-372-3205. Degrees granted: Associate; Bachelors; Masters; Doctorate. Adverse incident record source: Student Activities, 615-372-3237.

Attendance and degree information available by phone, FAX, mail. Search requires name only. Other helpful information: social security number, date of birth, approximate years of attendance. No fee for information.

Transcripts available by FAX, mail. Search requires name plus signed release. Other helpful information: social security number, date of birth, approximate years of attendance. No fee for transcripts.

Tennessee Temple University, Registrar, 1815 Union Ave, Chattanooga, TN 37404, 615-493-4100. Degrees granted: Associate; Bachelors; Masters.

Attendance information available by phone, FAX, mail. Search requires name plus approximate years of attendance. Other helpful information: exact years of attendance. No fee for information.

Degree information available by phone, FAX, mail. Search requires name plus approximate years of attendance. Other helpful information: social security number, date of birth, exact years of attendance. No fee for information.

Transcripts available by FAX, mail. Search requires name plus social security number, date of birth, approximate years of attendance, signed release. Other helpful information: exact years of attendance. Fee is $5.00.

Tennessee Wesleyan College, Registrar, PO Box 40, Athens, TN 37371, 615-745-7504 X5282 (FAX: 615-744-9968). Hours: 8:30AM-4:30PM. Degrees granted: Bachelors.

Attendance and degree information available by phone, FAX, mail. Search requires name only. Other helpful information: social security number, date of birth. No fee for information.

Transcripts available by FAX, mail. Search requires name plus signed release. Other helpful information: social security number, date of birth. Fee is $2.00.

Terra State Community College, Registrar, 2830 Napoleon Rd, Fremont, OH 43420, 419-334-8400 X333 (FAX: 419-324-3667). Hours: 8AM-5:30PM M-Th, 8AM-4:30PM. Records go back to 1970. Alumni records are maintained here also. Call 419-337-8400 X345. Degrees granted: Associate. Adverse incident record source: Student Services, 419-334-8400 X363.

Attendance and degree information available by phone, FAX, mail. Search requires name plus social security number, approximate years of attendance. No fee for information.

Transcripts available by FAX, mail. Search requires name plus social security number, approximate years of attendance, signed release. Fee is $2.00.

Texarkana College, Registrar, 2500 N Robinson Rd, Texarkana, TX 75599, 903-838-4541. Hours: 8AM-5PM. Records go back to 1927. Degrees granted: Associate.

Attendance and degree information available by FAX, mail. Search requires name plus social security number, approximate years of attendance. No fee for information.

Transcripts available by FAX, mail. Search requires name plus social security number, approximate years of attendance, signed release. Fee is $2.00.

Texas A&M International University, Registrar, One W End Washington St, Laredo, TX 78041, 210-722-8001. Hours: 8AM-4:30PM. Alumni records are maintained here at the same phone number. Degrees granted: Bachelors; Masters.

Attendance and degree information available by phone, mail. Search requires name plus social security number, date of birth, exact years of attendance. No fee for information.

Transcripts available by mail. Search requires name plus social security number, date of birth, exact years of attendance, signed release. Fee is $3.00.

Texas A&M University, Registrar, College Station, TX 77843, 409-845-1003 (FAX: 409-845-0727). Hours: 8AM-5PM. Records go back to 1876. Alumni records are maintained here also. Call 409-845-7514. Degrees granted: Bachelors; Masters; Doctorate.

Attendance and degree information available by phone, FAX, mail. Search requires name plus social security number, date of birth, exact years of attendance. No fee for information.

Transcripts available by FAX, mail. Search requires name plus social security number, date of birth, exact years of attendance, signed release. Fee is $5.00.

Texas A&M University at Galveston, Registrar, PO Box 1675, Galveston, TX 77553, 409-740-4414 (FAX: 409-740-4731). Hours: 8AM-5PM. Records go back to 1983. Official transcripts requested and produced from main campus at College Station. Degrees granted: Bachelors. Special programs- Corps of Cadets, 409-740-4588.

Attendance and degree information available by phone, FAX, mail. Search requires name only. Other helpful information: social

The Sourcebook of College and University Student Records **T**

security number, approximate years of attendance. No fee for information.

School does not provide transcripts. Search requires name plus social security number, signed release. Other helpful information: approximate years of attendance. Fee is $5.00.

Major credit cards accepted for payment.

Texas A&M University-Corpus Christi, Registrar, 6300 Ocean Dr, Corpus Christi, TX 78412, 512-991-6810. Hours: 8AM-4PM. Alumni records are maintained here at the same phone number. Degrees granted: Bachelors; Masters; Doctorate.

Attendance and degree information available by phone, mail. Search requires name plus social security number. No fee for information.

Transcripts available by phone, mail. Search requires name plus social security number, signed release. Fee is $3.00.

Texas A&M University-Kingsville, Registrar, Campus Box 101, Kingsville, TX 78363, 512-595-2111. Hours: 8AM-4PM. Alumni records are maintained here at the same phone number. Degrees granted: Bachelors; Masters; Doctorate.

Attendance and degree information available by phone, mail. Search requires name plus social security number, approximate years of attendance. No fee for information.

Transcripts available by written request only. Search requires name plus social security number, signed release. Fee is $3.00.

Texas Chiropractic College, Registrar, 5912 Spencer Hwy, Pasadena, TX 77505, 713-487-1170 (FAX: 713-487-2009). Hours: 8AM-5PM. Records go back to 1930. Alumni records are maintained here at the same phone number. Degrees granted: Bachelors; Doctorate.

Attendance and degree information available by phone, FAX, mail. Search requires name plus social security number, approximate years of attendance. Other helpful information: date of birth. No fee for information.

Transcripts available by mail. Search requires name plus social security number, date of birth, approximate years of attendance, signed release. Fee is $5.00. Expedited service available for $15.00.

Texas Christian University, Registrar, 2800 S University Dr, Fort Worth, TX 76129, 817-921-7828 (FAX: 817-921-7333). Hours: 8AM-5PM.

Attendance and degree information available by phone, FAX, mail. Search requires name plus approximate years of attendance. Other helpful information: social security number, date of birth, exact years of attendance. No fee for information. Include a stamped envelope.

Transcripts available by written request only. Search requires name plus approximate years of attendance, signed release. Other helpful information: social security number, date of birth, exact years of attendance. Fee is $2.00.

Texas College, Registrar, 2404 N Grand Ave, Tyler, TX 75712, 903-593-8311 X215 (FAX: 903-593-0588). Hours: 8AM-5PM. Records go back to 1900s. Degrees granted: Bachelors.

Attendance and degree information available by written request only. Search requires name plus social security number, date of birth, approximate years of attendance, signed release. No fee for information.

Transcripts available by written request only. Search requires name plus social security number, date of birth, approximate years of attendance, signed release. Fee is $3.00.

Texas Lutheran College, Registrar, 1000 W Court St, Seguin, TX 78155, 210-372-8040 (FAX: 210-372-8096). Hours: 8AM-5PM. Records go back to 1925. Degrees granted: Associate; Bachelors.

Attendance information available by phone, FAX, mail. Search requires name plus social security number, date of birth, exact years of attendance. Other helpful information: approximate years of attendance. No fee for information.

Degree information available by phone, FAX, mail. Search requires name plus social security number, date of birth. Other helpful information: approximate years of attendance. No fee for information.

Transcripts available by FAX, mail. Search requires name plus social security number, date of birth, signed release. Other helpful information: approximate years of attendance. Fee is $5.00. Expedited service available for $5.00.

Texas Southern University, Registrar, 3100 Cleburne St, Houston, TX 77004, 713-527-7080 (FAX: 713-639-1878). Hours: 8AM-5PM. Degrees granted: Bachelors; Masters; Doctorate. Adverse incident record source: TSU Police, 713-527-1000.

Attendance information available by phone, FAX, mail. Search requires name plus social security number, approximate years of attendance, signed release. No fee for information.

Degree information available by phone, FAX, mail. Search requires name plus signed release. Other helpful information: social security number, date of birth, approximate years of attendance. No fee for information.

Transcripts available by mail. Search requires name plus social security number, signed release. Other helpful information: date of birth. Fee is $3.00. Expedited service available for $5.00.

Include a stamped envelope.

Texas Southmost College, Registrar, 80 Fort Brown St, Brownsville, TX 78520, 210-544-8254 (FAX: 210-544-8832). Hours: 7:30AM-7PM M-Th; 7:30AM-1:30PM F. Records go back to 1926. Degrees granted: Associate.

Attendance and degree information available by FAX, mail. Search requires name plus date of birth, signed release. Other helpful information: social security number, approximate years of attendance. No fee for information.

Transcripts available by FAX, mail. Search requires name plus date of birth, signed release. Other helpful information: social security number, approximate years of attendance. Fee is $1.00.

Major credit cards accepted for payment.

Texas State Technical College-Amarillo, Registrar, PO Box 11197, Amarillo, TX 79111, 806-335-2316 X268. Hours: 8AM-5PM. Degrees granted: Associate.

Attendance and degree information available by mail. Search requires name plus social security number, exact years of attendance. No fee for information.

Transcripts available by mail. Search requires name plus social security number, exact years of attendance, signed release. Fee is $2.00.

Texas State Technical College-Harlingen, Registrar, 2424 Boxwood, Harlingen, TX 78550-3697, 210-425-0669 (FAX: 210-425-0698). Hours: 8AM-7PM. Records go back to 1974. Degrees granted: Associate. Adverse incident record source: Dean of Students, 210-425-0612: Security Dept., 210-425-0683

Attendance information available by phone, FAX, mail. Search requires name plus social security number. Other helpful information: exact years of attendance. No fee for information.

319 **DEGREE GRANTING INSTITUTIONS**

Degree information available by phone, mail. Search requires name plus social security number, approximate years of attendance. Other helpful information: exact years of attendance. No fee for information.

Transcripts available by written request only. Search requires name plus social security number, signed release. Other helpful information: approximate years of attendance. Fee is $3.00.

Major credit cards accepted for payment.

Texas State Technical College-Sweetwater, Registrar, 300 College Dr, Sweetwater, TX 79556, 915-235-7377 (FAX: 915-235-7416). Hours: 9AM-5PM. Records go back to founding date. Degrees granted: Associate. Adverse incident record source: Campus Security, 915-235-7400.

Attendance and degree information available by phone, FAX, mail. Search requires name plus signed release. Other helpful information: social security number, approximate years of attendance. No fee for information.

Transcripts available by written request only. Search requires name plus social security number, signed release. Other helpful information: approximate years of attendance. Fee is $3.00. Expedited service available for $3.00.

Written request must precede any release of information.

Texas State Technical College-Waco, Registrar, 3801 Campus Dr, Waco, TX 76705, 817-867-2363 (FAX: 817-867-2250). Hours: 8AM-5PM. Records go back to 1965. Degrees granted: Associate.

Attendance information available by mail. Search requires name plus social security number, signed release. Other helpful information: date of birth, approximate years of attendance. No fee for information.

Degree information available by phone, FAX, mail. Search requires name plus social security number, signed release. Other helpful information: date of birth, approximate years of attendance. No fee for information.

Transcripts available by mail. Search requires name plus social security number, signed release. Other helpful information: date of birth, approximate years of attendance. Fee is $3.00.

Major credit cards accepted for payment.

Texas Tech University Health Sciences Center, Registrar, 3601 Fourth St, Lubbock, TX 79430, 806-743-2300 (FAX: 806-743-3027). Hours: 8AM-5PM. Records go back to 1972. Alumni records are maintained here at the same phone number. Degrees granted: Bachelors; Masters; Doctorate. Certification: EMT.

Attendance information available by phone, FAX, mail. Search requires name only. Other helpful information: social security number, date of birth, approximate years of attendance. No fee for information.

Degree information available by phone, FAX, mail. Search requires name only. Other helpful information: social security number, date of birth, approximate years of attendance. No fee for information.

Transcripts available by mail. Search requires name plus signed release. Other helpful information: social security number, date of birth, approximate years of attendance. Fee is $2.00.

Texas Tech University, Registrar, PO Box 45015, Lubbock, TX 79409-5015, 806-742-1499. Hours: 8AM-5PM. Records go back to 1925. Degrees granted: Bachelors; Masters; Doctorate.

Attendance and degree information available by phone, mail. Search requires name only. Other helpful information: social security number, date of birth, approximate years of attendance. No fee for information.

Transcripts available by mail. Search requires name plus signed release. Other helpful information: social security number, date of birth, approximate years of attendance. Fee is $2.00.

Texas Wesleyan University, Registrar, 1201 Wesleyan St, Fort Worth, TX 76105-1536, 817-531-4414 (FAX: 817-531-4425). Hours: 8AM-5PM. Records go back to 1890s. Alumni records are maintained here at the same phone number. Degrees granted: Bachelors; Masters; Doctorate. Special programs- TX Wesleyan School of Law, 214-579-1071. Adverse incident record source: Dean of Students, 817-531-4859.

Attendance and degree information available by phone, FAX, mail. Search requires name plus social security number. Other helpful information: approximate years of attendance. No fee for information.

Transcripts available by FAX, mail. Search requires name plus social security number, signed release. Other helpful information: approximate years of attendance. Fee is $3.00. Expedited service available for $6.00.

Include a self addressed stamped envelope with mail request. Major credit cards accepted for payment.

Texas Women's University, Registrar, PO Box 425559, Denton, TX 76204, 817-898-3036 (FAX: 817-898-3072). Hours: 8AM-5PM. Records go back to 1901. Alumni Records Office: PO Box 425795, Denton, TX 76204 817-898-2586. Degrees granted: Bachelors; Masters; Doctorate. Adverse incident record source: Public Safety, 817-898-2911.

Attendance and degree information available by phone, FAX, mail. Search requires name plus social security number. Other helpful information: social security number, approximate years of attendance. No fee for information.

Transcripts available by mail. Search requires name plus signed release. Other helpful information: social security number, approximate years of attendance. Fee is $2.00.

Expedite: cost of FedEx.

Thaddeus Stevens State School of Technology, Registrar, 750 E King St, Lancaster, PA 17602, 717-299-7796. Hours: 8AM-4PM. Records go back to 1913. Degrees granted: Associate. Adverse incident record source: Dean of Students.

Attendance information available by phone, mail. Search requires name plus approximate years of attendance. Other helpful information: social security number, exact years of attendance. No fee for information.

Degree information available by phone, mail. Search requires name plus approximate years of attendance. Other helpful information: exact years of attendance. No fee for information.

Transcripts available by mail. Search requires name plus social security number, approximate years of attendance, signed release. Other helpful information: exact years of attendance. No fee for transcripts.

Thiel College, Registrar, 75 College Ave, Greenville, PA 16125, 412-589-2110 (FAX: 412-589-2850). Hours: 8AM-4:30PM. Records go back to 1866. Degrees granted: Associate; Bachelors. Adverse incident record source: Security, 412-589-2222.

Attendance and degree information available by phone, FAX, mail. Search requires name plus signed release. No fee for information.

Transcripts available by FAX, mail. Search requires name plus signed release. Fee is $2.00. Expedited service available for $5.00.

Thomas A. Edison State College, Registrar, 101 W State St, Trenton, NJ 08608-1176, 609-984-1186 (FAX: 609-777-0477). Hours: 8AM-4:30PM. Records go back to 1972. Alumni Records Office: 153 Halsey St 5th Flr, Newark, NJ 07102. Degrees granted: Associate; Bachelors.
Attendance and degree information available by phone, FAX, mail. Search requires name plus social security number. No fee for information.
Transcripts available by FAX, mail. Search requires name plus social security number, signed release. Fee is $5.00.

Thomas Aquinas College, Registrar, 10000 N Ojai Rd, Santa Paula, CA 93060, 805-525-4417 X308 (FAX: 805-525-0620). Hours: 8AM-5PM. Records go back to 1971. Alumni records are maintained here also. Call 805-525-4417. Degrees granted: Bachelors.
Attendance and degree information available by phone, FAX, mail. Search requires name plus social security number, signed release. No fee for information.
Transcripts available by FAX, mail. Search requires name plus social security number, signed release. No fee for transcripts.

Thomas College, Student Services, 1501 Millpond Rd, Thomasville, GA 31792, 912-226-1621 (FAX: 912-226-1653). Hours: 8AM-5PM. Records go back to 1950. Degrees granted: Associate; Bachelors.
Attendance and degree information available by phone, FAX, mail. Search requires name plus social security number, approximate years of attendance. Other helpful information: date of birth. No fee for information.
Transcripts available by FAX, mail. Search requires name plus approximate years of attendance, signed release. Other helpful information: social security number, date of birth. Fee is $3.00.
Major credit cards accepted for payment.

Thomas College, Registrar, 180 W River Rd, Waterville, ME 04901, 207-873-0771 (FAX: 207-877-0114). Hours: 8AM-4:30PM. Records go back to 1920s. Alumni records are maintained here at the same phone number. Degrees granted: Associate; Bachelors; Masters.
Attendance and degree information available by phone, FAX, mail. Search requires name plus social security number. Other helpful information: date of birth, approximate years of attendance. No fee for information.
Transcripts available by FAX, mail. Search requires name plus social security number, signed release. Other helpful information: approximate years of attendance. Fee is $3.00. Expedited service available for $5.00.

Thomas Jefferson University, Registrar, 11th and Walnut Sts, Philadelphia, PA 19107, 215-955-6748. Alumni records are maintained here at the same phone number. Degrees granted: Masters; Doctorate. Special programs- Graduate, 215-955-8982: Allied Health Sciences, 215-955-8893.
Attendance and degree information available by phone, mail. Search requires name plus exact years of attendance. No fee for information.
Transcripts available by mail. Search requires name plus exact years of attendance, signed release. Fee is $5.00.

Thomas M. Cooley Law School, Registrar, 507 Ceasar Chavez Ave, PO Box 13038, Lansing, MI 48901-3038, 517-371-5140. Records go back to 1976. Alumni records are maintained here also. Call 517-371-5140 X584. Adverse incident record source: Dean, 517-371-5140.
Attendance and degree information available by phone, FAX, mail. Search requires name only. Other helpful information: approximate years of attendance. Fee is $3.00.
Transcripts available by mail. Search requires name plus signed release. Other helpful information: approximate years of attendance. Fee is $3.00.
Student number helpful.

Thomas Moore College, Registrar, 333 Thomas More Pkwy, Crestview Hills, KY 41017, 606-344-3380 (FAX: 606-344-3345). Hours: 8:30AM-5PM. Records go back to 1921. Formerly Villa Madonna College (founded 1921). Alumni records are maintained here also. Call 606-344-3346. Degrees granted: Associate; Bachelors. Special programs- TAP Program, 606-341-4554. Adverse incident record source: Student Life, 606-344-3317.
Attendance and degree information available by mail. Search requires name plus social security number, date of birth, approximate years of attendance. Other helpful information: exact years of attendance. No fee for information.
Transcripts available by mail. Search requires name plus social security number, date of birth, approximate years of attendance, signed release. Other helpful information: exact years of attendance. Transcript fee is $3.00; $1.00 each additional on same order.
Inquiry policy may be changing.

Thomas Nelson Community College, Records Office, PO Box 9407, Hampton, VA 23670, 804-825-2843 (FAX: 804-825-2763). Hours: 8AM-7PM M-Th; 8AM-5PM F; 8AM-12:30PM Summer. Records go back to founding date. Degrees granted: Associate.
Attendance and degree information available by phone, FAX, mail. Search requires name plus social security number, approximate years of attendance. Other helpful information: exact years of attendance. No fee for information.
Transcripts available by FAX, mail. Search requires name plus social security number, approximate years of attendance, signed release. Other helpful information: exact years of attendance. No fee for transcripts.

Three Rivers Community College, Registrar, 2080 Three Rivers Blvd, Poplar Bluff, MO 63901, 314-840-9665 (FAX: 314-840-9604). Hours: 8AM-4PM. Records go back to 1967. Degrees granted: Associate.
Attendance information available by phone, FAX, mail. Search requires name plus social security number, signed release. Other helpful information: date of birth, exact years of attendance. No fee for information.
Degree information available by FAX, mail. Search requires name plus social security number, signed release. Other helpful information: date of birth, exact years of attendance. No fee for information.
Transcripts available by FAX. Search requires name plus social security number, signed release. Other helpful information: date of birth, exact years of attendance. Fee is $3.00.

Three Rivers Community-Technical College, Registrar, PO Box 629, Mahan Dr, Norwich, CT 06360, 203-823-2843 (FAX: 203-886-0691). Hours: 8:30AM-4:30PM. Degrees granted:

Associate. Adverse incident record source: Dean's Office, 203-823-2828

Attendance and degree information available by FAX, mail. Search requires name plus signed release. Other helpful information: social security number, date of birth, approximate years of attendance. No fee for information.

Transcripts available by FAX, mail. Search requires name plus signed release. Other helpful information: social security number, date of birth, approximate years of attendance. No fee for transcripts.

Three Rivers Community-Technical College, (Thames), Registrar, 574 New London Tpke, Norwich, CT 06360, 203-885-2301 (FAX: 203-886-4960). Hours: 8AM-4PM. Records go back 30 years. Alumni Records Office: Mahan Drive, Norwich, CT 06360. Degrees granted: Associate.

Attendance information available by FAX, mail. Search requires name plus social security number, signed release. Other helpful information: date of birth, approximate years of attendance. No fee for information.

Degree information available by phone, FAX, mail. Search requires name plus social security number, signed release. Other helpful information: date of birth, approximate years of attendance. No fee for information.

Transcripts available by FAX, mail. Search requires name plus social security number, signed release. Other helpful information: date of birth, approximate years of attendance. No fee for transcripts.

Tidewater Community College, Registrar, 7000 College Dr, Portsmouth, VA 23703, 804-484-2121. Hours: 9AM-6PM. Records go back to 1968. Alumni records are maintained here at the same phone number. Degrees granted: Associate.

Attendance and degree information available by mail. Search requires name plus social security number, signed release. No fee for information.

Transcripts available by mail. Search requires name plus social security number, signed release. No fee for transcripts.

Tiffin University, Registrar, 155 Miami St, Tiffin, OH 44883, 419-447-6442 X216 (FAX: 419-447-9605). Hours: 8AM-5PM. Records go back to 1924. Degrees granted: Associate; Bachelors; Masters. Adverse incident record source: Dean, 419-447-6442.

Attendance and degree information available by phone, FAX, mail. Search requires name plus social security number, approximate years of attendance. No fee for information.

Transcripts available by mail. Search requires name plus social security number, approximate years of attendance, signed release. Fee is $2.00.

Titusville Campus, Registrar, 504 E Main St, Titusville, PA 16354, 814-827-4482 (FAX: 814-827-4448). Hours: 8:30AM-5PM. Records go back to 1969. Degrees granted: Associate. Adverse incident record source: Student Affairs, 814-827-4460.

Attendance information available by phone, FAX, mail. Search requires name only. Other helpful information: social security number, approximate years of attendance. No fee for information.

Degree information available by phone, FAX, mail. Search requires name only. Other helpful information: social security number. No fee for information.

Transcripts available by mail. Search requires name plus signed release. Other helpful information: social security number, approximate years of attendance. Fee is $3.00.

Toccoa Falls College, Registrar's Office, PO Box 800896, Toccoa Falls, GA 30598, 706-886-6831 X5330 (FAX: 706-886-6412). Hours: 8:30AM-5PM. Records go back 84 years. Alumni Records Office: PO Box 800809, Toccoa Falls, GA 30598 706-886-6831 X5222. Degrees granted: Associate; Bachelors. Adverse incident record source: Student Affairs.

Attendance and degree information available by phone, FAX, mail. Search requires name only. Other helpful information: social security number, date of birth, approximate years of attendance. No fee for information.

Transcripts available by FAX, mail. Search requires name plus signed release. Other helpful information: social security number, date of birth, approximate years of attendance. Fee is $3.00.

Tomball College, Registrar, 30555 Tomball Pkwy, Tomball, TX 77375-4036, 713-351-3310 (FAX: 713-351-3384). Hours: 8AM-9:30PM M-Th; 8AM-4:30PM F. Degrees granted: Associate. Adverse incident record source: Student Services.

Attendance and degree information available by phone, mail. Search requires name plus social security number, signed release. No fee for information.

Transcripts available by phone, mail. Search requires name plus social security number, signed release. No fee for transcripts.

Tompkins Cortland Community College, Registrar, PO Box 139, 170 North St, Dryden, NY 13053, 607-844-3211 X4301 (FAX: 607-844-9665). Hours: 8:30AM-4PM. Records go back to 1968. Alumni records are maintained here also. Call 607-844-8211 X4366. Degrees granted: Associate. Adverse incident record source: Dean of Students.

Attendance information available by mail. Search requires name plus social security number, signed release. Other helpful information: date of birth, approximate years of attendance. No fee for information.

Degree information available by phone, mail. Search requires name plus social security number. Other helpful information: date of birth, approximate years of attendance. No fee for information.

Transcripts available by mail. Search requires name plus social security number, signed release. Other helpful information: date of birth, approximate years of attendance. Fee is $4.00. Expedited service available for $15.00.

Torah Temimah Talmudical Seminary, Registrar, 555 Ocean Pkwy, Brooklyn, NY 11218, 718-438-9860 (FAX: 718-438-5779). Degrees granted: Bachelors.

Attendance and degree information available by mail. Search requires name plus social security number, date of birth, exact years of attendance, signed release. No fee for information.

Transcripts available by mail. Search requires name plus social security number, date of birth, exact years of attendance, signed release. Fee is $2.00.

Tougaloo College, Registrar, 500 W County Line Rd, Tougaloo, MS 39174, 601-977-7700. Hours: 8AM-5PM. Records go back to 1869. Degrees granted: Associate; Bachelors.

Attendance information available by phone, FAX, mail. Search requires name only. Other helpful information: social security number, date of birth, approximate years of attendance. No fee for information.

Degree information available by phone, mail. Search requires name only. Other helpful information: social security number, date of birth, approximate years of attendance. No fee for information.

The Sourcebook of College and University Student Records

Transcripts available by written request only. Search requires name plus signed release. Other helpful information: social security number, date of birth, approximate years of attendance. No fee for transcripts.

Touro College, Registrar, Empire State Bldg Ste 5122, 350 Fifth Ave, New York, NY 10118, 212-463-0400 X611 (FAX: 212-627-9542). Records are not housed here. They are located at Touro College, Registrar, 844 6th Ave, New York, NY 10001.

Touro College, Registrar, 844 6th Ave, New York, NY 10001, 212-463-0400 X634 (FAX: 212-627-9542). Hours: 8AM-5PM. Records go back to 1971. Alumni Records Office: Touro College, 350 Fifth Ave, Empire State Bldg Ste 5122, New York, NY 10118. Degrees granted: Bachelors.
 Attendance and degree information available by phone, FAX, mail. Search requires name plus social security number, date of birth, exact years of attendance. No fee for information.
 Transcripts available by FAX, mail. Search requires name plus social security number, date of birth, exact years of attendance, signed release. Fee is $10.00.
 Major credit cards accepted for payment.

Touro College, **(Huntington Branch)**, Registrar, 300 Nassau Rd, Huntington, NY 11743, 516-421-2244. Hours: 9AM-7PM M-Th, 9AM-3PM F. Records go back to 1980. Alumni records are maintained here also. Call 516-421-2244 X315. Degrees granted: Masters; Doctorate. Adverse incident record source: Student Affairs, 516-421-2244.
 Attendance information available by phone, mail. Search requires name plus social security number. No fee for information.
 Degree information available by mail. Search requires name plus social security number, exact years of attendance. No fee for information.
 Transcripts available by mail. Search requires name plus social security number, exact years of attendance, signed release. Fee is $5.00.
 Proper letterhead required when confirming degree.

Towson State University, Records Office, 8000 York Rd, Towson, MD 21204, 410-830-3240 (FAX: 410-830-3443). Hours: 8:30AM-4:30PM. Records go back to 1920. Degrees granted: Bachelors; Masters. Adverse incident record source: Student Services.
 Attendance information available by phone, FAX, mail. Search requires name plus social security number, signed release. No fee for information.
 Degree information available by phone, FAX, mail. Search requires name plus social security number. Other helpful information: approximate years of attendance. No fee for information.
 Transcripts available by FAX, mail. Search requires name plus social security number, signed release. Other helpful information: approximate years of attendance. No fee for transcripts. Expedited service available for $10.00.
 Major credit cards accepted for payment.

Traditional Acupuncture Institute, Registrar, American City Bldg Ste 100, 10227 Wincopin Cir, Columbia, MD 21044, 410-997-4888/997-3770. Hours: 8AM-5PM. Records go back to 1981. Degrees granted: Masters.
 Attendance and degree information available by mail. Search requires name plus social security number, date of birth, exact years of attendance, signed release. No fee for information.

Transcripts available by mail. Search requires name plus social security number, date of birth, exact years of attendance, signed release. Fee is $5.00.

Transylvania University, Registrar, 300 N Broadway, Lexington, KY 40508, 606-233-8116. Hours: 8AM-5PM. Records go back to 1900. Alumni records are maintained here also. Call 606-233-8275. Degrees granted: Bachelors.
 Attendance information available by mail. Search requires name plus social security number. No fee for information.
 Degree information available by phone, mail. Search requires name plus social security number. No fee for information.
 Transcripts available by mail. Search requires name plus social security number. Fee is $3.00.

Treasure Valley Community College, Registrar, 650 College Blvd, Ontario, OR 97914, 503-889-6493 X234 (FAX: 503-881-2721). Hours: 8AM-5PM M-Th summer hours. Records go back to 1962. Degrees granted: Associate. Adverse incident record source: Dean, 503-889-6493.
 Attendance and degree information available by FAX, mail. Search requires name plus social security number, date of birth, approximate years of attendance, signed release. No fee for information.
 Transcripts available by mail. Search requires name plus social security number, date of birth, approximate years of attendance, signed release. Fee is $2.00.

Trenholm State Technical College, Registrar, 1225 Air Base Blvd, Montgomery, AL 36108, 334-832-9000 (FAX: 334-832-9777). Hours: 8AM-5PM. Records go back to 1966. Degrees granted: Associate.
 Attendance information available by phone, mail. Search requires name plus social security number, signed release. Other helpful information: date of birth, approximate years of attendance. No fee for information.
 Degree information available by mail. Search requires name plus social security number, signed release. Other helpful information: date of birth, approximate years of attendance. No fee for information.
 Transcripts available by mail. Search requires name plus social security number, signed release. Other helpful information: date of birth, approximate years of attendance. No fee for transcripts.

Trenton State College, Registrar, Hollywood Lakes, CN 4700, Trenton, NJ 08650, 609-771-1855. Hours: 8:30AM-4:30PM. Records go back to 1985. Alumni records are maintained here also. Call 609-771-2393. Degrees granted: Bachelors; Masters.
 Attendance and degree information available by phone, mail. Search requires name plus social security number, approximate years of attendance, signed release. No fee for information.
 Transcripts available by mail. Search requires name plus social security number, approximate years of attendance, signed release. Fee is $5.00.

Trevecca Nazarene College, Registrar, 333 Murfreesboro Rd, Nashville, TN 37210, 615-248-1267 (FAX: 615-248-7799). Hours: 8AM-4:30PM. Alumni records are maintained here also. Call 615-248-1350. Degrees granted: Associate; Bachelors; Masters. Adverse incident record source: Student Services, 615-248-1245.
 School will not confirm attendance information. Search requires name only. No fee for information.

Degree Granting Institutions

Degree information available by phone, FAX, mail. Search requires name only. Other helpful information: social security number, approximate years of attendance. No fee for information.

Transcripts available by FAX, mail. Search requires name plus social security number, signed release. Other helpful information: approximate years of attendance. Fee is $3.00.

Tri-College University, Registrar, 306 Ceres Hall, North Dakota State University, Fargo, ND 58105, 701-231-8170. Records are not housed here. They are located at North Dakota State College of Science, Registrar, 800 N Sixth St, Wahpeton, ND 58076.

Tri-County Community College, Registrar, 2300 Hwy 64 E, Murphy, NC 28906, 704-837-6810 (FAX: 704-837-3266). Hours: 8AM-6:30PM. Records go back 5 years. Degrees granted: Associate.

Attendance and degree information available by phone, FAX, mail. Search requires name plus social security number, signed release. Other helpful information: exact years of attendance. No fee for information.

Transcripts available by phone, FAX, mail. Search requires name plus social security number, signed release. Other helpful information: exact years of attendance. No fee for transcripts.

Tri-County Technical College, Student Records, PO Box 587, Pendleton, SC 29670, 803-646-8361 X2198 (FAX: 803-646-8256). Hours: 8AM-9PM. Records go back to 1961. Degrees granted: Associate.

Attendance information available by phone, FAX, mail. Search requires name only. Other helpful information: social security number, approximate years of attendance. No fee for information.

Degree information available by phone, FAX, mail. Search requires name only. Other helpful information: social security number, date of birth, approximate years of attendance. No fee for information.

Transcripts available by FAX, mail. Search requires name plus signed release. Other helpful information: social security number, date of birth, approximate years of attendance. Fee is $1.00. Expedite fee is based on cost of service.'

Major credit cards accepted for payment.

Tri-State Business Institute, Registrar, 5757 W 26th St, Erie, PA 16506, 814-88-7673. Hours: 8AM-5PM. Records go back to 1984. Degrees granted: Associate.

Attendance and degree information available by phone, mail. Search requires name plus social security number, exact years of attendance. No fee for information.

Transcripts available by mail. Search requires name plus social security number, exact years of attendance, signed release. Fee is $3.00.

Tri-State University, Registrar, Angola, IN 46703, 219-665-4240 (FAX: 219-665-4292). Hours: 8AM-5PM. Records go back to 1900. Degrees granted: Associate; Bachelors.

Attendance and degree information available by phone, FAX, mail. Search requires name only. Other helpful information: social security number, date of birth, approximate years of attendance. No fee for information.

Transcripts available by FAX, mail. Search requires name plus approximate years of attendance, signed release. Other helpful information: social security number, date of birth, exact years of attendance. Fee is $3.00.

Major credit cards accepted for payment.

Triangle Tech, Registrar, PO Box 551, Du Bois, PA 15801-0551, 814-371-2090. Hours: 8AM-5PM. Records go back to 1944. Alumni records are maintained here at the same phone number. Degrees granted: Associate.

Attendance and degree information available by phone, mail. Search requires name plus social security number, date of birth, exact years of attendance. No fee for information.

Transcripts available by mail. Search requires name plus social security number, date of birth, exact years of attendance, signed release. Fee is $2.00.

Need to know program of study.

Triangle Tech, Registrar, 2000 Liberty St, Erie, PA 16502-9987, 814-453-6016. Hours: 8AM-5PM. Alumni Records Office: 1940 Perrysville Ave, Pittsburgh, PA 15214-3897. Degrees granted: Associate.

Attendance and degree information available by mail. Search requires name plus social security number, exact years of attendance, signed release. No fee for information.

Transcripts available by mail. Search requires name plus social security number, exact years of attendance, signed release. Fee is $2.00.

Include a self addressed stamped envelope with mail request.

Triangle Tech, Registrar, 222 E Pittsburgh St, Greensburg, PA 15601-9944, 412-832-1050 (FAX: 412-834-0325). Hours: 7:30AM-4PM. Records go back to 1978. Degrees granted: Associate.

Attendance and degree information available by phone, FAX, mail. Search requires name only. Other helpful information: social security number, approximate years of attendance. No fee for information.

Transcripts available by phone, FAX, mail. Search requires name plus signed release. Other helpful information: social security number, approximate years of attendance. Fee is $2.00.

Major credit cards accepted for payment.

Triangle Tech, (Business Careers Institute), Registrar, 600 Blank School Rd, Greensburg, PA 15601, 412-832-1050 (FAX: 412-834-0325). Hours: 8AM-8PM. Records go back to 1944. Alumni Records Office: 1940 Perrysville Ave, Pittsburgh, PA 15214-3897. Degrees granted: Associate.

Attendance and degree information available by phone, mail. Search requires name plus social security number, exact years of attendance. No fee for information.

Transcripts available by mail. Search requires name plus social security number, exact years of attendance, signed release. Fee is $2.00.

Triangle Tech, (Main), Registrar, 1940 Perrysville Ave, Pittsburgh, PA 15214-3897, 412-359-1000 X197 (FAX: 412-359-1012). Hours: 8AM-5PM. Alumni records are maintained here at the same phone number. Degrees granted: Associate.

Attendance and degree information available by phone, FAX, mail. Search requires name plus social security number, date of birth, exact years of attendance. No fee for information.

Transcripts available by mail. Search requires name plus social security number, date of birth, exact years of attendance, signed release. Fee is $2.00.

Triangle Tech, (Monroeville School of Business), Registrar, 105 Mall Blvd Expo Mart 3rd Fl, Monroeville, PA 15146-2229, 412-856-8040. Hours: 8AM-6PM M-Th, 8AM-4PM F. Records go back to 1989. Degrees granted: Associate.

Attendance and degree information available by phone, mail. Search requires name plus exact years of attendance. No fee for information.

Transcripts available by mail. Search requires name plus exact years of attendance, signed release. Fee is $2.00.

Trident Technical College, Admissions & Records, AM-M, PO Box 118067, Charleston, SC 29423-8067, 803-572-6129 (FAX: 803-569-6483). Hours: 8AM-6:30PM M-Th; 8AM-1PM F. Records go back to 1970s. TTC from 1970's; Berkeley, Charlston, Dorchester Tech to 1950's; Palmer College from 1970's. Degrees granted: Associate. Adverse incident record source: Public Safety, 803-572-6024.

Attendance information available by phone, FAX, mail. Search requires name plus social security number, date of birth, signed release. Other helpful information: approximate years of attendance. No fee for information.

Degree information available by phone, FAX, mail. Search requires name plus social security number, date of birth, approximate years of attendance, signed release. No fee for information.

Transcripts available by FAX, mail. Search requires name plus social security number, date of birth, signed release. Other helpful information: approximate years of attendance. Fee is $1.00.

Trinidad State Junior College, Registrar, 600 Prospect St, Trinidad, CO 81082, 719-846-5621 (FAX: 719-846-5667). Hours: 8AM-5PM. Records go back to 1940. Degrees granted: Associate.

Attendance information available by phone, FAX, mail. Search requires name plus social security number. Other helpful information: date of birth, approximate years of attendance. Fee is $3.00.

Degree information available by phone, FAX, mail. Search requires name plus social security number, signed release. Other helpful information: date of birth, approximate years of attendance. Fee is $3.00.

Transcripts available by written request only. Search requires name plus social security number, signed release. Other helpful information: date of birth, approximate years of attendance. Fee is $3.00.

Major credit cards accepted for payment.

Trinity Bible College, Academic Records Office, 50 S Sixth St, Ellendale, ND 58436, 701-349-3621 X2034 (FAX: 701-349-5443). Hours: 8AM-5PM. Records go back to 1948. Alumni records are maintained here also. Call 701-349-5621 X2036. Degrees granted: Associate; Bachelors.

Attendance information available by phone, FAX, mail. Search requires name plus signed release. No fee for information.

Degree information available by phone, FAX, mail. Search requires name plus signed release. Other helpful information: social security number. No fee for information.

Transcripts available by FAX, mail. Search requires name plus signed release. Fee is $3.00. Expedited service available for $5.00.

Trinity Christian College, Registrar, 6601 W College Dr, Palos Heights, IL 60463, 708-597-3000 (FAX: 708-385-5665). Hours: 8AM-4:30PM. Records go back 36 years. Degrees granted: Bachelors.

Attendance and degree information available by phone, FAX, mail. Search requires name plus approximate years of attendance. Other helpful information: exact years of attendance. No fee for information.

Transcripts available by FAX, mail. Search requires name plus signed release. Fee is $2.00. Expedited service available for $2.00.

Trinity College, Registrar, 300 Summit St, Hartford, CT 06106, 203-297-2118 (FAX: 203-297-2257). Hours: 10AM-Noon, 1-3PM. Records go back to 1910. Alumni records are maintained here also. Call 203-297-2400. Degrees granted: Bachelors; Masters. Adverse incident record source: Dean of Students, 203-297-2156.

Attendance and degree information available by phone, FAX, mail. Search requires name only. Other helpful information: social security number, date of birth, approximate years of attendance. No fee for information.

Transcripts available by FAX, mail. Search requires name plus signed release. Other helpful information: social security number, date of birth, approximate years of attendance. Fee is $2.00.

Trinity College, Registrar, 125 Michigan Ave NE, Washington, DC 20017, 202-939-5031 (FAX: 202-939-5134). Hours: 9AM-5PM. Records go back to 1902. Degrees granted: Bachelors; Masters. Adverse incident record source: Mr. William Merritt, 202-939-5109.

Attendance and degree information available by phone, FAX. Search requires name plus social security number, signed release. Other helpful information: date of birth, approximate years of attendance. No fee for information.

Transcripts available by mail. Search requires name plus social security number, signed release. Other helpful information: date of birth, approximate years of attendance. No fee for transcripts. Expedited service available for $5.00.

Major credit cards accepted for payment.

Trinity College of Vermont, Registrar, 208 Colchester Ave, Burlington, VT 05401, 802-658-0337 X247 (FAX: 802-658-5446). Hours: 8AM-5PM. Records go back to 1925. Alumni records are maintained here at the same phone number. Degrees granted: Bachelors; Masters.

Attendance and degree information available by phone, FAX, mail. Search requires name plus social security number, date of birth. No fee for information.

Transcripts available by FAX, mail. Search requires name plus social security number, date of birth, signed release. No fee for transcripts.

Trinity Episcopal School for Ministry, Registrar, 311 Eleventh St, Ambridge, PA 15003, 412-266-3838 (FAX: 412-266-4617). Hours: 8:30AM-5PM. Records go back 20 years. Degrees granted: Masters; Basic Christian Studies, Aglican Studies.

Attendance and degree information available by phone, FAX, mail. Search requires name only. Other helpful information: approximate years of attendance. No fee for information.

Transcripts available by FAX, mail. Search requires name plus signed release. Other helpful information: approximate years of attendance. No fee for transcripts.

Trinity Evangelical Divinity School, Registrar, 2065 Half Day Dr, Deerfield, IL 60015, 708-317-8050 (FAX: 708-317-8097). Hours: 8AM-5PM. Records go back to 1897. Alumni records are maintained here at the same phone number. Degrees granted: Bachelors; Masters; Doctorate.

Attendance and degree information available by mail. Search requires name plus date of birth, exact years of attendance. No fee for information.

Transcripts available by mail. Search requires name plus date of birth, exact years of attendance, signed release. Fee is $2.00.

Trinity International University, Registrar, 500 NE First Ave, PO Box 019674, Miami, FL 33101-9674, 305-577-4600 X131 (FAX: 305-577-4612). Hours: 8AM-3PM. Degrees granted: Bachelors.

Attendance information available by phone, FAX, mail. Search requires name only. Other helpful information: social security number, date of birth, approximate years of attendance. No fee for information.

Degree information available by phone, FAX, mail. Search requires name plus signed release. Other helpful information: social security number, date of birth, approximate years of attendance. Fee is $2.00. Expedite service available for $2.00.

Transcripts available by FAX, mail. Search requires name only. Other helpful information: social security number, date of birth, approximate years of attendance. Fee is $2.00. Expedited service available for $2,00.

Major credit cards accepted for payment.

Trinity International University, (College of Liberal Arts), Records Office, 2065 Half Day Rd, Deerfield, IL 60015, 708-317-7050 (FAX: 708-317-7081). Hours: 9AM-4PM. Records go back to 1890. Alumni records are maintained here also. Call 708-317-8145. Degrees granted: Bachelors. Special programs- Continuing Education & Extension, 708-317-6550.

Attendance and degree information available by phone, FAX, mail. Search requires name only. Other helpful information: social security number, date of birth, approximate years of attendance. No fee for information.

Transcripts available by mail. Search requires name plus signed release. Other helpful information: social security number, date of birth, approximate years of attendance. Fee is $5.00. Expedited service available for $10.00.

Any former/previous names. Prefer to use their form.

Trinity Lutheran Seminary, Registrar, 2199 E Main St, Columbus, OH 43209-2334, 614-235-4136 (FAX: 614-238-0263). Hours: 8AM-4:30PM. Degrees granted: Masters.

Attendance and degree information available by phone, FAX, mail. Search requires name plus approximate years of attendance. Other helpful information: exact years of attendance. No fee for information.

Transcripts available by FAX, mail. Search requires name plus approximate years of attendance, signed release. Other helpful information: exact years of attendance. No fee for transcripts.

Trinity University, Registrar, 715 Stadium Dr, San Antonio, TX 78212, 210-736-7201 (FAX: 210-736-7206). Hours: 8AM-5PM. Records go back to 1895. Alumni records are maintained here at the same phone number. Degrees granted: Bachelors; Masters.

Attendance information available by phone, FAX, mail. Search requires name plus approximate years of attendance. Other helpful information: social security number, date of birth, exact years of attendance. No fee for information.

Degree information available by phone, FAX, mail. Search requires name plus approximate years of attendance. Other helpful information: social security number, date of birth. No fee for information.

Transcripts available by written request only. Search requires name plus approximate years of attendance, signed release. Other helpful information: social security number, date of birth, exact years of attendance. Fee is $2.00. Expedited service available for $10.00.

Trinity Valley Community College, Registrar, 500 S Prairieville, Athens, TX 75751, 903-675-6200. Degrees granted: Associate.

Attendance and degree information available by phone, FAX, mail. Search requires name only. Other helpful information: social security number, date of birth, approximate years of attendance. No fee for information.

Transcripts available by written request only. Search requires name plus signed release. Other helpful information: social security number, date of birth, approximate years of attendance. Fee is $2.00.

Triton College, Registrar, 2000 Fifth Ave, River Grove, IL 60171, 708-456-0300 X3213 (FAX: 708-456-0049). Hours: 8:30AM-7:30PM M-Th, 8:30AM-4PM F. Records go back to 1969. Degrees granted: Associate. Adverse incident record source: Police Dept, 708-456-0300 X2203.

Attendance and degree information available by phone, FAX, mail. Search requires name plus social security number, date of birth, signed release. No fee for information.

Transcripts available by mail. Search requires name plus social security number, date of birth, signed release. Fee is $2.00.

Trocaire College, Registrar, 110 Red Jacket Pkwy, Buffalo, NY 14220, 716-826-6110 (FAX: 716-826-4704). Hours: 8AM-7PM M-Th, 8AM-4PM F. Records go back to 1960. Alumni records are maintained here also. Call 716-826-1200 X306. Degrees granted: Associate. Adverse incident record source: Registrar, 716-826-1200 X224: Dean, 716-826-1200 X228

Attendance and degree information available by phone, FAX, mail. Search requires name plus date of birth. Other helpful information: social security number, approximate years of attendance. No fee for information.

Transcripts available by FAX, mail. Search requires name plus signed release. Other helpful information: social security number, date of birth, approximate years of attendance. Fee is $3.00. Expedited service available for $3.00.

To confirm attendance must specify which semester. Former names needed for transcript copies. Major credit cards accepted for payment.

Troy State University, University Records, University Ave, Troy, AL 36082, 334-670-3170 (FAX: 334-670-3538). Hours: 8AM-5PM. Records go back to 1887. Degrees granted: Associate; Bachelors; Masters.

Attendance and degree information available by phone, FAX, mail. Search requires name plus social security number, approximate years of attendance. No fee for information.

Transcripts available by written request only. Search requires name plus social security number, approximate years of attendance, signed release. Other helpful information: date of birth. Fee is $3.00.

Troy State University at Dothan, Registrar, PO Box 8368, 3601 US Hwy 231 N, Dothan, AL 36304-0368, 334-983-6556 X229 (FAX: 334-983-6322). Hours: 7:45AM-5:30PM M-Th; 8AM-Noon F. Records go back 14 years. Degrees granted: Associate; Bachelors; Masters.

Attendance and degree information available by phone, FAX, mail. Search requires name plus social security number, signed

release. Other helpful information: date of birth, approximate years of attendance. No fee for information.
 Transcripts available by mail. Search requires name plus social security number, signed release. Other helpful information: date of birth, approximate years of attendance. Fee is $3.00.

Troy State University in Montgomery, Registrar's Office, 231 Montgomery, PO Drawer 4415, Montgomery, AL 36103-4415, 334-241-9511 (FAX: 334-241-9714). Hours: 8AM-5:30PM. Records go back to 1972.
 Attendance and degree information available by phone, FAX, mail. Search requires name only. Other helpful information: social security number, date of birth, approximate years of attendance. No fee for information.
 Transcripts available by mail. Search requires name plus social security number, signed release. Other helpful information: date of birth, approximate years of attendance. Fee is $3.00. Expedited service available for $3.00.
 Major credit cards accepted for payment.

Truckee Meadows Community College, Registrar, 7000 Dandani Blvd, Reno, NV 89512, 702-673-7042 (FAX: 702-673-7028). Hours: 8AM-5PM M,Th,F; 8AM-7PM T,W. Records go back to 1972. Degrees granted: Associate. Adverse incident record source: 702-673-7000.
 Attendance and degree information available by mail. Search requires name plus social security number, signed release. Other helpful information: date of birth, approximate years of attendance. No fee for information.
 Transcripts available by mail. Search requires name plus social security number, signed release. Other helpful information: date of birth, approximate years of attendance. Fee is $2.00. Expedited service available for $2.00.
 Credit cards in person only.

Truett-McConnell College, Registrar, 100 Alumni Dr, Cleveland, GA 30528, 706-865-2134 (FAX: 706-865-5135). Hours: 8AM-4:30PM. Records go back to 1947. Alumni records are maintained here at the same phone number. Degrees granted: Associate.
 Attendance and degree information available by phone, FAX, mail. Search requires name only. Other helpful information: social security number, date of birth, approximate years of attendance. No fee for information.
 Transcripts available by mail. Search requires name plus signed release. Other helpful information: social security number, date of birth, approximate years of attendance. Fee is $3.00. Expedited service available for $5.00.

Trumbull Business College, Registrar, 3200 Ridge Rd, Warren, OH 44484, 216-369-3200 (FAX: 216-369-6792). Hours: 7:30AM-5PM. Records go back to 1972. Degrees granted: Associate.
 Attendance and degree information available by FAX, mail. Search requires name plus social security number, approximate years of attendance, signed release. No fee for information.
 Transcripts available by FAX, mail. Search requires name plus social security number, approximate years of attendance, signed release. Fee is $2.00.

Tufts University, Registrar, Medford, MA 02155, 617-627-3267 (FAX: 617-627-3267). Hours: 9AM-5PM. Records go back to 1856. Degrees granted: Bachelors; Masters; Doctorate.

Attendance and degree information available by phone, mail. Search requires name plus social security number, approximate years of attendance, signed release. Other helpful information: date of birth. No fee for information.
 Transcripts available by mail. Search requires name plus social security number, approximate years of attendance, signed release. Other helpful information: date of birth. Fee is $2.00.

Tulane University, Office of the Registrar, 110 Gibson Hall, New Orleans, LA 70118, 504-865-5231 (FAX: 504-865-6760). Hours: 8:30AM-5PM. Degrees granted: Associate; Bachelors; Masters; Doctorate. Special programs- School of Medicine, 504-588-5497: School of Public Health & Tropical Medicine, 504-588-5387.
 Attendance and degree information available by phone, FAX, mail. Search requires name plus approximate years of attendance. Other helpful information: social security number, date of birth, exact years of attendance. No fee for information.
 Transcripts available by FAX, mail. Search requires name plus approximate years of attendance, signed release. Other helpful information: social security number, exact years of attendance. Fee is $3.00. Expedited service available for $5.00.
 Major credit cards accepted for payment.

Tulsa Junior College, **(Metro)**, Registrar's Office, 909 S Boston, Tulsa, OK 74119, 918-631-7226. Hours: 8AM-7PM M-Th, 8AM-5PM F. Records go back to 1970. Degrees granted: Associate. Adverse incident record source: Security, 918-631-7263.
 Attendance information available by mail. Search requires name plus social security number, signed release. No fee for information.
 Degree information available by mail. Search requires name plus social security number, exact years of attendance, signed release. No fee for information.
 Transcripts available by mail. Search requires name plus social security number, exact years of attendance, signed release. No fee for transcripts.

Tunxis Community-Technical College, Registrar, 271 Scott Swamp Rd, Farmington, CT 06032, 203-679-9511 (FAX: 203-676-8906). Hours: 8:30AM-7:30PM. Records go back 25 years. Degrees granted: Associate.
 Attendance information available by FAX, mail. Search requires name plus social security number, date of birth, signed release. Other helpful information: exact years of attendance. No fee for information.
 Degree information available by mail. Search requires name plus social security number, date of birth, signed release. No fee for information.
 Transcripts available by mail. Search requires name plus social security number, date of birth, signed release. Other helpful information: exact years of attendance. No fee for transcripts.

Turtle Mountain Community College, Registrar, PO Box 340, Belcourt, ND 58316-0340, 701-477-5605 (FAX: 701-477-5028). Hours: 8AM-4:30PM. Records go back to 1973. Degrees granted: Associate. Adverse incident record source: Student Support Services.
 Attendance information available by phone, FAX, mail. Search requires name plus social security number, exact years of attendance. Other helpful information: date of birth, approximate years of attendance. No fee for information.

Degree information available by phone, FAX, mail. Search requires name plus social security number. Other helpful information: date of birth, approximate years of attendance. No fee for information.

Transcripts available by FAX, mail. Search requires name plus social security number, signed release. Other helpful information: date of birth, approximate years of attendance. Fee is $2.00.

Tusculum College, Registrar, PO Box 5050, Greeneville, TN 37743, 615-636-7300 (FAX: 615-638-5181). Hours: 8AM-5PM. Records go back to 1900. Degrees granted: Bachelors; Masters. Adverse incident record source: Campus Life, 615-636-7300 X315.

Attendance and degree information available by phone, FAX, mail. Search requires name plus social security number. Other helpful information: date of birth, approximate years of attendance. No fee for information.

Transcripts available by mail. Search requires name plus social security number, signed release. Other helpful information: date of birth, approximate years of attendance. Fee is $2.00. Expedited service available for $10.00.

Tusegee University, Registrar, Tuskegee, AL 36088, 334-727-8507. Hours: 8AM-4:30PM. Records go back to 1814. Alumni records are maintained here also. Call 205-727-8342. Degrees granted: Associate; Bachelors; Masters; Doctorate.

Attendance and degree information available by phone, mail. Search requires name plus social security number, date of birth, approximate years of attendance. No fee for information.

Transcripts available by mail. Search requires name plus social security number, date of birth, approximate years of attendance, signed release. Fee is $2.00. Expedited service available for $5.00.

Tyler Junior College, Registrar, PO Box 9020, Tyler, TX 75711, 903-510-2397 (FAX: 903-510-2634). Hours: 8AM-8PM M-Th; 8AM-5PM F. Records go back to 1926. Alumni records are maintained here also. Call 903-510-2497. Degrees granted: Associate. Adverse incident record source: Campus Safety, 903-510-2258.

Attendance and degree information available by FAX, mail. Search requires name plus social security number. Other helpful information: date of birth, approximate years of attendance. No fee for information.

Transcripts available by FAX, mail. Search requires name plus social security number, signed release. Other helpful information: date of birth, approximate years of attendance. Fee is $1.00. Major credit cards accepted for payment.

U

Ulster County Community College, Registrar, Stone Ridge, NY 12484, 914-687-5075. Hours: 8:30AM-7:30PM M-Th, 8:30AM-4:30PM F. Records go back to 1968. Alumni records are maintained here also. Call 914-687-5261. Degrees granted: Associate. Adverse incident record source: Dean, 914-687-5078.

Attendance information available by phone, mail. Search requires name plus social security number. No fee for information.

Degree information available by phone, mail. Search requires name plus social security number. Other helpful information: approximate years of attendance. No fee for information.

Transcripts available by mail. Search requires name plus social security number, signed release. Other helpful information: approximate years of attendance. Fee is $3.00. Major credit cards accepted for payment.

Umpqua Community College, Registrar, Roseburg, OR 97470, 503-440-4604 (FAX: 503-440-4612). Hours: 8AM-4PM. Records go back to 1964. Degrees granted: Associate.

School will not confirm attendance information. Search requires name only. No fee for information.

Degree information available by written request only. Search requires name only. No fee for information.

Transcripts available by written request only. Search requires name only. Fee is $2.00.

Uniformed Services University of the Health Sciences, Registrar, 4301 Jones Bridge Rd, Bethesda, MD 20814, 301-295-3197 (FAX: 301-295-3545). Hours: 7:30AM-4PM. Records go back to 1976. Alumni records are maintained here also. Call 301-295-3578. Degrees granted: Masters; Doctorate; Graduate Nursing. Special programs- Graduate School of Nursing, 301-295-1989.

Attendance and degree information available by phone, FAX, mail. Search requires name plus social security number. Other helpful information: date of birth, approximate years of attendance. No fee for information.

Transcripts available by FAX, mail. Search requires name plus social security number, signed release. Other helpful information: date of birth, approximate years of attendance. No fee for transcripts.

Union College, Registrar, 310 College St, Barbourville, KY 40906, 606-546-1208 (FAX: 606-546-1217). Hours: 8AM-4:30PM. Records go back to 1870. Alumni records are maintained here also. Call 606-546-1218. Degrees granted: Associate; Bachelors; Masters. Adverse incident record source: Dean of Students, 606-546-1208 X1230.

Attendance and degree information available by phone, FAX, mail. Search requires name plus social security number, approximate years of attendance, signed release. No fee for information.

Transcripts available by FAX, mail. Search requires name plus social security number, approximate years of attendance, signed release. Fee is $3.00.

Union College, Records, 3800 S 48th St, Lincoln, NE 68506, 402-486-2509 (FAX: 402-486-2895). Hours: 8:30AM-Noon, 1-5PM. Records go back to 1933. Degrees granted: Associate; Bachelors.

Attendance and degree information available by phone, FAX, mail. Search requires name only. Other helpful information: social security number, date of birth, approximate years of attendance. No fee for information.

Transcripts available by FAX, mail. Search requires name plus social security number, date of birth, signed release. Other helpful information: approximate years of attendance. Fee is $3.00. Expedited service available for $10.00.

Major credit cards accepted for payment.

Union College, Registrar, Whitaker House, Schenectady, NY 12308, 518-388-6109 (FAX: 518-388-6173). Hours: 8:30AM-5PM. Alumni records are maintained here also. Call 518-370-6000. Degrees granted: Bachelors; Masters; Doctorate. Special programs- Graduate, 518-388-6288.

Attendance and degree information available by phone, FAX, mail. Search requires name plus social security number, exact years of attendance. No fee for information.

Transcripts available by FAX, mail. Search requires name plus social security number, exact years of attendance, signed release. Fee is $2.00.

FAX requests for transcripts must be followed by written request and fee. Former names needed.

Union County College, Registrar, 1033 Springfield Ave, Cranford, NJ 07016, 908-709-7132 (FAX: 908-709-1392). Hours: 8:30AM-4:30PM. Records go back to 1933. Alumni records are maintained here also. Call 908-709-7113. Degrees granted: Associate. Adverse incident record source: Dean of Students, 908-709-7644.

Attendance information available by FAX, mail. Search requires name plus signed release. Other helpful information: social security number, date of birth, approximate years of attendance. No fee for information.

Degree information available by phone, FAX, mail. Search requires name only. Other helpful information: social security number, date of birth, approximate years of attendance. No fee for information.

Transcripts available by written request only. Search requires name plus signed release. Other helpful information: social security number, date of birth, approximate years of attendance. Fee is $4.00. Expedited service available for $4.00.

Major credit cards accepted for payment.

Union County College, (Elizabeth Campus), Registrar, 12 W Jersey St, Elizabeth, NJ 07206, 908-965-6050. Records are not housed here. They are located at Union County College, Registrar, 1033 Springfield Ave, Cranford, NJ 07016.

Union County College, (Plainfield Campus), Registrar, 232 E Second St, Plainfield, NJ 07060, 908-889-8500. Records are not housed here. They are located at Union County College, Registrar, 1033 Springfield Ave, Cranford, NJ 07016.

Union Institute, Registrar, 440 E McMillan St, Cincinnati, OH 45206-1947, 513-861-6400 (FAX: 513-861-0779). Hours: 9AM-5PM. Records go back to 1969. Alumni records are maintained here at the same phone number. Degrees granted: Bachelors; PhD. Adverse incident record source: Dean, 513-861-6400.

Attendance and degree information available by phone, FAX, mail. Search requires name plus social security number. No fee for information.

Transcripts available by mail. Search requires name plus social security number, signed release. Fee is $5.00.

Union Theological Seminary, Registrar, 3041 Broadway, New York, NY 10027, 212-280-1555 (FAX: 212-280-1416). Hours: 9AM-5PM. Records go back to 1935. Alumni records are maintained here also. Call 212-280-1591. Degrees granted: Bachelors; Masters; Doctorate. Special programs- Library (Pre 1935), 212-280-1501. Adverse incident record source: Dean, 212-280-1550.

Attendance and degree information available by phone, FAX, mail. Search requires name plus social security number, exact years of attendance. No fee for information.

Transcripts available by FAX, mail. Search requires name plus social security number, exact years of attendance, signed release. Fee is $3.00.

Union Theological Seminary in Virginia, Registrar, 3401 Brook Rd, Richmond, VA 23227, 804-355-0671 X233. Hours: 8AM-4:30PM. Records go back to 1898. Alumni records are maintained here at the same phone number. Degrees granted: Masters; Doctorate.

Attendance and degree information available by phone, mail. Search requires name plus social security number. No fee for information.

Transcripts available by mail. Search requires name plus social security number, signed release. Fee is $3.00.

Union University, Academic Center, 2447 Hwy 45 By-Pass N, Jackson, TN 38305, 901-661-5040 (FAX: 901-661-5187). Hours: 8AM-5PM. Records go back to 1925. Alumni records are maintained here also. Call 901-661-5208. Degrees granted: Associate; Bachelors; Masters.

Attendance and degree information available by phone, mail. Search requires name only. Other helpful information: social security number, date of birth, approximate years of attendance. No fee for information.

Transcripts available by FAX, mail. Search requires name plus signed release. Other helpful information: social security number, date of birth, approximate years of attendance. Fee is $1.00. Expedited service available for $5.00.

United States Air Force Academy, (Department of the Air Force), HQ USAFA/DFRR, 2354 Fairchild Dr Ste 6D106, USAF Academy, CO 80840-6210, 719-472-3970 (FAX: 719-472-2943). Hours: 7AM-4:30PM. Records go back to 1959. Degrees granted: Bachelors.

Attendance and degree information available by phone, FAX, mail. Search requires name only. Other helpful information: social security number, approximate years of attendance. No fee for information.

Transcripts available by mail. Search requires name plus social security number, signed release. Other helpful information: approximate years of attendance. Fee is $3.50.

Active duty military may FAX requests.

United States Army Command and General Staff College, Registrar, Reynolds Ave, Fort Leavenworth, KS 66027-1352, 913-684-2312 (FAX: 913-684-4648). Hours: 7PM-4:30PM. Records go back to 1881. Degrees granted: Masters.

Attendance and degree information available by phone, FAX, mail. Search requires name plus social security number, approximate years of attendance. Other helpful information: exact years of attendance. No fee for information.

Transcripts available by phone, FAX, mail. Search requires name plus social security number, approximate years of attendance. Other helpful information: exact years of attendance. No fee for transcripts.

United States Coast Guard Academy, Registrar, 15 Mohegan Ave, New London, CT 06320-4195, 203-444-8214 (FAX: 203-444-8216). Hours: 7:30AM-4:30PM. Records go back to 1930. Degrees granted: Bachelors.

Attendance and degree information available by phone, FAX, mail. Search requires name plus approximate years of attendance. No fee for information.

Transcripts available by written request only. Search requires name plus signed release. Other helpful information: approximate years of attendance. Fee is $1.50.

Strong preference for mail request, but will accept FAX.

United States International University, Registrar, 10455 Pomerado Rd, San Diego, CA 92131, 619-635-4580 (FAX: 619-693-8562). Hours: 8AM-5:30PM. Records go back to 1950. Degrees granted: Associate; Bachelors; Masters; Doctorate. Certification: Education.

Attendance information available by phone, FAX, mail. Search requires name plus approximate years of attendance. No fee for information.

Degree information available by phone, FAX, mail. Search requires name only. Other helpful information: approximate years of attendance. No fee for information.

Transcripts available by FAX, mail. Search requires name plus signed release. Other helpful information: date of birth, approximate years of attendance. Fee is $4.00.

United States Merchant Marine Academy, Registrar, Steamboat Rd, Kings Point, NY 11024, 516-773-5000.

United States Military Academy, Graduate Records Branch, Office of the Dean, West Point, NY 10996-5000, 914-938-3708. Hours: 7:45AM-4:30PM. Records go back to 1920. Degrees granted: Bachelors.

Attendance and degree information available by phone, FAX, mail. Search requires name plus signed release. Other helpful information: social security number, date of birth, exact years of attendance. No fee for information.

Transcripts available by mail. Search requires name plus social security number, exact years of attendance, signed release. Fee is $3.50.

United States Naval Academy, Registrar, 589 McNair Rd, Annapolis, MD 21402, 410-293-6389 (FAX: 410-293-2327). Hours: 8AM-4:30PM. Records go back to 1845. Alumni records are maintained here also. Call 410-293-1000. Degrees granted: Bachelors.

Attendance and degree information available by phone, FAX, mail. Search requires name plus social security number, date of birth, exact years of attendance, signed release. No fee for information.

Transcripts available by FAX, mail. Search requires name plus social security number, date of birth, exact years of attendance, signed release. No fee for transcripts.

United States Sports Academy, Registrar, One Academy Dr, Daphne, AL 36526, 334-626-3303 (FAX: 334-626-1149). Hours: 8AM-5PM. Records go back 22 years. Degrees granted: Bachelors; Masters.

Attendance and degree information available by phone, FAX, mail. Search requires name only. Other helpful information: social security number, date of birth. No fee for information.

Transcripts available by FAX, mail. Search requires name plus social security number, signed release. Other helpful information: date of birth, approximate years of attendance. Fee is $5.00. Major credit cards accepted for payment.

United Talmudical Academy, Registrar, 82 Lee Ave, Brooklyn, NY 11211, 718-963-9260. Hours: 9AM-5PM. Records go back to 1985. Alumni records are maintained here at the same phone number.

Attendance and degree information available by mail. Search requires name plus social security number, signed release. No fee for information.

Transcripts available by mail. Search requires name plus social security number, signed release. No fee for transcripts.

United Theological Seminary, Registrar, 1810 Harvard Blvd, Dayton, OH 45406, 513-278-5817 (FAX: 513-278-1218). Hours: 8:30AM-4:30pm. Records go back 122 years. Degrees granted: Masters; Doctorate.

Attendance and degree information available by phone, FAX, mail. Search requires name plus exact years of attendance. Other helpful information: social security number. No fee for information.

Transcripts available by written request only. Search requires name plus signed release. Other helpful information: social security number, exact years of attendance. Fee is $2.00.

United Theological Seminary of the Twin Cities, Registrar, 3000 Fifth St NW, New Brighton, MN 55112, 612-633-4311 (FAX: 612-633-4315). Hours: 8AM-5PM. Records go back 132 years. Degrees granted: Masters; Doctorate.

Attendance and degree information available by phone, FAX, mail. Search requires name only. Other helpful information: social security number, date of birth, approximate years of attendance. No fee for information.

Transcripts available by mail. Search requires name plus signed release. Other helpful information: social security number, date of birth, approximate years of attendance. No fee for transcripts.

United Tribes Technical College, Registrar, 3315 University Dr, Bismarck, ND 58504, 701-255-3285 X216 (FAX: 701-255-7718). Hours: 8AM-5PM. Records go back to 1969. Degrees granted: Associate.

Attendance information available by phone, FAX, mail. Search requires name plus social security number, date of birth, exact years of attendance, signed release. Fee is $2.00.

Degree information available by phone, FAX, mail. Search requires name plus social security number, date of birth, exact years of attendance, signed release. Fee is $2.

Transcripts available by phone, mail. Search requires name plus social security number, date of birth, exact years of attendance, signed release. Fee is $00,2.00.

Unity College, Registrar's Office, HC78 Box 1, Unity, ME 04988, 207-948-3131 X244 (FAX: 207-948-5626). Hours: 8:30AM-5PM. Records go back 30 years. Alumni records are maintained here at the same phone number. Degrees granted: Associate; Bachelors.

Attendance and degree information available by phone, FAX, mail. Search requires name only. Other helpful information: social security number, date of birth, approximate years of attendance. No fee for information.

Transcripts available by mail. Search requires name plus signed release. Other helpful information: social security number, date of birth, approximate years of attendance. Fee is $5.00.

Universidad Adventista de las Antillas, Registrar, PO Box 118, Mayaguez, PR 00681, 809-834-9595 (FAX: 809-834-9597). Hours: 7:30AM-Noon, 1-4PM M-Th; 7:30AM-12:30PM F. Records go back to 1981. Alumni records are maintained here at the same phone number. Degrees granted: Associate; Bachelors.

Attendance and degree information available by FAX, mail. Search requires name plus social security number, date of birth, signed release. Other helpful information: approximate years of attendance. No fee for information.

Transcripts available by mail. Search requires name plus social security number, date of birth, signed release. Other helpful information: approximate years of attendance. Fee is $3.00. Express mail is $3.00 plus expedite fee of $11.00.

Request for transcript should be made by student.

Universidad Metropolitana, Oficina Registraduria, PO Box 21150, San Juan, PR 00928-1150, 809-766-1717 X6548 (FAX: 809-766-1717 X6689). Hours: 8AM-5PM. Records go back to 1980s. Degrees granted: Associate; Bachelors; Masters. Certification: Accounting.

Attendance information available by FAX, mail. Search requires name plus social security number, exact years of attendance, signed release. No fee for information.

Degree information available by FAX, mail. Search requires name plus social security number, date of birth, approximate years of attendance, signed release. Fee is $70.00. Expedite service available for $70.00.

Transcripts available by mail. Search requires name plus social security number, date of birth, approximate years of attendance, signed release. Fee is $3.00. Expedited service available for $3.00. Include a stamped envelope.

Major credit cards accepted for payment.

Universidad Politecnica de Puerto Rico, Registrar, PO Box 2017, Hato Rey, PR 00918, 809-754-8000.

Universidad de Turapo, Registrar, PO Box 30303, Gurabo, PR 00778, 809-743-7979.

University of Akron, Registrar, Akron, OH 44325, 216-972-7844 (FAX: 216-972-7097). Hours: 8AM-5PM. Degrees granted: Associate; Bachelors; Masters; Doctorate.

Attendance and degree information available by phone, FAX, mail. Search requires name plus social security number, date of birth, approximate years of attendance, signed release. No fee for information.

School does not provide transcripts. Search requires name plus social security number, date of birth, approximate years of attendance, signed release. Fee is $4.00. Expedited service available for $10.00.

Include a self addressed stamped envelope with mail request. Major credit cards accepted for payment.

University of Alabama, Records Office, PO Box 870134, Tuscaloosa, AL 35487-0134, 205-348-4886 (FAX: 205-348-8187). Hours: 8AM-Noon, 1-4:45PM. Alumni Records Office: Alumni Hall, The University of Alabama, PO Box 1928, Tuscaloosa, AL 35486. Degrees granted: Bachelors; Masters; Doctorate. Adverse incident record source: Dept of Public Safety, 205-348-5454.

Attendance and degree information available by phone, FAX, mail. Search requires name plus social security number, date of birth. Other helpful information: approximate years of attendance. No fee for information.

Transcripts available by written request only. Search requires name plus social security number, date of birth, signed release. Other helpful information: approximate years of attendance. Fee is $4.00. Expedited service available for $15.50.

Major credit cards accepted for payment.

University of Alabama at Birmingham-Walker College, Registrar, 1411 Indiana Ave, Jasper, AL 35501, 205-387-0511 (FAX: 205-387-5175). Hours: 8AM-4:30PM. Records go back to 1938. Degrees granted: Associate.

Attendance and degree information available by phone. Search requires name plus social security number, signed release. No fee for information.

Transcripts available by phone, mail. Search requires name plus social security number, signed release. Fee is $4.00.

Major credit cards accepted for payment.

University of Alabama in Huntsville, Office of Records, University Center #116, Huntsville, AL 35899, 205-895-6750 (FAX: 205-895-6073). Hours: 8:15AM-5PM. Alumni records are maintained here at the same phone number. Degrees granted: Bachelors; Masters; Doctorate. Adverse incident record source: Student Affairs.

Attendance and degree information available by phone, FAX, mail. Search requires name plus social security number. Other helpful information: date of birth, approximate years of attendance. No fee for information.

Transcripts available by FAX, mail. Search requires name plus social security number, signed release. Other helpful information: date of birth, approximate years of attendance. Fee is $4.00. Expedited service available for $20.00.

Major credit cards accepted for payment.

University of Alaska Anchorage, Enrollment Services, 3211 Providence Dr, Anchorage, AK 99508, 907-786-1480 (FAX: 907-786-4888). Hours: 8AM-6PM. Records go back to 1950s. Alumni records are maintained here also. Call 907-786-1942. Degrees granted: Associate; Bachelors; Masters. Adverse incident record source: Dean of Students, 907-786-1214: Campus Police, 907-786-1120

Attendance information available by phone, FAX, mail. Search requires name plus social security number, date of birth, exact years of attendance. No fee for information.

Degree information available by phone, FAX, mail. Search requires name plus social security number, date of birth. Other helpful information: approximate years of attendance. No fee for information.

Transcripts available by written request only. Search requires name plus social security number, date of birth, approximate years of attendance, signed release. Other helpful information: exact years of attendance. Fee is $4.00. Expedite: $10.00 first copy; $5.00 each additional.

University of Alaska Anchorage, Records Dept., 3211 Providence Dr, Anchorage, AK 99508-8038, 907-786-1480 (FAX: 907-786-4888). Hours: 8AM-4:30PM. Records go back to 1950s. Degrees granted: Associate.

Attendance and degree information available by mail. Search requires name plus social security number, date of birth, signed notarized release. Other helpful information: approximate years of attendance. No fee for information.

Transcripts available by mail. Search requires name plus social security number, date of birth, signed notarized release. Other helpful information: approximate years of attendance. Fee is $4.00.

University of Alaska Fairbanks, Admissions & Records, PO Box 757480, Fairbanks, AK 99775-7480, 907-474-7500 (FAX: 907-474-5379). Hours: 8AM-5PM. Records go back to 1922. Alumni records are maintained here also. Call 907-474-7081. Degrees granted: Associate; Bachelors; Masters; Doctorate. Adverse incident record source: UAF Police, 907-474-5555.

Attendance and degree information available by phone, FAX, mail. Search requires name only. Other helpful information: social security number, date of birth, approximate years of attendance. No fee for information.

Transcripts available by FAX, mail. Search requires name plus signed release. Other helpful information: social security number, date of birth, approximate years of attendance. Fee is $5.00. Expedited service available for $10.00.

Major credit cards accepted for payment.

University of Alaska Fairbanks, (Chukchi), Registrar, PO Box 297, Kotzebue, AK 99752, 907-474-7521 (FAX: 907-474-5379). Records are not housed here. They are located at University of Alaska Fairbanks, Admissions & Records, PO Box 757480, Fairbanks, AK 99775-7480.

University of Alaska Southeast, Registrar, 11120 Glacier Hwy, Juneau, AK 99801, 907-465-6458. Hours: 9AM-5PM. Records go back to 1970s. Alumni records are maintained here also. Call 907-465-6457. Degrees granted: Bachelors; Masters.

Attendance and degree information available by mail. Search requires name plus social security number, date of birth, exact years of attendance, signed release. No fee for information.

Transcripts available by mail. Search requires name plus social security number, date of birth, exact years of attendance, signed release. Fee is $5.00.

University of Alaska Southeast, (Ketchikan), Registrar, Ketchikan, AK 99901, 907-225-6177 (FAX: 907-225-3624). Hours: 8AM-5PM. Records go back to 1980. Degrees granted: Associate. Certification: Welding, Tourism, Accounting, Business Office.

Attendance and degree information available by FAX, mail. Search requires name plus signed release. Other helpful information: social security number, date of birth, approximate years of attendance. No fee for information.

Transcripts available by FAX, mail. Search requires name plus signed release. Other helpful information: social security number, date of birth, approximate years of attendance. Fee is $5.00. Expedited service available for $10.00.

Major credit cards accepted for payment.

University of Alaska Southeast, (Sitka), Registrar, 1332 Seward Ave, Sitka, AK 99835, 907-465-6268 (FAX: 907-465-6365). Records are not housed here. They are located at University of Alaska Southeast, Registrar, 11120 Glacier Hwy, Juneau, AK 99801.

University of Alaska, (Kuskokwim), Registrar, Bethel, AK 99559, 907-543-4562 (FAX: 907-543-4527). Hours: 8AM-5PM. Records go back to 1972. Degrees granted: Associate; Bachelors.

Attendance and degree information available by phone, FAX, mail. Search requires name plus social security number. Other helpful information: date of birth, approximate years of attendance. No fee for information.

Transcripts available by mail. Search requires name plus social security number, signed release. Other helpful information: date of birth, approximate years of attendance. Fee is $3.00.

Major credit cards accepted for payment.

University of Alaska, (Northwest), Registrar, Pouch 400, Nome, AK 99762, 907-474-7521 (FAX: 907-474-5379). Records are not housed here. They are located at University of Alaska Fairbanks, Admissions & Records, PO Box 757480, Fairbanks, AK 99775-7480.

University of Arizona, Registrar, Tucson, AZ 85721, 602-621-3393. Hours: 8AM-5PM. Records go back to 1885. Alumni records are maintained here also. Call 602-621-2211. Degrees granted: Bachelors; Masters; Doctorate. Adverse incident record source: Registrar's Office, 602-621-3393.

Attendance and degree information available by phone, mail. Search requires name plus social security number, date of birth, exact years of attendance. No fee for information.

Transcripts available by mail. Search requires name plus social security number, date of birth, exact years of attendance, signed release. No fee for transcripts.

University of Arkansas at Little Rock, Registrar, 2801 S University Ave, Little Rock, AR 72204, 501-569-3111 (FAX: 501-569-8956). Hours: 8AM-5PM. Records go back to 1950. Degrees granted: Associate; Bachelors; Masters.

Attendance and degree information available by phone, FAX, mail. Search requires name plus social security number, date of birth, approximate years of attendance, signed release. No fee for information.

Transcripts available by mail. Search requires name plus social security number, date of birth, approximate years of attendance, signed release. Fee is $3.00. Include a stamped envelope.

Major credit cards accepted for payment.

University of Arkansas at Monticello, Registrar, Monticello, AR 71656, 501-460-1035 (FAX: 501-460-1935). Hours: 8AM-4:30PM. Records go back to 1950. Degrees granted: Bachelors.

Attendance and degree information available by phone, FAX, mail. Search requires name plus social security number, approximate years of attendance. No fee for information.

Transcripts available by mail. Search requires name plus social security number, approximate years of attendance, signed release. Fee is $2.00.

University of Arkansas at Pine Bluff, Registrar, 1200 N University Dr, Pine Bluff, AR 71601, 501-543-8486 (FAX: 501-543-8014). Hours: 8AM-5PM. Records go back to 1923. Alumni records are maintained here also. Call 501-543-8499. Degrees granted: Associate; Bachelors; Masters.

Attendance and degree information available by phone, FAX, mail. Search requires name plus social security number, approximate years of attendance, signed release. No fee for information.

Transcripts available by FAX, mail. Search requires name plus social security number, approximate years of attendance, signed release. Fee is $3.00. Expedited service available for $6.00.

University of Arkansas for Medical Sciences, Registrar, 4301 W Markham St, Little Rock, AR 72205, 501-686-5000. Hours: 8AM-4:30PM. Alumni records are maintained here also. Call 501-686-5000. Degrees granted: Associate; Bachelors; Masters; Doctorate; PhD, MD, Pharm.

Attendance information available by phone, FAX, mail. Search requires name plus social security number, approximate years of attendance. No fee for information.

Degree information available by phone, FAX, mail. Search requires name plus social security number. No fee for information.

Transcripts available by mail. Search requires name plus social security number, approximate years of attendance, signed release. No fee for transcripts.

University of Arkansas, Fayetteville, Registrar, Silas Hunt Hall, Fayetteville, AR 72701, 501-575-5451 (FAX: 501-575-4651). Hours: 8AM-5PM. Records go back to 1870. Degrees granted: Bachelors; Masters; Doctorate.

Attendance and degree information available by phone, FAX, mail. Search requires name plus signed release. Other helpful information: social security number, date of birth, approximate years of attendance. No fee for information.

Transcripts available by FAX, mail. Search requires name plus signed release. Other helpful information: social security number, date of birth, approximate years of attendance. Fee is $3.00.

University of Baltimore, Registrar, 1420 N Charles St, Baltimore, MD 21201, 410-837-4825. Hours: 8:30AM-8:30PM M-Th, 8:30AM-4:30PM F. Records go back to 1925. Alumni records are maintained here also. Call 410-837-6131. Degrees granted: Bachelors; Masters.

Attendance and degree information available by phone, mail. Search requires name plus social security number, date of birth, exact years of attendance. No fee for information.

Transcripts available by mail. Search requires name plus social security number, date of birth, exact years of attendance, signed release. Fee is $3.00.

University of Bridgeport, Registrar, 380 University Ave, Bridgeport, CT 06601, 203-576-4636 (FAX: 203-576-4941). Hours: 8:30AM-4:30PM. Records go back to 1927. Alumni records are maintained here also. Call 203-576-4508. Degrees granted: Associate; Bachelors; Masters; Doctorate. Certification: rt:Six year certificate.

Attendance and degree information available by phone, FAX, mail. Search requires name plus approximate years of attendance. Other helpful information: social security number, date of birth, exact years of attendance. No fee for information.

Transcripts available by FAX, mail. Search requires name plus approximate years of attendance, signed release. Other helpful information: social security number, date of birth, exact years of attendance. Fee is $5.00. Additional charge for FAX or FedEx.

Transcript copies are FAXed if fee is paid by credit card. Major credit cards accepted for payment.

University of California, Berkeley, Registrar, 123 Sproul Hall, Berkeley, CA 94720, 510-642-4814 (FAX: 510-643-8050). Hours: 8AM-5PM. Records go back to 1902. Degrees granted: Bachelors; Masters; Doctorate. Certification: Teaching Cred. Adverse incident record source: Student Conduct, 510-643-9069.

Attendance and degree information available by phone, FAX, mail. Search requires name plus approximate years of attendance. Other helpful information: social security number, date of birth, exact years of attendance. No fee for information.

Transcripts available by phone, FAX, mail. Search requires name plus approximate years of attendance. Other helpful information: social security number, date of birth, exact years of attendance. Fee is $4.00. Expedited service available for $10.00.

Major credit cards accepted for payment.

University of California, Davis, Office of the Registrar, 124 Mrak Hall, Davis, CA 95616, 916-752-2980 (FAX: 916-752-6906). Hours: 8AM-5PM. Records go back to 1960. Degrees granted: Bachelors; Masters; Doctorate.

Attendance and degree information available by phone, FAX, mail. Search requires name plus social security number, date of birth, signed release. Other helpful information: approximate years of attendance. No fee for information. Include stamped envelope.

School does not provide transcripts.

University of California, Hastings College of the Law, Registrar, 200 McAllister St, San Francisco, CA 94102, 415-565-4613 (FAX: 415-565-4863). Hours: 9AM-3:30PM. Records go back to 1975. Alumni records are maintained here also. Call 415-565-4667. Degrees granted: Doctorate.

Attendance and degree information available by phone, FAX, mail. Search requires name only. Other helpful information: social security number, approximate years of attendance. No fee for information. Expedited service available for $.

Transcripts available by mail. Search requires name plus signed release. Other helpful information: social security number, approximate years of attendance. Fee is $5.00. Expedited service available for $n/a.

University of California, Irvine, Registrar, Irvine, CA 92717-4975, 714-824-6124 (FAX: 714-824-7896). Hours: 8AM-5PM. Records go back to 1965. Degrees granted: Associate; Bachelors; Masters; Doctorate.

Attendance and degree information available by phone, mail. Search requires name plus social security number, date of birth, signed release. Fee is $3.00.

Transcripts available by mail. Search requires name plus social security number, date of birth, signed release. Fee is $3.00.

University of California, Los Angeles, Office of the Registrar, Transcripts, 405 Hilgard Ave, Rm 1105 Murphy House, Los Angeles, CA 90095-1429, 310-825-3801. Hours: 9AM-5PM. Records go back to 1898. Degrees granted: Bachelors; Masters; Doctorate.

Attendance and degree information available by phone, mail. Search requires name plus social security number, date of birth, signed release. Other helpful information: approximate years of attendance. No fee for information. Include stamped envelope.

Transcripts available by mail. Search requires name plus social security number, date of birth, signed release. Other helpful information: approximate years of attendance. Fee is $4.00.

University of California, Riverside, Registrar, Riverside, CA 92521, 909-787-7284 (FAX: 909-787-7368). Hours: 8AM-5PM. Records go back to founding date. Degrees granted: Bachelors; Masters; Doctorate. Certification: EDUC. Special programs-Extension Office, 909-787-7105.

Attendance information available by phone, FAX, mail. Search requires name plus social security number. Other helpful information: date of birth, approximate years of attendance. No fee for information.

Degree information available by phone, FAX, mail. Search requires name plus social security number. Other helpful information: date of birth, approximate years of attendance. No fee for information.

Transcripts available by mail. Search requires name plus social security number, signed release. Other helpful information: date of birth, approximate years of attendance. Fee is $3.00. Expedited service available for $13.00.

University of California, San Diego, Office of the Registrar, 9500 Gilman Dr, La Jolla, CA 92092, 619-534-3144 (FAX: 619-534-5723). Hours: 8AM-4:30PM. Records go back to 1960. Alumni records are maintained here at the same phone number. Degrees granted: Bachelors; Masters; Doctorate; MD. Adverse incident record source: Campus Police, 619-534-4357.

Attendance and degree information available by phone, mail. Search requires name plus social security number. Other helpful information: date of birth, approximate years of attendance. Fee is $4.00.

Transcripts available by FAX, mail. Search requires name plus social security number, date of birth, signed release. Other helpful information: approximate years of attendance. Fee is $4.00. Expedited service available for $10.00.

$10.00 for set of three transcripts.

University of California, San Francisco, Registrar, 513 Parnassus Ave, San Francisco, CA 94143, 415-476-4527. Hours: 8AM-5PM. Records go back to 1920. Alumni records are maintained here also. Call 415-476-1471.

Attendance and degree information available by phone, mail. Search requires name plus social security number, approximate years of attendance, signed release. No fee for information.

Transcripts available by mail. Search requires name only. Fee is $5.00.

University of California, Santa Barbara, Registrar, Santa Barbara, CA 93106, 805-893-4215 (FAX: 805-893-2985). Hours: 8AM-5PM. Records go back to 1900s. Alumni Records Office: 6550 Hollister Ave, Golita, CA 93117. Degrees granted: Bachelors; Masters; PhD.

Attendance and degree information available by phone, FAX, mail. Search requires name plus social security number, date of birth, signed release. No fee for information.

Transcripts available by mail. Search requires name plus social security number, date of birth, signed release. Fee is $5.00.

University of California, Santa Cruz, Registrar, 190 Hahn Student Services, Santa Cruz, CA 95064, 408-459-4412. Hours: 8AM-5PM. Records go back 30 years. Phone number for transcripts is 408-459-2902. Alumni Records Office: Carriage House, Santa Cruz, CA 95064 408-459-2530. Degrees granted: Bachelors; Masters; Doctorate. Certification: Post-Bac. Special programs- University Extension,740 Front St, Santa Cruz, CA 95060.

Attendance information available by mail. Search requires name plus signed release. Other helpful information: social security number, date of birth, approximate years of attendance. No fee for information. Include stamped envelope.

Degree information available by phone, mail. Search requires name plus approximate years of attendance. Other helpful information: social security number, date of birth, exact years of attendance. Fee is $5.00.

Transcripts available by mail. Search requires name plus approximate years of attendance, signed release. Other helpful information: social security number, date of birth, exact years of attendance. Fee is $10.00.

Current phone, college, major helpful. Also $5.00 for written confirmation of degree.

University of Central Arkansas, Registrar, 201 Donaghey Ave, Conway, AR 72035-0001, 501-450-5200 (FAX: 501-450-5734). Hours: 8AM-4:45PM. Records go back to 1908. Alumni records are maintained here also. Call 601-450-3114. Degrees granted: Associate; Bachelors; Masters; Ed. S. Adverse incident record source: Dean of Students, 501-450-3416.

Attendance and degree information available by phone, FAX, mail. Search requires name only. Other helpful information: social security number, date of birth, approximate years of attendance. No fee for information.

Transcripts available by FAX, mail. Search requires name plus signed release. Other helpful information: social security number, date of birth, approximate years of attendance. Fee is $3.00. Expedited service available for $5.00.

University of Central Florida, Registrar, 4000 Central Florida Blvd, PO Box 32816, Orlando, FL 32816, 407-823-2000. Hours: 8AM-5PM. Records go back to 1965. Alumni records are maintained here at the same phone number. Degrees granted: Bachelors; Masters; Doctorate.

Attendance and degree information available by phone, mail. Search requires name plus social security number, exact years of attendance. No fee for information.

Transcripts available by mail. Search requires name plus social security number, exact years of attendance, signed release. Fee is $2.00.

University of Central Oklahoma, Registrar, 100 N University Dr, Bos 158, Edmond, OK 73060, 405-341-2980 X2331 (FAX: 405-341-4964). Hours: 8AM-7:30PM M; 8AM-5PM T-F. Records go back 105 years. Alumni records are maintained here at the same phone number. Degrees granted: Bachelors; Masters. Adverse incident record source: Student Services.

Attendance and degree information available by phone, FAX. Search requires name plus social security number, approximate years of attendance, signed release. Other helpful information: date of birth, exact years of attendance. No fee for information.

Transcripts available by written request only. Search requires name plus social security number, approximate years of attendance, signed release. Other helpful information: date of birth, exact years of attendance. Fee is $3.00. Expedited service available for $2.90.

Credit cards: $25.00 minimum.

University of Central Texas, Records Office, PO Box 1416, Killeen, TX 76540, 817-526-8262 X253 (FAX: 817-526-8403). Hours: 8AM-7PM. Records go back to 1973. Degrees granted: Bachelors; Masters.

Attendance and degree information available by phone, FAX, mail. Search requires name only. Other helpful information: social security number, date of birth, approximate years of attendance. No fee for information.

Transcripts available by mail. Search requires name plus signed release. Other helpful information: social security number, date of birth, approximate years of attendance. Fee is $5.00.

University of Charleston, Registrar, 2300 MacCorkle Ave, Charleston, WV 25304, 304-357-4740. Degrees granted: Associate; Bachelors; Masters. Adverse incident record source: Security, 304-357-4857.

Attendance information available by phone, FAX, mail. Search requires name only. Other helpful information: social security number, date of birth, approximate years of attendance. No fee for information.

Degree information available by phone, FAX, mail. Search requires name only. Other helpful information: social security number, approximate years of attendance. No fee for information.

Transcripts available by mail. Search requires name plus signed release. Other helpful information: social security number, date of birth, approximate years of attendance. Fee is $4.00.

Major credit cards accepted for payment.

University of Chicago, Registrar, 5801 S Ellis Ave, Chicago, IL 60637, 312-702-7879 (FAX: 312-702-3562). Hours: 9AM-4PM. Records go back to 1897. Alumni records are maintained here also. Call 312-702-2150. Degrees granted: Bachelors; Masters.

Attendance and degree information available by phone, FAX, mail. Search requires name plus social security number, date of birth, approximate years of attendance, signed release. No fee for information.

Transcripts available by FAX, mail. Search requires name plus approximate years of attendance, signed release. Fee is $5.00.

University of Cincinnati, Registrar, 2624 Clifton Ave, Cincinnati, OH 45221, 513-556-9900. Hours: 8AM-5PM. Records go back to 1900. Alumni records are maintained here also. Call 513-556-4641 or 4344. Degrees granted: Associate; Bachelors; Masters; Doctorate; Ph.

Attendance and degree information available by phone, mail. Search requires name plus social security number, approximate years of attendance. No fee for information.

Transcripts available by mail. Search requires name plus social security number, approximate years of attendance, signed release. Fee is $4.00.

University of Cincinnati-Clermont College, Registrar, 4200 Clermont College Dr, Batavia, OH 45103, 513-732-5200 (FAX: 513-732-5303). Hours: 9AM-6PM M-Th, 9AM-5PM F. Records go back to 1920. Alumni Records Office: Alumni Association, University of Cincinnati, Alumni Center, PO Box 210024, Cincinnati, OH 45221-0024. Degrees granted: Associate. Adverse incident record source: Business office, 513-732-5200.

Attendance and degree information available by phone, FAX, mail. Search requires name plus social security number, signed release. No fee for information.

Transcripts available by mail. Search requires name plus social security number, signed release. Fee is $4.00.

University of Cincinnati-Raymond Walters College, Registrar, 9555 Plainfield Rd, Cincinnati, OH 45236, 513-745-5600 (FAX: 513-745-5768). Hours: 8AM-7PM M-Th, 8AM-5PM F. Alumni Records Office: Alumni Association, University of Cincinnati, PO Box 210024, Cincinnati, OH 45221-0024. Degrees granted: Associate. Special programs- University of Cincinnati, 513-556-9900.

Attendance and degree information available by phone, FAX, mail. Search requires name plus social security number, date of birth, exact years of attendance, signed release. No fee for information.

Transcripts available by mail. Search requires name plus social security number, date of birth, exact years of attendance, signed release. Fee is $4.00.

University of Colorado Health Sciences Center, Admissions & Records, 4200 E 9th Ave, Box A054, Denver, CO 80262, 303-399-1211 (FAX: 303-270-3358). Hours: 8AM-4:30PM. Alumni Records Office: Alumni Development, Box A065, Denver, CO 80262, 303-270-5271. Degrees granted: Bachelors; Masters; Doctorate.

Attendance and degree information available by phone, FAX, mail. Search requires name only. Other helpful information: social security number, date of birth, approximate years of attendance. No fee for information.

Transcripts available by mail. Search requires name plus social security number, signed release. Other helpful information: date of birth, approximate years of attendance. No fee for transcripts. Expedited service available for $5.00.

University of Colorado at Boulder, Office of the Registrar, Campus Box 68, Boulder, CO 80309, 303-492-6907 (FAX: 303-492-4884). Records go back 100+ years. Alumni Records Office: Campus Box 459, Boulder, CO 80309 303-492-8484. Degrees granted: Bachelors; Masters; Doctorate. Certification: Teacher. Adverse incident record source: Student Conduct, 303-492-5550.

Attendance and degree information available by phone, FAX, mail. Search requires name plus exact years of attendance, signed release. Other helpful information: social security number, date of birth, approximate years of attendance. No fee for information.

Transcripts available by phone, FAX, mail. Search requires name plus signed release. Other helpful information: social security number, date of birth, approximate years of attendance. No fee for transcripts. Expedite: $3.00 to $20.00.

Major credit cards accepted for payment.

University of Colorado at Colorado Springs, Registrar, PO Box 7150, Colorado Springs, CO 80933-7150, 719-593-3361 (FAX: 719-593-3116). Hours: 8AM-7PM M, 8AM-5PM T-F. Records go back 26 years. Degrees granted: Bachelors; Masters; Doctorate.

Attendance information available by FAX, mail. Search requires name plus social security number, date of birth, signed release. Other helpful information: approximate years of attendance. No fee for information.

Degree information available by phone, FAX, mail. Search requires name plus social security number, date of birth. No fee for information.

Transcripts available by FAX, mail. Search requires name plus social security number, date of birth, signed release. Other helpful information: approximate years of attendance. No fee for transcripts. Expedited service available for $5.00.

Major credit cards accepted for payment.

University of Colorado at Denver, Transcript Office, Campus Box 167, PO Box 173364, Denver, CO 80217-3364, 303-556-2389 (FAX: 303-556-4838). Hours: 8AM-5PM. Records go back to 1960. Alumni records are maintained here also. Call 303-556-2549. Degrees granted: Bachelors; Masters; Doctorate.

Attendance and degree information available by phone. Search requires name only. Other helpful information: social security number, date of birth, approximate years of attendance. No fee for information.

Transcripts available by mail. Search requires name plus signed release. Other helpful information: social security number, date of birth, approximate years of attendance. Fee is $5.00. Expedited service available for $15.00.

Major credit cards accepted for payment.

University of Connecticut School of Medicine, Registrar, UCONN School of Medicine, Farmington, CT 06030-1905, 203-679-2153 (FAX: 203-679-1282). Hours: 8AM-5PM. Records go back to 1968. Alumni records are maintained here also. Call 203-679-2819. Degrees granted: Doctorate.

Attendance and degree information available by phone, FAX, mail. Search requires name only. Other helpful information: social security number, date of birth. No fee for information.

Transcripts available by phone, FAX, mail. Search requires name plus signed release. Other helpful information: social security number, date of birth. No fee for transcripts.

Need to know degree awarded.

University of Connecticut, Office of the Registrar, Certifications Office, U-77E, 233 Glenbrook Rd, Wilbur Cross Bldg RM 153, Storrs, CT 06269, 203-486-3328 (FAX: 203-486-4199). Hours: 8:30AM-4:30PM. Records go back to 1900. Degrees granted: Bachelors; Masters; Doctorate. Special programs- School of Law, 203-241-5638: School of Social Work, 203-241-4737: School of Medicine, 203-679-3872: School of Dentistry, 203-679-2175. Adverse incident record source: Alumni Office, 203-486-2240.

Attendance information available by phone, FAX, mail. Search requires name plus approximate years of attendance. Other helpful information: social security number, date of birth, exact years of attendance. No fee for information.

Degree information available by phone, FAX, mail. Search requires name only. Other helpful information: social security number, date of birth, approximate years of attendance. No fee for information.

Transcripts available by mail. Search requires name plus social security number, date of birth, approximate years of attendance, signed release. Fee is $5.00. Expedited service available for $10.00.

University of Dallas, Registrar, 1845 E Northgate Dr, Irving, TX 75061-4799, 214-721-5221. Hours: 8AM-4:30PM. Degrees granted: Bachelors; Masters; Doctorate.

Attendance and degree information available by phone, mail. Search requires name plus social security number. No fee for information.

Transcripts available by mail. Search requires name plus social security number, signed release. Fee is $2.00.

University of Dayton, Registrar, 300 College Park Ave, Dayton, OH 45469, 513-229-4141. Hours: 8:30AM-4:30PM. Records go back 7 years. Alumni Records Office: Alumni Impaired Relations, Alumni House, Dayton, OH 45469-2710. Degrees granted: Bachelors; Masters; Doctorate. Adverse incident record source: Student Development, 513-229-3311.

Attendance and degree information available by phone, mail. Search requires name plus social security number, approximate years of attendance. No fee for information.

Transcripts available by mail. Search requires name plus social security number, approximate years of attendance. Fee is $2.00.

University of Delaware, Office of the Registrar, Student Services Bldg, Newark, DE 19716-6220, 302-831-2131 (FAX: 302-831-3005). Hours: 8AM-5PM. Alumni records are maintained here also. Call 302-831-8741. Degrees granted: Associate; Bachelors; Masters; PhD. Adverse incident record source: Dean of Students, 302-831-2116.

Attendance and degree information available by phone, FAX, mail. Search requires name only. Other helpful information: social security number, date of birth, approximate years of attendance. No fee for information.

Transcripts available by phone, FAX, mail. Search requires name plus signed release. Other helpful information: social security number, date of birth, approximate years of attendance. Fee is $4.00. Expedite: $4.00 plus FedEx.

University of Denver, Registrar, 2199 S University Blvd, Denver, CO 80208, 303-871-3989. Hours: 8AM-4:30PM. Records go back to 1910. Alumni records are maintained here also. Call 303-871-2701. Degrees granted: Bachelors; Masters; Doctorate.

Attendance and degree information available by mail. Search requires name plus social security number, exact years of attendance, signed release. No fee for information.

Transcripts available by mail. Search requires name plus social security number, exact years of attendance, signed release. Fee is $3.00.

University of Detroit Mercy, Registrar, 4001 W NcNichols Rd, PO Box 19900, Detroit, MI 48219, 313-993-3313 (FAX: 313-993-3317). Hours: 8:30AM-5PM. Records go back to 1877. Alumni records are maintained here also. Call 313-993-1250. Degrees granted: Associate; Bachelors; Masters; Doctorate.

Attendance and degree information available by phone, FAX, mail. Search requires name plus social security number, approximate years of attendance. Other helpful information: date of birth, exact years of attendance. No fee for information.

Transcripts available by phone, FAX, mail. Search requires name plus social security number, approximate years of attendance, signed release. Other helpful information: date of birth, exact years of attendance. Fee is $5.00. Expedite fee $10.00 for airborne or express delivery.

FAX and phone requests require credit card. SS# requirement depends on years of attendance. Signed release required unless paying by credit card. Major credit cards accepted for payment.

University of Dubuque, Registrar, 2000 University Ave, Dubuque, IA 52001, 319-589-3126 (FAX: 319-556-8633). Hours: 8AM-5PM. Records go back to founding date. Degrees granted: Associate; Bachelors; Masters; Doctorate.

Attendance and degree information available by phone, FAX, mail. Search requires name plus social security number, approximate years of attendance, signed release. Other helpful information: date of birth. No fee for information.

Transcripts available by FAX, mail. Search requires name plus social security number, approximate years of attendance, signed release. Other helpful information: date of birth. Fee is $5.00. Expedite fee is based on cost of service.'

Major credit cards accepted for payment.

University of Evansville, Registrar, 1800 Lincoln Ave, Evansville, IN 47722, 812-479-2267. Hours: 8AM-5PM. Records go back to 1854. Alumni records are maintained here also. Call 812-479-2000. Degrees granted: Bachelors; Masters. Adverse incident record source: Registrar, 812-479-2267.

Attendance and degree information available by phone, mail. Search requires name plus social security number. No fee for information.

Transcripts available by mail. Search requires name plus social security number, signed release. Fee is $1.00.

University of Findlay, Registrar, 1000 N Main St, Findlay, OH 45840, 419-424-4570 (FAX: 419-424-4822). Hours: 8:30AM-5PM. Records go back to 1983. Alumni records are maintained here also. Call 419-424-4516. Degrees granted: Associate; Bachelors; Masters. Adverse incident record source: Dean, 419-424-4570.

Attendance and degree information available by phone, FAX, mail. Search requires name plus social security number, approximate years of attendance, signed release. No fee for information.

Transcripts available by FAX, mail. Search requires name plus social security number, approximate years of attendance, signed release. Fee is $3.00.

University of Florida, Office of the Registrar, PO Box 114000, Gainesville, FL 32611-4000, 904-392-1374. Hours: 8AM-4:30PM. Records go back to 1800s. Alumni Records Office: 2012 W University Ave, Gainesville, FL 32611. Degrees granted: Associate; Bachelors; Masters; Doctorate; Specialist, Enginee. Adverse incident record source: University Police: Office for Judicial Affairs

Attendance and degree information available by phone, mail. Search requires name plus social security number, date of birth, exact years of attendance. Other helpful information: approximate years of attendance. No fee for information.

Transcripts available by mail. Search requires name plus social security number, date of birth, signed release. Other helpful information: approximate years of attendance. No fee for transcripts.

Will take phone transcript requests in emergency. Written request for confirmation necessary if student requests no release. Signed release for confirming not necessary unless student requests no release.

University of Georgia, Registrar's Office, 105 Academic Bldg, Athens, GA 30602-6113, 706-542-4040 (FAX: 706-542-6578). Hours: 8AM-5PM. Records go back to 1785. Limited records available back to 1785. Alumni records are maintained here at the same phone number. Degrees granted: Associate; Bachelors; Masters; Doctorate. Adverse incident record source: Student Judiciary, 706-542-1131.

Attendance and degree information available by phone, FAX, mail. Search requires name plus social security number. Other helpful information: date of birth, approximate years of attendance. No fee for information.

Transcripts available by FAX, mail. Search requires name plus social security number, signed release. Other helpful information: date of birth, approximate years of attendance. Fee is $2.00. Expedited service available for $6.00.

Confirmation assumes student has no restriction requested.

University of Guam, Registrar, UOG Station, Mangilao, 96923, 671-734-9340.

University of Hartford, Registrar, 200 Bloomfield Ave, West Hartford, CT 06117, 203-768-5589 (FAX: 203-768-4593). Hours: 8:30AM-7:30PM M-Th, 8:30AM-4:30PM F. Records go back to 1950. While the majority of the records date back to the 1950's, there may be records as old as the 1800's. Alumni Records Office: Alumni Relations, 312 Bloomfield Ave, West Hartford, CT 06117. Degrees granted: Associate; Bachelors; Masters; Doctorate; Engineerin. Adverse incident record source: Student Affairs, 203-768-4165.

Attendance and degree information available by phone, FAX, mail. Search requires name plus social security number. Other helpful information: date of birth, approximate years of attendance. No fee for information.

Transcripts available by FAX, mail. Search requires name plus social security number, signed release. Other helpful information: date of birth, approximate years of attendance. Fee is $3.00.

Major credit cards accepted for payment.

University of Hawaii at Hilo, Records Office, 200 W Kawili St, Hilo, HI 96720-4091, 808-933-3385 (FAX: 808-933-3691). Hours: 8AM-4:30PM. Records go back to 1941. Alumni records are maintained here also. Call 808-933-3567. Degrees granted: Bachelors.

Attendance and degree information available by phone, mail. Search requires name plus social security number, signed release. Other helpful information: date of birth, approximate years of attendance. No fee for information.

Transcripts available by mail. Search requires name plus social security number, signed release. Other helpful information: date of birth, approximate years of attendance. Fee is $1.00.

University of Hawaii at Manoa, Registrar, 2444 Dole St, Honolulu, HI 96822, 808-956-8010. Hours: 8:3AM-4:30PM. Records go back to 1907. Alumni records are maintained here also. Call 808-956-7547. Degrees granted: Bachelors; Masters; Doctorate.

Attendance and degree information available by phone, mail. Search requires name plus social security number, date of birth, exact years of attendance. No fee for information.

Transcripts available by mail. Search requires name plus social security number, date of birth, exact years of attendance, signed release. Fee is $3.00.

University of Hawaii at West Oahu, Student Services Office, 96-043 Ala Ike, Pearl City, HI 96782, 808-456-5921 (FAX: 808-456-5009). Hours: 8AM-6PM. Records go back to founding date. Degrees granted: Bachelors.

Attendance and degree information available by phone, FAX, mail. Search requires name only. Other helpful information: social security number, date of birth, approximate years of attendance. No fee for information.

Transcripts available by written request only. Search requires name plus signed release. Other helpful information: social security number, date of birth, approximate years of attendance. Fee is $1.00.

University of Hawaii, (Maui Community College), Registrar, 310 Kaahumanu Ave, Kahului, HI 96732, 808-242-1267 (FAX: 808-244-0268). Hours: 9AM-4:30PM. Records go back to 1931. Degrees granted: Associate.

Attendance and degree information available by FAX, mail. Search requires name plus social security number. No fee for information.

Transcripts available by FAX, mail. Search requires name plus social security number, signed release. Fee is $1.00.

University of Health Sciences, Registrar, 2105 Independence Blvd, Kansas City, MO 64124, 816-221-9698 (FAX: 816-283-2303). Hours: 8AM-4:30PM. Records go back to 1916. Alumni records are maintained here also. Call 816-283-2360. Degrees granted: Bachelors; Masters.

Attendance and degree information available by phone, FAX, mail. Search requires name plus social security number, exact years of attendance, signed release. No fee for information.

Transcripts available by FAX, mail. Search requires name plus social security number, exact years of attendance, signed release. Fee is $5.00.

Major credit cards accepted for payment.

University of Houston, Transcript Office, 4800 Calhoun Blvd, Houston, TX 77204-2161, 713-743-1010 (FAX: 713-743-9050). Hours: 8AM-7PM M,T; 8AM-5PM W-F. Records go back to 1927. Alumni records are maintained here also. Call 713-743-9550. Degrees granted: Bachelors; Masters; Doctorate. Adverse incident record source: Dean of Students, 713-743-5470.

Attendance and degree information available by phone, FAX, mail. Search requires name plus social security number, date of birth. Other helpful information: approximate years of attendance. No fee for information.

Transcripts available by FAX, mail. Search requires name plus social security number, date of birth, signed release. Other helpful information: approximate years of attendance. Fee is $5.00.

University of Houston-Clear Lake, Office of the Registrar-Transcripts, 2700 Bay Area Blvd, Box 13, Houston, TX 77058, 713-283-2534 (FAX: 713-283-2530). Hours: 10AM-7PM M-Th; 8AM-5PM F. Records go back to 1974. Alumni Records Office: Box 43, Houston, TX 77058 713-283-2023. Degrees granted: Bachelors; Masters.

Attendance and degree information available by phone, FAX, mail. Search requires name only. Other helpful information: social security number, date of birth, approximate years of attendance. No fee for information.

Transcripts available by FAX, mail. Search requires name plus signed release. Other helpful information: social security number, date of birth, approximate years of attendance. No fee for transcripts.

University of Houston-Downtown, Registrar, One Main St, Houston, TX 77002, 713-221-8999 (FAX: 713-221-8145). Hours: 8AM-6PM M-Th; 8AM-5PM F. Records go back to 1960. Degrees granted: Bachelors. Adverse incident record source: Student Affairs, 713-221-8100.

Attendance and degree information available by phone, FAX, mail. Search requires name only. Other helpful information: social security number, date of birth, approximate years of attendance. No fee for information.

Transcripts available by mail. Search requires name plus signed release. Other helpful information: social security number, date of birth, approximate years of attendance. Fee is $3.00. Expedited service available for $10.00.

Major credit cards accepted for payment.

University of Houston-Victoria, Registrar, 2506 E Red River, Victoria, TX 77901-4450, 512-788-6222 (FAX: 512-572-9377). Hours: 8AM-5PM. Records go back to 1973. Degrees granted: Bachelors; Masters.

Attendance and degree information available by phone, FAX, mail. Search requires name plus social security number. Other helpful information: date of birth, approximate years of attendance. No fee for information.

Transcripts available by mail. Search requires name plus social security number, signed release. Other helpful information: date of birth, approximate years of attendance. Fee is $4.00. Expedited service available for $10.00.

University of Idaho, Registrar, Moscow, ID 83844, 208-885-6731 (FAX: 208-885-9061). Hours: 8AM-6PM M-Th, 8AM-5PM F. Records go back to 1889. Alumni records are maintained here also. Call 208-885-6154. Degrees granted: Bachelors; Masters; Doctorate.

Attendance and degree information available by phone, FAX, mail. Search requires name plus social security number. No fee for information.

Transcripts available by FAX, mail. Search requires name plus social security number, signed release. Fee is $3.00.

University of Illinois at Chicago, Registrar, PO Box 5220, Chicago, IL 60680, 312-996-4350. Hours: 8:30AM-4:45PM. Records go back to 1936. Alumni records are maintained here at the same phone number. Degrees granted: Bachelors; Masters; Doctorate; MD,DDS,PharmD. Adverse incident record source: University Police, 312-996-2830.

Attendance and degree information available by phone, mail. Search requires name plus social security number. Other helpful information: date of birth, approximate years of attendance. Fee is $4.00.

Transcripts available by mail. Search requires name plus social security number, signed release. Other helpful information: date of birth, approximate years of attendance. Fee is $5.00.

University of Illinois at Urbana-Champaign, Transcript Department, Rm 10 Henry Admin. Bldg, 506 S Wright St, Urbana, IL 61801, 217-333-0210 (FAX: 217-333-3100). Hours: 8:30AM-5PM. Records go back to 1897. Alumni Records Office: 227 Illini Union, 1401 W Green St, Urbana, IL 61801. Degrees granted: Bachelors; Masters; Doctorate.

Attendance information available by phone, FAX, mail. Search requires name only. Other helpful information: social security number, date of birth, approximate years of attendance. Fee is $4.00.

Degree information available by phone, FAX, mail. Search requires name only. Other helpful information: social security number, date of birth, approximate years of attendance. Fee is $4.00.

Transcripts available by FAX, mail. Search requires name plus social security number, date of birth, approximate years of attendance, signed release. Fee is $5.00.

Will not FAX back results. Major credit cards accepted for payment.

University of Indianapolis, Registrar's Office, 1400 E Hanna Ave, Indianapolis, IN 46227, 317-788-3219 (FAX: 317-788-3300). Hours: 7:30AM09PM M-Th; 7:30AM-4:30PM F. Records go back to 1908. Alumni records are maintained here also. Call 317-788-3295. Degrees granted: Associate; Bachelors; Masters.

Attendance and degree information available by phone, FAX, mail. Search requires name only. Other helpful information: social security number, approximate years of attendance. No fee for information.

Transcripts available by written request only. Search requires name plus signed release. Other helpful information: social security number, approximate years of attendance. No fee for transcripts.

University of Iowa, Registrar, 1 Jessup Hall, Iowa City, IA 52242-1316, 319-335-0229 (FAX: 319-335-1999). Hours: 8:30AM-4:30PM. Records go back to 1965. Phone for transcripts is 319-335-0230. Records are on computer or film since 1965. Alumni records are maintained here at the same phone number. Degrees granted: Bachelors; Masters; Doctorate. Adverse incident record source: Campus Security, 319-335-5022.

Attendance and degree information available by phone, FAX, mail. Search requires name only. Other helpful information: social security number, approximate years of attendance. No fee for information. Expedited service available for $5.00.

Transcripts available by phone, FAX, mail. Search requires name plus signed release. Other helpful information: social security number, date of birth, approximate years of attendance. Fee is $3.00. Expedited service available for $14.75.

FAX may be used for request, but not for results. Phone for transcript by student only.

University of Judaism, Registrar, 15600 Mulholland Dr, Los Angeles, CA 90077, 310-476-9777 (FAX: 310-471-1278). Hours: 9AM-3PM. Records go back to 1947. Degrees granted: Bachelors; Masters.

Attendance and degree information available by phone, FAX, mail. Search requires name only. Other helpful information: social security number, approximate years of attendance. No fee for information.

Transcripts available by written request only. Search requires name plus signed release. Other helpful information: social security number, approximate years of attendance. Fee is $4.00.

University of Kansas, Registrar, Lawrence, KS 66045, 913-864-4422. Hours: 8AM-5PM. Records go back to 1860. Alumni records are maintained here also. Call 913-864-4760. Degrees granted: Bachelors; Masters; PhD. Adverse incident record source: Student Life, 913-864-4060.

Attendance information available by mail. Search requires name plus social security number, date of birth, approximate years of attendance, signed release. No fee for information.

Degree information available by phone, mail. Search requires name plus social security number, date of birth, approximate years of attendance, signed release. No fee for information.

Transcripts available by mail. Search requires name plus social security number, date of birth, approximate years of attendance, signed release. Fee is $5.00.

University of Kansas Medical Center, Registrar, 3901 St & Rainbow Blvd, Kansas City, KS 66160-7190, 913-588-4698 (FAX: 913-588-4697). Hours: 8AM-4:30PM. Records go back to 1902. Alumni records are maintained here also. Call 913-588-1255. Degrees granted: Bachelors; Masters; Doctorate.

Attendance and degree information available by phone, FAX, mail. Search requires name plus social security number, date of birth, signed release. No fee for information.

Transcripts available by mail. Search requires name plus social security number, date of birth, signed release. Fee is $5.00.

University of Kentucky, Registrar's Office, 10 Funkhouser Bldg, Lexington, KY 40506-0054, 606-257-3671 (FAX: 606-257-7160). Hours: 8AM-4:30PM. Records go back to 1900. Alumni Records Office: Alumni Association, 125 King, Lexington, KY 40506-0119. Degrees granted: Bachelors; Masters; Doctorate; Juris Doctor, MD, DD. Special programs- Dental School, 606-323-6071: Medical School, 606-323-5261. Adverse incident record source: Dean of Students, 606-257-3754.

Attendance and degree information available by phone, FAX, mail. Search requires name plus social security number. Other helpful information: date of birth, approximate years of attendance. No fee for information.

Transcripts available by FAX, mail. Search requires name plus social security number, signed release. Other helpful information: date of birth, approximate years of attendance. Transcript fee $3.00 for current student, $4.00 for others. Expedited service available for $8.00.

University of La Verne, Registrar, 1950 Third St, La Verne, CA 91750, 909-593-3511 (FAX: 909-593-2703). Hours: 8AM-5PM M,W,F; 8AM-7PM T,Th. Records go back to 1891. Degrees granted: Associate; Bachelors; Masters; Doctorate.

Attendance and degree information available by phone, FAX, mail. Search requires name plus signed release. Other helpful information: social security number, date of birth, approximate years of attendance. No fee for information.

Transcripts available by phone, FAX, mail. Search requires name plus signed release. Other helpful information: social security number, date of birth, approximate years of attendance. Fee is $5.00.

Major credit cards accepted for payment.

University of Louisville, Registrar, 2301 S Third St, Louisville, KY 40292, 502-852-6522 (FAX: 502-852-4776). Hours: 9AM-5PM. Records go back to 1900. Alumni records are maintained here also. Call 502-852-6186. Degrees granted: Bachelors; Masters. Adverse incident record source: Student Life, 502-852-5787.

Attendance and degree information available by phone, FAX, mail. Search requires name plus social security number, date of birth, approximate years of attendance, signed release. No fee for information.

Transcripts available by FAX, mail. Search requires name plus social security number, date of birth, approximate years of attendance, signed release. Transcript fee $4.00 for former students; $2.00 for current students.

University of Maine, Registrar, Orono, ME 04469, 207-581-1290 (FAX: 207-581-1314). Hours: 8AM-4:30PM. Records go back to 1865. Alumni records are maintained here also. Call 207-581-1138. Degrees granted: Associate; Bachelors; Masters; Doctorate. Adverse incident record source: Judicial Affairs, 207-581-1409.

Attendance and degree information available by phone, mail. Search requires name plus social security number, signed release. Other helpful information: date of birth, approximate years of attendance. No fee for information.

Transcripts available by FAX, mail. Search requires name plus social security number, signed release. Other helpful information: date of birth, approximate years of attendance. Fee is $3.00. Expedited service available for $8.00.

Will not send results by FAX.

University of Maine at Augusta, Admission & Records, 46 University Dr, Augusta, ME 04330, 207-621-3079 (FAX: 207-621-3116). Records go back to 1968. Degrees granted: Associate; Bachelors.

Attendance and degree information available by phone, FAX, mail. Search requires name plus social security number, signed release. Other helpful information: approximate years of attendance. No fee for information.

Transcripts available by FAX, mail. Search requires name plus social security number, signed release. Other helpful information: approximate years of attendance. Fee is $3.00. Expedited service available for $5.00.

Major credit cards accepted for payment.

University of Maine at Farmington, Registrar, 86 Main St, Farmington, ME 04938, 207-778-7000. Hours: 8AM-4:30PM. Records go back to 1864. Alumni records are maintained here at the same phone number. Degrees granted: Bachelors.

Attendance and degree information available by phone, mail. Search requires name plus social security number, exact years of attendance. No fee for information.

Transcripts available by mail. Search requires name plus social security number, exact years of attendance, signed release. Fee is $3.00.

University of Maine at Fort Kent, Registrar, Pleasant St, Fort Kent, ME 04743, 207-834-7521 (FAX: 207-834-7503). Hours: 8AM-4:30PM. Records go back to 1878. Alumni records are maintained here also. Call 207-834-7557.

Attendance information available by FAX, mail. Search requires name plus social security number, exact years of attendance. Other helpful information: date of birth. No fee for information.

Degree information available by FAX, mail. Search requires name plus social security number. Other helpful information: date of birth, exact years of attendance. No fee for information.

Transcripts available by FAX, mail. Search requires name plus social security number, signed release. Other helpful information: date of birth. Fee is $3.00. Expedited service available for $6.00. Major credit cards accepted for payment.

University of Maine at Machias, Registrar, Machias, ME 04654, 207-255-3313 (FAX: 207-255-4864). Hours: 8AM-5PM. Records go back to 1912. Degrees granted: Associate; Bachelors. Adverse incident record source: Student Services, 207-255-3313.

School will not confirm attendance or degree information. Search requires name only. No fee for information.

Transcripts available by FAX, mail. Search requires name plus signed release. Other helpful information: social security number, date of birth, approximate years of attendance. Fee is $3.00. Major credit cards accepted for payment.

University of Maine at Presque Isle, Registrar, 181 Main St, Presque Isle, ME 04769, 207-768-9400. Hours: 8AM-5PM. Records go back to 1903. Alumni records are maintained here also. Call 207-768-9400. Degrees granted: Bachelors.

Attendance and degree information available by phone, mail. Search requires name plus social security number. No fee for information.

Transcripts available by mail. Search requires name plus social security number, exact years of attendance, signed release. Fee is $2.00.

University of Mary, Registrar's Office, 7500 University Dr, Bismarck, ND 58504-9652, 701-255-7500 X411 (FAX: 701-255-7687). Hours: 8AM-4:30PM. Degrees granted: Associate; Bachelors; Masters.

Attendance and degree information available by phone, FAX, mail. Search requires name plus social security number. No fee for information. Expedited service available for $.

Transcripts available by FAX, mail. Search requires name plus social security number, signed release. Other helpful information: approximate years of attendance. Fee is $2.00. Expedite: $3.00 to $15.00.

University of Mary Hardin-Baylor, Registrar, Box 8425, Belton, TX 76513, 817-939-4512. Hours: 8AM-5PM. Records go back to 1845. Alumni records are maintained here at the same phone number. Alumni Records Office: Box 8427, Belton, TX 76513. Degrees granted: Bachelors; Masters.

Attendance information available by phone, FAX, mail. Search requires name plus exact years of attendance. Other helpful information: social security number, date of birth. No fee for information.

Degree information available by phone, FAX, mail. Search requires name only. Other helpful information: social security number, date of birth, exact years of attendance. No fee for information.

Transcripts available by mail. Search requires name plus signed release. Other helpful information: social security number, date of birth, exact years of attendance. Fee is $3.00. Major credit cards accepted for payment.

University of Maryland Baltimore County, Registrar, 5401 Wilkens Ave, Baltimore, MD 21228, 410-455-3727 (FAX: 410-455-1094). Hours: 8:30AM-4:30PM. Records go back to 1966. Alumni records are maintained here also. Call 410-455-2904. Degrees granted: Bachelors; Masters; Doctorate.

Attendance and degree information available by phone, FAX, mail. Search requires name plus social security number. No fee for information.

Transcripts available by FAX, mail. Search requires name plus social security number, exact years of attendance, signed release. No fee for transcripts.

University of Maryland College Park, Registrar, College Park, MD 20742, 301-314-1000 (FAX: 301-314-9568). Hours: 8:30AM-4:30PM. Records go back to 1900. Degrees granted: Bachelors; Masters; Doctorate. Special programs- Adult Ed Center, U of M, College Park, MD 20742. Adverse incident record source: Campus Police, 301-405-3555.

Attendance and degree information available by phone, FAX, mail. Search requires name plus social security number, date of birth, approximate years of attendance. No fee for information.

Transcripts available by FAX, mail. Search requires name plus social security number, date of birth, approximate years of attendance, signed release. No fee for transcripts.

Take credit cards for FedEx only.

University of Maryland Eastern Shore, Registrar, Princess Anne, MD 21853, 410-651-2200 X6410. Hours: 8:30AM-4:30PM. Records go back to 1886. Alumni records are maintained here also. Call 410-651-2200. Degrees granted: Bachelors; Masters; Doctorate.

Attendance and degree information available by phone, mail. Search requires name plus social security number, date of birth, exact years of attendance. No fee for information.

Transcripts available by mail. Search requires name plus social security number, date of birth, exact years of attendance, signed release. Fee is $2.00.

University of Maryland at Baltimore, Registrar, 621 W Lombard St Room 326, Baltimore, MD 21201, 410-706-7480 (FAX: 410-706-4053). Hours: 8AM-4:30PM. Records go back to 1886. Alumni Records Office: 666 W Baltimore St, Baltimore, MD 21201. Degrees granted: Masters; Doctorate. Adverse incident record source: Dean of Students, 410-706-7460.

Attendance and degree information available by phone, FAX, mail. Search requires name plus social security number. No fee for information.

Transcripts available by FAX, mail. Search requires name plus social security number, date of birth, exact years of attendance, signed release. No fee for transcripts.

Need to know program/degree.

University of Maryland, (College Park), Registrar, Mitchell Bldg Room 1101, College Park, MD 20742, 301-314-7934 (FAX: 301-314-9568). Hours: 9AM-5PM. Records go back to 1947. Alumni records are maintained here at the same phone number. Degrees granted: Doctorate.

Attendance and degree information available by phone, FAX, mail. Search requires name plus social security number. No fee for information.

Transcripts available by FAX, mail. Search requires name plus social security number, exact years of attendance, signed release. No fee for transcripts.

University of Massachusetts Boston, Registrar, 100 Morrisey Blvd, Boston, MA 02125-3393, 617-287-6200 (FAX: 617-287-6242). Records go back to 1965. Degrees granted: Bachelors; Masters; Doctorate.

Attendance and degree information available by phone, FAX, mail. Search requires name only. Other helpful information: social security number, date of birth, approximate years of attendance. No fee for information.

Transcripts available by FAX, mail. Search requires name plus signed release. Other helpful information: social security number, date of birth, approximate years of attendance. No fee for transcripts.

University of Massachusetts Dartmouth, Registrar, 285 Old Westport Rd, North Dartmouth, MA 02747, 508-999-8615 (FAX: 508-999-8901). Hours: 8AM-5PM. Records go back to 1950s. Degrees granted: Bachelors; Masters. Adverse incident record source: Campus Security, 508-999-8105.

Attendance information available by written request only. Search requires name plus social security number, exact years of attendance, signed release. Other helpful information: date of birth. No fee for information.

Degree information available by written request only. Search requires name plus social security number, exact years of attendance, signed release. Other helpful information: date of birth, approximate years of attendance. No fee for information.

Transcripts available by written request only. Search requires name plus social security number, exact years of attendance, signed release. Other helpful information: date of birth, approximate years of attendance. Fee is $2.00. Expedited service available for $5.00.

University of Massachusetts Lowell, Registrar, One University Ave, Lowell, MA 01854, 508-934-2550. Hours: 8:30AM-5PM. Records go back to 1890s. Alumni records are maintained here also. Call 508-454-6335. Degrees granted: Associate; Bachelors; Masters; Doctorate. Certification: C.E.

Attendance and degree information available by phone, mail. Search requires name plus social security number. No fee for information.

Transcripts available by mail. Search requires name plus social security number, approximate years of attendance, signed release. Other helpful information: date of birth. Fee is $1.00.

University of Massachusetts Medical Center at Worcester, Registrar, 55 Lake Ave N, Worcester, MA 01655, 508-856-2267 (FAX: 508-856-1899). Hours: 9AM-5PM. Records go back to 1974. Alumni records are maintained here also. Call 508-856-2129. Degrees granted: Doctorate; PhD.

Attendance and degree information available by phone, FAX, mail. Search requires name plus social security number, approximate years of attendance, signed release. No fee for information.

Transcripts available by phone, FAX, mail. Search requires name plus social security number, approximate years of attendance, signed release. No fee for transcripts.

University of Massachusetts at Amherst, Registrar, Amherst, MA 01003, 413-545-0555 (FAX: 413-545-4792). Hours: 8:30AM-5PM. Records go back to 1800s. Alumni records are maintained here also. Call 413-545-2317. Degrees granted: Bachelors. Adverse incident record source: Dean of Students, 413-545-2684.

Attendance and degree information available by phone, FAX, mail. Search requires name plus social security number, approximate years of attendance, signed release. No fee for information.

Transcripts available by mail. Search requires name plus social security number, approximate years of attendance, signed release. Fee is $3.00.

University of Medicine and Dentistry of New Jersey, Registrar, 30 Bergen St, Newark, NJ 07103-2714, 201-982-4300 (FAX: 201-982-6930). Hours: 8:30AM-4:30PM. Records go back to 1960. Alumni records are maintained here also. Call 201-982-6864. Degrees granted: Doctorate.

Attendance and degree information available by phone, FAX, mail. Search requires name only. No fee for information.

Transcripts available by mail. Search requires name plus signed release. Fee is $3.00.

University of Medicine and Dentistry of New Jersey, (**Dental School**), Registrar, 110 Bergen St, Newark, NJ 07103, 201-982-4728 (FAX: 201-982-3689). Hours: 8AM-4PM. Records go back to 1956. Degrees granted: Doctorate.

Attendance information available by phone, FAX, mail. Search requires name plus signed release. Other helpful information: social security number. No fee for information.

Degree information available by phone, FAX, mail. Search requires name only. Other helpful information: social security number. No fee for information.

Transcripts available by written request only. Search requires name plus signed release. Other helpful information: social security number. Fee is $5.00.

University of Medicine and Dentistry of New Jersey, (**Graduate School of Biomedical Sciences**), Registrar, 185 S Orange Ave, Newark, NJ 07103, 201-456-4511. Records are not housed here. They are located at University of Medicine and Dentistry of New Jersey, Registrar, 30 Bergen St, Newark, NJ 07103-2714.

University of Medicine and Dentistry of New Jersey, (**Medical School**), Registrar, 185 S Orange Ave, Newark, NJ 07103, 201-465-4539. Records are not housed here. They are located at University of Medicine and Dentistry of New Jersey, Registrar, 30 Bergen St, Newark, NJ 07103-2714.

University of Medicine and Dentistry of New Jersey, (**Robert Wood Johnson Medical School**), Registrar, 675 Hoes Lane, Piscataway, NJ 08854, 908-235-4565 (FAX: 908-235-5078). Hours: 8:30AM-5PM. Records go back to 1974. Alumni records are maintained here also. Call 908-235-4898. Degrees granted: Masters; Doctorate.

Attendance and degree information available by phone, FAX, mail. Search requires name only. Other helpful information: social security number. No fee for information.

Transcripts available by mail. Search requires name plus social security number, signed release. Fee is $3.00.

University of Medicine and Dentistry of New Jersey, (**School of Health-Related Professions**), Registrar, 65 Bergen St, Newark, NJ 07107, 201-456-5453. Records are not housed here. They are located at University of Medicine and Dentistry of New Jersey, Registrar, 30 Bergen St, Newark, NJ 07103-2714.

University of Medicine and Dentistry of New Jersey, (School of Osteopathic Medicine), Registrar, Academic Ctr, One Medical Center Dr, Stratford, NJ 08084, 609-566-6995. Records are not housed here. They are located at University of Medicine and Dentistry of New Jersey, Registrar, 30 Bergen St, Newark, NJ 07103-2714.

University of Memphis, Transcripts, Memphis, TN 38152, 901-678-3927 (FAX: 901-678-3249). Hours: 7:30AM-7PM M-Th; 7:30AM-4:30PM F; 8:30AM-Noon S. Records go back to 1912. Evening and Saturday phone number is 901-678-2671. Alumni records are maintained here also. Call 901-678-2586. Degrees granted: Bachelors; Masters; Doctorate. Certification: Paralegal. Adverse incident record source: Public Safety, 901-678-3848.

Attendance and degree information available by phone, FAX, mail. Search requires name only. Other helpful information: social security number, date of birth, approximate years of attendance. No fee for information.

Transcripts available by FAX, mail. Search requires name plus social security number, signed release. Other helpful information: date of birth, approximate years of attendance. No fee for transcripts.

University of Miami, Office of the Registrar, PO Box 248026, Coral Gables, FL 33124-4627, 305-284-5455 (FAX: 305-284-3144). Hours: 8:30AM-5PM. Records go back to 1926. Degrees granted: Bachelors; Masters; Doctorate. Certification: Continuing Studies. Special programs- Continuing Studies, 305-284-4000. Adverse incident record source: Public Safety, 305-284-6666.

Attendance information available by FAX, mail. Search requires name plus social security number, approximate years of attendance. Other helpful information: date of birth, exact years of attendance. No fee for information.

Degree information available by FAX, mail. Search requires name plus social security number, date of birth, approximate years of attendance. Other helpful information: exact years of attendance. No fee for information.

Transcripts available by FAX, mail. Search requires name plus social security number, date of birth, approximate years of attendance, signed release. Other helpful information: exact years of attendance. Fee is $5.00.

Credit cards in person only.

University of Michigan, Transcript Department, 555 LSA Building, Ann Arbor, MI 48109-1382, 313-763-9066 (FAX: 313-764-5556). Hours: 8AM-5PM. Records go back to 1817. Alumni Records Office: 200 Fletcher St, Ann Arbor, MI 48109-1007. Degrees granted: Bachelors; Masters; Doctorate. Special programs- Medical School, 313-764-0219: Dental School, 313-764-1512: Law, 313-764-6499.

Attendance and degree information available by phone, FAX, mail. Search requires name only. Other helpful information: social security number, date of birth, approximate years of attendance. No fee for information.

Transcripts available by FAX, mail. Search requires name plus signed release. Other helpful information: social security number, date of birth, approximate years of attendance. No fee for transcripts.

Major credit cards accepted for payment.

University of Michigan-Dearborn, 240 SSC, Transcripts, 4901 Evergreen Rd, Dearborn, MI 48128-1591, 313-593-5210 (FAX: 313-593-5697). Hours: 8AM-6:30PM M&Th; 8AM-5PM TWF. Records go back to 1959. Alumni records are maintained here also. Call 313-593-5131. Degrees granted: Bachelors; Masters. Special programs- Graduate/Master degrees, Ann Arbor, 313-763-9066. Adverse incident record source: Campus Safety, 313-593-5333.

Attendance and degree information available by phone, FAX, mail. Search requires name plus signed release. Other helpful information: social security number, date of birth, approximate years of attendance. No fee for information.

Transcripts available by phone, FAX, mail. Search requires name plus signed release. Other helpful information: social security number, date of birth, approximate years of attendance. Fee is $4.00. FAX is $10.00; Fed Ex $9.75; student copy $1.00.

FAX transcripts must be prepaid.

University of Michigan-Flint, Registrar, Flint, MI 48502, 810-762-3344 (FAX: 810-762-3346). Hours: 8AM-6:30PM M-Th; 8AM-5PM F. Records go back to 1956. Degrees granted: Bachelors; Masters.

Attendance and degree information available by phone, FAX, mail. Search requires name plus social security number. Other helpful information: date of birth, approximate years of attendance. No fee for information.

Transcripts available by mail. Search requires name plus social security number, signed release. Other helpful information: date of birth, approximate years of attendance. Fee is $4.00. Expedited service available for $4.00.

University of Minnesota-Crookston, Registrar, Hwys 2 and 75 N, Crookston, MN 56716, 218-281-8547 (FAX: 218-281-8050). Hours: 8AM-4:30PM. Records go back to 1966. Alumni records are maintained here at the same phone number. Degrees granted: Associate; Bachelors.

Attendance and degree information available by phone, FAX, mail. Search requires name plus social security number. No fee for information.

Transcripts available by mail. Search requires name plus social security number. Fee is $3.00.

University of Minnesota-Duluth, Registrar's Office, Attn: Transcripts, 10 University Dr, Duluth, MN 55812, 218-726-8805 (FAX: 218-726-6389). Hours: 8AM-4:30PM. Records go back to 1950. Degrees granted: Bachelors; Masters. Adverse incident record source: Campus Police, 218-726-7000.

Attendance information available by phone, FAX, mail. Search requires name plus social security number, date of birth. Other helpful information: approximate years of attendance. No fee for information.

Degree information available by phone, FAX, mail. Search requires name plus social security number, date of birth. Other helpful information: approximate years of attendance. No fee for information.

Transcripts available by mail. Search requires name plus social security number, date of birth, signed release. Other helpful information: approximate years of attendance. Fee is $5.00.

University of Minnesota-Morris, Registrar, 600 E Fourth St, Morris, MN 56267, 612-589-6030 (FAX: 612-589-3811). Hours: 8AM-4:30PM. Records go back to 1960. Alumni records are maintained here at the same phone number. Degrees granted: Bachelors.

Attendance and degree information available by phone, FAX, mail. Search requires name only. Other helpful information: social

security number, date of birth, approximate years of attendance. No fee for information.

Transcripts available by written request only. Search requires name plus signed release. Other helpful information: social security number, date of birth, approximate years of attendance. Fee is $3.00. Expedited service available for $9.00.

They will be adding FAX for transcripts within the next year. They plan to begin accepting credit cards within the next year.

University of Minnesota-Twin Cities, Office of the Registrar, 150 Williamson Hall, 231 Pillsbury Dr SE, Minneapolis, MN 55455, 612-625-5333. Hours: 9AM-5:30PM M; 8AM-4PM T-F. Records go back to 1880s. Alumni Records Office: 615 2nd Ave S, Minneapolis, MN 55402. Degrees granted: Associate; Bachelors; Masters; Doctorate. Adverse incident record source: University Police, 612-624-3550.

Attendance and degree information available by phone, mail. Search requires name plus social security number, signed release. Other helpful information: date of birth, approximate years of attendance. No fee for information.

Transcripts available by mail. Search requires name plus social security number, signed release. Other helpful information: date of birth, approximate years of attendance. Fee is $3.00. Expedited service available for $9.00.

University of Mississippi Medical Center, Registrar, 2500 N State St, Jackson, MS 39216-4505, 601-984-1080. Hours: 8AM-4:30PM. Records go back to 1955. Alumni records are maintained here at the same phone number. Degrees granted: Bachelors; Doctorate.

Attendance and degree information available by phone, mail. Search requires name plus social security number, date of birth, signed release. No fee for information.

Transcripts available by mail. Search requires name plus social security number, date of birth, signed release. Fee is $1.00.

University of Mississippi, Registrar, University, MS 38677, 601-232-7226 (FAX: 601-232-5869). Hours: 8AM-5PM. Records go back to 1848. Alumni records are maintained here also. Call 601-232-7375. Degrees granted: Bachelors; Masters; Doctorate; PhD. Adverse incident record source: Dean of Students, 601-232-7247.

Attendance and degree information available by phone, FAX, mail. Search requires name plus social security number, signed release. No fee for information.

Transcripts available by mail. Search requires name plus social security number, signed release. Fee is $4.00.

University of Missouri-Columbia, Registrar, Columbia, MO 65211, 314-882-7881. Alumni records are maintained here also. Call 314-882-6611. Degrees granted: Doctorate.

Attendance and degree information available by phone, mail. Search requires name only. Other helpful information: social security number. No fee for information.

Transcripts available by mail. Search requires name plus signed release. Other helpful information: social security number. No fee for transcripts.

University of Missouri-Kansas City, Records Office, 111 SSB, 4825 Troost, Kansas City, MO 64110, 816-235-1122 (FAX: 816-235-5513). Hours: 8AM-5PM. Records go back to 1933. Degrees granted: Bachelors; Masters; Doctorate. Adverse incident record source: Campus Police, 816-235-1515.

Attendance information available by FAX, mail. Search requires name plus signed release. Other helpful information: social security number, date of birth, approximate years of attendance. No fee for information.

Degree information available by phone, FAX, mail. Search requires name only. Other helpful information: social security number, date of birth, approximate years of attendance. No fee for information.

Transcripts available by FAX, mail. Search requires name plus signed release. Other helpful information: social security number, date of birth, approximate years of attendance. Fee is $3.00.

University of Missouri-Rolla, Registrar, 103 Parker Hall, Rolla, MO 65401, 314-341-4181 (FAX: 314-341-4362). Hours: 8AM-4PM. Records go back to 1930s. Alumni records are maintained here also. Call 314-341-4145. Degrees granted: Bachelors; Masters; Doctorate.

Attendance and degree information available by phone, FAX, mail. Search requires name only. Other helpful information: social security number, date of birth, approximate years of attendance. No fee for information. Expedited service available for $3.00.

Transcripts available by FAX, mail. Search requires name plus signed release. Other helpful information: social security number, date of birth, approximate years of attendance. Fee is $4.00.

Major credit cards accepted for payment.

University of Missouri-St. Louis, Registrar, 8001 Natural Bridge Rd, St Louis, MO 63121, 314-516-5676 (FAX: 314-516-5310). Hours: 8AM-5PM. Records go back to 1963. Degrees granted: Bachelors; Masters; Doctorate.

Attendance and degree information available by phone, FAX, mail. Search requires name plus social security number. Other helpful information: date of birth, approximate years of attendance. No fee for information.

Transcripts available by FAX, mail. Search requires name plus social security number, signed release. Other helpful information: date of birth, approximate years of attendance. Fee is $3.00.

Major credit cards accepted for payment.

University of Mobile, Registrar, PO Box 13220, Mobile, AL 36663-0220, 334-675-5990 X235 (FAX: 334-675-9816). Hours: 8AM-4:30PM. Records go back to 1963. Alumni records are maintained here also. Call 334-675-5990 X224. Degrees granted: Associate; Bachelors; Masters.

Attendance and degree information available by phone, FAX, mail. Search requires name plus social security number, approximate years of attendance. No fee for information.

Transcripts available by FAX, mail. Search requires name plus social security number, approximate years of attendance, signed release. Fee is $5.00.

University of Montana, Registrar, Missoula, MT 59812, 406-243-2995 (FAX: 406-243-4087). Hours: 9AM-4PM. Degrees granted: Associate; Bachelors; Masters; Doctorate. Certification: Elementary & Secondary Education. Adverse incident record source: Campus Police, 406-243-6131.

Attendance information available by phone, FAX, mail. Search requires name plus social security number, approximate years of attendance, signed release. Other helpful information: date of birth, exact years of attendance. No fee for information.

Degree information available by phone, FAX, mail. Search requires name plus social security number, approximate years of attendance. Other helpful information: date of birth, exact years of attendance. No fee for information.

Transcripts available by FAX, mail. Search requires name plus social security number, date of birth, approximate years of attendance, signed release. Other helpful information: exact years of attendance. Fee is $3.00. Expedite fee is based on cost of service.'

University of Montana-Missoula/College of Technology, Registrar, 909 South Ave W, Missoula, MT 59801, 406-243-7887.

Attendance and degree information available by phone, mail. Search requires name plus exact years of attendance. Other helpful information: date of birth, approximate years of attendance. No fee for information.

Transcripts available by written request only. Search requires name plus date of birth, exact years of attendance, signed release. Other helpful information: approximate years of attendance. No fee for transcripts.

University of Montevallo, Registrar, Station 6040, Montevallo, AL 35115-6001, 205-665-6040 (FAX: 205-665-6042). Hours: 8AM-5PM. Alumni records are maintained here at the same phone number. Alumni Records Office: Station 6215, Montevallo, AL 35115-6001. Degrees granted: Bachelors; Masters. Adverse incident record source: Student Affairs, Station 6020.

Attendance and degree information available by phone, FAX, mail. Search requires name only. Other helpful information: social security number, date of birth, approximate years of attendance. No fee for information.

Transcripts available by FAX, mail. Search requires name plus signed release. Other helpful information: social security number, date of birth, approximate years of attendance. Fee is $2.00. Expedited service available for $10.00.

University of Nebraska Medical Center, Registrar, 600 S 42nd St, Omaha, NE 68198-6605, 402-559-7391 (FAX: 402-559-6796). Hours: 8AM-4:30PM. Records go back to 1902. Alumni records are maintained here also. Call 402-559-4354. Degrees granted: Bachelors; Masters; Doctorate.

Attendance and degree information available by phone, FAX, mail. Search requires name only. Other helpful information: social security number, date of birth, approximate years of attendance. No fee for information.

Transcripts available by mail. Search requires name plus signed release. Other helpful information: social security number, date of birth, approximate years of attendance. Fee varies. Expedite fee varies.

University of Nebraska at Kearney, Registrar, Founders Hall, 905 W 25th St, Kearney, NE 68849, 308-865-8527. Hours: 8AM-5PM. Records go back to 1903. Alumni Records Office: 2222 9th Ave, Kearney, NE 68849. Degrees granted: Bachelors; Masters. Adverse incident record source: Campus Security, 308-865-8517.

Attendance information available by phone, FAX, mail. Search requires name plus social security number. Other helpful information: date of birth, approximate years of attendance. No fee for information.

Degree information available by phone, FAX, mail. Search requires name only. Other helpful information: social security number, date of birth, approximate years of attendance. No fee for information.

Transcripts available by FAX, mail. Search requires name plus social security number, signed release. Other helpful information: date of birth, approximate years of attendance. Fee is $3.00. Expedited service available for $8.00.

Accepts FAX requests for transcripts, but will not FAX back.

University of Nebraska at Omaha, Registrar, 60th and Dodge Sts, Omaha, NE 68182, 402-554-2314 (FAX: 402-554-3472). Hours: 8AM-5PM. Records go back to 1906. Degrees granted: Associate; Bachelors; Masters; Doctorate.

Attendance information available by phone, FAX, mail. Search requires name only. Other helpful information: social security number, date of birth, approximate years of attendance. No fee for information.

Degree information available by phone, FAX, mail. Search requires name only. Other helpful information: social security number, date of birth, approximate years of attendance. No fee for information.

Transcripts available by mail. Search requires name plus social security number, signed release. Other helpful information: date of birth, approximate years of attendance. Fee is $4.00.

University of Nebraska-Lincoln, Registration & Records, PO Box 880416, Lincoln, NE 68588-0416, 402-472-3684 (FAX: 402-472-8220). Hours: 8AM-5PM. Records go back to 1869. Alumni records are maintained here also. Call 402-472-2841. Degrees granted: Bachelors; Masters; Doctorate; Juris Doctor. Adverse incident record source: Student Judicial Affairs.

Attendance and degree information available by phone, mail. Search requires name plus social security number. Other helpful information: date of birth, approximate years of attendance. No fee for information.

Transcripts available by FAX, mail. Search requires name plus social security number, signed release. Other helpful information: date of birth, approximate years of attendance. Fee is $5.00. Expedited service available for $10.00.

University of Nevada, Las Vegas, Registrar, 4505 Maryland Pkwy, Las Vegas, NV 89154, 702-895-3371 (FAX: 702-895-4046). Hours: 8AM-5PM. Records go back to 1955. Alumni records are maintained here also. Call 702-895-3621. Degrees granted: Bachelors; Masters; Doctorate. Adverse incident record source: Public Safety, 702-895-3668.

Attendance and degree information available by phone, mail. Search requires name plus social security number. Other helpful information: date of birth. No fee for information.

Transcripts available by mail. Search requires name plus social security number, signed release. Other helpful information: date of birth. Fee is $2.00.

Must have signature for confirming if student has privacy request. Major credit cards accepted for payment.

University of Nevada, Reno, Registrar, Reno, NV 89557, 702-784-6865 (FAX: 702-784-4283). Hours: 8AM-4:30PM. Records go back to 1904. Alumni records are maintained here also. Call 704-784-6620. Degrees granted: Associate; Bachelors; Masters; Doctorate.

Attendance and degree information available by FAX, mail. Search requires name plus social security number, date of birth, approximate years of attendance, signed release. Other helpful information: exact years of attendance. No fee for information.

Transcripts available by written request only. Search requires name plus social security number, date of birth, approximate years of attendance, signed release. Other helpful information: exact years of attendance. Fee is $2.00.

Include a self addressed stamped envelope with mail request.

The Sourcebook of College and University Student Records

U

University of New England, Registrar, 11 Hills Beach Rd, Biddeford, ME 04005, 207-283-0171 X2473 (FAX: 207-282-6379). Hours: 9AM-4PM. Degrees granted: Associate; Bachelors; Masters; Doctorate.

Attendance information available by phone, FAX, mail. Search requires name plus social security number, date of birth, signed release. Other helpful information: exact years of attendance. No fee for information.

Degree information available by phone, FAX, mail. Search requires name plus social security number, signed release. Other helpful information: date of birth. No fee for information.

Transcripts available by FAX, mail. Search requires name plus social security number, signed release. Other helpful information: date of birth. Fee is $2.00.

University of New Hampshire, Registrar's Office, 11 Garrison Ave, Durham, NH 03824-3511, 603-862-1234 (FAX: 603-862-1817). Hours: 8AM-4:30PM. Records go back to 1866. Degrees granted: Associate; Bachelors; Masters; Doctorate.

Attendance and degree information available by phone, FAX, mail. Search requires name only. Other helpful information: social security number, date of birth, approximate years of attendance. No fee for information.

Transcripts available by FAX, mail. Search requires name plus signed release. Other helpful information: social security number, date of birth, approximate years of attendance. Fee is $3.00. Expedited service available for $5.00.

University of New Hampshire at Manchester, Registrar, RFD 4 Hackett Hill Rd, Manchester, NH 03102, 603-668-0700. Hours: 8AM-4:30PM. Records go back to 1988. Records older than 1988 are in Durham, NH (see above). Alumni records are maintained here also. Call 603-862-2040. Degrees granted: Associate; Bachelors.

Attendance and degree information available by phone, mail. Search requires name plus social security number, approximate years of attendance. Other helpful information: exact years of attendance. No fee for information.

Transcripts available by written request only. Search requires name plus social security number, approximate years of attendance, signed release. Other helpful information: exact years of attendance. Fee is $3.00.

University of New Haven, Registrar, West Haven, CT 06516, 203-932-7301 (FAX: 203-932-7429). Hours: 8:30AM-4:30PM. Records go back to 1920. Alumni records are maintained here also. Call 203-932-7268. Degrees granted: Associate; Bachelors; Masters; Doctorate. Adverse incident record source: Student Affairs, 203-932-7199.

Attendance and degree information available by phone, FAX, mail. Search requires name only. Other helpful information: social security number, date of birth, approximate years of attendance. No fee for information.

Transcripts available by written request only. Search requires name plus signed release. Other helpful information: social security number, date of birth, approximate years of attendance. Fee is $5.00. Expedite: Send postage paid envelope.

Major credit cards accepted for payment.

University of New Mexico, Records Office, Student Services Ctr Rm 250, Albuquerque, NM 87131-2039, 505-277-2917 (FAX: 505-277-6809). Hours: 8AM-5PM. Records go back to founding date. Alumni records are maintained here also. Call 505-277-5808. Degrees granted: Associate; Bachelors; Masters; Doctorate. Adverse incident record source: Dean of Students: Campus Police.

Attendance and degree information available by phone, FAX, mail. Search requires name plus social security number, approximate years of attendance. Other helpful information: date of birth. No fee for information.

Transcripts available by FAX, mail. Search requires name plus social security number, approximate years of attendance, signed release. Other helpful information: date of birth. Fee is $3.00. Expedited service available for $10.00.

Major credit cards accepted for payment.

University of New Mexico, (Gallup Branch), Registrar, 200 College Rd, Gallup, NM 87301, 505-722-7221. Records are not housed here. They are located at University of New Mexico, Records Office, Student Services Ctr Rm 250, Albuquerque, NM 87131-2039.

University of New Mexico, (Los Alamos Branch), Registrar, 400 University Dr, Los Alamos, NM 87544, 505-662-5919. Records are not housed here. They are located at University of New Mexico, Records Office, Student Services Ctr Rm 250, Albuquerque, NM 87131-2039.

University of New Mexico, (Valencia Branch), Registrar, 280 La Entrada, Los Lunas, NM 87031, 505-865-9596. Records are not housed here. They are located at University of New Mexico, Records Office, Student Services Ctr Rm 250, Albuquerque, NM 87131-2039.

University of New Orleans, Registrar, Lakefront, New Orleans, LA 70148, 504-286-6216 (FAX: 504-286-6217). Hours: 8AM-4:30PM. Records go back 37 years. Alumni records are maintained here also. Call 504-286-6368. Degrees granted: Bachelors; Masters; Doctorate. Adverse incident record source: Campus Police.

Attendance and degree information available by FAX, mail. Search requires name plus social security number, date of birth. Other helpful information: approximate years of attendance. No fee for information.

Transcripts available by written request only. Search requires name plus social security number, date of birth, signed release. Other helpful information: approximate years of attendance. Fee is $5.00.

University of North Alabama, Registrar, Box 5121, Florence, AL 35632-0001, 205-760-4316 (FAX: 205-760-4349). Hours: 8AM-4:30PM. Records go back to 1850. Alumni records are maintained here at the same phone number. Alumni Records Office: Box 5047, Florence, AL 35632-0001. Degrees granted: Bachelors; Masters.

Attendance and degree information available by phone, FAX, mail. Search requires name plus date of birth, signed notarized release. Other helpful information: social security number, approximate years of attendance. No fee for information.

Transcripts available by FAX, mail. Search requires name plus date of birth, signed release. Other helpful information: social security number, approximate years of attendance. No fee for transcripts.

Major credit cards accepted for payment.

University of North Carolina at Asheville, Registrar, One University Heights, Asheville, NC 28804, 704-251-6575

DEGREE GRANTING INSTITUTIONS

(FAX: 704-251-6841). Hours: 8AM-4:30PM. Records go back to 1930s. Degrees granted: Bachelors; Masters.

Attendance and degree information available by phone, FAX, mail. Search requires name plus social security number. Other helpful information: date of birth, approximate years of attendance. No fee for information.

Transcripts available by mail. Search requires name plus social security number, date of birth, approximate years of attendance, signed release. Other helpful information: exact years of attendance. Fee is $2.00.

University of North Carolina at Chapel Hill, Registrar, CB # 2100, 105 Hanes Hall, Chapel Hill, NC 27599-2100, 919-962-3954 (FAX: 919-962-3349). Hours: 8AM-4:30PM. Records go back to 1902. Alumni Records Office: Geo. Watts Hill Alumni Center, CB 9180, Chapel Hill, NC 27599-2100. Degrees granted: Bachelors; Masters. Adverse incident record source: Student Affairs, 919-962-4041.

Attendance and degree information available by mail. Search requires name plus social security number, signed release. Other helpful information: date of birth. No fee for information.

Transcripts available by mail. Search requires name plus social security number, signed release. Other helpful information: date of birth. Fee is $5.00.

University of North Carolina at Charlotte, Registrar, University City Blvd, Charlotte, NC 28223, 704-547-3481 (FAX: 704-547-3340). Hours: 8AM-5PM. Records go back to 1960. Alumni records are maintained here also. Call 704-547-2273. Degrees granted: Bachelors. Adverse incident record source: Dept. of Student Account, 704-547-2215: Dept. of Traffic, 704-547-4285

Attendance and degree information available by phone, mail. Search requires name plus social security number, approximate years of attendance, signed release. No fee for information.

Transcripts available by phone, mail. Search requires name plus social security number, approximate years of attendance, signed release. First transcript is free; $3.00 each additional.

University of North Carolina at Greensboro, Registrar, 1000 Spring Garden St, Greensboro, NC 27412, 910-334-5946 (FAX: 910-334-3649). Hours: 7:30AM-5:30PM. Alumni records are maintained here at the same phone number. Degrees granted: Doctorate.

Attendance and degree information available by phone, mail. Search requires name plus social security number. No fee for information.

Transcripts available by mail. Search requires name plus social security number, signed release. Fee is $5.00.

University of North Carolina at Wilmington, Registrar, 601 S College Rd, Wilmington, NC 28403-3297, 910-395-3125 (FAX: 910-395-3887). Hours: 8AM-5PM. Records go back to 1985. Degrees granted: Bachelors; Masters.

Attendance information available by mail. Search requires name plus social security number, date of birth, approximate years of attendance. No fee for information.

Degree information available by FAX, mail. Search requires name plus social security number, date of birth, approximate years of attendance. No fee for information.

Transcripts available by FAX, mail. Search requires name plus social security number, date of birth, approximate years of attendance. Fee is $2.00.

University of North Dakota (Lake Region), Registrar, N College Dr, Devils Lake, ND 58301, 701-662-1515 (FAX: 701-662-1570). Hours: 8AM-4:30PM. Records go back to 1941. Alumni records are maintained here also. Call 701-662-1520. Degrees granted: Associate.

Attendance and degree information available by phone, FAX, mail. Search requires name plus signed release. Other helpful information: social security number, date of birth, approximate years of attendance. No fee for information.

Transcripts available by FAX, mail. Search requires name plus signed release. Other helpful information: social security number, date of birth, approximate years of attendance. No fee for transcripts.

University of North Dakota (Williston), Registrar, PO Box 1326, Williston, ND 58801, 701-774-4212 (FAX: 701-774-4211). Hours: 8AM-5PM. Records go back to 1961. Degrees granted: Associate.

Attendance information available by written request only. Search requires name plus social security number, signed release. Other helpful information: date of birth, approximate years of attendance. No fee for information.

Degree information available by phone, FAX, mail. Search requires name only. Other helpful information: social security number, date of birth, approximate years of attendance. No fee for information.

Transcripts available by written request only. Search requires name plus social security number, date of birth, signed release. Other helpful information: approximate years of attendance. No fee for transcripts.

University of North Dakota, Records & Registration, Box 8232, University Station, Grand Forks, ND 58202-8232, 701-777-2711 (FAX: 701-777-2696). Hours: 8AM-4:30PM. Records go back to 1883. Alumni records are maintained here also. Call 701-777-2611. Degrees granted: Associate; Bachelors; Masters; Doctorate. Adverse incident record source: Affirmative Action, 701-777-4171.

Attendance and degree information available by phone, FAX, mail. Search requires name only. Other helpful information: social security number, date of birth, approximate years of attendance. No fee for information. Include a stamped envelope.

Transcripts available by FAX, mail. Search requires name plus signed release. Other helpful information: social security number, date of birth, approximate years of attendance. Fee is $2.00. Major credit cards accepted for payment.

University of North Florida, Registrar, 4567 St Johns Bluff Rd S, Jacksonville, FL 32224-2645, 904-646-2620 (FAX: 904-646-2703). Hours: 8AM-5PM. Records go back to 1972. Alumni records are maintained here also. Call 904-646-2513. Degrees granted: Bachelors; Masters; Doctorate.

Attendance and degree information available by mail. Search requires name plus social security number, signed release. No fee for information.

Transcripts available by mail. Search requires name plus social security number, signed release. Fee is $5.00.

University of North Texas, Registrar's Office, PO Box 13766, Denton, TX 76203, 817-565-2111. Hours: 8AM-5PM. Records go back to founding date. Degrees granted: Bachelors; Masters; Doctorate.

Attendance and degree information available by phone, mail. Search requires name only. Other helpful information: date of birth, approximate years of attendance. No fee for information.

Transcripts available by mail. Search requires name plus signed release. Other helpful information: date of birth, approximate years of attendance. Fee is $3.00.

Need student ID number.

University of North Texas Health Science Center at Fort Worth, Registrar, 3500 Camp Bowie Blvd, Fort Worth, TX 76107-2970, 817-735-2201. Hours: 8AM-5PM. Records go back to 1974. Degrees granted: Bachelors; Masters; Doctorate.

Attendance information available by phone, mail. Search requires name plus social security number, approximate years of attendance. Other helpful information: exact years of attendance. No fee for information.

Degree information available by phone, mail. Search requires name plus social security number, approximate years of attendance. Other helpful information: date of birth, exact years of attendance. No fee for information.

School does not provide transcripts. Search requires name plus social security number, approximate years of attendance, signed release. Other helpful information: exact years of attendance. No fee for transcripts.

University of Northern Colorado, Registrar's Office, Carter Hall 3002, Greeley, CO 80639, 303-351-2231 (FAX: 303-351-1870). Hours: 8AM-5PM. Records go back to 1890. Degrees granted: Bachelors; Masters; Doctorate. Certification: Teacher. Adverse incident record source: Police, 303-351-2245.

Attendance information available by phone, FAX, mail. Search requires name only. Other helpful information: social security number, date of birth, approximate years of attendance. No fee for information.

Degree information available by phone, FAX, mail. Search requires name only. Other helpful information: social security number, date of birth. No fee for information.

Transcripts available by FAX, mail. Search requires name plus social security number, signed release. Other helpful information: date of birth. Fee is $5.00. Expedited service available for $8.00. Major credit cards accepted for payment.

University of Northern Iowa, Registrar, Cedar Falls, IA 50614, 319-273-2241 (FAX: 319-273-6792). Hours: 8AM-5PM. Records go back to 1876. Alumni records are maintained here also. Call 319-273-2355. Degrees granted: Bachelors; Masters; Doctorate. Adverse incident record source: Student Services, 319-273-2332.

Attendance and degree information available by phone, FAX, mail. Search requires name plus social security number, approximate years of attendance, signed release. No fee for information.

Transcripts available by FAX, mail. Search requires name plus social security number, approximate years of attendance, signed release. Fee is $3.00.

University of Notre Dame, Registrar, Main Bldg Room 215, South Bend, IN 46556, 219-631-5000 (FAX: 219-631-5872). Hours: 8AM-5PM. Records go back to 1842. Alumni Records Office: 201 Main Bldg, South Bend, IN 46556 219-631-6000. Degrees granted: Bachelors; Masters; Doctorate.

Attendance and degree information available by phone, FAX, mail. Search requires name plus social security number, exact years of attendance. No fee for information.

Transcripts available by mail. Search requires name plus social security number, exact years of attendance, signed release. Fee is $2.00.

University of Oklahoma Health Sciences Center, Registrar, PO Box 26901, Oklahoma City, OK 73126-0901, 405-271-1537 (FAX: 405-271-2480). Hours: 8AM-5PM. Records go back to 1900s. Alumni records are maintained here at the same phone number. Degrees granted: Bachelors; Masters; Doctorate. Adverse incident record source: Campus Police, 405-271-4300.

Attendance and degree information available by phone, FAX, mail. Search requires name only. Other helpful information: social security number, date of birth, approximate years of attendance. No fee for information.

Transcripts available by mail. Search requires name plus signed release. Other helpful information: social security number, date of birth, approximate years of attendance. Fee is $3.00.

Confirming unless student asks no release.

University of Oklahoma, Registrar's Office, 1000 Asp Ave, Norman, OK 73019, 405-325-2012 (FAX: 405-325-7047). Hours: 8AM-5PM. Records go back to 1940. Alumni Records Office: Alumni Association, University of Oklahoma, 900 Asp Ave, Norman, OK 73019. Degrees granted: Bachelors. Adverse incident record source: Registrar, 405-325-2012.

Attendance information available by phone, FAX, mail. Search requires name plus social security number. No fee for information.

Degree information available by phone, FAX, mail. Search requires name plus social security number. Other helpful information: exact years of attendance. No fee for information.

Transcripts available by FAX, mail. Search requires name plus social security number, date of birth, exact years of attendance, signed release. No fee for transcripts.

University of Oregon, Office of Registrar, Eugene, OR 97403-5257, 503-346-3243 (FAX: 503-346-5815). Hours: 8AM-5PM. Records go back to 1875. Alumni records are maintained here also. Call 503-346-3036. Degrees granted: Bachelors; Masters; Doctorate. Adverse incident record source: Dean of Students, 503-346-3216.

Attendance information available by phone, FAX, mail. Search requires name plus social security number. No fee for information.

Degree information available by phone, FAX, mail. Search requires name plus social security number, exact years of attendance. No fee for information.

Transcripts available by FAX, mail. Search requires name plus social security number, exact years of attendance, signed release. Fee is $5.00.

Major credit cards accepted for payment.

University of Osteopathic Medicine and Health Sciences, Registrar, 3200 Grand Ave, Des Moines, IA 50313, 515-271-1460 (FAX: 515-271-1578). Hours: 8AM-4:30PM. Records go back to 1900. Degrees granted: Bachelors; Masters.

Attendance and degree information available by phone, FAX, mail. Search requires name only. Other helpful information: social security number. No fee for information.

Transcripts available by mail. Search requires name plus signed release. Other helpful information: social security number. Fee is $3.00. Expedited service available for $3.00.

$10.00 for overnight delivery.

University of Pennsylvania, Registrar, 3451 Walnut St, Franklin Bldg Room 221, Philadelphia, PA 19104, 215-898-1561. Hours: 8AM-5PM. Records go back to 1740. Alumni records are maintained here also. Call 215-898-7811. Degrees granted: Bachelors; Masters; Doctorate.

Attendance and degree information available by phone, mail. Search requires name plus social security number, exact years of attendance. No fee for information.

Transcripts available by mail. Search requires name plus social security number, exact years of attendance, signed release. Fee is $4.00.

University of Phoenix, Registrar, 4615 E Elwood St 3rd Flr, Phoenix, AZ 85072-2069, 602-966-9577 (FAX: 602-894-1758). Hours: 8AM-6PM. Records go back to 1979. Alumni records are maintained here at the same phone number. Degrees granted: Associate; Bachelors; Masters.

Attendance information available by phone, FAX, mail. Search requires name plus social security number. Other helpful information: date of birth. No fee for information. Expedited service available for $7.50.

Degree information available by phone, FAX, mail. Search requires name plus social security number. Other helpful information: date of birth, approximate years of attendance. No fee for information. Expedite service available for $7.50.

Transcripts available by FAX, mail. Search requires name plus social security number, signed release. Other helpful information: date of birth, approximate years of attendance. Fee is $5.00. Expedited service available for $7.50.

University of Phoenix, (Albuquerque Main), Registrar, 7471 Pan American Fwy NE, Albuquerque, NM 87109, 505-821-4800 (FAX: 505-821-5551). Hours: 8AM-6PM. Records go back 10 years. Transcript records are housed at University of Phoenix, Registrar, PO Box 52069, Phoenix, AZ 85072. Degrees granted: Associate; Bachelors; Masters.

Attendance and degree information available by written request only. Search requires name plus social security number, approximate years of attendance. No fee for information.

Transcripts available from the headquarters in Phoenix.

University of Phoenix, (Center for Distance Education), Registrar, PO Box 52069, Phoenix, AZ 85072, 602-921-8014 (FAX: 602-894-1758). Hours: 8AM-6PM. Records go back to 1980. Degrees granted: Bachelors; Masters; Nursing.

Attendance and degree information available by FAX, mail. Search requires name plus social security number, approximate years of attendance. No fee for information.

Transcripts available by FAX, mail. Search requires name plus social security number, approximate years of attendance, signed release. Transcript fee is $5.00 for official copy; unofficial copy is free.

University of Phoenix, (Denver Main), Registrar, 7800 E Dorado Pl, Englewood, CO 80111, 303-755-9090. Transcript records are housed at University of Phoenix, Registrar, PO Box 52069, Phoenix, AZ 85072.

Attendance and degree information available by written request only. Search requires name plus social security number, approximate years of attendance.

Transcripts available from the headquarters in Phoenix.

University of Phoenix, (Fountain Valley Main), Registrar, 10540 Talbert Ave, Fountain Valley, CA 92708, 714-968-2299. Transcript records are housed at University of Phoenix, Registrar, PO Box 52069, Phoenix, AZ 85072.

Attendance and degree information available by written request only. Search requires name plus social security number, approximate years of attendance.

Transcripts available from the headquarters in Phoenix.

University of Phoenix, (Hawaii Main), Registrar, 1585 Kapiolani Blvd #722, Honolulu, HI 96814, 808-949-0573. Transcript records are housed at University of Phoenix, Registrar, PO Box 52069, Phoenix, AZ 85072.

Attendance and degree information available by written request only. Search requires name plus social security number, approximate years of attendance.

Transcripts available from the headquarters in Phoenix.

University of Phoenix, (Online), Registrar, 100 Spear St #200, San Francisco, CA 94105, 415-956-2121. Transcript records are housed at University of Phoenix, Registrar, PO Box 52069, Phoenix, AZ 85072.

Attendance and degree information available by written request only. Search requires name plus social security number, approximate years of attendance.

Transcripts available from the headquarters in Phoenix.

University of Phoenix, (Phoenix Main), Registrar, 4605 E Elmwood St, PO Box 52076, Phoenix, AZ 85072-2076, 602-966-7400. Transcript records are housed at University of Phoenix, Registrar, PO Box 52069, Phoenix, AZ 85072.

Attendance and degree information available by written request only. Search requires name plus social security number, approximate years of attendance.

Transcripts available from the headquarters in Phoenix.

University of Phoenix, (Puerto Rico), Registrar, PO Box 3870, R D 177 KM2, Guaynabo, PR 00657-3870, 809-731-5400. Transcript records are housed at University of Phoenix, Registrar, PO Box 52069, Phoenix, AZ 85072.

Attendance and degree information available by written request only. Search requires name plus social security number, approximate years of attendance.

Transcripts available from the headquarters in Phoenix.

University of Phoenix, (Salt Lake City Main), Registrar, 5251 Green St, Salt Lake City, UT 84123, 801-263-1444. Transcript records are housed at University of Phoenix, Registrar, PO Box 52069, Phoenix, AZ 85072.

Attendance and degree information available by written request only. Search requires name plus social security number, approximate years of attendance.

Transcripts available from the headquarters in Phoenix.

University of Phoenix, (San Diego), Registrar, 3870 Murphy Canyon Rd Ste 200, San Diego, CA 92123, 619-576-7469. Transcript records are housed at University of Phoenix, Registrar, PO Box 52069, Phoenix, AZ 85072.

Attendance and degree information available by written request only. Search requires name plus social security number, approximate years of attendance.

Transcripts available from the headquarters in Phoenix.

University of Phoenix, (San Jose Main), Registrar, 3590 N 1st St, San Jose, CA 95134-1805, 408-435-8500. Transcript records are housed at University of Phoenix, Registrar, PO Box 52069, Phoenix, AZ 85072.

Attendance and degree information available by written request only. Search requires name plus social security number, approximate years of attendance.

Transcripts available from the headquarters in Phoenix.

University of Phoenix, (Tucson Main), Registrar, 3915 E Broadway, Tucson, AZ 85711, 520-881-6512. Transcript records are housed at University of Phoenix, Registrar, PO Box 52069, Phoenix, AZ 85072.

Attendance and degree information available by written request only. Search requires name plus social security number, approximate years of attendance.

Transcripts available from the headquarters in Phoenix.

University of Pittsburgh, Registrar, G-3 Thackerey Hall, Pittsburgh, PA 15260, 412-624-7660. Hours: 8AM-4:30PM. Records go back to 1787. Alumni records are maintained here also. Call 412-624-8222. Degrees granted: Bachelors; Masters; Doctorate.

Attendance and degree information available by phone, mail. Search requires name plus social security number, exact years of attendance. No fee for information.

Transcripts available by mail. Search requires name plus social security number, exact years of attendance, signed release. Fee is $3.00.

University of Pittsburgh, (Bradford Campus), Registrar, 300 Campus Dr, Bradford, PA 16701, 814-362-7600. Hours: 8AM-5PM. Records go back to 1963. Alumni records are maintained here also. Call 814-362-7655. Degrees granted: Bachelors.

Attendance and degree information available by phone, mail. Search requires name plus social security number. No fee for information.

Transcripts available by mail. Search requires name plus social security number, signed release. Fee is $3.00.

University of Pittsburgh, (Greensburg Campus), Registrar, 1150 Mount Pleasant Rd, Greensburg, PA 15601, 412-836-9900 (FAX: 412-836-9901). Hours: 8:30AM-7PM M-Th; 8:30AM-5PM F. Records go back to 1963. Alumni records are maintained here also. Call 412-836-9905. Degrees granted: Bachelors.

Attendance and degree information available by FAX, mail. Search requires name plus social security number, date of birth, signed release. Other helpful information: approximate years of attendance. Fee is $3.00. Expedited service available for $8.00.

Transcripts available by FAX, mail. Search requires name plus social security number, date of birth, signed release. Other helpful information: approximate years of attendance. Fee is $3.00. Expedited service available for $8.00.

Major credit cards accepted for payment.

University of Pittsburgh, (Johnstown Campus), Registrar, 6PJ, 132 Biddle Hall, Johnstown, PA 15956, 814-269-7060 (FAX: 814-269-7068). Hours: 8AM-4PM. Records go back to 1927. Degrees granted: Associate; Bachelors.

Attendance and degree information available by phone, FAX, mail. Search requires name plus signed release. Other helpful information: social security number, date of birth, approximate years of attendance. Fee is $3.00. Expedited service available for $10.00.

Transcripts available by FAX, mail. Search requires name plus signed release. Other helpful information: social security number, date of birth, approximate years of attendance. Fee is $3.00. Expedited service available for $10.00.

University of Portland, Registrar, 5000 N Willamette Blvd, Portland, OR 97203, 503-283-7321 (FAX: 503-283-7399). Hours: 8:30AM-4:30PM. Records go back to 1901. Alumni records are maintained here also. Call 602-283-7328. Degrees granted: Bachelors; Masters. Adverse incident record source: Student Services, 503-283-7207.

Attendance information available by phone, FAX, mail. Search requires name plus social security number. No fee for information.

Degree information available by phone, FAX, mail. Search requires name plus social security number. Other helpful information: approximate years of attendance. No fee for information.

Transcripts available by mail. Search requires name plus social security number, exact years of attendance, signed release. Fee is $3.00.

University of Puerto Rico Mayaguez Campus, Registrar, PO Box 5000, Mayaguez, PR 00681, 809-832-4040 (FAX: 809-832-7828). Hours: 7:45AM-11:45AM, 1-4:30PM. Records go back to 1915. Alumni records are maintained here also. Call 809-832-4040 X2376. Degrees granted: Associate; Bachelors; Masters; Doctorate.

Attendance information available by mail. Search requires name plus social security number, signed release. Other helpful information: date of birth. No fee for information.

Degree information available by written request only. Search requires name plus social security number, signed release. Other helpful information: date of birth. No fee for information.

Transcripts available by written request only. Search requires name plus social security number, signed release. Other helpful information: date of birth. Fee is $1.00.

Need student's father and mother last names.

University of Puerto Rico Medical Sciences Campus, Registrar, PO Box 365067, San Juan, PR 00936-5067, 809-758-2525.

University of Puerto Rico Rio Piedras Campus, Registrar, PO Box 23300, San Juan, PR 00931-3300, 809-764-0000.

University of Puget Sound, Office of the Registrar, Records Unit, 1500 N Warner, Tacoma, WA 98416, 206-756-3160 (FAX: 206-756-3500). Hours: 8:30AM-4:30PM. Records go back to 1888. Alumni records are maintained here also. Call 206-756-3245. Degrees granted: Bachelors; Masters. Adverse incident record source: Dean of Students, 206-756-3360: Security Services, 206-756-3311

Attendance and degree information available by phone, FAX, mail. Search requires name plus social security number. Other helpful information: date of birth, approximate years of attendance. No fee for information.

Transcripts available by mail. Search requires name plus social security number, signed release. Other helpful information: date of birth, approximate years of attendance. Fee is $3.00.

University of Redlands, Registrar, 1200 E Colton Ave, Redlands, CA 92373-0999, 909-793-2121. Hours: 8AM-5PM. Records go back to 1903. Degrees granted: Bachelors; Masters.

Attendance and degree information available by phone, mail. Search requires name only. Other helpful information: social security number. No fee for information.

Transcripts available by mail. Search requires name plus signed release. Other helpful information: social security number, date of birth, approximate years of attendance. Fee is $5.00. Expedited service available for $5.00.

Major credit cards accepted for payment.

University of Rhode Island, Registrar, Administration Bldg, Kingston, RI 02881-0806, 401-792-2835. Hours: 8AM-5PM. Records go back to 1892. Alumni records are maintained here also. Call 401-792-2242. Degrees granted: Bachelors; Masters; Doctorate.

Attendance and degree information available by phone, mail. Search requires name plus social security number, date of birth, exact years of attendance. No fee for information.

Transcripts available by mail. Search requires name plus social security number, date of birth, exact years of attendance, signed release. Fee is $4.00.

University of Richmond, Registrar, Richmond, VA 23173, 804-289-8639. Hours: 8AM-5PM. Records go back to 1830. Alumni records are maintained here also. Call 804-289-8473. Degrees granted: Bachelors; Masters; Doctorate.

Attendance and degree information available by phone, mail. Search requires name plus social security number, exact years of attendance. No fee for information.

Transcripts available by mail. Search requires name plus social security number, exact years of attendance, signed release. Fee is $2.00.

University of Rio Grande, Registrar, E College Ave, Rio Grande, OH 45674, 614-245-7368 (FAX: 614-245-7445). Hours: 8AM-5PM M,T,W,F; 8AM-6PM Th. Records go back to 1920. Alumni records are maintained here also. Call 614-245-7527. Degrees granted: Associate; Bachelors; Masters. Adverse incident record source: Student Development, 614-245-7234.

Attendance and degree information available by phone, FAX, mail. Search requires name plus social security number, approximate years of attendance, signed release. No fee for information.

Transcripts available by FAX, mail. Search requires name plus social security number, approximate years of attendance, signed release. Fee is $5.00.

University of Rochester, Registrar, River Campus, Administration Bldg, Rochester, NY 14627, 716-275-5131 (FAX: 716-275-2190). Hours: 8AM-5PM. Alumni records are maintained here also. Call 716-275-2121. Degrees granted: Bachelors; Masters; Doctorate.

Attendance and degree information available by phone, FAX, mail. Search requires name plus social security number, exact years of attendance. No fee for information.

Transcripts available by FAX, mail. Search requires name plus social security number, exact years of attendance, signed release. Fee is $2.00.

Need degree obtained and former names.

University of San Diego, Registrar, 5998 Alcala Park, San Diego, CA 92110-2492, 619-260-4557 (FAX: 619-260-4649). Hours: 8:30AM-5PM. Records go back to 1949. Alumni records are maintained here also. Call 619-260-4819. Degrees granted: Bachelors; Masters.

Attendance and degree information available by phone, FAX, mail. Search requires name plus social security number, approximate years of attendance. No fee for information.

Transcripts available by mail. Search requires name plus social security number, approximate years of attendance. Fee is $1.00. Include a self addressed stamped envelope with mail request.

University of San Francisco, Registrar, 2130 Fulton St, San Francisco, CA 94117-1080, 415-666-6316 (FAX: 415-666-6321). Hours: 8:30AM-5PM M-F, 10:30AM-3:30PM Sat. Records go back to 1986. Alumni records are maintained here also. Call 415-666-6431. Degrees granted: Bachelors; Masters; Doctorate.

Attendance and degree information available by phone, FAX, mail. Search requires name plus social security number, signed release. No fee for information.

Transcripts available by mail. Search requires name plus social security number, signed release. First transcript $5.00, each additional $1.00.

University of Sarasota, Registrar, 5250 17th St, Sarasota, FL 34235, 813-379-0404 (FAX: 813-379-9464). Hours: 10AM-4PM. Records go back to 1969. Alumni records are maintained here also. Call 813-379-0404. Degrees granted: Bachelors; Masters; Doctorate. Adverse incident record source: Dean of Students, 813-379-0404.

Attendance and degree information available by phone, FAX, mail. Search requires name plus social security number, exact years of attendance. No fee for information.

Transcripts available by mail. Search requires name plus social security number, exact years of attendance, signed release. Fee is $5.00.

University of Science and Arts of Oklahoma, Registrar, PO Box 82345, Chickasha, OK 73018, 405-224-3140 X204 (FAX: 405-521-6244). Hours: 8AM-5PM. Records go back to 1911. Alumni records are maintained here also. Call 405-224-3140 X290. Degrees granted: Bachelors.

Attendance and degree information available by phone, mail. Search requires name plus social security number. Fee is $1.00.

Transcripts available by mail. Search requires name plus social security number, signed release. Other helpful information: approximate years of attendance. Fee is $1.00.

University of Scranton, Registrar, 800 Linden St, Scranton, PA 18510-4501, 717-941-7720 (FAX: 717-941-4148). Hours: 8:30AM-4:30PM. Records go back to 1930. Degrees granted: Associate; Bachelors; Masters.

Attendance and degree information available by phone, FAX, mail. Search requires name only. Other helpful information: social security number, date of birth, approximate years of attendance. No fee for information.

Transcripts available by FAX, mail. Search requires name plus signed release. Other helpful information: social security number, date of birth, approximate years of attendance. Transcripts: $4.00 official; $2.00 student official; $0.50 unofficial.

University of Sioux Falls, Registrar, 1101 W 22nd St, Sioux Falls, SD 57105, 605-331-6650 (FAX: 605-331-6615). Hours: 8AM-5PM. Alumni records are maintained here also. Call 605-331-6608. Degrees granted: Associate; Bachelors; Masters. Adverse incident record source: Student Affairs, 605-331-6620.

Attendance and degree information available by phone, FAX, mail. Search requires name only. Other helpful information: social

security number, approximate years of attendance. No fee for information.

Transcripts available by mail. Search requires name plus signed release. Other helpful information: social security number, approximate years of attendance. Fee is $2.00. Expedited service available for $0.5.00.

Major credit cards accepted for payment.

University of South Alabama, Registrar, AD 165, Mobile, AL 36688, 334-460-6251 (FAX: 334-460-7738). Hours: 8AM-5PM. Records go back to 1963. Alumni Records Office: Plantation Creole House, Mobile, AL 36688. Degrees granted: Bachelors; Masters; Doctorate. Adverse incident record source: Campus Security, 334-460-6312: Dean of Students, 334-460-6171

Attendance information available by mail. Search requires name plus social security number, date of birth. Other helpful information: approximate years of attendance. No fee for information.

Degree information available by phone, mail. Search requires name plus social security number, date of birth. Other helpful information: approximate years of attendance. No fee for information.

Transcripts available by mail. Search requires name plus social security number, date of birth, signed release. Other helpful information: approximate years of attendance. Fee is $4.00.

Either SSN or DOB is sufficient. Take credit cards at Bursar's office only.

University of South Carolina-Aiken, Registrar, 171 University Pkwy, Aiken, SC 29801, 803-648-6851. Hours: 8AM-5PM. Transcript records are housed at University of South Carolina, Registrar, Columbia, SC, 29208. Degrees granted: Associate; Bachelors. Adverse incident record source: Public Safety, 803-648-6851.

Attendance information available by phone, FAX, mail. Search requires name only. No fee for information.

Degree information available by written request only. Search requires name plus social security number, signed release. No fee for information.

Transcripts available from main campus in Columbia.

University of South Carolina-Beaufort, Registrar, 801 Carteret St, Beaufort, SC 29902, 803-521-4101. Hours: 8AM-5PM. Transcript records are housed at University of South Carolina, Registrar, Columbia, SC, 29208.

Attendance information available by phone, FAX, mail. Search requires name only.

Degree information available by written request only. Search requires name plus social security number, signed release.

Transcripts available from main campus in Columbia.

University of South Carolina-Columbia, Registrar, Columbia, SC 29208, 803-777-3871 (FAX: 803-777-6349). Degrees granted: Associate.

Attendance information available by phone, FAX, mail. Search requires name only. Other helpful information: social security number. No fee for information.

Degree information available by FAX, mail. Search requires name plus social security number, signed release. Other helpful information: date of birth, approximate years of attendance. Fee is $5.00.

Transcripts available by FAX, mail. Search requires name plus social security number, signed release. Other helpful information: date of birth, approximate years of attendance. Fee is $5.00.

University of South Carolina-Lancaster, Registrar, PO Box 889, Lancaster, SC 29721, 803-285-7471 (FAX: 803-289-7116). Hours: 8:30AM-5PM. Transcript records are housed at University of South Carolina, Registrar, Columbia, SC, 29208. Degrees granted: Associate.

Attendance information available by phone, FAX, mail. Search requires name only. No fee for information.

Degree information available by written request only. Search requires name plus social security number, signed release. No fee for information.

Transcripts available from main campus in Columbia.

University of South Carolina-Salkehatchie, Registrar, PO Box 617, Allendale, SC 29810, 803-584-3446. Transcript records are housed at University of South Carolina, Registrar, Columbia, SC, 29208.

Attendance information available by phone, FAX, mail. Search requires name only.

Degree information available by written request only. Search requires name plus social security number, signed release.

Transcripts available from main campus in Columbia.

University of South Carolina-Spartanburg, Registrar, 800 University Wy, Spartanburg, SC 29303, 803-599-2220. Transcript records are housed at University of South Carolina, Registrar, Columbia, SC, 29208.

Attendance information available by phone, FAX, mail. Search requires name only.

Degree information available by written request only. Search requires name plus social security number, signed release.

Transcripts available from main campus in Columbia.

University of South Carolina-Sumter, Registrar, 200 Miller Rd, Sumter, SC 29150, 803-777-3871 (FAX: 803-777-6349). Hours: 8:30AM-5PM. Records go back to founding date. Transcript records are housed at University of South Carolina, Registrar, Columbia, SC, 29208. Alumni records are maintained here also. Call 803-775-6341. Degrees granted: Associate.

Attendance information available by phone, FAX, mail. Search requires name only. No fee for information.

Degree information available by written request only. Search requires name plus social security number, signed release. No fee for information.

Transcripts available from main campus in Columbia.

University of South Carolina-Union, Registrar, PO Drawer 729, Union, SC 29379, 803-429-8728. Transcript records are housed at University of South Carolina, Registrar, Columbia, SC, 29208.

Attendance information available by phone, FAX, mail. Search requires name only.

Degree information available by written request only. Search requires name plus social security number, signed release.

Transcripts available from main campus in Columbia.

University of South Dakota, Registrar, 414 E Clark St, Vermillion, SD 57069-2390, 605-677-5301 (FAX: 605-677-5073). Hours: 8AM-5PM. Alumni records are maintained here at the same phone number. Degrees granted: Bachelors; Masters; Doctorate.

Attendance and degree information available by phone, mail. Search requires name plus social security number, exact years of attendance. No fee for information.

Transcripts available by mail. Search requires name plus social security number, exact years of attendance, signed release. Fee is $5.00.

University of South Florida, Registrar's Office, SVC 1034, 4202 Fowler Ave, Tampa, FL 33620-6100, 813-974-2000 (FAX: 813-974-5271). Hours: 8AM-5PM. Records go back to 1956. Alumni records are maintained here also. Call 813-974-9127. Degrees granted: Associate; Bachelors; Masters; Doctorate. Adverse incident record source: Student Affairs, same address, ADM 151 USF.

Attendance and degree information available by phone, FAX, mail. Search requires name plus social security number. Other helpful information: date of birth, approximate years of attendance. No fee for information.

Transcripts available by FAX, mail. Search requires name plus social security number, signed release. Other helpful information: date of birth, approximate years of attendance. No fee for transcripts.

University of Southern California, Registrar, Los Angeles, CA 90089-0912, 213-740-2311 (FAX: 213-740-7254). Hours: 8:30AM-5PM. Records go back to founding date. Degrees granted: Bachelors; Masters; Doctorate. Adverse incident record source: Student Affairs, 213-740-2311.

Attendance and degree information available by phone, mail. Search requires name plus social security number, date of birth, exact years of attendance, signed release. No fee for information.

Transcripts available by mail. Search requires name plus date of birth, exact years of attendance, signed release. Transcript fee is $7.00. Written confirmation is $5.00.

Request by phone for years after 1979 only.

University of Southern Colorado, Registrar, 2200 Bonforte Blvd, Pueblo, CO 81001, 719-549-2261 (FAX: 719-549-2419). Hours: 8AM-5PM. Records go back to 1933. Degrees granted: Bachelors; Masters.

School will not confirm attendance information. Search requires name plus social security number, date of birth. No fee for information.

Degree information available by phone, FAX, mail. Search requires name plus social security number, date of birth, approximate years of attendance, signed release. No fee for information.

Transcripts available by phone, FAX, mail. Search requires name plus social security number, date of birth, signed release. Other helpful information: approximate years of attendance. Fee is $2.00.

Major credit cards accepted for payment.

University of Southern Indiana, Registrar, 8600 University Blvd, Evansville, IN 47712, 812-464-1763 (FAX: 812-464-1960). Hours: 8AM-4:30PM. Records go back to 1962. Degrees granted: Associate; Bachelors.

Attendance and degree information available by phone, FAX, mail. Search requires name plus signed release. Other helpful information: social security number. No fee for information.

Transcripts available by written request only. Search requires name plus signed release. Other helpful information: social security number. No fee for transcripts.

University of Southern Maine, Registrar, 96 Falmouth St, Portland, ME 04103, 207-780-5230. Hours: 8AM-4:30PM. Records go back 100 years. Alumni records are maintained here also. Call 207-780-4110. Degrees granted: Associate; Bachelors; Masters; L.L.D.

Attendance and degree information available by phone, mail. Search requires name only. Other helpful information: social security number, date of birth, approximate years of attendance. No fee for information.

Transcripts available by mail. Search requires name plus signed release. Other helpful information: social security number, date of birth, approximate years of attendance. Fee is $3.00. Expedited service available for $5.00.

University of Southern Mississippi, Registrar, Box 5006, Hattiesburg, MS 39406-5001, 601-266-5006 (FAX: 601-266-5816). Hours: 8AM-5PM. Records go back 50 years. Degrees granted: Bachelors; Masters; Doctorate.

School will not confirm attendance information. Search requires name only. No fee for information.

Degree information available by mail. Search requires name plus social security number, date of birth, exact years of attendance, signed release. No fee for information.

Transcripts available by mail. Search requires name plus social security number, date of birth, signed release. Other helpful information: approximate years of attendance. Fee is $4.00.

University of Southern Mississippi, (Gulf Park), Registrar, 730 E Beach Blvd, Long Beach, MS 39560, 601-865-4503 (FAX: 601-865-4587). Hours: 8AM-4:30PM. Records go back to 1984. Alumni Records Office: PO Box 5013, Hattiesburg, MS 39406. Degrees granted: Bachelors; Masters. Certification: Education.

Attendance and degree information available by phone, mail. Search requires name plus social security number. Other helpful information: date of birth, approximate years of attendance. No fee for information.

Transcripts available by mail. Search requires name plus social security number, approximate years of attendance, signed release. Other helpful information: date of birth, exact years of attendance. Fee is $4.00.

Major credit cards accepted for payment.

University of Southwestern Louisiana, Registrar, 200 E University Ave, Lafayette, LA 70503, 318-482-1000. Hours: 8AM-4:30PM. Records go back to 1901. Alumni records are maintained here also. Call 318-482-1000. Degrees granted: Bachelors; Masters; Doctorate.

Attendance and degree information available by phone, mail. Search requires name plus social security number, exact years of attendance. No fee for information.

Transcripts available by mail. Search requires name plus social security number, exact years of attendance, signed release. No fee for transcripts.

University of St. Mary of the Lake Mundelein Seminary, Registrar, 1000 E April Ave, Mundelein, IL 60060, 708-566-6401. Hours: 8AM-4:30PM. Records go back to 1929. Degrees granted: Masters.

Attendance and degree information available by mail. Search requires name plus social security number, date of birth, signed release. No fee for information.

Transcripts available by mail. Search requires name plus social security number, date of birth, signed release. Fee is $2.00.

University of St. Thomas, Registrar, 3800 Montrose Blvd, Houston, TX 77006-4696, 713-522-7911. Hours: 8AM-4:30PM.

Records go back to 1946. Alumni records are maintained here also. Call 713-525-3115. Degrees granted: Bachelors; Masters; Doctorate.

Attendance and degree information available by phone, mail. Search requires name plus social security number, signed release. Other helpful information: approximate years of attendance. No fee for information.

Transcripts available by mail. Search requires name plus social security number, signed release. Other helpful information: approximate years of attendance. Fee is $5.00.

Major credit cards accepted for payment.

University of St. Thomas, Registrar, 2115 Summit Ave, St Paul, MN 55105, 612-962-6707 (FAX: 612-962-6710). Hours: 8AM-4:30PM. Records go back to 1910. Alumni records are maintained here also. Call 612-962-6430. Degrees granted: Masters; Doctorate.

Attendance and degree information available by phone, FAX, mail. Search requires name plus social security number, signed release. No fee for information.

Transcripts available by FAX, mail. Search requires name plus social security number, signed release. Fee is $4.00.

University of Tampa, Registrar, 401 W Kennedy Blvd, Tampa, FL 33606-1490, 813-253-6251 (FAX: 813-258-7207). Hours: 8:30AM-5PM. Degrees granted: Associate; Bachelors; Masters.

Attendance and degree information available by phone, FAX, mail. Search requires name only. Other helpful information: social security number, date of birth, approximate years of attendance. No fee for information.

Transcripts available by FAX, mail. Search requires name plus signed release. Other helpful information: social security number, date of birth, approximate years of attendance. Fee is $5.00.

University of Tennessee at Chattanooga, Registrar, 615 McCallie Ave, Chattanooga, TN 37403-2598, 615-755-4416. Hours: 8AM-5PM. Alumni records are maintained here at the same phone number. Degrees granted: Bachelors; Masters.

Attendance and degree information available by phone, mail. Search requires name plus social security number, exact years of attendance. No fee for information.

Transcripts available by mail. Search requires name plus social security number, exact years of attendance, signed release. Fee is $2.00.

University of Tennessee at Martin, Registrar, University St, Martin, TN 38238, 901-587-7049 (FAX: 901-587-7048). Hours: 8AM-5PM. Records go back to 1927. Alumni records are maintained here also. Call 901-587-7610. Degrees granted: Bachelors; Masters.

Attendance and degree information available by phone, FAX, mail. Search requires name only. Other helpful information: social security number, date of birth, approximate years of attendance. No fee for information.

Transcripts available by FAX, mail. Search requires name plus signed release. Other helpful information: social security number, date of birth, approximate years of attendance. No fee for transcripts. Expedited service available for $5.00.

University of Tennessee, Knoxville, Registrar, 209 Student Services Bldg, Knoxville, TN 37796-0200, 615-974-2101 (FAX: 615-974-6341). Hours: 8AM-5PM. Records go back to 1880. Degrees granted: Bachelors; Masters; Doctorate. Adverse incident record source: Student Services, 615-974-3171.

Attendance information available by phone, FAX, mail. Search requires name plus social security number. Other helpful information: date of birth, exact years of attendance. No fee for information.

Degree information available by phone, FAX, mail. Search requires name plus social security number. Other helpful information: date of birth, approximate years of attendance. No fee for information.

Transcripts available by mail. Search requires name plus signed release. Other helpful information: social security number, date of birth, approximate years of attendance. No fee for transcripts.

University of Tennessee, Memphis, Registrar's Office, 119 Randolph Hall, Memphis, TN 38163, 901-448-5563. Hours: 8AM-5PM. Alumni records are maintained here at the same phone number. Degrees granted: Bachelors; Masters; Doctorate.

Attendance and degree information available by mail. Search requires name plus social security number, exact years of attendance. No fee for information.

Transcripts available by mail. Search requires name plus social security number, exact years of attendance, signed release. No fee for transcripts.

University of Texas Health Science Center at Houston, Registrar, PO Box 20036, 7000 Fannin Ste 2250, Houston, TX 77225, 713-792-7444 (FAX: 713-794-5701). Hours: 8AM-4:30PM. Alumni records are maintained here at the same phone number. Degrees granted: Bachelors; Masters; Doctorate.

Attendance and degree information available by phone, mail. Search requires name plus social security number, exact years of attendance. No fee for information.

Transcripts available by mail. Search requires name plus social security number, exact years of attendance, signed release. Fee is $5.00.

University of Texas Health Science Center at San Antonio, Registrar, 7703 Floyd Curl Dr, San Antonio, TX 78284, 210-567-2621 (FAX: 210-567-2685). Hours: 8AM-4:30PM. Alumni records are maintained here at the same phone number. Degrees granted: Bachelors; Masters; Doctorate.

Attendance and degree information available by mail. Search requires name plus social security number, exact years of attendance. No fee for information.

Transcripts available by mail. Search requires name plus social security number, exact years of attendance, signed release. Fee is $5.00.

University of Texas Medical Branch at Galveston, Registrar, 301 University Blvd, Galveston, TX 77555-1305, 409-772-1215 (FAX: 409-772-5056). Hours: 8AM-5PM. Records go back to founding date. Alumni records are maintained here also. Call 409-772-2772. Degrees granted: Bachelors; Masters; Doctorate.

Attendance and degree information available by phone, FAX, mail. Search requires name plus date of birth. Other helpful information: social security number, approximate years of attendance. No fee for information.

Transcripts available by FAX, mail. Search requires name plus date of birth, signed release. Other helpful information: social security number, approximate years of attendance. No fee for transcripts.

University of Texas Southwestern Medical Center at Dallas, Registrar, 5323 Harry Hines Blvd, Dallas, TX 75235, 214-648-2671 (FAX: 214-648-3289). Hours: 8AM-4:30PM. Alumni records are maintained here at the same phone number. Degrees granted: Doctorate.

Attendance and degree information available by phone, FAX, mail. Search requires name plus social security number. No fee for information.

Transcripts available by FAX, mail. Search requires name plus social security number, signed release. No fee for transcripts.

University of Texas at Arlington, Registrar, PO Box 19088, Arlington, TX 76019, 817-273-3719. Hours: 8AM-4:30PM. Alumni records are maintained here at the same phone number. Degrees granted: Bachelors; Masters; Doctorate.

Attendance and degree information available by phone, mail. Search requires name plus social security number. No fee for information.

Transcripts available by mail. Search requires name plus social security number, signed release. Fee is $5.00.

University of Texas at Austin, Registrar, Main Bldg Room 1, Austin, TX 78713-7389, 512-471-7701. Hours: 8AM-4:30PM. Alumni records are maintained here at the same phone number. Degrees granted: Bachelors; Masters; Doctorate.

Attendance and degree information available by phone, mail. Search requires name plus social security number, exact years of attendance. No fee for information.

Transcripts available by mail. Search requires name plus social security number, exact years of attendance, signed release. Fee is $5.00.

University of Texas at Brownsville, Registrar, 80 Fort Brown, Brownsville, TX 78520, 210-544-8254 (FAX: 210-544-8832). Hours: 7:30AM-7PM M-Th; 7:30AM-1:30PM F. Records go back to 1991. Degrees granted: Bachelors; Masters.

Attendance and degree information available by FAX, mail. Search requires name plus date of birth, signed release. Other helpful information: social security number, approximate years of attendance. No fee for information.

Transcripts available by FAX, mail. Search requires name plus date of birth, signed release. Other helpful information: social security number, approximate years of attendance. Fee is $1.00.

Major credit cards accepted for payment.

University of Texas at Dallas, Records & Registration, PO Box 830688 MCII, Richardson, TX 75083-0688, 214-883-2341 (FAX: 214-883-6335). Hours: 8AM-7PM M-Th; 8AM-5PM F. Records go back to 1969. Alumni records are maintained here at the same phone number. Degrees granted: Bachelors; Masters; Doctorate. Certification: Teacher Education. Adverse incident record source: Student Life, 214-883-2098.

Attendance and degree information available by phone, FAX, mail. Search requires name only. Other helpful information: social security number, date of birth, approximate years of attendance. No fee for information.

Transcripts available by FAX, mail. Search requires name plus signed release. Other helpful information: date of birth, approximate years of attendance. No fee for transcripts.

University of Texas at El Paso, Registrar, 500 W University Ave, El Paso, TX 79968, 915-747-5230 (FAX: 915-747-5012). Hours: 8AM-7PM M,T; 8AM-5PM W-F. Records go back to 1915. Degrees granted: Bachelors; Masters; Doctorate.

Attendance and degree information available by phone, FAX, mail. Search requires name plus date of birth. Other helpful information: social security number, approximate years of attendance. No fee for information.

Transcripts available by FAX, mail. Search requires name plus date of birth, signed release. Other helpful information: social security number, approximate years of attendance. Fee is $5.00. Expedited service available for $7.00.

University of Texas at San Antonio, Registrar, 6900 N Loop 1604 W, San Antonio, TX 78249-0617, 210-691-4530. Hours: 8AM-4:30PM. Alumni records are maintained here at the same phone number. Degrees granted: Bachelors; Masters; Doctorate.

Attendance and degree information available by phone, mail. Search requires name plus social security number, exact years of attendance. No fee for information.

Transcripts available by mail. Search requires name plus social security number, exact years of attendance, signed release. Fee is $5.00.

University of Texas at Tyler, Registrar, 3900 University Blvd, Tyler, TX 75799, 903-566-7439 (FAX: 903-566-7173). Hours: 8AM-5PM. Records go back to 1971. Alumni records are maintained here also. Call 903-566-7411. Degrees granted: Bachelors; Masters.

Attendance and degree information available by phone, FAX, mail. Search requires name plus social security number, signed release. Other helpful information: date of birth. No fee for information.

Transcripts available by FAX, mail. Search requires name plus social security number, signed release. Other helpful information: date of birth. Fee is $5.00.

Major credit cards accepted for payment.

University of Texas of the Permian Basin, Registrar, 4901 E University Blvd, Odessa, TX 79762, 915-552-2635 (FAX: 915-552-2374). Hours: 8AM-6PM M-Th; 8AM-5PM F. Records go back to 1972. Degrees granted: Bachelors; Masters.

Attendance information available by phone, FAX, mail. Search requires name only. Other helpful information: social security number. No fee for information.

Degree information available by phone, FAX, mail. Search requires name plus social security number. No fee for information.

Transcripts available by FAX, mail. Search requires name plus social security number, signed release. Fee is $5.00.

No information on confidential-tagged files. Expedite fee is $5.00 per page. Major credit cards accepted for payment.

University of Texas-Pan American, Registrar, 1201 W University Dr, Edinburg, TX 78539-2999, 210-381-2011. Hours: 8AM-5PM. Alumni records are maintained here at the same phone number. Degrees granted: Bachelors; Masters; Doctorate.

Attendance and degree information available by phone, mail. Search requires name plus social security number. No fee for information.

Transcripts available by written request only. Search requires name plus social security number, signed release. Fee is $3.00.

University of Toledo, Registrar, 2801 W Bancroft St, Toledo, OH 43606, 419-537-2701 (FAX: 419-537-7757). Hours: 9AM-5PM M,Th,F; 9AM-7PM T,W. Records go back to 1800s. Alumni records are maintained here also. Call 419-527-2601.

Degrees granted: Associate; Bachelors; Masters; Doctorate; Ph. Adverse incident record source: Dean, 419-527-2256.

Attendance and degree information available by phone, FAX, mail. Search requires name plus social security number, date of birth, exact years of attendance, signed release. No fee for information.

Transcripts available by FAX, mail. Search requires name plus social security number, date of birth, exact years of attendance, signed release. Fee is $4.00.

Major credit cards accepted for payment.

University of Tulsa, Registrar, 600 S College Ave, Tulsa, OK 74104, 918-631-2253 (FAX: 918-631-2622). Hours: 8AM-6PM M-Th; 8AM-5PM F. Degrees granted: Bachelors; Masters; Doctorate; J.D.

Attendance information available by phone, FAX, mail. Search requires name plus social security number, approximate years of attendance. Other helpful information: date of birth, exact years of attendance. No fee for information.

Degree information available by FAX, mail. Search requires name plus social security number, approximate years of attendance, signed release. Other helpful information: date of birth, exact years of attendance. No fee for information.

Transcripts available by FAX, mail. Search requires name plus social security number, approximate years of attendance, signed release. Other helpful information: date of birth, exact years of attendance. Fee is $2.00. Expedited service available for $5.00.

Major credit cards accepted for payment.

University of Utah, Registrar, Student Services Bldg Room 250, Salt Lake City, UT 84112, 801-581-8965 (FAX: 801-585-3034). Hours: 8:30AM-5PM. Records go back to 1850. Alumni records are maintained here at the same phone number. Degrees granted: Bachelors; Masters; Doctorate.

Attendance and degree information available by phone, mail. Search requires name plus social security number, date of birth, exact years of attendance. No fee for information.

Transcripts available by mail. Search requires name plus social security number, date of birth, exact years of attendance, signed release. Fee is $2.00.

University of Vermont, Academic Transcript, Burlington, VT 05405-0160, 802-656-2045 (FAX: 802-656-8230). Hours: 8AM-5PM. Records go back to 1791. Alumni records are maintained here also. Call 802-656-2010. Degrees granted: Bachelors; Masters; Doctorate.

Attendance and degree information available by phone, FAX, mail. Search requires name plus social security number, exact years of attendance. No fee for information.

Transcripts available by mail. Search requires name plus social security number, exact years of attendance, signed release. Fee is $5.00.

University of Virginia, Registrar, PO Box 9011, Charlottesville, VA 22906, 804-924-4122. Hours: 8AM-4:30PM. Records go back to 1819. Alumni records are maintained here also. Call 804-971-9721. Degrees granted: Bachelors; Masters; Doctorate.

Attendance and degree information available by mail. Search requires name plus social security number, exact years of attendance, signed release. No fee for information.

Transcripts available by mail. Search requires name plus social security number, exact years of attendance, signed release. Fee is $3.00.

University of Washington, Registrar, 1400 NE Campus Park Way, Seattle, WA 98195, 206-543-8580 (FAX: 206-543-9285). Hours: 8AM-4:30PM. Records go back to 1869. Alumni records are maintained here also. Call 206-543-0540. Degrees granted: Bachelors; Masters; Doctorate.

Attendance and degree information available by phone, FAX, mail. Search requires name plus social security number, date of birth, exact years of attendance, signed release. No fee for information.

Transcripts available by FAX, mail. Search requires name plus social security number, date of birth, exact years of attendance, signed release. Fee is $4.00.

University of West Florida, Registrar, 11000 University Pkwy, Pensacola, FL 32514-5750, 904-474-2244 (FAX: 904-474-3360). Hours: 8AM-5PM. Records go back to 1967. Alumni records are maintained here also. Call 904-474-2758. Degrees granted: Associate; Bachelors; Masters; Specialist. Special programs- Conferences & Continuing Ed, 904-474-2706. Adverse incident record source: Public Safety, 904-474-2415: Student Affairs, 904-474-2384

Attendance and degree information available by phone, FAX, mail. Search requires name plus signed release. Other helpful information: social security number, date of birth, approximate years of attendance. No fee for information.

Transcripts available by FAX, mail. Search requires name plus signed release. Other helpful information: social security number, date of birth, approximate years of attendance. Fee is $5.00.

University of West Los Angeles, Registrar, 1155 W Arbor Vitae St, Inglewood, CA 90301-2902, 310-215-3339 (FAX: 310-641-4736). Hours: 8:30AM-6:30PM. Alumni records are maintained here also. Call 310-215-3339. Degrees granted: Bachelors; Doctorate; Para-Legal. Adverse incident record source: Academic Office, 310-215-3339.

Attendance and degree information available by mail. Search requires name plus approximate years of attendance. No fee for information.

Transcripts available by mail. Search requires name plus approximate years of attendance, signed release. Fee is $5.00.

No fee for unofficial transcript copy.

University of Wisconsin, Registrar, PO Box 8680, Madison, WI 53708-8680, 608-262-1234. Hours: 8AM-5PM. Records go back to 1848. Alumni records are maintained here at the same phone number. Degrees granted: Associate.

Attendance and degree information available by phone, mail. Search requires name plus social security number. No fee for information.

Transcripts available by mail. Search requires name plus social security number, signed release. No fee for transcripts.

Include a self addressed stamped envelope with mail request.

University of Wisconsin-Baraboo-Sauk County, Registrar, 1006 Connie Rd, Baraboo, WI 53913, 608-356-8351. Hours: 8AM-5PM. Records go back to 1968. Degrees granted: Associate.

Attendance and degree information available by phone, mail. Search requires name plus social security number. No fee for information.

Transcripts available by written request only. Search requires name plus social security number, signed release. Fee is $3.00.

University of Wisconsin-Barron County, Registrar, 1800 College Dr, Rice Lake, WI 54868, 715-234-8176. Hours: 8AM-5PM. Records go back to 1968. Degrees granted: Associate.

Attendance and degree information available by phone, mail. Search requires name plus social security number. No fee for information.

Transcripts available by written request only. Search requires name plus social security number, signed release. Fee is $3.00.

University of Wisconsin-Eau Claire, Registrar, S 130, Eau Claire, WI 54702, 715-836-5912 (FAX: 715-836-2380). Hours: 7:45AM-4:30PM. Records go back to founding date. Degrees granted: Associate; Bachelors; Masters. Certification: Ed.

Attendance and degree information available by phone, FAX, mail. Search requires name plus social security number. Other helpful information: date of birth, approximate years of attendance. No fee for information.

Transcripts available by FAX, mail. Search requires name plus social security number, signed release. Other helpful information: date of birth, approximate years of attendance. No fee for transcripts. Expedite fee is based on cost of service.'

University of Wisconsin-Fond du Lac, Registrar, Campus Dr, Fond Du Lac, WI 54935, 414-929-3606 (FAX: 414-929-3626). Records are not housed here. They are located at University of Wisconsin, Registrar, PO Box 8680, Madison, WI 53708-8680.

University of Wisconsin-Fox Valley, Registrar, PO Box 8002, Menasha, WI 54952-8002, 414-832-2600. Hours: 8AM-5PM. Alumni records are maintained here at the same phone number. Degrees granted: Associate.

Attendance and degree information available by phone, mail. Search requires name plus social security number. No fee for information.

Transcripts available by written request only. Search requires name plus social security number, signed release. Fee is $3.00.

University of Wisconsin-Green Bay, Registrar, 2420 Nicolet Dr, Green Bay, WI 54311, 414-465-2055 (FAX: 414-465-2765). Hours: 9AM-4:30PM. Records go back to 1969. Alumni records are maintained here also. Call 414-465-2586. Degrees granted: Associate; Bachelors; Masters. Adverse incident record source: Dean of Students, 414-465-2152.

Attendance and degree information available by FAX, mail. Search requires name plus social security number. Other helpful information: approximate years of attendance. No fee for information.

Transcripts available by mail. Search requires name plus social security number, signed release. Other helpful information: date of birth, approximate years of attendance. Fee is $3.00. Expedited service available for $8.00.

University of Wisconsin-La Crosse, Registrar, 1725 State St, La Crosse, WI 54601, 608-785-8576 (FAX: 608-785-6695). Hours: 8AM-4:30PM. Records go back to 1906. Alumni records are maintained here also. Call 608-785-8489. Degrees granted: Associate; Bachelors; Masters.

Attendance and degree information available by phone, FAX, mail. Search requires name only. Other helpful information: social security number, date of birth, approximate years of attendance. No fee for information.

Transcripts available by FAX, mail. Search requires name plus social security number, signed release. Other helpful information: date of birth, approximate years of attendance. Fee is $3.00.

University of Wisconsin-Madison, Registrar, 750 University Ave, AW Peterson Ofc Bldg Room 60, Madison, WI 53706, 608-262-3722 (FAX: 608-262-0123). Hours: 8AM-5PM. Records go back to 1848. Alumni records are maintained here also. Call 608-262-2551. Degrees granted: Bachelors; Masters; Doctorate.

Attendance and degree information available by phone, mail. Search requires name plus social security number, date of birth, exact years of attendance. No fee for information.

Transcripts available by mail. Search requires name plus social security number, date of birth, exact years of attendance, signed release. No fee for transcripts.

University of Wisconsin-Manitowoc County, Registrar, 705 Viebahn St, Manitowoc, WI 54220-6699, 414-683-4700. Hours: 8AM-5PM. Alumni records are maintained here also. Call 414-683-4713. Degrees granted: Associate.

Attendance and degree information available by phone, mail. Search requires name plus social security number. No fee for information.

Transcripts available by written request only. Search requires name plus social security number, signed release. Fee is $3.00.

University of Wisconsin-Marathon County, Registrar, 518 S Seventh Ave, Wausau, WI 54401, 715-845-9602. Hours: 8AM-5PM. Degrees granted: Associate.

Attendance and degree information available by phone, mail. Search requires name plus social security number. No fee for information.

Transcripts available by written request only. Search requires name plus social security number, signed release. Fee is $3.00.

University of Wisconsin-Marinette County, Registrar, 750 W Bay Shore St, Marinette, WI 54143, 715-735-7477. Hours: 8AM-5PM. Records go back to 1968. Degrees granted: Associate.

Attendance and degree information available by phone, mail. Search requires name plus social security number. No fee for information.

Transcripts available by written request only. Search requires name plus social security number, signed release. Fee is $3.00.

University of Wisconsin-Marshfield-Wood County, Registrar, PO Box 150, Marshfield, WI 54449, 715-387-1147. Hours: 8AM-5PM. Records go back to 1968. Degrees granted: Associate.

Attendance and degree information available by phone, mail. Search requires name plus social security number. No fee for information.

Transcripts available by written request only. Search requires name plus social security number, signed release. Fee is $3.00.

University of Wisconsin-Milwaukee, Registrar, PO Box 729, Milwaukee, WI 53201, 414-229-4984 (Grad.) (FAX: 414-229-6940). Hours: 8AM-5PM. Records go back to 1956. Alumni records are maintained here at the same phone number. Degrees granted: Bachelors; Masters; Doctorate.

Attendance and degree information available by phone, mail. Search requires name plus social security number, exact years of attendance. No fee for information.

Transcripts available by mail. Search requires name plus social security number, exact years of attendance, signed release. Fee is $3.00.

University of Wisconsin-Oshkosh, Records Office, 800 Algoma Blvd, Oshkosh, WI 54901, 414-424-0325 (FAX: 414-424-7317). Hours: 8:30AM-3:30PM. Records go back to 1850s. Degrees granted: Associate; Bachelors; Masters. Adverse incident record source: Dean of Students, 414-424-3100.

Attendance and degree information available by phone, FAX, mail. Search requires name plus social security number. Other helpful information: date of birth. No fee for information.

Transcripts available by mail. Search requires name plus social security number, signed release. Other helpful information: date of birth, exact years of attendance. Fee is $3.00. Expedited service available for $5.00.

University of Wisconsin-Parkside, Registrar, Box 2000, Kenosha, WI 53141-2000, 414-595-2284. Hours: 8AM-5PM. Records go back to 1968. Alumni records are maintained here also. Call 414-595-2414. Degrees granted: Bachelors; Masters.

Attendance and degree information available by phone, mail. Search requires name plus social security number, date of birth, exact years of attendance. No fee for information.

Transcripts available by mail. Search requires name plus social security number, date of birth, exact years of attendance, signed release. Fee is $4.00.

University of Wisconsin-Platteville, Registrar, One University Plaza, Platteville, WI 53818-3099, 608-342-1321. Hours: 7:45AM-4:45PM. Records go back to 1800s. Alumni records are maintained here also. Call 608-342-1181. Degrees granted: Associate; Bachelors; Masters. Special programs- Masters Program Graduate Office, 608-342-1263. Adverse incident record source: Student Affairs, 608-342-1854.

Attendance information available by phone, mail. Search requires name plus social security number. Other helpful information: date of birth, approximate years of attendance. No fee for information.

Degree information available by phone, mail. Search requires name plus social security number, date of birth. Other helpful information: approximate years of attendance. No fee for information.

Transcripts available by mail. Search requires name plus social security number, date of birth, signed release. Other helpful information: approximate years of attendance. No fee for transcripts.

University of Wisconsin-Richland, Registrar, Hwy 14 W, Richland Center, WI 53581, 608-647-6186. Hours: 8AM-5PM. Records go back to 1967. Degrees granted: Associate.

Attendance and degree information available by phone, mail. Search requires name plus social security number. No fee for information.

Transcripts available by written request only. Search requires name plus social security number, signed release. Fee is $3.00.

University of Wisconsin-River Falls, Registrar, River Falls, WI 54022, 715-425-3342. Hours: 8AM-5PM. Records go back to 1874. Degrees granted: Bachelors; Masters.

Attendance and degree information available by phone, mail. Search requires name plus social security number, date of birth. No fee for information.

Transcripts available by mail. Search requires name plus social security number, date of birth, signed release. Fee is $2.00.

University of Wisconsin-Rock County, Registrar, 2909 Kellogg Ave, Janesville, WI 53546, 608-758-6522. Hours: 8AM-5PM. Records go back to 1968. Degrees granted: Associate.

Attendance and degree information available by phone, mail. Search requires name plus social security number. No fee for information.

Transcripts available by written request only. Search requires name plus social security number, signed release. Fee is $3.00.

University of Wisconsin-Sheboygan County, Registrar, One University Dr, Sheboygan, WI 53081, 414-459-6633 (FAX: 414-459-6602). Hours: 8AM-5PM. Records go back to 1950. Degrees granted: Associate.

Attendance and degree information available by phone, FAX, mail. Search requires name plus social security number, signed release. Other helpful information: date of birth, approximate years of attendance. No fee for information.

Transcripts available by written request only. Search requires name plus social security number, signed release. Other helpful information: date of birth, approximate years of attendance. Fee is $3.00.

University of Wisconsin-Stevens Point, Registrar, Stevens Point, WI 54481, 715-346-4301 (FAX: 715-346-2558). Hours: 7:45AM-4:30PM. Records go back to 1894. Degrees granted: Associate; Bachelors; Masters. Adverse incident record source: Student Rights & Responsibilities, 715-346-4566.

Attendance and degree information available by phone, FAX, mail. Search requires name only. Other helpful information: social security number, date of birth, approximate years of attendance. No fee for information.

Transcripts available by FAX, mail. Search requires name plus signed release. Other helpful information: social security number, date of birth, approximate years of attendance. Fee is $3.00. Expedited service available for $3.00.

University of Wisconsin-Stout, Registrar, Menomonie, WI 54751-0790, 715-232-2121 (FAX: 715-232-2436). Hours: 8AM-4:30PM. Records go back to 1893. Alumni records are maintained here also. Call 715-232-1151. Degrees granted: Bachelors; Masters. Special programs- Provosts Office, 715-232-2421.

Attendance and degree information available by phone, FAX, mail. Search requires name plus social security number. Other helpful information: date of birth, approximate years of attendance. No fee for information.

Transcripts available by mail. Search requires name plus social security number, signed release. Other helpful information: date of birth, approximate years of attendance. Fee is $3.00.

University of Wisconsin-Superior, Registrar, 1800 Grand Ave, Superior, WI 54880, 715-394-8228. Hours: 8AM-5PM. Records go back to 1922. Alumni records are maintained here also. Call 715-394-8101. Degrees granted: Bachelors; Masters.

Attendance and degree information available by phone, mail. Search requires name plus social security number, exact years of attendance. No fee for information.

Transcripts available by mail. Search requires name plus social security number, exact years of attendance, signed release. Fee is $3.00.

University of Wisconsin-Washington County, Registrar, 400 University Dr, West Bend, WI 53095, 414-335-5200. Records go back to 1968. Degrees granted: Associate.

Attendance and degree information available by phone, mail. Search requires name plus social security number. No fee for information.

Transcripts available by written request only. Search requires name plus social security number, signed release. Fee is $3.00.

University of Wisconsin-Waukesha County, Registrar, 1500 University Dr, Waukesha, WI 53188, 414-521-5200. Hours: 8AM-5PM. Records go back to 1966. Degrees granted: Associate.

Attendance and degree information available by phone, mail. Search requires name plus social security number. No fee for information.

Transcripts available by written request only. Search requires name plus social security number, signed release. Fee is $3.00.

University of Wisconsin-Whitewater, Registrar, 800 W Main St, Whitewater, WI 53190, 414-472-1580 (FAX: 414-472-1515). Hours: 7:45AM-4:30PM. Records go back to 1885. Alumni records are maintained here also. Call 414-472-1105. Degrees granted: Associate; Bachelors; Masters. Adverse incident record source: Student Affairs, 414-472-1051.

Attendance and degree information available by phone, FAX, mail. Search requires name only. Other helpful information: social security number, date of birth, approximate years of attendance. No fee for information. Include a stamped envelope.

Transcripts available by written request only. Search requires name plus social security number, signed release. Other helpful information: date of birth, approximate years of attendance. Fee is $3.00. Expedited service available for $3.00.

University of Wyoming, Registrar, PO Box 3964, University Station, Laramie, WY 82071, 307-766-5272. Hours: 8AM-5PM. Records go back to 1886. Alumni Records Office: PO Box 3137, Laramie, WY 82071 307-766-4166. Degrees granted: Bachelors; Masters; Doctorate.

Attendance and degree information available by phone, mail. Search requires name plus social security number, date of birth, exact years of attendance. No fee for information.

Transcripts available by mail. Search requires name plus social security number, date of birth, exact years of attendance, signed release. Fee is $3.00.

University of the Arts, Registrar, 320 S Broad St, Philadelphia, PA 19148, 215-875-4848. Hours: 9AM-5PM. Year records start varies depending on school. Alumni records are maintained here also. Call 215-875-4826. Degrees granted: Associate; Bachelors; Masters. Special programs- New Studies Center (now PIE), 215-875-3350. Adverse incident record source: Student Services, 215-875-2256.

Attendance and degree information available by phone, mail. Search requires name plus social security number, date of birth, approximate years of attendance. No fee for information.

Transcripts available by written request only. Search requires name plus social security number, date of birth, approximate years of attendance, signed release. Fee is $5.00. Major helpful. Credit card $25.00 minimum.

University of the District of Columbia, Registrar, 4200 Connecticut Ave NW, Washington, DC 20008, 202-274-6072 (FAX: 202-274-6073). Hours: 8AM-5PM M,W,F; 8AM-6PM T,Th. Records go back to 1800. Alumni Records Office: Alumni Affairs, 4250 Connecticut Ave, Washington, DC 20008 202-274-5117. Degrees granted: Masters; Undergrad. Adverse incident record source: Registrar, 202-274-6072.

Attendance and degree information available by mail. Search requires name plus social security number, exact years of attendance, signed release. Other helpful information: date of birth, approximate years of attendance. No fee for information.

Transcripts available by mail. Search requires name plus social security number, exact years of attendance, signed release. Other helpful information: date of birth, approximate years of attendance. Fee is $5.00.

University of the District of Columbia, (Georgia/Harvard Street), 11th and Harvard Sts NW, Washington, DC 20009, 202-673-7021. Records are not housed here. They are located at University of the District of Columbia, Registrar, 4200 Connecticut Ave NW, Washington, DC 20008.

University of the Ozarks, Registrar, 415 N College Ave, Clarksville, AR 72830, 501-979-1215 (FAX: 501-979-1355). Hours: 8AM-Noon,1-4:30PM. Records go back 80 years. Alumni records are maintained here also. Call 501-979-1237. Degrees granted: Associate; Bachelors; Masters. Adverse incident record source: Student Affairs, 501-979-1211.

Attendance and degree information available by phone, FAX, mail. Search requires name only. Other helpful information: social security number, approximate years of attendance. No fee for information.

Transcripts available by FAX, mail. Search requires name plus signed release. Other helpful information: social security number, date of birth, approximate years of attendance. Fee is $2.00. Expedite: $4.00 plus costs.

University of the Pacific, Registrar, 3601 Pacific Ave, Stockton, CA 95211, 209-946-2135 (FAX: 209-946-2596). Hours: 8AM-5PM. Records go back to 1900. Degrees granted: Bachelors; Masters; Doctorate.

Attendance and degree information available by phone, FAX, mail. Search requires name plus signed release. Other helpful information: social security number, date of birth, approximate years of attendance. No fee for information.

Transcripts available by phone, FAX, mail. Search requires name plus signed release. Other helpful information: social security number, date of birth, approximate years of attendance. Fee is $4.00. Expedited service available for $4.00.

University of the Sacred Heart, Registrar, Box 12383 Loiza Sta, Santurce, PR 00914, 809-728-1515.

University of the South, Registrar, 735 University Ave, Sewanee, TN 37375-1000, 615-598-1314. Hours: 8AM-4:30PM. Records go back to 1858. Alumni records are maintained here also. Call 615-598-1402. Degrees granted: Bachelors; Masters; Doctorate.

Attendance and degree information available by mail. Search requires name plus social security number, date of birth, exact years of attendance, signed release. No fee for information.

Transcripts available by mail. Search requires name plus social security number, date of birth, exact years of attendance, signed release. Fee is $2.00.

University of the Virgin Islands, Registrar, St Thomas, VI 00802, 809-776-9200.

University of the Virgin Islands, (Branch Campus), Registrar, St Croix, VI 00850, 809-778-1620.

Upper Iowa University, Registrar, Box 1857, College and Washington Sts, Fayette, IA 52142, 319-425-5268 (FAX: 319-425-5287). Hours: 8AM-5PM. Records go back to founding date. Degrees granted: Associate; Bachelors; Masters.
  Attendance information available by phone, FAX, mail. Search requires name plus social security number. Other helpful information: date of birth, approximate years of attendance. No fee for information.
  Degree information available by phone, FAX, mail. Search requires name plus social security number, date of birth. Other helpful information: approximate years of attendance. No fee for information.
  Transcripts available by FAX, mail. Search requires name plus social security number, signed release. Other helpful information: date of birth, approximate years of attendance. Fee is $2.00.

Urbana University, Registrar, One College Wy, Urbana, OH 43078, 513-484-1353. Hours: 8AM-4:30PM. Records go back to 1950. Degrees granted: Associate; Bachelors. Adverse incident record source: Dean of Students, 513-484-1378.
  Attendance and degree information available by phone, mail. Search requires name plus social security number, date of birth, approximate years of attendance, signed release. Other helpful information: exact years of attendance. No fee for information.
  Transcripts available by mail. Search requires name plus social security number, date of birth, approximate years of attendance, signed release. Other helpful information: exact years of attendance. Fee is $3.00.
  Major credit cards accepted for payment.

Ursinus College, Registrar, Box 1000, Main Street, Collegeville, PA 19426-1000, 610-489-4111 X2225. Hours: 8AM-5PM. Records go back to 1869. Alumni records are maintained here at the same phone number. Degrees granted: Bachelors.
  Attendance and degree information available by phone, mail. Search requires name only. No fee for information.
  Transcripts available by mail. Search requires name plus signed release. Fee is $2.00.

Ursuline College, Registrar, 2550 Lander Rd, Pepper Pike, OH 44124, 216-646-8131 (FAX: 216-646-8129). Hours: 8:30AM-5PM. Records go back to 1950. Alumni records are maintained here also. Call 216-646-8375. Degrees granted: Bachelors; Masters.
  Attendance and degree information available by phone, FAX, mail. Search requires name plus social security number. Other helpful information: date of birth, approximate years of attendance. No fee for information.
  Transcripts available by mail. Search requires name plus social security number. Other helpful information: date of birth, approximate years of attendance. Fee is $3.00.

Utah State University, Registrar, Logan, UT 84322-1400, 801-797-3988 (FAX: 801-797-3880). Alumni records are maintained here at the same phone number. Degrees granted: Bachelors; Masters; Doctorate.
  Attendance and degree information available by phone, FAX, mail. Search requires name plus social security number, exact years of attendance. No fee for information.
  Transcripts available by FAX, mail. Search requires name plus social security number, exact years of attendance, signed release. Fee is $3.00.

Utah Valley State College, Registrar, 1200 S 800 W, Orem, UT 84058, 801-222-8000 X8468. Hours: 8AM-5PM. Alumni records are maintained here at the same phone number. Degrees granted: Bachelors.
  Attendance and degree information available by phone, mail. Search requires name plus social security number, exact years of attendance. No fee for information.
  Transcripts available by mail. Search requires name plus social security number, exact years of attendance, signed release. Fee is $2.00.

Utica College of Syracuse University, Registrar, 1600 Burrstone Rd, Utica, NY 13502-4892, 315-792-3195. Hours: 8:30AM-5PM. Records go back 49 years. Alumni records are maintained here also. Call 315-792-3025. Degrees granted: Bachelors.
  Attendance and degree information available by phone, mail. Search requires name plus signed release. Other helpful information: social security number, date of birth, approximate years of attendance. No fee for information.
  Transcripts available by mail. Search requires name plus signed notarized release. Other helpful information: social security number, date of birth, approximate years of attendance. Fee is $4.00.
  Include a self addressed stamped envelope with mail request.

Utica School of Commerce, Registrar, 201 Bleecker St, Utica, NY 13501, 315-733-2307 (FAX: 315-733-9281). Hours: 7:30AM-4:30PM. Records go back to 1896. Alumni records are maintained here at the same phone number. Degrees granted: Associate.
  Attendance information available by FAX, mail. Search requires name plus social security number, exact years of attendance, signed release. No fee for information.
  Degree information available by FAX, mail. Search requires name plus social security number, exact years of attendance, signed release. No fee for information.
  Transcripts available by FAX, mail. Search requires name plus social security number, exact years of attendance, signed release. No fee for transcripts.

Utica School of Commerce, (Branch), Registrar, PO Box 462, Canastota, NY 13032, 315-697-8200. Records are not housed here. They are located at Utica School of Commerce, Registrar, 201 Bleecker St, Utica, NY 13501.

Utica School of Commerce, (Branch), Registrar, 17-19 Elm St, Oneonta, NY 13820, 607-432-7003. Records are not housed here. They are located at Utica School of Commerce, Registrar, 201 Bleecker St, Utica, NY 13501.

V

Valdosta State University, Registrar, 1500 N Patterson St, Valdosta, GA 31698, 912-333-5727 (FAX: 912-333-5475). Hours: 8AM-5:30PM M-Th, 8AM-3PM F. Records go back to 1919. Degrees granted: Associate; Bachelors; Masters. Adverse incident record source: Student Affairs, 912-333-5941: University Police, 912-333-7816

Attendance and degree information available by phone, FAX, mail. Search requires name plus social security number. Other helpful information: date of birth, approximate years of attendance. No fee for information. Expedited service available for $5.00.

Transcripts available by FAX, mail. Search requires name plus social security number, signed release. Other helpful information: date of birth, approximate years of attendance. Fee is $2.00. Expedited service available for $5.00.

Major credit cards accepted for payment.

Valencia Community College, (West), Registrar, PO Box 3028, 1800 S Kirkman Rd, Orlando, FL 32811, 407-299-5000 X1506. Hours: 7:30AM-9PM M-Th, 7:30AM-5PM F. Records go back to 1967. Alumni Records Office: Alumni Association, 190 N Orange Ave, Orlando, FL 32801. Degrees granted: Associate. Adverse incident record source: Provost, 407-299-5000 X1372.

Attendance information available by phone, mail. Search requires name plus social security number, date of birth, signed release. Other helpful information: approximate years of attendance. No fee for information.

Degree information available by phone, mail. Search requires name plus social security number, signed release. Other helpful information: approximate years of attendance. No fee for information.

Transcripts available by mail. Search requires name plus social security number, signed release. Other helpful information: approximate years of attendance. No fee for transcripts.

Valley City State University, Registrar, College St, Valley City, ND 58072, 701-845-7295 (FAX: 701-845-7245). Hours: 7:45AM-4:30PM. Records go back 104 years. Alumni records are maintained here also. Call 701-845-7411. Degrees granted: Bachelors.

Attendance and degree information available by phone, FAX, mail. Search requires name only. Other helpful information: social security number, date of birth, approximate years of attendance. No fee for information.

Transcripts available by FAX, mail. Search requires name plus signed release. Other helpful information: social security number, date of birth, approximate years of attendance. Fee is $2.00.

Fee increase scheduled.

Valley Forge Christian College, Registrar, 1401 Charlestown Rd, VFCC Box 51, Phoenixville, PA 19460, 610-935-0450 (FAX: 610-935-9353). Hours: 8AM-4:30PM. Records go back to 1938. Alumni records are maintained here at the same phone number. Degrees granted: Bachelors.

Attendance and degree information available by phone. Search requires name only. Other helpful information: social security number, approximate years of attendance. No fee for information.

Transcripts available by mail. Search requires name plus social security number, signed release. Other helpful information: approximate years of attendance. First transcript free; $5.00 each additional.

Valley Forge Military College, Registrar, 1001 Eagle Rd, Wayne, PA 19087-3695, 610-989-1455 (FAX: 610-989-1555). Hours: 8:30AM-4:30PM. Records go back to founding date. Alumni records are maintained here at the same phone number. Degrees granted: Associate.

Attendance and degree information available by phone, FAX, mail. Search requires name plus social security number. Other helpful information: approximate years of attendance. No fee for information.

Transcripts available by written request only. Search requires name plus social security number, signed release. Other helpful information: approximate years of attendance. Fee is $5.00.

Valparaiso University, Registrar, Valparaiso, IN 46383, 219-464-5212 (FAX: 219-464-5381). Hours: 8AM-5PM. Records go back to 1859. Alumni records are maintained here also. Call 219-464-5110. Degrees granted: Associate; Bachelors; Masters. Adverse incident record source: Registrar, 219-464-5212.

Attendance and degree information available by phone, FAX, mail. Search requires name plus social security number, date of birth, exact years of attendance. No fee for information.

Transcripts available by FAX, mail. Search requires name plus social security number, date of birth, exact years of attendance, signed release. No fee for transcripts.

Vance-Granville Community College, Registrar, PO Box 917, Poplar Creek Rd, Henderson, NC 27536, 919-492-2061 (FAX: 919-430-0460). Records go back to 1970. Degrees granted: Associate.

Attendance and degree information available by phone, FAX, mail. Search requires name plus social security number, date of birth, signed release. Other helpful information: exact years of attendance. Fee is $1.00.

Transcripts available by mail. Search requires name plus social security number, date of birth, signed release. Other helpful information: exact years of attendance. Fee is $1.00.

VanderCook College of Music, Registrar, 3209 S Michigan Ave, Chicago, IL 60616, 312-225-6288 (FAX: 312-225-5211). Hours: 9AM-5PM. Records go back to 1928. Alumni records are maintained here at the same phone number. Degrees granted: Bachelors; Masters.

Attendance and degree information available by phone, FAX, mail. Search requires name plus social security number, approximate years of attendance, signed release. No fee for information.

Transcripts available by mail. Search requires name plus social security number, approximate years of attendance, signed release. Fee is $3.00.

Vanderbilt University, Registrar, 242 Alexander Hall, Nashville, TN 37240, 615-322-7701 (FAX: 615-343-7709). Hours: 8AM-5PM. Records go back to 1875. Alumni records are maintained here also. Call 615-322-4219. Degrees granted: Bachelors; Masters; Doctorate.

Attendance and degree information available by phone, FAX, mail. Search requires name plus social security number. No fee for information.

Transcripts available by FAX, mail. Search requires name plus social security number, signed release. Fee is $2.00.

Need to know field of study. FAX fee is $5.00. Major credit cards accepted for payment.

Vassar College, Registrar, Raymond Ave, Box 1, Poughkeepsie, NY 12601, 914-437-5275 (FAX: 914-437-7187). Hours: 8AM-5PM. Records go back to 1865. Alumni records are maintained here also. Call 914-437-5445. Degrees granted: Bachelors; Masters. Adverse incident record source: Dean, 914-437-5255.

Attendance and degree information available by phone, FAX, mail. Search requires name plus social security number, date of birth, exact years of attendance. No fee for information.

Transcripts available by FAX, mail. Search requires name plus social security number, date of birth, exact years of attendance, signed release. Fee is $2.00.

Vennard College, Registrar, Eighth Ave E, PO Box 29, University Park, IA 52595, 515-673-8391 X205 (FAX: 515-673-8365). Hours: 8AM-5PM. Records go back to 1910. Alumni records are maintained here also. Call 515-673-8391 X209. Degrees granted: Associate; Bachelors. Adverse incident record source: Student Development, 515-673-8391 X250.

Attendance and degree information available by phone, FAX, mail. Search requires name plus social security number, signed release. No fee for information.

Transcripts available by mail. Search requires name plus social security number, signed release. Fee is $3.00.

Ventura College, Registrar, 4667 Telegraph Rd, Ventura, CA 93003, 805-654-6457 (FAX: 805-654-6466). Hours: 8AM-7:30PM M-Th, 9AM-5PM F. Records go back to 1945. Alumni records are maintained here also. Call 805-648-8927. Degrees granted: Associate. Adverse incident record source: Dean of Student Services, 805-654-6455.

Attendance and degree information available by phone, FAX, mail. Search requires name plus social security number, date of birth, approximate years of attendance. No fee for information.

Transcripts available by mail. Search requires name plus social security number, date of birth, approximate years of attendance, signed release. First two transcripts are free; $3.00 each additional.

Vermilion Community College, Registrar, 1900 E Camp St, Ely, MN 55731, 218-365-7223 (FAX: 218-365-7207). Hours: 8AM-4:30PM. Records go back to 1922. Degrees granted: Associate. Adverse incident record source: Student Services, 218-365-7249.

Attendance and degree information available by phone, FAX, mail. Search requires name plus social security number. Other helpful information: date of birth. No fee for information.

Transcripts available by phone, FAX, mail. Search requires name plus social security number. Other helpful information: date of birth. No fee for transcripts.

Transcripts other than to colleges require signature.

Vermont College of Norwich University, Registrar, College St, Montpelier, VT 05602, 802-828-8727 (FAX: 802-828-8855). Hours: 8AM-5PM. Records go back to 1934. Alumni records are maintained here also. Call 802-485-2100. Degrees granted: Bachelors; Masters.

Attendance and degree information available by phone, mail. Search requires name plus social security number, date of birth. No fee for information.

Transcripts available by mail. Search requires name plus social security number, date of birth, signed release. Fee is $4.00.

Vermont Law School, Registrar, PO Box 96, South Royalton, VT 05068, 802-763-8303 (FAX: 802-763-7071). Hours: 8:30AM-5PM. Records go back to 1973.

Attendance and degree information available by phone, FAX, mail. Search requires name only. Other helpful information: approximate years of attendance. No fee for information.

Transcripts available by phone, FAX, mail. Search requires name plus signed release. Other helpful information: approximate years of attendance. Fee is $2.00.

Student may request transcript by phone.

Vermont Technical College, Registrar, Randolph Center, VT 05061, 802-728-1302 (FAX: 802-728-1390). Hours: 8AM-4:30PM; 8AM-4PM Summers. Records go back to 1900. Alumni records are maintained here also. Call 802-728-1261. Degrees granted: Associate; Bachelors.

Attendance and degree information available by phone, FAX, mail. Search requires name only. Other helpful information: social security number, date of birth, approximate years of attendance. No fee for information.

Transcripts available by mail. Search requires name plus social security number, signed release. Other helpful information: date of birth, approximate years of attendance. Fee is $5.00. Expedited service available for $10.00.

Registrar reserves right to ask for written release for any request. Need to know maiden or other name. Major credit cards accepted for payment.

Vernon Regional Junior College, Registrar, 4400 College Dr, Vernon, TX 76384, 817-552-6291 X204 (FAX: 817-553-3902). Hours: 8AM-4:30PM. Degrees granted: Associate.

Attendance and degree information available by phone, FAX, mail. Search requires name plus social security number. No fee for information.

Transcripts available by FAX, mail. Search requires name plus social security number, signed release. Fee is $1.00.

Victor Valley College, Admissions & Records Dept, 18422 Bear Valley Rd, Victorville, CA 92392, 619-245-4271 (FAX: 619-245-9745). Hours: 8:30AM-5PM. Records go back to 1961. Alumni records are maintained here at the same phone number. Degrees granted: Associate. Certification: rt:Occupation. Adverse incident record source: Vice President, 619-245-4271 X271.

Attendance information available by phone, FAX. Search requires name plus social security number, date of birth. Other helpful information: approximate years of attendance. Fee is $2.00. Expedited service available for $2.00.

Degree information available by FAX. Search requires name plus social security number, date of birth. Other helpful information: approximate years of attendance. Fee is $2.00. Expedite service available for $2.00.

Transcripts available by FAX. Search requires name plus social security number, date of birth, signed release. Other helpful information: approximate years of attendance. Fee is $2.00. Expedited service available for $5.00.

Victoria College, Registrar, 2200 E Red River St, Victoria, TX 77901-4494, 512-572-6411 (FAX: 512-572-3850). Degrees granted: Associate.

Attendance and degree information available by phone, FAX, mail. Search requires name plus social security number. Other helpful information: date of birth, approximate years of attendance. No fee for information.

Transcripts available by phone, FAX, mail. Search requires name plus social security number. Other helpful information: date of birth, approximate years of attendance. Fee is $2.00.

Villa Julie College, Registrar, 1525 Green Spring Valley Rd, Stevenson, MD 21153, 410-486-7000 X2207. Hours: 8AM-4:30PM. Records go back to 1947. Alumni records are maintained here at the same phone number. Degrees granted: Bachelors.

Attendance and degree information available by phone, mail. Search requires name plus social security number, exact years of attendance. No fee for information.

Transcripts available by mail. Search requires name plus social security number, exact years of attendance, signed release. Fee is $3.00.

Villa Maria College of Buffalo, Registrar, 240 Pine Ridge Rd, Buffalo, NY 14225-3999, 716-896-0700 X337 (FAX: 716-896-0705). Hours: 8AM-4PM. Records go back to 1964. Alumni records are maintained here also. Call 716-896-0700 X327. Degrees granted: Associate.
 Attendance information available by FAX, mail. Search requires name plus signed release. Other helpful information: social security number, date of birth, approximate years of attendance. Fee is $2.00. Expedited service available for $2.00.
 Degree information available by phone, FAX, mail. Search requires name plus signed release. Other helpful information: social security number, date of birth, approximate years of attendance. Fee is $2.00. Expedite service available for $2.00.
 Transcripts available by mail. Search requires name plus signed release. Other helpful information: social security number, date of birth, approximate years of attendance. Fee is $2.00. Expedited service available for $2.00.
 Major credit cards accepted for payment.

Villanova University, Registrar, Lancaster Pike, Villanova, PA 19085, 610-519-4032 (FAX: 610-519-4033). Hours: 9AM-5PM. Records go back to 1855. Degrees granted: Associate; Bachelors; Masters; Doctorate.
 Attendance and degree information available by phone, FAX, mail. Search requires name plus social security number. Other helpful information: date of birth, approximate years of attendance. No fee for information.
 Transcripts available by FAX, mail. Search requires name plus social security number, signed release. Other helpful information: date of birth, approximate years of attendance. No fee for transcripts.

Vincennes University, Registrar, 1002 N First St, Vincennes, IN 47591, 812-885-4220 (FAX: 812-885-5868). Hours: 8AM-4:30PM. Records go back to 1806. Alumni records are maintained here also. Call 812-885-4354. Degrees granted: Associate.
 Attendance and degree information available by phone, FAX, mail. Search requires name plus social security number, exact years of attendance. No fee for information.
 Transcripts available by FAX, mail. Search requires name plus social security number, exact years of attendance, signed release. No fee for transcripts.

Virginia College, Registrar, 2163 Apperson Dr, Salem, VA 24153-7235, 703-776-0755. Hours: 9AM-6PM M-Th, 8AM-5PM F. Records go back to 1925. Degrees granted: Associate.
 Attendance and degree information available by phone, mail. Search requires name plus social security number, exact years of attendance. No fee for information.
 Transcripts available by mail. Search requires name plus social security number, exact years of attendance, signed release. Fee is $3.00.

Virginia College-Huntsville, Registrar, 2800-A Bob Wallace Ave, Huntsville, AL 35805, 205-533-7387 (FAX: 205-533-7785). Hours: 8AM-5PM. Records go back to 1993. Degrees granted: Associate.
 Attendance and degree information available by mail. Search requires name plus social security number, date of birth, signed release. Other helpful information: approximate years of attendance. No fee for information.
 Transcripts available by mail. Search requires name plus social security number, date of birth, signed release. Other helpful information: approximate years of attendance. Fee is $2.00.

Virginia College, **(Branch Campus)**, Registrar, 1900 28th Ave, Birmingham, AL 35209, 205-802-1200. Hours: 9AM-6PM M-Th, 9AM-4PM F. Records go back to 1993. Degrees granted: Associate.
 Attendance and degree information available by phone, mail. Search requires name plus social security number, exact years of attendance. No fee for information.
 Transcripts available by mail. Search requires name plus social security number, exact years of attendance, signed release. Fee is $3.00.

Virginia Commonwealth University, Registrar, 910 W Franklin St, PO Box 2520, Richmond, VA 23284, 804-367-1349. Degrees granted: Bachelors; Masters; Doctorate.
 Attendance and degree information available by phone, mail. Search requires name plus social security number, exact years of attendance. No fee for information.
 Transcripts available by mail. Search requires name plus social security number, exact years of attendance, signed release. No fee for transcripts.

Virginia Highlands Community College, Admissions Office, PO Box 828, Abingdon, VA 24210, 703-628-6094 (FAX: 703-628-7576). Hours: 8AM-5PM. Records go back to 1969. Degrees granted: AAS, AA&S.
 Attendance and degree information available by phone, FAX, mail. Search requires name plus social security number. Other helpful information: date of birth, approximate years of attendance. No fee for information.
 Transcripts available by FAX, mail. Search requires name plus social security number, signed release. Other helpful information: date of birth, approximate years of attendance. No fee for transcripts.

Virginia Intermont College, Registrar, 1013 Moore St, Bristol, VA 24201, 703-669-6101 (FAX: 703-669-5763). Hours: 8:30AM-Noon, 1-4:30PM. Records go back to 1800s. Degrees granted: Associate; Bachelors.
 Attendance and degree information available by phone, FAX, mail. Search requires name only. Other helpful information: social security number, date of birth, approximate years of attendance. No fee for information.
 Transcripts available by mail. Search requires name plus signed release. Other helpful information: social security number, date of birth, approximate years of attendance. Fee is $4.00.

Virginia Military Institute, Registrar, Lexington, VA 24450, 703-464-7000 (FAX: 703-464-7660). Degrees granted: Bachelors.
 Attendance and degree information available by phone, FAX, mail. Search requires name plus social security number, exact years of attendance. No fee for information.
 Transcripts available by mail. Search requires name plus social security number, exact years of attendance, signed release. No fee for transcripts.

Virginia Polytechnic Institute and State University, Office of the Registrar, Enrollment Services, 248 Burruss Hall, Blacksburg, VA 24061-0134, 703-231-5611 (FAX: 703-231-

5527). Hours: 8AM-5PM. Degrees granted: Bachelors; Masters; Doctorate.

Attendance information available by phone. Search requires name plus social security number, approximate years of attendance, signed release. Other helpful information: exact years of attendance. No fee for information.

Degree information available by phone, FAX, mail. Search requires name plus social security number, date of birth, exact years of attendance. No fee for information.

Transcripts available by FAX, mail. Search requires name plus social security number, signed release. Other helpful information: date of birth, approximate years of attendance. No fee for transcripts. Expedite fee is based on cost of service.'

Virginia State University, Registrar, PO Box 9217, One Hayden Dr, Petersburg, VA 23806, 804-524-5986. Hours: 8AM-4:30PM. Records go back to 1882. Alumni records are maintained here also. Call 804-524-5906. Degrees granted: Bachelors; Masters.

Attendance and degree information available by phone, mail. Search requires name plus social security number, exact years of attendance. No fee for information.

Transcripts available by mail. Search requires name plus social security number, exact years of attendance, signed release. Fee is $2.00.

Virginia Union University, Registrar, 1500 N Lombardy St, Richmond, VA 23220-1711, 804-257-5845. Hours: 8:30AM-4:30PM. Records go back to 1800s. Degrees granted: Bachelors; Masters; Doctorate. Adverse incident record source: Student Affairs, 804-257-5875.

Attendance and degree information available by phone, mail. Search requires name plus social security number, approximate years of attendance, signed release. No fee for information.

Transcripts available by mail. Search requires name plus social security number, approximate years of attendance, signed release. No fee for transcripts.

Virginia Wesleyan College, Office of the Registrar, 1584 Wesleyan Dr, Norfolk, VA 23502-5599, 804-455-3358 (FAX: 804-466-8526). Hours: 8:30AM-4:30PM. Records go back to 1966. Alumni records are maintained here also. Call 804-455-3298. Degrees granted: Bachelors. Adverse incident record source: Dean of Students, 804-455-3273: Campus Security, 804-455-3349

Attendance and degree information available by phone, FAX, mail. Search requires name plus social security number. Other helpful information: date of birth, approximate years of attendance. No fee for information.

Transcripts available by FAX, mail. Search requires name plus social security number, signed release. Other helpful information: date of birth, approximate years of attendance. Fee is $3.00.

Will accept FAX requests but original must be sent with fee.

Virginia Western Community College, Registrar, 3095 Colonial Ave SW, PO Box 14065, Roanoke, VA 24038, 703-857-7236 (FAX: 703-857-7544). Hours: 7:30AM-5PM. Records go back to 1966. Degrees granted: Associate; Career Studies.

Attendance and degree information available by phone, FAX, mail. Search requires name plus social security number. No fee for information.

Transcripts available by mail. Search requires name plus social security number, signed release. No fee for transcripts.

Vista College, Registrar, 2020 Milvia St, Berkeley, CA 94704, 510-841-8431 X245 (FAX: 510-841-7333). Hours: 9AM-7PM. Records go back to 1960. Alumni records are maintained here also. Call 510-841-8431 X267. Degrees granted: Associate.

Attendance and degree information available by FAX, mail. Search requires name plus social security number, approximate years of attendance. No fee for information.

Transcripts available by mail. Search requires name plus social security number, approximate years of attendance, signed release. Fee is $1.00.

Viterbo College, Registrar, 815 S Ninth St, La Crosse, WI 54601, 608-791-0412 (FAX: 608-791-0367). Hours: 8AM-4:30PM. Alumni records are maintained here also. Call 608-791-0471. Degrees granted: Bachelors; Masters.

Attendance information available by mail. Search requires name only. Other helpful information: social security number, date of birth. No fee for information.

Degree information available by phone, mail. Search requires name only. Other helpful information: social security number, date of birth. No fee for information.

Transcripts available by mail. Search requires name plus signed release. Other helpful information: social security number. Fee is $3.00. Expedited service available for $3.00.

Volunteer State Community College, Registrar, 1360 Nashville Pike, Gallatin, TN 37066, 615-452-8600 X461 (FAX: 615-452-8600 X645). Degrees granted: Associate.

Attendance and degree information available by phone, FAX, mail. Search requires name plus social security number, date of birth. Other helpful information: approximate years of attendance. No fee for information.

Transcripts available by FAX, mail. Search requires name plus social security number, date of birth, signed release. Other helpful information: approximate years of attendance. No fee for transcripts.

Voorhees College, Registrar, 1141 Voorhees Rd, Denmark, SC 29042, 803-793-3351 X7309 (FAX: 803-793-4584). Hours: 8AM-5PM. Records go back to 1897. Alumni records are maintained here also. Call 803-793-3351. Degrees granted: Bachelors.

Attendance and degree information available by phone, mail. Search requires name plus social security number, exact years of attendance. No fee for information.

Transcripts available by mail. Search requires name plus social security number, exact years of attendance, signed release. Fee is $5.00.

W

Wabash College, Registrar, 301 W Wabash Ave, Crawfordsville, IN 47933, 317-364-4245 (FAX: 317-364-4432). Hours: 8AM-4:30PM. Records go back to 1900. Degrees granted: Bachelors. Adverse incident record source: Dean of Students.

Attendance and degree information available by phone, FAX, mail. Search requires name only. Other helpful information: date of birth. No fee for information.

Transcripts available by FAX, mail. Search requires name plus signed release. Other helpful information: date of birth. Fee is $1.00.

Wabash Valley College, Admissions and Records, 2200 College Dr, Mount Carmel, IL 62863, 618-262-8641 (FAX: 618-262-8641). Hours: 8AM-5PM. Degrees granted: Associate.

Attendance information available by phone, FAX, mail. Search requires name plus social security number, date of birth, signed release. Other helpful information: approximate years of attendance. No fee for information.

Degree information available by phone, FAX, mail. Search requires name plus social security number, date of birth, exact years of attendance, signed release. Other helpful information: approximate years of attendance. No fee for information.

Transcripts available by FAX, mail. Search requires name plus social security number, date of birth, approximate years of attendance, signed release. Other helpful information: exact years of attendance. Fee is $1.00.

Wadhams Hall Seminary/College, Registrar, R D 4 Box 80, Ogdensburg, NY 13669, 315-393-4231 (FAX: 315-393-4249). Hours: 8AM-4PM. Records go back to 1924. Alumni records are maintained here at the same phone number. Degrees granted: Bachelors. Certification: Christian Leadership.

Attendance information available by phone. Search requires name plus social security number, signed release. Other helpful information: date of birth, approximate years of attendance. Fee is $4.00.

Degree information available by written request only. Search requires name plus social security number, signed release. Other helpful information: date of birth, approximate years of attendance. Fee is $4.00.

Transcripts available by written request only. Search requires name plus signed release. Other helpful information: social security number, date of birth, approximate years of attendance. Fee is $4.00.

Wagner College, Registrar, Howard Ave and Campus Rd, Staten Island, NY 10301, 718-390-3208 (FAX: 718-390-3344). Hours: 10AM-4PM. Records go back to founding date. Alumni records are maintained here also. Call 718-390-3240. Degrees granted: Bachelors; Masters. Certification: Nursing.

Attendance and degree information available by FAX, mail. Search requires name plus social security number. Other helpful information: date of birth, approximate years of attendance. No fee for information.

Transcripts available by FAX, mail. Search requires name plus social security number, signed release. Other helpful information: date of birth, approximate years of attendance. Fee is $5.00.

Major credit cards accepted for payment.

Wake Forest University, Registrar, PO Box 7207 Reynolds Station, Winston-Salem, NC 27109, 910-759-5206 (FAX: 910-759-6056). Hours: 8AM-5PM. Records go back to 1834. Alumni records are maintained here also. Call 910-759-5264. Degrees granted: Bachelors; Masters; Doctorate.

Attendance and degree information available by phone, FAX, mail. Search requires name plus social security number, exact years of attendance. No fee for information.

Transcripts available by FAX, mail. Search requires name plus social security number, exact years of attendance, signed release. Fee is $4.00.

Wake Technical Community College, Registrar, 9191 Fayetteville Rd, Raleigh, NC 27603-5696, 919-662-3240. Records go back to 1963. Degrees granted: Associate.

Attendance and degree information available by written request only. Search requires name plus social security number, date of birth. Other helpful information: approximate years of attendance. No fee for information.

Transcripts available by written request only. Search requires name plus social security number, date of birth, signed release. Other helpful information: approximate years of attendance. No fee for transcripts.

Walden University, Registrar, 155 S Fifth Ave, Minneapolis, MN 55401, 612-338-7224 (FAX: 612-338-5092). Hours: 8AM-5PM. Records go back to 1970. Degrees granted: Doctorate.

Attendance and degree information available by phone, FAX, mail. Search requires name plus signed release. Other helpful information: social security number, approximate years of attendance. No fee for information.

Transcripts available by mail. Search requires name plus social security number, signed release. Other helpful information: date of birth, approximate years of attendance. Fee is $5.00. Expedited service available for $5.00.

Major credit cards accepted for payment.

Waldorf College, Registrar, Forest City, IA 50436, 515-582-8139 (FAX: 515-582-8194). Hours: 8AM-5PM. Records go back to founding date. Degrees granted: Associate; Bachelors.

Attendance and degree information available by phone, FAX, mail. Search requires name plus social security number, approximate years of attendance. Other helpful information: date of birth. No fee for information. Include stamped envelope.

Transcripts available by phone, FAX, mail. Search requires name plus social security number, approximate years of attendance, signed release. Other helpful information: date of birth. First three free; $5.00 each additional.

Walla Walla College, Registrar, 204 S College Ave, College Place, WA 99324, 509-527-2811 (FAX: 509-527-2574). Hours: 8:30AM-Noon, 1-4:30PM. Records go back to 1905. Alumni records are maintained here also. Call 509-527-2093. Degrees granted: Associate; Bachelors; Masters.

Attendance and degree information available by phone, FAX, mail. Search requires name only. Other helpful information: social security number, date of birth, approximate years of attendance. No fee for information.

Transcripts available by mail. Search requires name plus social security number, date of birth, approximate years of attendance, signed release. Other helpful information: exact years of attendance. No fee for transcripts. Expedited service available for $5.00.

Walla Walla Community College, Registrar, 500 Tausick Way, Walla Walla, WA 99362, 509-527-4283 (FAX: 509-527-3661). Hours: 8AM-5PM. Records go back to 1967. Degrees granted: Associate.

Attendance and degree information available by phone, FAX, mail. Search requires name plus social security number, signed release. Other helpful information: date of birth. No fee for information.

Transcripts available by phone, FAX, mail. Search requires name plus social security number, signed release. Other helpful information: date of birth, approximate years of attendance. Fee is $3.00. Expedite fee is based on cost of service.'

Major credit cards accepted for payment.

Wallace State Community College, Registrar, 801 Main St, Hanceville, AL 35077, 205-352-6403 (FAX: 205-352-6400). Hours: 7:30AM-4PM. Records go back to 1966. Degrees granted: Associate.

Attendance and degree information available by phone, FAX, mail. Search requires name plus social security number, date of birth. Other helpful information: approximate years of attendance. No fee for information.

Transcripts available by mail. Search requires name plus social security number, date of birth, signed release. Other helpful information: approximate years of attendance. No fee for transcripts.

Walsh College of Accountancy and Business Administration, Registrar, 3838 Livernois Rd, PO Box 7006, Troy, MI 48007-7006, 810-689-8282 (FAX: 810-524-2520). Hours: 8:30AM-7PM. Records go back to 1922. Alumni records are maintained here at the same phone number. Degrees granted: Bachelors; Masters.

Attendance and degree information available by phone, FAX, mail. Search requires name only. Other helpful information: social security number, approximate years of attendance. No fee for information.

Transcripts available by written request only. Search requires name plus social security number, approximate years of attendance, signed release. Fee is $2.00.

Major credit cards accepted for payment.

Walsh University, Registrar, 2020 Easton St NW, Canton, OH 44720, 216-490-7194 (FAX: 216-490-7165). Hours: 8AM-4PM. Records go back to 1960. Degrees granted: Associate; Bachelors; Masters. Certification: Teacher Prep.

Attendance and degree information available by phone, FAX, mail. Search requires name plus social security number, date of birth. Other helpful information: approximate years of attendance. No fee for information.

Transcripts available by mail. Search requires name plus social security number, date of birth, signed release. Other helpful information: approximate years of attendance. Fee is $5.00.

Walters State Community College, Registrar, 500 S Davy Crockett Pkwy, Morristown, TN 37813-6899, 615-585-0828 (FAX: 615-585-2631). Hours: 8AM-4:30PM. Records go back to 1970. Degrees granted: Associate. Adverse incident record source: Student Affairs, 615-585-2680.

Attendance and degree information available by phone, FAX, mail. Search requires name plus social security number, signed release. Other helpful information: approximate years of attendance. No fee for information.

Transcripts available by FAX, mail. Search requires name plus social security number, signed release. Other helpful information: approximate years of attendance. No fee for transcripts.

Ward Stone College, Registrar, 9020 SW 137th Ave, Miami, FL 33186, 305-386-9900 (FAX: 305-388-1740). Hours: 8AM-4PM. Records go back 15 years. Degrees granted: Associate; SAD.

Attendance information available by phone, FAX, mail. Search requires name plus social security number, exact years of attendance, signed release. Other helpful information: approximate years of attendance. No fee for information.

Degree information available by FAX, mail. Search requires name plus social security number, signed release. Other helpful information: date of birth, approximate years of attendance. No fee for information.

Transcripts available by FAX, mail. Search requires name plus social security number, signed release. Other helpful information: date of birth, approximate years of attendance. Fee is $5.00. Expedited service available for $5.00.

Major credit cards accepted for payment.

Warner Pacific College, Registrar, 2219 SE 68th Ave, Portland, OR 97215, 503-775-4366 X611. Hours: 8AM-5PM. Records go back to 1937. Alumni records are maintained here also. Call 503-775-4366. Degrees granted: Bachelors; Masters.

Attendance and degree information available by phone, mail. Search requires name plus social security number. No fee for information.

Transcripts available by mail. Search requires name plus social security number, exact years of attendance, signed release. Fee is $5.00.

Warner Southern College, Registrar, 5301 US Hwy 27 S, Lake Wales, FL 33853-8725, 813-638-7204 (FAX: 813-638-1472). Records go back 27 years. Alumni records are maintained here at the same phone number. Degrees granted: Associate; Bachelors.

Attendance and degree information available by phone, FAX, mail. Search requires name plus social security number. Other helpful information: approximate years of attendance. No fee for information.

Transcripts available by FAX, mail. Search requires name plus social security number, signed release. Other helpful information: approximate years of attendance. Fee is $2.00.

Warren County Community College, Registrar, Box 55A Rte 57 W, Washington, NJ 07882, 908-689-1090 (FAX: 908-689-9262). Hours: 8:30AM-5PM. Records go back to 1981.

Attendance and degree information available by mail. Search requires name plus social security number, signed release. Other helpful information: approximate years of attendance. No fee for information.

Transcripts available by mail. Search requires name plus social security number, signed release. Other helpful information: approximate years of attendance. Fee is $3.00.

Major credit cards accepted for payment.

Warren Wilson College, Registrar, PO Box 9000, Asheville, NC 28815-9000, 704-298-3325 (FAX: 704-299-3326). Hours: 8AM-5PM. Records go back to 1894. Alumni records are maintained here at the same phone number. Degrees granted: Bachelors; Masters.

Attendance and degree information available by phone, FAX, mail. Search requires name plus social security number, date of birth, signed release. No fee for information.

Transcripts available by FAX, mail. Search requires name plus social security number, date of birth, signed release. Fee is $3.00.

Wartburg College, Registrar, 222 9th St NW, Waverly, IA 50677, 319-352-8272 (FAX: 319-352-8514). Hours: 8AM-4:30PM. Records go back to 1852. Alumni records are maintained here also. Call 319-352-8491. Degrees granted: Bachelors.

Attendance and degree information available by phone, FAX, mail. Search requires name only. Other helpful information: social security number, date of birth. No fee for information.

Transcripts available by written request only. Search requires name plus social security number, date of birth, signed release. Other helpful information: approximate years of attendance. Fee is $4.00.

Wartburg Theological Seminary, Registrar, 333 Wartburg Pl, Dubuque, IA 52003-7797, 319-589-0211 (FAX: 319-589-0333). Hours: 8AM-4:30PM. Degrees granted: Masters.

Attendance and degree information available by phone, FAX, mail. Search requires name only. Other helpful information: date of birth, approximate years of attendance. No fee for information.

Transcripts available by mail. Search requires name plus signed release. Other helpful information: date of birth, approximate years of attendance. Fee is $2.00.

Washburn University of Topeka, Registrar, 17th and College Sts, Topeka, KS 66621, 913-231-1010 X1580. Hours: 8AM-5PM. Degrees granted: Associate; Bachelors; Masters; J.D.

Attendance and degree information available by phone, mail. Search requires name plus social security number. Other helpful information: date of birth, approximate years of attendance. No fee for information.

Transcripts available by mail. Search requires name plus social security number, signed release. Other helpful information: date of birth, approximate years of attendance. Fee is $2.00.

Washington Bible College, Registrar, 6511 Princess Garden Pkwy, Lanham, MD 20706, 301-552-1400 (FAX: 301-552-2775). Hours: 8AM-4:30PM. Degrees granted: Associate; Bachelors.

Attendance and degree information available by phone, FAX, mail. Search requires name only. Other helpful information: approximate years of attendance. No fee for information.

Transcripts available by FAX, mail. Search requires name plus signed release. Other helpful information: social security number, date of birth, approximate years of attendance. Fee is $3.00. Expedite: $5.00 to $15.00

Washington College, Registrar, 300 Washington Ave, Chestertown, MD 21620, 410-778-7299 (FAX: 410-778-7850). Hours: 8:30AM-4:30PM. Records go back to 1930. Alumni records are maintained here also. Call 410-778-7812. Degrees granted: Bachelors; Masters.

Attendance and degree information available by phone, FAX, mail. Search requires name plus social security number, exact years of attendance. No fee for information.

Transcripts available by mail. Search requires name plus social security number, exact years of attendance, signed release. Fee is $2.00.

Washington County Technical College, Registrar, RR1 Box 22C, Calais, ME 04619, 207-454-1000 (FAX: 207-454-1026). Hours: 8AM-4:30PM. Records go back to 1969. Alumni records are maintained here also. Call 207-454-2144. Degrees granted: Associate. Adverse incident record source: Dean of Students, 207-454-2144.

Attendance and degree information available by phone, FAX, mail. Search requires name plus social security number, exact years of attendance. No fee for information.

Transcripts available by mail. Search requires name plus social security number, exact years of attendance, signed release. Fee is $3.00. Expedited service available for $5.00.

Washington State Community College, Records Office, 710 Colegate Dr, Marietta, OH 45750, 614-374-8716 (FAX: 614-373-7496). Hours: 7:30AM-4:30PM. Records go back to 1972. Degrees granted: Associate.

Attendance and degree information available by phone, FAX, mail. Search requires name plus social security number. No fee for information.

Transcripts available by FAX, mail. Search requires name plus social security number, signed release. Fee is $2.00.

Major credit cards accepted for payment.

Washington State University, Registrar, Pullman, WA 99164-1035, 509-335-5330 (FAX: 509-335-7823). Hours: 8AM-5PM. Records go back to 1890. Degrees granted: Bachelors; Masters; Doctorate; Vet Med. Adverse incident record source: Campus Police, 509-335-4555.

Attendance information available by phone, FAX, mail. Search requires name only. Other helpful information: social security number, date of birth, approximate years of attendance. No fee for information.

Degree information available by phone, FAX, mail. Search requires name plus signed release. Other helpful information: social security number, date of birth, approximate years of attendance. No fee for information.

Transcripts available by FAX, mail. Search requires name plus date of birth, signed release. Other helpful information: social security number, approximate years of attendance. Fee is $3.00. Expedited service available for $10.00.

Washington Theological Union, Registrar, 9001 New Hampshire Ave, Silver Spring, MD 20903, 301-439-0551 (FAX: 301-445-4929). Hours: 8AM-5PM. Records go back to 1970. Alumni records are maintained here at the same phone number. Degrees granted: Masters.

Attendance and degree information available by phone, FAX, mail. Search requires name plus approximate years of attendance. Other helpful information: social security number, date of birth. No fee for information.

Transcripts available by written request only. Search requires name plus social security number, signed release. Other helpful information: date of birth. No fee for transcripts.

Washington University, Registrar, One Brookings Dr, Box 1143, St Louis, MO 63130, 314-935-5933 (FAX: 314-935-4268). Hours: 8:30AM-5PM. Records go back to 1978. Alumni Records Office: Alumni Development, Box 1210, 1 Brookings, St Louis, MO 63130,. Degrees granted: Associate; Bachelors; Masters; Doctorate. Adverse incident record source: Academic Dean, 314-935-5994.

Attendance and degree information available by FAX, mail. Search requires name plus social security number, date of birth, approximate years of attendance, signed release. Other helpful information: exact years of attendance. Fee is $5.00.

Transcripts available by mail. Search requires name plus social security number, date of birth, approximate years of attendance, signed release. Other helpful information: exact years of attendance. Fee is $5.00.

Washington and Jefferson College, Registrar, 45 S Lincoln St, Washington, PA 15301, 412-223-6017. Hours: 9AM-Noon, 1-5PM. Records go back to 1901. Degrees granted: Associate; Bachelors.

Attendance information available by phone. Search requires name plus exact years of attendance. Other helpful information: social security number. No fee for information.

Degree information available by mail. Search requires name plus exact years of attendance. Other helpful information: social security number. No fee for information.

Transcripts available by mail. Search requires name plus exact years of attendance, signed release. Other helpful information: social security number. Fee is $2.00. Expedite: $12.00 to $18.00.

Washington and Lee University, Registrar's Office, Reid Hall, Lexington, VA 24450-0303, 504-463-8455 (FAX: 504-463-8045). Hours: 8:30AM-4:30PM. Records go back to 1945. Alumni records are maintained here also. Call 504-463-8464. Degrees granted: Bachelors; JD (Law).

Attendance and degree information available by phone, FAX, mail. Search requires name only. Other helpful information: social security number, date of birth, approximate years of attendance. No fee for information.

Transcripts available by mail. Search requires name plus signed release. Other helpful information: social security number, date of birth, approximate years of attendance. No fee for transcripts.

Washtenaw Community College, Registrar, 4800 E Huron River Dr, PO Box D-1, Ann Arbor, MI 48106, 313-973-3480. Hours: 8AM-7PM M-Th, 8AM-5PM F. Records go back to 1966. Alumni records are maintained here also. Call 313-973-3492. Degrees granted: Associate. Adverse incident record source: Dean of Students, 313-973-3536.

Attendance and degree information available by phone, mail. Search requires name plus social security number, signed release. No fee for information.

Transcripts available by mail. Search requires name plus social security number, signed release. No fee for transcripts.

Waubonsee Community College, Registrar, Illinois Rte 47 at Harter Rd, Sugar Grove, IL 60554, 708-466-4811 X373 (FAX: 708-466-4964). Hours: 8AM-8PM M-Th; 8AM-4PM F. Records go back to founding date. Alumni records are maintained here also. Call 708-892-3334 X149. Degrees granted: Associate.

Attendance and degree information available by phone, FAX, mail. Search requires name plus social security number, date of birth. Other helpful information: approximate years of attendance. No fee for information.

Transcripts available by FAX, mail. Search requires name plus social security number, date of birth, signed release. Other helpful information: approximate years of attendance. No fee for transcripts.

Waukesha County Technical College, Registrar, 800 Main St, Pewaukee, WI 53072, 414-691-5266 (FAX: 414-691-5123). Hours: 8AM-8:30PM. Records go back to 1960. Degrees granted: Associate.

Attendance information available by FAX, mail. Search requires name plus signed release. Other helpful information: social security number, approximate years of attendance. No fee for information.

Degree information available by phone, FAX, mail. Search requires name plus signed release. Other helpful information: social security number, approximate years of attendance. No fee for information.

Transcripts available by phone, FAX, mail. Search requires name plus signed release. Other helpful information: social security number, approximate years of attendance. Fee is $2.00.

Major credit cards accepted for payment.

Waycross College, Registrar, 2001 Francis St, Waycross, GA 31503, 912-285-6133 (FAX: 912-287-4909). Hours: 8AM-9PM. Records go back to 1976. Alumni records are maintained here at the same phone number. Degrees granted: Associate.

Attendance and degree information available by phone, mail. Search requires name plus social security number, signed release. Other helpful information: approximate years of attendance. No fee for information.

Transcripts available by mail. Search requires name plus social security number, signed release. Other helpful information: approximate years of attendance. Fee is $2.00.

Wayland Baptist University, Office of the Registrar, WBU #735, Plainview, TX 79072, 806-296-4706 (FAX: 806-296-4580). Hours: 8:30AM-5PM. Degrees granted: Associate; Bachelors; Masters. Certification: Secretarial. Adverse incident record source: Student Development, 806-296-4724.

Attendance and degree information available by phone, FAX, mail. Search requires name plus social security number, date of birth. Other helpful information: approximate years of attendance. No fee for information.

Transcripts available by mail. Search requires name plus social security number, date of birth, signed release. Other helpful information: approximate years of attendance. Fee is $3.00. Expedited service available for $5.00.

Major credit cards accepted for payment.

Wayne Community College, Admissions & Records, Caller Box 8002, Goldsboro, NC 27533-8002, 919-735-5151 (FAX: 919-736-3204). Hours: 8AM-5PM. Degrees granted: Associate. Adverse incident record source: Security: Student Development

Attendance and degree information available by phone, FAX, mail. Search requires name plus social security number. Other helpful information: date of birth, approximate years of attendance. No fee for information.

Transcripts available by FAX, mail. Search requires name plus social security number, signed release. Other helpful information: date of birth, approximate years of attendance. Fee is $1.00.

Wayne County Community College, Registrar, 801 W Fort St, Detroit, MI 48226-3010, 313-496-2862 (FAX: 313-961-2791). Hours: 9AM-4:30PM. Records go back to 1969. Degrees granted: Associate.

Attendance and degree information available by phone, mail. Search requires name plus social security number, date of birth, signed release. Other helpful information: approximate years of attendance. No fee for information.

Transcripts available by mail. Search requires name plus social security number, date of birth, signed release. Other helpful information: approximate years of attendance. Fee is $3.00.

Credit cards in person only.

Wayne State College, Registrar, 1111 Main St, Wayne, NE 68787, 402-375-7241 (FAX: 402-375-7204). Hours: 8AM-5PM. Records go back to 1891. Degrees granted: Bachelors; Masters; Ed Specialist. Adverse incident record source: Dean of Students, 402-375-7213.

Attendance and degree information available by phone, mail. Search requires name only. Other helpful information: social security number, approximate years of attendance. No fee for information.

Transcripts available by mail. Search requires name plus signed release. Other helpful information: social security number, approximate years of attendance. Fee is $2.00.

Wayne State University, Student Records, 2 W Helen Newberry Joy, SSC, Detroit, MI 48202, 313-577-3531 (FAX: 313-577-3769). Hours: 8:30AM-6PM M-Th; 8:30AM-5PM F. Degrees granted: Bachelors; Masters; Doctorate.

Attendance information available by phone, FAX, mail. Search requires name only. Other helpful information: social security number, date of birth, approximate years of attendance. No fee for information.

Degree information available by phone, FAX, mail. Search requires name only. Other helpful information: social security number, date of birth, approximate years of attendance. No fee for information.

Transcripts available by written request only. Search requires name plus signed release. Other helpful information: social security number, date of birth, approximate years of attendance. Fee is $2.00.

Waynesburg College, Registrar, 51 W College St, Waynesburg, PA 15370, 412-852-3252. Hours: 8AM-4:30PM. Records go back to 1849. Alumni records are maintained here also. Call 412-852-3300. Degrees granted: Bachelors; Masters.

Attendance and degree information available by phone, mail. Search requires name plus date of birth, exact years of attendance. No fee for information.

Transcripts available by mail. Search requires name plus date of birth, exact years of attendance, signed release. No fee for transcripts.

Weatherford College, Registrar, 308 E Park Ave, Weatherford, TX 76086, 817-594-5471 (FAX: 817-594-9435). Hours: 8AM-5PM M-Th; 8AM-4PM F. Records go back to 1920s. Degrees granted: Associate.

Attendance and degree information available by phone, FAX, mail. Search requires name plus social security number, signed release. Other helpful information: date of birth, exact years of attendance. No fee for information.

Transcripts available by written request only. Search requires name plus social security number, signed release. Other helpful information: date of birth, exact years of attendance. Fee is $4.00.

Webb Institute, Registrar, Crescent Beach Rd, Glen Cove, NY 11542, 516-671-2213 (FAX: 516-674-9838). Degrees granted: Bachelors.

Attendance and degree information available by phone, FAX, mail. Search requires name plus approximate years of attendance. Other helpful information: social security number. No fee for information.

Transcripts available by FAX, mail. Search requires name plus approximate years of attendance. Other helpful information: social security number. Fee is $3.00.

Webber College, Registrar, PO Box 96, Babson Park, FL 33827, 813-638-2929 (FAX: 813-638-2823). Hours: 8AM-5PM. Records go back to 1927. Degrees granted: Bachelors. Adverse incident record source: Registrars Office, 813-638-2929.

Attendance information available by phone, FAX, mail. Search requires name plus social security number, exact years of attendance. Other helpful information: date of birth, approximate years of attendance. No fee for information.

Degree information available by phone, FAX, mail. Search requires name plus social security number. Other helpful information: approximate years of attendance. No fee for information.

Transcripts available by FAX, mail. Search requires name plus social security number, exact years of attendance, signed release. Other helpful information: date of birth, approximate years of attendance. Fee is $3.00. Expedited service available for $6.00.

Weber State University, Registrar, 3750 Harrison Blvd, Ogden, UT 84408, 801-626-6751. Hours: 8AM-4:30PM. Degrees granted: Bachelors; Masters.

Attendance and degree information available by mail. Search requires name plus social security number, date of birth, exact years of attendance. No fee for information.

Transcripts available by mail. Search requires name plus social security number, date of birth, exact years of attendance, signed release. No fee for transcripts.

Webster College, Registrar, 412 Fairmont Ave, Fairmont, WV 26554, 304-363-8824. Hours: 8AM-4PM. Records go back to 1926. Degrees granted: Associate.

Attendance and degree information available by phone, mail. Search requires name plus social security number, exact years of attendance. No fee for information.

Transcripts available by mail. Search requires name plus social security number, exact years of attendance, signed release. Fee is $2.00.

Webster College, **(Branch Campus)**, Registrar, N Bridge Plaza, 2192 N US Rte 1, Fort Pierce, FL 34946, 407-464-7474. Hours: 8AM-5PM. Records go back to 1981. Degrees granted: Associate.

Attendance and degree information available by phone, mail. Search requires name plus social security number, exact years of attendance. No fee for information.

Transcripts available by mail. Search requires name plus social security number, exact years of attendance, signed release. Fee is $2.00.

Webster College, **(Branch Campus)**, Registrar, 2002 NW 13th St, Gainesville, FL 32601, 904-375-8014. Hours: 8AM-5PM. Records go back to 1984. Degrees granted: Associate.

Attendance and degree information available by phone, mail. Search requires name plus social security number, date of birth, exact years of attendance. No fee for information.

Transcripts available by mail. Search requires name plus social security number, date of birth, exact years of attendance, signed release. Fee is $3.00.

Webster College, **(Branch Campus)**, Registrar, 5623 US Hwy 19 Ste 300, New Port Richey, FL 34652, 813-849-4993. Hours: 8AM-5PM. Records go back to 1984. Degrees granted: Associate.

Attendance and degree information available by phone, mail. Search requires name plus social security number, exact years of attendance. No fee for information.

Transcripts available by mail. Search requires name plus social security number, exact years of attendance, signed release. Fee is $3.00.

Webster College, **(Branch Campus)**, Registrar, 1530 SW Third Ave, Ocala, FL 32671, 904-629-1941. Hours: 9AM-5PM. Records go back to 1986. Degrees granted: Associate.

Attendance and degree information available by phone, mail. Search requires name plus social security number, exact years of attendance. No fee for information.

Transcripts available by mail. Search requires name plus social security number, exact years of attendance, signed release. Fee is $3.00.

Webster University, Registrar, 470 E Lockwood Ave, St Louis, MO 63119, 314-968-7450 (FAX: 314-968-7112). Hours: 8:30AM-5:30PM. Records go back to 1915. Alumni records are maintained here also. Call 314-968-7141. Degrees granted: Bachelors; Masters; Doctorate.

Attendance and degree information available by phone, FAX, mail. Search requires name only. Other helpful information: social security number, date of birth, approximate years of attendance. No fee for information.

Transcripts available by mail. Search requires name plus signed release. Other helpful information: social security number, date of birth, approximate years of attendance. No fee for transcripts.

Wellesley College, Registrar, Wellesley, MA 02181, 617-283-2307 (FAX: 617-283-3680). Hours: 8:30AM-4:30PM. Records go back to 1920. Alumni records are maintained here also. Call 617-283-3331. Degrees granted: Bachelors.

Attendance and degree information available by phone, FAX, mail. Search requires name plus approximate years of attendance, signed release. No fee for information.

Transcripts available by FAX, mail. Search requires name plus approximate years of attendance, signed release. Fee is $3.00.

Wells College, Registrar, Aurora, NY 13026-0500, 315-364-3215 (FAX: 315-364-3229). Hours: 8:30AM-Noon, 1-4:30PM. Records go back to 1900. Alumni records are maintained here also. Call 315-364-3200. Degrees granted: Bachelors. Adverse incident record source: Dean of Students, 315-364-3311.

Attendance and degree information available by phone, FAX, mail. Search requires name plus social security number, date of birth. Other helpful information: approximate years of attendance. No fee for information.

Transcripts available by FAX, mail. Search requires name plus signed release. Other helpful information: social security number, date of birth, approximate years of attendance. Fee is $5.00. Expedited service available for $3.00.

SSN or DOB is either/or requirement. Minimum charge $10.00. Major credit cards accepted for payment.

Wenatchee Valley College, Registrar, 1300 Fifth St, Wenatchee, WA 98801, 509-662-1651 X2136 (FAX: 509-664-2576). Records go back to 1939. Alumni records are maintained here at the same phone number. Degrees granted: Associate.

Attendance and degree information available by phone, mail. Search requires name plus social security number, exact years of attendance. No fee for information.

Transcripts available by mail. Search requires name plus social security number, exact years of attendance, signed release. No fee for transcripts.

Wentworth Institute of Technology, Office of the Registrar, 550 Huntington Ave, Boston, MA 02115, 617-442-9010 X391 (FAX: 617-427-2852). Hours: 8:15AM-6PM M-Th; 8:15AM-4:45PM F; 9AM-1PM odd S. Records go back to 1920. Degrees granted: Associate; Bachelors.

Attendance and degree information available by phone, FAX, mail. Search requires name plus social security number. Other helpful information: approximate years of attendance. No fee for information.

Transcripts available by mail. Search requires name plus social security number, signed release. Other helpful information: date of birth, approximate years of attendance. Fee is $1.00.

Wentworth Military Academy and Junior College, Registrar, Washington Ave, Lexington, MO 64067, 816-259-2221 (FAX: 816-259-3395). Hours: 7AM-4:30PM. Records go back to 1890. Degrees granted: Associate.

Attendance and degree information available by phone, FAX, mail. Search requires name only. Other helpful information: social security number, date of birth, approximate years of attendance. No fee for information.

Transcripts available by FAX, mail. Search requires name plus signed release. Other helpful information: social security number, date of birth, approximate years of attendance. Fee is $2.00. Expedited service available for $5.00.

Major credit cards accepted for payment.

Weselyan University, Registrar, Middletown, CT 06459, 203-685-2748 (FAX: 203-685-2601). Hours: 9AM-4PM. Records go back to 1800s. Alumni records are maintained here also. Call 203-685-2110. Degrees granted: Bachelors. Adverse incident record source: Dean's Office, 203-685-2773.

Attendance and degree information available by phone, FAX, mail. Search requires name plus social security number. Other helpful information: approximate years of attendance. No fee for information.

Transcripts available by FAX, mail. Search requires name plus social security number, signed release. Other helpful information: approximate years of attendance. Fee is $3.00.

Wesley Biblical Seminary, Registrar, 5980 Floral Dr, Jackson, MS 39206, 601-957-1314 (FAX: 601-957-1314). Hours: 8AM-5PM. Records go back to 1974. Alumni records are maintained here also. Call 601-957-1314. Degrees granted: Masters.

Attendance and degree information available by phone, FAX, mail. Search requires name plus signed release. No fee for information.

Transcripts available by FAX, mail. Search requires name plus signed release. Fee is $4.00.

Wesley College, Registrar, 120 N State St, Dover, DE 19901, 302-736-2434 (FAX: 302-736-2301). Hours: 8:30AM-4:30PM. Records go back 50 years. Alumni records are maintained here also. Call 302-736-2355. Degrees granted: Associate; Bachelors; Masters.

Attendance information available by phone, FAX, mail. Search requires name plus approximate years of attendance. Fee is $4.00.

Degree information available by phone, FAX, mail. Search requires name only. Fee is $4.00.

Transcripts available by mail. Search requires name plus approximate years of attendance, signed release. Other helpful information: social security number, date of birth, exact years of attendance. Fee is $4.00.

Wesley College, Registrar, 111 Wesley Cir, PO Box 1070, Florence, MS 39073, 601-845-2265. Degrees granted: Bachelors.

Attendance and degree information available by phone, FAX, mail. Search requires name plus social security number. Other helpful information: date of birth, approximate years of attendance. No fee for information.

Transcripts available by mail. Search requires name plus social security number, exact years of attendance, signed release. Other helpful information: date of birth, approximate years of attendance. Fee is $5.00.

Wesley Theological Seminary, Registrar, 4500 Massachusetts Ave NW, Washington, DC 20016, 202-885-8650 (FAX: 202-885-8604). Hours: 9AM-4PM. Records go back to 1984. Degrees granted: Masters; Doctorate.

Attendance and degree information available by phone, FAX, mail. Search requires name only. No fee for information.

Transcripts available by mail. Search requires name plus signed release. Other helpful information: social security number, approximate years of attendance. Fee is $5.00.

Wesleyan College, Registrar, 4760 Forsyth Rd, Macon, GA 31297-4299, 912-477-1110 (FAX: 912-757-4030). Hours: 8:30AM-5PM. Records go back to 1836. Alumni records are maintained here at the same phone number. Degrees granted: Bachelors. Adverse incident record source: Student Life, 912-477-1110.

Attendance and degree information available by phone, FAX, mail. Search requires name plus social security number, approximate years of attendance, signed release. No fee for information.

Transcripts available by FAX, mail. Search requires name plus social security number, approximate years of attendance, signed release. Fee is $3.00.

West Chester University of Pennsylvania, Registrar, EO Bull Center Room 155, West Chester, PA 19383, 610-436-3541. Hours: 8AM-5PM. Records go back to 1971. Alumni records are maintained here also. Call 610-436-2813. Degrees granted: Bachelors; Masters.

Attendance and degree information available by phone, mail. Search requires name plus social security number, date of birth, exact years of attendance. No fee for information.

Transcripts available by mail. Search requires name plus social security number, date of birth, exact years of attendance, signed release. Fee is $3.00.

West Coast University, Records Department, 440 S Shatto Pl, Los Angeles, CA 90020-1765, 213-427-4400 (FAX: 213-380-4362). Hours: 9AM-5PM. Records go back to 1950. Some records go back to 1950. Alumni records are maintained here at the same phone number. Degrees granted: Associate; Bachelors; Masters. Certification: CEU.

Attendance information available by written request only. Search requires name plus social security number, signed release. Other helpful information: date of birth, approximate years of attendance. No fee for information.

Degree information available by phone, FAX, mail. Search requires name plus social security number, approximate years of attendance. Other helpful information: date of birth. No fee for information.

Transcripts available by mail. Search requires name plus social security number, date of birth, signed release. Other helpful information: approximate years of attendance. Fee is $5.00. Expedited service available for $20.00.

Major credit cards accepted for payment.

West Georgia College, Registrar, Carrollton, GA 30118-0001, 404-863-6438 (FAX: 404-836-6638). Hours: 8AM-5PM. Records go back to 1933. Alumni records are maintained here also. Call 404-836-6582. Degrees granted: Associate; Bachelors; Masters.

Attendance and degree information available by phone, FAX, mail. Search requires name plus social security number. Other helpful information: date of birth, approximate years of attendance. No fee for information.

Transcripts available by FAX, mail. Search requires name plus social security number, signed release. Other helpful information: date of birth, approximate years of attendance. Fee is $3.00. Expedited service available for $5.00.

Will not confirm attendance for obtaining credit cards.

West Hills Community College, Registrar, 300 Cherry Lane, Coalinga, CA 93210, 209-935-0801 (FAX: 209-935-5655). Hours: 8AM-5PM. Records go back to 1932. Degrees granted: Associate. Adverse incident record source: Local police, 209-935-1525.

Attendance information available by phone, FAX, mail. Search requires name only. Other helpful information: social security number, date of birth, approximate years of attendance. No fee for information.

Degree information available by phone, FAX, mail. Search requires name only. Other helpful information: social security number, date of birth, approximate years of attendance. No fee for information.

Transcripts available by FAX, mail. Search requires name plus signed release. Other helpful information: social security number, date of birth, approximate years of attendance. Fee is $2.00. Expedited service available for $10.00.

Major credit cards accepted for payment.

West Liberty State College, Registrar, West Liberty, WV 26074, 304-336-8007 (FAX: 304-336-8285). Hours: 8AM-4PM. Records go back to 1925. Alumni records are maintained here also. Call 304-336-8124. Degrees granted: Associate; Bachelors. Adverse incident record source: Dean of Students, 304-336-8016.

Attendance and degree information available by phone, FAX, mail. Search requires name only. Other helpful information: social security number, approximate years of attendance. No fee for information.

Transcripts available by FAX, mail. Search requires name plus signed release. Other helpful information: social security number, approximate years of attendance. Fee is $3.00.

West Los Angeles College, Attn: Admissions, 4800 Freshman Dr, Culver City, CA 90230, 310-287-4329 (FAX: 310-841-0396). Hours: 9AM-8PM M-Th; 9AM-3:30PM F. Records go back to founding date. Degrees granted: Associate.

Attendance and degree information available by FAX, mail. Search requires name plus social security number, signed release. Other helpful information: date of birth, approximate years of attendance. Fee is $1.00.

Transcripts available by mail. Search requires name plus social security number, signed release. Other helpful information: date of birth, approximate years of attendance. Fee is $6.00. Expedited service available for $6.00.

Major credit cards accepted for payment.

West Shore Community College, Student Records Office, 3000 N Stiles Rd, Scottville, MI 49454, 616-845-6211 (FAX: 616-845-0207). Hours: 8AM-4:30PM. Records go back to founding date. Alumni records are maintained here at the same phone number. Adverse incident record source: Business Office, 616-845-6211 X109.

School will not confirm attendance information.

Degree information available by mail. Search requires name plus social security number, exact years of attendance. Other helpful information: date of birth. Fee is $20.00.

Transcripts available by written request only. Search requires name plus social security number, signed release. Other helpful information: date of birth, approximate years of attendance. Fee is $2.00.

Major credit cards accepted for payment.

West Suburban College of Nursing, Registrar, Erie St at Austin Blvd, Oak Park, IL 60302, 708-383-3901 (FAX: 708-383-8783). Hours: 8:30AM-5:30PM. Degrees granted: Bachelors.

Attendance and degree information available by phone, mail. Search requires name plus social security number, date of birth, exact years of attendance. No fee for information.

Transcripts available by mail. Search requires name plus social security number, date of birth, exact years of attendance, signed release. Fee is $5.00.

Major credit cards accepted for payment.

West Texas A&M University, Registrar, 2501 Fourth Ave, PO Box 877 W.T. Station, Canyon, TX 79016, 806-656-2022 (FAX: 806-656-2936). Hours: 8AM-5PM. Records go back to 1911. Alumni records are maintained here at the same phone number. Degrees granted: Bachelors; Masters. Certification: Education/Teacher. Adverse incident record source: University Police, 806-656-2300.

Attendance and degree information available by phone, FAX, mail. Search requires name plus social security number. Other helpful information: date of birth, approximate years of attendance. No fee for information.

Transcripts available by FAX, mail. Search requires name plus social security number, signed release. Other helpful information: date of birth. Fee is $3.00.

Major credit cards accepted for payment.

West Valley College, Registrar, 14000 Fruitvale Ave, Saratoga, CA 95070, 408-867-2200. Hours: 10AM-7PM M-Th; 10PM-4PM F. Records go back to 1964. Degrees granted: Associate.

Attendance and degree information available by written request only. Search requires name plus social security number, date of birth, approximate years of attendance, signed release. Other helpful information: exact years of attendance. Fee is $2.00.

Transcripts available by written request only. Search requires name plus social security number, date of birth, approximate years of attendance, signed release. Other helpful information: exact years of attendance. Fee is $4.00. Expedited service available for $7.50.

Major credit cards accepted for payment.

West Virginia Business College, Registrar, 215 W Main St, Clarksburg, WV 26301, 304-624-7695. Hours: 8AM-5PM. Records go back to 1880. Degrees granted: Associate.

Attendance and degree information available by phone, mail. Search requires name plus social security number, exact years of attendance. No fee for information.

Transcripts available by mail. Search requires name plus social security number, exact years of attendance, signed release. Fee is $3.00.

West Virginia Business College, **(Branch Campus)**, Registrar, 1052 Main St, Wheeling, WV 26003, 304-232-0631. Hours: 8AM-5PM. Records go back to 1920. Degrees granted: Associate.

Attendance and degree information available by phone, mail. Search requires name plus social security number, exact years of attendance. No fee for information.

Transcripts available by mail. Search requires name plus social security number, exact years of attendance, signed release. Fee is $3.00.

West Virginia Career College, Registrar, 1000 Virginia St E, Charleston, WV 25301, 304-345-2820. Hours: 8AM-4PM. Degrees granted: Associate.

Attendance and degree information available by phone, mail. Search requires name plus exact years of attendance. Other helpful information: social security number, date of birth. No fee for information.

Transcripts available by written request only. Search requires name plus date of birth, exact years of attendance, signed release. Other helpful information: social security number. Fee is $2.00.

West Virginia Career College, Registrar, 148 Willey St, Morgantown, WV 26505, 304-296-8882. Hours: 8AM-4PM. Degrees granted: Associate.

Attendance and degree information available by phone, mail. Search requires name plus social security number, date of birth, exact years of attendance. No fee for information.

Transcripts available by written request only. Search requires name plus social security number, date of birth, exact years of attendance, signed release. Fee is $2.00.

West Virginia Career College, **(Branch Campus)**, Registrar, Nova Village Market Plaza, 1104 Beville Rd Ste J, Daytona Beach, FL 32114, 904-255-0175 (FAX: 904-255-6227). Hours: 8AM-7PM. Degrees granted: Associate.

Attendance and degree information available by FAX, mail. Search requires name plus social security number, exact years of attendance. No fee for information.

Transcripts available by mail. Search requires name plus social security number, exact years of attendance, signed release. No fee for transcripts.

Major credit cards accepted for payment.

West Virginia Career College, (Branch Campus), Registrar, 200 College Dr, Lemont Furnace, PA 15456, 412-437-4600. Records are not housed here. They are located at West Virginia Career College, Registrar, 148 Willey St, Morgantown, WV 26505.

West Virginia Graduate College, Registrar, PO Box 1003, Institute, WV 25112, 304-766-1903. Hours: 8AM-5PM. Records go back to 1958. They existed as a branch of another campus from 1958 to 1972, then became independent in 1972. Alumni records are maintained here at the same phone number. Degrees granted: Bachelors; Masters.

Attendance and degree information available by phone, mail. Search requires name plus social security number. No fee for information.

Transcripts available by mail. Search requires name plus social security number, signed release. Fee is $4.00.

West Virginia Institute of Technology, Registrar, Montgomery, WV 25136, 304-442-3151 (FAX: 304-442-3097). Hours: 8AM-4:30PM. Records go back to 1895. Degrees granted: Associate; Bachelors; Masters. Adverse incident record source: Dean of Students, 304-442-3158.

Attendance and degree information available by phone, FAX, mail. Search requires name only. Other helpful information: social security number. No fee for information.

Transcripts available by FAX, mail. Search requires name plus signed release. Other helpful information: approximate years of attendance. Fee is $3.00.

West Virginia Northern Community College, Registrar, 1704 Market St, Wheeling, WV 26003, 304-233-5900 X211 (FAX: 304-233-0965). Hours: 8:30AM-5PM. Records go back to 1972. Alumni records are maintained here also. Call 304-233-5900 X265. Degrees granted: Associate. Adverse incident record source: Institutional Research, 304-233-5900 X261.

Attendance and degree information available by mail. Search requires name plus social security number, signed release. Other helpful information: date of birth, approximate years of attendance. No fee for information.

Transcripts available by mail. Search requires name plus social security number, signed release. Other helpful information: date of birth, approximate years of attendance. Fee is $3.00.

Major credit cards accepted for payment.

West Virginia School of Osteopathic Medicine, Registrar, 400 N Lee St, Lewisburg, WV 24901, 304-647-6230 (FAX: 304-645-4859). Hours: 8AM-4:30PM. Records go back to 1974. Alumni records are maintained here also. Call 304-647-6382. Degrees granted: Bachelors; Masters; First Professional Degree.

Attendance and degree information available by phone, mail. Search requires name plus social security number, date of birth, exact years of attendance. No fee for information.

Transcripts available by mail. Search requires name plus social security number, date of birth, exact years of attendance, signed release. Fee is $3.00.

West Virginia State College, Registrar, Institute, WV 25112, 304-766-3137. Hours: 8AM-4:30PM. Records go back to 1958. Alumni records are maintained here at the same phone number. Degrees granted: Bachelors.

Attendance and degree information available by phone, mail. Search requires name plus social security number, date of birth, exact years of attendance. No fee for information.

Transcripts available by mail. Search requires name plus social security number, date of birth, exact years of attendance, signed release. Fee is $3.00.

West Virginia University, Admissions & Records, PO Box 6009, Morgantown, WV 26506-6009, 304-293-2124 (FAX: 304-293-3080). Hours: 8:15AM-4:45PM. Alumni Records Office: PO Box 4269, Morgantown, WV 26506-6009 304-293-4731 (FAX: 304-293-4733). Degrees granted: Bachelors; Masters; Doctorate. Adverse incident record source: Student Life, 304-293-5611.

Attendance information available by phone, FAX, mail. Search requires name plus social security number, signed release. Other helpful information: date of birth, approximate years of attendance. Fee is $5.00. Expedited service available for $8.00.

Degree information available by phone, FAX, mail. Search requires name plus social security number, signed release. Other helpful information: date of birth, approximate years of attendance. Fee is $5.00. Expedite service available for $8.00.

Transcripts available by FAX, mail. Search requires name plus social security number, signed release. Other helpful information: date of birth, approximate years of attendance. Fee is $5.00. Expedited service available for $8.00.

West Virginia University at Parkersburg, Registrar, Rte 5 Box 167-A, Parkersburg, WV 26101, 304-424-8220. Hours: 8AM-4:30PM. Records go back to 1961. Alumni records are maintained here at the same phone number. Degrees granted: Bachelors.

Attendance and degree information available by phone, mail. Search requires name plus social security number, date of birth, exact years of attendance. No fee for information.

Transcripts available by mail. Search requires name plus social security number, date of birth, exact years of attendance, signed release. Fee is $3.00.

West Virginia Wesleyan College, Registrar, College Ave, Buckhannon, WV 26201, 304-473-8470 (FAX: 304-473-8187). Hours: 8AM-4PM. Records go back to 1890. Degrees granted: Bachelors; Masters. Adverse incident record source: Dean of Students, 304-473-8440.

Attendance and degree information available by phone, FAX, mail. Search requires name only. Other helpful information: social security number, date of birth, approximate years of attendance. No fee for information.

Transcripts available by FAX, mail. Search requires name plus signed release. Other helpful information: social security number, date of birth, approximate years of attendance. Fee is $3.00. Expedited service available for $5.00.

Westark Community College, Registrar, PO Box 3649, Fort Smith, AR 72913, 501-788-7230 (FAX: 501-788-7016). Hours: 8AM-7PM M-Th, 8AM-4:30PM F. Records go back to 1928. Degrees granted: Associate. Adverse incident record source: Student Life, 501-788-7013: Security, 501-788-7140

Attendance and degree information available by phone, FAX, mail. Search requires name plus social security number, date of birth, approximate years of attendance. No fee for information.

Transcripts available by mail. Search requires name plus social security number, date of birth, approximate years of attendance, signed release. Fee is $1.00.

Westbrook College, Registrar, Stevens Ave, Portland, ME 04103, 207-797-7261. Hours: 8:30AM-5PM. Records go back to 1940. Alumni records are maintained here at the same phone number. Degrees granted: Associate; Bachelors. Certification: CNA (in past).

Attendance and degree information available by FAX, mail. Search requires name plus signed release. Other helpful information: social security number, date of birth, approximate years of attendance. No fee for information.

Transcripts available by FAX, mail. Search requires name plus signed release. Other helpful information: social security number, date of birth, approximate years of attendance. Fee is $3.00.

Name used while attending helpful.

Westchester Business Institute, Registrar, PO Box 710, 325 Central Ave, White Plains, NY 10600, 914-948-4442 (FAX: 914-948-8216). Hours: 8AM-11PM. Records go back to 1960. Alumni records are maintained here at the same phone number. Degrees granted: Associate.

Attendance and degree information available by FAX, mail. Search requires name plus social security number, signed release. No fee for information.

Transcripts available by FAX, mail. Search requires name plus social security number, signed release. Fee is $5.00.

Major credit cards accepted for payment.

Westchester Community College, Registrar, 75 Grasslands Rd, Valhalla, NY 10595, 914-785-6810. Hours: 9AM-8PM M-Th, 9AM-5PM F. Records go back to 1950. Alumni records are maintained here also. Call 914-785-6670. Degrees granted: Associate. Adverse incident record source: Student Affairs, 914-785-6731.

Attendance and degree information available by phone, mail. Search requires name plus social security number. No fee for information.

Transcripts available by mail. Search requires name plus social security number, exact years of attendance, signed release. Fee is $3.00.

Western Baptist College, Registrar, 5000 Deer Park Dr SE, Salem, OR 97301-9891, 503-375-7014 (FAX: 503-585-4316). Hours: 8AM-5PM. Records go back to 1935. Degrees granted: Associate; Bachelors.

Attendance and degree information available by phone, FAX, mail. Search requires name plus date of birth. Other helpful information: social security number, approximate years of attendance. No fee for information.

Transcripts available by FAX, mail. Search requires name plus date of birth, signed release. Other helpful information: social security number, approximate years of attendance. Fee is $5.00.

Western Carolina University, Registrar, Cullowhee, NC 28723, 704-227-7232 (FAX: 704-227-7217). Hours: 8AM-5pm. Records go back to 1920. Alumni records are maintained here also. Call 704-227-7335. Degrees granted: Bachelors; Masters. Adverse incident record source: Public Safety, 704-227-7301.

Attendance and degree information available by phone, FAX, mail. Search requires name only. Other helpful information: social security number, date of birth, approximate years of attendance. No fee for information.

Transcripts available by FAX, mail. Search requires name plus signed release. Other helpful information: social security number, date of birth, approximate years of attendance. No fee for transcripts.

Western Connecticut State University, Registrar, Danbury, CT 06810, 203-837-9200. Hours: 8AM-4:30PM. Records go back to 1904. Degrees granted: Associate; Bachelors; Masters.

Attendance and degree information available by phone, FAX, mail. Search requires name only. Other helpful information: social security number, date of birth, approximate years of attendance. No fee for information.

Transcripts available by FAX. Search requires name plus signed release. Other helpful information: social security number, date of birth, approximate years of attendance. Fee is $3.00.

Western Conservative Baptist Seminary, Registrar, 5511 SE Hawthorne Blvd, Portland, OR 97215, 503-233-8561 (FAX: 503-239-4216). Hours: 8:30AM-4PM. Records go back to 1926. Degrees granted: Masters; Doctorate.

School will not confirm attendance information. Search requires name only. Other helpful information: social security number, date of birth, approximate years of attendance. Fee is $10.00. Expedited service available for $10.00.

Degree information available by phone, FAX, mail. Search requires name only. Other helpful information: social security number, date of birth, approximate years of attendance. Fee is $10.00. Expedite service available for $10.00.

Transcripts available by written request only. Search requires name plus social security number, date of birth, signed release. Other helpful information: approximate years of attendance. Fee is $10.00. Expedited service available for $10.00.

Western Dakota Technical Institute, Registrar, 800 Mickelson Dr, Rapid City, SD 57701-4178, 605-394-4034 (FAX: 605-394-1789). Hours: 7:30AM-4PM. Records go back to 1968. Degrees granted: Associate.

Attendance information available by phone, FAX, mail. Search requires name only. Other helpful information: social security number, date of birth, approximate years of attendance. No fee for information.

Degree information available by phone, FAX, mail. Search requires name plus approximate years of attendance. Other helpful information: social security number, date of birth, exact years of attendance. No fee for information.

Transcripts available by mail. Search requires name plus social security number, date of birth, approximate years of attendance, signed release. Other helpful information: exact years of attendance. Fee is $3.00.

Western Evangelical Seminary, Registrar, 12753 SW 68th Ave, Tigard, OR 97223, 503-598-4309 (FAX: 503-598-4338). Hours: 8:30AM-4:30PM. Records go back 47 years. Alumni records are maintained here also. Call 503-639-0559. Degrees granted: Masters.

Attendance and degree information available by phone, FAX, mail. Search requires name only. Other helpful information: social security number, date of birth, approximate years of attendance. No fee for information.

Transcripts available by mail. Search requires name plus signed release. Other helpful information: social security number, date of birth, approximate years of attendance. Fee is $5.00.

Major credit cards accepted for payment.

Western Illinois University, Registrar, 1 University Circle, Macomb, IL 61455, 309-298-1891 (FAX: 309-298-2787). Hours: 8AM-4:30PM. Records go back to 1899. Alumni records are maintained here also. Call 309-298-1914. Degrees granted: Bachelors; Masters.

Attendance and degree information available by phone, FAX, mail. Search requires name plus social security number, date of birth. No fee for information.

Transcripts available by FAX, mail. Search requires name plus social security number, date of birth, signed release. No fee for transcripts.

Western International University, Registrar, 9215 N Black Canyon Rd, Phoenix, AZ 85021, 602-943-2311 (FAX: 602-371-8637). Hours: 9AM-6:30PM. Records go back to 1978. Degrees granted: Associate; Bachelors; Masters.

Attendance and degree information available by phone, FAX, mail. Search requires name only. Other helpful information: social security number, date of birth, approximate years of attendance. No fee for information.

Transcripts available by FAX, mail. Search requires name plus signed release. Other helpful information: social security number, date of birth, approximate years of attendance. Fee is $5.00.

Major credit cards accepted for payment.

Western Iowa Tech Community College, Registrar, 4647 Stone Ave, PO Box 265, Sioux City, IA 51102, 712-274-6400 (FAX: 712-274-6412). Hours: 8AM-5PM. Records go back to 1968. Degrees granted: Associate; GED. Special programs-GED's, 712-255-7632.

Attendance and degree information available by phone, FAX, mail. Search requires name plus approximate years of attendance. Other helpful information: social security number. No fee for information.

Transcripts available by mail. Search requires name plus social security number, approximate years of attendance, signed release. Other helpful information: date of birth. Fee is $1.00.

Western Kentucky University, Office of the Registrar, Potter Hall, #1 Big Red Wy, Bowling Green, KY 42101-3576, 502-745-3351 (FAX: 502-745-4830). Hours: 8AM-4:30PM. Records go back to founding date. Alumni records are maintained here also. Call 502-745-4395. Degrees granted: Associate; Bachelors; Masters. Adverse incident record source: Dean of Student Life, 502-745-2791.

Attendance and degree information available by phone, FAX, mail. Search requires name plus social security number. Other helpful information: date of birth, approximate years of attendance. No fee for information.

Transcripts available by FAX, mail. Search requires name plus social security number. Other helpful information: date of birth, approximate years of attendance. No fee for transcripts.

Western Maryland College, Registrar, 2 College Hill, Westminster, MD 21157, 410-857-2215 (FAX: 410-857-2752). Hours: 8:30AM-4:30PM. Alumni records are maintained here also. Call 410-857-2296. Degrees granted: Bachelors; Masters. Adverse incident record source: Campus Safety, 410-857-2202.

Attendance and degree information available by phone, FAX, mail. Search requires name only. Other helpful information: social security number, date of birth, approximate years of attendance. No fee for information.

Transcripts available by FAX, mail. Search requires name plus signed release. Other helpful information: social security number, date of birth, approximate years of attendance. Fee is $3.00.

Western Michigan University, Registrar, Kalamazoo, MI 49008, 616-387-4300. Hours: 8AM-5PM. Records go back to 1904. Alumni records are maintained here also. Call 616-387-8777. Degrees granted: Bachelors; Masters; PhD.

Attendance information available by mail. Search requires name plus social security number, date of birth, signed release. No fee for information.

Degree information available by phone, mail. Search requires name plus social security number, date of birth, signed release. No fee for information.

Transcripts available by mail. Search requires name plus social security number, date of birth, signed release. Fee is $3.00.

Western Montana College of the University of Montana, Registrar's Office, 710 S Atlantic St, Dillon, MT 59725-3598, 406-683-7371 (FAX: 406-683-7493). Hours: 9AM-3PM. Records go back to founding date. Degrees granted: Associate; Bachelors.

Attendance information available by written request only. Search requires name plus social security number, date of birth, signed release. Other helpful information: approximate years of attendance. No fee for information.

Degree information available by phone, FAX, mail. Search requires name plus social security number, signed release. Other helpful information: approximate years of attendance. No fee for information.

Transcripts available by written request only. Search requires name plus social security number, signed release. Other helpful information: approximate years of attendance. No fee for transcripts.

Western Nebraska Community College, Registrar, 1601 E 27th St, Scottsbluff, NE 69361, 308-635-6012 (FAX: 308-635-6100). Hours: 8AM-5PM. Records go back to 1926. Alumni records are maintained here also. Call 308-635-6080. Degrees granted: Associate. Adverse incident record source: Student Services, 308-635-3606.

Attendance and degree information available by phone, FAX, mail. Search requires name plus social security number, date of birth, signed release. Other helpful information: approximate years of attendance. No fee for information.

Transcripts available by mail. Search requires name plus social security number, date of birth, signed release. Other helpful information: approximate years of attendance. No fee for transcripts.

Western Nevada Community College, Registrar, 2201 W Nye Lane, Carson City, NV 89703, 702-887-3000 (FAX: 702-885-0642). Records go back to 1970s. Degrees granted: Associate.

Attendance and degree information available by phone, FAX, mail. Search requires name plus social security number, date of birth, approximate years of attendance. Other helpful information: exact years of attendance. No fee for information.

Transcripts available by written request only. Search requires name plus social security number, date of birth, approximate years of attendance, signed release. Other helpful information: exact years of attendance. Fee is $2.00.

Western New England College, Registrar, Springfield, MA 01119, 413-796-2080 (FAX: 413-796-2081). Hours: 8AM-

7PM M-Th, 8:30AM-4:30PM F. Records go back to 1970. Alumni records are maintained here also. Call 413-782-1539. Degrees granted: Bachelors; Masters.

Attendance and degree information available by phone, FAX, mail. Search requires name plus social security number, approximate years of attendance, signed release. No fee for information.

Transcripts available by mail. Search requires name plus social security number, approximate years of attendance, signed release. No fee for transcripts.

Western New Mexico University, Registrar, PO Box 680, 1000 W College Ave, Silver City, NM 88062, 505-538-6118 (FAX: 505-538-6155). Hours: 8AM-4:30PM. Alumni records are maintained here also. Call 505-538-6336. Degrees granted: Associate; Bachelors; Masters.

Attendance and degree information available by phone, FAX, mail. Search requires name plus social security number, approximate years of attendance. Other helpful information: date of birth. No fee for information.

Transcripts available by FAX, mail. Search requires name plus social security number, date of birth, approximate years of attendance, signed release. Other helpful information: exact years of attendance. Fee is $2.00. Expedited service available for $5.00. Major credit cards accepted for payment.

Western Oklahoma State College, Admissions and Registrar, 2801 N Main St, Altus, OK 73521, 405-477-2000 (FAX: 405-521-6154). Hours: 7:30AM-4:30PM. Records go back to 1926. Alumni records are maintained here at the same phone number. Degrees granted: Associate. Adverse incident record source: Student Affairs.

Attendance and degree information available by phone, FAX, mail. Search requires name plus social security number. No fee for information.

Transcripts available by FAX, mail. Search requires name plus social security number, signed release. Fee is $2.00.

Western Oregon State College, Registrar's Office, Monmouth, OR 97361, 503-838-8415 (FAX: 503-838-8144). Hours: 9AM-4PM. Degrees granted: Associate; Bachelors; Masters. Adverse incident record source: Dean of Students, 503-838-8221.

Attendance and degree information available by phone, FAX, mail. Search requires name only. Other helpful information: social security number, date of birth, approximate years of attendance. No fee for information.

Transcripts available by written request only. Search requires name plus social security number, signed release. Other helpful information: date of birth, approximate years of attendance. Fee is $5.00. Include a stamped envelope.

Western Piedmont Community College, Registrar, 1001 Burkemont Ave, Morganton, NC 28655-9978, 704-438-6041 (FAX: 704-438-6065). Hours: 8AM-5PM. Records go back to 1963. Degrees granted: Associate.

Attendance information available by phone, FAX, mail. Search requires name plus social security number, signed release. Other helpful information: date of birth, approximate years of attendance. No fee for information.

Degree information available by phone, FAX, mail. Search requires name plus signed release. Other helpful information: social security number, date of birth, approximate years of attendance. No fee for information.

Transcripts available by FAX, mail. Search requires name plus signed release. Other helpful information: date of birth, approximate years of attendance. First three transcripts per academic year are free; otherwise $3.00 each.

Western State College of Colorado, Registrar, Gunnison, CO 81231, 303-943-2047 (FAX: 303-943-7069). Hours: 8AM-5PM. Records go back to 1911. Alumni records are maintained here also. Call 303-943-2090. Degrees granted: Bachelors.

Attendance and degree information available by phone, FAX, mail. Search requires name plus social security number. No fee for information.

Transcripts available by mail. Search requires name plus social security number, signed release. Fee is $2.00.

Western State University College of Law of Orange County, Registrar, 1111 N State College Blvd, Fullerton, CA 92631, 714-738-1000 (FAX: 714-525-2786). Hours: 9AM-6PM. Degrees granted: Bachelors; Doctorate.

Attendance and degree information available by FAX, mail. Search requires name plus signed release. Other helpful information: social security number, date of birth, approximate years of attendance. No fee for information.

Transcripts available by mail. Search requires name plus signed release. Other helpful information: social security number, date of birth, approximate years of attendance. Fee is $3.00. Major credit cards accepted for payment.

Western State University College of Law of San Diego, Registrar, 2121 San Diego Ave, San Diego, CA 92110, 619-561-6574. Hours: 8AM-6PM. Records go back 25 years. Degrees granted: Doctorate.

Attendance and degree information available by mail. Search requires name plus signed release. Other helpful information: social security number, date of birth, approximate years of attendance. No fee for information.

Transcripts available by mail. Search requires name plus signed release. Other helpful information: social security number, date of birth, approximate years of attendance. Fee is $3.00.

Western States Chiropractic College, Registrar, 2900 NE 132nd Ave, Portland, OR 97230, 503-251-5706 (FAX: 503-251-5723). Hours: 8AM-4:30PM. Records go back to 1904. Alumni records are maintained here also. Call 503-251-5713. Degrees granted: Bachelors; Doctor of Chiropractic.

Attendance and degree information available by phone, FAX, mail. Search requires name only. Other helpful information: date of birth, approximate years of attendance. No fee for information.

Transcripts available by written request only. Search requires name plus signed release. Other helpful information: date of birth, approximate years of attendance. Fee is $5.00. Expedite: $15.00 to $20.00.

Western Texas College, Registrar, 6200 S College Ave, Snyder, TX 79549, 915-573-8511 (FAX: 915-573-9321). Hours: 8AM-Noon, 1-5PM. Records go back to 1970. Alumni records are maintained here at the same phone number. Degrees granted: Associate.

Attendance and degree information available by phone, FAX, mail. Search requires name plus social security number. Other helpful information: date of birth, approximate years of attendance. No fee for information.

Transcripts available by mail. Search requires name plus social security number, signed release. Other helpful information: date of birth, approximate years of attendance. Fee is $5.00.
Major credit cards accepted for payment.

Western Theological Seminary, Registrar, 85 E 13th St, Holland, MI 49423, 616-392-8555 (FAX: 616-392-7717). Hours: 8AM-5PM. Records go back to 1900. Alumni records are maintained here at the same phone number. Degrees granted: Masters; Doctorate.

Attendance and degree information available by phone, FAX, mail. Search requires name plus approximate years of attendance, signed release. No fee for information.

Transcripts available by mail. Search requires name plus approximate years of attendance, signed release. Fee is $3.00.

Western Washington University, Registrar, 516 High St, Bellingham, WA 98225, 206-650-3430 (FAX: 206-650-7327). Records go back to 1899. Alumni records are maintained here at the same phone number. Degrees granted: Bachelors; Masters.

Attendance and degree information available by phone, mail. Search requires name plus social security number, exact years of attendance. No fee for information.

Transcripts available by mail. Search requires name plus social security number, exact years of attendance, signed release. Fee is $5.00.

Western Wisconsin Technical College, Registrar, Box 908, 304 N Sixth St, La Crosse, WI 54602, 608-785-9149. Hours: 8AM-8PM. Records go back to 1917. Degrees granted: Associate. Special programs- Instructional Services, 608-785-9102. Adverse incident record source: 608-785-9444.

Attendance information available by mail. Search requires name plus signed release. Other helpful information: social security number, date of birth, approximate years of attendance. Fee is $3.00. Expedited service available for $10.00.

Degree information available by phone, FAX, mail. Search requires name only. Other helpful information: social security number, date of birth, approximate years of attendance. No fee for information.

Transcripts available by mail. Search requires name plus signed release. Other helpful information: social security number, date of birth, approximate years of attendance. Fee is $3.00. Expedited service available for $10.00.
Major credit cards accepted for payment.

Western Wyoming College, Registrar, PO Box 428, Rock Springs, WY 82901, 307-382-1641 (FAX: 307-382-1636). Hours: 8AM-5PM. Alumni records are maintained here also. Call 307-382-1600. Degrees granted: Associate.

Attendance and degree information available by phone, FAX, mail. Search requires name only. Other helpful information: social security number, date of birth, approximate years of attendance. No fee for information.

Transcripts available by phone, FAX, mail. Search requires name only. Other helpful information: social security number, date of birth, approximate years of attendance. Fee is $1.00. Expedited service available for $5.00.

Calls screened for right to know. Transcript request must come from student. Major credit cards accepted for payment.

Westfield State College, Registrar, Western Ave, Westfield, MA 01086, 413-572-5240 (FAX: 413-562-2613). Hours: 8AM-5PM. Records go back to 1957. Alumni records are maintained here also. Call 413-568-3311 X5210. Degrees granted: Bachelors. Adverse incident record source: Student Affairs, 413-568-5403.

Attendance and degree information available by phone, FAX, mail. Search requires name plus social security number, approximate years of attendance, signed release. No fee for information.

Transcripts available by mail. Search requires name plus social security number, approximate years of attendance, signed release. Fee is $2.00.

Westminster College, Registrar, 501 Westminster Ave, Fulton, MO 65251-1299, 314-592-1213 (FAX: 314-642-2176). Hours: 8AM-4:30PM. Records go back to 1800s. Alumni records are maintained here also. Call 314-592-1313. Degrees granted: Bachelors.

Attendance and degree information available by phone, FAX, mail. Search requires name plus approximate years of attendance. Other helpful information: exact years of attendance. No fee for information.

Transcripts available by FAX, mail. Search requires name plus approximate years of attendance, signed release. Other helpful information: social security number, exact years of attendance. Fee is $4.00.
Major credit cards accepted for payment.

Westminster College, Registrar's Office, South Market St, New Wilmington, PA 16172, 412-946-7136 (FAX: 412-946-7171). Hours: 8AM-4:30PM. Records go back to 1800s. Alumni records are maintained here also. Call 412-946-7008. Degrees granted: Bachelors; Masters. Adverse incident record source: Student Affairs, 412-946-7110.

Attendance and degree information available by phone, mail. Search requires name only. Other helpful information: social security number, date of birth, approximate years of attendance. No fee for information. Include a stamped envelope.

Transcripts available by mail. Search requires name plus approximate years of attendance, signed release. Other helpful information: social security number, date of birth. Fee is $3.00.

Westminster College of Salt Lake City, Registrar, 1840 S 1300 E, Salt Lake City, UT 84105, 801-488-4100 (FAX: 801-466-6916). Hours: 8AM-5PM M,W,F; 8AM-6PM T,Th. Degrees granted: Bachelors; Masters. Certification: Teaching. Adverse incident record source: 801-488-1665.

Attendance and degree information available by phone, FAX, mail. Search requires name only. Other helpful information: social security number, date of birth, approximate years of attendance. No fee for information.

Transcripts available by FAX, mail. Search requires name plus social security number, date of birth, approximate years of attendance, signed release. Other helpful information: exact years of attendance. Fee is $2.00.
Major credit cards accepted for payment.

Westminster Theological Seminary, Registrar, Church Rd and Willow Grove Ave, Glenside, PA 19038, 215-572-3809 (FAX: 215-887-5404). Hours: 8:30AM-4:30PM. Degrees granted: Masters; Doctorate.

Attendance and degree information available by phone, FAX, mail. Search requires name plus social security number. Other helpful information: date of birth, approximate years of attendance. No fee for information.

Transcripts available by FAX, mail. Search requires name plus social security number, signed release. Other helpful information: date of birth, approximate years of attendance. Fee is $2.00.

Westminster Theological Seminary in California, Registrar, 1725 Bear Valley Pkwy, Escondido, CA 92027, 619-480-8474 (FAX: 619-480-0252). Hours: 8AM-4:30PM. Records go back 5 years. Degrees granted: Masters; Doctorate.

Attendance and degree information available by phone, FAX, mail. Search requires name only. Other helpful information: social security number, date of birth, approximate years of attendance. No fee for information.

Transcripts available by FAX, mail. Search requires name plus signed release. Other helpful information: social security number, date of birth, approximate years of attendance. No fee for transcripts.

Westmont College, Registrar, 955 La Paz Rd, Santa Barbara, CA 93108-1089, 805-565-6060 (FAX: 805-565-6234). Hours: 8AM-4:30PM. Records go back to 1940. Degrees granted: Bachelors.

Attendance information available by phone, FAX, mail. Search requires name plus social security number. Other helpful information: date of birth, approximate years of attendance. No fee for information.

Degree information available by phone, FAX, mail. Search requires name only. Other helpful information: social security number, date of birth, approximate years of attendance. No fee for information.

Transcripts available by FAX, mail. Search requires name plus social security number, date of birth, signed release. Other helpful information: approximate years of attendance. Fee is $4.00. Expedited service available for $10.00.

Westmoreland County Community College, Registrar, Armbrust Rd, Youngwood, PA 15697-1895, 412-925-4069 (FAX: 412-925-4292). Hours: 8AM-5PM. Records go back to 1970. Degrees granted: Associate.

Attendance and degree information available by phone, FAX, mail. Search requires name plus social security number. No fee for information.

Transcripts available by FAX, mail. Search requires name plus social security number, signed release. Other helpful information: approximate years of attendance. No fee for transcripts.

Major credit cards accepted for payment.

Weston School of Theology, Registrar, 3 Phillips Pl, Cambridge, MA 02138, 617-492-1960 (FAX: 617-492-5833). Hours: 8:30AM-4:30PM. Records go back to 1950. Degrees granted: Masters.

Attendance and degree information available by FAX, mail. Search requires name plus social security number, approximate years of attendance, signed release. No fee for information.

Transcripts available by FAX, mail. Search requires name plus social security number, approximate years of attendance, signed release. Fee is $5.00.

Wharton County Junior College, Registrar, 911 Boling Hwy, Wharton, TX 77488, 409-532-6382. Hours: 8AM-5PM. Records go back to 1946. Alumni records are maintained here also. Call 409-532-6322. Degrees granted: Associate.

Attendance and degree information available by phone, mail. Search requires name plus social security number. Other helpful information: approximate years of attendance. No fee for information.

Transcripts available by mail. Search requires name plus social security number, signed release. Other helpful information: approximate years of attendance. No fee for transcripts.

Whatcom Community College, Registrar, 237 W Kellogg Rd, Bellingham, WA 98226, 360-676-2170 (FAX: 360-676-2171). Hours: 8AM-5PM. Records go back to 1970.

Attendance and degree information available by phone, FAX, mail. Search requires name only. Other helpful information: social security number, approximate years of attendance. No fee for information.

Transcripts available by written request only. Search requires name plus social security number, signed release. Other helpful information: approximate years of attendance. No fee for transcripts.

Wheaton College, Registrar, Norton, MA 02766, 508-285-8247 (FAX: 508-285-8276). Hours: 8:30AM-12:30PM, 1:30-4:30PM. Degrees granted: Bachelors.

Attendance information available by phone, FAX, mail. Search requires name only. Other helpful information: social security number, date of birth, approximate years of attendance. No fee for information.

Degree information available by phone, FAX, mail. Search requires name only. Other helpful information: social security number, date of birth, exact years of attendance. No fee for information.

Transcripts available by FAX, mail. Search requires name plus social security number, signed release. Other helpful information: date of birth, exact years of attendance. Fee is $2.00. Expedited service available for $5.00.

They will honor FAX request for transcripts with follow-up letter.

Wheaton College, Registrar, 501 E College Ave, Wheaton, IL 60187, 708-752-5045 (FAX: 708-752-5245). Hours: 9AM-4:30PM. Records go back to 1860. Alumni records are maintained here also. Call 708-752-5047. Degrees granted: Bachelors; Masters; Doctorate.

Attendance and degree information available by phone, FAX, mail. Search requires name only. Other helpful information: social security number, date of birth, approximate years of attendance. No fee for information.

Transcripts available by FAX, mail. Search requires name plus social security number, date of birth, signed release. Other helpful information: approximate years of attendance. No fee for transcripts.

Enrolled name helpful.

Wheeling Jesuit College, Registrar, 316 Washington Ave, Wheeling, WV 26003, 304-243-2238 (FAX: 304-243-2500). Hours: 8:30AM-5PM. Records go back to 1955. Alumni records are maintained here also. Call 304-243-2205. Degrees granted: Bachelors; Masters.

Attendance and degree information available by phone, FAX, mail. Search requires name plus date of birth, signed release. Other helpful information: social security number, exact years of attendance. No fee for information.

Transcripts available by FAX, mail. Search requires name plus date of birth, signed release. Other helpful information: social security number, exact years of attendance. No fee for transcripts.

Wheelock College, Registrar, 200 The Riverway, Boston, MA 02215-4176, 617-734-5200 X135 (FAX: 617-566-7369). Hours: 9AM-5PM. Records go back to 1900. Degrees granted: Associate; Bachelors; Masters; CAGS.

Attendance information available by phone, FAX, mail. Search requires name plus social security number, exact years of attendance. Other helpful information: approximate years of attendance. No fee for information.

Degree information available by phone, FAX, mail. Search requires name plus exact years of attendance. Other helpful information: social security number, approximate years of attendance. No fee for information.

Transcripts available by mail. Search requires name plus social security number, approximate years of attendance, signed release. Other helpful information: exact years of attendance. Fee is $2.00.

White Pines College, Registrar, Chester, NH 03036, 603-887-4401 (FAX: 603-887-1777). Hours: 8:30AM-4:30PM. Records go back to 1965. Degrees granted: Associate.

Attendance information available by phone, FAX, mail. Search requires name only. No fee for information.

Degree information available by FAX, mail. Search requires name plus signed release. No fee for information.

Transcripts available by FAX, mail. Search requires name plus signed release. Fee is $3.00.

Whitman College, Registrar, Walla Walla, WA 99362, 509-527-5179 (FAX: 509-527-4967). Hours: 8:30AM-Noon, 1-4:30PM. Records go back to 1859. Alumni records are maintained here also. Call 509-527-5167. Degrees granted: Bachelors. Adverse incident record source: Security, 509-527-5777.

Attendance and degree information available by phone, FAX, mail. Search requires name only. Other helpful information: social security number, date of birth, approximate years of attendance. No fee for information.

Transcripts available by FAX, mail. Search requires name plus signed release. Other helpful information: social security number, date of birth, approximate years of attendance. Fee is $5.00. Whitman ID# helpful.

Whittier College, Office of the Registrar, 13406 E Philadelphia St, Whittier, CA 90601, 310-907-4241 (FAX: 310-698-4067). Hours: 8AM-5PM. Records go back to 1902. Degrees granted: Bachelors; Masters. Adverse incident record source: Student Services, 310-907-4233.

Attendance information available by phone, FAX, mail. Search requires name only. Other helpful information: social security number, date of birth, exact years of attendance. No fee for information.

Degree information available by phone, FAX, mail. Search requires name only. Other helpful information: social security number, date of birth, approximate years of attendance. No fee for information.

Transcripts available by mail. Search requires name plus social security number, date of birth, signed release. Other helpful information: approximate years of attendance. Fee is $3.00.

Whitworth College, Academic Records, W 300 Hawthorne, Spokane, WA 99251, 509-466-3201 (FAX: 509-466-3773). Hours: 9AM-4PM. Degrees granted: Bachelors; Masters. Certification: Educ.

Attendance and degree information available by phone, FAX, mail. Search requires name plus exact years of attendance. Other helpful information: date of birth, approximate years of attendance. No fee for information.

Transcripts available by phone, mail. Search requires name plus date of birth, exact years of attendance, signed release. Other helpful information: approximate years of attendance. Fee is $4.00.

Major credit cards accepted for payment.

Wichita State University, Registrar, 1845 Fairmount, Wichita, KS 67260-0058, 316-689-3092 (FAX: 316-689-3795). Hours: 8AM-5PM. Records go back to 1892. Alumni records are maintained here also. Call 316-689-3290. Degrees granted: Associate; Bachelors; Masters; Doctorate. Adverse incident record source: Campus Police, 316-689-3450.

Attendance and degree information available by phone, FAX, mail. Search requires name plus social security number, date of birth, approximate years of attendance. Other helpful information: exact years of attendance. Fee is $3.00.

Transcripts available by FAX, mail. Search requires name plus social security number, date of birth, approximate years of attendance, signed release. Other helpful information: exact years of attendance. Fee is $3.00. Expedite fee is based on cost of service.'

Major credit cards accepted for payment.

Widener University, Registrar, One University Pl, Chester, PA 19013-5792, 610-499-4140. Hours: 8AM-4:30PM. Records go back to 1876. Alumni records are maintained here also. Call 610-499-1154. Degrees granted: Bachelors; Masters; Doctorate.

Attendance and degree information available by phone, mail. Search requires name plus social security number. No fee for information.

Transcripts available by mail. Search requires name plus social security number, signed release. Fee is $4.00.

Widener University at Harrisburg, (School of Law), Registrar, 3800 Vartan Way, Harrisburg, PA 17110-9450, 717-541-3904 (FAX: 717-541-1923). Hours: 8:30AM-6:50PM M,T; 8:30AM-5PM W-F. Records go back to 1989. Alumni Records Office: Alumni Office, Widener University, One University Place, Chester, PA 19013,. Degrees granted: Doctorate.

Attendance and degree information available by phone, FAX, mail. Search requires name plus approximate years of attendance. Other helpful information: social security number, exact years of attendance. No fee for information.

Transcripts available by written request only. Search requires name plus approximate years of attendance, signed release. Other helpful information: social security number, exact years of attendance. Fee is $2.00. Expedite: $2.00 plus cost of overnight mail.

Widener University, (School of Law), Registrar, 4601 Concord Pike, PO Box 7474, Wilmington, DE 19803-0474, 302-477-2149 (FAX: 302-477-2258). Hours: 9AM-5PM. Records go back to 1971. Degrees granted: Masters; Juris Doctor. Special programs- Legal Education Institute (Paralegal) prior 1989, 610-499-4000.

Attendance and degree information available by phone, FAX, mail. Search requires name plus social security number, exact years of attendance. Other helpful information: date of birth, approximate years of attendance. No fee for information.

Transcripts available by FAX, mail. Search requires name plus social security number, approximate years of attendance, signed release. Other helpful information: date of birth. Fee is $2.00.

Wilberforce University, Registrar, Wilberforce, OH 45384, 513-376-2911 (FAX: 513-376-2627). Hours: 8AM-4:30PM. Alumni records are maintained here also. Call 513-376-2911 X707. Degrees granted: Bachelors. Adverse incident record source: Campus Police, 513-376-2911 X701.

Attendance and degree information available by phone, FAX, mail. Search requires name only. Other helpful information: social security number, date of birth, approximate years of attendance. No fee for information.

Transcripts available by FAX, mail. Search requires name plus signed release. Other helpful information: social security number, date of birth, approximate years of attendance. Fee is $2.00.

Wilbur Wright College, Registrar, 4300 N Narragansett Ave, Chicago, IL 60634, 312-481-8060 (FAX: 312-481-8053). Hours: 9AM-8PM M-Th; 9AM-4PM F. Records go back 60 years. Degrees granted: Associate.

Attendance and degree information available by phone, FAX, mail. Search requires name plus social security number. Other helpful information: date of birth, approximate years of attendance. No fee for information.

Transcripts available by FAX, mail. Search requires name plus social security number, signed release. Other helpful information: date of birth, approximate years of attendance. Fee is $5.00. Expedited service available for $10.00.

Wilcox College of Nursing, Registrar, 28 Crescent St, Middletown, CT 06547, 203-344-6719 (FAX: 203-344-6999). Hours: 8AM-4:30PM. Records go back 85 years. Alumni records are maintained here also. Call 203-344-6401. Degrees granted: Associate.

Attendance and degree information available by phone, FAX, mail. Search requires name only. Other helpful information: social security number, approximate years of attendance. No fee for information.

Transcripts available by FAX, mail. Search requires name plus signed release. Other helpful information: social security number, approximate years of attendance. Fee is $3.00.

Wiley College, Registrar, 711 Wiley Ave, Marshall, TX 75670, 903-927-3221 (FAX: 903-938-8100). Hours: 8AM-5PM. Records go back to 1900s. Degrees granted: Bachelors. Adverse incident record source: Student Affairs, 903-927-3233.

Attendance and degree information available by mail. Search requires name plus social security number, date of birth, approximate years of attendance. No fee for information. Include stamped envelope.

Transcripts available by mail. Search requires name plus social security number, date of birth, approximate years of attendance, signed release. Fee is $2.00.

Wilkes Community College, Registrar, PO Box 120, Collegiate Dr, Wilkesboro, NC 28697-0120, 910-651-8642 (FAX: 910-651-8749). Hours: 8AM-5PM. Records go back 30 years. Degrees granted: Associate.

Attendance and degree information available by phone, FAX, mail. Search requires name plus social security number. Other helpful information: date of birth, exact years of attendance. No fee for information.

Transcripts available by FAX, mail. Search requires name plus social security number, signed release. Other helpful information: date of birth, exact years of attendance. No fee for transcripts.

Wilkes University, Registrar, 267 S Franklin St, Wilkes-Barre, PA 18766, 717-831-4856 (FAX: 717-823-9470). Hours: 8:30AM-4:30PM. Records go back to 1933. Alumni Records Office: Evans Alumni House, Wilkes University, 110 S River St, Wilkes-Barre, PA 18766,. Degrees granted: Bachelors; Masters. Adverse incident record source: Student Affairs, 717-831-4100.

Attendance and degree information available by phone, FAX, mail. Search requires name plus social security number, date of birth. Other helpful information: approximate years of attendance. No fee for information.

Transcripts available by FAX, mail. Search requires name plus signed release. Fee is $4.00.

Willamette University, Registrar, 900 State St, Salem, OR 97301, 503-370-6206 (FAX: 503-375-5395). Hours: 8AM-Noon, 1-5PM. Records go back to 1900s. Alumni records are maintained here also. Call 503-370-6340. Degrees granted: Bachelors; Masters; Doctorate.

Attendance information available by phone, FAX, mail. Search requires name plus social security number. No fee for information.

Degree information available by phone, FAX, mail. Search requires name plus social security number, exact years of attendance. No fee for information.

Transcripts available by FAX, mail. Search requires name plus social security number, exact years of attendance, signed release. Fee is $4.00.

William Carey College, Registrar, 498 Tuscan Ave, Hattiesburg, MS 39401-5499, 601-582-6195 (FAX: 601-582-6454). Hours: 8AM-5PM. Records go back to 1911. Degrees granted: Bachelors; Masters.

Attendance information available by phone, FAX, mail. Search requires name plus approximate years of attendance. Other helpful information: social security number, date of birth, exact years of attendance. No fee for information.

Degree information available by phone, FAX, mail. Search requires name only. Other helpful information: social security number, date of birth, approximate years of attendance. No fee for information.

Transcripts available by mail. Search requires name plus signed release. Other helpful information: social security number, date of birth, approximate years of attendance. No fee for transcripts. Expedite: Other than regular mail must be prepaid.

Major credit cards accepted for payment.

William Jewell College, Registrar's Office, 500 College Hill, Liberty, MO 64068, 816-781-7700 (FAX: 816-781-3164). Hours: 8AM-5PM. Alumni records are maintained here at the same phone number. Degrees granted: Bachelors.

Attendance and degree information available by phone, FAX, mail. Search requires name plus social security number, date of birth, approximate years of attendance, signed release. Other helpful information: exact years of attendance. No fee for information.

Transcripts available by FAX, mail. Search requires name plus social security number, date of birth, approximate years of attendance, signed release. Other helpful information: exact years of attendance. Fee is $2.00. Expedited service available for $7.00.

William Mitchell College of Law, Registrar, 875 Summit Ave, St Paul, MN 55105, 612-290-6363 (FAX: 612-290-6414). Hours: 8:30AM-7:30PM M-Th; 8:30AM-6PM F. Records go back to 1900. Alumni records are maintained here also. Call 612-290-6371. Degrees granted: Masters; 1st Prof. (JD).

Attendance and degree information available by phone, FAX, mail. Search requires name only. Other helpful information: social security number, approximate years of attendance. No fee for information.

Transcripts available by mail. Search requires name plus signed release. Other helpful information: social security number, approximate years of attendance. Fee is $3.00.

If student has placed hold on records, written request required for attendance & degree confirmation.

William Paterson College of New Jersey, Office of the Registrar, College Hall 358 Hamburg Tpk, PO Box 913, Wayne, NJ 07470-0913, 201-595-3119. Hours: 8:30AM-4:30PM. Records go back to founding date. Degrees granted: Bachelors; Masters. Certification: Education.

Attendance and degree information available by phone, mail. Search requires name plus social security number, date of birth, approximate years of attendance. No fee for information.

Transcripts available by mail. Search requires name plus social security number, date of birth, approximate years of attendance, signed release. Fee is $2.00.

William Penn College, Registrar, 201 Trueblood Ave, Oskaloosa, IA 52577, 515-673-1082 (FAX: 515-673-1396). Hours: 8AM-Noon, 1-5PM. Records go back to 1873. Degrees granted: Bachelors.

Attendance and degree information available by phone, FAX, mail. Search requires name only. Other helpful information: social security number, date of birth, approximate years of attendance. No fee for information.

Transcripts available by mail. Search requires name plus signed release. Other helpful information: social security number, date of birth, approximate years of attendance. Fee is $2.00. Expedite fee is based on cost of service.'

William Rainey Harper College, Registrar, 1200 W Algonquin Rd, Palatine, IL 60067-7398, 708-925-6501 (FAX: 708-925-6032). Hours: 8AM-8PM M-Th, 8AM-4:30PM F, 9AM-Noon Sat. Records go back to 1969. Degrees granted: Associate.

Attendance and degree information available by phone, FAX, mail. Search requires name plus social security number, signed release. No fee for information.

Transcripts available by mail. Search requires name plus social security number, signed release. Fee is $3.00.

William Tyndale College, Registrar, 35700 W Twelve Mile Rd, Farmington Hills, MI 48331, 810-553-7200 (FAX: 810-553-5963). Hours: 8AM-5PM. Records go back to 1945. Degrees granted: Associate; Bachelors.

Attendance and degree information available by FAX, mail. Search requires name plus social security number, exact years of attendance, signed release. Other helpful information: date of birth. No fee for information.

Transcripts available by FAX, mail. Search requires name plus social security number, signed release. Other helpful information: date of birth, exact years of attendance. Fee is $5.00.

Major credit cards accepted for payment.

William Woods University, Registrar, Fulton, MO 65251, 314-592-4248 (FAX: 314-592-1146). Hours: 8AM-4:30PM. Alumni records are maintained here also. Call 314-592-4219. Degrees granted: Associate; Bachelors; Masters. Adverse incident record source: Student Development, 314-592-4238.

Attendance and degree information available by phone, FAX, mail. Search requires name plus date of birth, approximate years of attendance. Other helpful information: social security number, exact years of attendance. No fee for information.

Transcripts available by FAX, mail. Search requires name plus approximate years of attendance, signed release. Other helpful information: social security number, date of birth, exact years of attendance. Fee is $5.00. Expedited service available for $5.00. Major credit cards accepted for payment.

Williams Baptist College, Registrar, Box 3667, Walnut Ridge, AR 72476, 501-886-6741 X104 (FAX: 501-886-3924). Hours: 8AM-4:30PM Winter, 9AM-4PM Summer. Records go back to 1941. Alumni records are maintained here also. Call 501-886-6741. Degrees granted: Bachelors. Adverse incident record source: Student Affairs, 501-886-6741.

Attendance and degree information available by phone, FAX, mail. Search requires name plus social security number, approximate years of attendance. No fee for information.

Transcripts available by mail. Search requires name plus social security number, approximate years of attendance, signed release. Fee is $3.00.

Williams College, Registrar, Williamstown, MA 01267, 413-597-4286 (FAX: 413-597-4010). Hours: 8:30AM-4:30PM. Records go back to 1795. Alumni records are maintained here also. Call 413-597-4151. Degrees granted: Bachelors; Masters.

Attendance information available by FAX, mail. Search requires name plus social security number, approximate years of attendance, signed release. No fee for information.

Degree information available by phone, FAX, mail. Search requires name plus social security number, approximate years of attendance, signed release. No fee for information.

Transcripts available by FAX, mail. Search requires name plus social security number, approximate years of attendance, signed release. No fee for transcripts.

Williamsburg Technical College, Registrar, 601 Martin Luther King Jr. Ave, Kingstree, SC 29556-4197, 803-354-2021 X165 (FAX: 803-354-7269). Hours: 8AM-4PM M,T,Th,F; Noon-8PM W. Records go back to 1969. Alumni records are maintained here at the same phone number. Degrees granted: Associate.

Attendance and degree information available by phone, FAX, mail. Search requires name plus social security number. Other helpful information: date of birth, exact years of attendance. No fee for information.

Transcripts available by written request only. Search requires name plus social security number, signed release. Other helpful information: date of birth, exact years of attendance. No fee for transcripts.

Williamsport School of Commerce, Registrar, 941 W Third St, Williamsport, PA 17701, 717-326-2869. Hours: 8AM-4PM. Records go back to 1955. Degrees granted: Associate.

Attendance and degree information available by phone, mail. Search requires name plus social security number. No fee for information.

The Sourcebook of College and University Student Records

Transcripts available by mail. Search requires name plus social security number, signed release. Fee is $1.00.

Willmar Community College, Registrar, PO Box 797, Willmar, MN 56201, 612-231-5108 (FAX: 612-231-6602). Hours: 8AM-4:30PM. Records go back to 1962. Degrees granted: Associate. Adverse incident record source: 612-231-5176.

Attendance and degree information available by phone, FAX, mail. Search requires name plus social security number. Other helpful information: approximate years of attendance. No fee for information.

Transcripts available by phone, mail. Search requires name plus social security number, date of birth, signed release. Other helpful information: approximate years of attendance. No fee for transcripts.

Will do occasional FAX with proper identification.

Wilmington College, Registrar, 320 Dupont Hwy, New Castle, DE 19720, 302-328-9401 X110 (FAX: 302-328-7918). Hours: 8:30AM-6PM M-Th, 8:30AM-4:30PM. Records go back to 1968. Alumni records are maintained here also. Call 302-328-9401 X101. Degrees granted: Associate; Bachelors; Masters; Doctorate.

Attendance and degree information available by phone, FAX, mail. Search requires name plus social security number, approximate years of attendance. No fee for information.

Transcripts available by mail. Search requires name plus social security number, approximate years of attendance, signed release. Fee is $3.00.

Wilmington College, Registrar, PO Box 1185, Wilmington, OH 45177, 513-382-6661 X512 (FAX: 513-382-7077). Hours: 8AM-5PM. Records go back to 1900. Alumni Records Office: Alumni Association, PO Box 1307, Pyle Center, Wilmington, OH 45177,. Degrees granted: Bachelors. Adverse incident record source: Student Services, 513-382-6661 X339.

Attendance and degree information available by phone, FAX, mail. Search requires name plus social security number, date of birth, exact years of attendance, signed release. No fee for information.

Transcripts available by phone, FAX, mail. Search requires name plus social security number, date of birth, exact years of attendance, signed release. First transcript is free; $2.00 each additional.

Wilson College, Registrar, 1015 Philadelphia Ave, Chambersburg, PA 17201-1285, 717-264-4141 X355 (FAX: 717-264-1578). Hours: 8AM-4:30PM. Records go back to 1869. Alumni records are maintained here also. Call 717-264-3182. Degrees granted: Bachelors.

Attendance and degree information available by phone, mail. Search requires name plus social security number, exact years of attendance. No fee for information.

Transcripts available by mail. Search requires name plus social security number, exact years of attendance, signed release. Fee is $3.00.

Wilson Technical Community College, Registrar, 902 Herring Ave, PO Box 4305, Wilson, NC 27893, 919-291-1195 X277 (FAX: 919-243-7148). Hours: 8AM-5PM. Records go back 40 years. Alumni records are maintained here also. Call 919-291-1195 X276. Degrees granted: Associate. Adverse incident record source: Dean of Fiscal Affairs, 919-291-1195 X221.

Attendance and degree information available by phone, FAX, mail. Search requires name only. Other helpful information: social security number, approximate years of attendance. No fee for information.

Transcripts available by FAX, mail. Search requires name plus social security number, approximate years of attendance, signed release. Other helpful information: exact years of attendance. No fee for transcripts.

Windward Community College, Registrar, 45-720 Keaahala Rd, Kaneohe, HI 96744, 808-235-7432. Hours: 8:30AM-4:30PM. Records go back to 1972. Degrees granted: Associate.

Attendance and degree information available by phone, mail. Search requires name plus social security number, exact years of attendance, signed release. No fee for information.

Transcripts available by mail. Search requires name plus social security number, exact years of attendance, signed release. Fee is $1.00.

Attendance confirmed by phone if release on file.

Winebrenner Theological Seminry, Registrar, 701 E Melrose Ave, PO Box 478, Findlay, OH 45839, 419-422-4824 (FAX: 419-424-3433). Hours: 8AM-5PM. Records go back to 1842. Alumni records are maintained here at the same phone number. Degrees granted: Masters.

Attendance and degree information available by phone, FAX, mail. Search requires name only. Other helpful information: approximate years of attendance. No fee for information.

Transcripts available by mail. Search requires name plus signed release. Other helpful information: approximate years of attendance. Fee is $4.00.

Former names needed.

Wingate College, Registrar, Wingate, NC 28174-0157, 704-233-8126 (FAX: 704-233-8125). Hours: 8:30AM-5PM. Records go back to 1896. Alumni records are maintained here also. Call 704-233-8114. Degrees granted: Associate; Bachelors; Masters.

Attendance and degree information available by phone, FAX, mail. Search requires name plus social security number. Other helpful information: date of birth, approximate years of attendance. No fee for information.

Transcripts available by mail. Search requires name plus signed release. Other helpful information: date of birth, approximate years of attendance. Fee is $2.00.

Winona State University, Registrar, Winona, MN 55987, 507-457-5030 (FAX: 507-457-5578). Hours: 7:30AM-4:30PM. Records go back to 1880. Alumni records are maintained here also. Call 507-457-5027. Degrees granted: Bachelors; Masters.

Attendance and degree information available by phone, FAX, mail. Search requires name only. Other helpful information: social security number, date of birth, approximate years of attendance. No fee for information.

Transcripts available by FAX, mail. Search requires name plus signed release. Other helpful information: social security number, date of birth, approximate years of attendance. No fee for transcripts.

Student can request that directory information not be released.

Winston-Salem State University, Registrar, 601 Martin Luther King,Jr. Dr, Winston-Salem, NC 27110, 910-750-2000. Degrees granted: Bachelors.

Attendance information available by phone, FAX, mail. Search requires name plus social security number, approximate years of attendance. Other helpful information: exact years of attendance. No fee for information.

Degree information available by phone, FAX, mail. Search requires name plus social security number, approximate years of attendance, signed release. No fee for information.

Transcripts available by mail. Search requires name plus social security number, approximate years of attendance, signed release.

Winthrop University, Records & Registration, 101 Tillman Hall, Rock Hill, SC 29733, 803-323-2194 (FAX: 803-323-4600). Hours: 8:30AM-5PM. Records go back to 1886. Alumni Records Office: 304 Tillman Hall, Rock Hill, SC 29733 803-323-2145. Degrees granted: Bachelors; Masters. Adverse incident record source: Public Safety, 803-323-3333.

Attendance information available by phone, FAX, mail. Search requires name plus social security number, approximate years of attendance. Other helpful information: exact years of attendance. No fee for information.

Degree information available by phone, FAX, mail. Search requires name plus social security number. Other helpful information: date of birth, approximate years of attendance. No fee for information.

Transcripts available by phone, FAX, mail. Search requires name plus social security number, approximate years of attendance, signed release. Other helpful information: exact years of attendance. No fee for transcripts. Expedite: up to $10.00. Major credit cards accepted for payment.

Wisconsin Indianhead Technical College, Registrar, HCR 69 Box 10B, Shell Lake, WI 54871, 715-468-2815. Hours: 8AM-5PM. Records go back to 1972. Degrees granted: Associate.

Attendance and degree information available by phone, mail. Search requires name plus social security number, exact years of attendance. No fee for information.

Transcripts available by mail. Search requires name plus social security number, exact years of attendance, signed release. Fee is $1.00.

Wisconsin Lutheran College, Registrar, 8800 W Bluemond Rd, Milwaukee, WI 53226, 414-774-8620 X17 (FAX: 414-774-9367). Hours: 7:30AM-3:30PM. Records go back to 1973. Alumni records are maintained here at the same phone number. Degrees granted: Bachelors.

Attendance and degree information available by phone, FAX, mail. Search requires name only. Other helpful information: social security number, date of birth, approximate years of attendance. No fee for information.

Transcripts available by written request only. Search requires name plus signed release. Other helpful information: social security number, date of birth, approximate years of attendance. Fee is $2.00. Expedited service available for $2.00.

Wisconsin School of Professional Psychology, Registrar, 9120 W Hampton Ave Ste 212, Milwaukee, WI 53225, 414-464-9777 (FAX: 414-358-5590). Hours: 9AM-5PM. Records go back to founding date. Degrees granted: Doctorate.

Attendance and degree information available by written request only. Search requires name plus social security number, date of birth, signed release. No fee for information.

Transcripts available by mail. Search requires name plus social security number, date of birth, signed release. Fee is $3.00. Expedited service available for $2.00.

Wittenberg University, Registrar, PO Box 720, Springfield, OH 45501, 513-327-6132 (FAX: 513-327-6340). Hours: 8AM-5PM. Records go back to 1900. Alumni Records Office: Alumni Association, PO Box 720, Springfield, OH 45501,. Degrees granted: Bachelors. Adverse incident record source: Dean, 513-327-7800.

Attendance information available by phone, FAX, mail. Search requires name plus social security number, date of birth, exact years of attendance. No fee for information.

Degree information available by phone, FAX, mail. Search requires name only. No fee for information.

Transcripts available by FAX, mail. Search requires name plus social security number, date of birth, signed release. Fee is $3.00.

Wofford College, Registrar, 429 N Church St, Spartanburg, SC 29303-3663, 803-597-4030 (FAX: 803-597-4019). Hours: 8:30AM-5PM. Records go back to 1854. Degrees granted: Bachelors. Adverse incident record source: Public Safety, 803-597-4350: Student Affairs, 803-592-4040

Attendance and degree information available by phone, FAX, mail. Search requires name only. No fee for information.

Transcripts available by FAX, mail. Search requires name plus signed release. Other helpful information: social security number, date of birth, approximate years of attendance. Fee is $2.00.

Wood College, Registrar, Wood College Rd, Mathiston, MS 39752, 601-263-5352 (FAX: 601-263-4964). Hours: 8AM-4:30PM. Records go back to 1886. Alumni records are maintained here at the same phone number. Degrees granted: Associate. Adverse incident record source: Dean of Students, 601-263-8000.

Attendance and degree information available by phone, FAX, mail. Search requires name plus social security number, signed release. No fee for information.

Transcripts available by mail. Search requires name plus social security number, signed release. Fee is $2.00.

Wood Tobe Coburn School, Registrar, 8 E 40th St, New York, NY 10016, 212-686-9040 X36 (FAX: 212-686-9171). Hours: 8AM-5PM. Records go back to 1954. Degrees granted: Associate.

Attendance and degree information available by phone, FAX, mail. Search requires name plus social security number, date of birth, exact years of attendance. No fee for information.

Transcripts available by mail. Search requires name plus social security number, date of birth, exact years of attendance, signed release. Fee is $5.00.

Woodbury College, Registrar, 660 Elm St, Montpelier, VT 05602, 802-229-0516. Hours: 8AM-5PM. Alumni records are maintained here at the same phone number. Degrees granted: Associate.

Attendance and degree information available by phone, mail. Search requires name plus social security number. Other helpful information: approximate years of attendance. No fee for information.

Transcripts available by written request only. Search requires name plus social security number, signed release. Other helpful information: approximate years of attendance. Fee is $2.00.

Woodbury University, Registrar's Office, PO Box 7846, Burbank, CA 91510-7846, 818-767-0888 X270 (FAX: 818-678-8628). Hours: 8AM-8PM M-Th; 8AM-5PM F. Records go back to 1930. Alumni records are maintained here at the same phone number. Degrees granted: Bachelors; Masters.

Attendance and degree information available by phone, FAX, mail. Search requires name plus social security number, date of birth, approximate years of attendance. Other helpful information: exact years of attendance. No fee for information.

Transcripts available by mail. Search requires name plus social security number, date of birth, approximate years of attendance, signed release. Other helpful information: exact years of attendance. Fee is $5.00.

Major credit cards accepted for payment.

Wor-Wic Community College, Registrar's Office Rm 109, 32000 Campus Dr, Salisbury, MD 21801, 410-334-2907 (FAX: 410-334-2954). Hours: 8:30PM-5PM Winter; 8AM-4:30PM Summer. Records go back to 1975. Degrees granted: Associate. Special programs- Continuing Education, 410-334-2815.

Attendance and degree information available by phone, FAX, mail. Search requires name plus social security number, approximate years of attendance. Other helpful information: date of birth, exact years of attendance. No fee for information.

Transcripts available by written request only. Search requires name plus social security number, approximate years of attendance, signed release. Other helpful information: date of birth, exact years of attendance. First transcript free; $2.00 each additional.

Worcester Polytechnic Institute, Registrar, 100 Institute Rd, Worcester, MA 01609-2280, 508-831-5211 (FAX: 508-831-5931). Hours: 9AM-4PM. Records go back to 1868. Alumni records are maintained here also. Call 508-831-5600. Degrees granted: Bachelors; Masters; PhD.

Attendance and degree information available by phone, FAX, mail. Search requires name plus social security number, signed release. No fee for information.

Transcripts available by FAX, mail. Search requires name plus social security number, signed release. Fee is $4.00. Expedited service available for $10.00.

Worcester State College, Registrar, 486 Chandler St, Worcester, MA 01602-2597, 508-793-8035 (FAX: 508-793-8196). Hours: 8:15AM-5PM. Records go back to 1874. Degrees granted: Bachelors; Masters.

Attendance information available by phone, FAX, mail. Search requires name plus social security number, date of birth, approximate years of attendance. Other helpful information: exact years of attendance. No fee for information.

Degree information available by phone, FAX, mail. Search requires name plus social security number, date of birth, exact years of attendance. No fee for information.

Transcripts available by mail. Search requires name plus social security number, date of birth, exact years of attendance, signed release. Fee is $2.00. Expedited service available for $4.00.

Worthington Community College, Registrar, 1450 Collegeway, Worthington, MN 56187, 507-372-3451 (FAX: 507-372-5801). Hours: 8AM-4:30PM. Records go back 59 years. Alumni records are maintained here at the same phone number. Degrees granted: Associate.

Attendance and degree information available by phone, FAX, mail. Search requires name plus social security number. Other helpful information: date of birth, approximate years of attendance. No fee for information.

Transcripts available by FAX, mail. Search requires name plus social security number, signed release. Other helpful information: date of birth, approximate years of attendance. No fee for transcripts.

Wright Institute, Registrar, 2728 Durant Ave, Berkeley, CA 94704, 310-841-9230. Records go back to 1969. Degrees granted: Doctorate.

Attendance and degree information available by phone, mail. Search requires name only. No fee for information.

Transcripts available by mail. Search requires name plus social security number, date of birth, signed release. Fee is $2.00.

Wright State University, Registrar, 3640 Colonel Glenn Hwy, Dayton, OH 45435, 513-873-5588 (FAX: 513-873-5795). Hours: 8:30AM-7PM M-Th, 8:30AM-5PM F. Records go back to 1964. Alumni records are maintained here also. Call 513-873-2251. Degrees granted: Associate; Bachelors; Masters; Doctorate; Medicine, Psy D. Special programs- School Medicine, 513-873-3013. Adverse incident record source: Public Safety, 513-873-2056.

Attendance and degree information available by phone, FAX, mail. Search requires name plus social security number, approximate years of attendance. No fee for information.

Transcripts available by FAX, mail. Search requires name plus social security number, approximate years of attendance, signed release. Fee is $3.00. Expedited service available for $15.00.

Wright State University, **(Lake)**, Registrar, 7600 State Rte 703, Celina, OH 45822, 419-586-0324 (FAX: 419-586-0358). Records are not housed here. They are located at Wright State University, Registrar, 3640 Colonel Glenn Hwy, Dayton, OH 45435.

Wytheville Community College, Registrar, 1000 E Main St, Wytheville, VA 24382, 703-228-5541 X316 (FAX: 703-228-6506). Hours: 8AM-5PM. Degrees granted: Associate.

Attendance information available by phone. Search requires name only. No fee for information.

Degree information available by phone, FAX, mail. Search requires name plus social security number. Other helpful information: date of birth, approximate years of attendance. No fee for information.

Transcripts available by FAX, mail. Search requires name plus social security number, signed release. Other helpful information: date of birth, approximate years of attendance. No fee for transcripts.

X,Y,Z

Xavier University, Registrar, 3800 Victory Pkwy, Cincinnati, OH 45207, 513-745-3941 (FAX: 513-745-2969). Hours: 8AM-7PM M-Th; 8AM-5PM F. Records go back to 1920s. Degrees granted: Associate; Bachelors; Masters. Adverse incident record source: Safety and Security, 513-745-1000.

Attendance and degree information available by phone, FAX, mail. Search requires name only. Other helpful information: social

security number, date of birth, approximate years of attendance. No fee for information.

School does not provide transcripts. Search requires name plus signed release. Other helpful information: social security number, date of birth, approximate years of attendance. Fee is $5.00. Expedited service available for $10.00.

Xavier University of Louisiana, Registrar, 7325 Palmetto St, New Orleans, LA 70125, 504-483-7583 (FAX: 504-486-4852). Hours: 8AM-5PM. Records go back to 1925. Alumni records are maintained here also. Call 504-483-7614. Degrees granted: Bachelors; Masters; Pharm D.

Attendance and degree information available by phone, FAX, mail. Search requires name only. Other helpful information: social security number, date of birth, approximate years of attendance. No fee for information. Expedited service available for $5.00.

Transcripts available by FAX, mail. Search requires name plus signed release. Other helpful information: social security number, date of birth, approximate years of attendance. First transcript is free; each additional $2.00. When ordering a group, $2.00 for first, then $1.00 each. Expedited service available for $5.00. Major credit cards accepted for payment.

Yakima Valley Community College, Registrar, PO Box 1647, Yakima, WA 98907, 509-575-2372 (FAX: 509-575-2461). Records go back to 1928. Alumni records are maintained here also. Call 509-575-2442. Degrees granted: Associate.

Attendance and degree information available by phone, FAX, mail. Search requires name plus social security number, date of birth, exact years of attendance. No fee for information.

Transcripts available by FAX, mail. Search requires name plus social security number, date of birth, exact years of attendance, signed release. Fee is $1.00.

FAX fee $2.00. Major credit cards accepted for payment.

Yale Divinity School, Registrar, 409 Prospect St, New Haven, CT 06511, 203-432-5312 (FAX: 203-432-5356). Hours: 9AM-5PM. Records go back to 1800s. Degrees granted: Masters.

Attendance and degree information available by phone, FAX, mail. Search requires name only. Other helpful information: date of birth, approximate years of attendance. No fee for information.

Transcripts available by written request only. Search requires name plus signed release. Other helpful information: date of birth, approximate years of attendance. Fee is $2.00.

Yale University, Registrar, New Haven, CT 06520, 203-432-2320 (FAX: 203-432-2324). Hours: 8:30AM-4:30PM. Records go back to 1700s. Alumni records are maintained here also. Call 203-432-2586. Degrees granted: Associate; Bachelors; Masters; Doctorate.

Attendance and degree information available by FAX, mail. Search requires name plus social security number, approximate years of attendance. No fee for information.

Transcripts available by mail. Search requires name plus social security number, approximate years of attendance, signed release. First transcript $5.00, each additional $1.00. Include stamped envelope.

Yavapai College, Registrar, 1100 E Sheldon St, Prescott, AZ 86301, 602-776-2150 (FAX: 602-776-2151). Hours: 8:30AM-4:30PM. Records go back 2 years. Degrees granted: Associate. Adverse incident record source: Campus Life, 602-776-7220.

Attendance and degree information available by phone, FAX, mail. Search requires name plus social security number, date of birth, approximate years of attendance. Other helpful information: exact years of attendance. No fee for information.

Transcripts available by FAX, mail. Search requires name plus social security number, date of birth, approximate years of attendance, signed release. Other helpful information: exact years of attendance. Fee is $3.00.

Yeshiva Beth Moshe, Registrar, 930 Hickory St, Scranton, PA 18505, 717-346-1747. Hours: 8AM-5PM. Records go back to 1965.

Attendance and degree information available by mail. Search requires name plus social security number, date of birth, exact years of attendance, signed release. No fee for information.

Transcripts available by mail. Search requires name plus social security number, date of birth, exact years of attendance, signed release. Fee is $5.00.

Yeshiva Beth Yehuda-Yeshiva Gedolah of Greater Detroit, Registrar, 24600 Greenfield St, Oak Park, MI 48237, 810-968-3360 (FAX: 810-968-8613). Hours: 8:30AM-5:30PM. Records go back to 1985. Degrees granted: Associate; Bachelors; Masters; Doctorate.

Attendance information available by phone, FAX, mail. Search requires name plus signed release. No fee for information.

Degree information available by FAX, mail. Search requires name plus signed release. No fee for information.

Transcripts available by FAX, mail. Search requires name plus signed release. No fee for transcripts.

Yeshiva Derech Chaim, Registrar, 1573 39th St, Brooklyn, NY 11218, 718-438-3070 (FAX: 718-435-9285).

Attendance and degree information available by mail. Search requires name plus social security number. No fee for information.

Transcripts available by mail. Search requires name plus social security number, exact years of attendance, signed release. No fee for transcripts.

Yeshiva Karlin Stolin Beth Aaron V'Israel Rabbinical Institute, Registrar, 1818 54th St, Brooklyn, NY 11204, 718-232-7800 (FAX: 718-331-4833).

Attendance and degree information available by mail. Search requires name plus social security number, signed release. No fee for information.

Transcripts available by mail. Search requires name plus social security number, signed release. No fee for transcripts.

Yeshiva Mikdash Melech, Registrar, 1326 Ocean Pkwy, Brooklyn, NY 11230-5655, 718-339-1090 (FAX: 718-998-9321).

Attendance and degree information available by phone, mail. Search requires name plus social security number, date of birth, exact years of attendance. No fee for information.

Transcripts available by mail. Search requires name plus social security number, date of birth, exact years of attendance, signed release. No fee for transcripts.

Yeshiva Ohr Elchonon-Chabad/West Coast Talmudic Seminary, Registrar, 7215 Waring Ave, Los Angeles, CA 90046, 213-937-3763 (FAX: 213-937-9456). Hours: 8:30AM-4PM. Records go back 40 years. Degrees granted: Bachelors.

Attendance and degree information available by phone, FAX, mail. Search requires name plus approximate years of attendance. Other helpful information: exact years of attendance. No fee for information.

Transcripts available by mail. Search requires name plus approximate years of attendance. Other helpful information: exact years of attendance. Fee is $36.00. Expedite: $50.00 plus overnight & postage. Reduced rate for simultaneous, multiple requests.

Yeshiva Shaar HaTorah Talmudic Research Institute, Registrar, 83-96 117th St, Kew Gardens, NY 11415, 718-846-1940 (FAX: 718-846-1942).

Attendance and degree information available by phone, mail. Search requires name plus exact years of attendance. No fee for information.

Transcripts available by mail. Search requires name plus social security number, exact years of attendance, signed release. No fee for transcripts.

Yeshiva Toras Chaim Talmudic Seminary, Registrar, 1400 Quitman St, PO Box 4067, Denver, CO 80204, 303-629-8200 (FAX: 303-623-5949). Hours: 8AM-5PM. Records go back to 1967. Degrees granted: Masters; 1st Professional Degree.

Attendance and degree information available by mail. Search requires name plus social security number, signed release. No fee for information.

Transcripts available by mail. Search requires name plus social security number, signed release. No fee for transcripts.

Yeshiva University, Registrar, 500 W 185th St, New York, NY 10033-3299, 212-960-5400. Hours: 9AM-5PM M,W; 1-5PM T,Th. Records go back to 1950. Degrees granted: Associate; Bachelors; Masters; Doctorate.

Attendance and degree information available by phone, mail. Search requires name plus social security number. Other helpful information: date of birth, approximate years of attendance. No fee for information.

Transcripts available by mail. Search requires name plus social security number, signed release. Other helpful information: date of birth, approximate years of attendance. Fee is $4.00. Expedited service available for $8.00.

Yeshiva of Nitra-Rabbinical College Yeshiva Farm Settlement, Registrar, Pines Bridge Rd, Mount Kisco, NY 10549, 718-387-0422 (FAX: 718-387-9400). Hours: 9AM-5PM. Degrees granted: Bachelors; Rabbinic Degree.

Attendance and degree information available by FAX, mail. Search requires name plus social security number, date of birth. No fee for information.

Transcripts available by FAX, mail. Search requires name plus social security number, date of birth, exact years of attendance, signed release. Fee is $15.00.

Major credit cards accepted for payment.

Yeshivas Novominsk, Registrar, 1569 47th St, Brooklyn, NY 11219, 718-438-2727 (FAX: 718-438-2472). Hours: 9AM-5PM.

Attendance information available by mail. Search requires name only. Other helpful information: social security number. No fee for information.

Degree information available by FAX, mail. Search requires name plus approximate years of attendance, signed release. Other helpful information: social security number. No fee for information.

Transcripts available by mail. Search requires name plus approximate years of attendance, signed release. Other helpful information: social security number. No fee for transcripts.

Include a self addressed stamped envelope with mail request.

Yeshivath Viznitz, Registrar, PO Box 446, Monsey, NY 10952, 914-356-1010 (FAX: 914-425-1730).

Attendance and degree information available by mail. Search requires name plus social security number, date of birth, exact years of attendance, signed release. No fee for information.

Transcripts available by mail. Search requires name plus social security number, date of birth, exact years of attendance, signed release. No fee for transcripts.

Yesivath Zichron Moshe, Registrar, Laurel Park Rd, PO Box 580, South Fallsburg, NY 12779, 914-434-5240 (FAX: 914-434-1009).

Attendance and degree information available by mail. Search requires name plus social security number, date of birth, exact years of attendance, signed release. No fee for information.

Transcripts available by mail. Search requires name plus social security number, date of birth, exact years of attendance, signed release. No fee for transcripts.

Yo San University of Traditional Chinese Medicine, Registrar, 1314 Second St, Santa Monica, CA 90401, 310-917-2202 (FAX: 310-917-2267). Hours: 9AM-7PM. Alumni records are maintained here also. Call 310-917-2202. Degrees granted: Masters.

Attendance and degree information available by phone, FAX, mail. Search requires name plus social security number, date of birth, approximate years of attendance, signed release. No fee for information.

Transcripts available by mail. Search requires name plus social security number, date of birth, approximate years of attendance, signed release. Fee is $5.00.

York College, Registrar, 9th & Kiplinger Ave, York, NY 68467-2699, 402-362-4441. Hours: 8AM-5PM. Records go back to 1890. Alumni records are maintained here also. Call 402-362-4441. Degrees granted: Bachelors.

Attendance and degree information available by phone, mail. Search requires name plus social security number, exact years of attendance. No fee for information.

Transcripts available by mail. Search requires name plus social security number, exact years of attendance, signed release. Fee is $5.00.

York College, Registrar, 912 Kiplinger Ave, York, NE 68467-2699, 402-363-5678 (FAX: 402-363-5623). Hours: 8-10:30AM, 11AM-Noon, 1-5PM. Records go back to 1956. Degrees granted: Associate; Bachelors. Adverse incident record source: Dean of Students, 402-363-5672.

Attendance information available by phone, FAX, mail. Search requires name only. Other helpful information: social security number, approximate years of attendance. No fee for information.

Degree information available by phone, FAX, mail. Search requires name only. Other helpful information: social security number, date of birth, approximate years of attendance. No fee for information. Expedite fee varies.

Transcripts available by FAX, mail. Search requires name plus approximate years of attendance, signed release. Other helpful information: social security number, date of birth, exact years of attendance. Fee is $5.00. Expedited service available for $20.00. Major credit cards accepted for payment.

York College of Pennsylvania, Records Office, Country Club Rd, York, PA 17405-7199, 717-846-7788. Hours: 8AM-5PM M-Th, 8-11:30AM F. Records go back to 1788. Alumni records are maintained here also. Call 717-846-7788 X1500. Degrees granted: Associate; Bachelors; Masters.

Attendance and degree information available by phone, mail. Search requires name plus social security number. Other helpful information: date of birth, approximate years of attendance. No fee for information.

Transcripts available by mail. Search requires name plus social security number, signed release. Other helpful information: date of birth, approximate years of attendance. Fee is $3.00.

York Technical College, Student Records, 452 S Anderson Rd, Rock Hill, SC 29730, 803-327-8002 (FAX: 803-327-8059). Hours: 8AM-7PM M-Th; 8AM-5PM F. Records go back to 1964. Degrees granted: Associate. Adverse incident record source: Security Office, 803-327-8013.

Attendance and degree information available by phone, FAX, mail. Search requires name plus social security number, signed release. Other helpful information: approximate years of attendance. No fee for information.

Transcripts available by FAX, mail. Search requires name plus social security number, signed release. Other helpful information: date of birth, approximate years of attendance. No fee for transcripts.

Yorktowne Business Institute, Registrar, W Seventh Ave, York, PA 17404, 717-846-5000 (FAX: 717-848-4584). Hours: 8AM-5PM. Records go back to 1977. Degrees granted: Associate.

Attendance and degree information available by phone, FAX, mail. Search requires name only. Other helpful information: social security number, date of birth, approximate years of attendance. No fee for information.

Transcripts available by FAX, mail. Search requires name plus signed release. Other helpful information: social security number, date of birth, approximate years of attendance. Fee is $3.00. Expedited service available for $3.00.

Young Harris College, Registrar, PO Box 96, Young Harris, GA 30582, 706-379-3111 X5699 (FAX: 706-379-4306). Hours: 8:30AM-4:30PM. Degrees granted: Associate. Adverse incident record source: Dean of Students.

Attendance and degree information available by phone, FAX, mail. Search requires name plus social security number. Other helpful information: date of birth, approximate years of attendance. No fee for information.

Transcripts available by mail. Search requires name plus social security number, signed release. Other helpful information: date of birth, approximate years of attendance. Fee is $2.00.

Youngstown State University, Records Office, 410 Wick Ave, Youngstown, OH 44555, 216-742-3182 (FAX: 216-742-1408). Hours: 8AM-5PM. Records go back to 1908. Degrees granted: Associate; Bachelors; Masters; Doctorate.

Attendance and degree information available by phone, FAX, mail. Search requires name plus social security number, date of birth. Other helpful information: approximate years of attendance. No fee for information.

Transcripts available by FAX, mail. Search requires name plus social security number, date of birth, signed release. Other helpful information: approximate years of attendance. Fee is $5.00. Expedited service available for $5.00.

Major credit cards accepted for payment.

Yuba College, Records Office, 2088 N Beale Rd, Marysville, CA 95901, 916-741-6871. Hours: 8AM-6PM M-Th; 8AM-5PM F. Records go back to 1926. Degrees granted: Associate. Adverse incident record source: Campus Police, 916-741-6771.

Attendance information available by mail. Search requires name plus signed release. Other helpful information: social security number, date of birth, approximate years of attendance. No fee for information.

Degree information available by phone, mail. Search requires name only. Other helpful information: social security number, date of birth, approximate years of attendance. No fee for information.

School does not provide transcripts. Search requires name plus signed release. Other helpful information: social security number, date of birth, approximate years of attendance. Fee is $3.00. Expedited service available for $6.00.

Section Two

Accredited, Non-Degree Granting Institution Profiles

Editor's Note: New Telephone Area Code Changes

- Southern Alabama • Effective 1/15/95, the southern half of Alabama (Montgomery area) switched from **Code 205** to **Code 334**. The end of the overlap period is 5/13/95.

- Washington • Effective 1/15/95, all **Code 206** outside Washington counties of King, Pierce, and Snohomish changed to **Code 360**. The end of the overlap period is 7/9/95.

- Arizona • Effective the Spring of 1995, all of Arizona, except for the Phoenix metro area of Maricopa County, changed from **Code 602** to **Code 520**. The overlap period will end 7/95.

- Southwest Florida • Effective May 28, 1995, **Code 941** was created from **Code 813**, except for Tampa which will remain 813. The overlap period ends March 3, 1996.

- Northern Virginia • Effective July 15, 1995, **Code 540** was created from **Code 703**. This will not include the DC Suburban area. The overlap period ends Jan. 27, 1996.

- Connecticut • Effective August 28, 1995, **Code 860** will be created from **Code 203**. The entire state will change except for New Haven and Fairfield counties. The overlap period ends Oct. 4, 1996.

- Southern California • Effective September 2, 1995, **Code 562** will overlay **Code 310** for cellular phones and pagers only.

- Eastern Tennessee • Effective September 11, 1995, **Code 423** will be created from **Code 615**. The overlap period ends Feb. 26, 1996.

- Oregon • Effective November 5, 1995, **Code 541** will be created from **Code 503**. The entire state will change except for the geographic region from Salem to Portland. The overlap period ends Feb. 26, 1996.

A

ABC Technical & Trade Schools
3761 E Technical Dr, Tucson, AZ 85713, 602-748-1762

ABS Training Center
7132 Garden Grove Blvd, Westminster, CA 92683, 714-895-9818

AEGIS Training Center
Dahlgren, VA 22448, 703-663-8531

AIMS Academy
1106 N Hwy 360 #305, Grand Prairie, TX 75050, 214-988-3202

AIMS Academy, (Branch Campus)
10830 N Central Expy, Dallas, TX 75231, 214-891-9672

ATI - American Trades Institutes
6627 Maple Ave, Dallas, TX 75235, 214-352-2222

ATI - American Trades Institutes, (Graphic Arts Institute)
11034 Shady Tr, Dallas, TX 75229, 214-353-9056

ATI - Hollywood
3024 Trinkle Ave, Roanoke, VA 24012, 703-362-9338

ATI - Hollywood, (Branch Campus)
1108 Brandon Ave SW, Roanoke, VA 24015, 703-343-0153

ATI - Hollywood, (Branch Campus)
109 E Main St, Salem, VA 24153, 703-389-1500

ATI Career Institute
7777 Leesburg Pike #100 S, Falls Church, VA 22043, 703-821-8570

ATI Career Institute, (Branch Campus)
Marine Corps Ed. Cmnd., Quantico, VA 22134, 703-640-2121

ATI Career Training Center
2351 W Northwest Hwy, Dallas, TX 75229, 214-688-0467

ATI Career Training Center Electronic Campus
2880 NW 62nd St, Fort Lauderdale, FL 33309, 305-973-4760

ATI Career Training Center
235 NE Loop 820 #110, Hurst, TX 76053, 817-589-1994

ATI Career Training Center
3501 NW 9th Ave, Oakland Park, FL 33309, 305-563-5899

ATI Career Training Center, (Branch Campus)
One NE 19th St, Miami, FL 33132, 305-573-1600

ATI-Health Education Center
1395 NW 167th St #200, Miami, FL 33169, 305-628-1000

Aaker's Business College
PO Box 876, Grand Forks, ND 58206, 701-772-6646

Abbeville Beauty Academy
1828 Veterans Memorial Dr, Abbeville, LA 70510, 318-893-1228

Abbie Business Institute
5310 Spectrum Dr, Frederick, MD 21701, 301-694-0211

Academy Education Center
3050 Metro Dr #200, Minneapolis, MN 55425, 612-851-0666

Academy Pacific Business and Travel College
1777 N Vine St, Hollywood, CA 90028, 213-462-3211

Academy for Career Education
55-05 Myrtle Ave, Ridgewood, NY 11385, 718-497-4900

Academy of Artistic Hair Design
314 Tenth St, North Wilkesboro, NC 28659, 919-838-4571

Academy of Creative Hair Design
2911 Jacksonville Rd, Ocala, FL 32670, 904-351-5900

Academy of Floral Design
837 Acoma St, Denver, CO 80204], 303-623-8855

Academy of Hair Design
1440 Whipple Ave, Canton, OH 44708, 216-477-6695

Academy of Hair Design
2150 Lafayette Rd, Indianapolis, IN 46222, 317-637-7227

Academy of Healing Arts, Message & Facial Skin Care
3141 S Military Tr, Lake Worth, FL 33463, 407-965-5550

Academy of Health Careers
27301 Dequindre Rd #200, Madison Heights, MI 48071, 313-547-8400

Academy of Medical Arts and Business
279 Boas St, Harrisburg, PA 17102, 717-233-2172

Academy of Medical Careers
5243 W Charleston Blvd #11, Las Vegas, NV 89102, 818-896-2272

Academy of Professional Development
98 Mayfield Ave, Edison, NJ 08837, 908-417-9100

Academy of Professional Development, (Branch Campus)
934 Parkway Ave, Ewing, NJ 08618, 609-538-0400

Acadian Technical Institute
1933 W Hutchinson Ave, Crowley, LA 70527, 318-788-7521

Acme Institute of Technology
102 Revere Dr, Manitowoc, WI 54220, 414-682-6144

Acme Institute of Technology
819 S 60th St, West Allis, WI 53214, 414-257-1011

Action Career Training
Rte 3 Box 41, Merkel, TX 79536, 915-676-3136

Acupuncture School of Maryland
4400 East-West Hwy #128, Bethesda, MD 20814, 301-907-8986

Advanced Career Training
8800 N Central Expy #120, Dallas, TX 75231, 214-692-5400

Advanced Hair Tech
4323 State Ave, Kansas City, KS 66101, 913-321-0214

Advanced Software Analysis
151 Lawrence St 2nd Fl, Brooklyn, NY 11201, 718-522-9073

Advertising Arts College
10025 Mesa Rim Rd, San Diego, CA 92121, 619-456-0602

Aero Mechanics School
Riverside, MO 64150, 816-741-7700

Air-Tech, Inc.
RR 1 Box 170, Limerick, ME 04048, 207-793-8020

Airman Proficiency Center
3565 NE Cornell Rd, Hillsboro, OR 97124, 503-648-2831

Akron Barber College
3200 S Arlington Rd #2, Akron, OH 44312, 216-644-9114

A

Akron Machining Institute, Inc.
2959 Barber Rd, Barberton Rd, OH 44203, 216-745-1111

Akron Machining Institute, Inc., (Cleveland Machining Institute)
2500 Brookpark Rd, Cleveland, OH 44134, 216-741-1100

Akron School of Practical Nursing
619 Sumner St, Akron, OH 44311, 216-376-4129

Akron-Medical-Dental Institute
733 W Market St, Akron, OH 44303, 216-762-9788

Al Collins Graphic Design School
1140 S Priest Dr, Tempe, AZ 85281, 602-966-3000

Al-Med Academy
10963 St Charles Rock Rd, St Louis, MO 63074, 314-739-4450

Alabama Reference Laboratories, Inc.
PO Box 4600, Montgomery, AL 36103, 205-263-5745

Alabama State College of Barber Styling
9480 Pkwy E, Birmingham, AL 35215-8308, 205-836-2404

Albany Technical Institute
1021 Lowe Rd, Albany, GA 31708, 912-888-1320

Albert I. Prince Regional Vocational-Technical School
500 Bookfield St, Hartford, CT 06106, 203-246-8594

Albuquerque Barber College
525 San Pedro Dr NE #104, Albuquerque, NM 87108, 505-266-4900

Alexandria Regional Technical Institute
4311 S MacArthur Dr, Alexandria, LA 71302, 318-487-5698

All-State Career School
501 Seminole St, Lester, PA 19029, 215-521-1818

All-State Career School, (Branch Campus)
201 S Arlington Ave, Baltimore, MD 21223, 410-566-7111

Allegheny Business Institute
239 Fourth Ave #617, Pittsburgh, PA 15222, 412-456-7100

Alliance Tractor Trailer Training Center
PO Box 883, Arden, NC 28704, 704-684-4454

Alliance Tractor Trailer Training Center
PO Box 1008, McDonough, GA 30253, 404-957-6401

Alliance Tractor Trailer Trining Centers II
PO Box 804, Wytheville, VA 24382, 703-228-6101

Alliance Tractor Trailer Trining Centers II, (Training Center V Campus)
PO Box 579, Benson, NC 27504, 919-892-8370

Allied Health Careers
5424 Hwy 29 W #105, Austin, TX 78735, 512-892-5210

Allied Medical Careers
104 Woodward Hill Rd, Edwardsville, PA 18704, 717-288-8400

Allied Medical Careers, (Branch Campus)
2901 Pittston Ave, Scranton, PA 18505, 717-342-8000

Allstate Hairstyling and Barber College
2546 Lorain Ave, Cleveland, OH 44113, 216-241-6684

Allstate Tractor Trailer Training School
2064 Main St, Bridgeport, CT 06004, 800-245-9422

Alpha Beauty School
10 Liberty Ln, Greenville, SC 29607, 803-271-0020

Alpha Beauty School, (Branch Campus)
2619 S Main St, Anderson, SC 29624, 803-224-8338

Alpha Beauty School, (Branch Campus)
Tunnell Rd, Asheville, SC 28805, 704-253-2875

Alpha Beauty School, (Branch Campus)
112 E North & Second Sts, Seneca, SC 29678, 803-882-0936

Alpha Beauty School, (Branch Campus)
653 N Church St, Spartanburg, SC 29301, 803-585-6666

Altamaha Technical Institute
1777 W Cherry St, Jessup, GA 31545, 912-427-5800

Altamaha Technical Institute, (Branch Campus)
Cromatie St, Hazlehurst, GA 31319, 912-375-5480

Alvin Ailey American Dance Center
211 W 61st St 3rd Fl, New York, NY 10023, 212-767-0940

American Academy of Nutrition
3408 Sausalito, Corona Del Mar, CA 92625, 714-760-5081

American Academy of Nutrition
1429 Cherokee Blvd, Knoxville, TN 37919, 615-524-8079

American Ballet Center/Joffrey Balley School
434 Ave of the Americas, New York, NY 10011, 212-254-8520

American Business Academy
66 Moore St, Hackensack, NJ 07601, 201-488-9400

American Business and Fashion Institute
1515 Mockingbird Ln #600, Charlotte, NC 28209, 704-523-3738

American Career Training
237 S State St, Chicago, IL 60604, 312-461-0700

American College of Optechs
4021 Rosewood Ave, Los Angeles, CA 90004, 213-383-2862

American College of Technology
1300 W Washington St, Bloomington, IL 61701, 309-828-5151

American Commercial College
402 Butternut St, Abilene, TX 79602, 915-672-8495

American Commercial College
2007 34th St, Lubbock, TX 79411, 806-747-4339

American Commercial College
2115 E Eighth St, Odessa, TX 79761, 915-332-0768

American Commercial College
3177 Executive Dr, San Angelo, TX 76904, 915-942-6797

American Diesel & Automotive College
1002 S Jason St, Denver, CO 80223, 303-778-5522

American Education Center
26075 Woodward Ave, Huntington Woods, MI 48070, 303-399-5522

American Education Institute of Cosmetology
415 Seventh Ave SW, Hickory, NC 29601, 704-327-2887

American Flyers College
5400 NW 21st Terr, Fort Lauderdale, FL 33309, 305-772-7500

American Health Information Management Association
919 N Michigan Ave #1400, Chicago, IL 60611, 312-787-2672

American Institute of Commerce
9330 LJB Fwy #350, Dallas, TX 75243, 214-690-1978

American Institute of Health Technology, Inc.
6600 Emerald St, Boise, ID 83704, 208-377-8080

The Sourcebook of College and University Student Records

A

American Institute of Medical-Dental Technolgy
1675 N Freedom Blvd #4, Provo, UT 84604, 801-377-2900

American Musical and Dramatic Academy
2109 Broadway, New York, NY 10023, 212-787-5300

American Nanny College
4650 Aroow Hwy Ste A10, Montclair, CA 91763, 909-624-7711

American School of Business
702 Professional Dr N, Shreveport, LA 71105, 318-798-3333

American School of Nail Techniques & Cosmetology
924 E Tallmadge Ave, Akron, OH 44310, 216-633-9427

American School of Technology
4599-4605 Morse Center Dr, Columbus, OH 43229, 614-436-4820

American Technical College for Career Training
191 S E St, San Bernardino, CA 92401, 714-885-3857

American Teller Schools
635 W Indian School Rd #201, Phoenix, AZ 85013, 602-248-0885

American Teller Schools, (Branch Campus)
1819 S Dobson Rd #215, Mesa, AZ 85202, 602-730-8191

American Teller Schools, (Branch Campus)
4023 E Grant Rd Ste A, Tucson, AZ 85712, 602-881-1541

Ameritech Colleges
6843 Lennox Ave, Van Nuys, CA 91405, 818-901-7311

Ameritech Colleges of Bakersfield
4300 Stine Rd Ste 700, Bakersfield, CA 93313, 805-835-9225

Amherst Career Center
201 W Park Ave, Greenwood, MS 38930, 601-453-0480

Amherst Career Center, (Branch Campus)
330 N Mart Plaza, Jackson, MS 38930, 601-336-0392

Amtech Institute
4011 E 31st St S, Wichita, KS 67210, 316-682-6548

Andon College at Modesto
1314 H St, Modesto, CA 95354, 209-571-8777

Andon College at Stockton
1201 N El Dorado St, Stockton, CA 95202, 209-462-8777

Anthony's Barber Styling College
1307 Jefferson Ave, Newport News, VA 23607, 804-244-2311

Antonelli Medical and Professional Institute
1700 Industrial Hwy, Pottstown, PA 19464, 215-323-7270

Apex Technical School
635 Ave of the Americas, New York, NY 10011, 212-645-3300

Apollo College - Phoenix, Inc.
8503 N 27th Ave, Phoenix, AZ 85051, 602-864-1571

Apollo College - Tri City, Inc.
630 W Southern Ave, Mesa, AZ 85210, 602-831-6585

Apollo College - Tucson, Inc.
3870 N Oracle Rd, Tucson, AZ 85705, 602-888-5885

Apollo College - Westridge, Inc.
7502 W Thomas Rd, Phoenix, AZ 85033, 602-849-9000

Apollo College of Medical-Dental Careers
2600 SE 98th St, Portland, OR 97266, 503-761-6100

Applied Career Training, Inc.
1101 N Wilson Blvd, Rosslyn, VA 22209, 703-527-6660

American Institute of Technology
440 S 54th Ave, Phoenix, AZ 85043, 602-233-2222

Apprentice School-Newport News Shipbuilding
4101 Washington Ave, Newport News, VA 23607, 804-380-2682

Aristotle College of Medical and Dental Technology
5425 S US 31, Indianapolis, IN 46227, 317-784-5400

Aristotle College of Medical and Dental Technology, (Branch Campus)
5255 Hohman Ave, Hammond, IN 46320, 219-931-1917

Aristotle Institute of Medical and Dental Technolgy
5900 Westerville Rd, Westerville, OH 43081, 614-891-1800

Arit Air Academy
5125 Voyager Dr, Dallas, TX 75376, 214-330-6060

Arkansas College of Barbering and Hair Design
200 Washington Ave, North Little Rock, AR 72114, 501-376-9696

Arkansas Valley Technical Institute
1311 S I St, Fort Smith, AR 72901, 501-441-5256

Arlington Court Reporting College
1201 N Watson Rd #270, Arlington, TX 76006, 817-640-8852

Arlington Court Reporting College, (Court Reporting Institute of Tennessee)
51 Century Blvd #350, Nashville, TN 37214, 615-885-9770

Armed Forces School of Music
1420 Gator Blvd, Norfolk, VA 23521, 804-464-7501

Armstrong University of Beauty
101 E Fourth St, Rome, GA 30161, 404-232-6565

Army Academy of Health Sciences
2250 Stanley Rd Bldg 2840, San Antonio, TX 78234, 512-221-8542

Army Academy of Health Sciences, (Medical Equipment and Optician School)
Aurora, CO 80045, 303-361-8898

Army Academy of Health Sciences, (School of Aviation Medicine)
Fort Rucker, AL 36362, 205-255-7393

Army Institute for Professional Development
US Army Training Support Ctr, Fort Eustis, VA 23604, 804-878-4774

Army Ordnance Center and School
Bldg 3071 #206, Aberdeen Proving Ground, MD 21005, 410-278-3373

Army Ordnance Missile and Munitions Center and School
Redstone Arsenal, Huntsville, AL 35897, 205-876-3349

Army Quartermaster Center and School
Fort Lee, VA 23801, 804-734-2555

Army Signal Center and School
Fort Gordon, GA 30905, 404-791-4588

Army Transportation and Aviation Logistics School
Bldg 2731, Fort Eustis, VA 23604, 804-878-4400

Non-Degree Granting Institutions

Arnold's Beauty College
3117 Shannon Rd, Durham, NC 27707, 919-493-9557

Arnold's Beauty School
1179 S Second St, Milan, TN 38358, 901-686-7351

Art Center, The
2525 N Country Club Rd, Tucson, AZ 85716, 602-325-0123

Art Center, The (Branch Campus)
2268 Wyoming Blvd NE, Albuquerque, NM 87112, 505-298-1828

Art Instruction Schools
500 S Fourth St, Minneapolis, MN 55415, 612-339-8721

Artiste School of Cosmetology
129 Springbrook Dr, Johnson City, TN 37601, 615-282-2279

Artistic Beauty College
1820 Hwy 20 #200, Conyers, GA 30208, 404-922-7653

Arundel Institute of Technology
1808 Edison Hwy, Baltimore, MD 21213, 410-327-6640

Ascension College
320 E Ascension St, Gonzales, LA 70737, 504-647-6609

Ascension Technical Institute
9697 Airline Hwy, Sorrento, LA 70778, 504-675-5397

Asher School of Business
100 Pinnacle Wy #110, Norcross, GA 30071, 404-368-0800

Associated Technical College
1177 N Magnolia Ave, Anaheim, CA 92801, 714-229-8785

Associated Technical College
1670 Wilshire Blvd, Los Angeles, CA 90017, 213-484-2444

Associated Technical College
395 N E St, San Bernardino, CA 92401, 714-885-1888

Associated Technical College
1475 Sixth Ave, San Diego, CA 92101, 619-234-2181

Atlanta Area Technical School
1560 Stewart Ave SW, Atlanta, GA 30310, 404-758-9451

Atlanta Area Technical School, (Branch Campus)
4191 Northside Dr NW, Atlanta, GA 30342, 404-842-3117

Atlanta Institute of Music
6145-D Northbelt Pkwy, Norcross, GA 30071, 404-242-7717

Atlanta Job Corps Center
239 W Lake Ave NW, Atlanta, GA 30314, 404-794-9512

Atlanta School of Massage
2300 Peachford Rd #3200, Atlanta, GA 30338, 404-454-7167

Atlantic Vocational-Technical Center
4700 Coconut Creek Pkwy, Coconut Creek, FL 33063, 305-977-2000

Atlantic Vocational-Technical Center, (Branch Campus)
1400 NE 6th St, Pompano Beach, FL 33060, 305-786-7630

Automation Academy
666 11th St NW #750, Washington, DC 20001, 202-638-6677

Automotive Training Center
114 Pickering Wy, Exton, PA 19341, 215-363-6716

Automotive Transmission School
453 E Okeechobee Rd, Hialeah, FL 33010, 305-888-4898

Avalon Vocational-Technical Institute
1407 Texas St, Fort Worth, TX 76102, 817-877-5511

Avalon Vocational-Technical Institute
4241 Tanglewood Ln, Odessa, TX 79762, 915-367-2622

Avalon Vocational-Technical Institute
One Eureka Cir, Wichita Falls, TX 76308, 817-692-6513

Avalon Vocational-Technical Institute, (Branch Campus)
3301 Marshall St, Longview, TX 76504, 903-295-2002

Avante School of Cosmetology
1650 White Bear Ave, St. Paul, MN 55106, 612-772-1417

Avanti Hair Tech
905 E Memorial Blvd, Lakeland, FL 33801, 813-686-2224

Avanti Hair Tech
8803 N Florida Ave, Tampa, FL 33604, 813-931-8500

Avanti Hair Tech
8851 N 56th St, Temple Terrace, FL 33617, 813-985-8785

Avanti Hair Tech, (Branch Campus)
5433 Lake Howell Rd, Winter Park, FL 32792, 305-657-0700

Avoyelles Technical Institute
Hwy 107, Cottonport, LA 71327, 318-876-2701

Ayers Institute
2924 Knight St #318, Shreveport, LA 71105, 318-868-3000

AzTech College
941 S Dobson Rd Ste 120, Mesa, AZ 85202, 602-967-7813

AzTech College, (Branch Campus)
2201 San Pedro Dr NE Bldg 3, Albuquerque, NM 87110, 505-888-5800

B

B.M. Spurr School of Practical Nursing
800 Wheeling Ave, Glen Dale, WV 26038, 304-845-3211

Ballard County Area Vocational Center
Rte 1, US Hwy 60, Box 214, Barlow, KY 42024, 502-665-5112

Bancroft School of Message Therapy
50 Franklin St, Worcester, MA 01608, 508-757-7923

Baran Institute of Technology
611 Day Hill Rd, Windsor, CT 06095, 203-688-3353

Barber Styling Institute
3433 Simpson Ferry Rd, Camp Hill, PA 17011, 717-763-4787

Barna Institute
1050 NE Fifth Terr, Fort Lauderdale, FL 33304, 305-525-5069

Barnes Business College
150 N Sheridan Blvd, Denver, CO 80226, 303-922-8454

Barrett & Company School of Hair Design
973 Kimberly Sq, Nicholasville, KY 40356, 606-885-9136

Basic Institute of Technology
4455 Chippewa Ave, St Louis, MO 63116, 314-771-1200

Bastrop Technical Institute
Kammell St, Bastrop, LA 71221, 318-283-0836

Bates Technical College
1101 S Yakima Ave, Tacoma, WA 98405, 206-596-1500

Batesville Job Corps Center
Hwy 51 S, Batesville, MS 38606, 601-563-4656

The Sourcebook of College and University Student Records **B**

Baton Rouge Regional Technical Institute
3250 N Acadian Thruway, Baton Rouge, LA 70805, 504-359-9201

Baton Rouge Regional Technical Institute, (J.M. Frazier Vo-Tech School)
555 Julia St, Baton Rouge, LA 70802, 504-359-9201

Bay Area Vocational-Technical School
1976 Lewis Turner Blvd, Fort Walton Beach, FL 32547, 904-833-3500

Bay State School of Appliances
225 Turnpike St, Canton, MA 02021, 617-828-3434

Beacon Career Institute
2900 NW 183rd St, Miami, FL 33056, 305-620-4637

Beauty Schools of America
7942 W Sample Rd, Margate, FL 33063, 305-755-2015

Beauty Schools of America, (Branch Campus)
1176 SW 67th Ave, Miami, FL 33144, 305-267-6604

Bellaire Beauty College
5014 Bellaire Blvd, Bellaire, TX 77401, 713-666-2318

Belleville Barber College
329 N Illinois St, Belleville, IL 62220, 618-234-4424

Bellingham Technical College
3028 Lindbergh Ave, Bellingham, WA 98225, 360-676-6490

Bemidji Technical College
905 Grant Ave SE, Bemidji, MN 56601, 218-759-3200

Ben Hill-Irwin Technical Institute
667 Perry House Rd, Fitzgerald, GA 31750, 912-468-7487

Berdan Institute
265 Rte 46 W, Totowa, NJ 07512, 201-256-3444

Berk TRade and Business School
311 W 35th St, New York, NY 10001, 212-629-3736

Berks Technical Institute
832 N Park Rd, Wyomissing, PA 19610, 215-372-1722

Betty Stevens Cosmetology Institute
301 Rainbow Dr, Florence, SC 29501, 803-669-4452

Bidwell Training Center
1815 Metropolitan St, Pittsburgh, PA 15233, 412-323-4000

Big Sky College of Barber Styling
750 Kensington Ave, Missoula, MT 59801, 406-721-5588

Bilingual Institute
601 Broad St, Newark, NJ 07102, 201-624-3883

Bilingual Institute, (Branch Campus)
2 W Broadway, Paterson, NJ 07505, 201-279-8988

Billings Business College
2520 Fifth Ave S, Billings, MT 59101, 406-256-1000

Billings School of Barbering and Hairstyling
206 N 13th St, Billings, MT 59101, 406-259-9369

Black Forest Hall
PO Box 140, Harbor Springs, MI 49740, 616-526-7066

Black World College of Hair Design
PO Box 669403, Charlotte, NC 28266, 704-372-8172

Blake Business School
PO Box 1052, New York, NY 10276, 212-254-1233

Blake Business School, (Branch Campus)
145A 4th Ave, New York, NY 10003, 212-995-1711

Boardwalk and Marina Casino Dealers School
2709 Atlantic Ave, Atlantic City, NJ 08401, 609-344-1986

Bobbie's School of Beauty Arts
108 Decatur Pike, Athens, TN 37371, 615-744-7251

Boone county Career Center
Box 50B, Danville, WV 25053, 304-369-4585

Boulder School of Massage Therapy
3285 30th St, Boulder, CO 80301, 303-443-5131

Boulder Valley Area Vocational-Technical Center
6600 E Arapahoe Ave, Boulder, CO 80303, 303-447-5247

Bradford School of Business
4669 Southwest Fwy #300, Houston, TX 77027, 713-629-8940

Branford Hall Career Institute
9 Business Park Dr, Branford, CT 06405, 203-488-2525

Braxton School
4917 Augusta Ave, Richmond, VA 23230, 804-353-4458

Brick Computer Science Institute
515 Hwy 70, Brick, NJ 08723, 908-477-0975

Broadcast Professionals Complete School of Radio Broadcasting
11507-D SW Pacific Hwy, Portland, OR 97223, 503-244-5113

Broadcasting Institute of Maryland
7200 Harford Rd, Baltimore, MD 21234, 410-254-2770

Brookstone College of Business
8307 Univers. Exec. Park Dr #240, Charlotte, NC 28262, 704-547-8600

Brookstone College of Business, (Branch Campus)
7815 National Service Rd, Greensboro, NC 27409, 919-668-2627

Brown College of Court Reporting & Medical Transcription
1100 Spring St NW #200, Atlanta, GA 30309, 404-867-1227

Brown College of Court Reporting & Medical Transcription, (Branch Campus)
501 Spur St #B-3, Longview, TX 75601, 903-757-4338

Bryan College of Court Reporting
2511 Beverly Blvd, Los Angeles, CA 90057, 213-484-8850

Bryan Institute
12184 Natural Bridge Rd, Bridgeton, MO 63044, 314-291-0241

Bryan Institute
2843 E 51st St, Tulsa, OK 74105, 918-749-6891

Bryan Institute
1004 S Oliver St, Wichita, KS 67214, 316-685-2284

Bryan Institute, (Branch Campus)
1719 W Pioneer Pkwy, Arlington, TX 76013, 817-265-5588

Bryan Travel College
520 W University St #B, Springfield, MO 65807, 417-862-5700

Bryan Travel College
1527 Fairlawn Rd, Topeka, KS 66604, 913-272-7511

Bryman School
4343 N 16th St, Phoenix, AZ 85016, 602-274-4300

Bryman School
1144 W 3300 S, Salt Lake City, UT 84119, 801-975-7000

Burdett School
745 Boylston St, Boston, MA 02116, 617-859-1900

Non-Degree Granting Institutions

Burdett School, (Branch Campus)
100 Front St, Worcester, MA 01608, 508-849-1900

Burke Academy of Cosmetic Art
304 W Union St, Morganton, NC 28655, 704-437-1028

Burke Academy of Cosmetic Art, (Branch Campus)
609 W 29th St, Newton, NC 28658, 704-465-7281

Business & Technology Institute
42 NW 27th Ave #323, Miami, FL 33125, 305-541-4463

Business Informatics Center
134 S Central Ave, Valley Stream, NY 11580, 516-561-0500

Business Skills Training Center
616 Fort Worth Dr #B, Denton, TX 76201, 817-382-7922

Business Training Institute
4 Forest Ave, Paramus, NJ 07652, 201-845-9300

Butera School of Art
111 Beacon St, Boston, MA 02116, 617-536-4623

Butler Business School
2710 North Ave, Bridgeport, CT 06604, 203-333-3601

C

CAD Institute
4100 E Broadway Rd Ste 150, Phoenix, AZ 85040, 602-437-0405

CARTI School of Radiation Therapy Technology
PO Box 5210, Little Rock, AR 72215, 501-664-8573

Cabot College
41 E 12th St, National City, CA 92050, 619-474-8017

Cain's Barber College
365 E 51st St, Chicago, IL 60615, 312-536-4623

California Academy of Merchandising, Art & Design
1333 Howe Ave Ste 150, Sacramento, CA 95825, 916-648-8168

California Career Schools
392 W Cerritos Ave, Anaheim, CA 92805, 714-635-6585

California Culinary Academy
625 Polk St, San Francisco, CA 94102, 415-771-3536

California Institute of Locksmithing
14721 Oxnard St, Van Nuys, CA 91411, 818-994-7426

California Nannie College
910 Howe Ave, Sacramento, CA 95825, 916-921-2400

California Paramedical & Technical College
3745 Long Beach Blvd, Long Beach, CA 90807, 310-595-6638

California Paramedical & Technical College
4550 LaSierra Ave, Riverside, CA 92505, 714-687-9006

California School of Court Reporting
3510 Adams St, Riverside, CA 92504, 714-359-0293

California School of Court Reporting
1201 N Main St, Santa Ana, CA 92701, 714-541-6892

Cambridge School of Culinary Arts
2020 Massachusetts Ave, Cambridge, MA 02140, 617-354-3836

Camden School of Hair Design
2630 N Broad St, Camden, SC 29020, 803-425-1011

Camelot Career College
2618 Wooddale Blvd #A, Baton Rouge, LA 70805, 504-928-3005

Cameron College
2740 Canal St, New Orleans, LA 70119, 504-821-5881

Cape Girardeau Area Vocational-Technical School
301 N Clark St, Cape Girardeau, MO 63701, 314-334-3358

Cape May County Technical Institute
188 Crest Haven Rd, Cape May Court House, NJ 08210, 609-465-3064

Capital Area Vocational Center
12201 Toronto Rd, Springfield, IL 62707, 217-529-5431

Capitol City Careers
4630 Westgate Blvd, Austin, TX 78749, 512-892-4270

Capitol City Trade & Technical School
205 E Riverside Dr, Austin, TX 78704, 512-444-3257

Capps College
3100 Cottage Hill Rd Bldg 4, Mobile, AL 36606, 205-473-1393

Capri Cosmetology College
PO Box 873, Dubuque, IA 52004, 319-588-4545

Career Academy
32 Oaklawn Village, Texarkana, TX 75501, 214-832-1021

Career Center, The
1750 45th St, West Palm Beach, FL 33407, 407-881-0220

Career Centers of Texas - El Paso
8375 Burnham Rd, El Paso, TX 79907, 915-595-1935

Career Development Center
413 S Chestnut St, Lufkin, TX 75901, 409-635-1740

Career Development Center
605 Thimble Shoals Blvd #209, Newport News, VA 23606, 804-873-2423

Career Development Institute
2233 Fourth Ave N, Birmingham, AL 35203, 205-252-6396

Career Development Institute
1060 Springhill Ave, Mobile, AL 36604, 205-433-5042

Career Development Institute
505 and 507 Montgomery St, Montgomery, AL 36101, 205-262-3131

Career Development Institute
516 14th St, Parkview Ctr, Tuscaloosa, AL 35401, 205-752-6025

Career Development Institute, (Branch Campus)
2314 Ninth Ave N, Bessemer, AL 35020, 205-425-6757

Career Floral Design Institute
13200 Northup Wy, Bellevue, WA 98005, 206-746-8340

Career Institute, The
1825 John F. Kennedy Blvd, Philadelphia, PA 19103, 215-561-7600

Career Institute, The, (Branch Campus)
711 Market St Mall, Wilmington, DE 19801, 302-575-1400

Career Management Institute
1855 W Katella Ave #150, Orange, CA 92667, 714-771-5077

Career Point Business School
485 Spencer Ln, San Antonio, TX 78201, 512-732-3000

The Sourcebook of College and University Student Records

C

Career Point Business School, (Branch Campus)
3138 S Garnett Rd, Tulsa, OK 74146, 918-622-4100

Career Training Academy
703 Fifth Ave, New Kensington, PA 15068, 412-337-1000

Career Training Academy, (Branch Campus)
244 Center Rd, Monroeville, PA 15146, 412-372-3900

Career Training Center
4000 W Broad St, Richmond, VA 23230, 804-342-1190

Career Training Center, (Branch Campus)
2600 Memorial Ave #201, Lynchburg, VA 24501, 804-845-7949

Career Training Center, (Branch Campus)
3223 Brandon Ave SW, Roanoke, VA 24018, 703-981-0925

Career Training Institute
101 W Main St, Leesburg, FL 34748, 904-326-5134

Career Training Institute
2120 W Colonial Dr, Orlando, FL 32804, 407-843-3984

Career Training Specialists
1611 Louisville Ave, Monroe, LA 71201, 318-323-2889

Career West Academy
2505B Zanella Wy, Chico, CA 95928, 916-893-1388

Careers Unlimited
335 S Bonner St, Tyler, TX 75702, 903-593-4424

Carl D. Perkins Job Corps Center
Box G-11, Bogle Roberts Rd, Prestonsburg, KY 41653, 606-886-1037

Carnegie Institute
550 Stephenson Hwy #100, Troy, MI 48083, 313-589-1078

Carolina Beauty College
801 English Rd, High Point, NC 27262, 919-886-4712

Carolina Beauty College, (Branch Campus)
244 E Front St, Burlington, NC 27215, 919-227-7658

Carolina Beauty College, (Branch Campus)
5430-0 N Tryon St, Charlotte, NC 28213, 704-597-5641

Carolina Beauty College, (Branch Campus)
5100 N Roxboro Rd, Durham, NC 22704, 919-477-4014

Carolina Beauty College, (Branch Campus)
1483-B E Franklin Blvd, Gastonia, NC 28053, 704-864-8723

Carolina Beauty College, (Branch Campus)
2001 E Wendover Ave, Greensboro, NC 27405, 919-272-2966

Carolina Beauty College, (Branch Campus)
930 Floyd St, Kannapolis, NC 28081, 704-932-5651

Carolina Beauty College, (Branch Campus)
338 N Main St, Kernersville, NC 27284, 919-993-6050

Carolina Beauty College, (Branch Campus)
810 E Winston Rd, Lexington, NC 27292, 704-249-1518

Carolina Beauty College, (Branch Campus)
1201 Stafford St #12, Monroe, NC 28110, 704-283-2514

Carolina Beauty College, (Branch Campus)
501 S South St, Mount Airy, NC 27030, 919-786-2791

Carolina Beauty College, (Branch Campus)
1902 S Main St, Salisbury, NC 28144, 704-637-7045

Carolina Beauty College, (Branch Campus)
231 N Lafayette St, Shelby, NC 28150, 704-487-0557

Carolina Beauty College, (Branch Campus)
123 Berry St, Statesville, NC 28677, 704-872-6662

Carolina Beauty College, (Branch Campus)
1253-24 Corporation Pkwy, Winston-Salem, NC 27127, 919-723-9510

Carroll Technical Institute
997 S Hwy 16, Carrollton, GA 30117, 404-834-6800

Carver Career and Technical Education Center
4799 Midland Dr, Charleston, WV 25306, 304-348-1965

Cashier Training Institute
500 Eighth Ave, New York, NY 10018, 212-564-0500

Catherine College
8155 Van Nuys Blvd #200, Panorama City, CA 91402, 818-989-9000

Catherine E. Hinds Institute of Esthetics
65 Riverside Pl, Woburn, MA 02155, 617-391-3733

Catholic Home Study Institute
781 Catoctin Ridge, Paeonian Springs, VA 22129, 703-883-3737

Cave Technical Institute
2842 S State St, Lockport, IL 60441, 815-727-1576

Cedar Rapids School of Hairstyling
1531 First Ave SE, Cedar Rapids, IA 52402, 515-362-1488

Center for Advanced Legal Studies
3015 Richmond Ave, Houston, TX 77098, 713-529-2778

Center for Creative Studies-Institute of Music and Dance
201 E Kirby St, Detroit, MI 48202, 313-872-3118

Center for Training in Business and Industry
2211 Silicon Ave, Lawrence, KS 66046, 913-841-9640

Central California School of Continuing Education
3195 McMillan St Ste F, San Luis Obispo, CA 93401, 805-543-9123

Central Oklahoma Area Vocational-Technical Center
3 CVT Cir, Drumright, OK 74030, 918-352-2551

Central School of Practical Nursing
3300 Chester Ave, Cleveland, OH 44114, 216-391-8434

Central School of Practical Nursing
1330 N Military Hwy, Norfolk, VA 23502, 804-441-5625

Central Texas Commercial College
PO Box 1324, Brownwood, TX 76801, 915-646-0521

Central Texas Commercial College, (Branch Campus)
9400 N Central Expy #200, Dallas, TX 75231, 214-368-3680

Century Business College
2665 Fifth Ave, San Diego, CA 92103, 619-233-0184

Century Business College, (Branch Campus)
3325 Wilshire Blvd, Los Angeles, CA 90010, 213-383-1585

Century Business College, (Century Schools)
3075 E Flamingo Rd Ste 114, Las Vegas, NV 89121, 702-451-6666

Champion Institute of Cosmetology
72261 Hwy 111, Palm Desert, CA 92260, 619-322-2227

Champion Institute of Cosmetology
559 S Palm Canyon Dr, Palm Springs, CA 92264, 619-322-2227

Non-Degree Granting Institutions

Charles B. Coreil Technical Institute
Industrial Park Ward I, Ville Platte, LA 70586, 318-363-2197

Charles H. McCann Technical School
Hodges Crossroad, North Adams, MA 01247, 413-663-5383

Charles Stuart School of Diamond Setting
1420 Kings Hwy, Brooklyn, NY 11229, 718-339-2640

Charleston Cosmetology Institute
8484 Dorchester Rd, Charleston, SC 29420, 803-552-3670

Charlotte Vocational-Technical Center
18300 Toledo Blade Blvd, Port Charlotte, FL 33948, 813-629-6819

Charzzanne Beauty College
1549 Hwy 72 E, Greenwood, SC 29649, 803-223-7321

Chattanooga Barber College
405 Market St, Chattanooga, TN 37402, 615-266-7013

Chauffeurs Training School
12 Railroad Ave, Albany, NY 12205, 518-482-8601

Chenier Business School
4320 Calder Ave, Beaumont, TX 77706, 409-899-3227

Chenier
6300 Richmond Ave #300, Houston, TX 77057, 713-886-3102

Chenier
2819 Loop 306, San Angelo, TX 76904, 915-944-4404

Cheryl Fell's School of Business
2541 Military Rd, Niagara Falls, NY 14304, 716-297-2750

Cheyenne Aero Tech
1204 Airport Pkwy, Cheyenne, WY 82001, 800-366-2376

Choctaw Training Institute
218 W Church St, Butler, AL 36904, 205-459-4331

Choffin Career Center
200 E Wood St, Youngstown, OH 44503, 216-744-8700

Chris Logan Career College
505 Seventh Ave N, Myrtle Beach, SC 29578, 803-448-6302

Chris Logan Career College, (Branch Campus)
3420 Clemson Blvd, Anderson, SC 29624, 803-226-8438

Chris Logan Career College, (Branch Campus)
1125 15-401 By-Pass #A, Bennettsville, SC 29512, 803-479-4076

Chris Logan Career College, (Branch Campus)
4830 Forest Dr, Columbia, SC 29206, 803-787-8621

Chris Logan Career College, (Branch Campus)
1810-B Second Loop Rd, Florence, SC 29501, 803-665-4602

Chris Logan Career College, (Branch Campus)
1235 S Pleasantburg Dr #A, Greenville, SC 29605, 803-299-0000

Chris Logan Career College, (Branch Campus)
Martintown Plaza, North Augusta, SC 29841, 803-278-1238

Chris Logan Career College, (Branch Campus)
1930 N Cherry Rd, Rock Hill, SC 29730, 803-328-1838

Chris Logan Career College, (Branch Campus)
256 S Pike Rd, Sumter, SC 29150, 803-773-8481

Chubb Institute
8 Sylvan Wy, Parsippany, NJ 07054, 201-682-4900

Chubb Institute, (Branch Campus)
40 Journal Sq, Jersey City, NJ 07306, 201-656-0330

Cincinnati School of Court Reporting and Business
35 E Seventh St, Cincinnati, OH 45202, 513-241-1011

Circle in the Square Theatre School
1633 Broadway, New York, NY 10019, 212-307-3732

Cittone Institute
1697 Oak Tree Rd, Edison, NJ 08820, 908-548-8798

Cittone Institute, (Branch Campus)
523 Fellowship Rd #625, Mount Laurel, NJ 08054, 609-722-9333

Cittone Institute, (Branch Campus)
100 Canal Pointe Blvd, Princeton, NJ 08540, 609-520-8798

Claiborne Technical Institute
3001 Minden Rd, Homer, LA 71040, 318-927-2034

Cleveland Institute of Dental-Medical Assistants, Inc.
1836 Euclid Ave #401, Cleveland, OH 44115, 216-241-2930

Cleveland Institute of Dental-Medical Assistants, Inc., (Branch Campus)
5564 Mayfield Rd, Lyndhurst, OH 44124, 216-473-6273

Cleveland Institute of Dental-Medical Assistants, Inc., (Branch Campus)
5733 Hopkins Rd, Mentor, OH 44060, 216-946-9530

Climate Control Institute
708 S Sheridan Rd, Tulsa, OK 74112, 918-836-6656

Climate Control Institute
3030 N Hillside St, Wichita, KS 67219, 316-686-7355

Climate Control Institute, (Travel Careers Division Campus)
568 Colonial Rd #102, Memphis, TN 38117, 901-761-5730

Clinton Technical Institute
2844 W Deer Valley Rd, Phoenix, AZ 85027, 602-869-9644

Clinton Technical Institute, (Motorcycle/Marine Mechanics Institute)
9751 Delegates Dr, Orlando, FL 32837, 407-240-2422

Clover Park Technical College
4500 Steilacoom Blvd SW, Tacoma, WA 98498, 206-589-5500

Cloyd's Beauty School No. 2
1311 Winnsboro Rd, Monroe, LA 71202, 318-322-5315

Cloyd's Beauty School No. 3
2514 Ferrand St, Monroe, LA 71201, 318-322-5314

Coastal College
2001 Canal St #300, New Orleans, LA 70112, 504-522-2400

Coastal College, (Branch Campus)
5520 Industrial Dr Ext, Bossier City, LA 71112, 318-746-8800

Coastal College, (Branch Campus)
119 Yokum Rd, Hammond, LA 70403, 504-345-3200

Coastal College, (Branch Campus)
2318 W Park Ave, Houma, LA 70346, 504-872-2800

Coastal College, (Branch Campus)
320 Howze Beach Rd, Slidell, LA 70461, 504-641-2121

Coastal Training Institute
5950 S Monticello Dr, Montgomery, AL 36117, 205-279-6241

Coastal Training Institute, (Branch Campus)
Calle Comercial #19 - 21, Aguadilla, PR 06003, 809-792-5915

Cobb Beauty College
3096 Cherokee St, Kennesaw, GA 30144, 404-424-6915

College for Recording Arts
665 Harrison St, San Francisco, CA 94107, 415-781-6306

College of Court Reporting
111 W 10th St #111, Hobart, IN 46342, 219-942-1459

College of Hair Design
304 S 11th St, Lincoln, NE 68508, 402-474-4244

College of Hair Design
810 LaPorte Rd, Waterloo, IA 50702, 319-232-9995

College of Legal Arts
527 SW Hall St #308, Portland, OR 97201, 503-223-5100

CollegeAmerica - Denver
720 S Colorado Blvd #260, Denver, CO 80222, 303-691-9756

CollegeAmerica - San Francisco
814 Mission St Ste 300, San Francisco, CA 94103, 415-882-4545

CollegeAmerica
921 SW Washington St #200, Portland, OR 97205, 503-242-9000

Colorado Aero Tech
10851 W 120th Ave, Broomfield, CO 80021, 800-888-3995

Colorado Association of Paramedical Education, Inc.
9191 Grant St, Thornton, CO 80229, 303-451-7800

Colorado Career Academy
13790 E Rice Pl, Aurora, CO 80015, 303-690-6900

Colorado Career Academy
95 S Wadsworth Blvd, Lakewood, CO 80226, 303-234-0401

Colorado School of Trades
1575 Hoyt St, Lakewood, CO 80215, 303-233-4697

Colorado School of Travel
608 Garrison St #J, Lakewood, CO 80215, 303-233-8654

Columbine College
5801 W 44th Ave, Denver, CO 80212, 303-935-2266

Columbine College, (Branch Campus)
3754 E LaSalle St, Colorado Springs, CO 80909, 719-574-8777

Columbus Para-Professional Institute
1077 Lexington Ave, Columbus, OH 43201, 614-299-0200

Combat Systems Technical Schools Command
Mare Island, Vallejo, CA 94592, 707-554-8550

Commercial College of Baton Rouge
5677 Florida Blvd, Baton Rouge, LA 70806, 504-927-3470

Commercial College of Shreveport
2640 Youree Dr, Shreveport, LA 71104, 318-865-6571

Commercial Driver Training
600 Patton Ave, West Babylon, NY 11704, 516-249-1330

Commercial Training Services
24325 Pacific Hwy S, Des Moines, WA 98198, 206-824-3970

Commercial Training Services
2416 N Marine Dr, Portland, OR 97217, 503-285-7542

Computer Career Center
6101 Montana, El Paso, TX 79925, 915-799-8031

Computer Career Center
474 Fulton Ave, Hempstead, NY 11550, 516-486-2526

Computer Career Center, (Branch Campus)
4121 Wyoming Blvd NE, Albuquerque, NM 87111, 505-271-8200

Computer Dynamics Institute
5361 Virginia Beach Blvd, Virginia Beach, VA 23452, 804-486-7300

Computer Education Services
981 S Third St #106, Louisville, KY 40203, 502-583-2860

Computer Learning Center
6295 Edsall Rd #210, Alexandria, VA 22312, 703-823-0300

Computer Learning Center
222 S Harbor Blvd, Anaheim, CA 92805, 714-956-8060

Computer Learning Center
200 S Michigan Ave 2nd Flr, Chicago, IL 60604, 312-427-2700

Computer Learning Center
3130 Wilshire Blvd, Los Angeles, CA 90010, 213-386-6311

Computer Learning Center
160 E Rte 4, Paramus, NJ 07652, 201-845-6868

Computer Learning Center
3600 Market St, Philadelphia, PA 19104, 215-222-6450

Computer Learning Center
661 Howard St, San Francisco, CA 94105, 415-498-0800

Computer Learning Center
111 N Market St, San Jose, CA 95113, 408-983-5950

Computer Learning Center
5 Middlesex Ave, Somerville, MA 02145, 617-776-3500

Computer Learning Center, (Branch Campus)
436 Broadway, Methuen, MA 01844, 508-794-0233

Computer Learning Network
1110 Fernwood Ave, Camp Hill, PA 17011, 717-761-1481

Computer Learning Network, (Branch Campus)
2900 Fairway Dr, Altoona, PA 16602, 814-944-5643

Computer Processing Institute
615 Massachusetts Ave, Cambridge, MA 02139, 617-354-6900

Computer School, The
820 Lane Allen Rd, Lexington, KY 40504, 606-276-1929

ConCorde Career Institute
1717 S Brookhurst St, Anaheim, CA 92804, 714-635-3450

ConCorde Career Institute
7960 Arlington Expy, Jacksonville, FL 32211, 904-725-0525

ConCorde Career Institute
3239 Broadway, Kansas City, MO 64111, 816-531-5223

ConCorde Career Institute
4000 N State Rd 7, Lauderdale Lakes, FL 33319, 305-731-8880

ConCorde Career Institute
12 N 12th St, Minneapolis, MN 55403, 612-341-3850

ConCorde Career Institute
4150 Lankershim Blvd, North Hollywood, CA 91602, 818-766-8151

ConCorde Career Institute
1827 NE 44th Ave, Portland, OR 97213, 503-281-4181

ConCorde Career Institute
600 N Sierra Wy, San Bernardino, CA 92410, 714-884-8891

ConCorde Career Institute
123 Camino de la Reina, San Diego, CA 92108, 619-280-5005

ConCorde Career Institute
1290 N First St, San Jose, CA 95112, 408-441-6411

ConCorde Career Institute
4202 W Spruce St, Tampa, FL 33607, 813-874-0094

ConCorde Career Institute, (Branch Campus)
285 NW 199th St, Miami, FL 33169, 305-652-0055

Concorde Career Institute
770 Grant St, Denver, CO 80203, 303-861-1151

Concorde Career Institute
5100 Poplar Ave #132, Memphis, TN 38137, 901-761-9494

Concordia Technical Institute
E.E. Wallace Blvd, Ferriday, LA 71334, 318-757-6501

Connecticut Business Institute
605 Broad St, Stratford, CT 06497, 203-377-1775

Connecticut Business Institute, (Branch Campus)
809 Main St, East Hartford, CT 06108, 203-291-2880

Connecticut Business Institute, (Branch Campus)
984 Chapel St, New Haven, CT 06510, 203-562-8114

Connecticut Center for Message Therapy
75 Kitts La, Newington, CT 06111, 203-562-8114

Connecticut Center for Message Therapy, (Branch Campus)
25 Sylvan Rd S, Westport, CT 06880, 203-221-7325

Connecticut Institute of Art
581 W Putnam Ave, Greenwich, CT 06830, 203-869-4430

Connecticut Institute of Hair Design
1681 Meriden Rd, Wolcott, CT 06716, 203-879-4247

Connecticut School of Broadcasting
4790 Red Bank Expy #102, Cincinnati, OH 45227, 216-271-6060

Connecticut School of Broadcasting
7601 Rockside Rd #204, Independence, OH 44131, 216-447-9117

Connecticut School of Broadcasting
200 W 22nd St #202, Lombard, IL 60148, 708-916-1700

Connecticut School of Electronics
586 Ella T. Grasso Blvd, New Haven, CT 06591, 203-624-2121

Conservatory of Recording Arts & Sciences
1110 E Missouri Ave #400, Phoenix, AZ 85014, 602-265-5566

Consolidated Welding Schools
4343 E Imperial Hwy, Lynwood, CA 90262, 310-638-0418

Continental Dental Assistant School
633 Jefferson Rd, Rochester, NY 14623, 716-272-8060

Cooking and Hospitality Institute of Chicago
361 W Chestnut St, Chicago, IL 60610, 312-944-2725

Coosa Valley Technical Institute
112 Hemlock St, Rome, GA 30161, 404-235-1142

Cope Institute
84 Williams St 4th Fl, New York, NY 10038, 718-436-1700

Cotton Boll Technical Institute
Box 36, Burdette, AR 72321, 501-763-1486

Court Reporting Academy & School of Professional Studies
1101 Kermit Dr #513, Nashville, TN 37217, 615-366-0566

Court Reporting Institute
929 N 130th St #2, Seattle, WA 98133, 206-363-8300

Court Reporting Institute of Dallas
8585 N Stemmons Fwy #200, Dallas, TX 75247, 214-350-9722

Court Reporting Institute, (Branch Campus)
1333 Camino del Rio S, San Diego, CA 92108, 619-294-5700

Coyne American Institute
1235 W Fullerton Ave, Chicago, IL 60614, 312-935-2520

Crown Academy
8739 S Hosmer St, Tacoma, WA 98444, 206-531-3123

Crown Business Institute
1223 SW Fourth St, Miami, FL 33135, 305-643-1600

Culinary Arts Institute of Louisiana
427 Lafayette St, Baton Rouge, LA 70802, 504-343-6233

Cumberland School of Technology
1065 E Tenth St, Cookeville, TN 38501, 615-526-3660

Cumberland School of Technology, (Branch Campus)
4173 Government St, Baton Rouge, LA 70806, 504-338-9085

D

David L. Carrasco Job Corps Center
11155 Gateway W, El Paso, TX 79935, 915-594-0022

Dalfort Aircraft Tech
7701 Lemmon Ave, Dallas, TX 75209, 214-358-7820

Dalfort Aircraft Tech, (Branch Campus)
990 Toffie Terr, Atlanta, GA 30320, 404-428-9056

Dallas Institute of Funeral Services
3909 S Buckner Blvd, Dallas, TX 75227, 214-388-5466

Dalton Vocational School of Health Occupations
1221 Elkwood Dr, Dalton, GA 30720, 404-278-8922

Dance Theatre of Harlem, Inc.
466 W 152nd St, New York, NY 10031, 212-690-2800

Data Institute
745 Burnside Ave, East Hartford, CT 06108, 203-528-4111

Data Institute, (Branch Campus)
101 Pierpont Rd, Waterbury, CT 06705, 203-765-5500

David G. Erwing Technical Center
2010 E Hollsborough Ave, Tampa, FL 33610, 813-238-8631

Davidson Technical College
212 Pavilion Blvd, Nashville, TN 37217, 615-360-3300

Davidson Technical College, (Branch Campus)
2424 Airway Dr, Bowling Green, KY 42103,

Davidson Technical College, (Branch Campus)
525 E Main St, Jackson, TN 38301, 901-424-6795

Dawn Training Institute
120 Old Churchmans Rd, New Castle, DE 19720, 302-328-9695

DeKalb Beauty College
6254 Memorial Dr #M, Stone Mountain, GA 30083, 404-879-6673

Defence Mapping School
5825 21st St #106, Fort Belvoir, VA 22060, 703-805-2557

Defense Equal Opportunity Management Institute
EOMI Library Bldg 560, Patrick Air Force Base, FL 32925, 305-494-6976

Defense Information School
Bldg 400, Fort Benjamin Harrison, IN 46216, 317-542-4046

Defense Language Institute
Presidio of Monterey, CA 93944, 408-647-5118

Delaware County Institute of Training
615 Ave of the States, Chester, PA 19013, 215-874-1888

Delaware Valley Academy of Medical and Dental Assistants
3330 Grant Ave, Philadelphia, PA 19114, 215-744-5300

Dell'Arte School of Physical Theatre
PO Box 816, Blue Lake, CA 95525, 707-668-5663

Delta Career College
1900 Cameron St, Lafayette, LA 70506, 318-235-1147

Delta Career College
1702 Hudson Ln, Monroe, LA 71201, 318-322-8870

Delta Career Institute
1310 Pennsylvania Ave, Beaumont, TX 77701, 409-833-6161

Delta Schools
4549 Johnston St, Lafayette, LA 70503, 318-988-2211

Delta Schools, (Branch Campus)
413 W Admiral Doyle St, New Iberia, LA 70560, 318-365-7348

Delta Technical Institute
323 Central Ave, Cleveland, MS 38732, 601-843-6063

Delta-Ouachita Regional Technical Institute
609 Vocational Pkwy, West Monroe, LA 71292, 318-396-7431

Denham Springs Beauty College
923 Florida Ave SE, Denham Springs, LA 70726, 504-665-6188

Dental Technology Institute
1937 W Chapman Ave #100, Orange, CA 92668, 714-937-3989

Denver Academy of Court Reporting
7290 Samuel Dr 2nd Flr, Denver, CO 80221, 303-629-1291

Denver Academy of Court Reporting, (Branch Campus)
220 Ruskin Dr, Colorado Springs, CO 80910, 719-574-5010

Denver Automotive and Diesel College
405 S Platte Rive Dr, Denver, CO 80223, 303-722-5724

Denver Paralegal Institute
1401 19th St, Denver, CO 80202, 800-848-0550

Denver Paralegal Institute, (Branch Campus)
105 E Vermijo Ave #415, Colorado Springs, CO 80903, 719-444-0190

Derma Clinic Academy
5600 Roswell Rd #110, Atlanta, GA 30066, 404-250-9600

Desert Institute of the Healing Arts
639 N Sixth Ave, Tucson, AZ 85705, 602-882-0879

Detroit Business Institute
1249 Washington Blvd #1200, Detroit, MI 48226, 313-962-6534

Detroit Business Institute-Downriver
19100 Fort St, Riverview, MI 48192, 313-479-0660

Detroit Institute of Ophthalmology
15415 E Jefferson Ave, Grosse Pointe Park, MI 48230, 313-824-4800

Diamond Council of America
9140 Ward Pkwy, Kansas City, MO 64114, 816-444-3500

Diana Ramsey's Specialty Beauty School
2245 W Hollsboro Blvd, Deerfield Beach, FL 33442, 305-429-8358

Dick Hill International Flight School
PO BOx 10603, Springfield, MO 65808, 417-485-3474

Dickinson-Warren Business College
1001 S 57th St, Richmond, CA 94804, 510-231-7555

Diesel Driving Academy
8136 Airline Hwy, Baton Rouge, LA 70815, 504-929-9990

Diesel Driving Academy
4309 Greenwood Rd, Shreveport, LA 71133, 318-636-6300

Diesel Institute of America
PO Box 69, Grantsville, MD 21536, 301-895-5139

Diesel Truck Driver Training School
90801 Hwy 99 N, Eugene, OR 97402, 800-888-7075

Diesel Truck Driver Training School
Hwy 151, Rte 2, Sun Prairie, WI 53590, 608-837-7800

Divers Academy of the Eastern Seaboard
2500 S Broadway, Camden, NJ 08104, 800-238-3483

Divers Institute of Technology
PO Box 70667, Seattle, WA 98107, 206-783-5542

Domestic Health Care Institute
4826 Jamestown Ave, Baton Rouge, LA 70808, 504-925-5312

Dominion Business School
933 Reservoir St, Harrisonburg, VA 22801, 703-433-6977

Dominion Business School
4142-1 Melrose Ave NW #1, Roanoke, VA 24017, 703-362-7738

Dominion Business School
825 Richmond Rd, Staunton, VA 24401, 703-886-3596

Dorsey Business School
30821 Barrington Ave, Madison Heights, MI 48071, 313-585-9200

Dorsey Business School
31542 Gratiot Ave, Roseville, MI 48066, 313-296-3225

Dorsey Business School
15755 Northline Rd, Southgate, MI 48195, 313-285-5400

Dorsey Business School
34841 Veteran's Plaza, Wayne, MI 48184, 313-595-1540

Dover Business College
15 E Blackwell St, Dover, NJ 07801, 201-366-6700

Dover Business College, (Branch Campus)
E 81 Rte 4 W, Paramus, NJ 07652, 201-843-8500

Dr. Welbes College of Message Therapy
2602 J St, Omaha, NE 68107, 402-731-6768

Drake Business School
2488 Grand Concourse, Bronx, NY 10458, 718-562-9700

Drake Business School
36-09 Main St 6th Fl, Flushing, NY 11354, 718-353-3535

Drake Business School
225 Broadway, New York, NY 10007, 212-349-7900

Drake Business School
25 Victory Blvd, Staten Island, NY 10301, 718-447-1515

Drake College of Business
9 Caldwell Pl, Elizabeth, NJ 07201, 201-352-5509

Drake College of Business, (Branch Campus)
60 Evergreen Pl, East Orange, NJ 07018, 201-673-6009

Draughons College
1430 W Peachtree St #101, Atlanta, GA 30309, 404-892-0814

Du Cret School of the Arts
1030 Central Ave, Plainfield, NJ 07060, 908-757-7171

Duluth Business University
412 W Superior St, Duluth, MN 55802, 218-722-3361

Durango Air Service
1300 County Rd 309, Durango, CO 81301, 303-247-5535

E

EDUTEK Professional Colleges
1541 Broadway, San Diego, CA 92101, 619-239-4138

EDUTEK Professional Colleges, (Branch Campus)
4560 Alvarado Canyon Rd, San Diego, CA 92120, 619-582-1319

EDUTEK Professional Colleges, (Branch Campus)
5952 El Cajon Blvd, San Diego, CA 92115, 619-582-1319

Earle C. Clements Job Corps Center
2302 Hwy 60 E, Morganfield, KY 42437, 502-389-2419

East Coast Aero Technical School
696 Virginia Rd, Concord, MA 01742, 508-371-9977

East Los Angeles Occupational Center
2100 Marengo St, Los Angeles, CA 90033, 213-223-1283

Eastern College of Health Vocations
6423 Forbing Rd, Little Rock, AR 72209, 501-568-0211

Eastern College of Health Vocations
3540 I-10 Service Rd S, Metairie, LA 70001, 504-834-8644

Eastern Jackson County College of Allied Health
808 S 15th St, Blue Springs, MO 64015, 816-229-4720

Echols International Tourism Institute
676 N St. Clair St #1950, Chicago, IL 60611, 800-342-2733

Educational Institute of the American Hotel and Motel Association
PO Box 1240, East Lansing, MI 48826, 517-353-5500

Educorp Career College
230 E Third St, Long Beach, CA 90802, 213-437-0501

Eldorado College
2204 El Camino Real, Oceanside, CA 92054, 619-433-3660

Eldorado College
1901 Pacific Ave, West Covina, CA 91790, 818-960-5173

Eldorado College, (Branch Campus)
385 N Escondido Blvd, Escondido, CA 92025, 619-743-2100

Eldorado College, (Branch Campus)
2255 Camino Del Rio, San Diego, CA 92108, 619-294-9256

Electronic Institute
1270 Queen Emma St #107, Honolulu, HI 96813, 808-521-5290

Elegance International
4929 Wilshire Blvd, Los Angeles, CA 90010, 213-937-4838

Eli Whitney Regional Vocational-Technical School
71 Jones Rd, Hamden, CT 06514, 203-397-4031

Elite Progressive School of Cosmetology
5522 Garfield Ave, Sacramento, CA 95841, 916-338-1885

Elkins Institute of Jacksonville
3947 Boulevard Center Dr #6, Jacksonville, FL 32207, 904-398-6211

Elmira Business Institute
180 Clemens Center Pkwy, Elmira, NY 14901, 607-733-7177

Emergency Management Institute
16825 S Seton Ave, Emmitsburg, MD 21727, 301-447-1172

Emil Fries Piano & Training Center
2510 E Evergreen Blvd, Vancouver, WA 98661, 206-693-1511

Emily Griffith Opportunity School
1250 Welton St, Denver, CO 80204, 303-572-8218

Empire Technical Schools of New Jersey
576 Central Ave, East Orange, NJ 07018, 201-675-0565

Engine City Technical Institute
Rte 22 W Box 3116, Union, NJ 07083, 201-964-1450

Environmental Technical Institue
1101 W Thorndale Ave, Itasca, IL 60143, 708-285-9100

Environmental Technical Institue, (Branch Campus)
13010 S Division St, Blue Island, IL 60406, 708-385-0707

Estelle Harman Actors Workshop
522 N La Brea Ave, Los Angeles, CA 90036, 213-931-8137

Eton Technical Institute
3649 Frontage Rd, Port Orchard, WA 98366, 206-479-3866

Eton Technical Institute, (Branch Campus)
209 E Casino Rd, Everett, WA 98208, 206-353-4888

Eton Technical Institute, (Branch Campus)
31919 Sixth Ave S, Federal Way, WA 98063, 206-941-5800

Euro Hair Design Institute
1964 W Tennessee St #14, Tallahassee, FL 32304, 904-576-2174

Euro Hair School
2301-A Morgan Ave, Corpus Christi, TX 78405, 512-887-8494

Euro-Skill Therapeutic Training Center
500 NE Spanish River Blvd #25-26, Boca Raton, FL 33431, 407-395-3089

European Health & Sciences Institute
1201 Airway A-2, El Paso, TX 79925, 915-772-4243

Evangeline Technical Institute
600 S M.L.K., Jr. Dr, Martinville, LA 70582, 318-394-6466

Executive Travel Institute
5775 Peachtree Dunwoody Rd #300E, Atlanta, GA 30342, 404-303-2929

Extension Course Institute of the United States Air Force
50 S Turner Blvd, Maxwell Afb, AL 36118, 205-416-4252

F

FAA Center for Management Development
4500 Palm Coast Pkwy SE, Palm Coast, FL 32137, 904-446-7136

FEGS Trades and Business School
17 Battery Pl #6N, New York, NY 10004, 212-440-8130

FEGS Trades and Business School, (Branch Campus)
199 Jay St, Brooklyn, NY 11201, 718-448-0120

Fairfield Career Center
4000 Columbus-Lancaster Rd, Carroll, OH 43112, 614-837-9443

Fanny Allen Memorial School of Practical Nursing
125 College Pkwy, Colchester, VT 05446, 802-655-2540

Farah's Beauty School
520 Bush River Rd, Columbia, SC 29210, 803-772-0101

Farah's Beauty School
107 Central Ave, Goose Creek, SC 29445, 803-572-5705

Fashion Careers of California
1923 Morena Blvd, San Diego, CA 92110, 619-275-4700

Fayetteville Beauty College
2018 Ft Bragg Rd, Fayetteville, NC 28303, 919-484-7191

Federal Correctional Institution
501 Capital Cir NE, Tallahassee, FL 32301, 904-878-2173

FinEd, School of Financial Education
5745 Essen Ln #207, Baton Rouge, LA 70810, 504-767-7983

Flatwoods Civilian Conservation Center
Rte 1 Box 211, Coeburn, VA 24230, 703-395-3384

Fleet Business School
2530 Riva Rd, Annapolis, MD 21401, 410-266-8500

FlightSafety International
PO Box 2708, Vero Beach, FL 32961, 407-567-5178

Flint Hills Technical School
3301 W 18th Ave, Emporia, KS 66801, 316-342-6404

Flint Institute of Barbering
3214 Flushing Rd, Flint, MI 48504, 313-232-4711

Flint River Technical Institute
1533 Hwy 19 S, Thomaston, GA 30286, 404-647-0928

Florida Institute of Message Therapy & Esthetics
5453 N University Dr, Lauderhill, FL 33351, 305-742-8399

Florida Institute of Ultrasound, Inc.
PO Box 15135, Pensacola, FL 32514, 904-478-7300

Florida Parishes Technical Institute
100 College Dr, Greensburg, LA 70441, 504-222-4251

Florida School of Business
2990 NW 81st Terrace, Miami, FL 33147, 305-696-6312

Florida School of Business
405 E Polk St, Tampa, FL 33602, 813-221-4200

Florida Technical College
1819 N Semoran Blvd, Orlando, FL 32807, 407-678-5600

Florida Technical College
4750 E Adamo Dr, Tampa, FL 33605, 813-247-1700

Florissant Upholstery School
1420 N Vandeventer St, St Louis, MO 63113, 314-534-1886

Folk Art Institute of the Museum of American Folk Art
61 W 62nd St, New York, NY 10023, 212-977-7170

Folkes Technical Institute
3337 Hwy 10 E, Jackson, LA 70748, 504-634-2636

Folkes Technical Institute, (Branch Campus)
Dixon Correctional Inst., Jackson, LA 70748, 504-634-2636

Forsyth School for Dental Hygienists
140 The Fenway, Boston, MA 02115, 617-262-5200

Fort Sanders School of Nursing
1915 White Ave, Knoxville, TN 37916, 615-541-1290

Fox Institute of Business
765 Asylum Ave, Hartford, CT 06105, 203-522-2888

Fox Secretarial College
4201 W 93rd St, Oak Lawn, IL 60453, 708-636-7700

Fox Travel Institute
520 Pike St #2800, Seattle, WA 98101, 206-224-7800

Francis Tuttle Vocational-Technical Center
12777 N Rockwell Ave, Oklahoma City, OK 73142, 405-722-7799

Franklin Academy
324 N Centre St, Pottsville, PA 17901, 717-622-8370

Franklin College of Court Reporting
1200 S Clearview Pkwy, New Orleans, LA 70123, 504-734-1000

French Culinary Institute
462 Broadway, New York, NY 10013, 212-219-8890

Fresno Institute of Technology
1545 N Fulton St, Fresno, CA 93720, 209-442-3574

Full Sail Center for the Recording Arts
3300 University Blvd, Winter Park, FL 32792, 407-679-6333

G

Gadsden Business College
PO Box 1544, Gadsden, AL 35901, 205-546-2863

Gadsden Business College, (Branch Campus)
PO Box 1575, Anniston, AL 36202, 205-237-7517

Galen College of Medical and Dental Assistants
1325 N Wishon Ave, Fresno, CA 93728, 209-264-9726

Galen College of Medical and Dental Assistants, (Branch Campus)
1604 Ford Ave #10, Modesto, CA 95350, 209-264-9726

Galen College of Medical and Dental Assistants, (Branch Campus)
3746 W Mineral King Ave Ste C, Visalia, CA 93291, 209-264-9726

Garces Commercial College
1301 SW First St, Miami, FL 33135, 305-643-1044

Garces Commercial College, (Branch Campus)
5385 NW 36th St, Miami Springs, FL 33166, 305-871-6535

Garfield Business Institute
709 Third Ave, New Brighton, PA 15066, 412-728-4050

Gary Job Corps Center
Hwy 21, San Marcos, TX 78667, 512-396-6652

Gateway Technical Institute
100 Seventh St, Pittsburgh, PA 15222, 412-281-4111

Geiger's School of Cosmetology
600 N 26th Ave, Hattiesburg, MS 39401, 601-583-2523

Gemological Institute of America
PO Box 2110, 1660 Teward St, Santa Monica, CA 90404-4088, 310-829-2991

Gemological Institute of America, (Branch Campus)
580 Fifth Ave, New York, CA 10036-4794, 212-944-5900

General Technical Institute Welding Trade School
1118 Baltimore Ave, Linden, NJ 07036, 201-486-9353

George Stone Vocational-Technical Center
2400 Longleaf Dr, Pensacola, FL 32526, 904-944-1424

George T. Baker Aviation School
3275 NW 42nd Ave, Miami, FL 33142, 305-871-3143

Georgia Institute of Cosmetology
3341 Lexington Rd, Athens, GA 30605, 706-549-6400

Georgia Medical Institute
40 Marietta St Flrs 5 & 13, Atlanta, GA 30303, 404-525-3272

Georgia Medical Institute, (Branch Campus)
1895 Phoenix Blvd #310, Atlanta, GA 30349, 404-994-1900

Georgia Medical Institute, (Branch Campus)
1355 S Marietta Pkwy #305, Marietta, GA 30067, 404-428-6303

Gleim Technical Institute
200 S Spring Garden St, Carlisle, PA 17013, 800-922-8399

Glendale Career College
1021 Grandview Ave, Glendale, CA 91201, 818-243-1131

Global Business Institute
1931 Mott Ave, Far Rockaway, NY 11691, 718-327-2220

Global Business Institute, (Branch Campus)
209 W 125th St, New York, NY 10027, 212-663-1500

Globe Institute of Technology
291 Broadway 4th Fl, New York, NY 10007, 212-234-9768

Golf Academy of San Diego
PO Box 3050, Rancho Santa Fe, CA 92067, 619-756-2486

Golf Academy of San Diego, (Golf Academy of the South)
PO Box 3609, Winter Springs, FL 32708, 407-669-1990

Grand Rapids Educational Center
1750 Woodworth St NE, Grand Rapids, MI 49505, 616-364-8464

Grand Rapids Educational Center, (Branch Campus)
5349 W Main St, Kalamazoo, MI 49009, 606-381-9616

Great Plains Area Vocational-Technical Center
4500 W Lee Blvd, Lawton, OK 73505, 405-355-6371

Greater Johnstown Area Vocational-Technical School
445 Schoolhouse Rd, Johnstown, PA 15904, 814-266-6073

Griffin Technical Institute
501 Varsity Rd, Griffin, GA 30223, 404-228-7365

Gulf Area Technical Institute
1115 Clover St, Abbeville, LA 70510, 318-893-4984

Gulf Coast Trades Center
FM 1375 W, New Waverly, TX 77358, 409-344-6677

Gulfport Job Corps Center
3300 20th St, Gulfport, MS 39501, 601-864-9691

Gwinnett College
4230 Hwy 29 Ste 11, Liburn, GA 30247, 404-381-7200

H

Hadley School for the Blind
700 Elm St, Winnetka, IL 60093, 708-446-8111

Hair Design School
5110 University Blvd Bldg C, Jacksonville, FL 32216, 904-731-7500

Hairstyling Institute of Charlotte
209-B S KIngs Dr, Charlotte, NC 28204, 704-334-5511

Hallmark Institute of Photography
PO Box 308, Turners Falls, MA 01376, 413-863-2478

Hammond Area Technical Institute
Hwy 190 & Pride Blvd, Hammond, LA 70404, 504-549-5063

Hamrick Truck Driving School
1156 Medina Rd, Medina, OH 44256, 216-239-2229

Hannah E. Mullins School of Practical Nursing
2094 E State St, Salem, OH 44460, 216-332-8940

Hannah Harrison Career Schools
4470 MacArthur Blvd NW, Washington, DC 20007, 202-333-3500

Hannibal Area Vocational-Technical School
4500 McMasters Ave, Hannibal, MO 63401, 314-221-4430

Harris School of Business
654 Longwood Ave, Cherry Hill, NJ 08002, 609-662-5300

Hartford Camerata Conservatory
834 Asylum Ave, Hartford, CT 06105, 203-246-2588

Hawaii Business College
111 N King Penthouse, Honolulu, HI 96817, 808-524-4014

Hawaii Institute of Hair Design
71 S Hotel St, Honolulu, HI 96813, 808-533-6596

Hawes Career Institute
47884 D St, Belleville, MI 48111, 800-447-1310

Health Care Training Institute
430 N Cleveland St, Memphis, TN 38104, 901-722-2288

Health Institute of Louisville
612 S Fourth St #400, Louisville, KY 40202, 502-580-3660

Health Institute of Louisville, (Branch Campus)
6800 Park Ten Blvd #160 S, San Antonio, TX 78213, 512-580-3660

Health Institute of Louisville, (Branch Campus)
11500 Ninth St N #140, St. Petersburg, FL 33716, 813-577-1497

Heart of Georgia Technical Institute
560 Pinehill Rd, Dublin, GA 31021, 912-275-6589

Heart of Georgia Technical Institute, (Branch Campus)
1124 College St, Eastman, GA 31023, 912-374-7122

The Sourcebook of College and University Student Records

Heartland School of Business
211 W State St #204, Jacksonville, IL 62650, 217-243-9001

Hemphill Schools
510 S Alvarado St, Los Angeles, CA 90057, 213-413-6323

Hennepin Technical College
9000 Brooklyn Blvd, Brooklyn Park, MN 55455, 612-425-3800

Henry W. Brewster Technical Center
2222 N Tampa St, Tampa, FL 33602, 813-273-9240

Heritage College of Health Careers
12 Lakeside La, Denver, CO 80212, 303-477-7240

Herzing Institute
1218 S 20th St, Birmingham, AL 35205, 205-933-8536

Hi-Tech School of Miami
10350 W Flagler St, Miami, FL 33174, 305-221-3423

Hialeah Technical Center
1780 E 4th Ave, Hialeah, FL 33012, 305-884-4387

Hickox School
200 Tremont St, Boston, MA 02116, 617-482-7655

High-Tech Institute
1515 E Indian School Rd, Phoenix, AZ 85014, 602-279-9700

High-Tech Institute, (Branch Campus)
1111 Howe Ave, Sacramento, CA 95825, 916-988-0986

HoHoKus School
50 S Frankling Tpke, Ramsey, NJ 07446, 201-327-8877

Hobart Institute of Welding Technology
Trade Sq E, Troy, OH 45373, 513-332-5214

Hollywood Cosmetology Center
PO Box 890488, Oklahoma City, OK 73189, 405-364-3375

Hospitality Training Center
220 N Main St, Hudson, OH 44236, 216-653-9151

Houston Allied Health Careers, Inc.
2800 San Jacinto St, Houston, TX 77004, 713-650-6155

Houston Ballet Academy
PO Box 130487, Houston, TX 77219, 713-523-6300

Houston Training School
701 Shotwell St, Houston, TX 77020, 713-672-9607

Houston Training School, (Branch Campus)
1260 Blalock, Houston, TX 77055, 713-464-1659

Houston Training School, (Branch Campus)
6969 Gulf Fwy #200, Houston, TX 77087, 713-649-5050

Huey P. Long Technical Institute
303 S Jones St, Winnfield, LA 71483, 318-628-4342

Huey P. Long Technical Institute, (Branch Campus)
E Bradford St, Jena, LA 71342, 318-992-2910

Humanities Center Institute of Allied Health/School of Message
4045 Park Blvd, Pinellas Park, FL 34665, 813-541-5200

Hunter Business School
3601 Hempstead Tpke, Levittown, NY 11756, 516-796-1000

Huntington College of Dental Technology
7466 Edinger Ave, Huntington Beach, CA 92647, 714-841-9500

Huntington Institute
193 Broadway, Norwich, CT 06360, 203-886-0507

Huntsville Business Institute School of Court Reporting
3315 S Memorial Pkwy #5, Huntsville, AL 35801, 205-880-7530

Hypnosis Motivation Institute
18607 Ventura Blvd #310, Tarzana, CA 91356, 818-344-4464

I

IHM Health Studies Center
2500 Abbott Pl, St Louis, MO 63143, 314-768-1234

ITT Technical Institute
4020 Sparks Dr SE, Grand Rapids, MI 49546, 616-956-1060

ITT Technical Institute, (Branch Campus)
600 Holiday Plaza Dr, Matteson, IL 60443,

Illinois School of Health Careers
1607 W Howard St #305, Chicago, IL 60626, 312-973-0299

Indian Meridian Vocational-Technical Center
1312 S Sangre St, Stillwater, OK 74074, 405-377-3333

Indiana Barber/Stylist College
121 S Ridgeview Dr, Indianapolis, IN 46219, 317-356-8222

Industrial Management and Training, Inc.
233 Mill St, Waterbury, CT 06706, 203-753-7910

Institute for Business & Technology
2550 Scott Blvd, Santa Clara, CA 95050, 408-727-1060

Institute for Business & Technology, (National Career Education)
6060 Sunrise Vista Dr #3000, Citrus Heights, CA 95160, 916-969-4900

Institute of Allied Medical Professions
106 Central Park S #23D, New York, NY 10019, 212-757-0520

Institute of Audio Research
64 University Pl, New York, NY 10003, 212-677-7580

Institute of Business and Medical Technology
20 E Main St #600, Mesa, AZ 85201, 602-833-1028

Institute of Business and Medical Technology
75-110 St Charles Pl, Palm Desert, CA 92260, 619-776-5873

Institute of Computer Science
808 S 74th Plaza #200, Omaha, NE 68114, 402-393-7064

Institute of Computer Technology
3200 Wilshire Blvd #400, Los Angeles, CA 90010, 213-381-3333

Institute of Medical and Dental Technology
375 Glensprings Dr #201, Cincinnati, OH 45246, 513-851-8500

Institute of Medical and Dental Technology, (Branch Campus)
4452 Eastgate Blvd #209, Cincinnati, OH 45244, 513-753-5030

Interactive Learning Systems
480 N Thomas St, Athens, GA 30622, 404-548-9800

Interactive Learning Systems
5600 Roswell Rd NE, Atlanta, GA 30342, 404-250-9000

Interactive Learning Systems
8585 N Stemmons Fwy #M50, Dallas, TX 75247, 214-637-3377

Non-Degree Granting Institutions

Interactive Learning Systems, (Branch Campus)
4814 Old National Hwy, College Park, GA 30337, 404-765-9777

Interactive Learning Systems, (Branch Campus)
11 S Main St, Day Ridge, KY 41097, 606-824-3573

Interactive Learning Systems, (Branch Campus)
6612 Dixie Hwy #2, Florence, KY 41042, 606-282-8989

Interactive Learning Systems, (Branch Campus)
10200 Richmond Ave, Houston, TX 77042, 713-782-5161

Interactive Learning Systems, (Branch Campus)
2759 Delk Rd #101, Marietta, GA 30067, 404-951-2367

Interactive Learning Systems, (Branch Campus)
2171 Northlake Pkwy #100, Tucker, GA 30084, 404-939-6008

Interior Design Institute
5225 S Easter Ave #4, Las Vegas, NV 89119, 702-369-9944

Intermountain College of Court Reporting
5980 S 300 E, Murray, UT 84107, 801-268-9271

International Air Academy
2901 E Mill Plain Blvd, Vancouver, WA 98661, 206-695-2500

International Air Academy, (Branch Campus)
2980 Inland Empire Blvd, Ontario, CA 91764, 714-989-5222

International Aviation and Travel Academy
300 W Arbrook Blvd, Arlington, TX 76014, 817-784-7000

International Aviation and Travel Academy
17340 Chanute Rd, Houston, TX 77032, 800-627-4379

International Aviation and Travel Academy, (Branch Campus)
5757 Alpha Rd #101, Dallas, TX 75240, 214-387-0553

International Business College
4121 Montana Ave, El Paso, TX 79903, 915-566-8644

International Business College
650 E Montana Ave #F, Las Cruces, NM 88001, 505-526-5579

International Business College
4630 50th St, Lubbock, TX 79414, 806-797-1933

International Business College, (Branch Campus)
1030 N Zaragosa Rd, El Paso, TX 79907, 915-859-3986

International Business College, (Business School - Denton)
3801 I-35N #138, Denton, TX 76205, 817-380-0024

International Business College, (Business School - Sherman)
4107 N Texoma Pkwy, Sherman, TX 75090, 806-893-6604

International College of Broadcasting
6 S Smithville Rd, Dayton, OH 45431, 513-258-8251

International Dealers School
6329 E Washington Blvd, Commerce, CA 90040, 213-890-0030

International Dealers School
503 E Fremont St, Las Vegas, NV 89101, 702-385-7665

International School of Skin & Nailcare
5600 Roswell Rd NE, Atlanta, GA 30342, 404-843-1005

Interstate Business College
2720 32nd Ave SW, Fargo, ND 58103, 701-232-2477

Interstate Business College, (Branch Campus)
520 E Main Ave, Bismarck, ND 58501, 701-255-0779

Iowa School of Barbering and Hairstyling
603 E Sixth St, Des Moines, IA 50309, 515-244-0971

Irvine College of Business
16591 Noyes Ave, Irvine, CA 92714, 714-863-1145

Isabella G. Hart School of Practical Nursing
1425 Portland Ave, Rochester, NY 14621, 716-338-4784

Island Drafting & Technical Institute
128 Broadway, Amityville, NY 11701, 516-691-8733

Iverson Institute of Court Reporting
1200 Copeland Rd #305, Arlington, TX 76011, 817-274-6465

J

J.H. Thompson Academies
2908 State St, Erie, PA 16508, 814-456-6217

J.R. Pittard Area Vocational School
22401 Alabama Hwy 21, Alpine, AL 35160, 205-539-8161

Jackson Academy of Beauty
2525 Robinson Rd, Jackson, MS 39209, 601-352-3003

James L. Walker Vocational-Technical Center
3702 Estey Ave, Naples, FL 33942, 813-643-0919

James Martin Adult Health Occupations
2600 Red Lion Rd, Philadelphia, PA 19114, 215-961-2131

Jefferson Davis Technical Institute
1230 N Main St, Jennings, LA 70546, 318-824-4811

Jefferson Technical Institute
5200 Blair Dr, Metairie, LA 70001, 504-736-7076

Jett College of Cosmetology & Barbering
3740 N Watkins St, Memphis, TN 38127, 901-357-0388

Jett College of Cosmetology & Barbering
524 S Cooper St, Memphis, TN 38104, 901-276-1721

Jett College of Cosmetology & Barbering
1286 Southbrook Mall, Memphis, TN 38116, 901-332-7330

Jocelyn Daspit Beauty College
3204 Independence St, Matairie, LA 70006, 504-888-8983

Jocelyn Daspit Beauty College, (Branch Campus)
507 Cypress St, Hammond, LA 70401, 504-345-6307

Jocelyn Daspit Beauty College, (Branch Campus)
1727 W Airline Hwy, La Place, LA 70068, 504-652-6807

Joe Kubert School of Cartoon and Graphic Art
37 Myrtle Ave, Dover, NJ 07801, 201-361-1327

John Pope Eden Area Vocational Education Center
Rte 2 Box 1855, Ashville, AL 35953, 205-594-7055

John Tracy Clinic
806 W Adams Blvd, Los Angeles, CA 90007, 213-748-5481

Johnston School of Practical Nursing
201 E University Pkwy, Baltimore, MD 21218, 410-554-2327

Joseph Donahue International School of Hairstyling
2485 Grant Ave, Philadelphia, PA 19114, 215-969-1313

Jumonville Memorial Technical Institute
Hwy 3131, Hospital Rd, New Roads, LA 70760, 504-638-8613

The Sourcebook of College and University Student Records

Jumonville Memorial Technical Institute, (Branch Campus)
Louisiana State Penentiary, Angola, LA 70712, 504-655-4411

Jumonville Memorial Technical Institute, (Branch Campus)
Hunt Corr. Ctr, PO Box 40, St. Gabriel, LA 70776, 504-642-3306

K

Kane Business Institute
206 Haddonfield Rd, Cherry Hill, NJ 08002, 609-488-1166

Kansas School of Hairstyling
1207 E Douglas Ave, Wichita, KS 67211, 316-264-4891

Kentucky College of Barbering and Hairstyling
1230 S Third St, Louisville, KY 40203, 502-634-0521

Kentucky Tech-Ashland State Vocational-Technical School
4818 Roberts Dr, Ashland, KY 41102, 606-928-6427

Kentucky Tech-Barren County Area Vocational Education Center
491 Trojan Tr, Glasgow, KY 42141, 502-651-2196

Kentucky Tech-Belfry Area Vocational Education Center
PO Box 280, Belfry, KY 41514, 606-353-4951

Kentucky Tech-Bell County Area Vocational Education Center
Box 199-A, Rte 7, Pineville, KY 40977, 606-337-3094

Kentucky Tech-Boone County Center
3320 Cougar Path, Hebron, KY 41048, 606-689-7855

Kentucky Tech-Bowling Green State Vocational-Technical School
1845 Loop Dr, Bowling Green, KY 42102, 502-843-5461

Kentucky Tech-Breathitt County Area Vocational Education Center
PO Box 786, Jackson, KY 41339, 606-666-5153

Kentucky Tech-Breckenridge County Area Vocational Education Ctr
PO Box 68, Harned, KY 40144, 502-756-2138

Kentucky Tech-Bullitt County Area Vocational Education Ctr
395 High School Dr, Shepherdsville, KY 40165, 502-543-7018

Kentucky Tech-Caldwell County Area Vocational Education Ctr
PO Box 350, Princeton, KY 42445, 502-365-5563

Kentucky Tech-Carroll County Area Center
1704 Highland Ave, Carrollton, KY 41008, 502-732-4479

Kentucky Tech-Casey County Area Vocational Education Center
Rte 4, Box 49, Liberty, KY 42539, 606-787-6241

Kentucky Tech-Central Campus
104 Vo-Tech Rd, Lexington, KY 40510, 606-255-8500

Kentucky Tech-Christian County Area Vocational Education Center
109 Hamond Plaza #2, Hopkinsville, KY 42240, 502-887-2524

Kentucky Tech-Clark County Center
650 Boone Ave, Winchester, KY 40391, 606-744-1250

Kentucky Tech-Clay County Area Vocational Education Center
Rte 2, Box 256, Manchester, KY 40962, 606-598-2194

Kentucky Tech-Clinton County Area Vocational Education Center
Rte 3 Box 8, Albany, KY 42602, 606-387-6448

Kentucky Tech-Corbin Area Vocational Education Center
1909 S Snyder Ave, Corbin, KY 40701, 606-528-5338

Kentucky Tech-Cumberland Valley Health Occupations Center
PO Box 187, Pineville, KY 40977, 606-337-3106

Kentucky Tech-Danville School of Health Occupations
448 S Third St, Danville, KY 40422, 606-236-2053

Kentucky Tech-Daviess County Vocational-Technical School
PO Box 1677, Owensboro, KY 42303, 502-686-3321

Kentucky Tech-Elizabethtown State Vocational-Technical School
505 University Dr, Elizabethtown, KY 42701, 502-765-2104

Kentucky Tech-Fulton County Area Vocational Education Center
Rte 4, Hickman, KY 42050, 502-236-2517

Kentucky Tech-Garth Area Vocational Education Center
HC79, Box 205, Martin, KY 41649, 606-285-3088

Kentucky Tech-Gerrard County Center
306 W Maple Ave, Lancaster, KY 40444, 606-792-2144

Kentucky Tech-Glasgow Health Occupations School
1215 N Race St, Glasgow, KY 42141, 502-651-5673

Kentucky Tech-Green County Area Vocational Education Center
PO Box 167, Greensburg, KY 42743, 502-932-4263

Kentucky Tech-Greenup County Area Vocational Education Center
PO Box 7, South Shore, KY 41175, 606-932-3107

Kentucky Tech-Harlan State Vocational-Technical School
21 Ballpark Rd, Harlan, KY 40831, 606-573-1506

Kentucky Tech-Harrison County Center
551 Webster Ave, Cynthiana, KY 41031, 606-234-5286

Kentucky Tech-Harrodsburg Center
PO Box 628, Harrodsburg, KY 40330, 606-734-9329

Kentucky Tech-Hazard State Vocational-Technical School
101 Vo-Tech Dr, Hazard, KY 41701, 606-436-3101

Kentucky Tech-Henderson County Area Vocational Education Center
2440 Zion Rd, Henderson, KY 42420, 502-827-3810

Non-Degree Granting Institutions

Kentucky Tech-Jefferson State Vocational-Technical Center
727 W Chestnut St, Louisville, KY 40203, 502-595-4136

Kentucky Tech-Kentucky Advanced Technology Center
1127 Morgantown Rd, Bowling Green, KY 42101, 502-843-5807

Kentucky Tech-Knott County Area Vocational Education Center
HCR 60, Box 1100, Hindman, KY 41822, 606-785-5350

Kentucky Tech-Knox County Area Vocational Education Center
210 Wall St, Barbourville, KY 40906, 606-546-5320

Kentucky Tech-Laurel County State Vocational-Technical School
1711 S Main St, London, KY 40741, 606-864-7311

Kentucky Tech-Lee County Area Vocational Education Center
PO Box B, Beattyville, KY 41311, 606-464-2475

Kentucky Tech-Leslie County Area Vocational Education Center
PO Box 902, Hyden, KY 41749, 606-672-2859

Kentucky Tech-Letcher County Area Vocational Education Center
610 Circle Dr, Whitesburg, KY 41858, 606-633-5053

Kentucky Tech-Madison County Center
PO Box 809, Richmond, KY 40476, 606-623-4061

Kentucky Tech-Madisonville Health Occupations School
701 N Laffoon, Madisonville, KY 42431, 502-825-6552

Kentucky Tech-Madisonville State Vocational-Technical School
150 School Ave, Madisonville, KY 42431, 502-825-6544

Kentucky Tech-Marion County Area Vocational Education Center
721 E Main, Lebanon, KY 40033, 502-692-3155

Kentucky Tech-Martin County Area Vocational Education Center
HC 68 Box 2177, Inez, KY 41224, 606-298-3879

Kentucky Tech-Mason County Area Vocational Education Center
646 Kent Station Rd, Maysville, KY 41056, 606-759-7101

Kentucky Tech-Mayfield Area Vocational Education Center
710 Doughtit Rd, Mayfield, KY 42066, 502-247-4710

Kentucky Tech-Mayo State Vocational-Technical School
513 Third St, Paintsville, KY 41240, 502-247-4710

Kentucky Tech-McCormick Center
50 Orchard Ln, Alexandria, KY 41001, 606-635-4101

Kentucky Tech-Meade County Area Vocational Education Center
110 Greer St, Brandenburg, KY 40108, 502-422-3955

Kentucky Tech-Millard Area Vocational Education Center
430 Millard Hwy, Pikeville, KY 41501, 606-437-6059

Kentucky Tech-Monroe County Area Vocational Education Center
4th and Emmerton Sts, Tompkinsville, KY 42167, 502-487-8261

Kentucky Tech-Montgomery County Area Vocational Education Center
682 Woodford Dr, Mount Sterling, KY 40353, 606-498-1103

Kentucky Tech-Morgan County Area Vocational Education Center
PO Box 249, West Liberty, KY 41472, 606-743-4321

Kentucky Tech-Muhlenberg County Area Vocational Education Center
RR Box 67, Greenville, KY 42345, 502-338-1271

Kentucky Tech-Murray Area Vocational Education Center
18th and Sycamore Sts, Murray, KY 42071, 502-753-1870

Kentucky Tech-Nelson County Area Vocational Education Center
1060 Bloomfield Rd, Bardstown, KY 40004, 502-348-9096

Kentucky Tech-Northern Campbell County Campus
90 Campbell Dr, Highland Heights, KY 41076, 606-441-2010

Kentucky Tech-Northern Kentucky Campus
1025 Amsterdam Rd, Covington, KY 41018, 606-431-2700

Kentucky Tech-Northern Kentucky Health Occupations Center
790 Thomas More Pkwy, Edgewood, KY 41017, 606-341-5200

Kentucky Tech-Ohio County Area Vocational Education Center
PO Box 1406, Hartford, KY 42347, 502-274-9612

Kentucky Tech-Oldham County Area Vocational Education Center
PO Box 127, Buckner, KY 40010, 502-222-0131

Kentucky Tech-Owensboro Vocational-Technical School
1501 Frederica St, Owensboro, KY 42301, 502-686-3255

Kentucky Tech-Paducah Area Vocational Education Center
2400 Adams St, Paducah, KY 42001, 502-443-6592

Kentucky Tech-Patton Center
3234 Turkeyfoot Rd, Fort Mitchell, KY 41017, 606-341-2266

Kentucky Tech-Phelps Area Vocational Education Center
HC67 #1002, Phelps, KY 41553, 606-456-8136

Kentucky Tech-Rockcastle County Area Vocational Education Center
PO Box 275, Mount Vernon, KY 40456, 606-256-4346

Kentucky Tech-Rowan State Vocational-Technical School
100 Vo-Tech Dr, 32 N, Morehead, KY 40351, 606-783-1538

Kentucky Tech-Russell Area Vocational Education Center
705 Red Devil Ln, Russell, KY 41169, 606-836-1256

Kentucky Tech-Russell County Area Vocational Education Center
PO Box 599, Russell Springs, KY 42642, 502-866-6175

Kentucky Tech-Russellville Area Vocational Education Center
1103 W 9th St, Russellville, KY 42276, 502-726-8433

Kentucky Tech-Shelby County Area Vocational Education Center
230 Rocket Ln, Shelbyville, KY 40065, 502-633-6554

Kentucky Tech-Somerset State Vocational Education Center
230 Airport Rd, Somerset, KY 42501, 606-679-4303

Kentucky Tech-Wayne County Area Vocational Education Center
150 Cardinal Wy, Monticello, KY 42633, 606-348-8424

Kentucky Tech-Webster County Area Vocational Education Center
PO Box 188, Dixon, KY 42409, 502-639-5035

Kentucky Tech-West Kentucky State Vocational-Technical School
Hwy 60 W, Paducah, KY 42002, 502-554-4991

Kerr Business College
PO Box 976, Lagrange, GA 30241, 706-884-1751

Kerr Business College, (Branch Campus)
PO Box 1986, Augusta, GA 30903, 404-738-5046

Kings College
322 Lamar Ave, Charlotte, NC 28204, 704-372-0266

Kinyon-Campbell Business School
59 Linden St, New Bedford, MA 02740, 508-992-5448

Kinyon-Campbell Business School, (Branch Campus)
1041 Pearl St, Brockton, MA 02401, 508-584-6869

Knox County Career Center
306 Martinsburg Rd, Mount Vernon, OH 43050, 614-397-5820

Knoxville Institute of Hair Design
1221 N Central St, Knoxville, TN 37917, 615-971-1529

Knoxville Job Corps Center
621 Dale Ave, Knoxville, TN 37921, 615-544-5600

Krissler Business Institute
166 Mansion Sq Park, Poughkeepsie, NY 12601, 914-471-0330

L

La Grande College of Business
10214 Wallowa Lake Hwy, La Grande, OR 97850, 503-963-6485

LaGrange Cosmetology School
1008 Colquitt St, Lagrange, GA 30240, 706-884-5750

Laban/Bartenieff Institute of Movement Studies, Inc.
11 E 4th St, New York, NY 10003, 212-477-4299

Lafayette Regional Technical Institute
1101 Bertrand Dr, Lafayette, LA 70506, 318-265-5962

Lake County Area Vocational-Technical Center
2001 Kurt St, Eustis, FL 32726, 904-357-8222

Lakeland Medical-Dental Academy
1402 W Lake St, Minneapolis, MN 55408, 612-827-5656

Lamar Salter Technical Institute
Hwy 171 S, Leesville, LA 71446, 318-537-3135

Landing School of Boat Building and Design
PO Box 1490, Kennebunkport, ME 04046, 207-985-7976

Lanier Technical Institute
2990 Landrum Education Dr, Oakwood, GA 30566, 404-531-6300

Lansing Computer Institute
501 N Marshall St #101, Lansing, MI 48912, 517-482-8896

Laural School
PO Box 5338, 2538 N Eighth St, Phoenix, AZ 85010, 602-994-3460

Lawton School
21800 Greenfield, Oak Park, MI 48237, 313-968-2421

Le Hair Design College
217 Pleasant Grove Shopping Ctr, Dallas, TX 75217, 214-398-5905

Le Hair Design College
505 Golden Triangle Shopping C, Dallas, TX 75224, 214-375-0592

Le Hair Design College
1125 E Seminary Dr, Fort Worth, TX 76115, 817-926-7555

Le Hair Design College
2410 W Walnut St, Garland, TX 75042, 214-272-8283

Le Hair Design College
5201 E Belknap, Haltom City, TX 76117, 817-831-7261

LeChef College of Hospitality Careers
6020 Dillard Cir, Austin, TX 78752, 512-323-2511

Learning Tree University
20916 Knapp St, Chatsworth, CA 91311, 818-882-5685

Learning and Evaluation Center
PO Box 616, Bloomsburg, PA 17815, 717-784-5220

Lederwolff Culinary Academy
3300 Stockton Blvd, Sacramento, CA 95820, 916-456-7002

Lee County Vocational High Tech Center
3800 Michigan Ave, Fort Myers, FL 33916, 813-334-4544

Leicester School
1106 W Olympic Blvd, Los Angeles, CA 90015, 212-746-7666

Levine School of Music
1690 36th St NW, Washington, DC 20007, 202-337-2227

Lewis A. Wilson Technical Center
17 Westminster Ave, Dix Hills, NY 11746, 516-667-6000

Lifetime Career Schools
101 Harrison St, Archbald, PA 18403, 717-876-6340

Lincoln Technical Institute
3200 Wilkens Ave, Baltimore, MD 21229, 410-646-5480

Lincoln Technical Institute
2501 E Arkansas Ln, Grand Prairie, TX 75051, 214-660-5701

Lincoln Technical Institute
7800 Central Ave, Landover, MD 20785, 301-336-7250

Lincoln Technical Institute
7320 W Agatite Ave, Norridge, IL 60656, 312-625-1535

Lincoln Technical Institute
8920 S Cicero Ave, Oak Lawn, IL 60453, 708-423-9000

Lincoln Technical Institute
Haddonfield Rd, Pennsauken, NJ 08110, 609-665-3010

Lincoln Technical Institute
9191 Torresdale Ave, Philadelphia, PA 19136, 215-335-0800

Lincoln Technical Institute
2299 Vauxhall Rd, Union, NJ 07083, 908-964-7800

Lindsey Hopkins Technical Education Center
750 NW 20th St, Miami, FL 33127, 305-324-6070

Lively Area Vocational-Technical Center
500 N Appleyard Dr, Tallahassee, FL 32304, 904-487-7401

Long Island Business Institute
6500 Jericho Tpke, Commack, NY 11725, 516-499-7100

Long Medical Institute
4126 N Black Canyon Hwy, Phoenix, AZ 85017, 602-279-9333

Longy School of Music, Inc.
One Follen St, Cambridge, MA 02138, 617-876-0956

Los Angeles ORT Technical Institute
635 S Harvard Blvd, Los Angeles, CA 90005, 213-387-4244

Los Angeles ORT Technical Institute, (Valley Branch)
15130 Ventura Blvd #250, Sherman Oaks, CA 91403, 818-788-7222

Louisiana Art Institute
7380 Exchange Pl, Baton Rouge, LA 70806, 504-928-7770

Louisiana Hair Design College
7909 Airline Hwy, Metairie, LA 70003, 504-737-2376

Louisiana Institute of Technology
3349 Masonic Dr, Alexandria, LA 71301, 318-442-1864

Louisiana Institute of Technology, (Branch Campus)
115 Henderson Rd, Lafayette, LA 70508, 318-233-0776

Louisiana Training Center
942-A Arizona St, Sulphur, LA 70663, 318-625-9469

Lyme Academy of Fine Arts
84 Lyme St, Old Lyme, CT 06371, 203-434-5232

Lyndon B. Johnson Civilian Conservation Center
466 Job Corps Dr, Franklin, NC 29734, 704-524-4446

M

M & M Word Processing Institute
5050 Westheimer Rd #300, Houston, TX 77056, 713-961-0500

M G Institute
40 E Delaware Pl, Chicago, IL 60611, 312-943-4190

M. Weeks Welding Laboratory Testing & School
4405 Hwy 347, Nederland, TX 77627, 409-727-7640

MBTI Business Training Institute
606 W Wisconsin Ave, Milwaukee, WI 53203, 414-272-2192

MBTI Business Training Institute, (Branch Campus)
237 South St, Waukesha, WI 53186, 414-257-3221

MTI Business College of Stockton Inc.
6006 N El Dorado St, Stockton, CA 95207, 209-957-3030

MTI College
2011 W Chapman Ave #100, Orange, CA 92668, 714-385-1132

MTI College, (Branch Campus)
760 Via Lata #300, Colton, CA 92324, 714-424-0123

MTI-Western Business College
2731 Capitol Ave, Sacramento, CA 95816, 916-442-8933

Mable Bailey Fashion College
3121 Cross Country Hill, Columbus, GA 31906, 404-324-4295

Macon Beauty School
630-J North Ave, Macon, GA 31211, 912-746-3243

Macon Technical Institute
3300 Macon Tech Dr, Macon, GA 31206, 912-781-0551

Macon Technical Institute, (Branch Campus)
940 Forsyth St, Macon, GA 31206, 912-744-4812

Madisonville Health Technology Center
PO Box 608, Madisonville, KY 42431, 502-825-6546

Management College of San Francisco
1255 Post St #450, San Francisco, CA 94109, 405-776-7244

Manatee Area Vocational-Technical Center
5603 34th St W, Bradenton, FL 34210, 813-755-2641

Mandl School
254 W 54th St, New York, NY 10019, 212-247-3434

Mansfield Technical Institute
1001 Oxford Rd, Mansfield, LA 71052, 318-872-2243

Margaret Murray Washington Vocational School
27 O St NW, Washington, DC 20001, 202-673-7224

Maria Parham Hospital, Inc.
PO Drawer 59, Henderson, NC 27536, 919-438-4143

Maric College of Medical Careers
7202 Princess View Dr, San Diego, CA 92120, 619-583-8232

Maric College of Medical Careers
1300 Rancheros Dr, San Marcos, CA 92069, 619-747-1555

Maric College of Medical Careers, (Vista Branch Campus)
1593-C E Vista Way, Vista, CA 92084, 619-758-8640

Marin Ballet School
100 Elm St, San Rafael, CA 94901, 415-453-6705

Marine Corps Institute
8th and Eye Sts SE, Washington, DC 20390, 202-433-2728

Marion County School of Radiologic Technology
438 SW Third St, Ocala, FL 32674, 904-629-7545

Marion S. Whelan School of Practical Nursing
196-198 North St, Geneva, NY 14456, 315-789-4222

Martha Graham School of Contemporary Dance, Inc.
316 E 63rd St, New York, NY 10021, 212-838-5886

Martin College
1901 NW Seventh St, Miami, FL 33125, 305-541-8140

Maryland Drafting Institute
2045 University Blvd E, Langley Park, MD 20783, 301-439-7776

Maryland Drafting Institute, (Branch Campus)
8001 Forbes Pl, North Springfield, VA 22151, 703-321-9777

The Sourcebook of College and University Student Records

M

Marymount School of Practical Nursing
12300 McCracken Rd, Garfield Heights, OH 44125, 216-587-8160

Massachusetts School of Barbering & Men's Hairstyling
152 Parkingway St, Quincy, MA 02169, 617-770-4444

Master Schools
824 SW 24th St, Fort Lauderdale, FL 33315, 305-467-8829

Master Schools
4315 NW Seventh St #36, Miami, FL 33126, 305-373-3036

Masters Institute
50 Airport Pkwy #8, San Jose, CA 95110, 408-441-1800

May Technical College
1306 Central Ave, Billings, MT 59102, 406-259-7000

May Technical College, (Branch Campus)
1807 Third St NW, Great Falls, MT 59404, 406-761-4000

McConnell School
831 Second Ave S, Minneapolis, MN 55402, 612-332-4238

McGraw-Hill Continuing Education Center
4401 Connecticut Ave NW, Washington, DC 20008, 202-244-1600

McGraw-Hill Continuing Education Center, (NRI Schools)
4401 Connecticut Ave NW, Washington, DC 20008, 202-244-1600

Med-Assist School of Hawaii
1149 Bethel St #605, Honolulu, HI 96813, 808-524-3363

Med-Help Training School
2702 Clayton Rd #201, Concord, CA 94519, 510-682-2030

Medical Arts Training Center, Inc.
441 S State Rd 7, Margate, FL 33068, 305-968-3500

Medical Career College
537 Main St, Nashville, TN 37206, 615-255-7531

Medical Careers Institute
116 S Michigan Ave 2nd Flr, Chicago, IL 60603, 312-782-9804

Medical Careers Training Center
4020 S College Ave, Fort Collins, CO 80524, 303-223-2669

Medical Institute of Minnesota
5503 Green Valley Dr, Bloomington, MN 55437, 612-884-0064

Medina County Career Center
1101 W Liberty St, Medina, OH 44256, 216-953-7118

Medix School
1017 York Rd, Towson, MD 21204, 410-337-5155

Medix School, (Branch Campus)
2480 Windy Hill Rd, Marietta, GA 30067, 404-980-0002

Memphis Aero Tech
8582 Hwy 51 N, Millington, TN 38083, 901-872-7117

Merce Cunningham Studio
55 Bethune St, New York, NY 10014, 212-255-313-

Merit College
7101 Sepulveda Blvd, Van Nuys, CA 91405, 818-988-6640

Merit College
7101 Sepulveda Blvd, Van Nuys, CA 91405, 818-988-6640

Metro Business College
1732 N Kingshighway Blvd, Cape Girardeau, MO 63701, 314-334-9181

Metro Business College, (Branch Campus)
1407 Southwest Blvd, Jefferson City, MO 65109, 314-635-6600

Metro Business College, (Branch Campus)
PO Box 839, Rolla, MO 65401, 314-364-8464

Metropolitan College of Business
4319 Covington Hwy #300, Decatur, GA 30032, 404-288-6241

Metropolitan College of Court Reporting
2201 San Pedro St NE, Albuquerque, NM 87110, 505-888-3400

Metropolitan College of Court Reporting
2525 Northwest Expy #215, Oklahoma City, OK 73112, 405-840-2181

Metropolitan College of Court Reporting
4640 E Elwood St, Phoenix, AZ 85040, 602-955-5900

Metropolitan College of Legal Studies
2865 E Skelly Dr, Tulsa, OK 74105, 918-745-9946

Metropolitan School of Hair Design
5481 Memorial Dr #E, Stone Mountain, GA 30083, 404-294-5697

Metropolitan Technical Institute
11 Daniel Rd, Fairfield, NJ 07004, 201-227-8191

Meyer Vocational Technical School
PO Box 2126, Minot, ND 58702, 701-852-0427

Miami Institute of Technology
1001 SW First St, Miami, FL 33130, 305-324-6781

Miami Job Corps Center
660 SW Third St, Miami, FL 33130, 305-325-1276

Miami Lakes Technical Education Center
5780 NW 158th St, Miami, FL 33014, 305-557-1100

Miami Technical Institute
14071 NW 7th Ave, North Miami, FL 33168, 305-688-8811

Miami Technical Institute, (Branch Campus)
7061 W Flagler St, Miami, FL 33144, 305-263-9832

Michigan Barber School, Inc.
8988-90 Grand River Ave, Detroit, MI 48204, 313-894-2300

Michigan Career Institute
14520 Gratiot Ave, Detroit, MI 48205, 313-526-6600

Microcomputer Technology Center
8303 Arlington Blvd #210, Fairfax, VA 22032, 703-573-1006

Mid-Del College
3420 S Sunny Ln, Del City, OK 73115, 405-677-8311

Mid-Florida Technical Institute
2900 W Oak Ridge Rd, Orlando, FL 32809, 305-855-5880

Mid-State Barber Styling College, Inc.
510 Jefferson St, Nashville, TN 37208, 615-242-9300

Middle Georgia Technical Institute
1311 Corder Rd, Warner Robins, GA 31088, 912-929-6800

Middle Georgia Technical Institute, (Branch Campus)
Robbins Air Force Museum, Robins Air Force Base, GA 31098, 912-929-6783

Midsouth School of Beauty
3974 Elvis Presley Blvd, Memphis, TN 38116, 901-332-6700

Non-Degree Granting Institutions

Midwest Center for the Study of Oriental Medicine
6226 Bankers Rd #5, Racine, WI 53403, 414-554-2010

Midwest Institute for Medical Assistants
112 W Jefferson St #120, Kirkwood, MO 63122, 314-965-8363

Mildred Elley Business School
2 Computer Dr S, Albany, NY 12205, 518-446-0595

Mildred Elley Business School, (Branch Campus)
400 Columbus Ave, Pittsfield, MA 01201, 413-499-8618

Mille-Motte Business College
1820 Business Park Dr, Clarksville, TN 37040, 615-553-0071

Mille-Motte Business College, (Branch Campus)
606 S College Rd, Wilmington, NC 28403, 910-392-4660

Minneapolis Business College
1711 W County Rd B, Roseville, MN 55113, 612-636-7406

Minneapolis Drafting School
5700 W Broadway, Minneapolis, MN 55428, 612-535-8843

Minneapolis Technical College
1415 Hennepin Ave S #446, Minneapolis, MN 55403, 612-370-9400

Minnesota School of Barbering
3615 E Lake St, Minneapolis, MN 55406, 612-722-1996

Minnesota School of Business
1401 W 76th St #500, Richfield, MN 55423, 612-861-2000

Minnesota School of Business, (Branch Campus)
6120 Earle Brown Dr, Brooklyn Center, MN 55430, 612-566-7777

Minot School for Allied Health
110 Burdick Expy W, Minot, ND 58701, 701-857-5620

Miss Shirley's Beauty College
309 SW 59th St #305, Oklahoma City, OK 73109, 405-631-0055

Mississippi Job Corps Center
501 Harmoney Rd, Crystal Springs, MS 39059, 601-892-3348

Missouri School of Barbering and Hairstyling
1125 N Hwy 67, Florissant, MO 63031, 314-839-0310

Missouri School of Barbering and Hairstyling
3740 Noland Rd, Independence, MO 64055, 816-836-4118

Mister Wayne's School of Unisex Hair Design
170 S Willow Ave, Cookeville, TN 38501, 615-526-1478

Modern Schools of America, Inc.
PO Box 5338, Phoenix, AZ 85010, 602-990-8346

Modern Technology School of X-Ray
1232 E Katella Ave, Anaheim, CA 92805, 714-978-7702

Modern Technology School of X-Ray
6180 Laurel Canyon Blvd, North Hollywood, CA 91606, 818-763-2563

Modern Welding School
1740 Broadway, Schenectady, NY 12306, 518-374-1216

Moler Barber College
3500 Broadway St, Oakland, CA 94611, 510-652-4177

Moler Barber College
517 SW Fourth St, Portland, OR 97204, 503-223-9818

Moler Barber College
727 J St, Sacramento, CA 95814, 916-441-0072

Moler Barber College
50 Mason St, San Francisco, CA 94102, 415-362-5885

Moler Barber College of Hairstyling
16 S Eighth St, Fargo, ND 58103, 701-232-6773

Moler Barber College, (Branch Campus)
2645 El Camino Ave, Sacramento, CA 95821, 916-482-0871

Moler Barber College, (Branch Campus)
410 E Weber Ave, Stockton, CA 95202, 209-465-3218

Moler Barber School of Hairstyling
1411 Nicollet Ave, Minneapolis, MN 55403, 612-871-3754

Moler Hairstyling College
5840 W Madison St, Chicago, IL 60644, 312-287-2552

Monongalia Country Technical Education Center
1000 Mississippi St, Morgantown, WV 26505, 304-291-9240

Moore Career College
2460 Terry Rd, Jackson, MS 39204, 601-371-2900

Moore Career College, (Branch Campus)
1500 N 31st Ave, Hattiesburg, MS 39401, 601-583-4100

Moore Career College, (Branch Campus)
1500 Hwy 19, Meridian, MS 39307, 601-693-2900

Moore Career College, (Branch Campus)
880 Cliff Gookin Blvd, Tupelo, MS 38801, 606-842-7600

Morse School of Business
275 Asylum St, Hartford, CT 06103, 203-522-2261

Motech Education Center
35155 Industrial Rd, Livonia, MI 48150, 313-522-9510

Moultrie Area Technical Institute
315 Industrial Park Dr, Moultrie, GA 31776, 912-985-2297

Moultrie Area Technical Institute, (Branch Campus)
314 E 14th St, Tifton, GA 31794, 912-382-2767

Mr. David's School of Hair Design
4348 Market St, Wilmington, NC 28403, 919-763-4418

Mundus Institute
4745 N Seventh St #100, Phoenix, AZ 85014, 602-248-8548

Munson-Williams-Proctor Institute
310 Genesee St, Utica, NY 13502, 315-797-8260

Music Center of the North Shore
300 Green Bay Rd, Winnetka, IL 60093, 708-446-3822

Music Tech
304 N Washington Ave, Minneapolis, MN 55401, 612-338-0175

Musicians Institute
1655 N McCadden Pl, Hollywood, CA 90028, 213-462-1384

Myotherapy Institute of Utah
3350 S 2300 E, Salt Lake City, UT 84109, 801-484-7624

N

NEI College of Technology
825 41st Ave NE, Columbia Heights, MN 55421, 612-781-4881

NHRAW Home Study Institute
PO Box 16790, Columbus, OH 43216, 614-488-1835

Napoleon Hill Foundation
1440 Paddock Dr, Northbrook, IL 60062, 708-998-0408

Nasson Institute
286 Main St, Pawtucket, RI 02860, 401-728-1570

Nasson Institute, (Branch Campus)
1276 Bald Hill Rd, Warwick, RI 02886, 401-823-3773

Nasson Institute, (Branch Campus)
191 Social St, Woonsocket, RI 02895, 401-769-2066

Natchitoches Technical Institute
200 Hwy 3110 S Bypass, Natchitoches, LA 71458, 318-357-3162

National Academy for Casino Dealers
557 S Sahara Ave #108, Las Vegas, NV 89104, 702-735-4884

National Aviation Academy
St Pete/Clearwater Airport #228, Clearwater, FL 34622, 813-531-2080

National Business Institute
243 W Ponce de Leon Ave, Decatur, GA 30030, 404-352-0800

National Career College
1351 McFarland Blvd E, Tuscaloosa, AL 35405, 205-758-9091

National Career Institute
17601-A E 40 Hwy, Independence, MO 64055, 816-373-6292

National Career Institute
3910 US Hwy 301 N #200, Tampa, FL 33619, 813-620-1446

National Career Institute, (Branch Campus)
1209 N Seventh St, Harlingen, TX 78550, 512-425-4183

National Conservatory of Dramatic Arts
1556 Wisconsin Ave NW, Washington, DC 20007, 202-333-2202

National Cryptologic School
9800 Savage Rd, Fort Meade, MD 20755, 410-859-6136

National Education Center - Arizona Automotive Institute
6829 N 46th Ave, Glendale, AZ 85301, 800-528-0717

National Education Center - Arkansas College of Technology
9720 Rodney Parham Rd, Little Rock, AR 72207, 501-224-8200

National Education Center - Bauder College Campus
4801 N Dixie Hwy, Fort Lauderdale, FL 33334, 305-491-7171

National Education Center - Bryman Campus
1120 N Brookhurst St, Anaheim, CA 92801, 714-778-6500

National Education Center - Bryman Campus
5350 Atlantic Ave, Long Beach, CA 90805, 310-422-6007

National Education Center - Bryman Campus
1017 Wilshire Blvd, Los Angeles, CA 90017, 213-481-1640

National Education Center - Bryman Campus
3505 N Hart Ave, Rosemead, CA 91770, 818-573-5470

National Education Center - Bryman Campus
731 Market St, San Francisco, CA 94103, 415-777-2500

National Education Center - Bryman Campus
2015 Naglee Ave, San Jose, CA 95128, 408-275-8800

National Education Center - Bryman Campus
4212 W Artesia Blvd, Torrance, CA 90504, 310-542-6951

National Education Center - Bryman Campus
20835 Sherman Way, Winnetka, CA 91306, 818-887-7911

National Education Center - Bryman Campus, (Branch Campus)
2322 Canal St, New Orleans, LA 70119, 504-822-4500

National Education Center - Bryman Campus, (Branch Campus)
1600 Broadway 3rd Flr, Oakland, CA 94612, 510-763-0800

National Education Center - Kee Business College
803 Dilligence Dr, Newport News, VA 23606, 804-873-1111

National Education Center - Tampa Technical Institute
2410 E Busch Blvd, Tampa, FL 33612, 813-935-5700

National Education Center Allentown Campus
1501 Lehigh St, Allentown, PA 18103, 215-791-5100

National Education Center Sawyer Campus
8475 Jackson Rd, Sacramento, CA 95826, 916-383-1909

National Education Center-Bryman Campus
40 Marietta St 8th Flr, Atlanta, GA 30303, 404-524-8800

National Education Center-Bryman Campus
323 Boylston St, Brookline, MA 02146, 617-232-6035

National Education Center-National Institute of Technology Campus
1225 Orlen Ave, Cuyahoga Falls, OH 44221, 216-923-9959

National Education Center-National Institute of Technology Campus
18000 Newburgh Rd, Livonia, MI 48152, 313-464-7387

National Education Center-National Institute of Technology Campus
3622 Fredericksburg Rd, San Antonio, TX 78201, 210-733-6000

National Education Center-National Institute of Technology Campus
2620 Remicl St SW, Wyoming, MI 49509, 616-538-3170

National Education Center-RETS Campus
103 Park Ave, Nutley, NJ 07110, 201-661-0600

National Education Center, (Branch Campus)
4244 Oakman Blvd, Detroit, MI 48204, 313-834-1400

National Education Center, (Branch Campus)
7955 NW 12th St #300, Miami, FL 33126, 305-477-0251

National Education Center, (Fort Worth Campus)
300 E Loop 820, Fort Worth, TX 76112, 817-451-0017

National Education Center, (San Jose Campus)
1302 N Fourth St, San Jose, CA 95112, 408-452-8800

National Hispanic University
135 E Gish Rd #201, San Jose, CA 95112, 408-441-2000

National Hispanic University, (Branch Campus)
262 Grand Ave 2nd Flr, Oakland, CA 94601, 510-451-0511

National School of Technology
16150 NE 17th Ave, N Miami Beach, FL 33162, 305-949-9500

National School of Technology, (Branch Campus)
4355 W 16th Ave, Hialeah, FL 33012, 305-558-9500

National Shakespeare Conservatory
591 Broadway, New York, NY 10012, 212-219-9874

National Tax Training School
PO Box 382, Monsey, NY 10952, 914-352-3634

National Tractor Trailer School
PO Box 208, Liverpool, NY 13088, 315-451-2430

National Tractor Trailer School, (Branch Campus)
175 Katherine St, Buffalo, NY 14210, 716-849-6886

National Training, Inc.
PO Box 1899, Orange Park, FL 32067, 904-272-4000

Naval Air Technical Training Center
Naval Air Station, Memphis, Millington, TN 38054, 901-872-5306

Naval Air Technical Training Center, (Branch Campus)
Hanger 1, Lakehurst, NJ 08733, 908-323-2300

Naval Amphibious School
Bldg 401, San Diego, CA 92155, 619-437-2236

Naval Construction Training Center
Port Hueneme, CA 93043, 805-982-5556

Naval Constructions Training Center
5510 CBC 8th St, Gulfport, MS 39501, 601-865-2531

Naval Damage Control Training Center
Naval Base, Philadelphia, PA 19112, 215-897-5677

Naval Diving and Salvage Training Center
Panama City, FL 32407, 9040235-5207

Naval Guided Missiles School
2025 Tartar Ave, Virginia Beach, VA 23461, 804-433-6628

Naval Health Sciences Education and Training Command
8901 Wisconsin Ave, Bethesda, MD 20889, 301-295-0203

Naval Health Sciences Education and Training Command, (Aerospace Medical Institute)
Pensacola, FL 32508, 904-452-4554

Naval Health Sciences Education and Training Command, (Dental School-Maxillofacial)
Nat'l Naval Dental Ctr, Bethesda, MD 20889, 301-295-0064

Naval Health Sciences Education and Training Command, (Field Medical Service School)
Camp Lejeune, NC 28542, 919-451-0929

Naval Health Sciences Education and Training Command, (Field Medical Service School)
Camp Pendleton, CA 92055, 619-725-7139

Naval Health Sciences Education and Training Command, (Hospital Corps School)
Great Lakes, IL 60088, 708-688-5680

Naval Health Sciences Education and Training Command, (Opthalmis Support and Training)
Yorktown, VA 23691, 804-887-7611

Naval Health Sciences Education and Training Command, (School of Dental Assisting)
Naval Station, San Diego, CA 92136, 619-556-8262

Naval Health Sciences Education and Training Command, (School of Health Science)
Nat'l Naval Medical Ctr, Bethesda, MD 20889, 301-295-1204

Naval Health Sciences Education and Training Command, (School of Health Science)
Oakland, CA 94627, 510-633-6065

Naval Health Sciences Education and Training Command, (School of Health Science)
Portsmouth, VA 23708, 804-398-5032

Naval Health Sciences Education and Training Command, (School of Health Science)
San Diego, CA 92134, 619-532-7700

Naval Health Sciences Education and Training Command, (Undersea Medical Institute)
Groton, CT 06349, 203-449-3365

Naval Service School Command
Naval Training Center, Orlando, FL 32813, 407-646-4122

Naval Service School Command
Naval Training Ctr, San Diego, CA 92133, 619-524-4857

Naval Technical Training Center
740 Fletcher Rd #100, Meridian, MS 39309, 601-769-2724

Naval Technical Training Center
Corry St, 640 Roberts Ave #112, Pensacola, FL 32511, 904-452-6558

Naval Technical Training Center
Treasure Island, 1070 M Ave, San Francisco, CA 94130, 415-395-3073

Naval Transportation Management School
Oakland Army Base Bldg 790, Oakland, CA 94626, 510-466-2155

Navy Fleet and Mine Warfare Training Center
Charleston Naval Base, Charleston, SC 29408, 803-743-4722

Navy Supply Corps School
Athens, GA 30606, 404-354-7200

Navy and Marine Corps Intelligence Training Center
2088 Regulus Ave #420, Virginia Beach, VA 23461, 804-433-8001

Neighborhood Playhouse School of Theatre
340 E 54th St, New York, NY 10022, 212-688-3770

Nell Institute
2101 IH 35S 3rd Fl, Austin, TX 78741, 512-447-9415

New England Hair Academy
492-500 Main St, Malden, MA 02148, 617-324-6799

New England Institute of Technology at Palm Beach
1126 53rd Ct, West Palm Beach, FL 33407, 407-842-8324

New England School of Accounting
155 Ararat St, Worcester, MA 01606, 508-853-8972

New England School of Acupuncture
30 Common St, Watertown, MA 02172, 617-926-1788

New England School of Broadcasting
One College Cir, Bangor, ME 04401, 207-947-6083

New England School of Photography
537 Commonwealt Ave, Boston, MA 02215, 617-437-1868

New England Technical College
2500 Post Rd, Warwick, RI 02886, 401-739-5000

New England Technical Institute of Connecticut
200 John Downey Dr, New Britain, CT 06051, 203-225-8641

New England Tractor Trailer Training School
1410 Bush St, Baltimore, MD 21230, 410-783-0100

The Sourcebook of College and University Student Records

New England Tractor Trailer Training School
3715 E Thompson St, Philadelphia, PA 19137, 215-288-7800

New England Tractor Trailer Training School of Connecticut
32 Field Rd, Somers, CT 06071, 203-749-0711

New England Tractor Trailer Training School of Massachusetts
1093 N Montello St, Brockton, MA 02401, 508-587-1100

New England Tractor Trailer Training School of Rhode Island
10 Dunnell Ln, Pawtucket, RI 02860, 401-725-1220

New Image Careers
109 E Sixth St, Corbin, KY 40701, 606-528-1490

New Orleands Regional Technical Institute
980 Navarre Ave, New Orleans, LA 71024, 504-483-4666

New School of Contemporary Radio
50 Colvin Ave, Albany, NY 12206, 518-438-7682

New Tyler Barber College Inc.
1211 E Seventh St, North Little Rock, AR 72114, 501-375-0377

New World College of Business
1031 Noble St, Anniston, AL 36201, 205-236-7578

New York Food & Hotel Management School
154 W 14th St, New York, NY 10011, 212-675-6655

New York Institute of Business and Technology
401 Park Ave S 2nd Fl, New York, NY 10016, 212-725-9400

New York School for Medical/Dental Assistants
116-16 Queens Blvd, Forest Hills, NY 11375, 718-793-2330

New York School of Dog Grooming
248 E 34th St, New York, NY 10016, 212-685-3776

New York School of Dog Grooming, (Branch Campus)
265-17 Union Tpke, New Hyde Park, NY 11040, 718-343-3130

New York Technical Institute of Hawaii
1375 Dillingham Blvd, Honolulu, HI 96817, 808-841-5827

Newbridge College
700 El Camino Real, Tustin, CA 92680, 714-573-8787

Newschool of Architecture
1249 F St, San Diego, CA 92101, 619-235-4100

Nichols Career Center
609 Union St, Jefferson City, MO 65101, 314-659-3000

Nick Randazzo Vocational Training Institute
125 Lafayette St, Gretna, LA 70053, 504-366-5409

Nikolais and Louis Dance Lab
375 W Broadway 5th Fl, New York, NY 10012, 212-226-7000

Norfolk Skills Center
922 W 21st St, Norfolk, VA 23517, 804-441-2665

North American Institute of Aviation
PO Box 680, Conway, SC 29526, 803-397-9111

North Bennet Street School
39 N Bennet St, Boston, MA 02113, 617-227-0155

North Carolina Academy of Cosmetic Art
131 Sixth Ave E, Hendersonville, NC 28739, 919-876-9210

North Central Institute
2469 Fort Campbell Blvd, Clarksville, TN 37042, 615-552-6200

North Central Kansas Area Vocational-Technical School
PO Box 507, Beloit, KS 67420, 913-738-2276

North Central Kansas Area Vocational-Technical School, (Hays Campus)
2205 Wheatland, Hays, KS 67601, 913-625-2437

North Central Technical Institute
605 N Boundary, Farmerville, LA 71241, 318-368-3179

North Fulton Beauty College
10930 Crabapple Rd, Roswell, GA 30075, 404-552-9570

North Hills School of Health Occupations
1500 Northway Mall, Pittsburgh, PA 15237, 412-367-8003

North Metro Technical Institute
5198 Ross Rd, Acworth, GA 30102, 404-975-4010

North Mississippi EMS Authority
PO Box 377, Tupelo, MS 38802, 601-844-5870

North Park College
3956 30th St, San Diego, CA 92104, 619-297-3333

North Park College, (Branch Campus)
4718 Clairemont Mesa Blvd, San Diego, CA 92117, 619-297-3333

North Technical Education Center
7071 Garden Rd, Riviera Beach, FL 33404, 407-881-4600

North Valley Occupational Center
11450 Sharp Ave, Mission Hills, CA 91345, 818-365-9645

Northeast Broadcasting School
142 Berkeley St, Boston, MA 02116, 617-267-7910

Northeast Career Schools
749 E Industrial Park Dr, Manchester, NH 03109, 603-669-1151

Northeast Institute of Industrial Technology
41 Phillips St, Boston, MA 02114, 617-523-2869

Northeast Louisiana Technical Institute
1710 Warren St, Winnsboro, LA 71295, 318-435-2163

Northern Arizona College of Health Careers
2575 E Seventh Ave, Flagstaff, AZ 86004, 602-526-0763

Northern Arizona Institute of Technology
1120 Kaibab La, Flagstaff, AZ 86001, 602-779-4532

Northern Arizona Institute of Technology, (Branch Campus)
11300 Lomas Blvd NE, Albuquerque, NM 87112, 505-231-4097

Northern Hospital of Surry County School of Medical Technology
PO Box 1101, Mount Airy, NC 27030, 919-789-9541

Northwest College of Medical & Dental Assistants
530 E Union Ave, Pasadena, CA 91101, 818-796-5815

Northwest College of Medical & Dental Assistants
134 W Holt Ave, Pomona, CA 91768, 714-623-1552

Northwest College of Medical & Dental Assistants
2121 W Garvey Ave, West Covina, CA 91790, 818-960-5046

Northwest College of Medical & Dental Assistants, (Branch Campus)
124 S Glendale Ave, Glendale, CA 91205, 818-242-0205

Northwest Louisiana Technical Institute
814 Constable St, Minden, LA 71055, 318-371-3035

Non-Degree Granting Institutions

Northwest School of Wooden Boatbuilding
251 Otto St, Port Townsend, WA 98368, 206-385-4948

Nova Institute of Health Technolgy
3000 S Robertson Blvd, Los Angeles, CA 90034, 310-840-5777

Nova Institute of Health Technolgy
520 N Euclid Ave, Ontario, CA 91762, 714-984-5027

Nova Institute of Health Technolgy
11416 Whittier Blvd, Whittier, CA 90601, 310-695-0771

Nu-Tek Academy of Beauty
Mount Sterling Plaza, Mount Sterling, KY 40353, 606-498-4460

O

O.T. Autry Area Vocational-Technical Center
1201 W Willow St, Enid, OK 73703, 405-242-2750

Oakbridge Academy of Arts
401 Ninth St, New Kensington, PA 15068, 412-335-5336

Oakdale Technical Institute
Old Pelican Hwy, Oakdale, LA 71463, 318-335-3944

Occupational Education Center-Central
3075 Alton Rd, Chamblee, GA 30341, 404-457-3393

Occupational Education Center-North
1995 Womack Rd, Dunwoody, GA 30338, 404-394-0321

Occupational Education Center-South
3303 Pantherville Rd, Decatur, GA 30034, 404-241-9600

Occupational Safety Training Institute
8415 W Bellfort St #300, Houston, TX 77031, 713-270-6882

Ocean Corporation
10840 Rockley Rd, Houston, TX 77099, 713-530-0202

Ocean State Business Institute
140 Point Judith Rd, Narragansett, RI 02882, 401-789-0287

Ochsner School of Allied Health Sciences
880 Commerce Rd W, New Orleans, LA 70123, 504-838-3232

Oconaluftee Job Corps Civilian Conservation Center
200 Park Cir, Cherokee, NC 28719, 704-497-5411

Office Careers Centre
7001 Grapevine Hwy #202, Fort Worth, TX 76180, 817-284-8107

Ogeechee Technical Institute
One Joe Kennedy Blvd, Statesboro, GA 30458, 912-764-8530

Ohio Auto-Diesel Technical Institute
1421 E 49th St, Cleveland, OH 44103, 216-881-1700

Ohio State College of Barber Styling
329 Superior St, Toledo, OH 43604, 419-241-5618

Ohio State College of Barber Styling, (Branch Campus)
4614 E Broad St, Columbus, OH 43223, 614-868-1015

Ohio State College of Barber Styling, (Branch Campus)
4390 Karl Rd, Columbus, OH 43224, 614-267-4247

Okefenokee Technical Institute
1701 Carswell Ave, Waycross, GA 31503, 912-283-2002

Oklahoma Farrier's College
Rte 2 Box 88, Sperry, OK 74073, 918-288-7221

Oklahoma State Horseshoeing School
Rte 1 Box 28B, Ardmore, OK 73401, 405-223-0064

Omaha College of Health Careers
10845 Harney St, Omaha, NE 68154, 402-333-1400

Omaha Opportunities Industrialization Center
2724 N 24th St, Omaha, NE 68110, 402-457-4222

Omega Institute
Rte 130 S, Cinnaminson, NJ 08077, 609-786-2200

Omege Travel School
3102 Omega Office Park, Fairfax, VA 22031, 703-359-8830

Omni Technical School
2242 W Broward Blvd, Fortlauderdale, FL 33312, 305-584-4730

Omni Technical School
1710 NW Seventh St, Miami, FL 33125, 305-541-6200

Orange County Business College
2035 E Ball Rd, Anaheim, CA 92805, 714-722-6941

Oregon School of Arts and Crafts
824t SW Barnes Rd, Portland, OR 97225, 503-297-5544

Orlando Vocational-Technical Center
301 W Amelia St, Orlando, FL 32801, 305-425-2756

Orleans Technical Institute
1330 Rhawn St, Philadelphia, PA 19111, 215-728-4700

Orleans Technical Institute, (Court Reporting Institute)
1845 Walnut St #700, Philadelphia, PA 19103, 215-854-1823

P

PCI Dealers School
920 S Valley View Blvd, Las Vegas, NV 89107, 702-877-4724

PCI Health Training Center
8101 John Carpenter Fwy, Dallas, TX 75247, 214-630-0568

PHD Hair Academy
27380 US Hwy 19 N, Clearwater, FL 34621, 813-791-7438

PJ's College of Cosmetology
Russellville Rd, Bowling Green, KY 42101, 502-842-8149

PJ's College of Cosmetology
124 W Washington St, Glasgow, KY 42141, 502-651-6553

PJ's College of Cosmetology, (Branch Campus)
113 N Washington St, Crawfordsville, IN 47933, 800-627-2566

PJ's College of Cosmetology, (Branch Campus)
1400 W Main St, Greenfield, IN 46140, 800-627-2566

PJ's College of Cosmetology, (Branch Campus)
5539 S Madison Ave, Indianapolis, IN 46227, 800-627-2566

PJ's College of Cosmetology, (Branch Campus)
3023 S Lafountain St, Kokomo, IN 46902, 800-627-2566

PJ's College of Cosmetology, (Branch Campus)
2006 N Walnut St, Muncie, IN 47303, 800-627-2566

PJ's College of Cosmetology, (Branch Campus)
2026 Stafford Rd, Plainfield, IN 46168, 800-627-2566

PJA School
7900 W Chester Pike, Upper Darby, PA 19082, 215-789-6700

PPI Health Careers School
2345 N Academy Blvd, Colorado Springs, CO 80909, 719-596-7400

PTC Career Institute
529 14th St NW #350, Washington, DC 20004, 202-638-5300

Pacific Coast College
1261 Third Ave #B, Chula Vista, CA 91911, 619-691-0882

Pacific Coast College
118 W Fifth St, Santa Ana, CA 92701, 714-558-8700

Pacific Gateway College
3018 Carmel St, Los Angeles, CA 90065, 818-247-9544

Pacific Northwest Ballet School
4649 Sunnyside Ave N, Seattle, WA 98103, 206-547-5910

Pacific Travel School
2515 N Main St, Santa Ana, CA 92701, 714-543-9495

Palm Beach Beauty & Barber School
4645 Gun Club Rd, West Palm Beach, FL 33415, 407-638-1238

Paralegal Careers
1211 N Westshore Blvd #100, Tampa, FL 33607, 813-289-6025

Paramedic Training Institute
PO Box 1878, Beaverton, OR 97075, 503-297-5592

Pathfinder Training Institute
19 E 21st St, Chicago, IL 60616, 312-842-7272

Patricia Stevens College
1415 Olive St, St Louis, MO 63103, 314-421-0949

Payne-Pulliam School of Trade and Commerce
2345 Cass Ave, Detroit, MI 48201, 313-963-4710

Pedigree Career Institute
Harbor Mall, Lynn, MA 01901, 617-592-3647

Pedigree Career Institute
3037 W Clarendon Ave, Phoenix, AZ 85017, 602-264-3647

Pedigree Career Institute
3781 E Technical Dr #1, Tucson, AZ 85713, 602-745-3647

Penn Commercial College
82 S Main St, Washington, PA 15301, 412-222-5330

Pennco Tech
PO Box 1427, Blackwood, NJ 08012, 609-232-0310

Pennsylvania Gunsmith School
812 Ohio River Blvd, Pittsburgh, PA 15202, 412-766-1812

Pennsylvania Institute of Culinary Arts
717 LIberty Ave, Pittsburgh, PA 15222, 412-566-2433

Pennsylvania Institute of Taxidermy
rural Ret 3 Box 188, Ebensburg, PA 15931, 814-472-4510

Pennsylvania School of Art and Design
204 N Prince St, Lancaster, PA 17603, 717-396-7833

Perry Technical Institute
2011 W Washington Ave, Yakima, WA 98903, 509-453-0374

Philadelphia Wireless Technical Institute
1533 Pine St, Philadelphia, PA 19102, 215-546-0745

Phillips Business College
PO Box 169, Lynchburg, VA 24505, 804-847-7701

Phillips Junior College
1491 S Nova Rd, Daytona Beach, FL 32114, 904-255-1707

Phillips Junior College, (Branch Campus)
2401 N Harbor City Blvd, Melbourne, FL 32935, 407-254-6459

Pickens Technical Institute
100 Pickens Tech Dr, Jasper, GA 30143, 404-692-3411

Pima Medical Institute
1627 Eastlake Ave E, Seattle, WA 98102, 206-322-6100

Pinellas Technical Education Center
6100 154th Ave N, Clearwater, FL 34620, 813-531-3531

Pinellas Technical Education Center-St. Petersburg Campus
910 34th St, St. Petersburg, FL 33711, 813-327-3671

Pinellas Technical Education Center, (Branch Campus)
14400 49th St N, Clearwater, FL 34620, 813-531-3531

Pinellas Technical Education Center, (Branch Campus)
2375 Whitney Rd, Clearwater, FL 34620, 813-530-0617

Platt College
3100 S Parker Rd, Aurora, CO 80014, 303-369-5151

Platt College
10900 E 183rd St #290, Cerritos, CA 90701, 310-809-5100

Platt College
2361 McGaw Ave, Irvine, CA 92714, 714-833-2300

Platt College
7470 N Figueroa St, Los Angeles, CA 90041, 213-258-8050

Platt College
2920 Inland Empire Blvd #102, Ontario, CA 91764, 909-989-1187

Platt College
6250 El Cajon Blvd, San Diego, CA 92115, 619-265-0107

Platt College
301 Mission St #450, San Francisco, CA 94105, 415-495-4000

Platt College
4821 S 72nd E Ave, Tulsa, OK 74145, 918-663-9000

Platt College, (Branch Campus)
3737 N Portland Ave, Oklahoma City, OK 73112, 405-942-8683

Plaza School
Bergen Mall, Paramus, NJ 07652, 201-843-0344

Politechnical Institute
1405 SW 107th Ave #201-C, Miami, FL 33174, 305-226-8099

Polytechnic Institute
4625 North Fwy #109, Houston, TX 77022, 713-694-6027

Pompano Academy of Aeronautics
1006 NE 10th St, Pompano Beach, FL 33060, 800-545-7262

Pontiac Business Institute
PO Box 459, Oxford, MI 48371, 313-628-4846

Porter and Chester Institute
PO Box 364, Stratford, CT 06497, 203-375-4463

Porter and Chester Institute, (Branch Campus)
138 Weymouth St, Enfield, CT 06082, 800-870-6789

Porter and Chester Institute, (Branch Campus)
320 Sylvan Lake Rd, Watertown, CT 06779, 203-274-9294

Porter and Chester Institute, (Branch Campus)
125 Silas Deane Hwy, Wethersfield, CT 06109, 203-529-2519

Portfolio Center
125 Bennett St NW, Atlanta, GA 30309, 404-351-5055

Potomac Academy of Hair Design
9191 Center St, Manassas, VA 22110, 703-361-7775

Pounter Institute for Media Studies
801 Third St S, St. Petersburg, FL 33701, 813-821-9494

Practical Schools
900 E Ball Rd, Anaheim, CA 92805, 714-535-6000

Presbyterian-St. Luke Center for Health Science Foundation
1719 E 19th Ave, Denver, CO 80218, 303-839-6740

Prince Institute of Professional Studies
7735 Atlanta Hwy, Montgomery, AL 36117, 205-271-1670

Pro-Way Hair School
8-B Franklin Rd, Newnan, GA 30263, 404-251-4592

Pro-Way Hair School, (Branch Campus)
3099 S Perkins Rd, Memphis, TN 38118, 901-363-3553

Professional Business Institute
125 Canal St, New York, NY 10002, 212-226-7300

Professional Career Development Institute
3597 Parkway Ln #100, Norcross, GA 30092, 404-729-8400

Professional Careers Institute
2611 Waterfront Pkwy, Indianapolis, IN 46214, 317-299-6001

Professional Careers
3305 Spring Mountain Rd #7, Las Vegas, NV 89193, 702-368-2338

Professional Court Reporting School
1401 N Central Expy, Richardson, TX 75080, 214-231-9502

Professional Hair Design Academy
1540 Wade Hampton Blvd, Greenville, SC 29607, 803-232-2676

Professional Skills Institute
1232 Flaire Dr, Toledo, OH 43615, 419-531-9610

Professional Skills Institute, (Santa Barbara Campus)
4213 State St #302, Santa Barbara, CA 93110, 805-683-1902

Provo College
1450 W 820 N, Provo, UT 84601, 801-375-1861

Q

QUALTEC Institute for Competitive Advantage
11760 US Hwy 1, North Palm Beach, FL 33408, 800-247-9871

Quality Plus Office Skills and Motivational Training Center
1655 Peachtree St #450, Atlanta, GA 30309, 404-892-6669

Queen City College
1191 Fort Campbell Blvd, Clarksville, TN 37042, 615-645-2361

Queen City College, (Branch Campus)
800 Hwy 1 S, Greenville, MS 38701, 601-334-9120

Quincy Technical Schools
501 N Third St, Quincy, IL 62301, 800-438-5621

R

R/S Institute
7122 Lawndale Ave, Houston, TX 77023, 713-923-6968

RETS Electronic Schools
965 Commonwealth Ave, Boston, MA 02215, 617-783-1197

RHDC Hair Design College
3209 N Main St, Fort Worth, TX 76106, 817-624-0871

RTI Technical Institute
1412 W Fairfield Dr, Pensacola, FL 32501, 904-433-6547

Radford M. Locklin Vocational-Technical Center
5330 Berryhill Rd, Milton, FL 32570, 904-626-1918

Raedel College and Industrial Welding School
137 Sixth St NE, Canton, OH 44702, 216-454-9006

Ralph Amodei INternational Institute of Hair Design & Technology
4451 Frankford Ave, Philadelphia, PA 19124, 215-289-4433

Rasmussen College St. Cloud
245 N 37th Ave, St Cloud, MN 56303, 612-251-5600

Recreational Vehicle Service Academy
1127 Ellenton Gillette Rd, Ellenton, FL 34222, 813-722-7244

Red River Technical College
PO Box 140, Hope, AR 71801, 501-777-5722

Refrigeration School
4210 E Washington St, Phoenix, AZ 85034, 602-275-7133

Refrigeration School of New Orleans
1201 Mazant St, New Orleans, LA 70117, 504-949-2712

Reporting Academy of Virginia
Pembroke Five #128, Virginia Beach, VA 23462, 804-499-5447

Reporting Academy of Virginia, (Branch Campus)
1001 Boulders Pkwy #305, Richmond, VA 23225, 804-232-1020

Reporting Academy of Virginia, (Branch Campus)
5501 Backlick Rd #250, Springfield, VA 22151, 703-658-0588

Rice Aviation, a Division of A&J Enterprises
8880 Telephone Rd, Houston, TX 77061, 713-644-6616

Rice Aviation, a Division of A&J Enterprises, (Branch Campus)
701 Wilson Point Rd, Baltimore, MD 21220, 410-682-2226

Rice Aviation, a Division of A&J Enterprises, (Branch Campus)
5202 W Military Hwy Hanger 7, Chesapeake, VA 23321, 804-465-2813

Rice Aviation, a Division of A&J Enterprises, (Branch Campus)
7811 N Shepherd Dr #100, Houston, TX 77088, 713-591-2908

Rice Aviation, a Division of A&J Enterprises, (Branch Campus)
8911 Aviation Blvd, Inglewood, CA 90301, 310-337-4444

Rice Aviation, a Division of A&J Enterprises, (Branch Campus)
3201 E Broadway, Phoenix, AZ 85040, 602-243-6611

Rice College
2116 Bessemer Rd, Birmingham, AL 35208, 205-781-8600

Rice College
2485 Union Ave, Memphis, TN 38112, 901-324-7423

Rice College, (Branch Campus)
2525 Robinson Rd, Jackson, MS 39209, 601-355-8100

Rice College, (Branch Campus)
5430 Norwood Ave, Jacksonville, FL 32208, 904-765-7300

Rice College, (Branch Campus)
1515 Magnolia Ave, Knoxville, TN 37917, 615-637-9899

Richard M. Milburne High School
14416 Jefferson Davis Hwy #12, Woodbridge, VA 22191, 703-494-0147

Ridge Vocational-Technical Center
7700 State Rd 544, Winter Haven, FL 33881, 813-422-6402

Ridley-Lowell Business and Technical Institute
116 Front St, Binghamton, NY 13905, 607-724-2941

Ridley-Lowell Business and Technical Institute
PO Box 652, New London, CT 06320, 203-443-7441

Riley College
4129 Ross Clark Cir NW, Dothan, AL 36303, 205-794-4296

Riley College, (Branch Campus)
610 W Oglethorpe Blvd, Albany, GA 31701, 912-883-8048

Riley College, (Branch Campus)
901-A Jeff Davis St, Selma, AL 36701, 205-782-2904

River Parishes Technical Institute
251 Regala Park Rd, Reserve, LA 70084, 504-536-4418

Robert Morgan Vocational-Technical Center
18180 SW 122nd Ave, Miami, FL 33177, 305-253-9920

Roberto-Venn School of Luthiery
4011 S 16th St, Phoenix, AZ 85040, 602-243-1179

Rockford School of Practical Nursing
978 Haskell Ave, Rockford, IL 61103, 815-966-3716

Roffler Academy for Hairstylists
454 Park St, Hartford, CT 06106, 203-522-2359

Roffler Academy for Hairstylists, (Branch Campus)
709 Queen St, Southington, CT 06489, 203-620-9260

Roffler Moler Hairstyling College
PO Box 518, Forest Park, GA 30050, 404-366-2838

Roffler Moler Hairstyling College, (Branch Campus)
1311 Roswell Rd, Marietta, GA 30062, 404-565-3285

Rolla Area Vocational-Technical School
1304 E Tenth St, Rolla, MO 65401, 314-364-3726

Romar Beauty Academy
1608 S Federal Hwy, Boynton Beach, FL 33435, 407-737-3430

Rosedale Technical Institute
4634 Browns Hill Rd, Pittsburgh, PA 15217, 412-521-6200

Ross Business Institute
22293 Eureka Rd, Taylor, MI 48180, 313-374-2135

Ross Business Institute, (Branch Campus)
37065 Gratiot, Clinton Township, MI 48036, 313-954-3083

Ross Business Institute, (Branch Campus)
1285 N Telegraph Rd, Monroe, MI 48161, 313-243-5456

Ross Medical Education Center
1036 Gilbert Rd, Flint, MI 48532, 313-230-1100

Ross Medical Education Center
913 W Holmes Rd #260, Lansing, MI 48910, 517-887-0180

Ross Medical Education Center
26417 Hoover Rd, Warren, MI 48089, 313-758-7200

Ross Medical Education Center, (Branch Campus)
15670 E Eight Mile Rd, Detroit, MI 48205, 313-371-2131

Ross Medical Education Center, (Branch Campus)
2035 28th St SE #O, Grand Rapids, MI 49508, 616-243-3070

Ross Medical Education Center, (Branch Campus)
1188 N West Ave, Jackson, MI 49202, 517-782-7677

Ross Medical Education Center, (Branch Campus)
950 W Norton Ave, Roosevelt Park, MI 48441, 616-739-1531

Ross Medical Education Center, (Branch Campus)
4054 Bay Rd, Saginaw, MI 48603, 517-793-9800

Ross Medical Education Center, (Branch Campus)
253 Summit Dr, Waterford, MI 48328, 313-683-1166

Ross Medical Education Center, (Ross Technical Institute)
1490 S Military Tr #11, West Palm Beach, FL 33415, 407-433-1288

Ross Technical Institute
5757 Whitmore Lake Rd #800, Brighton, MI 48116, 313-227-0160

Ross Technical Institute
1553 Woodward Ave #650, Detroit, MI 48226, 313-965-7451

Ross Technical Institute, (Branch Campus)
4703 Washtenaw Ave, Ann Arbor, MI 48108, 313-434-7320

Ross Technical Institute, (Branch Campus)
20820 Greenfield Rd 1st Fl, Oak Park, MI 48237, 313-967-3100

Rosston School of Hair Design
673 W Fifth St, San Bernardino, CA 92410, 714-884-2719

Roy's of Louisville Beauty Academy
151 Chenoweth Ln, Louisville, KY 40207, 502-897-9401

Roy's of Louisville Beauty Academy, (Branch Campus)
5200 Dixie Hwy, Louisville, KY 40216, 502-448-1016

Royal Academy of Hair Design
200 W Main St, Clinton, SC 29325, 803-833-6976

Royal Barber & Beauty School
108-112 Broadway, Schenectady, NY 12305, 518-346-2288

Ruston Technical Institute
1010 James St, Ruston, LA 71270, 318-251-4145

S

S.W. School of Business & Technical Careers
100 Main St, Eagle Pass, TX 78852, 512-733-1373

S.W. School of Business & Technical Careers
505 E Travis, San Antonio, TX 78205, 512-225-7287

S.W. School of Business & Technical Careers
602 W Southcross Blvd, San Antonio, TX 78221, 512-921-0951

S.W. School of Business & Technical Careers, (Branch Campus)
122 W North St, Uvalde, TX 78801, 512-278-4103

SCS Business and Technical Institute
394 Bridge St, Brooklyn, NY 11201, 718-802-9500

SCS Business and Technical Institute
884 Flatbush Ave, Brooklyn, NY 11226, 718-856-6100

SCS Business and Technical Institute
516 Main St, East Orange, NJ 07017, 201-675-4300

SCS Business and Technical Institute
163-02 Jamaica Ave, Jamaica, NY 11432, 718-658-8855

SCS Business and Technical Institute
25 W 17th St, New York, NY 10022, 212-366-1666

SCS Business and Technical Institute
220 Bergenline Ave, Union City, NJ 07087, 201-867-3500

SER Business and Technical Institute
9301 Michigan Ave, Detroit, MI 48210, 313-846-2240

SER Business and Technical Institute, (Chicago Campus)
5150 W Roosevelt, Chicago, IL 60650, 312-379-1152

SER-IBM Business Institute
42 NW 27th Ave #421, Miami, FL 33125, 305-649-7500

SUTECH School of Vocational-Technical Training
3427 E Olympic Blvd, Los Angeles, CA 90023, 213-262-3210

SUTECH School of Vocational-Technical Training, (Branch Campus)
1815 S Lewis St, Anaheim, CA 90023, 213-262-3210

SYRIT Computer School Systems
1760 53rd St, Brooklyn, NY 11204, 718-853-1212

Sabine Valley Technical Institute
Hwy 171 S, Many, LA 71449, 318-256-5663

Saginaw Beauty Academy
PO Box 423, Saginaw, MI 48601, 517-752-9261

Salisbury Business College
1400 Jake Alexander Blvd W, Salisbury, NC 28147, 704-636-4071

Salter School
155 Ararat St, Worcester, MA 01606, 508-853-1074

Salter School, (Branch Campus)
458 Bridge St, Cambridge, MA 01103, 413-731-7353

SamVerly College
210 Edgewood Ave NE, Atlanta, GA 30303, 404-522-4370

San Antonio College of Medical & Dental Assistants
4205 San Pedro Ave, San Antonio, TX 78202, 512-733-0777

San Antonio College of Medical & Dental Assistants, (Branch Campus)
3900 N 23rd St, Mcallen, TX 78501, 210-360-1499

San Antonio College of Medical & Dental Assistants, (Branch Campus)
5280 Medical Dr #100, San Antonio, TX 78229, 210-692-3829

San Antonio Trade School
120 Playmoor St, San Antonio, TX 78210, 512-533-9126

San Antonio Trade School, (Branch Campus)
117 W Martin, Del Rio, TX 78840, 512-774-5646

San Antonio Training Division
9350 S Presa, San Antonio, TX 78223, 512-633-1000

San Antonio Training Division, (Branch Campus)
Kelly AFB Bldg 210, San Antonio, TX 78241, 210-925-7317

San Antonio Training Division, (Branch Campus)
Hemisfair Park Bldg 277, San Antonio, TX 78291, 512-277-8217

San Francisco Ballet School
455 Franklin St, San Francisco, CA 94102, 415-861-5600

San Francisco Barber College
64 Sixth St, San Francisco, CA 94103, 415-621-6802

San Joaquin Valley College
201 New Stine Rd, Bakersfield, CA 93309, 805-834-0126

San Joaquin Valley College
3333 N Bond St, Fresno, CA 93726, 209-229-7800

San Joaquin Valley College
8400 W Mineral King Ave, Visalia, CA 93291, 209-651-2500

San Joaquin Valley College of Aeronautics
4985 E Andersen Ave, Fresno, CA 93726, 209-229-7800

Sanford-Brown Business College
3237 W Chain of Rocks Rd, Granite City, IL 62040, 618-931-0300

Santa Barbara Business College
211 S Real Rd, Bakersfield, CA 93301, 805-322-3006

Santa Barbara Business College
4333 Hansen Ave, Fremont, CA 94536, 510-793-4342

Santa Barbara Business College
4025 Foothill Rd, Santa Barbara, CA 93110, 805-967-9677

Santa Barbara Business College
303 E Plaza Dr, Santa Maria, CA 93454, 805-922-8256

Sarasota County Technical Institute
4748 Beneva Rd, Sarasota, FL 34233, 813-924-1365

Sawyer College
441 W Trimble Rd, San Jose, CA 95131, 408-954-8200

Sawyer College at Pomona
1021 E Holt Ave, Pomona, CA 91767, 714-629-2534

Sawyer College at Ventura
2101 E gonzales Rd, Oxnard, CA 93030, 805-485-6000

Sawyer College of Business
13027 Lorain Ave, Cleveland, OH 44111, 216-941-7666

Sawyer College of Business
3150 Mayfield Rd, Cleveland Heights, OH 44118, 216-932-0911

Sawyer School
101 Main St, Pawtucket, RI 02860, 401-272-8400

Sawyer School of Business
26051 Hoover Rd, Warren, MI 48089, 313-758-2300

Sawyer School, (Branch Campus)
1125 Dixwell Ave, Hamden, CT 06514, 203-239-6200

Sawyer School, (Branch Campus)
1222 Warwick Ave, Warwick, RI 02888, 401-781-2887

Schnenck Civilian Conservation Center
98 Schenck Dr, Pisgah Forest, NC 28768, 704-877-3291

School of Advertising Art
2900 Acosta St, Kettering, OH 45420, 513-294-0592

School of Automotive Machinists
1911 Antoine Dr, Houston, TX 77055, 713-683-3817

School of Business and Banking
5045 Preston Hwy, Louisville, KY 40213, 502-451-7615

School of Communication Arts
2526 27th Ave S, Minneapolis, MN 55406, 612-721-5357

School of Communications Electronics
184 Second St, San Francisco, CA 94105, 415-896-0858

School of Health Care Sciences
917 Missile Rd, Sheppard Afb, TX 76311, 817-676-4033

School of Medical and Legal Secretarial Sciences
60 S Angell St, Providence, RI 02906, 401-331-1711

School of the Hartford Ballet
Hartford Courant Arts Ctr, 224 Farmington Ave, Hartford, CT 06105, 203-525-9396

Scottsdale Culinary Institute
8100 E Camelback Rd, Scottsdale, AZ 85251, 602-990-3773

Sebring Career Schools
2212 Ave I, Huntsville, TX 77340, 409-291-6299

Sebring Career Schools, (Branch Campus)
6715 Bissonnet St, Houston, TX 77074, 713-772-6209

Sebring Career Schools, (Branch Campus)
6672 Hwy 6S, Houston, TX 77413, 713-561-6352

Segal Institute of Court Reporting
18850 US Hwy 19 N #565, Clearwater, FL 34624, 813-535-0608

Seguin Beauty School
102 E Court St, Seguin, TX 78155, 512-372-0935

Seguin Beauty School, (Branch Campus)
214 W San Antonio St, New Braunfels, TX 78130, 512-620-1301

Seminary Extension Independent Study Institute
901 Commerce St #500, Nashville, TN 37203, 615-242-2453

Sequoia Institute
420 Whitney Pl, Fremont, CA 94539, 510-490-6900

Settlement Music School
416 Queen St, Philadelphia, PA 19147, 215-336-0400

Sharp's Academy of Hairstyling
115 Main St, Flushing, MI 48433, 313-659-3348

Sharp's Academy of Hairstyling, (Branch Campus)
8166 Holly Rd, Grand Blanc, MI 48433, 313-695-6742

Sheridan Vocational-Technical Center
5400 Sheridan St, Hollywood, FL 33021, 305-985-3233

Shirley Rock School of the Pennsylvania Ballet
1101 S Broad St, Philadelphia, PA 19147, 215-551-7000

Shreveport-Bossier Regional Technical Institute
2010 N Market St, Shreveport, LA 71137, 318-226-7811

Sidney N. Collier Technical Institute
3727 Louisa St, New Orleans, LA 70126, 504-942-8333

Sierra Academy of Aeronautics Technicians Institute
Oakland International Airport, Oakland, CA 94614, 510-568-6100

Sierra Valley Business College
4747 N First St Bldg D, Fresno, CA 93726, 209-222-0947

Silicon Valley College
41350 Christy St, Fremont, CA 94538, 510-623-9966

Simi Valley Adult School
3192 Los Angeles Ave, Simi Valley, CA 93065, 805-527-4840

Skyland Academy
170 Rosscraggon Rd, Skyland, NC 28776, 704-687-1643

Slidell Technical Institute
1000 Canulette Rd, Slidell, LA 70459, 504-646-6430

Sonia Moore Studio of the Theatre
485 Park Ave #6A, New York, NY 10022, 212-755-5120

Sotheby's Educational Studies
1334 York Ave, New York, NY 10021, 212-606-7822

South Carolina Criminal Justice Academy
5400 Broad River Rd, Columbia, SC 29210, 803-737-8400

South Central Career College
4500 W Commercial Dr, North Little Rock, AR 72116, 501-758-6800

South Central Career College
1614 Brentwood Dr, Pine Bluff, AR 71601, 501-535-6800

South Central Career College, (Branch Campus)
2311 E Nettleton #G, Jonesboro, AR 72401, 501-972-6999

South Central Technical College
2200 Tech Dr, Albert Lea, MN 56007, 507-373-0656

South Coast College of Court Reporting
1380 S Sanderson Ave, Anaheim, CA 92806, 714-897-6464

South Georgia Technical Institute
728 Sotherfield Rd, Americus, GA 31709, 912-928-0283

South Louisiana Beauty College
300 Howard Ave, Houma, LA 70363, 504-873-8978

South Louisiana Regional Technical Institute
201 St. Charles St, Houma, LA 70361, 504-857-3655

South Louisiana Regional Technical Institute, (Branch Campus)
Station 1 Box 10251, Houma, LA 70361, 504-857-3698

South Technical Education Center
1300 SW 30th Ave, Boynton Beach, FL 33426, 407-369-7000

South Texas Vo-Tech Institute
2255 N Coria St, Brownsville, TX 78520, 512-546-0353

South Texas Vo-Tech Institute
2901 N 23rd St, Mcallen, TX 78501, 512-631-1107

South Texas Vo-Tech Institute
2419 E Haggar Ave, Weslaco, TX 78596, 512-969-1564

Southeast College of Technology
828 Downtowner Loop W, Mobile, AL 36609, 205-343-8200

Southeastern Academy, Inc.
PO Box 421768, Kissimmee, FL 32742, 407-847-4444

Southeastern Academy, Inc., (Peoples College of Independent Studies)
PO Box 421768, Kissimmee, FL 32742, 407-847-4444

Southeastern Center for the Arts
1935 Cliff Valley Wy #210, Atlanta, GA 30329, 404-633-1990

Southeastern Paralegal Institute
5440 Harvest Hill Rd #200, Dallas, TX 75230, 214-385-1446

Southeastern Paralegal Institute
2416 21st Ave S #300, Nashville, TN 37212, 615-269-9900

Southeastern School fo Aeronautics
Herbert Smart Airport, Macon, GA 31201, 800-423-7510

Southeastern Technical Institute
250 Foundry St, South Easton, MA 02375, 508-238-4374

Southeastern Technical Institute
3001 E First St, Vidalia, GA 30474, 912-537-0386

Southern California College of Business and Law
595 W Lambert Rd, Brea, CA 92621, 714-529-1055

Southern California College of Court Reporting
1100 S Claudina Pl, Anaheim, CA 92805, 714-758-1500

Southern Careers Institute
2301 S Congress Ave #27, Austin, TX 78704, 512-326-1415

Southern Careers Institute, (Branch Campus)
5333 Everhart Rd #C, Corpus Christi, TX 78411, 512-702-2151

Southern Careers Institute, (Branch Campus)
3233 N 38th St, Mcallen, TX 78501, 210-687-1415

Southern Careers Institute, (Branch Campus)
840 N Cage, Pharr, TX 78577, 512-702-2151

Southern Driver's Academy
3906 I-55 S, Jackson, MS 39284, 601-371-1371

Southern Technical Center
19151 S Dixie Hwy, Miami, FL 33157, 305-254-0995

Southern Technical College
7601 Scott Hamilton Dr, Little Rock, AR 72209, 501-565-7000

Southern Technical College, (Branch Campus)
3348 N College St, Fayetteville, AR 72703, 501-442-2364

Southern Vocational College
205 S Main St, Tuskegee, AL 36083, 205-727-5220

Southside Training Skills Center
Hwy 460 E, Crewe, VA 23930, 804-645-7471

Southwest Academy of Technology
1660 S Alma School Rd #227, Mesa, AZ 85210, 602-820-3003

Southwest School of Broadcasting
1031 E Battlefield Rd #212B, Springfield, MO 65807, 417-883-4060

Southwestern Academy
1660 S Alma School Rd #223, Mesa, AZ 85210, 602-820-3956

Sowela Regional Technical Institute
3820 Legion St, Lake Charles, LA 70616, 318-491-2698

Sowela Regional Technical Institute, (Branch Campus)
PO Box 1056, Dequincy, LA 70633, 318-491-2688

Spanish-American Institute
215 W 43rd St, New York, NY 10036, 212-840-7111

Sparks College
131 S Morgan St, Shelbyville, IL 62565, 217-774-5112

Specs Howard School of Broadcast Arts, Inc.
16900 W Eight Mile Rd #115, Southfield, MI 48075, 313-569-0101

Spencer Business and Technical Institute
200 State St, Schenectady, NY 12305, 518-374-7619

Spencerian College
PO Box 16418, Louisville, KY 40216, 502-447-1000

St. Augustine Technical Center
2980 Collins Ave, St. Augustine, FL 32095, 904-824-4401

St. Augustine Technical Center, (Branch Campus)
113 Putnam County Blvd, East Palatka, FL 32131, 904-557-2468

St. Francis School of Practical Nursing
2221 W STate St, Olean, NY 14760, 716-375-7316

St. John's School of Business
PO Box 1190, West Springfield, MA 01090, 413-781-0390

St. Louis College of Health Careers
4484 W Pine Blvd, St Louis, MO 63108, 314-652-0300

St. Louis Symphony Community Music School
560 Trinity Ave, St Louis, MO 63130, 314-863-3033

St. Louis Tech
9741 St Charles Rock Rd, St Louis, MO 63114, 314-427-3600

Star Technical Institute
251 N Delsea Dr, Deptford, NJ 08096, 609-384-2888

Star Technical Institute
2224 US Hwy, Edgewater Park, NJ 08010, 609-877-2727

Star Technical Institute
Somerdale Sq #2, Somerdale, NJ 08083, 609-435-7827

Star Technical Institute
1386 S Delsea Dr, Vineland, NJ 08360, 609-696-0500

Star Technical Institute
631 W Newport Pike, Wilmington, DE 19804, 302-999-7826

Star Technical Institute, (Branch Campus)
212 Wyoming Ave, Kingston, PA 18704, 717-287-9777

Star Technical Institute, (Branch Campus)
1255 Rte 70 #12N, Lakewood, NJ 08701, 908-901-0001

Star Technical Institute, (Branch Campus)
2105 Hwy 35, Ocean Township, NJ 07712, 908-493-1660

Star Technical Institute, (Branch Campus)
1600 Nay Aug Ave, Scranton, PA 18509, 717-963-0144

Star Technical Institute, (Branch Campus)
1541 Ala Dr 1st Flr, Whitehall, PA 18052, 215-434-9963

State Area Vocational-Technical School - Jacksboro
Rte 1 Elkins Rd, Jacksboro, TN 37757, 615-562-8648

State Area Vocational-Technical School - Jackson
2468 Westover Rd, Jackson, TN 38305, 901-424-0691

State Area Vocational-Technical School - Knoxville
1100 Liberty St, Knoxville, TN 37919, 615-546-5567

State Area Vocational-Technical School - Livingston
Airport Rd, Livingston, TN 38570, 615-823-5525

State Area Vocational-Technical School - McKenzie
905 Highland Dr, McKenzie, TN 38201, 901-352-5364

State Area Vocational-Technical School - McMinnville
1507 Vo-Tech Dr, McMinnville, TN 37110, 615-473-5587

State Area Vocational-Technical School - Memphis
550 Alabama, Memphis, TN 38105, 901-543-6100

State Area Vocational-Technical School - Memphis, (Branch Campus)
2752 Winchester Rd, Memphis, TN 38116, 901-345-1995

State Area Vocational-Technical School - Morristown
821 W Louise Ave, Morristown, TN 37813, 615-586-5771

State Area Vocational-Technical School - Morristown, (Branch Campus)
316 E Main St, Rogersville, TN 37857, 615-272-2100

State Area Vocational-Technical School - Murfreesboro
1303 Old Fort Pkwy, Murfreesboro, TN 37129, 615-898-8010

State Area Vocational-Technical School - Nashville
100 White Bridge Rd, Nashville, TN 37209, 615-741-1241

State Area Vocational-Technical School - Nashville, (Branch Campus)
7204 Cockrill Bend Rd, Nashville, TN 37209, 615-350-6224

State Area Vocational-Technical School - Newbern
340 Washington St, Newbern, TN 38059, 901-627-2511

State Area Vocational-Technical School - Oneida
120 Eli Ln, Oneida, TN 37841, 615-569-8338

State Area Vocational-Technical School - Paris
312 S Wilson St, Paris, TN 38242, 901-642-7552

State Area Vocational-Technical School - Pulaski
1233 E College St, Pulaski, TN 38478, 615-363-1588

State Area Vocational-Technical School - Ripley
S Industrial Park, Ripley, TN 38063, 901-635-3368

State Area Vocational-Technical School - Savannah
Hwy 64 W, Crump, TN 38327, 901-632-3393

State Area Vocational-Technical School - Shelbyville
1405 Madison St, Shelbyville, TN 37160, 615-685-5013

State Area Vocational-Technical School - Whiteville
330 Hwy 100, Whiteville, TN 38075, 901-254-8521

State Area Vocational-Technical School-Athens
1634 Vo-Tech Dr, Athens, TN 37371, 615-744-2814

State Area Vocational-Technical School-Covington
1600 Hwy 51 S, Covington, TN 38019, 901-476-8634

State Area Vocational-Technical School-Crossville
715 N Miller Ave, Crossville, TN 38555, 615-484-7502

State Area Vocational-Technical School-Dickson
740 Hwy 46, Dickson, TN 37055, 615-446-4710

State Area Vocational-Technical School-Elizabethton
1500 Arney St, Elizabethton, TN 37641, 615-542-4174

State Area Vocational-Technical School-Harriman
Hwy 27 N, Harriman, TN 37748, 615-882-6703

State Area Vocational-Technical School-Hartsville
716 McMurry blvd, Hartsville, TN 37074, 615-374-2147

State Area Vocational-Technical School-Hohenwald
813 W Main St, Hohenwald, TN 38462, 615-796-5351

State Barber & Hair Design College, Inc.
2514 S Agnew Ave, Oklahoma City, OK 73108, 405-631-8621

Ste. Genevieve Beauty College
755 Market St, Ste. Genevieve, MO 63670, 314-883-5550

Stella Adler Conservatory of Acting
419 Lafayette St 6thFl, New York, NY 10003, 212-260-0525

Stenotopia, the World of Court Reporting
45 S Service Rd, Plainview, NY 11803, 516-777-1117

Stenotype Institute of Jacksonville
500 Ninth Ave N, Jacksonville Beach, FL 32250, 904-246-7466

Stenotype Institute of South Dakota
705 West Ave N, Sioux Falls, SD 57104, 605-336-1442

Sterling School
801 E Indian School Rd, Phoenix, AZ 85014, 602-277-5276

Stone Academy
1315 Dixwell Ave, Hamden, CT 06514, 203-288-7474

Stuart School of Business Administration
2400 Belmar Blvd, Wall, NJ 07719, 201-681-7200

Suburban Technical School
175 Fulton Ave, Hempstead, NY 11550, 416-481-6660

Suburban Technical School, (Branch Campus)
2650 Sunrise Hwy, East Islip, NY 11730, 516-224-5001

Sullivan Technical Institute
1710 Sullivan Dr, Bogalusa, LA 70427, 504-732-6640

Sullivan Technical Institute, (Branch Campus)
Rte 2 Box 500, Angie, LA 70426, 504-732-6640

Sumter Beauty College
921 Carolina Ave, Sumter, SC 29150, 803-773-7311

Suncoast Center for Natural Health/Suncoast School
4910 Cypress St, Tampa, FL 33607, 813-287-1099

Sunstate Academy of Hair Design
2418 Colonial Blvd, Fort Myers, FL 33907, 813-278-1311

Sunstate Academy of Hair Design
1825 Tamiami Tr #E6, Port Charlotte, FL 33948, 813-255-1366

Sunstate Academy of Hair Design
4424 Bee Ridge Rd, Sarasota, FL 34233, 813-377-4880

Superior Career Institute
116 W 14th St, New York, NY 10011, 212-675-2140

Suwanee-Hamilton Area Vocational-Technical & Adult Education Ctr
415 Pinewood Dr SW, Live Oak, FL 32060, 904-362-2751

Swainsboro Technical Institute
201 Kite Rd, Swainsboro, GA 30401, 912-237-6465

Swanson's Driving Schools, Inc.
9915 Frankstown Rd, Pittsburgh, PA 15235, 412-241-6963

Swedish Institute
226 W 26th St 5th FL, New York, NY 10001, 212-924-5900

Systems Programming Development Institute
4900 Triggs St, City of Commerce, CA 90022, 213-261-8181

T

T.H. Harris Technical Institute
337 E South St, Opelousas, LA 70570, 318-948-0239

T.H. Pickens Technical Center
500 Buckley Rd, Aurora, CO 80011, 303-344-4910

TAD Technical Institute
45 Spruce St, Chelsea, MA 02150, 617-889-3600

TAD Technical Institute
7910 Troost Ave, Kansas City, MO 64131, 816-361-5140

TDDS
1688 N Princetown Rd, Diamond, OH 44412, 216-538-2216

TESST Electronics and Computer Institute
1400 Duke St, Alexandria, VA 22314, 703-548-4800

TESST Electronics and Computer Institute
5122 Baltimore Ave, Hyattsville, MD 20781, 301-864-5750

Tallapoosa-Alexander City Area Vocational Center
100 E Junior College Dr, Alexander City, AL 35010, 205-329-8448

Tallulah Technical Institute
Old Hwy 65 S, Tallulah, LA 71284, 318-574-4820

Tallulah Technical Institute, (Branch Campus)
Hwy 883-1, Lake Providence, LA 71254, 318-559-0864

Tara Lara Academy of K-9 Hair Design
16307 SE McLoughlin Blvd, Portland, OR 97267, 503-653-7134

Taylor Technical Institute
3233 Hwy 19 S, Perry, FL 32347, 904-584-7603

Taylor's Institute of Cosmetology
842C W 7th Ave, Corsicana, TX 75110, 903-874-7312

Teche Area Technical Institute
Acadiana Airport, New Iberia, LA 70560, 318-373-0111

Technical Career Institute
720 NW 27th Ave, Miami, FL 33125, 305-442-4480

Technical Careers Institute
11 Kimberly Ave, West Haven, CT 06516, 203-932-2282

Technical Careers Institute, (Branch Campus)
605 Day Hill Rd, Windsor, CT 06095, 203-688-8351

Technical Institute of Camden County
343 Berlin-Cross Keys Rd, Sicklerville, NJ 08081, 609-767-7000

Technical Trades Institute
2315 E Pikes Peak Ave, Colorado Springs, CO 80909, 719-632-7626

Technical Trades Institute
772 Horizon Dr, Grand Junction, CO 81501, 303-245-8101

Technical Trades Institute, (Emery Aviation College)
1245A Aviation Way, Colorado Springs, CO 80916, 719-591-9488

Techno-Dent Training Center
101 W 31st St 4th Fl, New York, NY 10001, 212-695-1818

Technology Education Center
288 S Hamilton Rd, Columbus, OH 43213, 614-759-7700

Temple Academy of Cosmetology
5 S First St, Temple, TX 76501, 817-778-2221

Temple Academy of Cosmetology, (Branch Campus)
1408 W Marshall Ave, Longview, TX 75604, 903-753-4717

Teterboro School of Aeronautics
80 Moonachie Ave, Teterboro, NJ 07608, 201-288-6300

Texas Aero Tech
6911 Lemmon Ave, Dallas, TX 75209, 214-358-7295

Texas Barber College
531 W Jefferson Blvd, Dallas, TX 75208, 214-943-7255

Texas Barber College, (Branch Campus)
2406 Gus Thomason Rd, Dallas, TX 75228, 214-324-2851

Texas Barber College, (Branch Campus)
525 W Arapaho Rd, Richardson, TX 75080, 214-644-4106

Texas School of Business - Southwest
10250 Bissonnet St, Houston, TX 77036, 713-771-1177

Texas School of Business
711 Airtex Blvd, Houston, TX 77073, 713-876-2888

Texas Vocational School
Rte 2 Box 254, Pharr, TX 78577, 512-631-6181

Texas Vocational School
1913 S Flores St, San Antonio, TX 78204, 512-225-3253

Texas Vocational Schools
1921 E Red River, Victoria, TX 77901, 512-575-4768

Texas Vocational Schools, (Branch Campus)
201 E Rio Grande, Victoria, TX 77902, 512-575-4768

Thibodaux Area Technical Institute
1425 Tiger Dr, Thibodaux, LA 70302, 504-447-0924

Thomas Technical Institute
Hwy 19 at Rte 319, Thomasville, GA 31799, 912-225-4094

Thompson School of Practical Nursing
30 Maple St, Brattleboro, VT 05301, 802-254-5570

Tidewater Tech
2697 Dean Dr #100, Virginia Beach, VA 23452, 804-340-2121

Tidewater Tech, (Branch Campus)
932 B Ventures Wy #310, Chesapeake, VA 23320, 804-548-2828

Tidewater Tech, (Branch Campus)
616 Denbigh Blvd, Newport News, VA 23402, 804-874-2121

Tidewater Tech, (Branch Campus)
1760 E Little Creek Rd, Norfolk, VA 23518, 804-588-2121

Titan Helicopter Academy
Easterwood St Bldg 90, Millville, NJ 08332, 609-327-5203

Tom P. Haney Vocational-Technical Center
3016 Hwy 77, Panama City, FL 32405, 904-769-2191

Topeka Technical College
1620 NW Gage Blvd, Topeka, KS 66618, 913-232-5858

Total Technical Institute
6500 Pearl Rd, Parma Heights, OH 44130, 216-843-2323

Trans American School of Broadcasting
600 Williamson St, Madison, WI 53703, 608-257-4600

Trans World Travel Academy
11495 Natural Bridge Rd, St Louis, MO 63044, 314-895-6754

Travel Career Institute
218 N 4th St, Bismarck, ND 58504, 701-258-9419

Travel Education Center
100 Cambridge Park Dr, Cambridge, MA 02140, 617-547-7750

Travel Education Center, (Branch Campus)
402 Amherst St, Nashua, NH 03063, 603-880-7200

Travel Institute
15 Park Row #617, New York, NY 10038, 212-349-3331

Travel Institute of the Pacific
1314 S King St #1164, Honolulu, HI 96814, 808-591-2708

Travel School of America
1047 Commonwealth Ave, Boston, MA 02215, 617-787-1214

Travel Training Center
5003-05 Schaefer Rd, Dearborn, MI 48126, 313-584-5000

Travel University International
3655 Ruffin Rd N #225, San Diego, CA 92123, 619-292-9755

Travel University International, (Branch Campus)
1441 Kapiolani Blvd #1414, Honolulu, HI 96814, 808-946-3535

Travel and Trade Career Institute
3635 Atlantic Ave, Long Beach, CA 90807, 310-426-8841

Travel and Trade Career Institute, (Branch Campus)
12541 Brookhurst St #100, Garden Grove, CA 92640, 714-636-2611

Traviss Vocational-Technical Center
3225 Winter Lake Rd, Eaton Park, FL 33803, 813-665-1220

Tri-City Barber School
128 E Main St, Norristown, PA 19401, 215-279-4432

Tri-City Barber School
5901 N Broad St, Philadelphia, PA 19141, 215-927-3232

Tri-State Beauty Academy
219 W Main St, Morehead, KY 40351, 606-784-6725

Tri-State Institute of Traditional Chinese Acupuncture
Planetarium Sta Box 890, New York, NY 10024, 212-496-7869

Trident Training Facility
1040 USS Georgia Ave, Kings Bay, GA 31547, 912-922-8304

Trident Training Facility
Silverdale, WA 98315, 206-396-4068

Truck Driving Academy
5168 N Blythe Ave #102, Fresno, CA 93722, 209-276-5708

Truck Driving Academy
5711 Florin-Perkins Rd, Sacramento, CA 95828, 916-381-2285

Truck Marketing Institute
PO Box 5000, Carpinteria, CA 93014, 805-685-4558

Tucson College
7302-10 E 22nd St, Tucson, AZ 85710, 602-296-3261

Tulsa Technology Center
3420 S Memorial Dr, Tulsa, OK 74145, 918-627-7200

Tulsa Welding School
3038 Southwest Blvd, Tulsa, OK 74107, 918-587-6789

Turner Job Corps Center
2000 Schilling Ave, Albany, GA 31705, 912-431-1820

Tyler School of Secretarial Sciences
8030 S Kedzie Ave, Chicago, IL 60652, 312-436-5050

U

U.S. Schools
100 N Plaza, Miami, FL 33283, 305-836-7424

UCC Vocational Center
1322 Coranado Ave, Long Beach, CA 90804, 310-597-3798

USA Hair Academy
2525 N Laurent St, Victoria, TX 77901, 512-578-0035

Ultrasound Diagnostic School
One Old Country Rd, Carle Place, NY 11514, 516-248-6060

Ultrasound Diagnostic School
2269 Saw Mill River Rd, Elmsford, NY 10523, 914-347-6817

Ultrasound Diagnostic School
675 Rte 1, Iselin, NJ 08830, 908-634-1131

Ultrasound Diagnostic School
121 W 27th St #504, New York, NY 10001, 212-645-9116

Ultrasound Diagnostic School, (Branch Campus)
13 Corp Sq Office Park #140, Atlanta, GA 30329, 404-248-9070

Ultrasound Diagnostic School, (Branch Campus)
6575 W Loop S #200, Bellaire, TX 77401, 713-664-9632

Ultrasound Diagnostic School, (Branch Campus)
4700 Rockside Rd, Independence, OH 44131, 216-573-5833

Ultrasound Diagnostic School, (Branch Campus)
102 Decker Ct #205, Irving, TX 75062, 214-791-1120

Ultrasound Diagnostic School, (Branch Campus)
10199 Southside Blvd #106, Jacksonville, FL 32256, 904-363-6221

Ultrasound Diagnostic School, (Branch Campus)
33 Boston Post Rd W #140, Marlborough, MA 01752, 508-485-1213

Ultrasound Diagnostic School, (Branch Campus)
12901 Townsend Rd, Philadelphia, PA 19154, 215-624-8245

Ultrasound Diagnostic School, (Branch Campus)
5830 Ellsworth Ave #201, Pittsburgh, PA 15232, 412-362-9404

Ultrasound Diagnostic School, (Branch Campus)
2760 E Atlantic Blvd, Pompano Beach, FL 33062, 305-942-6551

Ultrasound Diagnostic School, (Branch Campus)
1320 Fenwick Ln, Silver Spring, MD 20910, 301-588-0786

Ultrasound Diagnostic School, (Branch Campus)
5804 E Breckenridge Pkwy, Tampa, FL 33610, 813-621-0072

United State Army Intelligence Center and Fort Huachuca
ATSI-TDI-S, Fort Huachuca, AZ 85613, 602-533-5648

United States Coast Guard Institute
PO Substation 18, Oklahoma City, OK 73169, 405-680-4262

Universal Business and Media School
220 E 106th St, New York, NY 10029, 212-360-1210

Universal Technical Institute
902 Capitol Ave, Omaha, NE 68102, 402-345-2422

Universal Technical Institute
3121 W Weldon Ave, Phoenix, AZ 85017, 602-264-4164

Universal Technical Institute, (Branch Campus)
601 Regency Dr, Glendale Heights, IL 60139, 708-529-2662

University of Beauty
1701-G S Lee Plaza, Cleveland, TN 37311, 615-472-1702

University of Beauty, (Branch Campus)
5798-A Brainerd Rd, Chattanooga, TN 37411, 615-899-0246

V

Valdosta Technical Institute
Val-Tech Rd, Valdosta, GA 31602, 912-333-2100

Valley Commercial College
910 Twelfth St, Modesto, CA 95354, 209-578-0616

Vanderschmidt School
4625 Lindell Blvd, St Louis, MO 63108, 314-361-6000

Vanguard Institute of Technology
221 N Eighth St, Edinburg, TX 78539, 210-380-3264

Vanguard Institute of Technology, (Branch Campus)
603 Ed Carey Dr, Harlingen, TX 78550, 210-428-4999

Vatterott Educational Centers
3854 Washington Ave, St Louis, MO 63108, 314-534-2586

Vegas Career School
2101 S Decatur Blvd, Las Vegas, NV 89102, 702-362-8488

Virginia Hair Academy
3312 Williamson Rd NW, Roanoke, VA 24012, 703-563-2015

Virginia School of Cosmetology
1516 Willow Lawn Dr, Richmond, VA 23226, 804-288-7923

Vocational Training Institute
6400M NE Hwy 99, Vancouver, WA 98665, 206-695-5186

W

Walker Technical Institute
265 Bicentennial Trl, Rock Spring, GA 30739, 404-764-1016

Washington Business School of Northern Virginia
1980 Gallows Rd, Vienna, VA 22182, 703-556-8888

Washington Conservatory of Music, Inc.
PO Box 5758, Washington, DC 20816, 301-320-2770

Washington County Adult Skill Center
848 Thompson Dr, Abingdon, VA 24210, 703-628-6641

Washington-Holmes Area Vocational-Technical Center
209 Hoyt St, Chipley, FL 32428, 904-638-1180

Watterson College Pacific
815 N Oxnard Blvd, Oxnard, CA 93030, 805-656-5566

Watterson College Pacific, (Branch Campus)
2030 University Dr, Vista, CA 92083, 619-724-1500

Watterson College
1165 E Colorado Blvd, Pasadena, CA 91106, 818-449-3990

Watterson College
1422 S Azusa Ave, West Covina, CA 91791, 818-919-8701

Welder Training and Testing Institute
100 Pennsylvania Ave, Selinsgrove, PA 17870, 800-326-9306

Wentworth Technical School
1919 Spring Ave, Lexington, MA 02173, 617-674-1000

West Coast Training
11919 N Jensen Ave #292, Portland, OR 97217, 503-289-8661

West Coast Training, (Branch Campus)
2525 SE Stubb St, Milwaukie, OR 97222, 503-659-5181

West Georgia Technical Institute
303 Fort Dr, Lagrange, GA 30240, 404-882-2518

West Jefferson Technical Institute
475 Manhattan Blvd, Harvey, LA 70058, 504-361-6464

West Technical Education Center
2625 State Rd #715, Belle Glade, FL 33430, 407-996-4930

West Tennessee Business College
1186 Hwy 45 By-Pass, Jackson, TN 38301, 901-668-7240

Westchester Conservatory of Music
20 Soundview Ave, White Plains, NY 10606, 914-761-3715

Westech College
500 W Mission Blvd, Pomona, CA 91766, 714-622-6486

Western Business College
425 SW Washington St, Portland, OR 97204, 503-222-3225

Western Business College, (Branch Campus)
6625 E Mill Plain Blvd, Vancouver, WA 98661, 206-694-3225

Western Business Institute
3200 N White Sands Blvd, Alamogordo, NM 88310, 505-437-1854

Western Career College
8909 Folsom Blvd, Sacramento, CA 95826, 916-361-1660

Western Career College
170 Bayfair Mall, San Leandro, CA 94578, 510-278-3888

Western Culinary Institute
1316 SW 13th Ave, Portland, OR 97201, 503-223-2245

Western School of Health and Business Careers
327 5th Ave 2nd Flr, Pittsburgh, PA 15222, 412-281-2600

Western School of Health and Business Careers, (Branch Campus)
One Monroeville Ctr, Monroeville, PA 15146, 412-373-6400

Western Truck School
4565 N Golden State Blvd, Fresno, CA 93722, 209-276-1220

Western Truck School
10510 SW Industrial Wy Bldg 1, Tualatin, OR 97062, 503-691-0113

Western Truck School
4612 E Nunes Rd, Turlock, CA 95308, 209-472-1500

Western Truck School
4521 W Capitol Ave, West Sacramento, CA 95691, 916-372-6500

Western Truck School, (Branch Campus)
5800 State Rd, Bakersfield, CA 93308, 805-399-0707

Western Truck School, (Branch Campus)
1835 S Black Canyon Hwy, Phoenix, AZ 85040, 602-437-5303

Western Truck School, (Branch Campus)
4757 Old Cliffs Rd, San Diego, CA 92120, 619-229-8301

Western Truck School, (Branch Campus)
1053 N Broadway, Stockton, CA 95205, 209-946-0569

Westlake Institute of Technology
31826A Village Center Rd, Westlake Village, CA 91361, 818-991-9992

Westlawn School of Marine Technology
733 Summer St, Stamford, CT 06901, 203-359-0500

Westside Technical Institute
59125 Bayou Rd, Plaquemine, LA 70765, 504-342-8228

Westside Vocational-Technical Center
731 E Story Rd, Winter Garden, FL 34787, 407-656-2851

Westside Vocational-Technical Center, (Branch Campus)
2499 Edgewood Ranch Rd, Orlando, FL 32811, 407-295-2464

Westside Vocational-Technical Center, (Branch Campus)
6628 Old Winter Garden Rd, Orlando, FL 32811, 407-292-8696

Wheeling College of Hair Design
1122 Main St, Wheeling, WV 26003, 304-232-1957

Wichita Area Vocational-Technical School
324 N Emporia St, Wichita, KS 67202, 316-833-4664

Wichita Business College
501 E Pawnee St#515, Wichita, KS 67211, 316-263-1261

Wilma Boyd Career Schools
One Chatham Ctr, Pittsburgh, PA 15219, 412-456-1800

Windham Regional Vocational-Technical School
210 Birch St, Willimantic, CT 06226, 203-456-3879

Winston County Technical Center
Holly Grove Rd, Double Springs, AL 35553, 205-489-2121

Winston-Salem Barber School
1531 Silas Creek Pkwy, Winston-Salem, NC 27127, 919-724-1459

Winter Park Adult Vocational Center
901 Webster Ave, Winter Park, FL 32789, 407-647-6366

Wisconsin Conservatory of Music, Inc.
1584 N Prospect Ave, Milwaukee, WI 53202, 414-276-5760

Wisconsin School of Professional Pet Grooming
34197 Wisconsin Ave, Okauchee, WI 53069, 414-569-9492

Withlacoochee Technical Institute
1201 W Main St, Inverness, FL 34450, 904-726-2430

Wood County Vocational School
1511 Blizzard Dr, Parkersburg, WV 26101, 304-420-9501

Woodbridge Business Institute
309 E Main St, Salisbury, MD 21801, 410-762-6700

Woodrow Wilson Rehabilitation Center
Fishersville, VA 22939, 703-332-7166

Worcester Technical Institute
251 Belmont St, Worcester, MA 01605, 508-799-1945

Worsham College of Mortuary Science
495 Northgate Pkwy, Wheeling, IL 60090, 708-808-8444

Wright Business School
9500 Marshall Dr, Lenexa, KS 66215, 913-492-2888

Wright Business School
2219 SW 74th St #122, Oklahoma City, OK 73159, 405-681-2300

Wright Business School, (Branch Campus)
5528 NE Antioch Rd, Kansas City, MO 64119, 816-452-4411

Wyoming Technical Institute
4373 N Third St, Laramie, WY 82070, 307-742-3776

Wichita Technical Institute
942 S West St, Wichita, KS 67213, 316-943-2241

William R. Moore School of Technology
1200 Poplar Ave, Memphis, TN 38104, 901-726-1977

William T. McFatter Vocational-Technical Center
6500 Nova Dr, Davie, FL 33317, 305-370-8324

William T. McFatter Vocational-Technical Center, (Branch Campus)
2600 SW 71 Terr, Davie, FL 33314, 305-474-8219

William T. McFatter Vocational-Technical Center, (Branch Campus)
3501 SW Davie Rd, Davie, FL 33314, 305-474-8219

Young Memorial Technical Institute
900 Youngs Rd, Morgan City, LA 70380, 504-380-2436

X,Y,Z

York Technical Institute
3351 Whiteford Rd, York, PA 17402, 717-757-1100

The Sourcebook of College and University Records

Section Three

State Cross Reference Index

Alabama

Alabama Agricultural and Mechanical University .... Normal
Alabama Aviation and Technical College............................. Ozark
Alabama Reference Laboratories, Inc. .... Montgomery
Alabama Southern Community College .... Monroeville
Alabama Southern Community College
   (Thomasville)... Thomasville
Alabama State College of Barber Styling .... Birmingham
Alabama State University .... Montgomery
Army Academy of Health Sciences
   (School of Aviation Medicine)....................................... Fort Rucker
Army Ordnance Missile and Munitions Center and School .. Huntsville
Athens State College .... Athens
Auburn University... Auburn University
Auburn University at Montgomery .... Montgomery
Bessemer State Technical College .... Bessemer
Bevill State Community College .... Sumiton
Bevill State Community College
   (Brewer) .... Fayette
Birmingham-Southern College..................................... Birmingham
Bishop State Community College ....Mobile
Bishop State Community College
   (Carver)...Mobile
Bishop State Community College
   (Southwest)..Mobile
Capps College ....Mobile
Career Development Institute .... Birmingham
Career Development Institute ....Mobile
Career Development Institute .... Montgomery
Career Development Institute ....Tuscaloosa
Career Development Institute
   (Branch Campus)...Bessemer
Central Alabama Community College .... Alexander City
Chattahoochee Valley State Community College .... Phenix City
Choctaw Training Institute..Butler
Coastal Training Institute .... Montgomery
Community College of the Air Force/RRR .Maxwell Air Force Base
Concordia College ....Selma
Douglas MacArthur State Technical College .... Opp
Draughons Junior College .... Montgomery
Enterprise State Junior College ....Enterprise
Extension Course Institute of the United States Air Force.Maxwell Afb
Faulkner University .... Montgomery
Gadsden Business College.. Gadsden
Gadsden Business College
   (Branch Campus)..Anniston
Gadsden State Community College................................. Gadsden
George C. Wallace State Community College .... Dothan
George Corley Wallace State Community College .... Selma
Harry M. Ayers State Technical College............................Anniston
Herzing Institute .... Birmingham
Huntingdon College... Montgomery
Huntsville Business Institute School of Court Reporting ...... Huntsville
International Bible College... Florence
J. F. Drake State Technical College .... Huntsville
J.R. Pittard Area Vocational School...Alpine
Jacksonville State University ....Jacksonville
James H. Faulkner State Community College .... Bay Minette
Jefferson Davis Community College..............................Brewton
Jefferson State Community College............................Birmingham
John C. Calhoun State Community College ....Decatur
John M. Patterson State Technical College............... Montgomery
John Pope Eden Area Vocational Education Center ....Ashville
Judson College .... Marion
Lawson State Community College................................Birmingham
Livingston University .... Livingston
Lurleen B. Wallace State Junior College .... Andalusia
Marion Military Institute .... Marion
Miles College ....Birmingham

National Career College .... Tuscaloosa
New World College of Business .... Anniston
Northeast Alabama State Community College............... Rainsville
Northwest Shoals Community College................... Muscle Shoals
Oakwood College .... Huntsville
Phillips Junior College.. Mobile
Phillips Junior College at Birmingham .... Mountain Brook
Phillips Junior College at Birmingham
   (Phillips Junior College)... Huntsville
Prince Institute of Professional Studies .... Montgomery
Reid State Technical College .... Evergreen
Rice College..Birmingham
Riley College .... Dothan
Riley College
   (Branch Campus)... Selma
Samford University .... Birmingham
Selma University .... Selma
Shelton State Community College .... Tuscaloosa
Snead State Community College.. Boaz
Southeast College of Technology .... Mobile
Southeastern Bible College... Birmingham
Southern Christian University ....Montgomery
Southern Union State Community College .... Wadley
Southern Vocational College... Tuskegee
Sparks State Technical College....................................... Eufaula
Spring Hill College .... Mobile
Stillman College .... Tuscaloosa
Talladega College.. Talladega
Tallapoosa-Alexander City Area Vocational Center........Alexander City
Trenholm State Technical College ....Montgomery
Troy State University .... Troy
Troy State University at Dothan .... Dothan
Troy State University in Montgomery.........................Montgomery
Tusegee University ....Tuskegee
United States Sports Academy.. Daphne
University of Alabama.. Tuscaloosa
University of Alabama at Birmingham-Walker College .... Jasper
University of Alabama in Huntsville .... Huntsville
University of Mobile... Mobile
University of Montevallo ....Montevallo
University of North Alabama ....Florence
University of South Alabama .... Mobile
Virginia College
   (Branch Campus).. Birmingham
Virginia College-Huntsville.. Huntsville
Wallace State Community College .... Hanceville
Winston County Technical Center .... Double Springs

Alaska

Alaska Bible College ....Glennallen
Alaska Junior College.. Anchorage
Alaska Pacific University .... Anchorage
Kenai Peninsula College... Soldotna
Kodiak College .... Kodiak
Prince William Sound Community College .... Valdez
Sheldon Jackson College.. Sitka
University of Alaska
   (Kuskokwim) .... Bethel
University of Alaska
   (Northwest) .... Nome
University of Alaska Anchorage .... Anchorage
University of Alaska Anchorage .... Anchorage
University of Alaska Fairbanks....................................... Fairbanks
University of Alaska Fairbanks
   (Chukchi)... Kotzebue
University of Alaska Southeast .... Juneau
University of Alaska Southeast
   (Ketchikan) .... Ketchikan
University of Alaska Southeast
   (Sitka) .... Sitka

American Samoa

American Samoa Community College..........................Pago Pago

Arizona

ABC Technical & Trade Schools.....................................Tucson
Academy of Business College......................................Phoenix
Al Collins Graphic Design School ....Tempe
American Graduate School of International Management Glendale
American Indian Bible College of the Assemblies of God Phoenix
American Institute..Phoenix
American Institute of Technology ....Phoenix
American Teller Schools ....Phoenix
American Teller Schools
  (Branch Campus)..Mesa
American Teller Schools
  (Branch Campus)...Tucson
Apollo College - Phoenix, Inc. ....Phoenix
Apollo College - Tri City, Inc. ....Mesa
Apollo College - Tucson, Inc. ....Tucson
Apollo College - Westridge, Inc. ....Phoenix
Arizona College of the Bible ....Phoenix
Arizona Institute of Business and Technology ....Phoenix
Arizona Institute of Business and Technology
  (Branch) ....Mesa
Arizona Institute of Business and Technology
  (Branch) ....Phoenix
Arizona State University ....Tempe
Arizona State University West...................................Phoenix
Arizona Western College ....Yuma
Art Center, The ....Tucson
AzTech College..Mesa
Bryman School ....Phoenix
CAD Institute..Phoenix
Central Arizona College ....Coolidge
Chandler-Gilbert Community College ....Chandler
Chaparral Career College..Tucson
Clinton Technical Institute ....Phoenix
Cochise College ....Douglas
Conservatory of Recording Arts & Sciences ....Phoenix
DeVry Institute of Technology, Phoenix........................Phoenix
Denver Business College
  (Branch) ....Mesa
Desert Institute of the Healing Arts..............................Tucson
Eastern Arizona College ....Thatcher
Embry-Riddle Aeronautical University
  (Branch)..Prescott
Frank Lloyd Wright School of Architecture ....Scottsdale
Gateway Community College ....Phoenix
Glendale Community College...................................Glendale
Grand Canyon University ....Phoenix
High-Tech Institute..Phoenix
ITT Technical Institute..Phoenix
ITT Technical Institute...Tucson
Institute of Business and Medical Technology ....Mesa
Keller Graduate School of Management
  (East Valley Center) ....Mesa
Keller Graduate School of Management
  (Phoenix/Northwest Center) ....Phoenix
Lamson Business College ....Tucson
Laural School..Phoenix
Long Medical Institute..Phoenix
Mesa Community College..Mesa
Metropolitan College of Court Reporting......................Phoenix
Modern Schools of America, Inc. ....Phoenix
Mohave Community College.....................................Kingman
Mundus Institute..Phoenix

National Education Center - Arizona Automotive Institute......Glendale
Navajo Community College..Tsaile
Northern Arizona College of Health Careers ....Flagstaff
Northern Arizona Institute of Technology..................Flagstaff
Northern Arizona University ....Flagstaff
Northland Pioneer College ....Holbrook
Paradise Valley Community College ....Phoenix
Paralegal Institute, Inc. ....Phoenix
Parks College
  (Branch Campus) ....Tucson
Pedigree Career Institute ....Phoenix
Pedigree Career Institute ....Tucson
Phoenix College..Phoenix
Pima County Community College District....................Tucson
Pima Medical Institute ....Tucson
Pima Medical Institute
  (Branch)..Mesa
Prescott College..Prescott
Refrigeration School ....Phoenix
Rice Aviation, a Division of A&J Enterprises
  (Branch Campus) ....Phoenix
Rio Salado Community College..................................Phoenix
Roberto-Venn School of Luthiery ....Phoenix
Scottsdale Community College ....Scottsdale
Scottsdale Culinary Institute ....Scottsdale
South Mountain Community College ....Phoenix
Southwest Academy of Technology..............................Mesa
Southwestern Academy...Mesa
Southwestern College...Phoenix
Sterling School..Phoenix
Tucson College...Tucson
United State Army Intelligence Center and Fort Huachuca..................
....Fort Huachuca
Universal Technical Institute.....................................Phoenix
University of Arizona ....Tucson
University of Phoenix..Phoenix
University of Phoenix
  (Center for Distance Education) ....Phoenix
University of Phoenix
  (Phoenix Main)...Phoenix
University of Phoenix
  (Tucson Main) ....Tucson
Western International University...............................Phoenix
Western Truck School
  (Branch Campus) ....Phoenix
Yavapai College..Prescott

Arkansas

Arkansas Baptist College ....Little Rock
Arkansas College of Barbering and Hair Design........North Little Rock
Arkansas State University.......................................State University
Arkansas State University
  (Beebe Branch) ....Beebe
Arkansas Tech University ....Russellville
Arkansas Valley Technical Institute ....Fort Smith
Black River Technical College ....Pocahontas
CARTI School of Radiation Therapy Technology ....Little Rock
Central Baptist College ....Conway
Cotton Boll Technical Institute ....Burdette
East Arkansas Community College...........................Forrest City
Eastern College of Health Vocations.........................Little Rock
Garland County Community College ....Hot Springs
Harding University ....Searcy
Henderson State University ....Arkadelphia
Hendrix College ....Conway
John Brown University ....Siloam Springs
Lyon College...Batesville
Mississippi County Community College ....Blytheville
National Education Center - Arkansas College of Technology
....Little Rock

State Cross Reference Index   430   (Bold print indicates degree granting institutions)

The Sourcebook of College and University Student Records   **California**

New Tyler Barber College Inc. .... North Little Rock
North Arkansas Community/Technical College .... Harrison
Northwest Arkansas Community College .... Bentonville
Ouachita Baptist University .... Arkadelphia
Philander Smith College .... Little Rock
Phillips County Community College .... Helena
Pulaski Technical College .... North Little Rock
Red River Technical College .... Hope
Rich Mountain Community College .... Mena
Shorter College .... North Little Rock
South Arkansas Community College .... El Dorado
South Central Career College .... North Little Rock
South Central Career College .... Pine Bluff
South Central Career College
   (Branch Campus) .... Jonesboro
Southern Arkansas University .... Magnolia
Southern Arkansas University Tech .... Camden
Southern Technical College .... Little Rock
Southern Technical College
   (Branch Campus) .... Fayetteville
University of Arkansas at Little Rock .... Little Rock
University of Arkansas at Monticello .... Monticello
University of Arkansas at Pine Bluff .... Pine Bluff
University of Arkansas for Medical Sciences .... Little Rock
University of Arkansas, Fayetteville .... Fayetteville
University of Central Arkansas .... Conway
University of the Ozarks .... Clarksville
Westark Community College .... Fort Smith
Williams Baptist College .... Walnut Ridge

California

ABS Training Center .... Westminster
Advertising Arts College .... San Diego
Academy Pacific Business and Travel College .... Hollywood
Academy of Art College .... San Francisco
Academy of Chinese Culture and Health Sciences .... Oakland
Allan Hancock College .... Santa Maria
American Academy of Dramatic Arts West .... Pasadena
American Academy of Nutrition .... Corona Del Mar
American Baptist Seminary of the West .... Berkeley
American College for the Applied Arts
   (Branch) .... Los Angeles
American College of Optechs .... Los Angeles
American College of Traditional Chinese Medicine San Francisco
American Conservatory Theater .... San Francisco
American Film Institute Center for Advanced Film/TV Studies
   .... Los Angeles
American Nanny College .... Montclair
American River College .... Sacramento
American Technical College for Career Training .... San Bernardino
Ameritech Colleges .... Van Nuys
Ameritech Colleges of Bakersfield .... Bakersfield
Andon College at Modesto .... Modesto
Andon College at Stockton .... Stockton
Antelope Valley College .... Lancaster
Antioch University
   (Southern California (Los Angeles)) .... Marina Del Rey
Antioch University
   (Southern California (Santa Barbara)) .... Santa Barbara
Armstrong University .... Berkeley
Art Center College of Design .... Pasadena
Art Institute of Southern California .... Laguna Beach
Associated Technical College .... Anaheim
Associated Technical College .... Los Angeles
Associated Technical College .... San Bernardino
Associated Technical College .... San Diego
Azusa Pacific University .... Azusa
Bakersfield College .... Bakersfield
Barstow College .... Barstow
Bethany College of the Assemblies of God .... Scotts Valley

Bethel Seminary College
   (West) .... San Diego
Biola University .... La Mirada
Brooks College .... Long Beach
Brooks Institute of Photography .... Santa Barbara
Bryan College of Court Reporting .... Los Angeles
Butte College .... Oroville
Cabot College .... National City
Cabrillo College .... Aptos
California Academy of Merchandising, Art & Design .... Sacramento
California Baptist College .... Riverside
California Career Schools .... Anaheim
California College for Health Sciences .... National City
California College of Arts and Crafts .... Oakland
California College of Podiatric Medicine .... San Francisco
California Culinary Academy .... San Francisco
California Family Study Center .... North Hollywood
California Institute of Integral Studies .... San Francisco
California Institute of Locksmithing .... Van Nuys
California Institute of Technology .... Pasadena
California Institute of the Arts .... Valencia
California Lutheran University .... Thousand Oaks
California Maritime Academy .... Vallejo
California Nannie College .... Sacramento
California Paramedical & Technical College .... Long Beach
California Paramedical & Technical College .... Riverside
California Polytechnic State University, San Luis Obispo
   .... San Luis Obispo
California School of Court Reporting .... Riverside
California School of Court Reporting .... Santa Ana
California School of Professional Psychology, Berkeley/Alameda
   .... Alameda
California School of Professional Psychology, Fresno ..... Fresno
California School of Professional Psychology, Los Angeles
   .... Alhambra
California School of Professional Psychology, San Diego
   .... San Diego
California State Polytechnic University, Pomona .... Pomona
California State University, Bakersfield .... Bakersfield
California State University, Chico .... Chico
California State University, Dominguez Hills .... Carson
California State University, Fresno .... Fresno
California State University, Fullerton .... Fullerton
California State University, Hayward .... Hayward
California State University, Long Beach .... Long Beach
California State University, Los Angeles .... Los Angeles
California State University, Northridge .... Northridge
California State University, Sacramento .... Sacramento
California State University, San Bernardino .... San Bernardino
California State University, San Marcos .... San Marcos
California State University, Stanislaus .... Turlock
California Western School of Law .... San Diego
Canada College .... Redwood City
Career Management Institute .... Orange
Career West Academy .... Chico
Catherine College .... Panorama City
Central California School of Continuing Education .... San Luis Obispo
Century Business College .... San Diego
Century Business College
   (Branch Campus) .... Los Angeles
Cerritos College .... Norwalk
Cerro Coso Community College .... Ridgecrest
Chabot College .... Hayward
Chaffey College .... Rancho Cucamonga
Champion Institute of Cosmetology .... Palm Desert
Champion Institute of Cosmetology .... Palm Springs
Chapman University .... Orange
Charles R. Drew University of Medicine and Science Los Angeles
Christian Heritage College .... El Cajon
Church Divinity School of the Pacific .... Berkeley
Citrus College .... Glendora
City College of San Francisco .... San Francisco
Claremont Graduate School .... Claremont

(Bold print indicates degree granting institutions)   431   **State Cross Reference Index**

California

Claremont McKenna College
  (Bauer Center) .... Claremont
Cleveland Chiropractic College .... Los Angeles
Coastline Community College .... Fountain Valley
Cogswell Polytechnical College .... Sunnyvale
Coleman College .... La Mesa
College for Recording Arts .... San Francisco
College of Alameda .... Alameda
College of Marin .... Novato
College of Notre Dame .... Belmont
College of Oceaneering .... Wilmington
College of Osteopathic Medicine of the Pacific .... Pomona
College of San Mateo .... San Mateo
College of the Canyons .... Santa Clarita
College of the Desert .... Palm Desert
College of the Redwoods .... Eureka
College of the Sequoias .... Visalia
College of the Siskiyous .... Weed
CollegeAmerica - San Francisco .... San Francisco
Columbia College .... Sonora
Columbia College Hollywood .... Los Angeles
Combat Systems Technical Schools Command .... Vallejo
Compton Community College .... Compton
Computer Learning Center .... Anaheim
Computer Learning Center .... Los Angeles
Computer Learning Center .... San Francisco
Computer Learning Center .... San Jose
ConCorde Career Institute .... Anaheim
ConCorde Career Institute .... North Hollywood
ConCorde Career Institute .... San Bernardino
ConCorde Career Institute .... San Diego
ConCorde Career Institute .... San Jose
Concordia University .... Irvine
Consolidated Welding Schools .... Lynwood
Contra Costa College .... San Pablo
Cosumnes River College .... Sacramento
Court Reporting Institute
  (Branch Campus) .... San Diego
Crafton Hills College .... Yucaipa
Cuesta College .... San Luis Obispo
Cuyamaca College .... El Cajon
Cypress College .... Cypress
D-Q University .... Davis
De Anza College .... Cupertino
DeVry Institute of Technology .... Pomona
Defense Language Institute .... Presidio of Monterey
Dell'Arte School of Physical Theatre .... Blue Lake
Dental Technology Institute .... Orange
Design Institute of San Diego .... San Diego
Diablo Valley College .... Pleasant Hill
Dickinson-Warren Business College .... Richmond
Dominican College of San Rafael .... San Rafael
Dominican School of Philosophy and Theology .... Berkeley
Don Bosco Technical Institute .... Rosemead
EDUTEK Professional Colleges .... San Diego
EDUTEK Professional Colleges
  (Branch Campus) .... San Diego
EDUTEK Professional Colleges
  (Branch Campus) .... San Diego
East Los Angeles College .... Monterey Park
East Los Angeles Occupational Center .... Los Angeles
Educorp Career College .... Long Beach
El Camino College .... Torrance
Eldorado College .... Oceanside
Eldorado College .... West Covina
Eldorado College
  (Branch Campus) .... Escondido
Eldorado College
  (Branch Campus) .... San Diego
Elegance International .... Los Angeles
Elite Progressive School of Cosmetology .... Sacramento
Emperor's College of Traditional Oriental Medicine Santa Monica
Emperor's College of Traditional Oriental Medicine
  (Branch) .... Los Angeles
Empire College .... Santa Rosa
Estelle Harman Actors Workshop .... Los Angeles
Evergreen Valley College .... San Jose
Fashion Careers of California .... San Diego
Fashion Institute of Design and Merchandising .... Los Angeles
Fashion Institute of Design and Merchandising
  (Branch) .... Costa Mesa
Fashion Institute of Design and Merchandising
  (Branch) .... San Diego
Fashion Institute of Design and Merchandising
  (Branch) .... San Francisco
Feather River College .... Quincy
Fielding Institute .... Santa Barbara
Foothill College .... Los Altos Hills
Franciscan School of Theology .... Berkeley
Fresno City College .... Fresno
Fresno Institute of Technology .... Fresno
Fresno Pacific College .... Fresno
Fuller Theological Seminary .... Pasadena
Fullerton College .... Fullerton
Galen College of Medical and Dental Assistants .... Fresno
Galen College of Medical and Dental Assistants
  (Branch Campus) .... Modesto
Galen College of Medical and Dental Assistants
  (Branch Campus) .... Visalia
Gavilan College .... Gilroy
Gemological Institute of America .... Santa Monica
Gemological Institute of America
  (Branch Campus) .... New York
Glendale Career College .... Glendale
Glendale Community College .... Glendale
Golden Gate Baptist Theological Seminary ..... Mill Valley
Golden Gate University .... San Francisco
Golden West College .... Huntington Beach
Golf Academy of San Diego .... Rancho Santa Fe
Graduate Theological Union .... Berkeley
Grossmont College .... El Cajon
Hartnell College .... Salinas
Harvey Mudd College .... Claremont
Heald Business College-Concord .... Concord
Heald Business College-Fresno .... Fresno
Heald Business College-Hayward .... Hayward
Heald Business College-Oakland .... Oakland
Heald Business College-Sacramento ..... Rancho Cordova
Heald Business College-Salinas .... Salinas
Heald Business College-San Francisco ..... San Francisco
Heald Business College-San Jose .... San Jose
Heald Business College-Santa Rosa .... Santa Rosa
Heald Business College-Stockton .... Stockton
Heald Institute of Technology-Hayward .... Hayward
Heald Institute of Technology-Martinez .... Martinez
Heald Institute of Technology-Sacramento .... Rancho Cordova
Heald Institute of Technology-San Francisco .... San Francisco
Heald Institute of Technology-San Jose .... San Jose
Hebrew Union College-Jewish Institute of Religion ... Los Angeles
Hemphill Schools .... Los Angeles
High-Tech Institute
  (Branch Campus) .... Sacramento
Holy Names College .... Oakland
Humboldt State University .... Arcata
Humphrey's College .... Stockton
Huntington College of Dental Technology .... Huntington Beach
Hypnosis Motivation Institute .... Tarzana
ITT Technical Institute .... Buena Park
ITT Technical Institute .... Carson
ITT Technical Institute .... Sacramento
ITT Technical Institute .... San Bernardino
ITT Technical Institute .... San Diego
ITT Technical Institute .... Van Nuys
ITT Technical Institute .... West Covina
Imperial Valley College .... Imperial
Institute for Business & Technology .... Santa Clara

Institute for Business & Technology
   (National Career Education) .... Citrus Heights
Institute of Business and Medical Technology .... Palm Desert
Institute of Computer Technology.................................... Los Angeles
Interior Designers Institute ....Newport Beach
International Air Academy
   (Branch Campus)... Ontario
International Dealers School... Commerce
Irvine College of Business .... Irvine
Irvine Valley College .... Irvine
Jesuit School of Theology at Berkeley............................ Berkeley
John F. Kennedy University .... Orinda
John Tracy Clinic... Los Angeles
Kelsey-Jenney College.. San Diego
Kings River Community College .... Reedley
L.I.F.E Bible College .... San Dimas
La Sierra University .... Riverside
Lake Tahoe Community College .... South Lake Tahoe
Laney College...Oakland
Las Positas College .... Livermore
Lassen College... Susanville
Learning Tree University...Chatsworth
Lederwolff Culinary Academy .... Sacramento
Leicester School .... Los Angeles
Life Chiropractic College-West .... San Lorenzo
Lincoln University.. San Francisco
Loma Linda University .... Loma Linda
Long Beach City College .... Long Beach
Los Angeles City College .... Los Angeles
Los Angeles College of Chiropractic.............................. Whittier
Los Angeles Harbor College ....Wilmington
Los Angeles Mission College ....Sylmar
Los Angeles ORT Technical Institute............................... Los Angeles
Los Angeles ORT Technical Institute
   (Valley Branch)... Sherman Oaks
Los Angeles Pierce College ....Woodland Hills
Los Angeles Southwest College .... Los Angeles
Los Angeles Trade-Technical College........................ Los Angeles
Los Angeles Valley College .... Van Nuys
Los Medanos College.. Pittsburg
Louise Salinger Academy of Fashion...................... San Francisco
Loyola Marymount University .... Los Angeles
MTI Business College of Stockton Inc. .... Stockton
MTI College .... Orange
MTI College
   (Branch Campus)..Colton
MTI-Western Business College ....Sacramento
Management College of San Francisco....................... San Francisco
Maric College of Medical Careers....................................... San Diego
Maric College of Medical Careers....................................... San Marcos
Maric College of Medical Careers
   (Vista Branch Campus).. Vista
Marin Ballet School... San Rafael
Marymount College .... Rancho Palos Verdes
Master's College .... Santa Clara
Masters Institute .... San Jose
Med-Help Training School .... Concord
Mendocino College... Ukiah
Menlo College... Atherton
Mennonite Brethren Biblical Seminary............................Fresno
Merced College .... Merced
Merit College .... Van Nuys
Merit College .... Van Nuys
Merritt College...Oakland
Mills College ....Oakland
Mira Costa College .... Oceanside
Mission College .... Santa Clara
Modern Technology School of X-Ray .... Anaheim
Modern Technology School of X-Ray .... North Hollywood
Modesto Junior College .... Modesto
Moler Barber College...Oakland
Moler Barber College... Sacramento
Moler Barber College..San Francisco

Moler Barber College
   (Branch Campus)... Sacramento
Moler Barber College
   (Branch Campus)...Stockton
Monterey Institute of International Studies.....................Monterey
Monterey Peninsula College ....Monterey
Moorpark College..Moorpark
Mount San Jacinto College .... San Jacinto
Mount St. Mary's College .... Los Angeles
Mount St. Mary's College
   (Doheny)... Los Angeles
Mt. San Antonio College...Walnut
Musicians Institute .... Hollywood
Napa Valley College .... Napa
National Education Center
   (Brydan) .... Rosemead
National Education Center
   (San Jose Campus)..San Jose
National Education Center
   (Skadron) .... San Bernardino
National Education Center - Bryman Campus .... Anaheim
National Education Center - Bryman Campus .... Long Beach
National Education Center - Bryman Campus ....Los Angeles
National Education Center - Bryman Campus .... Rosemead
National Education Center - Bryman Campus .... San Francisco
National Education Center - Bryman Campus ....San Jose
National Education Center - Bryman Campus .... Torrance
National Education Center - Bryman Campus .... Winnetka
National Education Center - Bryman Campus
   (Branch Campus).. Oakland
National Education Center Sawyer Campus .... Sacramento
National Hispanic University ....San Jose
National Hispanic University
   (Branch Campus).. Oakland
National University .... San Diego
Naval Amphibious School .... San Diego
Naval Construction Training Center..............................Port Hueneme
Naval Health Sciences Education and Training Command
   (Field Medical Service School) .... Camp Pendleton
Naval Health Sciences Education and Training Command
   (School of Dental Assisting)...San Diego
Naval Health Sciences Education and Training Command
   (School of Health Science) .... Oakland
Naval Health Sciences Education and Training Command
   (School of Health Science) .... San Diego
Naval Postgraduate School..Monterey
Naval Service School Command.. San Diego
Naval Technical Training Center.................................. San Francisco
Naval Transportation Management School .... Oakland
Nazarene Bible College
   (Emmanuel Bible College) ....Pasadena
Nazarene Bible College
   (Instituto Teologico Nazareno).......................................Pasadena
New College of California .... San Francisco
Newbridge College... Tustin
Newschool of Architecture ....San Diego
North Park College..San Diego
North Park College
   (Branch Campus)...San Diego
North Valley Occupational Center...................................Mission Hills
Northwest College of Medical & Dental Assistants ....Pasadena
Northwest College of Medical & Dental Assistants .... Pomona
Northwest College of Medical & Dental Assistants .... West Covina
Northwest College of Medical & Dental Assistants
   (Branch Campus).. Glendale
Nova Institute of Health Technolgy ....Los Angeles
Nova Institute of Health Technolgy ....Ontario
Nova Institute of Health Technolgy ....Whittier
Occidental College .... Los Angeles
Ohlone College.. Fremont
Orange Coast College... Costa Mesa
Orange County Business College .... Anaheim
Otis College of Art and Design .... Los Angeles

California

The Sourcebook of College and University Student Records

Oxnard College	Oxnard
Pacific Christian College	Fullerton
Pacific Coast College	Chula Vista
Pacific Coast College	Santa Ana
Pacific College of Oriental Medicine	San Diego
Pacific Gateway College	Los Angeles
Pacific Graduate School of Psychology	Palo Alto
Pacific Lutheran Theological Seminary	Berkeley
Pacific Oaks College	Pasadena
Pacific School of Religion	Berkeley
Pacific Travel School	Santa Ana
Pacific Union College	Angwin
Palmer College of Chiropractic-West	San Jose
Palo Verde College	Blythe
Palomar College	San Marcos
Pasadena City College	Pasadena
Patten College	Oakland
Pepperdine University	Malibu
Phillips College Inland Empire Campus	Riverside
Phillips Junior College	Van Nuys
Phillips Junior College (Branch)	Carson
Phillips Junior College Condie Campus	Campbell
Phillips Junior College Fresno Campus	Fresno
Pitzer College	Claremont
Platt College	Cerritos
Platt College	Irvine
Platt College	Los Angeles
Platt College	Ontario
Platt College	San Diego
Platt College	San Francisco
Point Loma Nazarene College	San Diego
Pomona College	Claremont
Porterville College	Porterville
Practical Schools	Anaheim
Professional Skills Institute (Santa Barbara Campus)	Santa Barbara
Queen of the Holy Rosary College	Mission San Jose
Rancho Santiago Community College	Santa Ana
Rand Graduate School of Policy Studies	Santa Monica
Rice Aviation, a Division of A&J Enterprises (Branch Campus)	Inglewood
Rio Hondo College	Whittier
Riverside Community College	Riverside
Rosston School of Hair Design	San Bernardino
SUTECH School of Vocational-Technical Training	Los Angeles
SUTECH School of Vocational-Technical Training (Branch Campus)	Anaheim
Sacramento City College	Sacramento
Saddleback College	Mission Viejo
Saint Mary's College of California	Moraga
Salvation Army School for Officers' Training	Rancho Palos Verdes
Samra University of Oriental Medicine	Los Angeles
Samuel Merritt College	Oakland
San Bernardino Valley College	San Bernardino
San Diego City College	San Diego
San Diego Mesa College	San Diego
San Diego Miramar College	San Diego
San Diego State University	San Diego
San Francisco Art Institute	San Francisco
San Francisco Ballet School	San Francisco
San Francisco Barber College	San Francisco
San Francisco College of Mortuary Science	San Francisco
San Francisco Conservatory of Music	San Francisco
San Francisco State University	San Francisco
San Francisco Theological Seminary	San Anselmo
San Joaquin College of Law	Fresno
San Joaquin Delta College	Stockton
San Joaquin Valley College	Bakersfield
San Joaquin Valley College	Fresno
San Joaquin Valley College	Visalia
San Joaquin Valley College of Aeronautics	Fresno
San Jose Christian College	San Jose
San Jose City College	San Jose
San Jose State University	San Jose
Santa Barbara Business College	Bakersfield
Santa Barbara Business College	Fremont
Santa Barbara Business College	Santa Barbara
Santa Barbara Business College	Santa Maria
Santa Barbara City College	Santa Barbara
Santa Clara University	Santa Clara
Santa Monica College	Santa Monica
Santa Rosa Junior College	Santa Rosa
Sawyer College	San Jose
Sawyer College at Pomona	Pomona
Sawyer College at Ventura	Oxnard
Saybrook Institute Graduate School & Research Center	San Francisco
School of Communications Electronics	San Francisco
School of Theology at Claremont	Claremont
Scripps College	Claremont
Scripps Research Institute	La Jolla
Sequoia Institute	Fremont
Shasta College	Redding
Sierra Academy of Aeronautics Technicians Institute	Oakland
Sierra College	Rocklin
Sierra Valley Business College	Fresno
Silicon Valley College	Fremont
Simi Valley Adult School	Simi Valley
Simpson College	Redding
Skyline College	San Bruno
Solano Community College	Suisun
Sonoma State University	Rohnert Park
South Baylo University	Anaheim
South Baylo University (Branch)	Los Angeles
South Coast College of Court Reporting	Anaheim
Southern California College	Costa Mesa
Southern California College of Business and Law	Brea
Southern California College of Court Reporting	Anaheim
Southern California College of Optometry	Fullerton
Southwestern College	Chula Vista
Southwestern University School of Law	Los Angeles
St. John's Seminary	Camarillo
St. John's Seminary College	Camarillo
St. Patrick's Seminary	Menlo Park
Stanford University	Stanford
Starr King School for the Ministry	Berkeley
Systems Programming Development Institute	City of Commerce
Taft College	Taft
Thomas Aquinas College	Santa Paula
Travel University International	San Diego
Travel and Trade Career Institute	Long Beach
Travel and Trade Career Institute (Branch Campus)	Garden Grove
Truck Driving Academy	Fresno
Truck Driving Academy	Sacramento
Truck Marketing Institute	Carpinteria
UCC Vocational Center	Long Beach
United States International University	San Diego
University of California, Berkeley	Berkeley
University of California, Davis	Davis
University of California, Hastings College of the Law	San Francisco
University of California, Irvine	Irvine
University of California, Los Angeles	Los Angeles
University of California, Riverside	Riverside
University of California, San Diego	La Jolla
University of California, San Francisco	San Francisco
University of California, Santa Barbara	Santa Barbara
University of California, Santa Cruz	Santa Cruz
University of Judaism	Los Angeles
University of La Verne	La Verne
University of Phoenix (Fountain Valley Main)	Fountain Valley
University of Phoenix	

State Cross Reference Index (Bold print indicates degree granting institutions)

(Online) .... San Francisco
University of Phoenix
 (San Diego) .... San Diego
University of Phoenix
 (San Jose Main) .... San Jose
University of Redlands .... Redlands
University of San Diego .... San Diego
University of San Francisco .... San Francisco
University of Southern California .... Los Angeles
University of West Los Angeles .... Inglewood
University of the Pacific .... Stockton
Valley Commercial College .... Modesto
Ventura College .... Ventura
Victor Valley College .... Victorville
Vista College .... Berkeley
Watterson College .... Pasadena
Watterson College .... West Covina
Watterson College Pacific .... Oxnard
Watterson College Pacific
 (Branch Campus) .... Vista
West Coast University .... Los Angeles
West Hills Community College .... Coalinga
West Los Angeles College .... Culver City
West Valley College .... Saratoga
Westech College .... Pomona
Western Career College .... Sacramento
Western Career College .... San Leandro
Western State University College of Law of Orange County
 .... Fullerton
Western State University College of Law of San Diego San Diego
Western Truck School .... Fresno
Western Truck School .... Turlock
Western Truck School .... West Sacramento
Western Truck School
 (Branch Campus) .... Bakersfield
Western Truck School
 (Branch Campus) .... San Diego
Western Truck School
 (Branch Campus) .... Stockton
Westlake Institute of Technology .... Westlake Village
Westminster Theological Seminary in California .... Escondido
Westmont College .... Santa Barbara
Whittier College .... Whittier
Woodbury University .... Burbank
Wright Institute .... Berkeley
Yeshiva Ohr Elchonon-Chabad/West Coast Talmudic Seminary
 .... Los Angeles
Yo San University of Traditional Chinese Medicine Santa Monica
Yuba College .... Marysville

Colorado

Academy of Floral Design .... Denver
Adams State College .... Alamosa
Aims Community College .... Greeley
American Diesel & Automotive College .... Denver
Arapahoe Community College .... Littleton
Army Academy of Health Sciences
 (Medical Equipment and Optician School) .... Aurora
Barnes Business College .... Denver
Bel-Rea Institute of Animal Technology .... Denver
Beth-El College of Nursing .... Colorado Springs
Blair Junior College .... Colorado Springs
Boulder School of Massage Therapy .... Boulder
Boulder Valley Area Vocational-Technical Center .... Boulder
CollegeAmerica - Denver .... Denver
Colorado Aero Tech .... Broomfield
Colorado Association of Paramedical Education, Inc. .... Thornton
Colorado Career Academy .... Aurora
Colorado Career Academy .... Lakewood
Colorado Christian University .... Lakewood

Colorado College .... Colorado Springs
Colorado Institute of Art .... Denver
Colorado Mountain College .... Glenwood Springs
Colorado Mountain College
 (Alpine) .... Steamboat Springs
Colorado Mountain College
 (Roaring Fork) .... Glenwood Springs
Colorado Mountain College
 (Timberline) .... Leadville
Colorado Northwestern Community College .... Rangely
Colorado School of Mines .... Golden
Colorado School of Trades .... Lakewood
Colorado School of Travel .... Lakewood
Colorado State University .... Fort Collins
Colorado Technical College .... Colorado Springs
Columbine College .... Denver
Columbine College
 (Branch Campus) .... Colorado Springs
Community College of Aurora .... Aurora
Community College of Denver .... Denver
Concorde Career Institute .... Denver
Denver Academy of Court Reporting .... Denver
Denver Academy of Court Reporting
 (Branch Campus) .... Colorado Springs
Denver Automotive and Diesel College .... Denver
Denver Business College .... Denver
Denver Conservative Baptist Seminary .... Denver
Denver Institute of Technology .... Denver
Denver Institute of Technology
 (Health Careers Division) .... Denver
Denver Paralegal Institute .... Denver
Denver Paralegal Institute
 (Branch Campus) .... Colorado Springs
Denver Technical College .... Denver
Denver Technical College at Colorado Springs .. Colorado Springs
Durango Air Service .... Durango
Emily Griffith Opportunity School .... Denver
Fort Lewis College .... Durango
Front Range Community College .... Westminster
Heritage College of Health Careers .... Denver
ITT Technical Institute .... Aurora
Iliff School of Theology .... Denver
Johnson & Wales University
 (Branch Campus) .... Vail
Lamar Community College .... Lamar
Medical Careers Training Center .... Fort Collins
Mesa State College .... Grand Junction
Metropolitan State College of Denver .... Denver
Morgan Community College .... Fort Morgan
Naropa Institute .... Boulder
National Technological University .... Fort Collins
National Theatre Conservatory .... Denver
Nazarene Bible College .... Colorado Springs
Northeastern Junior College .... Sterling
Otero Junior College .... La Junta
PPI Health Careers School .... Colorado Springs
Parks Junior College .... Denver
Parks Junior College
 (Branch) .... Aurora
Pikes Peak Community College .... Colorado Springs
Pima Medical Institute
 (Branch) .... Denver
Platt College .... Aurora
Presbyterian-St. Luke Center for Health Science Foundation ... Denver
Pueblo College of Business and Technology .... Pueblo
Pueblo Community College .... Pueblo
Red Rocks Community College .... Lakewood
Regis University .... Denver
Rocky Mountain College of Art and Design .... Denver
St. Thomas Theological Seminary .... Denver
T.H. Pickens Technical Center .... Aurora
Technical Trades Institute .... Colorado Springs
Technical Trades Institute .... Grand Junction

Connecticut

Technical Trades Institute
  (Emery Aviation College) .... Colorado Springs
Trinidad State Junior College .... Trinidad
United States Air Force Academy
  (Department of the Air Force) .... USAF Academy
University of Colorado Health Sciences Center .... Denver
University of Colorado at Boulder .... Boulder
University of Colorado at Colorado Springs ...... Colorado Springs
University of Colorado at Denver .... Denver
University of Denver .... Denver
University of Northern Colorado .... Greeley
University of Phoenix
  (Denver Main) .... Englewood
University of Southern Colorado .... Pueblo
Western State College of Colorado .... Gunnison
Yeshiva Toras Chaim Talmudic Seminary .... Denver

Connecticut

Albert I. Prince Regional Vocational-Technical School .... Hartford
Albertus Magnus College .... New Haven
Allstate Tractor Trailer Training School .... Bridgeport
Asnuntuck Community-Technical College .... Enfield
Baran Institute of Technology .... Windsor
Branford Hall Career Institute .... Branford
Briarwood College .... Southington
Butler Business School .... Bridgeport
Capital Community-Technical College .... Hartford
Capital Community-Technical College
  (Flatbush) .... Hartford
Central Connecticut State University .... New Britain
Charter Oak State College .... Newington
Connecticut Business Institute .... Stratford
Connecticut Business Institute
  (Branch Campus) .... East Hartford
Connecticut Business Institute
  (Branch Campus) .... New Haven
Connecticut Center for Message Therapy .... Newington
Connecticut Center for Message Therapy
  (Branch Campus) .... Westport
Connecticut College .... New London
Connecticut Institute of Art .... Greenwich
Connecticut Institute of Hair Design .... Wolcott
Connecticut School of Electronics .... New Haven
Data Institute .... East Hartford
Data Institute
  (Branch Campus) .... Waterbury
Eastern Connecticut State University .... Willimantic
Eli Whitney Regional Vocational-Technical School .... Hamden
Fairfield University .... Fairfield
Fox Institute of Business .... Hartford
Gateway Community-Technical College .... New Haven
Gateway Community-Technical College
  (North Haven) .... North Haven
Hartford Camerata Conservatory .... Hartford
Hartford Graduate Center .... Hartford
Hartford Seminary .... Hartford
Holy Apostles College and Seminary .... Cromwell
Housatonic Community-Technical College .... Bridgeport
Huntington Institute .... Norwich
Industrial Management and Training, Inc. .... Waterbury
Katharine Gibbs School .... Norwalk
Lyme Academy of Fine Arts .... Old Lyme
Manchester Community-Technical College .... Manchester
Middlesex Community-Technical College .... Middletown
Mitchell College .... New London
Morse School of Business .... Hartford
Naugatuck Valley Community-Technical College .... Waterbury
Naval Health Sciences Education and Training Command
  (Undersea Medical Institute) .... Groton
New England Technical Institute of Connecticut .... New Britain
New England Tractor Trailer Training School of Connecticut .. Somers
Northwestern Connecticut Community-Technical College Winsted
Norwalk Community-Technical College .... Norwalk
Paier College of Art .... Hamden
Porter and Chester Institute .... Stratford
Porter and Chester Institute
  (Branch Campus) .... Enfield
Porter and Chester Institute
  (Branch Campus) .... Watertown
Porter and Chester Institute
  (Branch Campus) .... Wethersfield
Quinebaug Valley Community-Technical College .... Danielson
Quinnipiac College .... Hamden
Ridley-Lowell Business and Technical Institute .... New London
Roffler Academy for Hairstylists .... Hartford
Roffler Academy for Hairstylists
  (Branch Campus) .... Southington
Sacred Heart University .... Fairfield
Sawyer School
  (Branch Campus) .... Hamden
School of the Hartford Ballet .... Hartford
Southern Connecticut State University .... New Haven
St. Joseph College .... West Hartford
Stone Academy .... Hamden
Technical Careers Institute .... West Haven
Technical Careers Institute
  (Branch Campus) .... Windsor
Teikyo Post University .... Waterbury
Three Rivers Community-Technical College .... Norwich
Three Rivers Community-Technical College
  (Thames) .... Norwich
Trinity College .... Hartford
Tunxis Community-Technical College .... Farmington
United States Coast Guard Academy .... New London
University of Bridgeport .... Bridgeport
University of Connecticut .... Storrs
University of Connecticut School of Medicine .... Farmington
University of Hartford .... West Hartford
University of New Haven .... West Haven
Weselyan University .... Middletown
Western Connecticut State University .... Danbury
Westlawn School of Marine Technology .... Stamford
Wilcox College of Nursing .... Middletown
Windham Regional Vocational-Technical School .... Willimantic
Yale Divinity School .... New Haven
Yale University .... New Haven

Delaware

Career Institute
  (Branch Campus) .... Wilmington
Dawn Training Institute .... New Castle
Delaware State University .... Dover
Delaware Technical & Community College
  (Stanton/Willington) .... Newark
Delaware Technical & Community College
  (Terry) .... Dover
Deleware Technical & Community College
  (Southern) .... Georgetown
Goldey-Beacom College .... Wilmington
Star Technical Institute .... Wilmington
University of Delaware .... Newark
Wesley College .... Dover
Widener University
  (School of Law) .... Wilmington
Wilmington College .... New Castle

District of Columbia

- **American University** .... Washington
- Automation Academy .... Washington
- **Catholic University of America** .... Washington
- **Corcoran School of Art** .... Washington
- De Sales School of Theology .... Washington
- **District of Columbia School of Law** .... Washington
- Dominican House of Studies .... Washington
- **Gallaudet University** .... Washington
- **George Washington University** .... Washington
- **Georgetown University** .... Washington
- Hannah Harrison Career Schools .... Washington
- **Howard University** .... Washington
- **Johns Hopkins University**
  (School of Advanced International Studies) .... Washington
- **Joint Military Intelligence College** .... Washington
- Levine School of Music .... Washington
- Margaret Murray Washington Vocational School ...... Washington
- Marine Corps Institute .... Washington
- McGraw-Hill Continuing Education Center .... Washington
- McGraw-Hill Continuing Education Center
  (NRI Schools) .... Washington
- **Mount Vernon College** .... Washington
- National Conservatory of Dramatic Arts .... Washington
- **Oblate College** .... Washington
- PTC Career Institute .... Washington
- **Southeastern University** .... Washington
- **Strayer College** .... Washington
- **Trinity College** .... Washington
- **University of the District of Columbia** .... Washington
- **University of the District of Columbia**
  (Georgia/Harvard Street) .... Washington
- Washington Conservatory of Music, Inc. .... Washington
- **Wesley Theological Seminary** .... Washington

Florida

- ATI Career Training Center .... Oakland Park
- ATI Career Training Center
  (Branch Campus) .... Miami
- ATI Career Training Center Electronic Campus .... Fort Lauderdale
- ATI-Health Education Center .... Miami
- Academy of Creative Hair Design .... Ocala
- Academy of Healing Arts, Message & Facial Skin Care .... Lake Worth
- American Flyers College .... Fort Lauderdale
- **Art Institute of Fort Lauderdale** .... Fort Lauderdale
- **Atlantic Coast Institute** .... Fort Lauderdale
- Atlantic Vocational-Technical Center .... Coconut Creek
- Atlantic Vocational-Technical Center
  (Branch Campus) .... Pompano Beach
- Automotive Transmission School .... Hialeah
- Avanti Hair Tech .... Lakeland
- Avanti Hair Tech .... Tampa
- Avanti Hair Tech .... Temple Terrace
- Avanti Hair Tech
  (Branch Campus) .... Winter Park
- Barna Institute .... Fort Lauderdale
- **Barry University** .... Miami Shores
- Bay Area Vocational-Technical School .... Fort Walton Beach
- Beacon Career Institute .... Miami
- Beauty Schools of America .... Margate
- Beauty Schools of America
  (Branch Campus) .... Miami
- **Bethune-Cookman College** .... Daytona Beach
- **Brevard Community College** .... Cocoa
- **Broward Community College** .... Fort Lauderdale
- Business & Technology Institute .... Miami
- Career Center .... West Palm Beach
- **Career College**
  (Branch) .... Gainesville
- Career Training Institute .... Leesburg
- Career Training Institute .... Orlando
- **Caribbean Center for Advanced Studies**
  (Miami Institute of Psychology) .... Miami
- **Central Florida Community College** .... Ocala
- Charlotte Vocational-Technical Center .... Port Charlotte
- **Chipola Junior College** .... Marianna
- **Clearwater Christian College** .... Clearwater
- Clinton Technical Institute
  (Motorcycle/Marine Mechanics Institute) .... Orlando
- ConCorde Career Institute .... Jacksonville
- ConCorde Career Institute .... Lauderdale Lakes
- ConCorde Career Institute .... Tampa
- ConCorde Career Institute
  (Branch Campus) .... Miami
- **Cooper Academy of Court Reporting** .... West Palm Beach
- Crown Business Institute .... Miami
- David G. Erwing Technical Center .... Tampa
- **Daytona Beach Community College** .... Daytona Beach
- Defense Equal Opportunity Management Institute
  .... Patrick Air Force Base
- Diana Ramsey's Specialty Beauty School .... Deerfield Beach
- **Eckerd College** .... St Petersburg
- **Edison Community College** .... Fort Myers
- **Edward Waters College** .... Jacksonville
- Elkins Institute of Jacksonville .... Jacksonville
- **Embry-Riddle Aeronautical University** .... Daytona Beach
- Euro Hair Design Institute .... Tallahassee
- Euro-Skill Therapeutic Training Center .... Boca Raton
- FAA Center for Management Development .... Palm Coast
- Federal Correctional Institution .... Tallahassee
- **Flagler Career Institute** .... Jacksonville
- **Flagler College** .... St Augustine
- FlightSafety International .... Vero Beach
- **Florida Agricultural and Mechanical University** .... Tallahassee
- **Florida Atlantic University** .... Boca Raton
- **Florida Baptist Theological College** .... Graceville
- **Florida Bible College** .... Kissimmee
- **Florida Christian College** .... Kissimmee
- **Florida College** .... Temple Terrace
- **Florida Community College at Jacksonville** .... Jacksonville
- **Florida Computer & Business School** .... Miami
- Florida Institute of Message Therapy & Esthetics .... Lauderhill
- **Florida Institute of Technology** .... Melbourne
- Florida Institute of Ultrasound, Inc. .... Pensacola
- **Florida International University** .... Miami
- **Florida Keys Community College** .... Key West
- **Florida Memorial College** .... Miami
- Florida School of Business .... Miami
- Florida School of Business .... Tampa
- **Florida Southern College** .... Lakeland
- **Florida State University** .... Tallahassee
- **Florida Technical College** .... Jacksonville
- Florida Technical College .... Orlando
- Florida Technical College .... Tampa
- **Fort Lauderdale College** .... Fort Lauderdale
- Full Sail Center for the Recording Arts .... Winter Park
- Garces Commercial College .... Miami
- Garces Commercial College
  (Branch Campus) .... Miami Springs
- George Stone Vocational-Technical Center .... Pensacola
- George T. Baker Aviation School .... Miami
- Golf Academy of San Diego
  (Golf Academy of the South) .... Winter Springs
- **Gulf Coast Community College** .... Panama City
- Hair Design School .... Jacksonville
- Health Institute of Louisville
  (Branch Campus) .... St. Petersburg
- Henry W. Brewster Technical Center .... Tampa
- Hi-Tech School of Miami .... Miami

Florida

The Sourcebook of College and University Student Records

Hialeah Technical Center .... Hialeah
Hillsborough Community College...Tampa
Hobe Sound Bible College .... Hobe Sound
Humanities Center Institute of Allied Health/School of Message Pinellas Park
ITT Technical Institute..Maitland
ITT Technical Institute..Tampa
ITT Technical Institute
    (Branch) .... Fort Lauderdale
ITT Technical Institute
    (Branch) ....Jacksonville
Indian River Community College .... Fort Pierce
International Academy of Merchandising and Design........Tampa
International College ....Naples
International College
    (Branch) .... Fort Myers
International Fine Arts College.. Miami
Jacksonville University ....Jacksonville
James L. Walker Vocational-Technical Center..........................Naples
Johnson & Wales University
    (Branch Campus)..North Miami
Jones College..Jacksonville
Jones College
    (Branch) .... South Miami
Keiser College .... Fort Lauderdale
Keiser College
    (Branch) .... Melbourne
Keiser College
    (Branch) ....Tallahassee
Lake City Community College... Lake City
Lake County Area Vocational-Technical Center ....Eustis
Lake-Sumter Community College .... Leesburg
Lee County Vocational High Tech Center............................ Fort Myers
Legal Career Institute
    (Branch) ....Riviera Beach
Lindsey Hopkins Technical Education Center .... Miami
Lively Area Vocational-Technical Center ....Tallahassee
Lynn University... Boca Raton
Manatee Area Vocational-Technical Center ....Bradenton
Manatee Community College ....Bradenton
Marion County School of Radiologic Technology ....Ocala
Martin College .... Miami
Master Schools.. Fort Lauderdale
Master Schools.. Miami
Medical Arts Training Center, Inc..Margate
Miami Institute of Technology.. Miami
Miami Job Corps Center... Miami
Miami Lakes Technical Education Center .... Miami
Miami Technical Institute.. North Miami
Miami Technical Institute
    (Branch Campus)... Miami
Miami-Dade Community College.. Miami
Mid-Florida Technical Institute .... Orlando
National Aviation Academy ....Clearwater
National Career Institute ....Tampa
National Education Center
    (Branch Campus) .... Miami
National Education Center - Bauder College Campus. Fort Lauderdale
National Education Center - Tampa Technical Institute ....Tampa
National School of Technology ....N Miami Beach
National School of Technology
    (Branch Campus)...Hialeah
National Training, Inc..Orange Park
Naval Diving and Salvage Training Center ....Panama City
Naval Health Sciences Education and Training Command
    (Aerospace Medical Institute).. Pensacola
Naval Service School Command .... Orlando
Naval Technical Training Center .... Pensacola
New England Institute of Technology at Palm Beach
    ....West Palm Beach
North Florida Junior College .... Madison
North Technical Education Center ....Riviera Beach
Northwood University

    (Branch) ....West Palm Beach
Nova University ....Fort Lauderdale
Okaloosa-Walton Community College .... Niceville
Omni Technical School..Fortlauderdale
Omni Technical School... Miami
Orlando College...Orlando
Orlando College
    (Branch) ....Orlando
Orlando Vocational-Technical Center .... Orlando
PHD Hair Academy.. Clearwater
Palm Beach Atlantic College ....West Palm Beach
Palm Beach Beauty & Barber School..................West Palm Beach
Palm Beach Community College .... Lake Worth
Paralegal Careers .... Tampa
Pasco-Hernando Community College..........................Dade City
Pensacola Junior College... Pensacola
Phillips Junior College... Daytona Beach
Phillips Junior College..Melbourne
Phillips Junior College
    (Branch) .... Daytona Beach
Phillips Junior College
    (Branch Campus)..Melbourne
Pinellas Technical Education Center .... Clearwater
Pinellas Technical Education Center
    (Branch Campus) .... Clearwater
Pinellas Technical Education Center
    (Branch Campus) .... Clearwater
Pinellas Technical Education Center-St. Petersburg Campus
    .... St. Petersburg
Politechnical Institute ....Miami
Polk Community College...Winter Haven
Pompano Academy of Aeronautics............................. Pompano Beach
Pounter Institute for Media Studies.............................. St. Petersburg
Prospect Hall School of Business .... Hollywood
QUALTEC Institute for Competitive Advantage .... North Palm Beach
RTI Technical Institute..Pensacola
Radford M. Locklin Vocational-Technical Center .... Milton
Recreational Vehicle Service Academy...................................Ellenton
Rice College
    (Branch Campus) .... Jacksonville
Ridge Vocational-Technical Center................................Winter Haven
Ringling School of Art and Design .... Sarasota
Robert Morgan Vocational-Technical Center .... Miami
Rollins College .... Winter Park
Romar Beauty Academy .... Boynton Beach
Ross Medical Education Center
    (Ross Technical Institute)...West Palm Beach
SER-IBM Business Institute .... Miami
Santa Fe Community College .... Gainesville
Sarasota County Technical Institute .... Sarasota
Segal Institute of Court Reporting .... Clearwater
Seminole Community College .... Sanford
Sheridan Vocational-Technical Center................................ Hollywood
South College ....West Palm Beach
South Florida Community College .... Avon Park
South Technical Education Center .... Boynton Beach
Southeastern Academy, Inc. .... Kissimmee
Southeastern Academy, Inc. .... Kissimmee
Southeastern Academy, Inc.
    (Peoples College of Independent Studies).....................Kissimmee
Southeastern Academy, Inc.
    (Peoples College of Independent Studies).....................Kissimmee
Southeastern College of the Assemblies of God............. Lakeland
Southeastern University of the Health Sciences
    .... North Miami Beach
Southern College..Orlando
Southern Technical Center .... Miami
Southwest Florida College of Business....................... Fort Myers
St. Augustine Technical Center .... St. Augustine
St. Augustine Technical Center
    (Branch Campus)..East Palatka
St. John Vianney College Seminary .... Miami
St. Johns River Community College .... Palatka

State Cross Reference Index   (Bold print indicates degree granting institutions)

St. Leo College	Saint Leo
St. Petersburg Junior College	St Petersburg
St. Thomas University	Miami
St. Vincent de Paul Regional Seminary	Boynton Beach
Stenotype Institute of Jacksonville	Jacksonville Beach
Stetson University	Deland
Suncoast Center for Natural Health/Suncoast School	Tampa
Sunstate Academy of Hair Design	Fort Myers
Sunstate Academy of Hair Design	Port Charlotte
Sunstate Academy of Hair Design	Sarasota
Suwanee-Hamilton Area Vocational-Technical & Adult Education Ctr	Live Oak
Tallahassee Community College	Tallahassee
Talmudic College of Florida	Miami Beach
Tampa College	Clearwater
Tampa College	Tampa
Tampa College (Branch)	Lakeland
Tampa College (Branch)	Tampa
Taylor Technical Institute	Perry
Technical Career Institute	Miami
Tom P. Haney Vocational-Technical Center	Panama City
Traviss Vocational-Technical Center	Eaton Park
Trinity International University	Miami
U.S. Schools	Miami
Ultrasound Diagnostic School (Branch Campus)	Jacksonville
Ultrasound Diagnostic School (Branch Campus)	Pompano Beach
Ultrasound Diagnostic School (Branch Campus)	Tampa
University of Central Florida	Orlando
University of Florida	Gainesville
University of Miami	Coral Gables
University of North Florida	Jacksonville
University of Sarasota	Sarasota
University of South Florida	Tampa
University of Tampa	Tampa
University of West Florida	Pensacola
Valencia Community College (West)	Orlando
Ward Stone College	Miami
Warner Southern College	Lake Wales
Washington-Holmes Area Vocational-Technical Center	Chipley
Webber College	Babson Park
Webster College (Branch Campus)	Fort Pierce
Webster College (Branch Campus)	Gainesville
Webster College (Branch Campus)	New Port Richey
Webster College (Branch Campus)	Ocala
West Technical Education Center	Belle Glade
West Virginia Career College (Branch Campus)	Daytona Beach
Westside Vocational-Technical Center	Winter Garden
Westside Vocational-Technical Center (Branch Campus)	Orlando
Westside Vocational-Technical Center (Branch Campus)	Orlando
William T. McFatter Vocational-Technical Center	Davie
William T. McFatter Vocational-Technical Center (Branch Campus)	Davie
William T. McFatter Vocational-Technical Center (Branch Campus)	Davie
Winter Park Adult Vocational Center	Winter Park
Withlacoochee Technical Institute	Inverness

Georgia

Abraham Baldwin Agricultural College	Tifton
Agnes Scott College	Decatur
Albany State College	Albany
Albany Technical Institute	Albany
Alliance Tractor Trailer Training Center	McDonough
Altamaha Technical Institute	Jessup
Altamaha Technical Institute (Branch Campus)	Hazlehurst
American College	Atlanta
American Schools of Professional Psychology (Georgia School of Professional Psychology)	Atlanta
Andrew College	Cuthbert
Armstrong State College	Savannah
Armstrong University of Beauty	Rome
Army Signal Center and School	Fort Gordon
Art Institute of Atlanta	Atlanta
Artistic Beauty College	Conyers
Asher School of Business	Norcross
Athens Area Technical Institute	Athens
Atlanta Area Technical School	Atlanta
Atlanta Area Technical School (Branch Campus)	Atlanta
Atlanta Christian College	East Point
Atlanta College of Art	Atlanta
Atlanta Institute of Music	Norcross
Atlanta Job Corps Center	Atlanta
Atlanta Metropolitan College	Atlanta
Atlanta School of Massage	Atlanta
Augusta Technical Institute	Augusta
Bainbridge College	Bainbridge
Bauder College	Atlanta
Ben Hill-Irwin Technical Institute	Fitzgerald
Berry College	Rome
Brenau University	Gainesville
Brewton Parker College	Mount Vernon
Brown College of Court Reporting & Medical Transcription	Atlanta
Brunswick College	Brunswick
Carroll Technical Institute	Carrollton
Chattahoochee Technical Institute	Marietta
Clark Atlanta University	Atlanta
Clayton State College	Morrow
Cobb Beauty College	Kennesaw
Columbia Theological Seminary	Decatur
Columbus College	Columbus
Columbus Technical Institute	Columbus
Coosa Valley Technical Institute	Rome
Covenant College	Lookout Mountain
Dalfort Aircraft Tech (Branch Campus)	Atlanta
Dalton College	Dalton
Dalton Vocational School of Health Occupations	Dalton
Darton College	Albany
DeKalb Beauty College	Stone Mountain
DeKalb College	Clarkston
DeKalb Technical Institute	Clarkston
DeVry Institute of Technology, Atlanta	Decatur
Derma Clinic Academy	Atlanta
Draughons College	Atlanta
East Georgia College	Swainsboro
Emmanuel College	Franklin Springs
Emory University	Atlanta
Executive Travel Institute	Atlanta
Flint River Technical Institute	Thomaston
Floyd College	Rome
Fort Valley State College	Fort Valley
Gainesville College	Gainesville
Georgia College	Milledgeville
Georgia Institute of Cosmetology	Athens
Georgia Institute of Technology	Atlanta

(Bold print indicates degree granting institutions)

Georgia Medical Institute..Atlanta
Georgia Medical Institute
 (Branch Campus)..Atlanta
Georgia Medical Institute
 (Branch Campus).. Marietta
Georgia Military College ....Milledgeville
Georgia Southern University........................Statesboro
Georgia Southwestern College ....Americus
Georgia State University......................................Atlanta
Gordon College...Barnesville
Griffin Technical Institute ....Griffin
Gupton-Jones College of Funeral Service.......Decatur
Gwinnett College ....Liburn
Gwinnett Technical Institute........................Lawrenceville
Heart of Georgia Technical Institute ....Dublin
Heart of Georgia Technical Institute
 (Branch Campus)...Eastman
Institute of Paper Science and Technology.......Atlanta
Interactive Learning Systems ....Athens
Interactive Learning Systems ....Atlanta
Interactive Learning Systems
 (Branch Campus)..College Park
Interactive Learning Systems
 (Branch Campus)... Marietta
Interactive Learning Systems
 (Branch Campus)...Tucker
Interdenominational Theological Center..............Atlanta
International School of Skin & Nailcare.................Atlanta
Kennesaw State College .... Marietta
Kerr Business College.. Lagrange
Kerr Business College
 (Branch Campus)..Augusta
LaGrange College .... Lagrange
LaGrange Cosmetology School .... Lagrange
Lanier Technical Institute ....Oakwood
Life College.. Marietta
Mable Bailey Fashion College..............................Columbus
Macon Beauty School... Macon
Macon College .... Macon
Macon Technical Institute... Macon
Macon Technical Institute
 (Branch Campus).. Macon
Massey College of Business & Technology ....Atlanta
Massey College of Business & Technology
 (Massey Institute)...Atlanta
Medical College of Georgia ....Augusta
Medix School
 (Branch Campus)... Marietta
Mercer University ....Macon
Metropolitan College of Business ....Decatur
Metropolitan School of Hair Design ....Stone Mountain
Middle Georgia College ....Cochran
Middle Georgia Technical Institute ....Warner Robins
Middle Georgia Technical Institute
 (Branch Campus)...........................Robins Air Force Base
Morehouse College..Atlanta
Morehouse School of Medicine ....Atlanta
Morris Brown College...Atlanta
Moultrie Area Technical Institute .... Moultrie
Moultrie Area Technical Institute
 (Branch Campus)..Tifton
National Business Institute.......................................Decatur
National Education Center-Bryman Campus...........Atlanta
Navy Supply Corps School..Athens
North Fulton Beauty College..................................... Roswell
North Georgia College.......................................Dahlonega
North Metro Technical Institute ....Acworth
Occupational Education Center-Central ....Chamblee
Occupational Education Center-North ....Dunwoody
Occupational Education Center-South ....Decatur
Ogeechee Technical Institute ....Statesboro
Oglethorpe University ....Atlanta
Okefenokee Technical Institute ....Waycross

Paine College...Augusta
Pickens Technical Institute...Jasper
Piedmont College ....Demorest
Portfolio Center... Atlanta
Pro-Way Hair School .... Newnan
Professional Career Development Institute ....Norcross
Quality Plus Office Skills and Motivational Training Center ...... Atlanta
Reinhardt College..Waleska
Riley College
 (Branch Campus)..Albany
Roffler Moler Hairstyling College..........................Forest Park
Roffler Moler Hairstyling College
 (Branch Campus)... Marietta
SamVerly College .... Atlanta
Savannah College of Art and Design ....Savannah
Savannah State College ....Savannah
Savannah Technical Institute...........................Savannah
Shorter College... Rome
South College..Savannah
South Georgia College .... Douglas
South Georgia Technical Institute.......................... Americus
Southeastern Center for the Arts .... Atlanta
Southeastern School fo Aeronautics.......................Macon
Southeastern Technical Institute............................. Vidalia
Southern College of Technology.......................Marietta
Spelman College .... Atlanta
Swainsboro Technical Institute ....Swainsboro
Thomas College..Thomasville
Thomas Technical Institute................................Thomasville
Toccoa Falls College.................................... Toccoa Falls
Trident Training Facility .... Kings Bay
Truett-McConnell College ....Cleveland
Turner Job Corps Center..Albany
Ultrasound Diagnostic School
 (Branch Campus)... Atlanta
University of Georgia.. Athens
Valdosta State University ....Valdosta
Valdosta Technical Institute...................................Valdosta
Walker Technical Institute ....Rock Spring
Waycross College .... Waycross
Wesleyan College..Macon
West Georgia College .... Carrollton
West Georgia Technical Institute...........................Lagrange
Young Harris College....................................Young Harris

Guam

Guam Community College................................ Main Island
University of Guam... Mangilao

Hawaii

Brigham Young University
 (Hawaii) ....Laie
Chaminade University of Honolulu .... Honolulu
Denver Business College
 (Branch) .... Honolulu
Electronic Institute .... Honolulu
Hawaii Business College .... Honolulu
Hawaii Community College ....Hilo
Hawaii Institute of Hair Design................................ Honolulu
Hawaii Pacific University .... Honolulu
Honolulu Community College........................... Honolulu
Kansai Gaidai Hawaii College .... Honolulu
Kapiolani Community College .... Honolulu
Kauai Community College...Lihue
Leeward Community College......................... Pearl City
Med-Assist School of Hawaii .... Honolulu

New York Technical Institute of Hawaii .... Honolulu
Tai Hsuan Foundation College of Acupuncture and Herbal Medicine.. Honolulu
Travel Institute of the Pacific .... Honolulu
Travel University International
  (Branch Campus)... Honolulu
University of Hawaii
  (Maui Community College)..Kahului
University of Hawaii at Hilo..Hilo
University of Hawaii at Manoa..Honolulu
University of Hawaii at West Oahu..................................Pearl City
University of Phoenix
  (Hawaii Main) ....Honolulu
Windward Community College..Kaneohe

Idaho

Albertson College ....Caldwell
American Institute of Health Technology, Inc. .... Boise
Boise Bible College... Boise
Boise State University .... Boise
College of Southern Idaho .... Twin Falls
Eastern Idaho Technical College .... Idaho Falls
ITT Technical Institute.. Boise
Idaho State University .... Pocatello
Lewis-Clark State College..Lewiston
North Idaho College...Coeur D' Alene
Northwest Nazarene College .... Nampa
Ricks College ....Rexburg
University of Idaho ....Moscow

Illinois

Adler School of Professional Psychology ....Chicago
American Academy of Art ....Chicago
American Career Training ....Chicago
American College of Technology.................................Bloomington
American Conservatory of Music ....Chicago
American Health Information Management Association ....Chicago
American Schools of Professional Psychology ....Chicago
American Schools of Professional Psychology
  (Illinois School of Professional Psychology).......................Chicago
Augustana College .... Rock Island
Aurora University... Aurora
Barat College .... Lake Forest
Belleville Area College ....Belleville
Belleville Barber College ....Belleville
Black Hawk College ....Moline
Blackburn College ....Carlinville
Blessing-Rieman College of Nursing...............................Quincy
Bradley University ....Peoria
Cain's Barber College...Chicago
Capital Area Vocational Center..Springfield
Carl Sandburg College .... Galesburg
Catholic Theological Union ....Chicago
Cave Technical Institute ....Lockport
Chicago College of Commerce..Chicago
Chicago School of Professional Psychology ....Chicago
Chicago State University ....Chicago
Chicago Theological Seminary ....Chicago
College of DuPage ....Glen Ellyn
College of Lake County .... Grayslake
College of St. Francis ....Joliet
Columbia College...Chicago
Computer Learning Center ....Chicago
Concordia University... River Forest
Connecticut School of Broadcasting ....Lombard
Cooking and Hospitality Institute of Chicago ....Chicago
Coyne American Institute...Chicago
Danville Area Community College.................................. Danville
DePaul University ....Chicago
DeVry Institute of Technology, Chicago...........................Chicago
DeVry Institute of Technology, DuPage............................Addison
DeVry Institutes .... Oak Brook Terrace
Dr. William M. Scholl College of Podiatric Medicine .... Chicago
East-West University ....Chicago
Eastern Illinois University ....Charleston
Echols International Tourism Institute....................................Chicago
Elgin Community College.. Elgin
Elmhurst College ....Elmhurst
Environmental Technical Institue .... Itasca
Environmental Technical Institue
  (Branch Campus) ....Blue Island
Eureka College ....Eureka
Fox Secretarial College .... Oak Lawn
Frontier Community College.. Fairfield
Garrett-Evangelical Theological Seminary.....................Evanston
Gem City College .... Quincy
Governors State University..................................University Park
Greenville College...Greenville
Hadley School for the Blind.. Winnetka
Harold Washington College ....Chicago
Harrington Institute of Interior Design ....Chicago
Harry S. Truman College ....Chicago
Heartland School of Business..Jacksonville
Herman M. Finch University of Health Sciences
  (The Chicago Medical School) ....North Chicago
Highland Community College.. Freeport
ITT Technical Institute
  (Branch) ....Hoffman Estates
ITT Technical Institute
  (Branch Campus) ....Matteson
Illinois Benedictine College.. Lisle
Illinois Central College.. East Peoria
Illinois College ....Jacksonville
Illinois College of Optometry .... Chicago
Illinois Institute of Technology ....Chicago
Illinois School of Health Careers ....Chicago
Illinois State University.. Normal
Illinois Valley Community College .... Oglesby
Illinois Wesleyan University.....................................Bloomington
International Academy of Merchandising and Design ..... Chicago
John A. Logan College ....Carterville
John Marshall Law School ....Chicago
John Wood Community College .... Quincy
Joliet Junior College ....Joliet
Judson College... Elgin
Kankakee Community College...................................... Kankakee
Kaskaskia College.. Centralia
Keller Graduate School of Management........................ Chicago
Keller Graduate School of Management
  (North Suburban Center).. Lincolnshire
Keller Graduate School of Management
  (Northwest Suburban Center)...................................... Schaumburg
Keller Graduate School of Management
  (South Suburban Center) .... Orland Park
Keller Graduate School of Management
  (West Suburban Center) ....Downers Grove
Kendall College ....Evanston
Kennedy-King College ....Chicago
Kishwaukee College.. Malta
Knowledge Systems Institute .... Skokie
Knox College .... Galesburg
Lake Forest College ....Lake Forest
Lake Forest Graduate School of Management ....Lake Forest
Lake Land College .... Mattoon
Lewis University .... Romeoville
Lewis and Clark Community College ....Godfrey
Lexington Institute of Hospitality Careers....................... Chicago
Lincoln Christian College and Seminary .... Lincoln
Lincoln College... Lincoln

Indiana

The Sourcebook of College and University Student Records

Lincoln Land Community College	Springfield
Lincoln Technical Institute	Norridge
Lincoln Technical Institute	Oak Lawn
Lincoln Trail College	Robinson
Loyola University of Chicago	Chicago
Lutheran School of Theology at Chicago	Chicago
M G Institute	Chicago
MacCormac Junior College	Chicago
MacMurray College	Jacksonville
Malcolm X College	Chicago
McCormick Theological Seminary	Chicago
McHenry County College	Crystal Lake
McKendree College	Lebanon
Meadville/Lombard Theological School	Chicago
Medical Careers Institute	Chicago
Mennonite College of Nursing	Bloomington
Midstate College	Peoria
Midwestern University	Downers Grove
Millikin University	Decatur
Moler Hairstyling College	Chicago
Monmouth College	Monmouth
Montay College	Chicago
Moody Bible Institute	Chicago
Moraine Valley Community College	Palos Hills
Morrison Institute of Technology	Morrison
Morton College	Cicero
Music Center of the North Shore	Winnetka
NAES College	Chicago
Napoleon Hill Foundation	Northbrook
National College of Chiropractic	Lombard
National-Louis University	Wheeling
Naval Health Sciences Education and Training Command (Hospital Corps School)	Great Lakes
North Central College	Naperville
North Park College and Theological Seminary	Chicago
Northeastern Illinois University	Chicago
Northern Baptist Theological Seminary	Lombard
Northern Illinois University	De Kalb
Northwestern Business College	Chicago
Northwestern Business College (Southwestern)	Hickory Hills
Northwestern University	Evanston
Oakton Community College	Des Plaines
Olive-Harvey College	Chicago
Olivet Nazarene University	Kankakee
Olney Central College	Olney
Parkland College	Champaign
Pathfinder Training Institute	Chicago
Prairie State College	Chicago Heights
Principia College	Elsah
Quincy Technical Schools	Quincy
Quincy University	Quincy
Ray College of Design	Chicago
Ray College of Design (Branch)	Schaumburg
Rend Lake College	Ina
Richard J. Daley College	Chicago
Richland Community College	Decatur
Robert Morris College	Chicago
Rock Valley College	Rockford
Rockford Business College	Rockford
Rockford College	Rockford
Rockford School of Practical Nursing	Rockford
Roosevelt University	Chicago
Rosary College	River Forest
Rush University	Chicago
SER Business and Technical Institute (Chicago Campus)	Chicago
Sanford-Brown Business College	Granite City
Sangamon State University	Springfield
Sauk Valley Community College	Dixon
School of the Art Institute of Chicago	Chicago
Seabury-Western Theological Seminary	Evanston
Shawnee Community College	Ullin
Shimer College	Waukegan
South Suburban College of Cook County	South Holland
Southern Illinois University at Carbondale	Carbondale
Southern Illinois University at Edwardsville	Edwardsville
Southeastern Illinois College	Harrisburg
Sparks College	Shelbyville
Spertus Institute of Jewish Studies	Chicago
Spoon River College	Canton
Springfield College in Illinois	Springfield
St. Augustine College	Chicago
St. Francis Medical Center College of Nursing	Peoria
St. Joseph College of Nursing	Joliet
St. Louis University (Parks College)	Cahokia
St. Xavier University	Chicago
State Community College of East St. Louis	East St Louis
Taylor Business Institute	Chicago
Telshe Yeshiva-Chicago	Chicago
Trinity Christian College	Palos Heights
Trinity Evangelical Divinity School	Deerfield
Trinity International University (College of Liberal Arts)	Deerfield
Triton College	River Grove
Tyler School of Secretarial Sciences	Chicago
Universal Technical Institute (Branch Campus)	Glendale Heights
University of Chicago	Chicago
University of Illinois at Chicago	Chicago
University of Illinois at Urbana-Champaign	Urbana
University of St. Mary of the Lake Mundelein Seminary	Mundelein
VanderCook College of Music	Chicago
Wabash Valley College	Mount Carmel
Waubonsee Community College	Sugar Grove
West Suburban College of Nursing	Oak Park
Western Illinois University	Macomb
Wheaton College	Wheaton
Wilbur Wright College	Chicago
William Rainey Harper College	Palatine
Worsham College of Mortuary Science	Wheeling

Indiana

Academy of Hair Design	Indianapolis
Ancilla College	Donaldson
Anderson University	Anderson
Aristotle College of Medical and Dental Technology	Indianapolis
Aristotle College of Medical and Dental Technology (Branch Campus)	Hammond
Associated Mennonite Biblical Seminary	Elkhart
Ball State University	Muncie
Bethany Theological Seminary	Richmond
Bethel College	Mishawaka
Butler University	Indianapolis
Calumet College of St. Joseph	Whiting
Christian Theological Seminary	Indianapolis
College of Court Reporting	Hobart
Commonwealth Business College	Merrillville
Commonwealth Business College (Branch)	Moline
Commonwealth Business College (LaPorte)	La Porte
Concordia Theological Seminary	Fort Wayne
Davenport College of Business (Branch)	Granger
Davenport College of Business (Branch)	Merrillville
DePauw University	Greencastle
Defense Information School	Fort Benjamin Harrison
Earlham College	Richmond

State Cross Reference Index (Bold print indicates degree granting institutions)

The Sourcebook of College and University Student Records **Iowa**

Franklin College of Indiana .... Franklin
Goshen College .... Goshen
Grace College .... Winona Lake
Grace Theological Seminary .... Winona Lake
Hanover College .... Hanover
Holy Cross College .... Notre Dame
Huntington College .... Huntington
ITT Technical Institute .... Evansville
ITT Technical Institute .... Fort Wayne
ITT Technical Institute .... Indianapolis
Indiana Barber/Stylist College .... Indianapolis
Indiana Business College .... Indianapolis
Indiana Business College
(Branch) .... Anderson
Indiana Business College
(Branch) .... Columbus
Indiana Business College
(Branch) .... Evansville
Indiana Business College
(Branch) .... Indianapolis
Indiana Business College
(Branch) .... Lafayette
Indiana Business College
(Branch) .... Marion
Indiana Business College
(Branch) .... Muncie
Indiana Business College
(Branch) .... Terre Haute
Indiana Business College
(Branch) .... Vincennes
Indiana Institute of Technology .... Fort Wayne
Indiana State University .... Terre Haute
Indiana University East .... Richmond
Indiana University Northwest .... Gary
Indiana University Southeast .... New Albany
Indiana University at Bloomington .... Bloomington
Indiana University at Kokomo .... Kokomo
Indiana University at South Bend .... South Bend
Indiana University-Purdue University at Fort Wayne . Fort Wayne
Indiana University-Purdue University at Indianapolis Indianapolis
**Indiana Vocational Tech. College-Columbus/Bloomington Tech.
Inst.** .... Columbus
Indiana Vocational Tech. College-Eastcentral Technical Institute
.... Muncie
Indiana Wesleyan University .... Marion
International Business College .... Fort Wayne
International Business College .... Indianapolis
Ivy Tech State College .... Indianapolis
Ivy Tech State College-Kokomo Technical Institute .... Kokomo
Ivy Tech State College-Lafayette Technical Inst. .... Lafayette
Ivy Tech State College-Northcentral Technical Inst. .. South Bend
Ivy Tech State College-Northeast Technical Inst. .... Fort Wayne
Ivy Tech State College-Northwest Technical Inst. .... Gary
Ivy Tech State College-Northwest Technical Inst.
(Branch) .... Gary
Ivy Tech State College-Southcentral Tech. Inst. .... Sellersburg
Ivy Tech State College-Southeast Tech. Inst. .... Madison
Ivy Tech State College-Southwest Tech. Inst. .... Evansville
Ivy Tech State College-Wabash Valley Tech. Inst. ...... Terre Haute
Ivy Tech State College-Whitewater Tech. Inst. .... Richmond
Lutheran College of Health Professions .... Fort Wayne
Manchester College .... North Manchester
Marian College .... Indianapolis
Martin University .... Indianapolis
Michiana College .... South Bend
Michiana College
(Branch) .... Fort Wayne
Mid-America College of Funeral Service .... Jeffersonville
Oakland City College .... Oakland City
PJ's College of Cosmetology
(Branch Campus) .... Crawfordsville
PJ's College of Cosmetology
(Branch Campus) .... Greenfield
PJ's College of Cosmetology
(Branch Campus) .... Indianapolis
PJ's College of Cosmetology
(Branch Campus) .... Kokomo
PJ's College of Cosmetology
(Branch Campus) .... Muncie
PJ's College of Cosmetology
(Branch Campus) .... Plainfield
Professional Careers Institute .... Indianapolis
Purdue University .... West Lafayette
Purdue University Calumet .... Hammond
Purdue University North Central .... Westville
Rose-Hulman Institute of Technology .... Terre Haute
Saint Joseph's College .... Rensselaer
Saint Mary's College .... Notre Dame
Sawyer College, Inc. .... Hammond
Sawyer College, Inc.
(Branch) .... Merrillville
St. Francis College .... Fort Wayne
St. Mary-Of-The-Woods College .... St. Mary-of-the-Woods
St. Meinrad College .... St Meinrad
St. Meinrad School of Theology .... St Meinrad
Taylor University .... Upland
Taylor University
(Fort Wayne) .... Fort Wayne
Tri-State University .... Angola
University of Evansville .... Evansville
University of Indianapolis .... Indianapolis
University of Notre Dame .... South Bend
University of Southern Indiana .... Evansville
Valparaiso University .... Valparaiso
Vincennes University .... Vincennes
Wabash College .... Crawfordsville

Iowa

American Institute of Business .... Des Moines
American Institute of Commerce .... Davenport
American Institute of Commerce
(Branch) .... Cedar Falls
Briar Cliff College .... Sioux City
Buena Vista College .... Storm Lake
Capri Cosmetology College .... Dubuque
Cedar Rapids School of Hairstyling .... Cedar Rapids
Central College .... Pella
Clarke College .... Dubuque
Clinton Community College .... Clinton
Coe College .... Cedar Rapids
College of Hair Design .... Waterloo
Cornell College .... Mount Vernon
Des Moines Area Community College .... Ankeny
Divine Word College .... Epworth
Dordt College .... Sioux Center
Drake University .... Des Moines
Ellsworth Community College .... Iowa Falls
Emmaus Bible College .... Dubuque
Faith Baptist Bible College and Theological Seminary ...... Ankeny
Graceland College .... Lamoni
Grand View College .... Des Moines
Grinnell College .... Grinnell
Hamilton Technical College .... Davenport
Hawkeye Community College .... Waterloo
Indian Hills Community College .... Ottumwa
Indian Hills Community College
(Centerville) .... Centerville
Iowa Central Community College .... Fort Dodge
Iowa Lakes Community College
(Emmetsburg Campus) .... Emmetsburg
Iowa Lakes Community College
(Estherville) .... Estherville
Iowa School of Barbering and Hairstyling .... Des Moines

(Bold print indicates degree granting institutions) 443 **State Cross Reference Index**

Kansas

The Sourcebook of College and University Student Records

Iowa State University	Ames
Iowa Wesleyan College	Mount Pleasant
Iowa Western Community College	Council Bluffs
Kirkwood Community College	Cedar Rapids
Loras College	Dubuque
Luther College	Decorah
Maharishi International University	Fairfield
Marshalltown Community College	Marshalltown
Morningside College	Sioux City
Mount Mercy College	Cedar Rapids
Mount St. Clare College	Clinton
Muscatine Community College	Muscatine
North Iowa Area Community College	Mason City
Northeast Iowa Community College	Calmar
Northwest Iowa Community College	Sheldon
Northwestern College	Orange City
Palmer College of Chiropractic	Davenport
Scott Community College	Bettendorf
Simpson College	Indianola
Southeastern Community College	West Burlington
Southwestern Community College	Creston
Spencer College	Spencer
St. Ambrose University	Davenport
Teikyo Marycrest University	Davenport
Teikyo Westmar University	Le Mars
University of Dubuque	Dubuque
University of Iowa	Iowa City
University of Northern Iowa	Cedar Falls
University of Osteopathic Medicine and Health Sciences	Des Moines
Upper Iowa University	Fayette
Vennard College	University Park
Waldorf College	Forest City
Wartburg College	Waverly
Wartburg Theological Seminary	Dubuque
Western Iowa Tech Community College	Sioux City
William Penn College	Oskaloosa
Highland Community College	Highland
Hutchinson Community College	Hutchinson
Independence Community College	Independence
Johnson County Community College	Overland Park
Kansas City Kansas Community College	Kansas City
Kansas Newman College	Wichita
Kansas School of Hairstyling	Wichita
Kansas State University	Manhattan
Kansas State University (Salina College of Technology)	Salina
Kansas Wesleyan University	Salina
Labette Community College	Parsons
Manhattan Christian College	Manhattan
McPherson College	McPherson
MidAmerica Nazarene College	Olathe
Neosho County Community College	Chanute
North Central Kansas Area Vocational-Technical School	Beloit
North Central Kansas Area Vocational-Technical School (Hays Campus)	Hays
Ottawa University	Ottawa
Pittsburg State University	Pittsburg
Pratt Community College	Pratt
Seward County Community College	Liberal
Southwestern College	Winfield
St. Mary College	Leavenworth
Sterling College	Sterling
Tabor College	Hillsboro
Topeka Technical College	Topeka
United States Army Command and General Staff College	Fort Leavenworth
University of Kansas	Lawrence
University of Kansas Medical Center	Kansas City
Washburn University of Topeka	Topeka
Wichita Area Vocational-Technical School	Wichita
Wichita Business College	Wichita
Wichita State University	Wichita
Wichita Technical Institute	Wichita
Wright Business School	Lenexa

Kansas

Advanced Hair Tech	Kansas City
Allen County Community College	Iola
Amtech Institute	Wichita
Baker University	Baldwin City
Barclay College	Haviland
Barton County Community College	Great Bend
Benedictine College	Atchison
Bethany College	Lindsborg
Bethel College	North Newton
Brown Mackie College	Salina
Bryan Institute	Wichita
Bryan Travel College	Topeka
Butler County Community College	El Dorado
Center for Training in Business and Industry	Lawrence
Central Baptist Theological Seminary	Kansas City
Central College	McPherson
Climate Control Institute	Wichita
Cloud County Community College	Concordia
Coffeyville Community College	Coffeyville
Colby Community College	Colby
Cowley County Community College	Arkansas City
Dodge City Community College	Dodge City
Donnelly College	Kansas City
Emporia State University	Emporia
Flint Hills Technical School	Emporia
Fort Hays State University	Hays
Fort Scott Community College	Fort Scott
Friends University	Wichita
Garden City Community College	Garden City
Haskell Indian Junior College	Lawrence
Hesston College	Hesston

Kentucky

Alice Lloyd College	Pippa Passes
Asbury College	Wilmore
Asbury Theological Seminary	Wilmore
Ashland Community College	Ashland
Ballard County Area Vocational Center	Barlow
Barrett & Company School of Hair Design	Nicholasville
Bellarmine College	Louisville
Berea College	Berea
Brescia College	Owensboro
Campbellsville College	Campbellsville
CareerCom Junior College of Business	Hopkinsville
Carl D. Perkins Job Corps Center	Prestonsburg
Centre College	Danville
Clear Creek Baptist Bible College	Pineville
Computer Education Services	Louisville
Computer School	Lexington
Cumberland College	Williamsburg
Davidson Technical College (Branch Campus)	Bowling Green
Draughons Junior College (Branch Campus)	Bowling Green
Earle C. Clements Job Corps Center	Morganfield
Eastern Kentucky University	Richmond
Elizabethtown Community College	Elizabethtown
Fugazzi College	Lexington
Georgetown College	Georgetown
Hazard Community College	Hazard
Health Institute of Louisville	Louisville
Henderson Community College	Henderson
Hopkinsville Community College	Hopkinsville

State Cross Reference Index (Bold print indicates degree granting institutions)

The Sourcebook of College and University Student Records **Kentucky**

ITT Technical Institute
   (Branch) .... Louisville
Institute of Electronic Technology .... Paducah
Institute of Electronic Technology
   (Lexington Electronics Institute) .... Lexington
Interactive Learning Systems
   (Branch Campus) .... Day Ridge
Interactive Learning Systems
   (Branch Campus) .... Florence
Jefferson Community College .... Louisville
Kentucky Christian College .... Grayson
Kentucky College of Barbering and Hairstyling .... Louisville
Kentucky College of Business .... Lexington
Kentucky College of Business
   (Branch) .... Danville
Kentucky College of Business
   (Branch) .... Florence
Kentucky College of Business
   (Branch) .... Louisville
Kentucky College of Business
   (Branch) .... Pikeville
Kentucky College of Business
   (Branch) .... Richmond
Kentucky State University .... Frankfort
Kentucky Tech-Ashland State Vocational-Technical School ... Ashland
Kentucky Tech-Barren County Area Vocational Education Center
 .... Glasgow
Kentucky Tech-Belfry Area Vocational Education Center .... Belfry
Kentucky Tech-Bell County Area Vocational Education Center
 .... Pineville
Kentucky Tech-Boone County Center .... Hebron
Kentucky Tech-Bowling Green State Vocational-Technical School
 .... Bowling Green
Kentucky Tech-Breathitt County Area Vocational Education Center
 .... Jackson
Kentucky Tech-Breckenridge County Area Vocational Education Ctr
 .... Harned
Kentucky Tech-Bullitt County Area Vocational Education Ctr
 .... Shepherdsville
Kentucky Tech-Caldwell County Area Vocational Education Ctr
 .... Princeton
Kentucky Tech-Carroll County Area Center .... Carrollton
Kentucky Tech-Casey County Area Vocational Education Center
 .... Liberty
Kentucky Tech-Central Campus .... Lexington
Kentucky Tech-Christian County Area Vocational Education Center
 .... Hopkinsville
Kentucky Tech-Clark County Center .... Winchester
Kentucky Tech-Clay County Area Vocational Education Center
 .... Manchester
Kentucky Tech-Clinton County Area Vocational Education Center
 .... Albany
Kentucky Tech-Corbin Area Vocational Education Center .... Corbin
Kentucky Tech-Cumberland Valley Health Occupations Center
 .... Pineville
Kentucky Tech-Danville School of Health Occupations .... Danville
Kentucky Tech-Daviess County Vocational-Technical School
 .... Owensboro
Kentucky Tech-Elizabethtown State Vocational-Technical School
 .... Elizabethtown
Kentucky Tech-Fulton County Area Vocational Education Center
 .... Hickman
Kentucky Tech-Garth Area Vocational Education Center .... Martin
Kentucky Tech-Gerrard County Center .... Lancaster
Kentucky Tech-Glasgow Health Occupations School .... Glasgow
Kentucky Tech-Green County Area Vocational Education Center
 .... Greensburg
Kentucky Tech-Greenup County Area Vocational Education Center
 .... South Shore
Kentucky Tech-Harlan State Vocational-Technical School .... Harlan
Kentucky Tech-Harrison County Center .... Cynthiana
Kentucky Tech-Harrodsburg Center .... Harrodsburg
Kentucky Tech-Hazard State Vocational-Technical School ...... Hazard

Kentucky Tech-Henderson County Area Vocational Education Center
 .... Henderson
Kentucky Tech-Jefferson State Vocational-Technical Center
 .... Louisville
Kentucky Tech-Kentucky Advanced Technology Center
 .... Bowling Green
Kentucky Tech-Knott County Area Vocational Education Center
 .... Hindman
Kentucky Tech-Knox County Area Vocational Education Center
 .... Barbourville
Kentucky Tech-Laurel County State Vocational-Technical School
 .... London
Kentucky Tech-Lee County Area Vocational Education Center
 .... Beattyville
Kentucky Tech-Leslie County Area Vocational Education Center
 .... Hyden
Kentucky Tech-Letcher County Area Vocational Education Center
 .... Whitesburg
Kentucky Tech-Madison County Center .... Richmond
Kentucky Tech-Madisonville Health Occupations School . Madisonville
Kentucky Tech-Madisonville State Vocational-Technical School
 .... Madisonville
Kentucky Tech-Marion County Area Vocational Education Center
 .... Lebanon
Kentucky Tech-Martin County Area Vocational Education Center . Inez
Kentucky Tech-Mason County Area Vocational Education Center
 .... Maysville
Kentucky Tech-Mayfield Area Vocational Education Center ... Mayfield
Kentucky Tech-Mayo State Vocational-Technical School ..... Paintsville
Kentucky Tech-McCormick Center .... Alexandria
Kentucky Tech-Meade County Area Vocational Education Center
 .... Brandenburg
Kentucky Tech-Millard Area Vocational Education Center .... Pikeville
Kentucky Tech-Monroe County Area Vocational Education Center
 .... Tompkinsville
Kentucky Tech-Montgomery County Area Vocational Education Center
 .... Mount Sterling
Kentucky Tech-Morgan County Area Vocational Education Center
 .... West Liberty
Kentucky Tech-Muhlenberg County Area Vocational Education Center
 .... Greenville
Kentucky Tech-Murray Area Vocational Education Center .... Murray
Kentucky Tech-Nelson County Area Vocational Education Center
 .... Bardstown
Kentucky Tech-Northern Campbell County Campus Highland Heights
Kentucky Tech-Northern Kentucky Campus .... Covington
Kentucky Tech-Northern Kentucky Health Occupations Center
 .... Edgewood
Kentucky Tech-Ohio County Area Vocational Education Center
 .... Hartford
Kentucky Tech-Oldham County Area Vocational Education Center
 .... Buckner
Kentucky Tech-Owensboro Vocational-Technical School . Owensboro
Kentucky Tech-Paducah Area Vocational Education Center . Paducah
Kentucky Tech-Patton Center .... Fort Mitchell
Kentucky Tech-Phelps Area Vocational Education Center .... Phelps
Kentucky Tech-Rockcastle County Area Vocational Education Center
 .... Mount Vernon
Kentucky Tech-Rowan State Vocational-Technical School .. Morehead
Kentucky Tech-Russell Area Vocational Education Center ...... Russell
Kentucky Tech-Russell County Area Vocational Education Center
 .... Russell Springs
Kentucky Tech-Russellville Area Vocational Education Center
 .... Russellville
Kentucky Tech-Shelby County Area Vocational Education Center
 .... Shelbyville
Kentucky Tech-Somerset State Vocational Education Center
 .... Somerset
Kentucky Tech-Wayne County Area Vocational Education Center
 .... Monticello
Kentucky Tech-Webster County Area Vocational Education Center
 .... Dixon

(Bold print indicates degree granting institutions)   **State Cross Reference Index**

Louisiana

The Sourcebook of College and University Student Records

Kentucky Tech-West Kentucky State Vocational-Technical School ....Paducah
Kentucky Wesleyan College..Owensboro
Lees College..Jackson
Lexington Community College................................Lexington
Lexington Theological Seminary..........................Lexington
Lindsey Wilson College..Columbia
Louisville Presbyterian Theological Seminary................Louisville
Louisville Technical Institute....................................Louisville
Madisonville Community College.....................Madisonville
Madisonville Health Technology Center............................Madisonville
Maysville Community College................................Maysville
Mid-Continent Baptist Bible College..................Mayfield
Midway College..Midway
Morehead State University....................................Morehead
Murray State University...Murray
New Image Careers..Corbin
Northern Kentucky University..................Highland Heights
Nu-Tek Academy of Beauty...................................Mount Sterling
Owensboro Community College.........................Owensboro
Owensboro Junior College of Business...........Owensboro
PJ's College of Cosmetology..Bowling Green
PJ's College of Cosmetology..Glasgow
Paducah Community College....................................Paducah
Pikeville College...Pikeville
Prestonsburg Community College.....................Prestonsburg
Roy's of Louisville Beauty Academy..........................Louisville
Roy's of Louisville Beauty Academy
  (Branch Campus)...Louisville
School of Business and Banking...................................Louisville
Somerset Community College..................................Somerset
Southeast Community College..........................Cumberland
Southern Baptist Theological Seminary..........Louisville
Southern Ohio College
  (Northern Kentucky)...Fort Mitchell
Southwestern College Business..................Crestview Hills
Spalding University...Louisville
Spencerian College...Louisville
St. Catharine College...St Catharine
Sue Bennett College..London
Sullivan College..Louisville
Sullivan College
  (Branch)..Lexington
Thomas Moore College..................................Crestview Hills
Transylvania University...Lexington
Tri-State Beauty Academy..Morehead
Union College..Barbourville
University of Kentucky..Lexington
University of Louisville...Louisville
Western Kentucky University........................Bowling Green

Louisiana

Abbeville Beauty Academy...Abbeville
Acadian Technical Institute..Crowley
Alexandria Regional Technical Institute................Alexandria
American School of Business......................................Shreveport
Ascension College...Gonzales
Ascension Technical Institute..Sorrento
Avoyelles Technical Institute......................................Cottonport
Ayers Institute..Shreveport
Bastrop Technical Institute...Bastrop
Baton Rouge Regional Technical Institute.........Baton Rouge
Baton Rouge Regional Technical Institute
  (J.M. Frazier Vo-Tech School)...............................Baton Rouge
Bossier Parish Community College................Bossier City
Camelot Career College..Baton Rouge
Cameron College...New Orleans
Career Training Specialists..Monroe
Centenary College of Louisiana..........................Shreveport
Charles B. Coreil Technical Institute........................Ville Platte

Claiborne Technical Institute...Homer
Cloyd's Beauty School No. 2..Monroe
Cloyd's Beauty School No. 3..Monroe
Coastal College..New Orleans
Coastal College
  (Branch Campus)..Bossier City
Coastal College
  (Branch Campus)...Hammond
Coastal College
  (Branch Campus)..Houma
Coastal College
  (Branch Campus)...Slidell
Commercial College of Baton Rouge....................Baton Rouge
Commercial College of Shreveport..........................Shreveport
Concordia Technical Institute..Ferriday
Culinary Arts Institute of Louisiana....................Baton Rouge
Cumberland School of Technology
  (Branch Campus)...Baton Rouge
Delgado Community College................................New Orleans
Delta Career College...Lafayette
Delta Career College..Monroe
Delta Junior College..Baton Rouge
Delta Junior College
  (Branch)...Covington
Delta Junior College
  (Delta College)...Houma
Delta School of Business and Technology........Lake Charles
Delta Schools..Lafayette
Delta Schools
  (Branch Campus)..New Iberia
Delta-Ouachita Regional Technical Institute.......West Monroe
Denham Springs Beauty College..........................Denham Springs
Diesel Driving Academy...Baton Rouge
Diesel Driving Academy...Shreveport
Dillard University...New Orleans
Domestic Health Care Institute..................................Baton Rouge
Eastern College of Health Vocations..............................Metairie
Elaine P. Nunez Community College...................Chalmette
Elaine P. Nunez Community College
  (Branch)..Port Sulphur
Evangeline Technical Institute......................................Martinville
FinEd, School of Financial Education.....................Baton Rouge
Florida Parishes Technical Institute..........................Greensburg
Folkes Technical Institute...Jackson
Folkes Technical Institute
  (Branch Campus)...Jackson
Franklin College of Court Reporting.......................New Orleans
Grambling State University......................................Grambling
Grantham College of Engineering..............................Slidell
Gulf Area Technical Institute..Abbeville
Hammond Area Technical Institute..............................Hammond
Huey P. Long Technical Institute....................................Winnfield
Huey P. Long Technical Institute
  (Branch Campus)..Jena
Jefferson Davis Technical Institute.................................Jennings
Jefferson Technical Institute...Metairie
Jocelyn Daspit Beauty College...Matairie
Jocelyn Daspit Beauty College
  (Branch Campus)..Hammond
Jocelyn Daspit Beauty College
  (Branch Campus)...La Place
Jumonville Memorial Technical Institute..................New Roads
Jumonville Memorial Technical Institute
  (Branch Campus)..Angola
Jumonville Memorial Technical Institute
  (Branch Campus)..St. Gabriel
Lafayette Regional Technical Institute..........................Lafayette
Lamar Salter Technical Institute....................................Leesville
Louisiana Art Institute..Baton Rouge
Louisiana College..Pineville
Louisiana Hair Design College...Metairie
Louisiana Institute of Technology..............................Alexandria
Louisiana Institute of Technology

State Cross Reference Index   (Bold print indicates degree granting institutions)

(Branch Campus)	Lafayette
Louisiana State University Medical Center	New Orleans
Louisiana State University and Agricultural & Mechanical College	Baton Rouge
Louisiana State University at Alexandria	Alexandria
Louisiana State University at Eunice	Eunice
Louisiana State University at Shreveport	Shreveport
Louisiana Tech University	Ruston
Louisiana Training Center	Sulphur
Loyola University	New Orleans
Mansfield Technical Institute	Mansfield
McNeese State University	Lake Charles
Natchitoches Technical Institute	Natchitoches
National Education Center - Bryman Campus	
(Branch Campus)	New Orleans
New Orleands Regional Technical Institute	New Orleans
New Orleans Baptist Theological Seminary	New Orleans
Nicholls State University	Thibodaux
Nick Randazzo Vocational Training Institute	Gretna
North Central Technical Institute	Farmerville
Northeast Louisiana Technical Institute	Winnsboro
Northeast Louisiana University	Monroe
Northwest Louisiana Technical Institute	Minden
Northwestern State University	Natchitoches
Notre Dame Seminary Graduate School of Theology	New Orleans
Nunez Community College	
(Branch)	New Orleans
Oakdale Technical Institute	Oakdale
Ochsner School of Allied Health Sciences	New Orleans
Our Lady of Holy Cross College	New Orleans
Phillips Junior College	New Orleans
Refrigeration School of New Orleans	New Orleans
Remington College	Lafayette
River Parishes Technical Institute	Reserve
Ruston Technical Institute	Ruston
Sabine Valley Technical Institute	Many
Shreveport-Bossier Regional Technical Institute	Shreveport
Sidney N. Collier Technical Institute	New Orleans
Slidell Technical Institute	Slidell
South Louisiana Beauty College	Houma
South Louisiana Regional Technical Institute	Houma
South Louisiana Regional Technical Institute	
(Branch Campus)	Houma
Southeastern Louisiana University	Hammond
Southern University & Agricultural & Mech. College at Baton Rouge	Baton Rouge
Southern University at New Orleans	New Orleans
Southern University/Shreveport Bossier	Shreveport
Sowela Regional Technical Institute	Lake Charles
Sowela Regional Technical Institute	
(Branch Campus)	Dequincy
St. Joseph Seminary College	St Benedict
Sullivan Technical Institute	Bogalusa
Sullivan Technical Institute	
(Branch Campus)	Angie
T.H. Harris Technical Institute	Opelousas
Tallulah Technical Institute	Tallulah
Tallulah Technical Institute	
(Branch Campus)	Lake Providence
Teche Area Technical Institute	New Iberia
Thibodaux Area Technical Institute	Thibodaux
Tulane University	New Orleans
University of New Orleans	New Orleans
University of Southwestern Louisiana	Lafayette
West Jefferson Technical Institute	Harvey
Westside Technical Institute	Plaquemine
Xavier University of Louisiana	New Orleans
Young Memorial Technical Institute	Morgan City

Maine

Air-Tech, Inc.	Limerick
Andover College	Portland
Bangor Theological Seminary	Bangor
Bates College	Lewiston
Beal College	Bangor
Bowdoin College	Brunswick
Casco Bay College	Portland
Central Maine Medical Center School of Nursing	Lewiston
Central Maine Technical College	Auburn
Colby College	Waterville
College of the Atlantic	Bar Harbor
Eastern Maine Technical College	Bangor
Husson College	Bangor
Kennebec Valley Technical College	Fairfield
Landing School of Boat Building and Design	Kennebunkport
Maine College of Art	Portland
Maine Maritime Academy	Castine
Mid-State College	Auburn
Mid-State College	
(Branch)	Augusta
New England School of Broadcasting	Bangor
Northern Maine Technical College	Presque Isle
Southern Maine Technical College	South Portland
St. Joseph's College	Windham
Thomas College	Waterville
Unity College	Unity
University of Maine	Orono
University of Maine at Augusta	Augusta
University of Maine at Farmington	Farmington
University of Maine at Fort Kent	Fort Kent
University of Maine at Machias	Machias
University of Maine at Presque Isle	Presque Isle
University of New England	Biddeford
University of Southern Maine	Portland
Washington County Technical College	Calais
Westbrook College	Portland

Maryland

Abbie Business Institute	Frederick
Acupuncture School of Maryland	Bethesda
All-State Career School	
(Branch Campus)	Baltimore
Allegany Community College	Cumberland
Anne Arundel Community College	Arnold
Antioch University	
(George Meany Center for Labor Studies)	Silver Spring
Army Ordnance Center and School	Aberdeen Proving Ground
Arundel Institute of Technology	Baltimore
Baltimore City Community College	Baltimore
Baltimore City Community College	
(Harbor)	Baltimore
Baltimore Hebrew University	Baltimore
Baltimore International Culinary College	Baltimore
Bowie State University	Bowie
Broadcasting Institute of Maryland	Baltimore
Capitol College	Laurel
Catonsville Community College	Catonsville
Cecil Community College	North East
Charles County Community College	La Plata
Chesapeake College	Wye Mills
College of Notre Dame of Maryland	Baltimore
Columbia Union College	Takoma Park
Coppin State College	Baltimore
Diesel Institute of America	Grantsville
Dundalk Community College	Dundalk

(Bold print indicates degree granting institutions)

Massachusetts

Emergency Management Institute .... Emmitsburg
Essex Community College .... Baltimore
Fleet Business School .... Annapolis
Frederick Community College .... Frederick
Frostburg State University .... Frostburg
Garrett Community College .... McHenry
Goucher College .... Baltimore
Hagerstown Business College .... Hagerstown
Hagerstown Junior College .... Hagerstown
Harford Community College .... Bel Air
Home Study International .... Silver Spring
Home Study International
  (Griggs University) .... Silver Spring
Hood College .... Frederick
Howard Community College .... Columbia
Johns Hopkins University .... Baltimore
Johns Hopkins University
  (Columbia Center) .... Columbia
Johns Hopkins University
  (Peabody Institute of the Johns Hopkins University) .... Baltimore
Johnston School of Practical Nursing .... Baltimore
Lincoln Technical Institute .... Baltimore
Lincoln Technical Institute .... Landover
Loyola College in Maryland .... Baltimore
Maryland College of Art and Design .... Silver Spring
Maryland Drafting Institute .... Langley Park
Maryland Institute College of Art .... Baltimore
Medix School .... Towson
Montgomery College-Germantown Campus .... Germantown
Montgomery College-Rockville Campus .... Rockville
Montgomery College-Takoma Park Campus .... Takoma Park
Morgan State University .... Baltimore
Mount St. Mary's College and Seminary .... Emmitsburg
National Cryptologic School .... Fort Meade
Naval Health Sciences Education and Training Command ... Bethesda
Naval Health Sciences Education and Training Command
  (Dental School-Maxillofacial) .... Bethesda
Naval Health Sciences Education and Training Command
  (School of Health Science) .... Bethesda
Ner Israel Rabbinical College .... Baltimore
New England Tractor Trailer Training School .... Baltimore
Prince George's Community College .... Largo
Prince George's Community College
  (Branch) .... Andrews Air Force Base
Rice Aviation, a Division of A&J Enterprises
  (Branch Campus) .... Baltimore
Salisbury State University .... Salisbury
Sojourner-Douglass College .... Baltimore
St. John's College .... Annapolis
St. Mary's College of Maryland .... St. Mary's City
St. Mary's Seminary and University .... Baltimore
TESST Electronics and Computer Institute .... Hyattsville
Towson State University .... Towson
Traditional Acupuncture Institute .... Columbia
Ultrasound Diagnostic School
  (Branch Campus) .... Silver Spring
Uniformed Services University of the Health Sciences .. Bethesda
United States Naval Academy .... Annapolis
University of Baltimore .... Baltimore
University of Maryland
  (College Park) .... College Park
University of Maryland Baltimore County .... Baltimore
University of Maryland College Park .... College Park
University of Maryland Eastern Shore .... Princess Anne
University of Maryland at Baltimore .... Baltimore
Villa Julie College .... Stevenson
Washington Bible College .... Lanham
Washington College .... Chestertown
Washington Theological Union .... Silver Spring
Western Maryland College .... Westminster
Woodbridge Business Institute .... Salisbury
Wor-Wic Community College .... Salisbury

Massachusetts

American International College .... Springfield
Amherst College .... Amherst
Andover Newton Theological School .... Newton Centre
Anna Maria College .... Paxton
Aquinas College at Milton .... Milton
Aquinas College at Newton .... Newton
Art Institute of Boston .... Boston
Arthur D. Little Management Education Institute, Inc. .. Cambridge
Assumption College .... Worcester
Atlantic Union College .... South Lancaster
Babson College .... Wellesley
Bancroft School of Message Therapy .... Worcester
Bay Path College .... Longmeadow
Bay State College .... Boston
Bay State School of Appliances .... Canton
Becker College .... Worcester
Becker College
  (Branch) .... Leicester
Bentley College .... Waltham
Berklee College of Music .... Boston
Berkshire Community College .... Pittsfield
Boston College .... Chestnut Hill
Boston Conservatory .... Boston
Boston University .... Boston
Bradford College .... Bradford
Brandeis University .... Waltham
Bridgewater State College .... Bridgewater
Bristol Community College .... Fall River
Bunker Hill Community College .... Boston
Burdett School .... Boston
Burdett School
  (Branch Campus) .... Worcester
Butera School of Art .... Boston
Cambridge College .... Cambridge
Cambridge School of Culinary Arts .... Cambridge
Cape Cod Community College .... West Barnstable
Catherine E. Hinds Institute of Esthetics .... Woburn
Charles H. McCann Technical School .... North Adams
Clark University .... Worcester
College of Our Lady of the Elms .... Chicopee
College of the Holy Cross .... Worcester
Computer Learning Center .... Somerville
Computer Learning Center
  (Branch Campus) .... Methuen
Computer Processing Institute .... Cambridge
Conway School of Landscape Design .... Conway
Curry College .... Milton
Dean College .... Franklin
East Coast Aero Technical School .... Concord
Eastern Nazarene College .... Quincy
Emerson College .... Boston
Emmanuel College .... Boston
Endicott College .... Beverly
Episcopal Divinity School .... Cambridge
Essex Agricultural and Technical Institute .... Hathorne
Fisher College .... Boston
Fitchburg State College .... Fitchburg
Forsyth School for Dental Hygienists .... Boston
Framingham State College .... Framingham
Franklin Institute of Boston .... Boston
Gordon College .... Wenham
Gordon-Conwell Theological Seminary .... South Hamilton
Greenfield Community College .... Greenfield
Hallmark Institute of Photography .... Turners Falls
Hampshire College .... Amherst
Harvard University
  (Faculty of Arts and Sciences) .... Cambridge
Hebrew College .... Brookline

State Cross Reference Index   448   (Bold print indicates degree granting institutions)

Hellenic College/Holy Cross Greek Orthodox School of Theology .... Brookline
Hickox School .... Boston
Holyoke Community College .... Holyoke
ITT Technical Institute .... Framingham
Katharine Gibbs School .... Boston
Kinyon-Campbell Business School .... New Bedford
Kinyon-Campbell Business School
    (Branch Campus) .... Brockton
Laboure College .... Boston
Lasell College .... Newton
Lesley College .... Cambridge
Longy School of Music, Inc. .... Cambridge
MGH Institute of Health Professions .... Boston
Marian Court College .... Swampscott
Massachusetts Bay Community College .... Wellesley Hills
Massachusetts College of Art .... Boston
Massachusetts College of Pharmacy and Allied Health Services
    .... Boston
Massachusetts Institute of Technology .... Cambridge
Massachusetts Maritime Academy .... Buzzards Bay
Massachusetts School of Barbering & Men's Hairstyling .... Quincy
Massachusetts School of Professional Psychology .... Boston
Massasoit Community College .... Brockton
Merrimack College .... North Andover
Middlesex Community College .... Bedford
Middlesex Community College
    (Lowell) .... Lowell
Mildred Elley Business School
    (Branch Campus) .... Pittsfield
Montserrat College of Art .... Beverly
Mount Holyoke College .... South Hadley
Mount Ida College .... Newton Centre
Mount Wachusett Community College .... Gardner
National Education Center-Bryman Campus .... Brookline
New England Banking Institute .... Boston
New England College of Optometry .... Boston
New England Conservatory of Music .... Boston
New England Hair Academy .... Malden
New England School of Accounting .... Worcester
New England School of Acupuncture .... Watertown
New England School of Law .... Boston
New England School of Photography .... Boston
New England Tractor Trailer Training School of Massachusetts
    .... Brockton
Newbury College .... Brookline
Nichols College .... Dudley
North Adams State College .... North Adams
North Bennet Street School .... Boston
North Shore Community College .... Danvers
Northeast Broadcasting School .... Boston
Northeast Institute of Industrial Technology .... Boston
Northeastern University .... Boston
Northern Essex Community College .... Haverhill
Pedigree Career Institute .... Lynn
Pine Manor College .... Chestnut Hill
Pope John XXIII National Seminary .... Weston
Quincy College .... Quincy
Quinsigamond Community College .... Worcester
RETS Electronic Schools .... Boston
Radcliffe College .... Cambridge
Regis College .... Weston
Roxbury Community College .... Roxbury Crossing
Salem State College .... Salem
Salter School .... Worcester
Salter School
    (Branch Campus) .... Cambridge
School of the Museum of Fine Arts, Boston .... Boston
Simmons College .... Boston
Simon's Rock College of Bard .... Great Barrington
Smith College .... Northampton
Southeastern Technical Institute .... South Easton
Springfield College .... Springfield

Springfield Technical Community College .... Springfield
St. Hyacinth College and Seminary .... Granby
St. John's School of Business .... West Springfield
St. John's Seminary .... Brighton
Stonehill College .... North Easton
Suffolk University .... Boston
TAD Technical Institute .... Chelsea
Travel Education Center .... Cambridge
Travel School of America .... Boston
Tufts University .... Medford
Ultrasound Diagnostic School
    (Branch Campus) .... Marlborough
University of Massachusetts Boston .... Boston
University of Massachusetts Dartmouth ...... North Dartmouth
University of Massachusetts Lowell .... Lowell
University of Massachusetts Medical Center at Worcester
    .... Worcester
University of Massachusetts at Amherst .... Amherst
Wellesley College .... Wellesley
Wentworth Institute of Technology .... Boston
Wentworth Technical School .... Lexington
Western New England College .... Springfield
Westfield State College .... Westfield
Weston School of Theology .... Cambridge
Wheaton College .... Norton
Wheelock College .... Boston
Williams College .... Williamstown
Worcester Polytechnic Institute .... Worcester
Worcester State College .... Worcester
Worcester Technical Institute .... Worcester

Michigan

Academy of Court Reporting
    (Branch) .... Southfield
Academy of Health Careers .... Madison Heights
Adrian College .... Adrian
Albion College .... Albion
Alma College .... Alma
Alpena Community College .... Alpena
American Education Center .... Huntington Woods
Andrews University .... Berrien Springs
Aquinas College .... Grand Rapids
Baker College of Flint .... Flint
Baker College of Flint
    (Baker College of Muskegon) .... Muskegon
Baker College of Owosso .... Owosso
Bay de Noc Community College .... Escanaba
Black Forest Hall .... Harbor Springs
Calvin College .... Grand Rapids
Calvin Theological Seminary .... Grand Rapids
Carnegie Institute .... Troy
Center for Creative Studies-College of Art and Design ...... Detroit
Center for Creative Studies-Institute of Music and Dance .... Detroit
Center for Humanistic Studies .... Detroit
Central Michigan University .... Mount Pleasant
Charles Stewart Mott Community College .... Flint
Cleary College .... Ypsilanti
Concordia College .... Ann Arbor
Cornerstone College and Grand Rapids Baptist College and Seminary .... Grand Rapids
Cranbrook Academy of Art .... Bloomfield Hills
Davenport College of Business .... Grand Rapids
Davenport College of Business
    (Branch) .... Holland
Davenport College of Business
    (Branch) .... Kalamazoo
Davenport College of Business
    (Branch) .... Lansing
Delta College .... University Center
Detroit Business Institute .... Detroit

(Bold print indicates degree granting institutions)   449   State Cross Reference Index

Minnesota

The Sourcebook of College and University Student Records

Detroit Business Institute-Downriver	Riverview
Detroit College of Business	Dearborn
Detroit College of Law	Detroit
Detroit Institute of Ophthalmology	Grosse Pointe Park
Dorsey Business School	Madison Heights
Dorsey Business School	Roseville
Dorsey Business School	Southgate
Dorsey Business School	Wayne
Eastern Michigan University	Ypsilanti
Educational Institute of the American Hotel and Motel Association	East Lansing
Ferris State University	Big Rapids
Flint Institute of Barbering	Flint
GMI Engineering and Management Institute	Flint
Glen Oaks Community College	Centreville
Gogebic Community College	Ironwood
Grace Bible College	Grand Rapids
Grand Rapids Community College	Grand Rapids
Grand Rapids Educational Center	Grand Rapids
Grand Rapids Educational Center (Branch Campus)	Kalamazoo
Grand Valley State University	Allendale
Great Lakes Christian College	Lansing
Great Lakes Junior College	Saginaw
Hawes Career Institute	Belleville
Henry Ford Community College	Dearborn
Highland Park Community College	Highland Park
Hillsdale College	Hillsdale
Hope College	Holland
ITT Technical Institute	Grand Rapids
ITT Technical Institute (Branch)	Troy
Jackson Community College	Jackson
Kalamazoo College	Kalamazoo
Kalamazoo Valley Community College	Kalamazoo
Kellogg Community College	Battle Creek
Kendall College of Art and Design	Grand Rapids
Kirtland Community College	Roscommon
Lake Michigan College	Benton Harbor
Lake Superior State University	Sault Ste. Marie
Lansing Community College	Lansing
Lansing Computer Institute	Lansing
Lawrence Technological University	Southfield
Lawton School	Oak Park
Lewis College of Business	Detroit
Macomb Community College	Warren
Madonna University	Livonia
Marygrove College	Detroit
Michigan Barber School, Inc.	Detroit
Michigan Career Institute	Detroit
Michigan Christian College	Rochester Hills
Michigan State University	East Lansing
Michigan Technological University	Houghton
Mid Michigan Community College	Harrison
Monroe County Community College	Monroe
Montcalm Community College	Sidney
Motech Education Center	Livonia
Muskegon Community College	Muskegon
National Education Center (Branch Campus)	Detroit
National Education Center-National Institute of Technology Campus	Livonia
National Education Center-National Institute of Technology Campus	Wyoming
North Central Michigan College	Petoskey
Northern Michigan University	Marquette
Northwestern Michigan College	Traverse City
Northwood University	Midland
Oakland Community College	Bloomfield Hills
Oakland Community College (Auburn Hills)	Bloomfield Hills
Oakland Community College (Highland Lakes)	Waterford
Oakland Community College (Orchard Ridge)	Farmington Hills
Oakland Community College (Southfield)	Bloomfield Hills
Oakland University	Rochester
Olivet College	Olivet
Payne-Pulliam School of Trade and Commerce	Detroit
Pontiac Business Institute	Oxford
Reformed Bible College	Grand Rapids
Ross Business Institute	Taylor
Ross Business Institute (Branch Campus)	Clinton Township
Ross Business Institute (Branch Campus)	Monroe
Ross Medical Education Center	Flint
Ross Medical Education Center	Lansing
Ross Medical Education Center	Warren
Ross Medical Education Center (Branch Campus)	Detroit
Ross Medical Education Center (Branch Campus)	Grand Rapids
Ross Medical Education Center (Branch Campus)	Jackson
Ross Medical Education Center (Branch Campus)	Roosevelt Park
Ross Medical Education Center (Branch Campus)	Saginaw
Ross Medical Education Center (Branch Campus)	Waterford
Ross Technical Institute	Brighton
Ross Technical Institute	Detroit
Ross Technical Institute (Branch Campus)	Ann Arbor
Ross Technical Institute (Branch Campus)	Oak Park
SER Business and Technical Institute	Detroit
Sacred Heart Major Seminary	Detroit
Saginaw Beauty Academy	Saginaw
Saginaw Valley State University	University Center
Sawyer School of Business	Warren
Schoolcraft College	Livonia
Sharp's Academy of Hairstyling	Flushing
Sharp's Academy of Hairstyling (Branch Campus)	Grand Blanc
Siena Heights College	Adrian
Southwestern Michigan College	Dowagiac
Specs Howard School of Broadcast Arts, Inc.	Southfield
Spring Arbor College	Spring Arbor
St. Clair County Community College	Port Huron
St. Mary's College	Orchard Lake
Suomi College	Hancock
Thomas M. Cooley Law School	Lansing
Travel Training Center	Dearborn
University of Detroit Mercy	Detroit
University of Michigan	Ann Arbor
University of Michigan-Dearborn	Dearborn
University of Michigan-Flint	Flint
Walsh College of Accountancy and Business Administration	Troy
Washtenaw Community College	Ann Arbor
Wayne County Community College	Detroit
Wayne State University	Detroit
West Shore Community College	Scottville
Western Michigan University	Kalamazoo
Western Theological Seminary	Holland
William Tyndale College	Farmington Hills
Yeshiva Beth Yehuda-Yeshiva Gedolah of Greater Detroit	Oak Park

Minnesota

Academy Education Center	Minneapolis

State Cross Reference Index   (Bold print indicates degree granting institutions)

Alexandria Technical College .... Alexandria
Alfred Adler Institute of Minnesota .... Hopkins
American Schools of Professional Psychology
   (Minnesota School of Professional Psychology) .... Bloomington
Anoka Technical College .... Anoka
Anoka-Ramsey Community College .... Coon Rapids
Art Instruction Schools .... Minneapolis
Augsburg College .... Minneapolis
Austin Community College .... Austin
Avante School of Cosmetology .... St. Paul
Bemidji State University .... Bemidji
Bemidji Technical College .... Bemidji
Bethany Lutheran College .... Mankato
Bethel College .... St Paul
Bethel Theological Seminary .... St Paul
Brainerd Community College .... Brainerd
Carleton College .... Northfield
College of Associated Arts .... St Paul
College of St. Benedict .... St Joseph
College of St. Catherine .... St Paul
College of St. Catherine-Minneapolis
   (St. Mary's) .... Minneapolis
College of St. Scholastica .... Duluth
ConCorde Career Institute .... Minneapolis
Concordia College .... Moorhead
Concordia College .... St Paul
Crown College .... St Bonifacius
Dakota County Technical College .... Rosemount
Duluth Business University .... Duluth
Fergus Falls Community College .... Fergus Falls
Globe College of Business .... St Paul
Gustavus Adolphus College .... St Peter
Hamline University .... St Paul
Hennepin Technical College .... Brooklyn Park
Hibbing Community College .... Hibbing
Hutchinson-Willmar Regional Technical College .... Willmar
Inver Hills Community College .... Inver Grove Heights
Itasca Community College .... Grand Rapids
Lake Superior College .... Duluth
Lakeland Medical-Dental Academy .... Minneapolis
Lakewood Community College .... White Bear Lake
Lowthian College .... Minneapolis
Luther Seminary .... St Paul
Macalester College .... St Paul
Mankato State University .... Mankato
Martin Luther College .... New Ulm
Mayo Graduate School .... Rochester
Medical Institute of Minnesota .... Bloomington
Mesabi Community College .... Virginia
Metropolitan State University .... St Paul
Minneapolis Business College .... Roseville
Minneapolis College of Art and Design .... Minneapolis
Minneapolis Drafting School .... Minneapolis
Minneapolis Technical College .... Minneapolis
Minneapols Community College .... Minneapolis
Minnesota Bible College .... Rochester
Minnesota School of Barbering .... Minneapolis
Minnesota School of Business .... Richfield
Minnesota School of Business
   (Branch Campus) .... Brooklyn Center
Moler Barber School of Hairstyling .... Minneapolis
Moorhead State University .... Moorhead
Music Tech .... Minneapolis
NEI College of Technology .... Columbia Heights
Normandale Community College .... Bloomington
North Central Bible College .... Minneapolis
North Hennepin Community College .... Brooklyn Park
Northeast Metro Technical College .... White Bear Lake
Northland Community College .... Thief River Falls
Northwest Technical College .... East Grand Forks
Northwest Technical College-Moorhead .... Moorhead
Northwest Technical Institute .... Eden Prairie
Northwestern College .... St Paul

Northwestern College of Chiropractic .... Bloomington
Oak Hills Bible College .... Bemidji
Rainy River Community College .... International Falls
Range Technical College .... Hibbing
Rasmussen Business College .... Eagan
Rasmussen Business College .... Mankato
Rasmussen Business College .... Minnetonka
Rasmussen College St. Cloud .... St Cloud
Rochester Community College .... Rochester
School of Communication Arts .... Minneapolis
South Central Technical College .... Albert Lea
Southwest State University .... Marshall
Southwestern Technical College .... Granite Falls
St. Cloud State University .... St Cloud
St. Cloud Technical College .... St Cloud
St. John's University .... Collegeville
St. Mary's University of Minnesota .... Winona
St. Olaf College .... Northfield
St. Paul Technical College .... St Paul
The McConnell School .... Minneapolis
United Theological Seminary of the Twin Cities ...... New Brighton
University of Minnesota-Crookston .... Crookston
University of Minnesota-Duluth .... Duluth
University of Minnesota-Morris .... Morris
University of Minnesota-Twin Cities .... Minneapolis
University of St. Thomas .... St Paul
Vermilion Community College .... Ely
Walden University .... Minneapolis
William Mitchell College of Law .... St Paul
Willmar Community College .... Willmar
Winona State University .... Winona
Worthington Community College .... Worthington

Mississippi

Alcorn State University .... Lorman
Amherst Career Center .... Greenwood
Amherst Career Center
   (Branch Campus) .... Jackson
Batesville Job Corps Center .... Batesville
Belhaven College .... Jackson
Blue Mountain College .... Blue Mountain
Coahoma Community College .... Clarksdale
Copiah-Lincoln Community College .... Wesson
Delta State University .... Cleveland
Delta Technical Institute .... Cleveland
East Central Community College .... Decatur
East Mississippi Community College .... Scooba
Geiger's School of Cosmetology .... Hattiesburg
Gulfport Job Corps Center .... Gulfport
Hinds Community College .... Raymond
Holmes Community College .... Goodman
Itawamba Community College .... Fulton
Jackson Academy of Beauty .... Jackson
Jackson State University .... Jackson
Jones County Junior College .... Ellisville
Magnolia Bible College .... Kosciusko
Mary Holmes College .... West Point
Meridian Community College .... Meridian
Millsaps College .... Jackson
Mississippi College .... Clinton
Mississippi Delta Community College .... Moorhead
Mississippi Gulf Coast Community College .... Perkinston
Mississippi Job Corps Center .... Crystal Springs
Mississippi State University .... Mississippi State
Mississippi University for Women .... Columbus
Mississippi Valley State University .... Itta Bena
Moore Career College .... Jackson
Moore Career College
   (Branch Campus) .... Hattiesburg
Moore Career College

(Bold print indicates degree granting institutions)

Missouri

The Sourcebook of College and University Student Records

(Branch Campus)	Meridian
Moore Career College	
(Branch Campus)	Tupelo
Naval Constructions Training Center	Gulfport
Naval Technical Training Center	Meridian
North Mississippi EMS Authority	Tupelo
Northeast Mississippi Community College	Booneville
Northwest Mississippi Community College	Senatobia
Pearl River Community College	Poplarville
Phillips Junior College	Jackson
Queen City College	
(Branch Campus)	Greenville
Reformed Theological Seminary	Jackson
Rice College	
(Branch Campus)	Jackson
Rust College	Holly Springs
Southeastern Baptist College	Laurel
Southern Driver's Academy	Jackson
Southwest Mississippi Community College	Summit
Tougaloo College	Tougaloo
University of Mississippi	University
University of Mississippi Medical Center	Jackson
University of Southern Mississippi	Hattiesburg
University of Southern Mississippi	
(Gulf Park)	Long Beach
Wesley Biblical Seminary	Jackson
Wesley College	Florence
William Carey College	Hattiesburg
Wood College	Mathiston

Missouri

Aero Mechanics School	Riverside
Al-Med Academy	St Louis
Aquinas Institute of Theology	St Louis
Assemblies of God Theological Seminary	Springfield
Avila College	Kansas City
Baptist Bible College	Springfield
Basic Institute of Technology	St Louis
Basic Institute of Technology	St Louis
Bryan Institute	Bridgeton
Bryan Travel College	Springfield
Calvary Bible College	Kansas City
Cape Girardeau Area Vocational-Technical School	Cape Girardeau
Central Christian College of the Bible	Moberly
Central Methodist College	Fayette
Central Missouri State University	Warrensburg
Cleveland Chiropractic College	Kansas City
College of the Ozarks	Point Lookout
Columbia College	Columbia
ConCorde Career Institute	Kansas City
Conception Seminary College	Conception
Concordia Seminary	St Louis
Cottey College	Nevada
Covenant Theological Seminary	St Louis
Crowder College	Neosho
Culver-Stockton College	Canton
DeVry Institute of Technolgy, Kansas City	Kansas City
Deaconess College of Nursing	St Louis
Diamond Council of America	Kansas City
Dick Hill International Flight School	Springfield
Drury College	Springfield
East Central College	Union
Eastern Jackson County College of Allied Health	Blue Springs
Eden Theological Seminary	St Louis
Evangel College	Springfield
Florissant Upholstery School	St Louis
Fontbonne College	St Louis
Forest Institute of Professional Psychology	Springfield
Hannibal Area Vocational-Technical School	Hannibal
Hannibal-LaGrange College	Hannibal
Harris-Stowe State College	St Louis
Hickey School	St Louis
IHM Health Studies Center	St Louis
ITT Technical Institute	Earth City
Jefferson College	Hillsboro
Kansas City Art Institute	Kansas City
Keller Graduate School of Management	
(Kansas City Downtown)	Kansas City
Keller Graduate School of Management	
(Kansas City South)	Kansas City
Kemper Military School and College	Boonville
Kenrick-Glennon Seminary	St Louis
Kirksville College of Osteopathic Medicine	Kirksville
Lincoln University	Jefferson City
Lindenwood College	St Charles
Logan College of Chiropractic	Chesterfield
Longview Community College	Lee's Summit
Maple Woods Community College	Kansas City
Maryville University of St. Louis	St Louis
Metro Business College	Cape Girardeau
Metro Business College	
(Branch Campus)	Jefferson City
Metro Business College	
(Branch Campus)	Rolla
Midwest Institute for Medical Assistants	Kirkwood
Midwestern Baptist Theological Seminary	Kansas City
Mineral Area College	Park Hills
Missouri Baptist College	St Louis
Missouri School of Barbering and Hairstyling	Florissant
Missouri School of Barbering and Hairstyling	Independence
Missouri Southern State College	Joplin
Missouri Valley College	Marshall
Missouri Western State College	St Joseph
Moberly Area Community College	Moberly
National Career Institute	Independence
Nazarene Theological Seminary	Kansas City
Nichols Career Center	Jefferson City
North Central Missouri College	Trenton
Northeast Missouri State University	Kirksville
Northwest Missouri State University	Maryville
Ozark Christian College	Joplin
Ozarks Technical Community College	Springfield
Park College	Parkville
Patricia Stevens College	St Louis
Penn Valley Community College	Kansas City
Phillips Junior College	Springfield
Ranken Technical College	St Louis
Research College of Nursing	Kansas City
Rockhurst College	Kansas City
Rolla Area Vocational-Technical School	Rolla
Sanford-Brown Business College	Des Peres
Sanford-Brown Business College	
(Branch)	Hazelwood
Sanford-Brown Business College	
(Branch)	North Kansas City
Sanford-Brown Business College	
(Branch)	St Charles
Southeast Missouri State University	Cape Girardeau
Southwest Baptist University	Bolivar
Southwest Missouri State University	Springfield
Southwest School of Broadcasting	Springfield
St. Charles County Community College	St Peters
St. Louis Christian College	Florissant
St. Louis College of Health Careers	St Louis
St. Louis College of Pharmacy	St Louis
St. Louis Community College	St Louis
St. Louis Community College at Florissant Valley	St Louis
St. Louis Community College at Meramec	Kirkwood
St. Louis Symphony Community Music School	St Louis
St. Louis Tech	St Louis
St. Louis University	St Louis
St. Paul School of Theology	Kansas City
State Fair Community College	Sedalia

State Cross Reference Index 452 (Bold print indicates degree granting institutions)

The Sourcebook of College and University Student Records **Montana**

Ste. Genevieve Beauty College..................................Ste. Genevieve
Stephens College..Columbia
TAD Technical Institute..Kansas City
Three Rivers Community College..............................Poplar Bluff
Trans World Travel Academy..St Louis
University of Health Sciences....................................Kansas City
University of Missouri-Columbia...................................Columbia
University of Missouri-Kansas City...........................Kansas City
University of Missouri-Rolla..Rolla
University of Missouri-St. Louis......................................St Louis
Vanderschmidt School..St Louis
Vatterott Educational Centers...St Louis
Washington University...St Louis
Webster University..St Louis
Wentworth Military Academy and Junior College.........Lexington
Westminster College...Fulton
William Jewell College..Liberty
William Woods University..Fulton
Wright Business School
  (Branch Campus)..Kansas City

Montana

Big Sky College of Barber Styling..Missoula
Billings Business College..Billings
Billings School of Barbering and Hairstyling........................Billings
Blackfeet Community College.......................................Browning
Carroll College..Helena
College of Great Falls..Great Falls
Dawson Community College...Glendive
Flathead Valley Community College...............................Kalispell
Fort Belknap College...Harlem
Fort Peck Community College..Poplar
Little Big Horn College..Crow Agency
May Technical College...Billings
May Technical College
  (Branch Campus)..Great Falls
Miles Community College.. Miles City
Montana College of Technology of the University of Montana
  ....Helena
Montana State University College of Technology-Great Falls
  ....Great Falls
Montana State University-Billings...................................Billings
Montana State University-Bozeman..............................Bozeman
Montana Tech of the University of Montana......................Butte
**Montana Tech of the University of Montana-Division of
Technology**...Butte
Northern Montana College...Havre
Rocky Mountain College...Billings
Salish Kootenai College...Pablo
Stone Child Community College....................................Box Elder
University of Montana..Missoula
University of Montana-Missoula/College of Technology Missoula
Western Montana College of the University of Montana......Dillon

Nebraska

Bellevue University..Bellevue
Central Community College.......................................Grand Island
Central Technical Community College............................Hastings
Chadron State College..Chadron
Clarkson College...Omaha
College of Hair Design..Lincoln
College of St. Mary...Omaha
Concordia College..Seward
Creighton University..Omaha
Dana College..Blair
Doane College..Crete

Dr. Welbes College of Message Therapy ....Omaha
Grace University...Omaha
Hastings College...Hastings
ITT Technical Institute
  (Branch)..Omaha
Institute of Computer Science..Omaha
Lincoln School of Commerce..Lincoln
McCook Community College..McCook
Metropolitan Community College....................................Omaha
Mid-Plains Community College..................................North Platte
Midland Lutheran College..Fremont
Nebraska Christian College..Norfolk
Nebraska College of Business..Omaha
Nebraska College of Technical Agriculture........................Curtis
Nebraska Indian Community College..........................Winnebago
Nebraska Methodist College of Nursing and Allied Health Omaha
Nebraska Wesleyan University..Lincoln
Northeast Community College...Norfolk
Omaha College of Health Careers..Omaha
Omaha Opportunities Industrialization Center ....Omaha
Peru State College..Peru
Southeast Community College...Lincoln
Spencer School of Business.......................................Grand Island
Union College...Lincoln
Universal Technical Institute..Omaha
University of Nebraska Medical Center............................Omaha
University of Nebraska at Kearney..................................Kearney
University of Nebraska at Omaha.....................................Omaha
University of Nebraska-Lincoln...Lincoln
Wayne State College..Wayne
Western Nebraska Community College.....................Scottsbluff
York College...York

Nevada

Academy of Medical Careers..Las Vegas
Century Business College
  (Century Schools)..Las Vegas
Community College of Southern Nevada.............North Las Vegas
Deep Springs College...Dyer
Interior Design Institute...Las Vegas
International Dealers School ....Las Vegas
Morrison College-Reno...Reno
National Academy for Casino Dealers ....Las Vegas
Northern Nevada Community College...................................Elko
PCI Dealers School ....Las Vegas
Phillips Junior College of Las Vegas.............................Las Vegas
Professional Careers ....Las Vegas
Sierra Nevada College...Incline Village
Truckee Meadows Community College...............................Reno
University of Nevada, Las Vegas..................................Las Vegas
University of Nevada, Reno...Reno
Vegas Career School..Las Vegas
Western Nevada Community College.........................Carson City

New Hampshire

Antioch University
  (Antioch New England Graduate School)..............................Keene
Castle College..Windham
Colby-Sawyer College...New London
College for Lifelong Learning...Concord
Daniel Webster College..Nashua
Dartmouth College..Hanover
Franklin Pierce College...Rindge
Franklin Pierce Law Center..Concord
Hesser College...Manchester
Keene State College..Keene

(Bold print indicates degree granting institutions) **State Cross Reference Index**

New Jersey

McIntosh College .... Dover
New England College .... Henniker
New Hampshire College .... Manchester
New Hampshire Technical College .... Claremont
New Hampshire Technical College at Berlin .... Berlin
New Hampshire Technical College at Laconia .... Laconia
New Hampshire Technical College at Manchester ...... Manchester
New Hampshire Technical College at Nashua .... Nashua
New Hampshire Technical College at Stratham .... Stratham
New Hampshire Technical Institute .... Concord
Northeast Career Schools .... Manchester
Notre Dame College .... Manchester
Plymouth State College .... Plymouth
Rivier College .... Nashua
St. Anselm College .... Machester
Travel Education Center
 (Branch Campus) .... Nashua
University of New Hampshire .... Durham
University of New Hampshire at Manchester .... Manchester
White Pines College .... Chester

New Jersey

Academy of Professional Development .... Edison
Academy of Professional Development
 (Branch Campus) .... Ewing
American Business Academy .... Hackensack
Assumption College for Sisters .... Mendham
Atlantic Community College .... Mays Landing
Berdan Institute .... Totowa
Bergen Community College .... Paramus
Berkeley College of Business
 (Waldwick Campus) .... Waldwick
Berkeley College of Business
 (West Paterson Campus) .... West Paterson
Berkeley College of Business
 (Woodbridge Campus) .... Woodbridge
Beth Medrash Govoha .... Lakewood
Bilingual Institute .... Newark
Bilingual Institute
 (Branch Campus) .... Paterson
Bloomfield College .... Bloomfield
Boardwalk and Marina Casino Dealers School .... Atlantic City
Brick Computer Science Institute .... Brick
Brookdale Community College .... Freehold
Brookdale Community College .... Lincroft
Brookdale Community College
 (Asbury Park Learning Center) .... Asbury Park
Brookdale Community College
 (Bayshore Learning Center) .... West Keansburg
Brookdale Community College
 (Forth Monmouth Learning Center) .... Fort Monmouth
Brookdale Community College
 (Long Branch Learning Center) .... Long Branch
Burlington County College .... Pemberton
Business Training Institute .... Paramus
Caldwell College .... Caldwell
Camden County College .... Blackwood
Camden County College
 (Branch Campus) .... Camden
Cape May County Technical Institute .... Cape May Court House
Centenary College .... Hackettstown
Chubb Institute .... Parsippany
Chubb Institute
 (Branch Campus) .... Jersey City
Cittone Institute .... Edison
Cittone Institute
 (Branch Campus) .... Mount Laurel
Cittone Institute
 (Branch Campus) .... Princeton
College of St. Elizabeth .... Morristown

Computer Learning Center .... Paramus
County College of Morris .... Randolph
Cumberland County College .... Vineland
DeVry Technical Institute .... Woodbridge
Divers Academy of the Eastern Seaboard .... Camden
Dover Business College .... Dover
Dover Business College
 (Branch Campus) .... Paramus
Drake College of Business .... Elizabeth
Drake College of Business
 (Branch Campus) .... East Orange
Drew University .... Madison
Du Cret School of the Arts .... Plainfield
Empire Technical Schools of New Jersey .... East Orange
Engine City Technical Institute .... Union
Essex County College .... Newark
Essex County College
 (West Essex Branch Campus) .... West Caldwell
Fairleigh Dickinson University .... Teaneck
Fairleigh Dickinson University
 (Florham-Madison Campus) .... Madison
Fairleigh Dickinson University
 (Rutherford Campus) .... Rutherford
Fairleigh Dickinson University
 (Teaneck-Hackensack Campus) .... Hackensack
Felician College .... Lodi
General Technical Institute Welding Trade School .... Linden
Georgian Court College .... Lakewood
Gloucester County College .... Sewell
Harris School of Business .... Cherry Hill
HoHoKus School .... Ramsey
Hudson County Community College .... Jersey City
Immaculate Conception Seminary .... South Orange
Jersey City State College .... Jersey City
Joe Kubert School of Cartoon and Graphic Art .... Dover
Kane Business Institute .... Cherry Hill
Katherine Gibbs School .... Montclair
Katherine Gibbs School
 (Branch Campus) .... Piscataway
Kean College of New Jersey .... Union
Lincoln Technical Institute .... Pennsauken
Lincoln Technical Institute .... Union
Mercer County Community College .... Trenton
Mercer County Community College
 (James Kerney Campus) .... Trenton
Metropolitan Technical Institute .... Fairfield
Middlesex County College .... Edison
Monmouth University .... West Long Branch
Montclair State College .... Upper Montclair
National Education Center-RETS Campus .... Nutley
Naval Air Technical Training Center
 (Branch Campus) .... Lakehurst
New Brunswick Theological Seminary .... New Brusnwick
New Jersey Institute of Technology .... Newark
Ocean County College .... Toms River
Omega Institute .... Cinnaminson
Passiac County Community College .... Paterson
Pennco Tech .... Blackwood
Plaza School .... Paramus
Princeton Theological Seminary .... Princeton
Princeton University .... Princeton
Rabbinical College of America .... Morristown
Ramapo College of New Jersey .... Mahwah
Raritan Valley Community College .... Somerville
Rider College .... Lawrenceville
Rider College
 (Westminster Choir College) .... Princeton
Rowan College of New Jersey .... Glassboro
Rowan College of New Jersey
 (Camden Campus) .... Camden
Rutgers, The State University of New Jersey Camden Campus
 .... Camden

Rutgers, The State University of New Jersey New Brunswick Campus .... New Brunswick
Rutgers, The State University of New Jersey Newark Campus .... Newark
SCS Business and Technical Institute .... East Orange
SCS Business and Technical Institute .... Union City
Salem Community College .... Carneys Point
Seton Hall University .... South Orange
Seton Hall University
  (School of Law) .... Newark
St. Peter's College .... Jersey City
St. Peter's College
  (Englewood Cliffs Campus) .... Englewood Cliffs
Star Technical Institute .... Deptford
Star Technical Institute .... Edgewater Park
Star Technical Institute .... Somerdale
Star Technical Institute .... Vineland
Star Technical Institute
  (Branch Campus) .... Lakewood
Star Technical Institute
  (Branch Campus) .... Ocean Township
Stevens Institute of Technology .... Hoboken
Stockton College of New Jersey .... Pomona
Stockton State College .... Pomona
Stuart School of Business Administration .... Wall
Sussex County Community College .... Newton
Talmudical Academy of New Jersey .... Adelphia
Technical Institute of Camden County .... Sicklerville
Teterboro School of Aeronautics .... Teterboro
Thomas A. Edison State College .... Trenton
Titan Helicopter Academy .... Millville
Trenton State College .... Trenton
Ultrasound Diagnostic School .... Iselin
Union County College .... Cranford
Union County College
  (Elizabeth Campus) .... Elizabeth
Union County College
  (Plainfield Campus) .... Plainfield
University of Medicine and Dentistry of New Jersey .... Newark
University of Medicine and Dentistry of New Jersey
  (Dental School) .... Newark
University of Medicine and Dentistry of New Jersey
  (Graduate School of Biomedical Sciences) .... Newark
University of Medicine and Dentistry of New Jersey
  (Medical School) .... Newark
University of Medicine and Dentistry of New Jersey
  (Robert Wood Johnson Medical School) .... Piscataway
University of Medicine and Dentistry of New Jersey
  (School of Health-Related Professions) .... Newark
University of Medicine and Dentistry of New Jersey
  (School of Osteopathic Medicine) .... Stratford
Warren County Community College .... Washington
William Paterson College of New Jersey .... Wayne

New Mexico

Albuquerque Barber College .... Albuquerque
Albuquerque Technical-Vocational Institute .... Albuquerque
AzTech College
  (Branch Campus) .... Albuquerque
Clovis Community College .... Clovis
College of Santa Fe .... Santa Fe
College of the Southwest .... Hobbs
Computer Career Center
  (Branch Campus) .... Albuquerque
Dona Ana Branch Community College .... Las Cruces
Eastern New Mexico University .... Portales
Eastern New Mexico University-Roswell .... Roswell
ITT Technical Institute
  (Branch) .... Albuquerque

Institute of American Indian and Alaskan Native Culture and Arts
.... Santa Fe
International Business College .... Las Cruces
International Institute of Chinese Medicine .... Santa Fe
Luna Vocational Technical Institute .... Las Vegas
Metropolitan College of Court Reporting .... Albuquerque
Nazarene Bible College
  (Nazarene Indian Bible College) .... Albuquerque
New Mexico Highlands University .... Las Vegas
New Mexico Institute of Mining and Technology .... Socorro
New Mexico Junior College .... Hobbs
New Mexico Military Institute .... Roswell
New Mexico State University .... Las Cruces
New Mexico State University at Alamogordo .... Alamogordo
New Mexico State University at Carlsbad .... Carlsbad
New Mexico State University at Grants .... Grants
Northern Arizona Institute of Technology
  (Branch Campus) .... Albuquerque
Northern New Mexico Community College .... Espanola
Parks College .... Albuquerque
Pima Medical Institute
  (Branch) .... Albuquerque
San Juan College .... Farmington
Sante Fe Community College .... Santa Fe
Southwest Acupuncture College .... Santa Fe
Southwest Acupuncture College
  (Branch Campus) .... Albuquerque
Southwestern Indian Polytechnic Institute .... Albuquerque
St. John's College .... Santa Fe
The Art Center
  (Branch Campus) .... Albuquerque
University of New Mexico .... Albuquerque
University of New Mexico
  (Gallup Branch) .... Gallup
University of New Mexico
  (Los Alamos Branch) .... Los Alamos
University of New Mexico
  (Valencia Branch) .... Los Lunas
University of Phoenix
  (Albuquerque Main) .... Albuquerque
Western Business Institute .... Alamogordo
Western New Mexico University .... Silver City

New York

Academy for Career Education .... Ridgewood
Adelphi University .... Garden City
Adirondack Community College .... Queensbury
Advanced Software Analysis .... Brooklyn
Albany College of Pharmacy of Union University .... Albany
Albany Law School .... Albany
Albany Medical College of Union University .... Albany
Alfred University .... Alfred
Alfred University
  (New York State College of Ceramics) .... Alfred
Alvin Ailey American Dance Center .... New York
American Academy McAllister Institute of Funeral Service, Inc.
.... New York
American Academy of Dramatic Arts .... New York
American Ballet Center/Joffrey Balley School .... New York
American Musical and Dramatic Academy .... New York
Apex Technical School .... New York
Audrey Cohen College .... New York
Bank Street College of Education .... New York
Bard College .... Annandale-On-Hudson
Barnard College .... New York
Berk TRade and Business School .... New York
Berkeley College .... White Plains
Berkeley School of New York .... New York
Bernard M. Baruch College .... New York
Beth HaTalmud Rabbinical College .... Brooklyn

New York

The Sourcebook of College and University Student Records

Beth Hamedrash Shaarei Yosher	Brooklyn
Blake Business School	New York
Blake Business School (Branch Campus)	New York
Boricua College	New York
Borough of Manhattan Community College	New York
Briarcliffe School, Inc.	Woodbury
Briarcliffe School, Inc. (Branch Campus)	Lynbrook
Briarcliffe School, Inc. (Branch Campus)	Patchogue
Bronx Community College	Bronx
Brooklyn College	Brooklyn
Brooklyn Law School	Brooklyn
Broome Community College	Binghamton
Bryant & Stratton Business Institute	Albany
Bryant & Stratton Business Institute	Buffalo
Bryant & Stratton Business Institute	Rochester
Bryant & Stratton Business Institute	Syracuse
Bryant & Stratton Business Institute (Branch Campus)	Cicero
Bryant & Stratton Business Institute (Branch Campus)	Lackawanna
Bryant & Stratton Business Institute (Branch Campus)	Rochester
Bryant & Stratton Business Institute (Branch Campus)	Williamsville
Business Informatics Center	Valley Stream
Canisius College	Buffalo
Cashier Training Institute	New York
Cayuga County Community College	Auburn
Cazenovia College	Cazenovia
Central Yeshiva Tomchei Tmimim-Lubavitch	Brooklyn
Charles Stuart School of Diamond Setting	Brooklyn
Chauffeurs Training School	Albany
Cheryl Fell's School of Business	Niagara Falls
Christ the King Seminary	East Aurora
Circle in the Square Theatre School	New York
City College	New York
Clarkson University	Potsdam
Clinton Community College	Plattsburgh
Colgate Rochester Divinity School/Bexley Hall/Crozer Theo. Sem.	Rochester
Colgate University	Hamilton
College of Aeronautics	Flushing
College of Insurance	New York
College of Mount St. Vincent	Riverdale
College of New Rochelle	New Rochelle
College of New Rochelle (Brooklyn Campus)	Brooklyn
College of New Rochelle (Co-op City Campus)	Bronx
College of New Rochelle (DC 37 Campus)	New York
College of New Rochelle (New York Theological Seminary Campus)	New York
College of New Rochelle (Rosa Parks Campus)	New York
College of New Rochelle (South Bronx Campus)	Bronx
College of St. Rose	Albany
College of Staten Island	Staten Island
College of Staten Island (Sunnyside Campus)	Staten Island
Columbia University	New York
Columbia University Teachers College	New York
Columbia-Greene Community College	Hudson
Commercial Driver Training	West Babylon
Computer Career Center	Hempstead
Concordia College	Bronxville
Continental Dental Assistant School	Rochester
Cooper Union for the Advancement of Science and Art	New York
Cope Institute	New York
Cornell University	Ithaca
Corning Community College	Corning
D'Youville College	Buffalo
Daemen College	Amherst
Dance Theatre of Harlem, Inc.	New York
Darkei No'am Rabbinical College	Brooklyn
Dominican College of Blauvelt	Orangeburg
Dowling College	Oakdale
Drake Business School	Bronx
Drake Business School	Flushing
Drake Business School	New York
Drake Business School	Staten Island
Dutchess Community College	Poughkeepsie
Dutchess Community College (Branch Campus)	Poughkeepsie
Dutchess Community College (South Campus)	Wappingers Falls
Elmira Business Institute	Elmira
Elmira College	Elmira
Erie Community College City Campus	Buffalo
Erie Community College North (Amherst) Campus	Williamsville
Erie Community College South Campus	Orchard Park
FEGS Trades and Business School	New York
FEGS Trades and Business School (Branch Campus)	Brooklyn
Fashion Institute of Technology	New York
Finger Lakes Community College	Canandaigua
Five Towns College	Dix Hills
Folk Art Institute of the Museum of American Folk Art	New York
Fordham University	Bronx
French Culinary Institute	New York
Fulton-Montgomery Community College	Johnstown
General Theological Seminary	New York
Genesee Community College	Batavia
Global Business Institute	Far Rockaway
Global Business Institute (Branch Campus)	New York
Globe Institute of Technology	New York
Graduate School and University Center	New York
Hamilton College	Clinton
Hartwick College	Oneonta
Hebrew Union College-Jewish Institute of Religion	New York
Helene Fuld School of Nursing	New York
Herbert H. Lehman College	Bronx
Herkimer County Community College	Herkimer
Hilbert College	Hamburg
Hobart & William Smith College	Geneva
Hofstra University	Hempstead
Hostos Community College	Bronx
Houghton College	Houghton
Houghton College (Buffalo Suburban Campus)	West Seneca
Hudson Valley Community College	Troy
Hunter Business School	Levittown
Hunter College	New York
Institute of Allied Medical Professions	New York
Institute of Audio Research	New York
Interboro Institute	New York
Iona College	New Rochelle
Iona College (Manhattan Campus)	New York
Iona College (Rockland Campus)	Orangeburg
Iona College (Yonkers Campus)	Yonkers
Isabella G. Hart School of Practical Nursing	Rochester
Island Drafting & Technical Institute	Amityville
Ithaca College	Ithaca
Jamestown Business College	Jamestown
Jamestown Community College	Jamestown
Jamestown Community College (Cattaraugus County Campus)	Olean

State Cross Reference Index (Bold print indicates degree granting institutions)

Jefferson Community College	Watertown
Jewish Theological Seminary of America	New York
John Jay College of Criminal Justice	New York
Julliard School	New York
Katherine Gibbs School	Melville
Katherine Gibbs School	New York
Kehilath Yakov Rabbinical Seminary	Brooklyn
Keuka College	Keuka Park
King's College	Briarcliff Manor
Kingsborough Community College	Brooklyn
Krissler Business Institute	Poughkeepsie
La Guardia Community College	Long Island City
Laban/Bartenieff Institute of Movement Studies, Inc.	New York
Laboratory Institute of Merchandising	New York
LeMoyne College	Syracuse
Lewis A. Wilson Technical Center	Dix Hills
Long Island Business Institute	Commack
Long Island University	Brookville
Long Island University	Dobbs Ferry
Long Island University (Brentwood Campus)	Brentwood
Long Island University (Brooklyn Campus)	Brooklyn
Long Island University (C.W. Post Campus)	Brookville
Long Island University (Rockland Campus)	Orangeburg
Mandl School	New York
Manhattan College	Riverdale
Manhattan School of Music	New York
Manhattanville College	Purchase
Maria College of Albany	Albany
Marion S. Whelan School of Practical Nursing	Geneva
Marist College	Poughkeepsie
Martha Graham School of Contemporary Dance, Inc.	New York
Marymount College	Tarrytown
Marymount Manhattan College	New York
Mater Dei College	Ogdensburg
Medaille College	Buffalo
Medgar Evers College	Brooklyn
Merce Cunningham Studio	New York
Mercy College	Dobbs Ferry
Mercy College (Bronx Campus)	Bronx
Mercy College (White Plains Campus)	White Plains
Mercy College (Yorktown Campus)	Yorktown Heights
Mesivta Tifereth Jerusalem of America	New York
Mesivta Torah Vodaath Rabbinical Seminary	Brooklyn
Mesivta of Eastern Parkway Rabbinical Seminary	Brooklyn
Mildred Elley Business School	Albany
Mirrer Yeshiva Central Institute	Brooklyn
Modern Welding School	Schenectady
Mohawk Valley Community College	Utica
Mohawk Valley Community College (Branch Campus)	Rome
Molloy College	Rockville Centre
Monroe College	Bronx
Monroe College (New Rochelle Campus)	New Rochelle
Monroe Community College	Rochester
Mount Sinai School of Medicine	New York
Mount St. Mary College	Newburgh
Munson-Williams-Proctor Institute	Utica
Nassau Community College	Garden City
National Shakespeare Conservatory	New York
National Tax Training School	Monsey
National Tractor Trailer School	Liverpool
National Tractor Trailer School (Branch Campus)	Buffalo
Nazareth College of Rochester	Rochester
Neighborhood Playhouse School of Theatre	New York
New School for Social Research	New York
New School for Social Research (Parsons School of Design)	New York
New School of Contemporary Radio	Albany
New York Chiropractic College	Seneca Falls
New York City Technical College	Brooklyn
New York College of Podiatric Medicine	New York
New York Food & Hotel Management School	New York
New York Institute of Business and Technology	New York
New York Institute of Technology	Old Westbury
New York Institute of Technology (Central Islip Campus)	Central Islip
New York Institute of Technology (Manhattan Campus)	New York
New York Medical College	Valhalla
New York School for Medical/Dental Assistants	Forest Hills
New York School of Dog Grooming	New York
New York School of Dog Grooming (Branch Campus)	New Hyde Park
New York School of Interior Design	New York
New York School of Law	New York
New York Theological Seminary	New York
New York University	New York
Niagara County Community College	Sanborn
Niagara University	Niagara University
Nikolais and Louis Dance Lab	New York
North Country Community College	Saranac Lake
North Country Community College	Saranac Lake
North Country Community College (Branch Campus)	Malone
Nyack College	Nyack
Ohr Hameir Theological Seminary	Peekskill
Ohr Somayach Institutions	Monsey
Olean Business Institute	Olean
Onondaga Community College	Syracuse
Orange County Community College	Middletown
Pace University	New York
Pace University (Pleasantville/Briarcliff)	Pleasantville
Pace University (White Plains)	White Plains
Pacific College of Oriental Medicine (Branch)	New York
Paul Smith's College	Paul Smiths
Phillips Beth Israel School of Nursing	New York
Plaza Business Institute	Jackson Heights
Polytechnic University	Brooklyn
Polytechnic University (Long Island Center)	Farmingdale
Polytechnic University (Westchester Graduate Center)	Hawthorne
Pratt Institute	Brooklyn
Professional Business Institute	New York
Queens College	Flushing
Queensborough Community College	Bayside
Rabbinical Academy Mesivta Rabbi Chaim Berlin	Brooklyn
Rabbinical College Beth Shraga	Monsey
Rabbinical College Bobover Yeshiva B'nei Zion	Brooklyn
Rabbinical College Ch'san Sofer	Brooklyn
Rabbinical College of Long Island	Long Beach
Rabbinical Seminary Adas Yereim	Brooklyn
Rabbinical Seminary M'kor Chaim	Brooklyn
Rabbinical Seminary of America	Forest Hills
Regents College of the University of the State of New York	Albany
Rensselaer Polytechnic Institute	Troy
Ridley-Lowell Business and Technical Institute	Binghamton
Roberts Wesleyan College	Rochester
Rochester Business Institute	Rochester
Rochester Institute of Technology	Rochester
Rockland Community College	Suffern
Rockland Community College (Haverstraw Learning Center)	Haverstraw

(Bold print indicates degree granting institutions)

New York

Rockland Community College
 (Nyack Learning Center) .... Nyack
Rockland Community College
 (Spring Valley Learning Center) .... Spring Valley
Royal Barber & Beauty School .... Schenectady
SCS Business and Technical Institute .... Brooklyn
SCS Business and Technical Institute .... Brooklyn
SCS Business and Technical Institute .... Jamaica
SCS Business and Technical Institute .... New York
SYRIT Computer School Systems .... Brooklyn
Sage Colleges .... Troy
Sage Colleges
 (Sage Junior College of Albany) .... Albany
Sarah Lawrence College .... Bronxville
Schenectady County Community College .... Schenectady
School of Visual Arts .... New York
Seminary of the Immaculate Conception .... Huntington
Sh'or Yoshuv Rabbinical College .... Far Rockaway
Siena College .... Loudonville
Simmons Institute of Funeral Service .... Syracuse
Skidmore College .... Saratoga Springs
Sonia Moore Studio of the Theatre .... New York
Sotheby's Educational Studies .... New York
Southampton College of Long Island University ...... Southampton
Spanish-American Institute .... New York
Spencer Business and Technical Institute .... Schenectady
St. Bernard's Institute.. Rochester
St. Bonaventure University .... St Bonaventure
St. Francis College .... Brooklyn
St. Francis School of Practical Nursing .... Olean
St. John Fisher College .... Rochester
St. John's University .... Jamaica
St. John's University
 (Branch) .... Staten Island
St. Joseph's College .... Brooklyn
St. Joseph's College
 (Suffolk) ....Patchogue
St. Joseph's Seminary .... Yonkers
St. Lawrence University .... Canton
St. Thomas Aquinas College .... Sparkill
St. Vladimir's Orthodox Theological Seminary .... Crestwood
State University College at Brockport .... Brockport
State University College at Buffalo .... Buffalo
State University College at Cortland .... Cortland
State University College at Fredonia .... Fredonia
State University College at Geneseo .... Geneseo
State University College at Old Westbury .... Old Westbury
State University College at Oneonta .... Oneonta
State University College at Oswego .... Oswego
State University College at Plattsburgh .... Plattsburgh
State University College at Potsdam .... Potsdam
State University College at Purchase .... Purchase
State University of New York
 (College of Environmental Science and Forestry) .... Syracuse
State University of New York
 (College of Optometry at New York City) .... Manhattan
State University of New York College at Farmingdale
 .... Farmingdale
State University of New York College of Ag and Tech at Cobleskill .... Cobleskill
State University of New York College of Ag and Tech/Morrisville
 .... Morrisville
State University of New York College of Technology at Alfred
 .... Alfred
State University of New York College of Technology at Alfred
 (Branch) .... Alfred
State University of New York College of Technology at Canton
 .... Canton
State University of New York College of Technology at Delhi
 .... Delhi
State University of New York Empire State College
 .... Saratoga Springs
State University of New York Empire State College
 (Genesee Valley Regional Center) .... Rochester
State University of New York Empire State College
 (Hudson Valley Regional Center) .... Hartsdale
State University of New York Empire State College
 (Long Island Regional Center) .... Old Westbury
State University of New York Empire State College
 (Metropolitan Regional Center) .... New York
State University of New York Empire State College
 (Niagara Frontier Regional Center) .... Buffalo
State University of New York Empire State College
 (Northeast Center) .... Albany
State University of New York Health Science Center at Brooklyn
 .... Brooklyn
State University of New York Health Science Center at Syracuse
 .... Syracuse
State University of New York Institute of Technology / Utica/Rome .... Utica
State University of New York Maritime College .... Throggs Neck
State University of New York Maritime College
 (Stenotype Academy) .... New York
State University of New York at Albany .... Albany
State University of New York at Binghamton .... Binghamton
State University of New York at Buffalo .... Buffalo
State University of New York at New Paltz .... New Paltz
State University of New York at Stony Brook .... Stony Brook
Stella Adler Conservatory of Acting .... New York
Stenotopia, the World of Court Reporting .... Plainview
Suburban Technical School .... Hempstead
Suburban Technical School
 (Branch Campus) .... East Islip
Suffolk Community College
 (Ammerman) .... Selden
Suffolk Community College
 (Eastern) .... Riverhead
Suffolk Community College
 (Western) .... Brentwood
Sullivan County Community College .... Loch Sheldrake
Superior Career Institute .... New York
Swedish Institute .... New York
Syracuse University .... Syracuse
Talmudical Seminary Oholei Torah .... Brooklyn
Taylor Business Institute .... New York
Technical Career Institute .... New York
Techno-Dent Training Center .... New York
Tompkins Cortland Community College .... Dryden
Torah Temimah Talmudical Seminary .... Brooklyn
Touro College .... New York
Touro College .... New York
Touro College
 (Huntington Branch) .... Huntington
Travel Institute .... New York
Tri-State Institute of Traditional Chinese Acupuncture .... New York
Trocaire College .... Buffalo
Ulster County Community College .... Stone Ridge
Ultrasound Diagnostic School .... Carle Place
Ultrasound Diagnostic School .... Elmsford
Ultrasound Diagnostic School .... New York
Union College .... Schenectady
Union Theological Seminary .... New York
United States Merchant Marine Academy .... Kings Point
United States Military Academy .... West Point
United Talmudical Academy .... Brooklyn
Universal Business and Media School .... New York
University of Rochester .... Rochester
Utica College of Syracuse University .... Utica
Utica School of Commerce .... Utica
Utica School of Commerce
 (Branch) .... Canastota
Utica School of Commerce
 (Branch) .... Oneonta
Vassar College .... Poughkeepsie
Villa Maria College of Buffalo .... Buffalo
Wadhams Hall Seminary/College .... Ogdensburg

State Cross Reference Index 458 (Bold print indicates degree granting institutions)

The Sourcebook of College and University Student Records — **North Carolina**

Wagner College .... Staten Island
Webb Institute .... Glen Cove
Wells College .... Aurora
Westchester Business Institute .... White Plains
Westchester Community College .... Valhalla
Westchester Conservatory of Music .... White Plains
Wood Tobe Coburn School .... New York
Yeshiva Derech Chaim .... Brooklyn
Yeshiva Karlin Stolin Beth Aaron V'Israel Rabbinical Institute
.... Brooklyn
Yeshiva Mikdash Melech .... Brooklyn
Yeshiva Shaar HaTorah Talmudic Research Institute
.... Kew Gardens
Yeshiva University .... New York
Yeshiva of Nitra-Rabbinical College Yeshiva Farm Settlement
.... Mount Kisco
Yeshivas Novominsk .... Brooklyn
Yeshivath Viznitz .... Monsey
Yesivath Zichron Moshe .... South Fallsburg
York College .... York

North Carolina

Academy of Artistic Hair Design .... North Wilkesboro
Alamance Community College .... Graham
Alliance Tractor Trailer Training Center .... Arden
Alliance Tractor Trailer Trining Centers II
   (Training Center V Campus) .... Benson
American Business and Fashion Institute .... Charlotte
American Education Institute of Cosmetology .... Hickory
Anson Community College .... Polkton
Appalachian State University .... Boone
Arnold's Beauty College .... Durham
Asheville-Buncombe Technical Community College ..... Asheville
Barber-Scotia College .... Concord
Barton College .... Wilson
Beaufort County Community College .... Washington
Belmont Abbey College .... Belmont
Bennett College .... Greensboro
Black World College of Hair Design .... Charlotte
Bladen Community College .... Dublin
Blue Ridge Community College .... Flat Rock
Brevard College .... Brevard
Brookstone College of Business .... Charlotte
Brookstone College of Business
   (Branch Campus) .... Greensboro
Brunswick Community College .... Supply
Burke Academy of Cosmetic Art .... Morganton
Burke Academy of Cosmetic Art
   (Branch Campus) .... Newton
Caldwell Community College and Technical Institute .... Lenior
Campbell University .... Buies Creek
Cape Fear Community College .... Wilmington
Carolina Beauty College .... High Point
Carolina Beauty College
   (Branch Campus) .... Burlington
Carolina Beauty College
   (Branch Campus) .... Charlotte
Carolina Beauty College
   (Branch Campus) .... Durham
Carolina Beauty College
   (Branch Campus) .... Gastonia
Carolina Beauty College
   (Branch Campus) .... Greensboro
Carolina Beauty College
   (Branch Campus) .... Kannapolis
Carolina Beauty College
   (Branch Campus) .... Kernersville
Carolina Beauty College
   (Branch Campus) .... Lexington
Carolina Beauty College
   (Branch Campus) .... Monroe
Carolina Beauty College
   (Branch Campus) .... Mount Airy
Carolina Beauty College
   (Branch Campus) .... Salisbury
Carolina Beauty College
   (Branch Campus) .... Shelby
Carolina Beauty College
   (Branch Campus) .... Statesville
Carolina Beauty College
   (Branch Campus) .... Winston-Salem
Catawba College .... Salisbury
Catawba Valley Community College .... Hickory
Cateret Community College .... Morehead City
Cecil's College .... Asheville
Central Carolina Community College .... Sanford
Central Piedmont Community College .... Charlotte
Chowan College .... Murfreesboro
Cleveland Community College .... Shelby
Coastal Carolina Community College .... Jacksonville
College of the Albemarle .... Elizabeth City
Craven Community College .... New Bern
Davidson College .... Davidson
Davidson County Community College .... Lexington
Duke University .... Durham
Durham Technical Community College .... Durham
East Carolina University .... Greenville
East Coast Bible College .... Charlotte
Edgecombe Community College .... Tarboro
Elizabeth City State University .... Elizabeth City
Elon College .... Elon College
Fayetteville Beauty College .... Fayetteville
Fayetteville State University .... Fayetteville
Fayetteville Technical Community College .... Fayetteville
Forsyth Technical Community College .... Winston-Salem
Gardner-Webb University .... Boiling Springs
Gaston College .... Dallas
Greensboro College .... Greensboro
Guilford College .... Greensboro
Guilford Technical Community College .... Jamestown
Hairstyling Institute of Charlotte .... Charlotte
Halifax Community College .... Weldon
Haywood Community College .... Clyde
High Point University .... High Point
Isothermal Community College .... Spindale
James Sprunt Community College .... Kenansville
John Wesley College .... High Point
Johnson C. Smith University .... Charlotte
Johnston Community College .... Smithfield
Kings College .... Charlotte
Lees-McRae College .... Banner Elk
Lenoir Community College .... Kinston
Lenoir-Rhyne College .... Hickory
Livingstone College .... Salisbury
Louisburg College .... Louisburg
Lyndon B. Johnson Civilian Conservation Center .... Franklin
Maria Parham Hospital, Inc. .... Henderson
Mars Hill College .... Mars Hill
Martin Community College .... Williamston
Mayland Community College .... Spruce Pine
McDowell Technical Community College .... Marion
Meredith College .... Raleigh
Methodist College .... Fayetteville
Mille-Motte Business College
   (Branch Campus) .... Wilmington
Mitchell Community College .... Statesville
Montgomery Community College .... Troy
Montreat-Anderson College .... Montreat
Mount Olive College .... Mount Olive
Mr. David's School of Hair Design .... Wilmington
Nash Community College .... Rocky Mount
Naval Health Sciences Education and Training Command

(Bold print indicates degree granting institutions)

State Cross Reference Index

North Dakota

(Field Medical Service School) .... Camp Lejeune
North Carolina Academy of Cosmetic Art .... Hendersonville
North Carolina Agricultural and Technical State University
.... Greensboro
North Carolina Central University .... Durham
North Carolina School of the Arts .... Winston-Salem
North Carolina State University .... Raleigh
North Carolina Wesleyan College .... Rocky Mount
Northern Hospital of Surry County School of Medical Technology
.... Mount Airy
Oconaluftee Job Corps Civilian Conservation Center .... Cherokee
Pamlico Community College .... Grantsboro
Peace College .... Raleigh
Pembroke State University .... Pembroke
Pfeiffer College .... Misenheimer
Piedmont Bible College .... Winston-Salem
Piedmont Community College .... Roxboro
Pitt Community College .... Greenville
Queens College .... Charlotte
Randolph Community College .... Asheboro
Richmond Community College .... Hamlet
Roanoke Bible College .... Elizabeth City
Roanoke-Chowan Community College .... Ahoskie
Robeson Community College .... Lumberton
Rockingham Community College .... Wentworth
Rowan-Cabarrus Community College .... Salisbury
Salem College .... Winston-Salem
Salisbury Business College .... Salisbury
Sampson Community College .... Clinton
Sandhills Community College .... Pinehurst
Schnenck Civilian Conservation Center .... Pisgah Forest
Shaw University .... Raleigh
Skyland Academy .... Skyland
Southeastern Baptist Theological Seminary ...... Wake Forest
Southeastern Community College .... Whiteville
Southwestern Community College .... Sylva
St. Andrews Presbyterian College .... Laurinburg
St. Augustine's College .... Raleigh
St. Mary's College .... Raleigh
Stanly Community College .... Albemarle
Surry Community College .... Dobson
Tri-County Community College .... Murphy
University of North Carolina at Asheville .... Asheville
University of North Carolina at Chapel Hill ...... Chapel Hill
University of North Carolina at Charlotte .... Charlotte
University of North Carolina at Greensboro .... Greensboro
University of North Carolina at Wilmington .... Wilmington
Vance-Granville Community College .... Henderson
Wake Forest University .... Winston-Salem
Wake Technical Community College .... Raleigh
Warren Wilson College .... Asheville
Wayne Community College .... Goldsboro
Western Carolina University .... Cullowhee
Western Piedmont Community College .... Morganton
Wilkes Community College .... Wilkesboro
Wilson Technical Community College .... Wilson
Wingate College .... Wingate
Winston-Salem Barber School .... Winston-Salem
Winston-Salem State University .... Winston-Salem

North Dakota

Aaker's Business College .... Grand Forks
Bismarck State College .... Bismarck
Dickinson State University .... Dickinson
Fort Berthold Community College .... New Town
Interstate Business College .... Fargo
Interstate Business College
 (Branch Campus) .... Bismarck
Jamestown College .... Jamestown
Little Hoop Community College .... Fort Totten

Mayville State University .... Mayville
Medcenter One College of Nursing .... Bismarck
Meyer Vocational Technical School .... Minot
Minot School for Allied Health .... Minot
Minot State University .... Minot
Moler Barber College of Hairstyling .... Fargo
North Dakota State College of Science .... Wahpeton
North Dakota State University .... Fargo
North Dakota State University
 (Bottineau) .... Bottineau
Standing Rock College .... Fort Yates
Travel Career Institute .... Bismarck
Tri-College University .... Fargo
Trinity Bible College .... Ellendale
Turtle Mountain Community College .... Belcourt
United Tribes Technical College .... Bismarck
University of Mary .... Bismarck
University of North Dakota .... Grand Forks
University of North Dakota
 (Lake Region) .... Devils Lake
University of North Dakota
 (Williston) .... Williston
Valley City State University .... Valley City

Ohio

Academy of Court Reporting .... Cleveland
Academy of Court Reporting
 (Branch) .... Akron
Academy of Court Reporting
 (Branch) .... Columbus
Academy of Hair Design .... Canton
Air Force Institute of Technology .... Wright-Patterson AFB
Akron Barber College .... Akron
Akron Machining Institute, Inc .... Barberton Rd
Akron Machining Institute, Inc.
 (Cleveland Machining Institute) .... Cleveland
Akron School of Practical Nursing .... Akron
Akron-Medical-Dental Institute .... Akron
Allstate Hairstyling and Barber College .... Cleveland
American School of Nail Techniques & Cosmetology .... Akron
American School of Technology .... Columbus
Antioch University .... Yellow Springs
Antioch University
 (School for Adult and Experiential Learning) ...... Yellow Springs
Antonelli Institute of Art and Photography .... Cincinnati
Aristotle Institute of Medical and Dental Technolgy .... Westerville
Art Academy of Cincinnati .... Cincinnati
Ashland University .... Ashland
Athenaeum of Ohio .... Cincinnati
Baldwin-Wallace College .... Berea
Belmont Technical College .... St. Clairsville
Bluffton College .... Bluffton
Bohecker's Business College .... Ravenna
Bowling Green State University .... Bowling Green
Bowling Green State University
 (Firelands College) .... Huron
Bradford School .... Columbus
Bryant & Stratton Business Institute .... Parma
Bryant & Stratton Business Institute
 (Branch) .... Richmond Heights
Capital University .... Columbus
Case Western Reserve University .... Cleveland
Cedarville College .... Cedarville
Central Ohio Technical College .... Newark
Central School of Practical Nursing .... Cleveland
Central State University .... Wilberforce
Chatfield College .... St Martin
Choffin Career Center .... Youngstown
Cincinnati Bible College and Seminary .... Cincinnati
Cincinnati College of Mortuary Science .... Cincinnati

The Sourcebook of College and University Student Records **Ohio**

Cincinnati School of Court Reporting and Business............ Cincinnati
Cincinnati State Technical & Community College .... Cincinnati
Circleville Bible College .... Circleville
Clark State Community College .... Springfield
Cleveland College of Jewish Studies .... Beachwood
Cleveland Institute of Art .... Cleveland
Cleveland Institute of Dental-Medical Assistants, Inc........... Cleveland
Cleveland Institute of Dental-Medical Assistants, Inc.
    (Branch Campus) .... Lyndhurst
Cleveland Institute of Dental-Medical Assistants, Inc.
    (Branch Campus) .... Mentor
Cleveland Institute of Electronics, Inc. .... Cleveland
Cleveland Institute of Music .... Cleveland
Cleveland State University .... Cleveland
College of Mount St. Joseph .... Cincinnati
College of Wooster .... Wooster
Columbus College of Art and Design .... Columbus
Columbus Para-Professional Institute .... Columbus
Columbus Para-Professional Institute .... Columbus
Columbus State Community College .... Columbus
Connecticut School of Broadcasting .... Cincinnati
Connecticut School of Broadcasting .... Independence
Cuyahoga Community College
    (Eastern) .... Highland Hills
Cuyahoga Community College
    (Metropolitan) .... Cleveland
Cuyahoga Community College
    (Western) .... Parma
Davis College .... Toledo
DeVry Institute of Technology, Columbus .... Columbus
Defiance College .... Defiance
Denison University .... Granville
Dyke College .... Cleveland
ETI Technical College .... Cleveland
ETI Technical College .... North Canton
ETI Technical College
    (Niles) .... Niles
Edison State Community College .... Piqua
Fairfield Career Center .... Carroll
Franciscan University of Steubenville .... Steubenville
Franklin University .... Columbus
God's Bible College .... Cincinnati
Hamrick Truck Driving School .... Medina
Hannah E. Mullins School of Practical Nursing .... Salem
Hebrew Union College-Jewish Institute of Religion .... Cincinnati
Heidelberg College .... Tiffin
Hiram College .... Hiram
Hobart Institute of Welding Technology .... Troy
Hocking Technical College .... Nelsonville
Hospitality Training Center .... Hudson
ITT Technical Institute .... Dayton
ITT Technical Institute .... Youngstown
Institute of Medical and Dental Technology .... Cincinnati
Institute of Medical and Dental Technology
    (Branch Campus) .... Cincinnati
International College of Broadcasting .... Dayton
International College of Broadcasting .... Dayton
Jefferson Technical College .... Steubenville
John Carroll University .... University Heights
Kent State University .... Kent
Kent State University
    (Ashtabula) .... Ashtabula
Kent State University
    (East Liverpool) .... East Liverpool
Kent State University
    (Geauga) .... Burton Township
Kent State University
    (Salem) .... Salem
Kent State University
    (Stark) .... Canton
Kent State University
    (Trumbull) .... Warren
Kent State University
    (Tuscarawas) .... New Philadelphia
Kenyon College .... Gambier
Kettering College of Medical Arts .... Kettering
Knox County Career Center .... Mount Vernon
Lake Erie College .... Painesville
Lakeland Community College .... Mentor
Lima Technical College .... Lima
Lorain County Community College .... Elyria
Lourdes College .... Sylvania
MTI Business College .... Cleveland
Malone College .... Canton
Marietta College .... Marietta
Marion Technical College .... Marion
Marymount School of Practical Nursing .... Garfield Heights
Medical College of Ohio at Toledo .... Toledo
Medina County Career Center .... Medina
Methodist Theological School in Ohio .... Delaware
Miami University .... Oxford
Miami University
    (Hamilton) .... Hamilton
Miami University
    (Middletown) .... Middletown
Miami-Jacobs College .... Dayton
Mount Union College .... Alliance
Mount Vernon Nazarene College .... Mount Vernon
Muskingum Area Technical College .... Zanesville
Muskingum College .... New Concord
NHRAW Home Study Institute .... Columbus
National Education Center-National Institute of Technology Campus
    .... Cuyahoga Falls
North Central Technical College .... Mansfield
Northeastern Ohio Universities College of Medicine ....Rootstown
Northwest Technical College .... Archbold
Northwestern College .... Lima
Notre Dame College .... South Euclid
Oberlin College .... Oberlin
Ohio Auto-Diesel Technical Institute .... Cleveland
Ohio College of Podiatric Medicine .... Cleveland
Ohio Dominican College .... Columbus
Ohio Northern University .... Ada
Ohio State College of Barber Styling ....Toledo
Ohio State College of Barber Styling
    (Branch Campus) .... Columbus
Ohio State College of Barber Styling
    (Branch Campus) .... Columbus
Ohio State University .... Columbus
Ohio State University
    (Agricultural Technical Institute) .... Wooster
Ohio State University
    (Lima) .... Lima
Ohio State University
    (Mansfield) .... Mansfield
Ohio State University
    (Marion) .... Marion
Ohio State University
    (Newark) .... Newark
Ohio University .... Athens
Ohio University
    (Chillicothe) .... Chillicothe
Ohio University
    (Eastern) .... St Clairsville
Ohio University
    (Lancaster) .... Lancaster
Ohio University
    (Southern) .... Ironton
Ohio University
    (Zanesville) .... Zanesville
Ohio Valley Business College .... East Liverpool
Ohio Wesleyan University .... Delaware
Otterbein College .... Westerville
Owens Community College .... Toledo
Owens Community College
    (Branch) .... Findlay

(Bold print indicates degree granting institutions)   461   **State Cross Reference Index**

Pontifical College Josephinum	Columbus
Professional Skills Institute	Toledo
Rabbinical College of Telshe	Wickliffe
Raedel College and Industrial Welding School	Canton
Sawyer College of Business	Cleveland
Sawyer College of Business	Cleveland Heights
School of Advertising Art	Kettering
Shawnee State University	Portsmouth
Sinclair Community College	Dayton
Southeastern Business College	Chillicothe
Southeastern Business College	Gallipolis
Southeastern Business College	Lorain
Southeastern Business College (Branch)	Jackson
Southeastern Business College (Branch)	Lancaster
Southeastern Business College (Branch)	New Boston
Southeastern Business College (Branch)	Sandusky
Southern Ohio College	Cincinnati
Southern Ohio College (Branch)	Akron
Southern Ohio College (Branch)	Fairfield
Southern State Community College	Hillsboro
Southwestern College of Business	Cincinnati
Southwestern College of Business	Dayton
Southwestern College of Business (Branch)	Cincinnati
Southwestern College of Business (Branch)	Middletown
St. Mary Seminary	Wickliffe
Stark Technical College	Canton
Stautzenberger College (Central)	Toledo
Stautzenberger College (Findlay)	Findlay
TDDS	Diamond
Technology Education Center	Columbus
Terra State Community College	Fremont
Tiffin University	Tiffin
Total Technical Institute	Parma Heights
Trinity Lutheran Seminary	Columbus
Trumbull Business College	Warren
Ultrasound Diagnostic School (Branch Campus)	Independence
Union Institute	Cincinnati
United Theological Seminary	Dayton
University of Akron	Akron
University of Cincinnati	Cincinnati
University of Cincinnati-Clermont College	Batavia
University of Cincinnati-Raymond Walters College	Cincinnati
University of Dayton	Dayton
University of Findlay	Findlay
University of Rio Grande	Rio Grande
University of Toledo	Toledo
Urbana University	Urbana
Ursuline College	Pepper Pike
Walsh University	Canton
Washington State Community College	Marietta
Wilberforce University	Wilberforce
Wilmington College	Wilmington
Winebrenner Theological Seminry	Findlay
Wittenberg University	Springfield
Wright State University	Dayton
Wright State University (Lake)	Celina
Xavier University	Cincinnati
Youngstown State University	Youngstown

Oklahoma

Bacone College	Muskogee
Bartlesville Wesleyan College	Bartlesville
Bryan Institute	Tulsa
Cameron University	Lawton
Career Point Business School (Branch Campus)	Tulsa
Carl Albert State College	Poteau
Central Oklahoma Area Vocational-Technical Center	Drumright
Climate Control Institute	Tulsa
Connors State College	Warner
East Central University	Ada
Eastern Oklahoma State College	Wilburton
Francis Tuttle Vocational-Technical Center	Oklahoma City
Great Plains Area Vocational-Technical Center	Lawton
Hollywood Cosmetology Center	Oklahoma City
Indian Meridian Vocational-Technical Center	Stillwater
Langston University	Langston
Metropolitan College of Court Reporting	Oklahoma City
Metropolitan College of Legal Studies	Tulsa
Mid-America Bible College	Oklahoma City
Mid-Del College	Del City
Miss Shirley's Beauty College	Oklahoma City
Murray State College	Tishomingo
Northeastern Oklahoma A&M College	Miami
Northeastern State University	Tahlequah
Northern Oklahoma College	Tonkawa
Northwestern Oklahoma State University	Alva
O.T. Autry Area Vocational-Technical Center	Enid
Oklahoma Baptist University	Shawnee
Oklahoma Christian University of Science and Arts	Oklahoma City
Oklahoma City Community College	Oklahoma City
Oklahoma City University	Oklahoma City
Oklahoma Farrier's College	Sperry
Oklahoma Junior College	Oklahoma City
Oklahoma Panhandle State University	Goodwell
Oklahoma State Horseshoeing School	Ardmore
Oklahoma State University	Stillwater
Oklahoma State University (Oklahoma City)	Oklahoma City
Oklahoma State University (Okmulgee)	Okmulgee
Oklahoma State University College of Osteopathic Medicine	Tulsa
Oral Roberts University	Tulsa
Phillips Graduate Seminary	Enid
Phillips University	Enid
Platt College	Tulsa
Platt College (Branch Campus)	Oklahoma City
Redlands Community College	El Reno
Rogers State College	Claremore
Rose State College	Midwest City
Seminole Junior College	Seminole
Southeastern Oklahoma State University	Durant
Southern Nazarene University	Bethany
Southwestern College of Christian Ministries	Bethany
Southwestern Oklahoma State University	Weatherford
Southwestern Oklahoma State University (Sayre)	Sayre
St. Gregory's College	Shawnee
State Barber & Hair Design College, Inc.	Oklahoma City
Tulsa Junior College (Metro)	Tulsa
Tulsa Technology Center	Tulsa
Tulsa Welding School	Tulsa
United States Coast Guard Institute	Oklahoma City
University of Central Oklahoma	Edmond
University of Oklahoma	Norman
University of Oklahoma Health Sciences Center	Oklahoma City

The Sourcebook of College and University Student Records — **Oregon**

University of Science and Arts of Oklahoma .... Chickasha
University of Tulsa .... Tulsa
Western Oklahoma State College .... Altus
Wright Business School .... Oklahoma City

Oregon

Airman Proficiency Center .... Hillsboro
Apollo College of Medical-Dental Careers .... Portland
Bassist College .... Portland
Blue Mountain Community College .... Pendleton
Broadcast Professionals Complete School of Radio Broadcasting
.... Portland
Central Oregon Community College .... Bend
Chemeketa Community College .... Salem
Clackamas Community College .... Oregon City
Clatsop Community College .... Astoria
College of Legal Arts .... Portland
CollegeAmerica .... Portland
Commercial Training Services .... Portland
ConCorde Career Institute .... Portland
Concordia College .... Portland
Diesel Truck Driver Training School .... Eugene
Eastern Oregon State College .... La Grande
Eugene Bible College .... Eugene
George Fox College .... Newberg
ITT Technical Institute .... Portland
La Grande College of Business .... La Grande
Lane Community College .... Eugene
Lewis and Clark College .... Portland
Linfield College .... McMinnville
Linn-Benton Community College .... Albany
Marylhurst College .... Marylhurst
Moler Barber College .... Portland
Mount Angel Seminary .... St. Benedict
Mount Hood Community College .... Gresham
Multnomah Bible College .... Portland
Northwest Christian College .... Eugene
Oregon College of Oriental Medicine .... Portland
Oregon Graduate Institute of Science and Technology ... Portland
Oregon Health Sciences University .... Portland
Oregon Institute of Technology .... Klamath Falls
Oregon Polytechnic Institute .... Portland
Oregon School of Arts and Crafts .... Portland
Oregon State University .... Corvallis
Pacific Northwest College of Art .... Portland
Pacific University .... Forest Grove
Paramedic Training Institute .... Beaverton
Portland Community College .... Portland
Portland State University .... Portland
Reed College .... Portland
Rogue Community College .... Grants Pass
Southern Oregon State College .... Ashland
Southwestern Oregon Community College .... Coos Bay
Tara Lara Academy of K-9 Hair Design .... Portland
Treasure Valley Community College .... Ontario
Umpqua Community College .... Roseburg
University of Oregon .... Eugene
University of Portland .... Portland
Warner Pacific College .... Portland
West Coast Training .... Portland
West Coast Training
  (Branch Campus) .... Milwaukie
Western Baptist College .... Salem
Western Business College .... Portland
Western Conservative Baptist Seminary .... Portland
Western Culinary Institute .... Portland
Western Evangelical Seminary .... Tigard
Western Oregon State College .... Monmouth
Western States Chiropractic College .... Portland
Western Truck School .... Tualatin

Willamette University .... Salem

Pennsylvania

Academy of Medical Arts and Business .... Harrisburg
Academy of the New Church College .... Bryn Athyn
Albright College .... Reading
All-State Career School .... Lester
Allegheny Business Institute .... Pittsburgh
Allegheny College .... Meadville
Allentown College of St. Francis de Sales ...... Center Valley
Allied Medical Careers .... Edwardsville
Allied Medical Careers
  (Branch Campus) .... Scranton
Altoona School of Commerce .... Altoona
Alvernia College .... Reading
American College .... Bryn Mawr
American Institute of Design .... Philadelphia
Antonelli Institute .... Plymouth Meeting
Antonelli Medical and Professional Institute .... Pottstown
Art Institute of Philadelphia .... Philadelphia
Art Institute of Pittsburgh .... Pittsburgh
Automotive Training Center .... Exton
Baptist Bible College and Seminary .... Clarks Summit
Barber Styling Institute .... Camp Hill
Beaver College .... Glenside
Berean Institute .... Philadelphia
Berks Technical Institute .... Wyomissing
Biblical Theological Seminary .... Hatfield
Bidwell Training Center .... Pittsburgh
Bloomsburg University of Pennsylvania .... Bloomsburg
Bradford School .... Pittsburgh
Bradley Academy for the Visual Arts .... York
Bryn Mawr College .... Bryn Mawr
Bucknell University .... Lewisburg
Bucks County Community College .... Newtown
Butler County Community College .... Butler
Cabrini College .... Radnor
California Institute of Pennsylvania .... California
Cambria-Rowe Business College .... Johnstown
Cambria-Rowe Business College
  (Indiana) .... Indiana
Career Training Academy .... New Kensington
Career Training Academy
  (Branch Campus) .... Monroeville
Career Institute .... Philadelphia
Carlow College .... Pittsburgh
Carnegie Mellon University .... Pittsburgh
Cedar Crest College .... Allentown
Central Pennsylvania Business School .... Summerdale
Chatham College .... Pittsburgh
Chestnut Hill College .... Philadelphia
Cheyney University of Pennsylvania .... Cheyney
Chubb Institute-Keystone School .... Springfield
Churchman Business School .... Easton
Clarion University of Pennsylvania .... Clarion
Clarion University of Pennsylvania
  (Venango) .... Oil City
College Misericordia .... Dallas
Community College of Allegheny County
  (Allegheny) .... Pittsburgh
Community College of Allegheny County
  (Boyce) .... Monroeville
Community College of Allegheny County
  (North) .... Pittsburgh
Community College of Allegheny County
  (South) .... West Mifflin
Community College of Beaver County .... Monaca
Community College of Philadelphia .... Philadelphia
Computer Learning Center .... Philadelphia
Computer Learning Network .... Camp Hill

(Bold print indicates degree granting institutions)

State Cross Reference Index

Pennsylvania

The Sourcebook of College and University Student Records

Computer Learning Network
  (Branch Campus) .... Altoona
Computer Tech .... Pittsburgh
Consolidated School of Business .... Lancaster
Consolidated School of Business .... York
Curtis Institute of Music .... Philadelphia
Dean Institute of Technology .... Pittsburgh
Delaware County Community College .... Media
Delaware County Institute of Training .... Chester
Delaware Valley Academy of Medical and Dental Assistants
  .... Philadelphia
Delaware Valley College of Science and Agriculture ... Doylestown
Dickinson College .... Carlisle
Dickinson School of Law .... Carlisle
Douglas School of Business .... Monessen
Drexel University .... Philadelphia
DuBois Business College .... Du Bois
Duff's Business Institute .... Pittsburgh
Duquesne University .... Pittsburgh
East Stroudsburg University of Pennsylvania ... East Stroudsburg
Eastern Baptist Theological Seminary .... Wynnewood
Eastern College .... St Davids
Edinboro University of Pennsylvania .... Edinboro
Electronic Institutes .... Middletown
Electronic Institutes .... Pittsburgh
Elizabethtown College .... Elizabethtown
Erie Business Center .... Erie
Erie Business Center
  (Erie Business Center South) .... New Castle
Evangelical School of Theology .... Myerstown
Franklin & Marshall College .... Lancaster
Franklin Academy .... Pottsville
Gannon University .... Erie
Garfield Business Institute .... New Brighton
Gateway Technical Institute .... Pittsburgh
Geneva College .... Beaver Falls
Gettysburg College .... Gettysburg
Gleim Technical Institute .... Carlisle
Gratz College .... Melrose Park
Greater Johnstown Area Vocational-Technical School .... Johnstown
Grove City College .... Grove City
Gwynedd-Mercy College .... Gwynedd Valley
Harcum College .... Bryn Mawr
Harrisburg Area Community College .... Harrisburg
Harrisburg Area Community College
  (Lancaster) .... Lancaster
Harrisburg Area Community College
  (Lebanon) .... Lebanon
Haverford College .... Haverford
Holy Family College .... Philadelphia
Hussian School of Art .... Philadelphia
ICM School of Business .... Pittsburgh
ITT Technical Institute
  (Branch) .... Pittsburgh
Immaculata College .... Immaculata
Indiana University of Pennsylvania .... Indiana
Indiana University of Pennsylvania
  (Armstrong County) .... Kittanning
Indiana University of Pennsylvania
  (Punxsutawney) .... Punxsutawney
J.H. Thompson Academies .... Erie
James Martin Adult Health Occupations .... Philadelphia
Johnson Technical Institute .... Scranton
Johnson Technical Institute
  (Branch) .... Philipsburg
Joseph Donahue International School of Hairstyling .... Philadelphia
Juniata College .... Huntingdon
Keystone Junior College .... La Plume
King's College .... Wilkes-Barre
Kutztown University of Pennsylvania .... Kutztown
La Roche College .... Pittsburgh
La Salle University .... Philadelphia
Lackawanna Senior College .... Scranton

Lafayette College .... Easton
Lake Erie College of Osteopathic Medicine .... Erie
Lancaster Bible College .... Lancaster
Lancaster Theological Seminary .... Lancaster
Lansdale School of Business .... North Wales
Laurel Business Institute .... Uniontown
Learning and Evaluation Center .... Bloomsburg
Lebanon Valley College .... Annville
Lehigh Carbon Community College .... Schnecksville
Lehigh University .... Bethlehem
Lifetime Career Schools .... Archbald
Lincoln Technical Institute .... Philadelphia
Lincoln University .... Lincoln University
Lock Haven University .... Lock Haven
Lutheran Theological Seminary at Gettysburg .... Gettysburg
Lutheran Theological Seminary at Philadelphia ..... Philadelphia
Luzerne County Community College .... Nanticoke
Lycoming College .... Williamsport
Manor Junior College .... Jenkintown
Mansfield University of Pennsylvania .... Mansfield
Marywood College .... Scranton
McCann School of Business .... Mahanoy City
McCann School of Business
  (Branch) .... Wyoming
McCarrie Schools of Health Sciences and Technology Inc.
  .... Philadelphia
Median School of Allied Health Careers .... Pittsburgh
Medical College of Pennsylvania and Hahnemann University
  .... Philadelphia
Mercyhurst College .... Erie
Messiah College .... Grantham
Messiah College
  (City) .... Philadelphia
Millersville University of Pennsylvania .... Millersville
Montgomery County Community College .... Blue Bell
Moore College of Art and Design .... Philadelphia
Moravian College .... Bethlehem
Mount Aloysius College .... Cresson
Muhlenberg College .... Allentown
National Education Center Allentown Campus .... Allentown
National Education Center Thompson Campus .... Harrisburg
National Education Center Thompson Campus
  (Branch) .... Philadelphia
Naval Damage Control Training Center .... Philadelphia
Neumann College .... Aston
New England Tractor Trailer Training School .... Philadelphia
New Kensington Commercial School .... New Kensington
North Hills School of Health Occupations .... Pittsburgh
Northampton County Area Community College .... Bethlehem
Northeast Institute of Education .... Scranton
Northeast Institute of Education
  (Branch) .... Bartonsville
Oakbridge Academy of Arts .... New Kensington
Orleans Technical Institute .... Philadelphia
Orleans Technical Institute
  (Court Reporting Institute) .... Philadelphia
PJA School .... Upper Darby
Pace Institute .... Reading
Penn Commercial College .... Washington
Penn Technical Institute .... Pittsburgh
Pennco Tech .... Bristol
Pennsylvania Academy of the Fine Arts .... Philadelphia
Pennsylvania Business Institute .... Pottstown
Pennsylvania Business Institute
  (Branch) .... Nesquehoning
Pennsylvania College of Optometry .... Philadelphia
Pennsylvania College of Podiatric Medicine .... Philadelphia
Pennsylvania College of Technology .... Williamsport
Pennsylvania College of Technology .... Williamsport
Pennsylvania Gunsmith School .... Pittsburgh
Pennsylvania Institute of Culinary Arts .... Pittsburgh
Pennsylvania Institute of Taxidermy .... Ebensburg
Pennsylvania Institute of Technology .... Media

State Cross Reference Index   (Bold print indicates degree granting institutions)

The Sourcebook of College and University Student Records **Pennsylvania**

Pennsylvania School of Art and Design.................................Lancaster
Pennsylvania State University ....University Park
Pennsylvania State University
(Allentown).. Fogelsville
Pennsylvania State University
(Altoona)..Altoona
Pennsylvania State University
(Beaver) .... Monaca
Pennsylvania State University
(Berks)...Reading
Pennsylvania State University
(Delaware County) .... Media
Pennsylvania State University
(DuBois)...Du Bois
Pennsylvania State University
(Erie-Behrend College)..Erie
Pennsylvania State University
(Fayette) .... Uniontown
Pennsylvania State University
(Great Valley Graduate Center).. Malvern
Pennsylvania State University
(Harrisburg-Capital College) .... Middletown
Pennsylvania State University
(Hazleton)...Hazleton
Pennsylvania State University
(Hershey Medical Center) ....Hershey
Pennsylvania State University
(McKeesport Campus)..McKeesport
Pennsylvania State University
(Mont Alto Campus) ....Mont Alto
Pennsylvania State University
(New Kensington Campus).....................................New Kensington
Pennsylvania State University
(Ogontz Campus) ....Abington
Pennsylvania State University
(Schuylkill Campus) .... Schuylkill Haven
Pennsylvania State University
(Shenango Campus).. Sharon
Pennsylvania State University
(Wilkes-Barre Campus) .... Lehman
Pennsylvania State University
(Worthington-Scranton Campus)....................................... Dunmore
Pennsylvania State University
(York Campus)...York
Philadelphia College of Bible.. Langhorne
Philadelphia College of Osteopathic Medicine............Philadelphia
Philadelphia College of Pharmacy and Science..........Philadelphia
Philadelphia College of Textiles and Science..............Philadelphia
Philadelphia Wireless Technical Institute........................Philadelphia
Pierce Junior College .... Philadelphia
Pittsburgh Institute of Aeronautics................................Pittsburgh
Pittsburgh Institute of Mortuary Science ....Pittsburgh
Pittsburgh Technical Institute ....Pittsburgh
Pittsburgh Theological Seminary ....Pittsburgh
Point Park College ....Pittsburgh
Ralph Amodei INternational Institute of Hair Design & Technology
....Philadelphia
Reading Area Community College...................................Reading
Reconstructionist Rabbinical College..............................Wyncote
Robert Morris College .... Coraopolis
Robert Morris College
(Pittsburgh College) .... Coraopolis
Rosedale Technical Institute ....Pittsburgh
Rosemont College .... Rosemont
Sawyer School ....Pittsburgh
Schuylkill Business Institute ....Pottsville
Seton Hill College .... Greensburg
Settlement Music School...Philadelphia
Shenango Valley School of Business.................................. Sharon
Shenango Valley School of Business
(Branch Campus)... Pulaski
Shenango Valley School of Business
(Branch Campus) .... Titusville

Shippensburg University of Pennsylvania...............Shippensburg
Shirley Rock School of the Pennsylvania Ballet .... Philadelphia
Slippery Rock University of Pennsylvania............... Slippery Rock
South Hills Business School.................................... State College
St. Charles Borromeo Seminary ....Wynnewood
St. Francis College..Loretto
St. Joseph's University... Philadelphia
St. Vincent College and Seminary......................................Latrobe
Star Technical Institute
(Branch Campus)... Kingston
Star Technical Institute
(Branch Campus).. Scranton
Star Technical Institute
(Branch Campus)..Whitehall
Susquehanna University .... Selinsgrove
Swanson's Driving Schools, Inc... Pittsburgh
Swarthmore College... Swarthmore
Talmudical Yeshiva of Philadelphia .... Philadelphia
Temple University .... Philadelphia
Thaddeus Stevens State School of Technology ....Lancaster
Thiel College..Greenville
Thomas Jefferson University...................................... Philadelphia
Titusville Campus ....Titusville
Tri-City Barber School .... Norristown
Tri-City Barber School .... Philadelphia
Tri-State Business Institute... Erie
Triangle Tech...Du Bois
Triangle Tech...Erie
Triangle Tech .... Greensburg
Triangle Tech
(Business Careers Institute)... Greensburg
Triangle Tech
(Main) .... Pittsburgh
Triangle Tech
(Monroeville School of Business) ....Monroeville
Trinity Episcopal School for Ministry .... Ambridge
Ultrasound Diagnostic School
(Branch Campus) .... Philadelphia
Ultrasound Diagnostic School
(Branch Campus) .... Pittsburgh
University of Pennsylvania .... Philadelphia
University of Pittsburgh .... Pittsburgh
University of Pittsburgh
(Bradford Campus)...Bradford
University of Pittsburgh
(Greensburg Campus) .... Greensburg
University of Pittsburgh
(Johnstown Campus) .... Johnstown
University of Scranton.. Scranton
University of the Arts .... Philadelphia
Ursinus College ....Collegeville
Valley Forge Christian College .... Phoenixville
Valley Forge Military College ....Wayne
Villanova University.. Villanova
Washington and Jefferson College.............................. Washington
Waynesburg College.. Waynesburg
Welder Training and Testing Institute.............................. Selinsgrove
West Chester University of Pennsylvania................. West Chester
West Virginia Career College
(Branch Campus)...Lemont Furnace
Western School of Health and Business Careers................ Pittsburgh
Western School of Health and Business Careers
(Branch Campus)...Monroeville
Westminster College.. New Wilmington
Westminster Theological Seminary .... Glenside
Westmoreland County Community College................Youngwood
Widener University..Chester
Widener University at Harrisburg
(School of Law)..Harrisburg
Wilkes University..Wilkes-Barre
Williamsport School of Commerce........................Williamsport
Wilma Boyd Career Schools .... Pittsburgh
Wilson College...Chambersburg

(Bold print indicates degree granting institutions) **State Cross Reference Index**

Puerto Rico

Yeshiva Beth Moshe...Scranton
York College of Pennsylvania ....York
York Technical Institute ....York
Yorktowne Business Institute ....York

Puerto Rico

Aguadilla Regional College......................................Ramey
American University of Puerto Rico .... Bayamon
American University of Puerto Rico
    (Branch Campus)... Dorado
American University of Puerto Rico
    (Branch Campus).. Manati
Arecibo Technological University College.............Arecibo
Atlantic College...Guaynabo
Bayamon Central University .... Bayamon
Bayamon Technological University College.................. Bayamon
Caribbean Center for Advanced Studies.........................San Juan
Caribbean University .... Bayamon
Carolina Regional College .... Carolina
Cayey University College.. Cayey
Centro de Estudios Avanzados de Puerto Rico y El Caribe
    ....San Juan
Coastal Training Institute
    (Branch Campus)... Aguadilla
Colegio Biblico Pentecostal....................................St Just
Colegio Universitario del Este................................ Carolina
Columbia College...Caguas
Columbia College
    (Branch Campus)...Yauco
Conservatory of Music of Puerto Rico.............Santurce
Electronic Data Processing College .... Hato Rey
Electronic Data Processing College of PR, Inc.........San Sebastian
Evangelical Seminary of Puerto Rico ....San Juan
Huertas Junior College...Caguas
Humacao Community College............................Humacao
Humacao Community College
    (Branch Campus)... Fajardo
Humacao University College ....Humacao
Instituto Comercial de Puerto Rico Junior College......... Hato Rey
Instituto Comercial de Puerto Rico Junior College
    (Arecibo Campus)..Arecibo
Instituto Comercial de Puerto Rico Junior College
    (Mayaguez Campus)..Mayaguez
Inter American University of Puerto Rico
    (Fajardo Campus).. Fajardo
Inter American University of Puerto Rico Aguadilla Campus
    .... Aguadilla
Inter American University of Puerto Rico Arecibo Campus
    ....Arecibo
Inter American University of Puerto Rico Barranquitas Campus
    ....Barranquitas
Inter American University of Puerto Rico Bayamon Campus
    .... Bayamon
Inter American University of Puerto Rico Guayama Campus
    ....Guayama
Inter American University of Puerto Rico Metropolitan Campus
    .... Hato Rey
Inter American University of Puerto Rico Ponce Campus
    .... Mercedita
Inter American University of Puerto Rico San German Campus
    ....San German
Inter American University of Puerto Rico School of Law
    ....San Juan
Inter American University of Puerto Rico School of Optometry
    .... Hato Rey
International Business College ....San Juan
International College of Business & Technology
    (Branch Campus)..Caguas
International College of Business & Technology
    (Branch Campus).. Junacao
La Montana Regional College..................................Utuado
National College of Business & Technology..................Bayamon
National College of Business & Technology
    (Branch Campus).. Arecibo
Ponce School of Medicine....................................... Ponce
Ponce Technological University College.............. Ponce
Pontifical Catholic University of Puerto Rico...... Ponce
Pontifical Catholic University of Puerto Rico
    (Arecibo Branch Campus)................................... Arecibo
Pontifical Catholic University of Puerto Rico
    (Guayama Branch Campus)............................... Guayama
Pontifical Catholic University of Puerto Rico
    (Mayaguez Branch Campus).............................. Mayaguez
Ramirez College of Business and Technology............... Santurce
Technological College of the Municipality of San Juan.Hato Rey
Universidad Adventista de las Antillas ....Mayaguez
Universidad Metropolitana.................................... San Juan
Universidad Politecnica de Puerto Rico ....Hato Rey
Universidad de Turapo ....Gurabo
University of Phoenix
    (Puerto Rico) .... Guaynabo
University of Puerto Rico Mayaguez Campus .... Mayaguez
University of Puerto Rico Medical Sciences Campus.... San Juan
University of Puerto Rico Rio Piedras Campus .... San Juan
University of the Sacred Heart .... Santurce

Rhode Island

Brown University..Providence
Bryant College ....Smithfield
Community College of Rhode Island ....Warwick
Johnson & Wales University............................Providence
Katharine Gibbs School ....Providence
Nasson Institute..Pawtucket
Nasson Institute
    (Branch Campus)..Warwick
Nasson Institute
    (Branch Campus)...Woonsocket
Naval War College .... Newport
New England Institute of Technology...............Warwick
New England Technical College ....Warwick
New England Tractor Trailer Training School of Rhode Island
    ....Pawtucket
Ocean State Business Institute.........................Narragansett
Providence College ....Providence
Rhode Island College ....Providence
Rhode Island School of Design ....Providence
Roger Williams University................................... Bristol
Salve Regina University .... Newport
Sawyer School .... Pawtucket
Sawyer School
    (Branch Campus)..Warwick
School of Medical and Legal Secretarial Sciences.............Providence
University of Rhode Island................................... Kingston

South Carolina

Aiken Technical College ....Aiken
Allen University .... Columbia
Alpha Beauty School..Greenville
Alpha Beauty School
    (Branch Campus).. Anderson
Alpha Beauty School
    (Branch Campus).. Asheville
Alpha Beauty School
    (Branch Campus).. Seneca
Alpha Beauty School
    (Branch Campus).. Spartanburg

Anderson College	Anderson
Benedict College	Columbia
Betty Stevens Cosmetology Institute	Florence
Camden School of Hair Design	Camden
Central Carolina Technical College	Sumter
Central Wesleyan College	Central
Charleston Cosmetology Institute	Charleston
Charleston Southern University	Charleston
Charzzanne Beauty College	Greenwood
Chesterfield-Marlboro Technical College	Cheraw
Chris Logan Career College	Myrtle Beach
Chris Logan Career College (Branch Campus)	Anderson
Chris Logan Career College (Branch Campus)	Bennettsville
Chris Logan Career College (Branch Campus)	Columbia
Chris Logan Career College (Branch Campus)	Florence
Chris Logan Career College (Branch Campus)	Greenville
Chris Logan Career College (Branch Campus)	North Augusta
Chris Logan Career College (Branch Campus)	Rock Hill
Chris Logan Career College (Branch Campus)	Sumter
Citadel Military College of South Carolina	Charleston
Claflin College	Orangeburg
Clemson University	Clemson
Coastal Carolina University	Myrtle Beach
Coker College	Hartsville
College of Charleston	Charleston
Columbia College	Columbia
Columbia International University	Columbia
Columbia Junior College of Business	Columbia
Converse College	Spartanburg
Denmark Technical College	Denmark
Erskine College Seminary	Due West
Farah's Beauty School	Columbia
Farah's Beauty School	Goose Creek
Florence-Darlington Technical College	Florence
Forrest Junior College	Anderson
Francis Marion College	Florence
Furman University	Greenville
Greenville Technical College	Greenville
Horry-Georgetown Technical College	Conway
ITT Technical Institute	Greenville
Johnson & Wales University (Branch Campus)	Charleston
Lander University	Greenwood
Limestone College	Gaffney
Lutheran Theological Southern Seminary	Columbia
Medical University of South Carolina	Charleston
Midlands Technical College	Columbia
Morris College	Sumter
Navy Fleet and Mine Warfare Training Center	Charleston
Newberry College	Newberry
North American Institute of Aviation	Conway
North Greenville College	Tigerville
Orangeburg-Calhoun Technical College	Orangeburg
Piedmont Technical College	Greenwood
Presbyterian College	Clinton
Professional Hair Design Academy	Greenville
Royal Academy of Hair Design	Clinton
Sherman College of Straight Chiropractic	Spartanburg
South Carolina Criminal Justice Academy	Columbia
South Carolina State University	Orangeburg
Spartanburg Methodist College	Spartanburg
Spartanburg Technical College	Spartanburg
Sumter Beauty College	Sumter
Technical College of the Lowcountry	Beaufort
Tri-County Technical College	Pendleton
Trident Technical College	Charleston
University of South Carolina-Aiken	Aiken
University of South Carolina-Beaufort	Beaufort
University of South Carolina-Columbia	Columbia
University of South Carolina-Lancaster	Lancaster
University of South Carolina-Salkehatchie	Allendale
University of South Carolina-Spartanburg	Spartanburg
University of South Carolina-Sumter	Sumter
University of South Carolina-Union	Union
Voorhees College	Denmark
Williamsburg Technical College	Kingstree
Winthrop University	Rock Hill
Wofford College	Spartanburg
York Technical College	Rock Hill

South Dakota

Augustana College	Sioux Falls
Black Hills State University	Spearfish
Dakota State University	Madison
Dakota Wesleyan University	Mitchell
Huron University	Huron
Kilian Community College	Sioux Falls
Lake Area Vocational-Technical Institute	Watertown
Mitchell Technical Institute	Mitchell
Mount Marty College	Yankton
National College	Rapid City
Nettleton Junior College	Sioux Falls
North American Baptist Seminary	Sioux Falls
Northern State University	Aberdeen
Oglala Lakota College	Kyle
Presentation College	Aberdeen
Sinte Gleska University	Rosebud
Sisseton-Wahpeton Community College	Agency Village
South Dakota School of Mines and Technology	Rapid City
South Dakota State University	Brookings
Southeast Technical Institute	Sioux Falls
Stenotype Institute of South Dakota	Sioux Falls
University of Sioux Falls	Sioux Falls
University of South Dakota	Vermillion
Western Dakota Technical Institute	Rapid City

Tennessee

Aguinas College	Nashville
American Academy of Nutrition	Knoxville
American Baptist College	Nashville
American Technical Institute	Brunswick
Arlington Court Reporting College (Court Reporting Institute of Tennessee)	Nashville
Arnold's Beauty School	Milan
Artiste School of Cosmetology	Johnson City
Austin Peay State University	Clarksville
Belmont University	Nashville
Bethel College	McKenzie
Bobbie's School of Beauty Arts	Athens
Bryan College	Dayton
Carson-Newman College	Jefferson City
Chattanooga Barber College	Chattanooga
Chattanooga State Technical Community College	Chattanooga
Christian Brothers University	Memphis
Church of God School of Theology	Cleveland
Cleveland State Community College	Cleveland
Climate Control Institute (Travel Careers Division Campus)	Memphis
Columbia State Community College	Columbia
Concorde Career Institute	Memphis
Court Reporting Academy & School of Professional Studies	Nashville

(Bold print indicates degree granting institutions)

Texas

The Sourcebook of College and University Student Records

Crichton College	Memphis
Cumberland School of Technology	Cookeville
Cumberland University	Lebanon
David Lipscomb University	Nashville
Davidson Technical College	Nashville
Davidson Technical College (Branch Campus)	Jackson
Draughons Junior College	Nashville
Draughons Junior College (Branch Campus)	Clarksville
Dyersburg State Community College	Dyersburg
East Tennessee State University	Johnson City
Emmanuel School of Religion	Johnson City
Fisk University	Nashville
Fort Sanders School of Nursing	Knoxville
Free Will Baptist Bible College	Nashville
Freed-Hardeman University	Henderson
Fugazzi College (Branch)	Nashville
Harding University Graduate School of Religion	Memphis
Health Care Training Institute	Memphis
Hiwassee College	Madisonville
ITT Technical Institute	Knoxville
ITT Technical Institute	Nashville
Jackson State Community College	Jackson
Jett College of Cosmetology & Barbering	Memphis
Jett College of Cosmetology & Barbering	Memphis
Jett College of Cosmetology & Barbering	Memphis
John A. Gupton College	Nashville
Johnson Bible College	Knoxville
King College	Bristol
Knoxville Business College	Knoxville
Knoxville College (Morristown)	Knoxville
Knoxville Institute of Hair Design	Knoxville
Knoxville Job Corps Center	Knoxville
Lambuth University	Jackson
Lane College	Jackson
LeMoyne-Owen College	Memphis
Lee College	Cleveland
Lincoln Memorial University	Harrogate
Martin Methodist College	Pulaski
Maryville College	Maryville
Medical Career College	Nashville
Meharry Medical College	Nashville
Memphis Aero Tech	Millington
Memphis College of Art	Memphis
Memphis Theological Seminary	Memphis
Mid-America Baptist Theological Seminary	Memphis
Mid-State Barber Styling College, Inc.	Nashville
Middle Tennessee State University	Murfreesboro
Midsouth School of Beauty	Memphis
Mille-Motte Business College	Clarksville
Milligan College	Milligan College
Mister Wayne's School of Unisex Hair Design	Cookeville
Motlow State Community College	Tullahoma
Nashville State Technical Institute	Nashville
Naval Air Technical Training Center	Millington
North Central Institute	Clarksville
Northeast State Technical Community College	Blountville
O'More College of Design	Franklin
Pellissippi State Technical Community College	Knoxville
Pro-Way Hair School (Branch Campus)	Memphis
Queen City College	Clarksville
Rhodes College	Memphis
Rice College	Memphis
Rice College (Branch Campus)	Knoxville
Roane State Community College	Harriman
Seminary Extension Independent Study Institute	Nashville
Shelby State Community College	Memphis
Southeastern Paralegal Institute	Nashville
Southern College of Optometry	Memphis
Southern College of Seventh-Day Adventists	Collegedale
State Area Vocational-Technical School - Jacksboro	Jacksboro
State Area Vocational-Technical School - Jackson	Jackson
State Area Vocational-Technical School - Knoxville	Knoxville
State Area Vocational-Technical School - Livingston	Livingston
State Area Vocational-Technical School - McKenzie	McKenzie
State Area Vocational-Technical School - McMinnville	McMinnville
State Area Vocational-Technical School - Memphis	Memphis
State Area Vocational-Technical School - Memphis (Branch Campus)	Memphis
State Area Vocational-Technical School - Morristown	Morristown
State Area Vocational-Technical School - Morristown (Branch Campus)	Rogersville
State Area Vocational-Technical School - Murfreesboro	Murfreesboro
State Area Vocational-Technical School - Nashville	Nashville
State Area Vocational-Technical School - Nashville (Branch Campus)	Nashville
State Area Vocational-Technical School - Newbern	Newbern
State Area Vocational-Technical School - Oneida	Oneida
State Area Vocational-Technical School - Paris	Paris
State Area Vocational-Technical School - Pulaski	Pulaski
State Area Vocational-Technical School - Ripley	Ripley
State Area Vocational-Technical School - Savannah	Crump
State Area Vocational-Technical School - Shelbyville	Shelbyville
State Area Vocational-Technical School - Whiteville	Whiteville
State Area Vocational-Technical School-Athens	Athens
State Area Vocational-Technical School-Covington	Covington
State Area Vocational-Technical School-Crossville	Crossville
State Area Vocational-Technical School-Dickson	Dickson
State Area Vocational-Technical School-Elizabethton	Elizabethton
State Area Vocational-Technical School-Harriman	Harriman
State Area Vocational-Technical School-Hartsville	Hartsville
State Area Vocational-Technical School-Hohenwald	Hohenwald
State Technical Institute at Memphis	Memphis
Tennessee State University	Nashville
Tennessee Technological University	Cookeville
Tennessee Temple University	Chattanooga
Tennessee Wesleyan College	Athens
Trevecca Nazarene College	Nashville
Tusculum College	Greeneville
Union University	Jackson
University of Beauty	Cleveland
University of Beauty (Branch Campus)	Chattanooga
University of Memphis	Memphis
University of Tennessee at Chattanooga	Chattanooga
University of Tennessee at Martin	Martin
University of Tennessee, Knoxville	Knoxville
University of Tennessee, Memphis	Memphis
University of the South	Sewanee
Vanderbilt University	Nashville
Volunteer State Community College	Gallatin
Walters State Community College	Morristown
West Tennessee Business College	Jackson
William R. Moore School of Technology	Memphis

Texas

AIMS Academy	Grand Prairie
AIMS Academy (Branch Campus)	Dallas
ATI - American Trades Institutes	Dallas
ATI - American Trades Institutes (Graphic Arts Institute)	Dallas
ATI Career Training Center	Dallas
ATI Career Training Center	Hurst
Abilene Christian University	Abilene
Abilene Intercollegiate School of Nursing	Abilene
Action Career Training	Merkel
Advanced Career Training	Dallas

State Cross Reference Index   (Bold print indicates degree granting institutions)

Texas

The Sourcebook of College and University Student Records

Allied Health Careers	Austin
Alvin Community College	Alvin
Amarillo College	Amarillo
Amber University	Garland
American Commercial College	Abilene
American Commercial College	Lubbock
American Commercial College	Odessa
American Commercial College	San Angelo
American Institute of Commerce	Dallas
Angelina College	Lufkin
Angelo State University	San Angelo
Arit Air Academy	Dallas
Arlington Baptist College	Arlington
Arlington Court Reporting College	Arlington
Army Academy of Health Sciences	San Antonio
Austin College	Sherman
Austin Community College	Austin
Austin Presbyterian Theological Seminary	Austin
Avalon Vocational-Technical Institute	Fort Worth
Avalon Vocational-Technical Institute	Odessa
Avalon Vocational-Technical Institute	Wichita Falls
Avalon Vocational-Technical Institute (Branch Campus)	Longview
Baptist Missionary Association Theological Seminary	Jacksonville
Bauder Fashion College-Arlington	Arlington
Baylor College of Dentistry	Dallas
Baylor College of Medicine	Houston
Baylor University	Waco
Bee County College	Beeville
Bellaire Beauty College	Bellaire
Blinn College	Brenham
Bradford School of Business	Houston
Brazosport College	Lake Jackson
Brookhaven College	Farmers Branch
Brown College of Court Reporting & Medical Transcription (Branch Campus)	Longview
Bryan Institute (Branch Campus)	Arlington
Business Skills Training Center	Denton
Capitol City Careers	Austin
Capitol City Trade & Technical School	Austin
Career Academy	Texarkana
Career Centers of Texas - El Paso	El Paso
Career Development Center	Lufkin
Career Point Business School	San Antonio
Careers Unlimited	Tyler
Cedar Valley College	Lancaster
Center for Advanced Legal Studies	Houston
Central Texas College	Killeen
Central Texas Commercial College	Brownwood
Central Texas Commercial College (Branch Campus)	Dallas
Chenier	Houston
Chenier	San Angelo
Chenier Business School	Beaumont
Cisco Junior College	Cisco
Clarendon College	Clarendon
College of the Mainland	Texas City
Collin County Community College	McKinney
Commonwealth Institute of Funeral Service	Houston
Community College of the Air Force	Sheppard AFB
Computer Career Center	El Paso
Concordia Lutheran College	Austin
Court Reporting Institute of Dallas	Dallas
Criswell College	Dallas
Dalfort Aircraft Tech	Dallas
Dallas Baptist University	Dallas
Dallas Christian College	Dallas
Dallas Institute of Funeral Services	Dallas
Dallas Theological Seminary	Dallas
David L. Carrasco Job Corps Center	El Paso
DeVry Institute of Technology, Dallas	Irving
Del Mar College	Corpus Christi
Delta Career Institute	Beaumont
East Texas Baptist University	Marshall
East Texas State University	Commerce
East Texas State University at Texarkana	Texarkana
Eastfield College	Mesquite
El Centro College	Dallas
El Paso Community College	El Paso
Episcopal Theological Seminary of the Southwest	Austin
Euro Hair School	Corpus Christi
European Health & Sciences Institute	El Paso
Frank Phillips College	Borger
Galveston College	Galveston
Gary Job Corps Center	San Marcos
Grayson County College	Denison
Gulf Coast Trades Center	New Waverly
Hardin-Simmons University	Abilene
Health Institute of Louisville (Branch Campus)	San Antonio
Hill College	Hillsboro
Houston Allied Health Careers, Inc.	Houston
Houston Ballet Academy	Houston
Houston Baptist University	Houston
Houston Community College	Houston
Houston Community College (Central College)	Houston
Houston Community College (College Without Walls)	Houston
Houston Community College (Northeast College)	Houston
Houston Community College (Southeast College)	Houston
Houston Community College (Southwest College)	Houston
Houston Community College System	Houston
Houston Graduate School of Theology	Houston
Houston Training School	Houston
Houston Training School (Branch Campus)	Houston
Houston Training School (Branch Campus)	Houston
Howard College	Big Spring
Howard Payne University	Brownwood
Huston-Tillotson College	Austin
ICI University	Irving
ITT Technical Institute	Arlington
ITT Technical Institute	Garland
ITT Technical Institute	Houston
ITT Technical Institute	San Antonio
ITT Technical Institute (Branch)	Austin
ITT Technical Institute (Branch)	Houston
Incarnate Word College	San Antonio
Institute for Christian Studies	Austin
Interactive Learning Systems	Dallas
Interactive Learning Systems (Branch Campus)	Houston
International Aviation and Travel Academy	Arlington
International Aviation and Travel Academy	Houston
International Aviation and Travel Academy (Branch Campus)	Dallas
International Business College	El Paso
International Business College	Lubbock
International Business College (Branch Campus)	El Paso
International Business College (Business School - Denton)	Denton
International Business College (Business School - Sherman)	Sherman
Iverson Institute of Court Reporting	Arlington
Jacksonville College	Jacksonville
Jarvis Christian College	Hawkins
KD Studio	Dallas

(Bold print indicates degree granting institutions)

State Cross Reference Index

Texas

The Sourcebook of College and University Student Records

Kilgore College..Kilgore
Kingwood College..Kingwood
Lamar University at Beaumont........................Beaumont
Lamar University at Orange................................Orange
Lamar University at Port Arthur.....................Port Arthur
Laredo Community College................................Laredo
Le Hair Design College..Dallas
Le Hair Design College..Dallas
Le Hair Design College....................................Fort Worth
Le Hair Design College..Garland
Le Hair Design College...................................Haltom City
LeChef College of Hospitality Careers......................Austin
LeTourneau University....................................Longview
Lee College..Baytown
Lincoln Technical Institute............................Grand Prairie
Lon Morris College....................................Jacksonville
Lubbock Christian University..........................Lubbock
M & M Word Processing Institute..........................Houston
M. Weeks Welding Laboratory Testing & School.....Nederland
McLennan Community College..............................Waco
McMurry University..Abilene
Midland College...Midland
Midwestern State University......................Wichita Falls
Miss Wade's Fashion Merchandising College.........Dallas
Mountain View College......................................Dallas
National Career Institute
 (Branch Campus)..Harlingen
National Education Center
 (Fort Worth Campus)..................................Fort Worth
National Education Center-National Institute of Technology Campus
 ....San Antonio
Navarro College...Corsicana
Nell Institute...Austin
North Central Texas College........................Gainesville
North Harris Montgomery Community College.......Houston
North Lake College..Irving
Northeast Texas Community College......Mount Pleasant
Northwood University
 (Branch)..Cedar Hill
Oblate School of Theology..........................San Antonio
Ocean Corporation..Houston
Occupational Safety Training Institute..................Houston
Odessa College...Odessa
Office Careers Centre......................................Fort Worth
Our Lady of the Lake University.................San Antonio
PCI Health Training Center....................................Dallas
Palo Alto College..San Antonio
Panola College..Carthage
Paris Junior College..Paris
Parker College of Chiropractic................................Dallas
Paul Quinn College..Dallas
Polytechnic Institute..Houston
Prairie View A&M University......................Prairie View
Professional Court Reporting School..................Richardson
R/S Institute..Houston
RHDC Hair Design College................................Fort Worth
Ranger College..Ranger
Rice Aviation, a Division of A&J Enterprises.........Houston
Rice Aviation, a Division of A&J Enterprises
 (Branch Campus)..Houston
Rice University..Houston
Richland College...Dallas
S.W. School of Business & Technical Careers......Eagle Pass
S.W. School of Business & Technical Careers....San Antonio
S.W. School of Business & Technical Careers....San Antonio
S.W. School of Business & Technical Careers
 (Branch Campus)..Uvalde
Sam Houston State University........................Huntsville
San Antonio College..................................San Antonio
San Antonio College of Medical & Dental Assistants.....San Antonio
San Antonio College of Medical & Dental Assistants
 (Branch Campus)...Mcallen
San Antonio College of Medical & Dental Assistants
 (Branch Campus)..San Antonio
San Antonio Trade School................................San Antonio
San Antonio Trade School
 (Branch Campus)..Del Rio
San Antonio Training Division..........................San Antonio
San Antonio Training Division
 (Branch Campus)......................................San Antonio
San Antonio Training Division
 (Branch Campus)......................................San Antonio
San Jacinto College.......................................Pasadena
School of Automotive Machinists..........................Houston
School of Health Care Sciences.....................Sheppard Afb
Schreiner College...Kerrville
Sebring Career Schools.....................................Huntsville
Sebring Career Schools
 (Branch Campus)..Houston
Sebring Career Schools
 (Branch Campus)..Houston
Seguin Beauty School...Seguin
Seguin Beauty School
 (Branch Campus)..................................New Braunfels
South Plains College......................................Levelland
South Texas College of Law............................Houston
South Texas Vo-Tech Institute..........................Brownsville
South Texas Vo-Tech Institute...............................Mcallen
South Texas Vo-Tech Institute..............................Weslaco
Southeastern Paralegal Institute..............................Dallas
Southern Careers Institute.....................................Austin
Southern Careers Institute
 (Branch Campus)...................................Corpus Christi
Southern Careers Institute
 (Branch Campus)...Mcallen
Southern Careers Institute
 (Branch Campus)...Pharr
Southern Methodist University............................Dallas
Southwest Texas Junior College........................Uvalde
Southwest Texas State University................San Marcos
Southwestern Adventist College..........................Keene
Southwestern Assemblies of God University....Waxahachie
Southwestern Baptist Theological Seminary....Fort Worth
Southwestern Christian College..........................Terrell
Southwestern University..............................Georgetown
St. Edward's University......................................Austin
St. Mary's University................................San Antonio
St. Philip's College....................................San Antonio
Stephen F. Austin State University..............Nacogdoches
Sul Ross State University..................................Alpine
Sul Ross State University
 (Branch Campus)..Uvalde
Tarleton State University............................Stephenville
Tarrant County Junior College......................Fort Worth
Tarrant County Junior College
 (Northeast Campus)..Hurst
Tarrant County Junior College
 (Northwest Campus)..................................Fort Worth
Tarrant County Junior College
 (South Campus)...Fort Worth
Taylor's Institute of Cosmetology........................Corsicana
Temple Academy of Cosmetology...........................Temple
Temple Academy of Cosmetology
 (Branch Campus)..Longview
Temple Junior College......................................Temple
Texarkana College..Texarkana
Texas A&M International University..................Laredo
Texas A&M University..........................College Station
Texas A&M University at Galveston..............Galveston
Texas A&M University-Corpus Christi......Corpus Christi
Texas A&M University-Kingsville..................Kingsville
Texas Aero Tech..Dallas
Texas Barber College..Dallas
Texas Barber College
 (Branch Campus)..Dallas
Texas Barber College

State Cross Reference Index (Bold print indicates degree granting institutions)

(Branch Campus)	Richardson
Texas Chiropractic College	Pasadena
Texas Christian University	Fort Worth
Texas College	Tyler
Texas Lutheran College	Seguin
Texas School of Business	Houston
Texas School of Business - Southwest	Houston
Texas Southern University	Houston
Texas Southmost College	Brownsville
Texas State Technical College-Amarillo	Amarillo
Texas State Technical College-Harlingen	Harlingen
Texas State Technical College-Sweetwater	Sweetwater
Texas State Technical College-Waco	Waco
Texas Tech University	Lubbock
Texas Tech University Health Sciences Center	Lubbock
Texas Vocational School	Pharr
Texas Vocational School	San Antonio
Texas Vocational Schools	Victoria
Texas Vocational Schools	
(Branch Campus)	Victoria
Texas Wesleyan University	Fort Worth
Texas Women's University	Denton
Tomball College	Tomball
Trinity University	San Antonio
Trinity Valley Community College	Athens
Tyler Junior College	Tyler
USA Hair Academy	Victoria
Ultrasound Diagnostic School	
(Branch Campus)	Bellaire
Ultrasound Diagnostic School	
(Branch Campus)	Irving
University of Central Texas	Killeen
University of Dallas	Irving
University of Houston	Houston
University of Houston-Clear Lake	Houston
University of Houston-Downtown	Houston
University of Houston-Victoria	Victoria
University of Mary Hardin-Baylor	Belton
University of North Texas	Denton
University of North Texas Health Science Center at Fort Worth	Fort Worth
University of St. Thomas	Houston
University of Texas Health Science Center at Houston	Houston
University of Texas Health Science Center at San Antonio	San Antonio
University of Texas Medical Branch at Galveston	Galveston
University of Texas Southwestern Medical Center at Dallas	Dallas
University of Texas at Arlington	Arlington
University of Texas at Austin	Austin
University of Texas at Brownsville	Brownsville
University of Texas at Dallas	Richardson
University of Texas at El Paso	El Paso
University of Texas at San Antonio	San Antonio
University of Texas at Tyler	Tyler
University of Texas of the Permian Basin	Odessa
University of Texas-Pan American	Edinburg
Vanguard Institute of Technology	Edinburg
Vanguard Institute of Technology	
(Branch Campus)	Harlingen
Vernon Regional Junior College	Vernon
Victoria College	Victoria
Wayland Baptist University	Plainview
Weatherford College	Weatherford
West Texas A&M University	Canyon
Western Texas College	Snyder
Wharton County Junior College	Wharton
Wiley College	Marshall

United Kingdom

American College for the Applied Arts
 (Branch) ....London, England

Utah

American Institute of Medical-Dental Technolgy	Provo
Brigham Young University	Provo
College of Eastern Utah	Price
Dixie College	St George
ITT Technical Institute	Murray
Intermountain College of Court Reporting	Murray
LDS Business College	Salt Lake City
Myotherapy Institute of Utah	Salt Lake City
Phillips Junior College	Salt Lake City
Provo College	Provo
Salt Lake Community College	Salt Lake City
Snow College	Ephraim
Southern Utah University	Cedar City
Stevens College of Business	Ogden
Stevens-Henager College of Business	
(Branch Campus)	Provo
The Bryman School	Salt Lake City
University of Phoenix	
(Salt Lake City Main)	Salt Lake City
University of Utah	Salt Lake City
Utah State University	Logan
Utah Valley State College	Orem
Weber State University	Ogden
Westminster College of Salt Lake City	Salt Lake City

Vermont

Bennington College	Bennington
Burlington College	Burlington
Castleton State College	Castleton
Champlain College	Burlington
College of St. Joseph	Rutland
Community College of Vermont	Waterbury
Fanny Allen Memorial School of Practical Nursing	Colchester
Goddard College	Plainfield
Green Mountain College	Poultney
Johnson State College	Johnson
Landmark College	Putney
Lyndon State College	Lyndonville
Marlboro College	Marlboro
Middlebury College	Middlebury
Norwich University	Northfield
School for International Training	Brattleboro
Southern Vermont College	Bennington
St. Michael's College	Colchester
Sterling College	Craftsbury Common
Thompson School of Practical Nursing	Brattleboro
Trinity College of Vermont	Burlington
University of Vermont	Burlington
Vermont College of Norwich University	Montpelier
Vermont Law School	South Royalton
Vermont Technical College	Randolph Center
Woodbury College	Montpelier

(Bold print indicates degree granting institutions)

Virgin Islands

University of the Virgin Islands .... St Thomas
University of the Virgin Islands
  (Branch Campus) .... St Croix

Virginia

AEGIS Training Center .... Dahlgren
ATI - Hollywood .... Roanoke
ATI - Hollywood
  (Branch Campus) .... Roanoke
ATI - Hollywood
  (Branch Campus) .... Salem
ATI Career Institute .... Falls Church
ATI Career Institute
  (Branch Campus) .... Quantico
Alliance Tractor Trailer Trining Centers II .... Wytheville
Anthony's Barber Styling College .... Newport News
Applied Career Training, Inc. .... Rosslyn
Apprentice School-Newport News Shipbuilding ..... Newport News
Armed Forces School of Music .... Norfolk
Army Institute for Professional Development .... Fort Eustis
Army Quartermaster Center and School .... Fort Lee
Army Transportation and Aviation Logistics School ... Fort Eustis
Averett College .... Danville
Blue Ridge Community College .... Weyers Cave
Bluefield College .... Bluefield
Braxton School .... Richmond
Bridgewater College .... Bridgewater
Career Development Center .... Newport News
Career Training Center .... Richmond
Career Training Center
  (Branch Campus) .... Lynchburg
Career Training Center
  (Branch Campus) .... Roanoke
Catholic Home Study Institute .... Paeonian Springs
Central School of Practical Nursing .... Norfolk
Central Virginia Community College .... Lynchburg
Christendom College .... Front Royal
Christopher Newport College .... Newport News
Clinch Valley College of the University of Virginia .... Wise
College of William and Mary .... Williamsburg
Commonwealth College .... Virginia Beach
Commonwealth College
  (Branch Campus) .... Hampton
Commonwealth College
  (Branch Campus) .... Norfolk
Commonwealth College
  (Branch Campus) .... Portsmouth
Commonwealth College
  (Branch Campus) .... Richmond
**Community Hospital of Roanoke Valley College of Health
Sciences** .... Roanoke
Computer Dynamics Institute .... Virginia Beach
Computer Learning Center .... Alexandria
Dabney S. Lancaster Community College ..... Clifton Forge
Danville Community College .... Danville
Defence Mapping School .... Fort Belvoir
Dominion Business School .... Harrisonburg
Dominion Business School .... Roanoke
Dominion Business School .... Staunton
Eastern Mennonite College and Seminary .... Harrisonburg
Eastern Shore Community College .... Melfa
Eastern Virginia Medical School .... Norfolk
Emory and Henry College .... Emory
Ferrum College .... Ferrum
Flatwoods Civilian Conservation Center .... Coeburn

George Mason University .... Fairfax
Germanna Community College .... Locust Grove
Hampden-Sydney College .... Hampden-Sydney
Hampton University .... Hampton
Hollins College .... Roanoke
ITT Technical Institute
  (Branch) .... Norfolk
Institute of Textile Technology .... Charlottesville
J. Sargeant Reynolds Community College ..... Richmond
James Madison University .... Harrisonburg
John Tyler Community College .... Chester
Johnson & Wales University
  (Branch Campus) .... Norfolk
Judge Advocate General's School .... Charlottesville
Liberty University .... Lynchburg
Longwood College .... Farmville
Lord Fairfax Community College .... Middletown
Lynchburg College .... Lynchburg
Mary Baldwin College .... Staunton
Mary Washington College .... Fredericksburg
Maryland Drafting Institute
  (Branch Campus) .... North Springfield
Marymount University .... Arlington
Microcomputer Technology Center .... Fairfax
Mountain Empire Community College ..... Big Stone Gap
National Business College .... Roanoke
National Business College
  (Branch Campus) .... Bluefield
National Business College
  (Branch Campus) .... Bristol
National Business College
  (Branch Campus) .... Charlottesville
National Business College
  (Branch Campus) .... Danville
National Business College
  (Branch Campus) .... Harrisonburg
National Business College
  (Branch Campus) .... Lynchburg
National Business College
  (Corporate Office) .... Salem
National Education Center - Kee Business College ...... Newport News
Naval Guided Missiles School .... Virginia Beach
Naval Health Sciences Education and Training Command
  (Opthalmis Support and Training) .... Yorktown
Naval Health Sciences Education and Training Command
  (School of Health Science) .... Portsmouth
Navy and Marine Corps Intelligence Training Center .... Virginia Beach
New River Community College .... Dublin
Norfolk Skills Center .... Norfolk
Norfolk State University .... Norfolk
Northern Virginia Community College
  (Alexandria Campus) .... Alexandria
Northern Virginia Community College
  (Annandale Campus) .... Annandale
Northern Virginia Community College
  (Loudon Campus) .... Sterling
Northern Virginia Community College
  (Manassas Campus) .... Manassas
Northern Virginia Community College
  (Woodbridge Campus) .... Woodbridge
Old Dominion University .... Norfolk
Omege Travel School .... Fairfax
Paul D. Camp Community College .... Franklin
Phillips Business College .... Lynchburg
Piedmont Virginia Community College ..... Charlottesville
Potomac Academy of Hair Design .... Manassas
Presbyterian School of Christian Education ..... Richmond
Protestant Episcopal Theological Seminary in Virginia Alexandria
Radford University .... Radford
Randolph-Macon College .... Ashland
Randolph-Macon Woman's College .... Lynchburg
Rappahannock Community College .... Glenns
Regent University .... Virginia Beach

The Sourcebook of College and University Student Records — **Washington**

Reporting Academy of Virginia	Virginia Beach
Reporting Academy of Virginia (Branch Campus)	Richmond
Reporting Academy of Virginia (Branch Campus)	Springfield
Rice Aviation, a Division of A&J Enterprises (Branch Campus)	Chesapeake
Richard Bland College	Petersburg
Richard M. Milburne High School	Woodbridge
Roanoke College	Salem
Shenandoah University	Winchester
Southern Virginia College	Buena Vista
Southside Training Skills Center	Crewe
Southside Virginia Community College	Alberta
Southwest Virginia Community College	Richlands
St. Paul's College	Lawrenceville
Sweet Briar College	Sweet Briar
TESST Electronics and Computer Institute	Alexandria
Thomas Nelson Community College	Hampton
Tidewater Community College	Portsmouth
Tidewater Tech	Virginia Beach
Tidewater Tech (Branch Campus)	Chesapeake
Tidewater Tech (Branch Campus)	Newport News
Tidewater Tech (Branch Campus)	Norfolk
Union Theological Seminary in Virginia	Richmond
University of Richmond	Richmond
University of Virginia	Charlottesville
Virginia College	Salem
Virginia Commonwealth University	Richmond
Virginia Hair Academy	Roanoke
Virginia Highlands Community College	Abingdon
Virginia Intermont College	Bristol
Virginia Military Institute	Lexington
Virginia Polytechnic Institute and State University	Blacksburg
Virginia School of Cosmetology	Richmond
Virginia State University	Petersburg
Virginia Union University	Richmond
Virginia Wesleyan College	Norfolk
Virginia Western Community College	Roanoke
Washington Business School of Northern Virginia	Vienna
Washington County Adult Skill Center	Abingdon
Washington and Lee University	Lexington
Woodrow Wilson Rehabilitation Center	Fishersville
Wytheville Community College	Wytheville

Washington

Antioch University (Antioch Seattle)	Seattle
Art Institute of Seattle	Seattle
Bastyr University	Seattle
Bates Technical College	Tacoma
Bellevue Community College	Bellevue
Bellingham Technical College	Bellingham
Big Bend Community College	Moses Lake
Career Floral Design Institute	Bellevue
Central Washington University	Ellensburg
Centralia College	Centralia
City University	Bellevue
Clark College	Vancouver
Clover Park Technical College	Tacoma
Cogswell College North	Kirkland
Columbia Basin College	Pasco
Commercial Training Services	Des Moines
Cornish College of the Arts	Seattle
Court Reporting Institute	Seattle
Crown Academy	Tacoma
Divers Institute of Technology	Seattle
Eastern Washington University	Cheney
Edmonds Community College	Lynnwood
Emil Fries Piano & Training Center	Vancouver
Eton Technical Institute	Port Orchard
Eton Technical Institute (Branch Campus)	Everett
Eton Technical Institute (Branch Campus)	Federal Way
Everett Community College	Everett
Evergreen State College	Olympia
Fox Travel Institute	Seattle
Gonzaga University	Spokane
Grays Harbor College	Aberdeen
Green River Community College	Auburn
Heritage College	Toppenish
Highline Community College	Des Moines
ITT Technical Institute	Seattle
ITT Technical Institute	Spokane
International Air Academy	Vancouver
Lake Washington Technical College	Kirkland
Lower Columbia College	Longview
Lutheran Bible Institute of Seattle	Issaquah
North Seattle Community College	Seattle
Northwest College of the Assemblies of God	Kirkland
Northwest Indian College	Bellingham
Northwest Institute of Acupuncture and Oriental Medicine	Seattle
Northwest School of Wooden Boatbuilding	Port Townsend
Olympic College	Bremerton
Pacific Lutheran University	Tacoma
Pacific Northwest Ballet School	Seattle
Peninsula College	Port Angeles
Perry Technical Institute	Yakima
Pierce College	Tacoma
Pima Medical Institute	Seattle
Pima Medical Institute	Seattle
Puget Sound Christian College	Edmonds
Renton Technical College	Renton
Seattle Central Community College	Seattle
Seattle Pacific University	Seattle
Seattle University	Seattle
Shoreline Community College	Seattle
Skagit Valley College	Mount Vernon
South Puget Sound Community College	Olympia
South Seattle Community College	Seattle
Spokane Community College	Spokane
Spokane Falls Community College	Spokane
St. Martin's College	Lacey
Tacoma Community College	Tacoma
Trident Training Facility	Silverdale
University of Puget Sound	Tacoma
University of Washington	Seattle
Vocational Training Institute	Vancouver
Walla Walla College	College Place
Walla Walla Community College	Walla Walla
Washington State University	Pullman
Wenatchee Valley College	Wenatchee
Western Business College (Branch Campus)	Vancouver
Western Washington University	Bellingham
Whatcom Community College	Bellingham
Whitman College	Walla Walla
Whitworth College	Spokane
Yakima Valley Community College	Yakima

West Virginia

Alderson-Broaddus College	Philippi
Appalachian Bible College	Bradley
B.M. Spurr School of Practical Nursing	Glen Dale
Bethany College	Bethany

(Bold print indicates degree granting institutions)

State Cross Reference Index

Wisconsin

Bluefield State College	Bluefield
Boone county Career Center	Danville
Carver Career and Technical Education Center	Charleston
College of West Virginia	Beckley
Computer Tech	
(Branch)	Fairmont
Concord College	Athens
Davis & Elkins College	Elkins
Fairmont State College	Fairmont
Glenville State College	Glenville
Huntington Junior College	Huntington
Marshall University	Huntington
Monongalia Country Technical Education Center	Morgantown
Mountain State College	Parkersburg
Ohio Valley College	Parkersburg
Potomac State College of West Virginia University	Keyser
Salem-Teikyo University	Salem
Shepherd College	Shepherdstown
Southern West Virginia Community College	Logan
University of Charleston	Charleston
Webster College	Fairmont
West Liberty State College	West Liberty
West Virginia Business College	Clarksburg
West Virginia Business College	
(Branch Campus)	Wheeling
West Virginia Career College	Charleston
West Virginia Career College	Morgantown
West Virginia Graduate College	Institute
West Virginia Institute of Technology	Montgomery
West Virginia Northern Community College	Wheeling
West Virginia School of Osteopathic Medicine	Lewisburg
West Virginia State College	Institute
West Virginia University	Morgantown
West Virginia University at Parkersburg	Parkersburg
West Virginia Wesleyan College	Buckhannon
Wheeling College of Hair Design	Wheeling
Wheeling Jesuit College	Wheeling
Wood County Vocational School	Parkersburg

Wisconsin

Acme Institute of Technology	Manitowoc
Acme Institute of Technology	West Allis
Alverno College	Milwaukee
Bellin College of Nursing	Green Bay
Beloit College	Beloit
Blackhawk Technical College	Janesville
Cardinal Stritch College	Milwaukee
Carroll College	Waukesha
Carthage College	Kenosha
Chippewa Valley Technical College	Eau Claire
Columbia College of Nursing	Milwaukee
Concordia University Wisconsin	Mequon
Diesel Truck Driver Training School	Sun Prairie
Edgewood College	Madison
Fox Valley Technical Institute	Appleton
Gateway Technical College	Kenosha
ITT Technical Institute	Greenfield
Keller Graduate School of Management	
(Milwaukee Center)	Milwaukee
Keller Graduate School of Management	
(Waukesha Center)	Waukesha
LacCourte Oreilles Ojibwa Community College	Hayward
Lakeland College	Sheboygan
Lakeshore Technical College	Cleveland
Lawrence University	Appleton
MBTI Business Training Institute	Milwaukee
MBTI Business Training Institute	
(Branch Campus)	Waukesha
Madison Area Technical College	Madison
Madison Junior College of Business	Madison
Marantha Baptist Bible College	Watertown
Marian College of Fond du Lac	Fond Du Lac
Marquette University	Milwaukee
Medical College of Wisconsin	Milwaukee
Mid-State Technical College	Wisconsin Rapids
Midwest Center for the Study of Oriental Medicine	Racine
Milwaukee Area Technical College	Milwaukee
Milwaukee Institute of Art and Design	Milwaukee
Milwaukee School of Engineering	Milwaukee
Moraine Park Technical College	Fond Du Lac
Mount Mary College	Milwaukee
Mount Senario College	Ladysmith
Nashotah House	Nashotah
Nicolet Area Technical College	Rhinelander
North Central Technical College	Wausau
Northeast Wisconsin Technical College	Green Bay
Northland College	Ashland
Northwestern College	Watertown
Ripon College	Ripon
Sacred Heart School of Theology	Hales Corners
Silver Lake College	Manitowoc
Southwest Wisconsin Technical College	Fennimore
St. Francis Seminary	St Francis
St. Norbert College	De Pere
Stratton College	Milwaukee
Trans American School of Broadcasting	Madison
University of Wisconsin	Madison
University of Wisconsin-Baraboo-Sauk County	Baraboo
University of Wisconsin-Barron County	Rice Lake
University of Wisconsin-Eau Claire	Eau Claire
University of Wisconsin-Fond du Lac	Fond Du Lac
University of Wisconsin-Fox Valley	Menasha
University of Wisconsin-Green Bay	Green Bay
University of Wisconsin-La Crosse	La Crosse
University of Wisconsin-Madison	Madison
University of Wisconsin-Manitowoc County	Manitowoc
University of Wisconsin-Marathon County	Wausau
University of Wisconsin-Marinette County	Marinette
University of Wisconsin-Marshfield-Wood County	Marshfield
University of Wisconsin-Milwaukee	Milwaukee
University of Wisconsin-Oshkosh	Oshkosh
University of Wisconsin-Parkside	Kenosha
University of Wisconsin-Platteville	Platteville
University of Wisconsin-Richland	Richland Center
University of Wisconsin-River Falls	River Falls
University of Wisconsin-Rock County	Janesville
University of Wisconsin-Sheboygan County	Sheboygan
University of Wisconsin-Stevens Point	Stevens Point
University of Wisconsin-Stout	Menomonie
University of Wisconsin-Superior	Superior
University of Wisconsin-Washington County	West Bend
University of Wisconsin-Waukesha County	Waukesha
University of Wisconsin-Whitewater	Whitewater
Viterbo College	La Crosse
Waukesha County Technical College	Pewaukee
Western Wisconsin Technical College	La Crosse
Wisconsin Conservatory of Music, Inc.	Milwaukee
Wisconsin Indianhead Technical College	Shell Lake
Wisconsin Lutheran College	Milwaukee
Wisconsin School of Professional Pet Grooming	Okauchee
Wisconsin School of Professional Psychology	Milwaukee

Wyoming

Casper College	Casper
Central Wyoming College	Riverton
Cheyenne Aero Tech	Cheyenne
Eastern Wyoming College	Torrington
Laramie County Community College	Cheyenne
Northern Wyoming Community College District (Gillette Campus)	Gillette
Northwest College	Powell
Sheridan College	Sheridan
University of Wyoming	Laramie
Western Wyoming College	Rock Springs
Wyoming Technical Institute	Laramie

Make Your Library THE SOURCE for Public Record Researchers

Researchers, business, and libraries requiring public record retrieval information will find these works invaluable.

—Booklist, Reference Books Bulletin, 10/94

Introducing The New 2nd Edition... STATE PUBLIC RECORDS

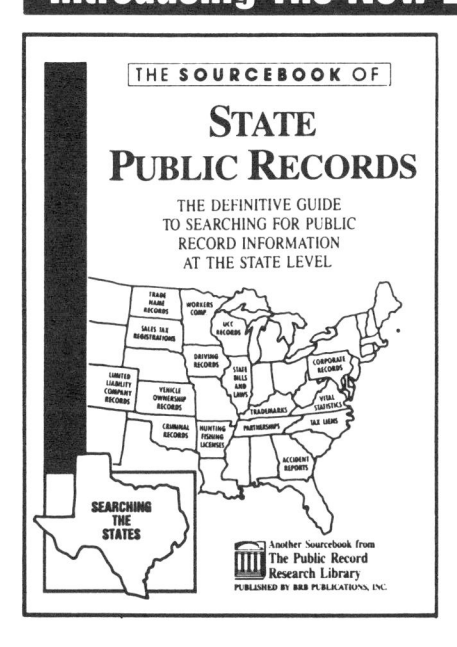

Uniquely Points the Searcher to All Major State Public Record Databases

The sourcebook gives the reader all the information needed for accurate, comprehensive public record searching at the state level. Each topic is covered in detail — where to locate, (i.e., address, telephone, office hours), search requirements, modes of access, costs, access and usage restrictions, how records are indexed, when records are available, and more, Additional information includes addresses and phone numbers for governors, attorneys general, state archives, and state-wide court administrators. Special attention is paid to on-line retrieval.

In addition, each state chapter contains a broad list of agencies involved in occupational licensing and business registration. Over 4,900 record centers of professional and business license addresses and telephone numbers are listed.

ISBN #1-879792-22-2   Publish Date 5/95
Price $33.00   Pages 360

Another Sourcebook from The Public Record Research Library
PUBLISHED BY BRB PUBLICATIONS, INC.

TURN THE PAGE FOR MORE PUBLIC RECORD SOURCEBOOKS!

ANNOUNCING NEW 2ND EDITION

THE SOURCEBOOK OF

LOCAL COURT AND COUNTY RECORD RETRIEVERS

THE NATIONAL GUIDE OF INFORMATION RETRIEVERS WHO PULL FILES AND DOCUMENTS FROM U.S., STATE, AND LOCAL COURTS AND FROM COUNTY AGENCIES.

THE SOURCEBOOK OF LOCAL COURT AND COUNTY RECORD RETRIEVERS

THE NATIONAL GUIDE OF INFORMATION RETRIEVERS WHO PULL FILES AND DOCUMENTS FROM US, STATE, AND LOCAL COURTS AND FROM COUNTY AGENCIES.

Another Sourcebook from The Public Record Research Library
PUBLISHED BY BRB PUBLICATIONS, INC.

ISBN #1-879892-21-4
Pages 544
Price $45.00
Published Date — 4/95

350 MORE RETRIEVERS!

3000 ADDITIONAL LISTINGS!

Now you can have at your fingertips a directory of more than 2,250 firms that regularly retrieve public records from courthouses and county offices. Shown on a county by county basis, "hands-on" document retrievers are highlighted by their search expertise in these categories:

- Local Court Civil Cases
- Local Court Criminal Cases
- Probate Cases
- US District Court Cases
- US Bankruptcy Court Cases
- Federal Records Centers
- UCC Liens and Records
- Real Property Liens, Recordings
  - Marriage, Divorce, Birth & Death Records
  - Voter Registration Records
  - Tax Assessor's Office
  - Service of Process

SPECIAL BONUS:

Included are the 328 Members of the **P**ublic **R**ecord **R**etrievers **N**etwork who abide by the PRRN Code of Professional Conduct.

Look for this logo.

MEMBER Public Record Retriever Network

FOR ORDERING INFORMATION:

Public Record Research Library

CALL 1-800-929-3764

BRB PUBLICATIONS, INC.
4653 South Lakeshore #3
Tempe, AZ 85282

THE SOURCEBOOK OF COUNTY ASSET/LIEN RECORDS

A National Guide to all County/City Government Agencies Where Real Estate Transactions, UCC Financing Statements, and Federal/State Tax Liens are Recorded.

Another Sourcebook from
The Public Record Research Library
PUBLISHED BY BRB PUBLICATIONS, INC.

ISBN #1-879792-17-6
Pages 460+
Price $29.00

Published 1/95

INTRODUCING

New First Edition

A National Guide to all County/City Government Agencies Where Real Estate Transactions, UCC Financing Statements, and Federal/State Tax Liens are Recorded.

This sourcebook, a companion to *County Court Records*, details how to obtain real estate, Uniform Commercial Code and tax lien records from 4,200+ city and county filing offices.

UCC records, federal and state tax lien records, four categories of real estate records (transfers, current ownership, unpaid taxes and mortgages and deeds) are examined in detail for search availability, how indexed, acceptable access methods (phone, mail, fax, etc.), required request forms, fees, copy costs, and more.

The Sourcebook also includes an extensive city to county cross index to locate the correct jurisdiction to contact.

FOR ORDERING INFORMATION:

Public Record Research Library

CALL 1-800-929-3764

BRB PUBLICATIONS, INC.
4653 South Lakeshore #3
Tempe, AZ 85282

INTRODUCING THE NEW EXPANDED MVR SOURCEBOOKS

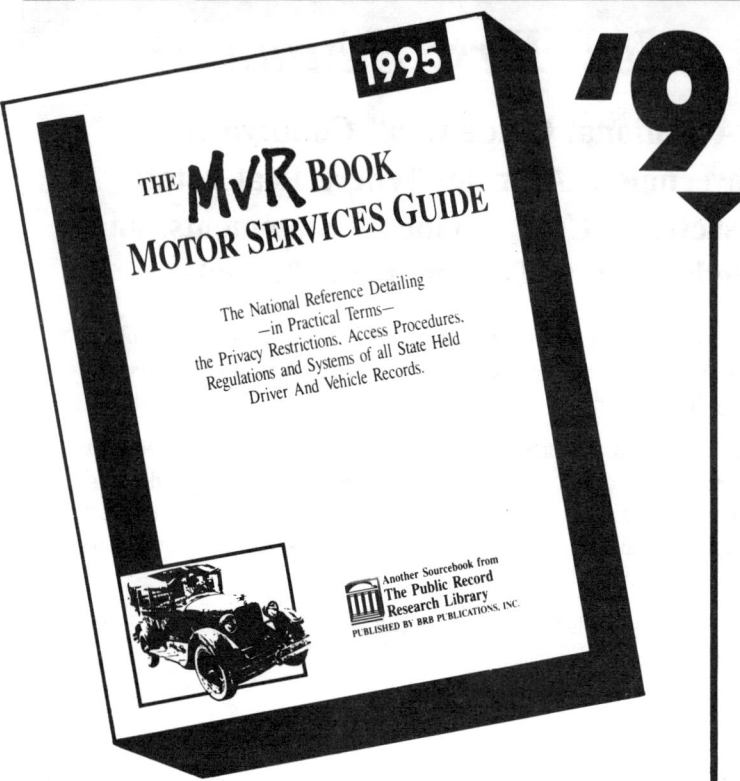

THE MVR BOOK MOTOR SERVICES GUIDE — 1995

The Comprehensive Reference Book for Professionals Using Driver History and Motor Vehicle Records

8½ x 11 • 272 Pages
Price $18.00 + S&H
ISBN 1-879792-19-2
Published 3/1995

The National Reference Detailing
—in Practical Terms—
the Privacy Restrictions, Access Procedures, Regulations and Systems of all State Held Driver and Vehicle Records.

Individual State Characteristics
- Latest in Privacy Laws and Access Restrictions
- Convictions That Do Not Appear on Driver History Records
- Commercial Access of Vehicle Ownership Records
- Driver License Format and Classification Facts

Appendix With These Research Tools
- Glossary of Related Professional Agencies and Institutions
- Glossary of Current Federal Programs and National Networks
- Reciprocity of Conviction Information Between the States

New Topics Explored For 1995
- Latest on PDPS (Problem Driver Pointer System)
- Copy of the Driver's Privacy Protection Act

THE MVR DECODER DIGEST — 1995

The Ideal Reference Book for Translating the Codes and Abbrevations Used on State Driver History Records

8½ x 11 • 288 Pages
Price $18.00 + S&H
ISBN 1-879792-20-6
Published 3/1995

The Companion to the MVR Book, Translating the Codes and Abbreviations Violations and Licensing Categories that Appear on Motor Vehicle Records For All States.

Including These Individual State Characteristics
- Violations and Codes
- Common Abbreviations
- Corresponding Points
- License Classifications
- Endorsements and Restrictions...
  for both CDL and Non-CDL Drivers

Additional Research Tools
- Compact and IRP Membership Table
- State License Format and Access Fee Table
- The AAMVA Conviction/Withdrawal Code Dictionary (ACD) as Mandated for 1995

SEE REVERSE FOR MORE DETAILS

Easy to Read Page Layouts

THE REVISED '95s ARE HERE!
Featuring 16 More Pages of Essential Information for Professionals Who Need Current and Concise Data

BOTH BOOK SPECIAL: $36.00 Postage Paid

ORDER: • FAX-800-929-4981 • TELEPHONE-800-929-3764 OR *MAIL TO:*
BRB PUBLICATIONS, INC. • 4653 S. Lakeshore #3 • Tempe, AZ 85282

☐ **Yes,** please send me the *Both Book Special* at $36 postage and shipping paid

OR...			
QTY	TITLE	PRICE EACH	TOTAL
	THE MVR BOOK	$18.00	
	DECODER DIGEST	$18.00	

*Arizona Sales — Please add 6.7% sales tax.
**Shipping & Handling = $3.25 for first book, $1.75 each additional book.

- SUBTOTAL
- DISCOUNT
- *TAX
- **S&H
- TOTAL

BOOK DISCOUNT SCHEDULES (MIX OR MATCH TITLES)
3-5 = 10%   6-10 = 15%   11-15 = 20%
16+ = 25%   Call for 100+ discount

Name _____
Title _____
Company _____
Address _____
City _____ State _____ Zip _____
Telephone _____

☐ MasterCard ☐ VISA ☐ AMEX ☐ Check   Expires _____
_____
Signature: _____

PLEASE MAKE CHECK PAYABLE TO BRB PUBLICATIONS
☐ PLEASE INVOICE P.O. # _____

INVOICE ORDERS MUST INCLUDE SIGNATURE, TELEPHONE NUMBER AND COMPANY PURCHASE ORDER NUMBER.

PUBLIC RECORDS SEARCHING • WHO • WHAT • WHERE • HOW

The Sourcebooks the Professionals Use

Searching at the Jurisdictions...

Unique Sources and Retrieval Aids...

"Wonderful reference books. We're expanding and need a set for each researcher in our offices."
— Pat Brent, Manager
Washington Document Service

"All volumes are written in a straightforward and succinct manner. Researchers, businesses, and libraries requiring public-record retrieval information will find these reference works invaluable." — BOOKLIST, October 1, 1994 issue

"This volume (Local Court and County Record Retrievers) is useful, accurate, and well arranged."
— BOOKLIST,
December 15, 1993 issue

- ☐ **CURRENT & UP TO DATE**
- ☐ **PRICES RANGE FROM $29 TO $45**
- ☐ **MONEY BACK GUARANTEE**
- ☐ **AVAILABLE ON CD-ROM**

Call For A FREE CATALOG Of All 10 Titles
1-800-929-3811

PUBLIC RECORD RESEARCH LIBRARY